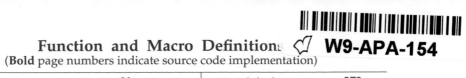

UNIX Network Programming

The Sockets Networking API

Addison-Wesley Professional Computing Series

Brian W. Kernighan and Craig Partridge, Consulting Editors

Visit www.awprofessional.com/series/professionalcomputing for more information about these titles.

UNIX Network Programming

The Sockets Networking API

Volume 1 • Third Edition

W. Richard Stevens
Bill Fenner
Andrew M. Rudoff

✦✦Addison-Wesley

Boston • San Francisco • New York • Toronto • Montreal
London • Munich • Paris • Madrid
Capetown • Sydney • Tokyo • Singapore • Mexico City

Many of the designations used by manufacturers and sellers to distinguish their products are claimed as trademarks. Where those designations appear in this book, and Addison-Wesley was aware of a trademark claim, the designations have been printed with initial capital letters or in all capitals.

The authors and publisher have taken care in the preparation of this book, but make no expressed or implied warranty of any kind and assume no responsibility for errors or omissions. No liability is assumed for incidental or consequential damages in connection with or arising out of the use of the information or programs contained herein.

The publisher offers discounts on this book when ordered in quantity for bulk purchases and special sales. For more information, please contact:

> U.S. Corporate and Government Sales
> (800) 382-3419
> corpsales@pearsontechgroup.com

For sales outside of the U.S., please contact:

> International Sales
> (317) 581-3793
> international@pearsontechgroup.com

Visit Addison-Wesley on the Web: www.awprofessional.com

Library of Congress Cataloging-in-Publication Data

A CIP catalog record for this book can be obtained from the Library of Congress.

ISBN: 0-13-141155-1

Text printed on recycled paper

First printing

To Rich.
Aloha nui loa.

Contents

Part 2. Elementary Sockets   65

Chapter 3.   Sockets Introduction   67

Chapter 4.   Elementary TCP Sockets   95

Chapter 5.   TCP Client/Server Example   121

Foreword

When the original text of this book arrived in 1990, it was quickly recognized as the definitive reference for programmers to learn network programming techniques. Since then, the art of computer networking has changed dramatically. All it takes is a look at the return address for comments from the original text ("uunet!hsi!netbook") to make this clear. (How many readers will even recognize this as an address in the UUCP dialup network that was commonplace in the 1980s?)

Today, UUCP networks are a rarity and new technologies such as wireless networks are becoming ubiquitous! With these changes, new network protocols and programming paradigms have been developed. But, programmers have lacked a good reference from which to learn the intricacies of these new techniques.

This book fills that void. Readers who have a dog-eared copy of the original book will want a new copy for the updated programming techniques and the substantial new material describing next-generation protocols such as IPv6. Everyone will want this book because it provides a great mix of practical experience, historical perspective, and a depth of understanding that only comes from being intimately involved in the field.

I've already enjoyed and learned from reading this book, and surely you will, too.

Sam Leffler

Preface

Introduction

This book is for people who want to write programs that communicate with each other using an application program interface (API) known as sockets. Some readers may be very familiar with sockets already, as that model has become synonymous with network programming. Others may need an introduction to sockets from the ground up. The goal of this book is to offer guidance on network programming for beginners as well as professionals, for those developing new network-aware applications as well as those maintaining existing code, and for people who simply want to understand how the networking components of their system function.

All the examples in this text are actual, runnable code tested on Unix systems. However, many non-Unix systems support the sockets API and the examples are largely operating system-independent, as are the general concepts we present. Virtually every operating system (OS) provides numerous network-aware applications such as Web browsers, email clients, and file-sharing servers. We discuss the usual partitioning of these applications into *client* and *server* and write our own small examples of these many times throughout the text.

Presenting this material in a Unix-oriented fashion has the natural side effect of providing background on Unix itself, and on TCP/IP as well. Where more extensive background may be interesting, we refer the reader to other texts. Four texts are so commonly mentioned in this book that we've assigned them the following abbreviations:

- APUE: *Advanced Programming in the UNIX Environment* [Stevens 1992]
- TCPv1: *TCP/IP Illustrated, Volume 1* [Stevens 1994]
- TCPv2: *TCP/IP Illustrated, Volume 2* [Wright and Stevens 1995]
- TCPv3: *TCP/IP Illustrated, Volume 3* [Stevens 1996]

TCPv2 contains a high level of detail very closely related to the material in this book, as it describes and presents the actual 4.4BSD implementation of the network programming functions for the sockets API (socket, bind, connect, and so on). If one understands the implementation of a feature, the use of that feature in an application makes more sense.

Changes from the Second Edition

Sockets have been around, more or less in their current form, since the 1980s, and it is a tribute to their initial design that they have continued to be the network API of choice. Therefore, it may come as a surprise to learn that quite a bit has changed since the second edition of this book was published in 1998. The changes we've made to the text are summarized as follows:

- This new edition contains updated information on IPv6, which was only in draft form at the time of publication of the second edition and has evolved somewhat.

- The descriptions of functions and the examples have all been updated to reflect the most recent POSIX specification (POSIX 1003.1-2001), also known as the *Single Unix Specification Version 3*.

- The coverage of the X/Open Transport Interface (XTI) has been dropped. That API has fallen out of common use and even the most recent POSIX specification does not bother to cover it.

- The coverage of TCP for transactions (T/TCP) has been dropped.

- Three chapters have been added to describe a relatively new transport protocol, SCTP. This reliable, message-oriented protocol provides multiple streams between endpoints and transport-level support for multihoming. It was originally designed for transport of telephony signaling across the Internet, but provides some features that many applications could take advantage of.

- A chapter has been added on *key management sockets*, which may be used with Internet Protocol Security (IPsec) and other network security services.

- The machines used, as well as the versions of their variants of Unix, have all been updated, and the examples have been updated to reflect how these machines behave. In many cases, examples were updated because OS vendors fixed bugs or added features, but as one might expect, we've discovered the occasional new bug here and there. The machines used for testing the examples in this book were:

  - Apple Power PC running MacOS/X 10.2.6
  - HP PA-RISC running HP-UX 11i
  - IBM Power PC running AIX 5.1
  - Intel x86 running FreeBSD 4.8
  - Intel x86 running Linux 2.4.7
  - Sun SPARC running FreeBSD 5.1
  - Sun SPARC running Solaris 9

See Figure 1.16 for details on how these machines were used.

Volume 2 of this *UNIX Network Programming* series, subtitled *Interprocess Communications*, builds on the material presented here to cover message passing, synchronization, shared memory, and remote procedure calls.

Using This Book

This text can be used as either a tutorial on network programming or as a reference for experienced programmers. When used as a tutorial or for an introductory class on network programming, the emphasis should be on Part 2, "Elementary Sockets" (Chapters 3 through 11), followed by whatever additional topics are of interest. Part 2 covers the basic socket functions for both TCP and UDP, along with SCTP, I/O multiplexing, socket options, and basic name and address conversions. Chapter 1 should be read by all readers, especially Section 1.4, which describes some wrapper functions used throughout the text. Chapter 2 and perhaps Appendix A should be referred to as necessary, depending on the reader's background. Most of the chapters in Part 3, "Advanced Sockets," can be read independently of the others in that part of the book.

To aid in the use of this book as a reference, a thorough index is provided, along with summaries on the end papers of where to find detailed descriptions of all the functions and structures. To help those reading topics in a random order, numerous references to related topics are provided throughout the text.

Source Code and Errata Availability

The source code for all the examples that appear in the book is available on the Web at www.unpbook.com. The best way to learn network programming is to take these programs, modify them, and enhance them. Actually writing code of this form is the *only* way to reinforce the concepts and techniques. Numerous exercises are also provided at the end of each chapter, and most answers are provided in Appendix E.

A current errata for the book is also available from the same Web site.

Acknowledgments

The first and second editions of this book were written solely by W. Richard Stevens, who passed away on September 1, 1999. His books have set a high standard and are largely regarded as concise, laboriously detailed, and extremely readable works of art. In providing this revision, the authors struggled to maintain the quality and thorough coverage of Rich's earlier editions and any shortcomings in this area are entirely the fault of the new authors.

The work of an author is only as good as the support from family members and friends. Bill Fenner would like to thank his dear wife, Peggy (beach ¼ mile champion), and their housemate, Christopher Boyd for letting him off all his household chores while working in the treehouse on this project. Thanks are also due to his friend, Jerry Winner, whose prodding and encouragement were invaluable. Likewise, Andy Rudoff wants to specifically thank his wife, Ellen, and girls, Jo and Katie, for their understanding and encouragement throughout this project. We simply could not have done this without all of you.

Randall Stewart with Cisco Systems, Inc. provided much of the SCTP material and deserves a special acknowledgment for this much-valued contribution. The coverage of this new and interesting topic simply would not exist without Randall's work.

The feedback from our reviewers was invaluable for catching errors, pointing out areas that required more explanation, and suggesting improvements to our text and code examples. The authors would like to thank: James Carlson, Wu-Chang Feng, Rick Jones, Brian Kernighan, Sam Leffler, John McCann, Craig Metz, Ian Lance Taylor, David Schwartz, and Gary Wright.

Numerous individuals and their organizations went beyond the normal call of duty to provide either a loaner system, software, or access to a system, all of which were used to test some of the examples in the text.

- Jessie Haug of IBM Austin provided an AIX system and compilers.
- Rick Jones and William Gilliam of Hewlett-Packard provided access to multiple systems running HP-UX.

The staff at Addison Wesley has been a true pleasure to work with: Noreen Regina, Kathleen Caren, Dan DePasquale, Anthony Gemellaro, and a very special thanks to our editor, Mary Franz.

In a trend that Rich Stevens instituted (but contrary to popular fads), we produced camera-ready copy of the book using the wonderful Groff package written by James Clark, created the illustrations using the `gpic` program (using many of Gary Wright's macros), produced the tables using the `gtbl` program, performed all the indexing, and did the final page layout. Dave Hanson's `loom` program and some scripts by Gary Wright were used to include the source code in the book. A set of `awk` scripts written by Jon Bentley and Brian Kernighan helped in producing the final index.

The authors welcome electronic mail from any readers with comments, suggestions, or bug fixes.

Bill Fenner   Andrew M. Rudoff
Woodside, California   *Boulder, Colorado*

October 2003
authors@unpbook.com
http://www.unpbook.com

Part 1

Introduction and TCP/IP

1

Introduction

1.1   Introduction

When writing programs that communicate across a computer network, one must first invent a *protocol*, an agreement on how those programs will communicate. Before delving into the design details of a protocol, high-level decisions must be made about which program is expected to initiate communication and when responses are expected. For example, a Web server is typically thought of as a long-running program (or *daemon*) that sends network messages only in response to requests coming in from the network. The other side of the protocol is a Web client, such as a browser, which always initiates communication with the server. This organization into *client* and *server* is used by most network-aware applications. Deciding that the client always initiates requests tends to simplify the protocol as well as the programs themselves. Of course, some of the more complex network applications also require *asynchronous callback* communication, where the server initiates a message to the client. But it is far more common for applications to stick to the basic client/server model shown in Figure 1.1.

Figure 1.1   Network application: client and server.

Clients normally communicate with one server at a time, although using a Web browser as an example, we might communicate with many different Web servers over, say, a 10-minute time period. But from the server's perspective, at any given point in time, it is not unusual for a server to be communicating with multiple clients. We show this in Figure 1.2. Later in this text, we will cover several different ways for a server to handle multiple clients at the same time.

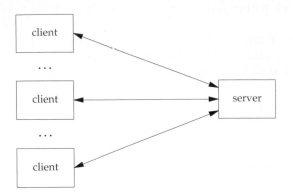

Figure 1.2 Server handling multiple clients at the same time.

The client application and the server application may be thought of as communicating via a network protocol, but actually, multiple layers of network protocols are typically involved. In this text, we focus on the TCP/IP protocol suite, also called the Internet protocol suite. For example, Web clients and servers communicate using the Transmission Control Protocol, or TCP. TCP, in turn, uses the Internet Protocol, or IP, and IP communicates with a datalink layer of some form. If the client and server are on the same Ethernet, we would have the arrangement shown in Figure 1.3.

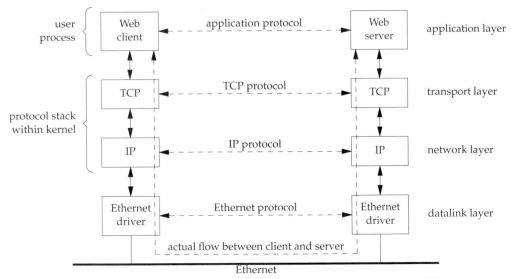

Figure 1.3 Client and server on the same Ethernet communicating using TCP.

Even though the client and server communicate using an application protocol, the transport layers communicate using TCP. Note that the actual flow of information between the client and server goes down the protocol stack on one side, across the network, and up the protocol stack on the other side. Also note that the client and server are typically user processes, while the TCP and IP protocols are normally part of the protocol stack within the kernel. We have labeled the four layers on the right side of Figure 1.3.

TCP and IP are not the only protocols that we will discuss. Some clients and servers use the User Datagram Protocol (UDP) instead of TCP, and we will discuss both protocols in more detail in Chapter 2. Furthermore, we have used the term "IP," but the protocol, which has been in use since the early 1980s, is officially called *IP version 4* (IPv4). A new version, *IP version 6* (IPv6) was developed during the mid-1990s and could potentially replace IPv4 in the years to come. This text covers the development of network applications using both IPv4 and IPv6. Appendix A provides a comparison of IPv4 and IPv6, along with other protocols that we will discuss.

The client and server need not be attached to the same *local area network* (LAN) as we show in Figure 1.3. For instance, in Figure 1.4, we show the client and server on different LANs, with both LANs connected to a *wide area network* (WAN) using *routers*.

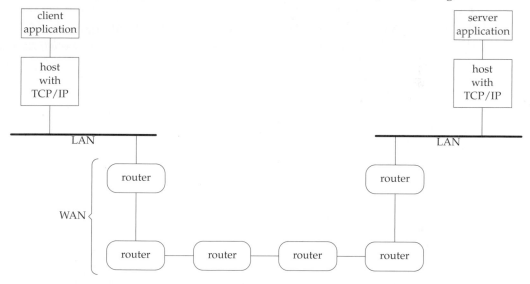

Figure 1.4 Client and server on different LANs connected through a WAN.

Routers are the building blocks of WANs. The largest WAN today is the *Internet*. Many companies build their own WANs and these private WANs may or may not be connected to the Internet.

The remainder of this chapter provides an introduction to the various topics that are covered in detail later in the text. We start with a complete example of a TCP client, albeit a simple one, that demonstrates many of the function calls and concepts that we will encounter throughout the text. This client works with IPv4 only, and we show the changes required to work with IPv6. A better solution is to write protocol-independent clients and servers, and we will discuss this in Chapter 11. This chapter also shows a complete TCP server that works with our client.

To simplify all our code, we define our own wrapper functions for most of the system functions that we call throughout the text. We can use these wrapper functions

most of the time to check for an error, print an appropriate message, and terminate
when an error occurs. We also show the test network, hosts, and routers used for most
examples in the text, along with their hostnames, IP addresses, and operating systems.

Most discussions of Unix these days include the term "X," which is the standard
that most vendors have adopted. We describe the history of POSIX and how it affects
the Application Programming Interfaces (APIs) that we describe in this text, along with
the other players in the standards arena.

1.2 A Simple Daytime Client

Let's consider a specific example to introduce many of the concepts and terms that we
will encounter throughout the book. Figure 1.5 is an implementation of a TCP time-of-
day client. This client establishes a TCP connection with a server and the server simply
sends back the current time and date in a human-readable format.

intro/daytimetcpcli.c

```
 1 #include      "unp.h"

 2 int
 3 main(int argc, char **argv)
 4 {
 5     int        sockfd, n;
 6     char       recvline[MAXLINE + 1];
 7     struct sockaddr_in servaddr;

 8     if (argc != 2)
 9         err_quit("usage: a.out <IPaddress>");

10     if ( (sockfd = socket(AF_INET, SOCK_STREAM, 0)) < 0)
11         err_sys("socket error");

12     bzero(&servaddr, sizeof(servaddr));
13     servaddr.sin_family = AF_INET;
14     servaddr.sin_port = htons(13);   /* daytime server */
15     if (inet_pton(AF_INET, argv[1], &servaddr.sin_addr) <= 0)
16         err_quit("inet_pton error for %s", argv[1]);

17     if (connect(sockfd, (SA *) &servaddr, sizeof(servaddr)) < 0)
18         err_sys("connect error");

19     while ( (n = read(sockfd, recvline, MAXLINE)) > 0) {
20         recvline[n] = 0;          /* null terminate */
21         if (fputs(recvline, stdout) == EOF)
22             err_sys("fputs error");
23     }
24     if (n < 0)
25         err_sys("read error");

26     exit(0);
27 }
```

intro/daytimetcpcli.c

Figure 1.5 TCP daytime client.

This is the format that we will use for all the source code in the text. Each nonblank line is numbered. The text describing portions of the code notes the starting and ending line numbers in the left margin, as shown shortly. Sometimes a paragraph is preceded by a short, descriptive, bold heading, providing a summary statement of the code being described.

The horizontal rules at the beginning and end of a code fragment specify the source code filename: the file `daytimetcpcli.c` in the directory `intro` for this example. Since the source code for all the examples in the text is freely available (see the Preface), this lets you locate the appropriate source file. Compiling, running, and especially modifying these programs while reading this text is an excellent way to learn the concepts of network programming.

Throughout the text, we will use indented, parenthetical notes such as this to describe implementation details and historical points.

If we compile the program into the default `a.out` file and execute it, we will have the following output:

```
solaris % a.out 206.168.112.96          our input
Mon May 26 20:58:40 2003                the program's output
```

Whenever we display interactive input and output, we will show our typed input in **bold** and the computer output `like this`. *Comments are added on the right side in italics.* We will always include the name of the system as part of the shell prompt (`solaris` in this example) to show on which host the command was run. Figure 1.16 shows the systems used to run most of the examples in this book. The hostnames usually describe the operating system (OS) as well.

There are many details to consider in this 27-line program. We mention them briefly here, in case this is your first encounter with a network program, and provide more information on these topics later in the text.

Include our own header

1   We include our own header, `unp.h`, which we will show in Section D.1. This header includes numerous system headers that are needed by most network programs and defines various constants that we use (e.g., `MAXLINE`).

Command-line arguments

2–3   This is the definition of the `main` function along with the command-line arguments. We have written the code in this text assuming an American National Standards Institute (ANSI) C compiler (also referred to as an ISO C compiler).

Create TCP socket

10–11   The `socket` function creates an Internet (`AF_INET`) stream (`SOCK_STREAM`) socket, which is a fancy name for a TCP socket. The function returns a small integer descriptor that we can use to identify the socket in all future function calls (e.g., the calls to `connect` and `read` that follow).

The `if` statement contains a call to the `socket` function, an assignment of the return value to the variable named `sockfd`, and then a test of whether this assigned value is less than 0. While we could break this into two C statements,

```
sockfd = socket(AF_INET, SOCK_STREAM, 0);
if (sockfd < 0)
```

it is a common C idiom to combine the two lines. The set of parentheses around the function call and assignment is required, given the precedence rules of C (the less-than operator has a higher precedence than assignment). As a matter of coding style, the authors always place a space between the two opening parentheses, as a visual indicator that the left-hand side of the comparison is also an assignment. (This style is copied from the Minix source code [Tanenbaum 1987].) We use this same style in the `while` statement later in the program.

We will encounter many different uses of the term "socket." First, the API that we are using is called the *sockets API*. In the preceding paragraph, we referred to a function named `socket` that is part of the sockets API. In the preceding paragraph, we also referred to a TCP socket, which is synonymous with a TCP endpoint.

If the call to `socket` fails, we abort the program by calling our own `err_sys` function. It prints our error message along with a description of the system error that occurred (e.g., "Protocol not supported" is one possible error from `socket`) and terminates the process. This function, and a few others of our own that begin with `err_`, are called throughout the text. We will describe them in Section D.3.

Specify server's IP address and port

12–16   We fill in an Internet socket address structure (a `sockaddr_in` structure named `servaddr`) with the server's IP address and port number. We set the entire structure to 0 using `bzero`, set the address family to `AF_INET`, set the port number to 13 (which is the well-known port of the daytime server on any TCP/IP host that supports this service, as shown in Figure 2.18), and set the IP address to the value specified as the first command-line argument (`argv[1]`). The IP address and port number fields in this structure must be in specific formats: We call the library function `htons` ("host to network short") to convert the binary port number, and we call the library function `inet_pton` ("presentation to numeric") to convert the ASCII command-line argument (such as `206.62.226.35` when we ran this example) into the proper format.

> `bzero` is not an ANSI C function. It is derived from early Berkeley networking code. Nevertheless, we use it throughout the text, instead of the ANSI C `memset` function, because `bzero` is easier to remember (with only two arguments) than `memset` (with three arguments). Almost every vendor that supports the sockets API also provides `bzero`, and if not, we provide a macro definition of it in our `unp.h` header.

> Indeed, the author of TCPv3 made the mistake of swapping the second and third arguments to `memset` in 10 occurrences in the first printing. A C compiler cannot catch this error because both arguments are of the same type. (Actually, the second argument is an `int` and the third argument is `size_t`, which is typically an `unsigned int`, but the values specified, 0 and 16, respectively, are still acceptable for the other type of argument.) The call to `memset` still worked, but did nothing. The number of bytes to initialize was specified as 0. The programs still worked, because only a few of the socket functions actually require that the final 8 bytes of an Internet socket address structure be set to 0. Nevertheless, it was an error, and one that could be avoided by using `bzero`, because swapping the two arguments to `bzero` will always be caught by the C compiler if function prototypes are used.

This may be your first encounter with the inet_pton function. It is new with IPv6 (which we will talk more about in Appendix A). Older code uses the inet_addr function to convert an ASCII dotted-decimal string into the correct format, but this function has numerous limitations that inet_pton corrects. Do not worry if your system does not (yet) support this function; we will provide an implementation of it in Section 3.7.

Establish connection with server

17–18   The connect function, when applied to a TCP socket, establishes a TCP connection with the server specified by the socket address structure pointed to by the second argument. We must also specify the length of the socket address structure as the third argument to connect, and for Internet socket address structures, we always let the compiler calculate the length using C's sizeof operator.

> In the unp.h header, we #define SA to be struct sockaddr, that is, a generic socket address structure. Everytime one of the socket functions requires a pointer to a socket address structure, that pointer must be cast to a pointer to a generic socket address structure. This is because the socket functions predate the ANSI C standard, so the void * pointer type was not available in the early 1980s when these functions were developed. The problem is that "struct sockaddr" is 15 characters and often causes the source code line to extend past the right edge of the screen (or page, in the case of a book), so we shorten it to SA. We will talk more about generic socket address structures when explaining Figure 3.3.

Read and display server's reply

19–25   We read the server's reply and display the result using the standard I/O fputs function. We must be careful when using TCP because it is a *byte-stream* protocol with no record boundaries. The server's reply is normally a 26-byte string of the form

```
Mon May 26 20:58:40 2003\r\n
```

where \r is the ASCII carriage return and \n is the ASCII linefeed. With a byte-stream protocol, these 26 bytes can be returned in numerous ways: a single TCP segment containing all 26 bytes of data, in 26 TCP segments each containing 1 byte of data, or any other combination that totals to 26 bytes. Normally, a single segment containing all 26 bytes of data is returned, but with larger data sizes, we cannot assume that the server's reply will be returned by a single read. Therefore, when reading from a TCP socket, we *always* need to code the read in a loop and terminate the loop when either read returns 0 (i.e., the other end closed the connection) or a value less than 0 (an error).

In this example, the end of the record is being denoted by the server closing the connection. This technique is also used by version 1.0 of the Hypertext Transfer Protocol (HTTP). Other techniques are available. For example, the Simple Mail Transfer Protocol (SMTP) marks the end of a record with the two-byte sequence of an ASCII carriage return followed by an ASCII linefeed. Sun Remote Procedure Call (RPC) and the Domain Name System (DNS) place a binary count containing the record length in front of each record that is sent when using TCP. The important concept here is that TCP itself provides no record markers: If an application wants to delineate the ends of records, it must do so itself and there are a few common ways to accomplish this.

Terminate program

26   exit terminates the program. Unix always closes all open descriptors when a process terminates, so our TCP socket is now closed.

As we mentioned, the text will go into much more detail on all the points we just described.

1.3 Protocol Independence

Our program in Figure 1.5 is *protocol-dependent* on IPv4. We allocate and initialize a
sockaddr_in structure, we set the family of this structure to AF_INET, and we specify
the first argument to socket as AF_INET.

To modify the program to work under IPv6, we must change the code. Figure 1.6
shows a version that works under IPv6, with the changes highlighted in bold.

intro/daytimetcpcliv6.c

```
 1 #include    "unp.h"

 2 int
 3 main(int argc, char **argv)
 4 {
 5     int     sockfd, n;
 6     char    recvline[MAXLINE + 1];
 7     struct sockaddr_in6 servaddr;

 8     if (argc != 2)
 9         err_quit("usage: a.out <IPaddress>");

10     if ( (sockfd = socket(AF_INET6, SOCK_STREAM, 0)) < 0)
11         err_sys("socket error");

12     bzero(&servaddr, sizeof(servaddr));
13     servaddr.sin6_family = AF_INET6;
14     servaddr.sin6_port = htons(13);     /* daytime server */
15     if (inet_pton(AF_INET6, argv[1], &servaddr.sin6_addr) <= 0)
16         err_quit("inet_pton error for %s", argv[1]);

17     if (connect(sockfd, (SA *) &servaddr, sizeof(servaddr)) < 0)
18         err_sys("connect error");

19     while ( (n = read(sockfd, recvline, MAXLINE)) > 0) {
20         recvline[n] = 0;       /* null terminate */
21         if (fputs(recvline, stdout) == EOF)
22             err_sys("fputs error");
23     }
24     if (n < 0)
25         err_sys("read error");

26     exit(0);
27 }
```

intro/daytimetcpcliv6.c

Figure 1.6 Version of Figure 1.5 for IPv6.

Only five lines are changed, but what we now have is another protocol-dependent program; this time, it is dependent on IPv6. It is better to make a program
protocol-independent. Figure 11.11 will show a version of this client that is protocol-independent by using the getaddrinfo function (which is called by tcp_connect).

Another deficiency in our programs is that the user must enter the server's IP address as a dotted-decimal number (e.g., 206.168.112.219 for the IPv4 version). Humans work better with names instead of numbers (e.g., `www.unpbook.com`). In Chapter 11, we will discuss the functions that convert between hostnames and IP addresses, and between service names and ports. We purposely put off the discussion of these functions and continue using IP addresses and port numbers so we know exactly what goes into the socket address structures that we must fill in and examine. This also avoids complicating our discussion of network programming with the details of yet another set of functions.

1.4   Error Handling: Wrapper Functions

In any real-world program, it is essential to check *every* function call for an error return. In Figure 1.5, we check for errors from `socket`, `inet_pton`, `connect`, `read`, and `fputs`, and when one occurs, we call our own functions, `err_quit` and `err_sys`, to print an error message and terminate the program. We find that most of the time, this is what we want to do. Occasionally, we want to do something other than terminate when one of these functions returns an error, as in Figure 5.12, when we must check for an interrupted system call.

Since terminating on an error is the common case, we can shorten our programs by defining a *wrapper function* that performs the actual function call, tests the return value, and terminates on an error. The convention we use is to capitalize the name of the function, as in

```
sockfd = Socket(AF_INET, SOCK_STREAM, 0);
```

Our wrapper function is shown in Figure 1.7.

lib/wrapsock.c

```
236 int
237 Socket(int family, int type, int protocol)
238 {
239     int     n;

240     if ( (n = socket(family, type, protocol)) < 0)
241         err_sys("socket error");
242     return (n);
243 }
```
lib/wrapsock.c

Figure 1.7 Our wrapper function for the `socket` function.

Whenever you encounter a function name in the text that begins with an uppercase letter, that is one of our wrapper functions. It calls a function whose name is the same but begins with the lowercase letter.

When describing the source code that is presented in the text, we always refer to the lowest level function being called (e.g., `socket`), not the wrapper function (e.g., `Socket`).

While these wrapper functions might not seem like a big savings, when we discuss threads in Chapter 26, we will find that thread functions do not set the standard Unix `errno` variable when an error occurs; instead, the `errno` value is the return value of the function. This means that every time we call one of the `pthread_` functions, we must allocate a variable, save the return value in that variable, and then set `errno` to this value before calling `err_sys`. To avoid cluttering the code with braces, we can use C's comma operator to combine the assignment into `errno` and the call of `err_sys` into a single statement, as in the following:

```
int     n;

if ( (n = pthread_mutex_lock(&ndone_mutex)) != 0)
    errno = n, err_sys("pthread_mutex_lock error");
```

Alternately, we could define a new error function that takes the system's error number as an argument. But, we can make this piece of code much easier to read as just

```
Pthread_mutex_lock(&ndone_mutex);
```

by defining our own wrapper function, as shown in Figure 1.8.

—— *lib/wrappthread.c*
```
72 void
73 Pthread_mutex_lock(pthread_mutex_t *mptr)
74 {
75     int     n;

76     if ( (n = pthread_mutex_lock(mptr)) == 0)
77         return;
78     errno = n;
79     err_sys("pthread_mutex_lock error");
80 }
```
—— *lib/wrappthread.c*

Figure 1.8 Our wrapper function for `pthread_mutex_lock`.

> With careful C coding, we could use macros instead of functions, providing a little run-time efficiency, but these wrapper functions are rarely the performance bottleneck of a program.
>
> Our choice of capitalizing the first character of a function name is a compromise. Many other styles were considered: prefixing the function name with an "e" (as done on p. 182 of [Kernighan and Pike 1984]), appending "_e" to the function name, and so on. Our style seems the least distracting while still providing a visual indication that some other function is really being called.
>
> This technique has the side benefit of checking for errors from functions whose error returns are often ignored: `close` and `listen`, for example.

Throughout the rest of this book, we will use these wrapper functions unless we need to check for an explicit error and handle it in some way other than terminating the process. We do not show the source code for all our wrapper functions, but the code is freely available (see the Preface).

Unix `errno` Value

When an error occurs in a Unix function (such as one of the socket functions), the global variable `errno` is set to a positive value indicating the type of error and the function normally returns –1. Our `err_sys` function looks at the value of `errno` and prints the corresponding error message string (e.g., "Connection timed out" if `errno` equals `ETIMEDOUT`).

The value of `errno` is set by a function only if an error occurs. Its value is undefined if the function does not return an error. All of the positive error values are constants with all-uppercase names beginning with "E," and are normally defined in the `<sys/errno.h>` header. No error has a value of 0.

Storing `errno` in a global variable does not work with multiple threads that share all global variables. We will talk about solutions to this problem in Chapter 26.

Throughout the text, we will use phrases such as "the `connect` function returns `ECONNREFUSED`" as shorthand to mean that the function returns an error (typically with a return value of –1), with `errno` set to the specified constant.

1.5   A Simple Daytime Server

We can write a simple version of a TCP daytime server, which will work with the client from Section 1.2. We use the wrapper functions that we described in the previous section and show this server in Figure 1.9.

Create a TCP socket

10   The creation of the TCP socket is identical to the client code.

Bind server's well-known port to socket

11–15   The server's well-known port (13 for the daytime service) is bound to the socket by filling in an Internet socket address structure and calling `bind`. We specify the IP address as `INADDR_ANY`, which allows the server to accept a client connection on any interface, in case the server host has multiple interfaces. Later we will see how we can restrict the server to accepting a client connection on just a single interface.

Convert socket to listening socket

16   By calling `listen`, the socket is converted into a listening socket, on which incoming connections from clients will be accepted by the kernel. These three steps, `socket`, `bind`, and `listen`, are the normal steps for any TCP server to prepare what we call the *listening descriptor* (`listenfd` in this example).

The constant `LISTENQ` is from our `unp.h` header. It specifies the maximum number of client connections that the kernel will queue for this listening descriptor. We say much more about this queueing in Section 4.5.

intro/daytimetcpsrv.c

```
 1 #include     "unp.h"
 2 #include     <time.h>

 3 int
 4 main(int argc, char **argv)
 5 {
 6     int      listenfd, connfd;
 7     struct sockaddr_in servaddr;
 8     char     buff[MAXLINE];
 9     time_t  ticks;

10     listenfd = Socket(AF_INET, SOCK_STREAM, 0);

11     bzero(&servaddr, sizeof(servaddr));
12     servaddr.sin_family = AF_INET;
13     servaddr.sin_addr.s_addr = htonl(INADDR_ANY);
14     servaddr.sin_port = htons(13);   /* daytime server */

15     Bind(listenfd, (SA *) &servaddr, sizeof(servaddr));

16     Listen(listenfd, LISTENQ);

17     for ( ; ; ) {
18         connfd = Accept(listenfd, (SA *) NULL, NULL);

19         ticks = time(NULL);
20         snprintf(buff, sizeof(buff), "%.24s\r\n", ctime(&ticks));
21         Write(connfd, buff, strlen(buff));

22         Close(connfd);
23     }
24 }
```

intro/daytimetcpsrv.c

Figure 1.9   TCP daytime server.

Accept client connection, send reply

17–21   Normally, the server process is put to sleep in the call to accept, waiting for a client connection to arrive and be accepted. A TCP connection uses what is called a *three-way handshake* to establish a connection. When this handshake completes, accept returns, and the return value from the function is a new descriptor (connfd) that is called the *connected descriptor*. This new descriptor is used for communication with the new client. A new descriptor is returned by accept for each client that connects to our server.

> The style used throughout the book for an infinite loop is
> ```
> for ( ; ; ) {
>     . . .
> }
> ```

The current time and date are returned by the library function time, which returns the number of seconds since the Unix Epoch: 00:00:00 January 1, 1970, Coordinated

Universal Time (UTC). The next library function, `ctime`, converts this integer value into a human-readable string such as

```
Mon May 26 20:58:40 2003
```

A carriage return and linefeed are appended to the string by `snprintf`, and the result is written to the client by `write`.

> If you're not already in the habit of using `snprintf` instead of the older `sprintf`, now's the time to learn. Calls to `sprintf` cannot check for overflow of the destination buffer. `snprintf`, on the other hand, requires that the second argument be the size of the destination buffer, and this buffer will not overflow.
>
> `snprintf` was a relatively late addition to the ANSI C standard, introduced in the version referred to as *ISO C99*. Virtually all vendors provide it as part of the standard C library, and many freely available versions are also available. We use `snprintf` throughout the text, and we recommend using it instead of `sprintf` in all your programs for reliability.
>
> It is remarkable how many network break-ins have occurred by a hacker sending data to cause a server's call to `sprintf` to overflow its buffer. Other functions that we should be careful with are `gets`, `strcat`, and `strcpy`, normally calling `fgets`, `strncat`, and `strncpy` instead. Even better are the more recently available functions `strlcat` and `strlcpy`, which ensure the result is a properly terminated string. Additional tips on writing secure network programs are found in Chapter 23 of [Garfinkel, Schwartz, and Spafford 2003].

Terminate connection

22   The server closes its connection with the client by calling `close`. This initiates the normal TCP connection termination sequence: a FIN is sent in each direction and each FIN is acknowledged by the other end. We will say much more about TCP's three-way handshake and the four TCP packets used to terminate a TCP connection in Section 2.6.

As with the client in the previous section, we have only examined this server briefly, saving all the details for later in the book. Note the following points:

- As with the client, the server is protocol-dependent on IPv4. We will show a protocol-independent version that uses the `getaddrinfo` function in Figure 11.13.

- Our server handles only one client at a time. If multiple client connections arrive at about the same time, the kernel queues them, up to some limit, and returns them to `accept` one at a time. This daytime server, which requires calling two library functions, `time` and `ctime`, is quite fast. But if the server took more time to service each client (say a few seconds or a minute), we would need some way to overlap the service of one client with another client.

The server that we show in Figure 1.9 is called an *iterative server* because it iterates through each client, one at a time. There are numerous techniques for writing a *concurrent server*, one that handles multiple clients at the same time. The simplest technique for a concurrent server is to call the Unix `fork` function (Section 4.7), creating one child process for each client. Other techniques are to use threads instead of `fork` (Section 26.4), or to pre-`fork` a fixed number of children when the server starts (Section 30.6).

- If we start a server like this from a shell command line, we might want the server to run for a long time, since servers often run for as long as the system is up. This requires that we add code to the server to run correctly as a Unix *daemon*: a process that can run in the background, unattached to a terminal. We will cover this in Section 13.4.

1.6 Roadmap to Client/Server Examples in the Text

Two client/server examples are used predominantly throughout the text to illustrate the various techniques used in network programming:

- A daytime client/server (which we started in Figures 1.5, 1.6, and 1.9)
- An echo client/server (which will start in Chapter 5)

To provide a roadmap for the different topics that are covered in this text, we will summarize the programs that we will develop, and give the starting figure number and page number in which the source code appears. Figure 1.10 lists the versions of the daytime client, two versions of which we have already seen. Figure 1.11 lists the versions of the daytime server. Figure 1.12 lists the versions of the echo client, and Figure 1.13 lists the versions of the echo server.

Figure	Page	Description
1.5	6	TCP/IPv4, protocol-dependent
1.6	10	TCP/IPv6, protocol-dependent
11.4	313	TCP/IPv4, protocol-dependent, calls `gethostbyname` and `getservbyname`
11.11	328	TCP, protocol-independent, calls `getaddrinfo` and `tcp_connect`
11.16	336	UDP, protocol-independent, calls `getaddrinfo` and `udp_client`
16.11	450	TCP, uses nonblocking `connect`
31.8	859	TCP, protocol-dependent, uses TPI instead of sockets
E.1	917	TCP, protocol-dependent, generates `SIGPIPE`
E.5	920	TCP, protocol-dependent, prints socket receive buffer sizes and MSS
E.11	931	TCP, protocol-dependent, allows hostname (`gethostbyname`) or IP address
E.12	932	TCP, protocol-independent, allows hostname (`gethostbyname`)

Figure 1.10 Different versions of the daytime client developed in the text.

Figure	Page	Description
1.9	14	TCP/IPv4, protocol-dependent
11.13	332	TCP, protocol-independent, calls `getaddrinfo` and `tcp_listen`
11.14	334	TCP, protocol-independent, calls `getaddrinfo` and `tcp_listen`
11.19	339	UDP, protocol-independent, calls `getaddrinfo` and `udp_server`
13.5	371	TCP, protocol-independent, runs as standalone daemon
13.12	378	TCP, protocol-independent, spawned from `inetd` daemon

Figure 1.11　Different versions of the daytime server developed in the text.

Figure	Page	Description
5.4	124	TCP/IPv4, protocol-dependent
6.9	168	TCP, uses `select`
6.13	174	TCP, uses `select` and operates on buffers
8.7	244	UDP/IPv4, protocol-dependent
8.9	247	UDP, verifies server's address
8.17	256	UDP, calls `connect` to obtain asynchronous errors
14.2	384	UDP, times out when reading server's reply using `SIGALRM`
14.4	386	UDP, times out when reading server's reply using `select`
14.5	387	UDP, times out when reading server's reply using `SO_RCVTIMEO`
15.4	418	Unix domain stream, protocol-dependent
15.6	419	Unix domain datagram, protocol-dependent
16.3	438	TCP, uses nonblocking I/O
16.10	447	TCP, uses two processes (`fork`)
16.21	462	TCP, establishes connection then sends RST
14.15	404	TCP, uses `/dev/poll` for multiplexing
14.18	407	TCP, uses `kqueue` for multiplexing
20.5	537	UDP, broadcasts with race condition
20.6	540	UDP, broadcasts with race condition
20.7	542	UDP, broadcasts, race condition fixed by using `pselect`
20.9	544	UDP, broadcasts, race condition fixed by using `sigsetjmp` and `siglongjmp`
20.10	547	UDP, broadcasts, race condition fixed by using IPC from signal handler
22.6	600	UDP, reliable using timeout, retransmit, and sequence number
26.2	680	TCP, uses two threads
27.6	716	TCP/IPv4, specifies a source route
27.13	729	UDP/IPv6, specifies a source route

Figure 1.12　Different versions of the echo client developed in the text.

Figure	Page	Description
5.2	123	TCP/IPv4, protocol-dependent
5.12	139	TCP/IPv4, protocol-dependent, reaps terminated children
6.21	178	TCP/IPv4, protocol-dependent, uses `select`, one process handles all clients
6.25	186	TCP/IPv4, protocol-dependent, uses `poll`, one process handles all clients
8.3	242	UDP/IPv4, protocol-dependent
8.24	263	TCP and UDP/IPv4, protocol-dependent, uses `select`
14.14	400	TCP, uses standard I/O library
15.3	417	Unix domain stream, protocol-dependent
15.5	418	Unix domain datagram, protocol-dependent
15.15	431	Unix domain stream, with credential passing from client
22.4	593	UDP, receives destination address and received interface; truncated datagrams
22.15	609	UDP, binds all interface addresses
25.4	668	UDP, uses signal-driven I/O
26.3	682	TCP, one thread per client
26.4	684	TCP, one thread per client, portable argument passing
27.6	716	TCP/IPv4, prints received source route
27.14	730	UDP/IPv6, prints and reverses received source route
28.31	773	UDP, uses `icmpd` to receive asynchronous errors
E.15	943	UDP, binds all interface addresses

Figure 1.13 Different versions of the echo server developed in the text.

1.7 OSI Model

A common way to describe the layers in a network is to use the International Organization for Standardization (ISO) *open systems interconnection* (OSI) model for computer communications. This is a seven-layer model, which we show in Figure 1.14, along with the approximate mapping to the Internet protocol suite.

We consider the bottom two layers of the OSI model as the device driver and networking hardware that are supplied with the system. Normally, we need not concern ourselves with these layers other than being aware of some properties of the datalink, such as the 1500-byte Ethernet maximum transfer unit (MTU), which we describe in Section 2.11.

The network layer is handled by the IPv4 and IPv6 protocols, both of which we will describe in Appendix A. The transport layers that we can choose from are TCP and UDP, and we will describe these in Chapter 2. We show a gap between TCP and UDP in Figure 1.14 to indicate that it is possible for an application to bypass the transport layer and use IPv4 or IPv6 directly. This is called a *raw socket*, and we will talk about this in Chapter 28.

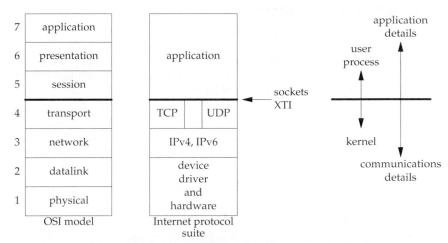

Figure 1.14 Layers in OSI model and Internet protocol suite.

The upper three layers of the OSI model are combined into a single layer called the application. This is the Web client (browser), Telnet client, Web server, FTP server, or whatever application we are using. With the Internet protocols, there is rarely any distinction between the upper three layers of the OSI model.

The sockets programming interfaces described in this book are interfaces from the upper three layers (the "application") into the transport layer. This is the focus of this book: how to write applications using sockets that use either TCP or UDP. We already mentioned raw sockets, and in Chapter 29 we will see that we can even bypass the IP layer completely to read and write our own datalink-layer frames.

Why do sockets provide the interface from the upper three layers of the OSI model into the transport layer? There are two reasons for this design, which we note on the right side of Figure 1.14. First, the upper three layers handle all the details of the application (FTP, Telnet, or HTTP, for example) and know little about the communication details. The lower four layers know little about the application, but handle all the communication details: sending data, waiting for acknowledgments, sequencing data that arrives out of order, calculating and verifying checksums, and so on. The second reason is that the upper three layers often form what is called a *user process* while the lower four layers are normally provided as part of the operating system (OS) kernel. Unix provides this separation between the user process and the kernel, as do many other contemporary operating systems. Therefore, the interface between layers 4 and 5 is the natural place to build the API.

1.8   BSD Networking History

The sockets API originated with the 4.2BSD system, released in 1983. Figure 1.15 shows the development of the various BSD releases, noting the major TCP/IP developments. A few changes to the sockets API also took place in 1990 with the 4.3BSD Reno release, when the OSI protocols went into the BSD kernel.

The path down the figure from 4.2BSD through 4.4BSD shows the releases from the Computer Systems Research Group (CSRG) at Berkeley, which required the recipient to already have a source code license for Unix. But all the networking code, both the kernel support (such as the TCP/IP and Unix domain protocol stacks and the socket interface), along with the applications (such as the Telnet and FTP clients and servers), were developed independently from the AT&T-derived Unix code. Therefore, starting in 1989, Berkeley provided the first of the BSD networking releases, which contained all the networking code and various other pieces of the BSD system that were not constrained by the Unix source code license requirement. These releases were "publicly available" and eventually became available by anonymous FTP to anyone.

The final releases from Berkeley were 4.4BSD-Lite in 1994 and 4.4BSD-Lite2 in 1995. We note that these two releases were then used as the base for other systems: BSD/OS, FreeBSD, NetBSD, and OpenBSD, most of which are still being actively developed and enhanced. More information on the various BSD releases, and on the history of the various Unix systems in general, can be found in Chapter 1 of [McKusick et al. 1996].

Many Unix systems started with some version of the BSD networking code, including the sockets API, and we refer to these implementations as *Berkeley-derived implementations*. Many commercial versions of Unix are based on System V Release 4 (SVR4). Some of these versions have Berkeley-derived networking code (e.g., UnixWare 2.x), while the networking code in other SVR4 systems has been independently derived (e.g., Solaris 2.x). We also note that Linux, a popular, freely available implementation of Unix, does *not* fit into the Berkeley-derived classification: Its networking code and sockets API were developed from scratch.

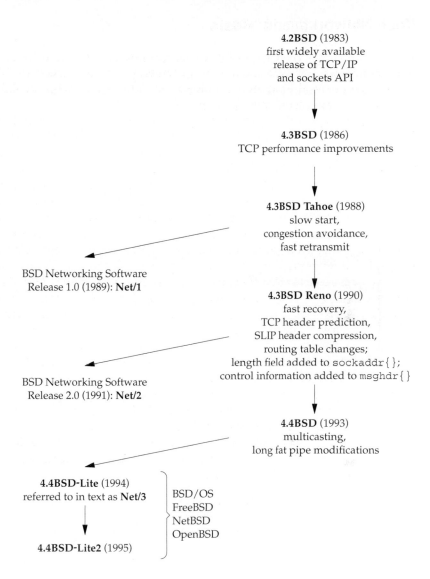

Figure 1.15 History of various BSD releases.

1.9   Test Networks and Hosts

Figure 1.16 shows the various networks and hosts used in the examples throughout the text. For each host, we show the OS and the type of hardware (since some of the operating systems run on more than one type of hardware). The name within each box is the hostname that appears in the text.

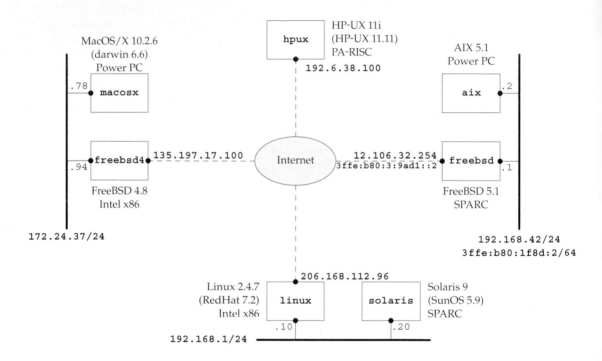

Figure 1.16 Networks and hosts used for most examples in the text.

The topology shown in Figure 1.16 is interesting for the sake of our examples, but the machines are largely spread out across the Internet and the physical topology becomes less interesting in practice. Instead, virtual private networks (VPNs) or secure shell (SSH) connections provide connectivity between these machines regardless of where they live physically.

The notation "/24" indicates the number of consecutive bits starting from the leftmost bit of the address used to identify the network and subnet. Section A.4 will talk about the /n notation used today to designate subnet boundaries.

> The real name of the Sun OS is SunOS 5.x and not Solaris 2.x, but everyone refers to it as Solaris, the name given to the sum of the OS and other software bundled with the base OS.

Discovering Network Topology

We show the network topology in Figure 1.16 for the hosts used for the examples throughout this text, but you may need to know your own network topology to run the examples and exercises on your own network. Although there are no current Unix standards with regard to network configuration and administration, two basic commands are provided by most Unix systems and can be used to discover some details of a network: `netstat` and `ifconfig`. Check the manual (man) pages for these commands on your system to see the details on the information that is output. Also be aware that some vendors place these commands in an administrative directory, such as /sbin or /usr/sbin, instead of the normal /usr/bin, and these directories might not be in your normal shell search path (PATH).

1. `netstat -i` provides information on the interfaces. We also specify the `-n` flag to print numeric addresses, instead of trying to find names for the networks. This shows us the interfaces and their names.

```
linux % netstat -ni
Kernel Interface table
Iface   MTU Met   RX-OK RX-ERR RX-DRP RX-OVR   TX-OK TX-ERR TX-DRP TX-OVR Flg
eth0    1500      049211085      0      0    040540958      0      0      0 BMRU
lo      16436     098613572      0      0    098613572      0      0      0 LRU
```

The loopback interface is called `lo` and the Ethernet is called `eth0`. The next example shows a host with IPv6 support.

```
freebsd % netstat -ni
Name    Mtu Network      Address          Ipkts Ierrs    Opkts Oerrs   Coll
hme0    1500 <Link#1>     08:00:20:a7:68:6b 29100435    35 46561488      0      0
hme0    1500 12.106.32/24 12.106.32.254    28746630     - 46617260      -      -
hme0    1500 fe80:1::a00:20ff:fea7:686b/64
                         fe80:1::a00:20ff:fea7:686b
                                               0       -        0      -      -
hme0    1500 3ffe:b80:1f8d:1::1/64
                         3ffe:b80:1f8d:1::1     0       -        0      -      -
hme1    1500 <Link#2>     08:00:20:a7:68:6b    51092     0    31537      0      0
hme1    1500 fe80:2::a00:20ff:fea7:686b/64
                         fe80:2::a00:20ff:fea7:686b
                                               0       -       90      -      -
hme1    1500 192.168.42   192.168.42.1        43584     -    24173      -      -
hme1    1500 3ffe:b80:1f8d:2::1/64
                         3ffe:b80:1f8d:2::1    78       -        8      -      -
lo0     16384 <Link#6>                        10198     0    10198      0      0
lo0     16384 ::1/128      ::1                  10       -       10      -      -
lo0     16384 fe80:6::1/64 fe80:6::1            0       -        0      -      -
lo0     16384 127          127.0.0.1         10167       -    10167      -      -
gif0    1280 <Link#8>                            6       0        5      0      0
gif0    1280 3ffe:b80:3:9ad1::2/128
                         3ffe:b80:3:9ad1::2     0       -        0      -      -
gif0    1280 fe80:8::a00:20ff:fea7:686b/64
                         fe80:8::a00:20ff:fea7:686b
                                               0       -        0      -      -
```

Note: We have wrapped some of the longer lines to align the output fields.

2. `netstat -r` shows the routing table, which is another way to determine the interfaces. We normally specify the `-n` flag to print numeric addresses. This also shows the IP address of the default router.

```
freebsd % netstat -nr
Routing tables

Internet:
Destination         Gateway              Flags   Refs      Use  Netif Expire
default             12.106.32.1          UGSc      10     6877  hme0
12.106.32/24        link#1               UC         3        0  hme0
12.106.32.1         00:b0:8e:92:2c:00    UHLW       9        7  hme0    1187
12.106.32.253       08:00:20:b8:f7:e0    UHLW       0        1  hme0     140
12.106.32.254       08:00:20:a7:68:6b    UHLW       0        2  lo0
127.0.0.1           127.0.0.1            UH         1    10167  lo0
192.168.42          link#2               UC         2        0  hme1
192.168.42.1        08:00:20:a7:68:6b    UHLW       0       11  lo0
192.168.42.2        00:04:ac:17:bf:38    UHLW       2    24108  hme1     210

Internet6:
Destination                             Gateway                  Flags      Netif Expire
::/96                                   ::1                      UGRSc      lo0 =>
default                                 3ffe:b80:3:9ad1::1       UGSc       gif0
::1                                     ::1                      UH         lo0
::ffff:0.0.0.0/96                       ::1                      UGRSc      lo0
3ffe:b80:3:9ad1::1                      3ffe:b80:3:9ad1::2       UH         gif0
3ffe:b80:3:9ad1::2                      link#8                   UHL        lo0
3ffe:b80:1f8d::/48                      lo0                      USc        lo0
3ffe:b80:1f8d:1::/64                    link#1                   UC         hme0
3ffe:b80:1f8d:1::1                      08:00:20:a7:68:6b        UHL        lo0
3ffe:b80:1f8d:2::/64                    link#2                   UC         hme1
3ffe:b80:1f8d:2::1                      08:00:20:a7:68:6b        UHL        lo0
3ffe:b80:1f8d:2:204:acff:fe17:bf38 00:04:ac:17:bf:38            UHLW       hme1
fe80::/10                               ::1                      UGRSc      lo0
fe80::%hme0/64                          link#1                   UC         hme0
fe80::a00:20ff:fea7:686b%hme0           08:00:20:a7:68:6b        UHL        lo0
fe80::%hme1/64                          link#2                   UC         hme1
fe80::a00:20ff:fea7:686b%hme1           08:00:20:a7:68:6b        UHL        lo0
fe80::%lo0/64                           fe80::1%lo0              Uc         lo0
fe80::1%lo0                             link#6                   UHL        lo0
fe80::%gif0/64                          link#8                   UC         gif0
fe80::a00:20ff:fea7:686b%gif0           link#8                   UHL        lo0
ff01::/32                               ::1                      U          lo0
ff02::/16                               ::1                      UGRS       lo0
ff02::%hme0/32                          link#1                   UC         hme0
ff02::%hme1/32                          link#2                   UC         hme1
ff02::%lo0/32                           ::1                      UC         lo0
ff02::%gif0/32                          link#8                   UC         gif0
```

3. Given the interface names, we execute `ifconfig` to obtain the details for each
    interface.

```
linux % ifconfig eth0
eth0      Link encap:Ethernet  HWaddr 00:C0:9F:06:B0:E1
          inet addr:206.168.112.96  Bcast:206.168.112.127  Mask:255.255.255.128
          UP BROADCAST RUNNING MULTICAST  MTU:1500  Metric:1
          RX packets:49214397 errors:0 dropped:0 overruns:0 frame:0
          TX packets:40543799 errors:0 dropped:0 overruns:0 carrier:0
          collisions:0 txqueuelen:100
          RX bytes:1098069974 (1047.2 Mb)  TX bytes:3360546472 (3204.8 Mb)
          Interrupt:11 Base address:0x6000
```

This shows the IP address, subnet mask, and broadcast address. The MULTICAST
flag is often an indication that the host supports multicasting. Some implementations provide a -a flag, which prints information on all configured interfaces.

4   One way to find the IP address of many hosts on the local network is to `ping` the
    broadcast address (which we found in the previous step).

```
linux % ping -b 206.168.112.127
WARNING: pinging broadcast address
PING 206.168.112.127 (206.168.112.127) from 206.168.112.96 : 56(84) bytes of data.
64 bytes from 206.168.112.96: icmp_seq=0 ttl=255 time=241 usec
64 bytes from 206.168.112.40: icmp_seq=0 ttl=255 time=2.566 msec (DUP!)
64 bytes from 206.168.112.118: icmp_seq=0 ttl=255 time=2.973 msec (DUP!)
64 bytes from 206.168.112.14: icmp_seq=0 ttl=255 time=3.089 msec (DUP!)
64 bytes from 206.168.112.126: icmp_seq=0 ttl=255 time=3.200 msec (DUP!)
64 bytes from 206.168.112.71: icmp_seq=0 ttl=255 time=3.311 msec (DUP!)
64 bytes from 206.168.112.31: icmp_seq=0 ttl=64 time=3.541 msec (DUP!)
64 bytes from 206.168.112.7: icmp_seq=0 ttl=255 time=3.636 msec (DUP!)
...
```

1.10 Unix Standards

At the time of this writing, the most interesting Unix standardization activity was being
done by The Austin Common Standards Revision Group (CSRG). Their efforts have
produced roughly 4,000 pages of specifications covering over 1,700 programming interfaces [Josey 2002]. These specifications carry both the IEEE POSIX designation as well as
The Open Group's Technical Standard designation. The net result is that you'll likely
encounter references to the same standard by various names: ISO/IEC 9945:2002, IEEE
Std 1003.1-2001, and the Single Unix Specification Version 3, for example. In this text,
we will refer to this standard as simply *The POSIX Specification*, except in sections like
this one where we are discussing specifics of various older standards.

The easiest way to acquire a copy of this consolidated standard is to either order it
on CD-ROM or access it via the Web (free of charge). The starting point for either of
these methods is

    http://www.UNIX.org/version3

Background on POSIX

POSIX is an acronym for Portable Operating System Interface. POSIX is not a single standard, but a family of standards being developed by the Institute for Electrical and Electronics Engineers, Inc., normally called the *IEEE*. The POSIX standards have also been adopted as international standards by ISO and the International Electrotechnical Commission (IEC), called ISO/IEC. The POSIX standards have an interesting history, which we cover only briefly here:

- IEEE Std 1003.1–1988 (317 pages) was the first POSIX standard. It specified the C language interface into a Unix-like kernel and covered the following areas: process primitives (`fork`, `exec`, signals, and timers), the environment of a process (user IDs and process groups), files and directories (all the I/O functions), terminal I/O, system databases (password file and group file), and the `tar` and `cpio` archive formats.

  > The first POSIX standard was a trial-use version in 1986 known as "IEEE-IX." The name "POSIX" was suggested by Richard Stallman.

- IEEE Std 1003.1–1990 (356 pages) was next, and it was also known as ISO/IEC 9945–1: 1990. Minimal changes were made from the 1988 to the 1990 version. Appended to the title was "Part 1: System Application Program Interface (API) [C Language]," indicating that this standard was the C language API.

- IEEE Std 1003.2–1992 came next in two volumes (about 1,300 pages). Its title contained "Part 2: Shell and Utilities." This part defined the shell (based on the System V Bourne shell) and about 100 utilities (programs normally executed from a shell, from `awk` and `basename` to `vi` and `yacc`). Throughout this text, we will refer to this standard as *POSIX.2*.

- IEEE Std 1003.1b–1993 (590 pages) was originally known as IEEE P1003.4. This was an update to the 1003.1–1990 standard to include the real-time extensions developed by the P1003.4 working group. The 1003.1b–1993 standard added the following items to the 1990 standard: file synchronization, asynchronous I/O, semaphores, memory management (`mmap` and shared memory), execution scheduling, clocks and timers, and message queues.

- IEEE Std 1003.1, 1996 Edition [IEEE 1996] (743 pages) came next and included 1003.1–1990 (the base API), 1003.1b–1993 (real-time extensions), 1003.1c–1995 (`pthreads`), and 1003.1i–1995 (technical corrections to 1003.1b). This standard was also called ISO/IEC 9945–1: 1996. Three chapters on threads were added, along with additional sections on thread synchronization (mutexes and condition variables), thread scheduling, and synchronization scheduling. Throughout this text, we will refer to this standard as *POSIX.1*. This standard also contains a Foreword stating that ISO/IEC 9945 consists of the following parts:

  - Part 1: System API (C language)
  - Part 2: Shell and utilities
  - Part 3: System administration (under development)

Parts 1 and 2 are what we call POSIX.1 and POSIX.2.

> Over one-quarter of the 743 pages are an appendix titled "Rationale and Notes." This appendix contains historical information and reasons why certain features were included or omitted. Often, the rationale is as informative as the official standard.

- IEEE Std 1003.1g: Protocol-independent interfaces (PII) became an approved standard in 2000. Until the introduction of The Single Unix Specification Version 3, this POSIX work was the most relevant to the topics covered in this book. This is the networking API standard and it defines two APIs, which it calls Detailed Network Interfaces (DNIs):

  1. DNI/Socket, based on the 4.4BSD sockets API

  2. DNI/XTI, based on the X/Open XPG4 specification
  Work on this standard started in the late 1980s as the P1003.12 working group (later renamed P1003.1g). Throughout this text, we will refer to this standard as *POSIX.1g*.

The current status of the various POSIX standards is available from

```
http://www.pasc.org/standing/sd11.html
```

Background on The Open Group

The Open Group was formed in 1996 by the consolidation of the X/Open Company (founded in 1984) and the Open Software Foundation (OSF, founded in 1988). It is an international consortium of vendors and end-user customers from industry, government, and academia. Here is a brief background on the standards they produced:

- X/Open published the *X/Open Portability Guide*, Issue 3 (XPG3) in 1989.

- Issue 4 was published in 1992, followed by Issue 4, Version 2 in 1994. This latest version was also known as "Spec 1170," with the magic number 1,170 being the sum of the number of system interfaces (926), the number of headers (70), and the number of commands (174). The latest name for this set of specifications is the "X/Open Single Unix Specification," although it is also called "Unix 95."

- In March 1997, Version 2 of the Single Unix Specification was announced. Products conforming to this specification were called "Unix 98." We will refer to this specification as just "Unix 98" throughout this text. The number of interfaces required by Unix 98 increases from 1,170 to 1,434, although for a workstation this jumps to 3,030, because it includes the Common Desktop Environment (CDE), which in turn requires the X Window System and the Motif user interface. Details are available in [Josey 1997] and at `http://www.UNIX.org/version2`. The networking services that are part of Unix 98 are defined for both the sockets and XTI APIs. This specification is nearly identical to POSIX.1g.

  > Unfortunately, Unix 98 referred to networking standards as XNS: X/Open Networking Services. The version of this document that defines sockets and XTI for Unix 98 ([Open Group 1997]) is called "XNS Issue 5." In the networking world XNS has always been an abbreviation

for the Xerox Network Systems architecture. We will avoid this use of XNS and refer to this X/Open document as just the Unix 98 network API standard.

Unification of Standards

The above brief backgrounds on POSIX and The Open Group both continue with The Austin Group's publication of The Single Unix Specification Version 3, as mentioned at the beginning of this section. Getting over 50 companies to agree on a single standard is certainly a landmark in the history of Unix. Most Unix systems today conform to some version of POSIX.1 and POSIX.2; many comply with The Single Unix Specification Version 3.

Historically, most Unix systems show either a Berkeley heritage or a System V heritage, but these differences are slowly disappearing as most vendors adopt the standards. The main differences still existing deal with system administration, one area that no standard currently addresses.

The focus of this book is on The Single Unix Specification Version 3, with our main focus on the sockets API. Whenever possible we will use the standard functions.

Internet Engineering Task Force (IETF)

The Internet Engineering Task Force (IETF) is a large, open, international community of network designers, operators, vendors, and researchers concerned with the evolution of the Internet architecture and the smooth operation of the Internet. It is open to any interested individual.

The Internet standards process is documented in RFC 2026 [Bradner 1996]. Internet standards normally deal with protocol issues and not with programming APIs. Nevertheless, two RFCs (RFC 3493 [Gilligan et al. 2003] and RFC 3542 [Stevens et al. 2003]) specify the sockets API for IPv6. These are informational RFCs, not standards, and were produced to speed the deployment of portable applications by the numerous vendors working on early releases of IPv6. Although standards bodies tend to take a long time, many APIs were standardized in The Single Unix Specification Version 3.

1.11 64-Bit Architectures

During the mid to late 1990s, the trend began toward 64-bit architectures and 64-bit software. One reason is for larger addressing within a process (i.e., 64-bit pointers), which can address large amounts of memory (more than 2^{32} bytes). The common programming model for existing 32-bit Unix systems is called the *ILP32* model, denoting that integers (I), long integers (L), and pointers (P) occupy 32 bits. The model that is becoming most prevalent for 64-bit Unix systems is called the *LP64* model, meaning only long integers (L) and pointers (P) require 64 bits. Figure 1.17 compares these two models.

Datatype	ILP32 model	LP64 model
char	8	8
short	16	16
int	32	32
long	32	64
pointer	32	64

Figure 1.17   Comparison of number of bits to hold various datatypes for the ILP32 and LP64 models.

From a programming perspective, the LP64 model means we cannot assume that a pointer can be stored in an integer. We must also consider the effect of the LP64 model on existing APIs.

ANSI C invented the `size_t` datatype, which is used, for example, as the argument to `malloc` (the number of bytes to allocate), and as the third argument to `read` and `write` (the number of bytes to read or write). On a 32-bit system, `size_t` is a 32-bit value, but on a 64-bit system, it must be a 64-bit value, to take advantage of the larger addressing model. This means a 64-bit system will probably contain a `typedef` of `size_t` to be an `unsigned long`. The networking API problem is that some drafts of POSIX.1g specified that function arguments containing the size of a socket address structures have the `size_t` datatype (e.g., the third argument to `bind` and `connect`). Some XTI structures also had members with a datatype of `long` (e.g., the `t_info` and `t_opthdr` structures). If these had been left as is, both would change from 32-bit values to 64-bit values when a Unix system changes from the ILP32 to the LP64 model. In both instances, there is no need for a 64-bit datatype: The length of a socket address structure is a few hundred bytes at most, and the use of `long` for the XTI structure members was a mistake.

The solution is to use datatypes designed specifically to handle these scenarios. The sockets API uses the `socklen_t` datatype for lengths of socket address structures, and XTI uses the `t_scalar_t` and `t_uscalar_t` datatypes. The reason for not changing these values from 32 bits to 64 bits is to make it easier to provide binary compatibility on the new 64-bit systems for applications compiled under 32-bit systems.

1.12 Summary

Figure 1.5 shows a complete, albeit simple, TCP client that fetches the current time and date from a specified server, and Figure 1.9 shows a complete version of the server. These two examples introduce many of the terms and concepts that are expanded on throughout the rest of the book.

Our client was protocol-dependent on IPv4 and we modified it to use IPv6 instead. But this just gave us another protocol-dependent program. In Chapter 11, we will develop some functions to let us write protocol-independent code, which will be important as the Internet starts using IPv6.

Throughout the text, we will use the wrapper functions developed in Section 1.4 to reduce the size of our code, yet still check every function call for an error return. Our wrapper functions all begin with a capital letter.

The Single Unix Specification Version 3, known by several other names and called simply *The POSIX Specification* by us, is the confluence of two long-running standards efforts, finally drawn together by The Austin Group.

Readers interested in the history of Unix networking should consult [Salus 1994] for a description of Unix history, and [Salus 1995] for the history of TCP/IP and the Internet.

Exercises

1.1 Go through the steps at the end of Section 1.9 to discover information about your network topology.

1.2 Obtain the source code for the examples in this text (see the Preface). Compile and test the TCP daytime client in Figure 1.5. Run the program a few times, specifying a different IP address as the command-line argument each time.

1.3 Modify the first argument to `socket` in Figure 1.5 to be 9999. Compile and run the program. What happens? Find the `errno` value corresponding to the error that is printed. How can you find more information on this error?

1.4 Modify Figure 1.5 by placing a counter in the `while` loop, counting the number of times `read` returns a value greater than 0. Print the value of the counter before terminating. Compile and run your new client.

1.5 Modify Figure 1.9 as follows: First, change the port number assigned to the `sin_port` member from 13 to 9999. Next, change the single call to `write` into a loop that calls `write` for each byte of the result string. Compile this modified server and start it running in the background. Next, modify the client from the previous exercise (which prints the counter before terminating), changing the port number assigned to the `sin_port` member from 13 to 9999. Start this client, specifying the IP address of the host on which the modified server is running as the command-line argument. What value is printed as the client's counter? If possible, also try to run the client and server on different hosts.

2

The Transport Layer:
TCP, UDP, and SCTP

2.1 Introduction

This chapter provides an overview of the protocols in the TCP/IP suite that are used in the examples throughout the book. Our goal is to provide enough detail from a network programming perspective to understand how to use the protocols and provide references to more detailed descriptions of their actual design, implementation, and history.

This chapter focuses on the transport layer: TCP, UDP, and Stream Control Transmission Protocol (SCTP). Most client/server applications use either TCP or UDP. SCTP is a newer protocol, originally designed for transport of telephony signaling across the Internet. These transport protocols use the network-layer protocol IP, either IPv4 or IPv6. While it is possible to use IPv4 or IPv6 directly, bypassing the transport layer, this technique, often called *raw sockets*, is used much less frequently. Therefore, we have a more detailed description of IPv4 and IPv6, along with ICMPv4 and ICMPv6, in Appendix A.

UDP is a simple, unreliable datagram protocol, while TCP is a sophisticated, reliable byte-stream protocol. SCTP is similar to TCP as a reliable transport protocol, but it also provides message boundaries, transport-level support for multihoming, and a way to minimize head-of-line blocking. We need to understand the services provided by these transport protocols to the application, so that we know what is handled by the protocol and what we must handle in the application.

There are features of TCP that, when understood, make it easier for us to write robust clients and servers. Also, when we understand these features, it becomes easier to debug our clients and servers using commonly provided tools such as `netstat`. We cover various topics in this chapter that fall into this category: TCP's three-way handshake, TCP's connection termination sequence, and TCP's TIME_WAIT state; SCTP's

31

four-way handshake and SCTP's connection termination; plus SCTP, TCP, and UDP buffering by the socket layer, and so on.

2.2   The Big Picture

Although the protocol suite is called "TCP/IP," there are more members of this family than just TCP and IP. Figure 2.1 shows an overview of these protocols.

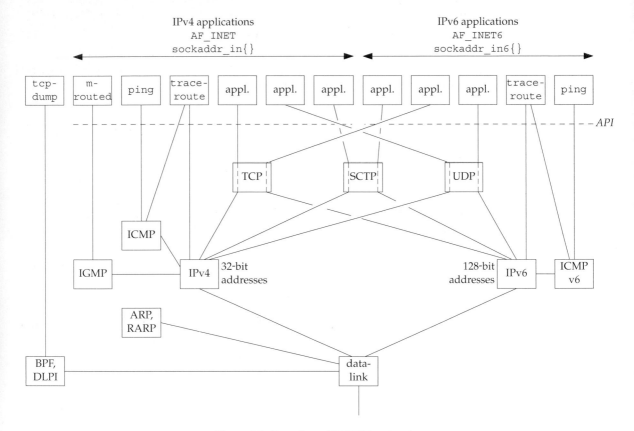

Figure 2.1 Overview of TCP/IP protocols.

We show both IPv4 and IPv6 in this figure. Moving from right to left, the rightmost five applications are using IPv6; we will talk about the AF_INET6 constant in Chapter 3, along with the sockaddr_in6 structure. The next six applications use IPv4.

The leftmost application, tcpdump, communicates directly with the datalink using either the BSD packet filter (BPF) or the datalink provider interface (DLPI). We mark the dashed line beneath the nine applications on the right as the *API*, which is normally sockets or XTI. The interface to either BPF or DLPI does not use sockets or XTI.

There is an exception to this, which we will describe in more detail in Chapter 28: Linux provides access to the datalink using a special type of socket called `SOCK_PACKET`.

We also note in Figure 2.1 that the `traceroute` program uses two sockets: one for IP and another for ICMP. In Chapter 28, we will develop IPv4 and IPv6 versions of both `ping` and `traceroute`.

We now describe each of the protocol boxes in this figure.

IPv4   *Internet Protocol version 4.* IPv4, which we often denote as just IP, has been the workhorse protocol of the IP suite since the early 1980s. It uses 32-bit addresses (Section A.4). IPv4 provides packet delivery service for TCP, UDP, SCTP, ICMP, and IGMP.

IPv6   *Internet Protocol version 6.* IPv6 was designed in the mid-1990s as a replacement for IPv4. The major change is a larger address comprising 128 bits (Section A.5), to deal with the explosive growth of the Internet in the 1990s. IPv6 provides packet delivery service for TCP, UDP, SCTP, and ICMPv6.

We often use the word *"IP"* as an adjective, as in *IP layer* and *IP address*, when the distinction between IPv4 and IPv6 is not needed.

TCP   *Transmission Control Protocol.* TCP is a connection-oriented protocol that provides a reliable, full-duplex byte stream to its users. TCP sockets are an example of *stream sockets*. TCP takes care of details such as acknowledgments, timeouts, retransmissions, and the like. Most Internet application programs use TCP. Notice that TCP can use either IPv4 or IPv6.

UDP   *User Datagram Protocol.* UDP is a connectionless protocol, and UDP sockets are an example of *datagram sockets*. There is no guarantee that UDP datagrams ever reach their intended destination. As with TCP, UDP can use either IPv4 or IPv6.

SCTP   *Stream Control Transmission Protocol.* SCTP is a connection-oriented protocol that provides a reliable full-duplex association. The word *"association"* is used when referring to a connection in SCTP because SCTP is multihomed, involving a set of IP addresses and a single port for each side of an association. SCTP provides a message service, which maintains record boundaries. As with TCP and UDP, SCTP can use either IPv4 or IPv6, but it can also use both IPv4 and IPv6 simultaneously on the same association.

ICMP   *Internet Control Message Protocol.* ICMP handles error and control information between routers and hosts. These messages are normally generated by and processed by the TCP/IP networking software itself, not user processes, although we show the `ping` and `traceroute` programs, which use ICMP. We sometimes refer to this protocol as ICMPv4 to distinguish it from ICMPv6.

IGMP   *Internet Group Management Protocol.* IGMP is used with multicasting (Chapter 21), which is optional with IPv4.

ARP   *Address Resolution Protocol.* ARP maps an IPv4 address into a hardware address (such as an Ethernet address). ARP is normally used on broadcast networks such as Ethernet, token ring, and FDDI, and is not needed on point-to-point networks.

RARP   *Reverse Address Resolution Protocol.* RARP maps a hardware address into an IPv4 address. It is sometimes used when a diskless node is booting.

ICMPv6   *Internet Control Message Protocol version 6.* ICMPv6 combines the functionality of ICMPv4, IGMP, and ARP.

BPF   *BSD packet filter.* This interface provides access to the datalink layer. It is normally found on Berkeley-derived kernels.

DLPI   *Datalink provider interface.* This interface also provides access to the datalink layer. It is normally provided with SVR4.

Each Internet protocol is defined by one or more documents called a *Request for Comments (RFC)*, which are their formal specifications. The solution to Exercise 2.1 shows how to obtain RFCs.

We use the terms *"IPv4/IPv6 host"* and *"dual-stack host"* to denote hosts that support both IPv4 and IPv6.

Additional details on the TCP/IP protocols themselves are in TCPv1. The 4.4BSD implementation of TCP/IP is described in TCPv2.

2.3   User Datagram Protocol (UDP)

UDP is a simple transport-layer protocol. It is described in RFC 768 [Postel 1980]. The application writes a message to a UDP socket, which is then *encapsulated* in a UDP *datagram*, which is then further encapsulated as an IP datagram, which is then sent to its destination. There is no guarantee that a UDP datagram will ever reach its final destination, that order will be preserved across the network, or that datagrams arrive only once.

The problem that we encounter with network programming using UDP is its lack of reliability. If a datagram reaches its final destination but the checksum detects an error, or if the datagram is dropped in the network, it is not delivered to the UDP socket and is not automatically retransmitted. If we want to be certain that a datagram reaches its destination, we can build lots of features into our application: acknowledgments from the other end, timeouts, retransmissions, and the like.

Each UDP datagram has a length. The length of a datagram is passed to the receiving application along with the data. We have already mentioned that TCP is a *byte-stream* protocol, without any record boundaries at all (Section 1.2), which differs from UDP.

We also say that UDP provides a *connectionless* service, as there need not be any long-term relationship between a UDP client and server. For example, a UDP client can create a socket and send a datagram to a given server and then immediately send another datagram on the same socket to a different server. Similarly, a UDP server can receive several datagrams on a single UDP socket, each from a different client.

2.4   Transmission Control Protocol (TCP)

The service provided by TCP to an application is different from the service provided by UDP. TCP is described in RFC 793 [Postel 1981c], and updated by RFC 1323 [Jacobson, Braden, and Borman 1992], RFC 2581 [Allman, Paxson, and Stevens 1999], RFC 2988 [Paxson and Allman 2000], and RFC 3390 [Allman, Floyd, and Partridge 2002]. First, TCP provides *connections* between clients and servers. A TCP client establishes a connection with a given server, exchanges data with that server across the connection, and then terminates the connection.

TCP also provides *reliability*. When TCP sends data to the other end, it requires an acknowledgment in return. If an acknowledgment is not received, TCP automatically retransmits the data and waits a longer amount of time. After some number of retransmissions, TCP will give up, with the total amount of time spent trying to send data typically between 4 and 10 minutes (depending on the implementation).

> Note that TCP does not guarantee that the data will be received by the other endpoint, as this is impossible. It delivers data to the other endpoint if possible, and notifies the user (by giving up on retransmissions and breaking the connection) if it is not possible. Therefore, TCP cannot be described as a 100% reliable protocol; it provides reliable delivery of data *or* reliable notification of failure.

TCP contains algorithms to estimate the *round-trip time* (RTT) between a client and server dynamically so that it knows how long to wait for an acknowledgment. For example, the RTT on a LAN can be milliseconds while across a WAN, it can be seconds. Furthermore, TCP continuously estimates the RTT of a given connection, because the RTT is affected by variations in the network traffic.

TCP also *sequences* the data by associating a sequence number with every byte that it sends. For example, assume an application writes 2,048 bytes to a TCP socket, causing TCP to send two segments, the first containing the data with sequence numbers 1–1,024 and the second containing the data with sequence numbers 1,025–2,048. (A *segment* is the unit of data that TCP passes to IP.) If the segments arrive out of order, the receiving TCP will reorder the two segments based on their sequence numbers before passing the data to the receiving application. If TCP receives duplicate data from its peer (say the peer thought a segment was lost and retransmitted it, when it wasn't really lost, the network was just overloaded), it can detect that the data has been duplicated (from the sequence numbers), and discard the duplicate data.

> There is no reliability provided by UDP. UDP itself does not provide anything like acknowledgments, sequence numbers, RTT estimation, timeouts, or retransmissions. If a UDP datagram is duplicated in the network, two copies can be delivered to the receiving host. Also, if a UDP client sends two datagrams to the same destination, they can be reordered by the network and arrive out of order. UDP applications must handle all these cases, as we will show in Section 22.5.

TCP provides *flow control*. TCP always tells its peer exactly how many bytes of data it is willing to accept from the peer at any one time. This is called the advertised *window*. At any time, the window is the amount of room currently available in the receive buffer, guaranteeing that the sender cannot overflow the receive buffer. The window changes dynamically over time: As data is received from the sender, the window size decreases, but as the receiving application reads data from the buffer, the window size increases. It is possible for the window to reach 0: when TCP's receive buffer for a socket is full and it must wait for the application to read data from the buffer before it can take any more data from the peer.

> UDP provides no flow control. It is easy for a fast UDP sender to transmit datagrams at a rate that the UDP receiver cannot keep up with, as we will show in Section 8.13.

Finally, a TCP connection is *full-duplex*. This means that an application can send and receive data in both directions on a given connection at any time. This means that TCP must keep track of state information such as sequence numbers and window sizes for each direction of data flow: sending and receiving. After a full-duplex connection is established, it can be turned into a simplex connection if desired (see Section 6.6).

> UDP can be full-duplex.

2.5 Stream Control Transmission Protocol (SCTP)

SCTP provides services similar to those offered by UDP and TCP. SCTP is described in RFC 2960 [Stewart et al. 2000], and updated by RFC 3309 [Stone, Stewart, and Otis 2002]. An introduction to SCTP is available in RFC 3286 [Ong and Yoakum 2002]. SCTP provides *associations* between clients and servers. SCTP also provides applications with reliability, sequencing, flow control, and full-duplex data transfer, like TCP. The word "*association*" is used in SCTP instead of "connection" to avoid the connotation that a connection involves communication between only two IP addresses. An association refers to a communication between two systems, which may involve more than two addresses due to multihoming.

Unlike TCP, SCTP is *message-oriented*. It provides sequenced delivery of individual records. Like UDP, the length of a record written by the sender is passed to the receiving application.

SCTP can provide multiple streams between connection endpoints, each with its own reliable sequenced delivery of messages. A lost message in one of these streams does not block delivery of messages in any of the other streams. This approach is in contrast to TCP, where a loss at any point in the single stream of bytes blocks delivery of all future data on the connection until the loss is repaired.

SCTP also provides a multihoming feature, which allows a single SCTP endpoint to support multiple IP addresses. This feature can provide increased robustness against network failure. An endpoint can have multiple redundant network connections, where each of these networks has a different connection to the Internet infrastructure. SCTP can work around a failure of one network or path across the Internet by switching to another address already associated with the SCTP association.

> Similar robustness can be obtained from TCP with help from routing protocols. For example, BGP connections within a domain (iBGP) often use addresses that are assigned to a virtual interface within the router as the endpoints of the TCP connection. The domain's routing

protocol ensures that if there is a route between two routers, it can be used, which would not be possible if the addresses used belonged to an interface that went down, for example. SCTP's multihoming feature allows *hosts* to multihome, not just routers, and allows this multihoming to occur across different service providers, which the routing-based TCP method cannot allow.

2.6   TCP Connection Establishment and Termination

To aid in our understanding of the `connect`, `accept`, and `close` functions and to help us debug TCP applications using the `netstat` program, we must understand how TCP connections are established and terminated, and TCP's state transition diagram.

Three-Way Handshake

The following scenario occurs when a TCP connection is established:

1. The server must be prepared to accept an incoming connection. This is normally done by calling `socket`, `bind`, and `listen` and is called a *passive open*.

2. The client issues an *active open* by calling `connect`. This causes the client TCP to send a "synchronize" (SYN) segment, which tells the server the client's initial sequence number for the data that the client will send on the connection. Normally, there is no data sent with the SYN; it just contains an IP header, a TCP header, and possible TCP options (which we will talk about shortly).

3. The server must acknowledge (ACK) the client's SYN and the server must also send its own SYN containing the initial sequence number for the data that the server will send on the connection. The server sends its SYN and the ACK of the client's SYN in a single segment.

4. The client must acknowledge the server's SYN.

The minimum number of packets required for this exchange is three; hence, this is called TCP's *three-way handshake*. We show the three segments in Figure 2.2.

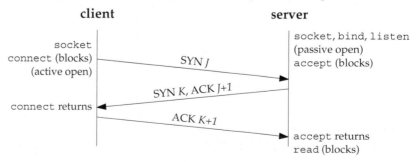

Figure 2.2   TCP three-way handshake.

We show the client's initial sequence number as *J* and the server's initial sequence number as *K*. The acknowledgment number in an ACK is the next expected sequence number for the end sending the ACK. Since a SYN occupies one byte of the sequence number space, the acknowledgment number in the ACK of each SYN is the initial sequence number plus one. Similarly, the ACK of each FIN is the sequence number of the FIN plus one.

> An everyday analogy for establishing a TCP connection is the telephone system [Nemeth 1997]. The socket function is the equivalent of having a telephone to use. bind is telling other people your telephone number so that they can call you. listen is turning on the ringer so that you will hear when an incoming call arrives. connect requires that we know the other person's phone number and dial it. accept is when the person being called answers the phone. Having the client's identity returned by accept (where the identify is the client's IP address and port number) is similar to having the caller ID feature show the caller's phone number. One difference, however, is that accept returns the client's identity only after the connection has been established, whereas the caller ID feature shows the caller's phone number before we choose whether to answer the phone or not. If the DNS is used (Chapter 11), it provides a service analogous to a telephone book. getaddrinfo is similar to looking up a person's phone number in the phone book. getnameinfo would be the equivalent of having a phone book sorted by telephone numbers that we could search, instead of a book sorted by name.

TCP Options

Each SYN can contain TCP options. Commonly used options include the following:

- MSS option. With this option, the TCP sending the SYN announces its *maximum segment size*, the maximum amount of data that it is willing to accept in each TCP segment, on this connection. The sending TCP uses the receiver's MSS value as the maximum size of a segment that it sends. We will see how to fetch and set this TCP option with the TCP_MAXSEG socket option (Section 7.9).

- Window scale option. The maximum window that either TCP can advertise to the other TCP is 65,535, because the corresponding field in the TCP header occupies 16 bits. But, high-speed connections, common in today's Internet (45 Mbits/sec and faster, as described in RFC 1323 [Jacobson, Braden, and Borman 1992]), or long delay paths (satellite links) require a larger window to obtain the maximum throughput possible. This newer option specifies that the advertised window in the TCP header must be scaled (left-shifted) by 0–14 bits, providing a maximum window of almost one gigabyte ($65,535 \times 2^{14}$). Both end-systems must support this option for the window scale to be used on a connection. We will see how to affect this option with the SO_RCVBUF socket option (Section 7.5).

> To provide interoperability with older implementations that do not support this option, the following rules apply. TCP can send the option with its SYN as part of an active open. But, it can scale its windows only if the other end also sends the option with its SYN. Similarly, the server's TCP can send this option only if it receives the option with the client's SYN. This logic assumes that implementations ignore options that they do not understand, which is required and common, but unfortunately, not guaranteed with all implementations.

- Timestamp option. This option is needed for high-speed connections to prevent possible data corruption caused by old, delayed, or duplicated segments. Since it is a newer option, it is negotiated similarly to the window scale option. As network programmers there is nothing we need to worry about with this option.

These common options are supported by most implementations. The latter two are sometimes called the "RFC 1323 options," as that RFC [Jacobson, Braden, and Borman 1992] specifies the options. They are also called the "long fat pipe options," since a network with either a high bandwidth or a long delay is called a *long fat pipe*. Chapter 24 of TCPv1 contains more details on these options.

TCP Connection Termination

While it takes three segments to establish a connection, it takes four to terminate a connection.

1. One application calls `close` first, and we say that this end performs the *active close*. This end's TCP sends a FIN segment, which means it is finished sending data.

2. The other end that receives the FIN performs the *passive close*. The received FIN is acknowledged by TCP. The receipt of the FIN is also passed to the application as an end-of-file (after any data that may have already been queued for the application to receive), since the receipt of the FIN means the application will not receive any additional data on the connection.

3. Sometime later, the application that received the end-of-file will `close` its socket. This causes its TCP to send a FIN.

4. The TCP on the system that receives this final FIN (the end that did the active close) acknowledges the FIN.

Since a FIN and an ACK are required in each direction, four segments are normally required. We use the qualifier "normally" because in some scenarios, the FIN in Step 1 is sent with data. Also, the segments in Steps 2 and 3 are both from the end performing the passive close and could be combined into one segment. We show these packets in Figure 2.3.

A FIN occupies one byte of sequence number space just like a SYN. Therefore, the ACK of each FIN is the sequence number of the FIN plus one.

Between Steps 2 and 3 it is possible for data to flow from the end doing the passive close to the end doing the active close. This is called a *half-close* and we will talk about this in detail with the `shutdown` function in Section 6.6.

The sending of each FIN occurs when a socket is closed. We indicated that the application calls `close` for this to happen, but realize that when a Unix process terminates, either voluntarily (calling `exit` or having the `main` function return) or involuntarily (receiving a signal that terminates the process), all open descriptors are closed, which will also cause a FIN to be sent on any TCP connection that is still open.

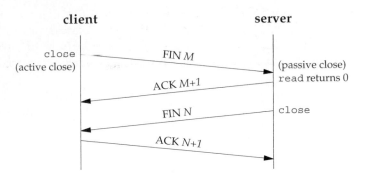

Figure 2.3 Packets exchanged when a TCP connection is closed.

Although we show the client in Figure 2.3 performing the active close, either end—the client or the server—can perform the active close. Often the client performs the active close, but with some protocols (notably HTTP/1.0), the server performs the active close.

TCP State Transition Diagram

The operation of TCP with regard to connection establishment and connection termination can be specified with a *state transition diagram*. We show this in Figure 2.4.

There are 11 different states defined for a connection and the rules of TCP dictate the transitions from one state to another, based on the current state and the segment received in that state. For example, if an application performs an active open in the CLOSED state, TCP sends a SYN and the new state is SYN_SENT. If TCP next receives a SYN with an ACK, it sends an ACK and the new state is ESTABLISHED. This final state is where most data transfer occurs.

The two arrows leading from the ESTABLISHED state deal with the termination of a connection. If an application calls close before receiving a FIN (an active close), the transition is to the FIN_WAIT_1 state. But if an application receives a FIN while in the ESTABLISHED state (a passive close), the transition is to the CLOSE_WAIT state.

We denote the normal client transitions with a darker solid line and the normal server transitions with a darker dashed line. We also note that there are two transitions that we have not talked about: a simultaneous open (when both ends send SYNs at about the same time and the SYNs cross in the network) and a simultaneous close (when both ends send FINs at the same time). Chapter 18 of TCPv1 contains examples and a discussion of both scenarios, which are possible but rare.

One reason for showing the state transition diagram is to show the 11 TCP states with their names. These states are displayed by netstat, which is a useful tool when debugging client/server applications. We will use netstat to monitor state changes in Chapter 5.

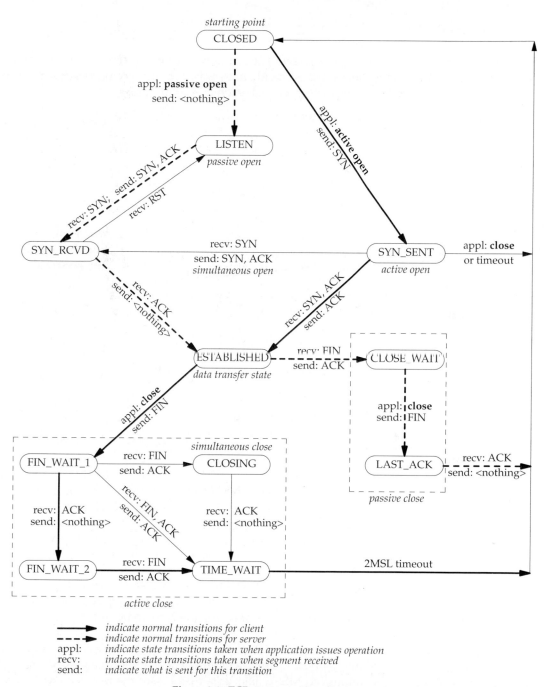

Figure 2.4 TCP state transition diagram.

Watching the Packets

Figure 2.5 shows the actual packet exchange that takes place for a complete TCP connection: the connection establishment, data transfer, and connection termination. We also show the TCP states through which each endpoint passes.

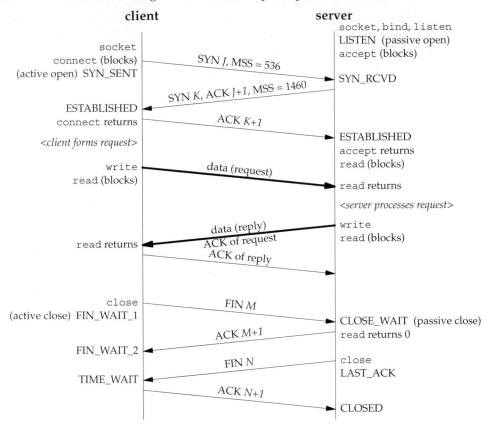

Figure 2.5 Packet exchange for TCP connection.

The client in this example announces an MSS of 536 (indicating that it implements only the minimum reassembly buffer size) and the server announces an MSS of 1,460 (typical for IPv4 on an Ethernet). It is okay for the MSS to be different in each direction (see Exercise 2.5).

Once a connection is established, the client forms a request and sends it to the server. We assume this request fits into a single TCP segment (i.e., less than 1,460 bytes given the server's announced MSS). The server processes the request and sends a reply, and we assume that the reply fits in a single segment (less than 536 in this example). We show both data segments as bolder arrows. Notice that the acknowledgment of the client's request is sent with the server's reply. This is called *piggybacking* and will normally happen when the time it takes the server to process the request and generate the reply is less than around 200 ms. If the server takes longer, say one second, we would see the acknowledgment followed later by the reply. (The dynamics of TCP data flow are covered in detail in Chapters 19 and 20 of TCPv1.)

We then show the four segments that terminate the connection. Notice that the end that performs the active close (the client in this scenario) enters the TIME_WAIT state. We will discuss this in the next section.

It is important to notice in Figure 2.5 that if the entire purpose of this connection was to send a one-segment request and receive a one-segment reply, there would be eight segments of overhead involved when using TCP. If UDP was used instead, only two packets would be exchanged: the request and the reply. But switching from TCP to UDP removes all the reliability that TCP provides to the application, pushing lots of these details from the transport layer (TCP) to the UDP application. Another important feature provided by TCP is congestion control, which must then be handled by the UDP application. Nevertheless, it is important to understand that many applications are built using UDP because the application exchanges small amounts of data and UDP avoids the overhead of TCP connection establishment and connection termination.

2.7   TIME_WAIT State

Undoubtedly, one of the most misunderstood aspects of TCP with regard to network programming is its TIME_WAIT state. We can see in Figure 2.4 that the end that performs the active close goes through this state. The duration that this endpoint remains in this state is twice the *maximum segment lifetime* (MSL), sometimes called 2MSL.

Every implementation of TCP must choose a value for the MSL. The recommended value in RFC 1122 [Braden 1989] is 2 minutes, although Berkeley-derived implementations have traditionally used a value of 30 seconds instead. This means the duration of the TIME_WAIT state is between 1 and 4 minutes. The MSL is the maximum amount of time that any given IP datagram can live in a network. We know this time is bounded because every datagram contains an 8-bit hop limit (the IPv4 TTL field in Figure A.1 and the IPv6 hop limit field in Figure A.2) with a maximum value of 255. Although this is a hop limit and not a true time limit, the assumption is made that a packet with the maximum hop limit of 255 cannot exist in a network for more than MSL seconds.

The way in which a packet gets "lost" in a network is usually the result of routing anomalies. A router crashes or a link between two routers goes down and it takes the routing protocols seconds or minutes to stabilize and find an alternate path. During that time period, routing loops can occur (router A sends packets to router B, and B sends them back to A) and packets can get caught in these loops. In the meantime, assuming the lost packet is a TCP segment, the sending TCP times out and retransmits the packet, and the retransmitted packet gets to the final destination by some alternate path. But sometime later (up to MSL seconds after the lost packet started on its journey), the routing loop is corrected and the packet that was lost in the loop is sent to the final destination. This original packet is called a *lost duplicate* or a *wandering duplicate*. TCP must handle these duplicates.

There are two reasons for the TIME_WAIT state:

1. To implement TCP's full-duplex connection termination reliably
2. To allow old duplicate segments to expire in the network

The first reason can be explained by looking at Figure 2.5 and assuming that the final ACK is lost. The server will resend its final FIN, so the client must maintain state information, allowing it to resend the final ACK. If it did not maintain this information, it would respond with an RST (a different type of TCP segment), which would be interpreted by the server as an error. If TCP is performing all the work necessary to terminate both directions of data flow cleanly for a connection (its full-duplex close), then it must correctly handle the loss of any of these four segments. This example also shows why the end that performs the active close is the end that remains in the TIME_WAIT state: because that end is the one that might have to retransmit the final ACK.

To understand the second reason for the TIME_WAIT state, assume we have a TCP connection between 12.106.32.254 port 1500 and 206.168.112.219 port 21. This connection is closed and then sometime later, we establish another connection between the same IP addresses and ports: 12.106.32.254 port 1500 and 206.168.112.219 port 21. This latter connection is called an *incarnation* of the previous connection since the IP addresses and ports are the same. TCP must prevent old duplicates from a connection from reappearing at some later time and being misinterpreted as belonging to a new incarnation of the same connection. To do this, TCP will not initiate a new incarnation of a connection that is currently in the TIME_WAIT state. Since the duration of the TIME_WAIT state is twice the MSL, this allows MSL seconds for a packet in one direction to be lost, and another MSL seconds for the reply to be lost. By enforcing this rule, we are guaranteed that when we successfully establish a TCP connection, all old duplicates from previous incarnations of the connection have expired in the network.

> There is an exception to this rule. Berkeley-derived implementations will initiate a new incarnation of a connection that is currently in the TIME_WAIT state if the arriving SYN has a sequence number that is "greater than" the ending sequence number from the previous incarnation. Pages 958–959 of TCPv2 talk about this in more detail. This requires the server to perform the active close, since the TIME_WAIT state must exist on the end that receives the next SYN. This capability is used by the rsh command. RFC 1185 [Jacobson, Braden, and Zhang 1990] talks about some pitfalls in doing this.

2.8   SCTP Association Establishment and Termination

SCTP is connection-oriented like TCP, so it also has association establishment and termination handshakes. However, SCTP's handshakes are different than TCP's, so we describe them here.

Four-Way Handshake

The following scenario, similar to TCP, occurs when an SCTP association is established:

1. The server must be prepared to accept an incoming association. This preparation is normally done by calling `socket`, `bind`, and `listen` and is called a *passive open*.

2. The client issues an *active open* by calling `connect` or by sending a message, which implicitly opens the association. This causes the client SCTP to send an INIT message (which stands for "initialization") to tell the server the client's list of IP addresses, initial sequence number, initiation tag to identify all packets in this association, number of outbound streams the client is requesting, and number of inbound streams the client can support.

3. The server acknowledges the client's INIT message with an INIT-ACK message, which contains the server's list of IP addresses, initial sequence number, initiation tag, number of outbound streams the server is requesting, number of inbound streams the server can support, and a state cookie. The state cookie contains all of the state that the server needs to ensure that the association is valid, and is digitally signed to ensure its validity.

4. The client echos the server's state cookie with a COOKIE-ECHO message. This message may also contain user data bundled within the same packet.

5. The server acknowledges that the cookie was correct and that the association was established with a COOKIE-ACK message. This message may also contain user data bundled within the same packet.

The minimum number of packets required for this exchange is four; hence, this process is called SCTP's *four-way handshake*. We show a picture of the four segments in Figure 2.6.

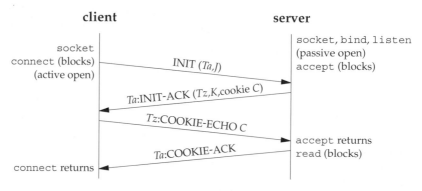

Figure 2.6 SCTP four-way handshake.

The SCTP four-way handshake is similar in many ways to TCP's three-way handshake, except for the cookie generation, which is an integral part. The INIT carries with it (along with its many parameters) a verification tag, Ta, and an initial sequence number, J. The tag Ta must be present in every packet sent by the peer for the life of the association. The initial sequence number J is used as the starting sequence number for DATA messages termed DATA chunks. The peer also chooses a verification tag, Tz, which must be present in each of its packets for the life of the association. Along with the verification tag and initial sequence number, K, the receiver of the INIT also sends a cookie, C. The cookie contains all the state needed to set up the SCTP association, so that the server's SCTP stack does not need to keep information about the associating client. Further details on SCTP's association setup can be found in Chapter 4 of [Stewart and Xie 2001].

At the conclusion of the four-way handshake, each side chooses a primary destination address. The primary destination address is used as the default destination to which data will be sent in the absence of network failure.

The four-way handshake is used in SCTP to avoid a form of denial-of-service attack we will discuss in Section 4.5.

> SCTP's four-way handshake using Cookies formalizes a method of protection against this attack. Many TCP implementations use a similar method; the big difference is that in TCP, the cookie state must be encoded into the initial sequence number, which is only 32 bits. SCTP provides an arbitrary-length field, and requires cryptographic security to prevent attacks.

Association Termination

Unlike TCP, SCTP does not permit a "half-closed" association. When one end shuts down an association, the other end must stop sending new data. The receiver of the shutdown request sends the data that was queued, if any, and then completes the shutdown. We show this exchange in Figure 2.7.

SCTP does not have a TIME_WAIT state like TCP, due to its use of verification tags. All chunks are tagged with the tag exchanged in the INIT chunks; a chunk from an old connection will arrive with an incorrect tag. Therefore, in lieu of keeping an entire connection in TIME_WAIT, SCTP instead places verification tag values in TIME_WAIT.

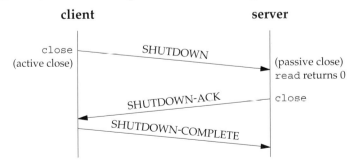

Figure 2.7 Packets exchanged when an SCTP association is closed.

SCTP State Transition Diagram

The operation of SCTP with regard to association establishment and termination can be specified with a *state transition diagram*. We show this in Figure 2.8.

As in Figure 2.4, the transitions from one state to another in the state machine are dictated by the rules of SCTP, based on the current state and the chunk received in that state. For example, if an application performs an active open in the CLOSED state, SCTP sends an INIT and the new state is COOKIE-WAIT. If SCTP next receives an INIT ACK, it sends a COOKIE ECHO and the new state is COOKIE-ECHOED. If SCTP then receives a COOKIE ACK, it moves to the ESTABLISHED state. This final state is where most data transfer occurs, although DATA chunks can be piggybacked on COOKIE ECHO and COOKIE ACK chunks.

The two arrows leading from the ESTABLISHED state deal with the termination of an association. If an application calls `close` before receiving a SHUTDOWN (an active close), the transition is to the SHUTDOWN-PENDING state. However, if an application receives a SHUTDOWN while in the ESTABLISHED state (a passive close), the transition is to the SHUTDOWN-RECEIVED state.

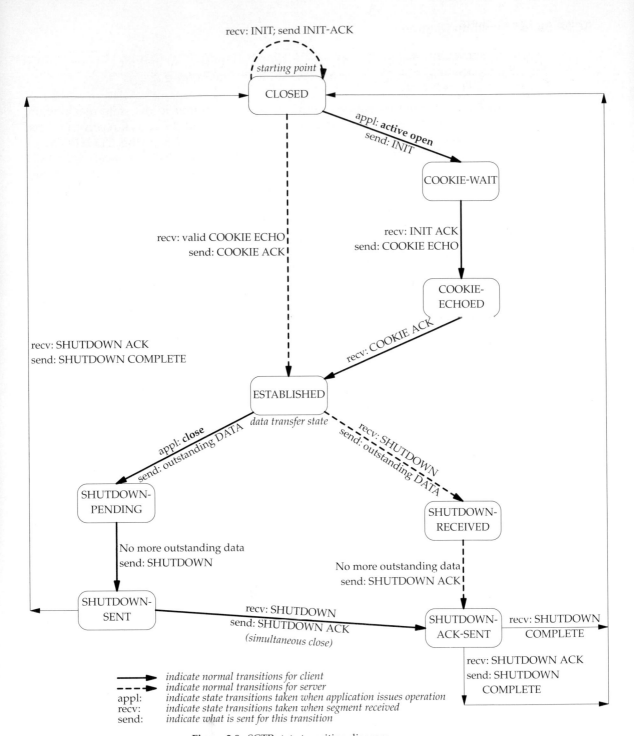

Figure 2.8   SCTP state transition diagram.

Watching the Packets

Figure 2.9 shows the actual packet exchange that takes place for a sample SCTP association: the association establishment, data transfer, and association termination. We also show the SCTP states through which each endpoint passes.

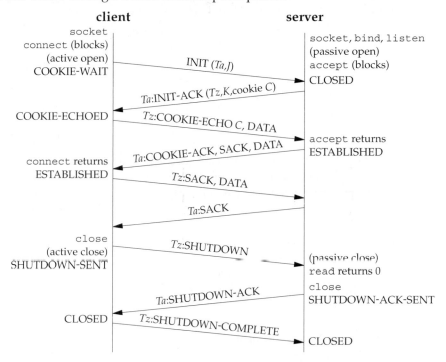

Figure 2.9 Packet exchange for SCTP association.

In this example, the client piggybacks its first data chunk on the COOKIE ECHO, and the server replies with data on the COOKIE ACK. In general, the COOKIE ECHO will often have one or more DATA chunks bundled with it when the application is using the one-to-many interface style (we will discuss the one-to-one and one-to-many interface styles in Section 9.2).

The unit of information within an SCTP packet is a "chunk." A "chunk" is self-descriptive and contains a chunk type, chunk flags, and a chunk length. This approach facilitates the bundling of chunks simply by combining multiple chunks into an SCTP outbound packet (details on chunk bundling and normal data transmission procedures can be found in Chapter 5 of [Stewart and Xie 2001]).

SCTP Options

SCTP uses parameters and chunks to facilitate optional features. New features are defined by adding either of these two items, and allowing normal SCTP processing rules to report unknown parameters and unknown chunks. The upper two bits of both the parameter space and the chunk space dictate what an SCTP receiver should do with an unknown parameter or chunk (further details can be found in Section 3.1 of [Stewart and Xie 2001]).

Currently, two extensions for SCTP are under development:

1. The dynamic address extension, which allows cooperating SCTP endpoints to dynamically add and remove IP addresses from an existing association.

2. The partial reliability extension, which allows cooperating SCTP endpoints, under application direction, to limit the retransmission of data. When a message becomes too old to send (according to the application's direction), the message will be skipped and thus no longer sent to the peer. This means that not all data is assured of arrival at the other end of the association.

2.9   Port Numbers

At any given time, multiple processes can be using any given transport: UDP, SCTP, or TCP. All three transport layers use 16-bit integer *port numbers* to differentiate between these processes.

When a client wants to contact a server, the client must identify the server with which it wants to communicate. TCP, UDP, and SCTP define a group of *well-known ports* to identify well-known services. For example, every TCP/IP implementation that supports FTP assigns the well-known port of 21 (decimal) to the FTP server. Trivial File Transfer Protocol (TFTP) servers are assigned the UDP port of 69.

Clients, on the other hand, normally use *ephemeral ports*, that is, short-lived ports. These port numbers are normally assigned automatically by the transport protocol to the client. Clients normally do not care about the value of the ephemeral port; the client just needs to be certain that the ephemeral port is unique on the client host. The transport protocol code guarantees this uniqueness.

The *Internet Assigned Numbers Authority* (IANA) maintains a list of port number assignments. Assignments were once published as RFCs; RFC 1700 [Reynolds and Postel 1994] is the last in this series. RFC 3232 [Reynolds 2002] gives the location of the online database that replaced RFC 1700: `http://www.iana.org/`. The port numbers are divided into three ranges:

1. The *well-known ports*: 0 through 1023. These port numbers are controlled and assigned by the IANA. When possible, the same port is assigned to a given service for TCP, UDP, and SCTP. For example, port 80 is assigned for a Web server, for both TCP and UDP, even though all implementations currently use only TCP.

> At the time that port 80 was assigned, SCTP did not yet exist. New port assignments are made for all three protocols, and RFC 2960 states that all existing TCP port numbers should be valid for the same service using SCTP.

2. The *registered ports*: 1024 through 49151. These are not controlled by the IANA, but the IANA registers and lists the uses of these ports as a convenience to the community. When possible, the same port is assigned to a given service for both TCP and UDP. For example, ports 6000 through 6063 are assigned for an X Window server for both protocols, even though all implementations currently use only TCP. The upper limit of 49151 for these ports was introduced to allow a range for ephemeral ports; RFC 1700 [Reynolds and Postel 1994] lists the upper range as 65535.

3. The *dynamic* or *private* ports, 49152 through 65535. The IANA says nothing about these ports. These are what we call *ephemeral* ports. (The magic number 49152 is three-fourths of 65536.)

Figure 2.10 shows this division, along with the common allocation of the port numbers.

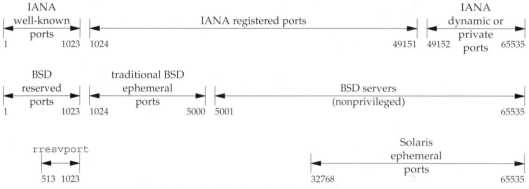

Figure 2.10 Allocation of port numbers.

We note the following points from this figure:

*   Unix systems have the concept of a *reserved port*, which is any port less than 1024. These ports can only be assigned to a socket by an appropriately privileged process. All the IANA well-known ports are reserved ports; hence, the server allocating this port (such as the FTP server) must have superuser privileges when it starts.

*   Historically, Berkeley-derived implementations (starting with 4.3BSD) have allocated ephemeral ports in the range 1024–5000. This was fine in the early 1980s, but it is easy today to find a host that can support more than 3977 connections at any given time. Therefore, many newer systems allocate ephemeral ports differently to provide more ephemeral ports, either using the IANA-defined ephemeral range or a larger range (e.g., Solaris as we show in Figure 2.10).

> As it turns out, the upper limit of 5000 for the ephemeral ports, which many older systems implement, was a typo [Borman 1997a]. The limit should have been 50,000.

- There are a few clients (not servers) that require a reserved port as part of the client/server authentication: the `rlogin` and `rsh` clients are common examples. These clients call the library function `rresvport` to create a TCP socket and assign an unused port in the range 513–1023 to the socket. This function normally tries to bind port 1023, and if that fails, it tries to bind 1022, and so on, until it either succeeds or fails on port 513.

> Notice that the BSD reserved ports and the `rresvport` function both overlap with the upper half of the IANA well-known ports. This is because the IANA well-known ports used to stop at 255. RFC 1340 (a previous "Assigned Numbers" RFC) in 1992 started assigning well-known ports between 256 and 1023. The previous "Assigned Numbers" document, RFC 1060 in 1990, called ports 256–1023 the *Unix Standard Services*. There are numerous Berkeley-derived servers that picked their well-known ports in the 1980s starting at 512 (leaving 256–511 untouched). The `rresvport` function chose to start at the top of the 512–1023 range and work down.

Socket Pair

The *socket pair* for a TCP connection is the four-tuple that defines the two endpoints of the connection: the local IP address, local port, foreign IP address, and foreign port. A socket pair uniquely identifies every TCP connection on a network. For SCTP, an association is identified by a set of local IP addresses, a local port, a set of foreign IP addresses, and a foreign port. In its simplest form, where neither endpoint is multihomed, this results in the same four-tuple socket pair used with TCP. However, when either of the endpoints of an association are multihomed, then multiple four-tuple sets (with different IP addresses but the same port numbers) may identify the same association.

The two values that identify each endpoint, an IP address and a port number, are often called a *socket*.

We can extend the concept of a socket pair to UDP, even though UDP is connectionless. When we describe the socket functions (`bind`, `connect`, `getpeername`, etc.), we will note which functions specify which values in the socket pair. For example, `bind` lets the application specify the local IP address and local port for TCP, UDP, and SCTP sockets.

2.10 TCP Port Numbers and Concurrent Servers

With a concurrent server, where the main server loop spawns a child to handle each new connection, what happens if the child continues to use the well-known port number while servicing a long request? Let's examine a typical sequence. First, the server is started on the host `freebsd`, which is multihomed with IP addresses 12.106.32.254 and 192.168.42.1, and the server does a passive open using its well-known port number (21, for this example). It is now waiting for a client request, which we show in Figure 2.11.

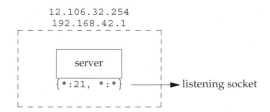

Figure 2.11 TCP server with a passive open on port 21.

We use the notation {*:21, *:*} to indicate the server's socket pair. The server is waiting for a connection request on any local interface (the first asterisk) on port 21. The foreign IP address and foreign port are not specified and we denote them as *:*. We also call this a *listening socket*.

> We use a colon to separate the IP address from the port number because that is what HTTP uses and is commonly seen elsewhere. The netstat program uses a period to separate the IP address and port, but this is sometimes confusing because decimal points are used in both domain names (freebsd.unpbook.com.21) and in IPv4 dotted-decimal notation (12.106.32.254.21).

When we specify the local IP address as an asterisk, it is called the *wildcard* character. If the host on which the server is running is multihomed (as in this example), the server can specify that it wants only to accept incoming connections that arrive destined to one specific local interface. This is a one-or-any choice for the server. The server cannot specify a list of multiple addresses. The wildcard local address is the "any" choice. In Figure 1.9, the wildcard address was specified by setting the IP address in the socket address structure to INADDR_ANY before calling bind.

At some later time, a client starts on the host with IP address 206.168.112.219 and executes an active open to the server's IP address of 12.106.32.254. We assume the ephemeral port chosen by the client TCP is 1500 for this example. This is shown in Figure 2.12. Beneath the client we show its socket pair.

When the server receives and accepts the client's connection, it forks a copy of itself, letting the child handle the client, as we show in Figure 2.13. (We will describe the fork function in Section 4.7.)

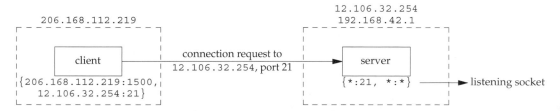

Figure 2.12 Connection request from client to server.

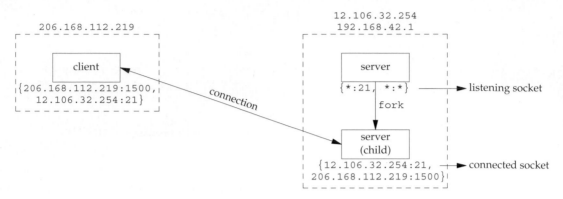

Figure 2.13 Concurrent server has child handle client.

At this point, we must distinguish between the listening socket and the connected socket on the server host. Notice that the connected socket uses the same local port (21) as the listening socket. Also notice that on the multihomed server, the local address is filled in for the connected socket (12.106.32.254) once the connection is established.

The next step assumes that another client process on the client host requests a connection with the same server. The TCP code on the client host assigns the new client socket an unused ephemeral port number, say 1501. This gives us the scenario shown in Figure 2.14. On the server, the two connections are distinct: the socket pair for the first connection differs from the socket pair for the second connection because the client's TCP chooses an unused port for the second connection (1501).

Notice from this example that TCP cannot demultiplex incoming segments by looking at just the destination port number. TCP must look at all four elements in the socket pair to determine which endpoint receives an arriving segment. In Figure 2.14, we have three sockets with the same local port (21). If a segment arrives from 206.168.112.219 port 1500 destined for 12.106.32.254 port 21, it is delivered to the first child. If a segment arrives from 206.168.112.219 port 1501 destined for 12.106.32.254 port 21, it is delivered to the second child. All other TCP segments destined for port 21 are delivered to the original server with the listening socket.

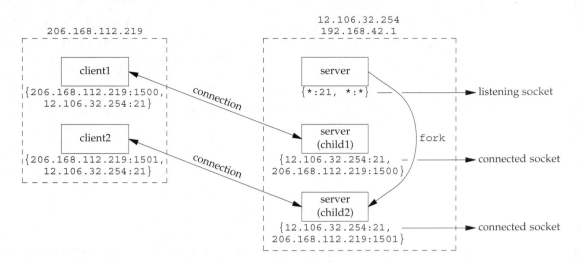

Figure 2.14 Second client connection with same server.

2.11 Buffer Sizes and Limitations

Certain limits affect the size of IP datagrams. We first describe these limits and then tie them all together with regard to how they affect the data an application can transmit.

- The maximum size of an IPv4 datagram is 65,535 bytes, including the IPv4 header. This is because of the 16-bit total length field in Figure A.1.

- The maximum size of an IPv6 datagram is 65,575 bytes, including the 40-byte IPv6 header. This is because of the 16-bit payload length field in Figure A.2. Notice that the IPv6 payload length field does not include the size of the IPv6 header, while the IPv4 total length field does include the header size.

  IPv6 has a jumbo payload option, which extends the payload length field to 32 bits, but this option is supported only on datalinks with a *maximum transmission unit* (MTU) that exceeds 65,535. (This is intended for host-to-host interconnects, such as HIPPI, which often have no inherent MTU.)

- Many networks have an *MTU* which can be dictated by the hardware. For example, the Ethernet MTU is 1,500 bytes. Other datalinks, such as point-to-point links using the Point-to-Point Protocol (PPP), have a configurable MTU. Older SLIP links often used an MTU of 1,006 or 296 bytes.

  The minimum link MTU for IPv4 is 68 bytes. This permits a maximum-sized IPv4 header (20 bytes of fixed header, 30 bytes of options) and minimum-sized fragment (the fragment offset is in units of 8 bytes). The minimum link MTU for IPv6 is 1,280 bytes. IPv6 can run over links with a smaller MTU, but requires link-specific fragmentation and reassembly to make the link appear to have an MTU of at least 1,280 bytes (RFC 2460 [Deering and Hinden 1998]).

- The smallest MTU in the path between two hosts is called the *path MTU*. Today, the Ethernet MTU of 1,500 bytes is often the path MTU. The path MTU need not be the same in both directions between any two hosts because routing in the Internet is often asymmetric [Paxson 1996]. That is, the route from A to B can differ from the route from B to A.

- When an IP datagram is to be sent out an interface, if the size of the datagram exceeds the link MTU, *fragmentation* is performed by both IPv4 and IPv6. The fragments are not normally *reassembled* until they reach the final destination. IPv4 hosts perform fragmentation on datagrams that they generate and IPv4 routers perform fragmentation on datagrams that they forward. But with IPv6, only hosts perform fragmentation on datagrams that they generate; IPv6 routers do not fragment datagrams that they are forwarding.

> We must be careful with our terminology. A box labeled as an IPv6 router may indeed perform fragmentation, but only on datagrams that the router itself generates, never on datagrams that it is forwarding. When this box generates IPv6 datagrams, it is really acting as a host. For example, most routers support the Telnet protocol and this is used for router configuration by administrators. The IP datagrams generated by the router's Telnet server are generated by the router, not forwarded by the router.
>
> You may notice that fields exist in the IPv4 header (Figure A.1) to handle IPv4 fragmentation, but there are no fields in the IPv6 header (Figure A.2) for fragmentation. Since fragmentation is the exception, rather than the rule, IPv6 contains an option header with the fragmentation information.
>
> Certain firewalls, which usually act as routers, may reassemble fragmented packets to allow inspection of the entire packet contents. This allows the prevention of certain attacks at the cost of additional complexity in the firewall device. It also requires the firewall device to be part of the only path to the network, reducing the opportunities for redundancy.

- If the "don't fragment" (DF) bit is set in the IPv4 header (Figure A.1), it specifies that this datagram must not be fragmented, either by the sending host or by any router. A router that receives an IPv4 datagram with the DF bit set whose size exceeds the outgoing link's MTU generates an ICMPv4 "destination unreachable, fragmentation needed but DF bit set" error message (Figure A.15).

  Since IPv6 routers do not perform fragmentation, there is an implied DF bit with every IPv6 datagram. When an IPv6 router receives a datagram whose size exceeds the outgoing link's MTU, it generates an ICMPv6 "packet too big" error message (Figure A.16).

  The IPv4 DF bit and its implied IPv6 counterpart can be used for *path MTU discovery* (RFC 1191 [Mogul and Deering 1990] for IPv4 and RFC 1981 [McCann, Deering, and Mogul 1996] for IPv6). For example, if TCP uses this technique with IPv4, then it sends all its datagrams with the DF bit set. If some intermediate router returns an ICMP "destination unreachable, fragmentation needed but DF bit set" error, TCP decreases the amount of data it sends per datagram and retransmits. Path MTU discovery is optional with IPv4, but IPv6 implementations all either support path MTU discovery or always send using the minimum MTU.

> Path MTU discovery is problematic in the Internet today; many firewalls drop all ICMP messages, including the fragmentation required message, meaning that TCP never gets the signal that it needs to decrease the amount of data it is sending. As of this writing, an effort is beginning in the IETF to define another method for path MTU discovery that does not rely on ICMP errors.

- IPv4 and IPv6 define a *minimum reassembly buffer size*, the minimum datagram size that we are guaranteed any implementation must support. For IPv4, this is 576 bytes. IPv6 raises this to 1,500 bytes. With IPv4, for example, we have no idea whether a given destination can accept a 577-byte datagram or not. Therefore, many IPv4 applications that use UDP (e.g., DNS, RIP, TFTP, BOOTP, SNMP) prevent applications from generating IP datagrams that exceed this size.

- TCP has a *maximum segment size* (MSS) that announces to the peer TCP the maximum amount of TCP data that the peer can send per segment. We saw the MSS option on the SYN segments in Figure 2.5. The goal of the MSS is to tell the peer the actual value of the reassembly buffer size and to try to avoid fragmentation. The MSS is often set to the interface MTU minus the fixed sizes of the IP and TCP headers. On an Ethernet using IPv4, this would be 1,460, and on an Ethernet using IPv6, this would be 1,440. (The TCP header is 20 bytes for both, but the IPv4 header is 20 bytes and the IPv6 header is 40 bytes.)

  The MSS value in the TCP MSS option is a 16-bit field, limiting the value to 65,535. This is fine for IPv4, since the maximum amount of TCP data in an IPv4 datagram is 65,495 (65,535 minus the 20-byte IPv4 header and minus the 20-byte TCP header). But with the IPv6 jumbo payload option, a different technique is used (RFC 2675 [Borman, Deering, and Hinden 1999]). First, the maximum amount of TCP data in an IPv6 datagram without the jumbo payload option is 65,515 (65,535 minus the 20-byte TCP header). Therefore, the MSS value of 65,535 is considered a special case that designates "infinity." This value is used only if the jumbo payload option is being used, which requires an MTU that exceeds 65,535. If TCP is using the jumbo payload option and receives an MSS announcement of 65,535 from the peer, the limit on the datagram sizes that it sends is just the interface MTU. If this turns out to be too large (i.e., there is a link in the path with a smaller MTU), then path MTU discovery will determine the smaller value.

- SCTP keeps a fragmentation point based on the smallest path MTU found to all the peer's addresses. This smallest MTU size is used to split large user messages into smaller pieces that can be sent in one IP datagram. The `SCTP_MAXSEG` socket option can influence this value, allowing the user to request a smaller fragmentation point.

TCP Output

Given all these terms and definitions, Figure 2.15 shows what happens when an application writes data to a TCP socket.

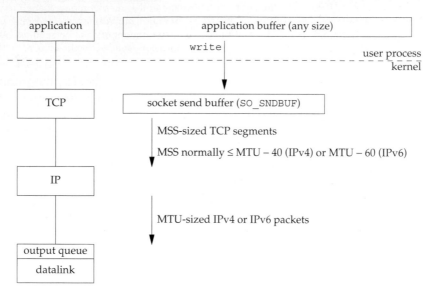

Figure 2.15 Steps and buffers involved when an application writes to a TCP socket.

Every TCP socket has a send buffer and we can change the size of this buffer with the SO_SNDBUF socket option (Section 7.5). When an application calls write, the kernel copies all the data from the application buffer into the socket send buffer. If there is insufficient room in the socket buffer for all the application's data (either the application buffer is larger than the socket send buffer, or there is already data in the socket send buffer), the process is put to sleep. This assumes the normal default of a blocking socket. (We will talk about nonblocking sockets in Chapter 16.) The kernel will not return from the write until the final byte in the application buffer has been copied into the socket send buffer. Therefore, the successful return from a write to a TCP socket only tells us that we can reuse our application buffer. It does *not* tell us that either the peer TCP has received the data or that the peer application has received the data. (We will talk about this more with the SO_LINGER socket option in Section 7.5.)

TCP takes the data in the socket send buffer and sends it to the peer TCP based on all the rules of TCP data transmission (Chapters 19 and 20 of TCPv1). The peer TCP must acknowledge the data, and as the ACKs arrive from the peer, only then can our TCP discard the acknowledged data from the socket send buffer. TCP must keep a copy of our data until it is acknowledged by the peer.

TCP sends the data to IP in MSS-sized or smaller chunks, prepending its TCP header to each segment, where the MSS is the value announced by the peer, or 536 if the peer did not send an MSS option. IP prepends its header, searches the routing table for the destination IP address (the matching routing table entry specifies the outgoing interface), and passes the datagram to the appropriate datalink. IP might perform fragmentation before passing the datagram to the datalink, but as we said earlier, one goal of the MSS option is to try to avoid fragmentation and newer implementations also use path MTU discovery. Each datalink has an output queue, and if this queue is full, the packet is discarded and an error is returned up the protocol stack: from the datalink to IP and then from IP to TCP. TCP will note this error and try sending the segment later. The application is not told of this transient condition.

UDP Output

Figure 2.16 shows what happens when an application writes data to a UDP socket.

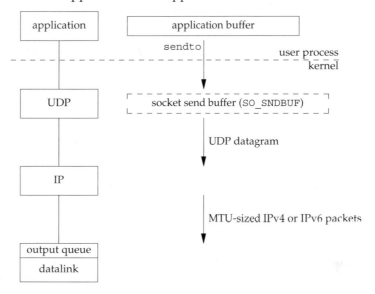

Figure 2.16   Steps and buffers involved when an application writes to a UDP socket.

This time, we show the socket send buffer as a dashed box because it doesn't really exist. A UDP socket has a send buffer size (which we can change with the SO_SNDBUF socket option, Section 7.5), but this is simply an upper limit on the maximum-sized UDP datagram that can be written to the socket. If an application writes a datagram larger than the socket send buffer size, EMSGSIZE is returned. Since UDP is unreliable, it does not need to keep a copy of the application's data and does not need an actual send buffer. (The application data is normally copied into a kernel buffer of some form as it passes down the protocol stack, but this copy is discarded by the datalink layer after the data is transmitted.)

UDP simply prepends its 8-byte header and passes the datagram to IP. IPv4 or IPv6 prepends its header, determines the outgoing interface by performing the routing function, and then either adds the datagram to the datalink output queue (if it fits within the MTU) or fragments the datagram and adds each fragment to the datalink output queue. If a UDP application sends large datagrams (say 2,000-byte datagrams), there is a much higher probability of fragmentation than with TCP, because TCP breaks the application data into MSS-sized chunks, something that has no counterpart in UDP.

The successful return from a `write` to a UDP socket tells us that either the datagram or all fragments of the datagram have been added to the datalink output queue. If there is no room on the queue for the datagram or one of its fragments, ENOBUFS is often returned to the application.

> Unfortunately, some implementations do not return this error, giving the application no indication that the datagram was discarded without even being transmitted.

SCTP Output

Figure 2.17 shows what happens when an application writes data to an SCTP socket.

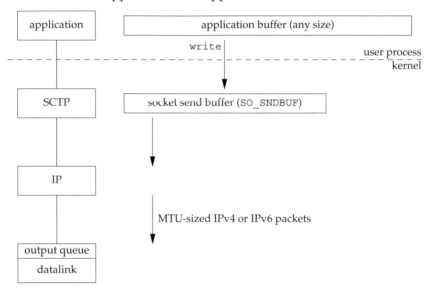

Figure 2.17 Steps and buffers involved when an application writes to an SCTP socket.

SCTP, since it is a reliable protocol like TCP, has a send buffer. As with TCP, an application can change the size of this buffer with the SO_SNDBUF socket option (Section 7.5). When the application calls `write`, the kernel copies all the data from the application buffer into the socket send buffer. If there is insufficient room in the socket buffer for all of the application's data (either the application buffer is larger than the socket send buffer, or there is already data in the socket send buffer), the process is put to sleep. This sleeping assumes the normal default of a blocking socket. (We will talk about non-blocking sockets in Chapter 16.) The kernel will not return from the `write` until the final byte in the application buffer has been copied into the socket send buffer. Therefore, the successful return from a `write` to an SCTP socket only tells the sender that it can reuse the application buffer. It does *not* tell us that either the peer SCTP has received the data, or that the peer application has received the data.

SCTP takes the data in the socket send buffer and sends it to the peer SCTP based on all the rules of SCTP data transmission (for details of data transfer, see Chapter 5 of [Stewart and Xie 2001]). The sending SCTP must await a SACK in which the cumulative acknowledgment point passes the sent data before that data can be removed from the socket buffer.

2.12 Standard Internet Services

Figure 2.18 lists several standard services that are provided by most implementations of TCP/IP. Notice that all are provided using both TCP and UDP and the port number is the same for both protocols.

Name	TCP port	UDP port	RFC	Description
echo	7	7	862	Server returns whatever the client sends.
discard	9	9	863	Server discards whatever the client sends.
daytime	13	13	867	Server returns the time and date in a human-readable format.
chargen	19	19	864	TCP server sends a continual stream of characters, until the connection is terminated by the client. UDP server sends a datagram containing a random number of characters (between 0 and 512) each time the client sends a datagram.
time	37	37	868	Server returns the time as a 32-bit binary number. This number represents the number of seconds since midnight January 1, 1900, UTC.

Figure 2.18 Standard TCP/IP services provided by most implementations.

Often these services are provided by the `inetd` daemon on Unix hosts (Section 13.5). These standard services provide an easy testing facility using the standard Telnet client. For example, the following tests both the daytime and echo servers:

```
aix % telnet freebsd daytime
Trying 12.106.32.254...                     output by Telnet client
Connected to freebsd.unpbook.com.           output by Telnet client
Escape character is '^]'.                    output by Telnet client
Mon Jul 28 11:56:22 2003                     output by daytime server
Connection closed by foreign host.           output by Telnet client (server closes connection)

aix % telnet freebsd echo
Trying 12.106.32.254...                     output by Telnet client
Connected to freebsd.unpbook.com.           output by Telnet client
Escape character is '^]'.                    output by Telnet client
hello, world                                 we type this
hello, world                                 and it is echoed back by the server
^]                                           we type control and right bracket to talk to Telnet client
telnet> quit                                 and tell client we are done
Connection closed.                           client closes the connection this time
```

In these two examples, we type the name of the host and the name of the service (`daytime` and `echo`). These service names are mapped into the port numbers shown in Figure 2.18 by the `/etc/services` file, as we will describe in Section 11.5.

Notice that when we connect to the `daytime` server, the server performs the active close, while with the `echo` server, the client performs the active close. Recall from Figure 2.4 that the end performing the active close is the end that goes through the TIME_WAIT state.

These "simple services" are often disabled by default on modern systems due to denial-of-service and other resource utilization attacks against them.

2.13 Protocol Usage by Common Internet Applications

Figure 2.19 summarizes the protocol usage of various common Internet applications.

Application	IP	ICMP	UDP	TCP	SCTP
ping		•			
traceroute		•	•		
OSPF (routing protocol)	•				
RIP (routing protocol)			•		
BGP (routing protocol)				•	
BOOTP (bootstrap protocol)			•		
DHCP (bootstrap protocol)			•		
NTP (time protocol)			•		
TFTP			•		
SNMP (network management)			•		
SMTP (electronic mail)				•	
Telnet (remote login)				•	
SSH (secure remote login)				•	
FTP				•	
HTTP (the Web)				•	
NNTP (network news)				•	
LPR (remote printing)				•	
DNS			•	•	
NFS (network filesystem)			•	•	
Sun RPC			•	•	
DCE RPC			•	•	
IUA (ISDN over IP)					•
M2UA,M3UA (SS7 telephony signaling)					•
H.248 (media gateway control)			•	•	•
H.323 (IP telephony)			•	•	•
SIP (IP telephony)			•	•	•

Figure 2.19 Protocol usage of various common Internet applications.

The first two applications, `ping` and `traceroute`, are diagnostic applications that use ICMP. `traceroute` builds its own UDP packets to send and reads ICMP replies.

The three popular routing protocols demonstrate the variety of transport protocols used by routing protocols. OSPF uses IP directly, employing a raw socket, while RIP uses UDP and BGP uses TCP.

The next five are UDP-based applications, followed by seven TCP applications and four that use both UDP and TCP. The final five are IP telephony applications that use SCTP exclusively or optionally UDP, TCP, or SCTP.

2.14   Summary

UDP is a simple, unreliable, connectionless protocol, while TCP is a complex, reliable, connection-oriented protocol. SCTP combines some of the features of both protocols, providing additional features beyond those found in TCP. While most applications on the Internet use TCP (the Web, Telnet, FTP, and email), there is a need for all three transport layers. In Section 22.4, we will discuss the reasons to choose UDP instead of TCP. In Section 23.12, we will discuss the reasons to choose SCTP instead of TCP.

TCP establishes connections using a three-way handshake and terminates connections using a four-packet exchange. When a TCP connection is established, it goes from the CLOSED state to the ESTABLISHED state, and when it is terminated, it goes back to the CLOSED state. There are 11 states in which a TCP connection can be, and a state transition diagram gives the rules on how to go between the states. Understanding this diagram is essential to diagnosing problems using the `netstat` command and understanding what happens when an application calls functions such as `connect`, `accept`, and `close`.

TCP's TIME_WAIT state is a continual source of confusion with network programmers. This state exists to implement TCP's full-duplex connection termination (i.e., to handle the case of the final ACK being lost), and to allow old duplicate segments to expire in the network.

SCTP establishes an association by using a four-way handshake and terminates connections using a three-packet exchange. When an SCTP association is established, it goes from the CLOSED state to the ESTABLISHED state, and when it is terminated, it goes back to the CLOSED state. There are eight states in which an SCTP association can be, and a state transition diagram gives the rules on how to go between the states. SCTP does not need the TIME_WAIT state as TCP does due to its use of verification tags.

Exercises

2.1   We have mentioned IP versions 4 and 6. What happened to version 5 and what were versions 0, 1, 2, and 3? (*Hint*: Find the IANA's "Internet Protocol" registry. Feel free to skip ahead to the solution if you cannot visit http://www.iana.org.)

2.2   Where would you look to find more information about the protocol that is assigned IP version 5?

2.3   With Figure 2.15, we said that TCP assumes an MSS of 536 if it does not receive an MSS option from the peer. Why is this value used?

2.4   Draw a figure like Figure 2.5 for the daytime client/server in Chapter 1, assuming the server returns the 26 bytes of data in a single TCP segment.

2.5   A connection is established between a host on an Ethernet, whose TCP advertises an MSS of 1,460, and a host on a Token Ring, whose TCP advertises an MSS of 4,096. Neither host implements path MTU discovery. Watching the packets, we never see more than 1,460 bytes of data in either direction. Why?

2.6   In Figure 2.19, we said that OSPF uses IP directly. What is the value of the protocol field in the IPv4 header (Figure A.1) for these OSPF datagrams?

2.7   In discussing SCTP output, we said that the SCTP sender must wait for the cumulative acknowledgment point to pass sent data before the data could be freed from the socket buffer. If a selective acknowledgment shows that data is acknowledged beyond the cumulative acknowledgment point, why can't the data be freed?

Part 2

Elementary Sockets

3

Sockets Introduction

3.1 Introduction

This chapter begins the description of the sockets API. We begin with socket address structures, which will be found in almost every example in the text. These structures can be passed in two directions: from the process to the kernel, and from the kernel to the process. The latter case is an example of a value-result argument, and we will encounter other examples of these arguments throughout the text.

The address conversion functions convert between a text representation of an address and the binary value that goes into a socket address structure. Most existing IPv4 code uses `inet_addr` and `inet_ntoa`, but two new functions, `inet_pton` and `inet_ntop`, handle both IPv4 and IPv6.

One problem with these address conversion functions is that they are dependent on the type of address being converted: IPv4 or IPv6. We will develop a set of functions whose names begin with `sock_` that work with socket address structures in a protocol-independent fashion. We will use these throughout the text to make our code protocol-independent.

3.2 Socket Address Structures

Most socket functions require a pointer to a socket address structure as an argument. Each supported protocol suite defines its own socket address structure. The names of these structures begin with `sockaddr_` and end with a unique suffix for each protocol suite.

IPv4 Socket Address Structure

An IPv4 socket address structure, commonly called an "Internet socket address structure," is named `sockaddr_in` and is defined by including the `<netinet/in.h>` header. Figure 3.1 shows the POSIX definition.

```
struct in_addr {
  in_addr_t   s_addr;              /* 32-bit IPv4 address */
                                   /* network byte ordered */
};

struct sockaddr_in {
  uint8_t        sin_len;          /* length of structure (16) */
  sa_family_t    sin_family;       /* AF_INET */
  in_port_t      sin_port;         /* 16-bit TCP or UDP port number */
                                   /* network byte ordered */
  struct in_addr sin_addr;         /* 32-bit IPv4 address */
                                   /* network byte ordered */
  char           sin_zero[8];      /* unused */
};
```

Figure 3.1 The Internet (IPv4) socket address structure: `sockaddr_in`.

There are several points we need to make about socket address structures in general using this example:

- The length member, `sin_len`, was added with 4.3BSD-Reno, when support for the OSI protocols was added (Figure 1.15). Before this release, the first member was `sin_family`, which was historically an `unsigned short`. Not all vendors support a length field for socket address structures and the POSIX specification does not require this member. The datatype that we show, `uint8_t`, is typical, and POSIX-compliant systems provide datatypes of this form (Figure 3.2).

  Having a length field simplifies the handling of variable-length socket address structures.

- Even if the length field is present, we need never set it and need never examine it, unless we are dealing with routing sockets (Chapter 18). It is used within the kernel by the routines that deal with socket address structures from various protocol families (e.g., the routing table code).

  The four socket functions that pass a socket address structure from the process to the kernel, `bind`, `connect`, `sendto`, and `sendmsg`, all go through the `sockargs` function in a Berkeley-derived implementation (p. 452 of TCPv2). This function copies the socket address structure from the process and explicitly sets its `sin_len` member to the size of the structure that was passed as an argument to these four functions. The five socket functions that pass a socket address structure from the kernel to the process, `accept`, `recvfrom`, `recvmsg`, `getpeername`, and `getsockname`, all set the `sin_len` member before returning to the process.

  Unfortunately, there is normally no simple compile-time test to determine whether an implementation defines a length field for its socket address structures. In our code, we test our own `HAVE_SOCKADDR_SA_LEN` constant (Figure D.2), but whether to define this constant or not requires trying to compile a simple test program that uses this optional structure member and seeing if the compilation succeeds or not. We will see in Figure 3.4 that IPv6 implementations are required to define `SIN6_LEN` if socket address structures have a length field. Some IPv4 implementations provide the length field of the socket address structure to the application based on a compile-time option (e.g., `_SOCKADDR_LEN`). This feature provides compatibility for older programs.

- The POSIX specification requires only three members in the structure: `sin_family`, `sin_addr`, and `sin_port`. It is acceptable for a POSIX-compliant implementation to define additional structure members, and this is normal for an Internet socket address structure. Almost all implementations add the `sin_zero` member so that all socket address structures are at least 16 bytes in size.

- We show the POSIX datatypes for the `s_addr`, `sin_family`, and `sin_port` members. The `in_addr_t` datatype must be an unsigned integer type of at least 32 bits, `in_port_t` must be an unsigned integer type of at least 16 bits, and `sa_family_t` can be any unsigned integer type. The latter is normally an 8-bit unsigned integer if the implementation supports the length field, or an unsigned 16-bit integer if the length field is not supported. Figure 3.2 lists these three POSIX-defined datatypes, along with some other POSIX datatypes that we will encounter.

Datatype	Description	Header
`int8_t`	Signed 8-bit integer	`<sys/types.h>`
`uint8_t`	Unsigned 8-bit integer	`<sys/types.h>`
`int16_t`	Signed 16-bit integer	`<sys/types.h>`
`uint16_t`	Unsigned 16-bit integer	`<sys/types.h>`
`int32_t`	Signed 32-bit integer	`<sys/types.h>`
`uint32_t`	Unsigned 32-bit integer	`<sys/types.h>`
`sa_family_t`	Address family of socket address structure	`<sys/socket.h>`
`socklen_t`	Length of socket address structure, normally `uint32_t`	`<sys/socket.h>`
`in_addr_t`	IPv4 address, normally `uint32_t`	`<netinet/in.h>`
`in_port_t`	TCP or UDP port, normally `uint16_t`	`<netinet/in.h>`

Figure 3.2 Datatypes required by the POSIX specification.

- You will also encounter the datatypes `u_char`, `u_short`, `u_int`, and `u_long`, which are all unsigned. The POSIX specification defines these with a note that they are obsolete. They are provided for backward compatibility.

- Both the IPv4 address and the TCP or UDP port number are always stored in the structure in network byte order. We must be cognizant of this when using these members. We will say more about the difference between host byte order and network byte order in Section 3.4.

- The 32-bit IPv4 address can be accessed in two different ways. For example, if `serv` is defined as an Internet socket address structure, then `serv.sin_addr` references the 32-bit IPv4 address as an `in_addr` structure, while `serv.sin_addr.s_addr` references the same 32-bit IPv4 address as an `in_addr_t` (typically an unsigned 32-bit integer). We must be certain that we are referencing the IPv4 address correctly, especially when it is used as an argument to a function, because compilers often pass structures differently from integers.

> The reason the `sin_addr` member is a structure, and not just an `in_addr_t`, is historical. Earlier releases (4.2BSD) defined the `in_addr` structure as a union of various structures, to allow access to each of the 4 bytes and to both of the 16-bit values contained within the 32-bit IPv4 address. This was used with class A, B, and C addresses to fetch the appropriate bytes of the address. But with the advent of subnetting and then the disappearance of the various address classes with classless addressing (Section A.4), the need for the union disappeared. Most systems today have done away with the union and just define `in_addr` as a structure with a single `in_addr_t` member.

- The `sin_zero` member is unused, but we *always* set it to 0 when filling in one of these structures. By convention, we always set the entire structure to 0 before filling it in, not just the `sin_zero` member.

  > Although most uses of the structure do not require that this member be 0, when binding a non-wildcard IPv4 address, this member must be 0 (pp. 731–732 of TCPv2).

- Socket address structures are used only on a given host: The structure itself is not communicated between different hosts, although certain fields (e.g., the IP address and port) are used for communication.

Generic Socket Address Structure

A socket address structures is *always* passed by reference when passed as an argument to any socket functions. But any socket function that takes one of these pointers as an argument must deal with socket address structures from *any* of the supported protocol families.

A problem arises in how to declare the type of pointer that is passed. With ANSI C, the solution is simple: `void *` is the generic pointer type. But, the socket functions predate ANSI C and the solution chosen in 1982 was to define a *generic* socket address structure in the `<sys/socket.h>` header, which we show in Figure 3.3.

```
struct sockaddr {
  uint8_t      sa_len;
  sa_family_t  sa_family;    /* address family: AF_xxx value */
  char         sa_data[14];  /* protocol-specific address */
};
```

Figure 3.3 The generic socket address structure: `sockaddr`.

The socket functions are then defined as taking a pointer to the generic socket address structure, as shown here in the ANSI C function prototype for the `bind` function:

```
int bind(int, struct sockaddr *, socklen_t);
```

This requires that any calls to these functions must cast the pointer to the protocol-specific socket address structure to be a pointer to a generic socket address structure. For example,

```
struct sockaddr_in   serv;      /* IPv4 socket address structure */

/* fill in serv{} */

bind(sockfd, (struct sockaddr *) &serv, sizeof(serv));
```

If we omit the cast "(struct sockaddr *)," the C compiler generates a warning of the form "warning: passing arg 2 of 'bind' from incompatible pointer type," assuming the system's headers have an ANSI C prototype for the bind function.

From an application programmer's point of view, the *only* use of these generic socket address structures is to cast pointers to protocol-specific structures.

> Recall in Section 1.2 that in our unp.h header, we define SA to be the string "struct sockaddr" just to shorten the code that we must write to cast these pointers.

> From the kernel's perspective, another reason for using pointers to generic socket address structures as arguments is that the kernel must take the caller's pointer, cast it to a struct sockaddr *, and then look at the value of sa_family to determine the type of the structure. But from an application programmer's perspective, it would be simpler if the pointer type was void *, omitting the need for the explicit cast.

IPv6 Socket Address Structure

The IPv6 socket address is defined by including the <netinet/in.h> header, and we show it in Figure 3.4.

```
struct in6_addr {
  uint8_t   s6_addr[16];         /* 128-bit IPv6 address */
                                 /* network byte ordered */
};

#define SIN6_LEN      /* required for compile-time tests */

struct sockaddr_in6 {
  uint8_t         sin6_len;      /* length of this struct (28) */
  sa_family_t     sin6_family;   /* AF_INET6 */
  in_port_t       sin6_port;     /* transport layer port# */
                                 /* network byte ordered */
  uint32_t        sin6_flowinfo; /* flow information, undefined */
  struct in6_addr sin6_addr;     /* IPv6 address */
                                 /* network byte ordered */
  uint32_t        sin6_scope_id; /* set of interfaces for a scope */
};
```

Figure 3.4 IPv6 socket address structure: sockaddr_in6.

The extensions to the sockets API for IPv6 are defined in RFC 3493 [Gilligan et al. 2003].

Note the following points about Figure 3.4:

- The `SIN6_LEN` constant must be defined if the system supports the length member for socket address structures.
- The IPv6 family is `AF_INET6`, whereas the IPv4 family is `AF_INET`.
- The members in this structure are ordered so that if the `sockaddr_in6` structure is 64-bit aligned, so is the 128-bit `sin6_addr` member. On some 64-bit processors, data accesses of 64-bit values are optimized if stored on a 64-bit boundary.
- The `sin6_flowinfo` member is divided into two fields:
  □ The low-order 20 bits are the flow label
  □ The high-order 12 bits are reserved

  The flow label field is described with Figure A.2. The use of the flow label field is still a research topic.
- The `sin6_scope_id` identifies the scope zone in which a scoped address is meaningful, most commonly an interface index for a link-local address (Section A.5).

New Generic Socket Address Structure

A new generic socket address structure was defined as part of the IPv6 sockets API, to overcome some of the shortcomings of the existing `struct sockaddr`. Unlike the `struct sockaddr`, the new `struct sockaddr_storage` is large enough to hold any socket address type supported by the system. The `sockaddr_storage` structure is defined by including the `<netinet/in.h>` header, which we show in Figure 3.5.

```
struct sockaddr_storage {
    uint8_t       ss_len;        /* length of this struct (implementation dependent) *
    sa_family_t   ss_family;     /* address family: AF_xxx value */
    /* implementation-dependent elements to provide:
     * a) alignment sufficient to fulfill the alignment requirements of
     *     all socket address types that the system supports.
     * b) enough storage to hold any type of socket address that the
     *     system supports.
     */
};
```

Figure 3.5 The storage socket address structure: `sockaddr_storage`.

The `sockaddr_storage` type provides a generic socket address structure that is different from `struct sockaddr` in two ways:

a) If any socket address structures that the system supports have alignment requirements, the `sockaddr_storage` provides the strictest alignment requirement.

b) The sockaddr_storage is large enough to contain any socket address structure that the system supports.

Note that the fields of the sockaddr_storage structure are opaque to the user, except
for ss_family and ss_len (if present). The sockaddr_storage must be cast or
copied to the appropriate socket address structure for the address given in ss_family
to access any other fields.

Comparison of Socket Address Structures

Figure 3.6 shows a comparison of the five socket address structures that we will
encounter in this text: IPv4, IPv6, Unix domain (Figure 15.1), datalink (Figure 18.1), and
storage. In this figure, we assume that the socket address structures all contain a one-
byte length field, that the family field also occupies one byte, and that any field that
must be at least some number of bits is exactly that number of bits.

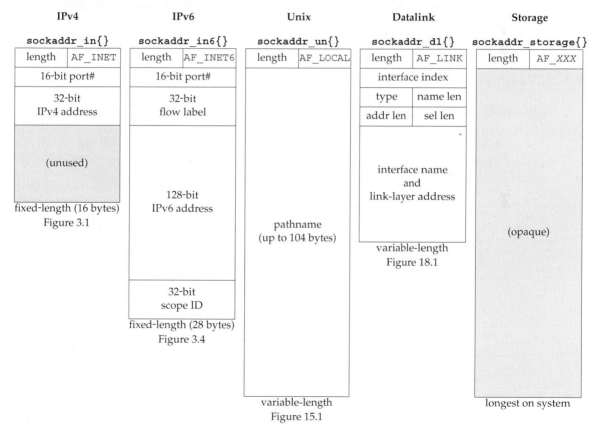

Figure 3.6 Comparison of various socket address structures.

Two of the socket address structures are fixed-length, while the Unix domain structure and the datalink structure are variable-length. To handle variable-length structures, whenever we pass a pointer to a socket address structure as an argument to one of the socket functions, we pass its length as another argument. We show the size in bytes (for the 4.4BSD implementation) of the fixed-length structures beneath each structure.

> The sockaddr_un structure itself is not variable-length (Figure 15.1), but the amount of infor-
> mation—the pathname within the structure—is variable-length. When passing pointers to
> these structures, we must be careful how we handle the length field, both the length field in
> the socket address structure itself (if supported by the implementation) and the length to and
> from the kernel.
>
> This figure shows the style that we follow throughout the text: structure names are always
> shown in a bolder font, followed by braces, as in **sockaddr_in{}**.
>
> We noted earlier that the length field was added to all the socket address structures with the
> 4.3BSD Reno release. Had the length field been present with the original release of sockets,
> there would be no need for the length argument to all the socket functions: the third argument
> to bind and connect, for example. Instead, the size of the structure could be contained in the
> length field of the structure.

3.3   Value-Result Arguments

We mentioned that when a socket address structure is passed to any socket function, it is always passed by reference. That is, a pointer to the structure is passed. The length of the structure is also passed as an argument. But the way in which the length is passed depends on which direction the structure is being passed: from the process to the kernel, or vice versa.

1. Three functions, bind, connect, and sendto, pass a socket address structure from the process to the kernel. One argument to these three functions is the pointer to the socket address structure and another argument is the integer size of the structure, as in

    ```
    struct sockaddr_in  serv;

    /* fill in serv{} */
    connect(sockfd, (SA *) &serv, sizeof(serv));
    ```

    Since the kernel is passed both the pointer and the size of what the pointer points to, it knows exactly how much data to copy from the process into the kernel. Figure 3.7 shows this scenario.

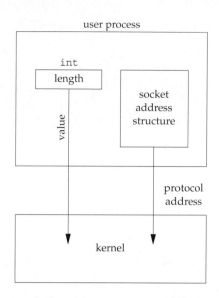

Figure 3.7 Socket address structure passed from process to kernel.

We will see in the next chapter that the datatype for the size of a socket address structure is actually `socklen_t` and not `int`, but the POSIX specification recommends that `socklen_t` be defined as `uint32_t`.

2. Four functions, `accept`, `recvfrom`, `getsockname`, and `getpeername`, pass a socket address structure from the kernel to the process, the reverse direction from the previous scenario. Two of the arguments to these four functions are the pointer to the socket address structure along with a pointer to an integer containing the size of the structure, as in

    ```
    struct sockaddr_un  cli;    /* Unix domain */
    socklen_t  len;

    len = sizeof(cli);          /* len is a value */
    getpeername(unixfd, (SA *) &cli, &len);
    /* len may have changed */
    ```

The reason that the size changes from an integer to be a pointer to an integer is because the size is both a *value* when the function is called (it tells the kernel the size of the structure so that the kernel does not write past the end of the structure when filling it in) and a *result* when the function returns (it tells the process how much information the kernel actually stored in the structure). This type of argument is called a *value-result* argument. Figure 3.8 shows this scenario.

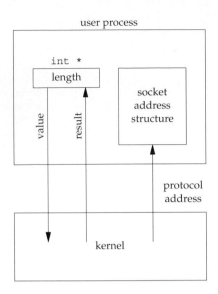

Figure 3.8 Socket address structure passed from kernel to process.

We will see an example of value-result arguments in Figure 4.11.

We have been talking about socket address structures being passed between the process and the kernel. For an implementation such as 4.4BSD, where all the socket functions are system calls within the kernel, this is correct. But in some implementations, notably System V, socket functions are just library functions that execute as part of a normal user process. How these functions interface with the protocol stack in the kernel is an implementation detail that normally does not affect us. Nevertheless, for simplicity, we will continue to talk about these structures as being passed between the process and the kernel by functions such as bind and connect. (We will see in Section C.1 that System V implementations do indeed pass socket address structures between processes and the kernel, but as part of STREAMS messages.)

Two other functions pass socket address structures: recvmsg and sendmsg (Section 14.5). But, we will see that the length field is not a function argument but a structure member.

When using value-result arguments for the length of socket address structures, if the socket address structure is fixed-length (Figure 3.6), the value returned by the kernel will always be that fixed size: 16 for an IPv4 sockaddr_in and 28 for an IPv6 sockaddr_in6, for example. But with a variable-length socket address structure (e.g., a Unix domain sockaddr_un), the value returned can be less than the maximum size of the structure (as we will see with Figure 15.2).

With network programming, the most common example of a value-result argument is the length of a returned socket address structure. But, we will encounter other value-result arguments in this text:

- The middle three arguments for the select function (Section 6.3)
- The length argument for the getsockopt function (Section 7.2)

- The `msg_namelen` and `msg_controllen` members of the `msghdr` structure, when used with `recvmsg` (Section 14.5)
- The `ifc_len` member of the `ifconf` structure (Figure 17.2)
- The first of the two length arguments for the `sysctl` function (Section 18.4)

3.4   Byte Ordering Functions

Consider a 16-bit integer that is made up of 2 bytes. There are two ways to store the two bytes in memory: with the low-order byte at the starting address, known as *little-endian* byte order, or with the high-order byte at the starting address, known as *big-endian* byte order. We show these two formats in Figure 3.9.

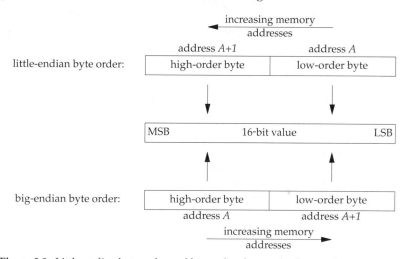

Figure 3.9 Little-endian byte order and big-endian byte order for a 16-bit integer.

In this figure, we show increasing memory addresses going from right to left in the top, and from left to right in the bottom. We also show the most significant bit (MSB) as the leftmost bit of the 16-bit value and the least significant bit (LSB) as the rightmost bit.

> The terms "little-endian" and "big-endian" indicate which end of the multibyte value, the little end or the big end, is stored at the starting address of the value.

Unfortunately, there is no standard between these two byte orderings and we encounter systems that use both formats. We refer to the byte ordering used by a given system as the *host byte order*. The program shown in Figure 3.10 prints the host byte order.

————————————————————————————————————— *intro/byteorder.c*

```
 1 #include    "unp.h"

 2 int
 3 main(int argc, char **argv)
 4 {
 5     union {
 6         short   s;
 7         char    c[sizeof(short)];
 8     } un;

 9     un.s = 0x0102;
10     printf("%s: ", CPU_VENDOR_OS);
11     if (sizeof(short) == 2) {
12         if (un.c[0] == 1 && un.c[1] == 2)
13             printf("big-endian\n");
14         else if (un.c[0] == 2 && un.c[1] == 1)
15             printf("little-endian\n");
16         else
17             printf("unknown\n");
18     } else
19         printf("sizeof(short) = %d\n", sizeof(short));

20     exit(0);
21 }
```

————————————————————————————————————— *intro/byteorder.c*

Figure 3.10 Program to determine host byte order.

We store the two-byte value `0x0102` in the short integer and then look at the two consecutive bytes, `c[0]` (the address *A* in Figure 3.9) and `c[1]` (the address *A+1* in Figure 3.9), to determine the byte order.

The string `CPU_VENDOR_OS` is determined by the GNU `autoconf` program when the software in this book is configured, and it identifies the CPU type, vendor, and OS release. We show some examples here in the output from this program when run on the various systems in Figure 1.16.

```
freebsd4 % byteorder
i386-unknown-freebsd4.8: little-endian

macosx % byteorder
powerpc-apple-darwin6.6: big-endian

freebsd5 % byteorder
sparc64-unknown-freebsd5.1: big-endian

aix % byteorder
powerpc-ibm-aix5.1.0.0: big-endian

hpux % byteorder
hppa1.1-hp-hpux11.11: big-endian

linux % byteorder
i586-pc-linux-gnu: little-endian

solaris % byteorder
sparc-sun-solaris2.9: big-endian
```

We have talked about the byte ordering of a 16-bit integer; obviously, the same discussion applies to a 32-bit integer.

> There are currently a variety of systems that can change between little-endian and big-endian byte ordering, sometimes at system reset, sometimes at run-time.

We must deal with these byte ordering differences as network programmers because networking protocols must specify a *network byte order*. For example, in a TCP segment, there is a 16-bit port number and a 32-bit IPv4 address. The sending protocol stack and the receiving protocol stack must agree on the order in which the bytes of these multibyte fields will be transmitted. The Internet protocols use big-endian byte ordering for these multibyte integers.

In theory, an implementation could store the fields in a socket address structure in host byte order and then convert to and from the network byte order when moving the fields to and from the protocol headers, saving us from having to worry about this detail. But, both history and the POSIX specification say that certain fields in the socket address structures must be maintained in network byte order. Our concern is therefore converting between host byte order and network byte order. We use the following four functions to convert between these two byte orders.

```
#include <netinet/in.h>

uint16_t htons(uint16_t host16bitvalue);

uint32_t htonl(uint32_t host32bitvalue);

                                                    Both return: value in network byte order

uint16_t ntohs(uint16_t net16bitvalue);

uint32_t ntohl(uint32_t net32bitvalue);

                                                    Both return: value in host byte order
```

In the names of these functions, h stands for *host*, n stands for *network*, s stands for *short*, and l stands for *long*. The terms "short" and "long" are historical artifacts from the Digital VAX implementation of 4.2BSD. We should instead think of s as a 16-bit value (such as a TCP or UDP port number) and l as a 32-bit value (such as an IPv4 address). Indeed, on the 64-bit Digital Alpha, a long integer occupies 64 bits, yet the htonl and ntohl functions operate on 32-bit values.

When using these functions, we do not care about the actual values (big-endian or little-endian) for the host byte order and the network byte order. What we must do is call the appropriate function to convert a given value between the host and network byte order. On those systems that have the same byte ordering as the Internet protocols (big-endian), these four functions are usually defined as null macros.

We will talk more about the byte ordering problem, with respect to the data contained in a network packet as opposed to the fields in the protocol headers, in Section 5.18 and Exercise 5.8.

We have not yet defined the term "byte." We use the term to mean an 8-bit quantity since almost all current computer systems use 8-bit bytes. Most Internet standards use the term *octet* instead of byte to mean an 8-bit quantity. This started in the early days of TCP/IP because much of the early work was done on systems such as the DEC-10, which did not use 8-bit bytes.

Another important convention in Internet standards is bit ordering. In many Internet standards, you will see "pictures" of packets that look similar to the following (this is the first 32 bits of the IPv4 header from RFC 791):

```
 0                   1                   2                   3
 0 1 2 3 4 5 6 7 8 9 0 1 2 3 4 5 6 7 8 9 0 1 2 3 4 5 6 7 8 9 0 1
+-+-+-+-+-+-+-+-+-+-+-+-+-+-+-+-+-+-+-+-+-+-+-+-+-+-+-+-+-+-+-+-+
|Version|  IHL  |Type of Service|         Total Length          |
+-+-+-+-+-+-+-+-+-+-+-+-+-+-+-+-+-+-+-+-+-+-+-+-+-+-+-+-+-+-+-+-+
```

This represents four bytes in the order in which they appear on the wire; the leftmost bit is the most significant. However, the numbering starts with zero assigned to the most significant bit. This is a notation that you should become familiar with to make it easier to read protocol definitions in RFCs.

> A common network programming error in the 1980s was to develop code on Sun workstations (big-endian Motorola 68000s) and forget to call any of these four functions. The code worked fine on these workstations, but would not work when ported to little-endian machines (such as VAXes).

3.5   Byte Manipulation Functions

There are two groups of functions that operate on multibyte fields, without interpreting the data, and without assuming that the data is a null-terminated C string. We need these types of functions when dealing with socket address structures because we need to manipulate fields such as IP addresses, which can contain bytes of 0, but are not C character strings. The functions beginning with str (for string), defined by including the <string.h> header, deal with null-terminated C character strings.

The first group of functions, whose names begin with b (for byte), are from 4.2BSD and are still provided by almost any system that supports the socket functions. The second group of functions, whose names begin with mem (for memory), are from the ANSI C standard and are provided with any system that supports an ANSI C library.

We first show the Berkeley-derived functions, although the only one we use in this text is bzero. (We use it because it has only two arguments and is easier to remember than the three-argument memset function, as explained on p. 8.) You may encounter the other two functions, bcopy and bcmp, in existing applications.

```
#include <strings.h>

void bzero(void *dest, size_t nbytes);

void bcopy(const void *src, void *dest, size_t nbytes);

int bcmp(const void *ptr1, const void *ptr2, size_t nbytes);
```

                                           Returns: 0 if equal, nonzero if unequal

> This is our first encounter with the ANSI C const qualifier. In the three uses here, it indicates
> that what is pointed to by the pointer with this qualification, *src*, *ptr1*, and *ptr2*, is not modified
> by the function. Worded another way, the memory pointed to by the const pointer is read but
> not modified by the function.

bzero sets the specified number of bytes to 0 in the destination. We often use this
function to initialize a socket address structure to 0. bcopy moves the specified number
of bytes from the source to the destination. bcmp compares two arbitrary byte strings.
The return value is zero if the two byte strings are identical; otherwise, it is nonzero.

The following functions are the ANSI C functions:

```
#include <string.h>

void *memset(void *dest, int c, size_t len);

void *memcpy(void *dest, const void *src, size_t nbytes);

int memcmp(const void *ptr1, const void *ptr2, size_t nbytes);
```

                                    Returns: 0 if equal, <0 or >0 if unequal (see text)

memset sets the specified number of bytes to the value *c* in the destination. memcpy is
similar to bcopy, but the order of the two pointer arguments is swapped. bcopy correctly handles overlapping fields, while the behavior of memcpy is undefined if the
source and destination overlap. The ANSI C memmove function must be used when the
fields overlap.

> One way to remember the order of the two pointers for memcpy is to remember that they are
> written in the same left-to-right order as an assignment statement in C:
>
>   *dest* = *src*;
>
> One way to remember the order of the final two arguments to memset is to realize that all of
> the ANSI C memXXX functions require a length argument, and it is always the final argument.

memcmp compares two arbitrary byte strings and returns 0 if they are identical. If
not identical, the return value is either greater than 0 or less than 0, depending on
whether the first unequal byte pointed to by *ptr1* is greater than or less than the corresponding byte pointed to by *ptr2*. The comparison is done assuming the two unequal
bytes are unsigned chars.

3.6   `inet_aton`, `inet_addr`, and `inet_ntoa` **Functions**

We will describe two groups of address conversion functions in this section and the next. They convert Internet addresses between ASCII strings (what humans prefer to use) and network byte ordered binary values (values that are stored in socket address structures).

1. `inet_aton`, `inet_ntoa`, and `inet_addr` convert an IPv4 address from a dot-ted-decimal string (e.g., `"206.168.112.96"`) to its 32-bit network byte ordered binary value. You will probably encounter these functions in lots of existing code.

2. The newer functions, `inet_pton` and `inet_ntop`, handle both IPv4 and IPv6 addresses. We describe these two functions in the next section and use them throughout the text.

```
#include <arpa/inet.h>

int inet_aton(const char *strptr, struct in_addr *addrptr);
```

                                                Returns: 1 if string was valid, 0 on error

```
in_addr_t inet_addr(const char *strptr);
```

              Returns: 32-bit binary network byte ordered IPv4 address; INADDR_NONE if error

```
char *inet_ntoa(struct in_addr inaddr);
```

                                                Returns: pointer to dotted-decimal string

---

The first of these, `inet_aton`, converts the C character string pointed to by *strptr* into its 32-bit binary network byte ordered value, which is stored through the pointer *addrptr*. If successful, 1 is returned; otherwise, 0 is returned.

> An undocumented feature of `inet_aton` is that if *addrptr* is a null pointer, the function still performs its validation of the input string but does not store any result.

`inet_addr` does the same conversion, returning the 32-bit binary network byte ordered value as the return value. The problem with this function is that all 2^{32} possible binary values are valid IP addresses (0.0.0.0 through 255.255.255.255), but the function returns the constant INADDR_NONE (typically 32 one-bits) on an error. This means the dotted-decimal string 255.255.255.255 (the IPv4 limited broadcast address, Section 20.2) cannot be handled by this function since its binary value appears to indicate failure of the function.

> A potential problem with `inet_addr` is that some man pages state that it returns −1 on an error, instead of INADDR_NONE. This can lead to problems, depending on the C compiler, when comparing the return value of the function (an unsigned value) to a negative constant.

Today, inet_addr is deprecated and any new code should use inet_aton instead. Better still is to use the newer functions described in the next section, which handle both IPv4 and IPv6.

The inet_ntoa function converts a 32-bit binary network byte ordered IPv4 address into its corresponding dotted-decimal string. The string pointed to by the return value of the function resides in static memory. This means the function is not re-entrant, which we will discuss in Section 11.18. Finally, notice that this function takes a structure as its argument, not a pointer to a structure.

> Functions that take actual structures as arguments are rare. It is more common to pass a pointer to the structure.

3.7   inet_pton and inet_ntop Functions

These two functions are new with IPv6 and work with both IPv4 and IPv6 addresses. We use these two functions throughout the text. The letters "p" and "n" stand for *presentation* and *numeric*. The presentation format for an address is often an ASCII string and the numeric format is the binary value that goes into a socket address structure.

```
#include   <arpa/inet.h>

int inet_pton(int family, const char *strptr, void *addrptr);
```

                              Returns: 1 if OK, 0 if input not a valid presentation format, –1 on error

```
const char *inet_ntop(int family, const void *addrptr, char *strptr, size_t len);
```

                                              Returns: pointer to result if OK, NULL on error

The *family* argument for both functions is either AF_INET or AF_INET6. If *family* is not supported, both functions return an error with errno set to EAFNOSUPPORT.

The first function tries to convert the string pointed to by *strptr*, storing the binary result through the pointer *addrptr*. If successful, the return value is 1. If the input string is not a valid presentation format for the specified *family*, 0 is returned.

inet_ntop does the reverse conversion, from numeric (*addrptr*) to presentation (*strptr*). The *len* argument is the size of the destination, to prevent the function from overflowing the caller's buffer. To help specify this size, the following two definitions are defined by including the <netinet/in.h> header:

```
#define  INET_ADDRSTRLEN    16    /* for IPv4 dotted-decimal */
#define  INET6_ADDRSTRLEN   46    /* for IPv6 hex string */
```

If *len* is too small to hold the resulting presentation format, including the terminating null, a null pointer is returned and errno is set to ENOSPC.

The *strptr* argument to inet_ntop cannot be a null pointer. The caller must allocate memory for the destination and specify its size. On success, this pointer is the return value of the function.

Figure 3.11 summarizes the five functions that we have described in this section and the previous section.

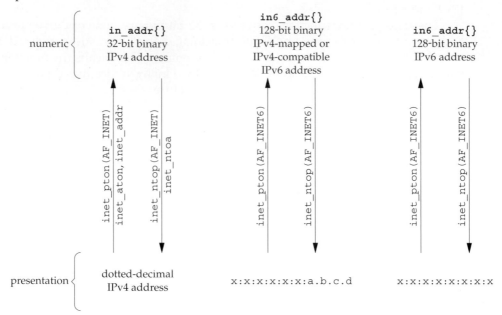

Figure 3.11 Summary of address conversion functions.

Example

Even if your system does not yet include support for IPv6, you can start using these newer functions by replacing calls of the form

```
foo.sin_addr.s_addr = inet_addr(cp);
```

with

```
inet_pton(AF_INET, cp, &foo.sin_addr);
```

and replacing calls of the form

```
ptr = inet_ntoa(foo.sin_addr);
```

with

```
char  str[INET_ADDRSTRLEN];
ptr = inet_ntop(AF_INET, &foo.sin_addr, str, sizeof(str));
```

Figure 3.12 shows a simple definition of inet_pton that supports only IPv4. Similarly, Figure 3.13 shows a simple version of inet_ntop that supports only IPv4.

── libfree/inet_pton_ipv4.c
```
10 int
11 inet_pton(int family, const char *strptr, void *addrptr)
12 {
13     if (family == AF_INET) {
14         struct in_addr in_val;

15         if (inet_aton(strptr, &in_val)) {
16             memcpy(addrptr, &in_val, sizeof(struct in_addr));
17             return (1);
18         }
19         return (0);
20     }
21     errno = EAFNOSUPPORT;
22     return (-1);
23 }
```
── libfree/inet_pton_ipv4.c

Figure 3.12 Simple version of inet_pton that supports only IPv4.

── libfree/inet_ntop_ipv4.c
```
 8 const char *
 9 inet_ntop(int family, const void *addrptr, char *strptr, size_t len)
10 {
11     const u_char *p = (const u_char *) addrptr;

12     if (family == AF_INET) {
13         char    temp[INET_ADDRSTRLEN];

14         snprintf(temp, sizeof(temp), "%d.%d.%d.%d", p[0], p[1], p[2], p[3]);
15         if (strlen(temp) >= len) {
16             errno = ENOSPC;
17             return (NULL);
18         }
19         strcpy(strptr, temp);
20         return (strptr);
21     }
22     errno = EAFNOSUPPORT;
23     return (NULL);
24 }
```
── libfree/inet_ntop_ipv4.c

Figure 3.13 Simple version of inet_ntop that supports only IPv4.

3.8   `sock_ntop` and Related Functions

A basic problem with `inet_ntop` is that it requires the caller to pass a pointer to a binary address. This address is normally contained in a socket address structure, requiring the caller to know the format of the structure and the address family. That is, to use it, we must write code of the form

```
struct sockaddr_in    addr;

inet_ntop(AF_INET, &addr.sin_addr, str, sizeof(str));
```

for IPv4, or

```
struct sockaddr_in6    addr6;

inet_ntop(AF_INET6, &addr6.sin6_addr, str, sizeof(str));
```

for IPv6. This makes our code protocol-dependent.

To solve this, we will write our own function named `sock_ntop` that takes a pointer to a socket address structure, looks inside the structure, and calls the appropriate function to return the presentation format of the address.

```
#include "unp.h"

char *sock_ntop(const struct sockaddr *sockaddr, socklen_t addrlen);

                                        Returns: non-null pointer if OK, NULL on error
```

> This is the notation we use for functions of our own (nonstandard system functions) that we use throughout the book: the box around the function prototype and return value is dashed. The header is included at the beginning is usually our unp.h header.

sockaddr points to a socket address structure whose length is *addrlen*. The function uses its own static buffer to hold the result and a pointer to this buffer is the return value.

> Notice that using static storage for the result prevents the function from being *re-entrant* or *thread-safe*. We will talk more about this in Section 11.18. We made this design decision for this function to allow us to easily call it from the simple examples in the book.

The presentation format is the dotted-decimal form of an IPv4 address or the hex string form of an IPv6 address surrounded by brackets, followed by a terminator (we use a colon, similar to URL syntax), followed by the decimal port number, followed by a null character. Hence, the buffer size must be at least `INET_ADDRSTRLEN` plus 6 bytes for IPv4 (16 + 6 = 22), or `INET6_ADDRSTRLEN` plus 8 bytes for IPv6 (46 + 8 = 54).

We show the source code for only the `AF_INET` case in Figure 3.14.

lib/sock_ntop.c

```
 5 char *
 6 sock_ntop(const struct sockaddr *sa, socklen_t salen)
 7 {
 8     char    portstr[8];
 9     static char str[128];        /* Unix domain is largest */

10     switch (sa->sa_family) {
11     case AF_INET:{
12         struct sockaddr_in *sin = (struct sockaddr_in *) sa;

13         if (inet_ntop(AF_INET, &sin->sin_addr, str, sizeof(str)) == NULL)
14             return (NULL);
15         if (ntohs(sin->sin_port) != 0) {
16             snprintf(portstr, sizeof(portstr), ":%d",
17                     ntohs(sin->sin_port));
18             strcat(str, portstr);
19         }
20         return (str);
21     }
```

lib/sock_ntop.c

Figure 3.14 Our sock_ntop function.

There are a few other functions that we define to operate on socket address structures, and these will simplify the portability of our code between IPv4 and IPv6.

```
#include "unp.h"

int sock_bind_wild(int sockfd, int family);

                                                    Returns: 0 if OK, −1 on error

int sock_cmp_addr(const struct sockaddr *sockaddr1,
                  const struct sockaddr *sockaddr2, socklen_t addrlen);

                        Returns: 0 if addresses are of the same family and equal, else nonzero

int sock_cmp_port(const struct sockaddr *sockaddr1,
                  const struct sockaddr *sockaddr2, socklen_t addrlen);

                        Returns: 0 if addresses are of the same family and ports are equal, else nonzero

int sock_get_port(const struct sockaddr *sockaddr, socklen_t addrlen);

                        Returns: non-negative port number for IPv4 or IPv6 address, else −1

char *sock_ntop_host(const struct sockaddr *sockaddr, socklen_t addrlen);

                                            Returns: non-null pointer if OK, NULL on error

void sock_set_addr(const struct sockaddr *sockaddr, socklen_t addrlen, void *ptr);

void sock_set_port(const struct sockaddr *sockaddr, socklen_t addrlen, int port);

void sock_set_wild(struct sockaddr *sockaddr, socklen_t addrlen);
```

sock_bind_wild binds the wildcard address and an ephemeral port to a socket. sock_cmp_addr compares the address portion of two socket address structures, and sock_cmp_port compares the port number of two socket address structures. sock_get_port returns just the port number, and sock_ntop_host converts just the host portion of a socket address structure to presentation format (not the port number). sock_set_addr sets just the address portion of a socket address structure to the value pointed to by *ptr*, and sock_set_port sets just the port number of a socket address structure. sock_set_wild sets the address portion of a socket address structure to the wildcard. As with all the functions in the text, we provide a wrapper function whose name begins with "S" for all of these functions that return values other than void and normally call the wrapper function from our programs. We do not show the source code for all these functions, but it is freely available (see the Preface).

3.9   readn, writen, and readline Functions

Stream sockets (e.g., TCP sockets) exhibit a behavior with the read and write functions that differs from normal file I/O. A read or write on a stream socket might input or output fewer bytes than requested, but this is not an error condition. The reason is that buffer limits might be reached for the socket in the kernel. All that is required to input or output the remaining bytes is for the caller to invoke the read or write function again. Some versions of Unix also exhibit this behavior when writing more than 4,096 bytes to a pipe. This scenario is always a possibility on a stream socket with read, but is normally seen with write only if the socket is nonblocking. Nevertheless, we always call our writen function instead of write, in case the implementation returns a short count.

We provide the following three functions that we use whenever we read from or write to a stream socket:

```
#include "unp.h"

ssize_t readn(int filedes, void *buff, size_t nbytes);

ssize_t writen(int filedes, const void *buff, size_t nbytes);

ssize_t readline(int filedes, void *buff, size_t maxlen);

                              All return: number of bytes read or written, –1 on error
```

Figure 3.15 shows the readn function, Figure 3.16 shows the writen function, and Figure 3.17 shows the readline function.

lib/readn.c
```
 1 #include    "unp.h"

 2 ssize_t                          /* Read "n" bytes from a descriptor. */
 3 readn(int fd, void *vptr, size_t n)
 4 {
 5     size_t  nleft;
 6     ssize_t nread;
 7     char    *ptr;

 8     ptr = vptr;
 9     nleft = n;
10     while (nleft > 0) {
11         if ( (nread = read(fd, ptr, nleft)) < 0) {
12             if (errno == EINTR)
13                 nread = 0;        /* and call read() again */
14             else
15                 return (-1);
16         } else if (nread == 0)
17             break;                /* EOF */

18         nleft -= nread;
19         ptr += nread;
20     }
21     return (n - nleft);           /* return >= 0 */
22 }
```
lib/readn.c

Figure 3.15 readn function: Read *n* bytes from a descriptor.

lib/writen.c
```
 1 #include    "unp.h"

 2 ssize_t                          /* Write "n" bytes to a descriptor. */
 3 writen(int fd, const void *vptr, size_t n)
 4 {
 5     size_t  nleft;
 6     ssize_t nwritten;
 7     const char *ptr;

 8     ptr = vptr;
 9     nleft = n;
10     while (nleft > 0) {
11         if ( (nwritten = write(fd, ptr, nleft)) <= 0) {
12             if (nwritten < 0 && errno == EINTR)
13                 nwritten = 0;    /* and call write() again */
14             else
15                 return (-1);      /* error */
16         }

17         nleft -= nwritten;
18         ptr += nwritten;
19     }
20     return (n);
21 }
```
lib/writen.c

Figure 3.16 writen function: Write *n* bytes to a descriptor.

―― *test/readline1.c*
```
 1 #include    "unp.h"

 2 /* PAINFULLY SLOW VERSION -- example only */
 3 ssize_t
 4 readline(int fd, void *vptr, size_t maxlen)
 5 {
 6     ssize_t n, rc;
 7     char    c, *ptr;

 8     ptr = vptr;
 9     for (n = 1; n < maxlen; n++) {
10       again:
11         if ( (rc = read(fd, &c, 1)) == 1) {
12             *ptr++ = c;
13             if (c == '\n')
14                 break;          /* newline is stored, like fgets() */
15         } else if (rc == 0) {
16             *ptr = 0;
17             return (n - 1);     /* EOF, n - 1 bytes were read */
18         } else {
19             if (errno == EINTR)
20                 goto again;
21             return (-1);        /* error, errno set by read() */
22         }
23     }

24     *ptr = 0;                   /* null terminate like fgets() */
25     return (n);
26 }
```
―― *test/readline1.c*

Figure 3.17 readline function: Read a text line from a descriptor, one byte at a time.

Our three functions look for the error EINTR (the system call was interrupted by a caught signal, which we will discuss in more detail in Section 5.9) and continue reading or writing if the error occurs. We handle the error here, instead of forcing the caller to call readn or writen again, since the purpose of these three functions is to prevent the caller from having to handle a short count.

In Section 14.3, we will mention that the MSG_WAITALL flag can be used with the recv function to replace the need for a separate readn function.

Note that our readline function calls the system's read function once for every byte of data. This is very inefficient, and why we've commented the code to state it is "PAINFULLY SLOW." When faced with the desire to read lines from a socket, it is quite tempting to turn to the standard I/O library (referred to as "stdio"). We will discuss this approach at length in Section 14.8, but it can be a dangerous path. The same stdio buffering that solves this performance problem creates numerous logistical problems that can lead to well-hidden bugs in your application. The reason is that the state of the stdio buffers is not exposed. To explain this further, consider a line-based protocol between a client and a server, where several clients and servers using that protocol may be implemented over time (really quite common; for example, there are many Web browsers and Web servers independently written to the HTTP specification). Good "defensive programming" techniques require these programs to not only expect their counterparts to follow the network protocol, but to check for unexpected network traffic as well. Such protocol violations should be reported as errors so that bugs are noticed and fixed (and malicious attempts are detected as well), and also so that network applications can recover from problem traffic and continue working if possible. Using stdio to buffer data for performance flies in the face of these goals since the application has no way to tell if unexpected data is being held in the stdio buffers at any given time.

There are many line-based network protocols such as SMTP, HTTP, the FTP control connection protocol, and finger. So, the desire to operate on lines comes up again and again. But our advice is to think in terms of buffers and not lines. Write your code to read buffers of data, and if a line is expected, check the buffer to see if it contains that line.

Figure 3.18 shows a faster version of the readline function, which uses its own buffering rather than stdio buffering. Most importantly, the state of readline's internal buffer is exposed, so callers have visibility into exactly what has been received. Even with this feature, readline can be problematic, as we'll see in Section 6.3. System functions like select still won't know about readline's internal buffer, so a carelessly written program could easily find itself waiting in select for data already received and stored in readline's buffers. For that matter, mixing readn and readline calls will not work as expected unless readn is modified to check the internal buffer as well.

lib/readline.c

```
 1 #include    "unp.h"

 2 static int read_cnt;
 3 static char *read_ptr;
 4 static char read_buf[MAXLINE];

 5 static ssize_t
 6 my_read(int fd, char *ptr)
 7 {

 8    if (read_cnt <= 0) {
 9      again:
10        if ( (read_cnt = read(fd, read_buf, sizeof(read_buf))) < 0) {
11            if (errno == EINTR)
12                goto again;
13            return (-1);
14        } else if (read_cnt == 0)
15            return (0);
16        read_ptr = read_buf;
17    }

18    read_cnt--;
19    *ptr = *read_ptr++;
20    return (1);
21 }
```

```
22 ssize_t
23 readline(int fd, void *vptr, size_t maxlen)
24 {
25     ssize_t n, rc;
26     char    c, *ptr;

27     ptr = vptr;
28     for (n = 1; n < maxlen; n++) {
29         if ( (rc = my_read(fd, &c)) == 1) {
30             *ptr++ = c;
31             if (c == '\n')
32                 break;              /* newline is stored, like fgets() */
33         } else if (rc == 0) {
34             *ptr = 0;
35             return (n - 1);       /* EOF, n - 1 bytes were read */
36         } else
37             return (-1);          /* error, errno set by read() */
38     }

39     *ptr = 0;                     /* null terminate like fgets() */
40     return (n);
41 }

42 ssize_t
43 readlinebuf(void **vptrptr)
44 {
45     if (read_cnt)
46         *vptrptr = read_ptr;
47     return (read_cnt);
48 }
```
—— *lib/readline.c*

Figure 3.18 Better version of readline function.

2–21   The internal function my_read reads up to MAXLINE characters at a time and then returns them, one at a time.

29   The only change to the readline function itself is to call my_read instead of read.

42–48   A new function, readlinebuf, exposes the internal buffer state so that callers can check and see if more data was received beyond a single line.

> Unfortunately, by using static variables in readline.c to maintain the state information across successive calls, the functions are not *re-entrant* or *thread-safe*. We will discuss this in Sections 11.18 and 26.5. We will develop a thread-safe version using thread-specific data in Figure 26.11.

3.10 Summary

Socket address structures are an integral part of every network program. We allocate them, fill them in, and pass pointers to them to various socket functions. Sometimes we pass a pointer to one of these structures to a socket function and it fills in the contents. We always pass these structures by reference (that is, we pass a pointer to the structure, not the structure itself), and we always pass the size of the structure as another argument. When a socket function fills in a structure, the length is also passed by reference, so that its value can be updated by the function. We call these value-result arguments.

Socket address structures are self-defining because they always begin with a field (the "family") that identifies the address family contained in the structure. Newer implementations that support variable-length socket address structures also contain a length field at the beginning, which contains the length of the entire structure.

The two functions that convert IP addresses between presentation format (what we write, such as ASCII characters) and numeric format (what goes into a socket address structure) are `inet_pton` and `inet_ntop`. Although we will use these two functions in the coming chapters, they are protocol-dependent. A better technique is to manipulate socket address structures as opaque objects, knowing just the pointer to the structure and its size. We used this method to develop a set of `sock_` functions that helped to make our programs protocol-independent. We will complete the development of our protocol-independent tools in Chapter 11 with the `getaddrinfo` and `getnameinfo` functions.

TCP sockets provide a byte stream to an application: There are no record markers. The return value from a `read` can be less than what we asked for, but this does not indicate an error. To help read and write a byte stream, we developed three functions, `readn`, `writen`, and `readline`, which we will use throughout the text. However, network programs should be written to act on buffers rather than lines.

Exercises

3.1 Why must value-result arguments such as the length of a socket address structure be passed by reference?

3.2 Why do both the `readn` and `writen` functions copy the void* pointer into a char* pointer?

3.3 The `inet_aton` and `inet_addr` functions have traditionally been liberal in what they accept as a dotted-decimal IPv4 address string: allowing from one to four numbers separated by decimal points, and allowing a leading 0x to specify a hexadecimal number, or a leading 0 to specify an octal number. (Try `telnet 0xe` to see this behavior.) `inet_pton` is much stricter with IPv4 address and requires exactly four numbers separated by three decimal points, with each number being a decimal number between 0 and 255. `inet_pton` does not allow a dotted-decimal number to be specified when the address family is `AF_INET6`, although one could argue that these should be allowed and the return value should be the IPv4-mapped IPv6 address for the dotted-decimal string (Figure A.10).

Write a new function named `inet_pton_loose` that handles these scenarios: If the address family is `AF_INET` and `inet_pton` returns 0, call `inet_aton` and see if it succeeds. Similarly, if the address family is `AF_INET6` and `inet_pton` returns 0, call `inet_aton` and if it succeeds, return the IPv4-mapped IPv6 address.

4

Elementary TCP Sockets

4.1 Introduction

This chapter describes the elementary socket functions required to write a complete TCP client and server. We will first describe all the elementary socket functions that we will be using and then develop the client and server in the next chapter. We will work with this client and server throughout the text, enhancing it many times (Figures 1.12 and 1.13).

We will also describe concurrent servers, a common Unix technique for providing concurrency when numerous clients are connected to the same server at the same time. Each client connection causes the server to fork a new process just for that client. In this chapter, we consider only the one-*process*-per-client model using fork, but we will consider a different one-*thread*-per-client model when we describe threads in Chapter 26.

Figure 4.1 shows a timeline of the typical scenario that takes place between a TCP client and server. First, the server is started, then sometime later, a client is started that connects to the server. We assume that the client sends a request to the server, the server processes the request, and the server sends a reply back to the client. This continues until the client closes its end of the connection, which sends an end-of-file notification to the server. The server then closes its end of the connection and either terminates or waits for a new client connection.

4.2 socket Function

To perform network I/O, the first thing a process must do is call the socket function, specifying the type of communication protocol desired (TCP using IPv4, UDP using IPv6, Unix domain stream protocol, etc.).

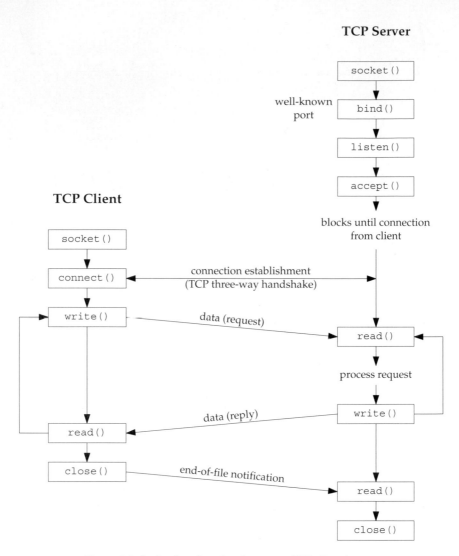

Figure 4.1 Socket functions for elementary TCP client/server.

```
#include <sys/socket.h>

int socket(int family, int type, int protocol);
```
                                         Returns: non-negative descriptor if OK, −1 on error

family specifies the protocol family and is one of the constants shown in Figure 4.2. This argument is often referred to as *domain* instead of *family*. The socket *type* is one of the constants shown in Figure 4.3. The *protocol* argument to the socket function should be set to the specific protocol type found in Figure 4.4, or 0 to select the system's default for the given combination of *family* and *type*.

Not all combinations of socket *family* and *type* are valid. Figure 4.5 shows the valid combinations, along with the actual protocols that are valid for each pair. The boxes marked "Yes" are valid but do not have handy acronyms. The blank boxes are not supported.

family	Description
AF_INET	IPv4 protocols
AF_INET6	IPv6 protocols
AF_LOCAL	Unix domain protocols (Chapter 15)
AF_ROUTE	Routing sockets (Chapter 18)
AF_KEY	Key socket (Chapter 19)

Figure 4.2 Protocol *family* constants for socket function.

type	Description
SOCK_STREAM	stream socket
SOCK_DGRAM	datagram socket
SOCK_SEQPACKET	sequenced packet socket
SOCK_RAW	raw socket

Figure 4.3 *type* of socket for socket function.

Protocol	Description
IPPROTO_TCP	TCP transport protocol
IPPROTO_UDP	UDP transport protocol
IPPROTO_SCTP	SCTP transport protocol

Figure 4.4 *protocol* of sockets for AF_INET or AF_INET6.

	AF_INET	AF_INET6	AF_LOCAL	AF_ROUTE	AF_KEY
SOCK_STREAM	TCP|SCTP	TCP|SCTP	Yes		
SOCK_DGRAM	UDP	UDP	Yes		
SOCK_SEQPACKET	SCTP	SCTP	Yes		
SOCK_RAW	IPv4	IPv6		Yes	Yes

Figure 4.5 Combinations of *family* and *type* for the socket function.

You may also encounter the corresponding PF_*xxx* constant as the first argument to socket. We will say more about this at the end of this section.

We note that you may encounter AF_UNIX (the historical Unix name) instead of AF_LOCAL (the POSIX name), and we will say more about this in Chapter 15.

There are other values for the *family* and *type* arguments. For example, 4.4BSD supports both AF_NS (the Xerox NS protocols, often called XNS) and AF_ISO (the OSI protocols). Similarly, the *type* of SOCK_SEQPACKET, a sequenced-packet socket, is implemented by both the Xerox NS protocols and the OSI protocols, and we will describe its use with SCTP in Section 9.2. But, TCP is a byte stream protocol, and supports only SOCK_STREAM sockets.

Linux supports a new socket type, SOCK_PACKET, that provides access to the datalink, similar to BPF and DLPI in Figure 2.1. We will say more about this in Chapter 29.

The key socket, AF_KEY, is newer than the others. It provides support for cryptographic security. Similar to the way that a routing socket (AF_ROUTE) is an interface to the kernel's routing table, the key socket is an interface into the kernel's key table. See Chapter 19 for details.

On success, the socket function returns a small non-negative integer value, similar to a file descriptor. We call this a *socket descriptor*, or a *sockfd*. To obtain this socket descriptor, all we have specified is a protocol family (IPv4, IPv6, or Unix) and the socket type (stream, datagram, or raw). We have not yet specified either the local protocol address or the foreign protocol address.

AF_*xxx* versus PF_*xxx*

The "AF_" prefix stands for "address family" and the "PF_" prefix stands for "protocol family." Historically, the intent was that a single protocol family might support multiple address families and that the PF_ value was used to create the socket and the AF_ value was used in socket address structures. But in actuality, a protocol family supporting multiple address families has never been supported and the <sys/socket.h> header defines the PF_ value for a given protocol to be equal to the AF_ value for that protocol. While there is no guarantee that this equality between the two will always be true, should anyone change this for existing protocols, lots of existing code would break. To conform to existing coding practice, we use only the AF_ constants in this text, although you may encounter the PF_ value, mainly in calls to socket.

Looking at 137 programs that call socket in the BSD/OS 2.1 release shows 143 calls that specify the AF_ value and only 8 that specify the PF_ value.

Historically, the reason for the similar sets of constants with the AF_ and PF_ prefixes goes back to 4.1cBSD [Lanciani 1996] and a version of the socket function that predates the one we are describing (which appeared with 4.2BSD). The 4.1cBSD version of socket took four arguments, one of which was a pointer to a sockproto structure. The first member of this structure was named sp_family and its value was one of the PF_ values. The second member, sp_protocol, was a protocol number, similar to the third argument to socket today. Specifying this structure was the only way to specify the protocol family. Therefore, in this early system, the PF_ values were used as structure tags to specify the protocol family in the sockproto structure, and the AF_ values were used as structure tags to specify the address family in the socket address structures. The sockproto structure is still in 4.4BSD (pp. 626–627 of TCPv2), but is only used internally by the kernel. The original definition had the comment "protocol family" for the sp_family member, but this has been changed to "address family" in the 4.4BSD source code.

To confuse this difference between the AF_ and PF_ constants even more, the Berkeley kernel data structure that contains the value that is compared to the first argument to socket (the dom_family member of the domain structure, p. 187 of TCPv2) has the comment that it contains an AF_ value. But, some of the domain structures within the kernel are initialized to the corresponding AF_ value (p. 192 of TCPv2) while others are initialized to the PF_ value (p. 646 of TCPv2 and p. 229 of TCPv3).

As another historical note, the 4.2BSD man page for socket, dated July 1983, calls its first argument *af* and lists the possible values as the AF_ constants.

Finally, we note that the POSIX standard specifies that the first argument to socket be a PF_ value, and the AF_ value be used for a socket address structure. But, it then defines only one family value in the addrinfo structure (Section 11.6), intended for use in either a call to socket or in a socket address structure!

4.3 connect **Function**

The connect function is used by a TCP client to establish a connection with a TCP server.

```
#include <sys/socket.h>
int connect(int sockfd, const struct sockaddr *servaddr, socklen_t addrlen);
                                                   Returns: 0 if OK, −1 on error
```

sockfd is a socket descriptor returned by the socket function. The second and third arguments are a pointer to a socket address structure and its size, as described in Section 3.3. The socket address structure must contain the IP address and port number of the server. We saw an example of this function in Figure 1.5.

The client does not have to call bind (which we will describe in the next section) before calling connect: the kernel will choose both an ephemeral port and the source IP address if necessary.

In the case of a TCP socket, the connect function initiates TCP's three-way handshake (Section 2.6). The function returns only when the connection is established or an error occurs. There are several different error returns possible.

1. If the client TCP receives no response to its SYN segment, ETIMEDOUT is returned. 4.4BSD, for example, sends one SYN when connect is called, another 6 seconds later, and another 24 seconds later (p. 828 of TCPv2). If no response is received after a total of 75 seconds, the error is returned.

    Some systems provide administrative control over this timeout; see Appendix E of TCPv1.

2. If the server's response to the client's SYN is a reset (RST), this indicates that no process is waiting for connections on the server host at the port specified (i.e., the server process is probably not running). This is a *hard error* and the error ECONNREFUSED is returned to the client as soon as the RST is received.

An RST is a type of TCP segment that is sent by TCP when something is wrong. Three conditions that generate an RST are: when a SYN arrives for a port that has no listening server (what we just described), when TCP wants to abort an existing connection, and when TCP receives a segment for a connection that does not exist. (TCPv1 [pp. 246–250] contains additional information.)

3. If the client's SYN elicits an ICMP "destination unreachable" from some intermediate router, this is considered a *soft error*. The client kernel saves the message but keeps sending SYNs with the same time between each SYN as in the first scenario. If no response is received after some fixed amount of time (75 seconds for 4.4BSD), the saved ICMP error is returned to the process as either EHOSTUNREACH or ENETUNREACH. It is also possible that the remote system is not reachable by any route in the local system's forwarding table, or that the connect call returns without waiting at all.

> Many earlier systems, such as 4.2BSD, incorrectly aborted the connection establishment attempt when the ICMP "destination unreachable" was received. This is wrong because this ICMP error can indicate a transient condition. For example, it could be that the condition is caused by a routing problem that will be corrected.

> Notice that ENETUNREACH is not listed in Figure A.15, even when the error indicates that the destination network is unreachable. Network unreachables are considered obsolete, and applications should just treat ENETUNREACH and EHOSTUNREACH as the same error.

We can see these different error conditions with our simple client from Figure 1.5. We first specify the local host (127.0.0.1), which is running the daytime server, and see the output.

```
solaris % daytimetcpcli 127.0.0.1
Sun Jul 27 22:01:51 2003
```

To see a different format for the returned reply, we specify a different machine's IP address (in this example, the IP address of the HP-UX machine).

```
solaris % daytimetcpcli 192.6.38.100
Sun Jul 27 22:04:59 PDT 2003
```

Next, we specify an IP address that is on the local subnet (192.168.1/24) but the host ID (100) is nonexistent. That is, there is no host on the subnet with a host ID of 100, so when the client host sends out ARP requests (asking for that host to respond with its hardware address), it will never receive an ARP reply.

```
solaris % daytimetcpcli 192.168.1.100
connect error: Connection timed out
```

We only get the error after the connect times out (around four minutes with Solaris 9). Notice that our err_sys function prints the human-readable string associated with the ETIMEDOUT error.

Our next example is to specify a host (a local router) that is not running a daytime server.

```
solaris % daytimetcpcli 192.168.1.5
connect error: Connection refused
```

The server responds immediately with an RST.

Our final example specifies an IP address that is not reachable on the Internet. If we watch the packets with `tcpdump`, we see that a router six hops away returns an ICMP host unreachable error.

```
solaris % daytimetcpcli 192.3.4.5
connect error: No route to host
```

As with the `ETIMEDOUT` error, in this example, `connect` returns the `EHOSTUNREACH` error only after waiting its specified amount of time.

In terms of the TCP state transition diagram (Figure 2.4), `connect` moves from the CLOSED state (the state in which a socket begins when it is created by the `socket` function) to the SYN_SENT state, and then, on success, to the ESTABLISHED state. If `connect` fails, the socket is no longer usable and must be closed. We cannot call `connect` again on the socket. In Figure 11.10, we will see that when we call `connect` in a loop, trying each IP address for a given host until one works, each time `connect` fails, we must `close` the socket descriptor and call `socket` again.

4.4   bind **Function**

The `bind` function assigns a local protocol address to a socket. With the Internet protocols, the protocol address is the combination of either a 32-bit IPv4 address or a 128-bit IPv6 address, along with a 16-bit TCP or UDP port number.

```
#include <sys/socket.h>

int bind(int sockfd, const struct sockaddr *myaddr, socklen_t addrlen);
```
Returns: 0 if OK, −1 on error

> Historically, the man page description of `bind` has said "bind assigns a name to an unnamed socket." The use of the term "name" is confusing and gives the connotation of domain names (Chapter 11) such as `foo.bar.com`. The bind function has nothing to do with names. bind assigns a protocol address to a socket, and what that protocol address means depends on the protocol.

The second argument is a pointer to a protocol-specific address, and the third argument is the size of this address structure. With TCP, calling `bind` lets us specify a port number, an IP address, both, or neither.

- Servers bind their well-known port when they start. We saw this in Figure 1.9. If a TCP client or server does not do this, the kernel chooses an ephemeral port for the socket when either `connect` or `listen` is called. It is normal for a TCP client to let the kernel choose an ephemeral port, unless the application requires a reserved port (Figure 2.10), but it is rare for a TCP server to let the kernel choose an ephemeral port, since servers are known by their well-known port.

Exceptions to this rule are Remote Procedure Call (RPC) servers. They normally let the kernel choose an ephemeral port for their listening socket since this port is then registered with the RPC port mapper. Clients have to contact the port mapper to obtain the ephemeral port before they can connect to the server. This also applies to RPC servers using UDP.

- A process can bind a specific IP address to its socket. The IP address must belong to an interface on the host. For a TCP client, this assigns the source IP address that will be used for IP datagrams sent on the socket. For a TCP server, this restricts the socket to receive incoming client connections destined only to that IP address.

Normally, a TCP client does not bind an IP address to its socket. The kernel chooses the source IP address when the socket is connected, based on the outgoing interface that is used, which in turn is based on the route required to reach the server (p. 737 of TCPv2).

If a TCP server does not bind an IP address to its socket, the kernel uses the destination IP address of the client's SYN as the server's source IP address (p. 943 of TCPv2).

As we said, calling bind lets us specify the IP address, the port, both, or neither. Figure 4.6 summarizes the values to which we set sin_addr and sin_port, or sin6_addr and sin6_port, depending on the desired result.

Process specifies		Result
IP address	port	
Wildcard	0	Kernel chooses IP address and port
Wildcard	nonzero	Kernel chooses IP address, process specifies port
Local IP address	0	Process specifies IP address, kernel chooses port
Local IP address	nonzero	Process specifies IP address and port

Figure 4.6 Result when specifying IP address and/or port number to bind.

If we specify a port number of 0, the kernel chooses an ephemeral port when bind is called. But if we specify a wildcard IP address, the kernel does not choose the local IP address until either the socket is connected (TCP) or a datagram is sent on the socket (UDP).

With IPv4, the *wildcard* address is specified by the constant INADDR_ANY, whose value is normally 0. This tells the kernel to choose the IP address. We saw the use of this in Figure 1.9 with the assignment

```
struct sockaddr_in    servaddr;

servaddr.sin_addr.s_addr = htonl(INADDR_ANY);    /* wildcard */
```

While this works with IPv4, where an IP address is a 32-bit value that can be represented as a simple numeric constant (0 in this case), we cannot use this technique with IPv6, since the 128-bit IPv6 address is stored in a structure. (In C we cannot represent a constant structure on the right-hand side of an assignment.) To solve this problem, we write

```
struct sockaddr_in6     serv;

serv.sin6_addr = in6addr_any;    /* wildcard */
```

The system allocates and initializes the `in6addr_any` variable to the constant `IN6ADDR_ANY_INIT`. The `<netinet/in.h>` header contains the `extern` declaration for `in6addr_any`.

The value of `INADDR_ANY` (0) is the same in either network or host byte order, so the use of `htonl` is not really required. But, since all the `INADDR_` constants defined by the `<netinet/in.h>` header are defined in host byte order, we should use `htonl` with any of these constants.

If we tell the kernel to choose an ephemeral port number for our socket, notice that `bind` does not return the chosen value. Indeed, it cannot return this value since the second argument to `bind` has the `const` qualifier. To obtain the value of the ephemeral port assigned by the kernel, we must call `getsockname` to return the protocol address.

A common example of a process binding a non-wildcard IP address to a socket is a host that provides Web servers to multiple organizations (Section 14.2 of TCPv3). First, each organization has its own domain name, such as www.*organization*.com. Next, each organization's domain name maps into a different IP address, but typically on the same subnet. For example, if the subnet is 198.69.10, the first organization's IP address could be 198.69.10.128, the next 198.69.10.129, and so on. All these IP addresses are then *aliased* onto a single network interface (using the `alias` option of the `ifconfig` command on 4.4BSD, for example) so that the IP layer will accept incoming datagrams destined for any of the aliased addresses. Finally, one copy of the HTTP server is started for each organization and each copy `bind`s only the IP address for that organization.

> An alternative technique is to run a single server that binds the wildcard address. When a connection arrives, the server calls `getsockname` to obtain the destination IP address from the client, which in our discussion above could be 198.69.10.128, 198.69.10.129, and so on. The server then handles the client request based on the IP address to which the connection was issued.

> One advantage in binding a non-wildcard IP address is that the demultiplexing of a given destination IP address to a given server process is then done by the kernel.

> We must be careful to distinguish between the interface on which a packet arrives versus the destination IP address of that packet. In Section 8.8, we will talk about the weak end system model and the strong end system model. Most implementations employ the former, meaning it is okay for a packet to arrive with a destination IP address that identifies an interface other than the interface on which the packet arrives. (This assumes a multihomed host.) Binding a non-wildcard IP address restricts the datagrams that will be delivered to the socket based only on the destination IP address. It says nothing about the arriving interface, unless the host employs the strong end system model.

A common error from `bind` is `EADDRINUSE` ("Address already in use"). We will say more about this in Section 7.5 when we talk about the `SO_REUSEADDR` and `SO_REUSEPORT` socket options.

4.5   `listen` Function

The `listen` function is called only by a TCP server and it performs two actions:

1. When a socket is created by the `socket` function, it is assumed to be an active socket, that is, a client socket that will issue a `connect`. The `listen` function converts an unconnected socket into a passive socket, indicating that the kernel should accept incoming connection requests directed to this socket. In terms of the TCP state transition diagram (Figure 2.4), the call to `listen` moves the socket from the CLOSED state to the LISTEN state.

2. The second argument to this function specifies the maximum number of connections the kernel should queue for this socket.

```
#include <sys/socket.h>

int listen(int sockfd, int backlog);
```
                                                              Returns: 0 if OK, –1 on error

This function is normally called after both the `socket` and `bind` functions and must be called before calling the `accept` function.

To understand the *backlog* argument, we must realize that for a given listening socket, the kernel maintains two queues:

1. An *incomplete connection queue*, which contains an entry for each SYN that has arrived from a client for which the server is awaiting completion of the TCP three-way handshake. These sockets are in the SYN_RCVD state (Figure 2.4).

2. A *completed connection queue*, which contains an entry for each client with whom the TCP three-way handshake has completed. These sockets are in the ESTAB-LISHED state (Figure 2.4).

Figure 4.7 depicts these two queues for a given listening socket.

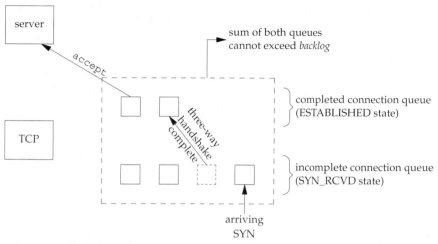

Figure 4.7 The two queues maintained by TCP for a listening socket.

When an entry is created on the incomplete queue, the parameters from the listen socket are copied over to the newly created connection. The connection creation mechanism is completely automatic; the server process is not involved. Figure 4.8 depicts the packets exchanged during the connection establishment with these two queues.

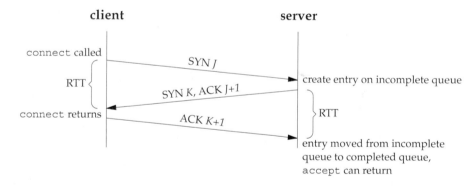

Figure 4.8 TCP three-way handshake and the two queues for a listening socket.

When a SYN arrives from a client, TCP creates a new entry on the incomplete queue and then responds with the second segment of the three-way handshake: the server's SYN with an ACK of the client's SYN (Section 2.6). This entry will remain on the incomplete queue until the third segment of the three-way handshake arrives (the client's ACK of the server's SYN), or until the entry times out. (Berkeley-derived implementations have a timeout of 75 seconds for these incomplete entries.) If the three-way handshake completes normally, the entry moves from the incomplete queue to the end of the completed queue. When the process calls accept, which we will describe in the next section, the first entry on the completed queue is returned to the process, or if the queue is empty, the process is put to sleep until an entry is placed onto the completed queue.

There are several points to consider regarding the handling of these two queues.

- The *backlog* argument to the `listen` function has historically specified the maximum value for the sum of both queues.

  > There has never been a formal definition of what the *backlog* means. The 4.2BSD man page says that it "defines the maximum length the queue of pending connections may grow to." Many man pages and even the POSIX specification copy this definition verbatim, but this definition does not say whether a pending connection is one in the SYN_RCVD state, one in the ESTABLISHED state that has not yet been accepted, or either. The historical definition in this bullet is the Berkeley implementation, dating back to 4.2BSD, and copied by many others.

- Berkeley-derived implementations add a fudge factor to the *backlog*: It is multiplied by 1.5 (p. 257 of TCPv1 and p. 462 of TCPv2). For example, the commonly specified *backlog* of 5 really allows up to 8 queued entries on these systems, as we show in Figure 4.10.

  > The reason for adding this fudge factor appears lost to history [Joy 1994]. But if we consider the *backlog* as specifying the maximum number of completed connections that the kernel will queue for a socket ([Borman 1997b], as discussed shortly), then the reason for the fudge factor is to take into account incomplete connections on the queue.

- Do not specify a *backlog* of 0, as different implementations interpret this differently (Figure 4.10). If you do not want any clients connecting to your listening socket, close the listening socket.

- Assuming the three-way handshake completes normally (i.e., no lost segments and no retransmissions), an entry remains on the incomplete connection queue for one RTT, whatever that value happens to be between a particular client and server. Section 14.4 of TCPv3 shows that for one Web server, the median RTT between many clients and the server was 187 ms. (The median is often used for this statistic, since a few large values can noticeably skew the mean.)

- Historically, sample code always shows a *backlog* of 5, as that was the maximum value supported by 4.2BSD. This was adequate in the 1980s when busy servers would handle only a few hundred connections per day. But with the growth of the World Wide Web (WWW), where busy servers handle millions of connections per day, this small number is completely inadequate (pp. 187–192 of TCPv3). Busy HTTP servers must specify a much larger *backlog*, and newer kernels must support larger values.

  > Many current systems allow the administrator to modify the maximum value for the *backlog*.

- A problem is: What value should the application specify for the *backlog*, since 5 is often inadequate? There is no easy answer to this. HTTP servers now specify a larger value, but if the value specified is a constant in the source code, to increase the constant requires recompiling the server. Another method is to assume some default but allow a command-line option or an environment variable to override the default. It is always acceptable to specify a value that is larger than supported by the kernel, as the kernel should silently truncate the value to the maximum value that it supports, without returning an error (p. 456 of TCPv2).

We can provide a simple solution to this problem by modifying our wrapper function for the listen function. Figure 4.9 shows the actual code. We allow the environment variable LISTENQ to override the value specified by the caller.

——— *lib/wrapsock.c*
```
137 void
138 Listen(int fd, int backlog)
139 {
140     char    *ptr;

141         /* can override 2nd argument with environment variable */
142     if ( (ptr = getenv("LISTENQ")) != NULL)
143         backlog = atoi(ptr);

144     if (listen(fd, backlog) < 0)
145         err_sys("listen error");
146 }
```
——— *lib/wrapsock.c*

Figure 4.9 Wrapper function for listen that allows an environment variable to specify *backlog*.

- Manuals and books have historically said that the reason for queuing a fixed number of connections is to handle the case of the server process being busy between successive calls to accept. This implies that of the two queues, the completed queue should normally have more entries than the incomplete queue. Again, busy Web servers have shown that this is false. The reason for specifying a large *backlog* is because the incomplete connection queue can grow as client SYNs arrive, waiting for completion of the three-way handshake.

- If the queues are full when a client SYN arrives, TCP ignores the arriving SYN (pp. 930–931 of TCPv2); it does not send an RST. This is because the condition is considered temporary, and the client TCP will retransmit its SYN, hopefully finding room on the queue in the near future. If the server TCP immediately responded with an RST, the client's connect would return an error, forcing the application to handle this condition instead of letting TCP's normal retransmission take over. Also, the client could not differentiate between an RST in response to a SYN meaning "there is no server at this port" versus "there is a server at this port but its queues are full."

  > Some implementations do send an RST when the queue is full. This behavior is incorrect for the reasons stated above, and unless your client specifically needs to interact with such a server, it's best to ignore this possibility. Coding to handle this case reduces the robustness of the client and puts more load on the network in the normal RST case, where the port really has no server listening on it.

- Data that arrives after the three-way handshake completes, but before the server calls `accept`, should be queued by the server TCP, up to the size of the connected socket's receive buffer.

Figure 4.10 shows the actual number of queued connections provided for different values of the *backlog* argument for the various operating systems in Figure 1.16. For seven different operating systems there are five distinct columns, showing the variety of interpretations about what *backlog* means!

backlog	Maximum actual number of queued connections				
	MacOS 10.2.6 AIX 5.1	Linux 2.4.7	HP-UX 11.11	FreeBSD 4.8 FreeBSD 5.1	Solaris 2.9
0	1	3	1	1	1
1	2	4	1	2	2
2	4	5	3	3	4
3	5	6	4	4	5
4	7	7	6	5	6
5	8	8	7	6	8
6	10	9	9	7	10
7	11	10	10	8	11
8	13	11	12	9	13
9	14	12	13	10	14
10	16	13	15	11	16
11	17	14	16	12	17
12	19	15	18	13	19
13	20	16	19	14	20
14	22	17	21	15	22

Figure 4.10   Actual number of queued connections for values of *backlog*.

AIX and MacOS have the traditional Berkeley algorithm, and Solaris seems very close to that algorithm as well. FreeBSD just adds one to *backlog*.

The program to measure these values is shown in the solution for Exercise 15.4.

As we said, historically the *backlog* has specified the maximum value for the sum of both queues. During 1996, a new type of attack was launched on the Internet called *SYN flooding* [CERT 1996b]. The hacker writes a program to send SYNs at a high rate to the victim, filling the incomplete connection queue for one or more TCP ports. (We use the term *hacker* to mean the attacker, as described in [Cheswick, Bellovin, and Rubin 2003].) Additionally, the source IP address of each SYN is set to a random number (this is called *IP spoofing*) so that the server's SYN/ACK goes nowhere. This also prevents the server from knowing the real IP address of the hacker. By filling the incomplete queue with bogus SYNs, legitimate SYNs are not queued, providing a *denial of service* to legitimate clients. There are two commonly used methods of handling these attacks, summarized in [Borman 1997b]. But what is most interesting in this note is revisiting what the `listen` *backlog* really means. It should specify the maximum number of *completed* connections for a given socket that the kernel will queue. The purpose of having a limit on these completed connections is to stop the kernel from accepting new connection requests for a given socket when the application is not accepting them (for whatever reason). If a system implements this interpretation, as does BSD/OS 3.0, then the application need not specify huge *backlog* values just because the server handles lots of client requests (e.g., a busy

Web server) or to provide protection against SYN flooding. The kernel handles lots of incomplete connections, regardless of whether they are legitimate or from a hacker. But even with this interpretation, scenarios do occur where the traditional value of 5 is inadequate.

4.6   accept **Function**

accept is called by a TCP server to return the next completed connection from the front of the completed connection queue (Figure 4.7). If the completed connection queue is empty, the process is put to sleep (assuming the default of a blocking socket).

```
#include <sys/socket.h>

int accept(int sockfd, struct sockaddr *cliaddr, socklen_t *addrlen);
```
Returns: non-negative descriptor if OK, –1 on error

The *cliaddr* and *addrlen* arguments are used to return the protocol address of the connected peer process (the client). *addrlen* is a value-result argument (Section 3.3): Before the call, we set the integer value referenced by *addrlen* to the size of the socket address structure pointed to by *cliaddr*; on return, this integer value contains the actual number of bytes stored by the kernel in the socket address structure.

If accept is successful, its return value is a brand-new descriptor automatically created by the kernel. This new descriptor refers to the TCP connection with the client. When discussing accept, we call the first argument to accept the *listening socket* (the descriptor created by socket and then used as the first argument to both bind and listen), and we call the return value from accept the *connected socket*. It is important to differentiate between these two sockets. A given server normally creates only one listening socket, which then exists for the lifetime of the server. The kernel creates one connected socket for each client connection that is accepted (i.e., for which the TCP three-way handshake completes). When the server is finished serving a given client, the connected socket is closed.

This function returns up to three values: an integer return code that is either a new socket descriptor or an error indication, the protocol address of the client process (through the *cliaddr* pointer), and the size of this address (through the *addrlen* pointer). If we are not interested in having the protocol address of the client returned, we set both *cliaddr* and *addrlen* to null pointers.

Figure 1.9 shows these points. The connected socket is closed each time through the loop, but the listening socket remains open for the life of the server. We also see that the second and third arguments to accept are null pointers, since we were not interested in the identity of the client.

Example: Value-Result Arguments

We will now show how to handle the value-result argument to accept by modifying the code from Figure 1.9 to print the IP address and port of the client. We show this in Figure 4.11.

———————————————————————————— intro/daytimetcpsrv1.c

```
 1 #include    "unp.h"
 2 #include    <time.h>

 3 int
 4 main(int argc, char **argv)
 5 {
 6     int     listenfd, connfd;
 7     socklen_t len;
 8     struct sockaddr_in servaddr, cliaddr;
 9     char    buff[MAXLINE];
10     time_t  ticks;

11     listenfd = Socket(AF_INET, SOCK_STREAM, 0);

12     bzero(&servaddr, sizeof(servaddr));
13     servaddr.sin_family = AF_INET;
14     servaddr.sin_addr.s_addr = htonl(INADDR_ANY);
15     servaddr.sin_port = htons(13);  /* daytime server */

16     Bind(listenfd, (SA *) &servaddr, sizeof(servaddr));

17     Listen(listenfd, LISTENQ);

18     for ( ; ; ) {
19         len = sizeof(cliaddr);
20         connfd = Accept(listenfd, (SA *) &cliaddr, &len);
21         printf("connection from %s, port %d\n",
22                 Inet_ntop(AF_INET, &cliaddr.sin_addr, buff, sizeof(buff)),
23                 ntohs(cliaddr.sin_port));

24         ticks = time(NULL);
25         snprintf(buff, sizeof(buff), "%.24s\r\n", ctime(&ticks));
26         Write(connfd, buff, strlen(buff));

27         Close(connfd);
28     }
29 }
```

———————————————————————————— intro/daytimetcpsrv1.c

Figure 4.11 Daytime server that prints client IP address and port.

New declarations

7–8   We define two new variables: len, which will be a value-result variable, and cliaddr, which will contain the client's protocol address.

Accept connection and print client's address

19–23   We initialize len to the size of the socket address structure and pass a pointer to the cliaddr structure and a pointer to len as the second and third arguments to accept. We call inet_ntop (Section 3.7) to convert the 32-bit IP address in the socket address structure to a dotted-decimal ASCII string and call ntohs (Section 3.4) to convert the 16-bit port number from network byte order to host byte order.

> Calling sock_ntop instead of inet_ntop would make our server more protocol-independent, but this server is already dependent on IPv4. We will show a protocol-independent version of this server in Figure 11.13.

If we run our new server and then run our client on the same host, connecting to our server twice in a row, we have the following output from the client:

```
solaris % daytimetcpcli 127.0.0.1
Thu Sep 11 12:44:00 2003
solaris % daytimetcpcli 192.168.1.20
Thu Sep 11 12:44:09 2003
```

We first specify the server's IP address as the loopback address (127.0.0.1) and then as its own IP address (192.168.1.20). Here is the corresponding server output:

```
solaris # daytimetcpsrv1
connection from 127.0.0.1, port 43388
connection from 192.168.1.20, port 43389
```

Notice what happens with the client's IP address. Since our daytime client (Figure 1.5) does not call bind, we said in Section 4.4 that the kernel chooses the source IP address based on the outgoing interface that is used. In the first case, the kernel sets the source IP address to the loopback address; in the second case, it sets the address to the IP address of the Ethernet interface. We can also see in this example that the ephemeral port chosen by the Solaris kernel is 43388, and then 43389 (recall Figure 2.10).

As a final point, our shell prompt for the server script changes to the pound sign (#), the commonly used prompt for the superuser. Our server must run with superuser privileges to bind the reserved port of 13. If we do not have superuser privileges, the call to bind will fail:

```
solaris % daytimetcpsrv1
bind error: Permission denied
```

4.7   fork and exec Functions

Before describing how to write a concurrent server in the next section, we must describe the Unix fork function. This function (including the variants of it provided by some systems) is the only way in Unix to create a new process.

```
#include <unistd.h>

pid_t fork(void);
```
Returns: 0 in child, process ID of child in parent, −1 on error

If you have never seen this function before, the hard part in understanding fork is that it is called *once* but it returns *twice*. It returns once in the calling process (called the parent) with a return value that is the process ID of the newly created process (the child). It also returns once in the child, with a return value of 0. Hence, the return value tells the process whether it is the parent or the child.

The reason fork returns 0 in the child, instead of the parent's process ID, is because a child has only one parent and it can always obtain the parent's process ID by calling getppid. A parent, on the other hand, can have any number of children, and there is no way to obtain the process IDs of its children. If a parent wants to keep track of the process IDs of all its children, it must record the return values from `fork`.

All descriptors open in the parent before the call to `fork` are shared with the child after `fork` returns. We will see this feature used by network servers: The parent calls `accept` and then calls `fork`. The connected socket is then shared between the parent and child. Normally, the child then reads and writes the connected socket and the parent closes the connected socket.

There are two typical uses of `fork`:

1. A process makes a copy of itself so that one copy can handle one operation while the other copy does another task. This is typical for network servers. We will see many examples of this later in the text.

2. A process wants to execute another program. Since the only way to create a new process is by calling `fork`, the process first calls `fork` to make a copy of itself, and then one of the copies (typically the child process) calls `exec` (described next) to replace itself with the new program. This is typical for programs such as shells.

The only way in which an executable program file on disk can be executed by Unix is for an existing process to call one of the six `exec` functions. (We will often refer generically to "the `exec` function" when it does not matter which of the six is called.) `exec` replaces the current process image with the new program file, and this new program normally starts at the `main` function. The process ID does not change. We refer to the process that calls `exec` as the *calling process* and the newly executed program as the *new program*.

> Older manuals and books incorrectly refer to the new program as the *new process*, which is wrong, because a new process is not created.

The differences in the six `exec` functions are: (a) whether the program file to execute is specified by a *filename* or a *pathname*; (b) whether the arguments to the new program are listed one by one or referenced through an array of pointers; and (c) whether the environment of the calling process is passed to the new program or whether a new environment is specified.

```
#include <unistd.h>

int execl(const char *pathname, const char *arg0, ... /* (char *) 0 */ );

int execv(const char *pathname, char *const argv[]);

int execle(const char *pathname, const char *arg0, ...
            /* (char *) 0, char *const envp[] */ );

int execve(const char *pathname, char *const argv[], char *const envp[]);

int execlp(const char *filename, const char *arg0, ... /* (char *) 0 */ );

int execvp(const char *filename, char *const argv[]);
```

All six return: −1 on error, no return on success

These functions return to the caller only if an error occurs. Otherwise, control passes to the start of the new program, normally the main function.

The relationship among these six functions is shown in Figure 4.12. Normally, only execve is a system call within the kernel and the other five are library functions that call execve.

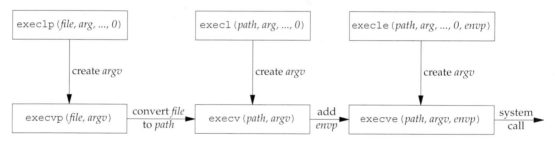

Figure 4.12 Relationship among the six exec functions.

Note the following differences among these six functions:

1. The three functions in the top row specify each argument string as a separate argument to the exec function, with a null pointer terminating the variable number of arguments. The three functions in the second row have an *argv* array, containing pointers to the argument strings. This *argv* array must contain a null pointer to specify its end, since a count is not specified.

2. The two functions in the left column specify a *filename* argument. This is converted into a *pathname* using the current PATH environment variable. If the *filename* argument to execlp or execvp contains a slash (/) anywhere in the string, the PATH variable is not used. The four functions in the right two columns specify a fully qualified *pathname* argument.

3. The four functions in the left two columns do not specify an explicit environment pointer. Instead, the current value of the external variable environ is

used for building an environment list that is passed to the new program. The two functions in the right column specify an explicit environment list. The *envp* array of pointers must be terminated by a null pointer.

Descriptors open in the process before calling exec normally remain open across the exec. We use the qualifier "normally" because this can be disabled using fcntl to set the FD_CLOEXEC descriptor flag. The inetd server uses this feature, as we will describe in Section 13.5.

4.8 Concurrent Servers

The server in Figure 4.11 is an *iterative server*. For something as simple as a daytime server, this is fine. But when a client request can take longer to service, we do not want to tie up a single server with one client; we want to handle multiple clients at the same time. The simplest way to write a *concurrent server* under Unix is to fork a child process to handle each client. Figure 4.13 shows the outline for a typical concurrent server.

```
pid_t  pid;
int    listenfd, connfd;

listenfd = Socket( ... );

    /* fill in sockaddr_in{} with server's well-known port */
Bind(listenfd, ... );
Listen(listenfd, LISTENQ);

for ( ; ; ) {
    connfd = Accept(listenfd, ... );       /* probably blocks */

    if ( (pid = Fork()) == 0) {
        Close(listenfd);     /* child closes listening socket */
        doit(connfd);        /* process the request */
        Close(connfd);       /* done with this client */
        exit(0);             /* child terminates */
    }

    Close(connfd);           /* parent closes connected socket */
}
```

Figure 4.13 Outline for typical concurrent server.

When a connection is established, accept returns, the server calls fork, and the child process services the client (on connfd, the connected socket) and the parent process waits for another connection (on listenfd, the listening socket). The parent closes the connected socket since the child handles the new client.

In Figure 4.13, we assume that the function doit does whatever is required to service the client. When this function returns, we explicitly close the connected socket in the child. This is not required since the next statement calls exit, and part of process termination is to close all open descriptors by the kernel. Whether to include this explicit call to close or not is a matter of personal programming taste.

We said in Section 2.6 that calling `close` on a TCP socket causes a FIN to be sent, followed by the normal TCP connection termination sequence. Why doesn't the `close` of connfd in Figure 4.13 by the parent terminate its connection with the client? To understand what's happening, we must understand that every file or socket has a reference count. The reference count is maintained in the file table entry (pp. 57–60 of APUE). This is a count of the number of descriptors that are currently open that refer to this file or socket. In Figure 4.13, after `socket` returns, the file table entry associated with `listenfd` has a reference count of 1. After `accept` returns, the file table entry associated with `connfd` has a reference count of 1. But, after `fork` returns, both descriptors are shared (i.e., duplicated) between the parent and child, so the file table entries associated with both sockets now have a reference count of 2. Therefore, when the parent closes `connfd`, it just decrements the reference count from 2 to 1 and that is all. The actual cleanup and de-allocation of the socket does not happen until the reference count reaches 0. This will occur at some time later when the child closes `connfd`.

We can also visualize the sockets and connection that occur in Figure 4.13 as follows. First, Figure 4.14 shows the status of the client and server while the server is blocked in the call to `accept` and the connection request arrives from the client.

Figure 4.14   Status of client/server before call to `accept` returns.

Immediately after `accept` returns, we have the scenario shown in Figure 4.15. The connection is accepted by the kernel and a new socket, `connfd`, is created. This is a connected socket and data can now be read and written across the connection.

The next step in the concurrent server is to call `fork`. Figure 4.16 shows the status after `fork` returns.

Figure 4.15   Status of client/server after return from `accept`.

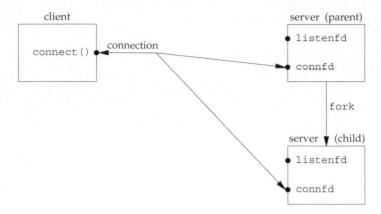

Figure 4.16 Status of client/server after `fork` returns.

Notice that both descriptors, `listenfd` and `connfd`, are shared (duplicated) between the parent and child.

The next step is for the parent to close the connected socket and the child to close the listening socket. This is shown in Figure 4.17.

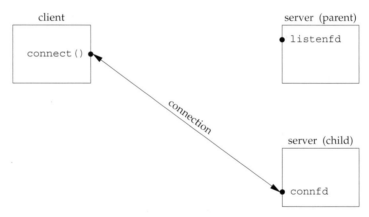

Figure 4.17 Status of client/server after parent and child close appropriate sockets.

This is the desired final state of the sockets. The child is handling the connection with the client and the parent can call `accept` again on the listening socket, to handle the next client connection.

4.9 `close` Function

The normal Unix `close` function is also used to close a socket and terminate a TCP connection.

```
#include <unistd.h>

int close(int sockfd);
```
Returns: 0 if OK, –1 on error

The default action of `close` with a TCP socket is to mark the socket as closed and return to the process immediately. The socket descriptor is no longer usable by the process: It cannot be used as an argument to `read` or `write`. But, TCP will try to send any data that is already queued to be sent to the other end, and after this occurs, the normal TCP connection termination sequence takes place (Section 2.6).

In Section 7.5, we will describe the `SO_LINGER` socket option, which lets us change this default action with a TCP socket. In that section, we will also describe what a TCP application must do to be guaranteed that the peer application has received any outstanding data.

Descriptor Reference Counts

At the end of Section 4.8, we mentioned that when the parent process in our concurrent server `closes` the connected socket, this just decrements the reference count for the descriptor. Since the reference count was still greater than 0, this call to `close` did not initiate TCP's four-packet connection termination sequence. This is the behavior we want with our concurrent server with the connected socket that is shared between the parent and child.

If we really want to send a FIN on a TCP connection, the `shutdown` function can be used (Section 6.6) instead of `close`. We will describe the motivation for this in Section 6.5.

We must also be aware of what happens in our concurrent server if the parent does not call `close` for each connected socket returned by `accept`. First, the parent will eventually run out of descriptors, as there is usually a limit to the number of descriptors that any process can have open at any time. But more importantly, none of the client connections will be terminated. When the child closes the connected socket, its reference count will go from 2 to 1 and it will remain at 1 since the parent never `closes` the connected socket. This will prevent TCP's connection termination sequence from occurring, and the connection will remain open.

4.10 `getsockname` and `getpeername` Functions

These two functions return either the local protocol address associated with a socket (getsockname) or the foreign protocol address associated with a socket (getpeername).

```
#include <sys/socket.h>

int getsockname(int sockfd, struct sockaddr *localaddr, socklen_t *addrlen);

int getpeername(int sockfd, struct sockaddr *peeraddr, socklen_t *addrlen);
```
Both return: 0 if OK, −1 on error

Notice that the final argument for both functions is a value-result argument. That is, both functions fill in the socket address structure pointed to by *localaddr* or *peeraddr*.

> We mentioned in our discussion of bind that the term "name" is misleading. These two functions return the protocol address associated with one of the two ends of a network connection, which for IPv4 and IPv6 is the combination of an IP address and port number. These functions have nothing to do with domain names (Chapter 11).

These two functions are required for the following reasons:

- After connect successfully returns in a TCP client that does not call bind, getsockname returns the local IP address and local port number assigned to the connection by the kernel.

- After calling bind with a port number of 0 (telling the kernel to choose the local port number), getsockname returns the local port number that was assigned.

- getsockname can be called to obtain the address family of a socket, as we show in Figure 4.19.

- In a TCP server that binds the wildcard IP address (Figure 1.9), once a connection is established with a client (accept returns successfully), the server can call getsockname to obtain the local IP address assigned to the connection. The socket descriptor argument in this call must be that of the connected socket, and not the listening socket.

- When a server is execed by the process that calls accept, the only way the server can obtain the identity of the client is to call getpeername. This is what happens whenever inetd (Section 13.5) forks and execs a TCP server. Figure 4.18 shows this scenario. inetd calls accept (top left box) and two values are returned: the connected socket descriptor, connfd, is the return value of the function, and the small box we label "peer's address" (an Internet socket address structure) contains the IP address and port number of the client. fork is called and a child of inetd is created. Since the child starts with a copy of the parent's memory image, the socket address structure is available to the child, as is the connected socket descriptor (since the descriptors are shared between the parent and child). But when the child execs the real server (say the Telnet server that we show), the memory image of the child is replaced with the new program file for the Telnet server (i.e., the socket address structure containing the peer's address is lost), and the connected socket descriptor remains open across the exec. One of the first function calls performed by the Telnet server is getpeername to obtain the IP address and port number of the client.

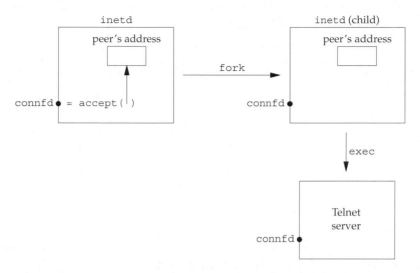

Figure 4.18 Example of inetd spawning a server.

Obviously the Telnet server in this final example must know the value of connfd when it starts. There are two common ways to do this. First, the process calling exec can format the descriptor number as a character string and pass it as a command-line argument to the newly execed program. Alternately, a convention can be established that a certain descriptor is always set to the connected socket before calling exec. The latter is what inetd does, always setting descriptors 0, 1, and 2 to be the connected socket.

Example: Obtaining the Address Family of a Socket

The sockfd_to_family function shown in Figure 4.19 returns the address family of a socket.

lib/sockfd_to_family.c

```
 1 #include    "unp.h"

 2 int
 3 sockfd_to_family(int sockfd)
 4 {
 5     struct sockaddr_storage ss;
 6     socklen_t len;

 7     len = sizeof(ss);
 8     if (getsockname(sockfd, (SA *) &ss, &len) < 0)
 9         return (-1);
10     return (ss.ss_family);
11 }
```

lib/sockfd_to_family.c

Figure 4.19 Return the address family of a socket.

Allocate room for largest socket address structure

5   Since we do not know what type of socket address structure to allocate, we use a `sockaddr_storage` value, since it can hold any socket address structure supported by the system.

Call `getsockname`

7–10   We call `getsockname` and return the address family.

Since the POSIX specification allows a call to `getsockname` on an unbound socket, this function should work for any open socket descriptor.

4.11 Summary

All clients and servers begin with a call to `socket`, returning a socket descriptor. Clients then call `connect`, while servers call `bind`, `listen`, and `accept`. Sockets are normally closed with the standard `close` function, although we will see another way to do this with the `shutdown` function (Section 6.6), and we will also examine the effect of the `SO_LINGER` socket option (Section 7.5).

Most TCP servers are concurrent, with the server calling `fork` for every client connection that it handles. We will see that most UDP servers are iterative. While these two models have been used successfully for many years, in Chapter 30 we will look at other server design options that use threads and processes.

Exercises

4.1   In Section 4.4, we stated that the `INADDR_` constants defined by the `<netinet/in.h>` header are in host byte order. How can we tell this?

4.2   Modify Figure 1.5 to call `getsockname` after `connect` returns successfully. Print the local IP address and local port assigned to the TCP socket using `sock_ntop`. In what range (Figure 2.10) are your system's ephemeral ports?

4.3   In a concurrent server, assume the child runs first after the call to `fork`. The child then completes the service of the client before the call to `fork` returns to the parent. What happens in the two calls to `close` in Figure 4.13?

4.4   In Figure 4.11, first change the server's port from 13 to 9999 (so that we do not need superuser privileges to start the program). Remove the call to `listen`. What happens?

4.5   Continue the previous exercise. Remove the call to `bind`, but allow the call to `listen`. What happens?

5

TCP Client/Server Example

5.1   Introduction

We will now use the elementary functions from the previous chapter to write a complete TCP client/server example. Our simple example is an echo server that performs the following steps:

1. The client reads a line of text from its standard input and writes the line to the server.

2. The server reads the line from its network input and echoes the line back to the client.

3. The client reads the echoed line and prints it on its standard output.

Figure 5.1 depicts this simple client/server along with the functions used for input and output.

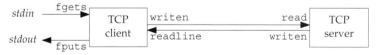

Figure 5.1 Simple echo client and server.

We show two arrows between the client and server, but this is really one full-duplex TCP connection. The `fgets` and `fputs` functions are from the standard I/O library and the `writen` and `readline` functions were shown in Section 3.9.

While we will develop our own implementation of an echo server, most TCP/IP implementations provide such a server, using both TCP and UDP (Section 2.12). We will also use this server with our own client.

A client/server that echoes input lines is a valid, yet simple, example of a network application. All the basic steps required to implement any client/server are illustrated by this example. To expand this example into your own application, all you need to do is change what the server does with the input it receives from its clients.

Besides running our client and server in their normal mode (type in a line and watch it echo), we examine lots of boundary conditions for this example: what happens when the client and server are started; what happens when the client terminates normally; what happens to the client if the server process terminates before the client is done; what happens to the client if the server host crashes; and so on. By looking at all these scenarios and understanding what happens at the network level, and how this appears to the sockets API, we will understand more about what goes on at these levels and how to code our applications to handle these scenarios.

In all these examples, we have "hard-coded" protocol-specific constants such as addresses and ports. There are two reasons for this. First, we must understand exactly what needs to be stored in the protocol-specific address structures. Second, we have not yet covered the library functions that can make this more portable. These functions will be covered in Chapter 11.

We note now that we will make many changes to both the client and server in successive chapters as we learn more about network programming (Figures 1.12 and 1.13).

5.2   TCP Echo Server: `main` Function

Our TCP client and server follow the flow of functions that we diagrammed in Figure 4.1. We show the concurrent server program in Figure 5.2.

Create socket, bind server's well-known port

9-15   A TCP socket is created. An Internet socket address structure is filled in with the wildcard address (INADDR_ANY) and the server's well-known port (SERV_PORT, which is defined as 9877 in our unp.h header). Binding the wildcard address tells the system that we will accept a connection destined for any local interface, in case the system is multihomed. Our choice of the TCP port number is based on Figure 2.10. It should be greater than 1023 (we do not need a reserved port), greater than 5000 (to avoid conflict with the ephemeral ports allocated by many Berkeley-derived implementations), less than 49152 (to avoid conflict with the "correct" range of ephemeral ports), and it should not conflict with any registered port. The socket is converted into a listening socket by `listen`.

Wait for client connection to complete

17-18   The server blocks in the call to `accept`, waiting for a client connection to complete.

Concurrent server

19-24   For each client, `fork` spawns a child, and the child handles the new client. As we discussed in Section 4.8, the child closes the listening socket and the parent closes the connected socket. The child then calls `str_echo` (Figure 5.3) to handle the client.

―― *tcpcliserv/tcpserv01.c*

```
 1 #include     "unp.h"

 2 int
 3 main(int argc, char **argv)
 4 {
 5     int      listenfd, connfd;
 6     pid_t    childpid;
 7     socklen_t clilen;
 8     struct sockaddr_in cliaddr, servaddr;

 9     listenfd = Socket(AF_INET, SOCK_STREAM, 0);

10     bzero(&servaddr, sizeof(servaddr));
11     servaddr.sin_family = AF_INET;
12     servaddr.sin_addr.s_addr = htonl(INADDR_ANY);
13     servaddr.sin_port = htons(SERV_PORT);

14     Bind(listenfd, (SA *) &servaddr, sizeof(servaddr));

15     Listen(listenfd, LISTENQ);

16     for ( ; ; ) {
17         clilen = sizeof(cliaddr);
18         connfd = Accept(listenfd, (SA *) &cliaddr, &clilen);

19         if ( (childpid = Fork()) == 0) { /* child process */
20             Close(listenfd);    /* close listening socket */
21             str_echo(connfd);   /* process the request */
22             exit(0);
23         }
24         Close(connfd);          /* parent closes connected socket */
25     }
26 }
```

―― *tcpcliserv/tcpserv01.c*

Figure 5.2 TCP echo server (improved in Figure 5.12).

5.3   TCP Echo Server: `str_echo` Function

The function `str_echo`, shown in Figure 5.3, performs the server processing for each client: It reads data from the client and echoes it back to the client.

Read a buffer and echo the buffer

8-9   `read` reads data from the socket and the line is echoed back to the client by `writen`. If the client closes the connection (the normal scenario), the receipt of the client's FIN causes the child's `read` to return 0. This causes the `str_echo` function to return, which terminates the child in Figure 5.2.

5.4 TCP Echo Client: `main` Function

Figure 5.4 shows the TCP client `main` function.

——————————————————————— lib/str_echo.c

```
 1 #include    "unp.h"

 2 void
 3 str_echo(int sockfd)
 4 {
 5     ssize_t n;
 6     char    buf[MAXLINE];

 7   again:
 8     while ( (n = read(sockfd, buf, MAXLINE)) > 0)
 9         Writen(sockfd, buf, n);

10     if (n < 0 && errno == EINTR)
11         goto again;
12     else if (n < 0)
13         err_sys("str_echo: read error");
14 }
```

——————————————————————— lib/str_echo.c

Figure 5.3 `str_echo` function: echoes data on a socket.

——————————————————————— tcpcliserv/tcpcli01.c

```
 1 #include    "unp.h"

 2 int
 3 main(int argc, char **argv)
 4 {
 5     int     sockfd;
 6     struct sockaddr_in servaddr;

 7     if (argc != 2)
 8         err_quit("usage: tcpcli <IPaddress>");

 9     sockfd = Socket(AF_INET, SOCK_STREAM, 0);

10     bzero(&servaddr, sizeof(servaddr));
11     servaddr.sin_family = AF_INET;
12     servaddr.sin_port = htons(SERV_PORT);
13     Inet_pton(AF_INET, argv[1], &servaddr.sin_addr);

14     Connect(sockfd, (SA *) &servaddr, sizeof(servaddr));

15     str_cli(stdin, sockfd);     /* do it all */

16     exit(0);
17 }
```

——————————————————————— tcpcliserv/tcpcli01.c

Figure 5.4 TCP echo client.

Create socket, fill in Internet socket address structure

9–13   A TCP socket is created and an Internet socket address structure is filled in with the server's IP address and port number. We take the server's IP address from the

command-line argument and the server's well-known port (SERV_PORT) is from our
unp.h header.

Connect to server

14-15   connect establishes the connection with the server. The function str_cli (Figure 5.5) handles the rest of the client processing.

5.5   TCP Echo Client: `str_cli` Function

This function, shown in Figure 5.5, handles the client processing loop: It reads a line of
text from standard input, writes it to the server, reads back the server's echo of the line,
and outputs the echoed line to standard output.

―――――――――――――――――――――――――――――― lib/str_cli.c
```
 1 #include      "unp.h"

 2 void
 3 str_cli(FILE *fp, int sockfd)
 4 {
 5     char    sendline[MAXLINE], recvline[MAXLINE];

 6     while (Fgets(sendline, MAXLINE, fp) != NULL) {

 7         Writen(sockfd, sendline, strlen(sendline));

 8         if (Readline(sockfd, recvline, MAXLINE) == 0)
 9             err_quit("str_cli: server terminated prematurely");

10         Fputs(recvline, stdout);
11     }
12 }
```
―――――――――――――――――――――――――――――― lib/str_cli.c

Figure 5.5 `str_cli` function: client processing loop.

Read a line, write to server

6-7   fgets reads a line of text and writen sends the line to the server.

Read echoed line from server, write to standard output

8-10   readline reads the line echoed back from the server and fputs writes it to standard output.

Return to main

11-12   The loop terminates when fgets returns a null pointer, which occurs when it
encounters either an end-of-file (EOF) or an error. Our Fgets wrapper function checks
for an error and aborts if one occurs, so Fgets returns a null pointer only when an end-
of-file is encountered.

5.6   Normal Startup

Although our TCP example is small (about 150 lines of code for the two `main` functions, `str_echo`, `str_cli`, `readline`, and `writen`), it is essential that we understand how the client and server start, how they end, and most importantly, what happens when something goes wrong: the client host crashes, the client process crashes, network connectivity is lost, and so on. Only by understanding these boundary conditions, and their interaction with the TCP/IP protocols, can we write robust clients and servers that can handle these conditions.

We first start the server in the background on the host `linux`.

```
linux % tcpserv01 &
[1] 17870
```

When the server starts, it calls `socket`, `bind`, `listen`, and `accept`, blocking in the call to `accept`. (We have not started the client yet.) Before starting the client, we run the `netstat` program to verify the state of the server's listening socket.

```
linux % netstat -a
Active Internet connections (servers and established)
Proto Recv-Q Send-Q Local Address           Foreign Address         State
tcp        0      0 *:9877                  *:*                     LISTEN
```

Here we show only the first line of output (the heading), plus the line that we are interested in. This command shows the status of *all* sockets on the system, which can be lots of output. We must specify the `-a` flag to see listening sockets.

The output is what we expect. A socket is in the LISTEN state with a wildcard for the local IP address and a local port of 9877. `netstat` prints an asterisk for an IP address of 0 (`INADDR_ANY`, the wildcard) or for a port of 0.

We then start the client on the same host, specifying the server's IP address of 127.0.0.1 (the loopback address). We could have also specified the server's normal (non-loopback) IP address.

```
linux % tcpcli01 127.0.0.1
```

The client calls `socket` and `connect`, the latter causing TCP's three-way handshake to take place. When the three-way handshake completes, `connect` returns in the client and `accept` returns in the server. The connection is established. The following steps then take place:

1. The client calls `str_cli`, which will block in the call to `fgets`, because we have not typed a line of input yet.

2. When `accept` returns in the server, it calls `fork` and the child calls `str_echo`. This function calls `readline`, which calls `read`, which blocks while waiting for a line to be sent from the client.

3. The server parent, on the other hand, calls `accept` again, and blocks while waiting for the next client connection.

We have three processes, and all three are asleep (blocked): client, server parent, and server child.

> When the three-way handshake completes, we purposely list the client step first, and then the server steps. The reason can be seen in Figure 2.5: connect returns when the second segment of the handshake is received by the client, but accept does not return until the third segment of the handshake is received by the server, one-half of the RTT after connect returns.

We purposely run the client and server on the same host because this is the easiest way to experiment with client/server applications. Since we are running the client and server on the same host, netstat now shows two additional lines of output, corresponding to the TCP connection:

```
linux % netstat -a
Active Internet connections (servers and established)
Proto Recv-Q Send-Q Local Address        Foreign Address      State
tcp        0      0 localhost:9877       localhost:42758      ESTABLISHED
tcp        0      0 localhost:42758      localhost:9877       ESTABLISHED
tcp        0      0 *:9877               *:*                  LISTEN
```

The first of the ESTABLISHED lines corresponds to the server child's socket, since the local port is 9877. The second of the ESTABLISHED lines is the client's socket, since the local port is 42758. If we were running the client and server on different hosts, the client host would display only the client's socket, and the server host would display only the two server sockets.

We can also use the ps command to check the status and relationship of these processes.

```
linux % ps -t pts/6 -o pid,ppid,tty,stat,args,wchan
  PID  PPID TT       STAT COMMAND            WCHAN
22038 22036 pts/6    S    -bash              wait4
17870 22038 pts/6    S    ./tcpserv01        wait_for_connect
19315 17870 pts/6    S    ./tcpserv01        tcp_data_wait
19314 22038 pts/6    S    ./tcpcli01 127.0   read_chan
```

(We have used very specific arguments to ps to only show us the information that pertains to this discussion.) In this output, we ran the client and server from the same window (pts/6, which stands for pseudo-terminal number 6). The PID and PPID columns show the parent and child relationships. We can tell that the first tcpserv01 line is the parent and the second tcpserv01 line is the child since the PPID of the child is the parent's PID. Also, the PPID of the parent is the shell (bash).

The STAT column for all three of our network processes is "S," meaning the process is sleeping (waiting for something). When a process is asleep, the WCHAN column specifies the condition. Linux prints wait_for_connect when a process is blocked in either accept or connect, tcp_data_wait when a process is blocked on socket input or output, or read_chan when a process is blocked on terminal I/O. The WCHAN values for our three network processes therefore make sense.

5.7   Normal Termination

At this point, the connection is established and whatever we type to the client is echoed back.

```
linux % tcpcli01 127.0.0.1        we showed this line earlier
hello, world                      we now type this
hello, world                      and the line is echoed
good bye
good bye
^D                                Control-D is our terminal EOF character
```

We type in two lines, each one is echoed, and then we type our terminal EOF character (Control-D), which terminates the client. If we immediately execute netstat, we have

```
linux % netstat -a | grep 9877
tcp        0        0 *:9877                *:*                       LISTEN
tcp        0        0 localhost:42758       localhost:9877            TIME_WAIT
```

The client's side of the connection (since the local port is 42758) enters the TIME_WAIT state (Section 2.7), and the listening server is still waiting for another client connection. (This time we pipe the output of netstat into grep, printing only the lines with our server's well-known port. Doing this also removes the heading line.)

We can follow through the steps involved in the normal termination of our client and server:

1. When we type our EOF character, fgets returns a null pointer and the function str_cli (Figure 5.5) returns.

2. When str_cli returns to the client main function (Figure 5.4), the latter terminates by calling exit.

3. Part of process termination is the closing of all open descriptors, so the client socket is closed by the kernel. This sends a FIN to the server, to which the server TCP responds with an ACK. This is the first half of the TCP connection termination sequence. At this point, the server socket is in the CLOSE_WAIT state and the client socket is in the FIN_WAIT_2 state (Figures 2.4 and 2.5).

4. When the server TCP receives the FIN, the server child is blocked in a call to readline (Figure 5.3), and readline then returns 0. This causes the str_echo function to return to the server child main.

5. The server child terminates by calling exit (Figure 5.2).

6. All open descriptors in the server child are closed. The closing of the connected socket by the child causes the final two segments of the TCP connection termination to take place: a FIN from the server to the client, and an ACK from the client (Figure 2.5). At this point, the connection is completely terminated. The client socket enters the TIME_WAIT state.

7. Finally, the SIGCHLD signal is sent to the parent when the server child terminates. This occurs in this example, but we do not catch the signal in our code,

and the default action of the signal is to be ignored. Thus, the child enters the zombie state. We can verify this with the ps command.

```
linux % ps -t pts/6 -o pid,ppid,tty,stat,args,wchan
  PID  PPID TT        STAT COMMAND           WCHAN
22038 22036 pts/6     S    -bash             read_chan
17870 22038 pts/6     S    ./tcpserv01       wait_for_connect
19315 17870 pts/6     Z    [tcpserv01 <defu  do_exit
```

The STAT of the child is now Z (for zombie).

We need to clean up our zombie processes and doing this requires dealing with Unix signals. In the next section, we will give an overview of signal handling.

5.8 POSIX Signal Handling

A *signal* is a notification to a process that an event has occurred. Signals are sometimes called *software interrupts*. Signals usually occur *asynchronously*. By this we mean that a process doesn't know ahead of time exactly when a signal will occur.

Signals can be sent

- By one process to another process (or to itself)
- By the kernel to a process

The SIGCHLD signal that we described at the end of the previous section is one that is sent by the kernel whenever a process terminates, to the parent of the terminating process.

Every signal has a *disposition*, which is also called the *action* associated with the signal. We set the disposition of a signal by calling the sigaction function (described shortly) and we have three choices for the disposition:

1. We can provide a function that is called whenever a specific signal occurs. This function is called a *signal handler* and this action is called *catching* a signal. The two signals SIGKILL and SIGSTOP cannot be caught. Our function is called with a single integer argument that is the signal number and the function returns nothing. Its function prototype is therefore

    ```
    void handler(int signo);
    ```

    For most signals, calling sigaction and specifying a function to be called when the signal occurs is all that is required to catch a signal. But we will see later that a few signals, SIGIO, SIGPOLL, and SIGURG, all require additional actions on the part of the process to catch the signal.

2. We can *ignore* a signal by setting its disposition to SIG_IGN. The two signals SIGKILL and SIGSTOP cannot be ignored.

3. We can set the *default* disposition for a signal by setting its disposition to SIG_DFL. The default is normally to terminate a process on receipt of a signal, with certain signals also generating a core image of the process in its current

working directory. There are a few signals whose default disposition is to be ignored: SIGCHLD and SIGURG (sent on the arrival of out-of-band data, Chapter 24) are two that we will encounter in this text.

signal **Function**

The POSIX way to establish the disposition of a signal is to call the sigaction function. This gets complicated, however, as one argument to the function is a structure that we must allocate and fill in. An easier way to set the disposition of a signal is to call the signal function. The first argument is the signal name and the second argument is either a pointer to a function or one of the constants SIG_IGN or SIG_DFL. But, signal is an historical function that predates POSIX. Different implementations provide different signal semantics when it is called, providing backward compatibility, whereas POSIX explicitly spells out the semantics when sigaction is called. The solution is to define our own function named signal that just calls the POSIX sigaction function. This provides a simple interface with the desired POSIX semantics. We include this function in our own library, along with our err_XXX functions and our wrapper functions, for example, that we specify when building any of our programs in this text. This function is shown in Figure 5.6 (the corresponding wrapper function, Signal, is not shown here as it would be the same whether it called our function or a vendor-supplied signal function).

lib/signal.c

```
 1 #include    "unp.h"

 2 Sigfunc *
 3 signal(int signo, Sigfunc *func)
 4 {
 5      struct sigaction act, oact;

 6      act.sa_handler = func;
 7      sigemptyset(&act.sa_mask);
 8      act.sa_flags = 0;
 9      if (signo == SIGALRM) {
10 #ifdef   SA_INTERRUPT
11          act.sa_flags |= SA_INTERRUPT;    /* SunOS 4.x */
12 #endif
13      } else {
14 #ifdef   SA_RESTART
15          act.sa_flags |= SA_RESTART; /* SVR4, 4.4BSD */
16 #endif
17      }
18      if (sigaction(signo, &act, &oact) < 0)
19          return (SIG_ERR);
20      return (oact.sa_handler);
21 }
```

lib/signal.c

Figure 5.6   signal function that calls the POSIX sigaction function.

Simplify function prototype using `typedef`

2-3   The normal function prototype for `signal` is complicated by the level of nested parentheses.

```
void (*signal(int signo, void (*func)(int)))(int);
```

To simplify this, we define the `Sigfunc` type in our `unp.h` header as

```
typedef  void  Sigfunc(int);
```

stating that signal handlers are functions with an integer argument and the function returns nothing (`void`). The function prototype then becomes

```
Sigfunc *signal(int signo, Sigfunc *func);
```

A pointer to a signal handling function is the second argument to the function, as well as the return value from the function.

Set handler

6   The `sa_handler` member of the `sigaction` structure is set to the *func* argument.

Set signal mask for handler

7   POSIX allows us to specify a set of signals that will be *blocked* when our signal handler is called. Any signal that is blocked cannot be *delivered* to a process. We set the `sa_mask` member to the empty set, which means that no additional signals will be blocked while our signal handler is running. POSIX guarantees that the signal being caught is always blocked while its handler is executing.

Set `SA_RESTART` flag

8-17   `SA_RESTART` is an optional flag. When the flag is set, a system call interrupted by this signal will be automatically restarted by the kernel. (We will talk more about interrupted system calls in the next section when we continue our example.) If the signal being caught is not `SIGALRM`, we specify the `SA_RESTART` flag, if defined. (The reason for making a special case for `SIGALRM` is that the purpose of generating this signal is normally to place a timeout on an I/O operation, as we will show in Section 14.2, in which case, we want the blocked system call to be interrupted by the signal.) Some older systems, notably SunOS 4.x, automatically restart an interrupted system call by default and then define the complement of this flag as `SA_INTERRUPT`. If this flag is defined, we set it if the signal being caught is `SIGALRM`.

Call `sigaction`

18-20   We call `sigaction` and then return the old action for the signal as the return value of the `signal` function.

Throughout this text, we will use the `signal` function from Figure 5.6.

POSIX Signal Semantics

We summarize the following points about signal handling on a POSIX-compliant system:

- Once a signal handler is installed, it remains installed. (Older systems removed the signal handler each time it was executed.)

- While a signal handler is executing, the signal being delivered is blocked. Furthermore, any additional signals that were specified in the sa_mask signal set passed to sigaction when the handler was installed are also blocked. In Figure 5.6, we set sa_mask to the empty set, meaning no additional signals are blocked other than the signal being caught.

- If a signal is generated one or more times while it is blocked, it is normally delivered only one time after the signal is unblocked. That is, by default, Unix signals are not *queued*. We will see an example of this in the next section. The POSIX real-time standard, 1003.1b, defines some reliable signals that are queued, but we do not use them in this text.

- It is possible to selectively block and unblock a set of signals using the sigprocmask function. This lets us protect a critical region of code by preventing certain signals from being caught while that region of code is executing.

5.9   Handling SIGCHLD Signals

The purpose of the zombie state is to maintain information about the child for the parent to fetch at some later time. This information includes the process ID of the child, its termination status, and information on the resource utilization of the child (CPU time, memory, etc.). If a process terminates, and that process has children in the zombie state, the parent process ID of all the zombie children is set to 1 (the init process), which will inherit the children and clean them up (i.e., init will wait for them, which removes the zombie). Some Unix systems show the COMMAND column for a zombie process as <defunct>.

Handling Zombies

Obviously we do not want to leave zombies around. They take up space in the kernel and eventually we can run out of processes. Whenever we fork children, we must wait for them to prevent them from becoming zombies. To do this, we establish a signal handler to catch SIGCHLD, and within the handler, we call wait. (We will describe the wait and waitpid functions in Section 5.10.) We establish the signal handler by adding the function call

```
Signal(SIGCHLD, sig_chld);
```

in Figure 5.2, after the call to listen. (It must be done sometime before we fork the first child and needs to be done only once.) We then define the signal handler, the function sig_chld, which we show in Figure 5.7.

```
                                                              tcpcliserv/sigchldwait.c
 1 #include     "unp.h"

 2 void
 3 sig_chld(int signo)
 4 {
 5     pid_t   pid;
 6     int     stat;

 7     pid = wait(&stat);
 8     printf("child %d terminated\n", pid);
 9     return;
10 }
                                                              tcpcliserv/sigchldwait.c
```

Figure 5.7 Version of SIGCHLD signal handler that calls wait (improved in Figure 5.11).

> *Warning*: Calling standard I/O functions such as printf in a signal handler is not recommended, for reasons that we will discuss in Section 11.18. We call printf here as a diagnostic tool to see when the child terminates.

> Under System V and Unix 98, the child of a process does not become a zombie if the process sets the disposition of SIGCHLD to SIG_IGN. Unfortunately, this works only under System V and Unix 98. POSIX explicitly states that this behavior is unspecified. The portable way to handle zombies is to catch SIGCHLD and call wait or waitpid.

If we compile this program—Figure 5.2, with the call to Signal, with our sig_chld handler—under Solaris 9 and use the signal function from the system library (not our version from Figure 5.6), we have the following:

```
solaris % tcpserv02 &                    start server in background
[2]    16939
solaris % tcpcli01 127.0.0.1             then start client in foreground
hi there                                 we type this
hi there                                 and this is echoed
^D                                       we type our EOF character
child 16942 terminated                   output by printf in signal handler
accept error: Interrupted system call    main function aborts
```

The sequence of steps is as follows:

1. We terminate the client by typing our EOF character. The client TCP sends a FIN to the server and the server responds with an ACK.

2. The receipt of the FIN delivers an EOF to the child's pending readline. The child terminates.

3. The parent is blocked in its call to accept when the SIGCHLD signal is delivered. The sig_chld function executes (our signal handler), wait fetches the child's PID and termination status, and printf is called from the signal handler. The signal handler returns.

4. Since the signal was caught by the parent while the parent was blocked in a

slow system call (`accept`), the kernel causes the `accept` to return an error of
`EINTR` (interrupted system call). The parent does not handle this error (Figure 5.2), so it aborts.

The purpose of this example is to show that when writing network programs that
catch signals, we must be cognizant of interrupted system calls, and we must handle
them. In this specific example, running under Solaris 9, the `signal` function provided
in the standard C library does not cause an interrupted system call to be automatically
restarted by the kernel. That is, the `SA_RESTART` flag that we set in Figure 5.6 is not set
by the `signal` function in the system library. Some other systems automatically restart
the interrupted system call. If we run the same example under 4.4BSD, using its library
version of the `signal` function, the kernel restarts the interrupted system call and
`accept` does not return an error. To handle this potential problem between different
operating systems is one reason we define our own version of the `signal` function that
we use throughout the text (Figure 5.6).

As part of the coding conventions used in this text, we always code an explicit
`return` in our signal handlers (Figure 5.7), even though falling off the end of the function does the same thing for a function returning `void`. When reading the code, the
unnecessary return statement acts as a reminder that the return may interrupt a system
call.

Handling Interrupted System Calls

We used the term "slow system call" to describe `accept`, and we use this term for any
system call that can block forever. That is, the system call need never return. Most networking functions fall into this category. For example, there is no guarantee that a
server's call to `accept` will ever return, if there are no clients that will connect to the
server. Similarly, our server's call to `read` in Figure 5.3 will never return if the client
never sends a line for the server to echo. Other examples of slow system calls are reads
and writes of pipes and terminal devices. A notable exception is disk I/O, which usually returns to the caller (assuming no catastrophic hardware failure).

The basic rule that applies here is that when a process is blocked in a slow system
call *and* the process catches a signal *and* the signal handler returns, the system call *can*
return an error of `EINTR`. *Some* kernels automatically restart *some* interrupted system
calls. For portability, when we write a program that catches signals (most concurrent
servers catch `SIGCHLD`), we must be prepared for slow system calls to return `EINTR`.
Portability problems are caused by the qualifiers "can" and "some," which were used
earlier, and the fact that support for the POSIX `SA_RESTART` flag is optional. Even if an
implementation supports the `SA_RESTART` flag, not all interrupted system calls may
automatically be restarted. Most Berkeley-derived implementations, for example, never
automatically restart `select`, and some of these implementations never restart `accept`
or `recvfrom`.

To handle an interrupted `accept`, we change the call to `accept` in Figure 5.2, the beginning of the `for` loop, to the following:

```
for ( ; ; ) {
    clilen = sizeof(cliaddr);
    if ( (connfd = accept(listenfd, (SA *) &cliaddr, &clilen)) < 0) {
        if (errno == EINTR)
            continue;          /* back to for() */
        else
            err_sys("accept error");
    }
```

Notice that we call `accept` and not our wrapper function `Accept`, since we must handle the failure of the function ourselves.

What we are doing in this piece of code is restarting the interrupted system call. This is fine for `accept`, along with functions such as `read`, `write`, `select`, and `open`. But there is one function that we cannot restart: `connect`. If this function returns `EINTR`, we cannot call it again, as doing so will return an immediate error. When `connect` is interrupted by a caught signal and is not automatically restarted, we must call `select` to wait for the connection to complete, as we will describe in Section 16.3.

5.10 `wait` and `waitpid` Functions

In Figure 5.7, we called the `wait` function to handle the terminated child.

```
#include <sys/wait.h>

pid_t wait(int *statloc);

pid_t waitpid(pid_t pid, int *statloc, int options);
```

                                Both return: process ID if OK, 0 or –1 on error

`wait` and `waitpid` both return two values: the return value of the function is the process ID of the terminated child, and the termination status of the child (an integer) is returned through the *statloc* pointer. There are three macros that we can call that examine the termination status and tell us if the child terminated normally, was killed by a signal, or was just stopped by job control. Additional macros let us then fetch the exit status of the child, or the value of the signal that killed the child, or the value of the job-control signal that stopped the child. We will use the WIFEXITED and WEXITSTATUS macros in Figure 15.10 for this purpose.

If there are no terminated children for the process calling `wait`, but the process has one or more children that are still executing, then `wait` blocks until the first of the existing children terminates.

`waitpid` gives us more control over which process to wait for and whether or not to block. First, the *pid* argument lets us specify the process ID that we want to wait for. A value of –1 says to wait for the first of our children to terminate. (There are other options, dealing with process group IDs, but we do not need them in this text.) The

options argument lets us specify additional options. The most common option is
WNOHANG. This option tells the kernel not to block if there are no terminated children.

Difference between `wait` and `waitpid`

We now illustrate the difference between the `wait` and `waitpid` functions when used
to clean up terminated children. To do this, we modify our TCP client as shown in Figure 5.9. The client establishes five connections with the server and then uses only the
first one (`sockfd[0]`) in the call to `str_cli`. The purpose of establishing multiple
connections is to spawn multiple children from the concurrent server, as shown in Figure 5.8.

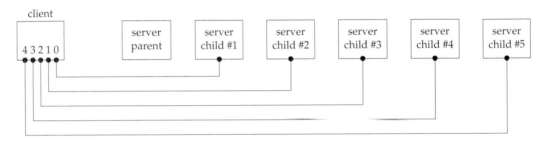

Figure 5.8 Client with five established connections to same concurrent server.

tcpcliserv/tcpcli04.c

```
 1 #include    "unp.h"

 2 int
 3 main(int argc, char **argv)
 4 {
 5     int     i, sockfd[5];
 6     struct sockaddr_in servaddr;

 7     if (argc != 2)
 8         err_quit("usage: tcpcli <IPaddress>");

 9     for (i = 0; i < 5; i++) {
10         sockfd[i] = Socket(AF_INET, SOCK_STREAM, 0);

11         bzero(&servaddr, sizeof(servaddr));
12         servaddr.sin_family = AF_INET;
13         servaddr.sin_port = htons(SERV_PORT);
14         Inet_pton(AF_INET, argv[1], &servaddr.sin_addr);

15         Connect(sockfd[i], (SA *) &servaddr, sizeof(servaddr));
16     }

17     str_cli(stdin, sockfd[0]);  /* do it all */

18     exit(0);
19 }
```

tcpcliserv/tcpcli04.c

Figure 5.9 TCP client that establishes five connections with server.

When the client terminates, all open descriptors are closed automatically by the kernel (we do not call `close`, only `exit`), and all five connections are terminated at about the same time. This causes five FINs to be sent, one on each connection, which in turn causes all five server children to terminate at about the same time. This causes five SIGCHLD signals to be delivered to the parent at about the same time, which we show in Figure 5.10.

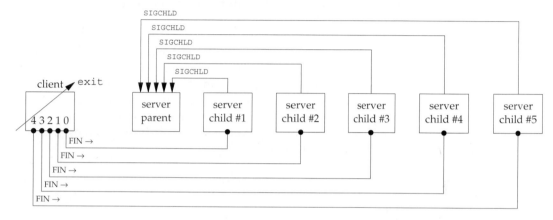

Figure 5.10 Client terminates, closing all five connections, terminating all five children.

It is this delivery of multiple occurrences of the same signal that causes the problem we are about to see.

We first run the server in the background and then our new client. Our server is Figure 5.2, modified to call `signal` to establish Figure 5.7 as a signal handler for SIGCHLD.

```
linux % tcpserv03 &
[1] 20419
linux % tcpcli04 127.0.0.1
hello                           we type this
hello                           and it is echoed
^D                              we then type our EOF character
child 20426 terminated          output by server
```

The first thing we notice is that only one `printf` is output, when we expect all five children to have terminated. If we execute `ps`, we see that the other four children still exist as zombies.

```
PID TTY          TIME CMD
20419 pts/6    00:00:00 tcpserv03
20421 pts/6    00:00:00 tcpserv03 <defunct>
20422 pts/6    00:00:00 tcpserv03 <defunct>
20423 pts/6    00:00:00 tcpserv03 <defunct>
```

Establishing a signal handler and calling `wait` from that handler are insufficient for preventing zombies. The problem is that all five signals are generated before the signal handler is executed, and the signal handler is executed only one time because Unix signals are normally not *queued*. Furthermore, this problem is nondeterministic. In the example we just ran, with the client and server on the same host, the signal handler is executed once, leaving four zombies. But if we run the client and server on different hosts, the signal handler is normally executed two times: once as a result of the first signal being generated, and since the other four signals occur while the signal handler is executing, the handler is called only one more time. This leaves three zombies. But sometimes, probably dependent on the timing of the FINs arriving at the server host, the signal handler is executed three or even four times.

The correct solution is to call `waitpid` instead of `wait`. Figure 5.11 shows the version of our `sig_chld` function that handles SIGCHLD correctly. This version works because we call `waitpid` within a loop, fetching the status of any of our children that have terminated. We must specify the WNOHANG option: This tells `waitpid` not to block if there are running children that have not yet terminated. In Figure 5.7, we cannot call `wait` in a loop, because there is no way to prevent `wait` from blocking if there are running children that have not yet terminated.

Figure 5.12 shows the final version of our server. It correctly handles a return of EINTR from `accept` and it establishes a signal handler (Figure 5.11) that calls `waitpid` for all terminated children.

————————————————————————————————— *tcpcliserv/sigchldwaitpid.c*

```
 1 #include      "unp.h"

 2 void
 3 sig_chld(int signo)
 4 {
 5      pid_t    pid;
 6      int      stat;

 7      while ( (pid = waitpid(-1, &stat, WNOHANG)) > 0)
 8          printf("child %d terminated\n", pid);
 9      return;
10 }
```

————————————————————————————————— *tcpcliserv/sigchldwaitpid.c*

Figure 5.11   Final (correct) version of `sig_chld` function that calls `waitpid`.

————————————————————————————————— *tcpcliserv/tcpserv04.c*

```
 1 #include      "unp.h"

 2 int
 3 main(int argc, char **argv)
 4 {
 5      int      listenfd, connfd;
 6      pid_t    childpid;
 7      socklen_t clilen;
 8      struct sockaddr_in cliaddr, servaddr;
 9      void     sig_chld(int);
10      listenfd = Socket(AF_INET, SOCK_STREAM, 0);

11      bzero(&servaddr, sizeof(servaddr));
12      servaddr.sin_family = AF_INET;
13      servaddr.sin_addr.s_addr = htonl(INADDR_ANY);
```

```
14        servaddr.sin_port = htons(SERV_PORT);
15        Bind(listenfd, (SA *) &servaddr, sizeof(servaddr));
16        Listen(listenfd, LISTENQ);
17        Signal(SIGCHLD, sig_chld);  /* must call waitpid() */
18        for ( ; ; ) {
19            clilen = sizeof(cliaddr);
20            if ( (connfd = accept(listenfd, (SA *) &cliaddr, &clilen)) < 0) {
21                if (errno == EINTR)
22                    continue;          /* back to for() */
23                else
24                    err_sys("accept error");
25            }
26            if ( (childpid = Fork()) == 0) { /* child process */
27                Close(listenfd);      /* close listening socket */
28                str_echo(connfd);     /* process the request */
29                exit(0);
30            }
31            Close(connfd);             /* parent closes connected socket */
32        }
33  }
```
—— *tcpcliserv/tcpserv04.c*

Figure 5.12 Final (correct) version of TCP server that handles an error of EINTR from accept.

The purpose of this section has been to demonstrate three scenarios that we can encounter with network programming:

1. We must catch the SIGCHLD signal when forking child processes.
2. We must handle interrupted system calls when we catch signals.
3. A SIGCHLD handler must be coded correctly using waitpid to prevent any zombies from being left around.

The final version of our TCP server (Figure 5.12), along with the SIGCHLD handler in Figure 5.11, handles all three scenarios.

5.11 Connection Abort before accept Returns

There is another condition similar to the interrupted system call example in the previous section that can cause accept to return a nonfatal error, in which case we should just call accept again. The sequence of packets shown in Figure 5.13 has been seen on busy servers (typically busy Web servers).

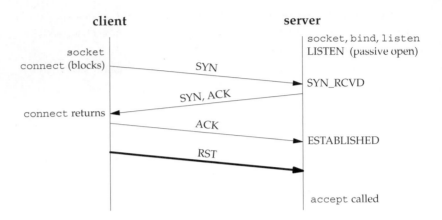

Figure 5.13   Receiving an RST for an ESTABLISHED connection before accept is called.

Here, the three-way handshake completes, the connection is established, and then the client TCP sends an RST (reset). On the server side, the connection is queued by its TCP, waiting for the server process to call accept when the RST arrives. Sometime later, the server process calls accept.

> An easy way to simulate this scenario is to start the server, have it call socket, bind, and listen, and then go to sleep for a short period of time before calling accept. While the server process is asleep, start the client and have it call socket and connect. As soon as connect returns, set the SO_LINGER socket option to generate the RST (which we will describe in Section 7.5 and show an example of in Figure 16.21) and terminate.

Unfortunately, what happens to the aborted connection is implementation-dependent. Berkeley-derived implementations handle the aborted connection completely within the kernel, and the server process never sees it. Most SVR4 implementations, however, return an error to the process as the return from accept, and the error depends on the implementation. These SVR4 implementations return an errno of EPROTO ("protocol error"), but POSIX specifies that the return must be ECONNABORTED ("software caused connection abort") instead. The reason for the POSIX change is that EPROTO is also returned when some fatal protocol-related events occur on the streams subsystem. Returning the same error for the nonfatal abort of an established connection by the client makes it impossible for the server to know whether to call accept again or not. In the case of the ECONNABORTED error, the server can ignore the error and just call accept again.

> The steps involved in Berkeley-derived kernels that never pass this error to the process can be followed in TCPv2. The RST is processed on p. 964, causing tcp_close to be called. This function calls in_pcbdetach on p. 897, which in turn calls sofree on p. 719. sofree (p. 473) finds that the socket being aborted is still on the listening socket's completed connection queue and removes the socket from the queue and frees the socket. When the server gets around to calling accept, it will never know that a connection that was completed has since been removed from the queue.

We will return to these aborted connections in Section 16.6 and see how they can present a problem when combined with `select` and a listening socket in the normal blocking mode.

5.12 Termination of Server Process

We will now start our client/server and then kill the server child process. This simulates the crashing of the server process, so we can see what happens to the client. (We must be careful to distinguish between the crashing of the server *process*, which we are about to describe, and the crashing of the server *host*, which we will describe in Section 5.14.) The following steps take place:

1. We start the server and client and type one line to the client to verify that all is okay. That line is echoed normally by the server child.

2. We find the process ID of the server child and `kill` it. As part of process termination, all open descriptors in the child are closed. This causes a FIN to be sent to the client, and the client TCP responds with an ACK. This is the first half of the TCP connection termination.

3. The `SIGCHLD` signal is sent to the server parent and handled correctly (Figure 5.12).

4. Nothing happens at the client. The client TCP receives the FIN from the server TCP and responds with an ACK, but the problem is that the client process is blocked in the call to `fgets` waiting for a line from the terminal.

5. Running `netstat` at this point shows the state of the sockets.

```
linux % netstat -a | grep 9877
tcp        0      0 *:9877                  *:*                     LISTEN
tcp        0      0 localhost:9877          localhost:43604         FIN_WAIT2
tcp        1      0 localhost:43604         localhost:9877          CLOSE_WAIT
```

From Figure 2.4, we see that half of the TCP connection termination sequence has taken place.

6. We can still type a line of input to the client. Here is what happens at the client starting from Step 1:

```
linux % tcpcli01 127.0.0.1          start client
hello                               the first line that we type
hello                               is echoed correctly
                                    here we kill the server child on the server host
another line                        we then type a second line to the client
str_cli: server terminated prematurely
```

When we type "another line," `str_cli` calls `writen` and the client TCP sends the data to the server. This is allowed by TCP because the receipt of the FIN by the client TCP only indicates that the server process has closed its end of the connection and will not be sending any more data. The receipt of the FIN does *not* tell the client TCP that the server process has terminated (which in this case, it has). We will cover this again in Section 6.6 when we talk about TCP's half-close.

When the server TCP receives the data from the client, it responds with an RST since the process that had that socket open has terminated. We can verify that the RST was sent by watching the packets with `tcpdump`.

7. The client process will not see the RST because it calls `readline` immediately after the call to `writen` and `readline` returns 0 (EOF) immediately because of the FIN that was received in Step 2. Our client is not expecting to receive an EOF at this point (Figure 5.5) so it quits with the error message "server terminated prematurely."

8. When the client terminates (by calling `err_quit` in Figure 5.5), all its open descriptors are closed.

> What we have described also depends on the timing of the example. The client's call to `readline` may happen before the server's RST is received by the client, or it may happen after. If the `readline` happens before the RST is received, as we've shown in our example, the result is an unexpected EOF in the client. But if the RST arrives first, the result is an ECONNRESET ("Connection reset by peer") error return from `readline`.

The problem in this example is that the client is blocked in the call to `fgets` when the FIN arrives on the socket. The client is really working with two descriptors—the socket and the user input—and instead of blocking on input from only one of the two sources (as `str_cli` is currently coded), it should block on input from either source. Indeed, this is one purpose of the `select` and `poll` functions, which we will describe in Chapter 6. When we recode the `str_cli` function in Section 6.4, as soon as we `kill` the server child, the client is notified of the received FIN.

5.13   `SIGPIPE` Signal

What happens if the client ignores the error return from `readline` and writes more data to the server? This can happen, for example, if the client needs to perform two writes to the server before reading anything back, with the first write eliciting the RST.

The rule that applies is: When a process writes to a socket that has received an RST, the `SIGPIPE` signal is sent to the process. The default action of this signal is to terminate the process, so the process must catch the signal to avoid being involuntarily terminated.

If the process either catches the signal and returns from the signal handler, or ignores the signal, the write operation returns `EPIPE`.

> A frequently asked question (FAQ) on Usenet is how to obtain this signal on the first write, and not the second. This is not possible. Following our discussion above, the first write elicits the RST and the second write elicits the signal. It is okay to write to a socket that has received a FIN, but it is an error to write to a socket that has received an RST.

To see what happens with `SIGPIPE`, we modify our client as shown in Figure 5.14.

```
                                                           ──────────── tcpcliserv/str_cli11.c
 1 #include     "unp.h"

 2 void
 3 str_cli(FILE *fp, int sockfd)
 4 {
 5     char     sendline[MAXLINE], recvline[MAXLINE];

 6     while (Fgets(sendline, MAXLINE, fp) != NULL) {

 7         Writen(sockfd, sendline, 1);
 8         sleep(1);
 9         Writen(sockfd, sendline + 1, strlen(sendline) - 1);

10         if (Readline(sockfd, recvline, MAXLINE) == 0)
11             err_quit("str_cli: server terminated prematurely");

12         Fputs(recvline, stdout);
13     }
14 }
```
─── tcpcliserv/str_cli11.c

Figure 5.14 `str_cli` that calls `writen` twice.

7–9   All we have changed is to call `writen` two times: the first time the first byte of data
is written to the socket, followed by a pause of one second, followed by the remainder
of the line. The intent is for the first `writen` to elicit the RST and then for the second
`writen` to generate `SIGPIPE`.

If we run the client on our Linux host, we get:

```
linux % tcpcli11 127.0.0.1
hi there                              we type this line
hi there                              this is echoed by the server
                                      here we kill the server child
bye                                   then we type this line
Broken pipe                           this is printed by the shell
```

We start the client, type in one line, see that line echoed correctly, and then terminate
the server child on the server host. We then type another line ("bye") and the shell tells
us the process died with a `SIGPIPE` signal (some shells do not print anything when a
process dies without dumping core, but the shell we're using for this example, `bash`,
tells us what we want to know).

The recommended way to handle `SIGPIPE` depends on what the application wants
to do when this occurs. If there is nothing special to do, then setting the signal disposition to `SIG_IGN` is easy, assuming that subsequent output operations will catch the
error of `EPIPE` and terminate. If special actions are needed when the signal occurs
(writing to a log file perhaps), then the signal should be caught and any desired actions
can be performed in the signal handler. Be aware, however, that if multiple sockets are
in use, the delivery of the signal will not tell us which socket encountered the error. If
we need to know which `write` caused the error, then we must either ignore the signal
or return from the signal handler and handle `EPIPE` from the `write`.

5.14 Crashing of Server Host

This scenario will test to see what happens when the server host crashes. To simulate this, we must run the client and server on different hosts. We then start the server, start the client, type in a line to the client to verify that the connection is up, disconnect the server host from the network, and type in another line at the client. This also covers the scenario of the server host being unreachable when the client sends data (i.e., some intermediate router goes down after the connection has been established).

The following steps take place:

1. When the server host crashes, nothing is sent out on the existing network connections. That is, we are assuming the host crashes and is not shut down by an operator (which we will cover in Section 5.16).

2. We type a line of input to the client, it is written by `writen` (Figure 5.5), and is sent by the client TCP as a data segment. The client then blocks in the call to `readline`, waiting for the echoed reply.

3. If we watch the network with `tcpdump`, we will see the client TCP continually retransmitting the data segment, trying to receive an ACK from the server. Section 25.11 of TCPv2 shows a typical pattern for TCP retransmissions: Berkeley-derived implementations retransmit the data segment 12 times, waiting for around 9 minutes before giving up. When the client TCP finally gives up (assuming the server host has not been rebooted during this time, or if the server host has not crashed but was unreachable on the network, assuming the host was still unreachable), an error is returned to the client process. Since the client is blocked in the call to `readline`, it returns an error. Assuming the server host crashed and there were no responses at all to the client's data segments, the error is ETIMEDOUT. But if some intermediate router determined that the server host was unreachable and responded with an ICMP "destination unreachable" message, the error is either EHOSTUNREACH or ENETUNREACH.

Although our client discovers (eventually) that the peer is down or unreachable, there are times when we want to detect this quicker than having to wait nine minutes. The solution is to place a timeout on the call to `readline`, which we will discuss in Section 14.2.

The scenario that we just discussed detects that the server host has crashed only when we send data to that host. If we want to detect the crashing of the server host even if we are not actively sending it data, another technique is required. We will discuss the SO_KEEPALIVE socket option in Section 7.5.

5.15 Crashing and Rebooting of Server Host

In this scenario, we will establish a connection between the client and server and then assume the server host crashes and reboots. In the previous section, the server host was still down when we sent it data. Here, we will let the server host reboot before sending it data. The easiest way to simulate this is to establish the connection, disconnect the server from the network, shut down the server host and then reboot it, and then reconnect the server host to the network. We do not want the client to see the server host shut down (which we will cover in Section 5.16).

As stated in the previous section, if the client is not actively sending data to the server when the server host crashes, the client is not aware that the server host has crashed. (This assumes we are not using the SO_KEEPALIVE socket option.) The following steps take place:

1. We start the server and then the client. We type a line to verify that the connection is established.

2. The server host crashes and reboots.

3. We type a line of input to the client, which is sent as a TCP data segment to the server host.

4. When the server host reboots after crashing, its TCP loses all information about connections that existed before the crash. Therefore, the server TCP responds to the received data segment from the client with an RST.

5. Our client is blocked in the call to readline when the RST is received, causing readline to return the error ECONNRESET.

If it is important for our client to detect the crashing of the server host, even if the client is not actively sending data, then some other technique (such as the SO_KEEPALIVE socket option or some client/server heartbeat function) is required.

5.16 Shutdown of Server Host

The previous two sections discussed the crashing of the server host, or the server host being unreachable across the network. We now consider what happens if the server host is shut down by an operator while our server process is running on that host.

When a Unix system is shut down, the init process normally sends the SIGTERM signal to all processes (we can catch this signal), waits some fixed amount of time (often between 5 and 20 seconds), and then sends the SIGKILL signal (which we cannot catch) to any processes still running. This gives all running processes a short amount of time to clean up and terminate. If we do not catch SIGTERM and terminate, our server will be terminated by the SIGKILL signal. When the process terminates, all open descriptors are closed, and we then follow the same sequence of steps discussed in Section 5.12. As stated there, we must use the select or poll function in our client to have the client detect the termination of the server process as soon as it occurs.

5.17 Summary of TCP Example

Before any TCP client and server can communicate with each other, each end must specify the socket pair for the connection: the local IP address, local port, foreign IP address, and foreign port. In Figure 5.15, we show these four values as bullets. This figure is from the client's perspective. The foreign IP address and foreign port must be specified by the client in the call to `connect`. The two local values are normally chosen by the kernel as part of the `connect` function. The client has the option of specifying either or both of the local values, by calling `bind` before `connect`, but this is not common.

As we mentioned in Section 4.10, the client can obtain the two local values chosen by the kernel by calling `getsockname` after the connection is established.

Figure 5.16 shows the same four values, but from the server's perspective.

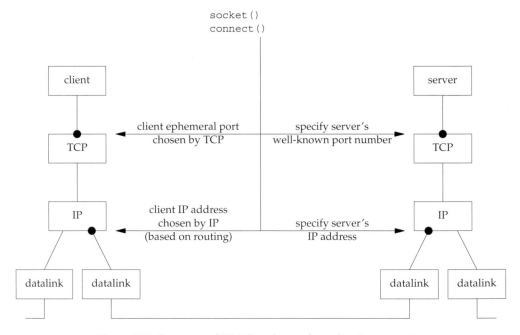

Figure 5.15 Summary of TCP client/server from client's perspective.

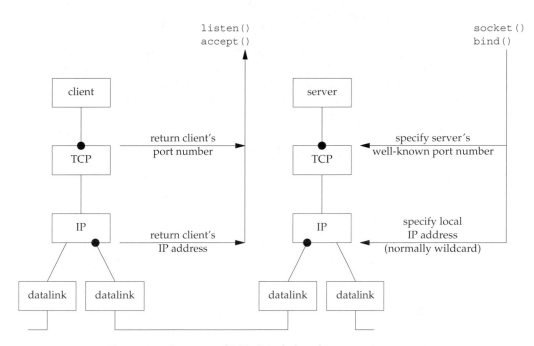

Figure 5.16 Summary of TCP client/server from server's perspective.

   The local port (the server's well-known port) is specified by `bind`. Normally, the server also specifies the wildcard IP address in this call. If the server binds the wildcard IP address on a multihomed host, it can determine the local IP address by calling `getsockname` after the connection is established (Section 4.10). The two foreign values are returned to the server by `accept`. As we mentioned in Section 4.10, if another program is `exec`ed by the server that calls `accept`, that program can call `getpeername` to determine the client's IP address and port, if necessary.

5.18   Data Format

In our example, the server never examines the request that it receives from the client. The server just reads all the data up through and including the newline and sends it back to the client, looking for only the newline. This is an exception, not the rule, and normally we must worry about the format of the data exchanged between the client and server.

Example: Passing Text Strings between Client and Server

Let's modify our server so that it still reads a line of text from the client, but the server now expects that line to contain two integers separated by white space, and the server returns the sum of those two integers. Our client and server `main` functions remain the same, as does our `str_cli` function. All that changes is our `str_echo` function, which we show in Figure 5.17.

```
                                                              ———————— tcpcliserv/str_echo08.c
 1 #include    "unp.h"

 2 void
 3 str_echo(int sockfd)
 4 {
 5     long    arg1, arg2;
 6     ssize_t n;
 7     char    line[MAXLINE];

 8     for ( ; ; ) {
 9         if ( (n = Readline(sockfd, line, MAXLINE)) == 0)
10             return;              /* connection closed by other end */

11         if (sscanf(line, "%ld%ld", &arg1, &arg2) == 2)
12             snprintf(line, sizeof(line), "%ld\n", arg1 + arg2);
13         else
14             snprintf(line, sizeof(line), "input error\n");

15         n = strlen(line);
16         Writen(sockfd, line, n);
17     }
18 }
                                                              ———————— tcpcliserv/str_echo08.c
```

Figure 5.17 str_echo function that adds two numbers.

11–14   We call sscanf to convert the two arguments from text strings to long integers,
and then snprintf is called to convert the result into a text string.

This new client and server work fine, regardless of the byte ordering of the client
and server hosts.

Example: Passing Binary Structures between Client and Server

We now modify our client and server to pass binary values across the socket, instead of
text strings. We will see that this does not work when the client and server are run on
hosts with different byte orders, or on hosts that do not agree on the size of a long integer (Figure 1.17).

Our client and server main functions do not change. We define one structure for
the two arguments, another structure for the result, and place both definitions in our
sum.h header, shown in Figure 5.18. Figure 5.19 shows the str_cli function.

```
                                                              ———————— tcpcliserv/sum.h
 1 struct args {
 2     long    arg1;
 3     long    arg2;
 4 };

 5 struct result {
 6     long    sum;
 7 };
                                                              ———————— tcpcliserv/sum.h
```

Figure 5.18 sum.h header.

——————————————————————————————— tcpcliserv/str_cli09.c
```
 1 #include    "unp.h"
 2 #include    "sum.h"

 3 void
 4 str_cli(FILE *fp, int sockfd)
 5 {
 6     char    sendline[MAXLINE];
 7     struct args args;
 8     struct result result;

 9     while (Fgets(sendline, MAXLINE, fp) != NULL) {

10         if (sscanf(sendline, "%ld%ld", &args.arg1, &args.arg2) != 2) {
11             printf("invalid input: %s", sendline);
12             continue;
13         }
14         Writen(sockfd, &args, sizeof(args));

15         if (Readn(sockfd, &result, sizeof(result)) == 0)
16             err_quit("str_cli: server terminated prematurely");

17         printf("%ld\n", result.sum);
18     }
19 }
```
——————————————————————————————— tcpcliserv/str_cli09.c

Figure 5.19 str_cli function which sends two binary integers to server.

10–14   sscanf converts the two arguments from text strings to binary, and we call
writen to send the structure to the server.

15–17   We call readn to read the reply, and print the result using printf.
     Figure 5.20 shows our str_echo function.

——————————————————————————————— tcpcliserv/str_echo09.c
```
 1 #include    "unp.h"
 2 #include    "sum.h"

 3 void
 4 str_echo(int sockfd)
 5 {
 6     ssize_t n;
 7     struct args args;
 8     struct result result;

 9     for ( ; ; ) {
10         if ( (n = Readn(sockfd, &args, sizeof(args))) == 0)
11             return;              /* connection closed by other end */

12         result.sum = args.arg1 + args.arg2;
13         Writen(sockfd, &result, sizeof(result));
14     }
15 }
```
——————————————————————————————— tcpcliserv/str_echo09.c

Figure 5.20 str_echo function that adds two binary integers.

9-14 We read the arguments by calling `readn`, calculate and store the sum, and call `writen` to send back the result structure.

If we run the client and server on two machines of the same architecture, say two SPARC machines, everything works fine. Here is the client interaction:

```
solaris % tcpcli09 12.106.32.254
11 22                              we type this
33                                 this is the server's reply
-11 -44
-55
```

But when the client and server are on two machines of different architectures (say the server is on the big-endian SPARC system `freebsd` and the client is on the little-endian Intel system `linux`), it does not work.

```
linux % tcpcli09 206.168.112.96
1 2                                we type this
3                                  and it works
-22 -77                            then we type this
-16777314                          and it does not work
```

The problem is that the two binary integers are sent across the socket in little-endian format by the client, but interpreted as big-endian integers by the server. We see that it appears to work for positive integers but fails for negative integers (see Exercise 5.8). There are really three potential problems with this example:

1. Different implementations store binary numbers in different formats. The most common formats are big-endian and little-endian, as we described in Section 3.4.

2. Different implementations can store the same C datatype differently. For example, most 32-bit Unix systems use 32 bits for a `long` but 64-bit systems typically use 64 bits for the same datatype (Figure 1.17). There is no guarantee that a `short`, `int`, or `long` is of any certain size.

3. Different implementations pack structures differently, depending on the number of bits used for the various datatypes and the alignment restrictions of the machine. Therefore, it is never wise to send binary structures across a socket.

There are two common solutions to this data format problem:

1. Pass all numeric data as text strings. This is what we did in Figure 5.17. This assumes that both hosts have the same character set.

2. Explicitly define the binary formats of the supported datatypes (number of bits, big- or little-endian) and pass all data between the client and server in this format. RPC packages normally use this technique. RFC 1832 [Srinivasan 1995] describes the *External Data Representation* (XDR) standard that is used with the Sun RPC package.

5.19 Summary

The first version of our echo client/server totaled about 150 lines (including the `readline` and `writen` functions), yet provided lots of details to examine. The first problem we encountered was zombie children and we caught the `SIGCHLD` signal to handle this. Our signal handler then called `waitpid` and we demonstrated that we must call this function instead of the older `wait` function, since Unix signals are not queued. This led us into some of the details of POSIX signal handling (additional information on this topic is provided in Chapter 10 of APUE).

The next problem we encountered was the client not being notified when the server process terminated. We saw that our client's TCP was notified, but we did not receive that notification since we were blocked, waiting for user input. We will use the `select` or `poll` function in Chapter 6 to handle this scenario, by waiting for any one of multiple descriptors to be ready, instead of blocking on a single descriptor.

We also discovered that if the server host crashes, we do not detect this until the client sends data to the server. Some applications must be made aware of this fact sooner; in Section 7.5, we will look at the `SO_KEEPALIVE` socket option.

Our simple example exchanged lines of text, which was okay since the server never looked at the lines it echoed. Sending numeric data between the client and server can lead to a new set of problems, as shown.

Exercises

5.1   Build the TCP server from Figures 5.2 and 5.3 and the TCP client from Figures 5.4 and 5.5. Start the server and then start the client. Type in a few lines to verify that the client and server work. Terminate the client by typing your EOF character and note the time. Use `netstat` on the client host to verify that the client's end of the connection goes through the TIME_WAIT state. Execute `netstat` every five seconds or so to see when the TIME_WAIT state ends. What is the MSL for this implementation?

5.2   What happens with our echo client/server if we run the client and redirect standard input to a binary file?

5.3   What is the difference between our echo client/server and using the Telnet client to communicate with our echo server?

5.4   In our example in Section 5.12, we verified that the first two segments of the connection termination are sent (the FIN from the server that is then ACKed by the client) by looking at the socket states using `netstat`. Are the final two segments exchanged (a FIN from the client that is ACKed by the server)? If so, when, and if not, why?

5.5   What happens in the example outlined in Section 5.14 if between Steps 2 and 3 we restart our server application on the server host?

5.6   To verify what we claimed happens with SIGPIPE in Section 5.13, modify Figure 5.4 as follows: Write a signal handler for SIGPIPE that just prints a message and returns. Establish this signal handler before calling connect. Change the server's port number to 13, the daytime server. When the connection is established, sleep for two seconds, write a few bytes to the socket, sleep for another two seconds, and write a few more bytes to the socket. Run the program. What happens?

5.7   What happens in Figure 5.15 if the IP address of the server host that is specified by the client in its call to connect is the IP address associated with the rightmost datalink on the server, instead of the IP address associated with the leftmost datalink on the server?

5.8   In our example output from Figure 5.20, when the client and server were on different endian systems, the example worked for small positive numbers, but not for small negative numbers. Why? (*Hint*: Draw a picture of the values exchanged across the socket, similar to Figure 3.9.)

5.9   In our example in Figures 5.19 and 5.20, can we solve the byte ordering problem by having the client convert the two arguments into network byte order using htonl, having the server then call ntohl on each argument before doing the addition, and then doing a similar conversion on the result?

5.10   What happens in Figures 5.19 and 5.20 if the client is on a SPARC that stores a long in 32 bits, but the server is on a Digital Alpha that stores a long in 64 bits? Does this change if the client and server are swapped between these two hosts?

5.11   In Figure 5.15, we say that the client IP address is chosen by IP based on routing. What does this mean?

6

I/O Multiplexing: The select *and* poll *Functions*

6.1 Introduction

In Section 5.12, we saw our TCP client handling two inputs at the same time: standard input and a TCP socket. We encountered a problem when the client was blocked in a call to fgets (on standard input) and the server process was killed. The server TCP correctly sent a FIN to the client TCP, but since the client process was blocked reading from standard input, it never saw the EOF until it read from the socket (possibly much later). What we need is the capability to tell the kernel that we want to be notified if one or more I/O conditions are ready (i.e., input is ready to be read, or the descriptor is capable of taking more output). This capability is called *I/O multiplexing* and is provided by the select and poll functions. We will also cover a newer POSIX variation of the former, called pselect.

> Some systems provide more advanced ways for processes to wait for a list of events. A *poll device* is one mechanism provided in different forms by different vendors. This mechanism will be described in Chapter 14.

I/O multiplexing is typically used in networking applications in the following scenarios:

- When a client is handling multiple descriptors (normally interactive input and a network socket), I/O multiplexing should be used. This is the scenario we described previously.

- It is possible, but rare, for a client to handle multiple sockets at the same time. We will show an example of this using select in Section 16.5 in the context of a Web client.

- If a TCP server handles both a listening socket and its connected sockets, I/O multiplexing is normally used, as we will show in Section 6.8.

- If a server handles both TCP and UDP, I/O multiplexing is normally used. We will show an example of this in Section 8.15.

- If a server handles multiple services and perhaps multiple protocols (e.g., the inetd daemon that we will describe in Section 13.5), I/O multiplexing is normally used.

I/O multiplexing is not limited to network programming. Many nontrivial applications find a need for these techniques.

6.2   I/O Models

Before describing `select` and `poll`, we need to step back and look at the bigger picture, examining the basic differences in the five I/O models that are available to us under Unix:

- blocking I/O
- nonblocking I/O
- I/O multiplexing (`select` and `poll`)
- signal driven I/O (`SIGIO`)
- asynchronous I/O (the POSIX `aio_` functions)

You may want to skim this section on your first reading and then refer back to it as you encounter the different I/O models described in more detail in later chapters.

As we show in all the examples in this section, there are normally two distinct phases for an input operation:

1. Waiting for the data to be ready
2. Copying the data from the kernel to the process

For an input operation on a socket, the first step normally involves waiting for data to arrive on the network. When the packet arrives, it is copied into a buffer within the kernel. The second step is copying this data from the kernel's buffer into our application buffer.

Blocking I/O Model

The most prevalent model for I/O is the *blocking I/O model*, which we have used for all our examples so far in the text. By default, all sockets are blocking. Using a datagram socket for our examples, we have the scenario shown in Figure 6.1.

We use UDP for this example instead of TCP because with UDP, the concept of data being "ready" to read is simple: either an entire datagram has been received or it has not. With TCP it gets more complicated, as additional variables such as the socket's low-water mark come into play.

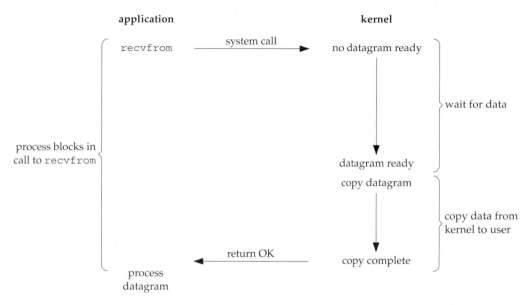

Figure 6.1 Blocking I/O model.

In the examples in this section, we also refer to `recvfrom` as a system call because we are differentiating between our application and the kernel. Regardless of how `recvfrom` is implemented (as a system call on a Berkeley-derived kernel or as a function that invokes the `getmsg` system call on a System V kernel), there is normally a switch from running in the application to running in the kernel, followed at some time later by a return to the application.

In Figure 6.1, the process calls `recvfrom` and the system call does not return until the datagram arrives and is copied into our application buffer, or an error occurs. The most common error is the system call being interrupted by a signal, as we described in Section 5.9. We say that our process is *blocked* the entire time from when it calls `recvfrom` until it returns. When `recvfrom` returns successfully, our application processes the datagram.

Nonblocking I/O Model

When we set a socket to be nonblocking, we are telling the kernel "when an I/O operation that I request cannot be completed without putting the process to sleep, do not put the process to sleep, but return an error instead." We will describe nonblocking I/O in Chapter 16, but Figure 6.2 shows a summary of the example we are considering.

The first three times that we call `recvfrom`, there is no data to return, so the kernel immediately returns an error of EWOULDBLOCK instead. The fourth time we call `recvfrom`, a datagram is ready, it is copied into our application buffer, and `recvfrom` returns successfully. We then process the data.

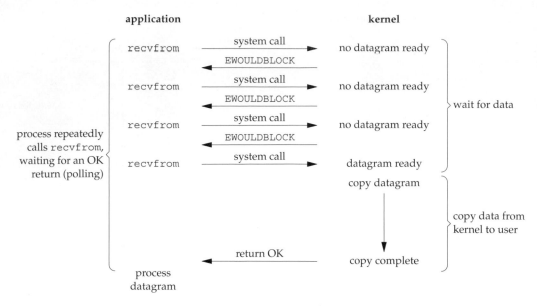

Figure 6.2 Nonblocking I/O model.

When an application sits in a loop calling `recvfrom` on a nonblocking descriptor like this, it is called *polling*. The application is continually polling the kernel to see if some operation is ready. This is often a waste of CPU time, but this model is occasionally encountered, normally on systems dedicated to one function.

I/O Multiplexing Model

With *I/O multiplexing*, we call `select` or `poll` and block in one of these two system calls, instead of blocking in the actual I/O system call. Figure 6.3 is a summary of the I/O multiplexing model.

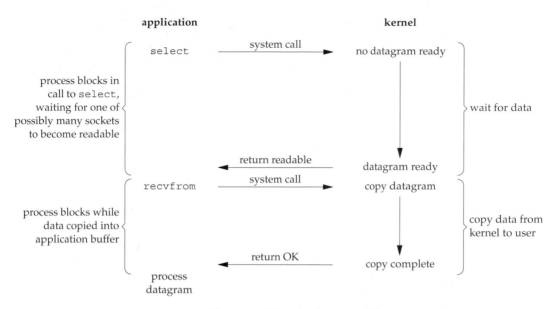

Figure 6.3 I/O multiplexing model.

We block in a call to `select`, waiting for the datagram socket to be readable. When `select` returns that the socket is readable, we then call `recvfrom` to copy the datagram into our application buffer.

Comparing Figure 6.3 to Figure 6.1, there does not appear to be any advantage, and in fact, there is a slight disadvantage because using `select` requires two system calls instead of one. But the advantage in using `select`, which we will see later in this chapter, is that we can wait for more than one descriptor to be ready.

> Another closely related I/O model is to use multithreading with blocking I/O. That model very closely resembles the model described above, except that instead of using `select` to block on multiple file descriptors, the program uses multiple threads (one per file descriptor), and each thread is then free to call blocking system calls like `recvfrom`.

Signal-Driven I/O Model

We can also use signals, telling the kernel to notify us with the `SIGIO` signal when the descriptor is ready. We call this *signal-driven I/O* and show a summary of it in Figure 6.4.

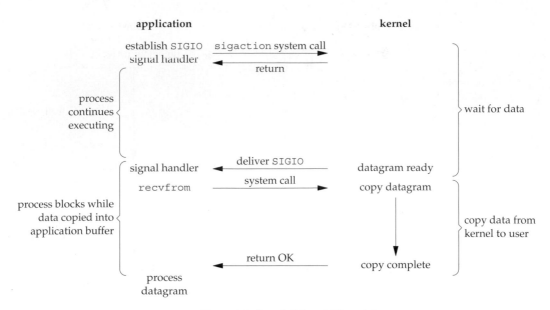

Figure 6.4 Signal-Driven I/O model.

We first enable the socket for signal-driven I/O (as we will describe in Section 25.2) and install a signal handler using the sigaction system call. The return from this system call is immediate and our process continues; it is not blocked. When the datagram is ready to be read, the SIGIO signal is generated for our process. We can either read the datagram from the signal handler by calling recvfrom and then notify the main loop that the data is ready to be processed (this is what we will do in Section 25.3), or we can notify the main loop and let it read the datagram.

Regardless of how we handle the signal, the advantage to this model is that we are not blocked while waiting for the datagram to arrive. The main loop can continue executing and just wait to be notified by the signal handler that either the data is ready to process or the datagram is ready to be read.

Asynchronous I/O Model

Asynchronous I/O is defined by the POSIX specification, and various differences in the *real-time* functions that appeared in the various standards which came together to form the current POSIX specification have been reconciled. In general, these functions work by telling the kernel to start the operation and to notify us when the entire operation (including the copy of the data from the kernel to our buffer) is complete. The main difference between this model and the signal-driven I/O model in the previous section is that with signal-driven I/O, the kernel tells us when an I/O operation can be *initiated*, but with asynchronous I/O, the kernel tells us when an I/O operation is *complete*. We show an example in Figure 6.5.

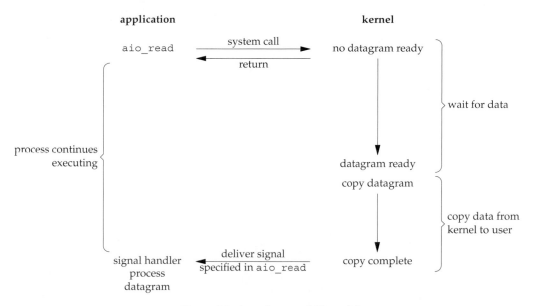

Figure 6.5 Asynchronous I/O model.

We call `aio_read` (the POSIX asynchronous I/O functions begin with `aio_` or `lio_`) and pass the kernel the descriptor, buffer pointer, buffer size (the same three arguments for `read`), file offset (similar to `lseek`), and how to notify us when the entire operation is complete. This system call returns immediately and our process is not blocked while waiting for the I/O to complete. We assume in this example that we ask the kernel to generate some signal when the operation is complete. This signal is not generated until the data has been copied into our application buffer, which is different from the signal-driven I/O model.

> As of this writing, few systems support POSIX asynchronous I/O. We are not certain, for example, if systems will support it for sockets. Our use of it here is as an example to compare against the signal-driven I/O model.

Comparison of the I/O Models

Figure 6.6 is a comparison of the five different I/O models. It shows that the main difference between the first four models is the first phase, as the second phase in the first four models is the same: the process is blocked in a call to `recvfrom` while the data is copied from the kernel to the caller's buffer. Asynchronous I/O, however, handles both phases and is different from the first four.

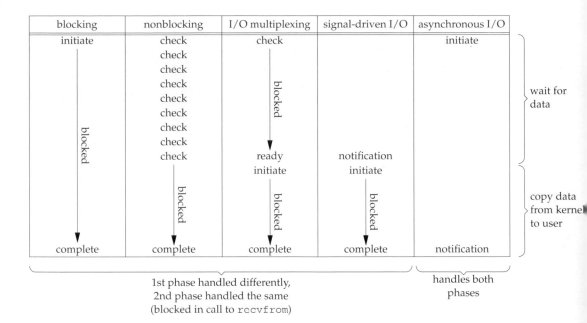

Figure 6.6 Comparison of the five I/O models.

Synchronous I/O versus Asynchronous I/O

POSIX defines these two terms as follows:

- A *synchronous I/O operation* causes the requesting process to be blocked until that I/O operation completes.
- An *asynchronous I/O operation* does not cause the requesting process to be blocked.

Using these definitions, the first four I/O models—blocking, nonblocking, I/O multiplexing, and signal-driven I/O—are all synchronous because the actual I/O operation (recvfrom) blocks the process. Only the asynchronous I/O model matches the asynchronous I/O definition.

6.3   select Function

This function allows the process to instruct the kernel to wait for any one of multiple events to occur and to wake up the process only when one or more of these events occurs or when a specified amount of time has passed.

As an example, we can call `select` and tell the kernel to return only when:

- Any of the descriptors in the set {1, 4, 5} are ready for reading
- Any of the descriptors in the set {2, 7} are ready for writing
- Any of the descriptors in the set {1, 4} have an exception condition pending
- 10.2 seconds have elapsed

That is, we tell the kernel what descriptors we are interested in (for reading, writing, or an exception condition) and how long to wait. The descriptors in which we are interested are not restricted to sockets; any descriptor can be tested using `select`.

> Berkeley-derived implementations have always allowed I/O multiplexing with any descriptor. SVR3 originally limited I/O multiplexing to descriptors that were STREAMS devices (Chapter 31), but this limitation was removed with SVR4.

```
#include <sys/select.h>
#include <sys/time.h>

int select(int maxfdp1, fd_set *readset, fd_set *writeset, fd_set *exceptset,
           const struct timeval *timeout);
```
                    Returns: positive count of ready descriptors, 0 on timeout, −1 on error

We start our description of this function with its final argument, which tells the kernel how long to wait for one of the specified descriptors to become ready. A `timeval` structure specifies the number of seconds and microseconds.

```
struct timeval {
  long   tv_sec;     /* seconds */
  long   tv_usec;    /* microseconds */
};
```

There are three possibilities:

1. Wait forever—Return only when one of the specified descriptors is ready for I/O. For this, we specify the *timeout* argument as a null pointer.

2. Wait up to a fixed amount of time—Return when one of the specified descriptors is ready for I/O, but do not wait beyond the number of seconds and microseconds specified in the `timeval` structure pointed to by the *timeout* argument.

3. Do not wait at all—Return immediately after checking the descriptors. This is called *polling*. To specify this, the *timeout* argument must point to a `timeval` structure and the timer value (the number of seconds and microseconds specified by the structure) must be 0.

The wait in the first two scenarios is normally interrupted if the process catches a signal and returns from the signal handler.

> Berkeley-derived kernels never automatically restart `select` (p. 527 of TCPv2), while SVR4 will if the `SA_RESTART` flag is specified when the signal handler is installed. This means that for portability, we must be prepared for `select` to return an error of `EINTR` if we are catching signals.

Although the `timeval` structure lets us specify a resolution in microseconds, the actual resolution supported by the kernel is often more coarse. For example, many Unix kernels round the timeout value up to a multiple of 10 ms. There is also a scheduling latency involved, meaning it takes some time after the timer expires before the kernel schedules this process to run.

> On some systems, `select` will fail with `EINVAL` if the `tv_sec` field in the timeout is over 100 million seconds. Of course, that's a very large timeout (over three years) and likely not very useful, but the point is that the `timeval` structure can represent values that are not supported by `select`.

The `const` qualifier on the *timeout* argument means it is not modified by `select` on return. For example, if we specify a time limit of 10 seconds, and `select` returns before the timer expires with one or more of the descriptors ready or with an error of `EINTR`, the `timeval` structure is not updated with the number of seconds remaining when the function returns. If we wish to know this value, we must obtain the system time before calling `select`, and then again when it returns, and subtract the two (any robust program will take into account that the system time may be adjusted by either the administrator or by a daemon like `ntpd` occasionally).

> Some Linux versions modify the `timeval` structure. Therefore, for portability, assume the `timeval` structure is undefined upon return, and initialize it before each call to `select`. POSIX specifies the `const` qualifier.

The three middle arguments, *readset*, *writeset*, and *exceptset*, specify the descriptors that we want the kernel to test for reading, writing, and exception conditions. There are only two exception conditions currently supported:

1. The arrival of out-of-band data for a socket. We will describe this in more detail in Chapter 24.

2. The presence of control status information to be read from the master side of a pseudo-terminal that has been put into packet mode. We do not talk about pseudo-terminals in this book.

A design problem is how to specify one or more descriptor values for each of these three arguments. `select` uses *descriptor sets*, typically an array of integers, with each bit in each integer corresponding to a descriptor. For example, using 32-bit integers, the first element of the array corresponds to descriptors 0 through 31, the second element of the array corresponds to descriptors 32 through 63, and so on. All the implementation details are irrelevant to the application and are hidden in the `fd_set` datatype and the following four macros:

```
void FD_ZERO(fd_set *fdset);        /* clear all bits in fdset */
void FD_SET(int fd, fd_set *fdset); /* turn on the bit for fd in fdset */
void FD_CLR(int fd, fd_set *fdset); /* turn off the bit for fd in fdset */
int  FD_ISSET(int fd, fd_set *fdset); /* is the bit for fd on in fdset ? */
```

We allocate a descriptor set of the `fd_set` datatype, we set and test the bits in the set using these macros, and we can also assign it to another descriptor set across an equals sign (=) in C.

> What we are describing, an array of integers using one bit per descriptor, is just one possible way to implement `select`. Nevertheless, it is common to refer to the individual descriptors within a descriptor set as *bits*, as in "turn on the bit for the listening descriptor in the read set."

> We will see in Section 6.10 that the `poll` function uses a completely different representation: a variable-length array of structures with one structure per descriptor.

For example, to define a variable of type `fd_set` and then turn on the bits for descriptors 1, 4, and 5, we write

```
fd_set  rset;

FD_ZERO(&rset);      /* initialize the set: all bits off */
FD_SET(1, &rset);    /* turn on bit for fd 1 */
FD_SET(4, &rset);    /* turn on bit for fd 4 */
FD_SET(5, &rset);    /* turn on bit for fd 5 */
```

It is important to initialize the set, since unpredictable results can occur if the set is allocated as an automatic variable and not initialized.

Any of the middle three arguments to `select`, *readset*, *writeset*, or *exceptset*, can be specified as a null pointer if we are not interested in that condition. Indeed, if all three pointers are null, then we have a higher precision timer than the normal Unix `sleep` function (which sleeps for multiples of a second). The `poll` function provides similar functionality. Figures C.9 and C.10 of APUE show a `sleep_us` function implemented using both `select` and `poll` that sleeps for multiples of a microsecond.

The *maxfdp1* argument specifies the number of descriptors to be tested. Its value is the maximum descriptor to be tested plus one (hence our name of *maxfdp1*). The descriptors 0, 1, 2, up through and including *maxfdp1−1* are tested.

The constant FD_SETSIZE, defined by including <sys/select.h>, is the number of descriptors in the `fd_set` datatype. Its value is often 1024, but few programs use that many descriptors. The *maxfdp1* argument forces us to calculate the largest descriptor that we are interested in and then tell the kernel this value. For example, given the previous code that turns on the indicators for descriptors 1, 4, and 5, the *maxfdp1* value is 6. The reason it is 6 and not 5 is that we are specifying the number of descriptors, not the largest value, and descriptors start at 0.

> The reason this argument exists, along with the burden of calculating its value, is purely for efficiency. Although each `fd_set` has room for many descriptors, typically 1,024, this is much more than the number used by a typical process. The kernel gains efficiency by not copying unneeded portions of the descriptor set between the process and the kernel, and by not testing bits that are always 0 (Section 16.13 of TCPv2).

`select` modifies the descriptor sets pointed to by the *readset*, *writeset*, and *exceptset* pointers. These three arguments are value-result arguments. When we call the function, we specify the values of the descriptors that we are interested in, and on return, the result indicates which descriptors are ready. We use the `FD_ISSET` macro on return to test a specific descriptor in an `fd_set` structure. Any descriptor that is not ready on return will have its corresponding bit cleared in the descriptor set. To handle this, we turn on all the bits in which we are interested in all the descriptor sets each time we call `select`.

> The two most common programming errors when using `select` are to forget to add one to the largest descriptor number and to forget that the descriptor sets are value-result arguments. The second error results in `select` being called with a bit set to 0 in the descriptor set, when we think that bit is 1.

The return value from this function indicates the total number of bits that are ready across all the descriptor sets. If the timer value expires before any of the descriptors are ready, a value of 0 is returned. A return value of −1 indicates an error (which can happen, for example, if the function is interrupted by a caught signal).

> Early releases of SVR4 had a bug in their implementation of `select`: If the same bit was on in multiple sets, say a descriptor was ready for both reading and writing, it was counted only once. Current releases fix this bug.

Under What Conditions Is a Descriptor Ready?

We have been talking about waiting for a descriptor to become ready for I/O (reading or writing) or to have an exception condition pending on it (out-of-band data). While readability and writability are obvious for descriptors such as regular files, we must be more specific about the conditions that cause `select` to return "ready" for sockets (Figure 16.52 of TCPv2).

1. A socket is ready for reading if any of the following four conditions is true:

   a. The number of bytes of data in the socket receive buffer is greater than or equal to the current size of the low-water mark for the socket receive buffer. A read operation on the socket will not block and will return a value greater than 0 (i.e., the data that is ready to be read). We can set this low-water mark using the `SO_RCVLOWAT` socket option. It defaults to 1 for TCP and UDP sockets.

   b. The read half of the connection is closed (i.e., a TCP connection that has received a FIN). A read operation on the socket will not block and will return 0 (i.e., EOF).

c. The socket is a listening socket and the number of completed connections is nonzero. An accept on the listening socket will normally not block, although we will describe a timing condition in Section 16.6 under which the accept can block.

d. A socket error is pending. A read operation on the socket will not block and will return an error (–1) with errno set to the specific error condition. These *pending errors* can also be fetched and cleared by calling getsockopt and specifying the SO_ERROR socket option.

2. A socket is ready for writing if any of the following four conditions is true:

a. The number of bytes of available space in the socket send buffer is greater than or equal to the current size of the low-water mark for the socket send buffer *and* either: (i) the socket is connected, or (ii) the socket does not require a connection (e.g., UDP). This means that if we set the socket to non-blocking (Chapter 16), a write operation will not block and will return a positive value (e.g., the number of bytes accepted by the transport layer). We can set this low-water mark using the SO_SNDLOWAT socket option. This low-water mark normally defaults to 2048 for TCP and UDP sockets.

b. The write half of the connection is closed. A write operation on the socket will generate SIGPIPE (Section 5.12).

c. A socket using a non-blocking connect has completed the connection, or the connect has failed.

d. A socket error is pending. A write operation on the socket will not block and will return an error (–1) with errno set to the specific error condition. These *pending errors* can also be fetched and cleared by calling getsockopt with the SO_ERROR socket option.

3. A socket has an exception condition pending if there is out-of-band data for the socket or the socket is still at the out-of-band mark. (We will describe out-of-band data in Chapter 24.)

> Our definitions of "readable" and "writable" are taken directly from the kernel's soreadable and sowriteable macros on pp. 530–531 of TCPv2. Similarly, our definition of the "exception condition" for a socket is from the soo_select function on these same pages.

Notice that when an error occurs on a socket, it is marked as both readable and writable by select.

The purpose of the receive and send low-water marks is to give the application control over how much data must be available for reading or how much space must be available for writing before select returns a readable or writable status. For example, if we know that our application has nothing productive to do unless at least 64 bytes of data are present, we can set the receive low-water mark to 64 to prevent select from waking us up if less than 64 bytes are ready for reading.

As long as the send low-water mark for a UDP socket is less than the send buffer size (which should always be the default relationship), the UDP socket is always writable, since a connection is not required.

Figure 6.7 summarizes the conditions just described that cause a socket to be ready for select.

Condition	Readable?	Writable?	Exception?
Data to read	•		
Read half of the connection closed	•		
New connection ready for listening socket	•		
Space available for writing		•	
Write half of the connection closed		•	
Pending error	•	•	
TCP out-of-band data			•

Figure 6.7 Summary of conditions that cause a socket to be ready for select.

Maximum Number of Descriptors for select

We said earlier that most applications do not use lots of descriptors. It is rare, for example, to find an application that uses hundreds of descriptors. But, such applications do exist, and they often use select to multiplex the descriptors. When select was originally designed, the OS normally had an upper limit on the maximum number of descriptors per process (the 4.2BSD limit was 31), and select just used this same limit. But, current versions of Unix allow for a virtually unlimited number of descriptors per process (often limited only by the amount of memory and any administrative limits), so the question is: How does this affect select?

Many implementations have declarations similar to the following, which are taken from the 4.4BSD <sys/types.h> header:

```
/*
 * Select uses bitmasks of file descriptors in longs.   These macros
 * manipulate such bit fields (the filesystem macros use chars).
 * FD_SETSIZE may be defined by the user, but the default here should
 * be enough for most uses.
 */
#ifndef FD_SETSIZE
#define FD_SETSIZE      256
#endif
```

This makes us think that we can just #define FD_SETSIZE to some larger value before including this header to increase the size of the descriptor sets used by select. Unfortunately, this normally does not work.

> To see what is wrong, notice that Figure 16.53 of TCPv2 declares three descriptor sets within the kernel and also uses the kernel's definition of FD_SETSIZE as the upper limit. The only way to increase the size of the descriptor sets is to increase the value of FD_SETSIZE and then recompile the kernel. Changing the value without recompiling the kernel is inadequate.

Some vendors are changing their implementation of select to allow the process to define FD_SETSIZE to a larger value than the default. BSD/OS has changed the kernel implementation to allow larger descriptor sets, and it also provides four new FD_*xxx* macros to dynamically allocate and manipulate these larger sets. From a portability standpoint, however, beware of using large descriptor sets.

6.4   str_cli **Function (Revisited)**

We can now rewrite our str_cli function from Section 5.5, this time using select, so we are notified as soon as the server process terminates. The problem with that earlier version was that we could be blocked in the call to fgets when something happened on the socket. Our new version blocks in a call to select instead, waiting for either standard input or the socket to be readable. Figure 6.8 shows the various conditions that are handled by our call to select.

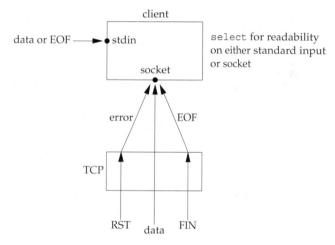

Figure 6.8   Conditions handled by select in str_cli.

Three conditions are handled with the socket:

1. If the peer TCP sends data, the socket becomes readable and read returns greater than 0 (i.e., the number of bytes of data).

2. If the peer TCP sends a FIN (the peer process terminates), the socket becomes readable and read returns 0 (EOF).

3. If the peer TCP sends an RST (the peer host has crashed and rebooted), the socket becomes readable, read returns −1, and errno contains the specific error code.

Figure 6.9 shows the source code for this new version.

—————————————————————————————— select/strcliselect01.c

```
 1 #include    "unp.h"

 2 void
 3 str_cli(FILE *fp, int sockfd)
 4 {
 5     int     maxfdp1;
 6     fd_set  rset;
 7     char    sendline[MAXLINE], recvline[MAXLINE];

 8     FD_ZERO(&rset);
 9     for ( ; ; ) {
10         FD_SET(fileno(fp), &rset);
11         FD_SET(sockfd, &rset);
12         maxfdp1 = max(fileno(fp), sockfd) + 1;
13         Select(maxfdp1, &rset, NULL, NULL, NULL);

14         if (FD_ISSET(sockfd, &rset)) {  /* socket is readable */
15             if (Readline(sockfd, recvline, MAXLINE) == 0)
16                 err_quit("str_cli: server terminated prematurely");
17             Fputs(recvline, stdout);
18         }

19         if (FD_ISSET(fileno(fp), &rset)) {  /* input is readable */
20             if (Fgets(sendline, MAXLINE, fp) == NULL)
21                 return;            /* all done */
22             Writen(sockfd, sendline, strlen(sendline));
23         }
24     }
25 }
```

—————————————————————————————— select/strcliselect01.c

Figure 6.9 Implementation of `str_cli` function using `select` (improved in Figure 6.13).

Call `select`

8–13   We only need one descriptor set—to check for readability. This set is initialized by
FD_ZERO and then two bits are turned on using FD_SET: the bit corresponding to the
standard I/O file pointer, fp, and the bit corresponding to the socket, sockfd. The
function fileno converts a standard I/O file pointer into its corresponding descriptor.
select (and poll) work only with descriptors.

select is called after calculating the maximum of the two descriptors. In the call,
the write-set pointer and the exception-set pointer are both null pointers. The final
argument (the time limit) is also a null pointer since we want the call to block until
something is ready.

Handle readable socket

14–18   If, on return from select, the socket is readable, the echoed line is read with
readline and output by fputs.

Handle readable input

19–23   If the standard input is readable, a line is read by fgets and written to the socket
using writen.

Notice that the same four I/O functions are used as in Figure 5.5, `fgets`, `writen`, `readline`, and `fputs`, but the order of flow within the function has changed. Instead of the function flow being driven by the call to `fgets`, it is now driven by the call to `select`. With only a few additional lines of code in Figure 6.9, compared to Figure 5.5, we have added greatly to the robustness of our client.

6.5 Batch Input and Buffering

Unfortunately, our `str_cli` function is still not correct. First, let's go back to our original version, Figure 5.5. It operates in a stop-and-wait mode, which is fine for interactive use: It sends a line to the server and then waits for the reply. This amount of time is one RTT plus the server's processing time (which is close to 0 for a simple echo server). We can therefore estimate how long it will take for a given number of lines to be echoed if we know the RTT between the client and server.

The `ping` program is an easy way to measure RTTs. If we run `ping` to the host `connix.com` from our host `solaris`, the average RTT over 30 measurements is 175 ms. Page 89 of TCPv1 shows that these `ping` measurements are for an IP datagram whose length is 84 bytes. If we take the first 2,000 lines of the Solaris `termcap` file, the resulting file size is 98,349 bytes, for an average of 49 bytes per line. If we add the sizes of the IP header (20 bytes) and the TCP header (20), the average TCP segment will be about 89 bytes, nearly the same as the `ping` packet sizes. We can therefore estimate that the total clock time will be around 350 seconds for 2,000 lines ($2,000 \times 0.175sec$). If we run our TCP echo client from Chapter 5, the actual time is about 354 seconds, which is very close to our estimate.

If we consider the network between the client and server as a full-duplex pipe, with requests going from the client to the server and replies in the reverse direction, then Figure 6.10 shows our stop-and-wait mode.

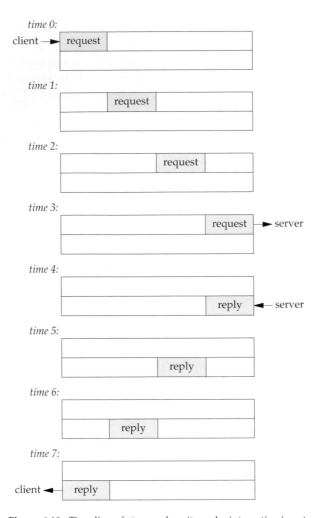

Figure 6.10 Time line of stop-and-wait mode: interactive input.

A request is sent by the client at time 0 and we assume an RTT of 8 units of time. The reply sent at time 4 is received at time 7. We also assume that there is no server processing time and that the size of the request is the same as the reply. We show only the data packets between the client and server, ignoring the TCP acknowledgments that are also going across the network.

Since there is a delay between sending a packet and that packet arriving at the other end of the pipe, and since the pipe is full-duplex, in this example, we are only using one-eighth of the pipe's capacity. This stop-and-wait mode is fine for interactive input, but since our client reads from standard input and writes to standard output, and since it is trivial under the Unix shells to redirect the input and output, we can easily run our client in a batch mode. When we redirect the input and output, however, the resulting output file is always smaller than the input file (and they should be identical for an echo server).

To see what's happening, realize that in a batch mode, we can keep sending requests as fast as the network can accept them. The server processes them and sends back the replies at the same rate. This leads to the full pipe at time 7, as shown in Figure 6.11.

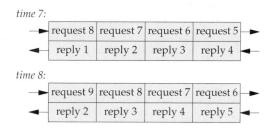

Figure 6.11 Filling the pipe between the client and server: batch mode.

Here we assume that after sending the first request, we immediately send another, and then another. We also assume that we can keep sending requests as fast as the network can accept them, along with processing replies as fast as the network supplies them.

> There are numerous subtleties dealing with TCP's bulk data flow that we are ignoring here, such as its slow-start algorithm, which limits the rate at which data is sent on a new or idle connection, and the returning ACKs. These are all covered in Chapter 20 of TCPv1.

To see the problem with our revised `str_cli` function in Figure 6.9, assume that the input file contains only nine lines. The last line is sent at time 8, as shown in Figure 6.11. But we cannot close the connection after writing this request because there are still other requests and replies in the pipe. The cause of the problem is our handling of an EOF on input: The function returns to the `main` function, which then terminates. But in a batch mode, an EOF on input does not imply that we have finished reading from the socket; there might still be requests on the way to the server, or replies on the way back from the server.

What we need is a way to close one-half of the TCP connection. That is, we want to send a FIN to the server, telling it we have finished sending data, but leave the socket descriptor open for reading. This is done with the `shutdown` function, which is described in the next section.

In general, buffering for performance adds complexity to a network application, and the code in Figure 6.9 suffers from this complexity. Consider the case when several lines of input are available from the standard input. `select` will cause the code at line 20 to read the input using `fgets` and that, in turn, will read the available lines into a buffer used by stdio. But, `fgets` only returns a single line and leaves any remaining data sitting in the stdio buffer. The code at line 22 of Figure 6.9 writes that single line to the server and then `select` is called again to wait for more work, even if there are additional lines to consume in the stdio buffer. The reason for this is that `select` knows nothing of the buffers used by stdio—it will only show readability from the viewpoint of the `read` system call, not calls like `fgets`. For this reason, mixing stdio and `select` is considered very error-prone and should only be done with great care.

The same problem exists with the call to readline in the example in Figure 6.9. Instead of data being hidden from select in a stdio buffer, it is hidden in readline's buffer. Recall that in Section 3.9 we provided a function that gives visibility into readline's buffer, so one possible solution is to modify our code to use that function *before* calling select to see if data has already been read but not consumed. But again, the complexity grows out of hand quickly when we have to handle the case where the readline buffer contains a partial line (meaning we still need to read more) as well as when it contains one or more complete lines (which we can consume).

We will address these buffering concerns in the improved version of str_cli shown in Section 6.7.

6.6   shutdown **Function**

The normal way to terminate a network connection is to call the close function. But, there are two limitations with close that can be avoided with shutdown:

1.   close decrements the descriptor's reference count and closes the socket only if the count reaches 0. We talked about this in Section 4.8. With shutdown, we can initiate TCP's normal connection termination sequence (the four segments beginning with a FIN in Figure 2.5), regardless of the reference count.

2.   close terminates both directions of data transfer, reading and writing. Since a TCP connection is full-duplex, there are times when we want to tell the other end that we have finished sending, even though that end might have more data to send us. This is the scenario we encountered in the previous section with batch input to our str_cli function. Figure 6.12 shows the typical function calls in this scenario.

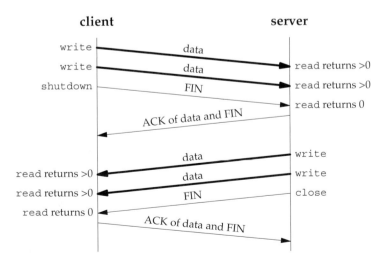

Figure 6.12 Calling shutdown to close half of a TCP connection.

```
#include <sys/socket.h>

int shutdown(int sockfd, int howto);
```

Returns: 0 if OK, −1 on error

The action of the function depends on the value of the *howto* argument.

SHUT_RD   The read half of the connection is closed—No more data can be received on the socket and any data currently in the socket receive buffer is discarded. The process can no longer issue any of the read functions on the socket. Any data received after this call for a TCP socket is acknowledged and then silently discarded.

> By default, everything written to a routing socket (Chapter 18) loops back as possible input to all routing sockets on the host. Some programs call shutdown with a second argument of SHUT_RD to prevent the loopback copy. An alternative way to prevent this loopback copy is to clear the SO_USELOOPBACK socket option.

SHUT_WR   The write half of the connection is closed—In the case of TCP, this is called a *half-close* (Section 18.5 of TCPv1). Any data currently in the socket send buffer will be sent, followed by TCP's normal connection termination sequence. As we mentioned earlier, this closing of the write half is done regardless of whether or not the socket descriptor's reference count is currently greater than 0. The process can no longer issue any of the write functions on the socket.

SHUT_RDWR The read half and the write half of the connection are both closed—This is equivalent to calling shutdown twice: first with SHUT_RD and then with SHUT_WR.

Figure 7.12 will summarize the different possibilities available to the process by calling shutdown and close. The operation of close depends on the value of the SO_LINGER socket option.

> The three SHUT_*xxx* names are defined by the POSIX specification. Typical values for the *howto* argument that you will encounter will be 0 (close the read half), 1 (close the write half), and 2 (close the read half and the write half).

6.7 `str_cli` Function (Revisited Again)

Figure 6.13 shows our revised (and correct) version of the `str_cli` function. This version uses select and shutdown. The former notifies us as soon as the server closes its end of the connection and the latter lets us handle batch input correctly. This version also does away with line-centric code and operates instead on buffers, eliminating the complexity concerns raised in Section 6.5.

── *select/strcliselect02.c*

```
 1 #include    "unp.h"

 2 void
 3 str_cli(FILE *fp, int sockfd)
 4 {
 5     int      maxfdp1, stdineof;
 6     fd_set   rset;
 7     char     buf[MAXLINE];
 8     int      n;

 9     stdineof = 0;
10     FD_ZERO(&rset);
11     for ( ; ; ) {
12         if (stdineof == 0)
13             FD_SET(fileno(fp), &rset);
14         FD_SET(sockfd, &rset);
15         maxfdp1 = max(fileno(fp), sockfd) + 1;
16         Select(maxfdp1, &rset, NULL, NULL, NULL);

17         if (FD_ISSET(sockfd, &rset)) {   /* socket is readable */
18             if ( (n = Read(sockfd, buf, MAXLINE)) == 0) {
19                 if (stdineof == 1)
20                     return;      /* normal termination */
21                 else
22                     err_quit("str_cli: server terminated prematurely");
23             }

24             Write(fileno(stdout), buf, n);
25         }

26         if (FD_ISSET(fileno(fp), &rset)) {   /* input is readable */
27             if ( (n = Read(fileno(fp), buf, MAXLINE)) == 0) {
28                 stdineof = 1;
29                 Shutdown(sockfd, SHUT_WR);   /* send FIN */
30                 FD_CLR(fileno(fp), &rset);
31                 continue;
32             }

33             Writen(sockfd, buf, n);
34         }
35     }
36 }
```

── *select/strcliselect02.c*

Figure 6.13   str_cli function using select that handles EOF correctly.

5–8   stdineof is a new flag that is initialized to 0. As long as this flag is 0, each time around the main loop, we select on standard input for readability.

17–25   When we read the EOF on the socket, if we have already encountered an EOF on standard input, this is normal termination and the function returns. But if we have not yet encountered an EOF on standard input, the server process has prematurely terminated. We now call read and write to operate on buffers instead of lines and allow select to work for us as expected.

26-34   When we encounter the EOF on standard input, our new flag, stdineof, is set and
we call shutdown with a second argument of SHUT_WR to send the FIN. Here also,
we've changed to operating on buffers instead of lines, using read and writen.

We are not finished with our str_cli function. We will develop a version using
nonblocking I/O in Section 16.2 and a version using threads in Section 26.3.

6.8   TCP Echo Server (Revisited)

We can revisit our TCP echo server from Sections 5.2 and 5.3 and rewrite the server as a
single process that uses select to handle any number of clients, instead of forking
one child per client. Before showing the code, let's look at the data structures that we
will use to keep track of the clients. Figure 6.14 shows the state of the server before the
first client has established a connection.

Figure 6.14   TCP server before first client has established a connection.

The server has a single listening descriptor, which we show as a bullet.

The server maintains only a read descriptor set, which we show in Figure 6.15. We
assume that the server is started in the foreground, so descriptors 0, 1, and 2 are set to
standard input, output, and error. Therefore, the first available descriptor for the listening socket is 3. We also show an array of integers named client that contains the connected socket descriptor for each client. All elements in this array are initialized to –1.

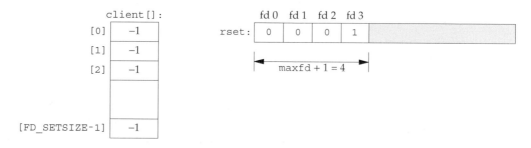

Figure 6.15   Data structures for TCP server with just a listening socket.

The only nonzero entry in the descriptor set is the entry for the listening sockets and the
first argument to select will be 4.

When the first client establishes a connection with our server, the listening descriptor becomes readable and our server calls accept. The new connected descriptor returned by accept will be 4, given the assumptions of this example. Figure 6.16 shows the connection from the client to the server.

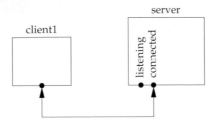

Figure 6.16   TCP server after first client establishes connection.

From this point on, our server must remember the new connected socket in its client array, and the connected socket must be added to the descriptor set. These updated data structures are shown in Figure 6.17.

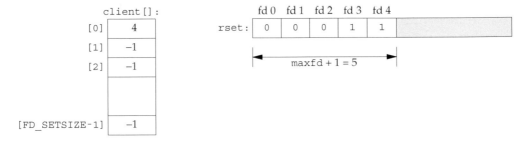

Figure 6.17   Data structures after first client connection is established.

Sometime later a second client establishes a connection and we have the scenario shown in Figure 6.18.

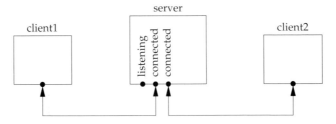

Figure 6.18   TCP server after second client connection is established.

The new connected socket (which we assume is 5) must be remembered, giving the data structures shown in Figure 6.19.

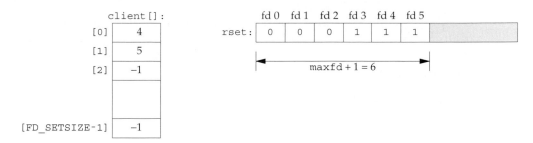

Figure 6.19 Data structures after second client connection is established.

Next, we assume the first client terminates its connection. The client TCP sends a FIN, which makes descriptor 4 in the server readable. When our server reads this connected socket, `read` returns 0. We then close this socket and update our data structures accordingly. The value of `client[0]` is set to −1 and descriptor 4 in the descriptor set is set to 0. This is shown in Figure 6.20. Notice that the value of `maxfd` does not change.

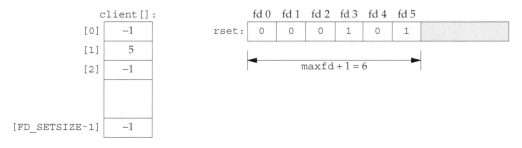

Figure 6.20 Data structures after first client terminates its connection.

In summary, as clients arrive, we record their connected socket descriptor in the first available entry in the `client` array (i.e., the first entry with a value of −1). We must also add the connected socket to the read descriptor set. The variable `maxi` is the highest index in the `client` array that is currently in use and the variable `maxfd` (plus one) is the current value of the first argument to `select`. The only limit on the number of clients that this server can handle is the minimum of the two values `FD_SETSIZE` and the maximum number of descriptors allowed for this process by the kernel (which we talked about at the end of Section 6.3).

Figure 6.21 shows the first half of this version of the server.

————————————————————————————————— tcpcliserv/tcpservselect01.c

```
 1 #include    "unp.h"

 2 int
 3 main(int argc, char **argv)
 4 {
 5     int     i, maxi, maxfd, listenfd, connfd, sockfd;
 6     int     nready, client[FD_SETSIZE];
 7     ssize_t n;
 8     fd_set  rset, allset;
 9     char    buf[MAXLINE];
10     socklen_t clilen;
11     struct sockaddr_in cliaddr, servaddr;

12     listenfd = Socket(AF_INET, SOCK_STREAM, 0);

13     bzero(&servaddr, sizeof(servaddr));
14     servaddr.sin_family = AF_INET;
15     servaddr.sin_addr.s_addr = htonl(INADDR_ANY);
16     servaddr.sin_port = htons(SERV_PORT);

17     Bind(listenfd, (SA *) &servaddr, sizeof(servaddr));

18     Listen(listenfd, LISTENQ);

19     maxfd = listenfd;            /* initialize */
20     maxi = -1;                   /* index into client[] array */
21     for (i = 0; i < FD_SETSIZE; i++)
22         client[i] = -1;          /* -1 indicates available entry */
23     FD_ZERO(&allset);
24     FD_SET(listenfd, &allset);
```

————————————————————————— tcpcliserv/tcpservselect01.c

Figure 6.21 TCP server using a single process and select: initialization.

Create listening socket and initialize for select

12-24   The steps to create the listening socket are the same as seen earlier: socket, bind, and listen. We initialize our data structures assuming that the only descriptor that we will select on initially is the listening socket.

The last half of the function is shown in Figure 6.22

—————————————————————————— tcpcliserv/tcpservselect01.c

```
25    for ( ; ; ) {
26        rset = allset;          /* structure assignment */
27        nready = Select(maxfd + 1, &rset, NULL, NULL, NULL);

28        if (FD_ISSET(listenfd, &rset)) {     /* new client connection */
29            clilen = sizeof(cliaddr);
30            connfd = Accept(listenfd, (SA *) &cliaddr, &clilen);

31            for (i = 0; i < FD_SETSIZE; i++)
32                if (client[i] < 0) {
33                    client[i] = connfd; /* save descriptor */
34                    break;
35                }
36            if (i == FD_SETSIZE)
37                err_quit("too many clients");

38            FD_SET(connfd, &allset);     /* add new descriptor to set */
39            if (connfd > maxfd)
40                maxfd = connfd; /* for select */
41            if (i > maxi)
42                maxi = i;          /* max index in client[] array */

43            if (--nready <= 0)
44                continue;          /* no more readable descriptors */
45        }

46        for (i = 0; i <= maxi; i++) {    /* check all clients for data */
47            if ( (sockfd = client[i]) < 0)
48                continue;
49            if (FD_ISSET(sockfd, &rset)) {
50                if ( (n = Read(sockfd, buf, MAXLINE)) == 0) {
51                        /* connection closed by client */
52                    Close(sockfd);
53                    FD_CLR(sockfd, &allset);
54                    client[i] = -1;
55                } else
56                    Writen(sockfd, buf, n);

57                if (--nready <= 0)
58                    break;         /* no more readable descriptors */
59            }
60        }
61    }
62 }
```

—————————————————————————— tcpcliserv/tcpservselect01.c

Figure 6.22 TCP server using a single process and `select` loop.

Block in `select`

26-27   `select` waits for something to happen: either the establishment of a new client connection or the arrival of data, a FIN, or an RST on an existing connection.

`accept` new connections

28-45   If the listening socket is readable, a new connection has been established. We call accept and update our data structures accordingly. We use the first unused entry in the client array to record the connected socket. The number of ready descriptors is decremented, and if it is 0, we can avoid the next for loop. This lets us use the return value from select to avoid checking descriptors that are not ready.

Check existing connections

46–60   A test is made for each existing client connection as to whether or not its descriptor is in the descriptor set returned by select. If so, a line is read from the client and echoed back to the client. If the client closes the connection, read returns 0 and we update our data structures accordingly.

We never decrement the value of maxi, but we could check for this possibility each time a client closes its connection.

This server is more complicated than the one shown in Figures 5.2 and 5.3, but it avoids all the overhead of creating a new process for each client and it is a nice example of select. Nevertheless, in Section 16.6, we will describe a problem with this server that is easily fixed by making the listening socket nonblocking and then checking for, and ignoring, a few errors from accept.

Denial-of-Service Attacks

Unfortunately, there is a problem with the server that we just showed. Consider what happens if a malicious client connects to the server, sends one byte of data (other than a newline), and then goes to sleep. The server will call read, which will read the single byte of data from the client and then block in the next call to read, waiting for more data from this client. The server is then blocked ("hung" may be a better term) by this one client and will not service any other clients (either new client connections or existing clients' data) until the malicious client either sends a newline or terminates.

The basic concept here is that when a server is handling multiple clients, the server can *never* block in a function call related to a single client. Doing so can hang the server and deny service to all other clients. This is called a *denial-of-service* attack. It does something to the server that prevents it from servicing other legitimate clients. Possible solutions are to: (i) use nonblocking I/O (Chapter 16), (ii) have each client serviced by a separate thread of control (e.g., either spawn a process or a thread to service each client), or (iii) place a timeout on the I/O operations (Section 14.2).

6.9   pselect **Function**

The pselect function was invented by POSIX and is now supported by many of the Unix variants.

```
#include <sys/select.h>
#include <signal.h>
#include <time.h>

int pselect(int maxfdp1, fd_set *readset, fd_set *writeset, fd_set *exceptset,
            const struct timespec *timeout, const sigset_t *sigmask);
```
                                    Returns: count of ready descriptors, 0 on timeout, −1 on error

pselect contains two changes from the normal select function:

1. pselect uses the timespec structure, another POSIX invention, instead of the timeval structure.

    ```
    struct timespec {
      time_t tv_sec;      /* seconds */
      long   tv_nsec;     /* nanoseconds */
    };
    ```

    The difference in these two structures is with the second member: The tv_nsec member of the newer structure specifies nanoseconds, whereas the tv_usec member of the older structure specifies microseconds.

2. pselect adds a sixth argument: a pointer to a signal mask. This allows the program to disable the delivery of certain signals, test some global variables that are set by the handlers for these now-disabled signals, and then call pselect, telling it to reset the signal mask.

With regard to the second point, consider the following example (discussed on pp. 308–309 of APUE). Our program's signal handler for SIGINT just sets the global intr_flag and returns. If our process is blocked in a call to select, the return from the signal handler causes the function to return with errno set to EINTR. But when select is called, the code looks like the following:

```
    if (intr_flag)
        handle_intr();     /* handle the signal */
    if ( (nready = select( ... )) < 0) {
        if (errno == EINTR) {
            if (intr_flag)
                handle_intr();
        }
        ...
    }
```

The problem is that between the test of intr_flag and the call to select, if the signal occurs, it will be lost if select blocks forever. With pselect, we can now code this example reliably as

```
sigset_t  newmask, oldmask, zeromask;

sigemptyset(&zeromask);
sigemptyset(&newmask);
sigaddset(&newmask, SIGINT);

sigprocmask(SIG_BLOCK, &newmask, &oldmask); /* block SIGINT */
if (intr_flag)
    handle_intr();     /* handle the signal */
if ( (nready = pselect( ... , &zeromask)) < 0) {
    if (errno == EINTR) {
        if (intr_flag)
            handle_intr();
    }
    ...
}
```

Before testing the intr_flag variable, we block SIGINT. When pselect is called, it replaces the signal mask of the process with an empty set (i.e., zeromask) and then checks the descriptors, possibly going to sleep. But when pselect returns, the signal mask of the process is reset to its value before pselect was called (i.e., SIGINT is blocked).

We will say more about pselect and show an example of it in Section 20.5. We will use pselect in Figure 20.7 and show a simple, albeit incorrect, implementation of pselect in Figure 20.8.

> There is one other slight difference between the two select functions. The first member of the timeval structure is a signed long integer, while the first member of the timespec structure is a time_t. The signed long in the former should also be a time_t, but was not changed retroactively to avoid breaking existing code. The brand new function, however, could make this change.

6.10 poll Function

The poll function originated with SVR3 and was originally limited to STREAMS devices (Chapter 31). SVR4 removed this limitation, allowing poll to work with any descriptor. poll provides functionality that is similar to select, but poll provides additional information when dealing with STREAMS devices.

```
#include <poll.h>

int poll(struct pollfd *fdarray, unsigned long nfds, int timeout);
```
                                    Returns: count of ready descriptors, 0 on timeout, −1 on error

The first argument is a pointer to the first element of an array of structures. Each element of the array is a `pollfd` structure that specifies the conditions to be tested for a given descriptor, `fd`.

```
struct pollfd {
  int     fd;       /* descriptor to check */
  short   events;   /* events of interest on fd */
  short   revents;  /* events that occurred on fd */
};
```

The conditions to be tested are specified by the `events` member, and the function returns the status for that descriptor in the corresponding `revents` member. (Having two variables per descriptor, one a value and one a result, avoids value-result arguments. Recall that the middle three arguments for `select` are value-result.) Each of these two members is composed of one or more bits that specify a certain condition. Figure 6.23 shows the constants used to specify the `events` flag and to test the `revents` flag against.

Constant	Input to *events* ?	Result from *revents* ?	Description
POLLIN	•	•	Normal or priority band data can be read
POLLRDNORM	•	•	Normal data can be read
POLLRDBAND	•	•	Priority band data can be read
POLLPRI	•	•	High-priority data can be read
POLLOUT	•	•	Normal data can be written
POLLWRNORM	•	•	Normal data can be written
POLLWRBAND	•	•	Priority band data can be written
POLLERR		•	Error has occurred
POLLHUP		•	Hangup has occurred
POLLNVAL		•	Descriptor is not an open file

Figure 6.23 Input *events* and returned *revents* for `poll`.

We have divided this figure into three sections: The first four constants deal with input, the next three deal with output, and the final three deal with errors. Notice that the final three cannot be set in `events`, but are always returned in `revents` when the corresponding condition exists.

There are three classes of data identified by `poll`: *normal*, *priority band*, and *high-priority*. These terms come from the STREAMS-based implementations (Figure 31.5).

> POLLIN can be defined as the logical OR of POLLRDNORM and POLLRDBAND. The POLLIN constant exists from SVR3 implementations that predated the priority bands in SVR4, so the constant remains for backward compatibility. Similarly, POLLOUT is equivalent to POLLWRNORM, with the former predating the latter.

With regard to TCP and UDP sockets, the following conditions cause `poll` to return the specified *revent*. Unfortunately, POSIX leaves many holes (i.e., optional ways to return the same condition) in its definition of `poll`.

- All regular TCP data and all UDP data is considered normal.

- TCP's out-of-band data (Chapter 24) is considered priority band.

- When the read half of a TCP connection is closed (e.g., a FIN is received), this is also considered normal data and a subsequent read operation will return 0.

- The presence of an error for a TCP connection can be considered either normal data or an error (POLLERR). In either case, a subsequent `read` will return –1 with `errno` set to the appropriate value. This handles conditions such as the receipt of an RST or a timeout.

- The availability of a new connection on a listening socket can be considered either normal data or priority data. Most implementations consider this normal data.

- The completion of a nonblocking `connect` is considered to make a socket writable.

The number of elements in the array of structures is specified by the *nfds* argument.

> Historically, this argument has been an `unsigned long`, which seems excessive. An `unsigned int` would be adequate. Unix 98 defines a new datatype for this argument: `nfds_t`.

The *timeout* argument specifies how long the function is to wait before returning. A positive value specifies the number of milliseconds to wait. Figure 6.24 shows the possible values for the *timeout* argument.

timeout value	Description
INFTIM	Wait forever
0	Return immediately, do not block
> 0	Wait specified number of milliseconds

Figure 6.24 *timeout* values for `poll`.

The constant INFTIM is defined to be a negative value. If the system does not provide a timer with millisecond accuracy, the value is rounded up to the nearest supported value.

> The POSIX specification requires that INFTIM be defined by including `<poll.h>`, but many systems still define it in `<sys/stropts.h>`.

> As with `select`, any timeout set for `poll` is limited by the implementation's clock resolution (often 10 ms).

The return value from `poll` is –1 if an error occurred, 0 if no descriptors are ready before the timer expires, otherwise it is the number of descriptors that have a nonzero `revents` member.

If we are no longer interested in a particular descriptor, we just set the `fd` member of the `pollfd` structure to a negative value. Then the `events` member is ignored and the `revents` member is set to 0 on return.

Recall our discussion at the end of Section 6.3 about `FD_SETSIZE` and the maximum number of descriptors per descriptor set versus the maximum number of descriptors per process. We do not have that problem with `poll` since it is the caller's responsibility to allocate an array of `pollfd` structures and then tell the kernel the number of elements in the array. There is no fixed-size datatype similar to `fd_set` that the kernel knows about.

> The POSIX specification requires both `select` and `poll`. But, from a portability perspective today, more systems support `select` than `poll`. Also, POSIX defines `pselect`, an enhanced version of `select` that handles signal blocking and provides increased time resolution. Nothing similar is defined for `poll`.

6.11   TCP Echo Server (Revisited Again)

We now redo our TCP echo server from Section 6.8 using `poll` instead of `select`. In the previous version using `select`, we had to allocate a `client` array along with a descriptor set named `rset` (Figure 6.15). With `poll`, we must allocate an array of `pollfd` structures to maintain the client information instead of allocating another array. We handle the `fd` member of this array the same way we handled the `client` array in Figure 6.15: a value of −1 means the entry is not in use; otherwise, it is the descriptor value. Recall from the previous section that any entry in the array of `pollfd` structures passed to `poll` with a negative value for the `fd` member is just ignored.

Figure 6.25 shows the first half of our server.

tcpcliserv/tcpservpoll01.c

```
 1 #include    "unp.h"
 2 #include    <limits.h>            /* for OPEN_MAX */

 3 int
 4 main(int argc, char **argv)
 5 {
 6     int     i, maxi, listenfd, connfd, sockfd;
 7     int     nready;
 8     ssize_t n;
 9     char    buf[MAXLINE];
10     socklen_t clilen;
11     struct pollfd client[OPEN_MAX];
12     struct sockaddr_in cliaddr, servaddr;

13     listenfd = Socket(AF_INET, SOCK_STREAM, 0);

14     bzero(&servaddr, sizeof(servaddr));
15     servaddr.sin_family = AF_INET;
16     servaddr.sin_addr.s_addr = htonl(INADDR_ANY);
17     servaddr.sin_port = htons(SERV_PORT);

18     Bind(listenfd, (SA *) &servaddr, sizeof(servaddr));

19     Listen(listenfd, LISTENQ);

20     client[0].fd = listenfd;
21     client[0].events = POLLRDNORM;
22     for (i = 1; i < OPEN_MAX; i++)
23         client[i].fd = -1;       /* -1 indicates available entry */
24     maxi = 0;                     /* max index into client[] array */
```

tcpcliserv/tcpservpoll01.c

Figure 6.25 First half of TCP server using poll.

Allocate array of pollfd structures

11   We declare OPEN_MAX elements in our array of pollfd structures. Determining the maximum number of descriptors that a process can have open at any one time is difficult. We will encounter this problem again in Figure 13.4. One way is to call the POSIX sysconf function with an argument of _SC_OPEN_MAX (as described on pp. 42–44 of APUE) and then dynamically allocate an array of the appropriate size. But one of the possible returns from sysconf is "indeterminate," meaning we still have to guess a value. Here, we just use the POSIX OPEN_MAX constant.

Initialize

20–24   We use the first entry in the client array for the listening socket and set the descriptor for the remaining entries to −1. We also set the POLLRDNORM event for this descriptor, to be notified by poll when a new connection is ready to be accepted. The variable maxi contains the largest index of the client array currently in use.

The second half of our function is shown in Figure 6.26.

—————————————————————————————————————— tcpcliserv/tcpservpoll01.c
```
25      for ( ; ; ) {
26          nready = Poll(client, maxi + 1, INFTIM);
27          if (client[0].revents & POLLRDNORM) {    /* new client connection */
28              clilen = sizeof(cliaddr);
29              connfd = Accept(listenfd, (SA *) &cliaddr, &clilen);
30              for (i = 1; i < OPEN_MAX; i++)
31                  if (client[i].fd < 0) {
32                      client[i].fd = connfd;  /* save descriptor */
33                      break;
34                  }
35              if (i == OPEN_MAX)
36                  err_quit("too many clients");
37              client[i].events = POLLRDNORM;
38              if (i > maxi)
39                  maxi = i;            /* max index in client[] array */
40              if (--nready <= 0)
41                  continue;            /* no more readable descriptors */
42          }
43          for (i = 1; i <= maxi; i++) {    /* check all clients for data */
44              if ( (sockfd = client[i].fd) < 0)
45                  continue;
46              if (client[i].revents & (POLLRDNORM | POLLERR)) {
47                  if ( (n = read(sockfd, buf, MAXLINE)) < 0) {
48                      if (errno == ECONNRESET) {
49                              /* connection reset by client */
50                          Close(sockfd);
51                          client[i].fd = -1;
52                      } else
53                          err_sys("read error");
54                  } else if (n == 0) {
55                          /* connection closed by client */
56                      Close(sockfd);
57                      client[i].fd = -1;
58                  } else
59                      Writen(sockfd, buf, n);
60                  if (--nready <= 0)
61                      break;          /* no more readable descriptors */
62              }
63          }
64      }
65  }
```
—————————————————————————————————————— tcpcliserv/tcpservpoll01.c

Figure 6.26 Second half of TCP server using poll.

Call poll, check for new connection

26–42   We call poll to wait for either a new connection or data on existing connection.
When a new connection is accepted, we find the first available entry in the client

array by looking for the first one with a negative descriptor. Notice that we start the search with the index of 1, since client[0] is used for the listening socket. When an available entry is found, we save the descriptor and set the POLLRDNORM event.

Check for data on an existing connection

43–63   The two return events that we check for are POLLRDNORM and POLLERR. The second of these we did not set in the events member because it is always returned when the condition is true. The reason we check for POLLERR is because some implementations return this event when an RST is received for a connection, while others just return POLLRDNORM. In either case, we call read and if an error has occurred, it will return an error. When an existing connection is terminated by the client, we just set the fd member to −1.

6.12 Summary

There are five different models for I/O provided by Unix:

- Blocking
- Nonblocking
- I/O multiplexing
- Signal-driven I/O
- Asynchronous I/O

The default is blocking I/O, which is also the most commonly used. We will cover nonblocking I/O and signal-driven I/O in later chapters and have covered I/O multiplexing in this chapter. True asynchronous I/O is defined by the POSIX specification, but few implementations exist.

The most commonly used function for I/O multiplexing is select. We tell the select function what descriptors we are interested in (for reading, writing, and exceptions), the maximum amount of time to wait, and the maximum descriptor number (plus one). Most calls to select specify readability, and we noted that the only exception condition when dealing with sockets is the arrival of out-of-band data (Chapter 24). Since select provides a time limit on how long a function blocks, we will use this feature in Figure 14.3 to place a time limit on an input operation.

We used our echo client in a batch mode using select and discovered that even though the end of the user input is encountered, data can still be in the pipe to or from the server. To handle this scenario requires the shutdown function, and it lets us take advantage of TCP's half-close feature.

The dangers of mixing stdio buffering (as well as our own readline buffering) with select caused us to produce versions of the echo client and server that operated on buffers instead of lines.

POSIX defines the function pselect, which increases the time precision from microseconds to nanoseconds and takes a new argument that is a pointer to a signal set. This lets us avoid race conditions when signals are being caught and we talk more about this in Section 20.5.

The `poll` function from System V provides functionality similar to `select` and provides additional information on STREAMS devices. POSIX requires both `select` and `poll`, but the former is used more often.

Exercises

6.1   We said that a descriptor set can be assigned to another descriptor set across an equals sign in C. How is this done if a descriptor set is an array of integers? (*Hint*: Look at your system's `<sys/select.h>` or `<sys/types.h>` header.)

6.2   When describing the conditions for which `select` returns "writable" in Section 6.3, why did we need the qualifier that the socket had to be nonblocking for a write operation to return a positive value?

6.3   What happens in Figure 6.9 if we prepend the word "`else`" before the word "`if`" on line 19?

6.4   In our example in Figure 6.21 add code to allow the server to be able to use as many descriptors as currently allowed by the kernel. (*Hint*: Look at the `setrlimit` function.)

6.5   Let's see what happens when the second argument to `shutdown` is SHUT_RD. Start with the TCP client in Figure 5.4 and make the following changes: Change the port number from SERV_PORT to 19, the `chargen` server (Figure 2.18); then, replace the call to `str_cli` with a call to the `pause` function. Run this program specifying the IP address of a local host that runs the `chargen` server. Watch the packets with a tool such as `tcpdump` (Section C.5). What happens?

6.6   Why would an application call `shutdown` with an argument of SHUT_RDWR instead of just calling `close`?

6.7   What happens in Figure 6.22 when the client sends an RST to terminate the connection?

6.8   Recode Figure 6.25 to call `sysconf` to determine the maximum number of descriptors and allocate the `client` array accordingly.

7

Socket Options

7.1 Introduction

There are various ways to get and set the options that affect a socket:

- The `getsockopt` and `setsockopt` functions
- The `fcntl` function
- The `ioctl` function

This chapter starts by covering the `setsockopt` and `getsockopt` functions, followed by an example that prints the default value of all the options, and then a detailed description of all the socket options. We divide the detailed descriptions into the following categories: generic, IPv4, IPv6, TCP, and SCTP. This detailed coverage can be skipped during a first reading of this chapter, and the individual sections referred to when needed. A few options are discussed in detail in a later chapter, such as the IPv4 and IPv6 multicasting options, which we will describe with multicasting in Section 21.6.

We also describe the `fcntl` function, because it is the POSIX way to set a socket for nonblocking I/O, signal-driven I/O, and to set the owner of a socket. We save the `ioctl` function for Chapter 17.

7.2 `getsockopt` **and** `setsockopt` **Functions**

These two functions apply only to sockets.

```
#include <sys/socket.h>

int getsockopt(int sockfd, int level, int optname, void *optval, socklen_t *optlen);

int setsockopt(int sockfd, int level, int optname, const void *optval,
               socklen_t optlen);
```
Both return: 0 if OK, −1 on error

sockfd must refer to an open socket descriptor. *level* specifies the code in the system that interprets the option: the general socket code or some protocol-specific code (e.g., IPv4, IPv6, TCP, or SCTP).

optval is a pointer to a variable from which the new value of the option is fetched by `setsockopt`, or into which the current value of the option is stored by `getsockopt`. The size of this variable is specified by the final argument, as a value for `setsockopt` and as a value-result for `getsockopt`.

Figures 7.1 and 7.2 summarize the options that can be queried by `getsockopt` or set by `setsockopt`. The "Datatype" column shows the datatype of what the *optval* pointer must point to for each option. We use the notation of two braces to indicate a structure, as in `linger{ }` to mean a `struct linger`.

There are two basic types of options: binary options that enable or disable a certain feature (flags), and options that fetch and return specific values that we can either set or examine (values). The column labeled "Flag" specifies if the option is a flag option. When calling `getsockopt` for these flag options, *optval* is an integer. The value returned in *optval* is zero if the option is disabled, or nonzero if the option is enabled. Similarly, `setsockopt` requires a nonzero *optval* to turn the option on, and a zero value to turn the option off. If the "Flag" column does not contain a "•," then the option is used to pass a value of the specified datatype between the user process and the system.

Subsequent sections of this chapter will give additional details on the options that affect a socket.

level	optname	get	set	Description	Flag	Datatype
SOL_SOCKET	SO_BROADCAST	•	•	Permit sending of broadcast datagrams	•	int
	SO_DEBUG	•	•	Enable debug tracing	•	int
	SO_DONTROUTE	•	•	Bypass routing table lookup	•	int
	SO_ERROR	•		Get pending error and clear		int
	SO_KEEPALIVE	•	•	Periodically test if connection still alive	•	int
	SO_LINGER	•	•	Linger on close if data to send		linger{}
	SO_OOBINLINE	•	•	Leave received out-of-band data inline	•	int
	SO_RCVBUF	•	•	Receive buffer size		int
	SO_SNDBUF	•	•	Send buffer size		int
	SO_RCVLOWAT	•	•	Receive buffer low-water mark		int
	SO_SNDLOWAT	•	•	Send buffer low-water mark		int
	SO_RCVTIMEO	•	•	Receive timeout		timeval{}
	SO_SNDTIMEO	•	•	Send timeout		timeval{}
	SO_REUSEADDR	•	•	Allow local address reuse	•	int
	SO_REUSEPORT	•	•	Allow local port reuse	•	int
	SO_TYPE	•		Get socket type		int
	SO_USELOOPBACK	•	•	Routing socket gets copy of what it sends	•	int
IPPROTO_IP	IP_HDRINCL	•	•	IP header included with data	•	int
	IP_OPTIONS	•	•	IP header options		(see text)
	IP_RECVDSTADDR	•	•	Return destination IP address	•	int
	IP_RECVIF	•	•	Return received interface index	•	int
	IP_TOS	•	•	Type-of-service and precedence		int
	IP_TTL	•	•	TTL		int
	IP_MULTICAST_IF	•	•	Specify outgoing interface		in_addr{}
	IP_MULTICAST_TTL	•	•	Specify outgoing TTL		u_char
	IP_MULTICAST_LOOP	•	•	Specify loopback		u_char
	IP_{ADD,DROP}_MEMBERSHIP		•	Join or leave multicast group		ip_mreq{}
	IP_{BLOCK,UNBLOCK}_SOURCE		•	Block or unblock multicast source		ip_mreq_source{}
	IP_{ADD,DROP}_SOURCE_MEMBERSHIP		•	Join or leave source-specific multicast		ip_mreq_source{}
IPPROTO_ICMPV6	ICMP6_FILTER	•	•	Specify ICMPv6 message types to pass		icmp6_filter{}
IPPROTO_IPV6	IPV6_CHECKSUM	•	•	Offset of checksum field for raw sockets		int
	IPV6_DONTFRAG	•	•	Drop instead of fragment large packets	•	int
	IPV6_NEXTHOP	•	•	Specify next-hop address		sockaddr_in6{}
	IPV6_PATHMTU	•		Retrieve current path MTU		ip6_mtuinfo{}
	IPV6_RECVDSTOPTS	•	•	Receive destination options	•	int
	IPV6_RECVHOPLIMIT	•	•	Receive unicast hop limit	•	int
	IPV6_RECVHOPOPTS	•	•	Receive hop-by-hop options	•	int
	IPV6_RECVPATHMTU	•	•	Receive path MTU	•	int
	IPV6_RECVPKTINFO	•	•	Receive packet information	•	int
	IPV6_RECVRTHDR	•	•	Receive source route	•	int
	IPV6_RECVTCLASS	•	•	Receive traffic class	•	int
	IPV6_UNICAST_HOPS	•	•	Default unicast hop limit		int
	IPV6_USE_MIN_MTU	•	•	Use minimum MTU	•	int
	IPV6_V6ONLY	•	•	Disable v4 compatibility	•	int
	IPV6_XXX	•	•	Sticky ancillary data		(see text)
	IPV6_MULTICAST_IF	•	•	Specify outgoing interface		u_int
	IPV6_MULTICAST_HOPS	•	•	Specify outgoing hop limit		int
	IPV6_MULTICAST_LOOP	•	•	Specify loopback	•	u_int
	IPV6_JOIN_GROUP		•	Join multicast group		ipv6_mreq{}
	IPV6_LEAVE_GROUP		•	Leave multicast group		ipv6_mreq{}
IPPROTO_IP *or* IPPROTO_IPV6	MCAST_JOIN_GROUP		•	Join multicast group		group_req{}
	MCAST_LEAVE_GROUP		•	Leave multicast group		group_source_req{}
	MCAST_BLOCK_SOURCE		•	Block multicast source		group_source_req{}
	MCAST_UNBLOCK_SOURCE		•	Unblock multicast source		group_source_req{}
	MCAST_JOIN_SOURCE_GROUP		•	Join source-specific multicast		group_source_req{}
	MCAST_LEAVE_SOURCE_GROUP		•	Leave source-specific multicast		group_source_req{}

Figure 7.1 Summary of socket and IP-layer socket options for getsockopt and setsockopt.

level	optname	get	set	Description	Flag	Datatype
IPPROTO_TCP	TCP_MAXSEG	•	•	TCP maximum segment size		int
	TCP_NODELAY	•	•	Disable Nagle algorithm	•	int
IPPROTO_SCTP	SCTP_ADAPTION_LAYER	•	•	Adaption layer indication		sctp_setadaption{}
	SCTP_ASSOCINFO	†	•	Examine and set association info		sctp_assocparams{}
	SCTP_AUTOCLOSE	•	•	Autoclose operation		int
	SCTP_DEFAULT_SEND_PARAM	•	•	Default send parameters		sctp_sndrcvinfo{}
	SCTP_DISABLE_FRAGMENTS	•	•	SCTP fragmentation	•	int
	SCTP_EVENTS	•	•	Notification events of interest		sctp_event_subscribe{}
	SCTP_GET_PEER_ADDR_INFO	†		Retrieve peer address status		sctp_paddrinfo{}
	SCTP_I_WANT_MAPPED_V4_ADDR	•	•	Mapped v4 addresses	•	int
	SCTP_INITMSG	•	•	Default INIT parameters		sctp_initmsg{}
	SCTP_MAXBURST	•	•	Maximum burst size		int
	SCTP_MAXSEG	•	•	Maximum fragmentation size		int
	SCTP_NODELAY	•	•	Disable Nagle algorithm	•	int
	SCTP_PEER_ADDR_PARAMS	†	•	Peer address parameters		sctp_paddrparams{}
	SCTP_PRIMARY_ADDR	†	•	Primary destination address		sctp_setprim{}
	SCTP_RTOINFO	†	•	RTO information		sctp_rtoinfo{}
	SCTP_SET_PEER_PRIMARY_ADDR		•	Peer primary destination address		sctp_setpeerprim{}
	SCTP_STATUS	†		Get association status		sctp_status{}

Figure 7.2 Summary of transport-layer socket options.

7.3   Checking if an Option Is Supported and Obtaining the Default

We now write a program to check whether most of the options defined in Figures 7.1 and 7.2 are supported, and if so, print their default value. Figure 7.3 contains the declarations for our program.

Declare `union` of possible values

3–8   Our `union` contains one member for each possible return value from `getsockopt`.

Define function prototypes

9–12   We define function prototypes for four functions that are called to print the value for a given socket option.

Define structure and initialize array

13–52   Our `sock_opts` structure contains all the information necessary to call `getsockopt` for each socket option and then print its current value. The final member, `opt_val_str`, is a pointer to one of our four functions that will print the option value. We allocate and initialize an array of these structures, one element for each socket option.

> Not all implementations support all socket options. The way to determine if a given option is supported is to use an #ifdef or a #if defined, as we show for SO_REUSEPORT. For completeness, *every* element of the array should be compiled similarly to what we show for SO_REUSEPORT, but we omit these because the #ifdefs just lengthen the code that we show and add nothing to the discussion.

———————————————— sockopt/checkopts.c

```
 1 #include      "unp.h"
 2 #include      <netinet/tcp.h>      /* for TCP_xxx defines */
 3 union val {
 4   int              i_val;
 5   long             l_val;
 6   struct linger    linger_val;
 7   struct timeval   timeval_val;
 8 } val;
 9 static char *sock_str_flag(union val *, int);
10 static char *sock_str_int(union val *, int);
11 static char *sock_str_linger(union val *, int);
12 static char *sock_str_timeval(union val *, int);
13 struct sock_opts {
14   const char      *opt_str;
15   int        opt_level;
16   int        opt_name;
17   char   *(*opt_val_str)(union val *, int);
18 } sock_opts[] = {
19     { "SO_BROADCAST",        SOL_SOCKET, SO_BROADCAST,    sock_str_flag },
20     { "SO_DEBUG",            SOL_SOCKET, SO_DEBUG,        sock_str_flag },
21     { "SO_DONTROUTE",        SOL_SOCKET, SO_DONTROUTE,    sock_str_flag },
22     { "SO_ERROR",            SOL_SOCKET, SO_ERROR,        sock_str_int },
23     { "SO_KEEPALIVE",        SOL_SOCKET, SO_KEEPALIVE,    sock_str_flag },
24     { "SO_LINGER",           SOL_SOCKET, SO_LINGER,       sock_str_linger },
25     { "SO_OOBINLINE",        SOL_SOCKET, SO_OOBINLINE,    sock_str_flag },
26     { "SO_RCVBUF",           SOL_SOCKET, SO_RCVBUF,       sock_str_int },
27     { "SO_SNDBUF",           SOL_SOCKET, SO_SNDBUF,       sock_str_int },
28     { "SO_RCVLOWAT",         SOL_SOCKET, SO_RCVLOWAT,     sock_str_int },
29     { "SO_SNDLOWAT",         SOL_SOCKET, SO_SNDLOWAT,     sock_str_int },
30     { "SO_RCVTIMEO",         SOL_SOCKET, SO_RCVTIMEO,     sock_str_timeval },
31     { "SO_SNDTIMEO",         SOL_SOCKET, SO_SNDTIMEO,     sock_str_timeval },
32     { "SO_REUSEADDR",        SOL_SOCKET, SO_REUSEADDR,    sock_str_flag },
33 #ifdef  SO_REUSEPORT
34     { "SO_REUSEPORT",        SOL_SOCKET, SO_REUSEPORT,    sock_str_flag },
35 #else
36     { "SO_REUSEPORT",        0,          0,              NULL },
37 #endif
38     { "SO_TYPE",             SOL_SOCKET, SO_TYPE,         sock_str_int },
39     { "SO_USELOOPBACK",      SOL_SOCKET, SO_USELOOPBACK, sock_str_flag },
40     { "IP_TOS",              IPPROTO_IP, IP_TOS,          sock_str_int },
41     { "IP_TTL",              IPPROTO_IP, IP_TTL,          sock_str_int },
42     { "IPV6_DONTFRAG",       IPPROTO_IPV6,IPV6_DONTFRAG, sock_str_flag },
43     { "IPV6_UNICAST_HOPS",   IPPROTO_IPV6,IPV6_UNICAST_HOPS,sock_str_int },
44     { "IPV6_V6ONLY",         IPPROTO_IPV6,IPV6_V6ONLY,    sock_str_flag },
45     { "TCP_MAXSEG",          IPPROTO_TCP,TCP_MAXSEG,      sock_str_int },
46     { "TCP_NODELAY",         IPPROTO_TCP,TCP_NODELAY,     sock_str_flag },
47     { "SCTP_AUTOCLOSE",      IPPROTO_SCTP,SCTP_AUTOCLOSE,sock_str_int },
48     { "SCTP_MAXBURST",       IPPROTO_SCTP,SCTP_MAXBURST, sock_str_int },
49     { "SCTP_MAXSEG",         IPPROTO_SCTP,SCTP_MAXSEG,    sock_str_int },
50     { "SCTP_NODELAY",        IPPROTO_SCTP,SCTP_NODELAY,   sock_str_flag },
51     { NULL,                  0,          0,              NULL }
52 };
```

———————————————— sockopt/checkopts.c

Figure 7.3 Declarations for our program to check the socket options.

Figure 7.4 shows our `main` function.

———————————————————————— sockopt/checkopts.c

```
53 int
54 main(int argc, char **argv)
55 {
56     int     fd;
57     socklen_t len;
58     struct sock_opts *ptr;

59     for (ptr = sock_opts; ptr->opt_str != NULL; ptr++) {
60         printf("%s: ", ptr->opt_str);
61         if (ptr->opt_val_str == NULL)
62             printf("(undefined)\n");
63         else {
64             switch (ptr->opt_level) {
65             case SOL_SOCKET:
66             case IPPROTO_IP:
67             case IPPROTO_TCP:
68                 fd = Socket(AF_INET, SOCK_STREAM, 0);
69                 break;
70 #ifdef  IPV6
71             case IPPROTO_IPV6:
72                 fd = Socket(AF_INET6, SOCK_STREAM, 0);
73                 break;
74 #endif
75 #ifdef  IPPROTO_SCTP
76             case IPPROTO_SCTP:
77                 fd = Socket(AF_INET, SOCK_SEQPACKET, IPPROTO_SCTP);
78                 break;
79 #endif
80             default:
81                 err_quit("Can't create fd for level %d\n", ptr->opt_level);
82             }

83             len = sizeof(val);
84             if (getsockopt(fd, ptr->opt_level, ptr->opt_name,
85                     &val, &len) == -1) {
86                 err_ret("getsockopt error");
87             } else {
88                 printf("default = %s\n", (*ptr->opt_val_str) (&val, len));
89             }
90             close(fd);
91         }
92     }
93     exit(0);
94 }
```

———————————————————————— sockopt/checkopts.c

Figure 7.4 `main` function to check all socket options.

Go through all options

59–63   We go through all elements in our array. If the `opt_val_str` pointer is null, the option is not defined by the implementation (which we showed for SO_REUSEPORT).

Create socket

63-82   We create a socket on which to try the option. To try socket, IPv4, and TCP layer socket options, we use an IPv4 TCP socket. To try IPv6 layer socket options, we use an IPv6 TCP socket, and to try SCTP layer socket options, we use an IPv4 SCTP socket.

Call `getsockopt`

83-87   We call `getsockopt` but do not terminate if an error is returned. Many implementations define some of the socket option names even though they do not support the option. Unsupported options should elicit an error of `ENOPROTOOPT`.

Print option's default value

88-89   If `getsockopt` returns success, we call our function to convert the option value to a string and print the string.

In Figure 7.3, we showed four function prototypes, one for each type of option value that is returned. Figure 7.5 shows one of these four functions, `sock_str_flag`, which prints the value of a flag option. The other three functions are similar.

```
                                                       ——— sockopt/checkopts.c
 95 static char strres[128];

 96 static char *
 97 sock_str_flag(union val *ptr, int len)
 98 {
 99     if (len != sizeof(int))
100         snprintf(strres, sizeof(strres), "size (%d) not sizeof(int)", len);
101     else
102         snprintf(strres, sizeof(strres),
103                 "%s", (ptr->i_val == 0) ? "off" : "on");
104     return(strres);
105 }
                                                       ——— sockopt/checkopts.c
```

Figure 7.5 `sock_str_flag` function: convert flag option to a string.

99-104   Recall that the final argument to `getsockopt` is a value-result argument. The first check we make is that the size of the value returned by `getsockopt` is the expected size. The string returned is `off` or `on`, depending on whether the value of the flag option is zero or nonzero, respectively.

Running this program under FreeBSD 4.8 with KAME SCTP patches gives the following output:

```
freebsd % checkopts
SO_BROADCAST: default = off
SO_DEBUG: default = off
SO_DONTROUTE: default = off
SO_ERROR: default = 0
SO_KEEPALIVE: default = off
SO_LINGER: default = l_onoff = 0, l_linger = 0
SO_OOBINLINE: default = off
SO_RCVBUF: default = 57344
```

```
SO_SNDBUF: default = 32768
SO_RCVLOWAT: default = 1
SO_SNDLOWAT: default = 2048
SO_RCVTIMEO: default = 0 sec, 0 usec
SO_SNDTIMEO: default = 0 sec, 0 usec
SO_REUSEADDR: default = off
SO_REUSEPORT: default = off
SO_TYPE: default = 1
SO_USELOOPBACK: default = off
IP_TOS: default = 0
IP_TTL: default = 64
IPV6_DONTFRAG: default = off
IPV6_UNICAST_HOPS: default = -1
IPV6_V6ONLY: default = off
TCP_MAXSEG: default = 512
TCP_NODELAY: default = off
SCTP_AUTOCLOSE: default = 0
SCTP_MAXBURST: default = 4
SCTP_MAXSEG: default = 1408
SCTP_NODELAY: default = off
```

The value of 1 returned for the SO_TYPE option corresponds to SOCK_STREAM for this implementation.

7.4   Socket States

Some socket options have timing considerations about when to set or fetch the option versus the state of the socket. We mention these with the affected options.

The following socket options are inherited by a connected TCP socket from the listening socket (pp. 462–463 of TCPv2): SO_DEBUG, SO_DONTROUTE, SO_KEEPALIVE, SO_LINGER, SO_OOBINLINE, SO_RCVBUF, SO_RCVLOWAT, SO_SNDBUF, SO_SND LOWAT, TCP_MAXSEG, and TCP_NODELAY. This is important with TCP because the connected socket is not returned to a server by accept until the three-way handshake is completed by the TCP layer. To ensure that one of these socket options is set for the connected socket when the three-way handshake completes, we must set that option for the listening socket.

7.5   Generic Socket Options

We start with a discussion of the generic socket options. These options are protocol-independent (that is, they are handled by the protocol-independent code within the kernel, not by one particular protocol module such as IPv4), but some of the options apply to only certain types of sockets. For example, even though the SO_BROADCAST socket option is called "generic," it applies only to datagram sockets.

SO_BROADCAST **Socket Option**

This option enables or disables the ability of the process to send broadcast messages. Broadcasting is supported for only datagram sockets and only on networks that support the concept of a broadcast message (e.g., Ethernet, token ring, etc.). You cannot broadcast on a point-to-point link or any connection-based transport protocol such as SCTP or TCP. We will talk more about broadcasting in Chapter 20.

   Since an application must set this socket option before sending a broadcast datagram, it prevents a process from sending a broadcast when the application was never designed to broadcast. For example, a UDP application might take the destination IP address as a command-line argument, but the application never intended for a user to type in a broadcast address. Rather than forcing the application to try to determine if a given address is a broadcast address or not, the test is in the kernel: If the destination address is a broadcast address and this socket option is not set, EACCES is returned (p. 233 of TCPv2).

SO_DEBUG **Socket Option**

This option is supported only by TCP. When enabled for a TCP socket, the kernel keeps track of detailed information about all the packets sent or received by TCP for the socket. These are kept in a circular buffer within the kernel that can be examined with the trpt program. Pages 916–920 of TCPv2 provide additional details and an example that uses this option.

SO_DONTROUTE **Socket Option**

This option specifies that outgoing packets are to bypass the normal routing mechanisms of the underlying protocol. For example, with IPv4, the packet is directed to the appropriate local interface, as specified by the network and subnet portions of the destination address. If the local interface cannot be determined from the destination address (e.g., the destination is not on the other end of a point-to-point link, or is not on a shared network), ENETUNREACH is returned.

   The equivalent of this option can also be applied to individual datagrams using the MSG_DONTROUTE flag with the send, sendto, or sendmsg functions.

   This option is often used by routing daemons (e.g., routed and gated) to bypass the routing table and force a packet to be sent out a particular interface.

SO_ERROR **Socket Option**

When an error occurs on a socket, the protocol module in a Berkeley-derived kernel sets a variable named so_error for that socket to one of the standard Unix E*xxx* values. This is called the *pending error* for the socket. The process can be immediately notified of the error in one of two ways:

   1. If the process is blocked in a call to select on the socket (Section 6.3), for either readability or writability, select returns with either or both conditions set.

2. If the process is using signal-driven I/O (Chapter 25), the SIGIO signal is gener-
    ated for either the process or the process group.

The process can then obtain the value of so_error by fetching the SO_ERROR socket
option. The integer value returned by getsockopt is the pending error for the socket.
The value of so_error is then reset to 0 by the kernel (p. 547 of TCPv2).

If so_error is nonzero when the process calls read and there is no data to return,
read returns –1 with errno set to the value of so_error (p. 516 of TCPv2). The value
of so_error is then reset to 0. If there is data queued for the socket, that data is
returned by read instead of the error condition. If so_error is nonzero when the process calls write, –1 is returned with errno set to the value of so_error (p. 495 of
TCPv2) and so_error is reset to 0.

> There is a bug in the code shown on p. 495 of TCPv2 in that so_error is not reset to 0. This
> has been fixed in most modern releases. Anytime the pending error for a socket is returned, it
> must be reset to 0.

This is the first socket option that we have encountered that can be fetched but cannot be set.

SO_KEEPALIVE Socket Option

When the keep-alive option is set for a TCP socket and no data has been exchanged
across the socket in either direction for two hours, TCP automatically sends a *keep-alive
probe* to the peer. This probe is a TCP segment to which the peer must respond. One of
three scenarios results:

1. The peer responds with the expected ACK. The application is not notified (since
    everything is okay). TCP will send another probe following another two hours
    of inactivity.

2. The peer responds with an RST, which tells the local TCP that the peer host has
    crashed and rebooted. The socket's pending error is set to ECONNRESET and the
    socket is closed.

3. There is no response from the peer to the keep-alive probe. Berkeley-derived
    TCPs send 8 additional probes, 75 seconds apart, trying to elicit a response.
    TCP will give up if there is no response within 11 minutes and 15 seconds after
    sending the first probe.

> HP-UX 11 treats the keep-alive probes in the same way as it would treat data, sending the
> second probe after a retransmission timeout and doubling the timeout for each packet
> until the configured maximum interval, with a default of 10 minutes.

If there is no response at all to TCP's keep-alive probes, the socket's pending
error is set to ETIMEDOUT and the socket is closed. But if the socket receives an
ICMP error in response to one of the keep-alive probes, the corresponding error
(Figures A.15 and A.16) is returned instead (and the socket is still closed). A
common ICMP error in this scenario is "host unreachable," indicating that the

peer host is unreachable, in which case, the pending error is set to
EHOSTUNREACH. This can occur either because of a network failure or because
the remote host has crashed and the last-hop router has detected the crash.

Chapter 23 of TCPv1 and pp. 828–831 of TCPv2 contain additional details on the keep-
alive option.

Undoubtedly the most common question regarding this option is whether the timing parameters can be modified (usually to reduce the two-hour period of inactivity to
some shorter value). Appendix E of TCPv1 discusses how to change these timing
parameters for various kernels, but be aware that most kernels maintain these parameters on a per-kernel basis, not on a per-socket basis, so changing the inactivity period
from 2 hours to 15 minutes, for example, will affect *all* sockets on the host that enable
this option. However, such questions usually result from a misunderstanding of the
purpose of this option.

The purpose of this option is to detect if the peer *host* crashes or becomes unreachable (e.g., dial-up modem connection drops, power fails, etc.). If the peer *process*
crashes, its TCP will send a FIN across the connection, which we can easily detect with
select. (This was why we used select in Section 6.4.) Also realize that if there is no
response to any of the keep-alive probes (scenario 3), we are not guaranteed that the
peer host has crashed, and TCP may well terminate a valid connection. It could be that
some intermediate router has crashed for 15 minutes, and that period of time just happens to completely overlap our host's 11-minute and 15-second keep-alive probe period.
In fact, this function might more properly be called "make-dead" rather than "keep-
alive" since it can terminate live connections.

This option is normally used by servers, although clients can also use the option.
Servers use the option because they spend most of their time blocked waiting for input
across the TCP connection, that is, waiting for a client request. But if the client host's
connection drops, is powered off, or crashes, the server process will never know about
it, and the server will continually wait for input that can never arrive. This is called a
half-open connection. The keep-alive option will detect these half-open connections and
terminate them.

Some servers, notably FTP servers, provide an application timeout, often on the
order of minutes. This is done by the application itself, normally around a call to read,
reading the next client command. This timeout does not involve this socket option.
This is often a better method of eliminating connections to missing clients, since the
application has complete control if it implements the timeout itself.

> SCTP has a *heartbeat* mechanism that is similar to TCP's "keep-alive" mechanism. The heart-
> beat mechanism is controlled through parameters of the SCTP_SET_PEER_ADDR_PARAMS
> socket option discussed later in this chapter, rather than the SO_KEEPALIVE socket option.
> The settings made by SO_KEEPALIVE on a SCTP socket are ignored and do not affect the
> SCTP heartbeat mechanism.

Figure 7.6 summarizes the various methods that we have to detect when something
happens on the other end of a TCP connection. When we say "using select for readability," we mean calling select to test whether a socket is readable.

Scenario	Peer process crashes	Peer host crashes	Peer host is unreachable
Our TCP is actively sending data	Peer TCP sends a FIN, which we can detect immediately using `select` for readability. If TCP sends another segment, peer TCP responds with an RST. If the application attempts to write to the socket after TCP has received an RST, our socket implementation sends us `SIGPIPE`.	Our TCP will time out and our socket's pending error will be set to `ETIMEDOUT`.	Our TCP will time out and our socket's pending error will be set to `EHOSTUNREACH`.
Our TCP is actively receiving data	Peer TCP will send a FIN, which we will read as a (possibly premature) EOF.	We will stop receiving data.	We will stop receiving data.
Connection is idle, keep-alive set	Peer TCP sends a FIN, which we can detect immediately using `select` for readability.	Nine keep-alive probes are sent after two hours of inactivity and then our socket's pending error is set to `ETIMEDOUT`.	Nine keep-alive probes are sent after two hours of inactivity and then our socket's pending error is set to `EHOSTUNREACH`.
Connection is idle, keep-alive not set	Peer TCP sends a FIN, which we can detect immediately using `select` for readability.	(Nothing)	(Nothing)

Figure 7.6 Ways to detect various TCP conditions.

`SO_LINGER` Socket Option

This option specifies how the `close` function operates for a connection-oriented protocol (e.g., for TCP and SCTP, but not for UDP). By default, `close` returns immediately, but if there is any data still remaining in the socket send buffer, the system will try to deliver the data to the peer.

The `SO_LINGER` socket option lets us change this default. This option requires the following structure to be passed between the user process and the kernel. It is defined by including `<sys/socket.h>`.

```
struct linger {
  int    l_onoff;    /* 0=off, nonzero=on */
  int    l_linger;   /* linger time, POSIX specifies units as seconds */
};
```

Calling `setsockopt` leads to one of the following three scenarios, depending on the values of the two structure members:

1. If `l_onoff` is 0, the option is turned off. The value of `l_linger` is ignored and the previously discussed TCP default applies: `close` returns immediately.

2. If `l_onoff` is nonzero and `l_linger` is zero, TCP aborts the connection when it is closed (pp. 1019–1020 of TCPv2). That is, TCP discards any data still

remaining in the socket send buffer and sends an RST to the peer, not the normal four-packet connection termination sequence (Section 2.6). We will show an example of this in Figure 16.21. This avoids TCP's TIME_WAIT state, but in doing so, leaves open the possibility of another incarnation of this connection being created within 2MSL seconds (Section 2.7) and having old duplicate segments from the just-terminated connection being incorrectly delivered to the new incarnation.

SCTP will also do an abortive close of the socket by sending an ABORT chunk to the peer (see Section 9.2 of [Stewart and Xie 2001]) when `l_onoff` is nonzero and `l_linger` is zero.

> Occasional USENET postings advocate the use of this feature just to avoid the TIME_WAIT state and to be able to restart a listening server even if connections are still in use with the server's well-known port. This should NOT be done and could lead to data corruption, as detailed in RFC 1337 [Braden 1992]. Instead, the SO_REUSEADDR socket option should always be used in the server before the call to `bind`, as we will describe shortly. The TIME_WAIT state is our friend and is there to help us (i.e., to let old duplicate segments expire in the network). Instead of trying to avoid the state, we should understand it (Section 2.7).

> There are certain circumstances which warrant using this feature to send an abortive close. One example is an RS-232 terminal server, which might hang forever in CLOSE_WAIT trying to deliver data to a stuck terminal port, but would properly reset the stuck port if it got an RST to discard the pending data.

3. If `l_onoff` is nonzero and `l_linger` is nonzero, then the kernel will *linger* when the socket is closed (p. 472 of TCPv2). That is, if there is any data still remaining in the socket send buffer, the process is put to sleep until either: (i) all the data is sent and acknowledged by the peer TCP, or (ii) the linger time expires. If the socket has been set to nonblocking (Chapter 16), it will not wait for the `close` to complete, even if the linger time is nonzero. When using this feature of the SO_LINGER option, it is important for the application to check the return value from `close`, because if the linger time expires before the remaining data is sent and acknowledged, `close` returns EWOULDBLOCK and any remaining data in the send buffer is discarded.

We now need to see exactly when a `close` on a socket returns given the various scenarios we looked at. We assume that the client writes data to the socket and then calls `close`. Figure 7.7 shows the default situation.

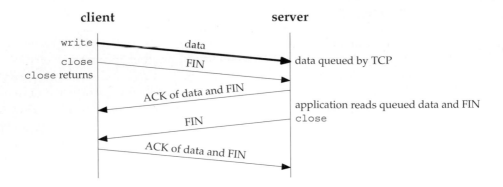

Figure 7.7 Default operation of `close`: it returns immediately.

We assume that when the client's data arrives, the server is temporarily busy, so the data is added to the socket receive buffer by its TCP. Similarly, the next segment, the client's FIN, is also added to the socket receive buffer (in whatever manner the implementation records that a FIN has been received on the connection). But by default, the client's `close` returns immediately. As we show in this scenario, the client's `close` can return before the server reads the remaining data in its socket receive buffer. Therefore, it is possible for the server host to crash before the server application reads this remaining data, and the client application will never know.

The client can set the `SO_LINGER` socket option, specifying some positive linger time. When this occurs, the client's `close` does not return until all the client's data and its FIN have been acknowledged by the server TCP. We show this in Figure 7.8.

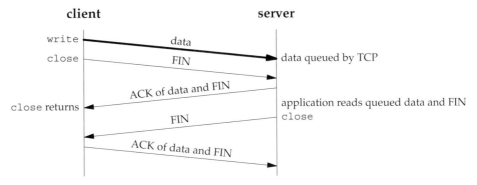

Figure 7.8 `close` with `SO_LINGER` socket option set and `l_linger` a positive value.

But we still have the same problem as in Figure 7.7: The server host can crash before the server application reads its remaining data, and the client application will never know. Worse, Figure 7.9 shows what can happen when the `SO_LINGER` option is set to a value that is too low.

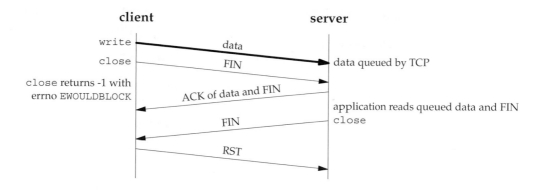

Figure 7.9 close with SO_LINGER socket option set and l_linger a small positive value.

The basic principle here is that a successful return from close, with the SO_LINGER socket option set, only tells us that the data we sent (and our FIN) have been acknowledged by the peer TCP. This does *not* tell us whether the peer application has read the data. If we do not set the SO_LINGER socket option, we do not know whether the peer TCP has acknowledged the data.

One way for the client to know that the server has read its data is to call shutdown (with a second argument of SHUT_WR) instead of close and wait for the peer to close its end of the connection. We show this scenario in Figure 7.10.

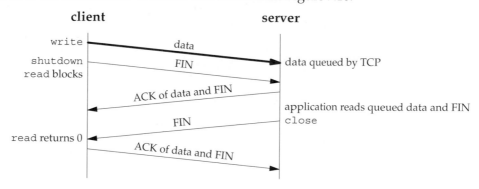

Figure 7.10 Using shutdown to know that peer has received our data.

Comparing this figure to Figures 7.7 and 7.8 we see that when we close our end of the connection, depending on the function called (close or shutdown) and whether the SO_LINGER socket option is set, the return can occur at three different times:

1. close returns immediately, without waiting at all (the default; Figure 7.7).

2. close lingers until the ACK of our FIN is received (Figure 7.8).

3. shutdown followed by a read waits until we receive the peer's FIN (Figure 7.10).

Another way to know that the peer application has read our data is to use an *application-level acknowledgment*, or *application ACK*. For example, in the following, the client sends its data to the server and then calls read for one byte of data:

```
char   ack;

Write(sockfd, data, nbytes);      /* data from client to server */
n = Read(sockfd, &ack, 1);        /* wait for application-level ACK */
```

The server reads the data from the client and then sends back the one-byte application-level ACK:

```
nbytes = Read(sockfd, buff, sizeof(buff));   /* data from client */
          /* server verifies it received correct
             amount of data from client */
Write(sockfd, "", 1);                      /* server's ACK back to client */
```

We are guaranteed that when the read in the client returns, the server process has read the data we sent. (This assumes that either the server knows how much data the client is sending, or there is some application-defined end-of-record marker, which we do not show here.) Here, the application-level ACK is a byte of 0, but the contents of this byte could be used to signal other conditions from the server to the client. Figure 7.11 shows the possible packet exchange.

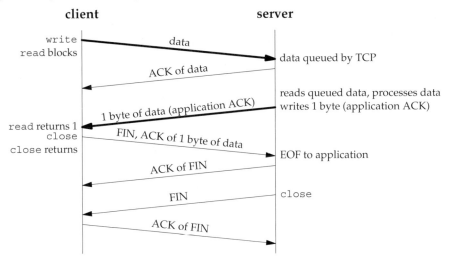

Figure 7.11 Application ACK.

Figure 7.12 summarizes the two possible calls to shutdown and the three possible calls to close, and the effect on a TCP socket.

Function	Description
shutdown, SHUT_RD	No more receives can be issued on socket; process can still send on socket; socket receive buffer discarded; any further data received is discarded by TCP (Exercise 6.5); no effect on socket send buffer.
shutdown, SHUT_WR	No more sends can be issued on socket; process can still receive on socket; contents of socket send buffer sent to other end, followed by normal TCP connection termination (FIN); no effect on socket receive buffer.
close, l_onoff = 0 (default)	No more receives or sends can be issued on socket; contents of socket send buffer sent to other end. If descriptor reference count becomes 0: normal TCP connection termination (FIN) sent following data in send buffer and socket receive buffer discarded.
close, l_onoff = 1 l_linger = 0	No more receives or sends can be issued on socket. If descriptor reference count becomes 0: RST sent to other end; connection state set to CLOSED (no TIME_WAIT state); socket send buffer and socket receive buffer discarded.
close, l_onoff = 1 l_linger != 0	No more receives or sends can be issued on socket; contents of socket send buffer sent to other end. If descriptor reference count becomes 0: normal TCP connection termination (FIN) sent following data in send buffer; socket receive buffer discarded; and if linger time expires before connection CLOSED, close returns EWOULDBLOCK.

Figure 7.12 Summary of shutdown and SO_LINGER scenarios.

SO_OOBINLINE Socket Option

When this option is set, out-of-band data will be placed in the normal input queue (i.e., inline). When this occurs, the MSG_OOB flag to the receive functions cannot be used to read the out-of-band data. We will discuss out-of-band data in more detail in Chapter 24.

SO_RCVBUF and SO_SNDBUF Socket Options

Every socket has a send buffer and a receive buffer. We described the operation of the send buffers with TCP, UDP, and SCTP in Figures 2.15, 2.16, and 2.17.

The receive buffers are used by TCP, UDP, and SCTP to hold received data until it is read by the application. With TCP, the available room in the socket receive buffer limits the window that TCP can advertise to the other end. The TCP socket receive buffer cannot overflow because the peer is not allowed to send data beyond the advertised window. This is TCP's flow control, and if the peer ignores the advertised window and sends data beyond the window, the receiving TCP discards it. With UDP, however, when a datagram arrives that will not fit in the socket receive buffer, that datagram is discarded. Recall that UDP has no flow control: It is easy for a fast sender to overwhelm a slower receiver, causing datagrams to be discarded by the receiver's UDP, as we will show in Section 8.13. In fact, a fast sender can overwhelm its own network interface, causing datagrams to be discarded by the sender itself.

These two socket options let us change the default sizes. The default values differ widely between implementations. Older Berkeley-derived implementations would default the TCP send and receive buffers to 4,096 bytes, but newer systems use larger values, anywhere from 8,192 to 61,440 bytes. The UDP send buffer size often defaults to a value around 9,000 bytes if the host supports NFS, and the UDP receive buffer size often defaults to a value around 40,000 bytes.

When setting the size of the TCP socket receive buffer, the ordering of the function calls is important. This is because of TCP's window scale option (Section 2.6), which is exchanged with the peer on the SYN segments when the connection is established. For a client, this means the SO_RCVBUF socket option must be set before calling connect. For a server, this means the socket option must be set for the listening socket before calling listen. Setting this option for the connected socket will have no effect whatsoever on the possible window scale option because accept does not return with the connected socket until TCP's three-way handshake is complete. That is why this option must be set for the listening socket. (The sizes of the socket buffers are always inherited from the listening socket by the newly created connected socket: pp. 462–463 of TCPv2.)

The TCP socket buffer sizes should be at least four times the MSS for the connection. If we are dealing with unidirectional data transfer, such as a file transfer in one direction, when we say "socket buffer sizes," we mean the socket send buffer size on the sending host and the socket receive buffer size on the receiving host. For bidirectional data transfer, we mean both socket buffer sizes on the sender and both socket buffer sizes on the receiver. With typical default buffer sizes of 8,192 bytes or larger, and a typical MSS of 512 or 1,460, this requirement is normally met.

> The minimum MSS multiple of four is a result of the way that TCP's fast recovery algorithm works. The TCP sender uses three duplicate acknowledgments to detect that a packet was lost (RFC 2581 [Allman, Paxson, and Stevens 1999]). The receiver sends a duplicate acknowledgment for each segment it receives after a lost segment. If the window size is smaller than four segments, there cannot be three duplicate acknowledgments, so the fast recovery algorithm cannot be invoked.

To avoid wasting potential buffer space, the TCP socket buffer sizes should also be an even multiple of the MSS for the connection. Some implementations handle this detail for the application, rounding up the socket buffer size after the connection is established (p. 902 of TCPv2). This is another reason to set these two socket options before establishing a connection. For example, using the default 4.4BSD size of 8,192 and assuming an Ethernet with an MSS of 1,460, both socket buffers are rounded up to 8,760 (6 × 1,460) when the connection is established. This is not a crucial requirement; the additional space in the socket buffer above the multiple of the MSS is simply unused.

Another consideration in setting the socket buffer sizes deals with performance. Figure 7.13 shows a TCP connection between two endpoints (which we call a *pipe*) with a capacity of eight segments.

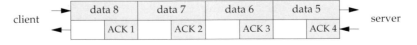

Figure 7.13 TCP connection (pipe) with a capacity of eight segments.

We show four data segments on the top and four ACKs on the bottom. Even though there are only four segments of data in the pipe, the client must have a send buffer capacity of at least eight segments, because the client TCP must keep a copy of each segment until the ACK is received from the server.

> We are ignoring some details here. First, TCP's slow-start algorithm limits the rate at which segments are initially sent on an idle connection. Next, TCP often acknowledges every other segment, not every segment as we show. All these details are covered in Chapters 20 and 24 of TCPv1.

What is important to understand is the concept of the full-duplex pipe, its capacity, and how that relates to the socket buffer sizes on both ends of the connection. The capacity of the pipe is called the *bandwidth-delay product* and we calculate this by multiplying the bandwidth (in bits/sec) times the RTT (in seconds), converting the result from bits to bytes. The RTT is easily measured with the ping program.

The bandwidth is the value corresponding to the slowest link between two endpoints and must somehow be known. For example, a T1 line (1,536,000 bits/sec) with an RTT of 60 ms gives a bandwidth-delay product of 11,520 bytes. If the socket buffer sizes are less than this, the pipe will not stay full, and the performance will be less than expected. Large socket buffers are required when the bandwidth gets larger (e.g., T3 lines at 45 Mbits/sec) or when the RTT gets large (e.g., satellite links with an RTT around 500 ms). When the bandwidth-delay product exceeds TCP's maximum normal window size (65,535 bytes), both endpoints also need the TCP *long fat pipe* options that we mentioned in Section 2.6.

> Most implementations have an upper limit for the sizes of the socket send and receive buffers, and sometimes this limit can be modified by the administrator. Older Berkeley-derived implementations had a hard upper limit of around 52,000 bytes, but newer implementations have a default limit of 256,000 bytes or more, and this can usually be increased by the administrator. Unfortunately, there is no simple way for an application to determine this limit. POSIX defines the fpathconf function, which most implementations support, and using the _PC_SOCK_MAXBUF constant as the second argument, we can retrieve the maximum size of the socket buffers. Alternately, an application can try setting the socket buffers to the desired value, and if that fails, cut the value in half and try again until it succeeds. Finally, an application should make sure that it's not actually making the socket buffer smaller when it sets it to a preconfigured "large" value; calling getsockopt first to retrieve the system's default and seeing if that's large enough is often a good start.

SO_RCVLOWAT and SO_SNDLOWAT Socket Options

Every socket also has a receive low-water mark and a send low-water mark. These are used by the select function, as we described in Section 6.3. These two socket options, SO_RCVLOWAT and SO_SNDLOWAT, let us change these two low-water marks.

The receive low-water mark is the amount of data that must be in the socket receive buffer for select to return "readable." It defaults to 1 for TCP, UDP, and SCTP sockets. The send low-water mark is the amount of available space that must exist in the socket send buffer for select to return "writable." This low-water mark normally defaults to 2,048 for TCP sockets. With UDP, the low-water mark is used, as we described in Section 6.3, but since the number of bytes of available space in the send

buffer for a UDP socket never changes (since UDP does not keep a copy of the datagrams sent by the application), as long as the UDP socket send buffer size is greater
than the socket's low-water mark, the UDP socket is always writable. Recall from Figure 2.16 that UDP does not have a send buffer; it has only a send buffer size.

SO_RCVTIMEO and SO_SNDTIMEO Socket Options

These two socket options allow us to place a timeout on socket receives and sends.
Notice that the argument to the two sockopt functions is a pointer to a timeval structure, the same one used with select (Section 6.3). This lets us specify the timeouts in
seconds and microseconds. We disable a timeout by setting its value to 0 seconds and 0
microseconds. Both timeouts are disabled by default.

The receive timeout affects the five input functions: read, readv, recv,
recvfrom, and recvmsg. The send timeout affects the five output functions: write,
writev, send, sendto, and sendmsg. We will talk more about socket timeouts in Section 14.2.

> These two socket options and the concept of inherent timeouts on socket receives and sends
> were added with 4.3BSD Reno.
>
> In Berkeley-derived implementations, these two values really implement an inactivity timer
> and not an absolute timer on the read or write system call. Pages 496 and 516 of TCPv2 talk
> about this in more detail.

SO_REUSEADDR and SO_REUSEPORT Socket Options

The SO_REUSEADDR socket option serves four different purposes:

1. SO_REUSEADDR allows a listening server to start and bind its well-known port,
   even if previously established connections exist that use this port as their local
   port. This condition is typically encountered as follows:

   (a) A listening server is started.

   (b) A connection request arrives and a child process is spawned to handle that
        client.

   (c) The listening server terminates, but the child continues to service the client
        on the existing connection.

   (d) The listening server is restarted.

   By default, when the listening server is restarted in (d) by calling socket,
   bind, and listen, the call to bind fails because the listening server is trying to
   bind a port that is part of an existing connection (the one being handled by the
   previously spawned child). But if the server sets the SO_REUSEADDR socket
   option between the calls to socket and bind, the latter function will succeed.
   All TCP servers should specify this socket option to allow the server to be
   restarted in this situation.

   This scenario is one of the most frequently asked questions on USENET.

2. SO_REUSEADDR allows a new server to be started on the same port as an existing server that is bound to the wildcard address, as long as each instance binds
   a different local IP address. This is common for a site hosting multiple HTTP
   servers using the IP alias technique (Section A.4). Assume the local host's primary IP address is 198.69.10.2 but it has two aliases: 198.69.10.128 and
   198.69.10.129. Three HTTP servers are started. The first HTTP server would call
   bind with the wildcard as the local IP address and a local port of 80 (the well-
   known port for HTTP). The second server would call bind with a local IP
   address of 198.69.10.128 and a local port of 80. But, this second call to bind fails
   unless SO_REUSEADDR is set before the call. The third server would bind
   198.69.10.129 and port 80. Again, SO_REUSEADDR is required for this final call
   to succeed. Assuming SO_REUSEADDR is set and the three servers are started,
   incoming TCP connection requests with a destination IP address of
   198.69.10.128 and a destination port of 80 are delivered to the second server,
   incoming requests with a destination IP address of 198.69.10.129 and a destination port of 80 are delivered to the third server, and all other TCP connection
   requests with a destination port of 80 are delivered to the first server. This
   "default" server handles requests destined for 198.69.10.2 in addition to any
   other IP aliases that the host may have configured. The wildcard means "everything that doesn't have a better (more specific) match." Note that this scenario
   of allowing multiple servers for a given service is handled automatically if the
   server always sets the SO_REUSEADDR socket option (as we recommend).

   With TCP, we are never able to start multiple servers that bind the same IP
   address and the same port: a *completely duplicate binding*. That is, we cannot start
   one server that binds 198.69.10.2 port 80 and start another that also binds
   198.69.10.2 port 80, even if we set the SO_REUSEADDR socket option for the second server.

   For security reasons, some operating systems prevent *any* "more specific" bind
   to a port that is already bound to the wildcard address, that is, the series of
   binds described here would not work with or without SO_REUSEADDR. On
   such a system, the server that performs the wildcard bind must be started last.
   This is to avoid the problem of a rogue server binding to an IP address and port
   that are being served already by a system service and intercepting legitimate
   requests. This is a particular problem for NFS, which generally does not use a
   privileged port.

3. SO_REUSEADDR allows a single process to bind the same port to multiple sockets, as long as each bind specifies a different local IP address. This is common
   for UDP servers that need to know the destination IP address of client requests
   on systems that do not provide the IP_RECVDSTADDR socket option. This technique is normally not used with TCP servers since a TCP server can always
   determine the destination IP address by calling getsockname after the connection is established. However, a TCP server wishing to serve connections to
   some, but not all, addresses belonging to a multihomed host should use this
   technique.

4. SO_REUSEADDR allows *completely duplicate bindings*: a bind of an IP address and port, when that same IP address and port are already bound to another socket, if the transport protocol supports it. Normally this feature is supported only for UDP sockets.

   This feature is used with multicasting to allow the same application to be run multiple times on the same host. When a UDP datagram is received for one of these multiply bound sockets, the rule is that if the datagram is destined for either a broadcast address or a multicast address, one copy of the datagram is delivered to each matching socket. But if the datagram is destined for a unicast address, the datagram is delivered to only one socket. If, in the case of a unicast datagram, there are multiple sockets that match the datagram, the choice of which socket receives the datagram is implementation-dependent. Pages 777–779 of TCPv2 talk more about this feature. We will talk more about broadcasting and multicasting in Chapters 20 and 21.

Exercises 7.5 and 7.6 show some examples of this socket option.

4.4BSD introduced the SO_REUSEPORT socket option when support for multicasting was added. Instead of overloading SO_REUSEADDR with the desired multicast semantics that allow completely duplicate bindings, this new socket option was introduced with the following semantics:

1. This option allows completely duplicate bindings, but only if each socket that wants to bind the same IP address and port specify this socket option.

2. SO_REUSEADDR is considered equivalent to SO_REUSEPORT if the IP address being bound is a multicast address (p. 731 of TCPv2).

The problem with this socket option is that not all systems support it, and on those that do not support the option but do support multicasting, SO_REUSEADDR is used instead of SO_REUSEPORT to allow completely duplicate bindings when it makes sense (i.e., a UDP server that can be run multiple times on the same host at the same time and that expects to receive either broadcast or multicast datagrams).

We can summarize our discussion of these socket options with the following recommendations:

1. Set the SO_REUSEADDR socket option before calling bind in all TCP servers.

2. When writing a multicast application that can be run multiple times on the same host at the same time, set the SO_REUSEADDR socket option and bind the group's multicast address as the local IP address.

Chapter 22 of TCPv2 talks about these two socket options in more detail.

There is a potential security problem with SO_REUSEADDR. If a socket exists that is bound to, say, the wildcard address and port 5555, if we specify SO_REUSEADDR, we can bind that same port to a different IP address, say the primary IP address of the host. Any future datagrams that arrive destined to port 5555 and the IP address that we bound to our socket are delivered to our socket, not to the other socket bound to the wildcard address. These could be TCP SYN segments, SCTP INIT chunks, or UDP datagrams. (Exercise 11.9 shows this feature with UDP.) For most well-known services, HTTP, FTP, and Telnet, for example, this is not a problem because these servers all bind a reserved port. Hence, any process that comes along later and tries to bind a more specific instance of that port (i.e., steal the port) requires superuser privileges. NFS, however, can be a problem since its normal port (2049) is not reserved.

> One underlying problem with the sockets API is that the setting of the socket pair is done with two function calls (bind and connect) instead of one. [Torek 1994] proposes a single function that solves this problem.
>
> ```
>         int bind_connect_listen(int sockfd,
>                                 const struct sockaddr *laddr, int laddrlen,
>                                 const struct sockaddr *faddr, int faddrlen,
>                                 int listen);
> ```
>
> *laddr* specifies the local IP address and local port, *faddr* specifies the foreign IP address and foreign port, and *listen* specifies a client (zero) or a server (nonzero; same as the backlog argument to listen). Then, bind would be a library function that calls this function with *faddr* a null pointer and *faddrlen* 0, and connect would be a library function that calls this function with *laddr* a null pointer and *laddrlen* 0. There are a few applications, notably TFTP, that need to specify both the local pair and the foreign pair, and they could call bind_connect_listen directly. With such a function, the need for SO_REUSEADDR disappears, other than for multicast UDP servers that explicitly need to allow completely duplicate bindings of the same IP address and port. Another benefit of this new function is that a TCP server could restrict itself to servicing connection requests that arrive from one specific IP address and port, something which RFC 793 [Postel 1981c] specifies but is impossible to implement with the existing sockets API.

SO_TYPE Socket Option

This option returns the socket type. The integer value returned is a value such as SOCK_STREAM or SOCK_DGRAM. This option is typically used by a process that inherits a socket when it is started.

SO_USELOOPBACK Socket Option

This option applies only to sockets in the routing domain (AF_ROUTE). This option defaults to ON for these sockets (the only one of the SO_*xxx* socket options that defaults to ON instead of OFF). When this option is enabled, the socket receives a copy of everything sent on the socket.

> Another way to disable these loopback copies is to call shutdown with a second argument of SHUT_RD.

7.6   IPv4 Socket Options

These socket options are processed by IPv4 and have a *level* of `IPPROTO_IP`. We defer discussion of the multicasting socket options until Section 21.6.

`IP_HDRINCL` Socket Option

If this option is set for a raw IP socket (Chapter 28), we must build our own IP header for all the datagrams we send on the raw socket. Normally, the kernel builds the IP header for datagrams sent on a raw socket, but there are some applications (notably `traceroute`) that build their own IP header to override values that IP would place into certain header fields.

When this option is set, we build a complete IP header, with the following exceptions:

- IP always calculates and stores the IP header checksum.
- If we set the IP identification field to 0, the kernel will set the field.
- If the source IP address is `INADDR_ANY`, IP sets it to the primary IP address of the outgoing interface.
- Setting IP options is implementation-dependent. Some implementations take any IP options that were set using the `IP_OPTIONS` socket option and append these to the header that we build, while others require our header to also contain any desired IP options.
- Some fields must be in host byte order, and some in network byte order. This is implementation-dependent, which makes writing raw packets with `IP_HDRINCL` not as portable as we'd like.

We show an example of this option in Section 29.7. Pages 1056–1057 of TCPv2 provide additional details on this socket option.

`IP_OPTIONS` Socket Option

Setting this option allows us to set IP options in the IPv4 header. This requires intimate knowledge of the format of the IP options in the IP header. We will discuss this option with regard to IPv4 source routes in Section 27.3.

`IP_RECVDSTADDR` Socket Option

This socket option causes the destination IP address of a received UDP datagram to be returned as ancillary data by `recvmsg`. We will show an example of this option in Section 22.2.

`IP_RECVIF` Socket Option

This socket option causes the index of the interface on which a UDP datagram is received to be returned as ancillary data by `recvmsg`. We will show an example of this option in Section 22.2.

`IP_TOS` Socket Option

This option lets us set the type-of-service (TOS) field (which contains the DSCP and ECN fields, Figure A.1) in the IP header for a TCP, UDP, or SCTP socket. If we call `getsockopt` for this option, the current value that would be placed into the DSCP and ECN fields in the IP header (which defaults to 0) is returned. There is no way to fetch the value from a received IP datagram.

An application can set the DSCP to a value negotiated with the network service provider to receive prearranged services, e.g., low delay for IP telephony or higher throughput for bulk data transfer. The diffserv architecture, defined in RFC 2474 [Nichols et al. 1998], provides for only limited backward compatibility with the historical TOS field definition (from RFC 1349 [Almquist 1992]). Applications that set `IP_TOS` to one of the contents from `<netinet/ip.h>`, for instance, `IPTOS_LOWDELAY` or `IPTOS_THROUGHPUT`, should instead use a user-specified DSCP value. The only TOS values that diffserv retains are precedence levels 6 ("internetwork control") and 7 ("network control"); this means that applications that set `IP_TOS` to `IPTOS_PREC_NETCONTROL` or `IPTOS_PREC_INTERNETCONTROL` *will* work in a diffserv network.

RFC 3168 [Ramakrishnan, Floyd, and Black 2001] contains the definition of the ECN field. Applications should generally leave the setting of the ECN field to the kernel, and should specify zero values in the low two bits of the value set with `IP_TOS`.

`IP_TTL` Socket Option

With this option, we can set and fetch the default TTL (Figure A.1) that the system will use for unicast packets sent on a given socket. (The multicast TTL is set using the `IP_MULTICAST_TTL` socket option, described in Section 21.6.) 4.4BSD, for example, uses the default of 64 for both TCP and UDP sockets (specified in the IANA's "IP Option Numbers" registry [IANA]) and 255 for raw sockets. As with the TOS field, calling `getsockopt` returns the default value of the field that the system will use in outgoing datagrams—there is no way to obtain the value from a received datagram. We will set this socket option with our `traceroute` program in Figure 28.19.

7.7   ICMPv6 Socket Option

This socket option is processed by ICMPv6 and has a *level* of IPPROTO_ICMPV6.

ICMP6_FILTER Socket Option

This option lets us fetch and set an icmp6_filter structure that specifies which of the 256 possible ICMPv6 message types will be passed to the process on a raw socket. We will discuss this option in Section 28.4.

7.8   IPv6 Socket Options

These socket options are processed by IPv6 and have a *level* of IPPROTO_IPV6. We defer discussion of the multicasting socket options until Section 21.6. We note that many of these options make use of *ancillary data* with the recvmsg function, and we will describe this in Section 14.6. All the IPv6 socket options are defined in RFC 3493 [Gilligan et al. 2003] and RFC 3542 [Stevens et al. 2003].

IPV6_CHECKSUM Socket Option

This socket option specifies the byte offset into the user data where the checksum field is located. If this value is non-negative, the kernel will: (i) compute and store a checksum for all outgoing packets, and (ii) verify the received checksum on input, discarding packets with an invalid checksum. This option affects all IPv6 raw sockets, except ICMPv6 raw sockets. (The kernel always calculates and stores the checksum for ICMPv6 raw sockets.) If a value of −1 is specified (the default), the kernel will not calculate and store the checksum for outgoing packets on this raw socket and will not verify the checksum for received packets.

> All protocols that use IPv6 should have a checksum in their own protocol header. These checksums include a pseudoheader (RFC 2460 [Deering and Hinden 1998]) that includes the source IPv6 address as part of the checksum (which differs from all the other protocols that are normally implemented using a raw socket with IPv4). Rather than forcing the application using the raw socket to perform source address selection, the kernel will do this and then calculate and store the checksum incorporating the standard IPv6 pseudoheader.

IPV6_DONTFRAG Socket Option

Setting this option disables the automatic insertion of a fragment header for UDP and raw sockets. When this option is set, output packets larger than the MTU of the outgoing interface will be dropped. No error needs to be returned from the system call that sends the packet, since the packet might exceed the path MTU en-route. Instead, the application should enable the IPV6_RECVPATHMTU option (Section 22.9) to learn about path MTU changes.

`IPV6_NEXTHOP` **Socket Option**

This option specifies the next-hop address for a datagram as a socket address structure, and is a privileged operation. We will say more about this feature in Section 22.8.

`IPV6_PATHMTU` **Socket Option**

This option cannot be set, only retrieved. When this option is retrieved, the current MTU as determined by path-MTU discovery is returned (see Section 22.9).

`IPV6_RECVDSTOPTS` **Socket Option**

Setting this option specifies that any received IPv6 destination options are to be returned as ancillary data by `recvmsg`. This option defaults to OFF. We will describe the functions that are used to build and process these options in Section 27.5.

`IPV6_RECVHOPLIMIT` **Socket Option**

Setting this option specifies that the received hop limit field is to be returned as ancillary data by `recvmsg`. This option defaults to OFF. We will describe this option in Section 22.8.

> There is no way with IPv4 to obtain the received TTL field.

`IPV6_RECVHOPOPTS` **Socket Option**

Setting this option specifies that any received IPv6 hop-by-hop options are to be returned as ancillary data by `recvmsg`. This option defaults to OFF. We will describe the functions that are used to build and process these options in Section 27.5.

`IPV6_RECVPATHMTU` **Socket Option**

Setting this option specifies that the path MTU of a path is to be returned as ancillary data by `recvmsg` (without any accompanying data) when it changes. We will describe this option in Section 22.9.

`IPV6_RECVPKTINFO` **Socket Option**

Setting this option specifies that the following two pieces of information about a received IPv6 datagram are to be returned as ancillary data by `recvmsg`: the destination IPv6 address and the arriving interface index. We will describe this option in Section 22.8.

`IPV6_RECVRTHDR` Socket Option

Setting this option specifies that a received IPv6 routing header is to be returned as ancillary data by `recvmsg`. This option defaults to OFF. We will describe the functions that are used to build and process an IPv6 routing header in Section 27.6.

`IPV6_RECVTCLASS` Socket Option

Setting this option specifies that the received traffic class (containing the DSCP and ECN fields) is to be returned as ancillary data by `recvmsg`. This option defaults to OFF. We will describe this option in Section 22.8.

`IPV6_UNICAST_HOPS` Socket Option

This IPv6 option is similar to the IPv4 `IP_TTL` socket option. Setting the socket option specifies the default hop limit for outgoing datagrams sent on the socket, while fetching the socket option returns the value for the hop limit that the kernel will use for the socket. The actual hop limit field from a received IPv6 datagram is obtained by using the `IPV6_RECVHOPLIMIT` socket option. We will set this socket option with our `traceroute` program in Figure 28.19.

`IPV6_USE_MIN_MTU` Socket Option

Setting this option to 1 specifies that path MTU discovery is not to be performed and that packets are sent using the minimum IPv6 MTU to avoid fragmentation. Setting it to 0 causes path MTU discovery to occur for all destinations. Setting it to −1 specifies that path MTU discovery is performed for unicast destinations but the minimum MTU is used when sending to multicast destinations. This option defaults to −1. We will describe this option in Section 22.9.

`IPV6_V6ONLY` Socket Option

Setting this option on an `AF_INET6` socket restricts it to IPv6 communication only. This option defaults to OFF, although some systems have an option to turn it ON by default. We will describe IPv4 and IPv6 communication using `AF_INET6` sockets in Sections 12.2 and 12.3.

`IPV6_XXX` Socket Options

Most of the IPv6 options for header modification assume a UDP socket with information being passed between the kernel and the application using ancillary data with `recvmsg` and `sendmsg`. A TCP socket fetches and stores these values using `getsockopt` and `setsockopt` instead. The socket option is the same as the type of the ancillary data, and the buffer contains the same information as would be present in the ancillary data. We will describe this in Section 27.7.

7.9   TCP Socket Options

There are two socket options for TCP. We specify the *level* as `IPPROTO_TCP`.

`TCP_MAXSEG` Socket Option

This socket option allows us to fetch or set the MSS for a TCP connection. The value returned is the maximum amount of data that our TCP will send to the other end; often, it is the MSS announced by the other end with its SYN, unless our TCP chooses to use a smaller value than the peer's announced MSS. If this value is fetched before the socket is connected, the value returned is the default value that will be used if an MSS option is not received from the other end. Also be aware that a value smaller than the returned value can actually be used for the connection if the timestamp option, for example, is in use, because this option occupies 12 bytes of TCP options in each segment.

The maximum amount of data that our TCP will send per segment can also change during the life of a connection if TCP supports path MTU discovery. If the route to the peer changes, this value can go up or down.

We note in Figure 7.1 that this socket option can also be set by the application. This is not possible on all systems; it was originally a read-only option. 4.4BSD limits the application to *decreasing* the value: We cannot increase the value (p. 1023 of TCPv2). Since this option controls the amount of data that TCP sends per segment, it makes sense to forbid the application from increasing the value. Once the connection is established, this value is the MSS option announced by the peer, and we cannot exceed that value. Our TCP, however, can always send less than the peer's announced MSS.

`TCP_NODELAY` Socket Option

If set, this option disables TCP's *Nagle algorithm* (Section 19.4 of TCPv1 and pp. 858–859 of TCPv2). By default, this algorithm is enabled.

The purpose of the Nagle algorithm is to reduce the number of small packets on a WAN. The algorithm states that if a given connection has outstanding data (i.e., data that our TCP has sent, and for which it is currently awaiting an acknowledgment), then no small packets will be sent on the connection in response to a user write operation until the existing data is acknowledged. The definition of a "small" packet is any packet smaller than the MSS. TCP will always send a full-sized packet if possible; the purpose of the Nagle algorithm is to prevent a connection from having multiple small packets outstanding at any time.

The two common generators of small packets are the Rlogin and Telnet clients, since they normally send each keystroke as a separate packet. On a fast LAN, we normally do not notice the Nagle algorithm with these clients, because the time required for a small packet to be acknowledged is typically a few milliseconds—far less than the time between two successive characters that we type. But on a WAN, where it can take a second for a small packet to be acknowledged, we can notice a delay in the character echoing, and this delay is often exaggerated by the Nagle algorithm.

Consider the following example: We type the six-character string "hello!" to either an Rlogin or Telnet client, with exactly 250 ms between each character. The RTT to the server is 600 ms and the server immediately sends back the echo of each character. We assume the ACK of the client's character is sent back to the client along with the character echo and we ignore the ACKs that the client sends for the server's echo. (We will talk about delayed ACKs shortly.) Assuming the Nagle algorithm is disabled, we have the 12 packets shown in Figure 7.14.

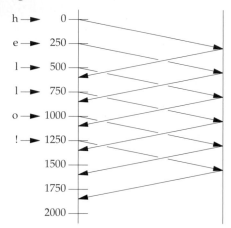

Figure 7.14 Six characters echoed by server with Nagle algorithm disabled.

Each character is sent in a packet by itself: the data segments from left to right, and the ACKs from right to left.

If the Nagle algorithm is enabled (the default), we have the eight packets shown in Figure 7.15. The first character is sent as a packet by itself, but the next two characters are not sent, since the connection has a small packet outstanding. At time 600, when the ACK of the first packet is received, along with the echo of the first character, these two characters are sent. Until this packet is ACKed at time 1200, no more small packets are sent.

The Nagle algorithm often interacts with another TCP algorithm: the *delayed ACK* algorithm. This algorithm causes TCP to not send an ACK immediately when it receives data; instead, TCP will wait some small amount of time (typically 50–200 ms) and only then send the ACK. The hope is that in this small amount of time, there will be data to send back to the peer, and the ACK can piggyback with the data, saving one TCP segment. This is normally the case with the Rlogin and Telnet clients, because the servers typically echo each character sent by the client, so the ACK of the client's character piggybacks with the server's echo of that character.

The problem is with other clients whose servers do not generate traffic in the reverse direction on which ACKs can piggyback. These clients can detect noticeable delays because the client TCP will not send any data to the server until the server's delayed ACK timer expires. These clients need a way to disable the Nagle algorithm, hence the TCP_NODELAY option.

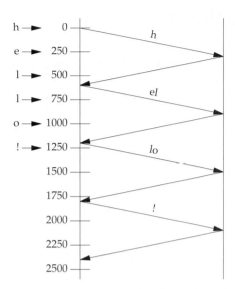

Figure 7.15 Six characters echoed by server with Nagle algorithm enabled.

Another type of client that interacts badly with the Nagle algorithm and TCP's delayed ACKs is a client that sends a single logical request to its server in small pieces. For example, assume a client sends a 400-byte request to its server, but this is a 4-byte request type followed by 396 bytes of request data. If the client performs a 4-byte `write` followed by a 396-byte `write`, the second write will not be sent by the client TCP until the server TCP acknowledges the 4-byte write. Also, since the server application cannot operate on the 4 bytes of data until it receives the remaining 396 bytes of data, the server TCP will delay the ACK of the 4 bytes of data (i.e., there will not be any data from the server to the client on which to piggyback the ACK). There are three ways to fix this type of client:

1. Use `writev` (Section 14.4) instead of two calls to `write`. A single call to `writev` ends up with one call to TCP output instead of two calls, resulting in one TCP segment for our example. This is the preferred solution.

2. Copy the 4 bytes of data and the 396 bytes of data into a single buffer and call `write` once for this buffer.

3. Set the `TCP_NODELAY` socket option and continue to call `write` two times. This is the least desirable solution, and is harmful to the network, so it generally should not even be considered.

Exercises 7.8 and 7.9 continue this example.

7.10   SCTP Socket Options

The relatively large number of socket options for SCTP (17 at present writing) reflects the finer grain of control SCTP provides to the application developer. We specify the *level* as `IPPROTO_SCTP`.

Several options used to get information about SCTP require that data be passed into the kernel (e.g., association ID and/or peer address). While some implementations of `getsockopt` support passing data both into and out of the kernel, not all do. The SCTP API defines a `sctp_opt_info` function (Section 9.11) that hides this difference. On systems on which `getsockopt` does support this, it is simply a wrapper around `getsockopt`. Otherwise, it performs the required action, perhaps using a custom `ioctl` or a new system call. We recommend always using `sctp_opt_info` when retrieving these options for maximum portability. These options are marked with a dagger (†) in Figure 7.2 and include `SCTP_ASSOCINFO`, `SCTP_GET_PEER_ADDR_INFO`, `SCTP_PEER_ADDR_PARAMS`,   `SCTP_PRIMARY_ADDR`,   `SCTP_RTOINFO`,   and `SCTP_STATUS`.

`SCTP_ADAPTION_LAYER` Socket Option

During association initialization, either endpoint may specify an adaption layer indication. This indication is a 32-bit unsigned integer that can be used by the two applications to coordinate any local application adaption layer. This option allows the caller to fetch or set the adaption layer indication that this endpoint will provide to peers.

When fetching this value, the caller will only retrieve the value the local socket will provide to all future peers. To retrieve the peer's adaption layer indication, an application must subscribe to adaption layer events.

`SCTP_ASSOCINFO` Socket Option

The `SCTP_ASSOCINFO` socket option can be used for three purposes: (i) to retrieve information about an existing association, (ii) to change the parameters of an existing association, and/or (iii) to set defaults for future associations. When retrieving information about an existing association, the `sctp_opt_info` function should be used instead of `getsockopt`. This option takes as input the `sctp_assocparams` structure.

```
struct sctp_assocparams {
  sctp_assoc_t sasoc_assoc_id;
  u_int16_t sasoc_asocmaxrxt;
  u_int16_t sasoc_number_peer_destinations;
  u_int32_t sasoc_peer_rwnd;
  u_int32_t sasoc_local_rwnd;
  u_int32_t sasoc_cookie_life;
};
```

These fields have the following meaning:

- `sasoc_assoc_id` holds the identification for the association of interest. If this value   is   set   to   0   when   calling   the   `setsockopt`   function,   then sasoc_asocmaxrxt and sasoc_cookie_life represent values that are to be set as defaults on the socket. Calling getsockopt will return association-specific information if the association ID is supplied; otherwise, if this field is 0, the default endpoint settings will be returned.

- sasoc_asocmaxrxt holds the maximum number of retransmissions an association will make without acknowledgment before giving up, reporting the peer unusable and closing the association.

- sasoc_number_peer_destinations holds the number of peer destination addresses. It cannot be set, only retrieved.

- sasoc_peer_rwnd holds the peer's current calculated receive window. This value represents the total number of data bytes that can yet be sent. This field is dynamic; as the local endpoint sends data, this value decreases. As the remote application reads data that has been received, this value increases. This value cannot be changed by this socket option call.

- sasoc_local_rwnd represents the local receive window the SCTP stack is currently reporting to the peer. This value is dynamic as well and is influenced by the SO_SNDBUF socket option. This value cannot be changed by this socket option call.

- sasoc_cookie_life represents the number of milliseconds for which a cookie, given to a remote peer, is valid. Each state cookie sent to a peer has a lifetime associated with it to prevent replay attacks. The default value of 60,000 milliseconds can be changed by setting this option with a sasoc_assoc_id value of 0.

We will provide advice on tuning the value of sasoc_asocmaxrxt for performance in Section 23.11. The sasoc_cookie_life can be reduced for greater protection against cookie replay attacks but less robustness to network delay during association initiation. The other values are useful for debugging.

SCTP_AUTOCLOSE Socket Option

This option allows us to fetch or set the autoclose time for an SCTP endpoint. The autoclose time is the number of seconds an SCTP association will remain open when idle. Idle is defined by the SCTP stack as neither endpoint sending or receiving user data. The default is for the autoclose function to be disabled.

The autoclose option is intended to be used in the one-to-many-style SCTP interface (Chapter 9). When this option is set, the integer passed to the option is the number of seconds before an idle connection should be closed; a value of 0 disables autoclose. Only future associations created by this endpoint will be affected by this option; existing associations retain their current setting.

Autoclose can be used by a server to force the closing of idle associations without the server needing to maintain additional state. A server using this feature needs to carefully assess the longest idle time expected on all its associations. Setting the autoclose value smaller than needed results in the premature closing of associations.

SCTP_DEFAULT_SEND_PARAM Socket Option

SCTP has many optional send parameters that are often passed as ancillary data or used with the `sctp_sendmsg` function call (which is often implemented as a library call that passes ancillary data for the user). An application that wishes to send a large number of messages, all with the same parameters, can use this option to set up the default parameters and thus avoid using ancillary data or the `sctp_sendmsg` call. This option takes as input the `sctp_sndrcvinfo` structure.

```
struct sctp_sndrcvinfo {
  u_int16_t sinfo_stream;
  u_int16_t sinfo_ssn;
  u_int16_t sinfo_flags;
  u_int32_t sinfo_ppid;
  u_int32_t sinfo_context;
  u_int32_t sinfo_timetolive;
  u_int32_t sinfo_tsn;
  u_int32_t sinfo_cumtsn;
  sctp_assoc_t sinfo_assoc_id;
};
```

These fields are defined as follows:

- `sinfo_stream` specifies the new default stream to which all messages will be sent.

- `sinfo_ssn` is ignored when setting the default options. When receiving a message with the `recvmsg` function or `sctp_recvmsg` function, this field will hold the value the peer placed in the stream sequence number (SSN) field in the SCTP DATA chunk.

- `sinfo_flags` dictates the default flags to apply to all future message sends. Allowable flag values can be found in Figure 7.16.

- `sinfo_pid` provides the default value to use when setting the SCTP payload protocol identifier in all data transmissions.

- `sinfo_context` specifies the default value to place in the `sinfo_context` field, which is provided as a local tag when messages that could not be sent to a peer are retrieved.

- `sinfo_timetolive` dictates the default lifetime that will be applied to all message sends. The lifetime field is used by SCTP stacks to know when to discard an outgoing message due to excessive delay (prior to its first transmission). If the two endpoints support the partial reliability option, then the lifetime is also used to specify how long a message is valid after its first transmission.

- `sinfo_tsn` is ignored when setting the default options. When receiving a message with the `recvmsg` function or `sctp_recvmsg` function, this field will hold the value the peer placed in the transport sequence number (TSN) field in the SCTP DATA chunk.

- `sinfo_cumtsn` is ignored when setting the default options. When receiving a message with the `recvmsg` function or `sctp_recvmsg` function, this field will hold the current cumulative TSN the local SCTP stack has associated with its remote peer.

- `sinfo_assoc_id` specifies the association identification that the requester wishes the default parameters to be set against. For one-to-one sockets, this field is ignored.

Constant	Description
MSG_ABORT	Invoke ABORTIVE termination of the association
MSG_ADDR_OVER	Specify that SCTP should override the primary address and use the provided address instead
MSG_EOF	Invoke graceful termination after the sending of this message
MSG_PR_BUFFER	Enable the buffer-based profile of the partial reliability feature (if available)
MSG_PR_SCTP	Enable the partial reliability (if available) feature on this message
MSG_UNORDERED	Specify that this message uses the unordered message service

Figure 7.16 Allowable SCTP flag values for the `sinfo_flags` field.

Note that all default settings will only affect messages sent without their own `sctp_sndrcvinfo` structure. Any send that provides this structure (e.g., `sctp_sendmsg` or `sendmsg` function with ancillary data) will override the default settings. Besides setting the default values, this option may be used to retrieve the current default parameters by using the `sctp_opt_info` function.

`SCTP_DISABLE_FRAGMENTS` Socket Option

SCTP normally fragments any user message that does not fit in a single SCTP packet into multiple DATA chunks. Setting this option disables this behavior on the sender. When disabled by this option, SCTP will return the error `EMSGSIZE` and not send the message. The default behavior is for this option to be disabled; SCTP will normally fragment user messages.

This option may be used by applications that wish to control message sizes, ensuring that every user application message will fit in a single IP packet. An application that enables this option must be prepared to handle the error case (i.e., its message was too big) by either providing application-layer fragmentation of the message or a smaller message.

`SCTP_EVENTS` Socket Option

This socket option allows a caller to fetch, enable, or disable various SCTP notifications. An SCTP notification is a message that the SCTP stack will send to the application. The message is read as normal data, with the `msg_flags` field of the `recvmsg` function being set to `MSG_NOTIFICATION`. An application that is not prepared to use either `recvmsg` or `sctp_recvmsg` should not enable events. Eight different types of events can be subscribed to by using this option and passing an `sctp_event_subscribe` structure. Any value of 0 represents a non-subscription and a value of 1 represents a subscription.

The `sctp_event_subscribe` structure takes the following form:

```
struct sctp_event_subscribe {
  u_int8_t sctp_data_io_event;
  u_int8_t sctp_association_event;
  u_int8_t sctp_address_event;
  u_int8_t sctp_send_failure_event;
  u_int8_t sctp_peer_error_event;
  u_int8_t sctp_shutdown_event;
  u_int8_t sctp_partial_delivery_event;
  u_int8_t sctp_adaption_layer_event;
};
```

Figure 7.17 summarizes the various events. Further details on notifications can be found in Section 9.14.

Constant	Description
`sctp_data_io_event`	Enable/disable `sctp_sndrcvinfo` to come with each `recvmsg`
`sctp_association_event`	Enable/disable association notifications
`sctp_address_event`	Enable/disable address notifications
`sctp_send_failure_event`	Enable/disable message send failure notifications
`sctp_peer_error_event`	Enable/disable peer protocol error notifications
`sctp_shutdown_event`	Enable/disable shutdown notifications
`sctp_partial_delivery_event`	Enable/disable partial-delivery API notifications
`sctp_adaption_layer_event`	Enable/disable adaption layer notification

Figure 7.17 SCTP event subscriptions.

`SCTP_GET_PEER_ADDR_INFO` Socket Option

This option retrieves information about a peer address, including the congestion window, smoothed RTT and MTU. This option may only be used to retrieve information about a specific peer address. The caller provides a `sctp_paddrinfo` structure with the `spinfo_address` field filled in with the peer address of interest, and should use `sctp_opt_info` instead of `getsockopt` for maximum portability. The sctp_paddrinfo structure has the following format:

```
struct sctp_paddrinfo {
  sctp_assoc_t spinfo_assoc_id;
  struct sockaddr_storage spinfo_address;
  int32_t spinfo_state;
  u_int32_t spinfo_cwnd;
  u_int32_t spinfo_srtt;
  u_int32_t spinfo_rto;
  u_int32_t spinfo_mtu;
};
```

The data returned to the caller provides the following:

- `spinfo_assoc_id` contains association identification information, also provided in the "communication up" notification (SCTP_COMM_UP). This unique value can be used as a shorthand method to represent the association for almost all SCTP operations.

- `spinfo_address` is set by the caller to inform the SCTP socket on which address to return information. On return, its value should be unchanged.

- `spinfo_state` holds one or more of the values seen in Figure 7.18.

Constant	Description
SCTP_ACTIVE	Address is active and reachable
SCTP_INACTIVE	Address cannot currently be reached
SCTP_ADDR_UNCONFIRMED	No heartbeat or data has confirmed this address

Figure 7.18 SCTP peer address states.

An *unconfirmed address* is one that the peer had listed as a valid address, but the local SCTP endpoint has not been able to confirm that the peer holds that address. An SCTP endpoint confirms an address when a heartbeat or user data, sent to that address, is acknowledged. Note that an unconfirmed address will also not have a valid retransmission timeout (RTO) value. Active addresses represent addresses that are considered available for use.

- `spinfo_cwnd` represents the current congestion window recorded for the peer address. A description of how the the `cwnd` value is managed can be found on page 177 of [Stewart and Xie 2001].

- `spinfo_srtt` represents the current estimate of the smoothed RTT for this address.

- `spinfo_rto` represents the current retransmission timeout in use for this address.

- `spinfo_mtu` represents the current path MTU as discovered by path MTU discovery.

One interesting use for this option is to translate an IP address structure into an association identification that can be used in other calls. We will illustrate the use of this socket option in Chapter 23. Another possibility is for the application to track performance to each address of a multihomed peer and update the primary address of the association to the peer's best address. These values are also useful for logging and debugging.

`SCTP_I_WANT_MAPPED_V4_ADDR` Socket Option

This flag can be used to enable or disable IPv4-mapped addresses on an `AF_INET6`-type socket. Note that when enabled (which is the default behavior), all IPv4 addresses will be mapped to a IPv6 address before sending to the application. If this option is disabled, the SCTP socket will *not* map IPv4 addresses and will instead pass them as a `sockaddr_in` structure.

`SCTP_INITMSG` Socket Option

This option can be used to get or set the default initial parameters used on an SCTP socket when sending out the INIT message. The option uses the `sctp_initmsg` structure, which is defined as:

```
struct sctp_initmsg {
  uint16_t sinit_num_ostreams;
  uint16_t sinit_max_instreams;
  uint16_t sinit_max_attempts;
  uint16_t sinit_max_init_timeo;
};
```

These fields are defined as follows:

- `sinit_num_ostreams` represents the number of outbound SCTP streams an application would like to request. This value is not confirmed until after the association finishes the initial handshake, and may be negotiated downward via peer endpoint limitations.

- `sinit_max_instreams` represents the maximum number of inbound streams the application is prepared to allow. This value will be overridden by the SCTP stack if it is greater than the maximum allowable streams the SCTP stack supports.

- `sinit_max_attempts` expresses how many times the SCTP stack should send the initial INIT message before considering the peer endpoint unreachable.

- `sinit_max_init_timeo` represents the maximum RTO value for the INIT timer. During exponential backoff of the initial timer, this value replaces `RTO.max` as the ceiling for retransmissions. This value is expressed in milliseconds.

Note that when setting these fields, any value set to 0 will be ignored by the SCTP socket. A user of the one-to-many-style socket (described in Section 9.2) may also pass an `sctp_initmsg` structure in ancillary data during implicit association setup.

`SCTP_MAXBURST` Socket Option

This socket option allows the application to fetch or set the *maximum burst size* used when sending packets. When an SCTP implementation sends data to a peer, no more than `SCTP_MAXBURST` packets are sent at once to avoid flooding the network with packets. An implementation may apply this limit by either: (i) reducing its congestion window to the current flight size plus the maximum burst size times the path MTU, or (ii) using this value as a separate micro-control, sending at most maximum burst packets at any single send opportunity.

`SCTP_MAXSEG` **Socket Option**

This socket option allows the application to fetch or set the *maximum fragment size* used during SCTP fragmentation. This option is similar to the TCP option `TCP_MAXSEG` described in Section 7.9.

When an SCTP sender receives a message from an application that is larger than this value, the SCTP sender will break the message into multiple pieces for transport to the peer endpoint. The size that the SCTP sender normally uses is the smallest MTU of all addresses associated with the peer. This option overrides this value downward to the value specified. Note that the SCTP stack may fragment a message at a smaller boundary than requested by this option. This smaller fragmentation will occur when one of the paths to the peer endpoint has a smaller MTU than the value requested in the `SCTP_MAXSEG` option.

This value is an endpoint-wide setting and may affect more than one association in the one-to-many interface style.

`SCTP_NODELAY` **Socket Option**

If set, this option disables SCTP's *Nagle algorithm*. This option is OFF by default (i.e., the Nagle algorithm is ON by default). SCTP's Nagle algorithm works identically to TCP's except that it is trying to coalesce multiple DATA chunks as opposed to simply coalescing bytes on a stream. For a further discussion of the Nagle algorithm, see `TCP_MAXSEG`.

`SCTP_PEER_ADDR_PARAMS` **Socket Option**

This socket option allows an application to fetch or set various parameters on an association. The caller provides the `sctp_paddrparams` structure, filling in the association identification. The `sctp_paddrparams` structure has the following format:

```
struct sctp_paddrparams {
  sctp_assoc_t spp_assoc_id;
  struct sockaddr_storage spp_address;
  u_int32_t spp_hbinterval;
  u_int16_t spp_pathmaxrxt;
};
```

These fields are defined as follows:

- `spp_assoc_id` holds the association identification for the information being requested or set. If this value is set to 0, the endpoint default values are set or retrieved instead of the association-specific values.

- `spp_address` specifies the IP address for which these parameters are being requested or set. If the `spp_assoc_id` field is set to 0, then this field is ignored.

- `spp_hbinterval` is the interval between heartbeats. A value of

SCTP_NO_HB disables heartbeats. A value of SCTP_ISSUE_HB requests an on-demand heartbeat. Any other value changes the heartbeat interval to this value in milliseconds. When setting the default parameters, the value of SCTP_ISSUE_HB is not allowed.

- spp_hbpathmaxrxt holds the number of retransmissions that will be attempted on this destination before it is declared INACTIVE. When an address is declared INACTIVE, if it is the primary address, an alternate address will be chosen as the primary.

SCTP_PRIMARY_ADDR Socket Option

This socket option fetches or sets the address that the local endpoint is using as primary. The primary address is used, by default, as the destination address for all messages sent to a peer. To set this value, the caller fills in the association identification and the peer's address that should be used as the primary address. The caller passes this information in a sctp_setprim structure, which is defined as:

```
struct sctp_setprim {
  sctp_assoc_t            ssp_assoc_id;
  struct sockaddr_storage ssp_addr;
};
```

These fields are defined as follows:

- spp_assoc_id specifies the association identification on which the requester wishes to set or retrieve the current primary address. For the one-to-one style, this field is ignored.

- sspp_addr specifies the primary address, which must be an address belonging to the peer. If the operation is a setsockopt function call, then the value in this field represents the new peer address the requester would like to be made into the primary destination address.

Note that retrieving the value of this option on a one-to-one socket that has only one local address associated with it is the same as calling getsockname.

SCTP_RTOINFO Socket Option

This socket option can be used to fetch or set various RTO information on a specific association or the default values used by this endpoint. When fetching, the caller should use sctp_opt_info instead of getsockopt for maximum portability. The caller provides a sctp_rtoinfo structure of the following form:

```
struct sctp_rtoinfo {
  sctp_assoc_t    srto_assoc_id;
  uint32_t        srto_initial;
  uint32_t        srto_max;
  uint32_t        srto_min;
};
```

These fields are defined as follows:

- `srto_assoc_id` holds either the specific association of interest or 0. If this field contains the value 0, then the system's default parameters are affected by the call.

- `srto_initial` contains the initial RTO value used for a peer address. The initial RTO is used when sending an INIT chunk to the peer. This value is in milliseconds and has a default value of 3,000.

- `srto_max` contains the maximum RTO value that will be used when an update is made to the retransmission timer. If the updated value is larger than the RTO maximum, then the RTO maximum is used as the RTO instead of the calculated value. The default value for this field is 60,000 milliseconds.

- `srto_min` contains the minimum RTO value that will be used when starting a retransmission timer. Anytime an update is made to the RTO timer, the RTO minimum value is checked against the new value. If the new value is smaller than the minimum, the minimum replaces the new value. The default value for this field is 1,000 milliseconds.

A value of 0 for `srto_initial`, `srto_max`, or `srto_min` indicates that the default value currently set should not be changed. All time values are expressed in milliseconds. We provide guidance on setting these timers for performance in Section 23.11.

`SCTP_SET_PEER_PRIMARY_ADDR` **Socket Option**

Setting this option causes a message to be sent that requests that the peer set the specified local address as its primary address. The caller provides an `sctp_setpeerprim` structure and must fill in both the association identification and a local address to request the peer mark as its primary. The address provided must be one of the local endpoint's bound addresses. The `sctp_setpeerprim` structure is defined as follows:

```
struct sctp_setpeerprim {
  sctp_assoc_t            sspp_assoc_id;
  struct sockaddr_storage sspp_addr;
};
```

These fields are defined as follows:

- `sspp_assoc_id` specifies the association identification on which the requester wishes to set the primary address. For the one-to-one style, this field is ignored.

- `sspp_addr` holds the local address that the requester wishes to ask the peer system to set as the primary address.

This feature is optional, and must be supported by both endpoints to operate. If the local endpoint does not support the feature, an error of `EOPNOTSUPP` will be returned to the caller. If the remote endpoint does not support the feature, an error of `EINVAL` will be returned to the caller. Note that this value may only be set and cannot be retrieved.

`SCTP_STATUS` Socket Option

This socket option will retrieve the current state of an SCTP association. The caller should use `sctp_opt_info` instead of `getaddrinfo` for maximum portability. The caller provides an `sctp_status` structure, filling in the association identification field, `sstat_assoc_id`. The structure will be returned filled in with the information pertaining to the requested association. The `sctp_status` structure has the following format:

```
struct sctp_status {
  sctp_assoc_t sstat_assoc_id;
  int32_t sstat_state;
  u_int32_t sstat_rwnd;
  u_int16_t sstat_unackdata;
  u_int16_t sstat_penddata;
  u_int16_t sstat_instrms;
  u_int16_t sstat_outstrms;
  u_int32_t sstat_fragmentation_point;
  struct sctp_paddrinfo sstat_primary;
};
```

These fields are defined as follows:

- `sstat_assoc_id` holds the association identification.
- `sstat_state` holds one of the values found in Figure 7.19 and indicates the overall state of the association. A detailed depiction of the states an SCTP endpoint goes through during association setup or shutdown can be found in Figure 2.8.
- `sstat_rwnd` holds our endpoint's current estimate of the peer's receive window.
- `sstat_unackdata` holds the number of unacknowledged DATA chunks pending for the peer.
- `sstat_penddata` holds the number of unread DATA chunks that the local endpoint is holding for the application to read.
- `sstat_instrms` holds the number of streams the peer is using to send data to this endpoint.

- sstat_outstrms holds the number of allowable streams that this endpoint can use to send data to the peer.

- sstat_fragmentation_point contains the current value the local SCTP endpoint is using as the fragmentation point for user messages. This value is normally the smallest MTU of all destinations, or possibly a smaller value set by the local application with SCTP_MAXSEG.

- sstat_primary holds the current primary address. The primary address is the default address used when sending data to the peer endpoint.

These values are useful for diagnostics and for determining the characteristics of the session; for example, the sctp_get_no_strms function in Section 10.2 will use the sstat_outstrms member to determine how many streams are available for outbound use. A low sstat_rwnd and/or a high sstat_unackdata value can be used to determine that the peer's receive socket buffer is becoming full, which can be used as a cue to the application to slow down transmission if possible. The sstat_fragmentation_point can be used by some applications to reduce the number of fragments that SCTP has to create, by sending smaller application messages.

Constant	Description
SCTP_CLOSED	A closed association
SCTP_COOKIE_WAIT	An association that has sent an INIT
SCTP_COOKIE_ECHOED	An association that has echoed the COOKIE
SCTP_ESTABLISHED	An established association
SCTP_SHUTDOWN_PENDING	An association pending sending the shutdown
SCTP_SHUTDOWN_SENT	An association that has sent a shutdown
SCTP_SHUTDOWN_RECEIVED	An association that has received a shutdown
SCTP_SHUTDOWN_ACK_SENT	An association that is waiting for a SHUTDOWN-COMPLETE

Figure 7.19 SCTP states.

7.11 fcntl Function

fcntl stands for "file control" and this function performs various descriptor control operations. Before describing the function and how it affects a socket, we need to look at the bigger picture. Figure 7.20 summarizes the different operations performed by fcntl, ioctl, and routing sockets.

Operation	fcntl	ioctl	Routing socket	POSIX
Set socket for nonblocking I/O	F_SETFL, O_NONBLOCK	FIONBIO		fcntl
Set socket for signal-driven I/O	F_SETFL, O_ASYNC	FIOASYNC		fcntl
Set socket owner	F_SETOWN	SIOCSPGRP or FIOSETOWN		fcntl
Get socket owner	F_GETOWN	SIOCGPGRP or FIOGETOWN		fcntl
Get # bytes in socket receive buffer		FIONREAD		
Test for socket at out-of-band mark		SIOCATMARK		sockatmark
Obtain interface list		SIOCGIFCONF	sysctl	
Interface operations		SIOC[GS]IF*xxx*		
ARP cache operations		SIOC*x*ARP	RTM_*xxx*	
Routing table operations		SIOC*xxx*RT	RTM_*xxx*	

Figure 7.20 Summary of fcntl, ioctl, and routing socket operations.

The first six operations can be applied to sockets by any process; the second two (interface operations) are less common, but are still general-purpose; and the last two (ARP and routing table) are issued by administrative programs such as ifconfig and route. We will talk more about the various ioctl operations in Chapter 17 and routing sockets in Chapter 18.

There are multiple ways to perform the first four operations, but we note in the final column that POSIX specifies that fcntl is the preferred way. We also note that POSIX provides the sockatmark function (Section 24.3) as the preferred way to test for the out-of-band mark. The remaining operations, with a blank final column, have not been standardized by POSIX.

> We also note that the first two operations, setting a socket for nonblocking I/O and for signal-driven I/O, have been set historically using the FNDELAY and FASYNC commands with fcntl. POSIX defines the O_*xxx* constants.

The fcntl function provides the following features related to network programming:

- Nonblocking I/O—We can set the O_NONBLOCK file status flag using the F_SETFL command to set a socket as nonblocking. We will describe nonblocking I/O in Chapter 16.

- Signal-driven I/O—We can set the O_ASYNC file status flag using the F_SETFL command, which causes the SIGIO signal to be generated when the status of a socket changes. We will discuss this in Chapter 25.

- The F_SETOWN command lets us set the socket owner (the process ID or process group ID) to receive the SIGIO and SIGURG signals. The former signal is generated when signal-driven I/O is enabled for a socket (Chapter 25) and the latter signal is generated when new out-of-band data arrives for a socket

(Chapter 24). The F_GETOWN command returns the current owner of the socket.

> The term "socket owner" is defined by POSIX. Historically, Berkeley-derived implementations have called this "the process group ID of the socket" because the variable that stores this ID is the so_pgid member of the socket structure (p. 438 of TCPv2).

```
#include <fcntl.h>

int fcntl(int fd, int cmd, ... /* int arg */ );
```
                                  Returns: depends on *cmd* if OK, −1 on error

Each descriptor (including a socket) has a set of file flags that is fetched with the F_GETFL command and set with the F_SETFL command. The two flags that affect a socket are

O_NONBLOCK—nonblocking I/O
O_ASYNC—signal-driven I/O

We will describe both of these features in more detail later. For now, we note that typical code to enable nonblocking I/O, using fcntl, would be:

```
int     flags;

    /* Set a socket as nonblocking */
if ( (flags = fcntl(fd, F_GETFL, 0)) < 0)
    err_sys("F_GETFL error");
flags |= O_NONBLOCK;
if (fcntl(fd, F_SETFL, flags) < 0)
    err_sys("F_SETFL error");
```

Beware of code that you may encounter that simply sets the desired flag.

```
    /* Wrong way to set a socket as nonblocking */
if (fcntl(fd, F_SETFL, O_NONBLOCK) < 0)
    err_sys("F_SETFL error");
```

While this sets the nonblocking flag, it also clears all the other file status flags. The only correct way to set one of the file status flags is to fetch the current flags, logically OR in the new flag, and then set the flags.

The following code turns off the nonblocking flag, assuming flags was set by the call to fcntl shown above:

```
flags &= ~O_NONBLOCK;
if (fcntl(fd, F_SETFL, flags) < 0)
    err_sys("F_SETFL error");
```

The two signals SIGIO and SIGURG are different from other signals in that they are generated for a socket only if the socket has been assigned an owner with the F_SETOWN command. The integer *arg* value for the F_SETOWN command can be either a positive integer, specifying the process ID to receive the signal, or a negative integer whose absolute value is the process group ID to receive the signal. The

F_GETOWN command returns the socket owner as the return value from the `fcntl` function, either the process ID (a positive return value) or the process group ID (a negative value other than –1). The difference between specifying a process or a process group to receive the signal is that the former causes only a single process to receive the signal, while the latter causes all processes in the process group (perhaps more than one) to receive the signal.

When a new socket is created by `socket`, it has no owner. But when a new socket is created from a listening socket, the socket owner is inherited from the listening socket by the connected socket (as are many socket options [pp. 462–463 of TCPv2]).

7.12 Summary

Socket options run the gamut from the very general (`SO_ERROR`) to the very specific (IP header options). The most commonly used options that we might encounter are `SO_KEEPALIVE`, `SO_RCVBUF`, `SO_SNDBUF`, and `SO_REUSEADDR`. The latter should always be set for a TCP server before it calls `bind` (Figure 11.12). The `SO_BROADCAST` option and the 10 multicast socket options are only for applications that broadcast or multicast, respectively.

The `SO_KEEPALIVE` socket option is set by many TCP servers and automatically terminates a half-open connection. The nice feature of this option is that it is handled by the TCP layer, without requiring an application-level inactivity timer; its downside is that it cannot tell the difference between a crashed client host and a temporary loss of connectivity to the client. SCTP provides 17 socket options that are used by the application to control the transport. `SCTP_NODELAY` and `SCTP_MAXSEG` are similar to `TCP_NODELAY` and `TCP_MAXSEG` and perform equivalent functions. The other 15 options give the application finer control of the SCTP stack; we will discuss the use of many of these socket options in Chapter 23.

The `SO_LINGER` socket option gives us more control over when `close` returns and also lets us force an RST to be sent instead of TCP's four-packet connection termination sequence. We must be careful sending RSTs, because this avoids TCP's TIME_WAIT state. Much of the time, this socket option does not provide the information that we need, in which case, an application-level ACK is required.

Every TCP and SCTP socket has a send buffer and a receive buffer, and every UDP socket has a receive buffer. The `SO_SNDBUF` and `SO_RCVBUF` socket options let us change the sizes of these buffers. The most common use of these options is for bulk data transfer across long fat pipes: TCP connections with either a high bandwidth or a long delay, often using the RFC 1323 extensions. UDP sockets, on the other hand, might want to increase the size of the receive buffer to allow the kernel to queue more datagrams if the application is busy.

Exercises

7.1   Write a program that prints the default TCP, UDP, and SCTP send and receive buffer sizes and run it on the systems to which you have access.

7.2   Modify Figure 1.5 as follows: Before calling `connect`, call `getsockopt` to obtain the socket receive buffer size and MSS. Print both values. After `connect` returns success, fetch these same two socket options and print their values. Have the values changed? Why? Run the program connecting to a server on your local network and also run the program connecting to a server on a remote network. Does the MSS change? Why? You should also run the program on any different hosts to which you have access.

7.3   Start with our TCP server from Figures 5.2 and 5.3 and our TCP client from Figures 5.4 and 5.5. Modify the client `main` function to set the `SO_LINGER` socket option before calling `exit`, setting `l_onoff` to 1 and `l_linger` to 0. Start the server and then start the client. Type in a line or two at the client to verify the operation, and then terminate the client by entering your EOF character. What happens? After you terminate the client, run `netstat` on the client host and see if the socket goes through the TIME_WAIT state.

7.4   Assume two TCP clients start at about the same time. Both set the `SO_REUSEADDR` socket option and then call `bind` with the same local IP address and the same local port (say 1500). But, one client `connects` to 198.69.10.2 port 7000 and the second `connects` to 198.69.10.2 (same peer IP address) but port 8000. Describe the race condition that occurs.

7.5   Obtain the source code for the examples in this book (see the Preface) and compile the `sock` program (Section C.3). First, classify your host as (a) no multicast support, (b) multicast support but `SO_REUSEPORT` not provided, or (c) multicast support and `SO_REUSEPORT` provided. Try to start multiple instances of the `sock` program as a TCP server (`-s` command-line option) on the same port, binding the wildcard address, one of your host's interface addresses, and the loopback address. Do you need to specify the `SO_REUSEADDR` option (the `-A` command-line option)? Use `netstat` to see the listening sockets.

7.6   Continue the previous example, but start a UDP server (`-u` command-line option) and try to start two instances, both binding the same local IP address and port. If your implementation supports `SO_REUSEPORT`, try using it (`-T` command-line option).

7.7   Many versions of the `ping` program have a `-d` flag to enable the `SO_DEBUG` socket option. What does this do?

7.8   Continuing the example at the end of our discussion of the `TCP_NODELAY` socket option, assume that a client performs two `writes`: the first of 4 bytes and the second of 396 bytes. Also assume that the server's delayed ACK time is 100 ms, the RTT between the client and server is 100 ms, and the server's processing time for the client's request is 50 ms. Draw a timeline that shows the interaction of the Nagle algorithm with delayed ACKs.

7.9   Redo the previous exercise, assuming the `TCP_NODELAY` socket option is set.

7.10 Redo Exercise 7.8 assuming the process calls `writev` one time, for both the 4-byte buffer and the 396-byte buffer.

7.11 Read RFC 1122 [Braden 1989] to determine the recommended interval for delayed ACKs.

7.12 Where does our server in Figures 5.2 and 5.3 spend most of its time? Assume the server sets the SO_KEEPALIVE socket option, there is no data being exchanged across the connection, and the client host crashes and does not reboot. What happens?

7.13 Where does our client in Figures 5.4 and 5.5 spend most of its time? Assume the client sets the SO_KEEPALIVE socket option, there is no data being exchanged across the connection, and the server host crashes and does not reboot. What happens?

7.14 Where does our client in Figures 5.4 and 6.13 spend most of its time? Assume the client sets the SO_KEEPALIVE socket option, there is no data being exchanged across the connection, and the server host crashes and does not reboot. What happens?

7.15 Assume both a client and server set the SO_KEEPALIVE socket option. Connectivity is maintained between the two peers, but there is no application data exchanged across the connection. When the keep-alive timer expires every two hours, how many TCP segments are exchanged across the connection?

7.16 Almost all implementations define the constant SO_ACCEPTCONN in the <sys/socket.h> header, but we have not described this option. Read [Lanciani 1996] to find out why this option exists.

8

Elementary UDP Sockets

8.1   Introduction

There are some fundamental differences between applications written using TCP versus those that use UDP. These are because of the differences in the two transport layers: UDP is a connectionless, unreliable, datagram protocol, quite unlike the connection-oriented, reliable byte stream provided by TCP. Nevertheless, there are instances when it makes sense to use UDP instead of TCP, and we will go over this design choice in Section 22.4. Some popular applications are built using UDP: DNS, NFS, and SNMP, for example.

Figure 8.1 shows the function calls for a typical UDP client/server. The client does not establish a connection with the server. Instead, the client just sends a datagram to the server using the `sendto` function (described in the next section), which requires the address of the destination (the server) as a parameter. Similarly, the server does not accept a connection from a client. Instead, the server just calls the `recvfrom` function, which waits until data arrives from some client. `recvfrom` returns the protocol address of the client, along with the datagram, so the server can send a response to the correct client.

Figure 8.1 shows a timeline of the typical scenario that takes place for a UDP client/server exchange. We can compare this to the typical TCP exchange that was shown in Figure 4.1.

In this chapter, we will describe the new functions that we use with UDP sockets, `recvfrom` and `sendto`, and redo our echo client/server to use UDP. We will also describe the use of the `connect` function with a UDP socket, and the concept of asynchronous errors.

239

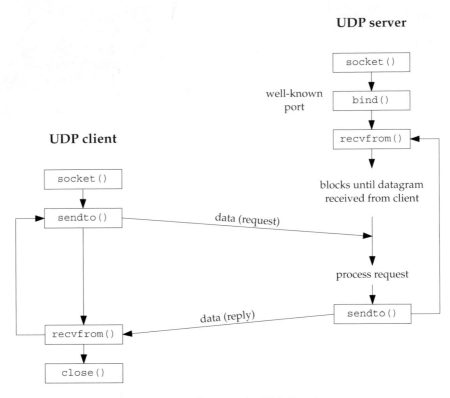

Figure 8.1 Socket functions for UDP client/server.

8.2   `recvfrom` and `sendto` Functions

These two functions are similar to the standard `read` and `write` functions, but three additional arguments are required.

```
#include <sys/socket.h>

ssize_t recvfrom(int sockfd, void *buff, size_t nbytes, int flags,
                 struct sockaddr *from, socklen_t *addrlen);

ssize_t sendto(int sockfd, const void *buff, size_t nbytes, int flags,
               const struct sockaddr *to, socklen_t addrlen);

                            Both return: number of bytes read or written if OK, −1 on error
```

The first three arguments, *sockfd*, *buff*, and *nbytes*, are identical to the first three arguments for `read` and `write`: descriptor, pointer to buffer to read into or write from, and number of bytes to read or write.

We will describe the *flags* argument in Chapter 14 when we discuss the `recv`, `send`, `recvmsg`, and `sendmsg` functions, since we do not need them with our simple UDP client/server example in this chapter. For now, we will always set the *flags* to 0.

The *to* argument for `sendto` is a socket address structure containing the protocol address (e.g., IP address and port number) of where the data is to be sent. The size of this socket address structure is specified by *addrlen*. The `recvfrom` function fills in the socket address structure pointed to by *from* with the protocol address of who sent the datagram. The number of bytes stored in this socket address structure is also returned to the caller in the integer pointed to by *addrlen*. Note that the final argument to `sendto` is an integer value, while the final argument to `recvfrom` is a pointer to an integer value (a value-result argument).

The final two arguments to `recvfrom` are similar to the final two arguments to `accept`: The contents of the socket address structure upon return tell us who sent the datagram (in the case of UDP) or who initiated the connection (in the case of TCP). The final two arguments to `sendto` are similar to the final two arguments to `connect`: We fill in the socket address structure with the protocol address of where to send the datagram (in the case of UDP) or with whom to establish a connection (in the case of TCP).

Both functions return the length of the data that was read or written as the value of the function. In the typical use of `recvfrom`, with a datagram protocol, the return value is the amount of user data in the datagram received.

Writing a datagram of length 0 is acceptable. In the case of UDP, this results in an IP datagram containing an IP header (normally 20 bytes for IPv4 and 40 bytes for IPv6), an 8-byte UDP header, and no data. This also means that a return value of 0 from `recvfrom` is acceptable for a datagram protocol: It does not mean that the peer has closed the connection, as does a return value of 0 from `read` on a TCP socket. Since UDP is connectionless, there is no such thing as closing a UDP connection.

If the *from* argument to `recvfrom` is a null pointer, then the corresponding length argument (*addrlen*) must also be a null pointer, and this indicates that we are not interested in knowing the protocol address of who sent us data.

Both `recvfrom` and `sendto` can be used with TCP, although there is normally no reason to do so.

8.3 UDP Echo Server: `main` Function

We will now redo our simple echo client/server from Chapter 5 using UDP. Our UDP client and server programs follow the function call flow that we diagrammed in Figure 8.1. Figure 8.2 depicts the functions that are used. Figure 8.3 shows the server `main` function.

Figure 8.2 Simple echo client/server using UDP.

—— *udpcliserv/udpserv01.c*

```
 1 #include    "unp.h"

 2 int
 3 main(int argc, char **argv)
 4 {
 5     int     sockfd;
 6     struct sockaddr_in servaddr, cliaddr;

 7     sockfd = Socket(AF_INET, SOCK_DGRAM, 0);

 8     bzero(&servaddr, sizeof(servaddr));
 9     servaddr.sin_family = AF_INET;
10     servaddr.sin_addr.s_addr = htonl(INADDR_ANY);
11     servaddr.sin_port = htons(SERV_PORT);

12     Bind(sockfd, (SA *) &servaddr, sizeof(servaddr));

13     dg_echo(sockfd, (SA *) &cliaddr, sizeof(cliaddr));
14 }
```
—— *udpcliserv/udpserv01.c*

Figure 8.3   UDP echo server.

Create UDP socket, bind server's well-known port

7–12   We create a UDP socket by specifying the second argument to socket as SOCK_DGRAM (a datagram socket in the IPv4 protocol). As with the TCP server example, the IPv4 address for the bind is specified as INADDR_ANY and the server's well-known port is the constant SERV_PORT from the unp.h header.

13   The function dg_echo is called to perform server processing.

8.4   UDP Echo Server: dg_echo Function

Figure 8.4 shows the dg_echo function.

—— *lib/dg_echo.c*

```
 1 #include    "unp.h"

 2 void
 3 dg_echo(int sockfd, SA *pcliaddr, socklen_t clilen)
 4 {
 5     int     n;
 6     socklen_t len;
 7     char    mesg[MAXLINE];

 8     for ( ; ; ) {
 9         len = clilen;
10         n = Recvfrom(sockfd, mesg, MAXLINE, 0, pcliaddr, &len);

11         Sendto(sockfd, mesg, n, 0, pcliaddr, len);
12     }
13 }
```
—— *lib/dg_echo.c*

Figure 8.4   dg_echo function: echo lines on a datagram socket.

Read datagram, echo back to sender

8–12   This function is a simple loop that reads the next datagram arriving at the server's port using `recvfrom` and sends it back using `sendto`.

Despite the simplicity of this function, there are numerous details to consider. First, this function never terminates. Since UDP is a connectionless protocol, there is nothing like an EOF as we have with TCP.

Next, this function provides an *iterative server*, not a concurrent server as we had with TCP. There is no call to `fork`, so a single server process handles any and all clients. In general, most TCP servers are concurrent and most UDP servers are iterative.

There is implied queuing taking place in the UDP layer for this socket. Indeed, each UDP socket has a receive buffer and each datagram that arrives for this socket is placed in that socket receive buffer. When the process calls `recvfrom`, the next datagram from the buffer is returned to the process in a first-in, first-out (FIFO) order. This way, if multiple datagrams arrive for the socket before the process can read what's already queued for the socket, the arriving datagrams are just added to the socket receive buffer. But, this buffer has a limited size. We discussed this size and how to increase it with the `SO_RCVBUF` socket option in Section 7.5.

Figure 8.5 summarizes our TCP client/server from Chapter 5 when two clients establish connections with the server.

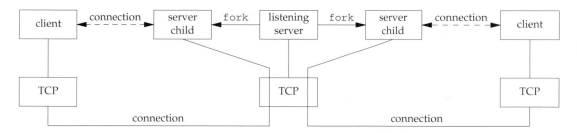

Figure 8.5 Summary of TCP client/server with two clients.

There are two connected sockets and each of the two connected sockets on the server host has its own socket receive buffer.

Figure 8.6 shows the scenario when two clients send datagrams to our UDP server.

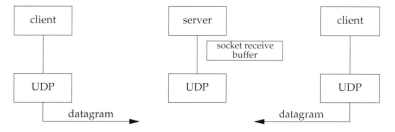

Figure 8.6 Summary of UDP client/server with two clients.

There is only one server process and it has a single socket on which it receives all arriving datagrams and sends all responses. That socket has a receive buffer into which all arriving datagrams are placed.

The main function in Figure 8.3 is *protocol-dependent* (it creates a socket of protocol AF_INET and allocates and initializes an IPv4 socket address structure), but the dg_echo function is *protocol-independent*. The reason dg_echo is protocol-independent is because the caller (the main function in our case) must allocate a socket address structure of the correct size, and a pointer to this structure, along with its size, are passed as arguments to dg_echo. The function dg_echo never looks inside this protocol-dependent structure: It simply passes a pointer to the structure to recvfrom and sendto. recvfrom fills this structure with the IP address and port number of the client, and since the same pointer (pcliaddr) is then passed to sendto as the destination address, this is how the datagram is echoed back to the client that sent the datagram.

8.5   UDP Echo Client: `main` Function

The UDP client main function is shown in Figure 8.7.

udpcliserv/udpcli01.c

```
1 #include     "unp.h"

2 int
3 main(int argc, char **argv)
4 {
5      int       sockfd;
6      struct sockaddr_in servaddr;

7      if (argc != 2)
8          err_quit("usage: udpcli <IPaddress>");

9      bzero(&servaddr, sizeof(servaddr));
10     servaddr.sin_family = AF_INET;
11     servaddr.sin_port = htons(SERV_PORT);
12     Inet_pton(AF_INET, argv[1], &servaddr.sin_addr);

13     sockfd = Socket(AF_INET, SOCK_DGRAM, 0);

14     dg_cli(stdin, sockfd, (SA *) &servaddr, sizeof(servaddr));

15     exit(0);
16 }
```

udpcliserv/udpcli01.c

Figure 8.7   UDP echo client.

Fill in socket address structure with server's address

9–12   An IPv4 socket address structure is filled in with the IP address and port number of the server. This structure will be passed to dg_cli, specifying where to send datagrams.

13–14   A UDP socket is created and the function dg_cli is called.

8.6 UDP Echo Client: `dg_cli` Function

Figure 8.8 shows the function `dg_cli`, which performs most of the client processing.

——— *lib/dg_cli.c*

```
1 #include     "unp.h"

2 void
3 dg_cli(FILE *fp, int sockfd, const SA *pservaddr, socklen_t servlen)
4 {
5     int     n;
6     char    sendline[MAXLINE], recvline[MAXLINE + 1];

7     while (Fgets(sendline, MAXLINE, fp) != NULL) {

8         Sendto(sockfd, sendline, strlen(sendline), 0, pservaddr, servlen);

9         n = Recvfrom(sockfd, recvline, MAXLINE, 0, NULL, NULL);

10        recvline[n] = 0;           /* null terminate */
11        Fputs(recvline, stdout);
12    }
13 }
```

——— *lib/dg_cli.c*

Figure 8.8 `dg_cli` function: client processing loop.

7–12   There are four steps in the client processing loop: read a line from standard input using `fgets`, send the line to the server using `sendto`, read back the server's echo using `recvfrom`, and print the echoed line to standard output using `fputs`.

Our client has not asked the kernel to assign an ephemeral port to its socket. (With a TCP client, we said the call to `connect` is where this takes place.) With a UDP socket, the first time the process calls `sendto`, if the socket has not yet had a local port bound to it, that is when an ephemeral port is chosen by the kernel for the socket. As with TCP, the client can call `bind` explicitly, but this is rarely done.

Notice that the call to `recvfrom` specifies a null pointer as the fifth and sixth arguments. This tells the kernel that we are not interested in knowing who sent the reply. There is a risk that any process, on either the same host or some other host, can send a datagram to the client's IP address and port, and that datagram will be read by the client, who will think it is the server's reply. We will address this in Section 8.8.

As with the server function `dg_echo`, the client function `dg_cli` is protocol-independent, but the client `main` function is protocol-dependent. The `main` function allocates and initializes a socket address structure of some protocol type and then passes a pointer to this structure, along with its size, to `dg_cli`.

8.7 Lost Datagrams

Our UDP client/server example is not reliable. If a client datagram is lost (say it is discarded by some router between the client and server), the client will block forever in its call to `recvfrom` in the function `dg_cli`, waiting for a server reply that will never arrive. Similarly, if the client datagram arrives at the server but the server's reply is lost, the client will again block forever in its call to `recvfrom`. A typical way to prevent this is to place a timeout on the client's call to `recvfrom`. We will discuss this in Section 14.2.

Just placing a timeout on the `recvfrom` is not the entire solution. For example, if we do time out, we cannot tell whether our datagram never made it to the server, or if the server's reply never made it back. If the client's request was something like "transfer a certain amount of money from account A to account B" (instead of our simple echo server), it would make a big difference as to whether the request was lost or the reply was lost. We will talk more about adding reliability to a UDP client/server in Section 22.5.

8.8 Verifying Received Response

At the end of Section 8.6, we mentioned that any process that knows the client's ephemeral port number could send datagrams to our client, and these would be intermixed with the normal server replies. What we can do is change the call to `recvfrom` in Figure 8.8 to return the IP address and port of who sent the reply and ignore any received datagrams that are not from the server to whom we sent the datagram. There are a few pitfalls with this, however, as we will see.

First, we change the client `main` function (Figure 8.7) to use the standard echo server (Figure 2.18). We just replace the assignment

```
servaddr.sin_port = htons(SERV_PORT);
```

with

```
servaddr.sin_port = htons(7);
```

We do this so we can use any host running the standard echo server with our client.

We then recode the `dg_cli` function to allocate another socket address structure to hold the structure returned by `recvfrom`. We show this in Figure 8.9.

Allocate another socket address structure

9   We allocate another socket address structure by calling `malloc`. Notice that the `dg_cli` function is still protocol-independent; because we do not care what type of socket address structure we are dealing with, we use only its size in the call to `malloc`.

Compare returned address

12-18   In the call to `recvfrom`, we tell the kernel to return the address of the sender of the datagram. We first compare the length returned by `recvfrom` in the value-result argument and then compare the socket address structures themselves using `memcmp`.

> Section 3.2 says that even if the socket address structure contains a length field, we need never set it or examine it. However, `memcmp` compares every byte of data in the two socket address structures, and the length field is set in the socket address structure that the kernel returns; so in this case we must set it when constructing the `sockaddr`. If we don't, the `memcmp` will compare a *0* (since we didn't set it) with a *16* (assuming `sockaddr_in`) and will not match.

——————————————————————————————— udpcliserv/dgcliaddr.c

```
 1 #include    "unp.h"

 2 void
 3 dg_cli(FILE *fp, int sockfd, const SA *pservaddr, socklen_t servlen)
 4 {
 5     int     n;
 6     char    sendline[MAXLINE], recvline[MAXLINE + 1];
 7     socklen_t len;
 8     struct sockaddr *preply_addr;

 9     preply_addr = Malloc(servlen);

10     while (Fgets(sendline, MAXLINE, fp) != NULL) {

11         Sendto(sockfd, sendline, strlen(sendline), 0, pservaddr, servlen);

12         len = servlen;
13         n = Recvfrom(sockfd, recvline, MAXLINE, 0, preply_addr, &len);
14         if (len != servlen || memcmp(pservaddr, preply_addr, len) != 0) {
15             printf("reply from %s (ignored)\n", Sock_ntop(preply_addr, len));
16             continue;
17         }

18         recvline[n] = 0;          /* null terminate */
19         Fputs(recvline, stdout);
20     }
21 }
```

——————————————————————————————— udpcliserv/dgcliaddr.c

Figure 8.9 Version of `dg_cli` that verifies returned socket address.

This new version of our client works fine if the server is on a host with just a single IP address. But this program can fail if the server is multihomed. We run this program to our host `freebsd4`, which has two interfaces and two IP addresses.

```
macosx % host freebsd4
freebsd4.unpbook.com has address 172.24.37.94
freebsd4.unpbook.com has address 135.197.17.100
macosx % udpcli02 135.197.17.100
hello
reply from 172.24.37.94:7 (ignored)
goodbye
reply from 172.24.37.94:7 (ignored)
```

We specified the IP address that does not share the same subnet as the client.

> This is normally allowed. Most IP implementations accept an arriving IP datagram that is destined for *any* of the host's IP addresses, regardless of the interface on which the datagram arrives (pp. 217–219 of TCPv2). RFC 1122 [Braden 1989] calls this the *weak end system model*. If a system implemented what this RFC calls the *strong end system model*, it would accept an arriving datagram only if that datagram arrived on the interface to which it was addressed.

The IP address returned by `recvfrom` (the source IP address of the UDP datagram) is not the IP address to which we sent the datagram. When the server sends its reply, the destination IP address is 172.24.37.78. The routing function within the kernel on `freebsd4` chooses 172.24.37.94 as the outgoing interface. Since the server has not bound an IP address to its socket (the server has bound the wildcard address to its socket, which is something we can verify by running `netstat` on `freebsd`), the kernel chooses the source address for the IP datagram. It is chosen to be the primary IP address of the outgoing interface (pp. 232–233 of TCPv2). Also, since it is the primary IP address of the interface, if we send our datagram to a nonprimary IP address of the interface (i.e., an alias), this will also cause our test in Figure 8.9 to fail.

One solution is for the client to verify the responding host's domain name instead of its IP address by looking up the server's name in the DNS (Chapter 11), given the IP address returned by `recvfrom`. Another solution is for the UDP server to create one socket for every IP address that is configured on the host, `bind` that IP address to the socket, use `select` across all these sockets (waiting for any one to become readable), and then reply from the socket that is readable. Since the socket used for the reply was bound to the IP address that was the destination address of the client's request (or the datagram would not have been delivered to the socket), this guaranteed that the source address of the reply was the same as the destination address of the request. We will show an example of this in Section 22.6.

> On a multihomed Solaris system, the source IP address for the server's reply is the destination IP address of the client's request. The scenario described in this section is for Berkeley-derived implementations that choose the source IP address based on the outgoing interface.

8.9   Server Not Running

The next scenario to examine is starting the client without starting the server. If we do so and type in a single line to the client, nothing happens. The client blocks forever in its call to `recvfrom`, waiting for a server reply that will never appear. But, this is an example where we need to understand more about the underlying protocols to understand what is happening to our networking application.

First we start `tcpdump` on the host `macosx`, and then we start the client on the same host, specifying the host `freebsd4` as the server host. We then type a single line, but the line is not echoed.

```
macosx % udpcli01 172.24.37.94
hello, world                              we type this line
                                          but nothing is echoed back
```

Figure 8.10 shows the `tcpdump` output.

```
1  0.0                    arp who-has freebsd4 tell macosx
2  0.003576 ( 0.0036)     arp reply freebsd4 is-at 0:40:5:42:d6:de

3  0.003601 ( 0.0000)     macosx.51139 > freebsd4.9877: udp 13
4  0.009781 ( 0.0062)     freebsd4 > macosx: icmp: freebsd4 udp port 9877 unreachable
```

Figure 8.10 `tcpdump` output when server process not started on server host.

First we notice that an ARP request and reply are needed before the client host can send the UDP datagram to the server host. (We left this exchange in the output to reiterate the potential for an ARP request-reply before an IP datagram can be sent to another host or router on the local network.)

In line 3, we see the client datagram sent but the server host responds in line 4 with an ICMP "port unreachable." (The length of 13 accounts for the 12 characters and the newline.) This ICMP error, however, is not returned to the client process, for reasons that we will describe shortly. Instead, the client blocks forever in the call to `recvfrom` in Figure 8.8. We also note that ICMPv6 has a "port unreachable" error, similar to ICMPv4 (Figures A.15 and A.16), so the results described here are similar for IPv6.

We call this ICMP error an *asynchronous error*. The error was caused by `sendto`, but `sendto` returned successfully. Recall from Section 2.11 that a successful return from a UDP output operation only means there was room for the resulting IP datagram on the interface output queue. The ICMP error is not returned until later (4 ms later in Figure 8.10), which is why it is called asynchronous.

The basic rule is that an asynchronous error is not returned for a UDP socket unless the socket has been connected. We will describe how to call `connect` for a UDP socket in Section 8.11. Why this design decision was made when sockets were first implemented is rarely understood. (The implementation implications are discussed on pp. 748–749 of TCPv2.)

Consider a UDP client that sends three datagrams in a row to three different servers (i.e., three different IP addresses) on a single UDP socket. The client then enters a loop that calls `recvfrom` to read the replies. Two of the datagrams are correctly delivered (that is, the server was running on two of the three hosts) but the third host was not running the server. This third host responds with an ICMP port unreachable. This ICMP error message contains the IP header and UDP header of the datagram that caused the error. (ICMPv4 and ICMPv6 error messages always contain the IP header and all of the UDP header or part of the TCP header to allow the receiver of the ICMP error to determine which socket caused the error. We will show this in Figures 28.21 and 28.22.) The client that sent the three datagrams needs to know the destination of the datagram that caused the error to distinguish which of the three datagrams caused the error. But how can the kernel return this information to the process? The only piece of information that `recvfrom` can return is an `errno` value; `recvfrom` has no way of returning the destination IP address and destination UDP port number of the datagram in error. The decision was made, therefore, to return these asynchronous errors to the process only if the process connected the UDP socket to exactly one peer.

Linux returns most ICMP "destination unreachable" errors even for unconnected sockets, as long as the SO_BSDCOMPAT socket option is not enabled. All the ICMP "destination unreachable" errors from Figure A.15 are returned, except codes 0, 1, 4, 5, 11, and 12.

We return to this problem of asynchronous errors with UDP sockets in Section 28.7 and show an easy way to obtain these errors on unconnected sockets using a daemon of our own.

8.10 Summary of UDP Example

Figure 8.11 shows as bullets the four values that must be specified or chosen when the
client sends a UDP datagram.

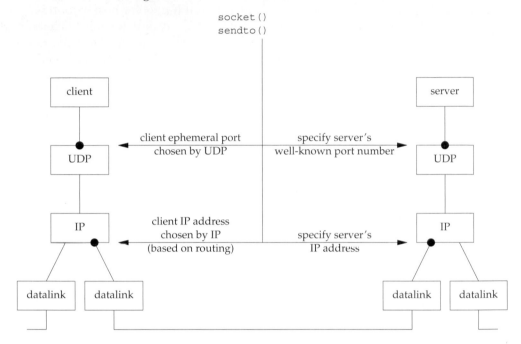

Figure 8.11 Summary of UDP client/server from client's perspective.

The client must specify the server's IP address and port number for the call to sendto.
Normally, the client's IP address and port are chosen automatically by the kernel,
although we mentioned that the client can call bind if it so chooses. If these two values
for the client are chosen by the kernel, we also mentioned that the client's ephemeral
port is chosen once, on the first sendto, and then it never changes. The client's IP
address, however, can change for every UDP datagram that the client sends, assuming
the client does not bind a specific IP address to the socket. The reason is shown in Figure 8.11: If the client host is multihomed, the client could alternate between two destinations, one going out the datalink on the left, and the other going out the datalink on the
right. In this worst-case scenario, the client's IP address, as chosen by the kernel based
on the outgoing datalink, would change for every datagram.

What happens if the client binds an IP address to its socket, but the kernel decides
that an outgoing datagram must be sent out some other datalink? In this case the IP
datagram will contain a source IP address that is different from the IP address of the
outgoing datalink (see Exercise 8.6).

Figure 8.12 shows the same four values, but from the server's perspective.

There are at least four pieces of information that a server might want to know from an arriving IP datagram: the source IP address, destination IP address, source port number, and destination port number. Figure 8.13 shows the function calls that return this information for a TCP server and a UDP server.

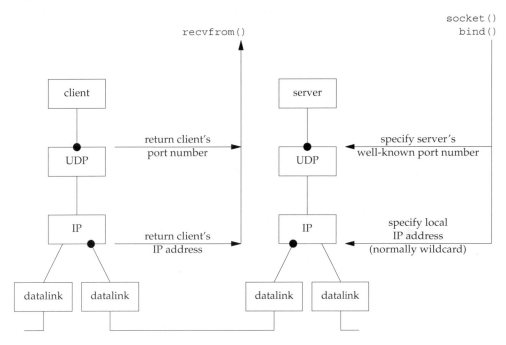

Figure 8.12 Summary of UDP client/server from server's perspective.

From client's IP datagram	TCP server	UDP server
Source IP address	`accept`	`recvfrom`
Source port number	`accept`	`recvfrom`
Destination IP address	`getsockname`	`recvmsg`
Destination port number	`getsockname`	`getsockname`

Figure 8.13 Information available to server from arriving IP datagram.

A TCP server always has easy access to all four pieces of information for a connected socket, and these four values remain constant for the lifetime of a connection. With a UDP socket, however, the destination IP address can only be obtained by setting the `IP_RECVDSTADDR` socket option for IPv4 or the `IPV6_PKTINFO` socket option for IPv6 and then calling `recvmsg` instead of `recvfrom`. Since UDP is connectionless, the destination IP address can change for each datagram that is sent to the server. A UDP server can also receive datagrams destined for one of the host's broadcast addresses or for a multicast address, as we will discuss in Chapters 20 and 21. We will show how to determine the destination address of a UDP datagram in Section 22.2, after we cover the `recvmsg` function.

8.11 `connect` **Function with UDP**

We mentioned at the end of Section 8.9 that an asynchronous error is not returned on a UDP socket unless the socket has been connected. Indeed, we are able to call `connect` (Section 4.3) for a UDP socket. But this does not result in anything like a TCP connection: There is no three-way handshake. Instead, the kernel just checks for any immediate errors (e.g., an obviously unreachable destination), records the IP address and port number of the peer (from the socket address structure passed to `connect`), and returns immediately to the calling process.

> Overloading the `connect` function with this capability for UDP sockets is confusing. If the convention that `sockname` is the local protocol address and `peername` is the foreign protocol address is used, then a better name would have been `setpeername`. Similarly, a better name for the `bind` function would be `setsockname`.

With this capability, we must now distinguish between

- An *unconnected UDP socket*, the default when we create a UDP socket
- A *connected UDP socket*, the result of calling `connect` on a UDP socket

With a connected UDP socket, three things change, compared to the default unconnected UDP socket:

1. We can no longer specify the destination IP address and port for an output operation. That is, we do not use `sendto`, but `write` or `send` instead. Anything written to a connected UDP socket is automatically sent to the protocol address (e.g., IP address and port) specified by `connect`.

   > Similar to TCP, we can call `sendto` for a connected UDP socket, but we cannot specify a destination address. The fifth argument to `sendto` (the pointer to the socket address structure) must be a null pointer, and the sixth argument (the size of the socket address structure) should be 0. The POSIX specification states that when the fifth argument is a null pointer, the sixth argument is ignored.

2. We do not need to use `recvfrom` to learn the sender of a datagram, but `read`, `recv`, or `recvmsg` instead. The only datagrams returned by the kernel for an input operation on a connected UDP socket are those arriving from the protocol address specified in `connect`. Datagrams destined to the connected UDP socket's local protocol address (e.g., IP address and port) but arriving from a protocol address other than the one to which the socket was connected are not passed to the connected socket. This limits a connected UDP socket to exchanging datagrams with one and only one peer.

   > Technically, a connected UDP socket exchanges datagrams with only one IP address, because it is possible to `connect` to a multicast or broadcast address.

3. Asynchronous errors are returned to the process for connected UDP sockets.

The corollary, as we previously described, is that unconnected UDP sockets do not receive asynchronous errors.

Figure 8.14 summarizes the first point in the list with respect to 4.4BSD.

Type of socket	write or send	sendto that does not specify a destination	sendto that specifies a destination
TCP socket	OK	OK	EISCONN
UDP socket, connected	OK	OK	EISCONN
UDP socket, unconnected	EDESTADDRREQ	EDESTADDRREQ	OK

Figure 8.14 TCP and UDP sockets: can a destination protocol address be specified?

The POSIX specification states that an output operation that does not specify a destination address on an unconnected UDP socket should return ENOTCONN, not EDESTADDRREQ.

Figure 8.15 summarizes the three points that we made about a connected UDP socket.

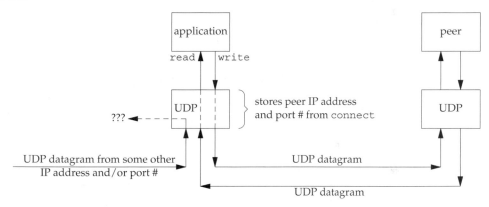

Figure 8.15 Connected UDP socket.

The application calls connect, specifying the IP address and port number of its peer. It then uses read and write to exchange data with the peer.

Datagrams arriving from any other IP address or port (which we show as "???" in Figure 8.15) are not passed to the connected socket because either the source IP address or source UDP port does not match the protocol address to which the socket is connected. These datagrams could be delivered to some other UDP socket on the host. If there is no other matching socket for the arriving datagram, UDP will discard it and generate an ICMP "port unreachable" error.

In summary, we can say that a UDP client or server can call connect only if that process uses the UDP socket to communicate with exactly one peer. Normally, it is a UDP client that calls connect, but there are applications in which the UDP server communicates with a single client for a long duration (e.g., TFTP); in this case, both the client and server can call connect.

The DNS provides another example, as shown in Figure 8.16.

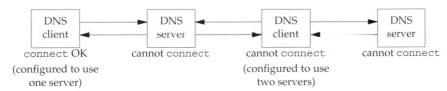

Figure 8.16 Example of DNS clients and servers and the `connect` function.

A DNS client can be configured to use one or more servers, normally by listing the IP addresses of the servers in the file /etc/resolv.conf. If a single server is listed (the leftmost box in the figure), the client can call `connect`, but if multiple servers are listed (the second box from the right in the figure), the client cannot call `connect`. Also, a DNS server normally handles any client request, so the servers cannot call `connect`.

Calling `connect` Multiple Times for a UDP Socket

A process with a connected UDP socket can call `connect` again for that socket for one of two reasons:

- To specify a new IP address and port
- To unconnect the socket

The first case, specifying a new peer for a connected UDP socket, differs from the use of `connect` with a TCP socket: `connect` can be called only one time for a TCP socket.

To unconnect a UDP socket, we call `connect` but set the family member of the socket address structure (`sin_family` for IPv4 or `sin6_family` for IPv6) to AF_UNSPEC. This might return an error of EAFNOSUPPORT (p. 736 of TCPv2), but that is acceptable. It is the process of calling `connect` on an already connected UDP socket that causes the socket to become unconnected (pp. 787–788 of TCPv2).

> The Unix variants seem to differ on exactly how to unconnect a socket, and you may encounter approaches that work on some systems and not others. For example, calling `connect` with NULL for the address works only on some systems (and on some, it only works if the third argument, the length, is nonzero). The POSIX specification and BSD man pages are not much help here, only mentioning that a *null address* should be used and not mentioning the error return (even on success) at all. The most portable solution is to zero out an address structure, set the family to AF_UNSPEC as mentioned above, and pass it to `connect`.
>
> Another area of disagreement is around the local binding of a socket during the unconnect process. AIX keeps both the chosen local IP address and the port, even from an implicit bind. FreeBSD and Linux set the local IP address back to all zeros, even if you previously called bind, but leave the port number intact. Solaris sets the local IP address back to all zeros if it was assigned by an implicit bind; but if the program called bind explicitly, then the IP address remains unchanged.

Performance

When an application calls `sendto` on an unconnected UDP socket, Berkeley-derived kernels temporarily connect the socket, send the datagram, and then unconnect the socket (pp. 762–763 of TCPv2). Calling `sendto` for two datagrams on an unconnected UDP socket then involves the following six steps by the kernel:

- Connect the socket
- Output the first datagram
- Unconnect the socket
- Connect the socket
- Output the second datagram
- Unconnect the socket

> Another consideration is the number of searches of the routing table. The first temporary connect searches the routing table for the destination IP address and saves (caches) that information. The second temporary connect notices that the destination address equals the destination of the cached routing table information (we are assuming two `sendto`s to the same destination) and we do not need to search the routing table again (pp. 737–738 of TCPv2).

When the application knows it will be sending multiple datagrams to the same peer, it is more efficient to connect the socket explicitly. Calling `connect` and then calling `write` two times involves the following steps by the kernel:

- Connect the socket
- Output first datagram
- Output second datagram

In this case, the kernel copies only the socket address structure containing the destination IP address and port one time, versus two times when `sendto` is called twice. [Partridge and Pink 1993] note that the temporary connecting of an unconnected UDP socket accounts for nearly one-third of the cost of each UDP transmission.

8.12   `dg_cli` **Function (Revisited)**

We now return to the `dg_cli` function from Figure 8.8 and recode it to call `connect`.
Figure 8.17 shows the new function.

—————————————————————————————————————— *udpcliserv/dgcliconnect.c*

```
 1 #include     "unp.h"

 2 void
 3 dg_cli(FILE *fp, int sockfd, const SA *pservaddr, socklen_t servlen)
 4 {
 5     int    n;
 6     char   sendline[MAXLINE], recvline[MAXLINE + 1];

 7     Connect(sockfd, (SA *) pservaddr, servlen);

 8     while (Fgets(sendline, MAXLINE, fp) != NULL) {

 9         Write(sockfd, sendline, strlen(sendline));

10         n = Read(sockfd, recvline, MAXLINE);

11         recvline[n] = 0;          /* null terminate */
12         Fputs(recvline, stdout);
13     }
14 }
```

—————————————————————————————————————— *udpcliserv/dgcliconnect.c*

Figure 8.17 `dg_cli` function that calls `connect`.

The changes are the new call to `connect` and replacing the calls to `sendto` and
`recvfrom` with calls to `write` and `read`. This function is still protocol-independent
since it doesn't look inside the socket address structure that is passed to `connect`. Our
client `main` function, Figure 8.7, remains the same.

If we run this program on the host `macosx`, specifying the IP address of the host
`freebsd4` (which is not running our server on port 9877), we have the following
output:

```
macosx % udpcli04 172.24.37.94
hello, world
read error: Connection refused
```

The first point we notice is that we do *not* receive the error when we start the client process. The error occurs only after we send the first datagram to the server. It is sending
this datagram that elicits the ICMP error from the server host. But when a TCP client
calls `connect`, specifying a server host that is not running the server process, `connect`
returns the error because the call to `connect` causes the TCP three-way handshake to
happen, and the first packet of that handshake elicits an RST from the server TCP (Section 4.3).

Figure 8.18 shows the `tcpdump` output.

```
macosx % tcpdump
1  0.0                            macosx.51139 > freebsd4.9877: udp 13
2  0.006180 ( 0.0062)     freebsd4 > macosx: icmp: freebsd4 udp port 9877 unreachable
```

Figure 8.18 `tcpdump` output when running Figure 8.17.

We also see in Figure A.15 that this ICMP error is mapped by the kernel into the error
ECONNREFUSED, which corresponds to the message string output by our `err_sys`
function: "Connection refused."

> Unfortunately, not all kernels return ICMP messages to a connected UDP socket, as we have
> shown in this section. Normally, Berkeley-derived kernels return the error, while System V
> kernels do not. For example, if we run the same client on a Solaris 2.4 host and `connect` to a
> host that is not running our server, we can watch with `tcpdump` and verify that the ICMP
> "port unreachable" error is returned by the server host, but the client's call to `read` never
> returns. This bug was fixed in Solaris 2.5. UnixWare does not return the error, while AIX, Dig-
> ital Unix, HP-UX, and Linux all return the error.

8.13 Lack of Flow Control with UDP

We now examine the effect of UDP not having any flow control. First, we modify our
`dg_cli` function to send a fixed number of datagrams. It no longer reads from standard input. Figure 8.19 shows the new version. This function writes 2,000 1,400-byte
UDP datagrams to the server.

We next modify the server to receive datagrams and count the number received.
This server no longer echoes datagrams back to the client. Figure 8.20 shows the new
`dg_echo` function. When we terminate the server with our terminal interrupt key
(SIGINT), it prints the number of received datagrams and terminates.

—— *udpcliserv/dgcliloop1.c*

```
 1 #include    "unp.h"

 2 #define NDG    2000          /* datagrams to send */
 3 #define DGLEN   1400          /* length of each datagram */

 4 void
 5 dg_cli(FILE *fp, int sockfd, const SA *pservaddr, socklen_t servlen)
 6 {
 7     int     i;
 8     char    sendline[DGLEN];

 9     for (i = 0; i < NDG; i++) {
10         Sendto(sockfd, sendline, DGLEN, 0, pservaddr, servlen);
11     }
12 }
```

—— *udpcliserv/dgcliloop1.c*

Figure 8.19 `dg_cli` function that writes a fixed number of datagrams to the server.

udpcliserv/dgecholoop1.c

```
 1 #include    "unp.h"

 2 static void recvfrom_int(int);
 3 static int count;

 4 void
 5 dg_echo(int sockfd, SA *pcliaddr, socklen_t clilen)
 6 {
 7     socklen_t len;
 8     char    mesg[MAXLINE];

 9     Signal(SIGINT, recvfrom_int);

10     for ( ; ; ) {
11         len = clilen;
12         Recvfrom(sockfd, mesg, MAXLINE, 0, pcliaddr, &len);

13         count++;
14     }
15 }

16 static void
17 recvfrom_int(int signo)
18 {
19     printf("\nreceived %d datagrams\n", count);
20     exit(0);
21 }
```

udpcliserv/dgecholoop1.c

Figure 8.20 dg_echo function that counts received datagrams.

We now run the server on the host freebsd, a slow SPARCStation. We run the client on the RS/6000 system aix, connected directly with 100Mbps Ethernet. Additionally, we run netstat -s on the server, both before and after, as the statistics that are output tell us how many datagrams were lost. Figure 8.21 shows the output on the server.

```
freebsd % netstat -s -p udp
udp:
        71208 datagrams received
        0 with incomplete header
        0 with bad data length field
        0 with bad checksum
        0 with no checksum
        832 dropped due to no socket
        16 broadcast/multicast datagrams dropped due to no socket
        1971 dropped due to full socket buffers
        0 not for hashed pcb
        68389 delivered
        137685 datagrams output
freebsd % udpserv06                     start our server
                                        we run the client here
^C                                      we type our interrupt key after the client is finished
received 30 datagrams
freebsd % netstat -s -p udp
udp:
        73208 datagrams received
        0 with incomplete header
        0 with bad data length field
        0 with bad checksum
        0 with no checksum
        832 dropped due to no socket
        16 broadcast/multicast datagrams dropped due to no socket
        3941 dropped due to full socket buffers
        0 not for hashed pcb
        68419 delivered
        137685 datagrams output
```

Figure 8.21 Output on server host.

The client sent 2,000 datagrams, but the server application received only 30 of these, for a 98% loss rate. There is *no* indication whatsoever to the server application or to the client application that these datagrams were lost. As we have said, UDP has no flow control and it is unreliable. It is trivial, as we have shown, for a UDP sender to overrun the receiver.

If we look at the netstat output, the total number of datagrams received by the server host (not the server application) is 2,000 (73,208 − 71,208). The counter "dropped due to full socket buffers" indicates how many datagrams were received by UDP but were discarded because the receiving socket's receive queue was full (p. 775 of TCPv2). This value is 1,970 (3,491 − 1,971), which when added to the counter output by the application (30), equals the 2,000 datagrams received by the host. Unfortunately, the netstat counter of the number dropped due to a full socket buffer is systemwide. There is no way to determine which applications (e.g., which UDP ports) are affected.

The number of datagrams received by the server in this example is not predictable. It depends on many factors, such as the network load, the processing load on the client host, and the processing load on the server host.

If we run the same client and server, but this time with the client on the slow Sun and the server on the faster RS/6000, no datagrams are lost.

```
aix % udpserv06
^?                                          we type our interrupt key after the client is finished
received 2000 datagrams
```

UDP Socket Receive Buffer

The number of UDP datagrams that are queued by UDP for a given socket is limited by the size of that socket's receive buffer. We can change this with the SO_RCVBUF socket option, as we described in Section 7.5. The default size of the UDP socket receive buffer under FreeBSD is 42,080 bytes, which allows room for only 30 of our 1,400-byte datagrams. If we increase the size of the socket receive buffer, we expect the server to receive additional datagrams. Figure 8.22 shows a modification to the dg_echo function from Figure 8.20 that sets the socket receive buffer to 240 KB.

udpcliserv/dgecholoop2.c
```
1 #include    "unp.h"

2 static void recvfrom_int(int);
3 static int count;

4 void
5 dg_echo(int sockfd, SA *pcliaddr, socklen_t clilen)
6 {
7     int    n;
8     socklen_t len;
9     char   mesg[MAXLINE];

10    Signal(SIGINT, recvfrom_int);

11    n = 220 * 1024;
12    Setsockopt(sockfd, SOL_SOCKET, SO_RCVBUF, &n, sizeof(n));

13    for ( ; ; ) {
14        len = clilen;
15        Recvfrom(sockfd, mesg, MAXLINE, 0, pcliaddr, &len);

16        count++;
17    }
18 }

19 static void
20 recvfrom_int(int signo)
21 {
22     printf("\nreceived %d datagrams\n", count);
23     exit(0);
24 }
```
udpcliserv/dgecholoop2.c

Figure 8.22 dg_echo function that increases the size of the socket receive queue.

If we run this server on the Sun and the client on the RS/6000, the count of received datagrams is now 103. While this is slightly better than the earlier example with the default socket receive buffer, it is no panacea.

Why do we set the receive socket buffer size to $220 \times 1{,}024$ in Figure 8.22? The maximum size of a socket receive buffer in FreeBSD 5.1 defaults to 262,144 bytes ($256 \times 1{,}024$), but due to the buffer allocation policy (described in Chapter 2 of TCPv2), the actual limit is 233,016 bytes. Many earlier systems based on 4.3BSD restricted the size of a socket buffer to around 52,000 bytes.

8.14 Determining Outgoing Interface with UDP

A connected UDP socket can also be used to determine the outgoing interface that will be used to a particular destination. This is because of a side effect of the `connect` function when applied to a UDP socket: The kernel chooses the local IP address (assuming the process has not already called `bind` to explicitly assign this). This local IP address is chosen by searching the routing table for the destination IP address, and then using the primary IP address for the resulting interface.

Figure 8.23 shows a simple UDP program that `connect`s to a specified IP address and then calls `getsockname`, printing the local IP address and port.

udpcliserv/udpcli09.c

```
 1 #include     "unp.h"

 2 int
 3 main(int argc, char **argv)
 4 {
 5     int      sockfd;
 6     socklen_t len;
 7     struct sockaddr_in cliaddr, servaddr;

 8     if (argc != 2)
 9         err_quit("usage: udpcli <IPaddress>");

10     sockfd = Socket(AF_INET, SOCK_DGRAM, 0);

11     bzero(&servaddr, sizeof(servaddr));
12     servaddr.sin_family = AF_INET;
13     servaddr.sin_port = htons(SERV_PORT);
14     Inet_pton(AF_INET, argv[1], &servaddr.sin_addr);

15     Connect(sockfd, (SA *) &servaddr, sizeof(servaddr));

16     len = sizeof(cliaddr);
17     Getsockname(sockfd, (SA *) &cliaddr, &len);
18     printf("local address %s\n", Sock_ntop((SA *) &cliaddr, len));

19     exit(0);
20 }
```

udpcliserv/udpcli09.c

Figure 8.23 UDP program that uses `connect` to determine outgoing interface.

If we run the program on the multihomed host `freebsd`, we have the following output:

```
freebsd % udpcli09 206.168.112.96
local address 12.106.32.254:52329

freebsd % udpcli09 192.168.42.2
local address 192.168.42.1:52330

freebsd % udpcli09 127.0.0.1
local address 127.0.0.1:52331
```

The first time we run the program, the command-line argument is an IP address that follows the default route. The kernel assigns the local IP address to the primary address of the interface to which the default route points. The second time, the argument is the IP address of a system connected to a second Ethernet interface, so the kernel assigns the local IP address to the primary address of this second interface. Calling connect on a UDP socket does not send anything to that host; it is entirely a local operation that saves the peer's IP address and port. We also see that calling connect on an unbound UDP socket also assigns an ephemeral port to the socket.

> Unfortunately, this technique does not work on all implementations, mostly SVR4-derived kernels. For example, this does not work on Solaris 2.5, but it works on AIX, HP-UX 11, MacOS X, FreeBSD, Linux, and Solaris 2.6 and later.

8.15 TCP and UDP Echo Server Using `select`

We now combine our concurrent TCP echo server from Chapter 5 with our iterative UDP echo server from this chapter into a single server that uses select to multiplex a TCP and UDP socket. Figure 8.24 is the first half of this server.

Create listening TCP socket

14–22   A listening TCP socket is created that is bound to the server's well-known port. We set the SO_REUSEADDR socket option in case connections exist on this port.

Create UDP socket

23–29   A UDP socket is also created and bound to the same port. Even though the same port is used for TCP and UDP sockets, there is no need to set the SO_REUSEADDR socket option before this call to bind, because TCP ports are independent of UDP ports.

Figure 8.25 shows the second half of our server.

Establish signal handler for SIGCHLD

30   A signal handler is established for SIGCHLD because TCP connections will be handled by a child process. We showed this signal handler in Figure 5.11.

Prepare for `select`

31–32   We initialize a descriptor set for select and calculate the maximum of the two descriptors for which we will wait.

udpcliserv/udpservselect01.c

```
1 #include    "unp.h"

2 int
3 main(int argc, char **argv)
4 {
5     int      listenfd, connfd, udpfd, nready, maxfdp1;
6     char     mesg[MAXLINE];
7     pid_t    childpid;
8     fd_set   rset;
9     ssize_t n;
10    socklen_t len;
11    const int on = 1;
12    struct sockaddr_in cliaddr, servaddr;
13    void     sig_chld(int);

14        /* create listening TCP socket */
15    listenfd = Socket(AF_INET, SOCK_STREAM, 0);

16    bzero(&servaddr, sizeof(servaddr));
17    servaddr.sin_family = AF_INET;
18    servaddr.sin_addr.s_addr = htonl(INADDR_ANY);
19    servaddr.sin_port = htons(SERV_PORT);

20    Setsockopt(listenfd, SOL_SOCKET, SO_REUSEADDR, &on, sizeof(on));
21    Bind(listenfd, (SA *) &servaddr, sizeof(servaddr));

22    Listen(listenfd, LISTENQ);

23        /* create UDP socket */
24    udpfd = Socket(AF_INET, SOCK_DGRAM, 0);

25    bzero(&servaddr, sizeof(servaddr));
26    servaddr.sin_family = AF_INET;
27    servaddr.sin_addr.s_addr = htonl(INADDR_ANY);
28    servaddr.sin_port = htons(SERV_PORT);

29    Bind(udpfd, (SA *) &servaddr, sizeof(servaddr));
```

udpcliserv/udpservselect01.c

Figure 8.24 First half of echo server that handles TCP and UDP using `select`.

Call `select`

34–41   We call `select`, waiting only for readability on the listening TCP socket or readability on the UDP socket. Since our `sig_chld` handler can interrupt our call to `select`, we handle an error of EINTR.

Handle new client connection

42–51   We `accept` a new client connection when the listening TCP socket is readable, `fork` a child, and call our `str_echo` function in the child. This is the same sequence of steps we used in Chapter 5.

—————————————————————————————— *udpcliserv/udpservselect01.c*

```
30      Signal(SIGCHLD, sig_chld);  /* must call waitpid() */

31      FD_ZERO(&rset);
32      maxfdp1 = max(listenfd, udpfd) + 1;
33      for ( ; ; ) {
34          FD_SET(listenfd, &rset);
35          FD_SET(udpfd, &rset);
36          if ( (nready = select(maxfdp1, &rset, NULL, NULL, NULL)) < 0) {
37              if (errno == EINTR)
38                  continue;       /* back to for() */
39              else
40                  err_sys("select error");
41          }

42          if (FD_ISSET(listenfd, &rset)) {
43              len = sizeof(cliaddr);
44              connfd = Accept(listenfd, (SA *) &cliaddr, &len);

45              if ( (childpid = Fork()) == 0) { /* child process */
46                  Close(listenfd);    /* close listening socket */
47                  str_echo(connfd);   /* process the request */
48                  exit(0);
49              }
50              Close(connfd);          /* parent closes connected socket */
51          }

52          if (FD_ISSET(udpfd, &rset)) {
53              len = sizeof(cliaddr);
54              n = Recvfrom(udpfd, mesg, MAXLINE, 0, (SA *) &cliaddr, &len);

55              Sendto(udpfd, mesg, n, 0, (SA *) &cliaddr, len);
56          }
57      }
58  }
```
—————————————————————————————— *udpcliserv/udpservselect01.c*

Figure 8.25 Second half of echo server that handles TCP and UDP using `select`.

Handle arrival of datagram

52–57   If the UDP socket is readable, a datagram has arrived. We read it with `recvfrom` and send it back to the client with `sendto`.

8.16 Summary

Converting our echo client/server to use UDP instead of TCP was simple. But lots of features provided by TCP are missing: detecting lost packets and retransmitting, verifying responses as being from the correct peer, and the like. We will return to this topic in Section 22.5 and see what it takes to add some reliability to a UDP application.

UDP sockets can generate asynchronous errors, that is, errors that are reported some time after a packet is sent. TCP sockets always report these errors to the application, but with UDP, the socket must be connected to receive these errors.

UDP has no flow control, and this is easy to demonstrate. Normally, this is not a problem, because many UDP applications are built using a request-reply model, and not for transferring bulk data.

There are still more points to consider when writing UDP applications, but we will save these until Chapter 22, after covering the interface functions, broadcasting, and multicasting.

Exercises

8.1 We have two applications, one using TCP and the other using UDP. 4,096 bytes are in the receive buffer for the TCP socket and two 2,048-byte datagrams are in the receive buffer for the UDP socket. The TCP application calls `read` with a third argument of 4,096 and the UDP application calls `recvfrom` with a third argument of 4,096. Is there any difference?

8.2 What happens in Figure 8.4 if we replace the final argument to `sendto` (which we show as `len`) with `clilen`?

8.3 Compile and run the UDP server in Figures 8.3 and 8.4 and then the UDP client in Figures 8.7 and 8.8. Verify that the client and server work together.

8.4 Run the `ping` program in one window, specifying the `-i 60` option (send one packet every 60 seconds; some systems use `-I` instead of `-i`), the `-v` option (print all received ICMP errors), and the loopback address (normally 127.0.0.1). We will use this program to see the ICMP port unreachable returned by the server host. Next, run our client from the previous exercise in another window, specifying the IP address of some host that is not running the server. What happens?

8.5 We said with Figure 8.5 that each connected TCP socket has its own socket receive buffer. What about the listening socket; do you think it has its own socket receive buffer?

8.6 Use the `sock` program (Section C.3) and a tool such as `tcpdump` (Section C.5) to test what we claimed in Section 8.10: If the client `binds` an IP address to its socket but sends a datagram that goes out some other interface, the resulting IP datagram still contains the IP address that was bound to the socket, even though this does not correspond to the outgoing interface.

8.7 Compile the programs from Section 8.13 and run the client and server on different hosts. Put a `printf` in the client each time a datagram is written to the socket. Does this change the percentage of received packets? Why? Put a `printf` in the server each time a datagram is read from the socket. Does this change the percentage of received packets? Why?

8.8 What is the largest length that we can pass to `sendto` for a UDP/IPv4 socket, that is, what is the largest amount of data that can fit into a UDP/IPv4 datagram? What changes with UDP/IPv6?

Modify Figure 8.8 to send one maximum-size UDP datagram, read it back, and print the number of bytes returned by `recvfrom`.

8.9 Modify Figure 8.25 to conform to RFC 1122 by using IP_RECVDSTADDR for the UDP socket.

9

Elementary SCTP Sockets

9.1 Introduction

SCTP is a newer transport protocol, standardized in the IETF in 2000 (compared with TCP, which was standardized in 1981). It was first designed to meet the needs of the growing IP telephony market; in particular, transporting telephony signaling across the Internet. The requirements it was designed to fulfill are described in RFC 2719 [Ong et al. 1999]. SCTP is a reliable, message-oriented protocol, providing multiple streams between endpoints and transport-level support for multihoming. Since it is a newer transport protocol, it does not have the same ubiquity as TCP or UDP; however, it provides some new features that may simplify certain application designs. We will discuss the reasons to consider using SCTP instead of TCP in Section 23.12.

Although there are some fundamental differences between SCTP and TCP, the *one-to-one* interface for SCTP provides very nearly the same application interface as TCP. This allows for trivial porting of applications, but does not permit use of some of SCTP's advanced features. The *one-to-many* interface provides full support for these features, but may require significant retooling of existing applications. The one-to-many interface is recommended for most new applications developed for SCTP.

This chapter describes additional elementary socket functions that can be used with SCTP. We first describe the two different interface models that are available to the application developer. We will develop a version of our echo server using the one-to-many model in Chapter 10. We also describe the new functions available for and used exclusively with SCTP. We look at the `shutdown` function and how its use with SCTP differs from TCP. We then briefly cover the use of *notifications* in SCTP. Notifications allow an application to be informed of significant protocol events other than the arrival of user data. We will see an example of how to use notifications in Section 23.4.

Since SCTP is a newer protocol, the interface for all its features has not yet completely stabilized. As of this writing, the interfaces described are believed to be stable, but are not yet as ubiquitous as the rest of the sockets API. Users of applications designed to use SCTP exclusively may need to be prepared to install kernel patches or otherwise upgrade their operating system, and applications which need to be ubiquitous need to be able to use TCP if SCTP is not available on the system they are running on.

9.2   Interface Models

There are two types of SCTP sockets: a *one-to-one* socket and a *one-to-many* socket. A one-to-one socket corresponds to exactly one SCTP association. (Recall from Section 2.5 that an SCTP association is a connection between two systems, but may involve more than two IP addresses due to multihoming.) This mapping is similar to the relationship between a TCP socket and a TCP connection. With a one-to-many socket, several SCTP associations can be active on a given socket simultaneously. This mapping is similar to the manner in which a UDP socket bound to a particular port can receive interleaved datagrams from several remote UDP endpoints that are all simultaneously sending data.

When deciding which style of interface to use, the application needs to consider several factors, including:

- What type of server is being written, *iterative* or *concurrent*?
- How many socket descriptors does the server wish to manage?
- Is it important to optimize the association setup to enable data on the third (and possibly fourth) packet of the four-way handshake?
- How much connection state does the application wish to maintain?

> When the sockets API for SCTP was under development, different terminology was used for the two styles of sockets, and readers may sometimes encounter these older terms in documentation or source code. The original term for the one-to-one socket was a "TCP-style" socket, and the original term for a one-to-many socket was a "UDP-style" socket.
>
> These style terms were later dropped because they tended to cause confusion by creating expectations that SCTP would behave more like TCP or UDP, depending on which style of socket was used. In fact, these terms referred to only one aspect of the differences between TCP and UDP sockets (i.e., whether a socket supports multiple concurrent transport-layer associations). The current terminology ("one-to-one" versus "one-to-many") focuses our attention on the key difference between the two socket styles. Finally, note that some writers use the term "many-to-one" instead of "one-to-many"; the terms are interchangeable.

The One-to-One Style

The one-to-one style was developed to ease the porting of existing TCP applications to SCTP. It provides nearly an identical model to that described in Chapter 4. There are some differences one should be aware of, especially when porting existing TCP applications to SCTP using this style.

1. Any socket options must be converted to the SCTP equivalent. Two commonly found options are `TCP_NODELAY` and `TCP_MAXSEG`. These can be easily mapped to `SCTP_NODELAY` and `SCTP_MAXSEG`.

2. SCTP preserves message boundaries; thus, application-layer message boundaries are not required. For example, an application protocol based on TCP might do a `write()` system call to write a two-byte message length field x, followed by a `write()` system call that writes x bytes of data. However, if this is done with SCTP, the receiving SCTP will receive two separate messages (i.e., the read call will return twice: once with a two-byte message, and then again with an x byte message).

3. Some TCP applications use a half-close to signal the end of input to the other side. To port such applications to SCTP, the application-layer protocol will need to be rewritten so that the application signals the end of input in the application data stream.

4. The `send` function can be used in the normal fashion. For the `sendto` and `sendmsg` functions, any address information included is treated as an override of the primary destination address (see Section 2.8).

A typical user of the one-to-one style will follow the timeline shown in Figure 9.1. When the server is started, it opens a socket, binds to an address, and waits for a client connection with the `accept` system call. Sometime later, the client is started, it opens a socket, and initiates an association with the server. We assume the client sends a request to the server, the server processes the request, and the server sends back a reply to the client. This cycle continues until the client initiates a shutdown of the association. This action closes the association, whereupon the server either exits or waits for a new association. As can be seen by comparison to a typical TCP exchange, an SCTP one-to-one socket exchange proceeds in a fashion similar to that shown in Figure 4.1.

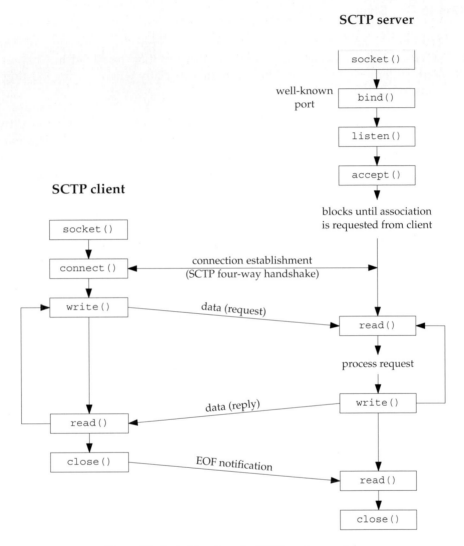

Figure 9.1 Socket functions for SCTP one-to-one style.

A one-to-one-style SCTP socket is an IP socket (family AF_INET or AF_INET6), with type SOCK_STREAM and protocol IPPROTO_SCTP.

The One-to-Many Style

The one-to-many style provides an application writer the ability to write a server without managing a large number of socket descriptors. A single socket descriptor will represent multiple associations, much the same way that a UDP socket can receive messages from multiple clients. An association identifier is used to identify a single association on a one-to-many-style socket. This association identifier is a value of type `sctp_assoc_t`; it is normally an integer. It is an opaque value; an application should not use an association identifier that it has not previously been given by the kernel. Users of the one-to-many style should keep the following issues in mind:

1. When the client closes the association, the server side will automatically close as well, thus removing any state for the association inside the kernel.

2. Using the one-to-many style is the only method that can be used to cause data to be piggybacked on the third or fourth packet of the four-way handshake (see Exercise 9.3).

3. Any `sendto`, `sendmsg`, or `sctp_sendmsg` to an address for which an association does not yet exist will cause an active open to be attempted, thus creating (if successful) a new association with that address. This behavior occurs even if the application doing the send has called the `listen` function to request a passive open.

4. The user must use the `sendto`, `sendmsg`, or `sctp_sendmsg` functions, and may not use the `send` or `write` function. (If the `sctp_peeloff` function is used to create a one-to-one-style socket, `send` or `write` may be used on it.)

5. Anytime one of the send functions is called, the primary destination address that was chosen by the system at association initiation time (Section 2.8) will be used unless the `MSG_ADDR_OVER` flag is set by the caller in a supplied `sctp_sndrcvinfo` structure. To supply this, the caller needs to use the `sendmsg` function with ancillary data, or the `sctp_sendmsg` function.

6. Association events (one of a number of SCTP notifications discussed in Section 9.14) may be enabled, so if an application does not wish to receive these events, it should disable them explicitly using the `SCTP_EVENTS` socket option. By default, the only event that is enabled is the `sctp_data_io_event`, which provides ancillary data to the `recvmsg` and `sctp_recvmsg` call. This default setting applies to both the one-to-one and one-to-many style.

> When the SCTP sockets API was first developed, the one-to-many-style interface was defined to have the association notification turned on by default as well. Later versions of the API document have since disabled all notifications except the `sctp_data_io_event` for both the one-to-one- and one-to-many-style interface. However not all implementations may have this behavior. It is always good practice for an application writer to explicitly disable (or enable) the notifications that are unwanted (or desired). This explicit approach assures the developer that the expected behavior will result no matter which OS the code is ported to.

A typical one-to-many style timeline is depicted in Figure 9.2. First, the server is started, creates a socket, binds to an address, calls `listen` to enable client associations, and calls `sctp_recvmsg`, which blocks waiting for the first message to arrive. A client opens a socket and calls `sctp_sendto`, which implicitly sets up the association and piggybacks the data request to the server on the third packet of the four-way hand-shake. The server receives the request, and processes and sends back a reply. The client receives the reply and closes the socket, thus closing the association. The server loops back to receive the next message.

This example shows an iterative server, where (possibly interleaved) messages from many associations (i.e., many clients) can be processed by a single thread of control. With SCTP, a one-to-many socket can also be used in conjunction with the `sctp_peeloff` function (see Section 9.12) to allow the iterative and concurrent server models to be combined as follows:

(1) The `sctp_peeloff` function can be used to peel off a particular association (for example, a long-running session) from a one-to-many socket into its own one-to-one socket.

(2) The one-to-one socket of the extracted association can then be dispatched to its own thread or forked process (as in the concurrent model).

(3) Meanwhile, the main thread continues to handle messages from any remaining associations in an iterative fashion on the original socket.

A one-to-many-style SCTP socket is an IP socket (family `AF_INET` or `AF_INET6`) with type `SOCK_SEQPACKET` and protocol `IPPROTO_SCTP`.

9.3   `sctp_bindx` Function

An SCTP server may wish to bind a subset of IP addresses associated with the host system. Traditionally, a TCP or UDP server can bind one or all addresses on a host, but they cannot bind a subset of addresses. The `sctp_bindx` function provides more flexibility by allowing an SCTP socket to bind a particular subset of addresses.

```
#include <netinet/sctp.h>

int sctp_bindx(int sockfd, const struct sockaddr *addrs, int addrcnt, int flags);
```

Returns: 0 if OK, –1 on error

The *sockfd* is a socket descriptor returned by the `socket` function. The second argument, *addrs*, is a pointer to a packed list of addresses. Each socket address structure is placed in the buffer immediately following the preceding socket address structure, with no intervening padding. See Figure 9.4 for an example.

The number of addresses being passed to `sctp_bindx` is specified by the *addrcnt* parameter. The *flags* parameter directs the `sctp_bindx` call to perform one of the two actions shown in Figure 9.3.

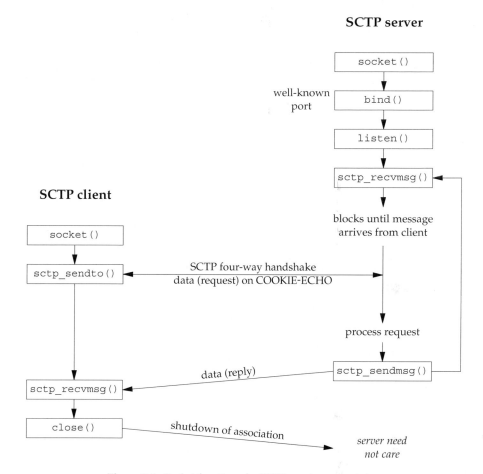

Figure 9.2 Socket functions for SCTP one-to-many style.

flags	Description
SCTP_BINDX_ADD_ADDR	Add the address(es) to the socket
SCTP_BINDX_REM_ADDR	Remove the address(es) from the socket

Figure 9.3 *flags* used with sctp_bindx function.

The sctp_bindx call can be used on a bound or unbound socket. For an unbound socket, a call to sctp_bindx will bind the given set of addresses to the socket descriptor. If sctp_bindx is used on a bound socket, the call can be used with SCTP_BINDX_ADD_ADDR to associate additional addresses with the socket descriptor or with SCTP_BINDX_REM_ADDR to remove a list of addresses associated with the socket descriptor. If sctp_bindx is performed on a listening socket, future associations will use the new address configuration; the change does not affect any existing associations. The two flags passed to sctp_bindx are mutually exclusive; if both are given,

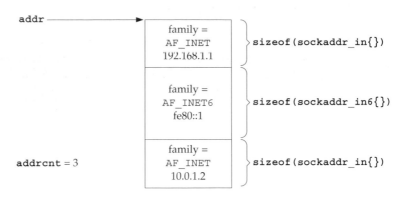

Figure 9.4 Packed address list format for SCTP calls.

sctp_bindx will fail, returning the error code EINVAL. The port number in all the socket address structures must be the same and must match any port number that is already bound; if it doesn't, then sctp_bindx will fail, returning the error code EINVAL.

If an endpoint supports the dynamic address feature, a call to sctp_bindx with the SCTP_BINDX_REM_ADDR or SCTP_BINDX_ADD_ADDR flag will cause the endpoint to send an appropriate message to the peer to change the peer's address lists. Since adding and removing addresses from a connected association is optional functionality, implementations that do not support this functionality will return EOPNOTSUPP. Note that both ends of an association must support this feature for proper operation. This feature can be useful if the system supports dynamic provisioning of interfaces; for example, if a new Ethernet interface is brought up, the application can use SCTP_BINDX_ADD_ADDR to start using the additional interface on an existing connection.

9.4   sctp_connectx **Function**

```
#include <netinet/sctp.h>

int sctp_connectx(int sockfd, const struct sockaddr *addrs, int addrcnt);
```

                                              Returns: 0 for success, −1 on error

The sctp_connectx function is used to connect to a multihomed peer. We specify *addrcnt* addresses, all belonging to the same peer, in the *addrs* parameter. The *addrs* parameter is a packed list of addresses, as in Figure 9.4. The SCTP stack uses one or more of the given addresses for establishing the association. All the addresses listed in *addrs* are considered to be valid, confirmed addresses.

9.5   `sctp_getpaddrs` **Function**

The `getpeername` function was not designed with the concept of a multihoming-aware transport protocol; when using SCTP, it only returns the primary address. When all the addresses are required, the `sctp_getpaddrs` function provides a mechanism for an application to retrieve all the addresses of a peer.

```
#include <netinet/sctp.h>

int sctp_getpaddrs(int sockfd, sctp_assoc_t id, struct sockaddr **addrs);
```
                               Returns: the number of peer addresses stored in *addrs*, −1 on error

The *sockfd* parameter is the socket descriptor returned by the `socket` function. The *id* is the association identification for a one-to-many-style socket. If the socket is using the one-to-one style, the *id* field is ignored. *addrs* is the address of a pointer that `sctp_getpaddrs` will fill in with a locally allocated, packed list of addresses. See Figures 9.4 and 23.12 for details on the structure of this return value. The caller should use `sctp_freepaddrs` to free resources allocated by `sctp_getpaddrs` when finished with them.

9.6   `sctp_freepaddrs` **Function**

The `sctp_freepaddrs` function frees resources allocated by the `sctp_getpaddrs` function. It is called as follows:

```
#include <netinet/sctp.h>

void sctp_freepaddrs(struct sockaddr *addrs);
```

addrs is the pointer to the array of addresses returned by `sctp_getpaddrs`.

9.7   `sctp_getladdrs` **Function**

The `sctp_getladdrs` function can be used to retrieve the local addresses that are part of an association. This function is often necessary when a local endpoint wishes to know exactly which local addresses are in use (which may be a proper subset of the system's addresses).

```
#include <netinet/sctp.h>

int sctp_getladdrs(int sockfd, sctp_assoc_t id, struct sockaddr **addrs);
```
                          Returns: the number of local addresses stored in *addrs*, −1 on error

The *sockfd* is the socket descriptor returned by the `socket` function. *id* is the association identification for a one-to-many-style socket. If the socket is using the one-to-one style, the *id* field is ignored. The *addrs* parameter is an address of a pointer that `sctp_getladdrs` will fill in with a locally allocated, packed list of addresses. See Figures 9.4 and 23.12 for details on the structure of this return value. The caller should use `sctp_freeladdrs` to free resources allocated by `sctp_getladdrs` when finished with them.

9.8   `sctp_freeladdrs` Function

The `sctp_freeladdrs` function frees resources allocated by the `sctp_getladdrs` function. It is called as follows:

```
#include <netinet/sctp.h>

void sctp_freeladdrs(struct sockaddr *addrs);
```

addrs is the pointer to the array of addresses returned by `sctp_getladdrs`.

9.9   `sctp_sendmsg` Function

An application can control various features of SCTP by using the `sendmsg` function along with ancillary data (described in Chapter 14). However, because the use of ancillary data may be inconvenient, many SCTP implementations provide an auxiliary library call (possibly implemented as a system call) that eases an application's use of SCTP's advanced features. The call takes the following form:

```
ssize_t sctp_sendmsg(int sockfd, const void *msg, size_t msgsz,
                     const struct sockaddr *to, socklen_t tolen,
                     uint32_t ppid,
                     uint32_t flags, uint16_t stream,
                     uint32_t timetolive, uint32_t context);
```
                                          Returns: the number of bytes written, −1 on error

The user of `sctp_sendmsg` has a greatly simplified sending method at the cost of more arguments. The *sockfd* field holds the socket descriptor returned from a `socket` system call. The *msg* field points to a buffer of *msgsz* bytes to be sent to the peer endpoint *to*. The *tolen* field holds the length of the address stored in *to*. The *ppid* field holds the payload protocol identifier that will be passed with the data chunk. The *flags* field will be passed to the SCTP stack to identify any SCTP options; valid values for this field may be found in Figure 7.16.

A caller specifies an SCTP stream number by filling in the *stream*. The caller may specify the lifetime of the message in milliseconds in the *lifetime* field, where 0 represents an infinite lifetime. A user context, if any, may be specified in *context*. A user context associates a failed message transmission, received via a message notification, with some local application-specific context. For example, to send a message to stream number 1, with the send flags set to MSG_PR_SCTP_TTL, the lifetime set to 1000 milliseconds, a payload protocol identifier of 24, and a context of 52, a user would formulate the following call:

```
ret = sctp_sendmsg(sockfd,
                    data, datasz, &dest, sizeof(dest),
                    24, MSG_PR_SCTP_TTL, 1, 1000, 52);
```

This approach is much easier than allocating the necessary ancillary data and setting up the appropriate structures in the msghdr structure. Note that if an implementation maps the sctp_sendmsg to a sendmsg function call, the *flags* field of the sendmsg call is set to 0.

9.10 sctp_recvmsg Function

Just like sctp_sendmsg, the sctp_recvmsg function provides a more user-friendly interface to the advanced SCTP features. Using this function allows a user to retrieve not only its peer's address, but also the msg_flags field that would normally accompany the recvmsg function call (e.g., MSG_NOTIFICATION, MSG_EOR, etc.). The function also allows the user to retrieve the sctp_sndrcvinfo structure that accompanies the message that was read into the message buffer. Note that if an application wishes to receive sctp_sndrcvinfo information, the sctp_data_io_event must be subscribed to with the SCTP_EVENTS socket option (ON by default). The sctp_recvmsg function takes the following form:

```
ssize_t sctp_recvmsg(int sockfd, void *msg, size_t msgsz,
                     struct sockaddr *from, socklen_t *fromlen,
                     struct sctp_sndrcvinfo *sinfo,
                     int *msg_flags);
                                       Returns: the number of bytes read, −1 on error
```

On return from this call, *msg* is filled with up to *msgsz* bytes of data. The message sender's address is contained in *from*, with the address size filled in the *fromlen* argument. Any message flags will be contained in the *msg_flags* argument. If the notification sctp_data_io_event has been enabled (the default), the sctp_sndrcvinfo structure will be filled in with detailed information about the message as well. Note that if an implementation maps the sctp_recvmsg to a recvmsg function call, the *flags* field of the call will be set to 0.

9.11 `sctp_opt_info` Function

The `sctp_opt_info` function is provided for implementations that cannot use the `getsockopt` functions for SCTP. This inability to use the `getsockopt` function is because some of the SCTP socket options, for example, `SCTP_STATUS`, need an in-out variable to pass the association identification. For systems that cannot provide an in-out variable to the `getsockopt` function, the user will need to use `sctp_opt_info`. For systems like FreeBSD that do allow in-out variables in the socket option call, the `sctp_opt_info` call is a library call that repackages the arguments into the appropriate `getsockopt` call. For portability's sake, applications should use `sctp_opt_info` for all the options that require in-out variables (Section 7.10).

The call has the following format:

```
int sctp_opt_info(int sockfd, sctp_assoc_t assoc_id, int opt,
                  void *arg, socklen_t *siz);
```

Returns: 0 for success, −1 on error

sockfd is the socket descriptor that the user would like the socket option to affect. *assoc_id* is the identification of the association (if any) on which the user is performing the option. *opt* is the socket option (as defined in Section 7.10) for SCTP. *arg* is the socket option argument, and *siz* is a pointer to a *socklen_t* which holds the size of the argument.

9.12 `sctp_peeloff` Function

As previously mentioned, it is possible to extract an association contained by a one-to-many socket into an individual one-to-one-style socket. The semantics are much like the `accept` function call with an additional argument. The caller passes the *sockfd* of the one-to-many socket and the association identification *id* that is being extracted. At the completion of the call, a new socket descriptor is returned. This new descriptor will be a one-to-one-style socket descriptor with the requested association. The function takes the following form:

```
int sctp_peeloff(int sockfd, sctp_assoc_t id);
```

Returns: a new socket descriptor on success, −1 on error

9.13 `shutdown` Function

The `shutdown` function that we discussed in Section 6.6 can be used with an SCTP endpoint using the one-to-one-style interface. Because SCTP's design does not provide a half-closed state, an SCTP endpoint reacts to a `shutdown` call differently than a TCP endpoint. When an SCTP endpoint initiates a shutdown sequence, both endpoints must complete transmission of any data currently in the queue and close the association. The endpoint that initiated the active open may wish to invoke shutdown instead of close so that the endpoint can be used to connect to a new peer. Unlike TCP, a close followed by the opening of a new socket is not required. SCTP allows the endpoint to issue a shutdown, and after the shutdown completes, the endpoint can reuse the socket to connect to a new peer. Note that the new connection will fail if the endpoint does not wait until the SCTP shutdown sequence completes. Figure 9.5 shows the typical function calls in this scenario.

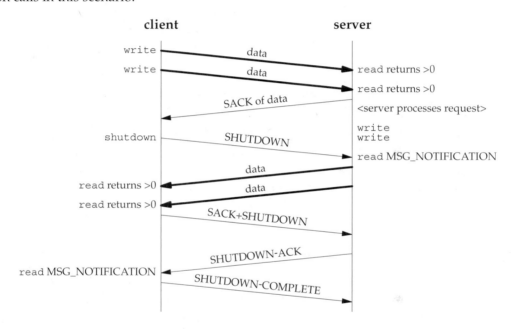

Figure 9.5 Calling shutdown to close an SCTP association.

Note that in Figure 9.5, we depict the user receiving the MSG_NOTIFICATION events. If the user had not subscribed to receive these events, then a read of length 0 would have been returned. The effects of the shutdown function for TCP were described in Section 6.6. The shutdown function *howto* holds the following semantics for SCTP:

SHUT_RD   The same semantics as for TCP discussed in Section 6.6; no SCTP protocol action is taken.

SHUT_WR   Disables further send operations and initiates the SCTP shutdown procedures, which will terminate the association. Note that this option does not provide a half-closed state, but does allow the local endpoint to read any queued data that the peer may have sent prior to receiving the SCTP SHUTDOWN message.

SHUT_RDWR   Disables all `read` and `write` operations, and initiates the SCTP shutdown procedure. Any queued data that was in transit to the local
endpoint will be acknowledged and then silently discarded.

9.14 Notifications

SCTP makes a variety of notifications available to the application programmer. The
SCTP user can track the state of its association(s) via these notifications. Notifications
communicate transport-level events, including network status change, association star-
tups, remote operational errors, and undeliverable messages. For both the one-to-one
and the one-to-many styles, all events are disabled by default with the exception of
`sctp_data_io_event`. We will see an example of using notifications in Section 23.7.

Eight events can be subscribed to using the `SCTP_EVENTS` socket option. Seven of
these events generate additional data—termed a notification—that a user will receive
via the normal socket descriptor. The notifications are added to the socket descriptor inline with data as the events that generate them occur. When reading from a socket with
notification subscriptions, user data and notifications will be interleaved on the socket
buffer. To differentiate between peer data and a notification, the user uses either the
`recvmsg` function or the `sctp_recvmsg` function. When the data returned is an event
notification, the `msg_flags` field of these two functions will contain the
`MSG_NOTIFICATION` flag. This flag tells the application that the message just read is
not data from the peer, but a notification from the local SCTP stack.

Each type of notification is in tag-length-value form, where the first eight bytes of
the message identify what type of notification has arrived and its total length. Enabling
the `sctp_data_io_event` event causes the receipt of `sctp_sndrcvinfo` structures
on every read of user data (this option is enabled by default for both interface styles).
This information is normally received in ancillary data using the `recvmsg` call. An
application can also use the `sctp_recvmsg` call, which will fill a pointer to the
`sctp_sndrcvinfo` structure with this information.

Two notifications contain an SCTP error cause code field. The values for this field
are listed in Section 3.3.10 of RFC 2960 [Stewart et al. 2000] and in the "CAUSE CODES"
section of `http://www.iana.org/assignments/sctp-parameters`.

Notifications have the following form:

```
struct sctp_tlv {
  u_int16_t sn_type;
  u_int16_t sn_flags;
  u_int32_t sn_length;
};

/* notification event */
union sctp_notification {
  struct sctp_tlv sn_header;
  struct sctp_assoc_change sn_assoc_change;
  struct sctp_paddr_change sn_paddr_change;
```

```
    struct sctp_remote_error sn_remote_error;
    struct sctp_send_failed sn_send_failed;
    struct sctp_shutdown_event sn_shutdown_event;
    struct sctp_adaption_event sn_adaption_event;
    struct sctp_pdapi_event sn_pdapi_event;
};
```

Note that the `sn_header` field is used to interpret the type value, to decode the actual message being sent. Figure 9.6 illustrates the value found in the `sn_header`. `sn_type` field and the corresponding subscription field used with the `SCTP_EVENTS` socket option.

sn_type	Subscription field
SCTP_ASSOC_CHANGE	sctp_association_event
SCTP_PEER_ADDR_CHANGE	sctp_address_event
SCTP_REMOTE_ERROR	sctp_peer_error_event
SCTP_SEND_FAILED	sctp_send_failure_event
SCTP_SHUTDOWN_EVENT	sctp_shutdown_event
SCTP_ADAPTION_INDICATION	sctp_adaption_layer_event
SCTP_PARTIAL_DELIVERY_EVENT	sctp_partial_delivery_event

Figure 9.6 *sn_type* and event subscription field.

Each notification has its own structure that gives further information about the event that has occurred on the transport.

SCTP_ASSOC_CHANGE
> This notification informs an application that a change has occurred to an association; either a new association has begun or an existing association has ended. The information provided with this event is defined as follows:

```
        struct sctp_assoc_change {
          u_int16_t sac_type;
          u_int16_t sac_flags;
          u_int32_t sac_length;
          u_int16_t sac_state;
          u_int16_t sac_error;
          u_int16_t sac_outbound_streams;
          u_int16_t sac_inbound_streams;
          sctp_assoc_t sac_assoc_id;
          uint8_t    sac_info[];
        };
```

> The *sac_state* describes the type of event that has occurred on the association, and will take one of the following values:

SCTP_COMM_UP   This state indicates that a new association has just been started. The inbound and outbound streams fields indicate how many streams are available in each direction. The association identification is filled with a unique value that can be used to communicate with the local SCTP stack regarding this association.

SCTP_COMM_LOST   This state indicates that the association specified by the association identification has closed due to either an unreachability threshold being triggered (i.e., the SCTP endpoint timed out multiple times and hit its threshold, which indicates the peer is no longer reachable), or the peer performed an abortive close (usually with the SO_LINGER option or by using sendmsg with a MSG_ABORT flag) of the association. Any user-specific information will be found in the sac_info field of the notification.

SCTP_RESTART   This state indicates that the peer has restarted. The most likely cause of this notification is a peer crash and restart. The application should verify the number of streams in each direction, since these values may change during a restart.

SCTP_SHUTDOWN_COMP
            This state indicates that a shutdown initiated by the local endpoint (via either a shutdown call or a sendmsg with a MSG_EOF flag) has completed. For the one-to-one style, after receiving this notification, the socket descriptor can be used again to connect to a different peer.

SCTP_CANT_STR_ASSOC
            This state indicates that a peer did not respond to an association setup attempt (i.e., the INIT message).

The *sac_error* field holds any SCTP protocol error cause code that may have caused an association change. The *sac_outbound_streams* and *sac_inbound_streams* fields inform the application how many streams in each direction have been negotiated on the association. *sac_assoc_id* holds a unique handle for an association that can be used to identify the association in both socket options and future notifications. *sac_info* holds any other information available to the user. For example, if an association was aborted by the peer with a user-defined error, that error would be found in this field.

SCTP_PEER_ADDR_CHANGE
        This notification indicates that one of the peer's addresses has experienced a change of state. This change may either be a failure, such as the destination is not responding when sent to, or a recovery, such as a destination that was in a failed state has recovered. The structure that accompanies an address change is as follows:

```
struct sctp_paddr_change {
  u_int16_t spc_type;
  u_int16_t spc_flags;
  u_int32_t spc_length;
  struct sockaddr_storage spc_aaddr;
  u_int32_t spc_state;
  u_int32_t spc_error;
  sctp_assoc_t spc_assoc_id;
};
```

The *spc_aaddr* field holds the address of the peer affected by this event. The `spc_state` field holds one of the values described in Figure 9.7.

spc_state	Description
SCTP_ADDR_ADDED	Address is now added to the association
SCTP_ADDR_AVAILABLE	Address is now reachable
SCTP_ADDR_CONFIRMED	Address has now been confirmed and is valid
SCTP_ADDR_MADE_PRIM	Address has now been made the primary destination
SCTP_ADDR_REMOVED	Address is no longer part of the association
SCTP_ADDR_UNREACHABLE	Address can no longer be reached

Figure 9.7 SCTP peer address state notifications.

When an address is declared `SCTP_ADDR_UNREACHABLE`, any data sent to that address will be rerouted to an alternate address. Note also that some of the states will only be available on SCTP implementations that support the dynamic address option (e.g., `SCTP_ADDR_ADDED` and `SCTP_ADDR_REMOVED`).

The *spc_error* field contains any notification error code to provide more information about the event, and *spc_assoc_id* holds the association identification.

`SCTP_REMOTE_ERROR`

A remote peer may send an operational error message to the local endpoint. These messages can indicate a variety of error conditions for the association. The entire error chunk will be passed to the application in wire format when this notification is enabled. The format of the message will be as follows:

```
struct sctp_remote_error {
 u_int16_t sre_type;
 u_int16_t sre_flags;
 u_int32_t sre_length;
 u_int16_t sre_error;
 sctp_assoc_t sre_assoc_id;
 u_int8_t  sre_data[];
};
```

The *sre_error* will hold one of the SCTP protocol error cause codes, *sre_assoc_id* will contain the association identification, and *sre_data* will hold the complete error in wire format.

SCTP_SEND_FAILED

When a message cannot be delivered to a peer, the message is sent back to the user through this notification. This notification is usually soon followed by an association failure notification. In most cases, the only way a message will not be delivered is if the association has failed. The only time a message failure will occur without an association failure is when the partial reliability extension of SCTP is being used.

When an error notification is sent, the following format will be read by the application:

```
struct sctp_send_failed {
  u_int16_t ssf_type;
  u_int16_t ssf_flags;
  u_int32_t ssf_length;
  u_int32_t ssf_error;
  struct sctp_sndrcvinfo ssf_info;
  sctp_assoc_t ssf_assoc_id;
  u_int8_t ssf_data[];
};
```

ssf_flags will be set to one of two values:

- SCTP_DATA_UNSENT, which indicates that the message could never be transmitted to the peer (e.g., flow control prevented the message from being sent before its lifetime expired), so the peer never received it

- SCTP_DATA_SENT, which indicates that the data was transmitted to the peer at least once, but was never acknowledged. In this case, the peer *may* have received the message, but it was unable to acknowledge it.

This distinction may be important to a transaction protocol, which might perform different actions to recover from a broken connection based on whether or not a given message might have been received. *ssf_error*, if not zero, holds an error code specific to this notification. The *ssf_info* field provides the information passed (if any) to the kernel when the data was sent (e.g., stream number, context, etc.). *ssf_assoc_id* holds the association identification, and *ssf_data* holds the undelivered message.

SCTP_SHUTDOWN_EVENT

This notification is passed to an application when a peer sends a SHUTDOWN chunk to the local endpoint. This notification informs the application that no new data will be accepted on the socket. All currently queued data will be transmitted, and at the completion of that transmission, the association will be shut down. The notification format is as follows:

```
struct sctp_shutdown_event {
  uint16_t sse_type;
  uint16_t sse_flags;
  uint32_t sse_length;
```

```
      sctp_assoc_t sse_assoc_id;
   };
```

sse_assoc_id holds the association identification for the association that is shutting down and can no longer accept data.

SCTP_ADAPTION_INDICATION

Some implementations support an adaption layer indication parameter. This parameter is exchanged in the INIT and INIT-ACK to inform each peer what type of application adaption is being performed. The notification will have the following form:

```
      struct sctp_adaption_event {
        u_int16_t    sai_type;
        u_int16_t    sai_flags;
        u_int32_t    sai_length;
        u_int32_t    sai_adaption_ind;
        sctp_assoc_t sai_assoc_id;
      };
```

The *sai_assoc_id* identifies of association that this adaption layer notification. *sai_adaption_ind* is the 32-bit integer that the peer communicates to the local host in the INIT or INIT-ACK message. The outgoing adaption layer is set with the SCTP_ADAPTION_LAYER socket option (Section 7.10). The adaption layer INIT/INIT-ACK option is described in [Stewart et al. 2003b], and a sample usage of the option for remote direct memory access/direct data placement is described in [Stewart et al. 2003a].

SCTP_PARTIAL_DELIVERY_EVENT

The partial delivery application interface is used to transport large messages to the user via the socket buffer. Consider a user writing a single message of 4MB. A message of this size would tax or exhaust system resources. An SCTP implementation would fail to handle such a message unless the implementation had a mechanism to begin delivering the message before all of it arrived. When an implementation does this form of delivery, it is termed *"the partial delivery API."* The partial delivery API is invoked by the SCTP implementation sending data with the msg_flags field remaining clear until the last piece of the message is ready to be delivered. The last piece of the message will have the msg_flags set to MSG_EOR. Note that if an application is going to receive large messages, it should use either recvmsg or sctp_recvmsg so that the msg_flags field can be examined for this condition.

In some instances, the partial delivery API will need to communicate a status to the application. For example, if the partial delivery API needs to be aborted, the SCTP_PARTIAL_DELIVERY_EVENT notification must be sent to the receiving application. This notification has the following format:

```
struct sctp_pdapi_event {
  uint16_t pdapi_type;
  uint16_t pdapi_flags;
  uint32_t pdapi length;
  uint32_t pdapi_indication;
  sctp_assoc_t pdapi_assoc_id;
};
```

The *pdapi_assoc_id* field identifies the association upon which the partial delivery API event has occurred. The *pdapi_indication* holds the event that has occurred. Currently, the only valid value found in this field is SCTP_PARTIAL_DELIVERY_ABORTED, which indicates that the currently active partial delivery has been aborted.

9.15 Summary

SCTP provides the application writer with two different interface styles: the one-to-one style, mostly compatible with existing TCP applications to ease migration to SCTP, and the one-to-many style, allowing access to all of SCTP's features. The sctp_peeloff function provides a method of extracting an association from one style to the other. SCTP also provides numerous notifications of transport events to which an application may wish to subscribe. These events can aid an application in better managing the associations it maintains.

Since SCTP is multihomed, not all the standard sockets functions introduced in Chapter 4 are adequate. Functions like sctp_bindx, sctp_connectx, sctp_getladdrs, and sctp_getpaddrs provide methods to better control and examine the multiple addresses that can make up an SCTP association. Utility functions such as sctp_sendmsg and sctp_recvmsg can simplify the use of these advanced features. We will explore many of the concepts introduced in this chapter in more detail through examples in Chapters 10 and 23.

Exercises

9.1 In what situation would an application programmer be most likely to use the *sctp_peeloff* function?

9.2 We say "the server side will automatically close as well" in our discussion of the one-to-many style; why is this true?

9.3 Why must the one-to-many style be used to cause data to be piggybacked on the third packet of the four-way handshake? (Hint: You must be able to send data at the time of association setup.)

9.4 In what scenario would you find data piggybacked on both the third and fourth packets of the four-way handshake?

9.5 Section 9.7 indicates that the local address set may be a proper subset of the bound addresses. In what circumstance would this occur?

10

SCTP Client/Server Example

10.1 Introduction

We will now use some of the elementary functions from Chapters 4 and 9 to write a complete one-to-many SCTP client/server example. Our simple example is similar to the echo server presented in Chapter 5, and performs the following steps:

1. A client reads a line of text from standard input and sends the line to the server. The line follows the form **[#] text**, where the number in brackets is the SCTP stream number on which the text message should be sent.

2. The server receives the text message from the network, increases the stream number on which the message arrived by one, and sends the text message back to the client on this new stream number.

3. The client reads the echoed line and prints it on its standard output, displaying the stream number, stream sequence number, and text string.

Figure 10.1 depicts this simple client/server along with the functions used for input and output.

Figure 10.1 Simple SCTP streaming echo client and server.

We show two arrows between the client and server depicting two unidirectional streams being used, even though the overall association is full-duplex. The fgets and fputs functions are from the standard I/O library. We do not use the writen and readline functions defined in Section 3.9 since they are unnecessary. Instead, we use the sctp_sendmsg and sctp_recvmsg functions defined in Sections 9.9 and 9.10, respectively.

For this example, we use a one-to-many-style server. We make this choice for one important reason. The examples in Chapter 5 can be modified to run over SCTP with one minor change: modify the socket function call to specify IPPROTO_SCTP instead of IPPROTO_TCP as the third argument. Simply making this change, however, would not take advantage of any of the additional features provided by SCTP except multi-homing. Using the one-to-many style allows us to exercise all of SCTP's features.

10.2   SCTP One-to-Many-Style Streaming Echo Server: main Function

Our SCTP client and server follow the flow of functions diagrammed in Figure 9.2. We show an iterative server program in Figure 10.2.

Set stream increment option

13-14 By default, our server responds using the next higher stream than the one on which the message was received. If an integer argument is passed on the command line, the server interprets the argument as the value of stream_increment, that is, it decides whether or not to increment the stream number of incoming messages. We will use this option in our discussion of head-of-line blocking in Section 10.5.

Create an SCTP socket

15 An SCTP one-to-many-style socket is created.

Bind an address

16-20 An Internet socket address structure is filled in with the wildcard address (INADDR_ANY) and the server's well-known port, SERV_PORT. Binding the wildcard address tells the system that this SCTP endpoint will use all available local addresses in any association that is set up. For multihomed hosts, this binding means that a remote endpoint will be able to make associations with and send packets to any of the local host's routeable addresses. Our choice of the SCTP port number is based on Figure 2.10. Note that the server makes the same considerations that were made earlier in our previous example found in Section 5.2.

Set up for notifications of interest

21-23 The server changes its notification subscription for the one-to-many SCTP socket. The server subscribes to just the sctp_data_io_event, which will allow the server to see the sctp_sndrcvinfo structure. From this structure, the server can determine the stream number on which the message arrived.

Enable incoming associations

24 The server enables incoming associations with the listen call. Then, control enters the main processing loop.

sctp/sctpserv01.c

```
 1 #include    "unp.h"

 2 int
 3 main(int argc, char **argv)
 4 {
 5     int     sock_fd, msg_flags;
 6     char    readbuf[BUFFSIZE];
 7     struct sockaddr_in servaddr, cliaddr;
 8     struct sctp_sndrcvinfo sri;
 9     struct sctp_event_subscribe evnts;
10     int     stream_increment = 1;
11     socklen_t len;
12     size_t  rd_sz;

13     if (argc == 2)
14         stream_increment = atoi(argv[1]);
15     sock_fd = Socket(AF_INET, SOCK_SEQPACKET, IPPROTO_SCTP);
16     bzero(&servaddr, sizeof(servaddr));
17     servaddr.sin_family = AF_INET;
18     servaddr.sin_addr.s_addr = htonl(INADDR_ANY);
19     servaddr.sin_port = htons(SERV_PORT);

20     Bind(sock_fd, (SA *) &servaddr, sizeof(servaddr));

21     bzero(&evnts, sizeof(evnts));
22     evnts.sctp_data_io_event = 1;
23     Setsockopt(sock_fd, IPPROTO_SCTP, SCTP_EVENTS, &evnts, sizeof(evnts));

24     Listen(sock_fd, LISTENQ);
25     for ( ; ; ) {
26         len = sizeof(struct sockaddr_in);
27         rd_sz = Sctp_recvmsg(sock_fd, readbuf, sizeof(readbuf),
28                         (SA *) &cliaddr, &len, &sri, &msg_flags);
29         if (stream_increment) {
30             sri.sinfo_stream++;
31             if (sri.sinfo_stream >=
32                 sctp_get_no_strms(sock_fd, (SA *) &cliaddr, len))
33                 sri.sinfo_stream = 0;
34         }
35         Sctp_sendmsg(sock_fd, readbuf, rd_sz,
36                     (SA *) &cliaddr, len,
37                     sri.sinfo_ppid,
38                     sri.sinfo_flags, sri.sinfo_stream, 0, 0);
39     }
40 }
```

sctp/sctpserv01.c

Figure 10.2 SCTP streaming echo server.

Wait for message

26–28   The server initializes the size of the client socket address structure, then blocks
while waiting for a message from any remote peer.

Increment stream number if desired

29–34   When a message arrives, the server checks the `stream_increment` flag to see if it should increment the stream number. If the flag is set (no arguments were passed on the command line), the server increments the stream number of the message. If that number grows larger than or equal to the maximum streams, which is obtained by calling our internal function call `sctp_get_no_strms`, the server resets the stream to 0. The function `sctp_get_no_strms` is not shown. It uses the `SCTP_STATUS` SCTP socket option discussed in Section 7.10 to find the number of streams negotiated.

Send back response

35–38   The server sends back the message using the payload protocol ID, flags, and the possibly modified stream number from the `sri` structure.

Notice that this server does not want association notification, so it disables all events that would pass messages up the socket buffer. The server relies on the information in the `sctp_sndrcvinfo` structure and the returned address found in *cliaddr* to locate the peer association and return the echo.

This program runs forever until the user shuts it down with an external signal.

10.3   SCTP One-to-Many-Style Streaming Echo Client: `main` Function

Figure 10.3 shows our SCTP client main function.

Validate arguments and create a socket

9–15   The client validates the arguments passed to it. First, the client verifies that the caller provided a host to send messages to. It then checks if the "echo to all" option is being enabled (we will see this used in Section 10.5). Finally, the client creates an SCTP one-to-many-style socket.

Set up server address

16–20   The client translates the server address, passed on the command line, using the `inet_pton` function. It combines that with the server's well-known port number and uses the resulting address as the destination for the requests.

Set up for notifications of interest

21–23   The client explicitly sets the notification subscription provided by our one-to-many SCTP socket. Again, it wants no `MSG_NOTIFICATION` events. Therefore, the client turns these off (as was done in the server) and only enables the receipt of the `sctp_sndrcvinfo` structure.

Call echo processing function

24–28   If the `echo_to_all` flag is not set, the client calls the `sctpstr_cli` function, discussed in Section 10.4. If the `echo_to_all` flag is set, the client calls the `sctpstr_cli_echoall` function. We will discuss this function in Section 10.5 as we explore uses for SCTP streams.

—————————————————————— sctp/sctpclient01.c

```
1 #include    "unp.h"

2 int
3 main(int argc, char **argv)
4 {
5      int     sock_fd;
6      struct sockaddr_in servaddr;
7      struct sctp_event_subscribe evnts;
8      int     echo_to_all = 0;

9      if (argc < 2)
10         err_quit("Missing host argument - use '%s host [echo]'\n", argv[0]);
11     if (argc > 2) {
12         printf("Echoing messages to all streams\n");
13         echo_to_all = 1;
14     }
15     sock_fd = Socket(AF_INET, SOCK_SEQPACKET, IPPROTO_SCTP);
16     bzero(&servaddr, sizeof(servaddr));
17     servaddr.sin_family = AF_INET;
18     servaddr.sin_addr.s_addr = htonl(INADDR_ANY);
19     servaddr.sin_port = htons(SERV_PORT);
20     Inet_pton(AF_INET, argv[1], &servaddr.sin_addr);

21     bzero(&evnts, sizeof(evnts));
22     evnts.sctp_data_io_event = 1;
23     Setsockopt(sock_fd, IPPROTO_SCTP, SCTP_EVENTS, &evnts, sizeof(evnts));
24     if (echo_to_all == 0)
25         sctpstr_cli(stdin, sock_fd, (SA *) &servaddr, sizeof(servaddr));
26     else
27         sctpstr_cli_echoall(stdin, sock_fd, (SA *) &servaddr,
28                             sizeof(servaddr));
29     Close(sock_fd);
30     return (0);
31 }
```

—————————————————————— sctp/sctpclient01.c

Figure 10.3 SCTP streaming echo client main.

Finish up

29–31   On return from processing, the client closes the SCTP socket, which shuts down any SCTP associations using the socket. The client then returns from main with a return code of 0, indicating that the program ran successfully.

10.4 SCTP Streaming Echo Client: `str_cli` Function

Figure 10.4 shows our SCTP default client processing function.

─────────────────────────────── sctp/sctp_strcli.c

```
 1 #include      "unp.h"

 2 void
 3 sctpstr_cli(FILE *fp, int sock_fd, struct sockaddr *to, socklen_t tolen)
 4 {
 5     struct sockaddr_in peeraddr;
 6     struct sctp_sndrcvinfo sri;
 7     char     sendline[MAXLINE], recvline[MAXLINE];
 8     socklen_t len;
 9     int      out_sz, rd_sz;
10     int      msg_flags;

11     bzero(&sri, sizeof(sri));
12     while (fgets(sendline, MAXLINE, fp) != NULL) {
13         if (sendline[0] != '[') {
14             printf("Error, line must be of the form '[streamnum]text'\n");
15             continue;
16         }
17         sri.sinfo_stream = strtol(&sendline[1], NULL, 0);
18         out_sz = strlen(sendline);
19         Sctp_sendmsg(sock_fd, sendline, out_sz,
20                     to, tolen, 0, 0, sri.sinfo_stream, 0, 0);

21         len = sizeof(peeraddr);
22         rd_sz = Sctp_recvmsg(sock_fd, recvline, sizeof(recvline),
23                         (SA *) &peeraddr, &len, &sri, &msg_flags);
24         printf("From str:%d seq:%d (assoc:0x%x):",
25                 sri.sinfo_stream, sri.sinfo_ssn, (u_int) sri.sinfo_assoc_id);
26         printf("%.*s", rd_sz, recvline);
27     }
28 }
```

─────────────────────────────── sctp/sctp_strcli.c

Figure 10.4 SCTP `sctp_strcli` function.

Initialize the `sri` structure and enter loop

11-12   The client starts by clearing the `sctp_sndrcvinfo` structure, `sri`. The client then enters a loop that reads from the `fp` passed by our caller with a blocking call to `fgets`. The main program passes `stdin` to this function, so user input is read and processed in the loop until the terminal EOF character (Control-D) is typed by the user. This user action ends the function and causes a return to the caller.

Validate input

13-16   The client examines the user input to make sure it is of the form **[#] text**. If the format is invalid, the client prints an error message and re-enters the blocking call to the `fgets` function.

Translate stream number

17   The client translates the user requested stream found in the input into the `sinfo_stream` field in the `sri` structure.

Send message

18-20   After initializing the appropriate lengths of the address and the size of the actual user data, the client sends the message using the `sctp_sendmsg` function.

Block while waiting for message

21-23   The client now blocks and waits for the echoed message from the server.

Display returned message and loop

24-26   The client displays the returned message echoed to it displaying the stream number, stream sequence number, as well as the text message. After displaying the message, the client loops back to get another request from the user.

Running the Code

A user starts the SCTP echo server with no arguments on a FreeBSD machine. The client is started with just the address of our server.

```
freebsd4% sctpclient01 10.1.1.5
[0]Hello                                                    Send a message on stream 0
From str:1 seq:0 (assoc:0xc99e15a0):[0]Hello                Server echoes on stream 1
[4]Message two                                              Send a message on stream 4
From str:5 seq:0 (assoc:0xc99e15a0):[4]Message two          Server echoes on stream 5
[4]Message three                                            Send a second message on stream 4
From str:5 seq:1 (assoc:0xc99e15a0):[4]Message three        Server echoes on stream 5
^D                                                          Control-D is our EOF character
freebsd4%
```

Notice that the client sends the message on streams 0 and 4 while our server sends the messages back on streams 1 and 5. This behavior is expected from our server with no arguments. Also notice that the stream sequence number incremented on the second message received on stream 5, as expected.

10.5   Exploring Head-of-Line Blocking

Our simple server provides a method to send text messages to any of a number of streams. A *stream* in SCTP is not a stream of bytes (as in TCP), but a sequence of messages that is ordered within the association. These sub-ordered streams are used to avoid the head-of-line blocking found in TCP.

Head-of-line blocking occurs when a TCP segment is lost and a subsequent TCP segment arrives out of order. That subsequent segment is held until the first TCP segment is retransmitted and arrives at the receiver. Delaying delivery of the subsequent segment assures that the receiving application sees all data in the order in which the sending application sent it. This delay to achieve complete ordering is quite useful, but it has a downside. Assume that semantically independent messages are being sent over a single TCP connection. For example, a server may send three different pictures for a Web browser to display. To make the pictures appear on the user's screen in parallel, a server sends a piece from the first picture, then a piece from the second picture, and finally a piece from the third picture. The server repeats this process until all three pictures are successfully transmitted to the browser. But what happens if a TCP packet holding a piece of the first picture is lost? The client will hold all data until that missing piece is retransmitted and arrives successfully, delaying all data for the second and third pictures, as well as data for the first picture. Figure 10.5 illustrates this problem.

> Although this is not how HTTP works, several extensions, such as SCP [Spero 1996] and SMUX [Gettys and Nielsen 1998], have been proposed to permit this type of parallel functionality on top of TCP. These multiplexing protocols have been proposed to avoid the harmful behavior of multiple parallel TCP connections that do not share state [Touch 1997]. Although creating one TCP connection per picture (as HTTP clients normally do) avoids the head-of-line blocking problem, each connection has to discover the RTT and available bandwidth independently; a loss on one connection (a signal of congestion on the path) does not necessarily cause the other connections to slow down. This leads to lower aggregate utilization of congested networks.

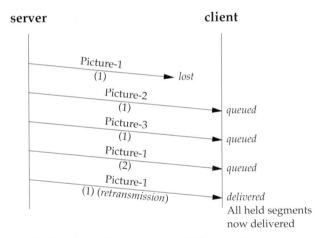

Figure 10.5 Sending three pictures over one TCP connection.

This blocking is not really what the application would like to occur. Ideally, only later pieces of the first picture would be delayed while pieces of the second and third pictures that arrive in order would be delivered immediately to the user.

Head-of-line blocking can be minimized by SCTP's multistream feature. In Figure 10.6, we see the same three pictures being sent. This time, the server uses streams so that head-of-line blocking only occurs where it is desired, allowing delivery of the second and third pictures but holding the partially received first picture until in-order delivery is possible.

We now complete our client code, including the missing function `sctpstr_cli_echoall` (Figure 10.7, p. 296), which we will use to demonstrate how SCTP minimizes head-of-line blocking. This function is similar to our previous `sctpstr_cli` function except the client no longer expects a stream number in brackets preceding each message. Instead, the function sends the user message to all `SERV_MAX_SCTP_STRM` streams. After sending the messages, the client waits for all the responses to arrive from the server. In running the code, we also pass an additional

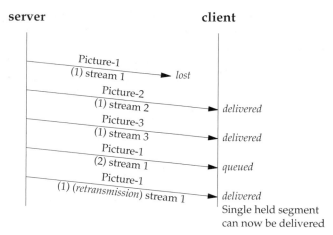

Figure 10.6 Sending three pictures over three SCTP streams.

argument to the server so that the server responds on the same stream on which a message was received. This way, the user can better track the responses sent and their order of arrival.

Initialize data structures and wait for input

13–15   As before, the client initializes the sri structure used to set up the stream it will be sending and receiving from. In addition, the client zeros out the data buffer from which it will collect user input. Then, the client enters the main loop, once again blocking on user input.

Pre-process message

16–20   The client sets up the message size and then deletes the newline character that is at the end of the buffer (if any).

Send message to each stream

21–26   The client sends the message using the sctp_sendmsg function, sending the whole buffer of SCTP_MAXLINE bytes. Before sending the message, it appends the string ".msg." and the stream number so that we can observe the order of the arriving messages. In this way, we can compare the arrival order to the order in which the client sent the actual messages. Note also the client sends the messages to a set number of streams without regard to how many were actually set up. It is possible that one or more of the sends may fail if the peer negotiates the number of streams downward.

> This code has the potential to fail if the send or receive windows are too small. If the peer's receive window is too small, it is possible that the client will block. Since the client does not read any information until all of its sends are complete, the server could also potentially block while waiting for the client to finish reading the responses the server already sent. The result of such a scenario would be a deadlock of the two endpoints. This code is not meant to be scalable, but instead to illustrate streams and head-of-line blocking in a simple, straightforward manner.

sctp/sctp_strcliecho.c

```
 1 #include    "unp.h"

 2 #define SCTP_MAXLINE    800

 3 void
 4 sctpstr_cli_echoall(FILE *fp, int sock_fd, struct sockaddr *to,
 5                     socklen_t tolen)
 6 {
 7     struct sockaddr_in peeraddr;
 8     struct sctp_sndrcvinfo sri;
 9     char    sendline[SCTP_MAXLINE], recvline[SCTP_MAXLINE];
10     socklen_t len;
11     int     rd_sz, i, strsz;
12     int     msg_flags;

13     bzero(sendline, sizeof(sendline));
14     bzero(&sri, sizeof(sri));
15     while (fgets(sendline, SCTP_MAXLINE - 9, fp) != NULL) {
16         strsz = strlen(sendline);
17         if (sendline[strsz - 1] == '\n') {
18             sendline[strsz - 1] = '\0';
19             strsz--;
20         }
21         for (i = 0; i < SERV_MAX_SCTP_STRM; i++) {
22             snprintf(sendline + strsz, sizeof(sendline) - strsz,
23                     ".msg.%d", i);
24             Sctp_sendmsg(sock_fd, sendline, sizeof(sendline),
25                         to, tolen, 0, 0, i, 0, 0);
26         }
27         for (i = 0; i < SERV_MAX_SCTP_STRM; i++) {
28             len = sizeof(peeraddr);
29             rd_sz = Sctp_recvmsg(sock_fd, recvline, sizeof(recvline),
30                         (SA *) &peeraddr, &len, &sri, &msg_flags);
31             printf("From str:%d seq:%d (assoc:0x%x):",
32                     sri.sinfo_stream, sri.sinfo_ssn,
33                     (u_int) sri.sinfo_assoc_id);
34             printf("%.*s\n", rd_sz, recvline);
35         }
36     }
37 }
```

sctp/sctp_strcliecho.c

Figure 10.7 sctp_strcliecho.

Read back echoed messages and display

27-35   We now block, reading all the response messages from our server and displaying each as we did before. After the last message is read, the client loops back for more user input.

Running the Code

We execute the client and server on two separate FreeBSD machines, separated by a configurable router, as illustrated in Figure 10.8. The router can be configured to insert both delay and loss. We execute the program first with no loss inserted by the router.

Figure 10.8 SCTP client/server lab.

We start the server with an additional argument of "0", forcing the server to not increment the stream number on its replies.

Next, we start the client, passing it the address of the echo server and an additional argument so that it will send a message to each stream.

```
freebsd4% sctpclient01 10.1.4.1 echo
Echoing messages to all streams
Hello
From str:0 seq:0 (assoc:0xc99e15a0):Hello.msg.0
From str:1 seq:0 (assoc:0xc99e15a0):Hello.msg.1
From str:2 seq:0 (assoc:0xc99e15a0):Hello.msg.2
From str:3 seq:0 (assoc:0xc99e15a0):Hello.msg.3
From str:4 seq:0 (assoc:0xc99e15a0):Hello.msg.4
From str:5 seq:0 (assoc:0xc99e15a0):Hello.msg.5
From str:6 seq:0 (assoc:0xc99e15a0):Hello.msg.6
From str:7 seq:0 (assoc:0xc99e15a0):Hello.msg.7
From str:8 seq:0 (assoc:0xc99e15a0):Hello.msg.8
From str:9 seq:0 (assoc:0xc99e15a0):Hello.msg.9
^D
freebsd4%
```

With no loss, the client sees the responses arrive back in the order in which the client sent them. We now change the parameters of our router to lose 10% of all packets traveling in both directions and restart our client.

```
freebsd4% sctpclient01 10.1.4.1 echo
Echoing messages to all streams
Hello
From str:0 seq:0 (assoc:0xc99e15a0):Hello.msg.0
From str:2 seq:0 (assoc:0xc99e15a0):Hello.msg.2
From str:3 seq:0 (assoc:0xc99e15a0):Hello.msg.3
From str:5 seq:0 (assoc:0xc99e15a0):Hello.msg.5
From str:1 seq:0 (assoc:0xc99e15a0):Hello.msg.1
From str:8 seq:0 (assoc:0xc99e15a0):Hello.msg.8
From str:4 seq:0 (assoc:0xc99e15a0):Hello.msg.4
From str:7 seq:0 (assoc:0xc99e15a0):Hello.msg.7
From str:9 seq:0 (assoc:0xc99e15a0):Hello.msg.9
From str:6 seq:0 (assoc:0xc99e15a0):Hello.msg.6
^D
freebsd4%
```

We can verify that the messages within a stream are properly being held for reordering by having the client send two messages to each stream. We also modify the client to add a suffix to its message number to help us identify each message duplicate. The modifications to the server are shown in Figure 10.9.

sctp/sctp_strcliecho2.c

```
21          for (i = 0; i < SERV_MAX_SCTP_STRM; i++) {
22              snprintf(sendline + strsz, sizeof(sendline) - strsz,
23                  ".msg.%d 1", i);
24              Sctp_sendmsg(sock_fd, sendline, sizeof(sendline),
25                      to, tolen, 0, 0, i, 0, 0);
26              snprintf(sendline + strsz, sizeof(sendline) - strsz,
27                  ".msg.%d 2", i);
28              Sctp_sendmsg(sock_fd, sendline, sizeof(sendline),
29                      to, tolen, 0, 0, i, 0, 0);
30          }
31          for (i = 0; i < SERV_MAX_SCTP_STRM * 2; i++) {
32              len = sizeof(peeraddr);
```

sctp/sctp_strcliecho2.c

Figure 10.9 sctp_strcliecho modifications.

Add additional message number and send

22–25   The client adds an additional message number, "1", to help us track which message is being sent. Then the client sends the message using the `sctp_sendmsg` function.

Change message number and send it again

26–29   The client now changes the number from "1" to "2" and sends this updated message to the same stream.

Read messages and display

31   Here the code requires only one small change: We double the number of messages the client expects to receive back from the echo server.

Running the Modified Code

We start our server and modified client, as before, and obtain the following output from the client:

```
freebsd4% sctpclient01 10.1.4.1 echo
Echoing messages to all streams
Hello
From str:0 seq:0 (assoc:0xc99e15a0):Hello.msg.0 1
From str:0 seq:1 (assoc:0xc99e15a0):Hello.msg.0 2
From str:1 seq:0 (assoc:0xc99e15a0):Hello.msg.1 1
From str:4 seq:0 (assoc:0xc99e15a0):Hello.msg.4 1
From str:5 seq:0 (assoc:0xc99e15a0):Hello.msg.5 1
From str:7 seq:0 (assoc:0xc99e15a0):Hello.msg.7 1
From str:8 seq:0 (assoc:0xc99e15a0):Hello.msg.8 1
From str:9 seq:0 (assoc:0xc99e15a0):Hello.msg.9 1
From str:3 seq:0 (assoc:0xc99e15a0):Hello.msg.3 1
From str:3 seq:1 (assoc:0xc99e15a0):Hello.msg.3 2
```

```
From str:1 seq:1 (assoc:0xc99e15a0):Hello.msg.1 2
From str:5 seq:1 (assoc:0xc99e15a0):Hello.msg.5 2
From str:2 seq:0 (assoc:0xc99e15a0):Hello.msg.2 1
From str:6 seq:0 (assoc:0xc99e15a0):Hello.msg.6 1
From str:6 seq:1 (assoc:0xc99e15a0):Hello.msg.6 2
From str:2 seq:1 (assoc:0xc99e15a0):Hello.msg.2 2
From str:7 seq:1 (assoc:0xc99e15a0):Hello.msg.7 2
From str:8 seq:1 (assoc:0xc99e15a0):Hello.msg.8 2
From str:9 seq:1 (assoc:0xc99e15a0):Hello.msg.9 2
From str:4 seq:1 (assoc:0xc99e15a0):Hello.msg.4 2
^D
freebsd4%
```

As we can see from the output, messages are lost, and yet only the messages in a particular stream are delayed. The other streams do not have their data delayed. SCTP streams can be a powerful mechanism to escape head-of-line blocking yet preserve order within a set of related messages.

10.6 Controlling the Number of Streams

We have seen how SCTP streams can be used, but how can we control the number of streams an endpoint requests at association initialization? Our previous examples used the system default for the number of outbound streams. For the FreeBSD KAME implementation of SCTP, this default is set to 10 streams. What if our application and server would like to use more than 10 streams? In Figure 10.10, we show a modification that allows a server to increase the number of streams the endpoint requests on association startup. Note that this change must be made on the socket before an association is created.

```
                                                               ──── sctp/sctpserv02.c
14      if (argc == 2)
15          stream_increment = atoi(argv[1]);
16      sock_fd = Socket(AF_INET, SOCK_SEQPACKET, IPPROTO_SCTP);
17      bzero(&initm, sizeof(initm));
18      initm.sinit_num_ostreams = SERV_MORE_STRMS_SCTP;
19      Setsockopt(sock_fd, IPPROTO_SCTP, SCTP_INITMSG, &initm, sizeof(initm));
                                                               ──── sctp/sctpserv02.c
```
Figure 10.10 Requesting more streams in our server.

Initial setup

14–16   As before, the server sets up the flags based on additional arguments and opens the socket.

Modifying the streams request

17–19   These lines contain the new code we have added to our server. The server first zeros out the `sctp_initmsg` structure. This change assures that the `setsockopt` call will not unintentionally change any other values. The server then sets the `sinit_max_ostreams` field to the number of streams it would like to request. Next, it sets the socket option with the initial message parameters.

An alternative to setting a socket option would be to use the sendmsg function and provide ancillary data to request different stream parameters from the default. This type of ancillary data is only effective on the one-to-many-style socket interface.

10.7 Controlling Termination

In our examples, we have depended on the client closing the socket to shut down the association. But the client application may not always wish to close the socket. For that matter, our server may not want to keep the association open after sending the reply message. In these cases, we need to look at two alternative mechanisms for shutting down an association. For the one-to-many-style interface, two possible methods are available to the application: one is graceful, while the other is disruptive.

If a server wishes to shut down an association after sending a message, we apply the MSG_EOF flag to the reply message in the sinfo_flags field of the sctp_sndrcvinfo structure. This flag forces an association to shut down after the message being sent is acknowledged. The other alternative is to apply the MSG_ABORT flag to the sinfo_flags field. This flag will force an immediate termination of the association with an ABORT chunk. An ABORT chunk is similar to a TCP RST segment, terminating any association without delay. Note that any data not yet transfered will be discarded. However, closing an SCTP session with an ABORT chunk does not have any negative side effects like preventing TCP's TIME_WAIT state; the ABORT chunk causes a "graceful" abortive close. Figure 10.11 shows the modifications needed to our echo server to initiate a graceful shutdown when the response message is sent to the peer. Figure 10.12 shows a modified client that sends an ABORT chunk before closing the socket.

—————————————————————————— sctp/sctpserv03.c

```
25    for ( ; ; ) {
26        len = sizeof(struct sockaddr_in);
27        rd_sz = Sctp_recvmsg(sock_fd, readbuf, sizeof(readbuf),
28                            (SA *) &cliaddr, &len, &sri, &msg_flags);
29        if (stream_increment) {
30            sri.sinfo_stream++;
31            if (sri.sinfo_stream >=
32                sctp_get_no_strms(sock_fd, (SA *) &cliaddr, len))
33                sri.sinfo_stream = 0;
34        }
35        Sctp_sendmsg(sock_fd, readbuf, rd_sz,
36                    (SA *) &cliaddr, len,
37                    sri.sinfo_ppid,
38                    (sri.sinfo_flags | MSG_EOF), sri.sinfo_stream, 0, 0);
39    }
```

—————————————————————————— sctp/sctpserv03.c

Figure 10.11 The server terminates an association on reply.

Send back response, but shut down association

38   We can see that the change in this line is simply OR'ing the `MSG_EOF` flag to the
`sctp_sendmsg` function. This flag value causes our server to shut down the association
after the reply message is successfully acknowledged.

—— *sctp/sctpclient02.c*
```
25      if (echo_to_all == 0)
26          sctpstr_cli(stdin, sock_fd, (SA *) &servaddr, sizeof(servaddr));
27      else
28          sctpstr_cli_echoall(stdin, sock_fd, (SA *) &servaddr,
29                          sizeof(servaddr));
30      strcpy(byemsg, "goodbye");
31      Sctp_sendmsg(sock_fd, byemsg, strlen(byemsg),
32                  (SA *) &servaddr, sizeof(servaddr), 0, MSG_ABORT, 0, 0, 0);
33      Close(sock_fd);
```
—— *sctp/sctpclient02.c*

Figure 10.12 The client aborts the association before closing.

Abort association before close

30-32   In these lines, the client prepares a message that is included with the abort as a user
error cause. The client then calls the `sctp_sendmsg` function with the `MSG_ABORT` flag.
This flag sends an ABORT chunk, which immediately terminates the association. The
ABORT chunk includes the user-initiated error cause with the message ("goodbye") in
the upper layer reason field.

Close socket descriptor

33   Even though the association has been aborted, we still need to close the socket
descriptor to free the system resources associated with it.

10.8   Summary

We have looked at a simple SCTP client and server spanning about 150 lines of code.
Both the client and server used the one-to-many-style SCTP interface. The server was
constructed in an iterative style, common when using the one-to-many-style interface,
receiving each message and responding on either the same stream the message was sent
on or on one stream higher. We then looked at the head-of-line blocking problem. We
modified our client to emphasize the problem and to show how SCTP streams can be
used to avoid this problem. We looked at how the number of streams can be manipulated using one of the many socket options available to control SCTP behavior. Finally,
we again modified our server and client so that they could be made to either abort an
association including a user upper layer reason code, or in our server's case, shut down
the association gracefully after sending a message.

We will examine SCTP more deeply in Chapter 23.

Exercises

10.1   In our client code shown in Figure 10.4, what will happen if SCTP returns an error? How would you correct this problem?

10.2   What will happen if our server exits before responding? Is there any way the client can be made aware of this?

10.3   In Figure 10.7 on line 22, we set `out_sz` to 800 bytes. Why do you think we do this? Is there a better way to find a more optimal size to set this to?

10.4   What effects will the Nagle algorithm (see Section 7.10) have on our client shown in Figure 10.7? Would turning off the Nagle algorithm be better for this program? Build the client and server code, then modify both of them to disable the Nagle algorithm.

10.5   In Section 10.6, we state that an application should change the number of streams before setting up an association. What happens if the application changes the number of streams afterwards?

10.6   When modifying the number of streams, we state that the one-to-many-style socket is the only style that can use ancillary data to request more streams. Why is this true? (*Hint:* The ancillary data must be sent with a message.)

10.7   Why can a server get away with not tracking the associations it has open? Is there any danger in not tracking associations?

10.8   In Section 10.7, we modified the server to terminate the association after replying to each message. Will this cause any problems? Is it a good design decision?

11

Name and
Address Conversions

11.1 Introduction

All the examples so far in this text have used numeric addresses for the hosts (e.g., 206.6.226.33) and numeric port numbers to identify the servers (e.g., port 13 for the standard daytime server and port 9877 for our echo server). We should, however, use names instead of numbers for numerous reasons: Names are easier to remember; the numeric address can change but the name can remain the same; and with the move to IPv6, numeric addresses become much longer, making it much more error-prone to enter an address by hand. This chapter describes the functions that convert between names and numeric values: `gethostbyname` and `gethostbyaddr` to convert between hostnames and IPv4 addresses, and `getservbyname` and `getservbyport` to convert between service names and port numbers. It also describes two protocol-independent functions: `getaddrinfo` and `getnameinfo`, which convert between hostnames and IP addresses *and* between service names and port numbers.

11.2 Domain Name System (DNS)

The DNS is used primarily to map between hostnames and IP addresses. A hostname can be either a *simple name*, such as `solaris` or `freebsd`, or a *fully qualified domain name* (FQDN), such as `solaris.unpbook.com`.

> Technically, an FQDN is also called an *absolute name* and must end with a period, but users often omit the ending period. The trailing period tells the resolver that this name is fully qualified and it doesn't need to search its list of possible domains.

In this section, we will cover only the basics of the DNS that we need for network programming. Readers interested in additional details should consult Chapter 14 of TCPv1 and [Albitz and Liu 2001]. The additions required for IPv6 are in RFC 1886 [Thomson and Huitema 1995] and RFC 3152 [Bush 2001].

Resource Records

Entries in the DNS are known as *resource records* (RRs). There are only a few types of RRs that we are interested in.

A
An A record maps a hostname into a 32-bit IPv4 address. For example, here are the four DNS records for the host `freebsd` in the `unpbook.com` domain, the first of which is an A record:

```
freebsd   IN   A      12.106.32.254
          IN   AAAA   3ffe:b80:1f8d:1:a00:20ff:fea7:686b
          IN   MX     5  freebsd.unpbook.com.
          IN   MX     10 mailhost.unpbook.com.
```

AAAA
A AAAA record, called a "quad A" record, maps a hostname into a 128-bit IPv6 address. The term "quad A" was chosen because a 128-bit address is four times larger than a 32-bit address.

PTR
PTR records (called "pointer records") map IP addresses into hostnames. For an IPv4 address, the 4 bytes of the 32-bit address are reversed, each byte is converted to its decimal ASCII value (0–255), and `in-addr.arpa` is then appended. The resulting string is used in the PTR query.

For an IPv6 address, the 32 4-bit nibbles of the 128-bit address are reversed, each nibble is converted to its corresponding hexadecimal ASCII value (0-9a-f), and `ip6.arpa` is appended.

For example, the two PTR records for our host `freebsd` would be `254.32.106.12.in-addr.arpa` and `b.6.8.6.7.a.e.f.f.f.0.2.0.0.a.0.1.0.0.0.d.8.f.1.0.8.b.0.e.f.f.3.ip6.arpa`.

> Earlier standards specified that IPv6 addresses were looked up in the `ip6.int` domain. This was changed to `ip6.arpa` for consistency with IPv4. There will be a transition period during which both zones will be populated.

MX
An MX record specifies a host to act as a "mail exchanger" for the specified host. In the example for the host `freebsd` above, two MX records are provided: The first has a preference value of 5 and the second has a preference value of 10. When multiple MX records exist, they are used in order of preference, starting with the smallest value.

> We do not use MX records in this text, but we mention them because they are used extensively in the real world.

CNAME CNAME stands for "canonical name." A common use is to assign CNAME records for common services, such as `ftp` and `www`. If people use these service names instead of the actual hostnames, it is transparent when a service is moved to another host. For example, the following could be CNAMEs for our host `linux`:

```
ftp        IN   CNAME   linux.unpbook.com.
www        IN   CNAME   linux.unpbook.com.
```

It is too early in the deployment of IPv6 to know what conventions administrators will use for hosts that support both IPv4 and IPv6. In our example earlier in this section, we specified both an A record and a AAAA record for our host `freebsd`. One possibility is to place both the A record and the AAAA record under the host's normal name (as shown earlier) and create another RR whose name ends in -4 containing the A record, another RR whose name ends in -6 containing the AAAA record, and another RR whose name ends in -6ll containing a AAAA record with the host's link-local address (which is sometimes handy for debugging purposes). All the records for another of our hosts are then

```
aix        IN   A       192.168.42.2
           IN   AAAA    3ffe:b80:1f8d:2:204:acff:fe17:bf38
           IN   MX      5  aix.unpbook.com.
           IN   MX      10 mailhost.unpbook.com.
aix-4      IN   A       192.168.42.2
aix-6      IN   AAAA    3ffe:b80:1f8d:2:204:acff:fe17:bf38
aix-6ll    IN   AAAA              fe80::204:acff:fe17:bf38
```

This gives us additional control over the protocol chosen by some applications, as we will see in the next chapter.

Resolvers and Name Servers

Organizations run one or more *name servers*, often the program known as BIND (Berkeley Internet Name Domain). Applications such as the clients and servers that we are writing in this text contact a DNS server by calling functions in a library known as the *resolver*. The common resolver functions are `gethostbyname` and `gethostbyaddr`, both of which are described in this chapter. The former maps a hostname into its IPv4 addresses, and the latter does the reverse mapping.

Figure 11.1 shows a typical arrangement of applications, resolvers, and name servers. We now write the application code. On some systems, the resolver code is contained in a system library and is link-edited into the application when the application is built. On others, there is a centralized resolver daemon that all applications share, and the system library code performs RPCs to this daemon. In either case, application code calls the resolver code using normal function calls, typically calling the functions `gethostbyname` and `gethostbyaddr`.

The resolver code reads its system-dependent configuration files to determine the location of the organization's name servers. (We use the plural "name servers" because most organizations run multiple name servers, even though we show only one local

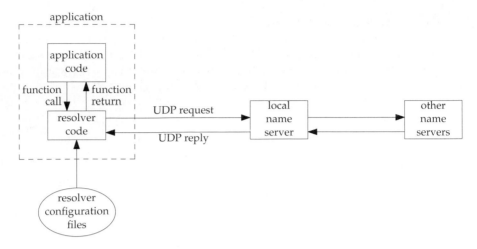

Figure 11.1 Typical arrangement of clients, resolvers, and name servers.

server in the figure. Multiple name servers are absolutely required for reliability and redundancy.) The file `/etc/resolv.conf` normally contains the IP addresses of the local name servers.

> It might be nice to use the names of the name servers in the `/etc/resolv.conf` file, since the names are easier to remember and configure, but this introduces a chicken-and-egg problem of where to go to do the name-to-address conversion for the server that will do the name and address conversion!

The resolver sends the query to the local name server using UDP. If the local name server does not know the answer, it will normally query other name servers across the Internet, also using UDP. If the answers are too large to fit in a UDP packet, the resolver will automatically switch to TCP.

DNS Alternatives

It is possible to obtain name and address information without using the DNS. Common alternatives are static host files (normally the file `/etc/hosts`, as we describe in Figure 11.21), the Network Information System (NIS) or Lightweight Directory Access Protocol (LDAP). Unfortunately, it is implementation-dependent how an administrator configures a host to use the different types of name services. Solaris 2.x, HP-UX 10 and later, and FreeBSD 5.x and later use the file `/etc/nsswitch.conf`, and AIX uses the file `/etc/netsvc.conf`. BIND 9.2.2 supplies its own version named the Information Retrieval Service (IRS), which uses the file `/etc/irs.conf`. If a name server is to be used for hostname lookups, then all these systems use the file `/etc/resolv.conf` to specify the IP addresses of the name servers. Fortunately, these differences are normally hidden to the application programmer, so we just call the resolver functions such as `gethostbyname` and `gethostbyaddr`.

11.3   `gethostbyname` **Function**

Host computers are normally known by human-readable names. All the examples that we have shown so far in this book have intentionally used IP addresses instead of names, so we know exactly what goes into the socket address structures for functions such as `connect` and `sendto`, and what is returned by functions such as `accept` and `recvfrom`. But, most applications should deal with names, not addresses. This is especially true as we move to IPv6, since IPv6 addresses (hex strings) are much longer than IPv4 dotted-decimal numbers. (The example AAAA record and `ip6.arpa` PTR record in the previous section should make this obvious.)

The most basic function that looks up a hostname is `gethostbyname`. If successful, it returns a pointer to a `hostent` structure that contains all the IPv4 addresses for the host. However, it is limited in that it can only return IPv4 addresses. See Section 11.6 for a function that handles both IPv4 and IPv6 addresses. The POSIX specification cautions that `gethostbyname` may be withdrawn in a future version of the spec.

> It is unlikely that `gethostbyname` implementations will actually disappear until the whole Internet is using IPv6, which will be far in the future. However, withdrawing the function from the POSIX specification is a way to assert that it should not be used in new code. We encourage the use of `getaddrinfo` (Section 11.6) in new programs.

```
#include <netdb.h>

struct hostent *gethostbyname(const char *hostname);
```
Returns: non-null pointer if OK, NULL on error with h_errno set

The non-null pointer returned by this function points to the following `hostent` structure:

```
struct hostent {
  char   *h_name;      /* official (canonical) name of host */
  char  **h_aliases;   /* pointer to array of pointers to alias names */
  int     h_addrtype;  /* host address type: AF_INET */
  int     h_length;    /* length of address: 4 */
  char  **h_addr_list; /* ptr to array of ptrs with IPv4 addrs */
};
```

In terms of the DNS, `gethostbyname` performs a query for an A record. This function can return only IPv4 addresses.

Figure 11.2 shows the arrangement of the `hostent` structure and the information that it points to assuming the hostname that is looked up has two alias names and three IPv4 addresses. Of these fields, the official hostname and all the aliases are null-terminated C strings.

The returned h_name is called the *canonical* name of the host. For example, given the CNAME records shown in the previous section, the canonical name of the host `ftp.unpbook.com` would be `linux.unpbook.com`. Also, if we call `gethostbyname` from the host `aix` with an unqualified hostname, say `solaris`, the FQDN (`solaris.unpbook.com`) is returned as the canonical name.

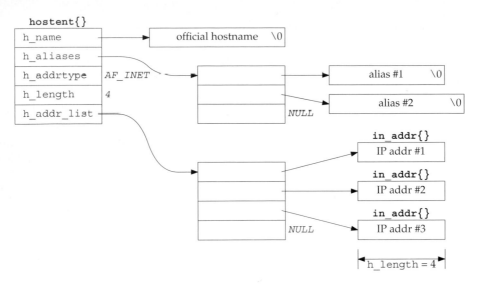

Figure 11.2 hostent structure and the information it contains.

Some versions of gethostbyname allow the *hostname* argument to be a dotted-decimal string. That is, a call of the form

```
hptr = gethostbyname("192.168.42.2");
```

will work. This code was added because the Rlogin client accepts only a hostname, calling get hostbyname, and will not accept a dotted-decimal string [Vixie 1996]. The POSIX specification permits, but does not require, this behavior, so a portable application cannot depend on it.

gethostbyname differs from the other socket functions that we have described in that it does not set errno when an error occurs. Instead, it sets the global integer h_errno to one of the following constants defined by including <netdb.h>:

- HOST_NOT_FOUND
- TRY_AGAIN
- NO_RECOVERY
- NO_DATA (identical to NO_ADDRESS)

The NO_DATA error means the specified name is valid, but it does not have an A record. An example of this is a hostname with only an MX record.

Most modern resolvers provide the function hstrerror, which takes an h_errno value as its only argument and returns a const char * pointer to a description of the error. We show some examples of the strings returned by this function in the next example.

Example

Figure 11.3 shows a simple program that calls gethostbyname for any number of command-line arguments and prints all the returned information.

——— names/hostent.c

```
 1 #include    "unp.h"

 2 int
 3 main(int argc, char **argv)
 4 {
 5     char    *ptr, **pptr;
 6     char     str[INET_ADDRSTRLEN];
 7     struct hostent *hptr;

 8     while (--argc > 0) {
 9         ptr = *++argv;
10         if ( (hptr = gethostbyname(ptr)) == NULL) {
11             err_msg("gethostbyname error for host: %s: %s",
12                     ptr, hstrerror(h_errno));
13             continue;
14         }
15         printf("official hostname: %s\n", hptr->h_name);

16         for (pptr = hptr->h_aliases; *pptr != NULL; pptr++)
17             printf("\talias: %s\n", *pptr);

18         switch (hptr->h_addrtype) {
19         case AF_INET:
20             pptr = hptr->h_addr_list;
21             for ( ; *pptr != NULL; pptr++)
22                 printf("\taddress: %s\n",
23                         Inet_ntop(hptr->h_addrtype, *pptr, str, sizeof(str)));
24             break;

25         default:
26             err_ret("unknown address type");
27             break;
28         }
29     }
30     exit(0);
31 }
```

——— names/hostent.c

Figure 11.3 Call gethostbyname and print returned information.

8–14   gethostbyname is called for each command-line argument.

15–17   The official hostname is output followed by a list of alias names.

18–24   pptr points to the array of pointers to the individual addresses. For each address, we call inet_ntop and print the returned string.

We first execute the program with the name of our host aix, which has just one IPv4 address.

```
freebsd % hostent aix
official hostname: aix.unpbook.com
        address: 192.168.42.2
```

Notice that the official hostname is the FQDN. Also notice that even though this host has an IPv6 address, only the IPv4 address is returned.

Next is a Web server with multiple IPv4 addresses.

```
freebsd % hostent cnn.com
official hostname: cnn.com
        address: 64.236.16.20
        address: 64.236.16.52
        address: 64.236.16.84
        address: 64.236.16.116
        address: 64.236.24.4
        address: 64.236.24.12
        address: 64.236.24.20
        address: 64.236.24.28
```

Next is a name that we showed in Section 11.2 as having a CNAME record.

```
freebsd % hostent www
official hostname: linux.unpbook.com
        alias: www.unpbook.com
        address: 206.168.112.219
```

As expected, the official hostname differs from our command-line argument.

To see the error strings returned by the `hstrerror` function, we first specify a non-existent hostname, and then a name that has only an MX record.

```
freebsd % hostent nosuchname.invalid
gethostbyname error for host: nosuchname.invalid: Unknown host
```

```
freebsd % hostent uunet.uu.net
gethostbyname error for host: uunet.uu.net: No address associated with name
```

11.4 `gethostbyaddr` Function

The function `gethostbyaddr` takes a binary IPv4 address and tries to find the hostname corresponding to that address. This is the reverse of `gethostbyname`.

```
#include <netdb.h>

struct hostent *gethostbyaddr(const char *addr, socklen_t len, int family);
```
                         Returns: non-null pointer if OK, NULL on error with h_errno set

This function returns a pointer to the same `hostent` structure that we described with `gethostbyname`. The field of interest in this structure is normally h_name, the canonical hostname.

The *addr* argument is not a `char*`, but is really a pointer to an `in_addr` structure containing the IPv4 address. *len* is the size of this structure: 4 for an IPv4 address. The *family* argument is `AF_INET`.

In terms of the DNS, `gethostbyaddr` queries a name server for a PTR record in the `in-addr.arpa` domain.

11.5 `getservbyname` and `getservbyport` **Functions**

Services, like hosts, are often known by names, too. If we refer to a service by its name in our code, instead of by its port number, and if the mapping from the name to port number is contained in a file (normally /etc/services), then if the port number changes, all we need to modify is one line in the /etc/services file instead of having to recompile the applications. The next function, getservbyname, looks up a service given its name.

> The canonical list of port numbers assigned to services is maintained by the IANA at http://www.iana.org/assignments/port-numbers (Section 2.9). A given /etc/services file is likely to contain a subset of the IANA assignments.

```
#include <netdb.h>

struct servent *getservbyname(const char *servname, const char *protoname);
```

                                        Returns: non-null pointer if OK, NULL on error

This function returns a pointer to the following structure:

```
struct servent {
  char   *s_name;      /* official service name */
  char   **s_aliases;  /* alias list */
  int     s_port;      /* port number, network-byte order */
  char   *s_proto;     /* protocol to use */
};
```

The service name *servname* must be specified. If a protocol is also specified (*protoname* is a non-null pointer), then the entry must also have a matching protocol. Some Internet services are provided using either TCP or UDP (for example, the DNS and all the services in Figure 2.18), while others support only a single protocol (e.g., FTP requires TCP). If *protoname* is not specified and the service supports multiple protocols, it is implementation-dependent as to which port number is returned. Normally this does not matter, because services that support multiple protocols often use the same TCP and UDP port number, but this is not guaranteed.

The main field of interest in the `servent` structure is the port number. Since the port number is returned in network byte order, we must not call `htons` when storing this into a socket address structure.

Typical calls to this function could be as follows:

```
struct servent  *sptr;

sptr = getservbyname("domain", "udp"); /* DNS using UDP */
sptr = getservbyname("ftp", "tcp");    /* FTP using TCP */
sptr = getservbyname("ftp", NULL);     /* FTP using TCP */
sptr = getservbyname("ftp", "udp");    /* this call will fail */
```

Since FTP supports only TCP, the second and third calls are the same, and the fourth call will fail. Typical lines from the /etc/services file are

```
freebsd % grep -e ^ftp -e ^domain /etc/services
ftp-data           20/tcp      #File Transfer [Default Data]
ftp                21/tcp      #File Transfer [Control]
domain             53/tcp      #Domain Name Server
domain             53/udp      #Domain Name Server
ftp-agent          574/tcp     #FTP Software Agent System
ftp-agent          574/udp     #FTP Software Agent System
ftps-data          989/tcp                 # ftp protocol, data, over TLS/SSL
ftps               990/tcp                 # ftp protocol, control, over TLS/SSL
```

The next function, `getservbyport`, looks up a service given its port number and an optional protocol.

```
#include <netdb.h>

struct servent *getservbyport(int port, const char *protoname);
```

Returns: non-null pointer if OK, NULL on error

The *port* value must be network byte ordered. Typical calls to this function could be as follows:

```
struct servent  *sptr;

sptr = getservbyport(htons(53), "udp");   /* DNS using UDP */
sptr = getservbyport(htons(21), "tcp");   /* FTP using TCP */
sptr = getservbyport(htons(21), NULL);    /* FTP using TCP */
sptr = getservbyport(htons(21), "udp");   /* this call will fail */
```

The last call fails because there is no service that uses port 21 with UDP.

Be aware that a few port numbers are used with TCP for one service, but the same port number is used with UDP for a totally different service. For example, the following:

```
freebsd % grep 514 /etc/services
shell              514/tcp     cmd         #like exec, but automatic
syslog             514/udp
```

shows that port 514 is used by the `rsh` command with TCP, but with the `syslog` daemon with UDP. Ports 512–514 have this property.

Example: Using `gethostbyname` and `getservbyname`

We can now modify our TCP daytime client from Figure 1.5 to use `gethostbyname` and `getservbyname` and take two command-line arguments: a hostname and a service name. Figure 11.4 shows our program. This program also shows the desired behavior of attempting to connect to all the IP addresses for a multihomed server, until one succeeds or all the addresses have been tried.

names/daytimetcpcli1.c

```
 1 #include     "unp.h"

 2 int
 3 main(int argc, char **argv)
 4 {
 5     int      sockfd, n;
 6     char     recvline[MAXLINE + 1];
 7     struct sockaddr_in servaddr;
 8     struct in_addr **pptr;
 9     struct in_addr *inetaddrp[2];
10     struct in_addr inetaddr;
11     struct hostent *hp;
12     struct servent *sp;
13     if (argc != 3)
14         err_quit("usage: daytimetcpcli1 <hostname> <service>");
15     if ( (hp = gethostbyname(argv[1])) == NULL) {
16         if (inet_aton(argv[1], &inetaddr) == 0) {
17             err_quit("hostname error for %s: %s", argv[1],
18                     hstrerror(h_errno));
19         } else {
20             inetaddrp[0] = &inetaddr;
21             inetaddrp[1] = NULL;
22             pptr = inetaddrp;
23         }
24     } else {
25         pptr = (struct in_addr **) hp->h_addr_list;
26     }
27     if ( (sp = getservbyname(argv[2], "tcp")) == NULL)
28         err_quit("getservbyname error for %s", argv[2]);
29     for ( ; *pptr != NULL; pptr++) {
30         sockfd = Socket(AF_INET, SOCK_STREAM, 0);
31         bzero(&servaddr, sizeof(servaddr));
32         servaddr.sin_family = AF_INET;
33         servaddr.sin_port = sp->s_port;
34         memcpy(&servaddr.sin_addr, *pptr, sizeof(struct in_addr));
35         printf("trying %s\n", Sock_ntop((SA *) &servaddr, sizeof(servaddr)));
36         if (connect(sockfd, (SA *) &servaddr, sizeof(servaddr)) == 0)
37             break;                  /* success */
38         err_ret("connect error");
39         close(sockfd);
40     }
41     if (*pptr == NULL)
42         err_quit("unable to connect");
43     while ( (n = Read(sockfd, recvline, MAXLINE)) > 0) {
44         recvline[n] = 0;            /* null terminate */
45         Fputs(recvline, stdout);
46     }
47     exit(0);
48 }
```

names/daytimetcpcli1.c

Figure 11.4 Our daytime client that uses gethostbyname and getservbyname.

Call `gethostbyname` and `getservbyname`

13-28   The first command-line argument is a hostname, which we pass as an argument to `gethostbyname`, and the second is a service name, which we pass as an argument to `getservbyname`. Our code assumes TCP, and that is what we use as the second argument to `getservbyname`. If `gethostbyname` fails to look up the name, we try using the `inet_aton` function (Section 3.6) to see if the argument was an ASCII-format address. If it was, we construct a single-element list consisting of the corresponding address.

Try each server address

29-35   We now code the calls to `socket` and `connect` in a loop that is executed for every server address until a `connect` succeeds or the list of IP addresses is exhausted. After calling `socket`, we fill in an Internet socket address structure with the IP address and port of the server. While we could move the call to `bzero` and the subsequent two assignments out of the loop, for efficiency, the code is easier to read as shown. Establishing the connection with the server is rarely a performance bottleneck for a network client.

Call `connect`

36-39   `connect` is called, and if it succeeds, `break` terminates the loop. If the connection establishment fails, we print an error and close the socket. Recall that a descriptor that fails a call to `connect` must be closed and is no longer usable.

Check for failure

41-42   If the loop terminates because no call to `connect` succeeded, the program terminates.

Read server's reply

43-47   Otherwise, we read the server's response, terminating when the server closes the connection.

If we run this program specifying one of our hosts that is running the daytime server, we get the expected output.

```
freebsd % daytimetcpcli1 aix daytime
trying 192.168.42.2:13
Sun Jul 27 22:44:19 2003
```

What is more interesting is to run the program to a multihomed system that is not running the daytime server.

```
freebsd % daytimetcpcli1 gateway.tuc.noao.edu daytime
trying 140.252.108.1:13
connect error: Operation timed out
trying 140.252.1.4:13
connect error: Operation timed out
trying 140.252.104.1:13
connect error: Connection refused
unable to connect
```

11.6 `getaddrinfo` **Function**

The `gethostbyname` and `gethostbyaddr` functions only support IPv4. The API for resolving IPv6 addresses went through several iterations, as will be described in Section 11.20; the final result is the `getaddrinfo` function. The `getaddrinfo` function handles both name-to-address and service-to-port translation, and returns `sockaddr` structures instead of a list of addresses. These `sockaddr` structures can then be used by the socket functions directly. In this way, the `getaddrinfo` function hides all the protocol dependencies in the library function, which is where they belong. The application deals only with the socket address structures that are filled in by `getaddrinfo`. This function is defined in the POSIX specification.

> The POSIX definition of this function comes from an earlier proposal by Keith Sklower for a function named `getconninfo`. This function was the result of discussions with Eric Allman, William Durst, Michael Karels, and Steven Wise, and from an early implementation written by Eric Allman. The observation that specifying a hostname and a service name would suffice for connecting to a service independent of protocol details was made by Marshall Rose in a proposal to X/Open.

```
#include <netdb.h>

int getaddrinfo(const char *hostname, const char *service,
                const struct addrinfo *hints, struct addrinfo **result);
```

Returns: 0 if OK, nonzero on error (see Figure 11.7)

This function returns through the *result* pointer a pointer to a linked list of `addrinfo` structures, which is defined by including `<netdb.h>`.

```
struct addrinfo {
    int          ai_flags;           /* AI_PASSIVE, AI_CANONNAME */
    int          ai_family;          /* AF_xxx */
    int          ai_socktype;        /* SOCK_xxx */
    int          ai_protocol;        /* 0 or IPPROTO_xxx for IPv4 and IPv6 */
    socklen_t    ai_addrlen;         /* length of ai_addr */
    char         *ai_canonname;      /* ptr to canonical name for host */
    struct sockaddr  *ai_addr;       /* ptr to socket address structure */
    struct addrinfo  *ai_next;       /* ptr to next structure in linked list */
};
```

The *hostname* is either a hostname or an address string (dotted-decimal for IPv4 or a hex string for IPv6). The *service* is either a service name or a decimal port number string. (See also Exercise 11.4, where we want to allow an address string for the host or a port number string for the service.)

hints is either a null pointer or a pointer to an `addrinfo` structure that the caller fills in with hints about the types of information the caller wants returned. For example, if the specified service is provided for both TCP and UDP (e.g., the `domain` service, which refers to a DNS server), the caller can set the `ai_socktype` member of the *hints* structure to `SOCK_DGRAM`. The only information returned will be for datagram sockets.

The members of the *hints* structure that can be set by the caller are:

- `ai_flags` (zero or more `AI_XXX` values *OR*'ed together)
- `ai_family` (an `AF_xxx` value)
- `ai_socktype` (a `SOCK_xxx` value)
- `ai_protocol`

The possible values for the `ai_flags` member and their meanings are:

`AI_PASSIVE`	The caller will use the socket for a passive open.
`AI_CANONNAME`	Tells the function to return the canonical name of the host.
`AI_NUMERICHOST`	Prevents any kind of name-to-address mapping; the *hostname* argument must be an address string.
`AI_NUMERICSERV`	Prevents any kind of name-to-service mapping; the *service* argument must be a decimal port number string.
`AI_V4MAPPED`	If specified along with an `ai_family` of `AF_INET6`, then returns IPv4-mapped IPv6 addresses corresponding to A records if there are no available AAAA records.
`AI_ALL`	If specified along with `AI_V4MAPPED`, then returns IPv4-mapped IPv6 addresses in addition to any AAAA records belonging to the name.
`AI_ADDRCONFIG`	Only looks up addresses for a given IP version if there is one or more interface that is not a loopback interface configured with an IP address of that version.

If the *hints* argument is a null pointer, the function assumes a value of 0 for `ai_flags`, `ai_socktype`, and `ai_protocol`, and a value of `AF_UNSPEC` for `ai_family`.

If the function returns success (0), the variable pointed to by the *result* argument is filled in with a pointer to a linked list of `addrinfo` structures, linked through the `ai_next` pointer. There are two ways that multiple structures can be returned:

1. If there are multiple addresses associated with the *hostname*, one structure is returned for each address that is usable with the requested address family (the `ai_family` hint, if specified).

2. If the service is provided for multiple socket types, one structure can be returned for each socket type, depending on the `ai_socktype` hint. (Note that most `getaddrinfo` implementations consider a port number string to be implemented only by the socket type requested in `ai_socktype`; if `ai_socktype` is not specified, an error is returned instead.)

For example, if no hints are provided and if the `domain` service is looked up for a host with two IP addresses, four `addrinfo` structures are returned:

- One for the first IP address and a socket type of SOCK_STREAM
- One for the first IP address and a socket type of SOCK_DGRAM
- One for the second IP address and a socket type of SOCK_STREAM
- One for the second IP address and a socket type of SOCK_DGRAM

We show this example in Figure 11.5. There is no guaranteed order of the structures when multiple items are returned; that is, we cannot assume that TCP services will be returned before UDP services.

> Although not guaranteed, an implementation should return the IP addresses in the same order as they are returned by the DNS. Some resolvers allow the administrator to specify an address sorting order in the /etc/resolv.conf file. IPv6 specifies address selection rules (RFC 3484 [Draves 2003]), which could affect the order of addresses returned by getaddrinfo.

The information returned in the addrinfo structures is ready for a call to socket and then either a call to connect or sendto (for a client), or bind (for a server). The arguments to socket are the members ai_family, ai_socktype, and ai_protocol. The second and third arguments to either connect or bind are ai_addr (a pointer to a socket address structure of the appropriate type, filled in by getaddrinfo) and ai_addrlen (the length of this socket address structure).

If the AI_CANONNAME flag is set in the *hints* structure, the ai_canonname member of the first returned structure points to the canonical name of the host. In terms of the DNS, this is normally the FQDN. Programs like telnet commonly use this flag to be able to print the canonical hostname of the system to which they are connecting, so that if the user supplied a shortcut or an alias, he or she knows what got looked up.

Figure 11.5 shows the returned information if we execute the following:

```
struct addrinfo      hints, *res;

bzero(&hints, sizeof(hints));
hints.ai_flags = AI_CANONNAME;
hints.ai_family = AF_INET;

getaddrinfo("freebsd4", "domain", &hints, &res);
```

In this figure, everything except the res variable is dynamically allocated memory (e.g., from malloc). We assume that the canonical name of the host freebsd4 is freebsd4.unpbook.com and that this host has two IPv4 addresses in the DNS.

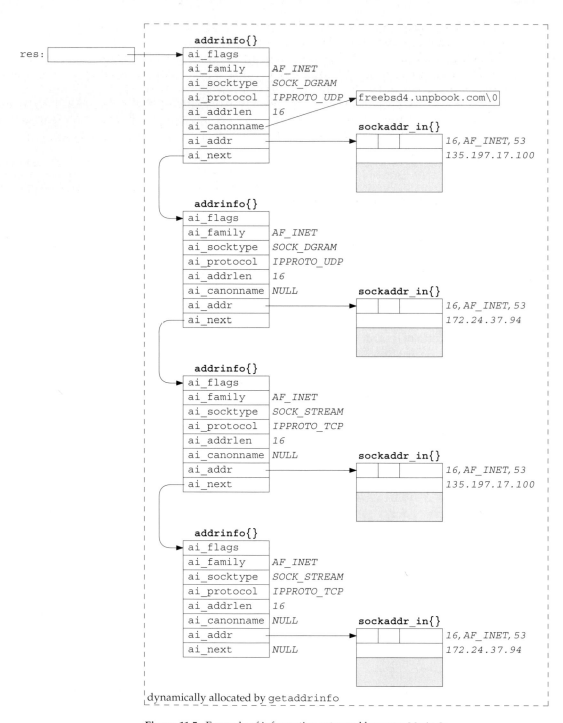

Figure 11.5 Example of information returned by `getaddrinfo`.

Port 53 is for the domain service. This port number will be in network byte order in the socket address structures. We also show the returned ai_protocol values as IPPROTO_TCP or IPPROTO_UDP. It would also be acceptable for getaddrinfo to return an ai_protocol of 0 for the two SOCK_STREAM structures if that is sufficient to specify TCP (it is not sufficient if the system implements SCTP, for example), and an ai_protocol of 0 for the two SOCK_DGRAM structures if the system doesn't implement any other SOCK_DGRAM protocols for IP (as of this writing, none are yet standardized, but two are in development in the IETF). It is safest for getaddrinfo to always return the specific protocol.

Figure 11.6 summarizes the number of addrinfo structures returned for each address that is being returned, based on the specified service name (which can be a decimal port number) and any ai_socktype hint.

ai_socktype hint	Service is a name, service provided by:						Service is a port number
	TCP only	UDP only	SCTP only	TCP and UDP	TCP and SCTP	TCP, UDP, and SCTP	
0	1	1	1	2	2	3	error
SOCK_STREAM	1	error	1	1	2	2	2
SOCK_DGRAM	error	1	error	1	error	1	1
SOCK_SEQPACKET	error	error	1	error	1	1	1

Figure 11.6 Number of addrinfo structures returned per IP address.

Multiple addrinfo structures are returned for each IP address only when no ai_socktype hint is provided and the service name is supported by multiple transport protocols (as indicated in the /etc/services file).

If we were to enumerate all 64 possible inputs to getaddrinfo (there are six input variables), many would be invalid and some would make little sense. Instead, we will look at the common cases.

- Specify the *hostname* and *service*. This is normal for a TCP or UDP client. On return, a TCP client loops through all returned IP addresses, calling socket and connect for each one, until the connection succeeds or until all addresses have been tried. We will show an example of this with our tcp_connect function in Figure 11.10.

  For a UDP client, the socket address structure filled in by getaddrinfo would be used in a call to sendto or connect. If the client can tell that the first address doesn't appear to work (either by receiving an error on a connected UDP socket or by experiencing a timeout on an unconnected socket), additional addresses can be tried.

  If the client knows it handles only one type of socket (e.g., Telnet and FTP clients handle only TCP; TFTP clients handle only UDP), then the ai_socktype member of the *hints* structure should be specified as either SOCK_STREAM or SOCK_DGRAM.

- A typical server specifies the *service* but not the *hostname*, and specifies the AI_PASSIVE flag in the *hints* structure. The socket address structures returned should contain an IP address of INADDR_ANY (for IPv4) or IN6ADDR_ANY_INIT (for IPv6). A TCP server then calls socket, bind, and listen. If the server wants to malloc another socket address structure to obtain the client's address from accept, the returned ai_addrlen value specifies this size.

  A UDP server would call socket, bind, and then recvfrom. If the server wants to malloc another socket address structure to obtain the client's address from recvfrom, the returned ai_addrlen value specifies this size.

  As with the typical client code, if the server knows it only handles one type of socket, the ai_socktype member of the *hints* structure should be set to either SOCK_STREAM or SOCK_DGRAM. This avoids having multiple structures returned, possibly with the wrong ai_socktype value.

- The TCP servers that we have shown so far create one listening socket, and the UDP servers create one datagram socket. That is what we assume in the previous item. An alternate server design is for the server to handle multiple sockets using select or poll. In this scenario, the server would go through the entire list of structures returned by getaddrinfo, create one socket per structure, and use select or poll.

  > The problem with this technique is that one reason for getaddrinfo returning multiple structures is when a service can be handled by IPv4 and IPv6 (Figure 11.8). But, these two protocols are not completely independent, as we will see in Section 12.2. That is, if we create a listening IPv6 socket for a given port, there is no need to also create a listening IPv4 socket for that same port, because connections arriving from IPv4 clients are automatically handled by the protocol stack and by the IPv6 listening socket, assuming that the IPV6_V6ONLY socket option is not set.

Despite the fact that getaddrinfo is "better" than the gethostbyname and getservbyname functions (it makes it easier to write protocol-independent code; one function handles both the hostname and the service; and all the returned information is dynamically allocated, not statically allocated), it is still not as easy to use as it could be. The problem is that we must allocate a *hints* structure, initialize it to 0, fill in the desired fields, call getaddrinfo, and then traverse a linked list trying each one. In the next sections, we will provide some simpler interfaces for the typical TCP and UDP clients and servers that we will write in the remainder of this text.

getaddrinfo solves the problem of converting hostnames and service names into socket address structures. In Section 11.17, we will describe the reverse function, get nameinfo, which converts socket address structures into hostnames and service names.

11.7 `gai_strerror` **Function**

The nonzero error return values from getaddrinfo have the names and meanings shown in Figure 11.7. The function gai_strerror takes one of these values as an argument and returns a pointer to the corresponding error string.

```
#include <netdb.h>

const char *gai_strerror(int error);
```

                                    Returns: pointer to string describing error message

Constant	Description
EAI_AGAIN	Temporary failure in name resolution
EAI_BADFLAGS	Invalid value for ai_flags
EAI_FAIL	Unrecoverable failure in name resolution
EAI_FAMILY	ai_family not supported
EAI_MEMORY	Memory allocation failure
EAI_NONAME	*hostname* or *service* not provided, or not known
EAI_OVERFLOW	User argument buffer overflowed (*getnameinfo*() only)
EAI_SERVICE	*service* not supported for ai_socktype
EAI_SOCKTYPE	ai_socktype not supported
EAI_SYSTEM	System error returned in errno

Figure 11.7 Nonzero error return constants from getaddrinfo.

11.8 `freeaddrinfo` Function

All the storage returned by getaddrinfo, the addrinfo structures, the ai_addr structures, and the ai_canonname string are obtained dynamically (e.g., from malloc). This storage is returned by calling freeaddrinfo.

```
#include <netdb.h>

void freeaddrinfo(struct addrinfo *ai);
```

ai should point to the first addrinfo structure returned by getaddrinfo. All the structures in the linked list are freed, along with any dynamic storage pointed to by those structures (e.g., socket address structures and canonical hostnames).

Assume we call getaddrinfo, traverse the linked list of addrinfo structures, and find the desired structure. If we then try to save a copy of the information by copying just the addrinfo structure and calling freeaddrinfo, we have a lurking bug. The reason is that the addrinfo structure itself points to dynamically allocated memory (for the socket address structure and possibly the canonical name), and memory pointed to by our saved structure is returned to the system when freeaddrinfo is called and can be used for something else.

> Making a copy of just the addrinfo structure and not the structures that it in turn points to is called a *shallow copy*. Copying the addrinfo structure and all the structures that it points to is called a *deep copy*.

11.9 `getaddrinfo` Function: IPv6

The POSIX specification defines the `getaddrinfo` function and the information it returns for both IPv4 and IPv6. We note the following points before summarizing these return values in Figure 11.8.

- `getaddrinfo` is dealing with two different inputs: the type of socket address structure the caller wants back and the type of records that should be searched for in the DNS or other database.

- The address family in the *hints* structure provided by the caller specifies the type of socket address structure that the caller expects to be returned. If the caller specifies AF_INET, the function must not return any `sockaddr_in6` structures; if the caller specifies AF_INET6, the function must not return any `sockaddr_in` structures.

- POSIX says that specifying AF_UNSPEC will return addresses that can be used with *any* protocol family that can be used with the hostname and service name. This implies that if a host has both AAAA records and A records, the AAAA records are returned as `sockaddr_in6` structures and the A records are returned as `sockaddr_in` structures. It makes no sense to also return the A records as IPv4-mapped IPv6 addresses in `sockaddr_in6` structures because no additional information is being returned: These addresses are already being returned in `sockaddr_in` structures.

- This statement in the POSIX specification also implies that if the AI_PASSIVE flag is specified without a hostname, then the IPv6 wildcard address (IN6ADDR_ANY_INIT or 0::0) should be returned as a `sockaddr_in6` structure, along with the IPv4 wildcard address (INADDR_ANY or 0.0.0.0), which is returned as a `sockaddr_in` structure. It also makes sense to return the IPv6 wildcard address first because we will see in Section 12.2 that an IPv6 server socket can handle both IPv6 and IPv4 clients on a dual-stack host.

- The address family specified in the *hint* structure's `ai_family` member, along with the flags such as AI_V4MAPPED and AI_ALL specified in the `ai_flags` member, dictate the type of records that are searched for in the DNS (A and/or AAAA) and what type of addresses are returned (IPv4, IPv6, and/or IPv4-mapped IPv6). We summarize this in Figure 11.8.

- The hostname can also be either an IPv6 hex string or an IPv4 dotted-decimal string. The validity of this string depends on the address family specified by the caller. An IPv6 hex string is not acceptable if AF_INET is specified, and an IPv4 dotted-decimal string is not acceptable if AF_INET6 is specified. But, if AF_UNSPEC is specified, either is acceptable and the appropriate type of socket address structure is returned.

> One could argue that if AF_INET6 is specified, then a dotted-decimal string should be returned as an IPv4-mapped IPv6 address in a `sockaddr_in6` structure. But, another way to obtain this result is to prefix the dotted-decimal string with `0::ffff:`.

Figure 11.8 summarizes how we expect `getaddrinfo` to handle IPv4 and IPv6 addresses. The "Result" column is what we want returned to the caller, given the variables in the first three columns. The "Action" column is how we obtain this result.

Hostname specified by caller	Address family specified by caller	Hostname string contains	Result	Action
non-null hostname string; active or passive	AF_UNSPEC	hostname	All AAAA records returned as sockaddr_in6{}s *and* all A records returned as sockaddr_in{}s	AAAA record search *and* A record search
		hex string	One sockaddr_in6{}	inet_pton(AF_INET6)
		dotted-decimal	One sockaddr_in{}	inet_pton(AF_INET)
	AF_INET6	hostname	All AAAA records returned as sockaddr_in6{}s	AAAA record search
			If ai_flags contains AI_V4MAPPED, all AAAA records returned as sockaddr_in6{}s *else* all A records returned as IPv4-mapped IPv6 sockaddr_in6{}s	AAAA record search if no results then A record search
			If ai_flags contains AI_V4MAPPED and AI_ALL, all AAAA records returned as sockaddr_in6{}s *and* all A records returned as IPv4-mapped IPv6 sockaddr_in6{}s	AAAA record search *and* A record search
		hex string	One sockaddr_in6{}	inet_pton(AF_INET6)
		dotted-decimal	Looked up as hostname	
	AF_INET	hostname	All A records returned as sockaddr_in{}s	A record search
		hex string	Looked up as hostname	
		dotted-decimal	One sockaddr_in{}	inet_pton(AF_INET)
null hostname string; passive	AF_UNSPEC	implied 0::0 implied 0.0.0.0	One sockaddr_in6{} and one sockaddr_in{}	inet_pton(AF_INET6) inet_pton(AF_INET)
	AF_INET6	implied 0::0	One sockaddr_in6{}	inet_pton(AF_INET6)
	AF_INET	implied 0.0.0.0	One sockaddr_in{}	inet_pton(AF_INET)
null hostname string; active	AF_UNSPEC	implied 0::1 implied 127.0.0.1	One sockaddr_in6{} and one sockaddr_in{}	inet_pton(AF_INET6) inet_pton(AF_INET)
	AF_INET6	implied 0::1	One sockaddr_in6{}	inet_pton(AF_INET6)
	AF_INET	implied 127.0.0.1	One sockaddr_in{}	inet_pton(AF_INET)

Figure 11.8 Summary of getaddrinfo and its actions and results.

Note that Figure 11.8 specifies only how getaddrinfo handles IPv4 and IPv6; that is, the number of addresses returned to the caller. The actual number of addrinfo structures returned to the caller also depends on the socket type specified and the service name, as summarized earlier in Figure 11.6.

11.10 `getaddrinfo` Function: Examples

We will now show some examples of `getaddrinfo` using a test program that lets us enter all the parameters: the hostname, service name, address family, socket type, and `AI_CANONNAME` and `AI_PASSIVE` flags. (We do not show this test program, as it is about 350 lines of uninteresting code. It is provided with the source code for the book, as described in the Preface.) The test program outputs information on the variable number of `addrinfo` structures that are returned, showing the arguments for a call to `socket` and the address in each socket address structure.

We first show the same example as in Figure 11.5.

```
freebsd % testga -f inet -c -h freebsd4 -s domain
socket(AF_INET, SOCK_DGRAM, 17), ai_canonname = freebsd4.unpbook.com
        address: 135.197.17.100:53

socket(AF_INET, SOCK_DGRAM, 17)
        address: 172.24.37.94:53

socket(AF_INET, SOCK_STREAM, 6), ai_canonname = freebsd4.unpbook.com
        address: 135.197.17.100:53

socket(AF_INET, SOCK_STREAM, 6)
        address: 172.24.37.94:53
```

The `-f inet` option specifies the address family, `-c` says to return the canonical name, `-h bsdi` specifies the hostname, and `-s domain` specifies the service name.

The common client scenario is to specify the address family, socket type (the `-t` option), hostname, and service name. The following example shows this for a multi-homed host with three IPv4 addresses:

```
freebsd % testga -f inet -t stream -h gateway.tuc.noao.edu -s daytime
socket(AF_INET, SOCK_STREAM, 6)
        address: 140.252.108.1:13

socket(AF_INET, SOCK_STREAM, 6)
        address: 140.252.1.4:13

socket(AF_INET, SOCK_STREAM, 6)
        address: 140.252.104.1:13
```

Next, we specify our host `aix`, which has both a AAAA record and an A record. We do not specify the address family, but we provide a service name of `ftp`, which is provided by TCP only.

```
freebsd % testga  -h aix  -s ftp -t stream
socket(AF_INET6, SOCK_STREAM, 6)
        address: [3ffe:b80:1f8d:2:204:acff:fe17:bf38]:21
socket(AF_INET, SOCK_STREAM, 6)
        address: 192.168.42.2:21
```

Since we didn't specify the address family, and since we ran this example on a host that supports both IPv4 and IPv6, two structures are returned: one for IPv4 and one for IPv6.

Next, we specify the AI_PASSIVE flag (the -p option); we do not specify an address family or hostname (implying the wildcard address). We also specify a port number of 8888 and a stream socket.

```
freebsd % testga  -p  -s 8888  -t stream

socket(AF_INET6, SOCK_STREAM, 6)
        address: [::]:8888

socket(AF_INET, SOCK_STREAM, 6)
        address: 0.0.0.0:8888
```

Two structures are returned. Since we ran this on a host that supports IPv6 and IPv4 without specifying an address family, getaddrinfo returns the IPv6 wildcard address and the IPv4 wildcard address. The IPv6 structure is returned before the IPv4 structure, because we will see in Chapter 12 that an IPv6 client or server on a dual-stack host can communicate with either IPv6 or IPv4 peers.

11.11 host_serv Function

Our first interface to getaddrinfo does not require the caller to allocate a *hints* structure and fill it in. Instead, the two fields of interest, the address family and the socket type, are arguments to our host_serv function.

```
#include "unp.h"

struct addrinfo *host_serv(const char *hostname, const char *service,
                           int family, int socktype);

                           Returns: pointer to addrinfo structure if OK, NULL on error
```

Figure 11.9 shows the source code for this function.

```
                                                                    ——— lib/host_serv.c
 1 #include    "unp.h"

 2 struct addrinfo *
 3 host_serv(const char *host, const char *serv, int family, int socktype)
 4 {
 5     int    n;
 6     struct addrinfo hints, *res;

 7     bzero(&hints, sizeof(struct addrinfo));
 8     hints.ai_flags = AI_CANONNAME;  /* always return canonical name */
 9     hints.ai_family = family;      /* AF_UNSPEC, AF_INET, AF_INET6, etc. */
10     hints.ai_socktype = socktype;   /* 0, SOCK_STREAM, SOCK_DGRAM, etc. */

11     if ( (n = getaddrinfo(host, serv, &hints, &res)) != 0)
12         return (NULL);

13     return (res);                  /* return pointer to first on linked list */
14 }
                                                                    ——— lib/host_serv.c
```

Figure 11.9 host_serv function.

7–13   The function initializes a *hints* structure, calls getaddrinfo, and returns a null pointer if an error occurs.

We will call this function from Figure 16.17 when we want to use getaddrinfo to obtain the host and service information, but we want to establish the connection ourself.

11.12 tcp_connect Function

We will now write two functions that use getaddrinfo to handle most scenarios for the TCP clients and servers that we write. The first function, tcp_connect, performs the normal client steps: create a TCP socket and connect to a server.

```
#include "unp.h"

int tcp_connect(const char *hostname, const char *service);

                            Returns: connected socket descriptor if OK, no return on error
```

Figure 11.10 shows the source code.

```
                                                                          lib/tcp_connect.c
 1 #include    "unp.h"

 2 int
 3 tcp_connect(const char *host, const char *serv)
 4 {
 5     int      sockfd, n;
 6     struct addrinfo hints, *res, *ressave;

 7     bzero(&hints, sizeof(struct addrinfo));
 8     hints.ai_family = AF_UNSPEC;
 9     hints.ai_socktype = SOCK_STREAM;

10     if ( (n = getaddrinfo(host, serv, &hints, &res)) != 0)
11         err_quit("tcp_connect error for %s, %s: %s",
12                  host, serv, gai_strerror(n));
13     ressave = res;

14     do {
15         sockfd = socket(res->ai_family, res->ai_socktype, res->ai_protocol);
16         if (sockfd < 0)
17             continue;              /* ignore this one */

18         if (connect(sockfd, res->ai_addr, res->ai_addrlen) == 0)
19             break;                 /* success */

20         Close(sockfd);             /* ignore this one */
21     } while ( (res = res->ai_next) != NULL);

22     if (res == NULL)               /* errno set from final connect() */
23         err_sys("tcp_connect error for %s, %s", host, serv);

24     freeaddrinfo(ressave);

25     return (sockfd);
26 }
                                                                          lib/tcp_connect.c
```

Figure 11.10 `tcp_connect` function: performs normal client steps.

Call `getaddrinfo`

7–13   `getaddrinfo` is called once and we specify the address family as `AF_UNSPEC` and the socket type as `SOCK_STREAM`.

Try each `addrinfo` structure until success or end of list

14–25   Each returned IP address is then tried. `socket` and `connect` are called. It is not a fatal error for `socket` to fail, as this could happen if an IPv6 address is returned but the host kernel does not support IPv6. If `connect` succeeds, a `break` is made out of the loop. Otherwise, when all the addresses have been tried, the loop also terminates. `freeaddrinfo` returns all the dynamic memory.

This function (and our other functions that provide a simpler interface to getaddrinfo in the following sections) terminates if either getaddrinfo fails or no call to connect succeeds. The only return is upon success. It would be hard to return an error code (one of the EAI_xxx constants) without adding another argument. This means that our wrapper function is trivial.

```
int
Tcp_connect(const char *host, const char *serv)
{
    return(tcp_connect(host, serv));
}
```

Nevertheless, we still call our wrapper function instead of tcp_connect, to maintain consistency with the remainder of the text.

> The problem with the return value is that descriptors are non-negative, but we do not know whether the EAI_xxx values are positive or negative. If these values were positive, we could return the negative of these values if getaddrinfo fails, but we also have to return some other negative value to indicate that all the structures were tried without success.

Example: Daytime Client

Figure 11.11 shows our daytime client from Figure 1.5 recoded to use tcp_connect.

—————————————————————————————————— names/daytimetcpcli.c

```
 1 #include    "unp.h"

 2 int
 3 main(int argc, char **argv)
 4 {
 5     int      sockfd, n;
 6     char     recvline[MAXLINE + 1];
 7     socklen_t len;
 8     struct sockaddr_storage ss;

 9     if (argc != 3)
10         err_quit
11             ("usage: daytimetcpcli <hostname/IPaddress> <service/port#>");

12     sockfd = Tcp_connect(argv[1], argv[2]);

13     len = sizeof(ss);
14     Getpeername(sockfd, (SA *) &ss, &len);
15     printf("connected to %s\n", Sock_ntop_host((SA *) &ss, len));

16     while ( (n = Read(sockfd, recvline, MAXLINE)) > 0) {
17         recvline[n] = 0;          /* null terminate */
18         Fputs(recvline, stdout);
19     }
20     exit(0);
21 }
```

—————————————————————————————————— names/daytimetcpcli.c

Figure 11.11 Daytime client recoded to use tcp_connect.

Command-line arguments

9–11   We now require a second command-line argument to specify either the service name or the port number, which allows our program to connect to other ports.

Connect to server

12   All the socket code for this client is now performed by tcp_connect.

Print server's address

13–15   We call getpeername to fetch the server's protocol address and print it. We do this to verify the protocol being used in the examples we are about to show.

Note that tcp_connect does not return the size of the socket address structure that was used for the connect. We could have added a pointer argument to return this value, but one design goal for this function was to reduce the number of arguments compared to getaddrinfo. What we do instead is use a sockaddr_storage socket address structure, which is large enough to hold and fulfills the alignment constraints of any socket address type the system supports.

This version of our client works with both IPv4 and IPv6, while the version in Figure 1.5 worked only with IPv4 and the version in Figure 1.6 worked only with IPv6. You should also compare our new version with Figure E.12, which we coded to use gethostbyname and getservbyname to support both IPv4 and IPv6.

We first specify the name of a host that supports only IPv4.

```
freebsd % daytimetcpcli linux daytime
connected to 206.168.112.96
Sun Jul 27 23:06:24 2003
```

Next, we specify the name of a host that supports both IPv4 and IPv6.

```
freebsd % daytimetcpcli aix daytime
connected to 3ffe:b80:1f8d:2:204:acff:fe17:bf38
Sun Jul 27 23:17:13 2003
```

The IPv6 address is used because the host has both a AAAA record and an A record, and as noted in Figure 11.8, since tcp_connect sets the address family to AF_UNSPEC, AAAA records are searched for first, and only if this fails is a search made for an A record.

In the next example, we force the use of the IPv4 address by specifying the hostname with our -4 suffix, which we noted in Section 11.2 is our convention for the hostname with only A records.

```
freebsd % daytimetcpcli aix-4 daytime
connected to 192.168.42.2
Sun Jul 27 23:17:48 2003
```

11.13 `tcp_listen` Function

Our next function, `tcp_listen`, performs the normal TCP server steps: create a TCP socket, `bind` the server's well-known port, and allow incoming connection requests to be accepted. Figure 11.12 shows the source code.

```
#include "unp.h"

int tcp_listen(const char *hostname, const char *service, socklen_t *addrlenp);
                                    Returns: connected socket descriptor if OK, no return on error
```

Call `getaddrinfo`

8–15   We initialize an `addrinfo` structure with our hints: `AI_PASSIVE`, since this function is for a server, `AF_UNSPEC` for the address family, and `SOCK_STREAM`. Recall from Figure 11.8 that if a hostname is not specified (which is common for a server that wants to bind the wildcard address), the `AI_PASSIVE` and `AF_UNSPEC` hints will cause two socket address structures to be returned: the first for IPv6 and the next for IPv4 (assuming a dual-stack host).

Create socket and bind address

16–25   The `socket` and `bind` functions are called. If either call fails, we just ignore this `addrinfo` structure and move on to the next one. As stated in Section 7.5, we always set the `SO_REUSEADDR` socket option for a TCP server.

Check for failure

26–27   If all the calls to `socket` and `bind` fail, we print an error and terminate. As with our `tcp_connect` function in the previous section, we do not try to return an error from this function.

28   The socket is turned into a listening socket by `listen`.

Return size of socket address structure

29–32   If the *addrlenp* argument is non-null, we return the size of the protocol addresses through this pointer. This allows the caller to allocate memory for a socket address structure to obtain the client's protocol address from `accept`. (See Exercise 11.7 also.)

Example: Daytime Server

Figure 11.13 shows our daytime server from Figure 4.11, recoded to use `tcp_listen`.

Require service name or port number as command-line argument

11–12   We require a command-line argument to specify either the service name or port number. This makes it easier to test our server, since binding port 13 for the daytime server requires superuser privileges.

Create listening socket

13   `tcp_listen` creates the listening socket. We pass a NULL pointer as the third argument because we don't care what size address structure the address family uses; we will use `sockaddr_storage`.

———————————————————————————————— lib/tcp_listen.c

```
 1 #include     "unp.h"

 2 int
 3 tcp_listen(const char *host, const char *serv, socklen_t *addrlenp)
 4 {
 5     int        listenfd, n;
 6     const int on = 1;
 7     struct addrinfo hints, *res, *ressave;

 8     bzero(&hints, sizeof(struct addrinfo));
 9     hints.ai_flags = AI_PASSIVE;
10     hints.ai_family = AF_UNSPEC;
11     hints.ai_socktype = SOCK_STREAM;

12     if ( (n = getaddrinfo(host, serv, &hints, &res)) != 0)
13         err_quit("tcp_listen error for %s, %s: %s",
14                 host, serv, gai_strerror(n));
15     ressave = res;

16     do {
17         listenfd =
18             socket(res->ai_family, res->ai_socktype, res->ai_protocol);
19         if (listenfd < 0)
20             continue;             /* error, try next one */

21         Setsockopt(listenfd, SOL_SOCKET, SO_REUSEADDR, &on, sizeof(on));
22         if (bind(listenfd, res->ai_addr, res->ai_addrlen) == 0)
23             break;                /* success */

24         Close(listenfd);          /* bind error, close and try next one */
25     } while ( (res = res->ai_next) != NULL);

26     if (res == NULL)              /* errno from final socket() or bind() */
27         err_sys("tcp_listen error for %s, %s", host, serv);

28     Listen(listenfd, LISTENQ);

29     if (addrlenp)
30         *addrlenp = res->ai_addrlen;    /* return size of protocol address */

31     freeaddrinfo(ressave);

32     return (listenfd);
33 }
```

———————————————————————————————— lib/tcp_listen.c

Figure 11.12 tcp_listen function: performs normal server steps.

Server loop

14–22   accept waits for each client connection. We print the client address by calling sock_ntop. In the case of either IPv4 or IPv6, this function prints the IP address and port number. We could use the function getnameinfo (Section 11.17) to try to obtain the hostname of the client, but that involves a PTR query in the DNS, which can take some time, especially if the PTR query fails. Section 14.8 of TCPv3 notes that on a busy Web server, almost 25% of all clients connecting to that server did not have PTR records

names/daytimetcpsrv1.c

```
 1 #include    "unp.h"
 2 #include    <time.h>

 3 int
 4 main(int argc, char **argv)
 5 {
 6     int     listenfd, connfd;
 7     socklen_t len;
 8     char    buff[MAXLINE];
 9     time_t  ticks;
10     struct sockaddr_storage cliaddr;

11     if (argc != 2)
12         err_quit("usage: daytimetcpsrv1 <service or port#>");

13     listenfd = Tcp_listen(NULL, argv[1], NULL);

14     for ( ; ; ) {
15         len = sizeof(cliaddr);
16         connfd = Accept(listenfd, (SA *) &cliaddr, &len);
17         printf("connection from %s\n", Sock_ntop((SA *) &cliaddr, len));

18         ticks = time(NULL);
19         snprintf(buff, sizeof(buff), "%.24s\r\n", ctime(&ticks));
20         Write(connfd, buff, strlen(buff));

21         Close(connfd);
22     }
23 }
```

names/daytimetcpsrv1.c

Figure 11.13 Daytime server recoded to use `tcp_listen` (see also Figure 11.14).

in the DNS. Since we do not want a server (especially an iterative server) to wait seconds for a PTR query, we just print the IP address and port.

Example: Daytime Server with Protocol Specification

There is a slight problem with Figure 11.13: The first argument to `tcp_listen` is a null pointer, which combined with the address family of `AF_UNSPEC` that `tcp_listen` specifies might cause `getaddrinfo` to return a socket address structure with an address family other than what is desired. For example, the first socket address structure returned will be for IPv6 on a dual-stack host (Figure 11.8), but we might want our server to handle only IPv4.

Clients do not have this problem since the client must always specify either an IP address or a hostname. Client applications normally allow the user to enter this as a command-line argument. This gives us the opportunity to specify a hostname that is associated with a particular type of IP address (recall our -4 and -6 hostnames in Section 11.2), or to specify either an IPv4 dotted-decimal string (forcing IPv4) or an IPv6 hex string (forcing IPv6).

But there is a simple technique for servers that lets us force a given protocol on a server, either IPv4 or IPv6: Allow the user to enter either an IP address or a hostname as a command-line argument to the program and pass this to getaddrinfo. In the case of an IP address, an IPv4 dotted-decimal string differs from an IPv6 hex string. The following calls to inet_pton either fail or succeed, as indicated:

```
inet_pton(AF_INET,  "0.0.0.0", &foo);      /* succeeds */
inet_pton(AF_INET,  "0::0",    &foo);      /* fails */
inet_pton(AF_INET6, "0.0.0.0", &foo);      /* fails */
inet_pton(AF_INET6, "0::0",    &foo);      /* succeeds */
```

Therefore, if we change our servers to accept an optional argument, and if we enter

```
% server
```

it defaults to IPv6 on a dual-stack host, but entering

```
% server 0.0.0.0
```

explicitly specifies IPv4 and

```
% server 0::0
```

explicitly specifies IPv6.

Figure 11.14 shows this final version of our daytime server.

Handle command-line arguments

11–16   The only change from Figure 11.13 is the handling of the command-line arguments, allowing the user to specify either a hostname or an IP address for the server to bind, in addition to a service name or port.

We first start this server with an IPv4 socket and then connect to the server from clients on two other hosts on the local subnet.

```
freebsd % daytimetcpsrv2 0.0.0.0 9999
connection from 192.168.42.2:32961
connection from 192.168.42.3:1389
```

Now we start the server with an IPv6 socket.

```
freebsd % daytimetcpsrv2 0::0 9999
connection from [3ffe:b80:1f8d:2:204:acff:fe17:bf38]:32964
connection from [3ffe:b80:1f8d:2:230:65ff:fe15:caa7]:49601
connection from [::ffff:192.168.42.2]:32967
connection from [::ffff:192.168.42.3]:49602
```

The first connection is from the host aix using IPv6 and the second is from the host macosx using IPv6. The next two connections are from the hosts aix and macosx, but using IPv4, not IPv6. We can tell this because the client's addresses returned by accept are both IPv4-mapped IPv6 addresses.

What we have just shown is that an IPv6 server running on a dual-stack host can handle either IPv4 or IPv6 clients. The IPv4 client addresses are passed to the IPv6 server as IPv4-mapped IPv6 addresses, as we will discuss in Section 12.2.

names/daytimetcpsrv2.c

```
 1 #include    "unp.h"
 2 #include    <time.h>

 3 int
 4 main(int argc, char **argv)
 5 {
 6     int      listenfd, connfd;
 7     socklen_t len;
 8     char     buff[MAXLINE];
 9     time_t   ticks;
10     struct sockaddr_storage cliaddr;

11     if (argc == 2)
12         listenfd = Tcp_listen(NULL, argv[1], &addrlen);
13     else if (argc == 3)
14         listenfd = Tcp_listen(argv[1], argv[2], &addrlen);
15     else
16         err_quit("usage: daytimetcpsrv2 [ <host> ] <service or port>");

17     for ( ; ; ) {
18         len = sizeof(cliaddr);
19         connfd = Accept(listenfd, (SA *) &cliaddr, &len);
20         printf("connection from %s\n", Sock_ntop((SA *) &cliaddr, len));

21         ticks = time(NULL);
22         snprintf(buff, sizeof(buff), "%.24s\r\n", ctime(&ticks));
23         Write(connfd, buff, strlen(buff));

24         Close(connfd);
25     }
26 }
```

names/daytimetcpsrv2.c

Figure 11.14 Protocol-independent daytime server that uses `tcp_listen`.

11.14 `udp_client` **Function**

Our functions that provide a simpler interface to `getaddrinfo` change with UDP because we provide one client function that creates an unconnected UDP socket, and another in the next section that creates a connected UDP socket.

```
#include "unp.h"

int udp_client(const char *hostname, const char *service,
               struct sockaddr **saptr, socklen_t *lenp);
```
Returns: unconnected socket descriptor if OK, no return on error

This function creates an unconnected UDP socket, returning three items. First, the return value is the socket descriptor. Second, *saptr* is the address of a pointer (declared by the caller) to a socket address structure (allocated dynamically by udp_client), and in that structure, the function stores the destination IP address and port for future calls to sendto. The size of the socket address structure is returned in the variable pointed to by *lenp*. This final argument cannot be a null pointer (as we allowed for the final argument to tcp_listen) because the length of the socket address structure is required in any calls to sendto and recvfrom.

Figure 11.15 shows the source code for this function.

lib/udp_client.c

```
 1 #include      "unp.h"

 2 int
 3 udp_client(const char *host, const char *serv, SA **saptr, socklen_t *lenp)
 4 {
 5     int       sockfd, n;
 6     struct addrinfo hints, *res, *ressave;

 7     bzero(&hints, sizeof(struct addrinfo));
 8     hints.ai_family = AF_UNSPEC;
 9     hints.ai_socktype = SOCK_DGRAM;

10     if ( (n = getaddrinfo(host, serv, &hints, &res)) != 0)
11         err_quit("udp_client error for %s, %s: %s",
12                 host, serv, gai_strerror(n));
13     ressave = res;

14     do {
15         sockfd = socket(res->ai_family, res->ai_socktype, res->ai_protocol);
16         if (sockfd >= 0)
17             break;              /* success */
18     } while ( (res = res->ai_next) != NULL);

19     if (res == NULL)            /* errno set from final socket() */
20         err_sys("udp_client error for %s, %s", host, serv);

21     *saptr = Malloc(res->ai_addrlen);
22     memcpy(*saptr, res->ai_addr, res->ai_addrlen);
23     *lenp = res->ai_addrlen;

24     freeaddrinfo(ressave);

25     return (sockfd);
26 }
```

lib/udp_client.c

Figure 11.15 udp_client function: creates an unconnected UDP socket.

getaddrinfo converts the *hostname* and *service* arguments. A datagram socket is created. Memory is allocated for one socket address structure, and the socket address structure corresponding to the socket that was created is copied into the memory.

Example: Protocol-Independent Daytime Client

We now recode our daytime client from Figure 11.11 to use UDP and our udp_client function. Figure 11.16 shows the protocol-independent source code.

names/daytimeudpcli1.c
```
 1 #include    "unp.h"

 2 int
 3 main(int argc, char **argv)
 4 {
 5     int     sockfd, n;
 6     char    recvline[MAXLINE + 1];
 7     socklen_t salen;
 8     struct sockaddr *sa;

 9     if (argc != 3)
10         err_quit
11             ("usage: daytimeudpcli1 <hostname/IPaddress> <service/port#>");

12     sockfd = Udp_client(argv[1], argv[2], (void **) &sa, &salen);

13     printf("sending to %s\n", Sock_ntop_host(sa, salen));

14     Sendto(sockfd, "", 1, 0, sa, salen);    /* send 1-byte datagram */

15     n = Recvfrom(sockfd, recvline, MAXLINE, 0, NULL, NULL);
16     recvline[n] = '\0';            /* null terminate */
17     Fputs(recvline, stdout);

18     exit(0);
19 }
```
names/daytimeudpcli1.c

Figure 11.16   UDP daytime client using our udp_client function.

12–17   We call our udp_client function and then print the IP address and port of the server to which we will send the UDP datagram. We send a one-byte datagram and then read and print the reply.

> We need to send only a zero-byte UDP datagram, as what triggers the daytime server's response is just the arrival of a datagram, regardless of its length and contents. But, many SVR4 implementations do not allow a zero-length UDP datagram.

We run our client specifying a hostname that has a AAAA record and an A record. Since the structure with the AAAA record is returned first by getaddrinfo, an IPv6 socket is created.

```
freebsd % daytimeudpcli1 aix daytime
sending to 3ffe:b80:1f8d:2:204:acff:fe17:bf38
Sun Jul 27 23:21:12 2003
```

Next, we specify the dotted-decimal address of the same host, resulting in an IPv4 socket.

```
freebsd % daytimeudpcli1 192.168.42.2 daytime
sending to 192.168.42.2
Sun Jul 27 23:21:40 2003
```

11.15 udp_connect **Function**

Our udp_connect function creates a connected UDP socket.

```
#include "unp.h"

int udp_connect(const char *hostname, const char *service);

                              Returns: connected socket descriptor if OK, no return on error
```

With a connected UDP socket, the final two arguments required by udp_client are no longer needed. The caller can call write instead of sendto, so our function need not return a socket address structure and its length.

Figure 11.17 shows the source code.

—————————————————————————— lib/udp_connect.c

```
 1 #include      "unp.h"

 2 int
 3 udp_connect(const char *host, const char *serv)
 4 {
 5     int     sockfd, n;
 6     struct addrinfo hints, *res, *ressave;

 7     bzero(&hints, sizeof(struct addrinfo));
 8     hints.ai_family = AF_UNSPEC;
 9     hints.ai_socktype = SOCK_DGRAM;

10     if ( (n = getaddrinfo(host, serv, &hints, &res)) != 0)
11         err_quit("udp_connect error for %s, %s: %s",
12                  host, serv, gai_strerror(n));
13     ressave = res;

14     do {
15         sockfd = socket(res->ai_family, res->ai_socktype, res->ai_protocol);
16         if (sockfd < 0)
17             continue;           /* ignore this one */

18         if (connect(sockfd, res->ai_addr, res->ai_addrlen) == 0)
19             break;              /* success */

20         Close(sockfd);          /* ignore this one */
21     } while ( (res = res->ai_next) != NULL);

22     if (res == NULL)            /* errno set from final connect() */
23         err_sys("udp_connect error for %s, %s", host, serv);

24     freeaddrinfo(ressave);

25     return (sockfd);
26 }
```

—————————————————————————— lib/udp_connect.c

Figure 11.17 udp_connect function: creates a connected UDP socket.

This function is nearly identical to tcp_connect. One difference, however, is that the call to connect with a UDP socket does not send anything to the peer. If something is wrong (the peer is unreachable or there is no server at the specified port), the caller does not discover that until it sends a datagram to the peer.

11.16 `udp_server` Function

Our final UDP function that provides a simpler interface to getaddrinfo is
udp_server.

```
#include "unp.h"

int udp_server(const char *hostname, const char *service, socklen_t *lenptr);
                                    Returns: unconnected socket descriptor if OK, no return on error
```

The arguments are the same as for `tcp_listen`: an optional *hostname*, a required *service*
(so its port number can be bound), and an optional pointer to a variable in which the
size of the socket address structure is returned.

Figure 11.18 shows the source code.

————————————————————————————————————— lib/udp_server.c
```
 1 #include     "unp.h"

 2 int
 3 udp_server(const char *host, const char *serv, socklen_t *addrlenp)
 4 {
 5     int      sockfd, n;
 6     struct addrinfo hints, *res, *ressave;

 7     bzero(&hints, sizeof(struct addrinfo));
 8     hints.ai_flags = AI_PASSIVE;
 9     hints.ai_family = AF_UNSPEC;
10     hints.ai_socktype = SOCK_DGRAM;
11     if ( (n = getaddrinfo(host, serv, &hints, &res)) != 0)
12         err_quit("udp_server error for %s, %s: %s",
13                   host, serv, gai_strerror(n));
14     ressave = res;

15     do {
16         sockfd = socket(res->ai_family, res->ai_socktype, res->ai_protocol);
17         if (sockfd < 0)
18             continue;           /* error - try next one */

19         if (bind(sockfd, res->ai_addr, res->ai_addrlen) == 0)
20             break;              /* success */

21         Close(sockfd);          /* bind error - close and try next one */
22     } while ( (res = res->ai_next) != NULL);

23     if (res == NULL)            /* errno from final socket() or bind() */
24         err_sys("udp_server error for %s, %s", host, serv);

25     if (addrlenp)
26         *addrlenp = res->ai_addrlen;    /* return size of protocol address */

27     freeaddrinfo(ressave);

28     return (sockfd);
29 }
```
————————————————————————————————————— lib/udp_server.c

Figure 11.18 `udp_server` function: creates an unconnected socket for a UDP server.

This function is nearly identical to `tcp_listen`, but without the call to `listen`. We set the address family to `AF_UNSPEC`, but the caller can use the same technique that we described with Figure 11.14 to force a particular protocol (IPv4 or IPv6).

We do not set the `SO_REUSEADDR` socket option for the UDP socket because this socket option can allow multiple sockets to bind the same UDP port on hosts that support multicasting, as we described in Section 7.5. Since there is nothing like TCP's TIME_WAIT state for a UDP socket, there is no need to set this socket option when the server is started.

Example: Protocol-Independent Daytime Server

Figure 11.19 shows our daytime server, modified from Figure 11.14 to use UDP.

names/daytimeudpsrv2.c
```
 1 #include     "unp.h"
 2 #include     <time.h>

 3 int
 4 main(int argc, char **argv)
 5 {
 6     int      sockfd;
 7     ssize_t n;
 8     char     buff[MAXLINE];
 9     time_t   ticks;
10     socklen_t len;
11     struct sockaddr_storage cliaddr;

12     if (argc == 2)
13         sockfd = Udp_server(NULL, argv[1], NULL);
14     else if (argc == 3)
15         sockfd = Udp_server(argv[1], argv[2], NULL);
16     else
17         err_quit("usage: daytimeudpsrv [ <host> ] <service or port>");

18     for ( ; ; ) {
19         len = sizeof(cliaddr);
20         n = Recvfrom(sockfd, buff, MAXLINE, 0, (SA *) &cliaddr, &len);
21         printf("datagram from %s\n", Sock_ntop((SA *) &cliaddr, len));

22         ticks = time(NULL);
23         snprintf(buff, sizeof(buff), "%.24s\r\n", ctime(&ticks));
24         Sendto(sockfd, buff, strlen(buff), 0, (SA *) &cliaddr, len);
25     }
26 }
```
names/daytimeudpsrv2.c

Figure 11.19 Protocol-independent UDP daytime server.

11.17 `getnameinfo` Function

This function is the complement of `getaddrinfo`: It takes a socket address and returns a character string describing the host and another character string describing the service. This function provides this information in a protocol-independent fashion; that is, the caller does not care what type of protocol address is contained in the socket address structure, as that detail is handled by the function.

```
#include <netdb.h>

int getnameinfo(const struct sockaddr *sockaddr, socklen_t addrlen,
                char *host, socklen_t hostlen,
                char *serv, socklen_t servlen, int flags);
```
                                        Returns: 0 if OK, nonzero on error (see Figure 11.7)

sockaddr points to the socket address structure containing the protocol address to be converted into a human-readable string, and *addrlen* is the length of this structure. This structure and its length are normally returned by `accept`, `recvfrom`, `getsockname`, or `getpeername`.

The caller allocates space for the two human-readable strings: *host* and *hostlen* specify the host string, and *serv* and *servlen* specify the service string. If the caller does not want the host string returned, a *hostlen* of 0 is specified. Similarly, a *servlen* of 0 specifies not to return information on the service.

The difference between `sock_ntop` and `getnameinfo` is that the former does not involve the DNS and just returns a printable version of the IP address and port number. The latter normally tries to obtain a name for both the host and service.

Figure 11.20 shows the six *flags* that can be specified to change the operation of `getnameinfo`.

Constant	Description
NI_DGRAM	Datagram service
NI_NAMEREQD	Return an error if name cannot be resolved from address
NI_NOFQDN	Return only hostname portion of FQDN
NI_NUMERICHOST	Return numeric string for hostname
NI_NUMERICSCOPE	Return numeric string for scope identifier
NI_NUMERICSERV	Return numeric string for service name

Figure 11.20 *flags* for `getnameinfo`.

`NI_DGRAM` should be specified when the caller knows it is dealing with a datagram socket. The reason is that given only the IP address and port number in the socket address structure, `getnameinfo` cannot determine the protocol (TCP or UDP). There are a few port numbers that are used for one service with TCP and a completely different service with UDP. An example is port 514, which is the `rsh` service with TCP, but the `syslog` service with UDP.

`NI_NAMEREQD` causes an error to be returned if the hostname cannot be resolved using the DNS. This can be used by servers that require the client's IP address to be mapped into a hostname. These servers then take this returned hostname and call `getaddrinfo`, and then verify that one of the returned addresses is the address in the socket address structure.

`NI_NOFQDN` causes the returned hostname to be truncated at the first period. For example, if the IP address in the socket address structure was 192.168.42.2, `gethostbyaddr` would return a name of `aix.unpbook.com`. But if this flag was specified to `getnameinfo`, it would return the hostname as just `aix`.

`NI_NUMERICHOST` tells `getnameinfo` not to call the DNS (which can take time). Instead, the numeric representation of the IP address is returned as a string, probably by calling `inet_ntop`. Similarly, `NI_NUMERICSERV` specifies that the decimal port number is to be returned as a string instead of looking up the service name, and `NI_NUMERICSCOPE` specifies that the numeric form of the scope identifier is to be returned instead of its name. Servers should normally specify `NI_NUMERICSERV` because the client port numbers typically have no associated service name—they are ephemeral ports.

The logical OR of multiple flags can be specified if they make sense together (e.g., `NI_DGRAM` and `NI_NUMERICHOST`).

11.18 Re-entrant Functions

The `gethostbyname` function from Section 11.3 presents an interesting problem that we have not yet examined in the text: It is not *re-entrant*. We will encounter this problem in general when we deal with threads in Chapter 26, but it is interesting to examine the problem now (without having to deal with the concept of threads) and to see how to fix it.

First, let us look at how the function works. If we look at its source code (which is easy since the source code for the entire BIND release is publicly available), we see that one file contains both `gethostbyname` and `gethostbyaddr`, and the file has the following general outline:

```
static struct hostent  host;    /* result stored here */

struct hostent *
gethostbyname(const char *hostname)
{
    return(gethostbyname2(hostname, family));
}

struct hostent *
gethostbyname2(const char *hostname, int family)
{
    /* call DNS functions for A or AAAA query */

    /* fill in host structure */

    return(&host);
}
```

```
struct hostent *
gethostbyaddr(const char *addr, socklen_t len, int family)
{
    /* call DNS functions for PTR query in in-addr.arpa domain */

    /* fill in host structure */

    return(&host);
}
```

We highlight the `static` storage class specifier of the result structure because that is the basic problem. The fact that these three functions share a single `host` variable presents yet another problem that we will discuss in Exercise 11.1. (`gethostbyname2` was introduced with the IPv6 support in BIND 4.9.4. It has since been deprecated; see Section 11.20 for more detail. We will ignore the fact that `gethostbyname2` is involved when we call `gethostbyname`, as that doesn't affect this discussion.)

The re-entrancy problem can occur in a normal Unix process that calls `gethostbyname` or `gethostbyaddr` from both the main flow of control and from a signal handler. When the signal handler is called (say it is a `SIGALRM` signal that is generated once per second), the main flow of control of the process is temporarily stopped and the signal handling function is called. Consider the following:

```
main()
{
    struct hostent   *hptr;

    ...
    signal(SIGALRM, sig_alrm);

    ...
    hptr = gethostbyname( ... );
    ...
}

void
sig_alrm(int signo)
{
    struct hostent   *hptr;

    ...
    hptr = gethostbyname( ... );
    ...
}
```

If the main flow of control is in the middle of `gethostbyname` when it is temporarily stopped (say the function has filled in the `host` variable and is about to return), and the signal handler then calls `gethostbyname`, since only one copy of the variable `host` exists in the process, it is reused. This overwrites the values that were calculated for the call from the main flow of control with the values calculated for the call from the signal handler.

If we look at the name and address conversion functions presented in this chapter, along with the inet_*XXX* functions from Chapter 4, we note the following:

- Historically, gethostbyname, gethostbyaddr, getservbyname, and get servbyport are not re-entrant because all return a pointer to a static structure.

  Some implementations that support threads (Solaris 2.x) provide re-entrant versions of these four functions with names ending with the _r suffix, which we will describe in the next section.

  Alternately, some implementations that support threads (HP-UX 10.30 and later) provide re-entrant versions of these functions using thread-specific data (Section 26.5).

- inet_pton and inet_ntop are always re-entrant.

- Historically, inet_ntoa is not re-entrant, but some implementations that support threads provide a re-entrant version that uses thread-specific data.

- getaddrinfo is re-entrant only if it calls re-entrant functions itself; that is, if it calls re-entrant versions of gethostbyname for the hostname and getservbyname for the service name. One reason that all the memory for the results is dynamically allocated is to allow it to be re-entrant.

- getnameinfo is re-entrant only if it calls re-entrant functions itself; that is, if it calls re-entrant versions of gethostbyaddr to obtain the hostname and getservbyport to obtain the service name. Notice that both result strings (for the hostname and the service name) are allocated by the caller to allow this re-entrancy.

A similar problem occurs with the variable errno. Historically, there has been a single copy of this integer variable per process. If a process makes a system call that returns an error, an integer error code is stored in this variable. For example, when the function named close in the standard C library is called, it might execute something like the following pseudocode:

- Put the argument to the system call (an integer descriptor) into a register
- Put a value in another register indicating the close system call is being called
- Invoke the system call (switch to the kernel with a special instruction)
- Test the value of a register to see if an error occurred
- If no error, return(0)
- Store the value of some other register into errno
- return(-1)

First, notice that if an error does not occur, the value of errno is not changed. That is why we cannot look at the value of errno unless we know that an error has occurred (normally indicated by the function returning –1).

Assume a program tests the return value of the close function and then prints the value of errno if an error occurred, as in the following:

```
if (close(fd) < 0) {
    fprintf(stderr, "close error, errno = %d\n", errno)
    exit(1);
}
```

There is a small window of time between the storing of the error code into errno when the system call returns and the printing of this value by the program, during which another thread of execution within this process (i.e., a signal handler) can change the value of errno. For example, if, when the signal handler is called, the main flow of control is between close and fprintf and the signal handler calls some other system call that returns an error (say write), then the errno value stored from the write system call overwrites the value stored by the close system call.

In looking at these two problems with regard to signal handlers, one solution to the problem with gethostbyname (returning a pointer to a static variable) is to *not* call nonre-entrant functions from a signal handler. The problem with errno (a single global variable that can be changed by the signal handler) can be avoided by coding the signal handler to save and restore the value of errno in the signal handler as follows:

```
void
sig_alrm(int signo)
{
    int   errno_save;

    errno_save = errno;        /* save its value on entry *
    if (write( ... ) != nbytes)
        fprintf(stderr, "write error, errno = %d\n", errno);
    errno = errno_save;        /* restore its value on return */
}
```

In this example code, we also call fprintf, a standard I/O function, from the signal handler. This is yet another re-entrancy problem because many versions of the standard I/O library are nonre-entrant: Standard I/O functions should not be called from signal handlers.

We will revisit this problem of re-entrancy in Chapter 26 and we will see how threads handle the problem of the errno variable. The next section describes some re-entrant versions of the hostname functions.

11.19 gethostbyname_r and gethostbyaddr_r Functions

There are two ways to make a nonre-entrant function such as gethostbyname re-entrant.

1. Instead of filling in and returning a static structure, the caller allocates the structure and the re-entrant function fills in the caller's structure. This is the technique used in going from the nonre-entrant gethostbyname to the re-entrant gethostbyname_r. But, this solution gets more complicated because not only

must the caller provide the hostent structure to fill in, but this structure also points to other information: the canonical name, the array of alias pointers, the alias strings, the array of address pointers, and the addresses (e.g., Figure 11.2). The caller must provide one large buffer that is used for this additional information and the hostent structure that is filled in then contains numerous pointers into this other buffer. This adds at least three arguments to the function: a pointer to the hostent structure to fill in, a pointer to the buffer to use for all the other information, and the size of this buffer. A fourth additional argument is also required: a pointer to an integer in which an error code can be stored, since the global integer h_errno can no longer be used. (The global integer h_errno presents the same re-entrancy problem that we described with errno.)

This technique is also used by getnameinfo and inet_ntop.

2. The re-entrant function calls malloc and dynamically allocates the memory. This is the technique used by getaddrinfo. The problem with this approach is that the application calling this function must also call freeaddrinfo to free the dynamic memory. If the free function is not called, a *memory leak* occurs: Each time the process calls the function that allocates the memory, the memory use of the process increases. If the process runs for a long time (a common trait of network servers), the memory usage just grows and grows over time.

We will now discuss the Solaris 2.x re-entrant functions for name-to-address and address-to-name resolution.

```
#include <netdb.h>

struct hostent *gethostbyname_r(const char *hostname,
                                struct hostent *result,
                                char *buf, int buflen, int *h_errnop);

struct hostent *gethostbyaddr_r(const char *addr, int len, int type,
                                struct hostent *result,
                                char *buf, int buflen, int *h_errnop);
```

Both return: non-null pointer if OK, NULL on error

Four additional arguments are required for each function. *result* is a hostent structure allocated by the caller. It is filled in by the function. On success, this pointer is also the return value of the function.

buf is a buffer allocated by the caller and *buflen* is its size. This buffer will contain the canonical hostname, the alias pointers, the alias strings, the address pointers, and the actual addresses. All the pointers in the structure pointed to by *result* point into this buffer. How big should this buffer be? Unfortunately, all that most man pages say is something vague like, "The buffer must be large enough to hold all of the data associated with the host entry." Current implementations of gethostbyname can return up to 35 alias pointers and 35 address pointers, and internally use an 8192-byte buffer to hold alias names and addresses. So, a buffer size of 8192 bytes should be adequate.

If an error occurs, the error code is returned through the *h_errnop* pointer, not through the global h_errno.

> Unfortunately, this problem of re-entrancy is even worse than it appears. First, there is no standard regarding re-entrancy and gethostbyname and gethostbyaddr. The POSIX specification says that gethostbyname and gethostbyaddr need not be re-entrant. Unix 98 just says that these two functions need not be thread-safe.
>
> Second, there is no standard for the _r functions. What we have shown in this section (for example purposes) are two of the _r functions provided by Solaris 2.x. Linux provides similar _r functions, except that instead of returning the hostent as the return value of the function, the hostent is returned using a value-result parameter as the next to last function argument. It returns the success of the lookup as the return value from the function as well as in the h_errno argument. Digital Unix 4.0 and HP-UX 10.30 have versions of these functions with different arguments. The first two arguments for gethostbyname_r are the same as the Solaris version, but the remaining three arguments for the Solaris version are combined into a new hostent_data structure (which must be allocated by the caller), and a pointer to this structure is the third and final argument. The normal functions gethostbyname and gethostbyaddr in Digital Unix 4.0 and HP-UX 10.30 are re-entrant by using thread-specific data (Section 26.5). An interesting history of the development of the Solaris 2.x _r functions is in [Maslen 1997].
>
> Lastly, while a re-entrant version of gethostbyname may provide safety from different threads calling it at the same time, this says nothing about the re-entrancy of the underlying resolver functions.

11.20 Obsolete IPv6 Address Lookup Functions

While IPv6 was being developed, the API to request the lookup of an IPv6 address went through several iterations. The resulting API was complicated and not sufficiently flexible, so it was deprecated in RFC 2553 [Gilligan et al. 1999]. RFC 2553 introduced its own new functions, which were finally simply replaced by getaddrinfo and getnameinfo in RFC 3493 [Gilligan et al. 2003]. This section briefly describes some of the old API to assist in the conversion of programs using the old API.

The RES_USE_INET6 Constant

Since gethostbyname doesn't have an argument to specify what address family is of interest (like getaddrinfo's hints.ai_family struct entry), the first revision of the API used the RES_USE_INET6 constant, which had to be added to the resolver flags using a private, internal interface. This API was not very portable since systems that used a different internal resolver interface had to mimic the BIND resolver interface to provide it.

Enabling RES_USE_INET6 caused gethostbyname to look up AAAA records first, and only look up A records if a name had no AAAA records. Since the hostent structure only has one address length field, gethostbyname could only return either IPv6 or IPv4 addresses, but not both.

Enabling RES_USE_INET6 also caused gethostbyname2 to return IPv4 addresses as IPv4-mapped IPv6 addresses. We will describe gethostbyname2 next.

The `gethostbyname2` Function

The `gethostbyname2` function adds an address family argument to `gethostbyname`.

```
#include <sys/socket.h>
#include <netdb.h>

struct hostent *gethostbyname2(const char *name, int af);
```
                    Returns: non-null pointer if OK, NULL on error with h_errno set

When the `af` argument is `AF_INET`, `gethostbyname2` behaves just like `gethostbyname`, looking up and returning IPv4 addresses. When the `af` argument is `AF_INET6`, `gethostbyname2` looks up and returns only AAAA records for IPv6 addresses.

The `getipnodebyname` Function

RFC 2553 [Gilligan et al. 1999] deprecated `RES_USE_INET6` and `gethostbyname2` because of the global nature of the `RES_USE_INET6` flag and the wish to provide more control over the returned information. It introduced the `getipnodebyname` function to solve some of these problems.

```
#include <sys/socket.h>
#include <netdb.h>

struct hostent *getipnodebyname(const char *name, int af,
                                int flags, int *error_num);
```
                    Returns: non-null pointer if OK, NULL on error with error_num set

This function returns a pointer to the same `hostent` structure that we described with `gethostbyname`. The `af` and `flags` arguments map directly to `getaddrinfo`'s `hints.ai_family` and `hints.ai_flags` arguments. For thread safety, the return value is dynamically allocated, so it must be freed with the `freehostent` function.

```
#include <netdb.h>

void freehostent(struct hostent *ptr);
```

The `getipnodebyname` and its matching `getipnodebyaddr` functions are deprecated by RFC 3493 [Gilligan et al. 2003] in favor of `getaddrinfo` and `getnameinfo`.

11.21 Other Networking Information

Our focus in this chapter has been on hostnames and IP addresses and service names and their port numbers. But looking at the bigger picture, there are four types of information (related to networking) that an application might want to look up: hosts, networks, protocols, and services. Most lookups are for hosts (gethostbyname and gethostbyaddr), with a smaller number for services (getservbyname and getservbyaddr), and an even smaller number for networks and protocols.

All four types of information can be stored in a file and three functions are defined for each of the four types:

1. A getXXXent function that reads the next entry in the file, opening the file if necessary.

2. A setXXXent function that opens (if not already open) and rewinds the file.

3. An endXXXent function that closes the file.

Each of the four types of information defines its own structure, and the following definitions are provided by including the <netdb.h> header: the hostent, netent, protoent, and servent structures.

In addition to the three get, set, and end functions, which allow sequential processing of the file, each of the four types of information provides some *keyed lookup* functions. These functions go through the file sequentially (calling the getXXXent function to read each line), but instead of returning each line to the caller, these functions look for an entry that matches an argument. These keyed lookup functions have names of the form getXXXbyYYY. For example, the two keyed lookup functions for the host information are gethostbyname (look for an entry that matches a hostname) and gethostbyaddr (look for an entry that matches an IP address). Figure 11.21 summarizes this information.

Information	Data file	Structure	Keyed lookup functions	
Hosts	/etc/hosts	hostent	gethostbyaddr,	gethostbyname
Networks	/etc/networks	netent	getnetbyaddr,	getnetbyname
Protocols	/etc/protocols	protoent	getprotobyname,	getprotobynumber
Services	/etc/services	servent	getservbyname,	getservbyport

Figure 11.21 Four types of network-related information.

How does this apply when the DNS is being used? First, only the host and network information is available through the DNS. The protocol and service information is always read from the corresponding file. We mentioned earlier in this chapter (with Figure 11.1) that different implementations employ different ways for the administrator to specify whether to use the DNS or a file for the host and network information.

Second, if the DNS is being used for the host and network information, then only the keyed lookup functions make sense. You cannot, for example, use gethostent and expect to sequence through all entries in the DNS! If gethostent is called, it reads only the /etc/hosts file and avoids the DNS.

> Although the network information can be made available through the DNS, few people set this up. [Albitz and Liu 2001] describes this feature. Typically, however, administrators build and maintain an /etc/networks file and it is used instead of the DNS. The netstat program with the -i option uses this file, if present, and prints the name for each network. However, classless addressing (Section A.4) makes these functions fairly useless, and these functions do not support IPv6 at all, so new applications should avoid using network names.

11.22 Summary

The set of functions that an application calls to convert a hostname into an IP address and vice versa is called the resolver. The two functions gethostbyname and gethostbyaddr are the historical entry points. With the move to IPv6 and threaded programming models, the getaddrinfo and getnameinfo functions are more useful, with the ability to resolve IPv6 addresses and their thread-safe calling conventions.

The commonly used function dealing with service names and port numbers is getservbyname, which takes a service name and returns a structure containing the port number. This mapping is normally contained in a text file. Additional functions exist to map protocol names into protocol numbers and network names into network numbers, but these are rarely used.

Another alternative that we have not mentioned is calling the resolver functions directly, instead of using gethostbyname and gethostbyaddr. One program that invokes the DNS this way is sendmail, which searches for an MX record, something that the gethostby*XXX* functions cannot do. The resolver functions have names that begin with res_; the res_init function is an example. A description of these functions and an example program that calls them can be found in Chapter 15 of [Albitz and Liu 2001] and typing man resolver should display the man pages for these functions.

Exercises

11.1   Modify the program in Figure 11.3 to call gethostbyaddr for each returned address, and then print the h_name that is returned. First run the program specifying a hostname with just one IP address and then run the program specifying a hostname that has more than one IP address. What happens?

11.2   Fix the problem shown in the preceding exercise.

11.3   Run Figure 11.4 specifying a service name of chargen.

11.4   Run Figure 11.4 specifying a dotted-decimal IP address as the hostname. Does your resolver allow this? Modify Figure 11.4 to allow a dotted-decimal IP address as the hostname and a decimal port number string as the service name. In testing the IP address for either a dotted-decimal string or a hostname, in what order should these two tests be performed?

11.5   Modify Figure 11.4 to work with either IPv4 or IPv6.

11.6   Modify Figure 8.9 to query the DNS and compare the returned IP address with all the destination host's IP addresses. That is, call `gethostbyaddr` using the IP address returned by `recvfrom`, followed by `gethostbyname` to find all the IP addresses for the host.

11.7   In Figure 11.12, the caller must pass a pointer to an integer to obtain the size of the protocol address. If the caller does not do this (i.e., passes a null pointer as the final argument), how can the caller still obtain the actual size of the protocol's addresses?

11.8   Modify Figure 11.14 to call `getnameinfo` instead of `sock_ntop`. What flags should you pass to `getnameinfo`?

11.9   In Section 7.5, we discussed port stealing with the SO_REUSEADDR socket option. To see how this works, build the protocol-independent UDP daytime server in Figure 11.19. Start one instance of the server in one window, binding the wildcard address and some port of your choosing. Start a client in another window and verify that this server is handling the client (note the `printf` in the server). Next, start another instance of the server in another window, this time binding one of the host's unicast addresses and the same port as the first server. What problem do you immediately encounter? Fix this problem and restart this second server. Start a client, send a datagram, and verify that the second server has stolen the port from the first server. If possible, start the second server again from a different login account on the first server to see if the stealing still succeeds. Some vendors will not allow the second bind unless the user ID is the same as that of the process that has already bound the port.

11.10   At the end of Section 2.12, we showed two `telnet` examples: to the daytime server and to the echo server. Knowing that a client goes through the two steps `gethostbyname` and `connect`, which lines output by the client indicate which steps?

11.11   `getnameinfo` can take a long time (up to 80 seconds) to return an error if a hostname cannot be found for an IP address. Write a new function named `getnameinfo_timeo` that takes an additional integer argument specifying the maximum number of seconds to wait for a reply. If the timer expires and the NI_NAMEREQD flag is not specified, just call `inet_ntop` and return an address string.

Part 3

Advanced Sockets

12

IPv4 and IPv6 Interoperability

12.1 Introduction

Over the coming years, there will probably be a gradual transition of the Internet from IPv4 to IPv6. During this transition phase, it is important that existing IPv4 applications continue to work with newer IPv6 applications. For example, a vendor cannot provide a `telnet` client that works only with IPv6 `telnet` servers but must provide one that works with IPv4 servers and one that works with IPv6 servers. Better yet would be one IPv6 `telnet` client that can work with both IPv4 and IPv6 servers, along with one `telnet` server that can work with both IPv4 and IPv6 clients. We will see how this is done in this chapter.

We assume throughout this chapter that the hosts are running *dual stacks*, that is, both an IPv4 protocol stack and an IPv6 protocol stack. Our example in Figure 2.1 is a dual-stack host. Hosts and routers will probably run like this for many years into the transition to IPv6. At some point, many systems will be able to turn off their IPv4 stack, but only time will tell when (and if) that will occur.

In this chapter, we will discuss how IPv4 applications and IPv6 applications can communicate with each other. There are four combinations of clients and servers using either IPv4 or IPv6 and we show these in Figure 12.1.

	IPv4 server	IPv6 server
IPv4 client	Almost all existing clients and servers	Discussed in Section 12.2
IPv6 client	Discussed in Section 12.3	Simple modifications to most existing clients and servers (e.g., Figure 1.5 to Figure 1.6)

Figure 12.1 Combinations of clients and servers using IPv4 or IPv6.

We will not say much more about the two scenarios where the client and server use the same protocol. The interesting cases are when the client and server use different protocols.

12.2 IPv4 Client, IPv6 Server

A general property of a dual-stack host is that IPv6 servers can handle both IPv4 and IPv6 clients. This is done using IPv4-mapped IPv6 addresses (Figure A.10). Figure 12.2 shows an example of this.

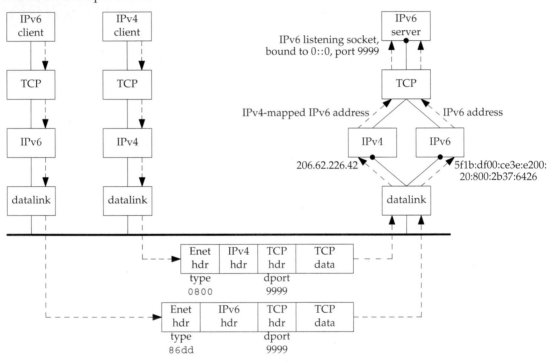

Figure 12.2 IPv6 server on dual-stack host serving IPv4 and IPv6 clients.

We have an IPv4 client and an IPv6 client on the left. The server on the right is written using IPv6 and it is running on a dual-stack host. The server has created an IPv6 listening TCP socket that is bound to the IPv6 wildcard address and TCP port 9999.

We assume the clients and server are on the same Ethernet. They could also be connected by routers, as long as all the routers support IPv4 and IPv6, but that adds nothing to this discussion. Section B.3 discusses a different case where IPv6 clients and servers are connected by IPv4-only routers.

We assume both clients send SYN segments to establish a connection with the server. The IPv4 client host will send the SYN in an IPv4 datagram and the IPv6 client host will send the SYN in an IPv6 datagram. The TCP segment from the IPv4 client appears on the wire as an Ethernet header followed by an IPv4 header, a TCP header, and the TCP data. The Ethernet header contains a type field of `0x0800`, which identifies the frame as an IPv4 frame. The TCP header contains the destination port of 9999. (Appendix A talks more about the formats and contents of these headers.) The destination IP address in the IPv4 header, which we do not show, would be 206.62.226.42.

The TCP segment from the IPv6 client appears on the wire as an Ethernet header followed by an IPv6 header, a TCP header, and the TCP data. The Ethernet header contains a type field of `0x86dd`, which identifies the frame as an IPv6 frame. The TCP header has the same format as the TCP header in the IPv4 packet and contains the destination port of 9999. The destination IP address in the IPv6 header, which we do not show, would be `5f1b:df00:ce3e:e200:20:800:2b37:6426`.

The receiving datalink looks at the Ethernet type field and passes each frame to the appropriate IP module. The IPv4 module, probably in conjunction with the TCP module, detects that the destination socket is an IPv6 socket, and the source IPv4 address in the IPv4 header is converted into the equivalent IPv4-mapped IPv6 address. That mapped address is returned to the IPv6 socket as the client's IPv6 address when `accept` returns to the server with the IPv4 client connection. All remaining datagrams for this connection are IPv4 datagrams.

When `accept` returns to the server with the IPv6 client connection, the client's IPv6 address does not change from whatever source address appears in the IPv6 header. All remaining datagrams for this connection are IPv6 datagrams.

We can summarize the steps that allow an IPv4 TCP client to communicate with an IPv6 server as follows:

1. The IPv6 server starts, creates an IPv6 listening socket, and we assume it `binds` the wildcard address to the socket.

2. The IPv4 client calls `gethostbyname` and finds an A record for the server. The server host will have both an A record and a AAAA record since it supports both protocols, but the IPv4 client asks for only an A record.

3. The client calls `connect` and the client's host sends an IPv4 SYN to the server.

4. The server host receives the IPv4 SYN directed to the IPv6 listening socket, sets a flag indicating that this connection is using IPv4-mapped IPv6 addresses, and responds with an IPv4 SYN/ACK. When the connection is established, the address returned to the server by `accept` is the IPv4-mapped IPv6 address.

5. When the server host sends to the IPv4-mapped IPv6 address, its IP stack generates IPv4 datagrams to the IPv4 address. Therefore, all communication between this client and server takes place using IPv4 datagrams.

6. Unless the server explicitly checks whether this IPv6 address is an IPv4-mapped IPv6 address (using the `IN6_IS_ADDR_V4MAPPED` macro described in Section 12.4), the server never knows that it is communicating with an IPv4 client. The dual-protocol stack handles this detail. Similarly, the IPv4 client has no idea that it is communicating with an IPv6 server.

An underlying assumption in this scenario is that the dual-stack server host has both an IPv4 address and an IPv6 address. This will work until all the IPv4 addresses are taken.

The scenario is similar for an IPv6 UDP server, but the address format can change for each datagram. For example, if the IPv6 server receives a datagram from an IPv4 client, the address returned by `recvfrom` will be the client's IPv4-mapped IPv6 address. The server responds to this client's request by calling `sendto` with the IPv4-mapped IPv6 address as the destination. This address format tells the kernel to send an IPv4 datagram to the client. But the next datagram received for the server could be an IPv6 datagram, and `recvfrom` will return the IPv6 address. If the server responds, the kernel will generate an IPv6 datagram.

Figure 12.3 summarizes how a received IPv4 or IPv6 datagram is processed, depending on the type of the receiving socket, for TCP and UDP, assuming a dual-stack host.

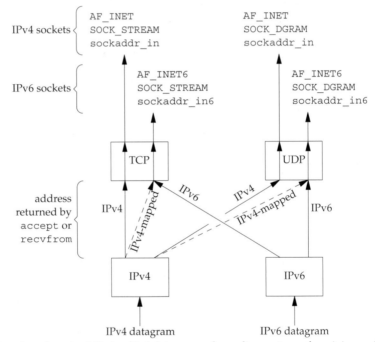

Figure 12.3 Processing of received IPv4 or IPv6 datagrams, depending on type of receiving socket.

- If an IPv4 datagram is received for an IPv4 socket, nothing special is done. These are the two arrows labeled "IPv4" in the figure: one to TCP and one to UDP. IPv4 datagrams are exchanged between the client and server.

- If an IPv6 datagram is received for an IPv6 socket, nothing special is done. These are the two arrows labeled "IPv6" in the figure: one to TCP and one to UDP. IPv6 datagrams are exchanged between the client and server.

- When an IPv4 datagram is received for an IPv6 socket, the kernel returns the corresponding IPv4-mapped IPv6 address as the address returned by `accept` (TCP) or `recvfrom` (UDP). These are the two dashed arrows in the figure. This mapping is possible because an IPv4 address can always be represented as an

IPv6 address. IPv4 datagrams are exchanged between the client and server.

- The converse of the previous bullet is false: In general, an IPv6 address cannot be represented as an IPv4 address; therefore, there are no arrows from the IPv6 protocol box to the two IPv4 sockets.

Most dual-stack hosts should use the following rules in dealing with listening sockets:

1. A listening IPv4 socket can accept incoming connections from only IPv4 clients.

2. If a server has a listening IPv6 socket that has bound the wildcard address and the `IPV6_V6ONLY` socket option (Section 7.8) is not set, that socket can accept incoming connections from either IPv4 clients or IPv6 clients. For a connection from an IPv4 client, the server's local address for the connection will be the corresponding IPv4-mapped IPv6 address.

3. If a server has a listening IPv6 socket that has bound an IPv6 address other than an IPv4-mapped IPv6 address, or has bound the wildcard address but has set the `IPV6_V6ONLY` socket option (Section 7.8), that socket can accept incoming connections from IPv6 clients only.

12.3 IPv6 Client, IPv4 Server

We now swap the protocols used by the client and server from the example in the previous section. First consider an IPv6 TCP client running on a dual-stack host.

1. An IPv4 server starts on an IPv4-only host and creates an IPv4 listening socket.

2. The IPv6 client starts and calls `getaddrinfo` asking for only IPv6 addresses (it requests the `AF_INET6` address family and sets the `AI_V4MAPPED` flag in its *hints* structure). Since the IPv4-only server host has only A records, we see from Figure 11.8 that an IPv4-mapped IPv6 address is returned to the client.

3. The IPv6 client calls `connect` with the IPv4-mapped IPv6 address in the IPv6 socket address structure. The kernel detects the mapped address and automatically sends an IPv4 SYN to the server.

4. The server responds with an IPv4 SYN/ACK, and the connection is established using IPv4 datagrams.

We can summarize this scenario in Figure 12.4.

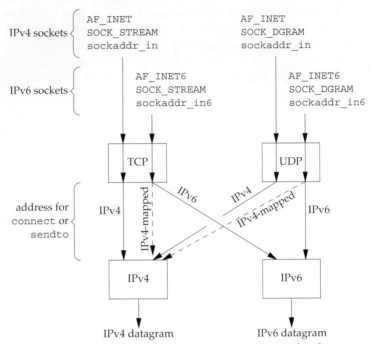

Figure 12.4 Processing of client requests, depending on address type and socket type.

- If an IPv4 TCP client calls `connect` specifying an IPv4 address, or if an IPv4 UDP client calls `sendto` specifying an IPv4 address, nothing special is done. These are the two arrows labeled "IPv4" in the figure.

- If an IPv6 TCP client calls `connect` specifying an IPv6 address, or if an IPv6 UDP client calls `sendto` specifying an IPv6 address, nothing special is done. These are the two arrows labeled "IPv6" in the figure.

- If an IPv6 TCP client specifies an IPv4-mapped IPv6 address to `connect` or if an IPv6 UDP client specifies an IPv4-mapped IPv6 address to `sendto`, the kernel detects the mapped address and causes an IPv4 datagram to be sent instead of an IPv6 datagram. These are the two dashed arrows in the figure.

- An IPv4 client cannot specify an IPv6 address to either `connect` or `sendto` because a 16-byte IPv6 address does not fit in the 4-byte `in_addr` structure within the IPv4 `sockaddr_in` structure. Therefore, there are no arrows from the IPv4 sockets to the IPv6 protocol box in the figure.

In the previous section (an IPv4 datagram arriving for an IPv6 server socket), the conversion of the received address to the IPv4-mapped IPv6 address is done by the kernel and returned transparently to the application by `accept` or `recvfrom`. In this section (an IPv4 datagram needing to be sent on an IPv6 socket), the conversion of the IPv4 address to the IPv4-mapped IPv6 address is done by the resolver according to the rules in Figure 11.8, and the mapped address is then passed transparently by the application to `connect` or `sendto`.

Summary of Interoperability

Figure 12.5 summarizes this section and the previous section, plus the combinations of clients and servers.

	IPv4 server IPv4-only host (A only)	IPv6 server IPv6-only host (AAAA only)	IPv4 server dual-stack host (A and AAAA)	IPv6 server dual-stack host (A and AAAA)
IPv4 client, IPv4-only host	IPv4	(no)	IPv4	IPv4
IPv6 client, IPv6-only host	(no)	IPv6	(no)	IPv6
IPv4 client, dual-stack host	IPv4	(no)	IPv4	IPv4
IPv6 client, dual-stack host	IPv4	IPv6	(no*)	IPv6

Figure 12.5 Summary of interoperability between IPv4 and IPv6 clients and servers.

Each box contains "IPv4" or "IPv6" if the combination is okay, indicating which protocol is used, or "(no)" if the combination is invalid. The third column on the final row is marked with an asterisk because interoperability depends on the address chosen by the client. Choosing the AAAA record and sending an IPv6 datagram will not work. But choosing the A record, which is returned to the client as an IPv4-mapped IPv6 address, causes an IPv4 datagram to be sent, which will work. By looping through all adresses that `getaddrinfo` returns, as shown in Figure 11.4, we can ensure that we will (perhaps after some timeouts) try the IPv4-mapped IPv6 address.

Although it appears that five entries in the table will not interoperate, in the real world for the foreseeable future, most implementations of IPv6 will be on dual-stack hosts and will not be IPv6-only implementations. If we therefore remove the second row and the second column, all of the "(no)" entries disappear and the only problem is the entry with the asterisk.

12.4 IPv6 Address-Testing Macros

There is a small class of IPv6 applications that must know whether they are talking to an IPv4 peer. These applications need to know if the peer's address is an IPv4-mapped IPv6 address. The following 12 macros are defined to test an IPv6 address for certain properties.

```
#include <netinet/in.h>

int IN6_IS_ADDR_UNSPECIFIED(const struct in6_addr *aptr);
int IN6_IS_ADDR_LOOPBACK(const struct in6_addr *aptr);
int IN6_IS_ADDR_MULTICAST(const struct in6_addr *aptr);
int IN6_IS_ADDR_LINKLOCAL(const struct in6_addr *aptr);
int IN6_IS_ADDR_SITELOCAL(const struct in6_addr *aptr);
int IN6_IS_ADDR_V4MAPPED(const struct in6_addr *aptr);
int IN6_IS_ADDR_V4COMPAT(const struct in6_addr *aptr);

int IN6_IS_ADDR_MC_NODELOCAL(const struct in6_addr *aptr);
int IN6_IS_ADDR_MC_LINKLOCAL(const struct in6_addr *aptr);
int IN6_IS_ADDR_MC_SITELOCAL(const struct in6_addr *aptr);
int IN6_IS_ADDR_MC_ORGLOCAL(const struct in6_addr *aptr);
int IN6_IS_ADDR_MC_GLOBAL(const struct in6_addr *aptr);
```

                     All return: nonzero if IPv6 address is of specified type, zero otherwise

The first seven macros test the basic type of IPv6 address. We show these various address types in Section A.5. The final five macros test the scope of an IPv6 multicast address (Section 21.2).

> IPv4-compatible addresses are used by a transition mechanism that has fallen out of favor. You're not likely to actually see this type of address or need to test for it.

An IPv6 client could call the `IN6_IS_ADDR_V4MAPPED` macro to test the IPv6 address returned by the resolver. An IPv6 server could call this macro to test the IPv6 address returned by `accept` or `recvfrom`.

As an example of an application that needs this macro, consider FTP and its `PORT` command. If we start an FTP client, log in to an FTP server, and issue an FTP `dir` command, the FTP client sends a `PORT` command to the FTP server across the control connection. This tells the server the client's IP address and port, to which the server then creates a data connection. (Chapter 27 of TCPv1 contains all the details of the FTP application protocol.) But, an IPv6 FTP client must know whether the server is an IPv4 server or an IPv6 server, because the former requires a command of the form `PORT a1,a2,a3,a4,p1,p2` where the first four numbers (each between 0 and 255) form the 4-byte IPv4 address and the last two numbers form the 2-byte port number. An IPv6 server, however, requires an `EPRT` command (RFC 2428 [Allman, Ostermann, and Metz 1998]), containing an address family, text format address, and text format port. Exercise 12.1 gives an example of IPv4 and IPv6 FTP protocol behavior.

12.5   Source Code Portability

Most existing network applications are written assuming IPv4. `sockaddr_in` structures are allocated and filled in and the calls to `socket` specify `AF_INET` as the first argument. We saw in the conversion from Figure 1.5 to Figure 1.6 that these IPv4 applications could be converted to use IPv6 without too much effort. Many of the changes that we showed could be done automatically using some editing scripts. Programs that are more dependent on IPv4, using features such as multicasting, IP options, or raw sockets, will take more work to convert.

If we convert an application to use IPv6 and distribute it in source code, we now have to worry about whether or not the recipient's system supports IPv6. The typical way to handle this is with `#ifdefs` throughout the code, using IPv6 when possible (since we have seen in this chapter that an IPv6 client can still communicate with IPv4 servers, and vice versa). The problem with this approach is that the code becomes littered with `#ifdefs` very quickly, and is harder to follow and maintain.

A better approach is to consider the move to IPv6 as a chance to make the program protocol-independent. The first step is to remove calls to `gethostbyname` and `gethostbyaddr` and use the `getaddrinfo` and `getnameinfo` functions that we described in the previous chapter. This lets us deal with socket address structures as opaque objects, referenced by a pointer and size, which is exactly what the basic socket functions do: `bind`, `connect`, `recvfrom`, and so on. Our sock_*XXX* functions from Section 3.8 can help manipulate these, independent of IPv4 or IPv6. Obviously these functions contain `#ifdefs` to handle IPv4 and IPv6, but hiding all of this protocol dependency in a few library functions makes our code simpler. We will develop a set of mcast_*XXX* functions in Section 21.7 that can make multicast applications independent of IPv4 or IPv6.

Another point to consider is what happens if we compile our source code on a system that supports both IPv4 and IPv6, distribute either executable code or object files (but not the source code), and someone runs our application on a system that does not support IPv6? There is a chance that the local name server supports AAAA records and returns both AAAA records and A records for some peer with which our application tries to connect. If our application, which is IPv6-capable, calls `socket` to create an IPv6 socket, it will fail if the host does not support IPv6. We handle this in the helper functions described in the previous chapter by ignoring the error from `socket` and trying the next address on the list returned by the name server. Assuming the peer has an A record, and that the name server returns the A record in addition to any AAAA records, the creation of an IPv4 socket will succeed. This is the type of functionality that belongs in a library function, and not in the source code of every application.

To enable passing socket descriptors to programs that were IPv4-only or IPv6-only, RFC 2133 [Gilligan et al. 1997] introduced the `IPV6_ADDRFORM` socket option, which could return or potentially change the address family associated with a socket. However, the semantics were never completely described, and it was only useful in very specific cases, so it was removed in the next revision of the API.

12.6 Summary

An IPv6 server on a dual-stack host can service both IPv4 clients and IPv6 clients. An IPv4 client still sends IPv4 datagrams to the server, but the server's protocol stack converts the client's address into an IPv4-mapped IPv6 address since the IPv6 server is dealing with IPv6 socket address structures.

Similarly, an IPv6 client on a dual-stack host can communicate with an IPv4 server. The client's resolver will return IPv4-mapped IPv6 addresses for all the server's A records, and calling `connect` for one of these addresses results in the dual stack sending an IPv4 SYN segment. Only a few special clients and servers need to know the protocol being used by the peer (e.g., FTP) and the `IN6_IS_ADDR_V4MAPPED` macro can be used to see if the peer is using IPv4.

Exercises

12.1 Start an IPv6 FTP client on a dual-stack host running IPv4 and IPv6. Connect to an IPv4 FTP server, make sure the client is in "active" mode (perhaps issuing the `passive` command to turn off "passive" mode), issue the `debug` command, and then the `dir` command. Next, perform the same operations, but to an IPv6 server, and compare the `PORT` commands issued as a result of the `dir` commands.

12.2 Write a program that requires one command-line argument that is an IPv4 dotted-decimal address. Create an IPv4 TCP socket and `bind` this address to the socket along with some port, say 9999. Call `listen` and then `pause`. Write a similar program that takes an IPv6 hex string as the command-line argument and creates a listening IPv6 TCP socket. Start the IPv4 program, specifying the wildcard address as the argument. Then, go to another window and start the IPv6 program, specifying the IPv6 wildcard address as the argument. Can you start the IPv6 program since the IPv4 program has already bound that port? Does the `SO_REUSEADDR` socket option make a difference? What if you start the IPv6 program first, and then try to start the IPv4 program?

13

Daemon Processes and the `inetd` *Superserver*

13.1 Introduction

A *daemon* is a process that runs in the background and is not associated with a controlling terminal. Unix systems typically have many processes that are daemons (on the order of 20 to 50), running in the background, performing different administrative tasks.

The lack of a controlling terminal is typically a side effect of being started by a system initialization script (e.g., at boot-time). But if a daemon is started by a user typing to a shell prompt, it is important for the daemon to disassociate itself from the controlling terminal to avoid any unwanted interraction with job control, terminal session management, or simply to avoid unexpected output to the terminal from the daemon as it runs in the background.

There are numerous ways to start a daemon:

1. During system startup, many daemons are started by the system initialization scripts. These scripts are often in the directory /etc or in a directory whose name begins with /etc/rc, but their location and contents are implementation-dependent. Daemons started by these scripts begin with superuser privileges.

    A few network servers are often started from these scripts: the `inetd` superserver (covered later in this chapter), a Web server, and a mail server (often `sendmail`). The `syslogd` daemon that we will describe in Section 13.2 is normally started by one of these scripts.

2. Many network servers are started by the `inetd` superserver. `inetd` itself is started from one of the scripts in Step 1. `inetd` listens for network requests

(Telnet, FTP, etc.), and when a request arrives, it invokes the actual server (Telnet server, FTP server, etc.).

3. The execution of programs on a regular basis is performed by the `cron` daemon, and programs that it invokes run as daemons. The `cron` daemon itself is started in Step 1 during system startup.

4. The execution of a program at one time in the future is specified by the `at` command. The `cron` daemon normally initiates these programs when their time arrives, so these programs run as daemons.

5. Daemons can be started from user terminals, either in the foreground or in the background. This is often done when testing a daemon, or restarting a daemon that was terminated for some reason.

Since a daemon does not have a controlling terminal, it needs some way to output messages when something happens, either normal informational messages or emergency messages that need to be handled by an administrator. The `syslog` function is the standard way to output these messages, and it sends the messages to the `syslogd` daemon.

13.2 `syslogd` Daemon

Unix systems normally start a daemon named `syslogd` from one of the system initializations scripts, and it runs as long as the system is up. Berkeley-derived implementations of `syslogd` perform the following actions on startup:

1. The configuration file, normally `/etc/syslog.conf`, is read, specifying what to do with each type of log message that the daemon can receive. These messages can be appended to a file (a special case of which is the file `/dev/console`, which writes the message to the console), written to a specific user (if that user is logged in), or forwarded to the `syslogd` daemon on another host.

2. A Unix domain socket is created and bound to the pathname `/var/run/log` (`/dev/log` on some systems).

3. A UDP socket is created and bound to port 514 (the `syslog` service).

4. The pathname `/dev/klog` is opened. Any error messages from within the kernel appear as input on this device.

The `syslogd` daemon runs in an infinite loop that calls `select`, waiting for any one of its three descriptors (from Steps 2, 3, and 4) to be readable; it reads the log message and does what the configuration file says to do with that message. If the daemon receives the `SIGHUP` signal, it rereads its configuration file.

We could send log messages to the `syslogd` daemon from our daemons by creating a Unix domain datagram socket and sending our messages to the pathname that the daemon has bound, but an easier interface is the `syslog` function that we will describe in the next section. Alternately, we could create a UDP socket and send our log messages to the loopback address and port 514.

> Newer implementations disable the creation of the UDP socket, unless specified by the administrator, as allowing anyone to send UDP datagrams to this port opens the system up to denial-of-service attacks, where someone could fill up the filesystem (e.g., by filling up log files) or cause log messages to be dropped (e.g., by overflowing syslog's socket receive buffer).

> Differences exist between the various implementations of syslogd. For example, Unix domain sockets are used by Berkeley-derived implementations, but System V implementations use a STREAMS log driver. Different Berkeley-derived implementations use different pathnames for the Unix domain socket. We can ignore all these details if we use the syslog function.

13.3 `syslog` Function

Since a daemon does not have a controlling terminal, it cannot just `fprintf` to `stderr`. The common technique for logging messages from a daemon is to call the `syslog` function.

```
#include <syslog.h>

void syslog(int priority, const char *message, ... );
```

Although this function was originally developed for BSD systems, it is provided by virtually all Unix vendors today. The description of `syslog` in the POSIX specification is consistent with what we describe here. RFC 3164 provides documentation of the BSD syslog protocol.

The *priority* argument is a combination of a *level* and a *facility*, which we show in Figures 13.1 and 13.2. Additional detail on the *priority* may be found in RFC 3164. The *message* is like a format string to `printf`, with the addition of a `%m` specification, which is replaced with the error message corresponding to the current value of `errno`. A newline can appear at the end of the *message*, but is not mandatory.

Log messages have a *level* between 0 and 7, which we show in Figure 13.1. These are ordered values. If no *level* is specified by the sender, `LOG_NOTICE` is the default.

level	Value	Description
LOG_EMERG	0	System is unusable (highest priority)
LOG_ALERT	1	Action must be taken immediately
LOG_CRIT	2	Critical conditions
LOG_ERR	3	Error conditions
LOG_WARNING	4	Warning conditions
LOG_NOTICE	5	Normal but significant condition (default)
LOG_INFO	6	Informational
LOG_DEBUG	7	Debug-level messages (lowest priority)

Figure 13.1 *level* of log messages.

Log messages also contain a *facility* to identify the type of process sending the message. We show the different values in Figure 13.2. If no *facility* is specified, LOG_USER is the default.

facility	Description
LOG_AUTH	Security/authorization messages
LOG_AUTHPRIV	Security/authorization messages (private)
LOG_CRON	cron daemon
LOG_DAEMON	System daemons
LOG_FTP	FTP daemon
LOG_KERN	Kernel messages
LOG_LOCAL0	Local use
LOG_LOCAL1	Local use
LOG_LOCAL2	Local use
LOG_LOCAL3	Local use
LOG_LOCAL4	Local use
LOG_LOCAL5	Local use
LOG_LOCAL6	Local use
LOG_LOCAL7	Local use
LOG_LPR	Line printer system
LOG_MAIL	Mail system
LOG_NEWS	Network news system
LOG_SYSLOG	Messages generated internally by syslogd
LOG_USER	Random user-level messages (default)
LOG_UUCP	UUCP system

Figure 13.2 *facility* of log messages.

For example, the following call could be issued by a daemon when a call to the `rename` function unexpectedly fails:

```
syslog(LOG_INFO|LOG_LOCAL2, "rename(%s, %s): %m", file1, file2);
```

The purpose of *facility* and *level* is to allow all messages from a given facility to be handled the same in the /etc/syslog.conf file, or to allow all messages of a given level to be handled the same. For example, the configuration file could contain the lines

```
kern.*              /dev/console
local7.debug        /var/log/cisco.log
```

to specify that all kernel messages get logged to the console and all `debug` messages from the `local7` facility get appended to the file `/var/log/cisco.log`.

When the application calls `syslog` the first time, it creates a Unix domain datagram socket and then calls `connect` to the well-known pathname of the socket created by the `syslogd` daemon (e.g., `/var/run/log`). This socket remains open until the process terminates. Alternately, the process can call `openlog` and `closelog`.

```
#include <syslog.h>

void openlog(const char *ident, int options, int facility);

void closelog(void);
```

`openlog` can be called before the first call to `syslog` and `closelog` can be called when the application is finished sending log messages.

ident is a string that will be prepended to each log message by `syslog`. Often this is the program name.

The *options* argument is formed as the logical OR of one or more of the constants in Figure 13.3.

options	Description
LOG_CONS	Log to console if cannot send to `syslogd` daemon
LOG_NDELAY	Do not delay open, create socket now
LOG_PERROR	Log to standard error as well as sending to `syslogd` daemon
LOG_PID	log the Process ID with each message

Figure 13.3 *options* for `openlog`.

Normally the Unix domain socket is not created when `openlog` is called. Instead, it is opened during the first call to `syslog`. The `LOG_NDELAY` option causes the socket to be created when `openlog` is called.

The *facility* argument to `openlog` specifies a default facility for any subsequent calls to `syslog` that do not specify a facility. Some daemons call `openlog` and specify the facility (which normally does not change for a given daemon). They then specify only the *level* in each call to `syslog` (since the *level* can change depending on the error).

Log messages can also be generated by the `logger` command. This can be used from within shell scripts, for example, to send messages to `syslogd`.

13.4 `daemon_init` Function

Figure 13.4 shows a function named `daemon_init` that we can call (normally from a server) to daemonize the process. This function should be suitable for use on all variants of Unix, but some offer a C library function called `daemon` that provides similar features. BSD offers the `daemon` function, as does Linux.

─── *daemon_init.c*

```
 1 #include    "unp.h"
 2 #include    <syslog.h>

 3 #define MAXFD    64

 4 extern int daemon_proc;          /* defined in error.c */

 5 int
 6 daemon_init(const char *pname, int facility)
 7 {
 8     int     i;
 9     pid_t   pid;

10     if ( (pid = Fork()) < 0)
11         return (-1);
12     else if (pid)
13         _exit(0);                /* parent terminates */

14     /* child 1 continues... */

15     if (setsid() < 0)            /* become session leader */
16         return (-1);

17     Signal(SIGHUP, SIG_IGN);
18     if ( (pid = Fork()) < 0)
19         return (-1);
20     else if (pid)
21         _exit(0);                /* child 1 terminates */

22     /* child 2 continues... */

23     daemon_proc = 1;             /* for err_XXX() functions */

24     chdir("/");                  /* change working directory */

25     /* close off file descriptors */
26     for (i = 0; i < MAXFD; i++)
27         close(i);

28     /* redirect stdin, stdout, and stderr to /dev/null */
29     open("/dev/null", O_RDONLY);
30     open("/dev/null", O_RDWR);
31     open("/dev/null", O_RDWR);

32     openlog(pname, LOG_PID, facility);

33     return (0);                  /* success */
34 }
```

─── *daemon_init.c*

Figure 13.4   daemon_init function: daemonizes the process.

fork

10–13   We first call fork and then the parent terminates, and the child continues. If the
process was started as a shell command in the foreground, when the parent terminates,
the shell thinks the command is done. This automatically runs the child process in the
background. Also, the child inherits the process group ID from the parent but gets its

own process ID. This guarantees that the child is not a process group leader, which is required for the next call to setsid.

setsid

15-16   setsid is a POSIX function that creates a new session. (Chapter 9 of APUE talks about process relationships and sessions in detail.) The process becomes the session leader of the new session, becomes the process group leader of a new process group, and has no controlling terminal.

Ignore SIGHUP and fork again

17-21   We ignore SIGHUP and call fork again. When this function returns, the parent is really the first child and it terminates, leaving the second child running. The purpose of this second fork is to guarantee that the daemon cannot automatically acquire a controlling terminal should it open a terminal device in the future. When a session leader without a controlling terminal opens a terminal device (that is not currently some other session's controlling terminal), the terminal becomes the controlling terminal of the session leader. But by calling fork a second time, we guarantee that the second child is no longer a session leader, so it cannot acquire a controlling terminal. We must ignore SIGHUP because when the session leader terminates (the first child), all processes in the session (our second child) receive the SIGHUP signal.

Set flag for error functions

23   We set the global daemon_proc to nonzero. This external is defined by our err_*XXX* functions (Section D.3), and when its value is nonzero, this tells them to call syslog instead of doing an fprintf to standard error. This saves us from having to go through all our code and call one of our error functions if the server is not being run as a daemon (i.e., when we are testing the server), but call syslog if it is being run as a daemon.

Change working directory

24   We change the working directory to the root directory, although some daemons might have a reason to change to some other directory. For example, a printer daemon might change to the printer's spool directory, where it does all its work. Should the daemon ever generate a core file, that file is generated in the current working directory. Another reason to change the working directory is that the daemon could have been started in any filesystem, and if it remains there, that filesystem cannot be unmounted (at least not without using some potentially destructive, forceful measures).

Close any open descriptors

25-27   We close any open descriptors that are inherited from the process that executed the daemon (normally a shell). The problem is determining the highest descriptor in use: There is no Unix function that provides this value. There are ways to determine the maximum number of descriptors that the process can open, but even this gets complicated (see p. 43 of APUE) because the limit can be infinite. Our solution is to close the first 64 descriptors, even though most of these are probably not open.

Solaris provides a function called closefrom for use by daemons to solve this problem.

Redirect `stdin`, `stdout`, and `stderr` to `/dev/null`

29–31

We `open /dev/null` for standard input, standard output, and standard error. This guarantees that these common descriptors are open, and a read from any of these descriptors returns 0 (EOF), and the kernel just discards anything written to them. The reason for opening these descriptors is so that any library function called by the daemon that assumes it can read from standard input or write to either standard output or standard error will not fail. Such a failure is potentially dangerous. If the daemon ends up opening a socket to a client, that socket descriptor ends up as `stdout` or `stderr` and some erroneous call to something like `perror` then sends unexpected data to a client.

Use `syslogd` for errors

32

`openlog` is called. The first argument is from the caller and is normally the name of the program (e.g., `argv[0]`). We specify that the process ID should be added to each log message. The *facility* is also specified by the caller, as one of the values from Figure 13.2 or 0 if the default of `LOG_USER` is acceptable.

We note that since a daemon runs without a controlling terminal, it should never receive the `SIGHUP` signal from the kernel. Therefore, many daemons use this signal as a notification from the administrator that the daemon's configuration file has changed, and the daemon should reread the file. Two other signals that a daemon should never receive are `SIGINT` and `SIGWINCH`, so daemons can safely use these signals as another way for administrators to indicate some change that the daemon should react to.

Example: Daytime Server as a Daemon

Figure 13.5 is a modification of our protocol-independent daytime server from Figure 11.14 that calls our `daemon_init` function to run as daemons.

There are only two changes: We call our `daemon_init` function as soon as the program starts, and we call our `err_msg` function, instead of `printf`, to print the client's IP address and port. Indeed, if we want our programs to be able to run as a daemon, we must avoid calling the `printf` and `fprintf` functions and use our `err_msg` function instead.

Note how we check `argc` and issue the appropriate usage message *before* calling `daemon_init`. This allows the user starting the daemon to get immediate feedback if the command has the incorrect number of arguments. After calling `daemon_init`, all subsequent error messages go to syslog.

If we run this program on our Linux host `linux` and then check the `/var/log/messages` file (where we send all `LOG_USER` messages) after connecting from the same machine (e.g., localhost), we have

```
Jun 10 09:54:37 linux daytimetcpsrv2[24288]:
connection from 127.0.0.1.55862
```

(We have wrapped the one long line.) The date, time, and hostname are prefixed automatically by the `syslogd` daemon.

inetd/daytimetcpsrv2.c

```
 1 #include     "unp.h"
 2 #include     <time.h>

 3 int
 4 main(int argc, char **argv)
 5 {
 6     int       listenfd, connfd;
 7     socklen_t addrlen, len;
 8     struct sockaddr *cliaddr;
 9     char      buff[MAXLINE];
10     time_t    ticks;

11     if (argc < 2 || argc > 3)
12         err_quit("usage: daytimetcpsrv2 [ <host> ] <service or port>");

13     daemon_init(argv[0], 0);

14     if (argc == 2)
15         listenfd = Tcp_listen(NULL, argv[1], &addrlen);
16     else
17         listenfd = Tcp_listen(argv[1], argv[2], &addrlen);

18     cliaddr = Malloc(addrlen);

19     for ( ; ; ) {
20         len = addrlen;
21         connfd = Accept(listenfd, cliaddr, &len);
22         err_msg("connection from %s", Sock_ntop(cliaddr, len));

23         ticks = time(NULL);
24         snprintf(buff, sizeof(buff), "%.24s\r\n", ctime(&ticks));
25         Write(connfd, buff, strlen(buff));

26         Close(connfd);
27     }
28 }
```

inetd/daytimetcpsrv2.c

Figure 13.5 Protocol-independent daytime server that runs as a daemon.

13.5 inetd **Daemon**

On a typical Unix system, there could be many servers in existence, just waiting for a client request to arrive. Examples are FTP, Telnet, Rlogin, TFTP, and so on. With systems before 4.3BSD, each of these services had a process associated with it. This process was started at boot-time from the file /etc/rc, and each process did nearly identical startup tasks: create a socket, bind the server's well-known port to the socket, wait for a connection (if TCP) or a datagram (if UDP), and then fork. The child process serviced the client and the parent waited for the next client request. There are two problems with this model:

1. All these daemons contained nearly identical startup code, first with respect to socket creation, and also with respect to becoming a daemon process (similar to our `daemon_init` function).

2. Each daemon took a slot in the process table, but each daemon was asleep most of the time.

The 4.3BSD release simplified this by providing an Internet *superserver*: the `inetd` daemon. This daemon can be used by servers that use either TCP or UDP. It does not handle other protocols, such as Unix domain sockets. This daemon fixes the two problems just mentioned:

1. It simplifies writing daemon processes since most of the startup details are handled by `inetd`. This obviates the need for each server to call our `daemon_init` function.

2. It allows a single process (`inetd`) to be waiting for incoming client requests for multiple services, instead of one process for each service. This reduces the total number of processes in the system.

The `inetd` process establishes itself as a daemon using the techniques that we described with our `daemon_init` function. It then reads and processes its configuration file, typically `/etc/inetd.conf`. This file specifies the services that the superserver is to handle, and what to do when a service request arrives. Each line contains the fields shown in Figure 13.6.

Field	Description
service-name	Must be in `/etc/services`
socket-type	`stream` (TCP) or `dgram` (UDP)
protocol	Must be in `/etc/protocols`: either `tcp` or `udp`
wait-flag	Typically `nowait` for TCP or `wait` for UDP
login-name	From `/etc/passwd`: typically `root`
server-program	Full pathname to `exec`
server-program-arguments	Arguments for `exec`

Figure 13.6 Fields in `inetd.conf` file.

Some sample lines are

```
ftp      stream  tcp  nowait  root    /usr/bin/ftpd      ftpd -l
telnet   stream  tcp  nowait  root    /usr/bin/telnetd   telnetd
login    stream  tcp  nowait  root    /usr/bin/rlogind   rlogind -s
tftp     dgram   udp  wait    nobody  /usr/bin/tftpd     tftpd -s /tftpboot
```

The actual name of the server is always passed as the first argument to a program when it is `exec`ed.

> This figure and the sample lines are just examples. Most vendors have added their own features to `inetd`. Examples are the ability to handle RPC servers, in addition to TCP and UDP servers, and the ability to handle protocols other than TCP and UDP. Also, the pathname to

exec and the command-line arguments to the server obviously depend on the implementation.

The *wait-flag* field can be a bit confusing. In general, it specifies whether the daemon started by inetd intends to take over the listening socket associated with the service. UDP services don't have separate listening and accepting sockets, and are virtually always configured as wait. TCP services could be handled either way, at the discretion of the person writing the daemon, but nowait is most common.

The interaction of IPv6 with /etc/inetd.conf depends on the vendor and special attention to detail is required to get what you want. Some use a *protocol* of tcp6 or udp6 to indicate that an IPv6 socket should be created for a service. Some allow *protocol* values of tcp46 or udp46 indicate the daemon wants sockets that allow both IPv6 and IPv4 connections. These special protocol names do not typically appear in the /etc/protocols file.

A picture of what the inetd daemon does is shown in Figure 13.7.

1. On startup, it reads the /etc/inetd.conf file and creates a socket of the appropriate type (stream or datagram) for all the services specified in the file. The maximum number of servers that inetd can handle depends on the maximum number of descriptors that inetd can create. Each new socket is added to a descriptor set that will be used in a call to select.

2. bind is called for the socket, specifying the port for the server and the wildcard IP address. This TCP or UDP port number is obtained by calling getservbyname with the *service-name* and *protocol* fields from the configuration file as arguments.

3. For TCP sockets, listen is called so that incoming connection requests are accepted. This step is not done for datagram sockets.

4. After all the sockets are created, select is called to wait for any of the sockets to become readable. Recall from Section 6.3 that a listening TCP socket becomes readable when a new connection is ready to be accepted and a UDP socket becomes readable when a datagram arrives. inetd spends most of its time blocked in this call to select, waiting for a socket to be readable.

5. When select returns that a socket is readable, if the socket is a TCP socket and the nowait flag is given, accept is called to accept the new connection.

6. The inetd daemon forks and the child process handles the service request. This is similar to a standard concurrent server (Section 4.8).

The child closes all descriptors except the socket descriptor it is handling: the new connected socket returned by accept for a TCP server or the original UDP socket. The child calls dup2 three times, duplicating the socket onto descriptors 0, 1, and 2 (standard input, standard output, and standard error). The original socket descriptor is then closed. By doing this, the only descriptors that are open in the child are 0, 1, and 2. If the child reads from standard input, it is reading from the socket and anything it writes to standard output or standard error is written to the socket. The child calls getpwnam to get the password file entry for the *login-name* specified in the configuration file. If this field is not root, then the child becomes the specified user by executing the setgid and setuid function calls. (Since the inetd process

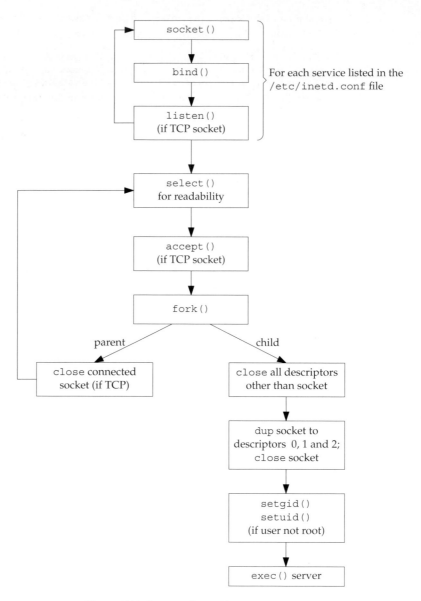

Figure 13.7 Steps performed by `inetd`.

is executing with a user ID of 0, the child process inherits this user ID across the `fork`, and is able to become any user that it chooses.)

The child process now does an `exec` to execute the appropriate *server-program* to handle the request, passing the arguments specified in the configuration file.

7. If the socket is a stream socket, the parent process must close the connected socket (like our standard concurrent server). The parent calls `select` again, waiting for the next socket to become readable.

If we look in more detail at the descriptor handling that is taking place, Figure 13.8 shows the descriptors in `inetd` when a new connection request arrives from an FTP client.

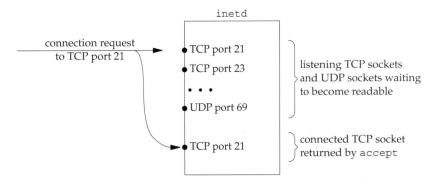

Figure 13.8   `inetd` descriptors when connection request arrives for TCP port 21.

The connection request is directed to TCP port 21, but a new connected socket is created by `accept`.

Figure 13.9 shows the descriptors in the child, after the call to `fork`, after the child has closed all the descriptors except the connected socket.

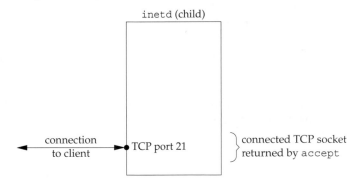

Figure 13.9   `inetd` descriptors in child.

The next step is for the child to duplicate the connected socket to descriptors 0, 1, and 2 and then close the connected socket. This gives us the descriptors shown in Figure 13.10.

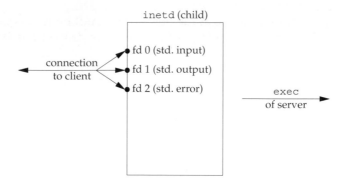

Figure 13.10   `inetd` descriptors after `dup2`.

The child then calls `exec`. Recall from Section 4.7 that all descriptors normally remain open across an `exec`, so the real server that is `exec`ed uses any of the descriptors, 0, 1, or 2, to communicate with the client. These should be the only descriptors open in the server.

The scenario we have described handles the case where the configuration file specifies `nowait` for the server. This is typical for all TCP services and it means that `inetd` need not wait for its child to terminate before accepting another connection for that service. If another connection request arrives for the same service, it is returned to the parent process as soon as it calls `select` again. Steps 4, 5, and 6 listed earlier are executed again, and another child process handles this new request.

Specifying the `wait` flag for a datagram service changes the steps done by the parent process. This flag says that `inetd` must wait for its child to terminate before selecting on this socket again. The following changes occur:

1. When `fork` returns in the parent, the parent saves the process ID of the child. This allows the parent to know when this specific child process terminates, by looking at the value returned by `waitpid`.

2. The parent disables the socket from future `select`s by using the `FD_CLR` macro to turn off the bit in its descriptor set. This means that the child process takes over the socket until it terminates.

3. When the child terminates, the parent is notified by a `SIGCHLD` signal, and the parent's signal handler obtains the process ID of the terminating child. It reenables `select` for the corresponding socket by turning on the bit in its descriptor set for this socket.

The reason that a datagram server must take over the socket until it terminates, preventing `inetd` from `select`ing on that socket for readability (awaiting another client datagram), is because there is only one socket for a datagram server, unlike a TCP server that has a listening socket and one connected socket per client. If inetd did not turn off readability for the datagram socket, and if the parent (inetd) executed before the child, then the datagram from the client would still be in the socket receive buffer, causing select to return readable again, causing inetd to fork another (unneeded) child. inetd must ignore the datagram socket until it knows that the child has read the datagram from the socket receive queue. The way that inetd knows when that child is finished with the socket is by receiving SIGCHLD, indicating that the child has terminated. We will show an example of this in Section 22.7.

The five standard Internet services that we described in Figure 2.18 are handled internally by inetd (see Exercise 13.2).

Since inetd is the process that calls accept for a TCP server, the actual server that is invoked by inetd normally calls getpeername to obtain the IP address and port number of the client. Recall Figure 4.18 where we showed that after a fork and an exec (which is what inetd does), the only way for the actual server to obtain the identify of the client is to call getpeername.

inetd is normally not used for high-volume servers, notably mail and Web servers. sendmail, for example, is normally run as a standard concurrent server, as we described in Section 4.8. In this mode, the process control cost for each client connection is just a fork, while the cost for a TCP server invoked by inetd is a fork and an exec. Web servers use a variety of techniques to minimize the process control overhead for each client connection, as we will discuss in Chapter 30.

> It is now common to find an extended Internet services daemon, called xinetd, on Linux and other systems. xinetd provides the same basic function as inetd, but also includes a long list of other interesting features. Those features include options for logging, accepting or rejecting connections based on the client's address, configuring services one-per-file instead of a single monolithic configuration, and many more. It is not described further here since the basic *superserver* idea behind them both is the same.

13.6 `daemon_inetd` Function

Figure 13.11 shows a function named daemon_inetd that we can call from a server we know is invoked by inetd.

daemon_inetd.c
```
1 #include    "unp.h"
2 #include    <syslog.h>

3 extern int daemon_proc;          /* defined in error.c */

4 void
5 daemon_inetd(const char *pname, int facility)
6 {
7     daemon_proc = 1;             /* for our err_XXX() functions */
8     openlog(pname, LOG_PID, facility);
9 }
```
daemon_inetd.c

Figure 13.11 daemon_inetd function: daemonizes process run by inetd.

This function is trivial compared to `daemon_init`, because all of the daemonization steps are performed by `inetd` when it starts. All that we do is set the `daemon_proc` flag for our error functions (Figure D.3) and call `openlog` with the same arguments as the call in Figure 13.4.

Example: Daytime Server as a Daemon Invoked by `inetd`

Figure 13.12 is a modification of our daytime server from Figure 13.5 that can be invoked by `inetd`.

———————————————————————————————————— *inetd/daytimetcpsrv3.c*

```
 1 #include    "unp.h"
 2 #include    <time.h>

 3 int
 4 main(int argc, char **argv)
 5 {
 6     socklen_t len;
 7     struct sockaddr *cliaddr;
 8     char    buff[MAXLINE];
 9     time_t  ticks;

10     daemon_inetd(argv[0], 0);

11     cliaddr = Malloc(sizeof(struct sockaddr_storage));
12     len = sizeof(struct sockaddr_storage);
13     Getpeername(0, cliaddr, &len);
14     err_msg("connection from %s", Sock_ntop(cliaddr, len));

15     ticks = time(NULL);
16     snprintf(buff, sizeof(buff), "%.24s\r\n", ctime(&ticks));
17     Write(0, buff, strlen(buff));

18     Close(0);                    /* close TCP connection */
19     exit(0);
20 }
```
———————————————————————————————————— *inetd/daytimetcpsrv3.c*

Figure 13.12 Protocol-independent daytime server that can be invoked by `inetd`.

There are two major changes in this program. First, all the socket creation code is gone: the calls to `tcp_listen` and to `accept`. Those steps are done by `inetd` and we reference the TCP connection using descriptor 0 (standard input). Second, the infinite `for` loop is gone because we are invoked once per client connection. After servicing this client, we terminate.

Call `getpeername`

11–14   Since we do not call `tcp_listen`, we do not know the size of the socket address structure it returns, and since we do not call `accept`, we do not know the client's protocol address. Therefore, we allocate a buffer for the socket address structure using `sizeof(struct sockaddr_storage)` and call `getpeername` with descriptor 0 as the first argument.

To run this example on our Solaris system, we first assign the service a name and port, adding the following line to `/etc/services`:

```
mydaytime       9999/tcp
```

We then add the following line to `/etc/inetd.conf`:

```
mydaytime   stream  tcp  nowait  andy
        /home/andy/daytimetcpsrv3  daytimetcpsrv3
```

(We have wrapped the long line.) We place the executable in the specified location and send the `SIGHUP` signal to `inetd`, telling it to reread its configuration file. The next step is to execute `netstat` to verify that a listening socket has been created on TCP port 9999.

```
solaris % netstat -na | grep 9999
    *.9999               *.*            0    0 49152    0 LISTEN
```

We then invoke the server from another host.

```
linux % telnet solaris 9999
Trying 192.168.1.20...
Connected to solaris.
Escape character is '^]'.
Tue Jun 10 11:04:02 2003
Connection closed by foreign host.
```

The `/var/adm/messages` file (where we have directed the `LOG_USER` facility messages to be logged in our `/etc/syslog.conf` file) contains the following entry:

```
Jun 10 11:04:02 solaris daytimetcpsrv3[28724]: connection from 192.168.1.10.58145
```

13.7 Summary

Daemons are processes that run in the background independent of control from all terminals. Many network servers run as daemons. All output from a daemon is normally sent to the `syslogd` daemon by calling the `syslog` function. The administrator then has complete control over what happens to these messages, based on the daemon that sent the message and the severity of the message.

To start an arbitrary program and have it run as a daemon requires a few steps: Call `fork` to run in the background, call `setsid` to create a new POSIX session and become the session leader, `fork` again to avoid obtaining a new controlling terminal, change the working directory and the file mode creation mask, and close all unneeded files. Our `daemon_init` function handles all these details.

Many Unix servers are started by the `inetd` daemon. It handles all the required daemonization steps, and when the actual server is started, the socket is open on standard input, standard output, and standard error. This lets us omit calls to `socket`, `bind`, `listen`, and `accept`, since all these steps are handled by `inetd`.

Exercises

13.1   What happens in Figure 13.5 if we move the call to `daemon_init` before the command-line arguments have been checked, so that the call to `err_quit` comes after it?

13.2   For the five services handled internally by `inetd` (Figure 2.18), considering the TCP version and the UDP version of each service, which of the 10 servers do you think are implemented with a call to `fork`, and which do not require a `fork`?

13.3   What happens if we create a UDP socket, bind port 7 to the socket (the standard `echo` server in Figure 2.18), and send a UDP datagram to a `chargen` server?

13.4   The Solaris 2.x man page for `inetd` describes a `-t` flag that causes `inetd` to call `syslog` (with a facility of `LOG_DAEMON` and a level of `LOG_NOTICE`) to log the client's IP address and port for any TCP service that `inetd` handles. How does `inetd` obtain this information?

This man page also says that `inetd` cannot do this for a UDP service. Why?

Is there a way around this limitation for UDP services?

14

Advanced I/O Functions

14.1 Introduction

This chapter covers a variety of functions and techniques that we lump into the category of "advanced I/O." First is setting a timeout on an I/O operation, which can be done in three different ways. Next are three more variations on the `read` and `write` functions: `recv` and `send`, which allow a fourth argument that contains flags from the process to the kernel, `readv` and `writev`, which let us specify a vector of buffers to input into or output from, and `recvmsg` and `sendmsg`, which combine all the features from the other I/O functions along with the new capability of receiving and sending ancillary data.

We also consider how to determine the amount of data in the socket receive buffer, how to use the C standard I/O library with sockets, and we discuss some advanced ways to wait for events.

14.2 Socket Timeouts

There are three ways to place a timeout on an I/O operation involving a socket:

1. Call `alarm`, which generates the `SIGALRM` signal when the specified time has expired. This involves signal handling, which can differ from one implementation to the next, and it may interfere with other existing calls to `alarm` in the process.

2. Block waiting for I/O in `select`, which has a time limit built-in, instead of blocking in a call to `read` or `write`.

3. Use the newer SO_RCVTIMEO and SO_SNDTIMEO socket options. The problem with this approach is that not all implementations support these two socket options.

All three techniques work with input and output operations (e.g., read, write, and other variations such as recvfrom and sendto), but we would also like a technique that we can use with connect, since a TCP connect can take a long time to time out (typically 75 seconds). select can be used to place a timeout on connect only when the socket is in a nonblocking mode (which we show in Section 16.3), and the two socket options do not work with connect. We also note that the first two techniques work with any descriptor, while the third technique works only with socket descriptors.

We now show examples of all three techniques.

connect with a Timeout Using SIGALRM

Figure 14.1 shows our function connect_timeo that calls connect with an upper limit specified by the caller. The first three arguments are the three required by connect and the fourth argument is the number of seconds to wait.

lib/connect_timeo.c

```
1 #include    "unp.h"

2 static void connect_alarm(int);

3 int
4 connect_timeo(int sockfd, const SA *saptr, socklen_t salen, int nsec)
5 {
6      Sigfunc *sigfunc;
7      int     n;

8      sigfunc = Signal(SIGALRM, connect_alarm);
9      if (alarm(nsec) != 0)
10         err_msg("connect_timeo: alarm was already set");

11     if ( (n = connect(sockfd, saptr, salen)) < 0) {
12         close(sockfd);
13         if (errno == EINTR)
14             errno = ETIMEDOUT;
15     }
16     alarm(0);                  /* turn off the alarm */
17     Signal(SIGALRM, sigfunc);  /* restore previous signal handler */

18     return (n);
19 }

20 static void
21 connect_alarm(int signo)
22 {
23     return;                    /* just interrupt the connect() */
24 }
```

lib/connect_timeo.c

Figure 14.1 connect with a timeout.

Establish signal handler

8   A signal handler is established for SIGALRM. The current signal handler (if any) is saved, so we can restore it at the end of the function.

Set alarm

9–10   The alarm clock for the process is set to the number of seconds specified by the caller. The return value from alarm is the number of seconds currently remaining in the alarm clock for the process (if one has already been set by the process) or 0 (if there is no current alarm). In the former case we print a warning message since we are wiping out that previously set alarm (see Exercise 14.2).

Call connect

11–15   connect is called and if the function is interrupted (EINTR), we set the errno value to ETIMEDOUT instead. The socket is closed to prevent the three-way handshake from continuing.

Turn off alarm and restore any previous signal handler

16–18   The alarm is turned off by setting it to 0 and the previous signal handler (if any) is restored.

Handle SIGALRM

20–24   The signal handler just returns, assuming this return will interrupt the pending connect, causing connect to return an error of EINTR. Recall our signal function (Figure 5.6) that does not set the SA_RESTART flag when the signal being caught is SIGALRM.

One point to make with this example is that we can always reduce the timeout period for a connect using this technique, but we cannot extend the kernel's existing timeout. That is, on a Berkeley-derived kernel the timeout for a connect is normally 75 seconds. We can specify a smaller value for our function, say 10, but if we specify a larger value, say 80, the connect itself will still time out after 75 seconds.

Another point with this example is that we use the interruptibility of the system call (connect) to return before the kernel's time limit expires. This is fine when we perform the system call and can handle the EINTR error return. But in Section 29.7, we will encounter a library function that performs the system call, and the library function reissues the system call when EINTR is returned. We can still use SIGALRM in this scenario, but we will see in Figure 29.10 that we also have to use sigsetjmp and siglongjmp to get around the library's ignoring of EINTR.

Although this example is fairly simple, signals are quite difficult to use correctly with multithreaded programs (see Chapter 26). So, the technique shown here is only recommended for single-threaded programs.

recvfrom with a Timeout Using SIGALRM

Figure 14.2 is a redo of our dg_cli function from Figure 8.8, but with a call to alarm to interrupt the recvfrom if a reply is not received within five seconds.

advio/dgclitimeo3.c

```
 1 #include    "unp.h"

 2 static void sig_alrm(int);

 3 void
 4 dg_cli(FILE *fp, int sockfd, const SA *pservaddr, socklen_t servlen)
 5 {
 6     int     n;
 7     char    sendline[MAXLINE], recvline[MAXLINE + 1];

 8     Signal(SIGALRM, sig_alrm);

 9     while (Fgets(sendline, MAXLINE, fp) != NULL) {

10         Sendto(sockfd, sendline, strlen(sendline), 0, pservaddr, servlen);

11         alarm(5);
12         if ( (n = recvfrom(sockfd, recvline, MAXLINE, 0, NULL, NULL)) < 0) {
13             if (errno == EINTR)
14                 fprintf(stderr, "socket timeout\n");
15             else
16                 err_sys("recvfrom error");
17         } else {
18             alarm(0);
19             recvline[n] = 0;    /* null terminate */
20             Fputs(recvline, stdout);
21         }
22     }
23 }

24 static void
25 sig_alrm(int signo)
26 {
27     return;                     /* just interrupt the recvfrom() */
28 }
```

advio/dgclitimeo3.c

Figure 14.2 dg_cli function with alarm to timeout recvfrom.

Handle timeout from recvfrom

8–22   We establish a signal handler for SIGALRM and then call alarm for a five-second timeout before each call to recvfrom. If recvfrom is interrupted by our signal handler, we print a message and continue. If a line is read from the server, we turn off the pending alarm and print the reply.

SIGALRM signal handler

24–28   Our signal handler just returns, to interrupt the blocked recvfrom.

This example works correctly because we are reading only one reply each time we establish an alarm. In Section 20.4, we will use the same technique, but since we are reading multiple replies for a given alarm, a race condition exists that we must handle.

recvfrom with a Timeout Using select

We demonstrate the second technique for setting a timeout (using select) in Figure 14.3. It shows our function named readable_timeo which waits up to a specified number of seconds for a descriptor to become readable.

——— lib/readable_timeo.c

```
 1 #include    "unp.h"

 2 int
 3 readable_timeo(int fd, int sec)
 4 {
 5     fd_set  rset;
 6     struct timeval tv;

 7     FD_ZERO(&rset);
 8     FD_SET(fd, &rset);

 9     tv.tv_sec = sec;
10     tv.tv_usec = 0;

11     return (select(fd + 1, &rset, NULL, NULL, &tv));
12         /* > 0 if descriptor is readable */
13 }
```
——— lib/readable_timeo.c

Figure 14.3 readable_timeo function: waits for a descriptor to become readable.

Prepare arguments for select

7-10   The bit corresponding to the descriptor is turned on in the read descriptor set. A timeval structure is set to the number of seconds that the caller wants to wait.

Block in select

11-12   select waits for the descriptor to become readable, or for the timeout to expire. The return value of this function is the return value of select: −1 on an error, 0 if a timeout occurs, or a positive value specifying the number of ready descriptors.

This function does not perform the read operation; it just waits for the descriptor to be ready for reading. Therefore, this function can be used with any type of socket, TCP or UDP.

It is trivial to create a similar function named writable_timeo that waits for a descriptor to become writable.

We use this function in Figure 14.4, which is a redo of our dg_cli function from Figure 8.8. This new version calls recvfrom only when our readable_timeo function returns a positive value.

We do not call recvfrom until the function readable_timeo tells us that the descriptor is readable. This guarantees that recvfrom will not block.

advio/dgclitimeo1.c

```
 1 #include    "unp.h"

 2 void
 3 dg_cli(FILE *fp, int sockfd, const SA *pservaddr, socklen_t servlen)
 4 {
 5     int     n;
 6     char    sendline[MAXLINE], recvline[MAXLINE + 1];

 7     while (Fgets(sendline, MAXLINE, fp) != NULL) {

 8         Sendto(sockfd, sendline, strlen(sendline), 0, pservaddr, servlen);

 9         if (Readable_timeo(sockfd, 5) == 0) {
10             fprintf(stderr, "socket timeout\n");
11         } else {
12             n = Recvfrom(sockfd, recvline, MAXLINE, 0, NULL, NULL);
13             recvline[n] = 0;      /* null terminate */
14             Fputs(recvline, stdout);
15         }
16     }
17 }
```

advio/dgclitimeo1.c

Figure 14.4   dg_cli function that calls readable_timeo to set a timeout.

recvfrom with a Timeout Using the SO_RCVTIMEO Socket Option

Our final example demonstrates the SO_RCVTIMEO socket option. We set this option once for a descriptor, specifying the timeout value, and this timeout then applies to all read operations on that descriptor. The nice thing about this method is that we set the option only once, compared to the previous two methods, which required doing something before every operation on which we wanted to place a time limit. But this socket option applies only to read operations, and the similar option SO_SNDTIMEO applies only to write operations; neither socket option can be used to set a timeout for a connect.

Figure 14.5 shows another version of our dg_cli function that uses the SO_RCVTIMEO socket option.

Set socket option

8-10   The fourth argument to setsockopt is a pointer to a timeval structure that is filled in with the desired timeout.

Test for timeout

15-17   If the I/O operation times out, the function (recvfrom, in this case) returns EWOULDBLOCK.

advio/dgclitimeo2.c
```
 1 #include    "unp.h"

 2 void
 3 dg_cli(FILE *fp, int sockfd, const SA *pservaddr, socklen_t servlen)
 4 {
 5     int      n;
 6     char     sendline[MAXLINE], recvline[MAXLINE + 1];
 7     struct timeval tv;

 8     tv.tv_sec = 5;
 9     tv.tv_usec = 0;
10     Setsockopt(sockfd, SOL_SOCKET, SO_RCVTIMEO, &tv, sizeof(tv));

11     while (Fgets(sendline, MAXLINE, fp) != NULL) {

12         Sendto(sockfd, sendline, strlen(sendline), 0, pservaddr, servlen);

13         n = recvfrom(sockfd, recvline, MAXLINE, 0, NULL, NULL);
14         if (n < 0) {
15             if (errno == EWOULDBLOCK) {
16                 fprintf(stderr, "socket timeout\n");
17                 continue;
18             } else
19                 err_sys("recvfrom error");
20         }

21         recvline[n] = 0;          /* null terminate */
22         Fputs(recvline, stdout);
23     }
24 }
```
advio/dgclitimeo2.c

Figure 14.5 dg_cli function that uses the SO_RCVTIMEO socket option to set a timeout.

14.3 recv and send Functions

These two functions are similar to the standard read and write functions, but one additional argument is required.

```
#include <sys/socket.h>

ssize_t recv(int sockfd, void *buff, size_t nbytes, int flags);

ssize_t send(int sockfd, const void *buff, size_t nbytes, int flags);
```
Both return: number of bytes read or written if OK, −1 on error

The first three arguments to recv and send are the same as the first three arguments to read and write. The *flags* argument is either 0 or is formed by logically OR'ing one or more of the constants shown in Figure 14.6.

flags	Description	recv	send
MSG_DONTROUTE	Bypass routing table lookup		•
MSG_DONTWAIT	Only this operation is nonblocking	•	•
MSG_OOB	Send or receive out-of-band data	•	•
MSG_PEEK	Peek at incoming message	•	
MSG_WAITALL	Wait for all the data	•	

Figure 14.6 *flags* for I/O functions.

MSG_DONTROUTE   This flag tells the kernel that the destination is on a locally attached network and not to perform a lookup of the routing table. We provided additional information on this feature with the SO_DONTROUTE socket option (Section 7.5). This feature can be enabled for a single output operation with the MSG_DONTROUTE flag, or enabled for all output operations for a given socket using the socket option.

MSG_DONTWAIT   This flag specifies nonblocking for a single I/O operation, without having to turn on the nonblocking flag for the socket, perform the I/O operation, and then turn off the nonblocking flag. We will describe nonblocking I/O in Chapter 16, along with turning the nonblocking flag on and off for all I/O operations on a socket.

This flag is newer than the others and might not be supported on all systems.

MSG_OOB   With send, this flag specifies that out-of-band data is being sent. With TCP, only one byte should be sent as out-of-band data, as we will describe in Chapter 24. With recv, this flag specifies that out-of-band data is to be read instead of normal data.

MSG_PEEK   This flag lets us look at the data that is available to be read, without having the system discard the data after the recv or recvfrom returns. We will talk more about this in Section 14.7.

MSG_WAITALL   This flag was introduced with 4.3BSD Reno. It tells the kernel not to return from a read operation until the requested number of bytes have been read. If the system supports this flag, we can then omit the readn function (Figure 3.15) and replace it with the following macro:

```
#define  readn(fd, ptr, n)  recv(fd, ptr, n, MSG_WAITALL)
```

Even if we specify MSG_WAITALL, the function can still

return fewer than the requested number of bytes if (i) a signal is caught, (ii) the connection is terminated, or (iii) an error is pending for the socket.

There are additional flags used by other protocols, but not TCP/IP. For example, the OSI transport layer is record-based (not a byte stream such as TCP) and supports the MSG_EOR flag for output operations to specify the end of a logical record.

There is a fundamental design problem with the *flags* argument: It is passed by value; it is not a value-result argument. Therefore, it can be used only to pass flags from the process to the kernel. The kernel cannot pass back flags to the process. This is not a problem with TCP/IP, because it is rare to need to pass flags back to the process from the kernel. But when the OSI protocols were added to 4.3BSD Reno, the need arose to return MSG_EOR to the process with an input operation. Thus, the decision was made with 4.3BSD Reno to leave the arguments to the commonly used input functions (recv and recvfrom) as-is and change the msghdr structure that is used with recvmsg and sendmsg. We will see in Section 14.5 that an integer msg_flags member was added to this structure, and since the structure is passed by reference, the kernel can modify these flags on return. This also means that if a process needs to have the flags updated by the kernel, the process must call recvmsg instead of either recv or recvfrom.

14.4 readv **and** writev **Functions**

These two functions are similar to read and write, but readv and writev let us read into or write from one or more buffers with a single function call. These operations are called *scatter read* (since the input data is scattered into multiple application buffers) and *gather write* (since multiple buffers are gathered for a single output operation).

```
#include <sys/uio.h>

ssize_t readv(int filedes, const struct iovec *iov, int iovcnt);

ssize_t writev(int filedes, const struct iovec *iov, int iovcnt);
```

Both return: number of bytes read or written, −1 on error

The second argument to both functions is a pointer to an array of iovec structures, which is defined by including the <sys/uio.h> header.

```
struct iovec {
  void   *iov_base;   /* starting address of buffer */
  size_t  iov_len;    /* size of buffer */
};
```

The datatypes shown for the members of the iovec structure are those specified by POSIX. You may encounter implementations that define iov_base to be a char *, and iov_len to be an int.

There is some limit to the number of elements in the array of `iovec` structures that an implementation allows. Linux, for example, allows up to 1,024, while HP-UX has a limit of 2,100. POSIX requires that the constant `IOV_MAX` be defined by including the `<sys/uio.h>` header and that its value be at least 16.

The `readv` and `writev` functions can be used with any descriptor, not just sockets. Also, `writev` is an atomic operation. For a record-based protocol such as UDP, one call to `writev` generates a single UDP datagram.

We mentioned one use of `writev` with the `TCP_NODELAY` socket option in Section 7.9. We said that a `write` of 4 bytes followed by a `write` of 396 bytes could invoke the Nagle algorithm and a preferred solution is to call `writev` for the two buffers.

14.5   `recvmsg` and `sendmsg` Functions

These two functions are the most general of all the I/O functions. Indeed, we could replace all calls to `read`, `readv`, `recv`, and `recvfrom` with calls to `recvmsg`. Similarly all calls to the various output functions could be replaced with calls to `sendmsg`.

```
#include <sys/socket.h>

ssize_t recvmsg(int sockfd, struct msghdr *msg, int flags);

ssize_t sendmsg(int sockfd, struct msghdr *msg, int flags);
```
Both return: number of bytes read or written if OK, −1 on error

Both functions package most arguments into a `msghdr` structure.

```
struct msghdr {
    void          *msg_name;        /* protocol address */
    socklen_t      msg_namelen;     /* size of protocol address */
    struct iovec *msg_iov;          /* scatter/gather array */
    int            msg_iovlen;      /* # elements in msg_iov */
    void          *msg_control;     /* ancillary data (cmsghdr struct) */
    socklen_t      msg_controllen;  /* length of ancillary data */
    int            msg_flags;       /* flags returned by recvmsg() */
};
```

> The `msghdr` structure that we show is the one specified in POSIX. Some systems still use an older `msghdr` structure that originated with 4.2BSD. This older structure does not have the `msg_flags` member, and the `msg_control` and `msg_controllen` members are named `msg_accrights` and `msg_accrightslen`. The newer form of the `msghdr` structure is often available using conditional compilation flags. The only form of ancillary data supported by the older structure is the passing of file descriptors (called access rights).

The `msg_name` and `msg_namelen` members are used when the socket is not connected (e.g., an unconnected UDP socket). They are similar to the fifth and sixth arguments to `recvfrom` and `sendto`: `msg_name` points to a socket address structure in which the caller stores the destination's protocol address for `sendmsg`, or in which `recvmsg` stores the sender's protocol address. If a protocol address does not need to be specified (e.g., a TCP socket or a connected UDP socket), msg_name should be set to a null pointer. msg_namelen is a value for sendmsg, but a value-result for recvmsg.

The msg_iov and msg_iovlen members specify the array of input or output buffers (the array of iovec structures), similar to the second and third arguments for readv or writev. The msg_control and msg_controllen members specify the location and size of the optional ancillary data. msg_controllen is a value-result argument for recvmsg. We will describe ancillary data in Section 14.6.

With recvmsg and sendmsg, we must distinguish between two flag variables: the *flags* argument, which is passed by value, and the msg_flags member of the msghdr structure, which is passed by reference (since the address of the structure is passed to the function).

- The msg_flags member is used only by recvmsg. When recvmsg is called, the *flags* argument is copied into the msg_flags member (p. 502 of TCPv2) and this value is used by the kernel to drive its receive processing. This value is then updated based on the result of recvmsg.

- The msg_flags member is ignored by sendmsg because this function uses the *flags* argument to drive its output processing. This means if we want to set the MSG_DONTWAIT flag in a call to sendmsg, we set the *flags* argument to this value; setting the msg_flags member to this value has no effect.

Figure 14.7 summarizes the flags that are examined by the kernel for both the input and output functions, as well as the msg_flags that might be returned by recvmsg. There is no column for sendmsg msg_flags because, as we mentioned, it is not used.

Flag	Examined by: send *flags* sendto *flags* sendmsg *flags*	Examined by: recv *flags* recvfrom *flags* recvmsg *flags*	Returned by: recvmsg msg_flags
MSG_DONTROUTE	•		
MSG_DONTWAIT	•	•	
MSG_PEEK		•	
MSG_WAITALL		•	
MSG_EOR	•		•
MSG_OOB	•	•	•
MSG_BCAST			•
MSG_MCAST			•
MSG_TRUNC			•
MSG_CTRUNC			•
MSG_NOTIFICATION			•

Figure 14.7 Summary of input and output flags by various I/O functions.

The first four flags are only examined and never returned; the next two are both examined and returned; and the last four are only returned. The following comments apply to the six flags returned by recvmsg:

MSG_BCAST   This flag is relatively new, supported by at least BSD, and is returned if the datagram was received as a link-layer broadcast or with a destination IP address that is a broadcast address. This flag is a better way of determining if a UDP datagram was sent to a broadcast address, compared to the IP_RECVDSTADDR socket option.

MSG_MCAST   This flag is also a fairly recent addition, supported by at least BSD, and is returned if the datagram was received as a link-layer multicast.

MSG_TRUNC   This flag is returned if the datagram was truncated; in other words, the kernel has more data to return than the process has allocated room for (the sum of all the iov_len members). We will discuss this more in Section 22.3.

MSG_CTRUNC   This flag is returned if the ancillary data was truncated; in other words, the kernel has more ancillary data to return than the process has allocated room for (msg_controllen).

MSG_EOR   This flag is cleared if the returned data does not end a logical record; the flag is turned on if the returned data ends a logical record. TCP does *not* use this flag since it is a byte-stream protocol.

MSG_OOB   This flag is *never* returned for TCP out-of-band data. This flag is returned by other protocol suites (e.g., the OSI protocols).

MSG_NOTIFICATON   This flag is returned for SCTP receivers to indicate that the message read is an event notification, not a data message.

Implementations might return some of the input *flags* in the msg_flags member, so we should examine only those flag values we are interested in (e.g., the last six in Figure 14.7).

Figure 14.8 shows a msghdr structure and the various information it points to. We assume in this figure that the process is about to call recvmsg for a UDP socket.

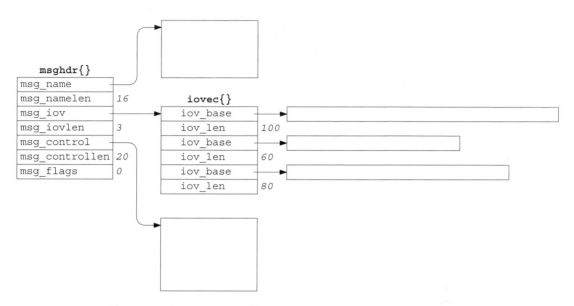

Figure 14.8 Data structures when recvmsg is called for a UDP socket.

Sixteen bytes are allocated for the protocol address and 20 bytes are allocated for the ancillary data. An array of three iovec structures is initialized: The first specifies a 100-byte buffer, the second a 60-byte buffer, and the third an 80-byte buffer. We also assume that the IP_RECVDSTADDR socket option has been set for the socket, to receive the destination IP address from the UDP datagram.

We next assume that a 170-byte UDP datagram arrives from 192.6.38.100, port 2000, destined for our UDP socket with a destination IP address of 206.168.112.96. Figure 14.9 shows all the information in the msghdr structure when recvmsg returns.

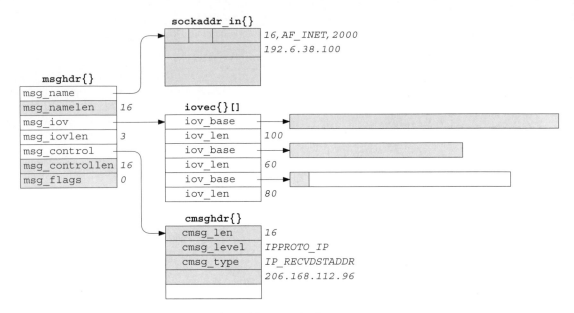

Figure 14.9 Update of Figure 14.8 when recvmsg returns.

The shaded fields are modified by recvmsg. The following items have changed from Figure 14.8 to Figure 14.9:

- The buffer pointed to by msg_name has been filled in as an Internet socket address structure, containing the source IP address and source UDP port from the received datagram.

- msg_namelen, a value-result argument, is updated with the amount of data stored in msg_name. Nothing changes since its value before the call was 16 and its value when recvmsg returns is also 16.

- The first 100 bytes of data are stored in the first buffer; the next 60 bytes are stored in the second buffer; and the final 10 bytes are stored in the third buffer. The last 70 bytes of the final buffer are not modified. The return value of the recvmsg function is the size of the datagram, 170.

- The buffer pointed to by msg_control is filled in as a cmsghdr structure. (We will say more about ancillary data in Section 14.6 and more about this particular socket option in Section 22.2.) The cmsg_len is 16; cmsg_level is IPPROTO_IP; cmsg_type is IP_RECVDSTADDR; and the next 4 bytes contain the destination IP address from the received UDP datagram. The final 4 bytes of the 20-byte buffer we supplied to hold the ancillary data are not modified.

- The msg_controllen member is updated with the actual amount of ancillary data that was stored. It is also a value-result argument and its result on return is 16.

- The msg_flags member is updated by recvmsg, but there are no flags to return to the process.

Figure 14.10 summarizes the differences among the five groups of I/O functions we described.

Function	Any descriptor	Only socket descriptor	Single read/write buffer	Scatter/gather read/write	Optional flags	Optional peer address	Optional control information
`read, write`	•		•				
`readv, writev`	•			•			
`recv, send`		•	•		•		
`recvfrom, sendto`		•	•		•	•	
`recvmsg, sendmsg`		•		•	•	•	•

Figure 14.10 Comparison of the five groups of I/O functions.

14.6 Ancillary Data

Ancillary data can be sent and received using the `msg_control` and `msg_controllen` members of the `msghdr` structure with the `sendmsg` and `recvmsg` functions. Another term for ancillary data is *control information*. In this section, we will describe the concept and show the structure and macros used to build and process ancillary data, but we will save the code examples for later chapters that describe the actual uses of ancillary data.

Figure 14.11 is a summary of the various uses of ancillary data we cover in this text.

Protocol	cmsg_level	cmsg_type	Description
IPv4	`IPPROTO_IP`	`IP_RECVDSTADDR` `IP_RECVIF`	Receive destination address with UDP datagram Receive interface index with UDP datagram

IPv6	`IPPROTO_IPV6`	`IPV6_DSTOPTS`
		`IPV6_HOPLIMIT`
		`IPV6_HOPOPTS`
		`IPV6_NEXTHOP`
		`IPV6_PKTINFO`
		`IPV6_RTHDR`
		`IPV6_TCLASS`
			Specify destination options
			Specify hop limit
			Specify hop-by-hop options
			Specify next-hop address
			Specify packet information
			Specify routing header
			Specify traffic class

Unix domain	`SOL_SOCKET`	`SCM_RIGHTS` `SCM_CREDS`	Send/receive descriptors Send/receive user credentials

Figure 14.11 Summary of uses for ancillary data.

The OSI protocol suite also uses ancillary data for various purposes we do not discuss in this text.

Ancillary data consists of one or more *ancillary data objects*, each one beginning with a `cmsghdr` structure, defined by including `<sys/socket.h>`.

```
struct cmsghdr {
  socklen_t  cmsg_len;   /* length in bytes, including this structure */
  int        cmsg_level; /* originating protocol */
  int        cmsg_type;  /* protocol-specific type */
      /* followed by unsigned char cmsg_data[] */
};
```

We have already seen this structure in Figure 14.9, when it was used with the `IP_RECVDSTADDR` socket option to return the destination IP address of a received UDP datagram. The ancillary data pointed to by `msg_control` must be suitably aligned for a `cmsghdr` structure . We will show one way to do this in Figure 15.11.

Figure 14.12 shows an example of two ancillary data objects in the control buffer.

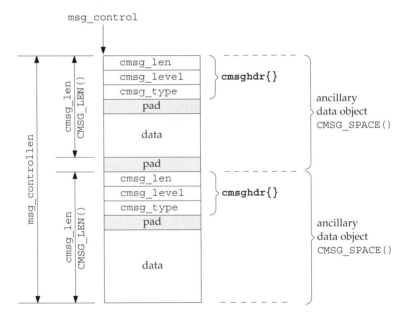

Figure 14.12 Ancillary data containing two ancillary data objects.

`msg_control` points to the first ancillary data object, and the total length of the ancillary data is specified by `msg_controllen`. Each object is preceded by a `cmsghdr` structure that describes the object. There can be padding between the `cmsg_type` member and the actual data, and there can also be padding at the end of the data, before the next ancillary data object. The five `CMSG_xxx` macros we describe shortly account for this possible padding.

> Not all implementations support multiple ancillary data objects in the control buffer.

Figure 14.13 shows the format of the `cmsghdr` structure when used with a Unix domain socket for descriptor passing (Section 15.7) or credential passing (Section 15.8).

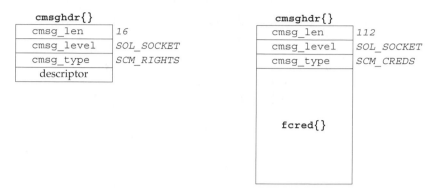

Figure 14.13 cmsghdr structure when used with Unix domain sockets.

In this figure, we assume each of the three members of the cmsghdr structure occupies four bytes and there is no padding between the cmsghdr structure and the actual data. When descriptors are passed, the contents of the cmsg_data array are the actual descriptor values. In this figure, we show only one descriptor being passed, but in general, more than one can be passed (in which case, the cmsg_len value will be 12 plus 4 times the number of descriptors, assuming each descriptor occupies 4 bytes).

Since the ancillary data returned by recvmsg can contain any number of ancillary data objects, and to hide the possible padding from the application, the following five macros are defined by including the <sys/socket.h> header to simplify the processing of the ancillary data:

```
#include <sys/socket.h>
#include <sys/param.h>    /* for ALIGN macro on many implementations */

struct cmsghdr *CMSG_FIRSTHDR(struct msghdr *mhdrptr);
```

                Returns: pointer to first cmsghdr structure or NULL if no ancillary data

```
struct cmsghdr *CMSG_NXTHDR(struct msghdr *mhdrptr, struct cmsghdr *cmsgptr);
```

            Returns: pointer to next cmsghdr structure or NULL if no more ancillary data objects

```
unsigned char *CMSG_DATA(struct cmsghdr *cmsgptr);
```

                Returns: pointer to first byte of data associated with cmsghdr structure

```
unsigned int CMSG_LEN(unsigned int length);
```

                    Returns: value to store in cmsg_len given the amount of data

```
unsigned int CMSG_SPACE(unsigned int length);
```

                Returns: total size of an ancillary data object given the amount of data

POSIX defines the first three macros; RFC 3542 [Stevens et al. 2003] defines the last two.

These macros would be used in the following pseudocode:

```
struct msghdr    msg;
struct cmsghdr  *cmsgptr;

/* fill in msg structure */

/* call recvmsg() */

for (cmsgptr = CMSG_FIRSTHDR(&msg); cmsgptr != NULL;
     cmsgptr = CMSG_NXTHDR(&msg, cmsgptr)) {
    if (cmsgptr->cmsg_level == ... &&
        cmsgptr->cmsg_type == ... ) {
        u_char  *ptr;

        ptr = CMSG_DATA(cmsgptr);
        /* process data pointed to by ptr */
    }
}
```

CMSG_FIRSTHDR returns a pointer to the first ancillary data object, or a null pointer if there is no ancillary data in the msghdr structure (either msg_control is a null pointer or cmsg_len is less than the size of a cmsghdr structure). CMSG_NXTHDR returns a null pointer when there is not another ancillary data object in the control buffer.

> Many existing implementations of CMSG_FIRSTHDR never look at msg_controllen and just return the value of cmsg_control. In Figure 22.2, we will test the value of msg_controllen before calling this macro.

The difference between CMSG_LEN and CMSG_SPACE is that the former does not account for any padding following the data portion of the ancillary data object and is therefore the value to store in cmsg_len, while the latter accounts for the padding at the end and is therefore the value to use if dynamically allocating space for the ancillary data object.

14.7   How Much Data Is Queued?

There are times when we want to see how much data is queued to be read on a socket, without reading the data. Three techniques are available:

1. If the goal is not to block in the kernel because we have something else to do when nothing is ready to be read, nonblocking I/O can be used. We will describe this in Chapter 16.

2. If we want to examine the data but still leave it on the receive queue for some other part of our process to read, we can use the MSG_PEEK flag (Figure 14.6). If we want to do this, but we are not sure that something is ready to be read, we can use this flag with a nonblocking socket or combine this flag with the MSG_DONTWAIT flag.

Be aware that the amount of data on the receive queue can change between two successive calls to recv for a stream socket. For example, assume we call recv for a TCP socket specifying a buffer length of 1,024 along with the MSG_PEEK flag, and the return value is 100. If we then call recv again, it is possible for more than 100 bytes to be returned (assuming we specify a buffer length greater than 100), because more data can be received by TCP between our two calls.

In the case of a UDP socket with a datagram on the receive queue, if we call recvfrom specifying MSG_PEEK, followed by another call without specifying MSG_PEEK, the return values from both calls (the datagram size, its contents, and the sender's address) will be the same, even if more datagrams are added to the socket receive buffer between the two calls. (We are assuming, of course, that some other process is not sharing the same descriptor and reading from this socket at the same time.)

3. Some implementations support the FIONREAD command of ioctl. The third argument to ioctl is a pointer to an integer, and the value returned in that integer is the current number of bytes on the socket's receive queue (p. 553 of TCPv2). This value is the total number of bytes queued, which for a UDP socket includes all queued datagrams. Also be aware that the count returned for a UDP socket by Berkeley-derived implementations includes the space required for the socket address structure containing the sender's IP address and port for each datagram (16 bytes for IPv4; 24 bytes for IPv6).

14.8 Sockets and Standard I/O

In all our examples so far, we have used what is sometimes called *Unix I/O*, the read and write functions and their variants (recv, send, etc.). These functions work with *descriptors* and are normally implemented as system calls within the Unix kernel.

Another method of performing I/O is the *standard I/O library*. It is specified by the ANSI C standard and is intended to be portable to non-Unix systems that support ANSI C. The standard I/O library handles some of the details that we must worry about ourselves when using the Unix I/O functions, such as automatically buffering the input and output streams. Unfortunately, its handling of a stream's buffering can present a new set of problems we must worry about. Chapter 5 of APUE covers the standard I/O library in detail, and [Plauger 1992] presents and discusses a complete implementation of the standard I/O library.

> The term *stream* is used with the standard I/O library, as in "we open an input stream" or "we flush the output stream." Do not confuse this with the STREAMS subsystem, which we will discuss in Chapter 31.

The standard I/O library can be used with sockets, but there are a few items to consider:

- A standard I/O stream can be created from any descriptor by calling the fdopen function. Similarly, given a standard I/O stream, we can obtain the corresponding descriptor by calling `fileno`. Our first encounter with `fileno` was in Figure 6.9 when we wanted to call `select` on a standard I/O stream. `select` works only with descriptors, so we had to obtain the descriptor for the standard I/O stream.

- TCP and UDP sockets are full-duplex. Standard I/O streams can also be full-duplex: we just open the stream with a type of `r+`, which means read-write. But on such a stream, an output function cannot be followed by an input function without an intervening call to `fflush`, `fseek`, `fsetpos`, or `rewind`. Similarly, an input function cannot be followed by an output function without an intervening call to `fseek`, `fsetpos`, or `rewind`, unless the input function encounters an EOF. The problem with these latter three functions is that they all call `lseek`, which fails on a socket.

- The easiest way to handle this read-write problem is to open two standard I/O streams for a given socket: one for reading and one for writing.

Example: `str_echo` Function Using Standard I/O

We now show an alternate version of our TCP echo server (Figure 5.3), which uses standard I/O instead of `read` and `writen`. Figure 14.14 is a version of our `str_echo` function that uses standard I/O. (This version has a problem that we will describe shortly.)

```
                                                         advio/str_echo_stdio02.c
1 #include    "unp.h"

2 void
3 str_echo(int sockfd)
4 {
5     char    line[MAXLINE];
6     FILE    *fpin, *fpout;

7     fpin = Fdopen(sockfd, "r");
8     fpout = Fdopen(sockfd, "w");

9     while (Fgets(line, MAXLINE, fpin) != NULL)
10         Fputs(line, fpout);
11 }
                                                         advio/str_echo_stdio02.c
```

Figure 14.14 `str_echo` function recoded to use standard I/O.

Convert descriptor into input stream and output stream

7–10   Two standard I/O streams are created by `fdopen`: one for input and one for output. The calls to `read` and `writen` are replaced with calls to `fgets` and `fputs`.

If we run our server with this version of `str_echo` and then run our client, we see the following:

```
hpux % tcpcli02 206.168.112.96
hello, world                    we type this line, but nothing is echoed
and hi                          and this one, still no echo
hello??                         and this one, still no echo
^D                              and our EOF character
hello, world                    and then the three echoed lines are output
and hi
hello??
```

There is a buffering problem here because nothing is echoed by the server until we enter our EOF character. The following steps take place:

- We type the first line of input and it is sent to the server.

- The server reads the line with `fgets` and echoes it with `fputs`.

- The server's standard I/O stream is *fully buffered* by the standard I/O library. This means the library copies the echoed line into its standard I/O buffer for this stream, but does not write the buffer to the descriptor, because the buffer is not full.

- We type the second line of input and it is sent to the server.

- The server reads the line with `fgets` and echoes it with `fputs`.

- Again, the server's standard I/O library just copies the line into its buffer, but does not write the buffer because it is still not full.

- The same scenario happens with the third line of input that we enter.

- We type our EOF character, and our `str_cli` function (Figure 6.13) calls `shutdown`, sending a FIN to the server.

- The server TCP receives the FIN, which `fgets` reads, causing `fgets` to return a null pointer.

- The `str_echo` function returns to the server `main` function (Figure 5.12) and the child terminates by calling `exit`.

- The C library function `exit` calls the standard I/O cleanup function (pp. 162–164 of APUE). The output buffer that was partially filled by our calls to `fputs` is now output.

- The server child process terminates, causing its connected socket to be closed, sending a FIN to the client, completing the TCP four-packet termination sequence.

- The three echoed lines are received by our `str_cli` function and output.

- `str_cli` then receives an EOF on its socket, and the client terminates.

The problem here is the buffering performed automatically by the standard I/O library on the server. There are three types of buffering performed by the standard I/O library:

1. *Fully buffered* means that I/O takes place only when the buffer is full, the process explicitly calls `fflush`, or the process terminates by calling `exit`. A common size for the standard I/O buffer is 8,192 bytes.

2. *Line buffered* means that I/O takes place when a newline is encountered, when the process calls fflush, or when the process terminates by calling exit.

3. *Unbuffered* means that I/O takes place each time a standard I/O output function is called.

Most Unix implementations of the standard I/O library use the following rules:

- Standard error is always unbuffered.

- Standard input and standard output are fully buffered, unless they refer to a terminal device, in which case, they are line buffered.

- All other streams are fully buffered unless they refer to a terminal device, in which case, they are line buffered.

Since a socket is not a terminal device, the problem seen with our str_echo function in Figure 14.14 is that the output stream (fpout) is fully buffered. One way around this is to force the output stream to be line buffered by calling setvbuf. Another is to force each echoed line to be output by calling fflush after each call to fputs. But in practice, either of these solutions is still error-prone and may interact badly with the Nagle algorithm described in Section 7.9. In most cases, the best solution is to avoid using the standard I/O library altogether for sockets and operate on buffers instead of lines, as described in Section 3.9. Using standard I/O on sockets may make sense when the convenience of standard I/O streams outweighs the concerns about bugs due to buffering, but these are rare cases.

> Be aware that some implementations of the standard I/O library still have a problem with descriptors greater than 255. This can be a problem with network servers that handle lots of descriptors. Check the definition of the FILE structure in your <stdio.h> header to see what type of variable holds the descriptor.

14.9 Advanced Polling

Earlier in this chapter, we discussed several ways to set a time limit on a socket operation. Many operating systems now offer another alternative, and provide the features of select and poll we described in Chapter 6 as well. Since none of these methods have been adopted by POSIX yet, and each implementation seems to be slightly different, code that uses these mechanisms should be considered nonportable. We'll describe two mechanisms here; other available mechanisms are similar.

/dev/poll Interface

Solaris provides a special file called /dev/poll, which provides a more scalable way to poll large numbers of file descriptors. The problem with select and poll is that the file descriptors of interest must be passed in with each call. The poll device maintains state between calls so that a program can set up the list of descriptors to poll and then loop, waiting for events, without setting up the list again each time around the loop.

After opening /dev/poll, the polling program must initialize an array of pollfd structures (the same structure used by the poll function, but the revents field is unused in this case). The array is then passed to the kernel by calling write to write the structured directly to the /dev/poll device. The program then uses an ioctl call, DP_POLL, to block, waiting for events. The following structure is passed into the ioctl call:

```
struct dvpoll {
    struct pollfd*  dp_fds;
    int             dp_nfds;
    int             dp_timeout;
}
```

The field dp_fds points to a buffer that is used to hold an array of pollfd structures returned from the ioctl call. The field dp_nfds field specifies the size of the buffer. The ioctl call blocks until there are interesting events on any of the polled file descriptors, or until dp_timeout milliseconds have passed. Using a value of zero for dp_timeout will cause the ioctl to return immediately, which provides a nonblocking way to use this interface. Passing in -1 for the timeout indicates that no timeout is desired.

We modify our str_cli function, which used select in Figure 6.13, to use /dev/poll in Figure 14.15.

—————————————————————————————————————— *advio/str_cli_poll03.c*

```
 1 #include    "unp.h"
 2 #include    <sys/devpoll.h>

 3 void
 4 str_cli(FILE *fp, int sockfd)
 5 {
 6     int     stdineof;
 7     char    buf[MAXLINE];
 8     int     n;
 9     int     wfd;
10     struct pollfd pollfd[2];
11     struct dvpoll dopoll;
12     int     i;
13     int     result;

14     wfd = Open("/dev/poll", O_RDWR, 0);

15     pollfd[0].fd = fileno(fp);
16     pollfd[0].events = POLLIN;
17     pollfd[0].revents = 0;

18     pollfd[1].fd = sockfd;
19     pollfd[1].events = POLLIN;
20     pollfd[1].revents = 0;

21     Write(wfd, pollfd, sizeof(struct pollfd) * 2);

22     stdineof = 0;
```

```
23      for ( ; ; ) {
24          /* block until /dev/poll says something is ready */
25          dopoll.dp_timeout = -1;
26          dopoll.dp_nfds = 2;
27          dopoll.dp_fds = pollfd;
28          result = Ioctl(wfd, DP_POLL, &dopoll);

29          /* loop through ready file descriptors */
30          for (i = 0; i < result; i++) {
31              if (dopoll.dp_fds[i].fd == sockfd) {
32                  /* socket is readable */
33                  if ( (n = Read(sockfd, buf, MAXLINE)) == 0) {
34                      if (stdineof == 1)
35                          return; /* normal termination */
36                      else
37                          err_quit("str_cli: server terminated prematurely");
38                  }

39                  Write(fileno(stdout), buf, n);
40              } else {
41                  /* input is readable */
42                  if ( (n = Read(fileno(fp), buf, MAXLINE)) == 0) {
43                      stdineof = 1;
44                      Shutdown(sockfd, SHUT_WR);   /* send FIN */
45                      continue;
46                  }

47                  Writen(sockfd, buf, n);
48              }
49          }
50      }
51  }
```
—— *advio/str_cli_poll03.c*

Figure 14.15 str_cli function using /dev/poll.

List descriptors for /dev/poll

14-21 After filling in an array of pollfd structures, we pass them to /dev/poll. Our example only requires two file descriptors, so we use a static array of structures. In practice, programs that use /dev/poll need to monitor hundreds or even thousands of file descriptors, so the array would likely be allocated dynamically.

Wait for work

24-28 Rather than calling select, this program blocks, waiting for work, in the ioctl call. The return is the number of file descriptors that are ready.

Loop through descriptors

30-49 The code in our example is simplified since we know the ready file descriptors will be sockfd, the input file descriptor, or both. In a large-scale program, this loop would be more complex, perhaps even dispatching the work to threads.

kqueue Interface

FreeBSD introduced the kqueue interface in FreeBSD version 4.1. This interface allows a process to register an "event filter" that describes the kqueue events it is interested in. Events include file I/O and timeouts like select, but also adds asynchronous I/O, file modification notification (e.g., notification when a file is removed or modified), process tracking (e.g., notification when a given process exits or calls fork), and signal handling. The kqueue interface includes the following two functions and macro:

```
#include <sys/types.h>
#include <sys/event.h>
#include <sys/time.h>

int kqueue(void);
int kevent(int kq, const struct kevent *changelist, int nchanges,
           struct kevent *eventlist, int nevents,
           const struct timespec *timeout);
void EV_SET(struct kevent *kev, uintptr_t ident, short filter,
           u_short flags, u_int fflags, intptr_t data, void *udata);
```

The kqueue function returns a new kqueue descriptor, which can be used with future calls to kevent. The kevent function is used to both register events of interest and determine if any events have occurred. The *changelist* and *nchanges* parameters describe the changes to be made to the events of interest, or are NULL and 0, respectively, if no changes are to be made. If *nchanges* is nonzero, each event filter change requested in the *changelist* array is performed. Any filters whose conditions have triggered, including those that may have just been added in the *changelist*, are returned through the *eventlist* parameter, which points to an array of *nevents* struct kevents. The kevent function returns the number of events that are returned, or zero if a timeout has occurred. The *timeout* argument holds the timeout, which is handled just like select: NULL to block, a nonzero timespec to specify an explicit timeout, and a zero timespec to perform a nonblocking check for events. Note that the *timeout* parameter is a struct timespec, which is different from select's struct timeval in that it has nanosecond instead of microsecond resolution.

The kevent structure is defined by including the <sys/event.h> header.

```
struct kevent {
  uintptr_t  ident;      /* identifier (e.g., file descriptor) */
  short      filter;     /* filter type (e.g., EVFILT_READ) */
  u_short    flags;      /* action flags (e.g., EV_ADD) */
  u_int      fflags;     /* filter-specific flags */
  intptr_t   data;       /* filter-specific data */
  void       *udata;     /* opaque user data */
};
```

The actions for changing a filter and the flag return values are shown in Figure 14.16.

flags	Description	change	return
EV_ADD	Add a new event; automatically enabled unless EV_DISABLE is specified	•	
EV_CLEAR	Reset event state after user retrieves it	•	
EV_DELETE	Delete event from filter	•	
EV_DISABLE	Disable event, but do not remove it from filter	•	
EV_ENABLE	Re-enable previously disabled event	•	
EV_ONESHOT	Delete event after it triggers once	•	
EV_EOF	An EOF condition occurred		•
EV_ERROR	An error occurred; errno is in the data element		•

Figure 14.16 *flags* for kevent operations.

Filter types are shown in Figure 14.17.

filter	Description
EVFILT_AIO	Asynchronous I/O events (Section 6.2)
EVFILT_PROC	Process exit, fork or exec events
EVFILT_READ	Descriptor is readable, similar to select
EVFILT_SIGNAL	Signal reception
EVFILT_TIMER	Periodic or one-shot timers
EVFILT_VNODE	File modification and deletion events
EVFILT_WRITE	Descriptor is writable, similar to select

Figure 14.17 *filters* for kevent operations.

We modify our str_cli function, which used select in Figure 6.13, to use kqueue in Figure 14.18.

Determine if file pointer points to a file

10-11   The behavior of kqueue on EOF is different depending on whether the file descriptor is associated with a file, a pipe, or a terminal, so we use the fstat call to determine if it is a file. We will use this determination later.

Set up kevent structures for kqueue

12-13   We use the EV_SET macro to set up two kevent structures; both specify a read filter (EVFILT_READ) and request to add this event to the filter (EV_ADD).

Create kqueue and add filters

14-16   We call kqueue to get a kqueue descriptor, set the timeout to zero to allow a non-blocking call to kevent, and call kevent with our array of kevents as the change request.

Loop forever, blocking in kevent

17-18   We loop forever, blocking in kevent. We pass a NULL change list, since we are only interested in the events we have already registered, and a NULL timeout to block forever.

Loop through returned events

19   We check each event that was returned and process it individually.

advio/str_cli_kqueue04.c

```
 1 #include    "unp.h"

 2 void
 3 str_cli(FILE *fp, int sockfd)
 4 {
 5     int     kq, i, n, nev, stdineof = 0, isfile;
 6     char    buf[MAXLINE];
 7     struct kevent kev[2];
 8     struct timespec ts;
 9     struct stat st;

10     isfile = ((fstat(fileno(fp), &st) == 0) &&
11               (st.st_mode & S_IFMT) == S_IFREG);

12     EV_SET(&kev[0], fileno(fp), EVFILT_READ, EV_ADD, 0, 0, NULL);
13     EV_SET(&kev[1], sockfd, EVFILT_READ, EV_ADD, 0, 0, NULL);

14     kq = Kqueue();
15     ts.tv_sec = ts.tv_nsec = 0;
16     Kevent(kq, kev, 2, NULL, 0, &ts);

17     for ( ; ; ) {
18         nev = Kevent(kq, NULL, 0, kev, 2, NULL);

19         for (i = 0; i < nev; i++) {
20             if (kev[i].ident == sockfd) {   /* socket is readable */
21                 if ( (n = Read(sockfd, buf, MAXLINE)) == 0) {
22                     if (stdineof == 1)
23                         return; /* normal termination */
24                     else
25                         err_quit("str_cli: server terminated prematurely");
26                 }

27                 Write(fileno(stdout), buf, n);
28             }

29             if (kev[i].ident == fileno(fp)) {   /* input is readable */
30                 n = Read(fileno(fp), buf, MAXLINE);
31                 if (n > 0)
32                     Writen(sockfd, buf, n);

33                 if (n == 0 || (isfile && n == kev[i].data)) {
34                     stdineof = 1;
35                     Shutdown(sockfd, SHUT_WR);   /* send FIN */
36                     kev[i].flags = EV_DELETE;
37                     Kevent(kq, &kev[i], 1, NULL, 0, &ts);   /* remove kevent */
38                     continue;
39                 }
40             }
41         }
42     }
43 }
```

advio/str_cli_kqueue04.c

Figure 14.18 str_cli function using kqueue.

Socket is readable

20–28   This code is exactly the same as in Figure 6.13.

Input is readable

29–40   This code is similar to Figure 6.13, but is structured slightly differently to handle how kqueue reports an EOF. On pipes and terminals, kqueue returns a readable indication that an EOF is pending, just like select. However, on files, kqueue simply returns the number of bytes left in the file in the data member of the struct kevent and assumes that the application will know when it reaches the end. Therefore, we restructure the loop to write the data to the network if a nonzero number of bytes were read. Next, we check our modified EOF condition: if we have read zero bytes or if it's a file and we've read as many bytes as are left in the file. The other modification from Figure 6.13 is that instead of using FD_CLR to remove the input descriptor from the file set, we set the flags to EV_DELETE and call kevent to remove this event from the filter in the kernel.

Suggestions

Care should be taken with these newly evolved interfaces to read the documentation specific to the OS release. These interfaces often change in subtle ways between releases while the vendors work through the details of how they should work.

While writing nonportable code is, in general, something to avoid, it is quite common to use any means possible to optimize a very heavily used network application for the specific server it runs on.

14.10 Summary

There are three main ways to set a time limit on a socket operation:

- Use the alarm function and the SIGALRM signal
- Use the time limit that is provided by select
- Use the newer SO_RCVTIMEO and SO_SNDTIMEO socket options

The first is easy to use, but involves signal handling, and as we will see in Section 20.5, can lead to race conditions. Using select means that we block in this function with its provided time limit instead of blocking in a call to read, write, or connect. The third alternative, to use the new socket options, is also easy, but is not provided by all implementations.

recvmsg and sendmsg are the most general of the five groups of I/O functions provided. They combine the ability to specify an MSG_xxx flag (from recv and send), plus employ the ability to return or specify the peer's protocol address (from recvfrom and sendto), with the ability to use multiple buffers (from readv and writev), along with two new features: returning flags to the application and receiving or sending ancillary data.

We describe ten different forms of ancillary data in the text, six of which are new with IPv6. Ancillary data consists of one or more ancillary data objects, each object preceded by a `cmsghdr` structure specifying its length, protocol level, and type of data. Five functions beginning with `CMSG_` are used to build and parse ancillary data.

Sockets can be used with the C standard I/O library, but doing this adds another level of buffering to that already being performed by TCP. Indeed, a lack of understanding of the buffering performed by the standard I/O library is the most common problem with the library. Since a socket is not a terminal device, the common solution to this potential problem is to set the standard I/O stream to unbuffered, or to simply avoid standard I/O on sockets completely.

Many vendors provide advanced ways to poll for many events without the overhead required by `select` and `poll`. While writing nonportable code should be avoided whenever possible, sometimes the benefits of performance improvements outweigh the risk of nonportability.

Exercises

14.1   What happens in Figure 14.1 when we reset the signal handler, and the process has not established a handler for `SIGALRM`?

14.2   In Figure 14.1, we print a warning if the process already has an `alarm` timer set. Modify the function to reset this `alarm` for the process after the `connect`, before the function returns.

14.3   Modify Figure 11.11 as follows: Before calling `read`, call `recv` specifying `MSG_PEEK`. When this returns, call `ioctl` with a command of `FIONREAD` and print the number of bytes queued on the socket's receive buffer. Then, call `read` to actually read the data.

14.4   What happens to the data in a standard I/O buffer that has not yet been output if the process falls off the end of the `main` function instead of calling `exit`?

14.5   Apply each of the two changes described following Figure 14.14 and verify that each one corrects the buffering problem.

15

Unix Domain Protocols

15.1 Introduction

The Unix domain protocols are not an actual protocol suite, but a way of performing client/server communication on a single host using the same API that is used for clients and servers on different hosts. The Unix domain protocols are an alternative to the interprocess communication (IPC) methods described in Volume 2 of this series, when the client and server are on the same host. Details on the actual implementation of Unix domain sockets in a Berkeley-derived kernel are provided in Part 3 of TCPv3.

Two types of sockets are provided in the Unix domain: stream sockets (similar to TCP) and datagram sockets (similar to UDP). Even though a raw socket is also provided, its semantics have never been documented, it is not used by any program that the authors are aware of, and it is not defined by POSIX.

Unix domain sockets are used for three reasons:

1. On Berkeley-derived implementations, Unix domain sockets are often twice as fast as a TCP socket when both peers are on the same host (pp. 223–224 of TCPv3). One application takes advantage of this: the X Window System. When an X11 client starts and opens a connection to the X11 server, the client checks the value of the DISPLAY environment variable, which specifies the server's hostname, window, and screen. If the server is on the same host as the client, the client opens a Unix domain stream connection to the server; otherwise the client opens a TCP connection to the server.

2. Unix domain sockets are used when passing descriptors between processes on the same host. We will provide a complete example of this in Section 15.7.

411

3. Newer implementations of Unix domain sockets provide the client's credentials (user ID and group IDs) to the server, which can provide additional security checking. We will describe this in Section 15.8.

The protocol addresses used to identify clients and servers in the Unix domain are pathnames within the normal filesystem. Recall that IPv4 uses a combination of 32-bit addresses and 16-bit port numbers for its protocol addresses, and IPv6 uses a combination of 128-bit addresses and 16-bit port numbers for its protocol addresses. These pathnames are not normal Unix files: We cannot read from or write to these files except from a program that has associated the pathname with a Unix domain socket.

15.2   Unix Domain Socket Address Structure

Figure 15.1 shows the Unix domain socket address structure, which is defined by including the `<sys/un.h>` header.

```
struct sockaddr_un {
  sa_family_t  sun_family;     /* AF_LOCAL */
  char         sun_path[104];  /* null-terminated pathname */
};
```

Figure 15.1   Unix domain socket address structure: `sockaddr_un`.

The POSIX specification does not define the length of the sun_path array and it specifically warns that applications should not assume a particular length. Use the `sizeof` operator to find the length at run-time and to verify that a pathname fits into the array. The length is likely to be between 92 and 108 rather than a larger value big enough to hold any pathname. The reason for these limits is an implementation artifact dating back to 4.2BSD requiring that this structure fit in a 128-byte mbuf (a kernel memory buffer).

The pathname stored in the `sun_path` array must be null-terminated. The macro `SUN_LEN` is provided and it takes a pointer to a `sockaddr_un` structure and returns the length of the structure, including the number of non-null bytes in the pathname. The unspecified address is indicated by a null string as the pathname, that is, a structure with `sun_path[0]` equal to 0. This is the Unix domain equivalent of the IPv4 `INADDR_ANY` constant and the IPv6 `IN6ADDR_ANY_INIT` constant.

POSIX renames the Unix domain protocols as "local IPC," to remove the dependence on the Unix OS. The historical constant `AF_UNIX` becomes `AF_LOCAL`. Nevertheless, we still use the term "Unix domain" as that has become its *de facto* name, regardless of the underlying OS. Also, even with POSIX attempting to make these OS-independent, the socket address structure still retains the _un suffix!

Example: `bind` of Unix Domain Socket

The program in Figure 15.2 creates a Unix domain socket, `binds` a pathname to it, and then calls `getsockname` and prints the bound pathname.

—————————————————————————————————— *unixdomain/unixbind.c*

```
 1 #include    "unp.h"

 2 int
 3 main(int argc, char **argv)
 4 {
 5     int       sockfd;
 6     socklen_t len;
 7     struct sockaddr_un addr1, addr2;

 8     if (argc != 2)
 9         err_quit("usage: unixbind <pathname>");

10     sockfd = Socket(AF_LOCAL, SOCK_STREAM, 0);

11     unlink(argv[1]);                /* OK if this fails */

12     bzero(&addr1, sizeof(addr1));
13     addr1.sun_family = AF_LOCAL;
14     strncpy(addr1.sun_path, argv[1], sizeof(addr1.sun_path) - 1);
15     Bind(sockfd, (SA *) &addr1, SUN_LEN(&addr1));

16     len = sizeof(addr2);
17     Getsockname(sockfd, (SA *) &addr2, &len);
18     printf("bound name = %s, returned len = %d\n", addr2.sun_path, len);

19     exit(0);
20 }
```

—————————————————————————————————— *unixdomain/unixbind.c*

Figure 15.2 bind of a pathname to a Unix domain socket.

Remove pathname first

11   The pathname that we `bind` to the socket is the command-line argument. But the `bind` will fail if the pathname already exists in the filesystem. Therefore, we call `unlink` to delete the pathname, in case it already exists. If it does not exist, `unlink` returns an error, which we ignore.

`bind` and then `getsockname`

12–18   We copy the command-line argument using `strncpy`, to avoid overflowing the structure if the pathname is too long. Since we initialize the structure to zero and then subtract one from the size of the `sun_path` array, we know the pathname is null-terminated. `bind` is called and we use the macro `SUN_LEN` to calculate the length argument for the function. We then call `getsockname` to fetch the name that was just bound and print the result.

If we run this program under Solaris, we obtain the following results:

```
solaris % umask                                       first print our umask value
022                                                   shells print this value in octal
solaris % unixbind /tmp/moose
bound name = /tmp/moose, returned len = 13
solaris % unixbind /tmp/moose                         run it again
bound name = /tmp/moose, returned len = 13
solaris % ls -l /tmp/moose
srwxr-xr-x   1 andy      staff           0 Aug 10 13:13 /tmp/moose
solaris % ls -lF /tmp/moose
srwxr-xr-x   1 andy      staff           0 Aug 10 13:13 /tmp/moose=
```

We first print our umask value because POSIX specifies that the file access permissions of the resulting pathname should be modified by this value. Our value of 22 turns off the group-write and other-write bits. We then run the program and see that the length returned by getsockname is 13: 2 bytes for the sun_family member and 11 bytes for the actual pathname (excluding the terminating null byte). This is an example of a value-result argument whose result when the function returns differs from its value when the function was called. We can output the pathname using the %s format of printf because the pathname is null-terminated in the sun_path member. We then run the program again, to verify that calling unlink removes the pathname.

We run ls -l to see the file permissions and file type. Under Solaris (and most Unix variants), the file type is a socket, which is printed as s. We also notice that the permission bits were modified as appropriate by the umask value. Finally, we run ls again, with the -F option, which causes Solaris to append an equals sign to the pathname.

> Historically, the umask value did not apply to the creation of Unix domain sockets, but over time, most Unix vendors have fixed this so the permissions fit expectations. Systems still exist where the file permission bits may show either all permissions or no permissions (regardless of the umask setting). In addition, some systems show the file as a FIFO, which is printed as p, and not all systems show the equals sign with ls -F. The behavior we show above is the most common.

15.3   socketpair Function

The socketpair function creates two sockets that are then connected together. This function applies only to Unix domain sockets.

```
#include <sys/socket.h>

int socketpair(int family, int type, int protocol, int sockfd[2]);

                                              Returns: nonzero if OK, −1 on error
```

The *family* must be AF_LOCAL and the *protocol* must be 0. The *type*, however, can be either SOCK_STREAM or SOCK_DGRAM. The two socket descriptors that are created are returned as *sockfd[0]* and *sockfd[1]*.

> This function is similar to the Unix `pipe` function: Two descriptors are returned, and each descriptor is connected to the other. Indeed, Berkeley-derived implementations employ `pipe` by performing the same internal operations as `socketpair` (pp. 253–254 of TCPv3).

The two created sockets are unnamed; that is, there is no implicit `bind` involved.

The result of `socketpair` with a *type* of SOCK_STREAM is called a *stream pipe*. It is similar to a regular Unix pipe (created by the `pipe` function), but a stream pipe is *full-duplex*; that is, both descriptors can be read and written. We show a picture of a stream pipe created by `socketpair` in Figure 15.7.

> POSIX does not require full-duplex pipes. On SVR4, `pipe` returns two full-duplex descriptors, while Berkeley-derived kernels traditionally return two half-duplex descriptors (Figure 17.31 of TCPv3).

15.4 Socket Functions

There are several differences and restrictions in the socket functions when using Unix domain sockets. We list the POSIX requirements when applicable, and note that not all implementations are currently at this level.

1. The default file access permissions for a pathname created by `bind` should be 0777 (read, write, and execute by user, group, and other), modified by the current `umask` value.

2. The pathname associated with a Unix domain socket should be an absolute pathname, not a relative pathname. The reason to avoid the latter is that its resolution depends on the current working directory of the caller. That is, if the server binds a relative pathname, then the client must be in the same directory as the server (or must know this directory) for the client's call to either `connect` or `sendto` to succeed.

    > POSIX says that binding a relative pathname to a Unix domain socket gives unpredictable results.

3. The pathname specified in a call to `connect` must be a pathname that is currently bound to an open Unix domain socket of the same type (stream or datagram). Errors occur if: (i) the pathname exists but is not a socket; (ii) the pathname exists and is a socket, but no open socket descriptor is associated with the pathname; or (iii) the pathname exists and is an open socket, but is of the wrong type (that is, a Unix domain stream socket cannot connect to a pathname associated with a Unix domain datagram socket, and vice versa).

4. The permission testing associated with the `connect` of a Unix domain socket is the same as if `open` had been called for write-only access to the pathname.

5. Unix domain stream sockets are similar to TCP sockets: They provide a byte stream interface to the process with no record boundaries.

6. If a call to `connect` for a Unix domain stream socket finds that the listening socket's queue is full (Section 4.5), `ECONNREFUSED` is returned immediately. This differs from TCP: The TCP listener ignores an arriving SYN if the socket's queue is full, and the TCP connector retries by sending the SYN several times.

7. Unix domain datagram sockets are similar to UDP sockets: They provide an unreliable datagram service that preserves record boundaries.

8. Unlike UDP sockets, sending a datagram on an unbound Unix domain datagram socket does not bind a pathname to the socket. (Recall that sending a UDP datagram on an unbound UDP socket causes an ephemeral port to be bound to the socket.) This means the receiver of the datagram will be unable to send a reply unless the sender has bound a pathname to its socket. Similarly, unlike TCP and UDP, calling `connect` for a Unix domain datagram socket does not bind a pathname to the socket.

15.5   Unix Domain Stream Client/Server

We now recode our TCP echo client/server from Chapter 5 to use Unix domain sockets. Figure 15.3 shows the server, which is a modification of Figure 5.12 to use the Unix domain stream protocol instead of TCP.

8   The datatype of the two socket address structures is now `sockaddr_un`.

10   The first argument to `socket` is `AF_LOCAL`, to create a Unix domain stream socket.

11-15   The constant `UNIXSTR_PATH` is defined in `unp.h` to be `/tmp/unix.str`. We first `unlink` the pathname, in case it exists from an earlier run of the server, and then initialize the socket address structure before calling `bind`. An error from `unlink` is acceptable.

Notice that this call to `bind` differs from the call in Figure 15.2. Here, we specify the size of the socket address structure (the third argument) as the total size of the `sockaddr_un` structure, not just the number of bytes occupied by the pathname. Both lengths are valid since the pathname must be null-terminated.

The remainder of the function is the same as Figure 5.12. The same `str_echo` function is used (Figure 5.3).

Figure 15.4 is the Unix domain stream protocol echo client. It is a modification of Figure 5.4.

6   The socket address structure to contain the server's address is now a `sockaddr_un` structure.

7   The first argument to `socket` is `AF_LOCAL`.

8-10   The code to fill in the socket address structure is identical to the code shown for the server: Initialize the structure to 0, set the family to `AF_LOCAL`, and copy the pathname into the `sun_path` member.

12   The function `str_cli` is the same as earlier (Figure 6.13 was the last version we developed).

———————————————————————————— *unixdomain/unixstrserv01.c*

```
 1 #include     "unp.h"

 2 int
 3 main(int argc, char **argv)
 4 {
 5     int      listenfd, connfd;
 6     pid_t    childpid;
 7     socklen_t clilen;
 8     struct sockaddr_un cliaddr, servaddr;
 9     void     sig_chld(int);

10     listenfd = Socket(AF_LOCAL, SOCK_STREAM, 0);

11     unlink(UNIXSTR_PATH);
12     bzero(&servaddr, sizeof(servaddr));
13     servaddr.sun_family = AF_LOCAL;
14     strcpy(servaddr.sun_path, UNIXSTR_PATH);

15     Bind(listenfd, (SA *) &servaddr, sizeof(servaddr));

16     Listen(listenfd, LISTENQ);

17     Signal(SIGCHLD, sig_chld);

18     for ( ; ; ) {
19         clilen = sizeof(cliaddr);
20         if ( (connfd = accept(listenfd, (SA *) &cliaddr, &clilen)) < 0) {
21             if (errno == EINTR)
22                 continue;        /* back to for() */
23             else
24                 err_sys("accept error");
25         }

26         if ( (childpid = Fork()) == 0) { /* child process */
27             Close(listenfd);     /* close listening socket */
28             str_echo(connfd);    /* process request */
29             exit(0);
30         }
31         Close(connfd);                  /* parent closes connected socket */
32     }
33 }
```

———————————————————————————— *unixdomain/unixstrserv01.c*

Figure 15.3 Unix domain stream protocol echo server.

15.6   Unix Domain Datagram Client/Server

We now recode our UDP client/server from Sections 8.3 and 8.5 to use Unix domain
datagram sockets. Figure 15.5 shows the server, which is a modification of Figure 8.3.

——————————————————————— unixdomain/unixstrcli01.c

```
 1 #include    "unp.h"

 2 int
 3 main(int argc, char **argv)
 4 {
 5     int     sockfd;
 6     struct sockaddr_un servaddr;

 7     sockfd = Socket(AF_LOCAL, SOCK_STREAM, 0);

 8     bzero(&servaddr, sizeof(servaddr));
 9     servaddr.sun_family = AF_LOCAL;
10     strcpy(servaddr.sun_path, UNIXSTR_PATH);

11     Connect(sockfd, (SA *) &servaddr, sizeof(servaddr));

12     str_cli(stdin, sockfd);     /* do it all */

13     exit(0);
14 }
```

——————————————————————— unixdomain/unixstrcli01.c

Figure 15.4 Unix domain stream protocol echo client.

——————————————————————— unixdomain/unixdgserv01.c

```
 1 #include    "unp.h"

 2 int
 3 main(int argc, char **argv)
 4 {
 5     int     sockfd;
 6     struct sockaddr_un servaddr, cliaddr;

 7     sockfd = Socket(AF_LOCAL, SOCK_DGRAM, 0);

 8     unlink(UNIXDG_PATH);
 9     bzero(&servaddr, sizeof(servaddr));
10     servaddr.sun_family = AF_LOCAL;
11     strcpy(servaddr.sun_path, UNIXDG_PATH);

12     Bind(sockfd, (SA *) &servaddr, sizeof(servaddr));

13     dg_echo(sockfd, (SA *) &cliaddr, sizeof(cliaddr));
14 }
```

——————————————————————— unixdomain/unixdgserv01.c

Figure 15.5 Unix domain datagram protocol echo server.

6   The datatype of the two socket address structures is now sockaddr_un.
7   The first argument to socket is AF_LOCAL, to create a Unix domain datagram
socket.

8-12   The constant UNIXDG_PATH is defined in unp.h to be /tmp/unix.dg. We first
unlink the pathname, in case it exists from an earlier run of the server, and then initialize the socket address structure before calling bind. An error from unlink is acceptable.

13   The same dg_echo function is used (Figure 8.4).

Figure 15.6 is the Unix domain datagram protocol echo client. It is a modification of
Figure 8.7.

```
                                                        unixdomain/unixdgcli01.c
 1 #include     "unp.h"

 2 int
 3 main(int argc, char **argv)
 4 {
 5     int      sockfd;
 6     struct sockaddr_un cliaddr, servaddr;

 7     sockfd = Socket(AF_LOCAL, SOCK_DGRAM, 0);

 8     bzero(&cliaddr, sizeof(cliaddr));   /* bind an address for us */
 9     cliaddr.sun_family = AF_LOCAL;
10     strcpy(cliaddr.sun_path, tmpnam(NULL));

11     Bind(sockfd, (SA *) &cliaddr, sizeof(cliaddr));

12     bzero(&servaddr, sizeof(servaddr)); /* fill in server's address */
13     servaddr.sun_family = AF_LOCAL;
14     strcpy(servaddr.sun_path, UNIXDG_PATH);

15     dg_cli(stdin, sockfd, (SA *) &servaddr, sizeof(servaddr));

16     exit(0);
17 }
                                                        unixdomain/unixdgcli01.c
```

Figure 15.6 Unix domain datagram protocol echo client.

6   The socket address structure to contain the server's address is now a sockaddr_un
structure. We also allocate one of these structures to contain the client's address, which
we will talk about shortly.

7   The first argument to socket is AF_LOCAL.

8-11   Unlike our UDP client, when using the Unix domain datagram protocol, we must
explicitly bind a pathname to our socket so that the server has a pathname to which it
can send its reply. We call tmpnam to assign a unique pathname that we then bind to
our socket. Recall from Section 15.4 that sending a datagram on an unbound Unix
domain datagram socket does not implicitly bind a pathname to the socket. Therefore,
if we omit this step, the server's call to recvfrom in the dg_echo function returns a
null pathname, which then causes an error when the server calls sendto.

12-14   The code to fill in the socket address structure with the server's well-known pathname is identical to the code shown earlier for the server.

15   The function dg_cli is the same as that shown in Figure 8.8.

15.7   Passing Descriptors

When we think of passing an open descriptor from one process to another, we normally think of either

- A child sharing all the open descriptors with the parent after a call to `fork`

- All descriptors normally remaining open when `exec` is called

In the first example, the process opens a descriptor, calls `fork`, and then the parent closes the descriptor, letting the child handle the descriptor. This passes an open descriptor from the parent to the child. But, we would also like the ability for the child to open a descriptor and pass it back to the parent.

Current Unix systems provide a way to pass any open descriptor from one process to any other process. That is, there is no need for the processes to be related, such as a parent and its child. The technique requires us to first establish a Unix domain socket between the two processes and then use `sendmsg` to send a special message across the Unix domain socket. This message is handled specially by the kernel, passing the open descriptor from the sender to the receiver.

> The black magic performed by the 4.4BSD kernel in passing an open descriptor across a Unix domain socket is described in detail in Chapter 18 of TCPv3.
>
> SVR4 uses a different technique within the kernel to pass an open descriptor, the `I_SENDFD` and `I_RECVFD` `ioctl` commands, described in Section 15.5.1 of APUE. But, the process can still access this kernel feature using a Unix domain socket. In this text, we describe the use of Unix domain sockets to pass open descriptors, since this is the most portable programming technique: It works under both Berkeley-derived kernels and SVR4, whereas using the `I_SENDFD` and `I_RECVFD` `ioctl`s works only under SVR4.
>
> The 4.4BSD technique allows multiple descriptors to be passed with a single `sendmsg`, whereas the SVR4 technique passes only a single descriptor at a time. All our examples pass one descriptor at a time.

The steps involved in passing a descriptor between two processes are then as follows:

1. Create a Unix domain socket, either a stream socket or a datagram socket.

   If the goal is to `fork` a child and have the child open the descriptor and pass the descriptor back to the parent, the parent can call `socketpair` to create a stream pipe that can be used to exchange the descriptor.

   If the processes are unrelated, the server must create a Unix domain stream socket and `bind` a pathname to it, allowing the client to `connect` to that socket. The client can then send a request to the server to open some descriptor and the server can pass back the descriptor across the Unix domain socket. Alternately, a Unix domain datagram socket can also be used between the client and server, but there is little advantage in doing this, and the possibility exists for a datagram to be discarded. We will use a stream socket between the client and server in an example presented later in this section.

2. One process opens a descriptor by calling any of the Unix functions that returns a descriptor: open, pipe, mkfifo, socket, or accept, for example. *Any* type of descriptor can be passed from one process to another, which is why we call the technique "descriptor passing" and not "file descriptor passing."

3. The sending process builds a msghdr structure (Section 14.5) containing the descriptor to be passed. POSIX specifies that the descriptor be sent as ancillary data (the msg_control member of the msghdr structure, Section 14.6), but older implementations use the msg_accrights member. The sending process calls sendmsg to send the descriptor across the Unix domain socket from Step 1. At this point, we say that the descriptor is "in flight." Even if the sending process closes the descriptor after calling sendmsg, but before the receiving process calls recvmsg (in the next step), the descriptor remains open for the receiving process. Sending a descriptor increments the descriptor's reference count by one.

4. The receiving process calls recvmsg to receive the descriptor on the Unix domain socket from Step 1. It is normal for the descriptor number in the receiving process to differ from the descriptor number in the sending process. Passing a descriptor is not passing a descriptor number, but involves creating a new descriptor in the receiving process that refers to the same file table entry within the kernel as the descriptor that was sent by the sending process.

The client and server must have some application protocol so that the receiver of the descriptor knows when to expect it. If the receiver calls recvmsg without allocating room to receive the descriptor, and a descriptor was passed and is ready to be read, the descriptor that was being passed is closed (p. 518 of TCPv2). Also, the MSG_PEEK flag should be avoided with recvmsg if a descriptor is expected, as the result is unpredictable.

Descriptor Passing Example

We now provide an example of descriptor passing. We will write a program named mycat that takes a pathname as a command-line argument, opens the file, and copies it to standard output. But instead of calling the normal Unix open function, we call our own function named my_open. This function creates a stream pipe and calls fork and exec to initiate another program that opens the desired file. This program must then pass the open descriptor back to the parent across the stream pipe.

Figure 15.7 shows the first step: our mycat program after creating a stream pipe by calling socketpair. We designate the two descriptors returned by socketpair as [0] and [1].

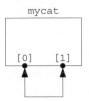

Figure 15.7 mycat program after creating stream pipe using socketpair.

The process then calls fork and the child calls exec to execute the openfile program. The parent closes the [1] descriptor and the child closes the [0] descriptor. (There is no difference in either end of the stream pipe; the child could close [1] and the parent could close [0].) This gives us the arrangement shown in Figure 15.8.

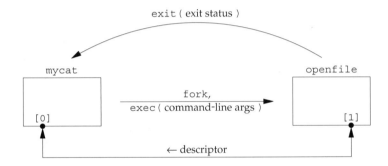

Figure 15.8 mycat program after invoking openfile program.

The parent must pass three pieces of information to the openfile program: (i) the pathname of the file to open, (ii) the open mode (read-only, read–write, or write-only), and (iii) the descriptor number corresponding to its end of the stream pipe (what we show as [1]). We choose to pass these three items as command-line arguments in the call to exec. An alternative method is to send these three items as data across the stream pipe. The openfile program sends back the open descriptor across the stream pipe and terminates. The exit status of the program tells the parent whether the file could be opened, and if not, what type of error occurred.

The advantage in executing another program to open the file is that the program could be a "set-user-ID" binary, which executes with root privileges, allowing it to open files that we normally do not have permission to open. This program could extend the concept of normal Unix permissions (user, group, and other) to any form of access checking it desires.

We begin with the mycat program, shown in Figure 15.9.

```
                                                                 ──── unixdomain/mycat.c
 1 #include    "unp.h"

 2 int     my_open(const char *, int);

 3 int
 4 main(int argc, char **argv)
 5 {
 6     int     fd, n;
 7     char    buff[BUFFSIZE];

 8     if (argc != 2)
 9         err_quit("usage: mycat <pathname>");

10     if ( (fd = my_open(argv[1], O_RDONLY)) < 0)
11         err_sys("cannot open %s", argv[1]);

12     while ( (n = Read(fd, buff, BUFFSIZE)) > 0)
13         Write(STDOUT_FILENO, buff, n);

14     exit(0);
15 }
                                                                 ──── unixdomain/mycat.c
```

Figure 15.9 mycat program: copies a file to standard output.

If we replace the call to my_open with a call to open, this simple program just copies a file to standard output.

The function my_open, shown in Figure 15.10, is intended to look like the normal Unix open function to its caller. It takes two arguments, a pathname and an open mode (such as O_RDONLY to mean read-only), opens the file, and returns a descriptor.

Create stream pipe

8   socketpair creates a stream pipe. Two descriptors are returned: sockfd[0] and sockfd[1]. This is the state we show in Figure 15.7.

fork and exec

9–16   fork is called, and the child then closes one end of the stream pipe. The descriptor number of the other end of the stream pipe is formatted into the argsockfd array and the open mode is formatted into the argmode array. We call snprintf because the arguments to exec must be character strings. The openfile program is executed. The execl function should not return unless it encounters an error. On success, the main function of the openfile program starts executing.

Parent waits for child

17–22   The parent closes the other end of the stream pipe and calls waitpid to wait for the child to terminate. The termination status of the child is returned in the variable status, and we first verify that the program terminated normally (i.e., it was not terminated by a signal). The WEXITSTATUS macro then converts the termination status into the exit status, whose value will be between 0 and 255. We will see shortly that if the `openfile` program encounters an error opening the requested file, it terminates with the corresponding errno value as its exit status.

unixdomain/myopen.c

```
1 #include    "unp.h"

2 int
3 my_open(const char *pathname, int mode)
4 {
5     int     fd, sockfd[2], status;
6     pid_t   childpid;
7     char    c, argsockfd[10], argmode[10];

8     Socketpair(AF_LOCAL, SOCK_STREAM, 0, sockfd);

9     if ( (childpid = Fork()) == 0) { /* child process */
10        Close(sockfd[0]);
11        snprintf(argsockfd, sizeof(argsockfd), "%d", sockfd[1]);
12        snprintf(argmode, sizeof(argmode), "%d", mode);
13        execl("./openfile", "openfile", argsockfd, pathname, argmode,
14              (char *) NULL);
15        err_sys("execl error");
16    }

17    /* parent process - wait for the child to terminate */
18    Close(sockfd[1]);              /* close the end we don't use */

19    Waitpid(childpid, &status, 0);
20    if (WIFEXITED(status) == 0)
21        err_quit("child did not terminate");
22    if ( (status = WEXITSTATUS(status)) == 0)
23        Read_fd(sockfd[0], &c, 1, &fd);
24    else {
25        errno = status;           /* set errno value from child's status */
26        fd = -1;
27    }

28    Close(sockfd[0]);
29    return (fd);
30 }
```

unixdomain/myopen.c

Figure 15.10 my_open function: opens a file and returns a descriptor.

Receive descriptor

23   Our function read_fd, shown next, receives the descriptor on the stream pipe. In addition to the descriptor, we read one byte of data, but do nothing with it.

> When sending and receiving a descriptor across a stream pipe, we always send at least one byte of data, even if the receiver does nothing with the data. Otherwise, the receiver cannot tell whether a return value of 0 from read_fd means "no data (but possibly a descriptor)" or "end-of-file."

Figure 15.11 shows the `read_fd` function, which calls `recvmsg` to receive data and a descriptor on a Unix domain socket. The first three arguments to this function are the same as for the `read` function, with a fourth argument being a pointer to an integer that will contain the received descriptor on return.

9–26   This function must deal with two versions of `recvmsg`: those with the `msg_control` member and those with the `msg_accrights` member. Our `config.h` header (Figure D.2) defines the constant `HAVE_MSGHDR_MSG_CONTROL` if the `msg_control` version is supported.

Make certain `msg_control` is suitably aligned

10–13   The `msg_control` buffer must be suitably aligned for a `cmsghdr` structure. Simply allocating a `char` array is inadequate. Here we declare a `union` of a `cmsghdr` structure with the character array, which guarantees that the array is suitably aligned. Another technique is to call `malloc`, but that would require freeing the memory before the function returns.

27–45   `recvmsg` is called. If ancillary data is returned, the format is as shown in Figure 14.13. We verify that the length, level, and type are correct, then fetch the newly created descriptor and return it through the caller's `recvfd` pointer. `CMSG_DATA` returns the pointer to the `cmsg_data` member of the ancillary data object as an `unsigned char` pointer. We cast this to an `int` pointer and fetch the integer descriptor that is pointed to.

─── *lib/read_fd.c*

```
 1 #include    "unp.h"

 2 ssize_t
 3 read_fd(int fd, void *ptr, size_t nbytes, int *recvfd)
 4 {
 5     struct msghdr msg;
 6     struct iovec iov[1];
 7     ssize_t n;

 8 #ifdef  HAVE_MSGHDR_MSG_CONTROL
 9     union {
10         struct cmsghdr cm;
11         char    control[CMSG_SPACE(sizeof(int))];
12     } control_un;
13     struct cmsghdr *cmptr;

14     msg.msg_control = control_un.control;
15     msg.msg_controllen = sizeof(control_un.control);
16 #else
17     int     newfd;

18     msg.msg_accrights = (caddr_t) & newfd;
19     msg.msg_accrightslen = sizeof(int);
20 #endif

21     msg.msg_name = NULL;
22     msg.msg_namelen = 0;

23     iov[0].iov_base = ptr;
24     iov[0].iov_len = nbytes;
25     msg.msg_iov = iov;
26     msg.msg_iovlen = 1;

27     if ( (n = recvmsg(fd, &msg, 0)) <= 0)
28         return (n);

29 #ifdef  HAVE_MSGHDR_MSG_CONTROL
30     if ( (cmptr = CMSG_FIRSTHDR(&msg)) != NULL &&
31         cmptr->cmsg_len == CMSG_LEN(sizeof(int))) {
32         if (cmptr->cmsg_level != SOL_SOCKET)
33             err_quit("control level != SOL_SOCKET");
34         if (cmptr->cmsg_type != SCM_RIGHTS)
35             err_quit("control type != SCM_RIGHTS");
36         *recvfd = *((int *) CMSG_DATA(cmptr));
37     } else
38         *recvfd = -1;           /* descriptor was not passed */
39 #else
40     if (msg.msg_accrightslen == sizeof(int))
41         *recvfd = newfd;
42     else
43         *recvfd = -1;        /* descriptor was not passed */
44 #endif

45     return (n);
46 }
```

─── *lib/read_fd.c*

Figure 15.11 read_fd function: receives data and a descriptor.

If the older `msg_accrights` member is supported, the length should be the size of an integer and the newly created descriptor is returned through the caller's `recvfd` pointer.

Figure 15.12 shows the `openfile` program. It takes the three command-line arguments that must be passed and calls the normal `open` function.

```
                                                                    unixdomain/openfile.c
 1 #include    "unp.h"

 2 int
 3 main(int argc, char **argv)
 4 {
 5     int     fd;

 6     if (argc != 4)
 7         err_quit("openfile <sockfd#> <filename> <mode>");

 8     if ( (fd = open(argv[2], atoi(argv[3]))) < 0)
 9         exit((errno > 0) ? errno : 255);

10     if (write_fd(atoi(argv[1]), "", 1, fd) < 0)
11         exit((errno > 0) ? errno : 255);

12     exit(0);
13 }
                                                                    unixdomain/openfile.c
```

Figure 15.12 `openfile` function: opens a file and passes back the descriptor.

Command-line arguments

7–12   Since two of the three command-line arguments were formatted into character strings by my_open, two are converted back into integers using `atoi`.

`open` the file

9–10   The file is opened by calling `open`. If an error is encountered, the `errno` value corresponding to the `open` error is returned as the exit status of the process.

Pass back descriptor

11–12   The descriptor is passed back by `write_fd`, which we show next. This process then terminates. But, recall that earlier in the chapter, we said that it was acceptable for the sending process to close the descriptor that was passed (which happens when we call `exit`), because the kernel knows that the descriptor is in flight, and keeps it open for the receiving process.

> The exit status must be between 0 and 255. The highest `errno` value is around 150. An alternate technique that doesn't require the `errno` values to be less than 256 would be to pass back an error indication as normal data in the call to `sendmsg`.

Figure 15.13 shows the final function, `write_fd`, which calls `sendmsg` to send a descriptor (and optional data, which we do not use) across a Unix domain socket.

lib/write_fd.c
```
 1 #include    "unp.h"

 2 ssize_t
 3 write_fd(int fd, void *ptr, size_t nbytes, int sendfd)
 4 {
 5     struct msghdr msg;
 6     struct iovec iov[1];

 7 #ifdef  HAVE_MSGHDR_MSG_CONTROL
 8     union {
 9         struct cmsghdr cm;
10         char    control[CMSG_SPACE(sizeof(int))];
11     } control_un;
12     struct cmsghdr *cmptr;

13     msg.msg_control = control_un.control;
14     msg.msg_controllen = sizeof(control_un.control);

15     cmptr = CMSG_FIRSTHDR(&msg);
16     cmptr->cmsg_len = CMSG_LEN(sizeof(int));
17     cmptr->cmsg_level = SOL_SOCKET;
18     cmptr->cmsg_type = SCM_RIGHTS;
19     *((int *) CMSG_DATA(cmptr)) = sendfd;
20 #else
21     msg.msg_accrights = (caddr_t) & sendfd;
22     msg.msg_accrightslen = sizeof(int);
23 #endif

24     msg.msg_name = NULL;
25     msg.msg_namelen = 0;

26     iov[0].iov_base = ptr;
27     iov[0].iov_len = nbytes;
28     msg.msg_iov = iov;
29     msg.msg_iovlen = 1;

30     return (sendmsg(fd, &msg, 0));
31 }
```
lib/write_fd.c

Figure 15.13 write_fd function: passes a descriptor by calling sendmsg.

As with read_fd, this function must deal with either ancillary data or older access rights. In either case, the msghdr structure is initialized and then sendmsg is called.

We will show an example of descriptor passing in Section 28.7 that involves unrelated processes. Additionally, we will show an example in Section 30.9 that involves related processes. We will use the read_fd and write_fd functions we just described.

15.8 Receiving Sender Credentials

In Figure 14.13, we showed another type of data that can be passed along a Unix domain socket as ancillary data: user credentials. Exactly how credentials are packaged up and sent as ancillary data tends to be OS-specific. We describe FreeBSD here, and other Unix variants are similar (usually the challenge is determining which structure to use for the credentials). We describe this feature, even though it is not uniform across systems, because it is an important, yet simple, addition to the Unix domain protocols. When a client and server communicate using these protocols, the server often needs a way to know exactly who the client is, to validate that the client has permission to ask for the service being requested.

FreeBSD passes credentials in a `cmsgcred` structure, which is defined by including the `<sys/socket.h>` header.

```
struct cmsgcred {
        pid_t    cmcred_pid;                    /* PID of sending process */
        uid_t    cmcred_uid;                    /* real UID of sending process */
        uid_t    cmcred_euid;                   /* effective UID of sending process */
        gid_t    cmcred_gid;                    /* real GID of sending process */
        short    cmcred_ngroups;                /* number of groups */
        gid_t    cmcred_groups[CMGROUP_MAX];     /* groups */
};
```

Normally, `CMGROUP_MAX` is 16. `cmcred_ngroups` is always at least 1, with the first element of the array the effective group ID.

This information is always available on a Unix domain socket, although there are often special arrangments the sender must make to have the information included when sending, and there are often special arrangements (e.g., socket options) the receiver must make to get the credentials. On our FreeBSD system, the receiver doesn't have to do anything special other than call `recvmsg` with an ancillary buffer large enough to hold the credentials, as we show in Figure 15.14. The sender, however, must include a `cmsgcred` structure when sending data using `sendmsg`. It is important to note that although FreeBSD requires the sender to include the structure, the contents are filled in by the kernel and cannot be forged by the sender. This makes the passing of credentials over a Unix domain socket a reliable way to verify the client's identity.

Example

As an example of credential passing, we modify our Unix domain stream server to ask for the client's credentials. Figure 15.14 shows a new function, `read_cred`, that is similar to `read`, but also returns a `cmsgcred` structure containing the sender's credentials.

3–4   The first three arguments are identical to `read`, with the fourth argument being a pointer to an `cmsgcred` structure that will be filled in.

22–31   If credentials were returned, the length, level, and type of the ancillary data are verified, and the resulting structure is copied back to the caller. If no credentials were returned, we set the structure to 0. Since the number of groups (`cmcred_ngroups`) is always 1 or more, the value of 0 indicates to the caller that no credentials were returned by the kernel.

The `main` function for our echo server, Figure 15.3, is unchanged. Figure 15.15 shows the new version of the `str_echo` function, modified from Figure 5.3. This function is called by the child after the parent has accepted a new client connection and called `fork`.

11–23   If credentials were returned, they are printed.

24–25   The remainder of the loop is unchanged. This code reads buffers from the client and writes them back to the client.

Our client from Figure 15.4 is only changed minimally to pass an empty `cmsgcred` structure that will be filled in when it calls `sendmsg`.

———————————————————————————————— unixdomain/readcred.c

```
 1 #include     "unp.h"

 2 #define CONTROL_LEN (sizeof(struct cmsghdr) + sizeof(struct cmsgcred))

 3 ssize_t
 4 read_cred(int fd, void *ptr, size_t nbytes, struct cmsgcred *cmsgcredptr)
 5 {
 6     struct msghdr msg;
 7     struct iovec iov[1];
 8     char    control[CONTROL_LEN];
 9     int     n;

10     msg.msg_name = NULL;
11     msg.msg_namelen = 0;
12     iov[0].iov_base = ptr;
13     iov[0].iov_len = nbytes;
14     msg.msg_iov = iov;
15     msg.msg_iovlen = 1;
16     msg.msg_control = control;
17     msg.msg_controllen = sizeof(control);
18     msg.msg_flags = 0;

19     if ( (n = recvmsg(fd, &msg, 0)) < 0)
20         return (n);

21     cmsgcredptr->cmcred_ngroups = 0;    /* indicates no credentials returned */
22     if (cmsgcredptr && msg.msg_controllen > 0) {
23         struct cmsghdr *cmptr = (struct cmsghdr *) control;

24         if (cmptr->cmsg_len < CONTROL_LEN)
25             err_quit("control length = %d", cmptr->cmsg_len);
26         if (cmptr->cmsg_level != SOL_SOCKET)
27             err_quit("control level != SOL_SOCKET");
28         if (cmptr->cmsg_type != SCM_CREDS)
29             err_quit("control type != SCM_CREDS");
30         memcpy(cmsgcredptr, CMSG_DATA(cmptr), sizeof(struct cmsgcred));
31     }

32     return (n);
33 }
```

———————————————————————————————— unixdomain/readcred.c

Figure 15.14   `read_cred` function: reads and returns sender's credentials.

———————————————————————————— unixdomain/strecho.c

```
 1 #include    "unp.h"

 2 ssize_t read_cred(int, void *, size_t, struct cmsgcred *);

 3 void
 4 str_echo(int sockfd)
 5 {
 6     ssize_t n;
 7     int     i;
 8     char    buf[MAXLINE];
 9     struct cmsgcred cred;
10   again:
11     while ( (n = read_cred(sockfd, buf, MAXLINE, &cred)) > 0) {
12         if (cred.cmcred_ngroups == 0) {
13             printf("(no credentials returned)\n");
14         } else {
15             printf("PID of sender = %d\n", cred.cmcred_pid);
16             printf("real user ID = %d\n", cred.cmcred_uid);
17             printf("real group ID = %d\n", cred.cmcred_gid);
18             printf("effective user ID = %d\n", cred.cmcred_euid);
19             printf("%d groups:", cred.cmcred_ngroups - 1);
20             for (i = 1; i < cred.cmcred_ngroups; i++)
21                 printf(" %d", cred.cmcred_groups[i]);
22             printf("\n");
23         }
24         Writen(sockfd, buf, n);
25     }

26     if (n < 0 && errno == EINTR)
27         goto again;
28     else if (n < 0)
29         err_sys("str_echo: read error");
30 }
```

———————————————————————————— unixdomain/strecho.c

Figure 15.15 str_echo function: asks for client's credentials.

Before running the client, we can see our current credentials using the id command.

```
freebsd % id
uid=1007(andy) gid=1007(andy) groups=1007(andy), 0(wheel)
```

Starting the server and then running the client one time in another window produces the following output from the server:

```
freebsd % unixstrserv02
PID of sender = 26881
real user ID = 1007
real group ID = 1007
effective user ID = 1007
2 groups: 1007 0
```

This information is output only after the client has sent data to the server. We see that the information matches what we saw with the id command.

15.9   Summary

Unix domain sockets are an alternative to IPC when the client and server are on the same host. The advantage in using Unix domain sockets over some form of IPC is that the API is nearly identical to a networked client/server. The advantage in using Unix domain sockets over TCP, when the client and server are on the same host, is the increased performance of Unix domain sockets over TCP on many implementations.

We modified our TCP and UDP echo clients and servers to use the Unix domain protocols and the only major difference was having to `bind` a pathname to the UDP client's socket, so that the UDP server had somewhere to send the replies.

Descriptor passing is a powerful technique between clients and servers on the same host and it takes place across a Unix domain socket. We showed an example in Section 15.7 that passed a descriptor from a child back to the parent. In Section 28.7, we will show an example in which the client and server are unrelated, and in Section 30.9, we will show another example that passes a descriptor from a parent to a child.

Exercises

15.1   What happens if a Unix domain server calls `unlink` after calling `bind`?

15.2   What happens if a Unix domain server does not `unlink` its well-known pathname when it terminates, and a client tries to `connect` to the server sometime after the server terminates?

15.3   Start with Figure 11.11 and modify it to call `sleep(5)` after the peer's protocol address is printed, and to also print the number of bytes returned by `read` each time `read` returns a positive value.

Start with Figure 11.14 and modify it to call `write` for each byte of the result that is sent to the client. (We discussed similar modifications in the solution to Exercise 1.5.) Run the client and server on the same host using TCP. How many bytes are `read` by the client?

Run the client and server on the same host using a Unix domain socket. Does anything change?

Now call `send` instead of `write` in the server and specify the `MSG_EOR` flag. (You need a Berkeley-derived implementation to finish this exercise.) Run the client and server on the same host using a Unix domain socket. Does anything change?

15.4   Write a program to determine the values shown in Figure 4.10. One approach is to create a stream pipe and then `fork` into a parent and child. The parent enters a `for` loop, incrementing the backlog from 0 through 14. Each time through the loop, the parent first writes the value of the backlog to the stream pipe. The child reads this value, creates a listening socket bound to the loopback address, and sets the backlog to that value. The child then writes to the stream pipe, just to tell the parent it is ready. The parent then attempts as many connections as possible, detecting when it has hit the backlog limit because the `connect` blocks. The parent may use an `alarm` set at two seconds to detect the blocking `connect`. The child never calls `accept` to let the kernel queue the connections from the parent. When the parent's `alarm` expires, it knows from the loop counter which `connect` hit the backlog limit. The parent then closes its sockets and writes the next new backlog value to the stream pipe for the child. When the child reads this next value, it closes its listening socket and creates a new listening socket, starting the procedure again.

15.5   Verify that omitting the call to `bind` in Figure 15.6 causes an error in the server.

16

Nonblocking I/O

16.1 Introduction

By default, sockets are blocking. This means that when we issue a socket call that cannot be completed immediately, our process is put to sleep, waiting for the condition to be true. We can divide the socket calls that may block into four categories:

1. Input operations—These include the `read`, `readv`, `recv`, `recvfrom`, and `recvmsg` functions. If we call one of these input functions for a blocking TCP socket (the default), and there is no data available in the socket receive buffer, we are put to sleep until some data arrives. Since TCP is a byte stream, we will be awakened when "some" data arrives: It could be a single byte of data, or it could be a full TCP segment of data. If we want to wait until some fixed amount of data is available, we can call our own function `readn` (Figure 3.15) or specify the `MSG_WAITALL` flag (Figure 14.6).

   Since UDP is a datagram protocol, if the socket receive buffer is empty for a blocking UDP socket, we are put to sleep until a UDP datagram arrives.

   With a nonblocking socket, if the input operation cannot be satisfied (at least one byte of data for a TCP socket or a complete datagram for a UDP socket), we see an immediate return with an error of `EWOULDBLOCK`.

2. Output operations—These include the `write`, `writev`, `send`, `sendto`, and `sendmsg` functions. For a TCP socket, we said in Section 2.11 that the kernel copies data from the application's buffer into the socket send buffer. If there is no room in the socket send buffer for a blocking socket, the process is put to sleep until there is room.

With a nonblocking TCP socket, if there is no room at all in the socket send buffer, we return immediately with an error of EWOULDBLOCK. If there is some room in the socket send buffer, the return value will be the number of bytes the kernel was able to copy into the buffer. (This is called a *short count*.)

We also said in Section 2.11 that there is no actual UDP socket send buffer. The kernel just copies the application data and moves it down the stack, prepending the UDP and IP headers. Therefore, an output operation on a blocking UDP socket (the default) will not block for the same reason as a TCP socket, but it is possible for output operations to block on some systems due to the buffering and flow control that happens within the networking code in the kernel.

3. Accepting incoming connections—This is the accept function. If accept is called for a blocking socket and a new connection is not available, the process is put to sleep.

   If accept is called for a nonblocking socket and a new connection is not available, the error EWOULDBLOCK is returned instead.

4. Initiating outgoing connections—This is the connect function for TCP. (Recall that connect can be used with UDP, but it does not cause a "real" connection to be established; it just causes the kernel to store the peer's IP address and port number.) We showed in Section 2.6 that the establishment of a TCP connection involves a three-way handshake and the connect function does not return until the client receives the ACK of its SYN. This means that a TCP connect always blocks the calling process for at least the RTT to the server.

   If connect is called for a nonblocking TCP socket and the connection cannot be established immediately, the connection establishment is initiated (e.g., the first packet of TCP's three-way handshake is sent), but the error EINPROGRESS is returned. Notice that this error differs from the error returned in the previous three scenarios. Also notice that some connections can be established immediately, normally when the server is on the same host as the client. So, even with a nonblocking connect, we must be prepared for connect to return successfully. We will show an example of a nonblocking connect in Section 16.3.

> Traditionally, System V has returned the error EAGAIN for a nonblocking I/O operation that cannot be satisfied, while Berkeley-derived implementations have returned the error EWOULDBLOCK. Because of this history, the POSIX specification says either may be returned for this case. Fortunately, most current systems define these two error codes to be the same (check your system's <sys/errno.h> header), so it doesn't matter which one we use. In this text, we use EWOULDBLOCK.

Section 6.2 summarized the different models available for I/O and compared nonblocking I/O to other models. In this chapter, we will provide examples of all four types of operations and develop a new type of client, similar to a Web client, that initiates multiple TCP connections at the same time using a nonblocking connect.

16.2 Nonblocking Reads and Writes: `str_cli` Function (Revisited)

We return once again to our `str_cli` function, which we discussed in Sections 5.5 and 6.4. The latter version, which uses `select`, still uses blocking I/O. For example, if a line is available on standard input, we read it with `read` and then send it to the server with `writen`. But the call to `writen` can block if the socket send buffer is full. While we are blocked in the call to `writen`, data could be available for reading from the socket receive buffer. Similarly, if a line of input is available from the socket, we can block in the subsequent call to `write`, if standard output is slower than the network. Our goal in this section is to develop a version of this function that uses nonblocking I/O. This prevents us from blocking while we could be doing something productive.

Unfortunately, the addition of nonblocking I/O complicates the function's buffer management noticeably, so we will present the function in pieces. As we discussed in Chapter 6, using standard I/O with sockets can be difficult, and that is very much the case with nonblocking I/O. So we continue to avoid standard I/O in this example.

We maintain two buffers: `to` contains data going from standard input to the server, and `fr` contains data arriving from the server going to standard output. Figure 16.1 shows the arrangement of the `to` buffer and the pointers into the buffer.

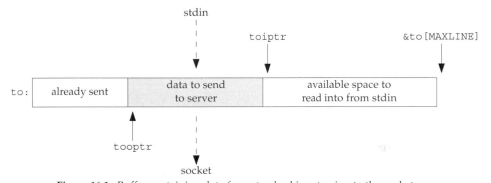

Figure 16.1 Buffer containing data from standard input going to the socket.

The pointer `toiptr` points to the next byte into which data can be read from standard input. `tooptr` points to the next byte that must be written to the socket. There are `toiptr` minus `tooptr` bytes to be written to the socket. The number of bytes that can be read from standard input is `&to[MAXLINE]` minus `toiptr`. As soon as `tooptr` reaches `toiptr`, both pointers are reset to the beginning of the buffer.

Figure 16.2 shows the corresponding arrangement of the `fr` buffer.

Figure 16.3 shows the first part of the function.

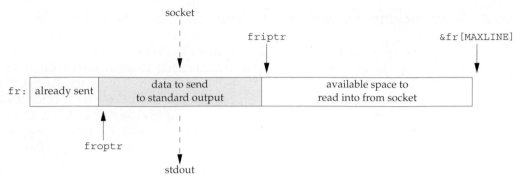

Figure 16.2   Buffer containing data from the socket going to standard output.

nonblock/strclinonb.c

```
 1 #include    "unp.h"

 2 void
 3 str_cli(FILE *fp, int sockfd)
 4 {
 5     int      maxfdp1, val, stdineof;
 6     ssize_t n, nwritten;
 7     fd_set   rset, wset;
 8     char     to[MAXLINE], fr[MAXLINE];
 9     char     *toiptr, *tooptr, *friptr, *froptr;

10     val = Fcntl(sockfd, F_GETFL, 0);
11     Fcntl(sockfd, F_SETFL, val | O_NONBLOCK);

12     val = Fcntl(STDIN_FILENO, F_GETFL, 0);
13     Fcntl(STDIN_FILENO, F_SETFL, val | O_NONBLOCK);

14     val = Fcntl(STDOUT_FILENO, F_GETFL, 0);
15     Fcntl(STDOUT_FILENO, F_SETFL, val | O_NONBLOCK);

16     toiptr = tooptr = to;        /* initialize buffer pointers */
17     friptr = froptr = fr;
18     stdineof = 0;

19     maxfdp1 = max(max(STDIN_FILENO, STDOUT_FILENO), sockfd) + 1;
20     for ( ; ; ) {
21         FD_ZERO(&rset);
22         FD_ZERO(&wset);
23         if (stdineof == 0 && toiptr < &to[MAXLINE])
24             FD_SET(STDIN_FILENO, &rset);    /* read from stdin */
25         if (friptr < &fr[MAXLINE])
26             FD_SET(sockfd, &rset);   /* read from socket */
27         if (tooptr != toiptr)
28             FD_SET(sockfd, &wset);   /* data to write to socket */
29         if (froptr != friptr)
30             FD_SET(STDOUT_FILENO, &wset);    /* data to write to stdout */

31         Select(maxfdp1, &rset, &wset, NULL, NULL);
```

nonblock/strclinonb.c

Figure 16.3   `str_cli` function, first part: initializes and calls `select`.

Set descriptors to nonblocking

10–15   All three descriptors are set to nonblocking using fcntl: the socket to and from the server, standard input, and standard output.

Initialize buffer pointers

16–19   The pointers into the two buffers are initialized and the maximum descriptor plus one is calculated, which will be used as the first argument for select.

Main loop: prepare to call select

20   As with the previous version of this function, Figure 6.13, the main loop of the function is a call to select followed by individual tests of the various conditions we are interested in.

Specify descriptors we are interested in

21–30   Both descriptor sets are set to 0 and then up to 2 bits are turned on in each set. If we have not yet read an EOF on standard input, and there is room for at least one byte of data in the to buffer, the bit corresponding to standard input is turned on in the read set. If there is room for at least one byte of data in the fr buffer, the bit corresponding to the socket is turned on in the read set. If there is data to write to the socket in the to buffer, the bit corresponding to the socket is turned on in the write set. Finally, if there is data in the fr buffer to send to standard output, the bit corresponding to standard output is turned on in the write set.

Call select

31   select is called, waiting for any one of the four possible conditions to be true. We do not specify a timeout for this function.

The next part of the function is shown in Figure 16.4. This code contains the first two tests (of four) that are made after select returns.

read from standard input

32–33   If standard input is readable, we call read. The third argument is the amount of available space in the to buffer.

Handle nonblocking error

34–35   If an error occurs and it is EWOULDBLOCK, nothing happens. Normally this condition "should not happen," that is, select telling us that the descriptor is readable and read returning EWOULDBLOCK, but we handle it nevertheless.

read returns EOF

36–40   If read returns 0, we are finished with the standard input. Our flag stdineof is set. If there is no more data in the to buffer to send (tooptr equals toiptr), shutdown sends a FIN to the server. If there is still data in the to buffer to send, the FIN cannot be sent until the buffer is written to the socket.

> We output a line to standard error noting the EOF, along with the current time, and we show how we use this output after describing this function. Similar calls to fprintf are found throughout this function.

nonblock/strclinonb.c

```
32              if (FD_ISSET(STDIN_FILENO, &rset)) {
33                  if ( (n = read(STDIN_FILENO, toiptr, &to[MAXLINE] - toiptr)) < 0) {
34                      if (errno !- EWOULDBLOCK)
35                          err_sys("read error on stdin");
36                  } else if (n == 0) {
37                      fprintf(stderr, "%s: EOF on stdin\n", gf_time());
38                      stdineof = 1;   /* all done with stdin */
39                      if (tooptr == toiptr)
40                          Shutdown(sockfd, SHUT_WR);   /* send FIN */
41                  } else {
42                      fprintf(stderr, "%s: read %d bytes from stdin\n", gf_time(),
43                              n);
44                      toiptr += n;    /* # just read */
45                      FD_SET(sockfd, &wset);  /* try and write to socket below */
46                  }
47              }

48              if (FD_ISSET(sockfd, &rset)) {
49                  if ( (n = read(sockfd, friptr, &fr[MAXLINE] - friptr)) < 0) {
50                      if (errno != EWOULDBLOCK)
51                          err_sys("read error on socket");
52                  } else if (n == 0) {
53                      fprintf(stderr, "%s: EOF on socket\n", gf_time());
54                      if (stdineof)
55                          return;     /* normal termination */
56                      else
57                          err_quit("str_cli: server terminated prematurely");
58                  } else {
59                      fprintf(stderr, "%s: read %d bytes from socket\n",
60                              gf_time(), n);
61                      friptr += n;    /* # just read */
62                      FD_SET(STDOUT_FILENO, &wset);   /* try and write below */
63                  }
64              }
```

nonblock/strclinonb.c

Figure 16.4 `str_cli` function, second part: reads from standard input or socket.

`read` **returns data**

41-45   When `read` returns data, we increment `toiptr` accordingly. We also turn on the
bit corresponding to the socket in the write set, to cause the test for this bit to be true
later in the loop, thus causing a `write` to be attempted to the socket.

> This is one of the hard design decisions when writing code. We have a few alternatives here.
> Instead of setting the bit in the write set, we could do nothing, in which case, `select` will test
> for writability of the socket the next time it is called. But this requires another loop around and
> another call to `select` when we already know that we have data to write to the socket.
> Another choice is to duplicate the code that writes to the socket here, but this seems wasteful
> and a potential source for error (in case there is a bug in that piece of duplicated code, and we

fix it in one location but not the other). Lastly, we could create a function that writes to the socket and call that function instead of duplicating the code, but that function needs to share three of the local variables with str_cli, which would necessitate making these variables global. The choice made is the authors' view on which alternative is best.

read **from socket**

48–64   These lines of code are similar to the if statement we just described when standard input is readable. If read returns EWOULDBLOCK, nothing happens. If we encounter an EOF from the server, this is okay if we have already encountered an EOF on the standard input, but it is not expected otherwise. If read returns some data, friptr is incremented and the bit for standard output is turned on in the write descriptor set, to try to write the data in the next part of the function.

Figure 16.5 shows the final portion of the function.

——————————————————————————— nonblock/strclinonb.c

```
65          if (FD_ISSET(STDOUT_FILENO, &wset) && ((n = friptr - froptr) > 0)) {
66              if ( (nwritten = write(STDOUT_FILENO, froptr, n)) < 0) {
67                  if (errno != EWOULDBLOCK)
68                      err_sys("write error to stdout");

69              } else {
70                  fprintf(stderr, "%s: wrote %d bytes to stdout\n",
71                          gf_time(), nwritten);
72                  froptr += nwritten; /* # just written */
73                  if (froptr == friptr)
74                      froptr = friptr = fr;   /* back to beginning of buffer */
75              }
76          }

77          if (FD_ISSET(sockfd, &wset) && ((n = toiptr - tooptr) > 0)) {
78              if ( (nwritten = write(sockfd, tooptr, n)) < 0) {
79                  if (errno != EWOULDBLOCK)
80                      err_sys("write error to socket");

81              } else {
82                  fprintf(stderr, "%s: wrote %d bytes to socket\n",
83                          gf_time(), nwritten);
84                  tooptr += nwritten; /* # just written */
85                  if (tooptr == toiptr) {
86                      toiptr = tooptr = to;   /* back to beginning of buffer */
87                      if (stdineof)
88                          Shutdown(sockfd, SHUT_WR);   /* send FIN */
89                  }
90              }
91          }
92      }
93  }
```

——————————————————————————— nonblock/strclinonb.c

Figure 16.5 str_cli function, third part: writes to standard output or socket.

write to standard output

65–68   If standard output is writable and the number of bytes to write is greater than 0, write is called. If EWOULDBLOCK is returned, nothing happens. Notice that this condition is entirely possible because the code at the end of the previous part of this function turns on the bit for standard output in the write set, without knowing whether the write will succeed or not.

write OK

69–75   If the write is successful, froptr is incremented by the number of bytes written. If the output pointer has caught up with the input pointer, both pointers are reset to point to the beginning of the buffer.

write to socket

77–91   This section of code is similar to the code we just described for writing to the standard output. The one difference is that when the output pointer catches up with the input pointer, not only are both pointers reset to the beginning of the buffer, but if we encountered an EOF on standard input, the FIN can be sent to the server.

We now examine the operation of this function and the overlapping of the nonblocking I/O. Figure 16.6 shows our gf_time function, which is called from our str_cli function.

―― lib/gf_time.c

```
 1 #include    "unp.h"
 2 #include    <time.h>

 3 char *
 4 gf_time(void)
 5 {
 6     struct timeval tv;
 7     static char str[30];
 8     char    *ptr;

 9     if (gettimeofday(&tv, NULL) < 0)
10         err_sys("gettimeofday error");

11     ptr = ctime(&tv.tv_sec);
12     strcpy(str, &ptr[11]);
13     /* Fri Sep 13 00:00:00 1986\n\0 */
14     /* 01234567890123456789012345 5 */
15     snprintf(str + 8, sizeof(str) - 8, ".%06ld", tv.tv_usec);

16     return (str);
17 }
```

―― lib/gf_time.c

Figure 16.6 gf_time function: returns pointer to time string.

This function returns a string containing the current time, including microseconds, in the following format:

```
12:34:56.123456
```

This is intentionally in the same format as the timestamps output by tcpdump. Also notice that all the calls to fprintf in our str_cli function write to standard error, allowing us to separate standard output (the lines echoed by the server) from our diagnostic output. We can then run our client and tcpdump and take this diagnostic output along with the tcpdump output and sort the two outputs together, ordered by the time. This lets us see what happens in our program and correlate it with the corresponding TCP action.

For example, we first run tcpdump on our host solaris, capturing only TCP segments to or from port 7 (the echo server), saving the output in the file named tcpd.

```
solaris % tcpdump -w tcpd tcp and port 7
```

We then run our TCP client on this host, specifying the server on the host linux.

```
solaris % tcpcli02 192.168.1.10 < 2000.lines > out 2> diag
```

Standard input is the file 2000.lines, the same file we used with Figure 6.13. Standard output is sent to the file out, and standard error is sent to the file diag. On completion, we run

```
solaris % diff 2000.lines out
```

to verify that the echoed lines are identical to the input lines. Finally, we terminate tcpdump with our interrupt key and then print the tcpdump records, sorting these records with the diagnostic output from the client. Figure 16.7 shows the first part of this result.

```
solaris % tcpdump -r tcpd -N | sort diag -
10:18:34.486392 solaris.33621 > linux.echo: S 1802738644:1802738644(0)
                                    win 8760 <mss 1460>
10:18:34.488278 linux.echo > solaris.33621: S 3212986316:3212986316(0)
                                    ack 1802738645 win 8760 <mss 1460>
10:18:34.488490 solaris.33621 > linux.echo: . ack 1 win 8760

10:18:34.491482: read 4096 bytes from stdin
10:18:34.518663 solaris.33621 > linux.echo: P 1:1461(1460) ack 1 win 8760
10:18:34.519016: wrote 4096 bytes to socket
10:18:34.528529 linux.echo > solaris.33621: P 1:1461(1460) ack 1461 win 8760
10:18:34.528785 solaris.33621 > linux.echo: . 1461:2921(1460) ack 1461 win 8760
10:18:34.528900 solaris.33621 > linux.echo: P 2921:4097(1176) ack 1461 win 8760
10:18:34.528958 solaris.33621 > linux.echo: . ack 1461 win 8760
10:18:34.536193 linux.echo > solaris.33621: . 1461:2921(1460) ack 4097 win 8760
10:18:34.536697 linux.echo > solaris.33621: P 2921:3509(588) ack 4097 win 8760
10:18:34.544636: read 4096 bytes from stdin
10:18:34.568505: read 3508 bytes from socket
10:18:34.580373 solaris.33621 > linux.echo: . ack 3509 win 8760
10:18:34.582244 linux.echo > solaris.33621: P 3509:4097(588) ack 4097 win 8760
10:18:34.593354: wrote 3508 bytes to stdout
10:18:34.617272 solaris.33621 > linux.echo: P 4097:5557(1460) ack 4097 win 8760
10:18:34.617610 solaris.33621 > linux.echo: P 5557:7017(1460) ack 4097 win 8760
10:18:34.617908 solaris.33621 > linux.echo: P 7017:8193(1176) ack 4097 win 8760
10:18:34.618062: wrote 4096 bytes to socket
10:18:34.623310 linux.echo > solaris.33621: . ack 8193 win 8760
10:18:34.626129 linux.echo > solaris.33621: . 4097:5557(1460) ack 8193 win 8760
10:18:34.626339 solaris.33621 > linux.echo: . ack 5557 win 8760
10:18:34.626611 linux.echo > solaris.33621: P 5557:6145(588) ack 8193 win 8760
10:18:34.628396 linux.echo > solaris.33621: . 6145:7605(1460) ack 8193 win 8760
10:18:34.643524: read 4096 bytes from stdin
10:18:34.667305: read 2636 bytes from socket
10:18:34.670324 solaris.33621 > linux.echo: . ack 7605 win 8760
10:18:34.672221 linux.echo > solaris.33621: P 7605:8193(588) ack 8193 win 8760
10:18:34.691039: wrote 2636 bytes to stdout
```

Figure 16.7 Sorted output from `tcpdump` and diagnostic output.

We wrapped the long lines containing the SYNs and we also removed the don't fragment (DF) notations from the Solaris segments, denoting that the DF bit is set (path MTU discovery).

Using this output, we can draw a timeline of what's happening. We show this in Figure 16.8, with time increasing down the page.

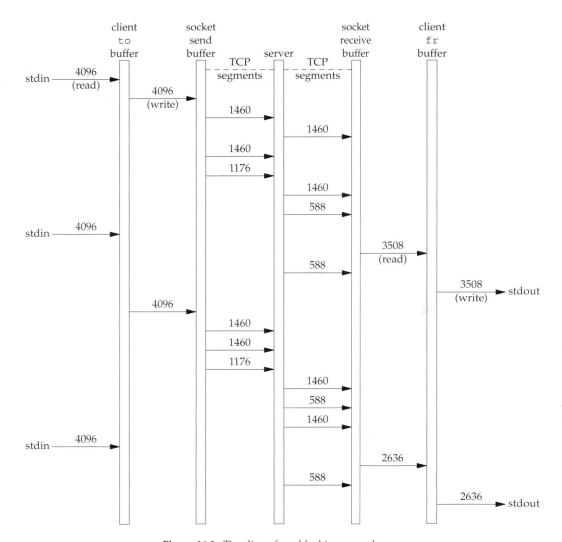

Figure 16.8 Timeline of nonblocking example.

In this figure, we do not show the ACK segments. Also realize that when the program outputs "wrote N bytes to stdout," the `write` has returned, possibly causing TCP to send one or more segments of data.

What we can see from this timeline are the dynamics of a client/server exchange. Using nonblocking I/O lets the program take advantage of these dynamics, reading or writing when the operation can take place. We let the kernel tell us when an I/O operation can occur by using the `select` function.

We can time our nonblocking version using the same 2,000-line file and the same server (a 175-ms RTT from the client) as in Section 6.7. The clock time is now 6.9 seconds, compared to 12.3 seconds for the version in Section 6.7. Therefore, nonblocking I/O reduces the overall time for this example that sends a file to the server.

A Simpler Version of `str_cli`

The nonblocking version of `str_cli` that we just showed is nontrivial: about 135 lines of code, compared to 40 lines for the version using `select` with blocking I/O in Figure 6.13, and 20 lines for our original stop-and-wait version (Figure 5.5). We know that doubling the size of the code from 20 to 40 lines was worth the effort, because the speed increased by almost a factor of 30 in a batch mode and using `select` with blocking descriptors was not overly complicated. But, is it worth the effort to code an application using nonblocking I/O, given the complexity of the resulting code? The answer is no. Whenever we find the need to use nonblocking I/O, it will usually be simpler to split the application into either processes (using `fork`) or threads (Chapter 26).

Figure 16.10 is yet another version of our `str_cli` function, with the function dividing itself into two processes using `fork`.

The function immediately calls `fork` to split into a parent and child. The child copies lines from the server to standard output and the parent copies lines from standard input to the server, as shown in Figure 16.9.

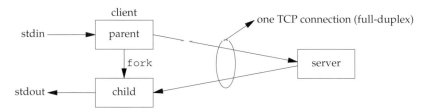

Figure 16.9 `str_cli` function using two processes.

We explicitly note that the TCP connection is full-duplex and that the parent and child are sharing the same socket descriptor: The parent writes to the socket and the child reads from the socket. There is only one socket, one socket receive buffer, and one socket send buffer, but this socket is referenced by two descriptors: one in the parent and one in the child.

We again need to worry about the termination sequence. Normal termination occurs when the EOF on standard input is encountered. The parent reads this EOF and calls `shutdown` to send a FIN. (The parent cannot call `close`. See Exercise 16.1.) But when this happens, the child needs to continue copying from the server to the standard output, until it reads an EOF on the socket.

It is also possible for the server process to terminate prematurely (Section 5.12); if this occurs, the child will read an EOF on the socket. If this happens, the child must tell the parent to stop copying from the standard input to the socket (see Exercise 16.2). In Figure 16.10, the child sends the SIGTERM signal to the parent, in case the parent is still running (see Exercise 16.3). Another way to handle this would be for the child to terminate and have the parent catch SIGCHLD, if the parent is still running.

————— nonblock/strclifork.c

```
 1 #include     "unp.h"

 2 void
 3 str_cli(FILE *fp, int sockfd)
 4 {
 5     pid_t   pid;
 6     char    sendline[MAXLINE], recvline[MAXLINE];

 7     if ( (pid = Fork()) == 0) {   /* child: server -> stdout */
 8         while (Readline(sockfd, recvline, MAXLINE) > 0)
 9             Fputs(recvline, stdout);

10         kill(getppid(), SIGTERM);   /* in case parent still running */
11         exit(0);
12     }

13     /* parent: stdin -> server */
14     while (Fgets(sendline, MAXLINE, fp) != NULL)
15         Writen(sockfd, sendline, strlen(sendline));

16     Shutdown(sockfd, SHUT_WR);   /* EOF on stdin, send FIN */
17     pause();
18     return;
19 }
```

————— nonblock/strclifork.c

Figure 16.10 Version of `str_cli` function that uses `fork`.

The parent calls `pause` when it has finished copying, which puts it to sleep until a signal is caught. Even though our parent does not catch any signals, this puts the parent to sleep until it receives the `SIGTERM` signal from the child. The default action of this signal is to terminate the process, which is fine for this example. The reason we make the parent wait for the child is to measure an accurate clock time for this version of `str_cli`. Normally, the child finishes after the parent, but since we measure the clock time using the shell's `time` command, the measurement ends when the parent terminates.

Notice the simplicity of this version compared to the nonblocking I/O version shown earlier in this section. Our nonblocking version managed four different I/O streams at the same time, and since all four were nonblocking, we had to concern ourselves with partial reads and writes for all four streams. But in the `fork` version, each process handles only two I/O streams, copying from one to the other. There is no need for nonblocking I/O because if there is no data to read from the input stream, there is nothing to write to the corresponding output stream.

Timing of `str_cli`

We have now shown four different versions of the `str_cli` function. We summarize the clock time required for these versions, along with a version using threads (Figure 26.2), when copying 2,000 lines from a Solaris client to a server with an RTT of 175 ms:

- 354.0 sec, stop-and-wait (Figure 5.5)
- 12.3 sec, `select` and blocking I/O (Figure 6.13)
- 6.9 sec, nonblocking I/O (Figure 16.3)
- 8.7 sec, `fork` (Figure 16.10)
- 8.5 sec, threaded version (Figure 26.2)

Our nonblocking I/O version is almost twice as fast as our version using blocking I/O with `select`. Our simple version using `fork` is slower than our nonblocking I/O version. Nevertheless, given the complexity of the nonblocking I/O code versus the `fork` code, we recommend the simple approach.

16.3   Nonblocking `connect`

When a TCP socket is set to nonblocking and then `connect` is called, `connect` returns immediately with an error of `EINPROGRESS` but the TCP three-way handshake continues. We then check for either a successful or unsuccessful completion of the connection's establishment using `select`. There are three uses for a nonblocking `connect`:

1. We can overlap other processing with the three-way handshake. A `connect` takes one RTT to complete (Section 2.6) and this can be anywhere from a few milliseconds on a LAN to hundreds of milliseconds or a few seconds on a WAN. There might be other processing we wish to perform during this time.

2. We can establish multiple connections at the same time using this technique. This has become popular with Web browsers, and we will show an example of this in Section 16.5.

3. Since we wait for the connection to be established using `select`, we can specify a time limit for `select`, allowing us to shorten the timeout for the `connect`. Many implementations have a timeout for `connect` that is between 75 seconds and several minutes. There are times when an application wants a shorter timeout, and using a nonblocking `connect` is one way to accomplish this. Section 14.2 talks about other ways to place timeouts on socket operations.

As simple as the nonblocking `connect` sounds, there are other details we must handle:

- Even though the socket is nonblocking, if the server to which we are connecting is on the same host, the connection is normally established immediately when we call `connect`. We must handle this scenario.

- Berkeley-derived implementations (and POSIX) have the following two rules regarding `select` and nonblocking `connect`s:

1. When the connection completes successfully, the descriptor becomes writable (p. 531 of TCPv2).

2. When the connection establishment encounters an error, the descriptor becomes both readable and writable (p. 530 of TCPv2).

These two rules regarding select fall out from our rules in Section 6.3 about the conditions that make a descriptor ready. A TCP socket is writable if there is available space in
the send buffer (which will always be the case for a connecting socket since we have not
yet written anything to the socket) *and* the socket is connected (which occurs only when
the three-way handshake completes). A pending error causes a socket to be both readable
and writable.

There are many portability problems with nonblocking connects that we mention in
the examples that follow.

16.4 Nonblocking connect: Daytime Client

Figure 16.11 shows our function connect_nonb, which performs a nonblocking
connect. We replace the call to connect in Figure 1.5 with

```
if (connect_nonb(sockfd, (SA *) &servaddr, sizeof(servaddr), 0) < 0)
    err_sys("connect error");
```

The first three arguments are the normal arguments to connect, and the fourth argument is the number of seconds to wait for the connection to complete. A value of 0
implies no timeout on the select; hence, the kernel will use its normal TCP connection
establishment timeout.

Set socket nonblocking

9–10   We call fcntl to set the socket to nonblocking.

11–14   We initiate the nonblocking connect. The error we expect is EINPROGRESS, indicating that the connection has started, but is not yet complete (p. 466 of TCPv2). Any
other error is returned to the caller.

Overlap processing with connection establishment

15   At this point, we can do whatever we want while we wait for the connection to
complete.

Check for immediate completion

16–17   If the nonblocking connect returns 0, the connection is complete. As we have said,
this can occur when the server is on the same host as the client.

Call select

18–24   We call select and wait for the socket to be ready for either reading or writing.
We zero out rset, turn on the bit corresponding to sockfd in this descriptor set, and
then copy rset into wset. This assignment is probably a structure assignment since
descriptor sets are normally represented as structures. We also initialize the timeval
structure and then call select. If the caller specifies a fourth argument of 0 (uses the
default timeout), we must specify a null pointer as the final argument to select and
not a timeval structure with a value of 0 (which means do not wait at all).

Handle timeouts

25–28   If select returns 0, the timer expired, and we return ETIMEDOUT to the caller. We
also close the socket, to prevent the three-way handshake from proceeding any further.

lib/connect_nonb.c

```
 1 #include    "unp.h"

 2 int
 3 connect_nonb(int sockfd, const SA *saptr, socklen_t salen, int nsec)
 4 {
 5     int     flags, n, error;
 6     socklen_t len;
 7     fd_set  rset, wset;
 8     struct timeval tval;

 9     flags = Fcntl(sockfd, F_GETFL, 0);
10     Fcntl(sockfd, F_SETFL, flags | O_NONBLOCK);

11     error = 0;
12     if ( (n = connect(sockfd, saptr, salen)) < 0)
13         if (errno != EINPROGRESS)
14             return (-1);

15     /* Do whatever we want while the connect is taking place. */

16     if (n == 0)
17         goto done;              /* connect completed immediately */

18     FD_ZERO(&rset);
19     FD_SET(sockfd, &rset);
20     wset = rset;
21     tval.tv_sec = nsec;
22     tval.tv_usec = 0;

23     if ( (n = Select(sockfd + 1, &rset, &wset, NULL,
24                   nsec ? &tval : NULL)) == 0) {
25         close(sockfd);          /* timeout */
26         errno = ETIMEDOUT;
27         return (-1);
28     }

29     if (FD_ISSET(sockfd, &rset) || FD_ISSET(sockfd, &wset)) {
30         len = sizeof(error);
31         if (getsockopt(sockfd, SOL_SOCKET, SO_ERROR, &error, &len) < 0)
32             return (-1);        /* Solaris pending error */
33     } else
34         err_quit("select error: sockfd not set");

35 done:
36     Fcntl(sockfd, F_SETFL, flags);  /* restore file status flags */

37     if (error) {
38         close(sockfd);          /* just in case */
39         errno = error;
40         return (-1);
41     }
42     return (0);
43 }
```

lib/connect_nonb.c

Figure 16.11 Issue a nonblocking connect.

Check for readability or writability

29-34   If the descriptor is readable or writable, we call `getsockopt` to fetch the socket's pending error (`SO_ERROR`). If the connection completed successfully, this value will be 0. If the connection encountered an error, this value is the `errno` value corresponding to the connection error (e.g., `ECONNREFUSED`, `ETIMEDOUT`, etc.). We also encounter our first portability problem. If an error occurred, Berkeley-derived implementations of `getsockopt` return 0 with the pending error returned in our variable `error`. But Solaris causes `getsockopt` itself to return –1 with `errno` set to the pending error. Our code handles both scenarios.

Turn off nonblocking and return

36-42   We restore the file status flags and return. If our `error` variable is nonzero from `getsockopt`, that value is stored in `errno` and the function returns –1.

As we said earlier, there are portability problems with various socket implementations and nonblocking connects. First, it is possible for a connection to complete and for data to arrive from a peer before `select` is called. In this case, the socket will be both readable and writable on success, the same as if the connection had failed. Our code in Figure 16.11 handles this scenario by calling `getsockopt` and checking the pending error for the socket.

Next is determining whether the connection completed successfully or not, if we cannot assume that writability is the only way success is returned. Various solutions have been posted to Usenet. These would replace our call to `getsockopt` in Figure 16.11.

1. Call `getpeername` instead of `getsockopt`. If this fails with `ENOTCONN`, the connection failed and we must then call `getsockopt` with `SO_ERROR` to fetch the pending error for the socket.

2. Call `read` with a length of 0. If the `read` fails, the `connect` failed and the `errno` from `read` indicates the reason for the connection failure. When a connection succeeds, `read` should return 0.

3. Call `connect` again. It should fail, and if the error is `EISCONN`, the socket is already connected and the first connection succeeded.

Unfortunately, nonblocking `connects` are one of the most nonportable areas of network programming. Be prepared for portability problems, especially with older implementations. A simpler technique is to create a thread (Chapter 26) to handle a connection.

Interrupted `connect`

What happens if our call to `connect` on a normal blocking socket is interrupted, say, by a caught signal, before TCP's three-way handshake completes? Assuming the `connect` is not automatically restarted, it returns `EINTR`. But, we cannot call `connect` again to wait for the connection to complete. Doing so will return `EADDRINUSE`.

What we must do in this scenario is call `select`, just as we have done in this section for a nonblocking `connect`. `select` returns when the connection completes successfully (making the socket writable) or when the connection fails (making the socket readable and writable).

16.5 Nonblocking `connect`: Web Client

A real-world example of nonblocking `connect`s started with the Netscape Web client (Section 13.4 of TCPv3). The client establishes an HTTP connection with a Web server and fetches a home page. Often, that page will have numerous references to other Web pages. Instead of fetching these other pages serially, one at a time, the client can fetch more than one at the same time using nonblocking `connect`s. Figure 16.12 shows an example of establishing multiple connections in parallel. The leftmost scenario shows all three connections performed serially. We assume that the first connection takes 10 units of time, the second 15, and the third 4, for a total of 29 units of time.

In the middle scenario, we perform two connections in parallel. At time 0, the first two connections are started, and when the first of these finishes, we start the third. The total time is almost halved, from 29 to 15, but realize that this is the ideal case. If the parallel connections are sharing a common link (say the client is behind a dialup modem link to the Internet), each can compete against each other for the limited resources and all the individual connection times might get longer. For example, the time of 10 might be 15, the time of 15 might be 20, and the time of 4 might be 6. Nevertheless, the total time would be 21, still shorter than the serial scenario.

In the third scenario, we perform three connections in parallel, and we again assume there is no interference between the three connections (the ideal case). But, the total time is the same (15 units) as the second scenario given the example times that we choose.

When dealing with Web clients, the first connection is done by itself, followed by multiple connections for the references found in the data from that first connection. We show this in Figure 16.13.

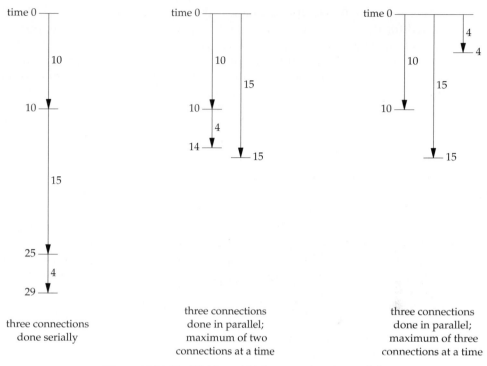

three connections
done serially

three connections
done in parallel;
maximum of two
connections at a time

three connections
done in parallel;
maximum of three
connections at a time

Figure 16.12 Establishing multiple connections in parallel.

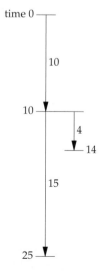

Figure 16.13 Complete first connection, then multiple connections in parallel.

To further optimize this sequence, the client can start parsing the data that is returned for the first connection before the first connection completes and initiate additional connections as soon as it knows that additional connections are needed.

Since we are doing multiple nonblocking connects at the same time, we cannot use our `connect_nonb` function from Figure 16.11 because it does not return until the connection is established. Instead, we must keep track of multiple connections ourself.

Our program will read up to 20 files from a Web server. We specify as command-line arguments the maximum number of parallel connections, the server's hostname, and each of the filenames to fetch from the server. A typical execution of our program is

```
solaris % web  3  www.foobar.com  /  image1.gif  image2.gif \
image3.gif  image4.gif  image5.gif \
image6.gif  image7.gif
```

The command-line arguments specify three simultaneous connections: the server's hostname, the filename for the home page (/, the server's root page), and seven files to then read (which in this example are all GIF images). These seven files would normally be referenced on the home page, and a Web client would read the home page and parse the HTML to obtain these filenames. We do not want to complicate this example with HTML parsing, so we just specify the filenames on the command line.

This is a larger example, so we will show it in pieces. Figure 16.14 is our `web.h` header that each file includes.

————————————————————————————— nonblock/web.h

```
 1 #include    "unp.h"

 2 #define MAXFILES     20
 3 #define SERV         "80"          /* port number or service name */

 4 struct file {
 5     char   *f_name;               /* filename */
 6     char   *f_host;               /* hostname or IPv4/IPv6 address */
 7     int     f_fd;                 /* descriptor */
 8     int     f_flags;              /* F_xxx below */
 9 } file[MAXFILES];

10 #define F_CONNECTING    1         /* connect() in progress */
11 #define F_READING       2         /* connect() complete; now reading */
12 #define F_DONE          4         /* all done */

13 #define GET_CMD     "GET %s HTTP/1.0\r\n\r\n"

14              /* globals */
15 int     nconn, nfiles, nlefttoconn, nlefttoread, maxfd;
16 fd_set  rset, wset;

17              /* function prototypes */
18 void    home_page(const char *, const char *);
19 void    start_connect(struct file *);
20 void    write_get_cmd(struct file *);
```
————————————————————————————— nonblock/web.h

Figure 16.14 `web.h` header.

Define `file` structure

2–13   The program reads up to MAXFILES files from the Web server. We maintain a `file` structure with information about each file: its name (copied from the command-line argument), the hostname or IP address of the server to read the file from, the socket descriptor being used for the file, and a set of flags to specify what we are doing with this file (connecting, reading, or done).

Define globals and function prototypes

14–20   We define the global variables and function prototypes for the functions that we will describe shortly.

Figure 16.15 shows the first part of the `main` program.

```
                                                        ─── nonblock/web.c
 1 #include     "web.h"

 2 int
 3 main(int argc, char **argv)
 4 {
 5     int     i, fd, n, maxnconn, flags, error;
 6     char    buf[MAXLINE];
 7     fd_set  rs, ws;

 8     if (argc < 5)
 9         err_quit("usage: web <#conns> <hostname> <homepage> <file1> ...");
10     maxnconn = atoi(argv[1]);

11     nfiles = min(argc - 4, MAXFILES);
12     for (i = 0; i < nfiles; i++) {
13         file[i].f_name = argv[i + 4];
14         file[i].f_host = argv[2];
15         file[i].f_flags = 0;
16     }
17     printf("nfiles = %d\n", nfiles);

18     home_page(argv[2], argv[3]);

19     FD_ZERO(&rset);
20     FD_ZERO(&wset);
21     maxfd = -1;
22     nlefttoread = nlefttoconn = nfiles;
23     nconn = 0;
                                                        ─── nonblock/web.c
```

Figure 16.15 First part of simultaneous connect: globals and start of main.

Process command-line arguments

11–17   The `file` structures are filled in with the relevant information from the command-line arguments.

Read home page

18   The function home_page, which we will show next, creates a TCP connection, sends a command to the server, and then reads the home page. This is the first connection, which is done by itself, before we start establishing multiple connections in parallel.

Initialize globals

19-23   Two descriptor sets, one for reading and one for writing, are initialized. `maxfd` is the maximum descriptor for `select` (which we initialize to –1 since descriptors are non-negative), `nlefttoread` is the number of files remaining to be read (when this reaches 0, we are finished), `nlefttoconn` is the number of files that still need a TCP connection, and `nconn` is the number of connections currently open (which can never exceed the first command-line argument).

Figure 16.16 shows the `home_page` function that is called once when the `main` function begins.

———————————————————————————————— *nonblock/home_page.c*
```
 1 #include    "web.h"

 2 void
 3 home_page(const char *host, const char *fname)
 4 {
 5     int     fd, n;
 6     char    line[MAXLINE];

 7     fd = Tcp_connect(host, SERV);    /* blocking connect() */

 8     n = snprintf(line, sizeof(line), GET_CMD, fname);
 9     Writen(fd, line, n);

10     for ( ; ; ) {
11         if ( (n = Read(fd, line, MAXLINE)) == 0)
12             break;                   /* server closed connection */

13         printf("read %d bytes of home page\n", n);
14         /* do whatever with data */
15     }
16     printf("end-of-file on home page\n");
17     Close(fd);
18 }
```
———————————————————————————————— *nonblock/home_page.c*

Figure 16.16 home_page function.

Establish connection with server

7   Our `tcp_connect` establishes a connection with the server.

Send HTTP command to server, read reply

8-17   An HTTP `GET` command is issued for the home page (often named /). The reply is read (we do not do anything with the reply) and the connection is closed.

The next function, `start_connect`, shown in Figure 16.17, initiates a nonblocking connect.

―――――――――――――――――――――――――――――――― *nonblock/start_connect.c*
```
 1 #include      "web.h"

 2 void
 3 start_connect(struct file *fptr)
 4 {
 5     int      fd, flags, n;
 6     struct addrinfo *ai;

 7     ai = Host_serv(fptr->f_host, SERV, 0, SOCK_STREAM);

 8     fd = Socket(ai->ai_family, ai->ai_socktype, ai->ai_protocol);
 9     fptr->f_fd = fd;
10     printf("start_connect for %s, fd %d\n", fptr->f_name, fd);

11         /* Set socket nonblocking */
12     flags = Fcntl(fd, F_GETFL, 0);
13     Fcntl(fd, F_SETFL, flags | O_NONBLOCK);

14         /* Initiate nonblocking connect to the server. */
15     if ( (n = connect(fd, ai->ai_addr, ai->ai_addrlen)) < 0) {
16         if (errno != EINPROGRESS)
17             err_sys("nonblocking connect error");
18         fptr->f_flags = F_CONNECTING;
19         FD_SET(fd, &rset);       /* select for reading and writing */
20         FD_SET(fd, &wset);
21         if (fd > maxfd)
22             maxfd = fd;

23     } else if (n >= 0)           /* connect is already done */
24         write_get_cmd(fptr);     /* write() the GET command */
25 }
```
―――――――――――――――――――――――――――――――― *nonblock/start_connect.c*

Figure 16.17 Initiate nonblocking connect.

Create socket, set to nonblocking

7–13   We call our `host_serv` function (Figure 11.9) to look up and convert the hostname and service name, returning a pointer to an array of `addrinfo` structures. We use only the first structure. A TCP socket is created and the socket is set to nonblocking.

Initiate nonblocking `connect`

14–22   The nonblocking `connect` is initiated and the file's flag is set to `F_CONNECTING`. The socket descriptor is turned on in both the read set and the write set since `select` will wait for either condition as an indication that the connection has finished. We also update `maxfd`, if necessary.

Handle connection complete

23–24   If `connect` returns successfully, the connection is already complete and the function `write_get_cmd` (shown next) sends a command to the server.

We set the socket to nonblocking for the connect, but never reset it to its default blocking mode. This is fine because we write only a small amount of data to the socket (the GET command in the next function) and we assume that this command is much smaller than the socket send buffer. Even if write returns a short count because of the nonblocking flag, our writen function handles this. Leaving the socket as nonblocking has no effect on the subsequent reads that are performed because we always call select to wait for the socket to become readable.

Figure 16.18 shows the function write_get_cmd, which sends an HTTP GET command to the server.

nonblock/write_get_cmd.c

```
 1 #include    "web.h"

 2 void
 3 write_get_cmd(struct file *fptr)
 4 {
 5     int     n;
 6     char    line[MAXLINE];

 7     n = snprintf(line, sizeof(line), GET_CMD, fptr->f_name);
 8     Writen(fptr->f_fd, line, n);
 9     printf("wrote %d bytes for %s\n", n, fptr->f_name);

10     fptr->f_flags = F_READING;   /* clears F_CONNECTING */

11     FD_SET(fptr->f_fd, &rset);   /* will read server's reply */
12     if (fptr->f_fd > maxfd)
13         maxfd = fptr->f_fd;
14 }
```

nonblock/write_get_cmd.c

Figure 16.18 Send an HTTP GET command to the server.

Build command and send it

7–9   The command is built and written to the socket.

Set flags

10–13   The file's F_READING flag is set, which also clears the F_CONNECTING flag (if set). This indicates to the main loop that this descriptor is ready for input. The descriptor is also turned on in the read set and maxfd is updated, if necessary.

We now return to the main function in Figure 16.19, picking up where we left off in Figure 16.15. This is the main loop of the program: As long as there are more files to process (nlefttoread is greater than 0), start another connection if possible and then use select on all active descriptors, handling both nonblocking connection completions and the arrival of data.

Initiate another connection, if possible

24–35   If we are not at the specified limit of simultaneous connections, and there are additional connections to establish, find a file that we have not yet processed (indicated by a f_flags of 0) and call start_connect to initiate the connection. The number of active connections is incremented (nconn) and the number of connections remaining to be established is decremented (nlefttoconn).

select: **wait for something to happen**

36-37   select waits for either readability or writability. Descriptors that have a non-blocking connect in progress will be enabled in both sets, while descriptors with a completed connection that are waiting for data from the server will be enabled in just the read set.

Handle all ready descriptors

39-55   We now process each element in the array of file structures to determine which descriptors need processing. If the F_CONNECTING flag is set and the descriptor is on in either the read set or the write set, the nonblocking connect is finished. As we described with Figure 16.11, we call getsockopt to fetch the pending error for the socket. If this value is 0, the connection completed successfully. In that case, we turn off the descriptor in the write set and call write_get_cmd to send the HTTP request to the server.

See if descriptor has data

56-67   If the F_READING flag is set and the descriptor is ready for reading, we call read. If the connection was closed by the other end, we close the socket, set the F_DONE flag, turn off the descriptor in the read set, and decrement the number of active connections and the total number of connections to be processed.

There are two optimizations that we do not perform in this example (to avoid complicating it even more). First, we could terminate the for loop in Figure 16.19 when we finish processing the number of descriptors that select said were ready. Next, we could decrease the value of maxfd when possible, to save select from examining descriptor bits that are no longer set. Since the number of descriptors this code deals with at any one time is probably less than 10, and not in the thousands, it is doubtful that either of these optimizations is worth the additional complications.

nonblock/web.c

```
24      while (nlefttoread > 0) {
25          while (nconn < maxnconn && nlefttoconn > 0) {
26                  /* find a file to read */
27              for (i = 0; i < nfiles; i++)
28                  if (file[i].f_flags == 0)
29                      break;
30              if (i == nfiles)
31                  err_quit("nlefttoconn = %d but nothing found", nlefttoconn);
32              start_connect(&file[i]);
33              nconn++;
34              nlefttoconn--;
35          }

36          rs = rset;
37          ws = wset;
38          n = Select(maxfd + 1, &rs, &ws, NULL, NULL);

39          for (i = 0; i < nfiles; i++) {
40              flags = file[i].f_flags;
41              if (flags == 0 || flags & F_DONE)
42                  continue;
43              fd = file[i].f_fd;
44              if (flags & F_CONNECTING &&
45                  (FD_ISSET(fd, &rs) || FD_ISSET(fd, &ws))) {
46                  n = sizeof(error);
47                  if (getsockopt(fd, SOL_SOCKET, SO_ERROR, &error, &n) < 0 ||
48                      error != 0) {
49                      err_ret("nonblocking connect failed for %s",
50                              file[i].f_name);
51                  }
52                      /* connection established */
53                  printf("connection established for %s\n", file[i].f_name);
54                  FD_CLR(fd, &wset);   /* no more writeability test */
55                  write_get_cmd(&file[i]);    /* write() the GET command */
56              } else if (flags & F_READING && FD_ISSET(fd, &rs)) {
57                  if ( (n = Read(fd, buf, sizeof(buf))) == 0) {
58                      printf("end-of-file on %s\n", file[i].f_name);
59                      Close(fd);
60                      file[i].f_flags = F_DONE;   /* clears F_READING */
61                      FD_CLR(fd, &rset);
62                      nconn--;
63                      nlefttoread--;
64                  } else {
65                      printf("read %d bytes from %s\n", n, file[i].f_name);
66                  }
67              }
68          }
69      }
70      exit(0);
71  }
```

nonblock/web.c

Figure 16.19 Main loop of main function.

Performance of Simultaneous Connections

What is the performance gain in establishing multiple connections at the same time? Figure 16.20 shows the clock time required to fetch a Web server's home page, followed by nine image files from that server. The RTT to the server is about 150 ms. The home page size was 4,017 bytes and the average size of the 9 image files was 1,621 bytes. TCP's segment size was 512 bytes. We also include in this figure, for comparison, values for a version of this program that we will develop in Section 26.9 using threads.

# simultaneous connections	Clock time (seconds), nonblocking	Clock time (seconds), threads
1	6.0	6.3
2	4.1	4.2
3	3.0	3.1
4	2.8	3.0
5	2.5	2.7
6	2.4	2.5
7	2.3	2.3
8	2.2	2.3
9	2.0	2.2

Figure 16.20 Clock time for various numbers of simultaneous connections.

Most of the improvement is obtained with three simultaneous connections (the clock time is halved), and the performance increase is much less with four or more simultaneous connections.

> We provide this example using simultaneous `connects` because it is a nice example using nonblocking I/O and one whose performance impact can be measured. It is also a feature used by a popular Web application, the Netscape browser. There are pitfalls in this technique if there is any congestion in the network. Chapter 21 of TCPv1 describes TCP's slow-start and congestion avoidance algorithms in detail. When multiple connections are established from a client to a server, there is no communication between the connections at the TCP layer. That is, if one connection encounters a packet loss, the other connections to the same server are not notified, and it is highly probable that the other connections will soon encounter packet loss unless they slow down. These additional connections are sending more packets into an already congested network. This technique also increases the load at any given time on the server.

16.6 Nonblocking `accept`

We stated in Chapter 6 that a listening socket is returned as readable by `select` when a completed connection is ready to be `accepted`. Therefore, if we are using `select` to wait for incoming connections, we should not need to set the listening socket to nonblocking because if `select` tells us that the connection is ready, `accept` should not block.

Unfortunately, there is a timing problem that can trip us up here [Gierth 1996]. To see this problem, we modify our TCP echo client (Figure 5.4) to establish the connection and then send an RST to the server. Figure 16.21 shows this new version.

nonblock/tcpcli03.c

```
 1 #include     "unp.h"

 2 int
 3 main(int argc, char **argv)
 4 {
 5     int      sockfd;
 6     struct linger ling;
 7     struct sockaddr_in servaddr;

 8     if (argc != 2)
 9         err_quit("usage: tcpcli <IPaddress>");

10     sockfd = Socket(AF_INET, SOCK_STREAM, 0);

11     bzero(&servaddr, sizeof(servaddr));
12     servaddr.sin_family = AF_INET;
13     servaddr.sin_port = htons(SERV_PORT);
14     Inet_pton(AF_INET, argv[1], &servaddr.sin_addr);

15     Connect(sockfd, (SA *) &servaddr, sizeof(servaddr));

16     ling.l_onoff = 1;              /* cause RST to be sent on close() */
17     ling.l_linger = 0;
18     Setsockopt(sockfd, SOL_SOCKET, SO_LINGER, &ling, sizeof(ling));
19     Close(sockfd);

20     exit(0);
21 }
```

nonblock/tcpcli03.c

Figure 16.21 TCP echo client that creates connection and sends an RST.

Set SO_LINGER socket option

16–19   Once the connection is established, we set the SO_LINGER socket option, setting the l_onoff flag to 1 and the l_linger time to 0. As stated in Section 7.5, this causes an RST to be sent on a TCP socket when the connection is closed. We then close the socket.

Next, we modify our TCP server from Figures 6.21 and 6.22 to pause after select returns that the listening socket is readable, but before calling accept. In the following code from the beginning of Figure 6.22, the two lines preceded by a plus sign are new:

```
      if (FD_ISSET(listenfd, &rset)) {    /* new client connection */
+         printf("listening socket readable\n");
+         sleep(5);
          clilen = sizeof(cliaddr);
          connfd = Accept(listenfd, (SA *) &cliaddr, &clilen);
```

What we are simulating here is a busy server that cannot call accept as soon as select returns that the listening socket is readable. Normally, this slowness on the part of the server is not a problem (indeed, this is why a queue of completed connections is maintained), but when combined with the RST from the client, after the connection is established, we can have a problem.

In Section 5.11, we noted that when the client aborts the connection before the server calls accept, Berkeley-derived implementations do not return the aborted connection to the server, while other implementations should return ECONNABORTED but often return EPROTO instead. Consider the following example of a Berkeley-derived implementation:

- The client establishes the connection and then aborts it as in Figure 16.21.

- select returns readable to the server process, but it takes the server a short time to call accept.

- Between the server's return from select and its calling accept, the RST is received from the client.

- The completed connection is removed from the queue and we assume that no other completed connections exist.

- The server calls accept, but since there are no completed connections, it blocks.

The server will remain blocked in the call to accept until some other client establishes a connection. But in the meantime, assuming a server like Figure 6.22, the server is blocked in the call to accept and will not handle any other ready descriptors.

> This problem is somewhat similar to the denial-of-service attack described in Section 6.8, but with this new bug, the server breaks out of the blocked accept as soon as another client establishes a connection.

The fix for this problem is as follows:

1. Always set a listening socket to nonblocking when you use select to indicate when a connection is ready to be accepted.

2. Ignore the following errors on the subsequent call to accept: EWOULDBLOCK (for Berkeley-derived implementations, when the client aborts the connection), ECONNABORTED (for POSIX implementations, when the client aborts the connection), EPROTO (for SVR4 implementations, when the client aborts the connection), and EINTR (if signals are being caught).

16.7 Summary

Our example of nonblocking reads and writes in Section 16.2 took our str_cli echo client and modified it to use nonblocking I/O on the TCP connection to the server. select is normally used with nonblocking I/O to determine when a descriptor is readable or writable. This version of our client is the fastest version that we show, although the code modifications are nontrivial. We then showed that it is simpler to divide the client into two pieces using `fork`; we will employ the same technique using threads in Figure 26.2.

Nonblocking connects let us do other processing while TCP's three-way hand shake takes place, instead of being blocked in the call to `connect`. Unfortunately, these are also nonportable, with different implementations having different ways of indicating that the connection completed successfully or encountered an error. We used non-blocking connects to develop a new client, which is similar to a Web client that opens multiple TCP connections at the same time to reduce the clock time required to fetch numerous files from a server. Initiating multiple connections like this can reduce the clock time, but is also "network-unfriendly" with regard to TCP's congestion avoidance.

Exercises

16.1 In our discussion of Figure 16.10, we mentioned that the parent must call `shutdown`, not `close`. Why?

16.2 What happens in Figure 16.10 if the server process terminates prematurely, plus the child receives the EOF and terminates, but the child does not notify the parent?

16.3 What happens in Figure 16.10 if the parent dies unexpectedly before the child, and the child then reads an EOF on the socket?

16.4 What happens in Figure 16.11 if we remove the two lines

```
if (n == 0)
    goto done;          /* connect completed immediately */
```

16.5 In Section 16.3 we said that it is possible for data to arrive for a socket before `connect` returns. How can this happen?

17

`ioctl` *Operations*

17.1 Introduction

The `ioctl` function has traditionally been the system interface used for everything that didn't fit into some other nicely defined category. POSIX is getting rid of `ioctl` for certain functionality by creating specific wrapper functions to replace `ioctl`s whose functionality is being standardized by POSIX. For example, the Unix terminal interface was traditionally accessed using `ioctl`, but POSIX created 12 new functions for terminals: `tcgetattr` to get the terminal attributes, `tcflush` to flush pending input or output, and so on. In a similar vein, POSIX has replaced one network `ioctl`: the new `sockatmark` function (Section 24.3) replaces the `SIOCATMARK` `ioctl`. Nevertheless, numerous `ioctl`s remain for implementation-dependent features related to network programming: obtaining interface information and accessing the routing table and ARP cache, for example.

This chapter provides an overview of the `ioctl` requests related to network programming, but many of these are implementation-dependent. Additionally, some implementations, including 4.4BSD-derived systems and Solaris 2.6 and later, use sockets in the `AF_ROUTE` domain (routing sockets) to accomplish many of these operations. We will cover routing sockets in Chapter 18.

A common use of `ioctl` by network programs (typically servers) is to obtain information on all the host's interfaces when the program starts: the interface addresses, whether the interface supports broadcasting, whether the interface supports multicasting, and so on. We will develop our own function to return this information and provide an implementation using `ioctl` in this chapter, and examine another implementation using routing sockets in Chapter 18.

17.2   `ioctl` **Function**

This function affects an open file referenced by the *fd* argument.

```
#include <unistd.h>

int ioctl(int fd, int request, ... /* void *arg */ );
```
                                                         Returns: 0 if OK, −1 on error

The third argument is always a pointer, but the type of pointer depends on the *request*.

> 4.4BSD defines the second argument to be an `unsigned long` instead of an `int`, but that is not a problem since header files define the constants that are used for this argument. As long as the prototype is in scope (i.e., the program using `ioctl` has included `<unistd.h>`), the correct type for the system will be used.

> Some implementations specify the third argument as a `void *` pointer instead of the ANSI C ellipsis notation.

> There is no standard for the header to include to define the function prototype for `ioctl` since it is not standardized by POSIX. Many systems define it in `<unistd.h>`, as we show, but traditional BSD systems define it in `<sys/ioctl.h>`.

We can divide the *request*s related to networking into six categories:

- Socket operations
- File operations
- Interface operations
- ARP cache operations
- Routing table operations
- STREAMS system (Chapter 31)

Recall from Figure 7.20 that not only do some of the `ioctl` operations overlap some of the `fcntl` operations (e.g., setting a socket to nonblocking), but there are also some operations that can be specified more than one way using `ioctl` (e.g., setting the process group ownership of a socket).

Figure 17.1 lists the *request*s, along with the datatype of what the *arg* address must point to. The following sections describe these requests in more detail.

17.3   **Socket Operations**

Three `ioctl` requests are explicitly used for sockets (pp. 551–553 of TCPv2). All three require that the third argument to `ioctl` be a pointer to an integer.

SIOCATMARK   Return through the integer pointed to by the third argument a nonzero value if the socket's read pointer is currently at the out-of-band mark, or a zero value if the read pointer is not at the out-of-band mark. We

Category	request	Description	Datatype
Socket	SIOCATMARK	At out-of-band mark ?	int
	SIOCSPGRP	Set process ID or process group ID of socket	int
	SIOCGPGRP	Get process ID or process group ID of socket	int
File	FIONBIO	Set/clear nonblocking flag	int
	FIOASYNC	Set/clear asynchronous I/O flag	int
	FIONREAD	Get # bytes in receive buffer	int
	FIOSETOWN	Set process ID or process group ID of file	int
	FIOGETOWN	Get process ID or process group ID of file	int
Interface	SIOCGIFCONF	Get list of all interfaces	struct ifconf
	SIOCSIFADDR	Set interface address	struct ifreq
	SIOCGIFADDR	Get interface address	struct ifreq
	SIOCSIFFLAGS	Set interface flags	struct ifreq
	SIOCGIFFLAGS	Get interface flags	struct ifreq
	SIOCSIFDSTADDR	Set point-to-point address	struct ifreq
	SIOCGIFDSTADDR	Get point-to-point address	struct ifreq
	SIOCGIFBRDADDR	Get broadcast address	struct ifreq
	SIOCSIFBRDADDR	Set broadcast address	struct ifreq
	SIOCGIFNETMASK	Get subnet mask	struct ifreq
	SIOCSIFNETMASK	Set subnet mask	struct ifreq
	SIOCGIFMETRIC	Get interface metric	struct ifreq
	SIOCSIFMETRIC	Set interface metric	struct ifreq
	SIOCGIFMTU	Get interface MTU	struct ifreq
	SIOC*xxx*	(many more; implementation-dependent)	
ARP	SIOCSARP	Create/modify ARP entry	struct arpreq
	SIOCGARP	Get ARP entry	struct arpreq
	SIOCDARP	Delete ARP entry	struct arpreq
Routing	SIOCADDRT	Add route	struct rtentry
	SIOCDELRT	Delete route	struct rtentry
STREAMS	I_*xxx*	(see Section 31.5)	

Figure 17.1 Summary of networking ioctl requests.

will describe out-of-band data in more detail in Chapter 24. POSIX replaces this request with the sockatmark function, and we will show an implementation of this new function using ioctl in Section 24.3.

SIOCGPGRP   Return through the integer pointed to by the third argument either the process ID or the process group ID that is set to receive the SIGIO or SIGURG signal for this socket. This request is identical to an fcntl of F_GETOWN, and we note in Figure 7.20 that POSIX standardizes the fcntl.

SIOCSPGRP   Set either the process ID or process group ID to receive the SIGIO or SIGURG signal for this socket from the integer pointed to by the third argument. This request is identical to an fcntl of F_SETOWN, and we note in Figure 7.20 that POSIX standardizes the fcntl.

17.4 File Operations

The next group of requests begin with `FIO` and may apply to certain types of files, in addition to sockets. We cover only the requests that apply to sockets (p. 553 of TCPv2). The following five requests all require that the third argument to `ioctl` point to an integer:

FIONBIO The nonblocking flag for the socket is cleared or turned on, depending on whether the third argument to `ioctl` points to a zero or nonzero value, respectively. This request has the same effect as the `O_NONBLOCK` file status flag, which can be set and cleared with the `F_SETFL` command to the `fcntl` function.

FIOASYNC The flag that governs the receipt of asynchronous I/O signals (`SIGIO`) for the socket is cleared or turned on, depending on whether the third argument to `ioctl` points to a zero or nonzero value, respectively. This flag has the same effect as the `O_ASYNC` file status flag, which can be set and cleared with the `F_SETFL` command to the `fcntl` function.

FIONREAD Return in the integer pointed to by the third argument to `ioctl` the number of bytes currently in the socket receive buffer. This feature also works for files, pipes, and terminals. We said more about this request in Section 14.7.

FIOSETOWN Equivalent to `SIOCSPGRP` for a socket.

FIOGETOWN Equivalent to `SIOCGPGRP` for a socket.

17.5 Interface Configuration

One of the first steps employed by many programs that deal with the network interfaces on a system is to obtain from the kernel all the interfaces configured on the system. This is done with the `SIOCGIFCONF` request, which uses the `ifconf` structure, which in turn uses the `ifreq` structure, both of which are shown in Figure 17.2.

Before calling `ioctl`, we allocate a buffer and an `ifconf` structure and then initialize the latter. We show a picture of this in Figure 17.3 (p. 470), assuming our buffer size is 1,024 bytes. The third argument to `ioctl` is a pointer to our `ifconf` structure.

If we assume that the kernel returns two `ifreq` structures, we could have the arrangement shown in Figure 17.4 (p. 470) when the `ioctl` returns. The shaded regions have been modified by `ioctl`. The buffer has been filled in with the two structures and the `ifc_len` member of the `ifconf` structure has been updated to reflect the amount of information stored in the buffer. We assume in this figure that each `ifreq` structure occupies 32 bytes.

A pointer to an `ifreq` structure is also used as an argument to the remaining interface `ioctl`s shown in Figure 17.1, which we will describe in Section 17.7. Notice that each `ifreq` structure contains a `union` and there are numerous #defines to hide the fact that these fields are members of a `union`. All references to individual members are

```
                                                                          ─── <net/if.h>
struct ifconf {
    int  ifc_len;                     /* size of buffer, value-result */
    union {
        caddr_t ifcu_buf;             /* input from user -> kernel */
        struct  ifreq *ifcu_req;      /* return from kernel -> user */
    } ifc_ifcu;
};
#define  ifc_buf  ifc_ifcu.ifcu_buf /* buffer address */
#define  ifc_req  ifc_ifcu.ifcu_req /* array of structures returned */

#define  IFNAMSIZ    16

struct ifreq {
    char    ifr_name[IFNAMSIZ];       /* interface name, e.g., "le0" */
    union {
        struct  sockaddr ifru_addr;
        struct  sockaddr ifru_dstaddr;
        struct  sockaddr ifru_broadaddr;
        short   ifru_flags;
        int     ifru_metric;
        caddr_t ifru_data;
    } ifr_ifru;
};
#define  ifr_addr       ifr_ifru.ifru_addr       /* address */
#define  ifr_dstaddr    ifr_ifru.ifru_dstaddr    /* other end of point-to-point link */
#define  ifr_broadaddr  ifr_ifru.ifru_broadaddr /* broadcast address */
#define  ifr_flags      ifr_ifru.ifru_flags      /* flags */
#define  ifr_metric     ifr_ifru.ifru_metric     /* metric */
#define  ifr_data       ifr_ifru.ifru_data       /* for use by interface */
                                                                          ─── <net/if.h>
```

Figure 17.2 ifconf and ifreq structures used with various interface ioctl requests.

made using defined names. Be aware that some systems have added many implementation-dependent members to the ifr_ifru union.

17.6 get_ifi_info **Function**

Since many programs need to know all the interfaces on a system, we will develop a function of our own named get_ifi_info that returns a linked list of structures, one for each interface that is currently "up." In this section, we will implement this function using the SIOCGIFCONF ioctl, and in Chapter 18, we will develop a version using routing sockets.

> FreeBSD provides a function named getifaddrs with similar functionality.

> Searching the entire FreeBSD 4.8 source tree shows that 12 programs issue the SIOCGIFCONF ioctl to determine the interfaces present.

We first define the ifi_info structure in a new header named unpifi.h, shown in Figure 17.5.

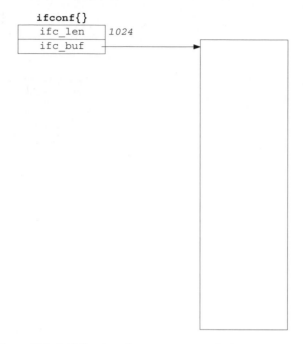

Figure 17.3   Initialization of ifconf structure before SIOCGIFCONF.

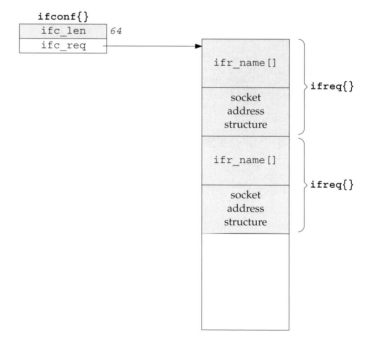

Figure 17.4   Values returned by SIOCGIFCONF.

———————————————————————————————— lib/unpifi.h
```
 1 /* Our own header for the programs that need interface configuration info.
 2    Include this file, instead of "unp.h". */

 3 #ifndef __unp_ifi_h
 4 #define __unp_ifi_h

 5 #include    "unp.h"
 6 #include    <net/if.h>

 7 #define IFI_NAME    16          /* same as IFNAMSIZ in <net/if.h> */
 8 #define IFI_HADDR    8          /* allow for 64-bit EUI-64 in future */

 9 struct ifi_info {
10     char    ifi_name[IFI_NAME]; /* interface name, null-terminated */
11     short   ifi_index;          /* interface index */
12     short   ifi_mtu;            /* interface MTU */
13     u_char  ifi_haddr[IFI_HADDR];  /* hardware address */
14     u_short ifi_hlen;           /* # bytes in hardware address: 0, 6, 8 */
15     short   ifi_flags;          /* IFF_xxx constants from <net/if.h> */
16     short   ifi_myflags;        /* our own IFI_xxx flags */
17     struct sockaddr *ifi_addr;  /* primary address */
18     struct sockaddr *ifi_brdaddr;   /* broadcast address */
19     struct sockaddr *ifi_dstaddr;   /* destination address */
20     struct ifi_info *ifi_next;  /* next of these structures */
21 };

22 #define IFI_ALIAS    1          /* ifi_addr is an alias */

23                     /* function prototypes */
24 struct ifi_info *get_ifi_info(int, int);
25 struct ifi_info *Get_ifi_info(int, int);
26 void    free_ifi_info(struct ifi_info *);

27 #endif  /* __unp_ifi_h */
```
———————————————————————————————— lib/unpifi.h

Figure 17.5 unpifi.h header.

9–21   A linked list of these structures is returned by our function, each structure's
ifi_next member pointing to the next one. We return in this structure just the information that a typical application is probably interested in: the interface name, the interface index, the MTU, the hardware address (e.g., an Ethernet address), the interface
flags (to let the application determine if the interface supports broadcasting or multicasting, or is a point-to-point interface), the interface address, the broadcast address,
and the destination address for a point-to-point link. All the memory used to hold the
ifi_info structures, along with the socket address structures contained within, are
obtained dynamically. Therefore, we also provide a free_ifi_info function to free
all this memory.

Before showing the implementation of our get_ifi_info function, we show a
simple program that calls this function and then outputs all the information. This program is a miniature version of the ifconfig program and is shown in Figure 17.6.

————————————————————————————————————— ioctl/prifinfo.c

```
 1 #include    "unpifi.h"

 2 int
 3 main(int argc, char **argv)
 4 {
 5     struct ifi_info *ifi, *ifihead;
 6     struct sockaddr *sa;
 7     u_char *ptr;
 8     int     i, family, doaliases;
 9     if (argc != 3)
10         err_quit("usage: prifinfo <inet4|inet6> <doaliases>");
11     if (strcmp(argv[1], "inet4") == 0)
12         family = AF_INET;
13     else if (strcmp(argv[1], "inet6") == 0)
14         family = AF_INET6;
15     else
16         err_quit("invalid <address-family>");
17     doaliases = atoi(argv[2]);
18     for (ifihead = ifi = Get_ifi_info(family, doaliases);
19          ifi != NULL; ifi = ifi->ifi_next) {
20         printf("%s: ", ifi->ifi_name);
21         if (ifi->ifi_index != 0)
22             printf("(%d) ", ifi->ifi_index);
23         printf("<");
24         if (ifi->ifi_flags & IFF_UP)           printf("UP ");
25         if (ifi->ifi_flags & IFF_BROADCAST)    printf("BCAST ");
26         if (ifi->ifi_flags & IFF_MULTICAST)    printf("MCAST ");
27         if (ifi->ifi_flags & IFF_LOOPBACK)     printf("LOOP ");
28         if (ifi->ifi_flags & IFF_POINTOPOINT)  printf("P2P ");
29         printf(">\n");
30         if ( (i = ifi->ifi_hlen) > 0) {
31             ptr = ifi->ifi_haddr;
32             do {
33                 printf("%s%x", (i == ifi->ifi_hlen) ? "  " : ":", *ptr++);
34             } while (--i > 0);
35             printf("\n");
36         }
37         if (ifi->ifi_mtu != 0)
38             printf("  MTU: %d\n", ifi->ifi_mtu);
39         if ( (sa = ifi->ifi_addr) != NULL)
40             printf("  IP addr: %s\n", Sock_ntop_host(sa, sizeof(*sa)));
41         if ( (sa = ifi->ifi_brdaddr) != NULL)
42             printf("  broadcast addr: %s\n",
43                     Sock_ntop_host(sa, sizeof(*sa)));
44         if ( (sa = ifi->ifi_dstaddr) != NULL)
45             printf("  destination addr: %s\n",
46                     Sock_ntop_host(sa, sizeof(*sa)));
47     }
48     free_ifi_info(ifihead);
49     exit(0);
50 }
```

————————————————————————————————————— ioctl/prifinfo.c

Figure 17.6 prifinfo program that calls our get_ifi_info function.

18-47   The program is a `for` loop that calls `get_ifi_info` once and then steps through
all the `ifi_info` structures that are returned.

20-36   The interface name, index, and flags are all printed. If the length of the hardware
address is greater than 0, it is printed as hexadecimal numbers. (Our `get_ifi_info`
function returns an `ifi_hlen` of 0 if it is not available.)

37-46   The MTU and three IP addresses are printed, if returned.

If we run this program on our host `macosx` (Figure 1.16), we have the following
output:

```
macosx % prifinfo inet4 0
lo0: <UP MCAST LOOP >
   MTU: 16384
   IP addr: 127.0.0.1
en1: <UP BCAST MCAST >
   MTU: 1500
   IP addr: 172.24.37.78
   broadcast addr: 172.24.37.95
```

The first command-line argument of `inet4` specifies IPv4 addresses, and the second
argument of 0 specifies that no address aliases are to be returned (we will describe IP
address aliases in Section A.4). Note that under MacOS X, the hardware address of the
Ethernet interface is not available using this method.

If we add three alias addresses to the Ethernet interface (`en1`) with host IDs of 79,
80, and 81, and if we change the second command-line argument to 1, we have the following:

```
macosx % prifinfo inet4 1
lo0: <UP MCAST LOOP >
   MTU: 16384
   IP addr: 127.0.0.1
en1: <UP BCAST MCAST >
   MTU: 1500
   IP addr: 172.24.37.78            primary IP address
   broadcast addr: 172.24.37.95
en1: <UP BCAST MCAST >
   MTU: 1500
   IP addr: 172.24.37.79            first alias
   broadcast addr: 172.24.37.95
en1: <UP BCAST MCAST >
   MTU: 1500
   IP addr: 172.24.37.80            second alias
   broadcast addr: 172.24.37.95
en1: <UP BCAST MCAST >
   MTU: 1500
   IP addr: 172.24.37.81            third alias
   broadcast addr: 172.24.37.95
```

If we run the same program under FreeBSD using the implementation of
`get_ifi_info` from Figure 18.16 (which can easily obtain the hardware address), we
have the following:

```
freebsd4 % prifinfo inet4 1
de0: <UP BCAST MCAST >
   0:80:c8:2b:d9:28
   IP addr: 135.197.17.100
   broadcast addr: 135.197.17.255
```

```
del: <UP BCAST MCAST >
  0:40:5:42:d6:de
  IP addr: 172.24.37.94              primary address
  broadcast addr: 172.24.37.95
del: <UP BCAST MCAST >
  0:40:5:42:d6:de
  IP addr: 172.24.37.93              alias
  broadcast addr: 172.24.37.93
lo0: <UP MCAST LOOP >
  IP addr: 127.0.0.1
```

For this example, we directed the program to print the aliases and we see that one alias is defined for the second Ethernet interface (del) with a host ID of 93.

We now show our implementation of get_ifi_info that uses the SIOCGIFCONF ioctl. Figure 17.7 shows the first part of the function, which obtains the interface configuration from the kernel.

lib/get_ifi_info.c

```
 1 #include      "unpifi.h"
 2 struct ifi_info *
 3 get_ifi_info(int family, int doaliases)
 4 {
 5     struct ifi_info *ifi, *ifihead, **ifipnext;
 6     int     sockfd, len, lastlen, flags, myflags, idx = 0, hlen = 0;
 7     char    *ptr, *buf, lastname[IFNAMSIZ], *cptr, *haddr, *sdlname;
 8     struct ifconf ifc;
 9     struct ifreq *ifr, ifrcopy;
10     struct sockaddr_in *sinptr;
11     struct sockaddr_in6 *sin6ptr;
12     sockfd = Socket(AF_INET, SOCK_DGRAM, 0);
13     lastlen = 0;
14     len = 100 * sizeof(struct ifreq);   /* initial buffer size guess */
15     for ( ; ; ) {
16         buf = Malloc(len);
17         ifc.ifc_len = len;
18         ifc.ifc_buf = buf;
19         if (ioctl(sockfd, SIOCGIFCONF, &ifc) < 0) {
20             if (errno != EINVAL || lastlen != 0)
21                 err_sys("ioctl error");
22         } else {
23             if (ifc.ifc_len == lastlen)
24                 break;             /* success, len has not changed */
25             lastlen = ifc.ifc_len;
26         }
27         len += 10 * sizeof(struct ifreq);   /* increment */
28         free(buf);
29     }
30     ifihead = NULL;
31     ifipnext = &ifihead;
32     lastname[0] = 0;
33     sdlname = NULL;
```

lib/get_ifi_info.c

Figure 17.7 Issue SIOCGIFCONF request to obtain interface configuration.

Create Internet socket

11   We create a UDP socket that will be used with `ioctl`s. Either a TCP or a UDP socket can be used (p. 163 of TCPv2).

Issue `SIOCGIFCONF` request in a loop

12-28   A fundamental problem with the `SIOCGIFCONF` request is that some implementations do not return an error if the buffer is not large enough to hold the result. Instead, the result is truncated and success is returned (a return value of 0 from `ioctl`). This means the only way we know that our buffer is large enough is to issue the request, save the return length, issue the request again with a larger buffer, and compare the length with the saved value. Only if the two lengths are the same is our buffer large enough.

> Berkeley-derived implementations do not return an error if the buffer is too small (pp. 118–119 of TCPv2); the result is just truncated to fit the available buffer. Solaris 2.5, on the other hand, returns `EINVAL` if the returned length would be greater than or equal to the buffer length. But, we cannot assume success if the returned length is less than the buffer size because Berkeley-derived implementations can return less than the buffer size if another structure does not fit.

> Some implementations provide a `SIOCGIFNUM` request that returns the number of interfaces. This allows the application to then allocate a buffer of sufficient size before issuing the `SIOCGIFCONF` request, but this new request is not widespread.

> Allocating a fixed-sized buffer for the result from the `SIOCGIFCONF` request has become a problem with the growth of the Web, because large Web servers are allocating many alias addresses to a single interface. Solaris 2.5, for example, had a limit of 256 aliases per interface, but this limit increases to 8,192 with 2.6. Sites with numerous aliases discovered that programs with fixed-size buffers for interface information started failing. Even though Solaris returns an error if a buffer is too small, these programs allocate their fixed-size buffer, issue the `ioctl`, but then die if an error is returned.

12-15   We dynamically allocate a buffer, starting with room for 100 `ifreq` structures. We also keep track of the length returned by the last `SIOCGIFCONF` request in `lastlen` and initialize this to 0.

19-20   If an error of `EINVAL` is returned by `ioctl`, and we have not yet had a successful return (i.e., `lastlen` is still 0), we have not yet allocated a buffer large enough and continue through the loop.

22-23   If `ioctl` returns success, and if the returned length equals `lastlen`, the length has not changed (our buffer is large enough) and we `break` out of the loop since we have all the information.

26-27   Each time around the loop, we increase the buffer size to hold 10 more `ifreq` structures.

Initialize linked list pointers

29-31   Since we will be returning a pointer to the head of a linked list of `ifi_info` structures, we use the two variables `ifihead` and `ifipnext` to hold pointers to the list as we build it.

The next part of our get_ifi_info function, the beginning of the main loop, is shown in Figure 17.8.

lib/get_ifi_info.c
```
34      for (ptr = buf; ptr < buf + ifc.ifc_len;) {
35          ifr = (struct ifreq *) ptr;

36 #ifdef  HAVE_SOCKADDR_SA_LEN
37          len = max(sizeof(struct sockaddr), ifr->ifr_addr.sa_len);
38 #else
39          switch (ifr->ifr_addr.sa_family) {
40 #ifdef  IPV6
41          case AF_INET6:
42              len = sizeof(struct sockaddr_in6);
43              break;
44 #endif
45          case AF_INET:
46          default:
47              len = sizeof(struct sockaddr);
48              break;
49          }
50 #endif  /* HAVE_SOCKADDR_SA_LEN */
51          ptr += sizeof(ifr->ifr_name) + len; /* for next one in buffer */

52 #ifdef  HAVE_SOCKADDR_DL_STRUCT
53          /* assumes that AF_LINK precedes AF_INET or AF_INET6 */
54          if (ifr->ifr_addr.sa_family == AF_LINK) {
55              struct sockaddr_dl *sdl = (struct sockaddr_dl *) &ifr->ifr_addr;
56              sdlname = ifr->ifr_name;
57              idx = sdl->sdl_index;
58              haddr = sdl->sdl_data + sdl->sdl_nlen;
59              hlen = sdl->sdl_alen;
60          }
61 #endif

62          if (ifr->ifr_addr.sa_family != family)
63              continue;            /* ignore if not desired address family */

64          myflags = 0;
65          if ( (cptr = strchr(ifr->ifr_name, ':')) != NULL)
66              *cptr = 0;          /* replace colon with null */
67          if (strncmp(lastname, ifr->ifr_name, IFNAMSIZ) == 0) {
68              if (doaliases == 0)
69                  continue;       /* already processed this interface */
70              myflags = IFI_ALIAS;
71          }
72          memcpy(lastname, ifr->ifr_name, IFNAMSIZ);

73          ifrcopy = *ifr;
74          Ioctl(sockfd, SIOCGIFFLAGS, &ifrcopy);
75          flags = ifrcopy.ifr_flags;
76          if ((flags & IFF_UP) == 0)
77              continue;            /* ignore if interface not up */
```
lib/get_ifi_info.c

Figure 17.8 Process interface configuration.

Step to next socket address structure

35–51   As we loop through all the `ifreq` structures, `ifr` points to each structure and we then increment `ptr` to point to the next one. But, we must deal with newer systems that provide a length field for socket address structures and older systems that do not provide this length. Even though the declaration in Figure 17.2 declares the socket address structure contained within the `ifreq` structure as a generic socket address structure, on newer systems, this can be any type of socket address structure. Indeed, on 4.4BSD, a datalink socket address structure is also returned for each interface (p. 118 of TCPv2). Therefore, if the length member is supported, we must use its value to update our pointer to the next socket address structure. Otherwise, we use a length based on the address family, using the size of the generic socket address structure (16 bytes) as the default.

> We put in a `case` for IPv6, for newer systems, just in case. The problem is that the `union` in the `ifreq` structure defines the returned addresses as generic 16-byte `sockaddr` structures, which are adequate for 16-byte IPv4 `sockaddr_in` structures, but too small for 28-byte IPv6 `sockaddr_in6` structures. This is not a problem on systems that have the `sa_len` field in the `sockaddr` since they can indicate variable-sized `sockaddr` structures easily.

Handle `AF_LINK`

52–60   If the system is one that returns `AF_LINK` sockaddrs in `SIOCGIFCONF`, copy the interface index and the hardware address information from the `AF_LINK sockaddr`.

62–63   We ignore any addresses from families except those desired by the caller.

Handle aliases

64–72   We must detect any aliases that may exist for the interface, that is, additional addresses that have been assigned to the interface. Note from our examples following Figure 17.6 that under Solaris, the interface name for an alias contains a colon, while under 4.4BSD, the interface name does not change for an alias. To handle both cases, we save the last interface name in `lastname` and only compare up to a colon, if present. If a colon is not present, we still ignore this interface if the name is equivalent to the last interface we processed.

Fetch interface flags

73–77   We issue an `ioctl` of `SIOCGIFFLAGS` (Section 17.5) to fetch the interface flags. The third argument to `ioctl` is a pointer to an `ifreq` structure that must contain the name of the interface for which we want the flags. We make a copy of the `ifreq` structure before issuing the `ioctl`, because if we didn't, this request would overwrite the IP address of the interface since both are members of the same `union` in Figure 17.2. If the interface is not up, we ignore it.

Figure 17.9 contains the third part of our function.

```
                                                                ── lib/get_ifi_info.c
78          ifi = Calloc(1, sizeof(struct ifi_info));
79          *ifipnext = ifi;          /* prev points to this new one */
80          ifipnext = &ifi->ifi_next;  /* pointer to next one goes here */

81          ifi->ifi_flags = flags; /* IFF_xxx values */
82          ifi->ifi_myflags = myflags; /* IFI_xxx values */
83 #if defined(SIOCGIFMTU) && defined(HAVE_STRUCT_IFREQ_IFR_MTU)
84          Ioctl(sockfd, SIOCGIFMTU, &ifrcopy);
85          ifi->ifi_mtu = ifrcopy.ifr_mtu;
86 #else
87          ifi->ifi_mtu = 0;
88 #endif
89          memcpy(ifi->ifi_name, ifr->ifr_name, IFI_NAME);
90          ifi->ifi_name[IFI_NAME - 1] = '\0';
91          /* If the sockaddr_dl is from a different interface, ignore it */
92          if (sdlname == NULL || strcmp(sdlname, ifr->ifr_name) != 0)
93              idx = hlen = 0;
94          ifi->ifi_index = idx;
95          ifi->ifi_hlen = hlen;
96          if (ifi->ifi_hlen > IFI_HADDR)
97              ifi->ifi_hlen = IFI_HADDR;
98          if (hlen)
99              memcpy(ifi->ifi_haddr, haddr, ifi->ifi_hlen);
                                                                ── lib/get_ifi_info.c
```

Figure 17.9 Allocate and initialize ifi_info structure.

Allocate and initialize ifi_info structure

78–99   At this point, we know that we will return this interface to the caller. We allocate memory for our ifi_info structure and add it to the end of the linked list we are building. We copy the interface flags, MTU, and name into the structure. We make certain that the interface name is null-terminated, and since calloc initializes the allocated region to all zero bits, we know that ifi_hlen is initialized to 0 and that ifi_next is initialized to a null pointer. We copy the saved interface index and hardware length; if the length is nonzero, we also copy the saved hardware address.

Figure 17.10 contains the last part of our function.

102–104   We copy the IP address that was returned from our original SIOCGIFCONF request in the structure we are building.

106–119   If the interface supports broadcasting, we fetch the broadcast address with an ioctl of SIOCGIFBRDADDR. We allocate memory for the socket address structure containing this address and add it to the ifi_info structure we are building. Similarly, if the interface is a point-to-point interface, the SIOCGIFDSTADDR returns the IP address of the other end of the link.

123–133   This is the IPv6 case; it is exactly the same as for IPv4 except that there is no call to SIOCGIFBRDADDR because IPv6 does not support broadcasting.

Figure 17.11 shows the free_ifi_info function, which takes a pointer that was returned by get_ifi_info and frees all the dynamic memory.

```
                                                            ——— lib/get_ifi_info.c
100         switch (ifr->ifr_addr.sa_family) {
101         case AF_INET:
102             sinptr = (struct sockaddr_in *) &ifr->ifr_addr;
103             ifi->ifi_addr = Calloc(1, sizeof(struct sockaddr_in));
104             memcpy(ifi->ifi_addr, sinptr, sizeof(struct sockaddr_in));
105 #ifdef   SIOCGIFBRDADDR
106             if (flags & IFF_BROADCAST) {
107                 Ioctl(sockfd, SIOCGIFBRDADDR, &ifrcopy);
108                 sinptr = (struct sockaddr_in *) &ifrcopy.ifr_broadaddr;
109                 ifi->ifi_brdaddr = Calloc(1, sizeof(struct sockaddr_in));
110                 memcpy(ifi->ifi_brdaddr, sinptr, sizeof(struct sockaddr_in));
111             }
112 #endif
113 #ifdef   SIOCGIFDSTADDR
114             if (flags & IFF_POINTOPOINT) {
115                 Ioctl(sockfd, SIOCGIFDSTADDR, &ifrcopy);
116                 sinptr = (struct sockaddr_in *) &ifrcopy.ifr_dstaddr;
117                 ifi->ifi_dstaddr = Calloc(1, sizeof(struct sockaddr_in));
118                 memcpy(ifi->ifi_dstaddr, sinptr, sizeof(struct sockaddr_in));
119             }
120 #endif
121             break;

122         case AF_INET6:
123             sin6ptr = (struct sockaddr_in6 *) &ifr->ifr_addr;
124             ifi->ifi_addr = Calloc(1, sizeof(struct sockaddr_in6));
125             memcpy(ifi->ifi_addr, sin6ptr, sizeof(struct sockaddr_in6));
126 #ifdef   SIOCGIFDSTADDR
127             if (flags & IFF_POINTOPOINT) {
128                 Ioctl(sockfd, SIOCGIFDSTADDR, &ifrcopy);
129                 sin6ptr = (struct sockaddr_in6 *) &ifrcopy.ifr_dstaddr;
130                 ifi->ifi_dstaddr = Calloc(1, sizeof(struct sockaddr_in6));
131                 memcpy(ifi->ifi_dstaddr, sin6ptr,
132                         sizeof(struct sockaddr_in6));
133             }
134 #endif
135             break;

136         default:
137             break;
138         }
139     }
140     free(buf);
141     return (ifihead);              /* pointer to first structure in linked list */
142 }
                                                            ——— lib/get_ifi_info.c
```

Figure 17.10 Fetch and return interface addresses.

```
                                                              ─── lib/get_ifi_info.c
143 void
144 free_ifi_info(struct ifi_info *ifihead)
145 {
146     struct ifi_info *ifi, *ifinext;

147     for (ifi = ifihead; ifi != NULL; ifi = ifinext) {
148         if (ifi->ifi_addr != NULL)
149             free(ifi->ifi_addr);
150         if (ifi->ifi_brdaddr != NULL)
151             free(ifi->ifi_brdaddr);
152         if (ifi->ifi_dstaddr != NULL)
153             free(ifi->ifi_dstaddr);
154         ifinext = ifi->ifi_next;    /* can't fetch ifi_next after free() */
155         free(ifi);                  /* the ifi_info{} itself */
156     }
157 }
                                                              ─── lib/get_ifi_info.c
```

Figure 17.11 free_ifi_info function: frees dynamic memory allocated by get_ifi_info.

17.7 Interface Operations

As we showed in the previous section, the SIOCGIFCONF request returns the name and a socket address structure for each interface that is configured. There are a multitude of other requests that we can then issue to set or get all the other characteristics of the interface. The *get* version of these requests (SIOCGxxx) is often issued by the netstat program, and the *set* version (SIOCSxxx) is often issued by the ifconfig program. Any user can get the interface information, while it takes superuser privileges to set the information.

These requests take or return an ifreq structure whose address is specified as the third argument to ioctl. The interface is always identified by its name: le0, lo0, ppp0, etc. in the ifr_name member.

Many of these requests use a socket address structure to specify or return an IP address or address mask with the application. For IPv4, the address or mask is contained in the sin_addr member of an Internet socket address structure; for IPv6, it is in the sin6_addr member of an IPv6 socket address structure.

SIOCGIFADDR	Return the unicast address in the ifr_addr member.
SIOCSIFADDR	Set the interface address from the ifr_addr member. The initialization function for the interface is also called.
SIOCGIFFLAGS	Return the interface flags in the ifr_flags member. The names of the various flags are IFF_xxx and are defined by including the <net/if.h> header. The flags indicate, for example, if the interface is up (IFF_UP), if the interface is a point-to-point interface (IFF_POINTOPOINT), if the interface supports broadcasting (IFF_BROADCAST), and so on.

SIOCSIFFLAGS   Set the interface flags from the `ifr_flags` member.

SIOCGIFDSTADDR   Return the point-to-point address in the `ifr_dstaddr` member.

SIOCSIFDSTADDR   Set the point-to-point address from the `ifr_dstaddr` member.

SIOCGIFBRDADDR   Return the broadcast address in the `ifr_broadaddr` member. The application must first fetch the interface flags and then issue the correct request: SIOCGIFBRDADDR for a broadcast interface or SIOCGIFDSTADDR for a point-to-point interface.

SIOCSIFBRDADDR   Set the broadcast address from the `ifr_broadaddr` member.

SIOCGIFNETMASK   Return the subnet mask in the `ifr_addr` member.

SIOCSIFNETMASK   Set the subnet mask from the `ifr_addr` member.

SIOCGIFMETRIC   Return the interface metric in the `ifr_metric` member. The interface metric is maintained by the kernel for each interface but is used by the routing daemon `routed`. The interface metric is added to the hop count (to make an interface less favorable).

SIOCSIFMETRIC   Set the interface routing metric from the `ifr_metric` member.

In this section, we described the generic interface requests. Many implementations have additional requests as well.

17.8 ARP Cache Operations

On some systems, the ARP cache is also manipulated with the `ioctl` function. Systems that use routing sockets (Chapter 18) usually use routing sockets instead of `ioctl` to access the ARP cache. These requests use an `arpreq` structure, shown in Figure 17.12 and defined by including the `<net/if_arp.h>` header.

```
——————————————————————————————————————————————————— <net/if_arp.h>
struct arpreq {
    struct  sockaddr  arp_pa;     /* protocol address */
    struct  sockaddr  arp_ha;     /* hardware address */
    int               arp_flags;  /* flags */
};

#define  ATF_INUSE       0x01  /* entry in use */
#define  ATF_COM         0x02  /* completed entry (hardware addr valid) */
#define  ATF_PERM        0x04  /* permanent entry */
#define  ATF_PUBL        0x08  /* published entry (respond for other host) */
——————————————————————————————————————————————————— <net/if_arp.h>
```

Figure 17.12 `arpreq` structure used with `ioctl` requests for ARP cache.

The third argument to `ioctl` must point to one of these structures. The following three *request*s are supported:

SIOCSARP   Add a new entry to the ARP cache or modify an existing entry. `arp_pa` is an Internet socket address structure containing the IP address, and arp_ha is a generic socket address structure with sa_family set to AF_UNSPEC and sa_data containing the hardware address (e.g., the 6-byte Ethernet address). The two flags, ATF_PERM and ATF_PUBL, can be specified by the application. The other two flags, ATF_INUSE and ATF_COM, are set by the kernel.

SIOCDARP   Delete an entry from the ARP cache. The caller specifies the Internet address for the entry to be deleted.

SIOCGARP   Get an entry from the ARP cache. The caller specifies the Internet address, and the corresponding Ethernet address is returned along with the flags.

Only the superuser can add or delete an entry. These three requests are normally issued by the arp program.

> These ARP-related ioctl requests are not supported on some newer systems, which use routing sockets for these ARP operations.

Notice that there is no way with ioctl to list all the entries in the ARP cache. On many systems, the arp command, when invoked with the -a flag (list all entries in the ARP cache), reads the kernel's memory (/dev/kmem) to obtain the current contents of the ARP cache. We will see an easier (and better) way to do this using sysctl, which only works on some systems (Section 18.4).

Example: Print Hardware Addresses of Host

We now use our get_ifi_info function to return all of a host's IP addresses, followed by an ioctl of SIOCGARP for each IP address to obtain and print the hardware addresses. We show our program in Figure 17.13.

Get list of addresses and loop through each one

12   We call get_ifi_info to obtain the host's IP addresses and then loop through each address.

Print IP address

13   We print the IP address using sock_ntop. We asked get_ifi_info to only return IPv4 addresses, since ARP is not used with IPv6.

Issue ioctl and check for error

14-19   We fill in the arp_pa structure as an IPv4 socket address structure containing the IPv4 address. ioctl is called, and if it returns an error (e.g., because the address supplied isn't on an interface that supports ARP), we print the error and loop to the next address.

Print hardware address

20-22   The hardware address returned from the ioctl is printed.

———————————————————————————— ioctl/prmac.c
```
 1 #include    "unpifi.h"
 2 #include    <net/if_arp.h>

 3 int
 4 main(int argc, char **argv)
 5 {
 6     int      sockfd;
 7     struct ifi_info *ifi;
 8     unsigned char *ptr;
 9     struct arpreq arpreq;
10     struct sockaddr_in *sin;

11     sockfd = Socket(AF_INET, SOCK_DGRAM, 0);
12     for (ifi = get_ifi_info(AF_INET, 0); ifi != NULL; ifi = ifi->ifi_next) {
13         printf("%s: ", Sock_ntop(ifi->ifi_addr, sizeof(struct sockaddr_in)));

14         sin = (struct sockaddr_in *) &arpreq.arp_pa;
15         memcpy(sin, ifi->ifi_addr, sizeof(struct sockaddr_in));

16         if (ioctl(sockfd, SIOCGARP, &arpreq) < 0) {
17             err_ret("ioctl SIOCGARP");
18             continue;
19         }

20         ptr = &arpreq.arp_ha.sa_data[0];
21         printf("%x:%x:%x:%x:%x:%x\n", *ptr, *(ptr + 1),
22                 *(ptr + 2), *(ptr + 3), *(ptr + 4), *(ptr + 5));
23     }
24     exit(0);
25 }
```
———————————————————————————— ioctl/prmac.c

Figure 17.13   Print a host's hardware addresses.

Running this program on our hpux host gives
```
hpux % prmac
192.6.38.100: 0:60:b0:c2:68:9b
192.168.1.1: 0:60:b0:b2:28:2b
127.0.0.1: ioctl SIOCGARP: Invalid argument
```

17.9 Routing Table Operations

On some systems, two ioctl requests are provided to operate on the routing table. These two requests require that the third argument to ioctl be a pointer to an rtentry structure, which is defined by including the <net/route.h> header. These requests are normally issued by the route program. Only the superuser can issue these requests. On systems with routing sockets (Chapter 18), these requests use routing sockets instead of ioctl.

SIOCADDRT   Add an entry to the routing table.

SIOCDELRT   Delete an entry from the routing table.

There is no way with `ioctl` to list all the entries in the routing table. This operation is usually performed by the `netstat` program when invoked with the `-r` flag.
This program obtains the routing table by reading the kernel's memory (`/dev/kmem`).
As with listing the ARP cache, we will see an easier (and better) way to do this using
`sysctl` in Section 18.4.

17.10 Summary

The `ioctl` commands that are used in network programs can be divided into six categories:

- Socket operations (Are we at the out-of-band mark?)
- File operations (set or clear the nonblocking flag)
- Interface operations (return interface list, obtain broadcast address)
- ARP table operations (create, modify, get, delete)
- Routing table operations (add or delete)
- STREAMS system (Chapter 31)

We will use the socket and file operations, and obtaining the interface list is such a common operation that we developed our own function to do this. We will use this function numerous times in the remainder of the text. Only a few specialized programs use
the `ioctl` operations with the ARP cache and routing table.

Exercises

17.1   In Section 17.7, we said that the broadcast address returned by the `SIOCGIFBRDADDR`
request is returned in the `ifr_broadaddr` member. But on p. 173 of TCPv2, notice that it
is returned in the `ifr_dstaddr` member. Does this matter?

17.2   Modify the `get_ifi_info` program to issue its first `SIOCGIFCONF` request for one
`ifreq` structure and then increment the length each time around the loop by the size of
one of these structures. Next, put some statements in the loop to print the buffer size each
time the request is issued, whether or not `ioctl` returns an error, and upon success print
the returned buffer length. Run the `prifinfo` program and see how your system handles
this request when the buffer size is too small. Also print the address family for any
returned structures whose address family is not the desired value to see what other structures are returned by your system.

17.3   Modify the `get_ifi_info` function to return information about an alias address if the
additional address is on a different subnet from the previous address for this interface.
That is, our version in Section 17.6 ignored the aliases 206.62.226.44 through 206.62.226.46,
which is acceptable since they are on the same subnet as the primary address for the interface, 206.62.226.33. But if, in this example, an alias is on a different subnet, say 192.3.4.5,
return an `ifi_info` structure with the information about the additional address.

17.4   If your system supports the `SIOCGIFNUM` ioctl, then modify Figure 17.7 to issue this
request and use the return value as the initial buffer size guess.

18

Routing Sockets

18.1 Introduction

Traditionally, the Unix routing table within the kernel has been accessed using `ioctl` commands. In Section 17.9, we described the two commands that are provided, `SIOCADDRT` and `SIOCDELRT`, to add or delete a route. We also mentioned that no command exists to dump the entire routing table, and instead programs such as `netstat` read the kernel memory to obtain the contents of the routing table. One additional piece to this hodgepodge is that routing daemons such as `gated` need to monitor ICMP redirect messages that are received by the kernel, and they often do this by creating a raw ICMP socket (Chapter 28) and listening on this socket to all received ICMP messages.

4.3BSD Reno cleaned up the interface to the kernel's routing subsystem by creating the `AF_ROUTE` domain. The only type of socket supported in the route domain is a raw socket. Three types of operations are supported on a routing socket:

1. A process can send a message to the kernel by writing to a routing socket. For example, this is how routes are added and deleted.

2. A process can read a message from the kernel on a routing socket. This is how the kernel notifies a process that an ICMP redirect has been received and processed, or how it requests a route resolution from an external routing process.

   Some operations involve both steps. For example, the process sends a message to the kernel on a routing socket asking for all the information on a given route, and the process reads back the response from the kernel on the routing socket.

3. A process can use the `sysctl` function (Section 18.4) to either dump the routing table or list all configured interfaces.

The first two operations require superuser privileges on most systems, while the last operation can be performed by any process.

> Some newer releases have relaxed the superuser requirement for opening a routing socket and instead restrict only routing socket messages that change the table. This allows any process to use, for instance, RTM_GET to look up a route without being the superuser.
>
> Technically, the third operation is not performed using a routing socket but invokes the generic sysctl function. We will see that one of the input parameters is the address family, which is AF_ROUTE for the operations we describe in this chapter, and the information returned is in the same format as the information returned by the kernel on a routing socket. Indeed, the sysctl processing for the AF_ROUTE family is part of the routing socket code in a 4.4BSD kernel (pp. 632–643 of TCPv2).
>
> The sysctl utility appeared in 4.4BSD. Unfortunately, not all implementations that support routing sockets provide sysctl. For example, AIX 5.1 and Solaris 9 support routing sockets, but neither supports sysctl.

18.2   Datalink Socket Address Structure

We will encounter datalink socket address structures as return values contained in some of the messages returned on a routing socket. Figure 18.1 shows the definition of the structure, which is defined by including <net/if_dl.h>.

```
struct sockaddr_dl {
  uint8_t     sdl_len;
  sa_family_t sdl_family;   /* AF_LINK */
  uint16_t    sdl_index;    /* system assigned index, if > 0 */
  uint8_t     sdl_type;     /* IFT_ETHER, etc. from <net/if_types.h> */
  uint8_t     sdl_nlen;     /* name length, starting in sdl_data[0] */
  uint8_t     sdl_alen;     /* link-layer address length */
  uint8_t     sdl_slen;     /* link-layer selector length */
  char        sdl_data[12]; /* minimum work area, can be larger;
                               contains i/f name and link-layer address */
};
```

Figure 18.1   Datalink socket address structure.

Each interface has a unique positive index, and we will see this returned by the if_nametoindex and if_nameindex functions later in this chapter, along with the IPv6 multicasting socket options in Chapter 21 and some advanced IPv4 and IPv6 socket options in Chapter 27.

The sdl_data member contains both the name and link-layer address (e.g., the 48-bit MAC address for an Ethernet interface). The name begins at sdl_data[0] and is not null-terminated. The link-layer address begins sdl_nlen bytes after the name. This header defines the following macro to return the pointer to the link-layer address:

```
#define LLADDR(s)  ((caddr_t)((s)->sdl_data + (s)->sdl_nlen))
```

These socket address structures are variable-length (p. 89 of TCPv2). If the link-layer address and name exceed 12 bytes, the structure will be larger than 20 bytes. The size is normally rounded up to the next multiple of 4 bytes on 32-bit systems. We will also see in Figure 22.3 that when one of these structures is returned by the `IP_RECVIF` socket option, all three lengths are 0 and there is no `sdl_data` member at all.

18.3 Reading and Writing

After a process creates a routing socket, it can send commands to the kernel by writing to the socket and read information from the kernel by reading from the socket. There are 12 different routing commands, 5 of which can be issued by the process. These commands are defined by including the `<net/route.h>` header and are shown in Figure 18.2.

Message type	To kernel?	From kernel?	Description	Structure type
RTM_ADD	•	•	Add route	rt_msghdr
RTM_CHANGE	•	•	Change gateway, metrics, or flags	rt_msghdr
RTM_DELADDR		•	Address being removed from interface	ifa_msghdr
RTM_DELETE	•	•	Delete route	rt_msghdr
RTM_DELMADDR		•	Multicast address being removed from interface	ifma_msghdr
RTM_GET	•	•	Report metrics and other route information	rt_msghdr
RTM_IFANNOUNCE		•	Interface being added or removed from system	if_announcemsghdr
RTM_IFINFO		•	Interface going up, down, etc.	if_msghdr
RTM_LOCK	•	•	Lock given metrics	rt_msghdr
RTM_LOSING		•	Kernel suspects route is failing	rt_msghdr
RTM_MISS		•	Lookup failed on this address	rt_msghdr
RTM_NEWADDR		•	Address being added to interface	ifa_msghdr
RTM_NEWMADDR		•	Multicast address being joined on interface	ifma_msghdr
RTM_REDIRECT		•	Kernel told to use different route	rt_msghdr
RTM_RESOLVE		•	Request to resolve destination to link-layer address	rt_msghdr

Figure 18.2 Types of messages exchanged across a routing socket.

Five different structures are exchanged across a routing socket, as shown in the final column of this figure: `rt_msghdr`, `if_announcemsghdr`, `if_msghdr`, `ifa_msghdr`, and `ifma_msghdr`, which we show in Figure 18.3.

```
struct rt_msghdr {     /* from <net/route.h> */
  u_short  rtm_msglen;   /* to skip over non-understood messages */
  u_char   rtm_version;  /* future binary compatibility */
  u_char   rtm_type;     /* message type */

  u_short  rtm_index;    /* index for associated ifp */
  int      rtm_flags;    /* flags, incl. kern & message, e.g., DONE */
  int      rtm_addrs;    /* bitmask identifying sockaddrs in msg */
  pid_t    rtm_pid;      /* identify sender */
  int      rtm_seq;      /* for sender to identify action */
  int      rtm_errno;    /* why failed */
  int      rtm_use;      /* from rtentry */
  u_long   rtm_inits;    /* which metrics we are initializing */
  struct rt_metrics  rtm_rmx; /* metrics themselves */
};
struct if_msghdr {     /* from <net/if.h> */
  u_short  ifm_msglen;   /* to skip over non-understood messages */
  u_char   ifm_version;  /* future binary compatibility */
  u_char   ifm_type;     /* message type */

  int      ifm_addrs;    /* like rtm_addrs */
  int      ifm_flags;    /* value of if_flags */
  u_short  ifm_index;    /* index for associated ifp */
  struct if_data  ifm_data;/* statistics and other data about if */
};
struct ifa_msghdr {    /* from <net/if.h> */
  u_short  ifam_msglen;  /* to skip over non-understood messages */
  u_char   ifam_version; /* future binary compatibility */
  u_char   ifam_type;    /* message type */

  int      ifam_addrs;   /* like rtm_addrs */
  int      ifam_flags;   /* value of ifa_flags */
  u_short  ifam_index;   /* index for associated ifp */
  int      ifam_metric;  /* value of ifa_metric */
};
struct ifma_msghdr {   /* from <net/if.h> */
  u_short ifmam_msglen;   /* to skip over non-understood messages */
  u_char  ifmam_version;  /* future binary compatibility */
  u_char  ifmam_type;     /* message type */

  int     ifmam_addrs;    /* like rtm_addrs */
  int     ifmam_flags;    /* value of ifa_flags */
  u_short ifmam_index;    /* index for associated ifp */
};
struct if_announcemsghdr {  /* from <net/if.h> */
  u_short ifan_msglen;    /* to skip over non-understood messages */
  u_char  ifan_version;   /* future binary compatibility */
  u_char  ifan_type;      /* message type */

  u_short ifan_index;     /* index for associated ifp */
  char    ifan_name[IFNAMSIZ]; /* if name, e.g. "en0" */
  u_short ifan_what;      /* what type of announcement */
};
```

Figure 18.3   The five structures returned with routing messages.

The first three members of each structure are the same: length, version, and type of message. The type is one of the constants from the first column in Figure 18.2. The length member allows an application to skip over message types it does not understand.

The members rtm_addrs, ifm_addrs, ifam_addrs, and ifmam_addrs are bitmasks that specify which of eight possible socket address structures follow the message. Figure 18.4 shows the constants and values for each bitmask, which are defined by including the <net/route.h> header.

Bitmask		Array index		Socket address structure containing
Constant	Value	Constant	Value	
RTA_DST	0x01	RTAX_DST	0	Destination address
RTA_GATEWAY	0x02	RTAX_GATEWAY	1	Gateway address
RTA_NETMASK	0x04	RTAX_NETMASK	2	Network mask
RTA_GENMASK	0x08	RTAX_GENMASK	3	Cloning mask
RTA_IFP	0x10	RTAX_IFP	4	Interface name
RTA_IFA	0x20	RTAX_IFA	5	Interface address
RTA_AUTHOR	0x40	RTAX_AUTHOR	6	Author of redirect
RTA_BRD	0x80	RTAX_BRD	7	Broadcast or point-to-point destination address
		RTAX_MAX	8	Max # elements

Figure 18.4 Constants used to refer to socket address structures in routing messages.

When multiple socket address structures are present, they are always in the order shown in the table.

Example: Fetch and Print a Routing Table Entry

We now show an example using routing sockets. Our program takes a command-line argument consisting of an IPv4 dotted-decimal address and sends an RTM_GET message to the kernel for this address. The kernel looks up the address in its IPv4 routing table and returns an RTM_GET message with information about the routing table entry. For example, if we execute

```
freebsd % getrt 206.168.112.219
dest: 0.0.0.0
gateway: 12.106.32.1
netmask: 0.0.0.0
```

on our host freebsd, we see that this destination address uses the default route (which is stored in the routing table with a destination IP address of 0.0.0.0 and a mask of 0.0.0.0). The next-hop router is this system's gateway to the Internet. If we execute

```
freebsd % getrt 192.168.42.0
dest: 192.168.42.0
gateway: AF_LINK, index=2
netmask: 255.255.255.0
```

specifying the secondary Ethernet as the destination, the destination is the network itself. The gateway is now the outgoing interface, returned as a sockaddr_dl structure with an interface index of 2.

Before showing the source code, we show what we write to the routing socket in Figure 18.5 along with what is returned by the kernel.

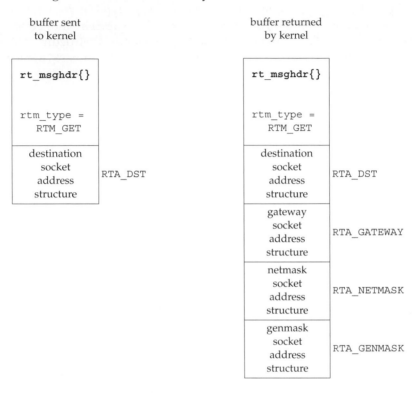

Figure 18.5 Data exchanged with kernel across routing socket for RTM_GET command.

We build a buffer containing an rt_msghdr structure, followed by a socket address structure containing the destination address for the kernel to look up. The rtm_type is RTM_GET and the rtm_addrs is RTA_DST (recall Figure 18.4), indicating that the only socket address structure following the rt_msghdr structure is one containing the desti-nation address. This command can be used with any protocol family (that provides a routing table), because the family of the address to look up is contained in the socket address structure.

After sending the message to the kernel, we read back the reply, and it has the for-mat shown at the right of Figure 18.5: an rt_msghdr structure followed by up to four socket address structures. Which of the four socket address structures gets returned depends on the routing table entry; we are told which of the four by the value in the rtm_addrs member of the returned rt_msghdr structure. The family of each socket address structure is contained in the sa_family member, and as we saw in our exam-ples earlier, one time the returned gateway was an IPv4 socket address structure and the next time it was a datalink socket address structure.

Figure 18.6 shows the first part of our program.

———————————————————————————— route/getrt.c

```
 1 #include    "unproute.h"

 2 #define BUFLEN  (sizeof(struct rt_msghdr) + 512)
 3                         /* sizeof(struct sockaddr_in6) * 8 = 192 */
 4 #define SEQ     9999

 5 int
 6 main(int argc, char **argv)
 7 {
 8     int     sockfd;
 9     char    *buf;
10     pid_t   pid;
11     ssize_t n;
12     struct rt_msghdr *rtm;
13     struct sockaddr *sa, *rti_info[RTAX_MAX];
14     struct sockaddr_in *sin;

15     if (argc != 2)
16         err_quit("usage: getrt <IPaddress>");

17     sockfd = Socket(AF_ROUTE, SOCK_RAW, 0); /* need superuser privileges */

18     buf = Calloc(1, BUFLEN);    /* and initialized to 0 */

19     rtm = (struct rt_msghdr *) buf;
20     rtm->rtm_msglen = sizeof(struct rt_msghdr) + sizeof(struct sockaddr_in);
21     rtm->rtm_version = RTM_VERSION;
22     rtm->rtm_type = RTM_GET;
23     rtm->rtm_addrs = RTA_DST;
24     rtm->rtm_pid = pid = getpid();
25     rtm->rtm_seq = SEQ;

26     sin = (struct sockaddr_in *) (rtm + 1);
27     sin->sin_len = sizeof(struct sockaddr_in);
28     sin->sin_family = AF_INET;
29     Inet_pton(AF_INET, argv[1], &sin->sin_addr);

30     Write(sockfd, rtm, rtm->rtm_msglen);

31     do {
32         n = Read(sockfd, rtm, BUFLEN);
33     } while (rtm->rtm_type != RTM_GET || rtm->rtm_seq != SEQ ||
34              rtm->rtm_pid != pid);
```

———————————————————————————— route/getrt.c

Figure 18.6 First half of program to issue RTM_GET command on routing socket.

1–3   Our unproute.h header includes some files that are needed and then includes our unp.h file. The constant BUFLEN is the size of the buffer that we allocate to hold our message to the kernel, along with the kernel's reply. We need room for one rt_msghdr structure and possibly eight socket address structures (the maximum number that is ever returned on a routing socket). Since an IPv6 socket address structure is 28 bytes in size, the value of 512 is more than adequate.

Create routing socket

17   We create a raw socket in the AF_ROUTE domain, and as we said earlier, this may require superuser privileges. A buffer is allocated and initialized to 0.

Fill in `rt_msghdr` structure

18–25   We fill in the structure with our request. We store our process ID and a sequence number of our choosing in the structure. We will compare these values in the responses that we read, looking for the correct reply.

Fill in Internet socket address structure with destination

26–29   Following the `rt_msghdr` structure, we build a `sockaddr_in` structure containing the destination IPv4 address for the kernel to look up in its routing table. All we set are the address length, the address family, and the address.

`write` message to kernel and `read` reply

30–34   We `write` the message to the kernel and `read` back the reply. Since other processes may have routing sockets open, and since the kernel passes a copy of all routing messages to all routing sockets, we must check the message type, sequence number, and process ID to verify that the message received is the one we are waiting for.

The last half of this program is shown in Figure 18.7. This half processes the reply.

———— route/getrt.c

```
35      rtm = (struct rt_msghdr *) buf;
36      sa = (struct sockaddr *) (rtm + 1);
37      get_rtaddrs(rtm->rtm_addrs, sa, rti_info);
38      if ( (sa = rti_info[RTAX_DST]) != NULL)
39          printf("dest: %s\n", Sock_ntop_host(sa, sa->sa_len));

40      if ( (sa = rti_info[RTAX_GATEWAY]) != NULL)
41          printf("gateway: %s\n", Sock_ntop_host(sa, sa->sa_len));

42      if ( (sa = rti_info[RTAX_NETMASK]) != NULL)
43          printf("netmask: %s\n", Sock_masktop(sa, sa->sa_len));

44      if ( (sa = rti_info[RTAX_GENMASK]) != NULL)
45          printf("genmask: %s\n", Sock_masktop(sa, sa->sa_len));

46      exit(0);
47  }
```

———— route/getrt.c

Figure 18.7 Last half of program to issue RTM_GET command on routing socket.

35–36   `rtm` points to the `rt_msghdr` structure and `sa` points to the first socket address structure that follows.

37   `rtm_addrs` is a bitmask of which of the eight possible socket address structures follow the `rt_msghdr` structure. Our `get_rtaddrs` function (which we will show next) takes this mask plus the pointer to the first socket address structure (`sa`) and fills in the array `rti_info` with pointers to the corresponding socket address structures. Assuming that all four socket address structures shown in Figure 18.5 are returned by the kernel, the resulting `rti_info` array will be as shown in Figure 18.8.

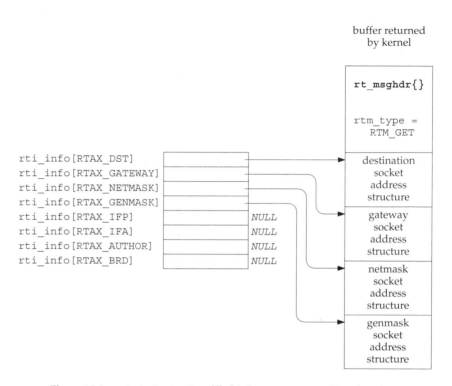

Figure 18.8 rti_info structure filled in by our get_rtaddrs function.

Our program then goes through the rti_info array, doing what it wants with all the non-null pointers in the array.

38-45   Each of the four possible addresses are printed, if present. We call our sock_ntop_host function to print the destination address and the gateway address, but we call our sock_masktop to print the two masks. We will show this new function shortly.

Figure 18.9 shows our get_rtaddrs function that we called from Figure 18.7.

Loop through eight possible pointers

17-23   RTAX_MAX is 8 in Figure 18.4, the maximum number of socket address structures returned in a routing message from the kernel. The loop in this function looks at each of the eight RTA_*xxx* bitmask constants from Figure 18.4 that can be set in the rtm_addrs, ifm_addrs, or ifam_addrs members of the structures in Figure 18.3. If the bit is set, the corresponding element in the rti_info array is set to the pointer to the socket address structure; otherwise, the array element is set to a null pointer.

Step to next socket address structure

2-12   The socket address structures are variable-length, but this code assumes that each has an sa_len field specifying its length. There are two complications that must be handled. First, the two masks, the network mask and the cloning mask, can be returned

---
libroute/get_rtaddrs.c

```
 1 #include    "unproute.h"

 2 /*
 3  * Round up 'a' to next multiple of 'size', which must be a power of 2
 4  */
 5 #define ROUNDUP(a, size) (((a) & ((size)-1)) ? (1 + ((a) | ((size)-1))) : (a))

 6 /*
 7  * Step to next socket address structure;
 8  * if sa_len is 0, assume it is sizeof(u_long).
 9  */
10 #define NEXT_SA(ap) ap = (SA *) \
11     ((caddr_t) ap + (ap->sa_len ? ROUNDUP(ap->sa_len, sizeof (u_long)) : \
12                                   sizeof(u_long)))

13 void
14 get_rtaddrs(int addrs, SA *sa, SA **rti_info)
15 {
16     int     i;

17     for (i = 0; i < RTAX_MAX; i++) {
18         if (addrs & (1 << i)) {
19             rti_info[i] = sa;
20             NEXT_SA(sa);
21         } else
22             rti_info[i] = NULL;
23     }
24 }
```
libroute/get_rtaddrs.c

Figure 18.9 Build array of pointers to socket address structures in routing message.

---

in a socket address structure with an sa_len of 0, but this really occupies the size of an unsigned long. (Chapter 19 of TCPv2 discusses the cloning feature of the 4.4BSD routing table.) This value represents a mask of all zero bits, which we printed as 0.0.0.0 for the network mask of the default route in our earlier example. Second, each socket address structure can be padded at the end so that the next one begins on a specific boundary, which in this case is the size of an unsigned long (e.g., a 4-byte boundary for a 32-bit architecture). Although sockaddr_in structures occupy 16 bytes, which requires no padding, the masks often have padding at the end.

The last function that we must show for our example program is sock_masktop in Figure 18.10, which returns the presentation string for one of the two mask values that can be returned. Masks are stored in socket address structures. The sa_family member is undefined, but the mask socket address structures do contain an sa_len of 0, 5, 6, 7, or 8 for 32-bit IPv4 masks. When the length is greater than 0, the actual mask starts at the same offset from the beginning as does the IPv4 address in a sockaddr_in structure: 4 bytes from the beginning of the structure (as shown in Figure 18.21, p. 577 of TCPv2), which is the sa_data[2] member of the generic socket address structure.

libroute/sock_masktop.c

```
 1 #include     "unproute.h"

 2 const char *
 3 sock_masktop(SA *sa, socklen_t salen)
 4 {
 5     static char str[INET6_ADDRSTRLEN];
 6     unsigned char *ptr = &sa->sa_data[2];

 7     if (sa->sa_len == 0)
 8         return ("0.0.0.0");
 9     else if (sa->sa_len == 5)
10         snprintf(str, sizeof(str), "%d.0.0.0", *ptr);
11     else if (sa->sa_len == 6)
12         snprintf(str, sizeof(str), "%d.%d.0.0", *ptr, *(ptr + 1));
13     else if (sa->sa_len == 7)
14         snprintf(str, sizeof(str), "%d.%d.%d.0", *ptr, *(ptr + 1),
15                 *(ptr + 2));
16     else if (sa->sa_len == 8)
17         snprintf(str, sizeof(str), "%d.%d.%d.%d",
18                 *ptr, *(ptr + 1), *(ptr + 2), *(ptr + 3));
19     else
20         snprintf(str, sizeof(str), "(unknown mask, len = %d, family = %d)",
21                 sa->sa_len, sa->sa_family);
22     return (str);
23 }
```

libroute/sock_masktop.c

Figure 18.10 Convert a mask value to its presentation format.

7-21   If the length is 0, the implied mask is 0.0.0.0. If the length is 5, only the first byte of the 32-bit mask is stored, with an implied value of 0 for the remaining 3 bytes. When the length is 8, all 4 bytes of the mask are stored.

In this example, we want to read the kernel's reply because the reply contains the information we are looking for. But in general, the return value from our `write` to the routing socket tells us if the command succeeded or not. If that is all the information we need, we can call `shutdown` with a second argument of `SHUT_RD` immediately after opening the socket to prevent a reply from being sent. For example, if we are deleting a route, a return of 0 from `write` means success, while an error return of `ESRCH` means the route could not be found (p. 608 of TCPv2). Similarly, an error return of `EEXIST` from `write` when adding a route means the entry already exists. In our example in Figure 18.6, if the routing table entry does not exist (say our host does not have a default route), then `write` returns an error of `ESRCH`.

18.4   `sysctl` Operations

Our main interest in routing sockets is the use of the `sysctl` function to examine both the routing table and interface list. Whereas the creation of a routing socket (a raw socket in the AF_ROUTE domain) requires superuser privileges, any process can examine the routing table and interface list using sysctl.

```
#include <sys/param.h>
#include <sys/sysctl.h>

int sysctl(int *name, u_int namelen, void *oldp, size_t *oldlenp,
           void *newp, size_t newlen);
```
                                                                              Returns: 0 if OK, −1 on error

This function uses names that look like SNMP management information base (MIB) names. Chapter 25 of TCPv1 talks about SNMP and its MIB in detail. These names are hierarchical.

The *name* argument is an array of integers specifying the name, and *namelen* specifies the number of elements in the array. The first element in the array specifies which subsystem of the kernel the request is directed to. The second element specifies some part of that subsystem, and so on. Figure 18.11 shows the hierarchical arrangement, with some of the constants used at the first three levels.

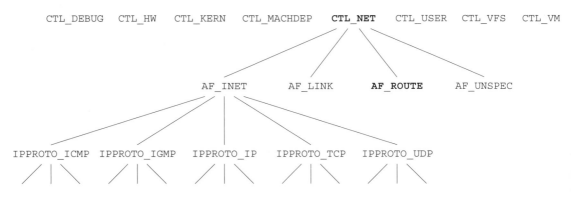

Figure 18.11 Hierarchical arrangement of sysctl names.

To fetch a value, *oldp* points to a buffer into which the kernel stores the value. *oldlenp* is a value-result argument: When the function is called, the value pointed to by *oldlenp* specifies the size of this buffer, and on return, the value contains the amount of data stored in the buffer by the kernel. If the buffer is not large enough, ENOMEM is returned. As a special case, *oldp* can be a null pointer and *oldlenp* a non-null pointer, and the kernel can determine how much data the call would have returned and returns this size through *oldlenp*.

To set a new value, *newp* points to a buffer of size *newlen*. If a new value is not being specified, *newp* should be a null pointer and *newlen* should be 0.

The sysctl man page details all the various system information that can be obtained with this function: information on the filesystems, virtual memory, kernel limits, hardware, and so on. Our interest is in the networking subsystem, designated by the first element of the *name* array being set to CTL_NET. (The CTL_*xxx* constants are defined by including the <sys/sysctl.h> header.) The second element can then be as follows:

- AF_INET—Get or set variables affecting the Internet protocols. The next level specifies the protocol using one of the IPPROTO_*xxx* constants. FreeBSD 5.0 provides about 75 variables at this level, controlling features such as whether the kernel should generate an ICMP redirect, whether TCP should use the RFC 1323 options, whether UDP checksums should be sent, and so on. We will show an example of this use of sysctl at the end of this section.

- AF_LINK—Get or set link-layer information such as the number of PPP interfaces.

- AF_ROUTE—Return information on either the routing table or interface list. We will describe this information shortly.

- AF_UNSPEC—Get or set some socket-layer variables such as the maximum size of a socket send or receive buffer.

When the second element of the *name* array is AF_ROUTE, the third element (a protocol number) is always 0 (since there are no protocols within the AF_ROUTE family, as there are within the AF_INET family, for example), the fourth element is an address family, and the fifth and sixth levels specify what to do. We will summarize this in Figure 18.12.

name[]	Return IPv4 routing table	Return IPv4 ARP cache	Return IPv6 routing table	Return interface list
0	CTL_NET	CTL_NET	CTL_NET	CTL_NET
1	AF_ROUTE	AF_ROUTE	AF_ROUTE	AF_ROUTE
2	0	0	0	0
3	AF_INET	AF_INET	AF_INET6	0
4	NET_RT_DUMP	NET_RT_FLAGS	NET_RT_DUMP	NET_RT_IFLIST
5	0	RTF_LLINFO	0	0

Figure 18.12 sysctl information returned for route domain.

Three operations are supported, specified by *name*[4]. (The NET_RT_*xxx* constants are defined by including the <sys/socket.h> header.) The information returned by these four operations is returned through the *oldp* pointer in the call to sysctl. This buffer contains a variable number of RTM_*xxx* messages (Figure 18.2).

1. NET_RT_DUMP returns the routing table for the address family specified by *name*[3]. If this address family is 0, the routing tables for all address families are returned.

   The routing table is returned as a variable number of RTM_GET messages, with each message followed by up to four socket address structures: the destination, gateway, network mask, and cloning mask of the routing table entry. We showed one of these messages on the right side of Figure 18.5 and our code in Figure 18.7 parsed one of these messages. All that changes with this `sysctl` operation is that one or more of these messages are returned by the kernel.

2. `NET_RT_FLAGS` returns the routing table for the address family specified by *name*[3], but only the routing table entries with an RTF_*xxx* flag value that contains the flag specified by *name*[5]. All ARP cache entries in the routing table have the `RTF_LLINFO` flag bit set.

   The information is returned in the same format as the previous item.

3. `NET_RT_IFLIST` returns information on all configured interfaces. If *name*[5] is nonzero, it is an interface index number, and only information on that interface is returned. (We will say more about interface indexes in Section 18.6.) All the addresses assigned to each interface are also returned, and if *name*[3] is nonzero, only addresses for that address family are returned.

   For each interface, one `RTM_IFINFO` message is returned, followed by one `RTM_NEWADDR` message for each address assigned to the interface. The `RTM_IFINFO` message is followed by one datalink socket address structure, and each `RTM_NEWADDR` message is followed by up to three socket address structures: the interface address, the network mask, and the broadcast address. These two messages are shown in Figure 18.14.

Example: Determine if UDP Checksums Are Enabled

We now provide a simple example of `sysctl` with the Internet protocols to check whether UDP checksums are enabled. Some UDP applications (e.g., BIND) check whether UDP checksums are enabled when they start, and if not, they try to enable them. Naturally, it takes superuser privileges to enable a feature such as this, but all we do now is check whether the feature is enabled or not. Figure 18.13 is our program.

route/checkudpsum.c
```
 1 #include    "unproute.h"
 2 #include    <netinet/udp.h>
 3 #include    <netinet/ip_var.h>
 4 #include    <netinet/udp_var.h> /* for UDPCTL_xxx constants */

 5 int
 6 main(int argc, char **argv)
 7 {
 8     int     mib[4], val;
 9     size_t  len;

10     mib[0] = CTL_NET;
11     mib[1] = AF_INET;
12     mib[2] = IPPROTO_UDP;
13     mib[3] = UDPCTL_CHECKSUM;

14     len = sizeof(val);
15     Sysctl(mib, 4, &val, &len, NULL, 0);
16     printf("udp checksum flag: %d\n", val);

17     exit(0);
18 }
```
route/checkudpsum.c

Figure 18.13 Check whether UDP checksums are enabled.

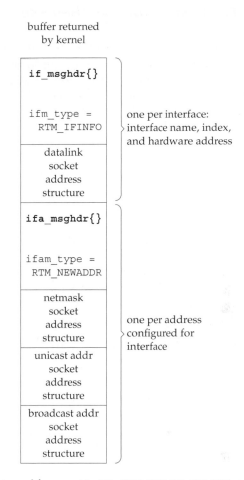

buffer returned
by kernel

```
if_msghdr{}


ifm_type =
    RTM_IFINFO
```
datalink
socket
address
structure

one per interface:
interface name, index,
and hardware address

```
ifa_msghdr{}


ifam_type =
    RTM_NEWADDR
```
netmask
socket
address
structure

unicast addr
socket
address
structure

broadcast addr
socket
address
structure

one per address
configured for
interface

Figure 18.14 Information returned for `sysctl`, `CTL_NET`, `NET_RT_IFLIST` command.

Include system headers

2–4   We must include the `<netinet/udp_var.h>` header to obtain the definition of the UDP `sysctl` constants. The two other headers are required for this header.

Call `sysctl`

10–16   We allocate an integer array with four elements and store the constants that correspond to the hierarchy shown in Figure 18.11. Since we are only fetching a variable and not setting a new value, we specify a null pointer for the *newp* argument to `sysctl` and a value of 0 for the *newlen* argument. *oldp* points to an integer variable of ours into which the result is stored and *oldlenp* points to a value-result variable for the size of this integer. The flag that we print will be either 0 (disabled) or 1 (enabled).

18.5 `get_ifi_info` Function (Revisited)

We now return to the example from Section 17.6: returning all the interfaces that are up as a linked list of `ifi_info` structures (Figure 17.5). The `prifinfo` program remains the same (Figure 17.6), but we now show a version of the `get_ifi_info` function that uses `sysctl` instead of the `SIOCGIFCONF` `ioctl` that was used in Figure 17.7.

We first show the function `net_rt_iflist` in Figure 18.15. This function calls `sysctl` with the `NET_RT_IFLIST` command to return the interface list for a specified address family.

libroute/net_rt_iflist.c

```
 1 #include     "unproute.h"

 2 char *
 3 net_rt_iflist(int family, int flags, size_t *lenp)
 4 {
 5     int     mib[6];
 6     char    *buf;

 7     mib[0] = CTL_NET;
 8     mib[1] = AF_ROUTE;
 9     mib[2] = 0;
10     mib[3] = family;            /* only addresses of this family */
11     mib[4] = NET_RT_IFLIST;
12     mib[5] = flags;             /* interface index or 0 */
13     if (sysctl(mib, 6, NULL, lenp, NULL, 0) < 0)
14         return (NULL);

15     if ( (buf = malloc(*lenp)) == NULL)
16         return (NULL);
17     if (sysctl(mib, 6, buf, lenp, NULL, 0) < 0) {
18         free(buf);
19         return (NULL);
20     }

21     return (buf);
22 }
```

libroute/net_rt_iflist.c

Figure 18.15 Call `sysctl` to return interface list.

7–14   The array `mib` is initialized as shown in Figure 18.12 to return the interface list and all configured addresses of the specified family. `sysctl` is then called twice. In the first call, the third argument is null, which returns the buffer size required to hold all the interface information in the variable pointed to by `lenp`.

15–21   Space is then allocated for the buffer and `sysctl` is called again, this time with a non-null third argument. This time, the variable pointed to by `lenp` will return with the amount of information stored in the buffer, and this variable is allocated by the caller. A pointer to the buffer is also returned to the caller.

> Since the size of the routing table or the number of interfaces can change between the two calls to `sysctl`, the value returned by the first call contains a 10% fudge factor (pp. 639–640 of TCPv2).

Figure 18.16 shows the first half of the get_ifi_info function.

route/get_ifi_info.c
```
 3 struct ifi_info *
 4 get_ifi_info(int family, int doaliases)
 5 {
 6     int     flags;
 7     char    *buf, *next, *lim;
 8     size_t  len;
 9     struct if_msghdr *ifm;
10     struct ifa_msghdr *ifam;
11     struct sockaddr *sa, *rti_info[RTAX_MAX];
12     struct sockaddr_dl *sdl;
13     struct ifi_info *ifi, *ifisave, *ifihead, **ifipnext;

14     buf = Net_rt_iflist(family, 0, &len);

15     ifihead = NULL;
16     ifipnext = &ifihead;

17     lim = buf + len;
18     for (next = buf; next < lim; next += ifm->ifm_msglen) {
19         ifm = (struct if_msghdr *) next;
20         if (ifm->ifm_type == RTM_IFINFO) {
21             if (((flags = ifm->ifm_flags) & IFF_UP) == 0)
22                 continue;        /* ignore if interface not up */

23             sa = (struct sockaddr *) (ifm + 1);
24             get_rtaddrs(ifm->ifm_addrs, sa, rti_info);
25             if ( (sa = rti_info[RTAX_IFP]) != NULL) {
26                 ifi = Calloc(1, sizeof(struct ifi_info));
27                 *ifipnext = ifi;   /* prev points to this new one */
28                 ifipnext = &ifi->ifi_next;  /* ptr to next one goes here */

29                 ifi->ifi_flags = flags;
30                 if (sa->sa_family == AF_LINK) {
31                     sdl = (struct sockaddr_dl *) sa;
32                     ifi->ifi_index = sdl->sdl_index;
33                     if (sdl->sdl_nlen > 0)
34                         snprintf(ifi->ifi_name, IFI_NAME, "%*s",
35                                 sdl->sdl_nlen, &sdl->sdl_data[0]);
36                     else
37                         snprintf(ifi->ifi_name, IFI_NAME, "index %d",
38                                 sdl->sdl_index);

39                     if ( (ifi->ifi_hlen = sdl->sdl_alen) > 0)
40                         memcpy(ifi->ifi_haddr, LLADDR(sdl),
41                                 min(IFI_HADDR, sdl->sdl_alen));
42                 }
43             }
```
route/get_ifi_info.c

Figure 18.16 get_ifi_info function, first half.

6-14   We declare the local variables and then call our net_rt_iflist function.

17-19   The for loop steps through each routing message in the buffer filled in by sysctl. We assume that the message is an if_msghdr structure and look at the ifm_type field. (Recall that the first three members of all three structures are identical, so it doesn't matter which of the three structures we use to look at the *type* member.)

Check if interface is up

20-22   An RTM_IFINFO structure is returned for each interface. If the interface is not up, it is ignored.

Determine which socket address structures are present

23-24   sa points to the first socket address structure following the if_msghdr structure. Our get_rtaddrs function initializes the rti_info array, depending on which socket address structures are present.

Handle interface name

25-43   If the socket address structure with the interface name is present, an ifi_info structure is allocated and the interface flags are stored. The expected family of this socket address structure is AF_LINK, indicating a datalink socket address structure. We store the interface index into the ifi_index member. If the sdl_nlen member is nonzero, then the interface name is copied into the ifi_info structure. Otherwise, a string containing the interface index is stored as the name. If the sdl_alen member is nonzero, then the hardware address (e.g., the Ethernet address) is copied into the ifi_info structure and its length is also returned as ifi_hlen.

Figure 18.17 shows the second half of our get_ifi_info function, which returns the IP addresses for the interface.

Return IP addresses

44-65   An RTM_NEWADDR message is returned by sysctl for each address associated with the interface: the primary address and all aliases. If we have already filled in the IP address for this interface, then we are dealing with an alias. In that case, if the caller wants the alias address, we must allocate memory for another ifi_info structure, copy the fields that have been filled in, and then fill in the addresses that have been returned.

Return broadcast and destination addresses

66-75   If the interface supports broadcasting, the broadcast address is returned, and if the interface is a point-to-point interface, the destination address is returned.

route/get_ifi_info.c
```
44              } else if (ifm->ifm_type == RTM_NEWADDR) {
45                  if (ifi->ifi_addr) {    /* already have an IP addr for i/f */
46                      if (doaliases == 0)
47                          continue;

48                          /* we have a new IP addr for existing interface */
49                      ifisave = ifi;
50                      ifi = Calloc(1, sizeof(struct ifi_info));
51                      *ifipnext = ifi;    /* prev points to this new one */
52                      ifipnext = &ifi->ifi_next;  /* ptr to next one goes here */
53                      ifi->ifi_flags = ifisave->ifi_flags;
54                      ifi->ifi_index = ifisave->ifi_index;
55                      ifi->ifi_hlen = ifisave->ifi_hlen;
56                      memcpy(ifi->ifi_name, ifisave->ifi_name, IFI_NAME);
57                      memcpy(ifi->ifi_haddr, ifisave->ifi_haddr, IFI_HADDR);
58                  }

59                  ifam = (struct ifa_msghdr *) next;
60                  sa = (struct sockaddr *) (ifam + 1);
61                  get_rtaddrs(ifam->ifam_addrs, sa, rti_info);

62                  if ( (sa = rti_info[RTAX_IFA]) != NULL) {
63                      ifi->ifi_addr = Calloc(1, sa->sa_len);
64                      memcpy(ifi->ifi_addr, sa, sa->sa_len);
65                  }

66                  if ((flags & IFF_BROADCAST) && (sa = rti_info[RTAX_BRD]) != NULL) {
67                      ifi->ifi_brdaddr = Calloc(1, sa->sa_len);
68                      memcpy(ifi->ifi_brdaddr, sa, sa->sa_len);
69                  }

70                  if ((flags & IFF_POINTOPOINT) &&
71                      (sa = rti_info[RTAX_BRD]) != NULL) {
72                      ifi->ifi_dstaddr = Calloc(1, sa->sa_len);
73                      memcpy(ifi->ifi_dstaddr, sa, sa->sa_len);
74                  }

75          } else
76              err_quit("unexpected message type %d", ifm->ifm_type);
77      }
78      /* "ifihead" points to the first structure in the linked list */
79      return (ifihead);           /* ptr to first structure in linked list */
80 }
```
route/get_ifi_info.c

Figure 18.17 get_ifi_info function, second half.

18.6   Interface Name and Index Functions

RFC 3493 [Gilligan et al. 2003] defines four functions that deal with interface names and indexes. These four functions are used in many places where it is necessary to describe an interface. They were introduced for use with the IPv6 API, as we will describe in Chapters 21 and 27, but we find interface indexes in the IPv4 API as well (e.g., in the IP_RECVIF call, or in AF_LINK sockaddrs seen on the routing socket). The basic concept is that each interface has a unique name and a unique positive index (0 is never used as an index).

```
#include <net/if.h>

unsigned int if_nametoindex(const char *ifname);
```

                                   Returns: positive interface index if OK, 0 on error

```
char *if_indextoname(unsigned int ifindex, char *ifname);
```

                                   Returns: pointer to interface name if OK, NULL on error

```
struct if_nameindex *if_nameindex(void);
```

                                   Returns: non-null pointer if OK, NULL on error

```
void if_freenameindex(struct if_nameindex *ptr);
```

if_nametoindex returns the index of the interface whose name is *ifname*. if_indextoname returns a pointer to the interface name given its *ifindex*. The *ifname* argument points to a buffer of size IFNAMSIZ (defined by including the <net/if.h> header; also shown in Figure 17.2) that the caller must allocate to hold the result, and this pointer is also the return value upon success.

if_nameindex returns a pointer to an array of if_nameindex structures as follows:

```
struct if_nameindex {
  unsigned int    if_index;  /* 1, 2, ... */
  char           *if_name;   /* null-terminated name: "le0", ... */
};
```

The final entry in this array contains a structure with an if_index of 0 and an if_name that is a null pointer. The memory for this array, along with the names pointed to by the array members, is dynamically obtained and is returned by calling if_freenameindex.

We now provide an implementation of these four functions using routing sockets.

`if_nametoindex` Function

Figure 18.18 shows the `if_nametoindex` function.

libroute/if_nametoindex.c

```
 1 #include    "unpifi.h"
 2 #include    "unproute.h"

 3 unsigned int
 4 if_nametoindex(const char *name)
 5 {
 6     unsigned int idx, namelen;
 7     char    *buf, *next, *lim;
 8     size_t  len;
 9     struct if_msghdr *ifm;
10     struct sockaddr *sa, *rti_info[RTAX_MAX];
11     struct sockaddr_dl *sdl;

12     if ( (buf = net_rt_iflist(0, 0, &len)) == NULL)
13         return (0);

14     namelen = strlen(name);
15     lim = buf + len;
16     for (next = buf; next < lim; next += ifm->ifm_msglen) {
17         ifm = (struct if_msghdr *) next;
18         if (ifm->ifm_type == RTM_IFINFO) {
19             sa = (struct sockaddr *) (ifm + 1);
20             get_rtaddrs(ifm->ifm_addrs, sa, rti_info);
21             if ( (sa = rti_info[RTAX_IFP]) != NULL) {
22                 if (sa->sa_family == AF_LINK) {
23                     sdl = (struct sockaddr_dl *) sa;
24                     if (sdl->sdl_nlen == namelen
25                         && strncmp(&sdl->sdl_data[0], name,
26                                 sdl->sdl_nlen) == 0) {
27                         idx = sdl->sdl_index;   /* save before free() */
28                         free(buf);
29                         return (idx);
30                     }
31                 }
32             }
33         }
34     }
35     free(buf);
36     return (0);                     /* no match for name */
37 }
```

libroute/if_nametoindex.c

Figure 18.18 Return an interface index given its name.

Get interface list

12-13 Our `net_rt_iflist` function returns the interface list.

Process only `RTM_IFINFO` messages

17-30 We process the messages in the buffer (Figure 18.14), looking only for the `RTM_IFINFO` messages. When we find one, we call our `get_rtaddrs` function to set up the pointers to the socket address structures, and if an interface name structure is present (the `RTAX_IFP` element of the `rti_info` array), the interface name is compared to the argument.

`if_indextoname` Function

The next function, `if_indextoname`, is shown in Figure 18.19.

```
                                                              —— libroute/if_indextoname.c
 1 #include     "unpifi.h"
 2 #include     "unproute.h"

 3 char *
 4 if_indextoname(unsigned int idx, char *name)
 5 {
 6     char    *buf, *next, *lim;
 7     size_t  len;
 8     struct if_msghdr *ifm;
 9     struct sockaddr *sa, *rti_info[RTAX_MAX];
10     struct sockaddr_dl *sdl;

11     if ( (buf = net_rt_iflist(0, idx, &len)) == NULL)
12         return (NULL);

13     lim = buf + len;
14     for (next = buf; next < lim; next += ifm->ifm_msglen) {
15         ifm = (struct if_msghdr *) next;
16         if (ifm->ifm_type == RTM_IFINFO) {
17             sa = (struct sockaddr *) (ifm + 1);
18             get_rtaddrs(ifm->ifm_addrs, sa, rti_info);
19             if ( (sa = rti_info[RTAX_IFP]) != NULL) {
20                 if (sa->sa_family == AF_LINK) {
21                     sdl = (struct sockaddr_dl *) sa;
22                     if (sdl->sdl_index == idx) {
23                         int    slen = min(IFNAMSIZ - 1, sdl->sdl_nlen);
24                         strncpy(name, sdl->sdl_data, slen);
25                         name[slen] = 0; /* null terminate */
26                         free(buf);
27                         return (name);
28                     }
29                 }
30             }
31         }
32     }
33     free(buf);
34     return (NULL);              /* no match for index */
35 }
```
—— libroute/if_indextoname.c

Figure 18.19 Return an interface name given its index.

This function is nearly identical to the previous function, but instead of looking for an interface name, we compare the interface index against the caller's argument. Also, the second argument to our `net_rt_iflist` function is the desired index, so the result should contain the information for only the desired interface. When a match is found, the interface name is returned and it is also null-terminated.

`if_nameindex` **Function**

The next function, `if_nameindex`, returns an array of `if_nameindex` structures containing all the interface names and indexes. It is shown in Figure 18.20.

── libroute/if_nameindex.c

```
 1 #include     "unpifi.h"
 2 #include     "unproute.h"

 3 struct if_nameindex *
 4 if_nameindex(void)
 5 {
 6     char   *buf, *next, *lim;
 7     size_t len;
 8     struct if_msghdr *ifm;
 9     struct sockaddr *sa, *rti_info[RTAX_MAX];
10     struct sockaddr_dl *sdl;
11     struct if_nameindex *result, *ifptr;
12     char   *namptr;

13     if ( (buf = net_rt_iflist(0, 0, &len)) == NULL)
14         return (NULL);

15     if ( (result = malloc(len)) == NULL) /* overestimate */
16         return (NULL);
17     ifptr = result;
18     namptr = (char *) result + len; /* names start at end of buffer */

19     lim = buf + len;
20     for (next = buf; next < lim; next += ifm->ifm_msglen) {
21         ifm = (struct if_msghdr *) next;
22         if (ifm->ifm_type == RTM_IFINFO) {
23             sa = (struct sockaddr *) (ifm + 1);
24             get_rtaddrs(ifm->ifm_addrs, sa, rti_info);
25             if ( (sa = rti_info[RTAX_IFP]) != NULL) {
26                 if (sa->sa_family == AF_LINK) {
27                     sdl = (struct sockaddr_dl *) sa;
28                     namptr -= sdl->sdl_nlen + 1;
29                     strncpy(namptr, &sdl->sdl_data[0], sdl->sdl_nlen);
30                     namptr[sdl->sdl_nlen] = 0;   /* null terminate */
31                     ifptr->if_name = namptr;
32                     ifptr->if_index = sdl->sdl_index;
33                     ifptr++;
34                 }
35             }
36         }
37     }
38     ifptr->if_name = NULL;        /* mark end of array of structs */
39     ifptr->if_index = 0;
40     free(buf);
41     return (result);             /* caller must free() this when done */
42 }
```

── libroute/if_nameindex.c

Figure 18.20 Return all the interface names and indexes.

Get interface list, allocate room for result

13–18   We call our `net_rt_iflist` function to return the interface list. We also use the returned size as the size of the buffer that we allocate to contain the array of `if_nameindex` structures we return. This is an overestimate, but it is simpler than making two passes through the interface list: one to count the number of interfaces and the total sizes of the names and another to fill in the information. We create the `if_nameindex` array at the beginning of this buffer and store the interface names starting at the end of the buffer.

Process only `RTM_IFINFO` messages

22–36   We process all the messages looking for `RTM_IFINFO` messages and the datalink socket address structures that follow. The interface name and index are stored in the array we are building.

Terminate array

38–39   The final entry in the array has a null `if_name` and an index of 0.

`if_freenameindex` Function

The final function, shown in Figure 18.21, frees the memory that was allocated for the array of `if_nameindex` structures and the names contained therein.

libroute/if_nameindex.c
```
43 void
44 if_freenameindex(struct if_nameindex *ptr)
45 {
46     free(ptr);
47 }
```
libroute/if_nameindex.c

Figure 18.21 Free the memory allocated by `if_nameindex`.

This function is trivial because we stored both the array of structures and the names in the same buffer. If we had called `malloc` for each name, to free the memory, we would have to go through the entire array, `free` the memory for each name, and then free the array.

18.7 Summary

The last socket address structure that we encounter in this text is the `sockaddr_dl` structure, the variable-length datalink socket address structure. Berkeley-derived kernels associate these with interfaces, returning the interface index, name, and hardware address in one of these structures.

Five types of messages can be written to a routing socket by a process and 15 different messages can be returned by the kernel asynchronously on a routing socket. We showed an example where the process asks the kernel for information on a routing table entry and the kernel responds with all the details. These kernel responses contain up to eight socket address structures and we have to parse this message to obtain each piece of information.

The `sysctl` function is a general way to fetch and store OS parameters. The information we are interested in with `sysctl` is

- Dumping the interface list
- Dumping the routing table
- Dumping the ARP cache

The changes required by IPv6 to the sockets API include four functions to map between interface names and their indexes. Each interface is assigned a unique positive index. Berkeley-derived implementations already associate an index with each interface, so we are easily able to implement these functions using `sysctl`.

Exercises

18.1 What would you expect the `sdl_len` field of a datalink socket address structure to contain for a device named `eth10` whose link-layer address is a 64-bit IEEE EUI-64 address?

18.2 In Figure 18.6 disable the `SO_USELOOPBACK` socket option before calling `write`. What happens?

19

Key Management Sockets

19.1 Introduction

With the introduction of the security architecture for IP (IPsec, described in RFC 2401 [Kent and Atkinson 1998a]), a standard mechanism was needed to manage secret encryption and authorization keys. RFC 2367 [McDonald, Metz, and Phan 1998] introduces a generic key management API that can be used for IPsec and other network security services. Similar to routing sockets (Chapter 18), this API creates a new protocol family, the PF_KEY domain. As with routing sockets, the only type of socket supported in the key domain is a raw socket.

> As described in Section 4.2, on most systems, AF_KEY would be defined to the same value as PF_KEY. However, RFC 2367 is quite specific that PF_KEY is the constant that must be used with key management sockets.

Opening a raw key management socket requires privileges. On systems where privileges are segmented, there must be an individual privilege for opening key management sockets. On regular UNIX systems, opening a key management socket is limited to the superuser.

IPsec provides security services to packets based on *security associations*, or SAs. An SA describes a combination of source and destination addresses (and optionally, transport protocol and ports), mechanism (e.g., authentication), and keying material. More than one SA (e.g., authentication and encryption) can apply to a single stream of traffic. The set of security associations stored for use on a system is called the security association database, or SADB.

The SADB on a system may be used for more than just IPsec; for instance, OSPFv2, RIPv2, RSVP, and Mobile-IP may also have entries in the SADB. For this reason, PF_KEY sockets are not specific to IPsec.

IPsec also requires a *security policy* database, or SPDB. The security policy database describes requirements for traffic; for example, traffic between host A and host B must be authorized using IPsec AH, and any that is not must be dropped. The SADB describes how to perform the required security steps, such as, if traffic between host A and host B is using IPsec AH, then the SADB contains the algorithm and key to use. Unfortunately, there is no standard mechanism to maintain the SPDB. PF_KEY allows maintenance of the SADB, but not the SPDB. KAME's IPsec implementation uses PF_KEY extensions for SPDB maintenance, but there is no standard for this.

Three types of operations are supported on key management sockets:

1. A process can send a message to the kernel and all other processes with open key management sockets by writing to a key management socket. This is how SADB entries are added and deleted, and how processes that do their own security like OSPFv2 can request a key from a key management daemon.

2. A process can read a message from the kernel (or another process) on a key management socket. The kernel can use this facility to request that a key management daemon install a security association for a new TCP session that policy requires be protected.

3. A process can send a dump request message to the kernel, and the kernel will reply with a dump of the current SADB. This is a debugging feature that may not be available on all systems.

19.2 Reading and Writing

All messages on a key management socket have the same basic header, shown in Figure 19.1. Each message may be followed by various extensions, depending on what additional information is available or required. All the appropriate structures are defined by including <net/pfkeyv2.h>. Each message and extension is 64-bit-aligned and is a multiple of 64 bits in length. All length fields are in units of 64 bits, that is, a length of 1 means 8 bytes. Any extension that does not require enough data to be a multiple of 64 bits in length is padded to the next multiple of 64 bits. The value of this padding is not defined.

The sadb_msg_type value determines which of the 10 key management commands is being invoked. These message types are listed in Figure 19.2. Each sadb_msg header will be followed by zero or more extensions. Most message types have required and optional extensions; we will describe these as we describe each message type. The 16 types of extensions, along with the name of the structure that defines each extension, are listed in Figure 19.4.

```
struct sadb_msg {
  u_int8_t sadb_msg_version;      /* PF_KEY_V2 */
  u_int8_t sadb_msg_type;         /* see Figure 19.2 */
  u_int8_t sadb_msg_errno;        /* error indication */
  u_int8_t sadb_msg_satype;       /* see Figure 19.3 */
  u_int16_t sadb_msg_len;         /* length of header + extensions / 8 */
  u_int16_t sadb_msg_reserved;    /* zero on transmit, ignored on receive */
  u_int32_t sadb_msg_seq;         /* sequence number */
  u_int32_t sadb_msg_pid;         /* process ID of source or dest */
};
```

Figure 19.1 Key management message header.

Message type	To kernel?	From kernel?	Description
SADB_ACQUIRE	•	•	Request creation of an SADB entry
SADB_ADD	•	•	Add a complete security database entry
SADB_DELETE	•	•	Delete an entry
SADB_DUMP	•	•	Dump the SADB (debugging)
SADB_EXPIRE		•	Notify of expiration of an entry
SADB_FLUSH	•	•	Flush the entire database
SADB_GET	•	•	Get an entry
SADB_GETSPI	•	•	Allocate an SPI to create an SADB entry
SADB_REGISTER	•		Register as a replier to SADB_ACQUIRE
SADB_UPDATE	•	•	Update a partial SADB entry

Figure 19.2 Types of messages exchanged across a PF_KEY socket.

Security Association Type	Description
SADB_SATYPE_AH	IPsec authentication header
SADB_SATYPE_ESP	IPsec encapsulating security payload
SADB_SATYPE_MIP	Mobile IP authentication
SADB_SATYPE_OSPFV2	OSPFv2 authentication
SADB_SATYPE_RIPV2	RIPv2 authentication
SADB_SATYPE_RSVP	RSVP authentication
SADB_SATYPE_UNSPECIFIED	Unspecified; only valid in requests

Figure 19.3 Types of SAs.

Extension header type	Description	Structure
SADB_EXT_ADDRESS_DST	SA destination address	sadb_address
SADB_EXT_ADDRESS_PROXY	SA proxy address	sadb_address
SADB_EXT_ADDRESS_SRC	SA source address	sadb_address
SADB_EXT_IDENTITY_DST	Destination identity	sadb_ident
SADB_EXT_IDENTITY_SRC	Source identity	sadb_ident
SADB_EXT_KEY_AUTH	Authentication key	sadb_key
SADB_EXT_KEY_ENCRYPT	Encryption key	sadb_key
SADB_EXT_LIFETIME_CURRENT	Current lifetime of SA	sadb_lifetime
SADB_EXT_LIFETIME_HARD	Hard lifetime limit of SA	sadb_lifetime
SADB_EXT_LIFETIME_SOFT	Soft lifetime limit of SA	sadb_lifetime
SADB_EXT_PROPOSAL	Proposed situation	sadb_prop
SADB_EXT_SA	SA	sadb_sa
SADB_EXT_SENSITIVITY	Sensitivity of SA	sadb_sens
SADB_EXT_SPIRANGE	Acceptable range of SPI values	sadb_spirange
SADB_EXT_SUPPORTED_AUTH	Supported authentication algorithms	sadb_supported
SADB_EXT_SUPPORTED_ENCRYPT	Supported encryption algorithms	sadb_supported

Figure 19.4 PF_KEY Extension Types.

We now show several examples and the messages and extensions involved in several common operations on key management sockets.

19.3 Dumping the Security Association Database (SADB)

To dump the current SADB, a process uses the SADB_DUMP message. This is the simplest message to send since the message does not require any extensions, simply the 16-byte sadb_msg header. After the process sends the SADB_DUMP message to the kernel on a key management socket, the kernel replies with a series of SADB_DUMP messages back to the same socket, each with one entry from the SADB. The end of the list is indicated by a message with a value of 0 for the sadb_msg_seq field.

The type of SA can be limited by setting the sadb_msg_satype field in the request to one of the values in Figure 19.3. If it is set to SADB_SATYPE_UNSPEC, then all SAs in the database are returned. Otherwise, only SAs of the specified type are returned. Not all types of security associations are supported by all implementations. The KAME implementation only supports IPsec SAs (SADB_SATYPE_AH and SADB_SATYPE_ESP), so an attempt to dump SADB_SATYPE_RIPV2 SADB entries will get an error reply with errno EINVAL. When requesting a specific type whose table is empty, the errno ENOENT is returned.

Our program to dump the SADB follows in Figure 19.5.

———————————————————————————————— key/dump.c

```
 1 void
 2 sadb_dump(int type)
 3 {
 4     int     s;
 5     char    buf[4096];
 6     struct sadb_msg msg;
 7     int     goteof;

 8     s = Socket(PF_KEY, SOCK_RAW, PF_KEY_V2);

 9     /* Build and write SADB_DUMP request */
10     bzero(&msg, sizeof(msg));
11     msg.sadb_msg_version = PF_KEY_V2;
12     msg.sadb_msg_type = SADB_DUMP;
13     msg.sadb_msg_satype = type;
14     msg.sadb_msg_len = sizeof(msg) / 8;
15     msg.sadb_msg_pid = getpid();
16     printf("Sending dump message:\n");
17     print_sadb_msg(&msg, sizeof(msg));
18     Write(s, &msg, sizeof(msg));

19     printf("\nMessages returned:\n");
20     /* Read and print SADB_DUMP replies until done */
21     goteof = 0;
22     while (goteof == 0) {
23         int     msglen;
24         struct sadb_msg *msgp;

25         msglen = Read(s, &buf, sizeof(buf));
26         msgp = (struct sadb_msg *) &buf;
27         print_sadb_msg(msgp, msglen);
28         if (msgp->sadb_msg_seq == 0)
29             goteof = 1;
30     }
31     close(s);
32 }

33 int
34 main(int argc, char **argv)
35 {
36     int     satype = SADB_SATYPE_UNSPEC;
37     int     c;

38     opterr = 0;                  /* don't want getopt() writing to stderr */
39     while ( (c = getopt(argc, argv, "t:")) != -1) {
40         switch (c) {
41         case 't':
42             if ( (satype = getsatypebyname(optarg)) == -1)
43                 err_quit("invalid -t option %s", optarg);
44             break;

45         default:
46             err_quit("unrecognized option: %c", c);
47         }
48     }
49     sadb_dump(satype);
50 }
```

———————————————————————————————— key/dump.c

Figure 19.5 Program to issue SADB_DUMP command on key management socket.

This is our first encounter with the POSIX getopt function. The third argument is a character string specifying the characters that we allow as command-line arguments, just t in this example. It is followed by a colon, indicating that the option takes an argument. In programs that take more than one option, they are concatenated together; for example, Figure 29.7 passes 0i:l:v to indicate that it accepts four options; i and l take an argument and 0 and v don't. This function works with four global variables that are defined by including <unistd.h>.

```
extern char  *optarg;
extern int    optind, opterr, optopt;
```

Before calling getopt, we set opterr to 0 to prevent the function from writing error messages to standard error in case of an error, because we want to handle these. POSIX states that if the first character of the third argument is a colon, this also prevents the function from writing to standard error, but not all implementations support this.

Open PF_KEY socket

1–8   We first open a PF_KEY socket. This requires system privileges, as described earlier, since this allows access to sensitive keying material.

Build SADB_DUMP request

9–15   We first zero out the sadb_msg struct so that we can skip initializing the fields that we wish to remain zero. We fill in each remaining field in the sadb_msg struct individually. All messages on sockets opened with PF_KEY_V2 as the third argument must also use PF_KEY_V2 as the message version. The message type is SADB_DUMP. We set the length to the length of the base header with no extensions since the dump message does not take extensions. Finally, we set the process ID (PID) to our own PID since all messages must be identified by the PID of the sender.

Display and write SADB_DUMP message

16–18   We display the message using our print_sadb_msg routine. We don't show this routine since it is long and uninteresting, but it is included in the freely available source code. This routine accepts a message that is being written to or has been received from a key management socket and prints all the information from the message in a human-readable form. We then write the message to the socket.

Read replies

19–30   We loop, reading replies and printing them using our print_sadb_msg function. The last message in the dump sequence has a message sequence number of zero, so we use this as our "end-of-file" indication.

Close PF_KEY socket

31   Finally, we close the socket that we opened.

Handle command-line arguments

38–48   The main function has very little work to do. This program takes a single optional argument, which is the type of SA to dump. By default, the type is SADB_SATYPE_UNSPEC, which dumps all SAs of any type. By specifying a command-line argument, the user can select which type of SAs to dump. This program uses our getsatypebyname function, which returns the type value for a text string.

Call sadb_dump routine

49   Finally, we call the sadb_dump function we defined above to do all the work.

Sample Run

The following is a sample run of the dump program on a system with two static SAs.

```
macosx % dump
Sending dump message:
SADB Message Dump, errno 0, satype Unspecified, seq 0, pid 20623

Messages returned:
SADB Message Dump, errno 0, satype IPsec AH, seq 1, pid 20623
 SA: SPI=258 Replay Window=0 State=Mature
  Authentication Algorithm: HMAC-MD5
  Encryption Algorithm: None
 [unknown extension 19]
 Current lifetime:
  0 allocations, 0 bytes
  added at Sun May 18 16:28:11 2003, never used
 Source address:   2.3.4.5/128 (IP proto 255)
 Dest address:   6.7.8.9/128 (IP proto 255)
 Authentication key, 128 bits: 0x20202020202020200202020202020202
SADB Message Dump, errno 0, satype IPsec AH, seq 0, pid 20623
 SA: SPI=257 Replay Window=0 State=Mature
  Authentication Algorithm: HMAC-MD5
  Encryption Algorithm: None
 [unknown extension 19]
 Current lifetime:
  0 allocations, 0 bytes
  added at Sun May 18 16:26:24 2003, never used
 Source address:   1.2.3.4/128 (IP proto 255)
 Dest address:   5.6.7.8/128 (IP proto 255)
 Authentication key, 128 bits: 0x10101010101010100101010101010101
```

19.4 Creating a Static Security Association (SA)

The most straightforward method of adding an SA is to send an SADB_ADD message with all parameters filled in, presumably manually specified. Although manual specification of keying material does not lead easily to key changes, which are crucial to avoid cryptanalysis attacks, it is quite easy to configure: Alice and Bob agree on a key and algorithms to use out-of-band, and proceed to use them. We show the steps needed to create and send an SADB_ADD message.

The SADB_ADD message requires three extensions: SA, address and key. It can also optionally contain other extensions: lifetime, identity, and sensitivity. We describe the required extensions first. The SA extension is described by the sadb_sa structure, shown in Figure 19.6.

```
struct sadb_sa {
  u_int16_t sadb_sa_len;      /* length of extension / 8 */
  u_int16_t sadb_sa_exttype;  /* SADB_EXT_SA */
  u_int32_t sadb_sa_spi;      /* Security Parameters Index (SPI) */
  u_int8_t  sadb_sa_replay;   /* replay window size, or zero */
  u_int8_t  sadb_sa_state;    /* SA state, see Figure 19.7 */
  u_int8_t  sadb_sa_auth;     /* authentication algorithm, see Figure 19.8 */
  u_int8_t  sadb_sa_encrypt;  /* encryption algorithm, see Figure 19.8 */
  u_int32_t sadb_sa_flags;    /* bitmask of flags */
};
```

Figure 19.6 SA Extension.

SA state	Description	Can be used?
SADB_SASTATE_LARVAL	In process of being created	No
SADB_SASTATE_MATURE	Fully formed	Yes
SADB_SASTATE_DYING	Soft lifetime has expired	Yes
SADB_SASTATE_DEAD	Hard lifetime has expired	No

Figure 19.7 Possible states for SAs.

Algorithm	Description	Reference
SADB_AALG_NONE	No authentication	
SADB_AALG_MD5HMAC	HMAC-MD5-96	RFC 2403
SADB_AALG_SHA1HMAC	HMAC-SHA-1-96	RFC 2404
SADB_EALG_NONE	No encryption	
SADB_EALG_DESCBC	DES-CBC	RFC 2405
SADB_EALG_3DESCBC	3DES-CBC	RFC 1851
SADB_EALG_NULL	NULL	RFC 2410

Figure 19.8 Authentication and Encryption algorithms.

The sadb_sa_spi field contains the *Security Parameters Index*, or SPI. This value, combined with the destination address and protocol in use (e.g., IPsec AH), uniquely identifies an SA. When receiving a packet, this value is used to look up the SA for that packet; when sending a packet, this value is inserted into the packet for the other end to use. It has no other meaning, so these values can be allocated sequentially, randomly, or using any method the destination system prefers. The sadb_sa_reply field specifies the window size for replay protection. Since static keying prevents replay protection, we will set this to zero. The sadb_sa_state field varies during the life cycle of a dynamically created SA, using the values in Figure 19.7. However, manually created SAs spend all their time in the SADB_SASTATE_MATURE state. We will see the other states in Section 19.5.

The sadb_sa_auth and sadb_sa_encrypt fields specify the authentication and encryption algorithms for this SA. Possible values for these fields are listed in Figure 19.8. There is only one flag value currently defined for the sadb_sa_flags field,

`SADB_SAFLAGS_PFS`. This flag requests *perfect forward security*, that is, the value of this key must not be dependent on any previous keys or some master key. This flag value is used when requesting keys from a key management application and is not used when adding static associations.

The next required extensions for an `SADB_ADD` command are the addresses. Source and destination addresses, specified with `SADB_EXT_ADDRESS_SRC` and `SADB_EXT_ADDRESS_DST`, respectively, are required. A proxy address, specified with `SADB_EXT_ADDRESS_PROXY`, is optional. For more details on proxy addresses, see RFC 2367 [McDonald, Metz, and Phan 1998]. Addresses are specified using a `sadb_address` extension, shown in Figure 19.9. The `sadb_address_exttype` field determines what type of address this extension is supplying. The `sadb_address_proto` field specifies the IP protocol to be matched for this SA, or 0 to match all protocols. The `sadb_address_prefixlen` field describes the prefix of the address that is significant. This permits an SA to match more than one address. A `sockaddr` of the appropriate family (e.g., `sockaddr_in`, `sockaddr_in6`) follows the `sadb_address` structure. The port number in this `sockaddr` is significant only if the `sadb_address_proto` specifies a protocol that supports port numbers (e.g., `IPPROTO_TCP`).

```
struct sadb_address {
  u_int16_t sadb_address_len;        /* length of extension + address / 8 */
  u_int16_t sadb_address_exttype;    /* SADB_EXT_ADDRESS_{SRC,DST,PROXY} */
  u_int8_t  sadb_address_proto;      /* IP protocol, or 0 for all */
  u_int8_t  sadb_address_prefixlen;  /* # significant bits in address */
  u_int16_t sadb_address_reserved;   /* reserved for extension */
};
                                     /* followed by appropriate sockaddr */
```

Figure 19.9 Address extension.

The final required extensions for the `SADB_ADD` message are the authentication and encryption keys, specified with the `SADB_EXT_KEY_AUTH` and `SADB_EXT_KEY_ENCRYPT` extensions, which are represented by a `sadb_key` structure (Figure 19.10). The key extension is very straightforward; the `sadb_key_exttype` member defines whether it is an authentication or encryption key, the `sadb_key_bits` member specifies the number of bits in the key, and the key itself follows the `sadb_key` structure.

```
struct sadb_key {
  u_int16_t sadb_key_len;        /* length of extension + key / 8 */
  u_int16_t sadb_key_exttype;    /* SADB_EXT_KEY_{AUTH,ENCRYPT} */
  u_int16_t sadb_key_bits;       /* # bits in key */
  u_int16_t sadb_key_reserved;   /* reserved for extension */
};
                                 /* followed by key data */
```

Figure 19.10 Key extension.

```
                                                                        key/add.c
33 void
34 sadb_add(struct sockaddr *src, struct sockaddr *dst, int type, int alg,
35          int spi, int keybits, unsigned char *keydata)
36 {
37     int     s;
38     char    buf[4096], *p;        /* XXX */
39     struct sadb_msg *msg;
40     struct sadb_sa *saext;
41     struct sadb_address *addrext;
42     struct sadb_key *keyext;
43     int     len;
44     int     mypid;

45     s = Socket(PF_KEY, SOCK_RAW, PF_KEY_V2);

46     mypid = getpid();

47     /* Build and write SADB_ADD request */
48     bzero(&buf, sizeof(buf));
49     p = buf;
50     msg = (struct sadb_msg *) p;
51     msg->sadb_msg_version = PF_KEY_V2;
52     msg->sadb_msg_type = SADB_ADD;
53     msg->sadb_msg_satype = type;
54     msg->sadb_msg_pid = getpid();
55     len = sizeof(*msg);
56     p += sizeof(*msg);

57     saext = (struct sadb_sa *) p;
58     saext->sadb_sa_len = sizeof(*saext) / 8;
59     saext->sadb_sa_exttype = SADB_EXT_SA;
60     saext->sadb_sa_spi = htonl(spi);
61     saext->sadb_sa_replay = 0;  /* no replay protection with static keys */
62     saext->sadb_sa_state = SADB_SASTATE_MATURE;
63     saext->sadb_sa_auth = alg;
64     saext->sadb_sa_encrypt = SADB_EALG_NONE;
65     saext->sadb_sa_flags = 0;
66     len += saext->sadb_sa_len * 8;
67     p += saext->sadb_sa_len * 8;

68     addrext = (struct sadb_address *) p;
69     addrext->sadb_address_len = (sizeof(*addrext) + salen(src) + 7) / 8;
70     addrext->sadb_address_exttype = SADB_EXT_ADDRESS_SRC;
71     addrext->sadb_address_proto = 0;    /* any protocol */
72     addrext->sadb_address_prefixlen = prefix_all(src);
73     addrext->sadb_address_reserved = 0;
74     memcpy(addrext + 1, src, salen(src));
75     len += addrext->sadb_address_len * 8;
76     p += addrext->sadb_address_len * 8;

77     addrext = (struct sadb_address *) p;
78     addrext->sadb_address_len = (sizeof(*addrext) + salen(dst) + 7) / 8;
79     addrext->sadb_address_exttype = SADB_EXT_ADDRESS_DST;
80     addrext->sadb_address_proto = 0;    /* any protocol */
81     addrext->sadb_address_prefixlen = prefix_all(dst);
82     addrext->sadb_address_reserved = 0;
```

```
83        memcpy(addrext + 1, dst, salen(dst));
84        len += addrext->sadb_address_len * 8;
85        p += addrext->sadb_address_len * 8;

86        keyext = (struct sadb_key *) p;
87        /* "+7" handles alignment requirements */
88        keyext->sadb_key_len = (sizeof(*keyext) + (keybits / 8) + 7) / 8;
89        keyext->sadb_key_exttype = SADB_EXT_KEY_AUTH;
90        keyext->sadb_key_bits = keybits;
91        keyext->sadb_key_reserved = 0;
92        memcpy(keyext + 1, keydata, keybits / 8);
93        len += keyext->sadb_key_len * 8;
94        p += keyext->sadb_key_len * 8;

95        msg->sadb_msg_len = len / 8;
96        printf("Sending add message:\n");
97        print_sadb_msg(buf, len);
98        Write(s, buf, len);

99        printf("\nReply returned:\n");
100       /* Read and print SADB_ADD reply, discarding any others */
101       for ( ; ; ) {
102           int     msglen;
103           struct sadb_msg *msgp;

104           msglen = Read(s, &buf, sizeof(buf));
105           msgp = (struct sadb_msg *) &buf;
106           if (msgp->sadb_msg_pid == mypid && msgp->sadb_msg_type == SADB_ADD) {
107               print_sadb_msg(msgp, msglen);
108               break;
109           }
110       }
111       close(s);
112   }
```
———————————————————————————————— key/add.c

Figure 19.11   Program to issue SADB_ADD command on key management socket.

We show our program to add a static SADB entry in Figure 19.11.

Open PF_KEY socket and save PID

55–56   As before, we open a PF_KEY socket and save our PID for later.

Build common message header

47–56   We build the common message header for the SADB_ADD message. We don't set the sadb_msg_len element until just before writing the message since it must reflect the entire length of the message. The len variable keeps a running length of the message, and the p pointer always points to the first unused byte in the buffer.

Append SA extension

57–67   Next, we add the required SA extension (Figure 19.6). The sadb_sa_spi field must be in network byte order, so we call htonl on the host order value that was passed to the function. We turn off replay protection and set the SA state (Figure 19.7) to SADB_SASTATE_MATURE. We set the authentication algorithm to the algorithm value specified on the command line, and specify no encryption with SADB_EALG_NONE.

Append source address

68-76 We add the source address to the message as an `SADB_EXT_ADDRESS_SRC` extension. We set the protocol to 0, meaning that this association applies to all protocols. We set the prefix length to the appropriate length for the IP version, that is, 32 bits for IPv4 and 128 bits for IPv6. The calculation of the length field adds 7 before dividing by 8, which ensures that the length reflects the padding required to pad out to a 64-bit boundary as required for all `PF_KEY` extensions. The `sockaddr` is copied after the extension header.

Append destination address

77-85 The destination address is added as an `SADB_EXT_ADDRESS_DST` extension in exactly the same way as the source address.

Append key

86-94 We add the authentication key to the message as an `SADB_EXT_KEY_AUTH` extension. We calculate the length field the same way as for the addresses, to add the required padding for the variable-length key. We set the number of bits and copy the key data to follow the extension header.

Write message

95-98 We print out the message with our `print_sadb_msg` function, and write it to the socket.

Read reply

99-111 We read messages from the socket until we receive one that is addressed to our PID and is an `SADB_ADD` message. We then print that message with the `print_sadb_msg` function and exit.

Example

We run our program to send an `SADB_ADD` message for traffic between 127.0.0.1 and 127.0.0.1; in other words, on the local system.

```
macosx % add 127.0.0.1 127.0.0.1 HMAC-SHA-1-96 160 \
                        0123456789abcdef0123456789abcdef01234567
Sending add message:
SADB Message Add, errno 0, satype IPsec AH, seq 0, pid 6246
 SA: SPI=39030 Replay Window=0 State=Mature
  Authentication Algorithm: HMAC-SHA-1
  Encryption Algorithm: None
  Source address:   127.0.0.1/32
  Dest address:   127.0.0.1/32
  Authentication key, 160 bits: 0x0123456789abcdef0123456789abcdef01234567

Reply returned:
SADB Message Add, errno 0, satype IPsec AH, seq 0, pid 6246
 SA: SPI=39030 Replay Window=0 State=Mature
  Authentication Algorithm: HMAC-SHA-1
  Encryption Algorithm: None
  Source address:   127.0.0.1/32
  Dest address:   127.0.0.1/32
```

Note that the reply echoes the request without the key. This is because the reply is sent to all `PF_KEY` sockets, but different `PF_KEY` sockets may belong to sockets in different protection domains, and keying data should not cross protection domains. After adding the SA to the database, we ping 127.0.0.1 to cause the SA to be used, then dump the database to see what was added.

```
macosx % dump
Sending dump message:
SADB Message Dump, errno 0, satype Unspecified, seq 0, pid 6283

Messages returned:
SADB Message Dump, errno 0, satype IPsec AH, seq 0, pid 6283
 SA: SPI=39030 Replay Window=0 State=Mature
  Authentication Algorithm: HMAC-SHA-1
  Encryption Algorithm: None
[unknown extension 19]
Current lifetime:
 36 allocations, 0 bytes
 added at Thu Jun  5 21:01:31 2003, first used at Thu Jun  5 21:15:07 2003
Source address:   127.0.0.1/128 (IP proto 255)
Dest address:   127.0.0.1/128 (IP proto 255)
Authentication key, 160 bits: 0x0123456789abcdef0123456789abcdef01234567
```

We see from this dump that the kernel has changed our IP protocol zero to 255. This is an artifact of this implementation, not a general property of `PF_KEY` sockets. In addition, we see that the kernel changed the prefix length from 32 to 128. This appears to be a confusing issue between IPv4 and IPv6 within the kernel. The kernel returns an extension (numbered 19) that our dump program doesn't understand. Unknown extensions are skipped using the length field. A lifetime extension (Figure 19.12) is returned containing the current lifetime information of the SA.

```
struct sadb_lifetime {
  u_int16_t sadb_lifetime_len;         /* length of extension / 8 */
  u_int16_t sadb_lifetime_exttype;     /* SADB_EXT_LIFETIME_{SOFT,HARD,CURRENT} */
  u_int32_t sadb_lifetime_allocations; /* # connections, endpoints, or flows */
  u_int64_t sadb_lifetime_bytes;       /* # bytes */
  u_int64_t sadb_lifetime_addtime;     /* time of creation, or time from
                                          creation to expiration */
  u_int64_t sadb_lifetime_usetime;     /* time first used, or time from
                                          first use to expiration */
};
```

Figure 19.12 Lifetime extension.

There are three different lifetime extensions. The `SADB_LIFETIME_SOFT` and `SADB_LIFETIME_HARD` extensions specify soft and hard lifetimes for an SA, respectively. The kernel sends an `SADB_EXPIRE` message when the soft lifetime has been reached; the SA will not be used after its hard lifetime has been reached. The `SADB_LIFETIME_CURRENT` extension is returned in `SADB_DUMP`, `SADB_EXPIRE`, and `SADB_GET` responses to describe the values for the current association.

19.5 Dynamically Maintaining SAs

For greater security, periodic rekeying is required. This is usually performed by a proto-col such as IKE (RFC 2409 [Harkins and Carrel 1998]).

> As of this writing, the IETF IPsec working group is working on a replacement for IKE.

To learn when an SA is required between a new pair of hosts, a daemon registers itself with the kernel using the SADB_REGISTER message, specifying the type of SA it can handle in the sadb_msg_satype field from the values in Figure 19.3. If a daemon can handle multiple SA types, it sends multiple SADB_REGISTER messages, each regis-tering a single type. In its SADB_REGISTER reply message, the kernel includes a sup-ported algorithms extension, indicating what encryption and/or authentication mechanisms are supported with what key lengths. The supported algorithms extension is described by an sadb_supported structure, shown in Figure 19.13; it simply con-tains a series of encryption or authentication algorithm descriptions in sadb_alg struc-tures following the extension header.

```
struct sadb_supported {
  u_int16_t sadb_supported_len;      /* length of extension ı algorithms / 8 */
  u_int16_t sadb_supported_exttype;  /* SADB_EXT_SUPPORTED_{AUTH,ENCRYPT} */
  u_int32_t sadb_supported_reserved; /* reserved for future expansion */
};
                                     /* followed by algorithm list */

struct sadb_alg {
  u_int8_t sadb_alg_id;              /* algorithm ID from Figure 19.8 */
  u_int8_t sadb_alg_ivlen;           /* IV length, or zero */
  u_int16_t sadb_alg_minbits;        /* minimum key length */
  u_int16_t sadb_alg_maxbits;        /* maximum key length */
  u_int16_t sadb_alg_reserved;       /* reserved for future expansion */
};
```

Figure 19.13 Supported algorithms extension.

One sadb_alg structure follows the sadb_supported extension header for each algorithm supported by the system. Figure 19.14 shows a possible reply to a message registering for SA type SADB_SATYPE_ESP.

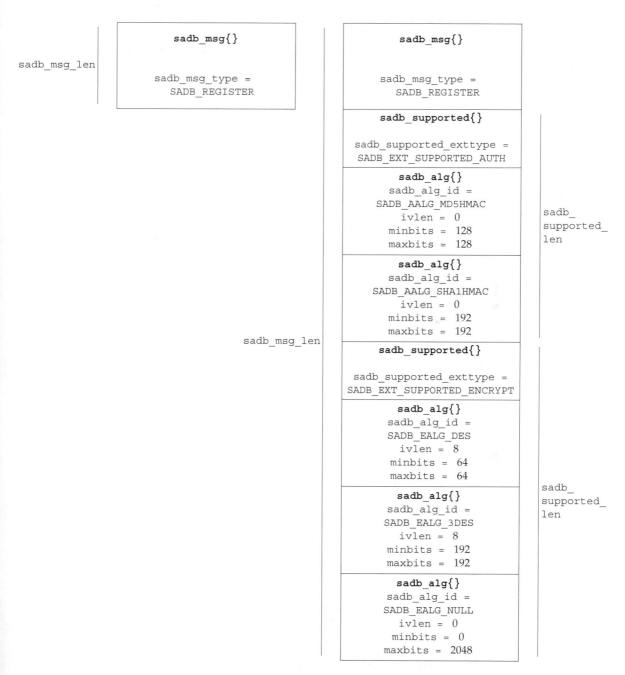

Figure 19.14 Data returned from kernel for `SADB_REGISTER` command.

Our first example program, shown in Figure 19.15, simply registers with the kernel for a given mechanism and prints the supported algorithms reply.

key/register.c

```
 1 void
 2 sadb_register(int type)
 3 {
 4     int     s;
 5     char    buf[4096];              /* XXX */
 6     struct sadb_msg msg;
 7     int     goteof;
 8     int     mypid;

 9     s = Socket(PF_KEY, SOCK_RAW, PF_KEY_V2);

10     mypid = getpid();

11     /* Build and write SADB_REGISTER request */
12     bzero(&msg, sizeof(msg));
13     msg.sadb_msg_version = PF_KEY_V2;
14     msg.sadb_msg_type = SADB_REGISTER;
15     msg.sadb_msg_satype = type;
16     msg.sadb_msg_len = sizeof(msg) / 8;
17     msg.sadb_msg_pid = mypid;
18     printf("Sending  message:\n");
19     print_sadb_msg(&msg, sizeof(msg));
20     Write(s, &msg, sizeof(msg));

21     printf("\nReply returned:\n");
22     /* Read and print SADB_REGISTER reply, discarding any others */
23     for ( ; ; ) {
24         int     msglen;
25         struct sadb_msg *msgp;

26         msglen = Read(s, &buf, sizeof(buf));
27         msgp = (struct sadb_msg *) &buf;
28         if (msgp->sadb_msg_pid == mypid &&
29             msgp->sadb_msg_type == SADB_REGISTER) {
30             print_sadb_msg(msgp, msglen);
31             break;
32         }
33     }
34     close(s);
35 }
```

key/register.c

Figure 19.15 Program to register on key management socket.

Open PF_KEY socket

1–9   We open the PF_KEY socket.

Store PID

10   Since messages will be addressed to us using our PID, we store it for comparison later.

Create SADB_REGISTER message

11–17   Just like SADB_DUMP, the SADB_REGISTER message does not require any extensions. We zero out the message and then fill in the individual fields needed.

Display and write message to socket

18-20   We display the message that we're sending using our `print_sadb_msg` function, and send the message to the socket.

Wait for reply

23-33   We read messages from the socket and wait for the reply to our register message. The reply is addressed to our PID and is a `SADB_REGISTER` message. It contains a list of supported algorithms, which we print with our `print_sadb_msg` function.

Example

We run the `register` program on a system that supports several more protocols than are described in RFC 2367.

```
macosx % register -t ah
Sending register message:
SADB Message Register, errno 0, satype IPsec AH, seq 0, pid 20746

Reply returned:
SADB Message Register, errno 0, satype IPsec AH, seq 0, pid 20746
 Supported authentication algorithms:
  HMAC-MD5 ivlen 0 bits 128-128
  HMAC-SHA-1 ivlen 0 bits 160-160
  Keyed MD5 ivlen 0 bits 128-128
  Keyed SHA-1 ivlen 0 bits 160-160
  Null ivlen 0 bits 0-2048
  SHA2-256 ivlen 0 bits 256-256
  SHA2-384 ivlen 0 bits 384-384
  SHA2-512 ivlen 0 bits 512-512
 Supported encryption algorithms:
  DES-CBC ivlen 8 bits 64-64
  3DES-CBC ivlen 8 bits 192-192
  Null ivlen 0 bits 0-2048
  Blowfish-CBC ivlen 8 bits 40-448
  CAST128-CBC ivlen 8 bits 40-128
  AES ivlen 16 bits 128-256
```

When the kernel needs to communicate with a peer and policy says that an SA is required but one is not available, the kernel sends an `SADB_ACQUIRE` message to key management sockets that have registered the SA type required, containing a proposal extension describing the kernel's proposed algorithms and key lengths. The proposal may be a combination of what is supported by the system and preconfigured policy that limits what is permitted for this communication. The proposal is a list of algorithms, key lengths, and lifetimes, in order of preference. When a key management daemon receives an `SADB_ACQUIRE` message, it performs the acts required to choose a key that fits one of the kernel's proposed combinations, and installs this key in the kernel. It uses the `SADB_GETSPI` message to ask the kernel to select an SPI from a desired range. The kernel's response to the `SADB_GETSPI` message includes creating an SA in the lar-val state. The daemon then negotiates security parameters with the remote end using the SPI supplied by the kernel, and uses the `SADB_UPDATE` message to complete the SA and cause it to enter the mature state. Dynamically created SAs generally have both a soft and a hard lifetime associated with them. When either lifetime expires, the kernel sends an SADB_EXPIRE message, indicating whether the soft or hard lifetime has expired. If the soft lifetime has expired, the SA has entered the dying state, during which it can still be used but a new SA must be obtained. If the hard lifetime has expired, the SA has entered the dead state, in which it is no longer used for security purposes and will be removed from the SADB.

19.6 Summary

Key management sockets are used to communicate SAs to the kernel, key management daemons, and to other security consumers such as routing daemons. SAs can be installed statically or dynamically via a key negotiation protocol. Dynamic keys can have associated lifetimes; when the soft lifetime is reached, the key management daemon is informed. If an SA is not replaced before the hard lifetime is reached, the SA can no longer be used.

Ten messages are exchanged between the process and kernel on key management sockets. Each message type has associated extensions, some required and some optional. Each message that is sent by a process is echoed to all other open key management sockets, removing any extensions containing sensitive data.

Exercises

19.1 Write a program that opens a PF_KEY socket and dumps all the messages that it receives.

19.2 Find out about the new protocol that the IETF IPsec working group has created to replace IKE by visiting the working group web page, http://www.ietf.org/html.charters/ipsec-charter.html

20

Broadcasting

20.1 Introduction

In this chapter, we will describe *broadcasting* and in the next chapter, we will describe *multicasting*. All the examples in the text so far have dealt with *unicasting*: a process talking to exactly one other process. Indeed, TCP works with only unicast addresses, although UDP and raw IP support other paradigms. Figure 20.1 shows a comparison of the different types of addressing.

Type	IPv4	IPv6	TCP	UDP	# IP interfaces identified	# IP interfaces delivered to
Unicast	•	•	•	•	One	One
Anycast	*	•	Not yet	•	A set	One in set
Multicast	opt.	•		•	A set	All in set
Broadcast	•			•	All	All

Figure 20.1 Different forms of addressing.

IPv6 has added *anycasting* to the addressing architecture. An IPv4 version of anycasting, which was never widely deployed, is described in RFC 1546 [Partridge, Mendez, and Milliken 1993]. IPv6 anycasting is defined in RFC 3513 [Hinden and Deering 2003]. Anycasting allows addressing one (usually the "closest" by some metric) system out of a set of systems that usually provides identical services. With an appropriate routing configuration, hosts can provide anycasting services in either IPv4 or IPv6 by injecting the same address into the routing protocol in multiple locations. However, RFC 3513's anycasting only permits routers to have anycast addresses; hosts may not provide anycasting services. As of this writing, there is no API defined for using anycast addresses. There is work in progress to refine the IPv6 anycast architecture, and hosts may be able to dynamically provide anycasting services in the future.

The important points in Figure 20.1 are:

- Multicasting support is optional in IPv4, but mandatory in IPv6.

- Broadcasting support is not provided in IPv6. Any IPv4 application that uses broadcasting must be recoded for IPv6 to use multicasting instead.

- Broadcasting and multicasting require datagram transport such as UDP or raw IP; they cannot work with TCP.

One use for broadcasting is to locate a server on the local subnet when the server is assumed to be on the local subnet but its unicast IP address is not known. This is sometimes called *resource discovery*. Another use is to minimize the network traffic on a LAN when there are multiple clients communicating with a single server. There are numerous examples of Internet applications that use broadcasting for this purpose. Some of these can also use multicasting.

- ARP—Although this is a protocol that lies underneath IPv4, and not a user application, ARP broadcasts a request on the local subnet that says, "Will the system with an IP address of a.b.c.d please identify yourself and tell me your hardware address?" ARP uses link-layer broadcast, not IP-layer, but is an example of a use of broadcasting.

- DHCP—The client assumes a server or relay is on the local subnet and sends its request to the broadcast address (often 255.255.255.255 since the client doesn't yet know its IP address, its subnet mask, or the limited broadcast address of the subnet).

- Network Time Protocol (NTP)—In one common scenario, an NTP client is configured with the IP address of one or more servers to use, and the client polls the servers at some frequency (every 64 seconds or longer). The client updates its clock using sophisticated algorithms based on the time-of-day returned by the servers and the RTT to the servers. But on a broadcast LAN, instead of making each of the clients poll a single server, the server can broadcast the current time every 64 seconds for all the clients on the local subnet, reducing the amount of network traffic.

- Routing daemons—The oldest routing daemon, `routed`, which implements RIP version 1, broadcasts its routing table on a LAN. This allows all other routers attached to the LAN to receive these routing announcements, without each router having to be configured with the IP addresses of all its neighboring routers. This feature can also be used by hosts on the LAN listening to these routing announcements and updating their routing tables accordingly. RIP version 2 permits the use of either multicast or broadcast.

We must note that multicasting can replace both uses of broadcasting (resource discovery and reducing network traffic) and we will describe the problems with broadcasting later in this chapter and the next chapter.

20.2 Broadcast Addresses

If we denote an IPv4 address as {*subnetid, hostid*}, where *subnetid* represents the bits that are covered by the network mask (or the CIDR prefix) and *hostid* represents the bits that are not, then we have two types of broadcast addresses. We denote a field containing all one bits as −1.

1. Subnet-directed broadcast address: {*subnetid*, −1}—This addresses all the interfaces on the specified subnet. For example, if we have the subnet 192.168.42/24, then 192.168.42.255 would be the subnet-directed broadcast address for all interfaces on the 192.168.42/24 subnet.

   Normally, routers do not forward these broadcasts (pp. 226–227 of TCPv2). In Figure 20.2, we show a router connected to the two subnets 192.168.42/24 and 192.168.123/24.

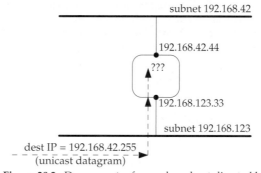

Figure 20.2 Does a router forward a subnet-directed broadcast?

The router receives a unicast IP datagram on the 192.168.123/24 subnet with a destination address of 192.168.42.255 (the subnet-directed broadcast address of another interface). The router normally does not forward the datagram on to the 192.168.42/24 subnet. Some systems have a configuration option that allows subnet-directed broadcasts to be forwarded (Appendix E of TCPv1).

> Forwarding subnet-directed broadcasts enables a class of denial-of-service attacks called "amplification" attacks; for instance, sending an ICMP echo request to a subnet-directed broadcast address can cause multiple replies to be sent for a single request. Combined with a forged IP source address, this results in a bandwidth utilization attack against the victim system, so it's advisable to leave this configuration option off.

> For this reason, it's inadvisable to design an application that relies on forwarding of subnet-directed broadcasts except in a controlled environment, where you know it's safe to turn them on.

2. Limited broadcast address: {−1, −1, −1} or 255.255.255.255—Datagrams destined
    to this address must never be forwarded by a router.

> 255.255.255.255 is to be used as the destination address during the bootstrap process by appli-
> cations such as BOOTP and DHCP, which do not yet know the node's IP address.

> The question is: What does a host do when an application sends a UDP datagram to
> 255.255.255.255? Most hosts allow this (assuming the process has set the SO_BROADCAST
> socket option) and convert the destination address to the subnet-directed broadcast address of
> the outgoing interface. It is often necessary to access the datalink directly (Chapter 29) to send
> a packet to 255.255.255.255.

> Another question is: What does a multihomed host do when the application sends a UDP data-
> gram to 255.255.255.255? Some systems send a single broadcast on the primary interface (the
> first interface that was configured) with the destination IP address set to the subnet-directed
> broadcast address of that interface (p. 736 of TCPv2). Other systems send one copy of the
> datagram out from each broadcast-capable interface. Section 3.3.6 of RFC 1122 [Braden 1989]
> "takes no stand" on this issue. For portability, however, if an application needs to send a
> broadcast out from all broadcast-capable interfaces, it should obtain the interface configuration
> (Section 17.6) and do one sendto for each broadcast-capable interface with the destination set
> to that interface's broadcast address.

20.3 Unicast versus Broadcast

Before looking at broadcasting, let's make certain we understand the steps that take
place when a UDP datagram is sent to a unicast address. Figure 20.3 shows three hosts
on an Ethernet.

The subnet address of the Ethernet is 192.168.42/24 with 24 bits in the network
mask, leaving 8 bits for the host ID. The application on the left host calls sendto on a
UDP socket, sending a datagram to 192.168.42.3, port 7433. The UDP layer prepends a
UDP header and passes the UDP datagram to the IP layer. IP prepends an IPv4 header,
determines the outgoing interface, and in the case of an Ethernet, ARP is invoked to
map the destination IP address to the corresponding Ethernet address: 00:0a:95:79:
bc:b4. The packet is then sent as an Ethernet frame with that 48-bit address as the destination Ethernet address. The frame type field of the Ethernet frame will be 0x0800,
specifying an IPv4 packet. The frame type for an IPv6 packet is 0x86dd.

The Ethernet interface on the host in the middle sees the frame pass by and compares the destination Ethernet address to its own Ethernet address 00:04:ac:17:bf:
38). Since they are not equal, the interface ignores the frame. With a unicast frame,
there is no overhead whatsoever to this host. The interface ignores the frame.

The Ethernet interface on the host on the right also sees the frame pass by, and
when it compares the destination Ethernet address with its own Ethernet address, they
are equal. This interface reads in the entire frame, probably generates a hardware interrupt when the frame is complete, and the device driver reads the frame from the interface memory. Since the frame type is 0x0800, the packet is placed on the IP input
queue.

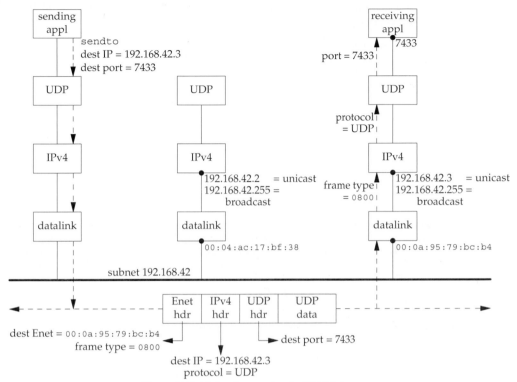

Figure 20.3 Unicast example of a UDP datagram.

When the IP layer processes the packet, it first compares the destination IP address (192.168.42.3) with all of its own IP addresses. (Recall that a host can be multihomed. Also recall our discussion of the strong end system model and the weak end system model in Section 8.8.) Since the destination address is one of the host's own IP addresses, the packet is accepted.

The IP layer then looks at the protocol field in the IPv4 header, and its value will be 17 for UDP. The IP datagram is passed to UDP.

The UDP layer looks at the destination port (and possibly the source port, too, if the UDP socket is connected), and in our example, places the datagram onto the appropriate socket receive queue. The process is awakened, if necessary, to read the newly received datagram.

The key point in this example is that a unicast IP datagram is received by only the one host specified by the destination IP address. No other hosts on the subnet are affected.

We now consider a similar example, on the same subnet, but with the sending application writing a UDP datagram to the subnet-directed broadcast address: 192.168.42.255. Figure 20.4 shows the arrangement.

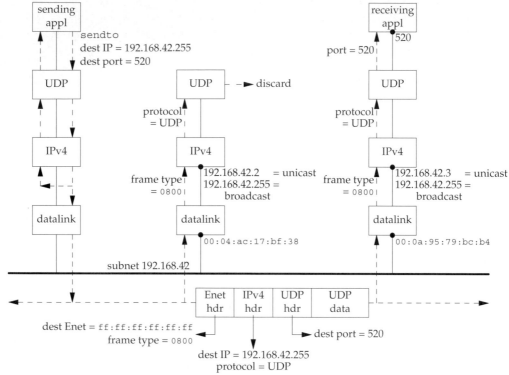

Figure 20.4 Example of a broadcast UDP datagram.

When the host on the left sends the datagram, it notices that the destination IP address is the subnet-directed broadcast address and maps this into the Ethernet address of 48 one bits: ff:ff:ff:ff:ff:ff. This causes *every* Ethernet interface on the subnet to receive the frame. The two hosts on the right of this figure that are running IPv4 will both receive the frame. Since the Ethernet frame type is 0x0800, both hosts pass the packet to the IP layer. Since the destination IP address matches the broadcast address for each of the two hosts, and since the protocol field is 17 (UDP), both hosts pass the packet up to UDP.

The host on the right passes the UDP datagram to the application that has bound UDP port 520. Nothing special needs to be done by an application to receive a broadcast UDP datagram: It just creates a UDP socket and binds the application's port number to the socket. (We assume the IP address bound is INADDR_ANY, which is typical.)

On the host in the middle, no application has bound UDP port 520. The host's UDP code then discards the received datagram. This host must *not* send an ICMP "port unreachable," as doing so could generate a *broadcast storm*: a condition where lots of hosts on the subnet generate a response at about the same time, leading to the network being unusable for a period of time. In addition, it's not clear what the sending host would do with an ICMP error: What if some receivers report errors and others don't?

In this example, we also show the datagram that is output by the host on the left being delivered to itself. This is a property of broadcasts: By definition, a broadcast goes to every host on the subnet, which includes the sender (pp. 109–110 of TCPv2). We also assume that the sending application has bound the port that it is sending to (520), so it will receive a copy of each broadcast datagram it sends. (In general, however, there is no requirement that a process bind a UDP port to which it sends datagrams.)

> In this example, we show a logical loopback performed by either the IP layer or the datalink layer making a copy (pp. 109–110 of TCPv2) and sending the copy up the protocol stack. A network could use a physical loopback, but this can lead to problems in the case of network faults (such as an unterminated Ethernet).

This example shows the fundamental problem with broadcasting: Every IPv4 host on the subnet that is not participating in the application must completely process the broadcast UDP datagram all the way up the protocol stack, through and including the UDP layer, before discarding the datagram. (Recall our discussion following Figure 8.21.) Also, every non-IP host on the subnet (say a host running Novell's IPX) must also receive the entire frame at the datalink layer before discarding the frame (assuming the host does not support the frame type, which would be `0x0800` for an IPv4 datagram). For applications that generate IP datagrams at a high rate (audio or video, for example), this unnecessary processing can severely affect these other hosts on the subnet. We will see in the next chapter how multicasting gets around this problem to some extent.

> Our choice of UDP port 520 in Figure 20.4 is intentional. This is the port used by the `routed` daemon to exchange RIP packets. All routers on a subnet that are using RIP version 1 will send a broadcast UDP datagram every 30 seconds. If there are 200 systems on the subnet, including two routers using RIP, 198 hosts will have to process (and discard) these broadcast datagrams every 30 seconds, assuming none of the 198 hosts is running `routed`. RIP version 2 uses multicast to avoid this very problem.

20.4 dg_cli **Function Using Broadcasting**

We modify our `dg_cli` function one more time, this time allowing it to broadcast to the standard UDP daytime server (Figure 2.18) and printing all replies. The only change we make to the `main` function (Figure 8.7) is to change the destination port number to 13.

```
servaddr.sin_port = htons(13);
```

We first compile this modified `main` function with the unmodified `dg_cli` function from Figure 8.8 and run it on the host `freebsd`.

```
freebsd % udpcli01 192.168.42.255
hi
sendto error: Permission denied
```

The command-line argument is the subnet-directed broadcast address for the secondary Ethernet. We type a line of input, the program calls `sendto`, and the error EACCES is returned. The reason we receive the error is that we are not allowed to send a datagram to a broadcast destination address unless we explicitly tell the kernel that we will be broadcasting. We do this by setting the SO_BROADCAST socket option (Section 7.5).

> Berkeley-derived implementations implement this sanity check. Solaris 2.5, on the other hand, accepts the datagram destined for the broadcast address even if we do not specify the socket option. The POSIX specification requires the SO_BROADCAST socket option to be set to send a broadcast packet.

> Broadcasting was a privileged operation with 4.2BSD and the SO_BROADCAST socket option did not exist. This option was added to 4.3BSD and any process was allowed to set the option.

We now modify our dg_cli function as shown in Figure 20.5. This version sets the SO_BROADCAST socket option and prints all the replies received within five seconds.

Allocate room for server's address, set socket option

11-13   malloc allocates room for the server's address to be returned by recvfrom. The SO_BROADCAST socket option is set and a signal handler is installed for SIGALRM.

Read line, send to socket, read all replies

14-24   The next two steps, fgets and sendto, are similar to previous versions of this function. But since we are sending a broadcast datagram, we can receive multiple replies. We call recvfrom in a loop and print all the replies received within five seconds. After five seconds, SIGALRM is generated, our signal handler is called, and recvfrom returns the error EINTR.

Print each received reply

25-29   For each reply received, we call sock_ntop_host, which in the case of IPv4 returns a string containing the dotted-decimal IP address of the server. This is printed along with the server's reply.

If we run the program specifying the subnet-directed broadcast address of 192.168.42.255, we see the following:

```
freebsd % udpcli01 192.168.42.255
hi
from 192.168.42.2: Sat Aug  2 16:42:45 2003
from 192.168.42.1: Sat Aug  2 14:42:45 2003
from 192.168.42.3: Sat Aug  2 14:42:45 2003
hello
from 192.168.42.3: Sat Aug  2 14:42:57 2003
from 192.168.42.2: Sat Aug  2 16:42:57 2003
from 192.168.42.1: Sat Aug  2 14:42:57 2003
```

Each time we must type a line of input to generate the output UDP datagram. Each time we receive three replies, and this includes the sending host. As we said earlier, the destination of a broadcast datagram is *all* the hosts on the attached network, including the sender. Each reply is unicast because the source address of the request, which is used by each server as the destination address of the reply, is a unicast address.

All the systems report the same time because all run NTP.

bcast/dgclibcast1.c

```
 1 #include    "unp.h"

 2 static void recvfrom_alarm(int);

 3 void
 4 dg_cli(FILE *fp, int sockfd, const SA *pservaddr, socklen_t servlen)
 5 {
 6     int      n;
 7     const int on = 1;
 8     char     sendline[MAXLINE], recvline[MAXLINE + 1];
 9     socklen_t len;
10     struct sockaddr *preply_addr;

11     preply_addr = Malloc(servlen);

12     Setsockopt(sockfd, SOL_SOCKET, SO_BROADCAST, &on, sizeof(on));

13     Signal(SIGALRM, recvfrom_alarm);

14     while (Fgets(sendline, MAXLINE, fp) != NULL) {

15         Sendto(sockfd, sendline, strlen(sendline), 0, pservaddr, servlen);

16         alarm(5);
17         for ( ; ; ) {
18             len = servlen;
19             n = recvfrom(sockfd, recvline, MAXLINE, 0, preply_addr, &len);
20             if (n < 0) {
21                 if (errno == EINTR)
22                     break;       /* waited long enough for replies */
23                 else
24                     err_sys("recvfrom error");
25             } else {
26                 recvline[n] = 0;    /* null terminate */
27                 printf("from %s: %s",
28                         Sock_ntop_host(preply_addr, len), recvline);
29             }
30         }
31     }
32     free(preply_addr);
33 }

34 static void
35 recvfrom_alarm(int signo)
36 {
37     return;                        /* just interrupt the recvfrom() */
38 }
```

bcast/dgclibcast1.c

Figure 20.5 dg_cli function that broadcasts.

IP Fragmentation and Broadcasts

Berkeley-derived kernels do not allow a broadcast datagram to be fragmented. If the size of an IP datagram that is being sent to a broadcast address exceeds the outgoing interface MTU, EMSGSIZE is returned (pp. 233–234 of TCPv2). This is a policy decision that has existed since 4.2BSD. There is nothing that prevents a kernel from fragmenting a broadcast datagram, but the feeling is that broadcasting puts enough load on the network as it is, so there is no need to multiply this load by the number of fragments.

We can see this scenario with our program in Figure 20.5. We redirect standard input from a file containing a 2,000-byte line, which will require fragmentation on an Ethernet.

```
freebsd % udpcli01 192.168.42.255 < 2000line
sendto error: Message too long
```

> AIX, FreeBSD, and MacOS implement this limitation. Linux, Solaris, and HP-UX fragment datagrams sent to a broadcast address. For portability, however, an application that needs to broadcast should determine the MTU of the outgoing interface using the SIOCGIFMTU ioctl, and then subtract the IP and transport header lengths to determine the maximum payload size. Alternately, it can pick a common MTU, like Ethernet's 1500, and use it as a constant.

20.5 Race Conditions

A *race condition* is usually when multiple processes are accessing data that is shared among them, but the correct outcome depends on the execution order of the processes. Since the execution order of processes on typical Unix systems depends on many factors that may vary between executions, sometimes the outcome is correct, but sometimes the outcome is wrong. The hardest type of race conditions to debug are those in which the outcome is normally correct and only occasionally is the outcome wrong. We will talk more about these types of race conditions in Chapter 26, when we discuss mutual exclusion variables and condition variables. Race conditions are always a concern with threads programming since so much data is shared among all the threads (e.g., all the global variables).

Race conditions of a different type often exist when dealing with signals. The problem occurs because a signal can normally be delivered at anytime while our program is executing. POSIX allows us to *block* a signal from being delivered, but this is often of little use while we are performing I/O operations.

An example is an easy way to see this problem. A race condition exists in Figure 20.5; take a few minutes and see if you can find it. (*Hint*: Where can we be executing when the signal is delivered?) You can also force the condition to occur as follows: Change the argument to `alarm` from 5 to 1, and add `sleep(1)` immediately before the `printf`.

When we make these changes to the function and then type the first line of input, the line is sent as a broadcast and we set the `alarm` for one second in the future. We block in the call to `recvfrom`, and the first reply then arrives for our socket, probably within a few milliseconds. The reply is returned by `recvfrom`, but we then go to sleep for one second. Additional replies are received, and they are placed into our socket's receive buffer. But while we are asleep, the `alarm` timer expires and the `SIGALRM` signal is generated: Our signal handler is called, and it just returns and interrupts the `sleep` in which we are blocked. We then loop around and read the queued replies with a one-second pause each time we print a reply. When we have read all the replies, we block again in the call to `recvfrom`, but the timer is not running. Thus, we will block forever in `recvfrom`. The fundamental problem is that our intent is for our signal handler to interrupt a blocked `recvfrom`, but the signal can be delivered at any time, and we can be executing anywhere in the infinite `for` loop when the signal is delivered.

We now examine four different solutions to this problem: one incorrect solution and three different correct solutions.

Blocking and Unblocking the Signal

Our first (incorrect) solution reduces the window of error by blocking the signal from being delivered while we are executing the remainder of the `for` loop. Figure 20.6 shows the new version.

——— *bcast/dgclibcast3.c*

```
 1 #include    "unp.h"

 2 static void recvfrom_alarm(int);

 3 void
 4 dg_cli(FILE *fp, int sockfd, const SA *pservaddr, socklen_t servlen)
 5 {
 6     int     n;
 7     const int on = 1;
 8     char    sendline[MAXLINE], recvline[MAXLINE + 1];
 9     sigset_t sigset_alrm;
10     socklen_t len;
11     struct sockaddr *preply_addr;

12     preply_addr = Malloc(servlen);

13     Setsockopt(sockfd, SOL_SOCKET, SO_BROADCAST, &on, sizeof(on));

14     Sigemptyset(&sigset_alrm);
15     Sigaddset(&sigset_alrm, SIGALRM);

16     Signal(SIGALRM, recvfrom_alarm);

17     while (Fgets(sendline, MAXLINE, fp) != NULL) {

18         Sendto(sockfd, sendline, strlen(sendline), 0, pservaddr, servlen);

19         alarm(5);
20         for ( ; ; ) {
21             len = servlen;
22             Sigprocmask(SIG_UNBLOCK, &sigset_alrm, NULL);
23             n = recvfrom(sockfd, recvline, MAXLINE, 0, preply_addr, &len);
24             Sigprocmask(SIG_BLOCK, &sigset_alrm, NULL);
25             if (n < 0) {
26                 if (errno == EINTR)
27                     break;      /* waited long enough for replies */
28                 else
29                     err_sys("recvfrom error");
30             } else {
31                 recvline[n] = 0;    /* null terminate */
32                 printf("from %s: %s",
33                         Sock_ntop_host(preply_addr, len), recvline);
34             }
35         }
36     }
37     free(preply_addr);
38 }

39 static void
40 recvfrom_alarm(int signo)
41 {
42     return;                      /* just interrupt the recvfrom() */
43 }
```
——— *bcast/dgclibcast3.c*

Figure 20.6 Block signals while executing within the `for` loop (incorrect solution).

Declare signal set and initialize

14–15   We declare a signal set, initialize it to the empty set (`sigemptyset`), and then turn on the bit corresponding to SIGALRM (`sigaddset`).

Unblock and block signal

21–24   Before calling `recvfrom`, we unblock the signal (so that it can be delivered while we are blocked) and then block it as soon as `recvfrom` returns. If the signal is generated (i.e., the timer expires) while it is blocked, the kernel remembers this fact, but cannot deliver the signal (i.e., call our signal handler) until it is unblocked. This is the fundamental difference between the *generation* of a signal and its *delivery*. Chapter 10 of APUE provides additional details on all these facets of POSIX signal handling.

If we compile and run this program, it appears to work fine, but then most programs with a race condition work most of the time! There is still a problem: The unblocking of the signal, the call to `recvfrom`, and the blocking of the signal are all independent system calls. Assume `recvfrom` returns with the final datagram reply and the signal is delivered between the `recvfrom` and the blocking of the signal. The next call to `recvfrom` will block forever. We have reduced the window, but the problem still exists.

A variation of this solution is to have the signal handler set a global flag when the signal is delivered.

```
static void
recvfrom_alarm(int signo)
{
    had_alarm = 1;
    return;
}
```

The flag is initialized to 0 each time `alarm` is called. Our `dg_cli` function checks this flag before calling `recvfrom` and does not call it if the flag is nonzero.

```
for ( ; ; ) {
    len = servlen;
    Sigprocmask(SIG_UNBLOCK, &sigset_alrm, NULL);
    if (had_alarm == 1)
        break;
    n = recvfrom(sockfd, recvline, MAXLINE, 0, preply_addr, &len);
```

If the signal was generated during the time it was blocked (after the previous return from `recvfrom`), and when the signal is unblocked in this piece of code, it will be delivered before `sigprocmask` returns, setting our flag. But there is still a small window of time between the testing of the flag and the call to `recvfrom` when the signal can be generated and delivered, and if this happens, the call to `recvfrom` will block forever (assuming, of course, no additional replies are received).

Blocking and Unblocking the Signal with `pselect`

One correct solution is to use `pselect` (Section 6.9), as shown in Figure 20.7.

bcast/dgclibcast4.c

```
1 #include    "unp.h"
2 static void recvfrom_alarm(int);
3 void
4 dg_cli(FILE *fp, int sockfd, const SA *pservaddr, socklen_t servlen)
5 {
6     int     n;
7     const int on = 1;
8     char    sendline[MAXLINE], recvline[MAXLINE + 1];
9     fd_set  rset;
10    sigset_t sigset_alrm, sigset_empty;
11    socklen_t len;
12    struct sockaddr *preply_addr;
13    preply_addr = Malloc(servlen);
14    Setsockopt(sockfd, SOL_SOCKET, SO_BROADCAST, &on, sizeof(on));
15    FD_ZERO(&rset);
16    Sigemptyset(&sigset_empty);
17    Sigemptyset(&sigset_alrm);
18    Sigaddset(&sigset_alrm, SIGALRM);
19    Signal(SIGALRM, recvfrom_alarm);
20    while (Fgets(sendline, MAXLINE, fp) != NULL) {
21        Sendto(sockfd, sendline, strlen(sendline), 0, pservaddr, servlen);
22        Sigprocmask(SIG_BLOCK, &sigset_alrm, NULL);
23        alarm(5);
24        for ( ; ; ) {
25            FD_SET(sockfd, &rset);
26            n = pselect(sockfd + 1, &rset, NULL, NULL, NULL, &sigset_empty);
27            if (n < 0) {
28                if (errno == EINTR)
29                    break;
30                else
31                    err_sys("pselect error");
32            } else if (n != 1)
33                err_sys("pselect error: returned %d", n);
34            len = servlen;
35            n = Recvfrom(sockfd, recvline, MAXLINE, 0, preply_addr, &len);
36            recvline[n] = 0;    /* null terminate */
37            printf("from %s: %s",
38                    Sock_ntop_host(preply_addr, len), recvline);
39        }
40    }
41    free(preply_addr);
42 }
43 static void
44 recvfrom_alarm(int signo)
45 {
46    return;                         /* just interrupt the recvfrom() */
47 }
```

bcast/dgclibcast4.c

Figure 20.7 Blocking and unblocking signals with `pselect`.

22-33   We block `SIGALRM` and call `pselect`. The final argument to `pselect` is a pointer to our `sigset_empty` variable, which is a signal set with no signals blocked, that is, all signals are unblocked. `pselect` will save the current signal mask (which has `SIGALRM` blocked), test the specified descriptors, and block if necessary with the signal mask set to the empty set. Before returning, the signal mask of the process is reset to its value when `pselect` was called. The key to `pselect` is that the setting of the signal mask, the testing of the descriptors, and the resetting of the signal mask are atomic operations with regard to the calling process.

34-38   If our socket is readable, we call `recvfrom`, knowing it will not block.

As we mentioned in Section 6.9, `pselect` is new with the POSIX specification; of all the systems in Figure 1.16, only FreeBSD and Linux support the function. Nevertheless, Figure 20.8 shows a simple, albeit incorrect, implementation. Our reason for showing this incorrect implementation is to show the three steps involved: setting the signal mask to the value specified by the caller along with saving the current mask, testing the descriptors, and resetting the signal mask.

—————————————————————————————————————— lib/pselect.c

```
 9 #include     "unp.h"

10 int
11 pselect(int nfds, fd_set *rset, fd_set *wset, fd_set *xset,
12          const struct timespec *ts, const sigset_t *sigmask)
13 {
14     int     n;
15     struct timeval tv;
16     sigset_t savemask;

17     if (ts != NULL) {
18         tv.tv_sec = ts->tv_sec;
19         tv.tv_usec = ts->tv_nsec / 1000;     /* nanosec -> microsec */
20     }

21     sigprocmask(SIG_SETMASK, sigmask, &savemask);   /* caller's mask */
22     n = select(nfds, rset, wset, xset, (ts == NULL) ? NULL : &tv);
23     sigprocmask(SIG_SETMASK, &savemask, NULL);  /* restore mask */

24     return (n);
25 }
```

—————————————————————————————————————— lib/pselect.c

Figure 20.8 Simple, incorrect implementation of `pselect`.

Using `sigsetjmp` and `siglongjmp`

Another correct way to solve our problem is not to use the ability of a signal handler to interrupt a blocked system call, but to call `siglongjmp` from the signal handler instead. This is called a *nonlocal goto* because we can use it to jump from one function back to another. Figure 20.9 demonstrates this technique.

```
                                                              —— bcast/dgclibcast5.c
 1 #include    "unp.h"
 2 #include    <setjmp.h>

 3 static void recvfrom_alarm(int);
 4 static sigjmp_buf jmpbuf;

 5 void
 6 dg_cli(FILE *fp, int sockfd, const SA *pservaddr, socklen_t servlen)
 7 {
 8     int     n;
 9     const int on = 1;
10     char    sendline[MAXLINE], recvline[MAXLINE + 1];
11     socklen_t len;
12     struct sockaddr *preply_addr;

13     preply_addr = Malloc(servlen);

14     Setsockopt(sockfd, SOL_SOCKET, SO_BROADCAST, &on, sizeof(on));

15     Signal(SIGALRM, recvfrom_alarm);

16     while (Fgets(sendline, MAXLINE, fp) != NULL) {

17         Sendto(sockfd, sendline, strlen(sendline), 0, pservaddr, servlen);

18         alarm(5);
19         for ( ; ; ) {
20             if (sigsetjmp(jmpbuf, 1) != 0)
21                 break;
22             len = servlen;
23             n = Recvfrom(sockfd, recvline, MAXLINE, 0, preply_addr, &len);
24             recvline[n] = 0;     /* null terminate */
25             printf("from %s: %s",
26                     Sock_ntop_host(preply_addr, len), recvline);
27         }
28     }
29     free(preply_addr);
30 }

31 static void
32 recvfrom_alarm(int signo)
33 {
34     siglongjmp(jmpbuf, 1);
35 }
```
                                                              —— bcast/dgclibcast5.c

Figure 20.9 Use of sigsetjmp and siglongjmp from signal handler.

Allocate jump buffer

4   We allocate a jump buffer that will be used by our function and its signal handler.

Call sigsetjmp

20–23   When we call sigsetjmp directly from our dg_cli function, it establishes the jump buffer and returns 0. We proceed on and call recvfrom.

Handle `SIGALRM` and call `siglongjmp`

31–35   When the signal is delivered, we call `siglongjmp`. This causes the `sigsetjmp` in the `dg_cli` function to return with a return value equal to the second argument (1), which must be a nonzero value. This will cause the `for` loop in `dg_cli` to terminate.

Using `sigsetjmp` and `siglongjmp` in this fashion guarantees that we will not block forever in `recvfrom` because of a signal delivered at an inopportune time. However, this introduces another potential problem: If the signal is delivered while `printf` is in the middle of its output, we will effectively jump out of the middle of `printf` and back to our `sigsetjmp`. This may leave `printf` with inconsistent private data structures, for example. To prevent this, we should combine the signal blocking and unblocking from Figure 20.6 with the nonlocal goto. This makes this solution unwieldy, as the signal blocking has to occur around any function that may behave poorly as a result of being interrupted in the middle.

Using IPC from Signal Handler to Function

There is yet another correct way to solve our problem. Instead of having the signal handler just return and hopefully interrupt a blocked `recvfrom`, we have the signal handler use IPC to notify our `dg_cli` function that the timer has expired. This is somewhat similar to the proposal we made earlier for the signal handler to set the global `had_alarm` when the timer expired, because that global variable was being used as a form of IPC (shared memory between our function and the signal handler). The problem with that solution, however, was our function had to test this variable, and this led to timing problems if the signal was delivered at about the same time.

What we use in Figure 20.10 is a pipe within our process, with the signal handler writing one byte to the pipe when the timer expires and our `dg_cli` function reading that byte to know when to terminate its `for` loop. What makes this such a nice solution is that the testing for the pipe being readable is done using `select`. We test for either the socket being readable or the pipe being readable.

Create pipe

15   We create a normal Unix pipe and two descriptors are returned. `pipefd[0]` is the read end and `pipefd[1]` is the write end.

> We could also use `socketpair` and get a full-duplex pipe. On some systems, notably SVR4, a normal Unix pipe is always full-duplex and we can read from either end and write to either end.

`select` on both socket and read end of pipe

23–30   We `select` on both `sockfd`, the socket, and `pipefd[0]`, the read end of the pipe.
47–52   When `SIGALRM` is delivered, our signal handler writes one byte to the pipe, making the read end readable. Our signal handler also returns, possibly interrupting `select`. Therefore, if `select` returns `EINTR`, we ignore the error, knowing that the read end of the pipe will also be readable, and that will terminate the `for` loop.

`read` from pipe

39–42   When the read end of the pipe is readable, we `read` the null byte that the signal handler wrote and ignore it. But this tells us that the timer expired, so we `break` out of the infinite `for` loop.

bcast/dgclibcast6.c

```
 1 #include      "unp.h"

 2 static void recvfrom_alarm(int);
 3 static int pipefd[2];

 4 void
 5 dg_cli(FILE *fp, int sockfd, const SA *pservaddr, socklen_t servlen)
 6 {
 7     int     n, maxfdp1;
 8     const int on = 1;
 9     char    sendline[MAXLINE], recvline[MAXLINE + 1];
10     fd_set  rset;
11     socklen_t len;
12     struct sockaddr *preply_addr;

13     preply_addr = Malloc(servlen);

14     Setsockopt(sockfd, SOL_SOCKET, SO_BROADCAST, &on, sizeof(on));

15     Pipe(pipefd);
16     maxfdp1 = max(sockfd, pipefd[0]) + 1;

17     FD_ZERO(&rset);

18     Signal(SIGALRM, recvfrom_alarm);

19     while (Fgets(sendline, MAXLINE, fp) != NULL) {
20         Sendto(sockfd, sendline, strlen(sendline), 0, pservaddr, servlen);

21         alarm(5);
22         for ( ; ; ) {
23             FD_SET(sockfd, &rset);
24             FD_SET(pipefd[0], &rset);
25             if ( (n = select(maxfdp1, &rset, NULL, NULL, NULL)) < 0) {
26                 if (errno == EINTR)
27                     continue;
28                 else
29                     err_sys("select error");
30             }

31             if (FD_ISSET(sockfd, &rset)) {
32                 len = servlen;
33                 n = Recvfrom(sockfd, recvline, MAXLINE, 0, preply_addr,
34                             &len);
35                 recvline[n] = 0;    /* null terminate */
36                 printf("from %s: %s",
37                         Sock_ntop_host(preply_addr, len), recvline);
38             }

39             if (FD_ISSET(pipefd[0], &rset)) {
40                 Read(pipefd[0], &n, 1); /* timer expired */
41                 break;
42             }
43         }
44     }
45     free(preply_addr);
46 }
```

```
47 static void
48 recvfrom_alarm(int signo)
49 {
50     Write(pipefd[1], "", 1);    /* write one null byte to pipe */
51     return;
52 }
```
bcast/dgclibcast6.c

Figure 20.10 Using a pipe as IPC from signal handler to our function.

20.6 Summary

Broadcasting sends a datagram that all hosts on the attached subnet receive. The disadvantage in broadcasting is that every host on the subnet must process the datagram, up through the UDP layer in the case of a UDP datagram, even if the host is not participating in the application. For high data rate applications, such as audio or video, this can place an excessive processing load on these hosts. We will see in the next chapter that multicasting solves this problem because only the hosts that are interested in the application receive the datagram.

Using a version of our UDP echo client that sends a broadcast to the daytime server and then prints all the replies that are received within five seconds, we looked at race conditions with the SIGALRM signal. Since the use of the alarm function and the SIGALRM signal is a common way to place a timeout on a read operation, this subtle error is common in networking applications. We showed one incorrect way to solve the problem, and three correct ways:

- Using pselect
- Using sigsetjmp and siglongjmp
- Using IPC (typically a pipe) from the signal handler to the main loop

Exercises

20.1 Run the UDP client using the dg_cli function that broadcasts (Figure 20.5). How many replies do you receive? Are the replies always in the same order? Do the hosts on your network have synchronized clocks?

20.2 Put some printfs in Figure 20.10 after select returns to see whether it returns an error or readability for one of the two descriptors. When the alarm expires, does your system return EINTR or readability on the pipe?

20.3 Run a tool such as tcpdump, if available, and look for broadcast packets on your LAN; tcpdump ether broadcast is the tcpdump command. To which protocol suites do the broadcasts belong?

21

Multicasting

21.1 Introduction

As shown in Figure 20.1, a unicast address identifies a *single* IP interface, a broadcast address identifies *all* IP interfaces on the subnet, and a multicast address identifies a *set* of IP interfaces. Unicasting and broadcasting are the extremes of the addressing spectrum (one or all) and the intent of multicasting is to allow addressing something in between. A multicast datagram should be received only by those interfaces interested in the datagram, that is, by the interfaces on the hosts running applications wishing to participate in the multicast group. Also, broadcasting is normally limited to a LAN, whereas multicasting can be used on a LAN or across a WAN. Indeed, applications multicast across a subset of the Internet on a daily basis.

The additions to the sockets API to support multicasting are simple; they comprise nine socket options: three that affect the sending of UDP datagrams to a multicast address and six that affect the host's reception of multicast datagrams.

21.2 Multicast Addresses

When describing multicast addresses, we must distinguish between IPv4 and IPv6.

IPv4 Class D Addresses

Class D addresses, in the range 224.0.0.0 through 239.255.255.255, are the multicast addresses in IPv4 (Figure A.3). The low-order 28 bits of a class D address form the multicast *group ID* and the 32-bit address is called the *group address*.

Figure 21.1 shows how IP multicast addresses are mapped into Ethernet multicast addresses. This mapping for IPv4 multicast addresses is described in RFC 1112 [Deering 1989] for Ethernets, in RFC 1390 [Katz 1993] for FDDI networks, and in RFC 1469 [Pusateri 1993] for token-ring networks. We also show the mapping for IPv6 multicast addresses to allow easy comparison of the resulting Ethernet addresses.

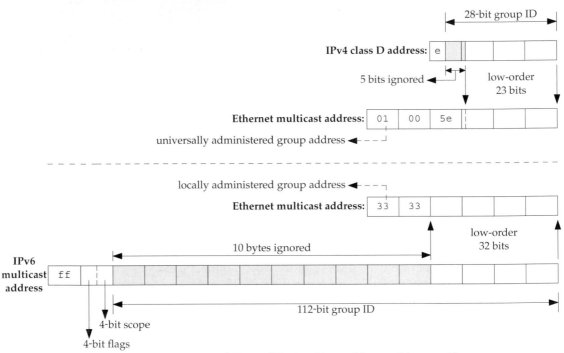

Figure 21.1 Mapping of IPv4 and IPv6 multicast address to Ethernet addresses.

Considering just the IPv4 mapping, the high-order 24 bits of the Ethernet address are always `01:00:5e`. The next bit is always 0, and the low-order 23 bits are copied from the low-order 23 bits of the multicast group address. The high-order 5 bits of the group address are ignored in the mapping. This means that 32 multicast addresses map to a single Ethernet address: The mapping is not one-to-one.

The low-order 2 bits of the first byte of the Ethernet address identify the address as a universally administered group address. *Universally administered* means the high-order 24 bits have been assigned by the IEEE and group addresses are recognized and handled specially by receiving interfaces.

There are a few special IPv4 multicast addresses:

- 224.0.0.1 is the *all-hosts* group. All multicast-capable nodes (hosts, routers, printers, etc.) on a subnet must join this group on all multicast-capable interfaces. (We will talk about what it means to join a multicast group shortly.)

- 224.0.0.2 is the *all-routers* group. All multicast-capable routers on a subnet must join this group on all multicast-capable interfaces.

The range 224.0.0.0 through 224.0.0.255 (which we can also write as 224.0.0.0/24) is called *link local*. These addresses are reserved for low-level topology discovery or maintenance protocols, and datagrams destined to any of these addresses are never forwarded by a multicast router. We will say more about the scope of various IPv4 multicast addresses after looking at IPv6 multicast addresses.

IPv6 Multicast Addresses

The high-order byte of an IPv6 multicast address has the value `ff`. Figure 21.1 shows the mapping from a 16-byte IPv6 multicast address into a 6-byte Ethernet address. The low-order 32 bits of the group address are copied into the low-order 32 bits of the Ethernet address. The high-order 2 bytes of the Ethernet address are `33:33`. This mapping for Ethernets is specified in RFC 2464 [Crawford 1998a], the same mapping for FDDI is in RFC 2467 [Crawford 1998b], and the token-ring mapping is in RFC 2470 [Crawford, Narten, and Thomas 1998].

The low-order two bits of the first byte of the Ethernet address specify the address as a locally administered group address. *Locally administered* means there is no guarantee that the address is unique to IPv6. There could be other protocol suites besides IPv6 sharing the network and using the same high-order two bytes of the Ethernet address. As we mentioned earlier, group addresses are recognized and handled specially by receiving interfaces.

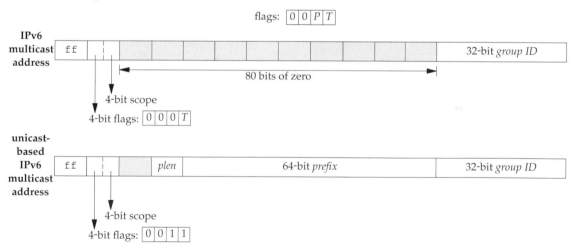

Figure 21.2   Format of IPv6 multicast addresses

Two formats are defined for IPv6 multicast addresses, as shown in Figure 21.2. When the *P* flag is 0, the *T* flag differentiates between a *well-known* multicast group (a value of 0) and a *transient* multicast group (a value of 1). A *P* value of 1 designates a multicast address that is assigned based on a unicast prefix (defined in RFC 3306 [Haberman and Thaler 2002]). If the *P* flag is 1, the *T* flag also must be 1 (i.e., unicast-based multicast addresses are always transient), and the *plen* and *prefix* fields are set to the prefix length and value of the unicast prefix, respectively. The upper two bits of this field are reserved. IPv6 multicast addresses also have a 4-bit *scope* field that we will discuss shortly. RFC 3307 [Haberman 2002] describes the allocation mechanism for the low-order 32 bits of an IPv6 group address (the *group ID*), independent of the setting of the *P* flag.

There are a few special IPv6 multicast addresses:

- `ff01::1` and `ff02::1` are the *all-nodes* groups at interface-local and link-local scope. All nodes (hosts, routers, printers, etc.) on a subnet must join these groups on all multicast-capable interfaces. This is similar to the IPv4 224.0.0.1 multicast address. However, since multicast is an integral part of IPv6, unlike IPv4, this is not optional.

  Although the IPv4 group is called the *all-hosts* group and the IPv6 group is called the *all-nodes* group, they serve the same purpose. The group was renamed in IPv6 to make it clear that it is intended to address routers, printers, and any other IP devices on the subnet as well as hosts.

- `ff01::2`, `ff02::2` and `ff05::2` are the *all-routers* groups at interface-local, link-local, and site-local scopes. All routers on a subnet must join these groups on all multicast-capable interfaces. This is similar to the IPv4 224.0.0.2 multicast address.

Scope of Multicast Addresses

IPv6 multicast addresses have an explicit 4-bit *scope* field that specifies how "far" the multicast packet will travel. IPv6 packets also have a *hop limit* field that limits the number of times the packet is forwarded by a router. The following values have been assigned to the scope field:

 1: interface-local
 2: link-local
 4: admin-local
 5: site-local
 8: organization-local
14: global

The remaining values are unassigned or reserved. An interface-local datagram must not be output by an interface and a link-local datagram must never be forwarded by a router. What defines an admin region, a site, or an organization is up to the administrators of the multicast routers at that site or organization. IPv6 multicast addresses that differ only in scope represent different groups.

IPv4 does not have a separate scope field for multicast packets. Historically, the IPv4 TTL field in the IP header has doubled as a multicast scope field: A TTL of 0 means interface-local; 1 means link-local; up through 32 means site-local; up through 64 means region-local; up through 128 means continent-local (meaning avoiding low-rate or highly congested links, intercontinental or not); and up through 255 are unrestricted in scope (global). This double usage of the TTL field has led to difficulties, as detailed in RFC 2365 [Meyer 1998].

Although use of the IPv4 TTL field for scoping is accepted and recommended practice, administrative scoping is preferred when possible. This defines the range 239.0.0.0 through 239.255.255.255 as the *administratively scoped IPv4 multicast space* (RFC 2365 [Meyer 1998]). This is the high end of the multicast address space. Addresses in this range are assigned locally by an organization, but are not guaranteed to be unique across organizational boundaries. An organization must configure its boundary routers (multicast routers at the boundary of the organization) not to forward multicast packets destined to any of these addresses.

Administratively scoped IPv4 multicast addresses are divided into local scope and organization-local scope, the former being similar (but not semantically equivalent) to IPv6 site-local scope. We summarize the different scoping rules in Figure 21.3.

Scope	IPv6 scope	IPv4	
		TTL scope	Administrative scope
Interface-local	1	0	
Link-local	2	1	224.0.0.0 to 224.0.0.255
Site-local	5	<32	239.255.0.0 to 239.255.255.255
Organization-local	8		239.192.0.0 to 239.195.255.255
Global	14	≤255	224.0.1.0 to 238.255.255.255

Figure 21.3 Scope of IPv4 and IPv6 multicast addresses.

Multicast Sessions

Especially in the case of streaming multimedia, the combination of an IP multicast address (either IPv4 or IPv6) and a transport-layer port (typically UDP) is referred to as a *session*. For example, an audio/video teleconference may comprise two sessions; one for audio and one for video. These sessions almost always use different ports and sometimes also use different groups for flexibility in choice when receiving. For example, one client may choose to receive only the audio session, and one client may choose to receive both the audio and the video session. If the sessions used the same group address, this choice would not be possible.

21.3 Multicasting versus Broadcasting on a LAN

We now return to the examples in Figures 20.3 and 20.4 to show what happens in the case of multicasting. We use IPv4 for the example shown in Figure 21.4, but the steps are similar for IPv6.

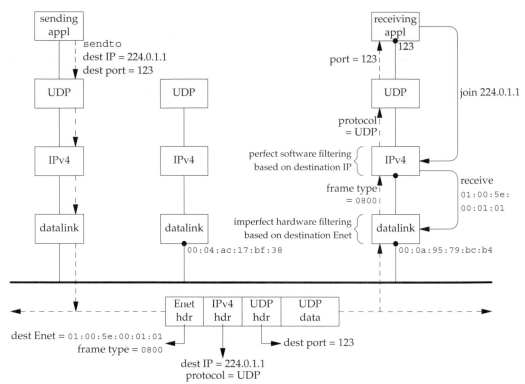

Figure 21.4 Multicast example of a UDP datagram.

The receiving application on the rightmost host starts and creates a UDP socket, binds port 123 to the socket, and then joins the multicast group 224.0.1.1. We will see shortly that this "join" operation is done by calling `setsockopt`. When this happens, the IPv4 layer saves the information internally and then tells the appropriate datalink to receive Ethernet frames destined to `01:00:5e:00:01:01` (Section 12.11 of TCPv2). This is the Ethernet address corresponding to the multicast address that the application has just joined using the mapping we showed in Figure 21.1.

The next step is for the sending application on the leftmost host to create a UDP socket and send a datagram to 224.0.1.1, port 123. Nothing special is required to send a multicast datagram: The application does not have to join the multicast group. The sending host converts the IP address into the corresponding Ethernet destination address and the frame is sent. Notice that the frame contains both the destination Ethernet address (which is examined by the interfaces) and the destination IP address (which is examined by the IP layers).

We assume that the host in the middle is not IPv4 multicast-capable (since support for IPv4 multicasting is optional). This host ignores the frame completely because: (i) the destination Ethernet address does not match the address of the interface; (ii) the destination Ethernet address is not the Ethernet broadcast address; and (iii) the interface has not been told to receive any group addresses (those with the low-order bit of the high-order byte set to 1, as in Figure 21.1).

The frame is received by the datalink on the right based on what we call *imperfect filtering*, which is done by the interface using the Ethernet destination address. We say this is imperfect because it is normally the case that when the interface is told to receive frames destined to one specific Ethernet multicast address, it can receive frames destined to other Ethernet multicast addresses, too.

When told to receive frames destined to a specific Ethernet multicast address, many current Ethernet interface cards apply a hash function to the address, calculating a value between 0 and 511. One of 512 bits in an array is then turned ON. When a frame passes by on the cable destined for a multicast address, the same hash function is applied by the interface to the destination address (which is the first field in the frame), calculating a value between 0 and 511. If the corresponding bit in the array is ON, the frame is received; otherwise, it is ignored. Older interface cards reduce the size of the bit array from 512 to 64, increasing the probability that an interface will receive frames in which it is not interested. Over time, as more and more applications use multicasting, this size will probably increase even more. Some interface cards today already have perfect filtering (the ability to filter out datagrams addressed to all but the desired multicast addresses). Other interface cards have no multicast filtering at all, and when told to receive a specific multicast address, must receive all multicast frames (sometimes called *multicast promiscuous* mode). One popular interface card does perfect filtering for 16 multicast addresses as well as having a 512-bit hash table. Another does perfect filtering for 80 multicast addresses, but then has to enter multicast promiscuous mode. Even if the interface performs perfect filtering, perfect software filtering at the IP layer is still required because the mapping from the IP multicast address to the hardware address is not one-to-one.

Assuming that the datalink on the right receives the frame, since the Ethernet frame type is IPv4, the packet is passed to the IP layer. Since the received packet was destined to a multicast IP address, the IP layer compares this address against all the multicast addresses that applications on this host have joined. We call this *perfect filtering* since it is based on the entire 32-bit class D address in the IPv4 header. In this example, the packet is accepted by the IP layer and passed to the UDP layer, which in turn passes the datagram to the socket that is bound to port 123.

There are three scenarios that we do not show in Figure 21.4:

1. A host running an application that has joined the multicast address 225.0.1.1. Since the upper five bits of the group address are ignored in the mapping to the Ethernet address, this host's interface will also be receiving frames with a destination Ethernet address of `01:00:5e:00:01:01`. In this case, the packet will be discarded by the perfect filtering in the IP layer.

2. A host running an application that has joined some multicast group whose corresponding Ethernet address just happens to be one that the interface receives when it is programmed to receive `01:00:5e:00:01:01` (i.e., the interface card performs imperfect filtering). This frame will be discarded either by the datalink layer or by the IP layer.

3. A packet destined to the same group, 224.0.1.1, but a different port, say 4000. The rightmost host in Figure 21.4 still receives the packet, which is accepted by the IP layer, but assuming a socket does not exist that has bound port 4000, the packet will be discarded by the UDP layer.

This demonstrates that for a process to receive a multicast datagram, the process must join the group and bind the port.

21.4 Multicasting on a WAN

Multicasting on a single LAN, as discussed in the previous section, is simple. One host sends a multicast packet and any interested host receives the packet. The benefit of multicasting over broadcasting is reducing the load on all the hosts not interested in the multicast packets.

Multicasting is also beneficial on WANs. Consider the WAN shown in Figure 21.5, which shows five LANs connected with five multicast routers.

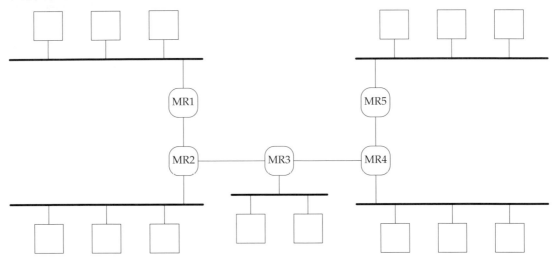

Figure 21.5 Five LANs connected with five multicast routers.

Next, assume that some program is started on five of the hosts (say a program that listens to a multicast audio session) and those five programs join a given multicast group. Each of the five hosts then joins that multicast group. We also assume that the multicast routers are all communicating with their neighbor multicast router using a *multicast routing protocol*, which we designate as just *MRP*. We show this in Figure 21.6.

When a process on a host joins a multicast group, that host sends an IGMP message to any attached multicast routers telling them that the host has just joined that group. The multicast routers then exchange this information using the MRP so that each multicast router knows what to do if it receives a packet destined to the multicast address.

Multicast routing is still a research topic and could easily consume a book on its own.

We now assume that a process on the host at the top left starts sending packets destined to the multicast address. Say this process is sending the audio packets that the multicast receivers are waiting to receive. We show these packets in Figure 21.7.

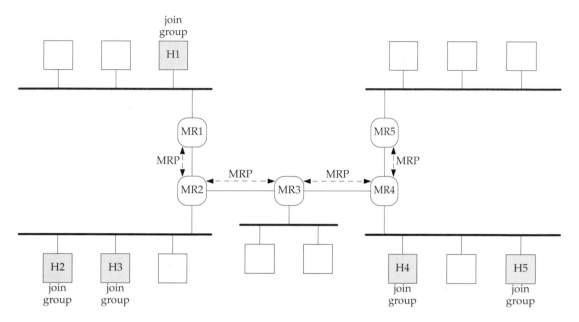

Figure 21.6   Five hosts join a multicast group on a WAN.

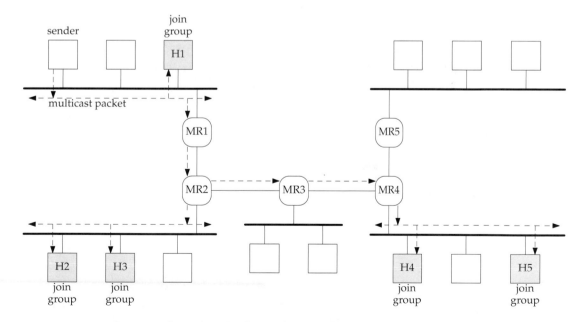

Figure 21.7   Sending multicast packets on a WAN.

We can follow the steps taken as the multicast packets go from the sender to all the receivers:

- The packets are multicast on the top left LAN by the sender. Receiver H1 receives these (since it has joined the group) as does MR1 (since a multicast router must receive all multicast packets).

- MR1 forwards the multicast packet to MR2, because the MRP has informed MR1 that MR2 needs to receive packets destined to this group.

- MR2 multicasts the packet on to its attached LAN, since hosts H2 and H3 belong to the group. It also makes a copy of the packet and sends it to MR3.

  Making a copy of the packet, as MR2 does here, is something unique to multicast forwarding. A unicast packet is never duplicated as it is forwarded by routers.

- MR3 sends the multicast packet to MR4, but MR3 does not multicast a copy on its attached LAN because we assume no host on the LAN has joined the group.

- MR4 multicasts the packet onto its attached LAN, since hosts H4 and H5 belong to the group. It does not make a copy and send it to MR5 because none of the hosts on MR5's attached LAN belong to the group and MR4 knows this based on the multicast routing information it has exchanged with MR5.

Two less desirable alternatives to multicasting on a WAN are *broadcast flooding* and sending individual copies to each receiver. In the first case, the packets would be broadcast by the sender, and each router would broadcast the packets out each of its interfaces, except the arriving interface. It should be obvious that this increases the number of uninterested hosts and routers that must deal with the packet.

In the second case, the sender must know the IP address of all the receivers and send each one a copy. With the five receivers we show in Figure 21.7, this would require five packets on the sender's LAN, four packets going from MR1 to MR2, and two packets going from MR2 to MR3 to MR4. Now just imagine the situation with a million receivers!

21.5 Source-Specific Multicast

Multicasting on a WAN has been difficult to deploy for several reasons. The biggest problem is that the *MRP*, described in Section 21.4, needs to get the data from all the senders, which may be located anywhere in the network, to all the receivers, which may similarly be located anywhere. Another large problem is multicast address allocation: There are not enough IPv4 multicast addresses to statically assign them to everyone who wants one, as is done with unicast addresses. To send wide-area multicast and not conflict with other multicast senders, you need a unique address, but there is not yet a global multicast address allocation mechanism.

Source-specific multicast, or *SSM* [Holbrook and Cheriton 1999], provides a pragmatic solution to these problems. It combines the group address with a system's source address, which solves the problems as follows:

- The receivers supply the sender's source address to the routers as part of joining the group. This removes the rendezvous problem from the network, as the network now knows exactly where the sender is. However, it retains the scaling properties of not requiring the sender to know who all the receivers are. This simplifies multicast routing protocols immensely.

- It redefines the identifier from simply being a multicast group address to being a combination of a unicast source and multicast destination (which SSM now calls a *channel*). This means that the source may pick any multicast address since it becomes the (source, destination) combination that must be unique, and the source already makes it unique. An SSM session is the combination of source, destination, and port.

SSM also provides a certain amount of anti-spoofing, that is, it is harder for source 2 to transmit on source 1's channel since source 1's channel includes source 1's source address. Spoofing is still possible, of course, but is much harder.

21.6 Multicast Socket Options

The API support for traditional multicasting requires only five new socket options. Source-filtering support, which is required for *SSM*, adds four more. Figure 21.8 shows the three nonmembership-related socket options, plus the datatype of the argument expected in the call to `getsockopt` or `setsockopt`. Figure 21.9 shows the six membership-related socket options for IPv4, IPv6, and the IP version-independent API. A pointer to a variable of the datatype shown is the fourth argument to `getsockopt` and `setsockopt`. All nine of these options are valid with `setsockopt`, but the six that join and leave a multicast group or source are not allowed with `getsockopt`.

Command	Datatype	Description
IP_MULTICAST_IF IP_MULTICAST_TTL IP_MULTICAST_LOOP	struct in_addr u_char u_char	Specify default interface for outgoing multicasts Specify TTL for outgoing multicasts Enable or disable loopback of outgoing multicasts
IPV6_MULTICAST_IF IPV6_MULTICAST_HOPS IPV6_MULTICAST_LOOP	u_int int u_int	Specify default interface for outgoing multicasts Specify hop limit for outgoing multicasts Enable or disable loopback of outgoing multicasts

Figure 21.8 Multicast socket options.

The IPv4 TTL and loopback options take a `u_char` argument, while the IPv6 hop limit and loopback options take an `int` and a `u_int` argument, respectively. A common programming error with the IPv4 multicast options is to call `setsockopt` with an `int` argument to specify the TTL or loopback (which is not allowed; pp. 354–355 of TCPv2), since most of the other socket options in Figure 7.1 have integer arguments. The change with IPv6 makes them more consistent with other options.

Command	Datatype	Description
`IP_ADD_MEMBERSHIP`	`struct ip_mreq`	Join a multicast group
`IP_DROP_MEMBERSHIP`	`struct ip_mreq`	Leave a multicast group
`IP_BLOCK_SOURCE`	`struct ip_mreq_source`	Block a source from a joined group
`IP_UNBLOCK_SOURCE`	`struct ip_mreq_source`	Unblock a previously blocked source
`IP_ADD_SOURCE_MEMBERSHIP`	`struct ip_mreq_source`	Join a source-specific group
`IP_DROP_SOURCE_MEMBERSHIP`	`struct ip_mreq_source`	Leave a source-specific group
`IPV6_JOIN_GROUP`	`struct ipv6_mreq`	Join a multicast group
`IPV6_LEAVE_GROUP`	`struct ipv6_mreq`	Leave a multicast group
`MCAST_JOIN_GROUP`	`struct group_req`	Join a multicast group
`MCAST_LEAVE_GROUP`	`struct group_req`	Leave a multicast group
`MCAST_BLOCK_SOURCE`	`struct group_source_req`	Block a source from a joined group
`MCAST_UNBLOCK_SOURCE`	`struct group_source_req`	Unblock a previously blocked source
`MCAST_JOIN_SOURCE_GROUP`	`struct group_source_req`	Join a source-specific group
`MCAST_LEAVE_SOURCE_GROUP`	`struct group_source_req`	Leave a source-specific group

Figure 21.9 Multicast group membership socket options.

We now describe each of these nine socket options in more detail. Notice that the nine options are conceptually identical between IPv4 and IPv6; only the name and argument type are different.

`IP_ADD_MEMBERSHIP`, `IPV6_JOIN_GROUP`, `MCAST_JOIN_GROUP`
> Join an any-source multicast group on a specified local interface. We specify the local interface with one of its unicast addresses for IPv4 or with the interface index for IPv6 and the protocol-independent API. The following three structures are used when joining or leaving a group:

```
struct ip_mreq {
  struct in_addr   imr_multiaddr;    /* IPv4 class D multicast addr */
  struct in_addr   imr_interface;    /* IPv4 addr of local interface */
};

struct ipv6_mreq {
  struct in6_addr  ipv6mr_multiaddr; /* IPv6 multicast addr */
  unsigned int     ipv6mr_interface; /* interface index, or 0 */
};

struct group_req {
  unsigned int            gr_interface;    /* interface index, or 0 */
  struct sockaddr_storage gr_group;        /* IPv4 or IPv6 multicast addr */
}
```

If the local interface is specified as the wildcard address for IPv4 (`INADDR_ANY`) or as an index of 0 for IPv6, then a single local interface is chosen by the kernel.

We say that a host belongs to a given multicast group on a given interface if one or more processes currently belongs to that group on that interface.

More than one join is allowed on a given socket, but each join must be for a different multicast address, or for the same multicast address but on a different interface from previous joins for that address on this socket. This can be used on a multihomed host where, for example, one socket is created and then for each interface, a join is performed for a given multicast address.

Recall from Figure 21.3 that IPv6 multicast addresses have an explicit scope field as part of the address. As we noted, IPv6 multicast addresses that differ only in scope represent different groups. Therefore, if an implementation of NTP wanted to receive all NTP packets, regardless of scope, it would have to join `ff01::101` (interface-local), `ff02::101` (link-local), `ff05::101` (site-local), `ff08::101` (organization-local), and `ff0e::101` (global). All the joins could be performed on a single socket, and the `IPV6_PKTINFO` socket option could be set (Section 22.8) to have `recvmsg` return the destination address of each datagram.

The IP protocol-independent socket option (`MCAST_JOIN_GROUP`) is the same as the IPv6 option except that it uses a `sockaddr_storage` instead of `in6_addr` to pass the group address to the kernel. A `sockaddr_storage` (Figure 3.5) is large enough to store any type of address the system supports.

> Most implementations have a limit on the number of joins that are allowed per socket. This limit is specified as `IP_MAX_MEMBERSHIPS` (20 for Berkeley-derived implementations), but some implementations have lifted this limitation or raised the maximum.

> When the interface on which to join is not specified, Berkeley-derived kernels look up the multicast address in the normal IP routing table and use the resulting interface (p. 357 of TCPv2). Some systems install a route for all multicast addresses (that is, a route with a destination of 224.0.0.0/8 for IPv4) upon initialization to handle this scenario.

> The change was made with the IPv6 and protocol-independent options to use an interface index to specify the interface instead of the local unicast address that is used with IPv4 to allow joins on unnumbered interfaces and tunnel endpoints.

> The original IPv6 multicast API definition used `IPV6_ADD_MEMBERSHIP` instead of `IPV6_JOIN_GROUP`. The API is otherwise the same. Our `mcast_join` function described later hides this difference.

`IP_DROP_MEMBERSHIP`, `IPV6_LEAVE_GROUP`, `MCAST_LEAVE_GROUP`

Leave an any-source multicast group on a specified local interface. The same structures that we just showed for joining a group are used with this socket option. If the local interface is not specified (that is, the value is `INADDR_ANY` for IPv4 or it has an interface index of 0 for IPv6), the first matching multicasting group membership is dropped.

If a process joins a group but never explicitly leaves the group, when the socket is closed (either explicitly or on process termination), the membership is dropped automatically. It is possible for multiple sockets on a host to each join the same group, in which case, the host remains a member of that group until the last socket leaves the group.

> The original IPv6 multicast API definition used `IPV6_DROP_MEMBERSHIP` instead of `IPV6_LEAVE_GROUP`. The API is otherwise the same. Our `mcast_leave` function described later hides this difference.

IP_BLOCK_SOURCE, MCAST_BLOCK_SOURCE

Block receipt of traffic on this socket from a source given an existing any-source group membership on a specified local interface. If all joined sockets have blocked the same source, the system can inform routers that this traffic is unwanted, possibly affecting multicast routing in the network. It can be used to ignore traffic from rogue senders, for example. We specify the local interface with one of its unicast addresses for IPv4 or with the interface index for the protocol-independent API. The following two structures are used when blocking or unblocking a source:

```
struct ip_mreq_source {
  struct in_addr    imr_multiaddr;      /* IPv4 class D multicast addr */
  struct in_addr    imr_sourceaddr;     /* IPv4 source addr */
  struct in_addr    imr_interface;      /* IPv4 addr of local interface */
};

struct group_source_req {
  unsigned int           gsr_interface;  /* interface index, or 0 */
  struct sockaddr_storage gsr_group;     /* IPv4 or IPv6 multicast addr */
  struct sockaddr_storage gsr_source;    /* IPv4 or IPv6 source addr */
}
```

If the local interface is specified as the wildcard address for IPv4 (INADDR_ANY) or as an index of 0 for the protocol-independent API, then the local interface is chosen by the kernel to match the first membership on this socket for the given group.

The block source request modifies an existing group membership, so the group must have already been joined on the specified interface with the IP_ADD_MEMBERSHIP, IPV6_JOIN_GROUP, or MCAST_JOIN_GROUP option.

IP_UNBLOCK_SOURCE, MCAST_UNBLOCK_SOURCE

Unblock a previously blocked source. The arguments must be the same as a previous IP_BLOCK_SOURCE or MCAST_BLOCK_SOURCE request on this socket.

If the local interface is specified as the wildcard address for IPv4 (INADDR_ANY) or as an index of 0 for the protocol-independent API, then the first matching blocked source is unblocked.

IP_ADD_SOURCE_MEMBERSHIP, MCAST_JOIN_SOURCE_GROUP

Join a source-specific group on a specified local interface. The same structures that we just showed for blocking or unblocking sources are used with this socket option. The group must not have already been joined using the any-source interface (IP_ADD_MEMBERSHIP, IPV6_JOIN_GROUP, or MCAST_JOIN_GROUP).

If the local interface is specified as the wildcard address for IPv4 (INADDR_ANY) or as an index of 0 for the protocol-independent API, then the local interface is chosen by the kernel.

IP_DROP_SOURCE_MEMBERSHIP, MCAST_LEAVE_SOURCE_GROUP

Leave a source-specific group on a specified local interface. The same structures that we just showed for joining a source-specific group are used with this socket option. If the local interface is not specified (that is, the value is INADDR_ANY for IPv4 or it has an interface index of 0 for the protocol-independent API), the first matching source-specific membership is dropped.

If a process joins a source-specific group but never explicitly leaves the group, when the socket is closed (either explicitly or on process termination), the membership is dropped automatically. It is possible for multiple processes on a host to each join the same source-specific group, in which case, the host remains a member of that group until the last process leaves the group.

IP_MULTICAST_IF, IPV6_MULTICAST_IF

Specify the interface for outgoing multicast datagrams sent on this socket. This interface is specified as either an in_addr structure for IPv4 or an interface index for IPv6. If the value specified is INADDR_ANY for IPv4 or is an interface index of 0 for IPv6, this removes any interface previously assigned by this socket option and the system will choose the interface each time a datagram is sent.

Be careful to distinguish between the local interface specified (or chosen) when a process joins a group (the interface on which arriving multicast datagrams will be received) and the local interface specified (or chosen) when a multicast datagram is output.

> Berkeley-derived kernels choose the default interface for an outgoing multicast datagram by searching the normal IP routing table for a route to the destination multicast address, and the corresponding interface is used. This is the same technique used to choose the receiving interface if the process does not specify one when joining a group. The assumption is that if a route exists for a given multicast address (perhaps the default route in the routing table), then the resulting interface should be used for input and output.

IP_MULTICAST_TTL, IPV6_MULTICAST_HOPS

Set the IPv4 TTL or the IPv6 hop limit for outgoing multicast datagrams. If this is not specified, both will default to 1, which restricts the datagram to the local subnet.

IP_MULTICAST_LOOP, IPV6_MULTICAST_LOOP

Enable or disable local loopback of multicast datagrams. By default, loopback is enabled: A copy of each multicast datagram sent by a process on the host will also be looped back and processed as a received datagram by that host, if the host belongs to that multicast group on the outgoing interface.

This is similar to broadcasting, where we saw that broadcasts sent on a host are also processed as a received datagram on that host (Figure 20.4). (With broadcasting, there is no way to disable this loopback.) This means that if a process belongs to the multicast group to which it is sending datagrams, it will receive its own transmissions.

> The loopback that is being described here is an internal loopback performed at the IP layer or higher. Should the interface hear its own transmissions, RFC 1112 [Deering 1989] requires that the driver discard these copies. This RFC also states that the loopback option defaults to ON as "a performance optimization for upper-layer protocols that restrict the membership of a group to one process per host (such as a routing protocol)."

The first six pairs of socket options (ADD_MEMBERSHIP/JOIN_GROUP, DROP_MEMBERSHIP/LEAVE_GROUP, BLOCK_SOURCE, UNBLOCK_SOURCE, ADD_SOURCE_MEMBERSHIP/JOIN_SOURCE_GROUP, and DROP_SOURCE_MEMBERSHIP/LEAVE_SOURCE_GROUP) affect the *receiving* of multicast datagrams, while the last three pairs affect the *sending* of multicast datagrams (outgoing interface, TTL or hop limit, and loopback). We mentioned earlier that nothing special is required to send a multicast datagram. If no multicast socket option is specified before sending a multicast datagram, the interface for the outgoing datagram will be chosen by the kernel, the TTL or hop limit will be 1, and a copy will be looped back.

To receive a multicast datagram, a process must join the multicast group and it must also `bind` a UDP socket to the port number that will be used as the destination port number for datagrams sent to the group. The two operations are distinct and both are required. Joining the group tells the host's IP layer and datalink layer to receive multicast datagrams sent to that group. Binding the port is how the application specifies to UDP that it wants to receive datagrams sent to that port. Some applications also `bind` the multicast address to the socket, in addition to the port. This prevents any other datagrams that might be received for that port to other unicast, broadcast, or multicast addresses from being delivered to the socket.

> Historically, the multicast service interface only required that *some* socket on the host join the multicast group, not necessarily the socket that binds the port and then receives the multicast datagrams. There is the potential, however, with these implementations for multicast datagrams to be delivered to applications that are not multicast-aware. Newer multicast kernels now require that the process bind the port and set any multicast socket option for the socket, the latter being an indication that the application is multicast-aware. The most common multicast socket option to set is a join of the group. Solaris differs slightly and only delivers received multicast datagrams to a socket that has both joined the group and bound the port. For portability, all multicast applications should join the group and bind the port.

> The newer multicast service interface requires that the IP layer only deliver multicast packets to a socket if that socket has joined the applicable group and/or source. This was introduced with IGMPv3 (RFC 3376 [Cain et al. 2002]) to permit source filtering and source-specific multicast. This reinforces the requirement to join the group, but relaxes the requirement to bind to the group address. However, for maximum portability to both the old and new multicast service interfaces, applications should both join the group and bind to the group address.

> Some older multicast-capable hosts do not allow the `bind` of a multicast address to a socket. For portability, an application may wish to ignore a `bind` error for a multicast address and try again using INADDR_ANY or in6addr_any.

21.7 `mcast_join` **and Related Functions**

Although the multicast socket options for IPv4 are similar to the multicast socket options for IPv6, there are enough differences that protocol-independent code using multicasting becomes complicated with lots of `#ifdef`s. A better solution is to hide the differences within the following eight functions:

```
#include "unp.h"

int mcast_join(int sockfd, const struct sockaddr *grp, socklen_t grplen,
               const char *ifname, u_int ifindex);

int mcast_leave(int sockfd, const struct sockaddr *grp, socklen_t grplen);

int mcast_block_source(int sockfd,
               const struct sockaddr *src, socklen_t srclen,
               const struct sockaddr *grp, socklen_t grplen);

int mcast_unblock_source(int sockfd,
               const struct sockaddr *src, socklen_t srclen,
               const struct sockaddr *grp, socklen_t grplen);

int mcast_join_source_group(int sockfd,
               const struct sockaddr *src, socklen_t srclen,
               const struct sockaddr *grp, socklen_t grplen,
               const char *ifname, u_int ifindex);

int mcast_leave_source_group(int sockfd,
               const struct sockaddr *src, socklen_t srclen,
               const struct sockaddr *grp, socklen_t grplen);

int mcast_set_if(int sockfd, const char *ifname, u_int ifindex);

int mcast_set_loop(int sockfd, int flag);

int mcast_set_ttl(int sockfd, int ttl);
```

                                        All above return: 0 if OK, −1 on error

```
int mcast_get_if(int sockfd);
```

                            Returns: non-negative interface index if OK, −1 on error

```
int mcast_get_loop(int sockfd);
```

                                Returns: current loopback flag if OK, −1 on error

```
int mcast_get_ttl(int sockfd);
```

                                Returns: current TTL or hop limit if OK, −1 on error

`mcast_join` joins the any-source multicast group whose IP address is contained within the socket address structure pointed to by *grp*, and whose length is specified by *grplen*. We can specify the interface on which to join the group by either the interface name (a non-null *ifname*) or a nonzero interface index (*ifindex*). If neither is specified, the kernel chooses the interface on which the group is joined. Recall that with IPv6, the interface is specified to the socket option by its index. If a name is specified for an IPv6 socket, we call `if_nametoindex` to obtain the index. With the IPv4 socket option, the interface is specified by its unicast IP address. If a name is specified for an IPv4 socket, we call `ioctl` with a request of `SIOCGIFADDR` to obtain the unicast IP address for the interface. If an index is specified for an IPv4 socket, we first call `if_indextoname` to obtain the name and then process the name as just described.

> An interface name, such as `le0` or `ether0`, is normally the way users specify interfaces, and not with either the IP address or the index. `tcpdump`, for example, is one of the few programs that lets the user specify an interface, and its `-i` option takes an interface name as the argument.

`mcast_leave` leaves the multicast group whose IP address is contained within the socket address structure pointed to by *grp*. Note that `mcast_leave` does not take an interface specification; it always deletes the first matching membership. This simplifies the library API, but means that programs that require direct control of per-interface membership need to use the `setsockopt` API directly.

`mcast_block_source` blocks reception on the given socket of the source and group whose IP addresses are contained within the socket address structures pointed to by *src* and *grp*, respectively, and whose lengths are specified by *srclen* and *grplen*. `mcast_join` must have already been called on this socket for the given group.

`mcast_unblock_source` unblocks reception of traffic from the given source to the given group. The *src*, *srclen*, *grp*, and *grplen* arguments must be the same as a previous call to `mcast_block_source`.

`mcast_join_source_group` joins the source-specific group where the source and group IP addresses are contained within the socket address structures pointed to by *src* and *grp*, respectively, and whose lengths are specified by *srclen* and *grplen*. We can specify the interface on which to join the group by either the interface name (a non-null *ifname*) or a nonzero interface index (*ifindex*). If neither is specified, the kernel chooses the interface on which the group is joined.

`mcast_leave_source_group` leaves the source-specific multicast group whose source and group IP addresses are contained within the socket address structures pointed to by *src* and *grp*, respectively, and whose lengths are specified by *srclen* and *grplen*. As with `mcast_leave`, `mcast_leave_source_group` does not take an interface specification; it always deletes the first matching membership.

`mcast_set_if` sets the default interface index for outgoing multicast datagrams. If *ifindex* is greater than 0, then it specifies the interface index; otherwise, if *ifname* is non-null, then it specifies the interface name. For IPv6, the name is mapped to an index using `if_nametoindex`. For IPv4, the mapping from either a name or an index into the interface's unicast IP address is done as described for `mcast_join`.

`mcast_set_loop` sets the loopback option to either 0 or 1, and `mcast_set_ttl` sets either the IPv4 TTL or the IPv6 hop limit. The three `mcast_get_XXX` functions return the corresponding value.

Example: `mcast_join` Function

Figure 21.10 shows the first third of our `mcast_join` function. This third shows how straightforward the protocol-independent API can be.

Handle index

9–17   If the caller supplied an index, then we just use it directly. Otherwise, if the caller supplied an interface name, the index is obtained by calling `if_nametoindex`. Otherwise, the interface is set to 0, telling the kernel to choose the interface.

Copy address and call setsockopt

18–22   The caller's socket address is copied directly into the request's group field. Recall that the group field is a `sockaddr_storage`, so it is big enough to handle any socket address type the system supports. However, to guard against buffer overruns caused by sloppy coding, we check the `sockaddr` size and return `EINVAL` if it is too large.

23–24   `setsockopt` performs the join. The *level* argument to `setsockopt` is determined using the family of the group address and our `family_to_level` function. Some systems support a mismatch between *level* and the socket's address family, for instance, using `IPPROTO_IP` with `MCAST_JOIN_GROUP`, even with an `AF_INET6` socket, but not all do, so we turn the address family into the appropriate level. We do not show this trivial function, but the source code is freely available (see the Preface).

lib/mcast_join.c

```
 1 #include    "unp.h"
 2 #include    <net/if.h>

 3 int
 4 mcast_join(int sockfd, const SA *grp, socklen_t grplen,
 5            const char *ifname, u_int ifindex)
 6 {
 7 #ifdef MCAST_JOIN_GROUP
 8     struct group_req req;
 9     if (ifindex > 0) {
10         req.gr_interface = ifindex;
11     } else if (ifname != NULL) {
12         if ( (req.gr_interface = if_nametoindex(ifname)) == 0) {
13             errno = ENXIO;        /* i/f name not found */
14             return (-1);
15         }
16     } else
17         req.gr_interface = 0;
18     if (grplen > sizeof(req.gr_group)) {
19         errno = EINVAL;
20         return -1;
21     }
22     memcpy(&req.gr_group, grp, grplen);
23     return (setsockopt(sockfd, family_to_level(grp->sa_family),
24                        MCAST_JOIN_GROUP, &req, sizeof(req)));
25 #else
```

lib/mcast_join.c

Figure 21.10 Join a multicast group: IP version-independent.

Figure 21.11 shows the second third of `mcast_join`, which handles IPv4 sockets.

Handle index

33–38   The IPv4 multicast address in the socket address structure is copied into an `ip_mreq` structure. If an index was specified, `if_indextoname` is called, storing the name into our `ifreq` structure. If this succeeds, we branch ahead to issue the `ioctl`.

Handle name

39–46   The caller's name is copied into an `ifreq` structure, and an `ioctl` of `SIOCGIFADDR` returns the unicast address associated with this name. Upon success the IPv4 address is copied into the `imr_interface` member of the `ip_mreq` structure.

Specify default

47–48   If an index was not specified and a name was not specified, the interface is set to the wildcard address, telling the kernel to choose the interface.

49–50   `setsockopt` performs the join.

─── *lib/mcast_join.c*
```
26      switch (grp->sa_family) {
27      case AF_INET:{
28              struct ip_mreq mreq;
29              struct ifreq ifreq;

30              memcpy(&mreq.imr_multiaddr,
31                      &((const struct sockaddr_in *) grp)->sin_addr,
32                      sizeof(struct in_addr));

33              if (ifindex > 0) {
34                  if (if_indextoname(ifindex, ifreq.ifr_name) == NULL) {
35                      errno = ENXIO;  /* i/f index not found */
36                      return (-1);
37                  }
38                  goto doioctl;
39              } else if (ifname != NULL) {
40                  strncpy(ifreq.ifr_name, ifname, IFNAMSIZ);
41              doioctl:
42                  if (ioctl(sockfd, SIOCGIFADDR, &ifreq) < 0)
43                      return (-1);
44                  memcpy(&mreq.imr_interface,
45                          &((struct sockaddr_in *) &ifreq.ifr_addr)->sin_addr,
46                          sizeof(struct in_addr));
47              } else
48                  mreq.imr_interface.s_addr = htonl(INADDR_ANY);

49              return (setsockopt(sockfd, IPPROTO_IP, IP_ADD_MEMBERSHIP,
50                              &mreq, sizeof(mreq)));
51      }
```
─── *lib/mcast_join.c*

Figure 21.11 Join a multicast group: IPv4 socket.

The final portion of the function, which handles IPv6 sockets, is shown in Figure 21.12.

Copy address

55–57   First the IPv6 multicast address is copied from the socket address structure into the
`ipv6_mreq` structure.

Handle index, name, or default

58–66   If an index was specified, it is stored in the `ipv6mr_interface` member; if a name
was specified, the index is obtained by calling `if_nametoindex`; otherwise, the interface index is set to 0 for `setsockopt`, telling the kernel to choose the interface.

67–68   The group is joined.

—————————————————————————————————— lib/mcast_join.c
```
52 #ifdef  IPV6
53     case AF_INET6:{
54             struct ipv6_mreq mreq6;

55             memcpy(&mreq6.ipv6mr_multiaddr,
56                     &((const struct sockaddr_in6 *) grp)->sin6_addr,
57                     sizeof(struct in6_addr));

58             if (ifindex > 0) {
59                 mreq6.ipv6mr_interface = ifindex;
60             } else if (ifname != NULL) {
61                 if ( (mreq6.ipv6mr_interface = if_nametoindex(ifname)) == 0) {
62                     errno = ENXIO;  /* i/f name not found */
63                     return (-1);
64                 }
65             } else
66                 mreq6.ipv6mr_interface = 0;

67             return (setsockopt(sockfd, IPPROTO_IPV6, IPV6_JOIN_GROUP,
68                             &mreq6, sizeof(mreq6)));
69         }
70 #endif

71     default:
72             errno = EAFNOSUPPORT;
73             return (-1);
74     }
75 #endif
76 }
```
—————————————————————————————————— lib/mcast_join.c

Figure 21.12   Join a multicast group: IPv6 socket.

Example: `mcast_set_loop` Function

Figure 21.13 shows our `mcast_set_loop` function.
Since the argument is a socket descriptor and not a socket address structure, we call
our `sockfd_to_family` function to obtain the address family of the socket. The
appropriate socket option is set.

We do not show the source code for all remaining `mcast_XXX` functions, but it is
freely available (see the Preface).

—————————————————————————————————————— *lib/mcast_set_loop.c*

```
 1 #include    "unp.h"

 2 int
 3 mcast_set_loop(int sockfd, int onoff)
 4 {
 5     switch (sockfd_to_family(sockfd)) {
 6     case AF_INET:{
 7             u_char  flag;

 8             flag = onoff;
 9             return (setsockopt(sockfd, IPPROTO_IP, IP_MULTICAST_LOOP,
10                               &flag, sizeof(flag)));
11         }

12 #ifdef  IPV6
13     case AF_INET6:{
14             u_int   flag;

15             flag = onoff;
16             return (setsockopt(sockfd, IPPROTO_IPV6, IPV6_MULTICAST_LOOP,
17                               &flag, sizeof(flag)));
18         }
19 #endif

20     default:
21         errno = EAFNOSUPPORT;
22         return (-1);
23     }
24 }
```

—————————————————————————————————————— *lib/mcast_set_loop.c*

Figure 21.13 Set the multicast loopback option.

21.8 `dg_cli` Function Using Multicasting

We modify our `dg_cli` function from Figure 20.5 by just removing the call to `setsockopt`. As we said earlier, none of the multicast socket options needs to be set to send a multicast datagram if the default settings for the outgoing interface, TTL, and loopback option are acceptable. We run a modified UDP echo server that joins the all-hosts group, then run our program specifying the all-hosts group as the destination address.

```
macosx % udpcli01 224.0.0.1
hi there
from 172.24.37.78: hi there              MacOS X
from 172.24.37.94: hi there              FreeBSD
```

We get a response from both systems on the subnet. They are each running the multi-cast echo server. Each reply is unicast because the source address of the request, which is used by each server as the destination address of the reply, is a unicast address.

IP Fragmentation and Multicasts

We mentioned at the end of Section 20.4 that most systems do not allow the fragmentation of a broadcast datagram as a policy decision. Fragmentation is fine to use with multicasting, as we can easily verify using the same file with a 2,000-byte line.

```
macosx % udpcli01 224.0.0.1 < 2000line
from 172.24.37.78: xxxxxxxxxx[...]
from 172.24.37.94: xxxxxxxxxx[...]
```

21.9 Receiving IP Multicast Infrastructure Session Announcements

The IP multicast infrastructure is the portion of the Internet with inter-domain multicast enabled. Multicast is not enabled on the entire Internet; the IP multicast infrastructure started life as the "MBone" in 1992 as an overlay network and moved toward being deployed as part of the Internet infrastructure in 1998. Multicast is widely deployed within enterprises, but being part of the inter-domain IP multicast infrastructure is less common.

To receive a multimedia conference on the IP multicast infrastructure, a site needs to know only the multicast address of the conference and the UDP ports for the conference's data streams (audio and video, for example). The *Session Announcement Protocol*, or SAP (RFC 2974 [Handley, Perkins, and Whelan 2000]), describes the way this is done (the packet headers and frequency with which these announcements are multicast to the IP multicast infrastructure), and the *Session Description Protocol*, or SDP (RFC 2327 [Handley and Jacobson 1998]), describes the contents of these announcements (how the multicast addresses and UDP port numbers are specified). A site wishing to announce a session on the IP multicast infrastructure periodically sends a multicast packet containing a description of the session to a well-known multicast group and UDP port. Sites on the IP multicast infrastructure run a program named `sdr` to receive these announcements. This program does a lot: Not only does it receive session announcements, but it also provides an interactive user interface that displays the information and lets the user send announcements.

In this section, we will develop a simple program that only receives these session announcements to show an example of a simple multicast receiving program. Our goal is to show the simplicity of a multicast receiver, not to delve into the details of this one application.

Figure 21.14 shows our `main` program that receives periodic SAP/SDP announcements.

Well-known name and well-known port

2-3   The multicast address assigned for SAP announcements is 224.2.127.254 and its name is `sap.mcast.net`. All the well-known multicast addresses (see `http://www.iana.org/assignments/multicast-addresses`) appear in the DNS under the `mcast.net` hierarchy. The well-known UDP port is 9875.

```
                                                              ── mysdr/main.c
 1 #include    "unp.h"

 2 #define SAP_NAME     "sap.mcast.net" /* default group name and port */
 3 #define SAP_PORT     "9875"

 4 void    loop(int, socklen_t);

 5 int
 6 main(int argc, char **argv)
 7 {
 8      int      sockfd;
 9      const int on = 1;
10      socklen_t salen;
11      struct sockaddr *sa;

12      if (argc == 1)
13          sockfd = Udp_client(SAP_NAME, SAP_PORT, (void **) &sa, &salen);
14      else if (argc == 4)
15          sockfd = Udp_client(argv[1], argv[2], (void **) &sa, &salen);
16      else
17          err_quit("usage: mysdr <mcast-addr> <port#> <interface-name>");

18      Setsockopt(sockfd, SOL_SOCKET, SO_REUSEADDR, &on, sizeof(on));
19      Bind(sockfd, sa, salen);

20      Mcast_join(sockfd, sa, salen, (argc == 4) ? argv[3] : NULL, 0);

21      loop(sockfd, salen);        /* receive and print */

22      exit(0);
23 }
                                                              ── mysdr/main.c
```

Figure 21.14 main program to receive SAP/SDP announcements.

Create UDP socket

12–17   We call our `udp_client` function to look up the name and port, and it fills in the appropriate socket address structure. We use the defaults if no command-line arguments are specified; otherwise, we take the multicast address, port, and interface name from the command-line arguments.

bind port

18–19   We set the `SO_REUSEADDR` socket option to allow multiple instances of this program to run on a host, and `bind` the port to the socket. By binding the multicast address to the socket, we prevent the socket from receiving any other UDP datagrams that may be received for the port. Binding this multicast address is not required, but it provides filtering by the kernel of packets in which we are not interested.

Join multicast group

20   We call our `mcast_join` function to join the group. If the interface name was specified as a command-line argument, it is passed to our function; otherwise, we let the kernel choose the interface on which the group is joined.

21   We call our `loop` function, shown in Figure 21.15, to read and print all the announcements.

—— mysdr/loop.c

```
 1 #include    "mysdr.h"

 2 void
 3 loop(int sockfd, socklen_t salen)
 4 {
 5     socklen_t len;
 6     ssize_t n;
 7     char    *p;
 8     struct sockaddr *sa;
 9     struct sap_packet {
10         uint32_t sap_header;
11         uint32_t sap_src;
12         char    sap_data[BUFFSIZE];
13     } buf;

14     sa = Malloc(salen);

15     for ( ; ; ) {
16         len = salen;
17         n = Recvfrom(sockfd, &buf, sizeof(buf) - 1, 0, sa, &len);
18         ((char *) &buf)[n] = 0; /* null terminate */
19         buf.sap_header = ntohl(buf.sap_header);

20         printf("From %s hash 0x%04x\n", Sock_ntop(sa, len),
21                 buf.sap_header & SAP_HASH_MASK);
22         if (((buf.sap_header & SAP_VERSION_MASK) >> SAP_VERSION_SHIFT) > 1) {
23             err_msg("... version field not 1 (0x%08x)", buf.sap_header);
24             continue;
25         }
26         if (buf.sap_header & SAP_IPV6) {
27             err_msg("... IPv6");
28             continue;
29         }
30         if (buf.sap_header & (SAP_DELETE | SAP_ENCRYPTED | SAP_COMPRESSED)) {
31             err_msg("... can't parse this packet type (0x%08x)",
32                     buf.sap_header);
33             continue;
34         }
35         p = buf.sap_data + ((buf.sap_header & SAP_AUTHLEN_MASK)
36                             >> SAP_AUTHLEN_SHIFT);
37         if (strcmp(p, "application/sdp") == 0)
38             p += 16;
39         printf("%s\n", p);
40     }
41 }
```

—— mysdr/loop.c

Figure 21.15 Loop that receives and prints SAP/SDP announcements.

Packet format

9–13   sap_packet describes the SDP packet: a 32-bit SAP header, followed by a 32-bit source address, followed by the actual announcement. The announcement is simply lines of ISO 8859–1 text and should not exceed 1,024 bytes. Only one session announcement is allowed in each UDP datagram.

Read UDP datagram, print sender and contents

15-21   `recvfrom` waits for the next UDP datagram destined to our socket. When one arrives, we place a null byte at the end of the buffer, fix the byte order of the header field, and print the source of the packet and SAP hash.

Check SAP header

22-34   We check the SAP header to see if it is a type that we handle. We don't handle SAP packets with IPv6 addresses in the header, or compressed or encrypted packets.

Find beginning of announcement and print

35-39   We skip over any authentication data that may be present, skip over the packet content type if it's present, and then print out the contents of the packet.

Figure 21.16 shows some typical output from our program.

```
freebsd % mysdr
From 128.223.83.33:1028 hash 0x0000
v=0
o=- 60345 0 IN IP4 128.223.214.198
s=UO Broadcast - NASA Videos - 25 Years of Progress
i=25 Years of Progress, parts 1-13. Broadcast with Cisco System's
 IP/TV using MPEG1 codec (6 hours 5 Minutes; repeats) More information
 about IP/TV and the client needed to view this program is available
 from http://videolab.uoregon.edu/download.html
u=http://videolab.uoregon.edu/
e=Hans Kuhn <multicast@lists.uoregon.edu>
p=Hans Kuhn <541/346-1758>
b=AS:1000
t=0 0
a=type:broadcast
a=tool:IP/TV Content Manager 3.2.24
a=x-iptv-file:1 name y:25yop1234567890123.mpg
m=video 63096 RTP/AVP 32 31 96
c=IN IP4 224.2.245.25/127
a=framerate:30
a=rtpmap:96 WBIH/90000
a=x-iptv-svr:video blaster2.uoregon.edu file 1 loop
m=audio 31954 RTP/AVP 14 96 0 3 5 97 98 99 100 101 102 10 11 103 104 105 106
c=IN IP4 224.2.216.85/127
a=rtpmap:96 X-WAVE/8000
a=rtpmap:97 L8/8000/2
a=rtpmap:98 L8/8000
a=rtpmap:99 L8/22050/2
a=rtpmap:100 L8/22050
a=rtpmap:101 L8/11025/2
a=rtpmap:102 L8/11025
a=rtpmap:103 L16/22050/2
a=rtpmap:104 L16/22050
a=rtpmap:105 L16/11025/2
a=rtpmap:106 L16/11025
a=x-iptv-svr:audio blaster2.uoregon.edu file 1 loop
```

Figure 21.16   Typical SAP/SDP announcement.

This announcement describes the NASA coverage on the IP Multicast Infrastructure of a space shuttle mission. The SDP session description consists of numerous lines of the form

   type=value

where the *type* is always one character and is case-significant. The *value* is a structured text string that depends on the *type*. Spaces are not allowed around the equals sign. v=0 is the version.

   o= is the origin. - indicates no particular username, 60345 is the session ID, 0 is the version number for this announcement, IN is the network type, IP4 is the address type, and 128.223.214.198 is the address. The five-tuple consisting of the username, session ID, network type, address type, and address form a globally unique identifier for the session.

   s= defines the session name, and i= is information about the session. We have wrapped the latter every 80 characters. u= provides a Uniform Resource Identifier (URI) for more information about the session, and e= and p= provide the email address and phone number of the person responsible for the conference.

   b= provides a measure of the expected bandwidth for this session. t= provides the starting time and stopping time, both in NTP units, which are seconds since January 1, 1900, UTC. In this case, this session is "permanent;" having no particular start or stop time, so both start and stop time are specified as 0.

   The a= lines are attributes; either of the session, if they appear before any m= lines, or of the media, if they appear after a m= line.

   The m= lines are the media announcements. The first of these two lines specifies that the video is on port 63096 and its format is RTP, using the Audio/Video Profile or AVP, with possible payload types 32, 31 or 96 (which are MPEG, H.261, and WBIH, respectively). The c= line that follows provides the connection information, which in this example, specifies that it is IP-based, using IPv4, with a multicast address of 224.2.245.25 and a TTL of 127. Although these are separated by a slash, like the CIDR prefix format, they are not meant to represent a prefix and a mask.

   The next m= line specifies that the audio is on port 31954 and may be in any of a number of RTP/AVP payload types, some of which are standard and some of which are specified below using a=rtpmap: attributes. The c= line that follows provides the connection information for the audio, which in this example specifies that it is IP-based, using IPv4, with a multicast address of 224.2.216.85 and a TTL of 127.

21.10 Sending and Receiving

The IP multicast infrastructure session announcement program in the previous section only received multicast datagrams. We will now develop a simple program that sends and receives multicast datagrams. Our program consists of two parts. The first part sends a multicast datagram to a specific group every five seconds and the datagram contains the sender's hostname and process ID. The second part is an infinite loop that joins the multicast group to which the first part is sending and prints every received datagram (containing the hostname and process ID of the sender). This allows us to start the program on multiple hosts on a LAN and easily see which host is receiving datagrams from which senders.

Figure 21.17 shows the `main` function for our program.

—— *mcast/main.c*
```
 1 #include    "unp.h"

 2 void    recv_all(int, socklen_t);
 3 void    send_all(int, SA *, socklen_t);

 4 int
 5 main(int argc, char **argv)
 6 {
 7     int     sendfd, recvfd;
 8     const int on = 1;
 9     socklen_t salen;
10     struct sockaddr *sasend, *sarecv;

11     if (argc != 3)
12         err_quit("usage: sendrecv <IP-multicast-address> <port#>");

13     sendfd = Udp_client(argv[1], argv[2], (void **) &sasend, &salen);

14     recvfd = Socket(sasend->sa_family, SOCK_DGRAM, 0);

15     Setsockopt(recvfd, SOL_SOCKET, SO_REUSEADDR, &on, sizeof(on));

16     sarecv = Malloc(salen);
17     memcpy(sarecv, sasend, salen);
18     Bind(recvfd, sarecv, salen);

19     Mcast_join(recvfd, sasend, salen, NULL, 0);
20     Mcast_set_loop(sendfd, 0);

21     if (Fork() == 0)
22         recv_all(recvfd, salen);    /* child -> receives */

23     send_all(sendfd, sasend, salen);    /* parent -> sends */
24 }
```
—— *mcast/main.c*

Figure 21.17   Create sockets, `fork`, and start sender and receiver.

We create two sockets, one for sending and one for receiving. We want the receiving socket to `bind` the multicast group and port, say 239.255.1.2 port 8888. (Recall that we could just `bind` the wildcard IP address and port 8888, but binding the multicast address prevents the socket from receiving any other datagrams that might arrive destined for port 8888.) We then want the receiving socket to join the multicast group. The sending socket will send datagrams to this same multicast address and port, say 239.255.1.2 port 8888. But if we try to use a single socket for sending and receiving, the source protocol address is 239.255.1.2:8888 from the `bind` (using `netstat` notation) and the destination protocol address for the `sendto` is also 239.255.1.2:8888. However, now the source protocol address that is bound to the socket becomes the source IP address of the UDP datagram, and RFC 1122 [Braden 1989] forbids an IP datagram from having a source IP address that is a multicast address or a broadcast address (see Exercise 21.2 also). Therefore, we must create two sockets: one for sending and one for receiving.

Create sending socket

13   Our udp_client function creates the sending socket, processing the two command-line arguments that specify the multicast address and port number. This function also returns a socket address structure that is ready for calls to sendto along with the length of this socket address structure.

Create receiving socket and bind multicast address and port

14-18   We create the receiving socket using the same address family that was used for the sending socket. We set the SO_REUSEADDR socket option to allow multiple instances of this program to run at the same time on a host. We then allocate room for a socket address structure for this socket, copy its contents from the sending socket address structure (whose address and port were taken from the command-line arguments), and bind the multicast address and port to the receiving socket.

Join multicast group and turn off loopback

19-20   We call our mcast_join function to join the multicast group on the receiving socket and our mcast_set_loop function to disable the loopback feature on the sending socket. For the join, we specify the interface name as a null pointer and the interface index as 0, telling the kernel to choose the interface.

fork and call appropriate functions

21-23   We fork and then the child is the receive loop and the parent is the send loop.

Our send_all function, which sends one multicast datagram every five seconds, is shown in Figure 21.18. The main function passes as arguments the socket descriptor, a pointer to a socket address structure containing the multicast destination and port, and the structure's length.

Obtain hostname and form datagram contents

9-11   We obtain the hostname from the uname function and build the output line containing it and the process ID.

Send datagram, then go to sleep

12-15   We send a datagram and then sleep for five seconds.

The recv_all function, which is the infinite receive loop, is shown in Figure 21.19.

Allocate socket address structure

9   A socket address structure is allocated to receive the sender's protocol address for each call to recvfrom.

Read and print datagrams

10-15   Each datagram is read by recvfrom, null-terminated, and printed.

```
                                                             ── mcast/send.c
 1 #include    "unp.h"
 2 #include    <sys/utsname.h>

 3 #define SENDRATE    5           /* send one datagram every five seconds */

 4 void
 5 send_all(int sendfd, SA *sadest, socklen_t salen)
 6 {
 7     char    line[MAXLINE];         /* hostname and process ID */
 8     struct utsname myname;

 9     if (uname(&myname) < 0)
10         err_sys("uname error");;
11     snprintf(line, sizeof(line), "%s, %d\n", myname.nodename, getpid());

12     for ( ; ; ) {
13         Sendto(sendfd, line, strlen(line), 0, sadest, salen);

14         sleep(SENDRATE);
15     }
16 }
                                                             ── mcast/send.c
```

Figure 21.18 Send a multicast datagram every five seconds.

```
                                                             ── mcast/recv.c
 1 #include    "unp.h"

 2 void
 3 recv_all(int recvfd, socklen_t salen)
 4 {
 5     int     n;
 6     char    line[MAXLINE + 1];
 7     socklen_t len;
 8     struct sockaddr *safrom;

 9     safrom = Malloc(salen);

10     for ( ; ; ) {
11         len = salen;
12         n = Recvfrom(recvfd, line, MAXLINE, 0, safrom, &len);

13         line[n] = 0;               /* null terminate */
14         printf("from %s: %s", Sock_ntop(safrom, len), line);
15     }
16 }
                                                             ── mcast/recv.c
```

Figure 21.19 Receive all multicast datagrams for a group we have joined.

Example

We run this program on our two systems, freebsd4 and macosx. We see that each system sees the packets that the other is sending.

```
freebsd4 % sendrecv 239.255.1.2 8888
from 172.24.37.78:51297: macosx, 21891
from 172.24.37.78:51297: macosx, 21891
from 172.24.37.78:51297: macosx, 21891
from 172.24.37.78:51297: macosx, 21891

macosx % sendrecv 239.255.1.2 8888
from 172.24.37.94.1215: freebsd4, 55372
from 172.24.37.94.1215: freebsd4, 55372
from 172.24.37.94.1215: freebsd4, 55372
from 172.24.37.94.1215: freebsd4, 55372
```

21.11 Simple Network Time Protocol (SNTP)

NTP is a sophisticated protocol for synchronizing clocks across a WAN or a LAN, and can often achieve millisecond accuracy. RFC 1305 [Mills 1992] describes the protocol in detail and RFC 2030 [Mills 1996] describes SNTP, a simplified but protocol-compatible version intended for hosts that do not need the complexity of a complete NTP implementation. It is common for a few hosts on a LAN to synchronize their clocks across the Internet to other NTP hosts and then redistribute this time on the LAN using either broadcasting or multicasting.

In this section, we will develop an SNTP client that listens for NTP broadcasts or multicasts on all attached networks and then prints the time difference between the NTP packet and the host's current time-of-day. We do not try to adjust the time-of-day, as that takes superuser privileges.

The file `ntp.h`, shown in Figure 21.20, contains some basic definitions of the NTP packet format.

—— *ssntp/ntp.h*

```
 1 #define JAN_1970    2208988800UL    /* 1970 - 1900 in seconds */

 2 struct l_fixedpt {                 /* 64-bit fixed-point */
 3     uint32_t int_part;
 4     uint32_t fraction;
 5 };

 6 struct s_fixedpt {                 /* 32-bit fixed-point */
 7     uint16_t int_part;
 8     uint16_t fraction;
 9 };

10 struct ntpdata {                   /* NTP header */
11     u_char   status;
12     u_char   stratum;
13     u_char   ppoll;
14     int      precision:8;
15     struct s_fixedpt distance;
16     struct s_fixedpt dispersion;
17     uint32_t refid;
18     struct l_fixedpt reftime;
19     struct l_fixedpt org;
20     struct l_fixedpt rec;
21     struct l_fixedpt xmt;
22 };

23 #define VERSION_MASK    0x38
24 #define MODE_MASK       0x07

25 #define MODE_CLIENT     3
26 #define MODE_SERVER     4
27 #define MODE_BROADCAST  5
```
—— *ssntp/ntp.h*

Figure 21.20 `ntp.h` header: NTP packet format and definitions.

2–22   `l_fixedpt` defines the 64-bit fixed-point values used by NTP for timestamps and `s_fixedpt` defines the 32-bit fixed-point values that are also used by NTP. The `ntpdata` structure is the 48-byte NTP packet format.

Figure 21.21 shows the `main` function.

Get multicast IP address

12–14   When the program is executed, the user must specify the multicast address to join as the command-line argument. With IPv4, this would be 224.0.1.1 or the name `ntp.mcast.net`. With IPv6, this would be `ff05::101` for the site-local scope NTP. Our `udp_client` function allocates space for a socket address structure of the correct type (either IPv4 or IPv6) and stores the multicast address and port in that structure. If this program is run on a host that does not support multicasting, any IP address can be specified, as only the address family and port are used from this structure. Note that

```
                                                                ——— ssntp/main.c
 1 #include    "sntp.h"

 2 int
 3 main(int argc, char **argv)
 4 {
 5     int      sockfd;
 6     char     buf[MAXLINE];
 7     ssize_t n;
 8     socklen_t salen, len;
 9     struct ifi_info *ifi;
10     struct sockaddr *mcastsa, *wild, *from;
11     struct timeval now;

12     if (argc != 2)
13         err_quit("usage: ssntp <IPaddress>");

14     sockfd = Udp_client(argv[1], "ntp", (void **) &mcastsa, &salen);

15     wild = Malloc(salen);
16     memcpy(wild, mcastsa, salen);   /* copy family and port */
17     sock_set_wild(wild, salen);
18     Bind(sockfd, wild, salen);  /* bind wildcard */

19 #ifdef  MCAST
20         /* obtain interface list and process each one */
21     for (ifi = Get_ifi_info(mcastsa->sa_family, 1); ifi != NULL;
22          ifi = ifi->ifi_next) {
23         if (ifi->ifi_flags & IFF_MULTICAST) {
24             Mcast_join(sockfd, mcastsa, salen, ifi->ifi_name, 0);
25             printf("joined %s on %s\n",
26                     Sock_ntop(mcastsa, salen), ifi->ifi_name);
27         }
28     }
29 #endif

30     from = Malloc(salen);
31     for ( ; ; ) {
32         len = salen;
33         n = Recvfrom(sockfd, buf, sizeof(buf), 0, from, &len);
34         Gettimeofday(&now, NULL);
35         sntp_proc(buf, n, &now);
36     }
37 }
                                                                ——— ssntp/main.c
```

Figure 21.21 main function.

our udp_client function does not bind the address to the socket; it just creates the
socket and fills in the socket address structure.

Bind wildcard address to socket

15–18   We allocate space for another socket address structure and fill it in by copying the
structure that was filled in by udp_client. This sets the address family and port. We call
our sock_set_wild function to set the IP address to the wildcard and then call bind.

Get interface list

20–22   Our get_ifi_info function returns information on all the interfaces and addresses. The address family that we ask for is taken from the socket address structure that was filled in by udp_client based on the command-line argument.

Join multicast group

23–27   We call our mcast_join function to join the multicast group specified by the command-line argument for each multicast-capable interface. All these joins are done on the one socket that this program uses. As we said earlier, there is normally a limit of IP_MAX_MEMBERSHIPS (often 20) joins per socket, but few multihomed hosts have that many interfaces.

Read and process all NTP packets

30–36   Another socket address structure is allocated to hold the address returned by recvfrom and the program enters an infinite loop, reading all the NTP packets that the host receives and calling our sntp_proc function (described next) to process the packet. Since the socket was bound to the wildcard address, and since the multicast group was joined on all multicast-capable interfaces, the socket should receive any unicast, broadcast, or multicast NTP packet that the host receives. Before calling sntp_proc, we call gettimeofday to fetch the current time, because sntp_proc calculates the difference between the time in the packet and the current time.

Our sntp_proc function, shown in Figure 21.22, processes the actual NTP packet.

Validate packet

10–21   We first check the size of the packet and then print the version, mode, and server stratum. If the mode is MODE_CLIENT, the packet is a client request, not a server reply, and we ignore it.

Obtain transmit time from NTP packet

22–33   The field in the NTP packet that we are interested in is xmt, the transmit timestamp, which is the 64-bit fixed-point time at which the packet was sent by the server. Since NTP timestamps count seconds beginning in 1900 and Unix timestamps count seconds beginning in 1970, we first subtract JAN_1970 (the number of seconds in these 70 years) from the integer part.

The fractional part is a 32-bit unsigned integer between 0 and 4,294,967,295, inclusive. This is copied from a 32-bit integer (useci) to a double-precision floating-point variable (usecf) and then divided by 4,294,967,296 (2^{32}). The result is greater than or equal to 0.0 and less than 1.0. We multiply this by 1,000,000, the number of microseconds in a second, storing the result as a 32-bit unsigned integer in the variable useci. This is the number of microseconds and will be between 0 and 999,999 (see Exercise 21.5). We convert to microseconds because the Unix timestamp returned by gettimeofday is returned as two integers: the number of seconds since January 1, 1970, UTC, along with the number of microseconds. We then calculate and print the difference between the host's time-of-day and the NTP server's time-of-day, in microseconds.

――― *ssntp/sntp_proc.c*

```
 1 #include    "sntp.h"

 2 void
 3 sntp_proc(char *buf, ssize_t n, struct timeval *nowptr)
 4 {
 5     int     version, mode;
 6     uint32_t nsec, useci;
 7     double  usecf;
 8     struct timeval diff;
 9     struct ntpdata *ntp;

10     if (n < (ssize_t) sizeof(struct ntpdata)) {
11         printf("\npacket too small: %d bytes\n", n);
12         return;
13     }

14     ntp = (struct ntpdata *) buf;
15     version = (ntp->status & VERSION_MASK) >> 3;
16     mode = ntp->status & MODE_MASK;
17     printf("\nv%d, mode %d, strat %d, ", version, mode, ntp->stratum);
18     if (mode == MODE_CLIENT) {
19         printf("client\n");
20         return;
21     }

22     nsec = ntohl(ntp->xmt.int_part) - JAN_1970;
23     useci = ntohl(ntp->xmt.fraction);    /* 32-bit integer fraction */
24     usecf = useci;              /* integer fraction -> double */
25     usecf /= 4294967296.0;      /* divide by 2**32 -> [0, 1.0) */
26     useci = usecf * 1000000.0;  /* fraction -> parts per million */

27     diff.tv_sec = nowptr->tv_sec - nsec;
28     if ( (diff.tv_usec = nowptr->tv_usec - useci) < 0) {
29         diff.tv_usec += 1000000;
30         diff.tv_sec--;
31     }
32     useci = (diff.tv_sec * 1000000) + diff.tv_usec; /* diff in microsec */
33     printf("clock difference = %d usec\n", useci);
34 }
```

――― *ssntp/sntp_proc.c*

Figure 21.22 sntp_proc function: processes the NTP packet.

One thing that our program does not take into account is the network delay between the server and the client. But we assume that the NTP packets are normally received as a broadcast or multicast on a LAN, in which case, the network delay should be only a few milliseconds.

If we run this program on our host `macosx` with an NTP server on our host `freebsd4`, which is multicasting NTP packets to the Ethernet every 64 seconds, we have the following output:

```
macosx # ssntp 224.0.1.1
joined 224.0.1.1.123 on lo0
joined 224.0.1.1.123 on en1

v4, mode 5, strat 3, clock difference = 661 usec

v4, mode 5, strat 3, clock difference = -1789 usec

v4, mode 5, strat 3, clock difference = -2945 usec

v4, mode 5, strat 3, clock difference = -3689 usec

v4, mode 5, strat 3, clock difference = -5425 usec

v4, mode 5, strat 3, clock difference = -6700 usec

v4, mode 5, strat 3, clock difference = -8520 usec
```

To run our program, we first terminated the normal NTP server running on this host, so when our program starts, the time is very close to the server's time. We see this host lost 9181 microseconds in the 384 seconds we ran the program, or about 2 seconds in 24 hours.

21.12 Summary

A multicast application starts by joining the multicast group assigned to the application. This tells the IP layer to join the group, which in turns tells the datalink layer to receive multicast frames that are sent to the corresponding hardware layer multicast address. Multicasting takes advantage of the hardware filtering present on most interface cards, and the better the filtering, the fewer the number of undesired packets received. Using this hardware filtering reduces the load on all the other hosts that are not participating in the application.

Multicasting on a WAN requires multicast-capable routers and a multicast routing protocol. Until all the routers on the Internet are multicast-capable, multicast is only available to a subset of Internet users. We use the term "IP multicast infrastructure" to describe the set of all multicast-capable systems on the Internet.

Nine socket options provide the API for multicasting:

- Join an any-source multicast group on an interface
- Leave a multicast group
- Block a source from a joined group
- Unblock a blocked source
- Join a source-specific multicast group on an interface
- Leave a source-specific multicast group
- Set the default interface for outgoing multicasts
- Set the TTL or hop limit for outgoing multicasts
- Enable or disable loopback of multicasts

The first six are for receiving, and the last three are for sending. There is enough difference between the IPv4 socket options and the IPv6 socket options that protocol-independent multicasting code becomes littered with #ifdefs very quickly. We developed 12 functions of our own, all beginning with mcast_, that can help in writing multicast applications that work with either IPv4 or IPv6.

Exercises

21.1 Build the program shown in Figure 20.9 and run it specifying an IP address on the command line of 224.0.0.1. What happens?

21.2 Modify the program in the previous example to bind 224.0.0.1 and port 0 to its socket. Run it. Are you allowed to bind a multicast address to the socket? If you have a tool such as tcpdump, watch the packets on the network. What is the source IP address of the datagram you send?

21.3 One way to tell which hosts on your subnet are multicast-capable is to ping the all-hosts group: 224.0.0.1. Try this.

21.4 One way to tell if your host is connected to the IP multicast infrastructure is to run our program from Section 21.9, wait a few minutes, and see if any session announcements appear. Try this and see if you receive any announcements.

21.5 Go through the calculations in Figure 21.22 when the fractional part of the NTP timestamp is 1,073,741,824 (one-quarter of 2^{32}).

Redo these calculations for the largest possible integer fraction ($2^{32} - 1$).

21.6 Modify the implementation of mcast_set_if for IPv4 to remember each interface name for which it obtains the IP address to prevent calling ioctl again for that interface.

22

Advanced UDP Sockets

22.1 Introduction

This chapter is a collection of various topics that affect applications using UDP sockets. First is determining the destination address of a UDP datagram and the interface on which the datagram was received, because a socket bound to a UDP port and the wild-card address can receive unicast, broadcast, and multicast datagrams on any interface.

TCP is a byte-stream protocol and it uses a sliding window, so there is no such thing as a record boundary or allowing the sender to overrun the receiver with data. With UDP, however, each input operation corresponds to a UDP datagram (a record), so a problem arises of what happens when the received datagram is larger than the application's input buffer.

UDP is unreliable but there are applications where it makes sense to use UDP instead of TCP. We will discuss the factors affecting when UDP can be used instead of TCP. In these UDP applications, we must include some features to make up for UDP's unreliability: a timeout and retransmission, to handle lost datagrams, and sequence numbers, to match the replies to the requests. We develop a set of functions that we can call from our UDP applications to handle these details.

If the implementation does not support the IP_RECVDSTADDR socket option, then one way to determine the destination IP address of a UDP datagram is to bind all the interface addresses and use select.

Most UDP servers are iterative, but there are applications that exchange multiple UDP datagrams between the client and server requiring some form of concurrency. TFTP is the common example, and we will discuss how this is done, both with and without inetd.

The final topic is the per-packet information that can be specified as ancillary data for an IPv6 datagram: the source IP address, the sending interface, the outgoing hop limit, and the next-hop address. Similar information can be returned with an IPv6 datagram: the destination IP address, received interface, and received hop limit.

22.2 Receiving Flags, Destination IP Address, and Interface Index

Historically, `sendmsg` and `recvmsg` have been used only to pass descriptors across Unix domain sockets (Section 15.7), and even this was rare. But the use of these two functions is increasing for two reasons:

1. The `msg_flags` member, which was added to the `msghdr` structure with 4.3BSD Reno, returns flags to the application. We summarized these flags in Figure 14.7.

2. Ancillary data is being used to pass more and more information between the application and the kernel. We will see in Chapter 27 that IPv6 continues this trend.

As an example of `recvmsg`, we will write a function named `recvfrom_flags`, which is similar to `recvfrom` but also returns the following:

- The returned `msg_flags` value

- The destination address of the received datagram (from the `IP_RECVDSTADDR` socket option)

- The index of the interface on which the datagram was received (the `IP_RECVIF` socket option)

To return the last two items, we define the following structure in our `unp.h` header:

```
struct unp_in_pktinfo {
  struct in_addr  ipi_addr;    /* destination IPv4 address */
  int             ipi_ifindex; /* received interface index */
};
```

We have purposely chosen the structure name and member names to be similar to the IPv6 `in6_pktinfo` structure that returns the same two items for an IPv6 socket (Section 22.8). Our `recvfrom_flags` function will take a pointer to an `unp_in_pktinfo` structure as an argument, and if this pointer is non-null, we will return the structure through the pointer.

A design problem with this structure is what to return if the `IP_RECVDSTADDR` information is not available (i.e., the implementation does not support the socket option). The interface index is easy to handle because a value of 0 can indicate that the index is not known. But all 32-bit values for an IP address are valid. What we have chosen is to return a value of all zeros (0.0.0.0) as the destination address when the actual value is not available. While this is a valid IP address, it is never allowed as the destination IP address (RFC 1122 [Braden 1989]); it is valid only as the source IP address when a host is bootstrapping and does not yet know its IP address.

> Unfortunately, Berkeley-derived kernels accept IP datagrams destined to 0.0.0.0 (pp. 218–219 of TCPv2). These are obsolete broadcasts generated by 4.2BSD-derived kernels.

We now show the first half of our `recvfrom_flags` function in Figure 22.1. This function is intended to be used with a UDP socket.

————————————————————————————— advio/recvfromflags.c
```
 1 #include    "unp.h"
 2 #include    <sys/param.h>        /* ALIGN macro for CMSG_NXTHDR() macro */

 3 ssize_t
 4 recvfrom_flags(int fd, void *ptr, size_t nbytes, int *flagsp,
 5                SA *sa, socklen_t *salenptr, struct unp_in_pktinfo *pktp)
 6 {
 7     struct msghdr msg;
 8     struct iovec iov[1];
 9     ssize_t n;

10 #ifdef  HAVE_MSGHDR_MSG_CONTROL
11     struct cmsghdr *cmptr;
12     union {
13         struct cmsghdr cm;
14         char    control[CMSG_SPACE(sizeof(struct in_addr)) +
15                         CMSG_SPACE(sizeof(struct unp_in_pktinfo))];
16     } control_un;

17     msg.msg_control = control_un.control;
18     msg.msg_controllen = sizeof(control_un.control);
19     msg.msg_flags = 0;
20 #else
21     bzero(&msg, sizeof(msg));   /* make certain msg_accrightslen = 0 */
22 #endif

23     msg.msg_name = sa;
24     msg.msg_namelen = *salenptr;
25     iov[0].iov_base = ptr;
26     iov[0].iov_len = nbytes;
27     msg.msg_iov = iov;
28     msg.msg_iovlen = 1;

29     if ( (n = recvmsg(fd, &msg, *flagsp)) < 0)
30         return (n);

31     *salenptr = msg.msg_namelen;    /* pass back results */
32     if (pktp)
33         bzero(pktp, sizeof(struct unp_in_pktinfo)); /* 0.0.0.0, i/f = 0 */
```
————————————————————————————— advio/recvfromflags.c

Figure 22.1 `recvfrom_flags` function: calls `recvmsg`.

Include files

1-2   The CMSG_NXTHDR macro requires the <sys/param.h> header.

Function arguments

3-5   The function arguments are similar to recvfrom, except the fourth argument is now a pointer to an integer flag (so that we can return the flags returned by recvmsg) and the seventh argument is new: It is a pointer to an unp_in_pktinfo structure that will contain the destination IPv4 address of the received datagram and the interface index on which the datagram was received.

Implementation differences

10-22   When dealing with the msghdr structure and the various MSG_*xxx* constants, we encounter lots of differences between various implementations. Our way of handling these differences is to use C's conditional inclusion feature (#ifdef). If the implementation supports the msg_control member, space is allocated to hold the values returned by both the IP_RECVDSTADDR and IP_RECVIF socket options, and the appropriate members are initialized.

Fill in `msghdr` structure and call `recvmsg`

23-33   A msghdr structure is filled in and recvmsg is called. The values of the msg_namelen and msg_flags members must be passed back to the caller; they are value-result arguments. We also initialize the caller's unp_in_pktinfo structure, setting the IP address to 0.0.0.0 and the interface index to 0.

Figure 22.2 shows the second half of our function.

34-37   If the implementation does not support the msg_control member, we just set the returned flags to 0 and return. The remainder of the function handles the msg_control information.

Return if no control information

38-41   We return the msg_flags value and then return to the caller if: (i) there is no control information; (ii) the control information was truncated; or (iii) the caller does not want an unp_in_pktinfo structure returned.

Process ancillary data

42-43   We process any number of ancillary data objects using the CMSG_FIRSTHDR and CMSG_NXTHDR macros.

Process `IP_RECVDSTADDR`

44-51   If the destination IP address was returned as control information (Figure 14.9), it is returned to the caller.

Process `IP_RECVIF`

52-59   If the index of the received interface was returned as control information, it is returned to the caller. Figure 22.3 shows the contents of the ancillary data object that is returned.

advio/recvfromflags.c
```
34 #ifndef HAVE_MSGHDR_MSG_CONTROL
35     *flagsp = 0;                  /* pass back results */
36     return (n);
37 #else

38     *flagsp = msg.msg_flags;    /* pass back results */
39     if (msg.msg_controllen < sizeof(struct cmsghdr) ||
40         (msg.msg_flags & MSG_CTRUNC) || pktp == NULL)
41         return (n);

42     for (cmptr = CMSG_FIRSTHDR(&msg); cmptr != NULL;
43          cmptr = CMSG_NXTHDR(&msg, cmptr)) {

44 #ifdef  IP_RECVDSTADDR
45         if (cmptr->cmsg_level == IPPROTO_IP &&
46             cmptr->cmsg_type == IP_RECVDSTADDR) {

47             memcpy(&pktp->ipi_addr, CMSG_DATA(cmptr),
48                    sizeof(struct in_addr));
49             continue;
50         }
51 #endif

52 #ifdef  IP_RECVIF
53         if (cmptr->cmsg_level == IPPROTO_IP && cmptr->cmsg_type == IP_RECVIF) {
54             struct sockaddr_dl *sdl;

55             sdl = (struct sockaddr_dl *) CMSG_DATA(cmptr);
56             pktp->ipi_ifindex = sdl->sdl_index;
57             continue;
58         }
59 #endif
60         err_quit("unknown ancillary data, len = %d, level = %d, type = %d",
61                  cmptr->cmsg_len, cmptr->cmsg_level, cmptr->cmsg_type);
62     }
63     return (n);
64 #endif  /* HAVE_MSGHDR_MSG_CONTROL */
65 }
```
advio/recvfromflags.c

Figure 22.2 `recvfrom_flags` function: returns flags and destination address.

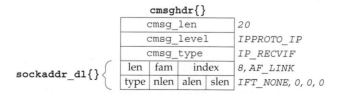

Figure 22.3 Ancillary data object returned for `IP_RECVIF`.

Recall the datalink socket address structure in Figure 18.1. The data returned in the ancillary data object is one of these structures, but the three lengths are 0 (name length, address length, and selector length). Therefore, there is no need for any of the data that follows these lengths, so the size of the structure should be 8 bytes, not the 20 that we show in Figure 18.1. The information we return is the interface index.

Example: Print Destination IP Address and Datagram-Truncated Flag

To test our function, we modify our `dg_echo` function (Figure 8.4) to call `recvfrom_flags` instead of `recvfrom`. We show this new version of `dg_echo` in Figure 22.4.

Change `MAXLINE`

2–3   We remove the existing definition of `MAXLINE` that occurs in our `unp.h` header and redefine it to be 20. We do this to see what happens when we receive a UDP datagram that is larger than the buffer that we pass to the input function (`recvmsg` in this case).

Set `IP_RECVDSTADDR` and `IP_RECVIF` socket options

14–21   If the `IP_RECVDSTADDR` socket option is defined, it is turned on. Similarly, the `IP_RECVIF` socket option is turned on.

```
                                                    ───────── advio/dgechoaddr.c
 1 #include    "unpifi.h"

 2 #undef  MAXLINE
 3 #define MAXLINE 20                  /* to see datagram truncation */

 4 void
 5 dg_echo(int sockfd, SA *pcliaddr, socklen_t clilen)
 6 {
 7     int      flags;
 8     const int on = 1;
 9     socklen_t len;
10     ssize_t n;
11     char     mesg[MAXLINE], str[INET6_ADDRSTRLEN], ifname[IFNAMSIZ];
12     struct in_addr in_zero;
13     struct unp_in_pktinfo pktinfo;

14 #ifdef  IP_RECVDSTADDR
15     if (setsockopt(sockfd, IPPROTO_IP, IP_RECVDSTADDR, &on, sizeof(on)) < 0)
16         err_ret("setsockopt of IP_RECVDSTADDR");
17 #endif
18 #ifdef  IP_RECVIF
19     if (setsockopt(sockfd, IPPROTO_IP, IP_RECVIF, &on, sizeof(on)) < 0)
20         err_ret("setsockopt of IP_RECVIF");
21 #endif
```

```
22        bzero(&in_zero, sizeof(struct in_addr));    /* all 0 IPv4 address */
23        for ( ; ; ) {
24            len = clilen;
25            flags = 0;
26            n = Recvfrom_flags(sockfd, mesg, MAXLINE, &flags,
27                            pcliaddr, &len, &pktinfo);
28            printf("%d-byte datagram from %s", n, Sock_ntop(pcliaddr, len));
29            if (memcmp(&pktinfo.ipi_addr, &in_zero, sizeof(in_zero)) != 0)
30                printf(", to %s", Inet_ntop(AF_INET, &pktinfo.ipi_addr,
31                                    str, sizeof(str)));
32            if (pktinfo.ipi_ifindex > 0)
33                printf(", recv i/f = %s",
34                        If_indextoname(pktinfo.ipi_ifindex, ifname));
35 #ifdef   MSG_TRUNC
36            if (flags & MSG_TRUNC)
37                printf(" (datagram truncated)");
38 #endif
39 #ifdef   MSG_CTRUNC
40            if (flags & MSG_CTRUNC)
41                printf(" (control info truncated)");
42 #endif
43 #ifdef   MSG_BCAST
44            if (flags & MSG_BCAST)
45                printf(" (broadcast)");
46 #endif
47 #ifdef   MSG_MCAST
48            if (flags & MSG_MCAST)
49                printf(" (multicast)");
50 #endif
51            printf("\n");

52            Sendto(sockfd, mesg, n, 0, pcliaddr, len);
53        }
54 }
```
—— *advio/dgechoaddr.c*

Figure 22.4 dg_echo function that calls our recvfrom_flags function.

Read datagram, print source IP address and port

24–28   The datagram is read by calling recvfrom_flags. The source IP address and port of the server's reply are converted to presentation format by sock_ntop.

Print destination IP address

29–31   If the returned IP address is not 0, it is converted to presentation format by inet_ntop and printed.

Print name of received interface

32–34   If the returned interface index is not 0, its name is obtained by calling if_indextoname and it is printed.

Test various flags

35–51   We test four additional flags and print a message if any are on.

22.3 Datagram Truncation

On BSD-derived systems, when a UDP datagram arrives that is larger than the application's buffer, recvmsg sets the MSG_TRUNC flag in the msg_flags member of the msghdr structure (Figure 14.7). All Berkeley-derived implementations that support the msghdr structure with the msg_flags member provide this notification.

> This is an example of a flag that must be returned from the kernel to the process. We mentioned in Section 14.3 that one design problem with the recv and recvfrom functions is that their *flags* argument is an integer, which allows flags to be passed from the process to the kernel, but not vice versa.

Unfortunately, not all implementations handle a larger-than-expected UDP datagram in this fashion. There are three possible scenarios:

1. Discard the excess bytes and return the MSG_TRUNC flag to the application. This requires that the application call recvmsg to receive the flag.

2. Discard the excess bytes, but do not tell the application.

3. Keep the excess bytes and return them in subsequent read operations on the socket.

> The POSIX specification specifies the first type of behavior: discarding the excess bytes and setting the MSG_TRUNC flag. Early releases of SVR4 exhibited the third type of behavior.

Since there are such variations in how implementations handle datagrams that are larger than the application's receive buffer, one way to detect the problem is to always allocate an application buffer that is one byte greater than the largest datagram the application should ever receive. If a datagram is ever received whose length equals this buffer, consider it an error.

22.4 When to Use UDP Instead of TCP

In Sections 2.3 and 2.4, we described the major differences between UDP and TCP. Given that TCP is reliable while UDP is not, the question arises: When should we use UDP instead of TCP, and why? We first list the advantages of UDP:

- As we show in Figure 20.1, UDP supports broadcasting and multicasting. Indeed, UDP *must* be used if the application uses broadcasting or multicasting. We discussed these two addressing modes in Chapters 20 and 21.

- UDP has no connection setup or teardown. With regard to Figure 2.5, UDP requires only two packets to exchange a request and a reply (assuming the size of each is less than the minimum MTU between the two end-systems). TCP requires about 10 packets, assuming that a new TCP connection is established for each request-reply exchange.

  Also important in this number-of-packet analysis is the number of packet round trips required to obtain the reply. This becomes important if the latency exceeds the bandwidth, as described in Appendix A of TCPv3. That text shows that the minimum *transaction time* for a UDP request-reply is RTT + server processing time (SPT). With TCP, however, if a new TCP connection is used for the request-reply, the minimum transaction time is $2 \times$ RTT + SPT, one RTT greater than the UDP time.

It should be obvious with regard to the second point that if a TCP connection is used for multiple request-reply exchanges, then the cost of the connection's establishment and teardown is amortized across all the requests and replies, and this is normally a better design than using a new connection for each request-reply. Nevertheless, there are applications that use a new TCP connection for each request-reply (e.g., the older versions of HTTP), and there are applications in which the client and server exchange one request-reply (e.g., the DNS) and then might not talk to each other for hours or days.

We now list the features of TCP that are not provided by UDP, which means that an application must provide these features itself, if they are necessary to the application. We use the qualifier "necessary" because not all features are needed by all applications. For example, dropped segments might not need to be retransmitted for a real-time audio application, if the receiver can interpolate the missing data. Also, for simple request-reply transactions, windowed flow control might not be needed if the two ends agree ahead of time on the size of the largest request and reply.

- Positive acknowledgments, retransmission of lost packets, duplicate detection, and sequencing of packets reordered by the network—TCP acknowledges all data, allowing lost packets to be detected. The implementation of these two features requires that every TCP data segment contain a sequence number that can then be acknowledged. It also requires that TCP estimate a retransmission time-out value for the connection and that this value be updated continually as network traffic between the two end-systems changes.

- Windowed flow control—A receiving TCP tells the sender how much buffer space it has allocated for receiving data, and the sender cannot exceed this. That is, the amount of unacknowledged data at the sender can never exceed the receiver's advertised window.

- Slow start and congestion avoidance—This is a form of flow control imposed by the sender to determine the current network capacity and to handle periods of congestion. All current TCPs must support these two features and we know from experience (before these algorithms were implemented in the late 1980s) that protocols that do not "back off" in the face of congestion just make the congestion worse (e.g., [Jacobson 1988]).

In summary, we can state the following recommendations:

- UDP *must* be used for broadcast or multicast applications. Any form of desired error control must be added to the clients and servers, but applications often use broadcasting or multicasting when some (assumed small) amount of error is acceptable (such as lost packets for audio or video). Multicast applications requiring reliable delivery have been built (e.g., multicast file transfer), but we must decide whether the performance gain in using multicasting (sending one packet to N destinations versus sending *N* copies of the packet across *N* TCP connections) outweighs the added complexity required within the application to provide reliable communications.

- UDP *can* be used for simple request-reply applications, but error detection must then be built into the application. Minimally, this involves acknowledgments, timeouts, and retransmission. Flow control is often not an issue for reasonably sized requests and responses. We will provide an example of these features in a UDP application in Section 22.5. The factors to consider here are how often the client and server communicate (Could a TCP connection be left up between the two?) and how much data is exchanged (if multiple packets are normally required, then the cost of the TCP connection's establishment and teardown becomes less of a factor).

- UDP *should not* be used for bulk data transfer (e.g., file transfer). The reason is that windowed flow control, congestion avoidance, and slow-start must all be built into the application, along with the features from the previous bullet point, which means we are reinventing TCP within the application. We should let the vendors focus on better TCP performance and concentrate our efforts on the application itself.

There are exceptions to these rules, especially in existing applications. TFTP, for example, uses UDP for bulk data transfer. UDP was chosen for TFTP because it is simpler to implement than TCP in bootstrap code (800 lines of C code for UDP versus 4500 lines for TCP in TCPv2, for example), and because TFTP is used only to bootstrap systems on a LAN, not for bulk data transfer across WANs. But this requires that TFTP include its own sequence number field for acknowledgments, along with a timeout and retransmission capability.

NFS is another exception to the rule: It also uses UDP for bulk data transfer (although some might claim it is really a request-reply application, albeit using large requests and replies). This is partly historical, because in the mid-1980s when it was designed, UDP implementations were faster than TCP, and NFS was used only on LANs, where packet loss is often orders of magnitude less than on WANs. But as NFS started being used across WANs in the early 1990s, and as TCP implementations passed UDP in terms of bulk data transfer performance, NFS version 3 was designed to support TCP, and most vendors are now providing NFS over both UDP and TCP. Similar reasoning (UDP being faster than TCP in the mid-1980s along with a predominance of LANs over WANs) led the precursor of the DCE RPC package (the Apollo NCS package) to also choose UDP over TCP, although current implementations support both UDP and TCP.

We might be tempted to say that UDP usage is decreasing compared to TCP, with good TCP implementations being as fast as the network today, and with fewer application designers wanting to reinvent TCP within their UDP application. But the predicted increase in multimedia applications over the next decade will see an increase in UDP usage, since multimedia usually implies multicasting, which requires UDP.

22.5 Adding Reliability to a UDP Application

If we are going to use UDP for a request-reply application, as mentioned in the previous section, then we *must* add two features to our client:

1. Timeout and retransmission to handle datagrams that are discarded

2. Sequence numbers so the client can verify that a reply is for the appropriate request

These two features are part of most existing UDP applications that use the simple request-reply paradigm: DNS resolvers, SNMP agents, TFTP, and RPC, for example. We are not trying to use UDP for bulk data transfer; our intent is for an application that sends a request and waits for a reply.

> By definition, a datagram is unreliable; therefore, we purposely do not call this a "reliable datagram service." Indeed, the term "reliable datagram" is an oxymoron. What we are showing is an application that adds reliability on top of an unreliable datagram service (UDP).

Adding sequence numbers is simple. The client prepends a sequence number to each request and the server must echo this number back to the client in the reply. This lets the client verify that a given reply is for the request that was issued.

The old-fashioned method for handling timeout and retransmission was to send a request and wait for N seconds. If no response was received, retransmit and wait another N seconds. After this had happened some number of times, the application gave up. This is an example of a linear retransmit timer. (Figure 6.8 of TCPv1 shows an example of a TFTP client that uses this technique. Many TFTP clients still use this method.)

The problem with this technique is that the amount of time required for a datagram to make a round trip on a network can vary from fractions of a second on a LAN to many seconds on a WAN. Factors affecting the RTT are distance, network speed, and congestion. Additionally, the RTT between a client and server can change rapidly with time, as network conditions change. We must use a timeout and retransmission algorithm that take into account the actual RTTs that we measure along with the changes in the RTT over time. Much work has been focused on this area, mostly relating to TCP, but the same ideas apply to any network application.

We want to calculate the RTO to use for every packet that we send. To calculate this, we measure the RTT: the actual round-trip time for a packet. Every time we measure an RTT, we update two statistical estimators: *srtt* is the smoothed RTT estimator and *rttvar* is the smoothed mean deviation estimator. The latter is a good approximation of the standard deviation, but easier to compute since it does not involve a square root. Given these two estimators, the *RTO* to use is *srtt* plus four times *rttvar*. [Jacobson 1988] provides all the details of these calculations, which we can summarize in the following four equations:

$$delta = measuredRTT - srtt$$

$$srtt \leftarrow srtt + g \times delta$$

$$rttvar \leftarrow rttvar + h(\,|\,delta\,|\, - rttvar)$$

$$RTO = srtt + 4 \times rttvar$$

delta is the difference between the measured RTT and the current smoothed RTT estimator (*srtt*). *g* is the gain applied to the RTT estimator and equals ⅛. *h* is the gain applied to the mean deviation estimator and equals ¼.

> The two gains and the multiplier 4 in the *RTO* calculation are purposely powers of 2 so they can be calculated using shift operations instead of multiplying or dividing. Indeed, the TCP kernel implementation (Section 25.7 of TCPv2) is normally performed using fixed-point arithmetic for speed, but for simplicity, we use floating-point calculations in our code that follows.

Another point made in [Jacobson 1988] is that when the retransmission timer expires, an *exponential backoff* must be used for the next *RTO*. For example, if our first *RTO* is 2 seconds and the reply is not received in this time, then the next *RTO* is 4 seconds. If there is still no reply, the next *RTO* is 8 seconds, and then 16, and so on.

Jacobson's algorithms tell us how to calculate the *RTO* each time we measure an RTT and how to increase the *RTO* when we retransmit. But, a problem arises when we have to retransmit a packet and then receive a reply. This is called the *retransmission ambiguity problem*. Figure 22.5 shows the following three possible scenarios when our retransmission timer expires:

- The request is lost
- The reply is lost
- The *RTO* is too small

When the client receives a reply to a request that was retransmitted, it cannot tell to which request the reply corresponds. In the example on the right, the reply corresponds to the original request, while in the two other examples, the reply corresponds to the retransmitted request.

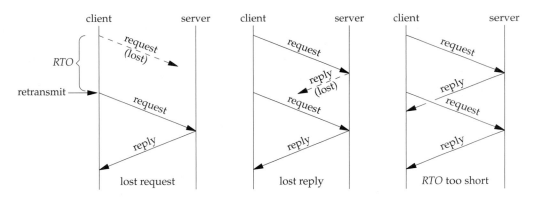

Figure 22.5 Three scenarios when retransmission timer expires.

Karn's algorithm [Karn and Partridge 1991] handles this scenario with the following rules that apply whenever a reply is received for a request that was retransmitted:

- If an RTT was measured, do not use it to update the estimators since we do not know to which request the reply corresponds.

- Since this reply arrived before our retransmission timer expired, reuse this *RTO* for the next packet. Only when we receive a reply to a request that is not retransmitted will we update the RTT estimators and recalculate the *RTO*.

It is not hard to take Karn's algorithm into account when coding our RTT functions, but it turns out that an even better and more elegant solution exists. This solution is from the TCP extensions for "long fat pipes" (networks with either a high bandwidth, a long RTT, or both), which are documented in RFC 1323 [Jacobson, Braden, and Borman 1992]. In addition to prepending a sequence number to each request, which the server must echo back, we also prepend a *timestamp* that the server must also echo. Each time we send a request, we store the current time in the timestamp. When a reply is received, we calculate the RTT of that packet as the current time minus the timestamp that was echoed by the server in its reply. Since every request carries a timestamp that is echoed by the server, we can calculate the RTT of *every* reply we receive. There is no longer any ambiguity at all. Furthermore, since all the server does is echo the client's timestamp, the client can use any units desired for the timestamps and there is no requirement at all that the client and server have synchronized clocks.

Example

We will now put all of this together in an example. We start with our UDP client `main` function from Figure 8.7 and just change the port number from `SERV_PORT` to 7 (the standard echo server, Figure 2.18).

Figure 22.6 is the `dg_cli` function. The only change from Figure 8.8 is to replace the calls to `sendto` and `recvfrom` with a call to our new function, `dg_send_recv`.

Before showing our `dg_send_recv` function and the RTT functions it calls, Figure 22.7 shows an outline of how we add reliability to a UDP client. All functions beginning with `rtt_` will be shown shortly.

—— rtt/dg_cli.c
```
 1 #include     "unp.h"

 2 ssize_t Dg_send_recv(int, const void *, size_t, void *, size_t,
 3                      const SA *, socklen_t);

 4 void
 5 dg_cli(FILE *fp, int sockfd, const SA *pservaddr, socklen_t servlen)
 6 {
 7     ssize_t n;
 8     char    sendline[MAXLINE], recvline[MAXLINE + 1];

 9     while (Fgets(sendline, MAXLINE, fp) != NULL) {

10         n = Dg_send_recv(sockfd, sendline, strlen(sendline),
11                          recvline, MAXLINE, pservaddr, servlen);

12         recvline[n] = 0;         /* null terminate */
13         Fputs(recvline, stdout);
14     }
15 }
```
—— rtt/dg_cli.c

Figure 22.6 dg_cli function that calls our dg_send_recv function.

```
static sigjmp_buf   jmpbuf;

{
    . . .
    form request

    signal(SIGALRM, sig_alrm); /* establish signal handler */
    rtt_newpack();             /* initialize rexmt counter to 0 */
sendagain:
    sendto();

    alarm(rtt_start());        /* set alarm for RTO seconds */
    if (sigsetjmp(jmpbuf, 1) != 0) {
        if (rtt_timeout())     /* double RTO, retransmitted enough? */
            give up
        goto sendagain;        /* retransmit */
    }
    do {
        recvfrom();
    } while (wrong sequence#);

    alarm(0);                  /* turn off alarm */
    rtt_stop();                /* calculate RTT and update estimators */

    process reply
    . . .
}

void
sig_alrm(int signo)
{
    siglongjmp(jmpbuf, 1);
}
```

Figure 22.7 Outline of RTT functions and when they are called.

When a reply is received but the sequence number is not the one expected, we call `recvfrom` again, but we do not retransmit the request and we do not restart the retransmission timer that is running. Notice in the rightmost example in Figure 22.5 that the final reply from the retransmitted request will be in the socket receive buffer the next time the client sends a new request. That is fine as the client will read this reply, notice that the sequence number is not the one expected, discard the reply, and call `recvfrom` again.

We call `sigsetjmp` and `siglongjmp` to avoid the race condition with the `SIGALRM` signal we described in Section 20.5.

Figure 22.8 shows the first half of our `dg_send_recv` function.

1–5   We include a new header, `unprtt.h`, shown in Figure 22.10, which defines the `rtt_info` structure that maintains the RTT information for a client. We define one of these structures and numerous other variables.

Define `msghdr` structures and `hdr` structure

6–10   We want to hide the fact from the caller that we prepend a sequence number and a timestamp to each packet. The easiest way to do this is to use `writev`, writing our header (the `hdr` structure), followed by the caller's data, as a single UDP datagram. Recall that the output for `writev` on a datagram socket is a single datagram. This is easier than forcing the caller to allocate room at the front of its buffer for our use and is also faster than copying our header and the caller's data into one buffer (that we would have to allocate) for a single `sendto`. But since we are using UDP and have to specify a destination address, we must use the `iovec` capability of `sendmsg` and `recvmsg`, instead of `sendto` and `recvfrom`. Recall from Section 14.5 that some systems have a newer `msghdr` structure with ancillary data, while older systems still have the access rights members at the end of the structure. To avoid complicating the code with #ifdefs to handle these differences, we declare two `msghdr` structures as `static`, forcing their initialization to all zero bits by C and then just ignore the unused members at the end of the structures.

Initialize first time we are called

20–24   The first time we are called, we call the `rtt_init` function.

Fill in `msghdr` structures

25–41   We fill in the two `msghdr` structures that are used for output and input. We increment the sending sequence number for this packet, but do not set the sending timestamp until we send the packet (since it might be retransmitted, and each retransmission needs the current timestamp).

The second half of the function, along with the `sig_alrm` signal handler, is shown in Figure 22.9.

rtt/dg_send_recv.c

```
 1 #include    "unprtt.h"
 2 #include    <setjmp.h>

 3 #define RTT_DEBUG

 4 static struct rtt_info rttinfo;
 5 static int rttinit = 0;
 6 static struct msghdr msgsend, msgrecv;  /* assumed init to 0 */
 7 static struct hdr {
 8     uint32_t seq;                /* sequence # */
 9     uint32_t ts;                 /* timestamp when sent */
10 } sendhdr, recvhdr;

11 static void sig_alrm(int signo);
12 static sigjmp_buf jmpbuf;

13 ssize_t
14 dg_send_recv(int fd, const void *outbuff, size_t outbytes,
15              void *inbuff, size_t inbytes,
16              const SA *destaddr, socklen_t destlen)
17 {
18     ssize_t n;
19     struct iovec iovsend[2], iovrecv[2];

20     if (rttinit == 0) {
21         rtt_init(&rttinfo);      /* first time we're called */
22         rttinit = 1;
23         rtt_d_flag = 1;
24     }

25     sendhdr.seq++;
26     msgsend.msg_name = destaddr;
27     msgsend.msg_namelen = destlen;
28     msgsend.msg_iov = iovsend;
29     msgsend.msg_iovlen = 2;
30     iovsend[0].iov_base = &sendhdr;
31     iovsend[0].iov_len = sizeof(struct hdr);
32     iovsend[1].iov_base = outbuff;
33     iovsend[1].iov_len = outbytes;

34     msgrecv.msg_name = NULL;
35     msgrecv.msg_namelen = 0;
36     msgrecv.msg_iov = iovrecv;
37     msgrecv.msg_iovlen = 2;
38     iovrecv[0].iov_base = &recvhdr;
39     iovrecv[0].iov_len = sizeof(struct hdr);
40     iovrecv[1].iov_base = inbuff;
41     iovrecv[1].iov_len = inbytes;
```

rtt/dg_send_recv.c

Figure 22.8 dg_send_recv function: first half.

rtt/dg_send_recv.c
```
42     Signal(SIGALRM, sig_alrm);
43     rtt_newpack(&rttinfo);        /* initialize for this packet */

44   sendagain:
45     sendhdr.ts = rtt_ts(&rttinfo);
46     Sendmsg(fd, &msgsend, 0);

47     alarm(rtt_start(&rttinfo)); /* calc timeout value & start timer */

48     if (sigsetjmp(jmpbuf, 1) != 0) {
49         if (rtt_timeout(&rttinfo) < 0) {
50             err_msg("dg_send_recv: no response from server, giving up");
51             rttinit = 0;           /* reinit in case we're called again */
52             errno = ETIMEDOUT;
53             return (-1);
54         }
55         goto sendagain;
56     }

57     do {
58         n = Recvmsg(fd, &msgrecv, 0);
59     } while (n < sizeof(struct hdr) || recvhdr.seq != sendhdr.seq);

60     alarm(0);                      /* stop SIGALRM timer */
61     /* calculate & store new RTT estimator values */
62     rtt_stop(&rttinfo, rtt_ts(&rttinfo) - recvhdr.ts);

63     return (n - sizeof(struct hdr));    /* return size of received datagram */
64 }

65 static void
66 sig_alrm(int signo)
67 {
68     siglongjmp(jmpbuf, 1);
69 }
```
rtt/dg_send_recv.c

Figure 22.9 dg_send_recv function: second half.

Establish signal handler

42–43   A signal handler is established for SIGALRM and rtt_newpack sets the retransmission counter to 0.

Send datagram

45–47   The current timestamp is obtained by rtt_ts and stored in the hdr structure prepended to the user's data. A single UDP datagram is sent by sendmsg. rtt_start returns the number of seconds for this timeout and the SIGALRM is scheduled by calling alarm.

Establish jump buffer

48   We establish a jump buffer for our signal handler with sigsetjmp. We wait for the next datagram to arrive by calling recvmsg. (We discussed the use of sigsetjmp and siglongjmp along with SIGALRM with Figure 20.9.) If the alarm timer expires, sigsetjmp returns 1.

Handle timeout

49–55   When a timeout occurs, `rtt_timeout` calculates the next *RTO* (the exponential backoff) and returns −1 if we should give up, or 0 if we should retransmit. If we give up, we set `errno` to `ETIMEDOUT` and return to the caller.

Call `recvmsg`, compare sequence numbers

57–59   We wait for a datagram to arrive by calling `recvmsg`. When it returns, the datagram's length must be at least the size of our `hdr` structure and its sequence number must equal the sequence number that was sent. If either comparison is false, `recvmsg` is called again.

Turn off alarm and update RTT estimators

60–62   When the expected reply is received, the pending `alarm` is turned off and `rtt_stop` updates the RTT estimators. `rtt_ts` returns the current timestamp and the timestamp from the received datagram is subtracted from this, giving the RTT.

`SIGALRM` handler

65–69   `siglongjmp` is called, causing the `sigsetjmp` in `dg_send_recv` to return 1.

We now look at the various RTT functions that were called by `dg_send_recv`. Figure 22.10 shows the `unprtt.h` header.

——————————————————————————————————— *lib/unprtt.h*

```
 1 #ifndef __unp_rtt_h
 2 #define __unp_rtt_h

 3 #include    "unp.h"

 4 struct rtt_info {
 5    float    rtt_rtt;         /* most recent measured RTT, in seconds */
 6    float    rtt_srtt;        /* smoothed RTT estimator, in seconds */
 7    float    rtt_rttvar;      /* smoothed mean deviation, in seconds */
 8    float    rtt_rto;         /* current RTO to use, in seconds */
 9    int      rtt_nrexmt;      /* # times retransmitted: 0, 1, 2, ... */
10    uint32_t rtt_base;        /* # sec since 1/1/1970 at start */
11 };

12 #define RTT_RXTMIN    2       /* min retransmit timeout value, in seconds */
13 #define RTT_RXTMAX    60      /* max retransmit timeout value, in seconds */
14 #define RTT_MAXNREXMT  3      /* max # times to retransmit */

15                 /* function prototypes */
16 void     rtt_debug(struct rtt_info *);
17 void     rtt_init(struct rtt_info *);
18 void     rtt_newpack(struct rtt_info *);
19 int      rtt_start(struct rtt_info *);
20 void     rtt_stop(struct rtt_info *, uint32_t);
21 int      rtt_timeout(struct rtt_info *);
22 uint32_t rtt_ts(struct rtt_info *);

23 extern int rtt_d_flag;       /* can be set to nonzero for addl info */

24 #endif  /* __unp_rtt_h */
```

——————————————————————————————————— *lib/unprtt.h*

Figure 22.10 `unprtt.h` header.

`rtt_info` **structure**

4-11   This structure contains the variables necessary to time the packets between a client and server. The first four variables are from the equations given near the beginning of this section.

12-14   These constants define the minimum and maximum retransmission timeouts and the maximum number of times we retransmitted.

Figure 22.11 shows a macro and the first two of our RTT functions.

lib/rtt.c

```
 1 #include    "unprtt.h"

 2 int     rtt_d_flag = 0;              /* debug flag; can be set by caller */

 3 /*
 4  * Calculate the RTO value based on current estimators:
 5  *        smoothed RTT plus four times the deviation
 6  */
 7 #define RTT_RTOCALC(ptr) ((ptr)->rtt_srtt + (4.0 * (ptr)->rtt_rttvar))

 8 static float
 9 rtt_minmax(float rto)
10 {
11     if (rto < RTT_RXTMIN)
12         rto = RTT_RXTMIN;
13     else if (rto > RTT_RXTMAX)
14         rto = RTT_RXTMAX;
15     return (rto);
16 }

17 void
18 rtt_init(struct rtt_info *ptr)
19 {
20     struct timeval tv;

21     Gettimeofday(&tv, NULL);
22     ptr->rtt_base = tv.tv_sec;   /* # sec since 1/1/1970 at start */

23     ptr->rtt_rtt    = 0;
24     ptr->rtt_srtt   = 0;
25     ptr->rtt_rttvar = 0.75;
26     ptr->rtt_rto = rtt_minmax(RTT_RTOCALC(ptr));
27     /* first RTO at (srtt + (4 * rttvar)) = 3 seconds */
28 }
```

lib/rtt.c

Figure 22.11 RTT_RTOCALC macro and `rtt_minmax` and `rtt_init` functions.

3–7   The RTT_RTOCALC macro calculates the *RTO* as the RTT estimator plus four times the mean deviation estimator.

8–16   rtt_minmax makes certain that the *RTO* is between the upper and lower limits in the unprtt.h header.

17–28   rtt_init is called by dg_send_recv the first time any packet is sent. gettimeofday returns the current time and date in the same timeval structure that we saw with select (Section 6.3). We save only the current number of seconds since the Unix Epoch, which is 00:00:00 January 1, 1970, UTC. The measured RTT is set to 0 and the RTT and mean deviation estimators are set to 0 and 0.75, respectively, giving an initial *RTO* of 3 seconds.

Figure 22.12 shows the next three RTT functions.

---
lib/rtt.c

```
34 uint32_t
35 rtt_ts(struct rtt_info *ptr)
36 {
37     uint32_t ts;
38     struct timeval tv;

39     Gettimeofday(&tv, NULL);
40     ts = ((tv.tv_sec - ptr->rtt_base) * 1000) + (tv.tv_usec / 1000);
41     return (ts);
42 }

43 void
44 rtt_newpack(struct rtt_info *ptr)
45 {
46     ptr->rtt_nrexmt = 0;
47 }

48 int
49 rtt_start(struct rtt_info *ptr)
50 {
51     return ((int) (ptr->rtt_rto + 0.5));    /* round float to int */
52         /* return value can be used as: alarm(rtt_start(&foo)) */
53 }
```
lib/rtt.c

Figure 22.12 rtt_ts, rtt_newpack, and rtt_start functions.

34–42   rtt_ts returns the current timestamp for the caller to store as an unsigned 32-bit integer in the datagram being sent. We obtain the current time and date from gettimeofday and then subtract the number of seconds when rtt_init was called (the value saved in rtt_base). We convert this to milliseconds and also convert the microsecond value returned by gettimeofday into milliseconds. The timestamp is then the sum of these two values in milliseconds.

The difference between two calls to rtt_ts is the number of milliseconds between the two calls. But, we store the millisecond timestamps in an unsigned 32-bit integer instead of a timeval structure.

43–47   rtt_newpack just sets the retransmission counter to 0. This function should be called whenever a new packet is sent for the first time.

48-53   rtt_start returns the current *RTO* in seconds. The return value can then be used
as the argument to alarm.

rtt_stop, shown in Figure 22.13, is called after a reply is received to update the
RTT estimators and calculate the new *RTO*.

————————————————————————————————————— lib/rtt.c
```
62 void
63 rtt_stop(struct rtt_info *ptr, uint32_t ms)
64 {
65     double  delta;

66     ptr->rtt_rtt = ms / 1000.0; /* measured RTT in seconds */

67     /*
68      * Update our estimators of RTT and mean deviation of RTT.
69      * See Jacobson's SIGCOMM '88 paper, Appendix A, for the details.
70      * We use floating point here for simplicity.
71      */

72     delta = ptr->rtt_rtt - ptr->rtt_srtt;
73     ptr->rtt_srtt += delta / 8; /* g = 1/8 */

74     if (delta < 0.0)
75         delta = -delta;          /* |delta| */

76     ptr->rtt_rttvar += (delta - ptr->rtt_rttvar) / 4;   /* h = 1/4 */

77     ptr->rtt_rto = rtt_minmax(RTT_RTOCALC(ptr));
78 }
```
————————————————————————————————————— lib/rtt.c

Figure 22.13 rtt_stop function: updates RTT estimators and calculates new *RTO*.

62-78   The second argument is the measured RTT, obtained by the caller by subtracting the
received timestamp in the reply from the current timestamp (rtt_ts). The equations
at the beginning of this section are then applied, storing new values for rtt_srtt,
rtt_rttvar, and rtt_rto.

The final function, rtt_timeout, is shown in Figure 22.14. This function is called
when the retransmission timer expires.

————————————————————————————————————— lib/rtt.c
```
83 int
84 rtt_timeout(struct rtt_info *ptr)
85 {
86     ptr->rtt_rto *= 2;              /* next RTO */

87     if (++ptr->rtt_nrexmt > RTT_MAXNREXMT)
88         return (-1);               /* time to give up for this packet */
89     return (0);
90 }
```
————————————————————————————————————— lib/rtt.c

Figure 22.14 rtt_timeout function: applies exponential backoff.

86   The current *RTO* is doubled: This is the exponential backoff.

87-89   If we have reached the maximum number of retransmissions, −1 is returned to tell the caller to give up; otherwise, 0 is returned.

As an example, our client was run twice to two different echo servers across the Internet in the morning on a weekday. Five hundred lines were sent to each server. Eight packets were lost to the first server and 16 packets were lost to the second server. Of the 16 lost to the second server, one packet was lost twice in a row: that is, the packet had to be retransmitted two times before a reply was received. All other lost packets were handled with a single retransmission. We could verify that these packets were really lost by printing the sequence number of each received packet. If a packet is just delayed and not lost, after the retransmission, two replies will be received by the client: one corresponding to the original transmission that was delayed and one corresponding to the retransmission. Notice we are unable to tell when we retransmit whether it was the client's request or the server's reply that was discarded.

> For the first edition of this book, the author wrote a UDP server that randomly discarded packets to test this client. That is no longer needed; all we have to do is run the client to a server across the Internet and we are almost guaranteed of some packet loss!

22.6 Binding Interface Addresses

One common use for our `get_ifi_info` function is with UDP applications that need to monitor all interfaces on a host to know when a datagram arrives, and on which interface it arrives. This allows the receiving program to know the destination address of the UDP datagram, since that address is what determines the socket to which a datagram is delivered, even if the host does not support the IP_RECVDSTADDR socket option.

> Recall our discussion at the end of Section 22.2. If the host employs the common weak end system model, the destination IP address may differ from the IP address of the receiving interface. In this case, all we can determine is the destination address of the datagram, which does not need to be an address assigned to the receiving interface. To determine the receiving interface requires either the IP_RECVIF or IPV6_PKTINFO socket option.

Figure 22.15 is the first part of a simple example of this technique with a UDP server that binds all the unicast addresses, all the broadcast addresses, and finally the wildcard address.

Call `get_ifi_info` to obtain interface information

11-12   `get_ifi_info` obtains all the IPv4 addresses, including aliases, for all interfaces. The program then loops through each returned `ifi_info` structure.

Create UDP socket and `bind` unicast address

13-20   A UDP socket is created and the unicast address is bound to it. We also set the SO_REUSEADDR socket option, as we are binding the same port (SERV_PORT) for all IP addresses.

```
                                                                            advio/udpserv03.c
 1 #include      "unpifi.h"

 2 void    mydg_echo(int, SA *, socklen_t, SA *);

 3 int
 4 main(int argc, char **argv)
 5 {
 6     int     sockfd;
 7     const int on = 1;
 8     pid_t   pid;
 9     struct ifi_info *ifi, *ifihead;
10     struct sockaddr_in *sa, cliaddr, wildaddr;

11     for (ifihead = ifi = Get_ifi_info(AF_INET, 1);
12          ifi != NULL; ifi = ifi->ifi_next) {

13             /* bind unicast address */
14         sockfd = Socket(AF_INET, SOCK_DGRAM, 0);

15         Setsockopt(sockfd, SOL_SOCKET, SO_REUSEADDR, &on, sizeof(on));

16         sa = (struct sockaddr_in *) ifi->ifi_addr;
17         sa->sin_family = AF_INET;
18         sa->sin_port = htons(SERV_PORT);
19         Bind(sockfd, (SA *) sa, sizeof(*sa));
20         printf("bound %s\n", Sock_ntop((SA *) sa, sizeof(*sa)));

21         if ( (pid = Fork()) == 0) {   /* child */
22             mydg_echo(sockfd, (SA *) &cliaddr, sizeof(cliaddr), (SA *) sa);
23             exit(0);                /* never executed */
24         }
```
                                                                            advio/udpserv03.c

Figure 22.15 First part of UDP server that binds all addresses.

Not all implementations require that this socket option be set. Berkeley-derived implementations, for example, do not require the option and allow a new bind of an already bound port if the new IP address being bound: (i) is not the wildcard, and (ii) differs from all the IP addresses that are already bound to the port.

`fork` **child for this address**

21–24   A child is forked and the function mydg_echo is called for the child. This function waits for any datagram to arrive on this socket and echoes it back to the sender.

Figure 22.16 shows the next part of the main function, which handles broadcast addresses.

Bind broadcast address

25–42   If the interface supports broadcasting, a UDP socket is created and the broadcast address is bound to it. This time, we allow the bind to fail with an error of EADDRINUSE because if an interface has multiple addresses (aliases) on the same subnet, then each of the different unicast addresses will have the same broadcast address. We showed an example of this following Figure 17.6. In this scenario, we expect only the first bind to succeed.

```
                                                            ──────── advio/udpserv03.c
 25          if (ifi->ifi_flags & IFF_BROADCAST) {
 26                  /* try to bind broadcast address */
 27              sockfd = Socket(AF_INET, SOCK_DGRAM, 0);
 28              Setsockopt(sockfd, SOL_SOCKET, SO_REUSEADDR, &on, sizeof(on));

 29              sa = (struct sockaddr_in *) ifi->ifi_brdaddr;
 30              sa->sin_family = AF_INET;
 31              sa->sin_port = htons(SERV_PORT);
 32              if (bind(sockfd, (SA *) sa, sizeof(*sa)) < 0) {
 33                  if (errno == EADDRINUSE) {
 34                      printf("EADDRINUSE: %s\n",
 35                              Sock_ntop((SA *) sa, sizeof(*sa)));
 36                      Close(sockfd);
 37                      continue;
 38                  } else
 39                      err_sys("bind error for %s",
 40                              Sock_ntop((SA *) sa, sizeof(*sa)));
 41              }
 42              printf("bound %s\n", Sock_ntop((SA *) sa, sizeof(*sa)));

 43              if ( (pid = Fork()) == 0) {  /* child */
 44                  mydg_echo(sockfd, (SA *) &cliaddr, sizeof(cliaddr),
 45                          (SA *) sa);
 46                  exit(0);            /* never executed */
 47              }
 48          }
 49      }
                                                            ──────── advio/udpserv03.c
```

Figure 22.16 Second part of UDP server that binds all addresses.

`fork` child

43-47   A child is spawned and it calls the function `mydg_echo`.

The final part of the `main` function is shown in Figure 22.17. This code binds the wildcard address to handle any destination addresses except the unicast and broadcast addresses we have already bound. The only datagrams that should arrive on this socket should be those destined to the limited broadcast address (255.255.255.255).

Create socket and bind wildcard address

50-62   A UDP socket is created, the `SO_REUSEADDR` socket option is set, and the wildcard IP address is bound. A child is spawned, which calls the `mydg_echo` function.

`main` function terminates

63   The `main` function terminates, and the server continues executing all the children that were spawned.

advio/udpserv03.c

```
50            /* bind wildcard address */
51        sockfd = Socket(AF_INET, SOCK_DGRAM, 0);
52        Setsockopt(sockfd, SOL_SOCKET, SO_REUSEADDR, &on, sizeof(on));

53        bzero(&wildaddr, sizeof(wildaddr));
54        wildaddr.sin_family = AF_INET;
55        wildaddr.sin_addr.s_addr = htonl(INADDR_ANY);
56        wildaddr.sin_port = htons(SERV_PORT);
57        Bind(sockfd, (SA *) &wildaddr, sizeof(wildaddr));
58        printf("bound %s\n", Sock_ntop((SA *) &wildaddr, sizeof(wildaddr)));

59        if ( (pid = Fork()) == 0) {   /* child */
60            mydg_echo(sockfd, (SA *) &cliaddr, sizeof(cliaddr), (SA *) sa);
61            exit(0);                  /* never executed */
62        }
63        exit(0);
64 }
```

advio/udpserv03.c

Figure 22.17 Final part of UDP server that binds all addresses.

The function `mydg_echo`, which is executed by all the children, is shown in Figure 22.18.

advio/udpserv03.c

```
65 void
66 mydg_echo(int sockfd, SA *pcliaddr, socklen_t clilen, SA *myaddr)
67 {
68     int      n;
69     char     mesg[MAXLINE];
70     socklen_t len;

71     for ( ; ; ) {
72         len = clilen;
73         n = Recvfrom(sockfd, mesg, MAXLINE, 0, pcliaddr, &len);
74         printf("child %d, datagram from %s", getpid(),
75                 Sock_ntop(pcliaddr, len));
76         printf(", to %s\n", Sock_ntop(myaddr, clilen));

77         Sendto(sockfd, mesg, n, 0, pcliaddr, len);
78     }
79 }
```

advio/udpserv03.c

Figure 22.18 `mydg_echo` function.

New argument

65–66   The fourth argument to this function is the IP address that was bound to the socket. This socket should receive only datagrams destined to that IP address. If the IP address is the wildcard, then the socket should receive only datagrams that are not matched by some other socket bound to the same port.

Read datagram and echo reply

71–78   The datagram is read with `recvfrom` and sent back to the client with `sendto`.

This function also prints the client's IP address and the IP address that was bound to the socket.

We now run this program on our host `solaris` after establishing an alias address for the `hme0` Ethernet interface. The alias address is host number 200 on 10.0.0/24.

```
solaris % udpserv03
bound 127.0.0.1:9877              loopback interface
bound 10.0.0.200:9877            unicast address of hme0:1 interface
bound 10.0.0.255:9877            broadcast address of hme0:1 interface
bound 192.168.1.20:9877         unicast address of hme0 interface
bound 192.168.1.255:9877       broadcast address of hme0 interface
bound 0.0.0.0.9877               wildcard
```

We can check that all these sockets are bound to the indicated IP address and port using `netstat`.

```
solaris % netstat -na | grep 9877
127.0.0.1.9877                              Idle
10.0.0.200.9877                             Idle
      *.9877                                Idle
192.129.100.100.9877                        Idle
      *.9877                                Idle
      *.9877                                Idle
```

We should note that our design of one child process per socket is for simplicity and other designs are possible. For example, to reduce the number of processes, the program could manage all the descriptors itself using `select`, never calling `fork`. The problem with this design is the added code complexity. While it is easy to use `select` for all the descriptors, we would have to maintain some type of mapping of each descriptor to its bound IP address (probably an array of structures) so we could print the destination IP address when a datagram was read from a socket. It is often simpler to use a single process or a single thread for one operation or descriptor instead of having a single process multiplex many different operations or descriptors.

22.7 Concurrent UDP Servers

Most UDP servers are iterative: The server waits for a client request, reads the request, processes the request, sends back the reply, and then waits for the next client request. But when the processing of the client request takes a long time, some form of concurrency is desired.

The definition of a "long time" is whatever is considered too much time for another client to wait while the current client is being serviced. For example, if two client requests arrive within 10 ms of each other, and it takes an average of 5 seconds of clock time to service a client, then the second client will have to wait about 10 seconds for its reply, instead of about 5 seconds if the request was handled as soon as it arrived.

With TCP, it is simple to just `fork` a new child (or create a new thread, as we will see in Chapter 26) and let the child handle the new client. What simplifies this server concurrency when TCP is being used is that every client connection is unique: The TCP socket pair is unique for every connection. But with UDP, we must deal with two different types of servers:

1. First is a simple UDP server that reads a client request, sends a reply, and is then finished with the client. In this scenario, the server that reads the client request can `fork` a child and let it handle the request. The "request," that is, the contents of the datagram and the socket address structure containing the client's protocol address, are passed to the child in its memory image from `fork`. The child then sends its reply directly to the client.

2. Second is a UDP server that exchanges multiple datagrams with the client. The problem is that the only port number the client knows for the server is its well-known port. The client sends the first datagram of its request to that port, but how does the server distinguish between subsequent datagrams from that client and new requests? The typical solution to this problem is for the server to create a new socket for each client, `bind` an ephemeral port to that socket, and use that socket for all its replies. This requires that the client look at the port number of the server's first reply and send subsequent datagrams for this request to that port.

An example of the second type of UDP server is TFTP. To transfer a file using TFTP normally requires many datagrams (hundreds or thousands, depending on the file size), because the protocol sends only 512 bytes per datagram. The client sends a datagram to the server's well-known port (69), specifying the file to send or receive. The server reads the request, but sends its reply from another socket that it creates and binds to an ephemeral port. All subsequent datagrams between the client and server for this file use the new socket. This allows the main TFTP server to continue to handle other client requests, which arrive at port 69, while this file transfer takes place (perhaps over seconds, or even minutes).

If we assume a standalone TFTP server (i.e., not invoked by `inetd`), we have the scenario shown in Figure 22.19. We assume that the ephemeral port bound by the child to its new socket is 2134.

If `inetd` is used, the scenario involves one more step. Recall from Figure 13.6 that most UDP servers specify the *wait-flag* as `wait`. In our description following Figure 13.10, we said that this causes `inetd` to stop selecting on the socket until its child terminates, allowing its child to read the datagram that has arrived on the socket. Figure 22.20 shows the steps involved.

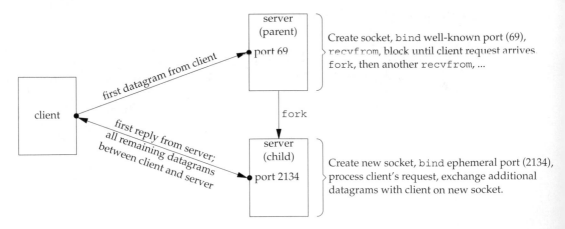

Figure 22.19 Processes involved in standalone concurrent UDP server.

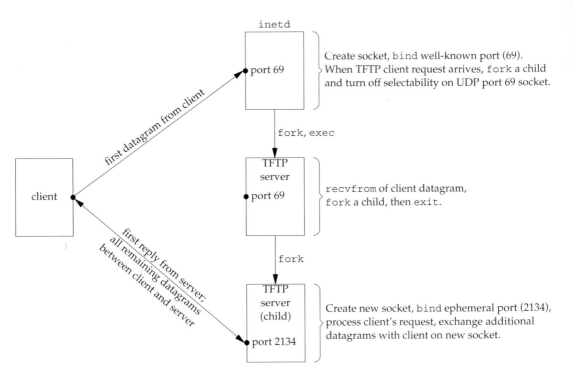

Figure 22.20 UDP concurrent server invoked by inetd.

The TFTP server that is the child of inetd calls recvfrom and reads the client request. It then forks a child of its own, and that child will process the client request. The TFTP server then calls exit, sending SIGCHLD to inetd, which tells inetd to again select on the socket bound to UDP port 69.

22.8 IPv6 Packet Information

IPv6 allows an application to specify up to five pieces of information for an outgoing datagram:

1. Source IPv6 address
2. Outgoing interface index
3. Outgoing hop limit
4. Next-hop address
5. Outgoing traffic class

This information is sent as ancillary data with `sendmsg`. "Sticky" values can be set for the socket, so that they apply to every packet sent, as described in Section 27.7. Four similar pieces of information can be returned for a received packet, and they are returned as ancillary data with `recvmsg`:

1. Destination IPv6 address
2. Arriving interface index
3. Arriving hop limit
4. Arriving traffic class

Figure 22.21 summarizes the contents of the ancillary data, which we will discuss shortly.

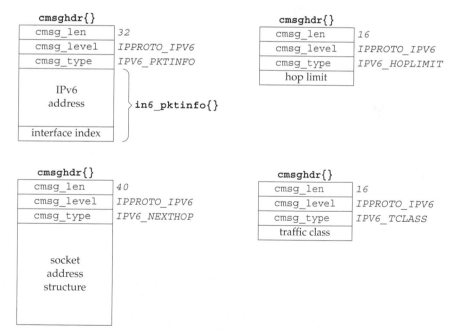

Figure 22.21 Ancillary data for IPv6 packet information.

An `in6_pktinfo` structure contains either the source IPv6 address and outgoing interface index for an outgoing datagram or the destination IPv6 address and arriving interface index for a received datagram.

```
struct in6_pktinfo {
    struct in6_addr ipi6_addr;    /* src/dst IPv6 address */
    int             ipi6_ifindex; /* send/recv interface index */
};
```

This structure is defined by including the `<netinet/in.h>` header. In the `cmsghdr` structure containing this ancillary data, the `cmsg_level` member will be `IPPROTO_IPV6`, the `cmsg_type` member will be `IPV6_PKTINFO`, and the first byte of data will be the first byte of the `in6_pktinfo` structure. In the example in Figure 22.21, we assume no padding between the `cmsghdr` structure and the data, and 4 bytes for an integer.

To specify this information for a given packet, just specify the control information as ancillary data for `sendmsg`. To specify this information for all packets sent on a socket, set the `IPV6_PKTINFO` socket option with the `in6_pktinfo` as the option value as described in Section 27.7. This information is returned as ancillary data by `recvmsg` only if the application has the `IPV6_RECVPKTINFO` socket option enabled.

Outgoing and Arriving Interface

Interfaces on an IPv6 node are identified by positive integers, as we discussed in Section 18.6. Recall that no interface is ever assigned an index of 0. When specifying the outgoing interface, if the `ipi6_ifindex` value is 0, the kernel will choose the outgoing interface. If the application specifies an outgoing interface for a multicast packet, the interface specified by the ancillary data overrides any interface specified by the `IPV6_MULTICAST_IF` socket option for this datagram only.

Source and Destination IPv6 Addresses

The source IPv6 address is normally specified by calling `bind`. Supplying the source address together with the data may require less overhead. This option also allows a server to guarantee that the source address of its reply equals the destination address of the client's request, a feature some clients require and that is harder to accomplish with IPv4 (Exercise 22.4).

When specifying the source IPv6 address as ancillary data, if the `ipi6_addr` member of the `in6_pktinfo` structure is `IN6ADDR_ANY_INIT`, then: (i) if an address is currently bound to the socket, it is used as the source address, or (ii) if no address is currently bound to the socket, the kernel will choose the source address. If the `ipi6_addr` member is not the unspecified address, but the socket has already bound a source address, then the `ipi6_addr` value overrides the already bound source address for this output operation only. The kernel will verify that the requested source address is indeed a unicast address assigned to the node.

When the `in6_pktinfo` structure is returned as ancillary data by `recvmsg`, the `ipi6_addr` member contains the destination IPv6 address from the received packet. This is similar in concept to the `IP_RECVDSTADDR` socket option for IPv4.

Specifying and Receiving the Hop Limit

The outgoing hop limit is normally specified with either the `IPV6_UNICAST_HOPS` socket option for unicast datagrams (Section 7.8) or the `IPV6_MULTICAST_HOPS` socket option for multicast datagrams (Section 21.6). Specifying the hop limit as ancillary data lets us override either the kernel's default or a previously specified value, for either a unicast destination or a multicast destination, for a single output operation. Returning the received hop limit is useful for programs such as `traceroute` and for a class of IPv6 applications that need to verify that the received hop limit is 255 (e.g., that the packet has not been forwarded).

The received hop limit is returned as ancillary data by `recvmsg` only if the application has enabled the `IPV6_RECVHOPLIMIT` socket option. In the `cmsghdr` structure containing this ancillary data, the `cmsg_level` member will be `IPPROTO_IPV6`, the `cmsg_type` member will be `IPV6_HOPLIMIT`, and the first byte of data will be the first byte of the (4-byte) integer hop limit. We showed this in Figure 22.21. Realize that the value returned as ancillary data is the actual value from the received datagram, while the value returned by a `getsockopt` of the `IPV6_UNICAST_HOPS` option is the default value the kernel will use for outgoing datagrams on the socket.

To control the outgoing hop limit for a given packet, just specify the control information as ancillary data for `sendmsg`. The normal values for the hop limit are between 0 and 255, inclusive, but if the integer value is –1, this tells the kernel to use its default.

> The hop limit is not contained in the `in6_pktinfo` structure for the following reason: Some UDP servers want to respond to client requests by sending their reply out the same interface on which the request was received and with the source IPv6 address of the reply equal to the destination IPv6 address of the request. To do this, the application can enable just the `IPV6_RECVPKTINFO` socket option and then use the received control information from `recvmsg` as the outgoing control information for `sendmsg`. The application need not examine or modify the `in6_pktinfo` structure at all. But if the hop limit was contained in this structure, the application would have to parse the received control information and change the hop limit member, since the received hop limit is not the desired value for an outgoing packet.

Specifying the Next-Hop Address

The `IPV6_NEXTHOP` ancillary data object specifies the next hop for the datagram as a socket address structure. In the `cmsghdr` structure containing this ancillary data, the `cmsg_level` member is `IPPROTO_IPV6`, the `cmsg_type` member is `IPV6_NEXTHOP`, and the first byte of data is the first byte of the socket address structure.

In Figure 22.21, we show an example of this ancillary data object, assuming the socket address structure is a 28-byte `sockaddr_in6` structure. In this case, the node identified by that address must be a neighbor of the sending host. If that address equals the destination IPv6 address of the datagram, then this is equivalent to the existing `SO_DONTROUTE` socket option. The next-hop address can be set for all packets on a socket by setting the `IPV6_NEXTHOP` socket option with the `sockaddr_in6` as the option value, as described in Section 27.7. Setting this option requires superuser privileges.

Specifying and Receiving the Traffic Class

The `IPV6_TCLASS` ancillary data object specifies the traffic class for the datagram. In the `cmsghdr` structure containing this ancillary data, the `cmsg_level` member will be `IPPROTO_IPV6`, the `cmsg_type` member will be `IPV6_TCLASS`, and the first byte of data will be the first byte of the (4-byte) integer traffic class. We showed this in Figure 22.21. As described in Section A.3, the traffic class is made up of the *DSCP* and *ECN* fields. These fields must be set together. The kernel may mask or ignore the user-specified value if it needs to control the value (e.g., if the kernel implements ECN, it may set the ECN bits to its own desired value, ignoring the two bits specified with the `IPV6_TCLASS` option). The traffic class specified may be in the normal range of 0 to 255, or −1 to allow the kernel to use its default value.

To specify the traffic class for a given packet, include the ancillary data with that packet. To specify the traffic class for all packets on a socket, specify the traffic class as an integer to the `IPV6_TCLASS` socket option, as described in Section 27.7. The received traffic class is returned as ancillary data by `recvmsg` only if the application has the `IPV6_RECVTCLASS` socket option enabled.

22.9 IPv6 Path MTU Control

IPv6 gives applications several controls over path MTU discovery (Section 2.11). The defaults are appropriate for the vast majority of applications, but special-purpose programs may want to modify the path MTU discovery behavior. Four socket options are provided for this purpose.

Sending with Minimum MTU

When performing path MTU discovery, packets are normally fragmented using the MTU of the outgoing interface or the path MTU, whichever is smaller. IPv6 defines a minimum MTU of 1,280 bytes, which must be supported by all paths. Fragmenting to this minimum MTU wastes opportunities for sending larger packets (which is more efficient), but avoids the drawbacks of path MTU discovery (dropped packets and delay while the MTU is being discovered).

Two classes of applications may want to use the minimum MTU: those that use multicast (to avoid an implosion of ICMP "packet too big" messages) and those that perform brief transactions to lots of destinations (such as the DNS). Learning the MTU for a multicast session may not be important enough to pay the cost of receiving and processing millions of ICMP "packet too big" messages, and applications such as the DNS generally don't talk to the same server often enough to make it worthwhile to risk the cost of dropped packets.

The use of the minimum MTU is controlled with the `IPV6_USE_MIN_MTU` socket option. It has three defined values: −1, the default, uses the minimum MTU for multicast destinations but performs path MTU discovery to unicast destinations; 0 performs path MTU discovery to all destinations; and 1 uses the minimum MTU for all destinations.

IPV6_USE_MIN_MTU can also be sent as ancillary data. In the cmsghdr structure containing this ancillary data, the cmsg_level member will be IPPROTO_IPV6, the cmsg_type member will be IPV6_USE_MIN_MTU, and the first byte of data will be the first byte of the (4-byte) integer value.

Receiving Path MTU Change Indications

To receive change notifications in the path MTU, an application can enable the IPV6_RECVPATHMTU socket option. This flag enables the reception of the path MTU as ancillary data anytime it changes. recvmsg will return a zero-length datagram, but there will be ancillary data indicating the path MTU. In the cmsghdr structure containing this ancillary data, the cmsg_level member will be IPPROTO_IPV6, the cmsg_type member will be IPV6_PATHMTU, and the first byte of data will be the first byte of an ip6_mtuinfo structure. This structure contains the destination for which the path MTU has changed and the new path MTU value in bytes.

```
struct ip6_mtuinfo {
    struct sockaddr_in6 ip6m_addr;    /* destination address */
    uint32_t            ip6m_mtu;     /* path MTU in host byte order */
};
```

This structure is defined by including the <netinet/in.h> header.

Determining the Current Path MTU

If an application has not been keeping track with the IPV6_RECVPATHMTU option, it can determine the current path MTU of a *connected* socket with the IPV6_PATHMTU socket option. This is a get-only option, which returns an ip6_mtuinfo structure (see above) containing the current path MTU. If no path MTU has been determined, it returns the MTU of the outgoing interface. The value of the returned address is undefined.

Avoiding Fragmentation

By default, the IPv6 stack will fragment outgoing packets to the path MTU. An application such as traceroute may not want this automatic fragmentation, to discover the path MTU on its own. The IPV6_DONTFRAG socket option is used to turn off automatic fragmentation; a value of 0 (the default) permits automatic fragmentation, while a value of 1 turns off automatic fragmentation.

When automatic fragmentation is off, a send call providing a packet that requires fragmentation *may* return EMSGSIZE; however, the implementation is not required to provide this. The only way to determine whether a packet requires fragmentation is to use the IPV6_RECVPATHMTU option, which was already described.

IPV6_DONTFRAG can also be sent as ancillary data. In the cmsghdr structure containing this ancillary data, the cmsg_level member will be IPPROTO_IPV6, the cmsg_type member will be IPV6_DONTFRAG, and the first byte of data will be the first byte of the (4-byte) integer value.

22.10 Summary

There are applications that want to know the destination IP address and the received interface for a UDP datagram. The IP_RECVDSTADDR and IP_RECVIF socket options can be enabled to return this information as ancillary data with each datagram. Similar information, along with the received hop limit, can be returned for IPv6 sockets by enabling the IPV6_RECVPKTINFO socket option.

Despite all the features provided by TCP that are not provided by UDP, there are times to use UDP. UDP must be used for broadcasting or multicasting. UDP can be used for simple request-reply scenarios, but some form of reliability must then be added to the application. UDP should not be used for bulk data transfer.

We added reliability to our UDP client in Section 22.5 by detecting lost packets using a timeout and retransmission. We modified our retransmission timeout dynamically by adding a timestamp to each packet and kept track of two estimators: the RTT and its mean deviation. We also added a sequence number to verify that a given reply was the one expected. Our client still employed a simple stop-and-wait protocol, but that is the type of application for which UDP can be used.

Exercises

22.1   In Figure 22.18, why are there two calls to printf?

22.2   Can dg_send_recv (Figures 22.8 and 22.9) ever return 0?

22.3   Recode dg_send_recv to use select and its timer instead of using alarm, SIGALRM, sigsetjmp, and siglongjmp.

22.4   How can an IPv4 server guarantee that the source address of its reply equals the destination address of the client's request (e.g., functionality similar to that provided by the IPV6_PKTINFO socket option)?

22.5   The main function in Section 22.6 is protocol-dependent on IPv4. Recode it to be protocol-independent. Require the user to specify one or two command-line arguments, the first being an optional IP address (e.g., 0.0.0.0 or 0::0) and the second being a required port number. Then call udp_client just to obtain the address family, port number, and length of the socket address structure.

What happens if you call udp_client, as suggested, without specifying a *hostname* argument because udp_client does not specify the AI_PASSIVE hint to getaddrinfo?

22.6   Run the client in Figure 22.6 to an echo server across the Internet after modifying the RTT functions to print each RTT. Also, modify the dg_send_recv function to print each received sequence number. Plot the resulting RTTs along with the estimators for the RTT and its mean deviation.

23

Advanced SCTP Sockets

23.1 Introduction

In this chapter, we will dig a bit deeper into SCTP, examining more of the features and socket options that SCTP provides to its users. We will discuss a number of topics, including control of failure detection, unordered data, and notifications. Throughout this chapter, we will provide examples of code so that the reader can see how to use some of SCTP's advanced features.

SCTP is a message-oriented protocol, delivering partial or complete messages to the user. Partial messages will only be delivered if the application chooses to send large messages (e.g., larger than half the socket buffer size) to its peer. When partial messages are delivered, SCTP will never mix two partial messages together. An application will either receive a whole message in one receive operation or it will receive a message in several consecutive receive operations. We will illustrate a method of dealing with this partial delivery mechanism through an example utility function.

SCTP servers can be either iterative or concurrent, depending on the style of interface the application developer chooses. SCTP also provides a method to extract an association from a one-to-many-style socket into a separate one-to-one-style socket. This method allows the construction of a server that is both iterative and concurrent.

23.2 An Autoclosing One-to-Many-Style Server

Recall the server program we wrote in Chapter 10. That program does not keep track of any associations. The server depends on the client to close the association, thereby removing the association state. But depending on the client to close the association leaves a weakness: What happens if a client opens an association and never sends any data? Resources would be allocated to a client that never uses them. This dependency could introduce an accidental denial-of-service attack to our SCTP implementation from lazy clients. To avoid this problem, an *autoclose* feature was added to SCTP.

Autoclose lets an SCTP endpoint specify a maximum number of seconds an association may remain idle. An association is considered idle when it is not transmitting user data in either direction. If an association is idle for more than this maximum time, the association is automatically closed by the SCTP implementation.

When using this option, care should be taken in choosing a value for autoclose. The server should not pick too small a value, otherwise it may find itself needing to send data on an association that has been closed. There would be extra overhead in re-opening the association to send back the data to the client, and it is unlikely that the client would have performed a `listen` to enable inbound associations. Figure 23.1 revisits our server code and inserts the necessary calls to make our server resistant to stale idle associations. As described in Section 7.10, autoclose defaults to disabled and must be explicitly enabled with the `SCTP_AUTOCLOSE` socket option.

————————————————————————————————— sctp/sctpserv04.c

```
14      if (argc == 2)
15          stream_increment = atoi(argv[1]);
16      sock_fd = Socket(AF_INET, SOCK_SEQPACKET, IPPROTO_SCTP);
17      close_time = 120;
18      Setsockopt(sock_fd, IPPROTO_SCTP, SCTP_AUTOCLOSE,
19                  &close_time, sizeof(close_time));

20      bzero(&servaddr, sizeof(servaddr));
21      servaddr.sin_family = AF_INET;
22      servaddr.sin_addr.s_addr = htonl(INADDR_ANY);
23      servaddr.sin_port = htons(SERV_PORT);
```

————————————————————————————————— sctp/sctpserv04.c

Figure 23.1 A server enabling autoclose.

Set autoclose option

17–19   The server selects a value of 120 seconds to shut down idle associations and places this value in the variable `close_time`. Next, the server calls the socket option that configures the autoclose time. All the remaining code in the server stays unchanged.

Now, SCTP will automatically close associations that remain idle for more than two minutes. By forcing the association to close automatically, we reduce the amount of server resources consumed by lazy clients.

23.3 Partial Delivery

Partial delivery will be used by the SCTP implementation any time a "large" message is being received, where "large" means the SCTP stack deems that it does not have the resources to dedicate to the message. The following considerations will be made by the receiving SCTP implementation before starting this API:

- The amount of buffer space being consumed by the message must meet or exceed some threshold.

- The stack can only deliver from the beginning of the message sequentially up to the first missing piece.

- Once invoked, no other messages may be made available for the user until the current message has been completely received and passed to the user. This means that the large message blocks all other messages that would normally be deliverable, including those in other streams.

The KAME implementation of SCTP uses a threshold of one-half the socket receive buffer. At this writing, the default receive buffer for the stack is 131,072 bytes. So, without changing the SO_RCVBUF, a single message must be larger than 65,536 bytes before the partial delivery API will be invoked. To further extend the new version of the server from Section 10.2, we write a utility function that wraps the sctp_recvmsg function call. We then create a modified server to use our new function. Figure 23.2 shows our wrapper function to handle the partial delivery API.

Prepare static buffer

12–15   If the function's static buffer has not been allocated, allocate it and set up the state associated with it.

Read message

16–18   Read in the first message using the sctp_recvmsg function.

Handle initial read error

19–22   If sctp_recvmsg returns an error or an EOF, we pass it directly back to the caller.

While there is more data for this message

23–24   While the message flags show that the function has not received a complete message, collect more data. The function starts by calculating how much is left in the static buffer.

See if we need to grow static buffer

25–34   Whenever the function no longer has a minimum amount of room left in its receive buffer, it must grow the buffer. We do this using the realloc function to allocate a new buffer of the current size, plus an increment amount, and copy the old data. If for some reason the function cannot grow its buffer any more, it exits with an error.

Receive more data

35–36   Gather more data with the sctp_recvmsg function.

Move forward

37–38   The function increments the buffer index and goes back to test if it has read all of the message.

At loop end

39–40   When the loop terminates, the function copies the number of bytes read into the pointer provided by the caller and returns a pointer to the allocated buffer.

sctp/sctp_pdapircv.c

```
 1 #include    "unp.h"

 2 static uint8_t *sctp_pdapi_readbuf = NULL;
 3 static int sctp_pdapi_rdbuf_sz = 0;

 4 uint8_t *
 5 pdapi_recvmsg(int sock_fd,
 6                  int *rdlen,
 7                  SA *from,
 8                  int *from_len, struct sctp_sndrcvinfo *sri, int *msg_flags)
 9 {
10     int     rdsz, left, at_in_buf;
11     int     frmlen = 0;

12     if (sctp_pdapi_readbuf == NULL) {
13         sctp_pdapi_readbuf = (uint8_t *) Malloc(SCTP_PDAPI_INCR_SZ);
14         sctp_pdapi_rdbuf_sz = SCTP_PDAPI_INCR_SZ;
15     }
16     at_in_buf =
17         Sctp_recvmsg(sock_fd, sctp_pdapi_readbuf, sctp_pdapi_rdbuf_sz, from,
18                      from_len, sri, msg_flags);
19     if (at_in_buf < 1) {
20         *rdlen = at_in_buf;
21         return (NULL);
22     }
23     while ((*msg_flags & MSG_EOR) == 0) {
24         left = sctp_pdapi_rdbuf_sz - at_in_buf;
25         if (left < SCTP_PDAPI_NEED_MORE_THRESHOLD) {
26             sctp_pdapi_readbuf =
27                 realloc(sctp_pdapi_readbuf,
28                         sctp_pdapi_rdbuf_sz + SCTP_PDAPI_INCR_SZ);
29             if (sctp_pdapi_readbuf == NULL) {
30                 err_quit("sctp_pdapi ran out of memory");
31             }
32             sctp_pdapi_rdbuf_sz += SCTP_PDAPI_INCR_SZ;
33             left = sctp_pdapi_rdbuf_sz - at_in_buf;
34         }
35         rdsz = Sctp_recvmsg(sock_fd, &sctp_pdapi_readbuf[at_in_buf],
36                             left, NULL, &frmlen, NULL, msg_flags);
37         at_in_buf += rdsz;
38     }
39     *rdlen = at_in_buf;
40     return (sctp_pdapi_readbuf);
41 }
```

sctp/sctp_pdapircv.c

Figure 23.2 Handling the partial delivery API.

We next modify our server in Figure 23.3 so that it uses the new function.

Read message

29–30   Here the server calls the new partial delivery utility function. The server calls this after nulling out any old data that may have been hanging around in the sri variable.

```
                                                                    sctp/sctpserv05.c
26    for ( ; ; ) {
27        len = sizeof(struct sockaddr_in);
28        bzero(&sri, sizeof(sri));
29        readbuf = pdapi_recvmsg(sock_fd, &rd_sz,
30                              (SA *) &cliaddr, &len, &sri, &msg_flags);
31        if (readbuf == NULL)
32            continue;
                                                                    sctp/sctpserv05.c
```

Figure 23.3 Our server using the partial delivery API.

Verify we read something

31-32   Note that now the server must test for NULL to see if the read was successful. If not, the server just continues.

23.4 Notifications

As we discussed in Section 9.14, an application can subscribe to seven notifications. Up to now, our application has ignored all events that may occur other than the receipt of new data. The examples in this section give an overview of how to receive and interpret SCTP's notifications of additional transport-layer events. Figure 23.4 shows a function that will display any notification that arrives from the transport. We will also modify our server to enable all events and call this new function when a notification is received. Note that our server is not really using the notification for any specific purpose.

Cast and switch

14-15   The function casts the incoming buffer to the overall union type. It dereferences the generic sn_header structure and the generic type sn_type, and switches on this value.

Process association change

16-40   If the function finds an association change notification in the buffer, it prints the type of association change that occurred.

Peer address change

41-66   If it was a peer address notification, the function prints the address event (after decoding) and the address.

Remote error

67-71   If the function finds a remote error, it displays this fact and the association ID on which it occurred. The function does not bother to decode and display the actual error reported by the remote peer. The information is available in the sre_data field of the sctp_remote_error structure.

—————————————————————————— sctp/sctp_displayevents.c

```
 1 #include     "unp.h"

 2 void
 3 print_notification(char *notify_buf)
 4 {
 5     union sctp_notification *snp;
 6     struct sctp_assoc_change *sac;
 7     struct sctp_paddr_change *spc;
 8     struct sctp_remote_error *sre;
 9     struct sctp_send_failed *ssf;
10     struct sctp_shutdown_event *sse;
11     struct sctp_adaption_event *ae;
12     struct sctp_pdapi_event *pdapi;
13     const char *str;

14     snp = (union sctp_notification *) notify_buf;
15     switch (snp->sn_header.sn_type) {
16     case SCTP_ASSOC_CHANGE:
17         sac = &snp->sn_assoc_change;
18         switch (sac->sac_state) {
19         case SCTP_COMM_UP:
20             str = "COMMUNICATION UP";
21             break;
22         case SCTP_COMM_LOST:
23             str = "COMMUNICATION LOST";
24             break;
25         case SCTP_RESTART:
26             str = "RESTART";
27             break;
28         case SCTP_SHUTDOWN_COMP:
29             str = "SHUTDOWN COMPLETE";
30             break;
31         case SCTP_CANT_STR_ASSOC:
32             str = "CAN'T START ASSOC";
33             break;
34         default:
35             str = "UNKNOWN";
36             break;
37         }                        /* end switch(sac->sac_state) */
38         printf("SCTP_ASSOC_CHANGE: %s, assoc=0x%x\n", str,
39                 (uint32_t) sac->sac_assoc_id);
40         break;
41     case SCTP_PEER_ADDR_CHANGE:
42         spc = &snp->sn_paddr_change;
43         switch (spc->spc_state) {
44         case SCTP_ADDR_AVAILABLE:
45             str = "ADDRESS AVAILABLE";
46             break;
47         case SCTP_ADDR_UNREACHABLE:
48             str = "ADDRESS UNREACHABLE";
49             break;
50         case SCTP_ADDR_REMOVED:
51             str = "ADDRESS REMOVED";
52             break;
```

```
53            case SCTP_ADDR_ADDED:
54                str = "ADDRESS ADDED";
55                break;
56            case SCTP_ADDR_MADE_PRIM:
57                str = "ADDRESS MADE PRIMARY";
58                break;
59            default:
60                str = "UNKNOWN";
61                break;
62            }                            /* end switch(spc->spc_state) */
63            printf("SCTP_PEER_ADDR_CHANGE: %s, addr=%s, assoc=0x%x\n", str,
64                    Sock_ntop((SA *) &spc->spc_aaddr, sizeof(spc->spc_aaddr)),
65                    (uint32_t) spc->spc_assoc_id);
66            break;
67        case SCTP_REMOTE_ERROR:
68            sre = &snp->sn_remote_error;
69            printf("SCTP_REMOTE_ERROR: assoc=0x%x error=%d\n",
70                    (uint32_t) sre->sre_assoc_id, sre->sre_error);
71            break;
72        case SCTP_SEND_FAILED:
73            ssf = &snp->sn_send_failed;
74            printf("SCTP_SEND_FAILED: assoc=0x%x error=%d\n",
75                    (uint32_t) ssf->ssf_assoc_id, ssf->ssf_error);
76            break;
77        case SCTP_ADAPTION_INDICATION:
78            ae = &snp->sn_adaption_event;
79            printf("SCTP_ADAPTION_INDICATION: 0x%x\n",
80                    (u_int) ae->sai_adaption_ind);
81            break;
82        case SCTP_PARTIAL_DELIVERY_EVENT:
83            pdapi = &snp->sn_pdapi_event;
84            if (pdapi->pdapi_indication == SCTP_PARTIAL_DELIVERY_ABORTED)
85                printf("SCTP_PARTIAL_DELIEVERY_ABORTED\n");
86            else
87                printf("Unknown SCTP_PARTIAL_DELIVERY_EVENT 0x%x\n",
88                        pdapi->pdapi_indication);
89            break;
90        case SCTP_SHUTDOWN_EVENT:
91            sse = &snp->sn_shutdown_event;
92            printf("SCTP_SHUTDOWN_EVENT: assoc=0x%x\n",
93                    (uint32_t) sse->sse_assoc_id);
94            break;
95        default:
96            printf("Unknown notification event type=0x%x\n",
97                    snp->sn_header.sn_type);
98        }
99 }
```
                                                            ———————— *sctp/sctp_displayevents.c*

Figure 23.4 A notifications display utility.

Failed message

72–76   If the function decodes a send failed notification, it knows that a message was not
sent to the peer. This means that either: (i) the association is coming down, and an

association notification will soon follow (if it has not already arrived), or (ii) the server is using the partial reliability extension and a message was not successfully sent (due to constraints placed on the transfer). The data actually sent is available to the function in the `ssf_data` field (which our function does not examine).

Adaption layer indication

77–81 If the function decodes an adaption layer indicator, it displays the 32-bit value passed in the setup message (INIT or INIT-ACK).

Partial delivery notification

82–89 If a partial delivery notification arrives, the function announces it. The only event defined as of this writing is that the partial delivery is aborted.

Shutdown notification

90–94 If the function decodes this notification, it knows that the peer has issued a graceful shutdown. This notification is usually soon followed by an association change notification when the shutdown sequence completes.

The modification to the server to use our new function can be seen in Figure 23.5.

———————————————————————————————— *sctp/sctpserv06.c*
```
21      bzero(&evnts, sizeof(evnts));
22      evnts.sctp_data_io_event = 1;
23      evnts.sctp_association_event = 1;
24      evnts.sctp_address_event = 1;
25      evnts.sctp_send_failure_event = 1;
26      evnts.sctp_peer_error_event = 1;
27      evnts.sctp_shutdown_event = 1;
28      evnts.sctp_partial_delivery_event = 1;
29      evnts.sctp_adaption_layer_event = 1;
30      Setsockopt(sock_fd, IPPROTO_SCTP, SCTP_EVENTS, &evnts, sizeof(evnts));

31      Listen(sock_fd, LISTENQ);
32      for ( ; ; ) {
33          len = sizeof(struct sockaddr_in);
34          rd_sz = Sctp_recvmsg(sock_fd, readbuf, sizeof(readbuf),
35                          (SA *) &cliaddr, &len, &sri, &msg_flags);
36          if (msg_flags & MSG_NOTIFICATION) {
37              print_notification(readbuf);
38              continue;
39          }
```
———————————————————————————————— *sctp/sctpserv06.c*

Figure 23.5 A modified server that uses notifications.

Set up to receive notifications

21–30 Here the server changes the event settings so that it will receive all notifications.

Normal receive code

31–35 This section of server code is unchanged.

Handle notification

36–39 Here the server checks the `msg_flags` field. If the server finds that the data is a notification, it calls our display function `sctp_print_notification` and loops around to read the next message.

Running the Code

We start the client and send one message as follows:

```
FreeBSD-lap: ./sctpclient01 10.1.1.5
[0]Hello
From str:1 seq:0 (assoc:c99e15a0):[0]Hello
Control-D
FreeBSD-lap:
```

When receiving the connection, message, and connection termination, our modified server displays each event as it occurs.

```
FreeBSD-lap: ./sctpserv06
SCTP_ADAPTION_INDICATION:0x504c5253
SCTP_ASSOC_CHANGE: COMMUNICATION UP, assoc=c99e2680h
SCTP_SHUTDOWN_EVENT: assoc=c99e2680h
SCTP_ASSOC_CHANGE: SHUTDOWN COMPLETE, assoc=c99e2680h
Control-C
```

As you can see, the server now announces the events as they occur on the transport.

23.5 Unordered Data

SCTP normally provides reliable ordered delivery of data. SCTP also provides a reliable unordered service. A message with the MSG_UNORDERED flag is sent with no order constraints and is made deliverable as soon as it arrives. Unordered data can be sent in any stream. No stream sequence number is assigned. Figure 23.6 shows the changes needed to our client program to send the request to the echo server with the unordered data service.

```
                                                              ─ sctp/sctp_strcli_un.c
18          out_sz = strlen(sendline);
19          Sctp_sendmsg(sock_fd, sendline, out_sz,
20                    to, tolen, 0, MSG_UNORDERED, sri.sinfo_stream, 0, 0);
                                                              ─ sctp/sctp_strcli_un.c
```

Figure 23.6 A sctp_strcli that sends unordered data.

Send data using unordered service

18-20   This is nearly the same as the sctpstr_cli function developed in Section 10.4. On line 21, we see the single change made: The client explicitly passes the MSG_UNORDERED flag to invoke the unordered service. Normally, all data within a given stream is ordered with sequence numbers. The MSG_UNORDERED flag causes the data sent with this flag to be sent unordered, with no sequence number, and can be delivered as soon as it arrives, even if other unordered data that was sent earlier on the same stream has not yet arrived.

23.6   Binding a Subset of Addresses

Some applications may want to bind a proper subset of the IP addresses of a machine to
a single socket. In TCP and UDP, traditionally, it was not possible to bind a subset of
addresses. The `bind` system call allows an application to bind a single address or the
wildcard address. Due to this restriction, the new function call `sctp_bindx` is provided to allow an application to bind to more than one address. Note that all the
addresses must use the same port number, and if `bind` was called, the port number
must be the same as that provided to `bind`. The `sctp_bindx` call will fail if a different
port is provided. Figure 23.7 shows a utility we will add to our server that will bind an
argument list.

```
                                                            ———————— sctp/sctp_bindargs.c
 1 #include    "unp.h"

 2 int
 3 sctp_bind_arg_list(int sock_fd, char **argv, int argc)
 4 {
 5     struct addrinfo *addr;
 6     char    *bindbuf, *p, portbuf[10];
 7     int      addrcnt = 0;
 8     int      i;

 9     bindbuf = (char *) Calloc(argc, sizeof(struct sockaddr_storage));
10     p = bindbuf;
11     sprintf(portbuf, "%d", SERV_PORT);
12     for (i = 0; i < argc; i++) {
13         addr = Host_serv(argv[i], portbuf, AF_UNSPEC, SOCK_SEQPACKET);
14         memcpy(p, addr->ai_addr, addr->ai_addrlen);
15         freeaddrinfo(addr);
16         addrcnt++;
17         p += addr->ai_addrlen;
18     }
19     Sctp_bindx(sock_fd, (SA *) bindbuf, addrcnt, SCTP_BINDX_ADD_ADDR);
20     free(bindbuf);
21     return (0);
22 }
                                                            ———————— sctp/sctp_bindargs.c
```

Figure 23.7 Function to bind a subset of addresses.

Allocate space for bind arguments

9–10   Our `sctp_bind_arg_list` function starts off by allocating space for the bind
arguments. Note that the `sctp_bindx` function can accept a mix of IPv6 and IPv4
addresses. We allocate enough space for a `sockaddr_storage` for each address, even
though the address list argument to `sctp_bindx` is a packed list of addresses (Figure 9.4). This results in some memory waste but is simpler than calculating the exact
space required by processing the argument list twice.

Process arguments

11–18   We set up the *portbuf* to be an ASCII representation of the port number, to prepare to
call our `getaddrinfo` wrapper function, `host_serv`. We pass each address and the

port number to `host_serv`, along with `AF_UNSPEC` to allow IPv4 or IPv6, and `SOCK_SEQPACKET` to specify that we're using SCTP. We copy the first `sockaddr` that is returned and ignore any others. Since the arguments to this function are meant to be literal address strings, as opposed to names that could have multiple addresses associated with them, this is safe. We free the return value from `getaddrinfo`, increment our count of addresses, and move the pointer to the next element in our packed array of `sockaddr` structures.

Call binding function

19   The function now resets its pointer to the top of the bind buffer and calls `sctp_bindx` with the subset of addresses decoded earlier.

Return success

20-21   If the function reaches here, we are successful, so clean up and return.

Figure 23.8 illustrates our modified echo server that now binds a list of addresses passed on the command line. Note that we have modified the server slightly so it always returns any echoed message on the stream on which it arrived.

```
────────────────────────────────────────────────────── sctp/sctpserv07.c
12     if (argc < 2)
13         err_quit("Error, use %s [list of addresses to bind]\n", argv[0]);
14     sock_fd = Socket(AF_INET6, SOCK_SEQPACKET, IPPROTO_SCTP);

15     if (sctp_bind_arg_list(sock_fd, argv + 1, argc - 1))
16         err_sys("Can't bind the address set");

17     bzero(&evnts, sizeof(evnts));
18     evnts.sctp_data_io_event = 1;
────────────────────────────────────────────────────── sctp/sctpserv07.c
```

Figure 23.8 Server using a variable set of addresses.

Server code using IPv6

14   Here we see the server we have been working on throughout this chapter, but with a slight modification. The server creates an `AF_INET6` socket. This way, the server can use both IPv4 and IPv6.

Use the new `sctp_bind_arg_list` function

15-16   The server calls the new `sctp_bind_arg_list` function, passing the argument list to it for processing.

23.7 Determining Peer and Local Address Information

Because SCTP is a multihomed protocol, different mechanisms are needed to find out what addresses are in use at both the remote as well as the local endpoints of an association. In this section, we will modify our client to receive the communication up notification. Our client will then use this notification to display the addresses of both the local and remote sides of the association. Figures 23.9 and 23.10 show the modifications to our client code. Figures 23.11 and 23.12 show the new code we add to the client.

```
16        bzero(&evnts, sizeof(evnts));
17        evnts.sctp_data_io_event = 1;
18        evnts.sctp_association_event = 1;
19        Setsockopt(sock_fd, IPPROTO_SCTP, SCTP_EVENTS, &evnts, sizeof(evnts));

20        sctpstr_cli(stdin, sock_fd, (SA *) &servaddr, sizeof(servaddr));
```
———————————————————————————————————— *sctp/sctpclient04*

Figure 23.9 Client set up for notifications.

Set events and call echo function

16-20   We see a slight change to our client's main routine. The client explicitly subscribes to association change notifications.

We now look at the modifications needed to `sctpstr_cli` so that it will use our new notification processing routine.

———————————————————————————————————— *sctp/sctp_strcli1.c*
```
21        do {
22            len = sizeof(peeraddr);
23            rd_sz = Sctp_recvmsg(sock_fd, recvline, sizeof(recvline),
24                            (SA *) &peeraddr, &len, &sri, &msg_flags);
25            if (msg_flags & MSG_NOTIFICATION)
26                check_notification(sock_fd, recvline, rd_sz);
27        } while (msg_flags & MSG_NOTIFICATION);
28        printf("From str:%d seq:%d (assoc:0x%x):",
29                sri.sinfo_stream, sri.sinfo_ssn, (u_int) sri.sinfo_assoc_id);
30        printf("%.*s", rd_sz, recvline);
```
———————————————————————————————————— *sctp/sctp_strcli1.c*

Figure 23.10 `sctp_strcli` that handles notifications.

Loop waiting for message

21-24   Here the client sets up the address length variable and calls the receive function to get the echoed message from the server.

Check for notifications

25-26   The client now checks to see if the message it just read is a notification. If it is, the client calls our notification processing routine shown in Figure 23.11.

Loop while waiting for data

27   If the message read was a notification, keep looping until we read actual data.

Display message

28-30   Next, the client displays the message and goes back to the top of its processing loop, waiting for user input.

Now let's look at the new function `sctp_check_notification`, which will display the addresses of both endpoints when an association notification event arrives.

```
                                                              — sctp/sctp_check_notify.c
 1 #include    "unp.h"

 2 void
 3 check_notification(int sock_fd, char *recvline, int rd_len)
 4 {
 5     union sctp_notification *snp;
 6     struct sctp_assoc_change *sac;
 7     struct sockaddr_storage *sal, *sar;
 8     int     num_rem, num_loc;

 9     snp = (union sctp_notification *) recvline;
10     if (snp->sn_header.sn_type == SCTP_ASSOC_CHANGE) {
11         sac = &snp->sn_assoc_change;
12         if ((sac->sac_state == SCTP_COMM_UP) ||
13             (sac->sac_state == SCTP_RESTART)) {
14             num_rem = sctp_getpaddrs(sock_fd, sac->sac_assoc_id, &sar);
15             printf("There are %d remote addresses and they are:\n", num_rem);
16             sctp_print_addresses(sar, num_rem);
17             sctp_freepaddrs(sar);

18             num_loc = sctp_getladdrs(sock_fd, sac->sac_assoc_id, &sal);
19             printf("There are %d local addresses and they are:\n", num_loc);
20             sctp_print_addresses(sal, num_loc);
21             sctp_freeladdrs(sal);
22         }
23     }
24 }
                                                              — sctp/sctp_check_notify.c
```

Figure 23.11 Process notifications.

Check if it is notification we want

9–13   The function casts the receive buffer to our generic notification pointer to find the notification type. If it is the notification the function is interested in, an association change notification, it then tests if the notification is a new or restarted association (SCTP_COMM_UP or SCTP_RESTART). We ignore all other notifications.

Gather and print peer addresses

14–17   We call `sctp_getpaddrs` to gather a list of remote addresses. We then print the number of addresses and use the address printing routine, `sctp_print_addresses`, shown in Figure 23.12, to display the addresses. When it finishes using the address pointer, the function calls the `sctp_freepaddrs` function to release the resources allocated by `sctp_getpaddrs`.

Gather and print local addresses

18–21   We call `sctp_getladdrs` to gather a list of local addresses, plus print the number of addresses and the addresses themselves. After the function finishes using the addresses, it calls the `sctp_freeladdrs` function to release the resources allocated by `sctp_getladdrs`.

Finally, we look at one last new function, sctp_print_addresses, which will print a list of addresses in the form that is returned by the sctp_getpaddrs and sctp_getladdrs functions.

——————————————————————————————————— sctp/sctp_print_addrs.c

```
 1 #include    "unp.h"

 2 void
 3 sctp_print_addresses(struct sockaddr_storage *addrs, int num)
 4 {
 5     struct sockaddr_storage *ss;
 6     int     i, salen;

 7     ss = addrs;
 8     for (i = 0; i < num; i++) {
 9         printf("%s\n", Sock_ntop((SA *) ss, salen));
10 #ifdef HAVE_SOCKADDR_SA_LEN
11         salen = ss->ss_len;
12 #else
13         switch (ss->ss_family) {
14         case AF_INET:
15             salen = sizeof(struct sockaddr_in);
16             break;
17 #ifdef IPV6
18         case AF_INET6:
19             salen = sizeof(struct sockaddr_in6);
20             break;
21 #endif
22         default:
23             err_quit("sctp_print_addresses: unknown AF");
24             break;
25         }
26 #endif
27         ss = (struct sockaddr_storage *) ((char *) ss + salen);
28     }
29 }
```

——————————————————————————————————— sctp/sctp_print_addrs.c

Figure 23.12 Print a list of addresses.

Process each address

7–8   The function loops through each address based on the number of addresses our caller specified.

Print address

9   We print the address using our sock_ntop function. Recall that this prints any socket address structure format the system supports.

Determine address size

10–26   The list of addresses is a packed list, not a simple array of sockaddr_storage structures. This is because the sockaddr_storage structure is quite large and it is too wasteful to use in passing addresses back and forth between the kernel and user space. On systems on which the sockaddr structure contains its own length, this is trivial: just extract the length from the current `sockaddr_storage` structure. On other systems, we choose the length based on the address family and quit with an error if the address family is unknown.

Move address pointer

27   The function now adds the size of the address to the base pointer to move forward through the list of addresses.

Running the Code

We run our modified client against the server as follows:

```
FreeBSD-lap: ./sctpclient01 10.1.1.5
[0]Hi
There are 2 remote addresses and they are:
10.1.1.5:9877
127.0.0.1:9877
There are 2 local addresses and they are:
10.1.1.5:1025
127.0.0.1:1025
From str:0 seq:0 (assoc:c99e2680):[0]Hi
Control-D
FreeBSD-lap:
```

23.8 Finding an Association ID Given an IP Address

In the recent changes we made to our client in Section 23.7, the client used the association notification to trigger retrieving the list of addresses. This notification was quite convenient since it held the association's identification in the `sac_assoc_id` field. But, if the application is not tracking association identifications and only has an address of a peer, how can it find an association's identification? In Figure 23.13, we illustrate a simple function that translates a peer's address into an association ID. The server will use this function later in Section 23.10.

Initialize

7–8   Our function first initializes its `sctp_paddrparams` structure.

Copy address

9   We copy the address, using the passed length, into the `sctp_paddrparams` structure.

Call socket option

10   The function now uses the `SCTP_PEER_ADDR_PARAMS` socket option to request peer address parameters. Note that we use `sctp_opt_info`, instead of `getsockopt`, since the `SCTP_PEER_ADDR_PARAMS` socket option requires copying arguments both into and out of the kernel. This call will return the current heartbeat interval, the maximum number of retransmissions before the SCTP implementation considers the peer address to have failed, and most importantly, the association ID. Note that we do not check the return value, since if the call fails, we want to return 0.

sctp/sctp_addr_to_associd.c

```
 1 #include     "unp.h"

 2 sctp_assoc_t
 3 sctp_address_to_associd(int sock_fd, struct sockaddr *sa, socklen_t salen)
 4 {
 5     struct sctp_paddrparams sp;
 6     int     siz;

 7     siz = sizeof(struct sctp_paddrparams);
 8     bzero(&sp, siz);
 9     memcpy(&sp.spp_address, sa, salen);
10     sctp_opt_info(sock_fd, 0, SCTP_PEER_ADDR_PARAMS, &sp, &siz);
11     return (sp.spp_assoc_id);
12 }
```

sctp/sctp_addr_to_associd.c

Figure 23.13 Translate an address to an association ID.

11   The function returns the association ID to the caller. Note that if the call fails, the earlier clearing of the structure will assure our caller of getting a 0 as the returned association ID. An association ID of 0 is not allowed and is used to indicate no association by the SCTP implementation as well.

23.9 Heartbeating and Address Failure

SCTP provides a heartbeat mechanism similar in concept to TCP's keep-alive option. In the case of SCTP, however, the option is enabled by default. The application can control the heartbeat and set the error threshold for an address by using the same socket option we saw in Section 23.8. The error threshold is the number of missed heartbeats or retransmission timeouts that must occur before a destination address is considered unreachable. When the destination address becomes reachable again, detected by heartbeats, the address becomes active.

The application can disable heartbeats, but without heartbeats, SCTP has no way to detect if a failed peer address has become reachable again. Such addresses cannot come back to an active state without user intervention.

The heartbeat parameter field of the `sctp_paddrparams` structure is `spp_hbinterval`. If an application sets the `spp_hbinterval` field to `SCTP_NO_HB` (0), heartbeats are disabled. A value of `SCTP_ISSUE_HB` (0xffffffff) requests an on-demand (immediate) heartbeat. Any other value sets the heartbeat delay in milliseconds. The heartbeat delay provides a set delay between heartbeats. This value, added to the current retransmission timer value plus a random jitter, will become the amount of time between heartbeats. In Figure 23.14 we show a small function that will either set the heartbeat delay, request an on-demand heartbeat, or disable the heartbeat for the specified destination. Note that by leaving the retransmissions parameter, the `spp_pathmaxrxt` field of the `sctp_paddrparams` structure, set to 0, we leave the current value unchanged.

sctp/sctp_modify_hb.c

```
 1 #include     "unp.h"

 2 int
 3 heartbeat_action(int sock_fd, struct sockaddr *sa, socklen_t salen,
 4                  u_int value)
 5 {
 6     struct sctp_paddrparams sp;
 7     int     siz;

 8     bzero(&sp, sizeof(sp));
 9     sp.spp_hbinterval = value;
10     memcpy((caddr_t) & sp.spp_address, sa, salen);
11     Setsockopt(sock_fd, IPPROTO_SCTP,
12                SCTP_PEER_ADDR_PARAMS, &sp, sizeof(sp));
13     return (0);
14 }
```

sctp/sctp_modify_hb.c

Figure 23.14 Heartbeat control utility function.

Zero `sctp_paddrparams` struct and copy interval

8–9   We zero out `struct sctp_paddrparams` to ensure that we won't change any parameters we don't want to. We then copy the user's desired heartbeat value: `SCTP_ISSUE_HB`, `SCTP_NO_HB`, or a heartbeat interval.

Set up address

10   The function sets up the address and copies it into the `sctp_paddrparams` structure so that the SCTP implementation will know the address to which we wish to send a heartbeat.

Perform action

11–12   Finally, the function issues the socket option call to cause the action the user has requested.

23.10 Peeling Off an Association

We have been focusing on the one-to-many-style interface provided by SCTP. This interface has several advantages over the more classic one-to-one style:

- There is only one file descriptor to maintain.
- It allows us to write a simple iterative server.
- It lets an application send data on the third and fourth packet of the four-way handshake by using `sendmsg` or `sctp_sendmsg` to implicitly establish the connection.
- There is no need to track transport state. In other words, the application just does a receive call on the socket descriptor and does not need to do any of the traditional `connect` or `accept` function calls before receiving messages.

However, there is one major drawback to this style. It makes it difficult to build a concurrent server (either using threads or by forking children). This drawback has brought about the addition of the `sctp_peeloff` function. `sctp_peeloff` takes a one-to-many socket descriptor and an association ID and returns a new socket descriptor with just that association (plus any queued notifications and data on that association) attached in a one-to-one style. The original socket remains open, and any other associations represented by the one-to-many socket are left unaffected.

This socket can then be handed off to either a thread or a child process to execute a concurrent server. Figure 23.15 illustrates a further modification to our server that processes the first message of a client, extracts the client socket descriptor using `sctp_peeloff`, forks a child, and calls our original TCP `str_echo` function introduced in Section 5.3. We use the address of the received message to call our function that gets us the association ID (Section 23.8). The association ID is also available in `sri.sinfo_assoc_id`; we show this method of determining the association ID from the IP address to illustrate another method. After forking the child, our server loops back to process the next message.

―― *sctp/sctpserv_fork.c*
```
23      for ( ; ; ) {
24          len = sizeof(struct sockaddr_in);
25          rd_sz = Sctp_recvmsg(sock_fd, readbuf, sizeof(readbuf),
26                              (SA *) &cliaddr, &len, &sri, &msg_flags);
27          Sctp_sendmsg(sock_fd, readbuf, rd_sz,
28                      (SA *) &cliaddr, len,
29                      sri.sinfo_ppid,
30                      sri.sinfo_flags, sri.sinfo_stream, 0, 0);
31          assoc = sctp_address_to_associd(sock_fd, (SA *) &cliaddr, len);
32          if ((int) assoc == 0) {
33              err_ret("Can't get association id");
34              continue;
35          }
36          connfd = sctp_peeloff(sock_fd, assoc);
37          if (connfd == -1) {
38              err_ret("sctp_peeloff fails");
39              continue;
40          }
41          if ( (childpid = fork()) == 0) {
42              Close(sock_fd);
43              str_echo(connfd);
44              exit(0);
45          } else {
46              Close(connfd);
47          }
48      }
```
―― *sctp/sctpserv_fork.c*

Figure 23.15 A concurrent SCTP server.

Receive and process first message from client

26–30   The server receives and processes the first message a client sends.

Translate address to association ID

31-35   The server next uses our function from Figure 23.13 to translate the address to an association ID. If for some reason the server cannot get an association ID, it skips this attempt to fork a child and instead will try with the next message.

Extract association

36-40   The server extracts the association into its own socket descriptor with `sctp_peeloff`. This results in a one-to-one socket that can be passed to our earlier TCP version of `str_echo`.

Delegate work to child

41-47   The server forks a child and lets the child perform all future work on this new socket descriptor.

23.11 Controlling Timing

SCTP has many controls that are user-tunable. All of these advanced controls are accessed via socket options we discussed in Section 7.10. In this section, we will highlight some of the specific controls that influence how long an SCTP endpoint will take to declare either an association or destination failure.

There are seven specific controls that dictate failure detection time in SCTP (Figure 23.16).

field	Description	default	unit
srto_min	Minimum retransmission timeout	1000	milliseconds
srto_max	Maximum retransmission timeout	60000	milliseconds
srto_initial	Initial retransmission timeout	3000	milliseconds
sinit_max_init_timeo	Maximum retransmission timeout during INIT	3000	milliseconds
sinit_max_attempts	Maximum retransmissions of INIT	8	attempts
spp_pathmaxrxt	Maximum retransmissions per address	5	attempts
sasoc_asocmaxrxt	Maximum retransmissions per association	10	attempts

Figure 23.16 Fields that control timing in SCTP.

Each of these parameters influences how quickly SCTP will detect failure or attempt retransmission. We can think of these as control knobs that either shorten or lengthen the time it takes for an endpoint to detect failure. We first examine two scenarios:

1. An SCTP endpoint tries to open an association to a peer that has been disconnected from the network.

2   Two multihomed SCTP endpoints are exchanging data, and one of them is powered down during the middle of the communication. No ICMP messages are being received due to filtering by a firewall.

In Scenario 1, the system trying to open the connection would first set its RTO timer to the `srto_initial` value of 3,000 ms. After a timeout, it would retransmit the INIT message and double the RTO timer to 6,000 ms. This behavior would continue until it had sent `sinit_max_attempts`, or eight INIT messages, and had subsequently timed out on each of the transmissions. The doubling of the RTO timer would be capped at `sinit_max_init_timeo`, or 60,000 ms. Therefore, it would take 3+6+12+24+48+60+60+60, or 273 seconds, to reach the point where the SCTP implementation would declare the potential peer unreachable.

There are a number of knobs and combinations of knobs we can tune to shorten or lengthen this time. First, let's focus on the influence of two specific parameters we can use to shorten the time from 270 seconds. One change we can make is to decrease the number of retransmissions by changing `sinit_max_attempts`. An alternative change that can also be made is to reduce the maximum RTO value for the INIT by changing `srto_max_init_timeo`. If we lower the number of attempts to 4, our detection time to failure drops drastically to 45 seconds, one-sixth of what the default value gives us. But this method has a drawback: We may experience a case where our peer is available, but due to loss in the network, or perhaps overload at the peer, we declare the peer to be unreachable.

Another approach is to lower the `srto_max_init_timeo` to 20 seconds. This decreases our failure detection time to 121 seconds, less than one-half of the original value, but this change also carries with it a tradeoff. If we pick a value that is too low, it is possible that excessive delay in the network would cause us to send many more INIT messages than needed.

Now let's turn our attention to Scenario 2, in which there are two multihomed peers communicating with each other. One endpoint has the addresses IP-A and IP-B, the other IP-X and IP-Y. If one of them becomes unreachable (assuming data was being sent by the peer that was not powered down), the sending endpoint sees successive timeouts to each destination starting at a value of `srto_min` (default 1 second) and doubling until both destinations reach `srto_max` (default 60 seconds). The endpoint would retransmit until it reached the association maximum `sasoc_asocmaxrxt` (default 10 retransmissions).

Now in our scenario, the sending endpoint would see timeouts at 1(IP-A) + 1(IP-B)+ 2(IP-A) + 2(IP-B) + 4(IP-A) + 4(IP-B) + 8(IP-A) + 8(IP-B) + 16(IP-A) + 16(IP-B), for a total of 62 seconds. The `srto_max` parameter does not influence a multihomed peer when left to its default value since we reach the default value of `sasoc_asocmaxrxt` before we reach `srto_max`. We again focus on two parameters we can use to affect these timeouts and the resulting failure detection. We can decrease the number of attempts by changing the `sasoc_asocmaxrxt` value (default 10), or we can decrease the maximum RTO by changing `srto_max` (default 60 seconds). If we set our `srto_max` time to 10 seconds, we can decrease the detection time by 12 seconds, reducing it to 50 seconds. An alternative, decreasing the maximum retransmissions to 8, would drop our detection time to 30 seconds. The same concerns we mentioned before apply to this scenario as well: A brief, survivable network problem or remote system overload could cause a working connection to be torn down.

Among the many alternatives, we do not recommend lowering the minimum RTO (`srto_min`). When communicating across the Internet, lowering this value could have dire consequences in that we would retransmit much more rapidly, straining the

Internet's infrastructure. In a private network, it may be acceptable to tune this value lower, but for most applications, this value should not be decreased.

Each application, when turning these timing knobs, must take into consideration several factors before making adjustments:

- How quickly does your application need to detect failure?
- Will the application be run in private networks where the conditions on the overall end-to-end path are well-known and less varying than the Internet?
- What are the consequences of false failure detection?

Only after carefully answering these questions will an application be able to properly tune the timing parameters of SCTP.

23.12 When to Use SCTP Instead of TCP

SCTP was originally developed for call control signaling to allow the transport of telephony signals across the Internet. However, during its development, its scope was expanded beyond that into a general-purpose transport protocol. It provides most of the features of TCP, and adds to those a wide range of new transport-layer services. There are few applications that could not benefit by the use of SCTP. So when should we use SCTP? Let's start by listing the benefits of SCTP:

1. SCTP is a protocol that directly supports multihoming. An endpoint can take advantage of multiple networks on a host to gain additional reliability. An added bonus is that the application does not need to take any action, other than moving to SCTP, to automatically take advantage of SCTP's multihomed service. For further details on SCTP's multihoming, see Section 7.4 of [Stewart and Xie 2001].

2. Head-of-line blocking can be eliminated. An application can use a single SCTP association and transport multiple data elements in parallel. A loss in one stream of information will not influence any of the other parallel streams of information flowing through the association (we discussed this concept in Section 10.5).

3. Application layer message boundaries are preserved. Many applications do not send streams of bytes; instead, they send messages. SCTP preserves message boundaries sent by an application and thus simplifies the application writer's task. No longer is it necessary to mark message boundaries within a stream of bytes and provide special handling code to deal with reconstructing messages from the information flow at the receiver.

4. An unordered message service is provided. For some applications, no ordering is needed. In the past, such an application may have used TCP for its reliability with the drawback that all data, even though unordered, would have to be delivered in order. Any loss would cause head-of-line blocking for all

subsequent messages flowing through the connection. With SCTP, an unordered service is available that avoids this issue and allows an application to match its needs directly to the transport.

5. A partially reliable service is available in some SCTP implementations. This feature allows an SCTP sender to specify a lifetime on each message, using the `sinfo_timetolive` field of the `struct sctp_sndrcvinfo`. (This is different from the IPv4 TTL or the IPv6 hop limit; it is actually a length of time.) When both endpoints support this feature, time-sensitive data can be discarded by the transport instead of the application, even if it has been transmitted and lost, thus optimizing data transport in the face of congestion.

6. An easy migration path from TCP is provided by SCTP with its one-to-one-style interface. This interface duplicates a typical TCP interface so that with one or two slight changes, a TCP application can be migrated to SCTP.

7. Many of the features of TCP, such as positive acknowledgment, retransmission of lost data, resequencing of data, windowed flow control, slow-start and congestion avoidance, and selective acknowledgments, are included in SCTP with two notable exceptions (the half-closed state and urgent data).

8. SCTP provides many hooks (as seen in this chapter and in Section 7.10) for an application to configure and tune the transport to match its needs on an association-by-association basis. This flexibility, along with a general set of good defaults (for the application that does not wish to tune the transport), provide the application with controls unavailable in TCP.

SCTP does not provide two features that TCP does provide. One is the half-closed state. This state is entered when an application closes its half of the connection but still allows the peer to send data to it (we discussed this in Section 6.6). An application enters the half-closed state to signal to the peer that it is finished transmitting data. Very few applications use this feature, so during SCTP development, it was considered not worth adding to the protocol. Applications that need this feature and want to move to SCTP will need to change their application-layer protocol to provide this signal in the application data stream. In some instances, this change may not be trivial.

Another TCP feature that SCTP does not provide is urgent data. Using a separate SCTP stream for urgent data has somewhat similar semantics, but cannot replicate the feature exactly.

Another type of application that may not benefit from SCTP is one that is truly byte stream-oriented, like `telnet`, `rlogin`, `rsh`, and `ssh`. For such an application, TCP can segment the stream of bytes into IP packets more efficiently than SCTP. SCTP will faithfully preserve the message boundaries, which may equate to a size that does not fit efficiently into IP datagrams, and thus may cause somewhat more overhead.

In summary, many applications could consider using SCTP as it becomes available on their Unix platform. However, it takes an eye toward SCTP's special features to truly benefit from them; until SCTP is ubiquitous, it could be advantageous to simply stick with TCP.

23.13 Summary

In this chapter, we looked at the SCTP autoclose facility, exploring how it can be used to limit idle associations in a one-to-many socket. We built a simple utility that an application can use to receive large messages with the partial delivery API. We examined how an application can decode events that occur on the transport with a simple utility that displays notifications. We briefly looked at how a user can send unordered data and bind a subset of addresses. We saw how to acquire the addresses of both the peer end of an association as well as the local end. We also examined a simple method an application can use to translate an address into an association ID.

Heartbeats (termed keep-alives in TCP) are exchanged by default on an SCTP association. We examined how to control this feature through a small utility we built. We looked at how to extract an association with the `sctp_peeloff` system call, and illustrated an example server that was both iterative and concurrent using this call. We also discussed considerations an application needs to make before tuning the SCTP timing parameters. We concluded with a look at when an application should consider using SCTP.

Exercises

23.1 Write a client that can test our server's partial delivery API we developed in Section 23.3.

23.2 Besides sending a very large message to the server illustrated in Section 23.3, what other method can be used to get the partial delivery API invoked in our server?

23.3 Rewrite the partial delivery API server to handle partial delivery API notifications.

23.4 What applications would benefit from the use of unordered data? What applications would not benefit from unordered data? Explain your choices.

23.5 How can you test the subset binding server?

23.6 Assume that your application is running on a private network where the endpoints are all connected via a local LAN. Also assume that all of your servers and clients are running on multihomed hosts. What parameters do you need to adjust to assure that you detect failure in two seconds or less?

24

Out-of-Band Data

24.1 Introduction

Many transport layers have the concept of *out-of-band* data, which is sometimes called *expedited data*. The idea is that something important occurs at one end of a connection and that end wants to tell its peer quickly. By "quickly" we mean that this notification should be sent before any "normal" (sometimes called "in-band") data that is already queued to be sent, and should be sent regardless of any flow control or blocking issues. That is, out-of-band data is considered higher priority than normal data. Instead of using two connections between the client and server, out-of-band data is mapped onto the existing connection.

Unfortunately, once we get beyond the general concepts and down to the real world, almost every transport layer has a different implementation of out-of-band data. As an extreme example, UDP has no implementation of out-of-band data. In this chapter, we will focus on TCP's model of out-of-band data, provide numerous small examples of how it is handled by the sockets API, and describe how it is used by applications like `telnet`, `rlogin`, and FTP. Other than remote interactive applications like these, it is rare to find any use for out-of-band data.

24.2 TCP Out-of-Band Data

TCP does not have true *out-of-band data*. Instead, TCP provides an *urgent mode*. Assume a process has written N bytes of data to a TCP socket and that data is queued by TCP in the socket send buffer, waiting to be sent to the peer. We show this in Figure 24.1 and have labeled the data bytes 1 through N.

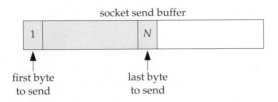

Figure 24.1   Socket send buffer containing data to send.

The process now writes a single byte of out-of-band data, containing the ASCII character a, using the send function and the MSG_OOB flag.

```
send(fd, "a", 1, MSG_OOB);
```

TCP places the data in the next available position in the socket send buffer and sets its *urgent pointer* for this connection to be the next available location. We show this in Figure 24.2 and have labeled the out-of-band byte "OOB."

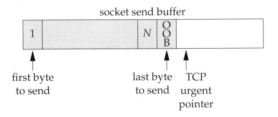

Figure 24.2   Socket send buffer after one byte of out-of-band data is written by application.

> TCP's urgent pointer has a sequence number one greater than the byte of data that is written with the MSG_OOB flag. As discussed on pp. 292–296 of TCPv1, this is an historical artifact that is now emulated by all implementations. As long as the sending TCP and the receiving TCP agree on the interpretation of TCP's urgent pointer, all is fine.

Given the state of the TCP socket send buffer shown in Figure 24.2, the next segment sent by TCP will have its URG flag set in the TCP header and the urgent offset field in the TCP header will point to the byte following the out-of-band byte. But this segment may or may not contain the byte that we have labeled as OOB. Whether the OOB byte is sent depends on the number of bytes ahead of it in the socket send buffer, the segment size that TCP is sending to the peer, and the current window advertised by the peer.

> We have used the terms *urgent pointer* and *urgent offset*. At the TCP level, the two are different. The 16-bit value in the TCP header is called the urgent offset and it must be added to the sequence number field in the header to obtain the 32-bit urgent pointer. TCP looks at the urgent offset only if another bit in the header is set, and this bit is called the *URG flag*. From a programming perspective, we need not worry about this detail and just refer to TCP's urgent pointer.

This is an important characteristic of TCP's urgent mode: The TCP header indicates that the sender has entered urgent mode (i.e., the URG flag is set along with the urgent offset), but the actual byte of data referred to by the urgent pointer need not be sent. Indeed, if the sending TCP is stopped by flow control (the receiver's socket receive buffer is full, so its TCP has advertised a window of 0 to the sending TCP), the urgent notification is sent without any data (pp. 1016–1017 of TCPv2), as we will show in Figures 24.10 and 24.11. This is one reason why applications use TCP's urgent mode (i.e., out-of-band data): The urgent notification is *always* sent to the peer TCP, even if the flow of data is stopped by TCP's flow control.

What happens if we send multiple bytes of out-of-band data, as in

```
send(fd, "abc", 3, MSG_OOB);
```

In this example, TCP's urgent pointer points one beyond the final byte; that is, the final byte (the c) is considered the out-of-band byte.

Now that we have covered the sending of out-of-band data, let's look at it from the receiver's side:

1. When TCP receives a segment with the URG flag set, the urgent pointer is examined to see whether it refers to *new* out-of-band data, that is, whether this is the first time TCP's urgent mode has referenced this particular byte in the stream of data from the sender to the receiver. It is common for the sending TCP to send multiple segments (typically over a short period of time) containing the URG flag, but with the urgent pointer pointing to the same byte of data. Only the first of these segments causes the receiving process to be notified that new out-of-band data has arrived.

2. The receiving process is notified when a new urgent pointer arrives. First the SIGURG signal is sent to the owner of the socket, assuming either fcntl or ioctl has been called to establish an owner for the socket (Figure 7.20). Second, if the process is blocked in a call to select waiting for this socket descriptor to have an exception condition, select returns.

   These two potential notifications to the receiving process take place when a new urgent pointer arrives, regardless of whether the actual byte of data pointed to by the urgent pointer has arrived at the receiving TCP.

   There is only one OOB mark; if a new OOB byte arrives before the old OOB byte was read, the old byte is discarded.

3. When the actual byte of data pointed to by the urgent pointer arrives at the receiving TCP, the data byte can be pulled out-of-band or left inline. By default, the SO_OOBINLINE socket option is *not* set for a socket, so the single byte of data is not placed into the socket receive buffer. Instead, the data byte is placed into a separate one-byte out-of-band buffer for this connection (pp. 986–988 of TCPv2). The only way for the process to read from this special one-byte buffer is to call recv, recvfrom, or recvmsg and specify the MSG_OOB flag. If a new OOB byte arrives before the old byte is read, the previous value in this buffer is discarded.

If, however, the process sets the SO_OOBINLINE socket option, then the single byte of data referred to by TCP's urgent pointer is left in the normal socket receive buffer. The process cannot specify the MSG_OOB flag to read the data byte in this case. The process will know when it reaches this byte of data by checking the *out-of-band mark* for this connection, as we will describe in Section 24.3.

Some of the following errors are possible:

1. If the process asks for out-of-band data (e.g., specifying the MSG_OOB flag), but the peer has not sent any, EINVAL is returned.

2. If the process has been notified that the peer has sent an out-of-band byte (e.g., by SIGURG or select), and the process tries to read it but that byte has not yet arrived, EWOULDBLOCK is returned. All the process can do at this point is read from the socket receive buffer (possibly discarding the data if it has no room to store the data), to make space in the buffer so that the peer TCP can send the out-of-band byte.

3. If the process tries to read the same out-of-band byte multiple times, EINVAL is returned.

4. If the process has set the SO_OOBINLINE socket option and then tries to read the out-of-band data by specifying MSG_OOB, EINVAL is returned.

Simple Example Using SIGURG

We now show a trivial example of sending and receiving out-of-band data. Figure 24.3 shows the sending program.

Nine bytes are sent, with a one-second sleep between each output operation. The purpose of the pause is to let each write or send be transmitted as a single TCP segment and received as such by the other end. We'll talk later about some of the timing considerations with out-of-band data. When we run this program, we see the expected output.

```
macosx % tcpsend01 freebsd4 9999
wrote 3 bytes of normal data
wrote 1 byte of OOB data
wrote 2 bytes of normal data
wrote 1 byte of OOB data
wrote 2 bytes of normal data
```

```
                                                                   oob/tcpsend01.c
 1 #include    "unp.h"

 2 int
 3 main(int argc, char **argv)
 4 {
 5     int    sockfd;

 6     if (argc != 3)
 7         err_quit("usage: tcpsend01 <host> <port#>");

 8     sockfd = Tcp_connect(argv[1], argv[2]);

 9     Write(sockfd, "123", 3);
10     printf("wrote 3 bytes of normal data\n");
11     sleep(1);

12     Send(sockfd, "4", 1, MSG_OOB);
13     printf("wrote 1 byte of OOB data\n");
14     sleep(1);

15     Write(sockfd, "56", 2);
16     printf("wrote 2 bytes of normal data\n");
17     sleep(1);

18     Send(sockfd, "7", 1, MSG_OOB);
19     printf("wrote 1 byte of OOB data\n");
20     sleep(1);

21     Write(sockfd, "89", 2);
22     printf("wrote 2 bytes of normal data\n");
23     sleep(1);

24     exit(0);
25 }
                                                                   oob/tcpsend01.c
```

Figure 24.3 Simple out-of-band sending program.

Figure 24.4 is the receiving program.

Establish signal handler and socket owner

16-17   The signal handler for SIGURG is established, and fcntl sets the owner of the connected socket.

> Notice that we do not establish the signal handler until accept returns. There is a small probability that out-of-band data can arrive after our TCP completes the three-way handshake, but before accept returns, which we would miss. But if we established the signal handler before calling accept and also set the owner of the listening socket (which carries over to the connected socket), then if out-of-band data arrives before accept returns, our signal handler won't yet have a value for connfd. If this scenario is important for the application, it should initialize connfd to −1, check for this value in the signal handler, and if true, just set a flag for the main loop to check after accept returns. Alternately, it could block the signal around the call to accept, but this is subject to all the signal race conditions we discussed in Section 20.5.

oob/tcprecv01.c

```
 1 #include    "unp.h"

 2 int     listenfd, connfd;

 3 void    sig_urg(int);

 4 int
 5 main(int argc, char **argv)
 6 {
 7     int     n;
 8     char    buff[100];

 9     if (argc == 2)
10         listenfd = Tcp_listen(NULL, argv[1], NULL);
11     else if (argc == 3)
12         listenfd = Tcp_listen(argv[1], argv[2], NULL);
13     else
14         err_quit("usage: tcprecv01 [ <host> ] <port#>");

15     connfd = Accept(listenfd, NULL, NULL);

16     Signal(SIGURG, sig_urg);
17     Fcntl(connfd, F_SETOWN, getpid());

18     for ( ; ; ) {
19         if ( (n = Read(connfd, buff, sizeof(buff) - 1)) == 0) {
20             printf("received EOF\n");
21             exit(0);
22         }
23         buff[n] = 0;                /* null terminate */
24         printf("read %d bytes: %s\n", n, buff);
25     }
26 }

27 void
28 sig_urg(int signo)
29 {
30     int     n;
31     char    buff[100];

32     printf("SIGURG received\n");
33     n = Recv(connfd, buff, sizeof(buff) - 1, MSG_OOB);
34     buff[n] = 0;                    /* null terminate */
35     printf("read %d OOB byte: %s\n", n, buff);
36 }
```

oob/tcprecv01.c

Figure 24.4 Simple out-of-band receiving program.

18-25   The process reads from the socket, printing each string that is returned by read. When the sender terminates the connection, the receiver then terminates.

SIGURG handler

27-36   Our signal handler calls printf, reads the out-of-band byte by specifying the MSG_OOB flag, and then prints the returned data. Notice that we ask for up to 100 bytes in the call to `recv`, but as we will see shortly, only 1 byte is ever returned as out-of-band data.

> As stated earlier, calling the unsafe `printf` function from a signal handler is not recommended. We do it just to see what's happening with our programs.

Here is the output when we run the receiving program, and then run the sending program from Figure 24.3:

```
freebsd4 % tcprecv01 9999
read 3 bytes: 123
SIGURG received
read 1 OOB byte: 4
read 2 bytes: 56
SIGURG received
read 1 OOB byte: 7
read 2 bytes: 89
received EOF
```

The results are as we expect. Each sending of out-of-band data by the sender generates `SIGURG` for the receiver, which then reads the single out-of-band byte.

Simple Example Using `select`

We now redo our out-of-band receiver to use `select` instead of the `SIGURG` signal. Figure 24.5 is the receiving program.

15–20   The process calls `select` while waiting for either normal data (the read set, `rset`) or out-of-band data (the exception set, `xset`). In each case, the received data is printed.

When we run this program and then run the same sending program as earlier (Figure 24.3), we encounter the following error:

```
freebsd4 % tcprecv02 9999
read 3 bytes: 123
read 1 OOB byte: 4
recv error: Invalid argument
```

The problem is that `select` indicates an exception condition until the process reads *beyond* the out-of-band data (pp. 530–531 of TCPv2). We cannot read the out-of-band data more than once because after we read it the first time, the kernel clears the one-byte out-of-band buffer. When we call `recv` specifying the `MSG_OOB` flag the second time, it returns `EINVAL`.

————————————————————————————— oob/tcprecv02.c
```
 1 #include    "unp.h"

 2 int
 3 main(int argc, char **argv)
 4 {
 5     int      listenfd, connfd, n;
 6     char     buff[100];
 7     fd_set   rset, xset;

 8     if (argc == 2)
 9         listenfd = Tcp_listen(NULL, argv[1], NULL);
10     else if (argc == 3)
11         listenfd = Tcp_listen(argv[1], argv[2], NULL);
12     else
13         err_quit("usage: tcprecv02 [ <host> ] <port#>");

14     connfd = Accept(listenfd, NULL, NULL);

15     FD_ZERO(&rset);
16     FD_ZERO(&xset);
17     for ( ; ; ) {
18         FD_SET(connfd, &rset);
19         FD_SET(connfd, &xset);

20         Select(connfd + 1, &rset, NULL, &xset, NULL);

21         if (FD_ISSET(connfd, &xset)) {
22             n = Recv(connfd, buff, sizeof(buff) - 1, MSG_OOB);
23             buff[n] = 0;          /* null terminate */
24             printf("read %d OOB byte: %s\n", n, buff);
25         }

26         if (FD_ISSET(connfd, &rset)) {
27             if ( (n = Read(connfd, buff, sizeof(buff) - 1)) == 0) {
28                 printf("received EOF\n");
29                 exit(0);
30             }
31             buff[n] = 0;          /* null terminate */
32             printf("read %d bytes: %s\n", n, buff);
33         }
34     }
35 }
```
————————————————————————————— oob/tcprecv02.c

Figure 24.5 Receiving program that (incorrectly) uses select to be notified of out-of-band data.

The solution is to select for an exception condition only after reading normal data. Figure 24.6 is a modification of Figure 24.5 that handles this scenario correctly.

5   We declare a new variable named justreadoob, which indicates whether we just read out-of-band data or not. This flag determines whether or not to select for an exception condition.

26-27   When we set the justreadoob flag, we must also clear the bit for this descriptor in the exception set.

The program now works as expected.

———————————————————————————— oob/tcprecv03.c

```
 1 #include    "unp.h"

 2 int
 3 main(int argc, char **argv)
 4 {
 5     int     listenfd, connfd, n, justreadoob = 0;
 6     char    buff[100];
 7     fd_set  rset, xset;

 8     if (argc == 2)
 9         listenfd = Tcp_listen(NULL, argv[1], NULL);
10     else if (argc == 3)
11         listenfd = Tcp_listen(argv[1], argv[2], NULL);
12     else
13         err_quit("usage: tcprecv03 [ <host> ] <port#>");

14     connfd = Accept(listenfd, NULL, NULL);

15     FD_ZERO(&rset);
16     FD_ZERO(&xset);
17     for ( ; ; ) {
18         FD_SET(connfd, &rset);
19         if (justreadoob == 0)
20             FD_SET(connfd, &xset);

21         Select(connfd + 1, &rset, NULL, &xset, NULL);

22         if (FD_ISSET(connfd, &xset)) {
23             n = Recv(connfd, buff, sizeof(buff) - 1, MSG_OOB);
24             buff[n] = 0;          /* null terminate */
25             printf("read %d OOB byte: %s\n", n, buff);
26             justreadoob = 1;
27             FD_CLR(connfd, &xset);
28         }

29         if (FD_ISSET(connfd, &rset)) {
30             if ( (n = Read(connfd, buff, sizeof(buff) - 1)) == 0) {
31                 printf("received EOF\n");
32                 exit(0);
33             }
34             buff[n] = 0;          /* null terminate */
35             printf("read %d bytes: %s\n", n, buff);
36             justreadoob = 0;
37         }
38     }
39 }
```

———————————————————————————— oob/tcprecv03.c

Figure 24.6 Modification of Figure 24.5 to `select` for an exception condition correctly.

24.3 `sockatmark` Function

Whenever out-of-band data is received, there is an associated *out-of-band mark*. This is the position in the normal stream of data *at the sender* when the sending process sent the out-of-band byte. The receiving process determines whether or not it is at the out-of-band mark by calling the `sockatmark` function while it reads from the socket.

```
#include <sys/socket.h>

int sockatmark(int sockfd);
                                    Returns: 1 if at out-of-band mark, 0 if not at mark, −1 on error
```

This function is an invention of POSIX. POSIX is replacing many `ioctl`s with functions.

Figure 24.7 shows an implementation of this function using the commonly found `SIOCATMARK ioctl`.

```
                                                                      lib/sockatmark.c
1 #include      "unp.h"

2 int
3 sockatmark(int fd)
4 {
5     int      flag;

6     if (ioctl(fd, SIOCATMARK, &flag) < 0)
7         return (-1);
8     return (flag != 0);
9 }
                                                                      lib/sockatmark.c
```

Figure 24.7 `sockatmark` function implemented using `ioctl`.

The out-of-band mark applies regardless of whether the receiving process is receiving the out-of-band data inline (the `SO_OOBINLINE` socket option) or out-of-band (the `MSG_OOB` flag). One common use of the out-of-band mark is for the receiver to treat all the data as special until the mark is passed.

Example

We now show a simple example to illustrate the following two features of the out-of-band mark:

1. The out-of-band mark always points one beyond the final byte of normal data. This means that, if the out-of-band data is received inline, `sockatmark` returns true if the next byte to be read is the byte that was sent with the `MSG_OOB` flag. Alternately, if the `SO_OOBINLINE` socket option is not enabled, then `sockatmark` returns true if the next byte of data is the first byte that was sent following the out-of-band data.

2. A read operation always stops at the out-of-band mark (pp. 519–520 of TCPv2). That is, if there are 100 bytes in the socket receive buffer, but only 5 bytes until the out-of-band mark, and the process performs a read asking for 100 bytes, only the 5 bytes up to the mark are returned. This forced stop at the mark is to allow the process to call sockatmark to determine if the buffer pointer is at the mark.

Figure 24.8 is our sending program. It sends three bytes of normal data, one byte of out-of-band data, followed by another byte of normal data. There are no pauses between each output operation.

Figure 24.9 is the receiving program. This program does not use the SIGURG signal or select. Instead, it calls sockatmark to determine when the out-of-band byte is encountered.

oob/tcpsend04.c

```
 1 #include    "unp.h"

 2 int
 3 main(int argc, char **argv)
 4 {
 5     int     sockfd;

 6     if (argc != 3)
 7         err_quit("usage: tcpsend04 <host> <port#>");

 8     sockfd = Tcp_connect(argv[1], argv[2]);

 9     Write(sockfd, "123", 3);
10     printf("wrote 3 bytes of normal data\n");

11     Send(sockfd, "4", 1, MSG_OOB);
12     printf("wrote 1 byte of OOB data\n");

13     Write(sockfd, "5", 1);
14     printf("wrote 1 byte of normal data\n");

15     exit(0);
16 }
```

oob/tcpsend04.c

Figure 24.8 Sending program.

oob/tcprecv04.c

```
 1 #include    "unp.h"

 2 int
 3 main(int argc, char **argv)
 4 {
 5     int     listenfd, connfd, n, on = 1;
 6     char    buff[100];

 7     if (argc == 2)
 8         listenfd = Tcp_listen(NULL, argv[1], NULL);
 9     else if (argc == 3)
10         listenfd = Tcp_listen(argv[1], argv[2], NULL);
11     else
12         err_quit("usage: tcprecv04 [ <host> ] <port#>");

13     Setsockopt(listenfd, SOL_SOCKET, SO_OOBINLINE, &on, sizeof(on));

14     connfd = Accept(listenfd, NULL, NULL);
15     sleep(5);

16     for ( ; ; ) {
17         if (Sockatmark(connfd))
18             printf("at OOB mark\n");

19         if ( (n = Read(connfd, buff, sizeof(buff) - 1)) == 0) {
20             printf("received EOF\n");
21             exit(0);
22         }
23         buff[n] = 0;                  /* null terminate */
24         printf("read %d bytes: %s\n", n, buff);
25     }
26 }
```

oob/tcprecv04.c

Figure 24.9 Receiving program that calls `sockatmark`.

Set `SO_OOBINLINE` socket option

13   We want to receive the out-of-band data inline, so we must set the `SO_OOBINLINE` socket option. But if we wait until `accept` returns and set the option on the connected socket, the three-way handshake is complete and out-of-band data may have already arrived. Therefore, we must set this option for the listening socket, knowing that all socket options carry over from the listening socket to the connected socket (Section 7.4).

`sleep` after connection accepted

14–15   The receiver sleeps after the connection is accepted to let all the data from the sender be received. This allows us to demonstrate that a `read` stops at the out-of-band mark, even though additional data is in the socket receive buffer.

Read all data from sender

16–25   The program calls `read` in a loop, printing the received data. But before calling `read`, `sockatmark` checks if the buffer pointer is at the out-of-band mark.

When we run this program, we get the following output:

```
freebsd4 % tcprecv04 6666
read 3 bytes: 123
at OOB mark
read 2 bytes: 45
received EOF
```

Even though all the data has been received by the receiving TCP when read is called the first time (because the receiving process calls sleep), only three bytes are returned because the mark is encountered. The next byte read is the out-of-band byte (with a value of 4), because we told the kernel to place the out-of-band data inline.

Example

We now show another simple example to illustrate two additional features of out-of-band data, both of which we mentioned earlier.

1. TCP sends notification of out-of-band data (its urgent pointer), even though it is stopped by flow control from sending data.

2. A receiving process can be notified that the sender has sent out-of-band data (with the SIGURG signal or by select) *before* the out-of-band data arrives. If the process then calls recv specifying MSG_OOB and the out-of-band data has not arrived, an error of EWOULDBLOCK is returned.

Figure 24.10 is the sending program.

9–19   This process sets the size of its socket send buffer to 32,768, writes 16,384 bytes of normal data, and then sleeps for 5 seconds. We will see shortly that the receiver sets the size of its socket receive buffer to 4,096, so these operations by the sender guarantee that the sending TCP fills the receiver's socket receive buffer. The sender then sends 1 byte of out-of-band data, followed by 1,024 bytes of normal data, and terminates.

oob/tcpsend05.c

```
 1 #include    "unp.h"

 2 int
 3 main(int argc, char **argv)
 4 {
 5     int     sockfd, size;
 6     char    buff[16384];

 7     if (argc != 3)
 8         err_quit("usage: tcpsend05 <host> <port#>");

 9     sockfd = Tcp_connect(argv[1], argv[2]);

10     size = 32768;
11     Setsockopt(sockfd, SOL_SOCKET, SO_SNDBUF, &size, sizeof(size));

12     Write(sockfd, buff, 16384);
13     printf("wrote 16384 bytes of normal data\n");
14     sleep(5);

15     Send(sockfd, "a", 1, MSG_OOB);
16     printf("wrote 1 byte of OOB data\n");

17     Write(sockfd, buff, 1024);
18     printf("wrote 1024 bytes of normal data\n");

19     exit(0);
20 }
```

oob/tcpsend05.c

Figure 24.10 Sending program.

Figure 24.11 shows the receiving program.

14–20   The receiving process sets the size of the listening socket's receive buffer to 4,096. This size will carry over to the connected socket after the connection is established. The process then accepts the connection, establishes a signal handler for SIGURG, and establishes the owner of the socket. The main loop calls pause in an infinite loop.

22–31   The signal handler calls recv to read the out-of-band data.

When we start the receiver and then the sender, here is the output from the sender:

```
macosx % tcpsend05 freebsd4 5555
wrote 16384 bytes of normal data
wrote 1 byte of OOB data
wrote 1024 bytes of normal data
```

As expected, all the data fits into the sender's socket send buffer, and then it terminates. Here is the output from the receiver:

```
freebsd4 % tcprecv05 5555
SIGURG received
recv error: Resource temporarily unavailable
```

The error string printed by our err_sys function corresponds to EAGAIN, which is the same as EWOULDBLOCK in FreeBSD. TCP sends the out-of-band notification to the receiving TCP, which then generates the SIGURG signal for the receiving process. But

oob/tcprecv05.c

```
 1 #include     "unp.h"

 2 int     listenfd, connfd;

 3 void    sig_urg(int);

 4 int
 5 main(int argc, char **argv)
 6 {
 7     int     size;

 8     if (argc == 2)
 9         listenfd = Tcp_listen(NULL, argv[1], NULL);
10     else if (argc == 3)
11         listenfd = Tcp_listen(argv[1], argv[2], NULL);
12     else
13         err_quit("usage: tcprecv05 [ <host> ] <port#>");

14     size = 4096;
15     Setsockopt(listenfd, SOL_SOCKET, SO_RCVBUF, &size, sizeof(size));

16     connfd = Accept(listenfd, NULL, NULL);

17     Signal(SIGURG, sig_urg);
18     Fcntl(connfd, F_SETOWN, getpid());

19     for ( ; ; )
20         pause();
21 }

22 void
23 sig_urg(int signo)
24 {
25     int     n;
26     char    buff[2048];

27     printf("SIGURG received\n");
28     n = Recv(connfd, buff, sizeof(buff) - 1, MSG_OOB);
29     buff[n] = 0;                    /* null terminate */
30     printf("read %d OOB byte\n", n);
31 }
```

oob/tcprecv05.c

Figure 24.11 Receiving program.

when recv is called specifying the MSG_OOB flag, the out-of-band byte cannot be read.

The solution is for the receiver to make room in its socket receive buffer by reading the normal data that is available. This will cause its TCP to advertise a nonzero window to the sender, which will eventually let the sender transmit the out-of-band byte.

> We note two related issues in Berkeley-derived implementations (pp. 1016–1017 of TCPv2). First, even if the socket send buffer is full, an out-of-band byte is always accepted by the kernel from the process for sending to the peer. Second, when the process sends an out-of-band byte, a TCP segment is immediately sent that contains the urgent notification. All the normal TCP output checks (Nagle algorithm, silly-window avoidance, etc.) are bypassed.

Example

Our next example demonstrates that there is only a single out-of-band mark for a given TCP connection, and if new out-of-band data arrives before the receiving process reads some existing out-of-band data, the previous mark is lost.

Figure 24.12 is the sending program, which is similar to Figure 24.8 with the addition of another `send` of out-of-band data, followed by one more `write` of normal data.

———————————————————————————————— oob/tcpsend06.c

```
 1 #include    "unp.h"

 2 int
 3 main(int argc, char **argv)
 4 {
 5     int     sockfd;

 6     if (argc != 3)
 7         err_quit("usage: tcpsend06 <host> <port#>");

 8     sockfd = Tcp_connect(argv[1], argv[2]);

 9     Write(sockfd, "123", 3);
10     printf("wrote 3 bytes of normal data\n");

11     Send(sockfd, "4", 1, MSG_OOB);
12     printf("wrote 1 byte of OOB data\n");

13     Write(sockfd, "5", 1);
14     printf("wrote 1 byte of normal data\n");

15     Send(sockfd, "6", 1, MSG_OOB);
16     printf("wrote 1 byte of OOB data\n");

17     Write(sockfd, "7", 1);
18     printf("wrote 1 byte of normal data\n");

19     exit(0);
20 }
```

———————————————————————————————— oob/tcpsend06.c

Figure 24.12 Sending two out-of-band bytes in rapid succession.

There are no pauses in the sending, allowing all the data to be sent to the receiving TCP quickly.

The receiving program is identical to Figure 24.9, which `sleeps` for five seconds after accepting the connection to allow the data to arrive at its TCP. Here is the receiving program's output:

```
freebsd4 % tcprecv06 5555
read 5 bytes: 12345
at OOB mark
read 2 bytes: 67
received EOF
```

The arrival of the second out-of-band byte (the 6) overwrites the mark that was stored when the first out-of-band byte arrived (the 4). As we said, there is at most one out-of-band mark per TCP connection.

24.4   TCP Out-of-Band Data Recap

All our examples using out-of-band data so far have been trivial. Unfortunately, out-of-band data gets messy when we consider the timing problems that may arise. The first point to consider is that the concept of out-of-band data really conveys three different pieces of information to the receiver:

1. The fact that the sender went into urgent mode. The receiving process can be notified of this with either the SIGURG signal or with select. This *notification* is transmitted immediately after the sender sends the out-of-band byte, because we saw in Figure 24.11 that TCP sends the notification even if it is stopped by flow control from sending any data to the receiver. This notification might cause the receiver to go into some special mode of processing for any subsequent data that it receives.

2. The *position* of the out-of-band byte, that is, where it was sent with regard to the rest of data from the sender: the out-of-band mark.

3. The actual *value* of the out-of-band byte. Since TCP is a byte stream protocol that does not interpret the data sent by the application, this can be any 8-bit value.

With TCP's urgent mode, we can think of the URG flag as being the notification, the urgent pointer as being the mark, and the byte of data as itself.

The problems with this concept of out-of-band data are that: (i) there is only one TCP urgent pointer per connection; (ii) there is only one out-of-band mark per connection; and (iii) there is only a single one-byte out-of-band buffer per connection (which is an issue only if the data is not being read inline). We saw with Figure 24.12 that an arriving mark overwrites any previous mark that the process has not yet encountered. If the data is being read inline, previous out-of-band bytes are not lost when new out-of-band data arrives, but the mark is lost.

One common use of out-of-band data is with rlogin, when the client interrupts the program that it is running on the server (pp. 393–394 of TCPv1). The server needs to tell the client to discard all queued output because up to one window's worth of output may be queued to send from the server to the client. The server sends a special byte to the client, telling it to flush all output, and this byte is sent as out-of-band data. When the client receives the SIGURG signal, it just reads from the socket until it encounters the mark, discarding everything up through the mark. (Pages 398–401 of TCPv1 contain an example of this use of out-of-band data, along with the corresponding tcpdump output.) In this scenario, if the server sent multiple out-of-band bytes in quick succession, it wouldn't affect the client, as the client just reads up through the final mark, discarding all the data.

In summary, the usefulness of out-of-band data depends on why it is being used by the application. If the purpose is to tell the peer to discard the normal data up through the mark, then losing an intermediate out-of-band byte and its corresponding mark is of no consequence. But if it is important that no out-of-band bytes be lost, then the data must be received inline. Furthermore, the data bytes that are sent as out-of-band data should be differentiated from normal data since intermediate marks can be overwritten when a new mark is received, effectively mixing out-of-band bytes with the normal data. `telnet`, for example, sends its own commands in the normal stream of data between the client and server, prefixing its commands with a byte of 255. (To send this value as data then requires two successive bytes of 255.) This lets it differentiate its commands from normal user data, but requires that the client and server process each byte of data looking for commands.

24.5 Summary

TCP does not have true out-of-band data. It provides an urgent pointer that is sent in the TCP header to the peer as soon as the sender goes into urgent mode. The receipt of this pointer by the other end of the connection tells that process that the sender has gone into urgent mode, and the pointer points to the final byte of urgent data. But all the data is still subject to TCP's normal flow control.

The sockets API maps TCP's urgent mode into what it calls out-of-band data. The sender goes into urgent mode by specifying the `MSG_OOB` flag in a call to `send`. The final byte of data in this call is considered the out-of-band byte. The receiver is notified when its TCP receives a new urgent pointer by either the `SIGURG` signal, or by an indication from `select` that the socket has an exception condition pending. By default, TCP takes the out-of-band byte out of the normal stream of data and places it into its own one-byte out-of-band buffer that the process reads by calling `recv` with the `MSG_OOB` flag. Alternately, the receiver can set the `SO_OOBINLINE` socket option, in which case, the out-of-band byte is left in the normal stream of data. Regardless of which method is used by the receiver, the socket layer maintains an out-of-band mark in the data stream and will not read through the mark with a single input operation. The receiver determines if it has reached the mark by calling the `sockatmark` function.

Out-of-band data is not heavily used. `telnet` and `rlogin` use it, as does FTP; they all use it to notify the remote end of an exceptional condition (e.g., client interrupt), and the servers discard all input received before the out-of-band mark.

Exercises

24.1   Is there a difference between the single function call

        send(fd, "ab", 2, MSG_OOB);

and the two function calls

        send(fd, "a", 1, MSG_OOB);
        send(fd, "b", 1, MSG_OOB);

24.2   Redo Figure 24.6 to use `poll` instead of `select`.

25

Signal-Driven I/O

25.1 Introduction

When using signal-driven I/O, the kernel notifies us with a signal when something happens on a descriptor. Historically, this has been called *asynchronous I/O*, but the signal-driven I/O that we will describe is not true asynchronous I/O. The latter is normally defined as the process performing the I/O operation (say a read or write), with the kernel returning immediately after the kernel initiates the I/O operation. The process continues executing while the I/O takes place. Some form of notification is then provided to the process when the operation is complete or encounters an error. We compared the various types of I/O that are normally available in Section 6.2 and showed the difference between signal-driven I/O and asynchronous I/O.

The nonblocking I/O we described in Chapter 16 is not asynchronous I/O either. With nonblocking I/O, the kernel does not return after initiating the I/O operation; the kernel returns immediately only if the operation cannot be completed without putting the process to sleep.

> POSIX provides true asynchronous I/O with its `aio_XXX` functions. These functions let the process specify whether or not a signal is generated when the I/O completes, and which signal to generate.

Berkeley-derived implementations support signal-driven I/O for sockets and terminal devices using the `SIGIO` signal. SVR4 supports signal-driven I/O for STREAMS devices using the `SIGPOLL` signal, which is then equated to `SIGIO`.

25.2 Signal-Driven I/O for Sockets

To use signal-driven I/O with a socket (SIGIO) requires the process to perform the following three steps:

1. A signal handler must be established for the SIGIO signal.

2. The socket owner must be set, normally with the F_SETOWN command of fcntl (Figure 7.20).

3. Signal-driven I/O must be enabled for the socket, normally with the F_SETFL command of fcntl to turn on the O_ASYNC flag (Figure 7.20).

> The O_ASYNC flag is a relatively late addition to the POSIX specification. Very few systems have implemented support for the flag. In Figure 25.4, we will enable signal-driven I/O with the FIOASYNC ioctl instead. Notice the bad choice of names by POSIX: The name O_SIGIO would have been a better choice for the new flag.

> We should establish the signal handler *before* setting the owner of the socket. Under Berkeley-derived implementations, the order of the two function calls does not matter because the default action is to ignore SIGIO. Therefore, if we were to reverse the order of the two function calls, there is a small chance that a signal could be generated after the call to fcntl but before the call to signal; if that happens, the signal is just discarded. Under SVR4, however, SIGIO is defined to be SIGPOLL in the <sys/signal.h> header and the default action of SIGPOLL is to terminate the process. Therefore, under SVR4, we want to be certain the signal handler is installed before setting the owner of the socket.

Although setting a socket for signal-driven I/O is easy, the hard part is determining what conditions cause SIGIO to be generated for the socket owner. This depends on the underlying protocol.

SIGIO with UDP Sockets

Using signal-driven I/O with UDP is simple. The signal is generated whenever

- A datagram arrives for the socket
- An asynchronous error occurs on the socket

Hence, when we catch SIGIO for a UDP socket, we call recvfrom to either read the datagram that arrived or to obtain the asynchronous error. We talked about asynchronous errors with regard to UDP sockets in Section 8.9. Recall that these are generated only if the UDP socket is connected.

> SIGIO is generated for these two conditions by the calls to sorwakeup on pp. 775, 779, and 784 of TCPv2.

SIGIO with TCP Sockets

Unfortunately, signal-driven I/O is next to useless with a TCP socket. The problem is that the signal is generated too often, and the occurrence of the signal does not tell us what happened. As noted on p. 439 of TCPv2, the following conditions all cause `SIGIO` to be generated for a TCP socket (assuming signal-driven I/O is enabled):

- A connection request has completed on a listening socket
- A disconnect request has been initiated
- A disconnect request has completed
- Half of a connection has been shut down
- Data has arrived on a socket
- Data has been sent from a socket (i.e., the output buffer has free space)
- An asynchronous error occurred

For example, if one is both reading from and writing to a TCP socket, `SIGIO` is generated when new data arrives and when data previously written is acknowledged, and there is no way to distinguish between the two in the signal handler. If `SIGIO` is used in this scenario, the TCP socket should be set to nonblocking to prevent a `read` or `write` from blocking. We should consider using `SIGIO` only with a listening TCP socket, because the only condition that generates `SIGIO` for a listening socket is the completion of a new connection.

The only real-world use of signal-driven I/O with sockets that the authors were able to find is the NTP server, which uses UDP. The main loop of the server receives a datagram from a client and sends a response. But, there is a non-negligible amount of processing to do for each client's request (more than our trivial echo server). It is important for the server to record accurate timestamps for each received datagram, since that value is returned to the client and then used by the client to calculate the RTT to the server. Figure 25.1 shows two ways to build such a UDP server.

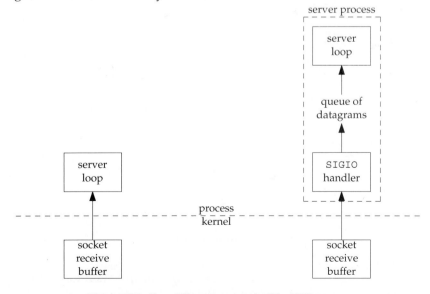

Figure 25.1 Two different ways to build a UDP server.

Most UDP servers (including our echo server from Chapter 8) are designed as shown at the left of this figure. But the NTP server uses the technique shown on the right side: When a new datagram arrives, it is read by the SIGIO handler, which also records the time at which the datagram arrived. The datagram is then placed on another queue within the process from which it will be removed by and processed by the main server loop. Although this complicates the server code, it provides accurate timestamps of arriving datagrams.

> Recall from Figure 22.4 that the process can set the IP_RECVDSTADDR socket option to receive the destination address of a received UDP datagram. One could argue that two additional pieces of information that should also be returned for a received UDP datagram are an indication of the received interface (which can differ from the destination address, if the host employs the common weak end system model) and the time at which the datagram arrived.

> For IPv6, the IPV6_PKTINFO socket option (Section 22.8) returns the received interface. For IPv4, we discussed the IP_RECVIF socket option in Section 22.2.

> FreeBSD also provides the SO_TIMESTAMP socket option, which returns the time at which the datagram was received as ancillary data in a timeval structure. Linux provides an SIOCGSTAMP ioctl that returns a timeval structure containing the time at which the datagram was received.

25.3 UDP Echo Server Using SIGIO

We now provide an example similar to the right side of Figure 25.1: a UDP server that uses the SIGIO signal to receive arriving datagrams. This example also illustrates the use of POSIX reliable signals.

We do not change the client at all from Figures 8.7 and 8.8, and the server main function does not change from Figure 8.3. The only changes that we make are to the dg_echo function, which we show in the next four figures. Figure 25.2 shows the global declarations.

Queue of received datagrams

3–12   The SIGIO signal handler places arriving datagrams onto a queue. This queue is an array of DG structures that we treat as a circular buffer. Each structure contains a pointer to the received datagram, its length, a pointer to a socket address structure containing the protocol address of the client, and the size of the protocol address. QSIZE of these structures are allocated, and we will see in Figure 25.4 that the dg_echo function calls malloc to allocate memory for all the datagrams and socket address structures. We also allocate a diagnostic counter, cntread, that we will examine shortly. Figure 25.3 shows the array of structures, assuming the first entry points to a 150-byte datagram and the length of its associated socket address structure is 16.

Array indexes

13–15   iget is the index of the next array entry for the main loop to process, and iput is the index of the next array entry for the signal handler to store into. nqueue is the total number of datagrams on the queue for the main loop to process.

sigio/dgecho01.c

```
 1 #include    "unp.h"

 2 static int sockfd;

 3 #define QSIZE     8              /* size of input queue */
 4 #define MAXDG   4096             /* max datagram size */
 5 typedef struct {
 6     void   *dg_data;            /* ptr to actual datagram */
 7     size_t  dg_len;             /* length of datagram */
 8     struct sockaddr *dg_sa;     /* ptr to sockaddr{} w/client's address */
 9     socklen_t dg_salen;         /* length of sockaddr{} */
10 } DG;
11 static DG dg[QSIZE];            /* queue of datagrams to process */
12 static long cntread[QSIZE + 1]; /* diagnostic counter */

13 static int iget;               /* next one for main loop to process */
14 static int iput;               /* next one for signal handler to read into */
15 static int nqueue;             /* # on queue for main loop to process */
16 static socklen_t clilen;       /* max length of sockaddr{} */

17 static void sig_io(int);
18 static void sig_hup(int);
```

sigio/dgecho01.c

Figure 25.2 Global declarations.

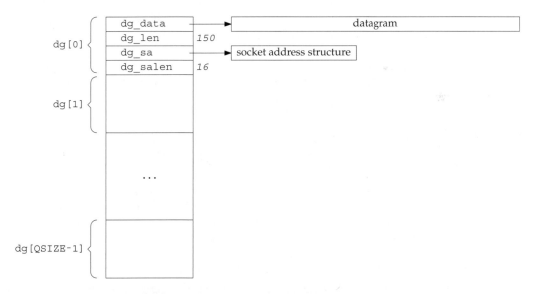

Figure 25.3 Data structures used to hold received datagrams and their socket address structures.

Figure 25.4 shows the main server loop, the dg_echo function.

```
                                                                ─── sigio/dgecho01.c
19 void
20 dg_echo(int sockfd_arg, SA *pcliaddr, socklen_t clilen_arg)
21 {
22     int     i;
23     const int on = 1;
24     sigset_t zeromask, newmask, oldmask;

25     sockfd = sockfd_arg;
26     clilen = clilen_arg;

27     for (i = 0; i < QSIZE; i++) {    /* init queue of buffers */
28         dg[i].dg_data = Malloc(MAXDG);
29         dg[i].dg_sa = Malloc(clilen);
30         dg[i].dg_salen = clilen;
31     }
32     iget = iput = nqueue = 0;

33     Signal(SIGHUP, sig_hup);
34     Signal(SIGIO, sig_io);
35     Fcntl(sockfd, F_SETOWN, getpid());
36     Ioctl(sockfd, FIOASYNC, &on);
37     Ioctl(sockfd, FIONBIO, &on);

38     Sigemptyset(&zeromask);       /* init three signal sets */
39     Sigemptyset(&oldmask);
40     Sigemptyset(&newmask);
41     Sigaddset(&newmask, SIGIO);   /* signal we want to block */

42     Sigprocmask(SIG_BLOCK, &newmask, &oldmask);
43     for ( ; ; ) {
44         while (nqueue == 0)
45             sigsuspend(&zeromask);   /* wait for datagram to process */

46             /* unblock SIGIO */
47         Sigprocmask(SIG_SETMASK, &oldmask, NULL);

48         Sendto(sockfd, dg[iget].dg_data, dg[iget].dg_len, 0,
49                 dg[iget].dg_sa, dg[iget].dg_salen);

50         if (++iget >= QSIZE)
51             iget = 0;

52             /* block SIGIO */
53         Sigprocmask(SIG_BLOCK, &newmask, &oldmask);
54         nqueue--;
55     }
56 }
                                                                ─── sigio/dgecho01.c
```

Figure 25.4 dg_echo function: server main processing loop.

Initialize queue of received datagrams

27–32   The socket descriptor is saved in a global variable since the signal handler needs it.
The queue of received datagrams is initialized.

Establish signal handlers and set socket flags

33–37   Signal handlers are established for `SIGHUP` (which we use for diagnostic purposes) and `SIGIO`. The socket owner is set using `fcntl` and the signal-driven and non-blocking I/O flags are set using `ioctl`.

> We mentioned earlier that the `O_ASYNC` flag with `fcntl` is the POSIX way to specify signal-driven I/O, but since most systems do not yet support it, we use `ioctl` instead. While most systems do support the `O_NONBLOCK` flag to set nonblocking, we show the `ioctl` method here.

Initialize signal sets

38–41   Three signal sets are initialized: `zeromask` (which never changes), `oldmask` (which contains the old signal mask when we block `SIGIO`), and `newmask`. `sigaddset` turns on the bit corresponding to `SIGIO` in `newmask`.

Block `SIGIO` and wait for something to do

42–45   `sigprocmask` stores the current signal mask of the process in `oldmask` and then logically ORs `newmask` into the current signal mask. This blocks `SIGIO` and returns the current signal mask. We then enter the `for` loop and test the `nqueue` counter. As long as this counter is 0, there is nothing to do and we can call `sigsuspend`. This POSIX function saves the current signal mask internally and then sets the current signal mask to the argument (`zeromask`). Since `zeromask` is an empty signal set, this enables all signals. `sigsuspend` returns after a signal has been caught and the signal handler returns. (It is an unusual function because it *always* returns an error, `EINTR`.) Before returning, `sigsuspend` always sets the signal mask to its value when the function was called, which in this case is the value of `newmask`, so we are guaranteed that when `sigsuspend` returns, `SIGIO` is blocked. That is why we can test the counter `nqueue`, knowing that while we are testing it, a `SIGIO` signal cannot be delivered.

> Consider what would happen if `SIGIO` was not blocked while we tested the variable `nqueue`, which is shared between the main loop and the signal handler. We could test `nqueue` and find it 0, but immediately after this test, the signal is delivered and `nqueue` gets set to 1. We then call `sigsuspend` and go to sleep, effectively missing the signal. We are never awakened from the call to `sigsuspend` unless another signal occurs. This is similar to the race condition we described in Section 20.5.

Unblock `SIGIO` and send reply

46–51   We unblock `SIGIO` by calling `sigprocmask` to set the signal mask of the process to the value that was saved earlier (`oldmask`). The reply is then sent by `sendto`. The `iget` index is incremented, and if its value is the number of elements in the array, its value is set back to 0. We treat the array as a circular buffer. Notice that we do not need `SIGIO` blocked while modifying `iget`, because this index is used only by the main loop; it is never modified by the signal handler.

Block `SIGIO`

52–54   `SIGIO` is blocked and the value of `nqueue` is decremented. We must block the signal while modifying this variable since it is shared between the main loop and the signal handler. Also, we need `SIGIO` blocked when we test `nqueue` at the top of the loop.

An alternate technique is to remove both calls to `sigprocmask` that are within the `for` loop, which avoids unblocking the signal and then blocking it later. The problem, however, is that this executes the entire loop with the signal blocked, which decreases the responsiveness of the signal handler. Datagrams should not get lost because of this change (assuming the socket receive buffer is large enough), but the delivery of the signal to the process will be delayed the entire time that the signal is blocked. One goal when coding applications that perform signal handling should be to block the signal for the minimum amount of time.

Figure 25.5 shows the SIGIO signal handler.

sigio/dgecho01.c
```
57 static void
58 sig_io(int signo)
59 {
60     ssize_t len;
61     int     nread;
62     DG      *ptr;

63     for (nread = 0;;) {
64         if (nqueue >= QSIZE)
65             err_quit("receive overflow");

66         ptr = &dg[iput];
67         ptr->dg_salen = clilen;
68         len = recvfrom(sockfd, ptr->dg_data, MAXDG, 0,
69                        ptr->dg_sa, &ptr->dg_salen);
70         if (len < 0) {
71             if (errno == EWOULDBLOCK)
72                 break;              /* all done; no more queued to read */
73             else
74                 err_sys("recvfrom error");
75         }
76         ptr->dg_len = len;

77         nread++;
78         nqueue++;
79         if (++iput >= QSIZE)
80             iput = 0;

81     }
82     cntread[nread]++;               /* histogram of # datagrams read per signal */
83 }
```
sigio/dgecho01.c

Figure 25.5 SIGIO handler.

The problem that we encounter when coding this signal handler is that POSIX signals are normally *not* queued. This means that, if we are in the signal handler, which guarantees that the signal is blocked, and the signal occurs two more times, the signal is delivered only one more time.

> POSIX provides some real-time signals that *are* queued, but other signals such as SIGIO are normally not queued.

Consider the following scenario: A datagram arrives and the signal is delivered. The signal handler reads the datagram and places it onto the queue for the main loop. But while the signal handler is executing, two more datagrams arrive, causing the signal to be generated two more times. Since the signal is blocked, when the signal handler returns, it is called only one more time. The second time the signal handler executes, it reads the second datagram, but the third datagram is left on the socket receive queue. This third datagram will be read only if and when a fourth datagram arrives. When a fourth datagram arrives, it is the third datagram that is read and placed on the queue for the main loop, not the fourth one.

Because signals are not queued, the descriptor that is set for signal-driven I/O is normally set to nonblocking also. We then code our SIGIO handler to read in a loop, terminating only when the read returns EWOULDBLOCK.

Check for queue overflow

64–65   If the queue is full, we terminate. There are other ways to handle this (e.g., additional buffers could be allocated), but for our simple example, we just terminate.

Read datagram

66–76   recvfrom is called on the nonblocking socket. The array entry indexed by iput is where the datagram is stored. If there are no datagrams to read, break jumps out of the for loop.

Increment counters and index

77–80   nread is a diagnostic counter of the number of datagrams read per signal. nqueue is the number of datagrams for the main loop to process.

82   Before the signal handler returns, it increments the counter corresponding to the number of datagrams read per signal. We print this array in Figure 25.6 when the SIGHUP signal is delivered as diagnostic information.

The final function (Figure 25.6) is the SIGHUP signal handler, which prints the cntread array. This counts the number of datagrams read per signal.

—————————————————————— sigio/dgecho01.c
```
84 static void
85 sig_hup(int signo)
86 {
87     int     i;

88     for (i = 0; i <= QSIZE; i++)
89         printf("cntread[%d] = %ld\n", i, cntread[i]);
90 }
```
—————————————————————— sigio/dgecho01.c

Figure 25.6 SIGHUP handler.

To illustrate that signals are not queued and that we must set the socket to nonblocking in addition to setting the signal-driven I/O flag, we will run this server with six clients simultaneously. Each client sends 3,645 lines for the server to echo, and each client is started from a shell script in the background so that all clients are started at about the same time. When all the clients have terminated, we send the SIGHUP signal to the server, causing it to print its cntread array.

```
linux % udpserv01
cntread[0]  =  0
cntread[1]  =  15899
cntread[2]  =  2099
cntread[3]  =  515
cntread[4]  =  57
cntread[5]  =  0
cntread[6]  =  0
cntread[7]  =  0
cntread[8]  =  0
```

Most of the time, the signal handler reads only one datagram, but there are times when more than one is ready. The nonzero counter for cntread[0] is when the signal is generated while the signal handler is executing, but before the signal handler returns, it reads all pending datagrams. When the signal handler is called again, there are no datagrams left to read. Finally, we can verify that the weighted sum of the array elements $(15899 \times 1 + 2099 \times 2 + 515 \times 3 + 57 \times 4 = 21870)$ equals 6 (the number of clients) times 3,645 lines per client.

25.4 Summary

Signal-driven I/O has the kernel notify us with the SIGIO signal when "something" happens on a socket.

- With a connected TCP socket, numerous conditions can cause this notification, making this feature of little use.

- With a listening TCP socket, this notification occurs when a new connection is ready to be accepted.

- With UDP, this notification means either a datagram has arrived or an asynchronous error has arrived; in both cases, we call recvfrom.

We modified our UDP echo server to use signal-driven I/O, using a technique similar to that used by NTP: read a datagram as soon as possible after it arrives to obtain an accurate timestamp for its arrival and then queue it for later processing.

Exercises

25.1   An alternate design for the loop in Figure 25.4 is the following:

```
for ( ; ; ) {
    Sigprocmask(SIG_BLOCK, &newmask, &oldmask);
    while (nqueue == 0)
        sigsuspend(&zeromask);  /* wait for datagram to process */
    nqueue--;

        /* unblock SIGGIO */
    Sigprocmask(SIG_SETMASK, &oldmask, NULL);

    Sendto(sockfd, dg[iget].dg_data, dg[iget].dg_len, 0,
            dg[iget].dg_sa, dg[iget].dg_salen);

    if (++iget >= QSIZE)
        iget = 0;
}
```

Is this modification acceptable?

26

Threads

26.1 Introduction

In the traditional Unix model, when a process needs something performed by another entity, it forks a child process and lets the child perform the processing. Most network servers under Unix are written this way, as we have seen in our concurrent server examples: The parent accepts the connection, forks a child, and the child handles the client.

While this paradigm has served well for many years, there are problems with fork:

- fork is expensive. Memory is copied from the parent to the child, all descriptors are duplicated in the child, and so on. Current implementations use a technique called *copy-on-write*, which avoids a copy of the parent's data space to the child until the child needs its own copy. But, regardless of this optimization, fork is expensive.

- IPC is required to pass information between the parent and child *after* the fork. Passing information from the parent to the child *before* the fork is easy, since the child starts with a copy of the parent's data space and with a copy of all the parent's descriptors. But, returning information from the child to the parent takes more work.

Threads help with both problems. Threads are sometimes called *lightweight processes* since a thread is "lighter weight" than a process. That is, thread creation can be 10–100 times faster than process creation.

All threads within a process share the same global memory. This makes the sharing of information easy between the threads, but along with this simplicity comes the problem of *synchronization*.

More than just the global variables are shared. All threads within a process share the following:

- Process instructions
- Most data
- Open files (e.g., descriptors)
- Signal handlers and signal dispositions
- Current working directory
- User and group IDs

But each thread has its own

- Thread ID
- Set of registers, including program counter and stack pointer
- Stack (for local variables and return addresses)
- `errno`
- Signal mask
- Priority

> One analogy is to think of signal handlers as a type of thread as we discussed in Section 11.18. That is, in the traditional Unix model, we have the main flow of execution (one thread) and a signal handler (another thread). If the main flow is in the middle of updating a linked list when a signal occurs, and the signal handler also tries to update the linked list, havoc normally results. The main flow and signal handler share the same global variables, but each has its own stack.

In this text, we cover POSIX threads, also called *Pthreads*. These were standardized in 1995 as part of the POSIX.1c standard and most versions of Unix will support them in the future. We will see that all the Pthread functions begin with `pthread_`. This chapter is an introduction to threads, so that we can use threads in our network programs. For additional details see [Butenhof 1997].

26.2   Basic Thread Functions: Creation and Termination

In this section, we will cover five basic thread functions and then use these in the next two sections to recode our TCP client/server using threads instead of `fork`.

`pthread_create` Function

When a program is started by `exec`, a single thread is created, called the *initial thread* or *main thread*. Additional threads are created by `pthread_create`.

```
#include <pthread.h>

int pthread_create(pthread_t *tid, const pthread_attr_t *attr,
                   void *(*func)(void *), void *arg);
```

Returns: 0 if OK, positive E*xxx* value on error

Each thread within a process is identified by a *thread ID*, whose datatype is `pthread_t` (often an `unsigned int`). On successful creation of a new thread, its ID is returned through the pointer *tid*.

Each thread has numerous *attributes*: its priority, its initial stack size, whether it should be a daemon thread or not, and so on. When a thread is created, we can specify these attributes by initializing a `pthread_attr_t` variable that overrides the default. We normally take the default, in which case, we specify the *attr* argument as a null pointer.

Finally, when we create a thread, we specify a function for it to execute. The thread starts by calling this function and then terminates either explicitly (by calling `pthread_exit`) or implicitly (by letting the function return). The address of the function is specified as the *func* argument, and this function is called with a single pointer argument, *arg*. If we need multiple arguments to the function, we must package them into a structure and then pass the address of this structure as the single argument to the start function.

Notice the declarations of *func* and *arg*. The function takes one argument, a generic pointer (`void *`), and returns a generic pointer (`void *`). This lets us pass one pointer (to anything we want) to the thread, and lets the thread return one pointer (again, to anything we want).

The return value from the Pthread functions is normally 0 if successful or nonzero on an error. But unlike the socket functions, and most system calls, which return −1 on an error and set `errno` to a positive value, the Pthread functions return the positive error indication as the function's return value. For example, if `pthread_create` cannot create a new thread because of exceeding some system limit on the number of threads, the function return value is `EAGAIN`. The Pthread functions do not set `errno`. The convention of 0 for success or nonzero for an error is fine since all the E*xxx* values in `<sys/errno.h>` are positive. A value of 0 is never assigned to one of the E*xxx* names.

`pthread_join` Function

We can wait for a given thread to terminate by calling `pthread_join`. Comparing threads to Unix processes, `pthread_create` is similar to `fork`, and `pthread_join` is similar to `waitpid`.

```
#include <pthread.h>

int pthread_join(pthread_t tid, void **status);
```

Returns: 0 if OK, positive E*xxx* value on error

We must specify the *tid* of the thread that we want to wait for. Unfortunately, there is no way to wait for any of our threads (similar to `waitpid` with a process ID argument of −1). We will return to this problem when we discuss Figure 26.14.

If the *status* pointer is non-null, the return value from the thread (a pointer to some object) is stored in the location pointed to by *status*.

pthread_self Function

Each thread has an ID that identifies it within a given process. The thread ID is returned by `pthread_create` and we saw it was used by `pthread_join`. A thread fetches this value for itself using `pthread_self`.

```
#include <pthread.h>

pthread_t pthread_self(void);
```
                                                        Returns: thread ID of calling thread

Comparing threads to Unix processes, `pthread_self` is similar to `getpid`.

pthread_detach Function

A thread is either *joinable* (the default) or *detached*. When a joinable thread terminates, its thread ID and exit status are retained until another thread calls `pthread_join`. But a detached thread is like a daemon process: When it terminates, all its resources are released and we cannot wait for it to terminate. If one thread needs to know when another thread terminates, it is best to leave the thread as joinable.

The `pthread_detach` function changes the specified thread so that it is detached.

```
#include <pthread.h>

int pthread_detach(pthread_t tid);
```
                                                Returns: 0 if OK, positive Exxx value on error

This function is commonly called by the thread that wants to detach itself, as in

```
pthread_detach(pthread_self());
```

pthread_exit Function

One way for a thread to terminate is to call `pthread_exit`.

```
#include <pthread.h>

void pthread_exit(void *status);
```
                                                                    Does not return to caller

If the thread is not detached, its thread ID and exit status are retained for a later pthread_join by some other thread in the calling process.

The pointer *status* must not point to an object that is local to the calling thread since that object disappears when the thread terminates.

There are two other ways for a thread to terminate:

- The function that started the thread (the third argument to pthread_create) can return. Since this function must be declared as returning a void pointer, that return value is the exit status of the thread.

- If the main function of the process returns or if any thread calls exit, the process terminates, including any threads.

26.3 str_cli Function Using Threads

Our first example using threads is to recode the str_cli function from Figure 16.10, which uses fork, to use threads. Recall that we have provided numerous other versions of this function: The original in Figure 5.5 used a stop-and-wait protocol, which we showed was far from optimal for batch input; Figure 6.13 used blocking I/O and the select function; and the version starting with Figure 16.3 used nonblocking I/O. Figure 26.1 shows the design of our threads version.

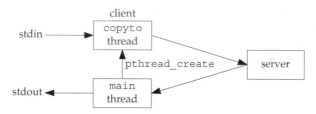

Figure 26.1 Recoding str_cli to use threads.

Figure 26.2 shows the str_cli function using threads.

unpthread.h header

1   This is the first time we have encountered the unpthread.h header. It includes our normal unp.h header, followed by the POSIX <pthread.h> header, and then defines the function prototypes for our wrapper versions of the pthread_*XXX* functions (Section 1.4), which all begin with Pthread_.

Save arguments in externals

10–11   The thread that we are about to create needs the values of the two arguments to str_cli: fp, the standard I/O FILE pointer for the input file, and sockfd, the TCP socket connected to the server. For simplicity, we store these two values in external variables. An alternative technique is to put the two values into a structure and then pass a pointer to the structure as the argument to the thread we are about to create.

———————————————————————————————— *threads/strclithread.c*

```
 1 #include    "unpthread.h"

 2 void    *copyto(void *);

 3 static int sockfd;                      /* global for both threads to access */
 4 static FILE *fp;

 5 void
 6 str_cli(FILE *fp_arg, int sockfd_arg)
 7 {
 8      char    recvline[MAXLINE];
 9      pthread_t tid;

10      sockfd = sockfd_arg;           /* copy arguments to externals */
11      fp = fp_arg;

12      Pthread_create(&tid, NULL, copyto, NULL);

13      while (Readline(sockfd, recvline, MAXLINE) > 0)
14          Fputs(recvline, stdout);
15 }

16 void *
17 copyto(void *arg)
18 {
19      char    sendline[MAXLINE];

20      while (Fgets(sendline, MAXLINE, fp) != NULL)
21          Writen(sockfd, sendline, strlen(sendline));

22      Shutdown(sockfd, SHUT_WR);   /* EOF on stdin, send FIN */

23      return (NULL);
24          /* return (i.e., thread terminates) when EOF on stdin */
25 }
```

———————————————————————————————— *threads/strclithread.c*

Figure 26.2 str_cli function using threads.

Create new thread

12   The thread is created and the new thread ID is saved in tid. The function executed by the new thread is copyto. No arguments are passed to the thread.

Main thread loop: copy socket to standard output

13–14   The main thread calls readline and fputs, copying from the socket to the standard output.

Terminate

15   When the str_cli function returns, the main function terminates by calling exit (Section 5.4). When this happens, *all* threads in the process are terminated. Normally, the copyto thread will have already terminated by the time the server's main function completes. But in the case where the server terminates prematurely (Section 5.12), calling exit when the server's main function completes will terminate the copyto thread, which is what we want.

`copyto` thread

16-25   This thread just copies from standard input to the socket. When it reads an EOF on standard input, a FIN is sent across the socket by `shutdown` and the thread returns. The `return` from this function (which started the thread) terminates the thread.

At the end of Section 16.2, we provided measurements for the five different implementation techniques that we have used with our `str_cli` function. The threads version we just presented took 8.5 seconds, which is slightly faster than the version using `fork` (which we expect), but slower than the nonblocking I/O version. Nevertheless, comparing the complexity of the nonblocking I/O version (Section 16.2) versus the simplicity of the threads version, we still recommend using threads instead of nonblocking I/O.

26.4   TCP Echo Server Using Threads

We now redo our TCP echo server from Figure 5.2 using one thread per client instead of one child process per client. We also make it protocol-independent, using our `tcp_listen` function. Figure 26.3 shows the server.

Create thread

17-21   When `accept` returns, we call `pthread_create` instead of `fork`. The single argument that we pass to the `doit` function is the connected socket descriptor, `connfd`.

> We cast the integer descriptor `connfd` to be a `void` pointer. ANSI C does not guarantee that this works. It works only on systems on which the size of an integer is less than or equal to the size of a pointer. Fortunately, most Unix implementations have this property (Figure 1.17). We will talk more about this shortly.

Thread function

23-30   `doit` is the function executed by the thread. The thread detaches itself since there is no reason for the main thread to wait for each thread it creates. The function `str_echo` does not change from Figure 5.3. When this function returns, we must `close` the connected socket since the thread shares all descriptors with the main thread. With `fork`, the child did not need to `close` the connected socket because when the child terminated, all open descriptors were closed on process termination (see Exercise 26.2).

Also notice that the main thread does not close the connected socket, which we always did with a concurrent server that calls `fork`. This is because all threads within a process share the descriptors, so if the main thread called `close`, it would terminate the connection. Creating a new thread does not affect the reference counts for open descriptors, which is different from `fork`.

There is a subtle error in this program, which we will describe in detail in Section 26.5. Can you spot the error (see Exercise 26.5)?

threads/tcpserv01.c

```
 1 #include    "unpthread.h"

 2 static void *doit(void *);       /* each thread executes this function */

 3 int
 4 main(int argc, char **argv)
 5 {
 6     int     listenfd, connfd;
 7     pthread_t tid;
 8     socklen_t addrlen, len;
 9     struct sockaddr *cliaddr;

10     if (argc == 2)
11         listenfd = Tcp_listen(NULL, argv[1], &addrlen);
12     else if (argc == 3)
13         listenfd = Tcp_listen(argv[1], argv[2], &addrlen);
14     else
15         err_quit("usage: tcpserv01 [ <host> ] <service or port>");

16     cliaddr = Malloc(addrlen);

17     for ( ; ; ) {
18         len = addrlen;
19         connfd = Accept(listenfd, cliaddr, &len);
20         Pthread_create(&tid, NULL, &doit, (void *) connfd);
21     }
22 }

23 static void *
24 doit(void *arg)
25 {
26     Pthread_detach(pthread_self());
27     str_echo((int) arg);          /* same function as before */
28     Close((int) arg);             /* done with connected socket */
29     return (NULL);
30 }
```

threads/tcpserv01.c

Figure 26.3   TCP echo server using threads (see also Exercise 26.5).

Passing Arguments to New Threads

We mentioned that in Figure 26.3, we cast the integer variable connfd to be a void pointer, but this is not guaranteed to work on all systems. To handle this correctly requires additional work.

First, notice that we cannot just pass the address of connfd to the new thread. That is, the following does not work:

```
int
main(int argc, char **argv)
{
    int     listenfd, connfd;
    ...

    for ( ; ; ) {
        len = addrlen;
        connfd = Accept(listenfd, cliaddr, &len);

        Pthread_create(&tid, NULL, &doit, &connfd);
    }
}
static void *
doit(void *arg)
{
    int   connfd;

    connfd = *((int *) arg);
    Pthread_detach(pthread_self());
    str_echo(connfd);       /* same function as before */
    Close(connfd);          /* done with connected socket */
    return(NULL);
}
```

From an ANSI C perspective this is acceptable: We are guaranteed that we can cast the integer pointer to be a void * and then cast this pointer back to an integer pointer. The problem is what this pointer points to.

There is one integer variable, connfd in the main thread, and each call to accept overwrites this variable with a new value (the connected descriptor). The following scenario can occur:

- accept returns, connfd is stored into (say the new descriptor is 5), and the main thread calls pthread_create. The pointer to connfd (not its contents) is the final argument to pthread_create.
- A thread is created and the doit function is scheduled to start executing.
- Another connection is ready and the main thread runs again (before the newly created thread). accept returns, connfd is stored into (say the new descriptor is now 6), and the main thread calls pthread_create.

Even though two threads are created, both will operate on the final value stored in connfd, which we assume is 6. The problem is that multiple threads are accessing a shared variable (the integer value in connfd) with no synchronization. In Figure 26.3, we solved this problem by passing the *value* of connfd to pthread_create instead of a pointer to the value. This is fine, given the way that C passes integer values to a called function (a copy of the value is pushed onto the stack for the called function).

Figure 26.4 shows a better solution to this problem.

threads/tcpserv02.c

```
 1 #include    "unpthread.h"

 2 static void *doit(void *);        /* each thread executes this function */

 3 int
 4 main(int argc, char **argv)
 5 {
 6     int     listenfd, *iptr;
 7     thread_t tid;
 8     socklen_t addrlen, len;
 9     struct sockaddr *cliaddr;

10     if (argc == 2)
11         listenfd = Tcp_listen(NULL, argv[1], &addrlen);
12     else if (argc == 3)
13         listenfd = Tcp_listen(argv[1], argv[2], &addrlen);
14     else
15         err_quit("usage: tcpserv01 [ <host> ] <service or port>");

16     cliaddr = Malloc(addrlen);

17     for ( ; ; ) {
18         len = addrlen;
19         iptr = Malloc(sizeof(int));
20         *iptr = Accept(listenfd, cliaddr, &len);
21         Pthread_create(&tid, NULL, &doit, iptr);
22     }
23 }

24 static void *
25 doit(void *arg)
26 {
27     int     connfd;

28     connfd = *((int *) arg);
29     free(arg);

30     Pthread_detach(pthread_self());
31     str_echo(connfd);               /* same function as before */
32     Close(connfd);                  /* done with connected socket */
33     return (NULL);
34 }
```

threads/tcpserv02.c

Figure 26.4 TCP echo server using threads with more portable argument passing.

17-22   Each time we call `accept`, we first call `malloc` and allocate space for an integer variable, the connected descriptor. This gives each thread its own copy of the connected descriptor.

28-29   The thread fetches the value of the connected descriptor and then calls `free` to release the memory.

Historically, the `malloc` and `free` functions have been nonre-entrant. That is, calling either function from a signal handler while the main thread is in the middle of one of these two functions has been a recipe for disaster, because of static data structures that are manipulated by these two functions. How can we call these two functions in

Figure 26.4? POSIX requires that these two functions, along with many others, be *thread-safe*. This is normally done by some form of synchronization performed within the library functions that is transparent to us.

Thread-Safe Functions

POSIX.1 requires that all the functions defined by POSIX.1 and by the ANSI C standard be thread-safe, with the exceptions listed in Figure 26.5.

Need not be thread-safe	Must be thread-safe	Comment
asctime	asctime_r	
	ctermid	Thread-safe only if non-null argument
ctime	ctime_r	
getc_unlocked		
getchar_unlocked		
getgrid	getgrid_r	
getgrnam	getgrnam_r	
getlogin	getlogin_r	
getpwnam	getpwnam_r	
getpwuid	getpwuid_r	
gmtime	gmtime_r	
localtime	localtime_r	
putc_unlocked		
putchar_unlocked		
rand	rand_r	
readdir	readdir_r	
strtok	strtok_r	
	tmpnam	Thread-safe only if non-null argument
ttyname	ttyname_r	
gethost*XXX*		
getnet*XXX*		
getproto*XXX*		
getserv*XXX*		
inet_ntoa		

Figure 26.5 Thread-safe functions.

Unfortunately, POSIX says nothing about thread safety with regard to the networking API functions. The last five lines in this table are from Unix 98. We talked about the nonre-entrant property of gethostbyname and gethostbyaddr in Section 11.18. We mentioned that even though some vendors have defined thread-safe versions whose names end in _r, there is no standard for these functions and they should be avoided. All of the nonre-entrant get*XXX* functions were summarized in Figure 11.21.

We see from Figure 26.5 that the common technique for making a function thread-safe is to define a new function whose name ends in _r. Two of the functions are thread-safe only if the caller allocates space for the result and passes that pointer as the argument to the function.

26.5 Thread-Specific Data

When converting existing functions to run in a threads environment, a common problem encountered is due to static variables. A function that keeps state in a private buffer, or one that returns a result in the form of a pointer to a static buffer, is not thread-safe because multiple threads cannot use the buffer to hold different things at the same time. When faced with this problem, there are various solutions:

- Use thread-specific data. This is nontrivial and then converts the function into one that works only on systems with threads support. The advantage to this approach is that the calling sequence does not change and all the changes go into the library function and not the applications that call the function. We show a version of readline that is thread-safe by using thread-specific data later in this section.

- Change the calling sequence so that the caller packages all the arguments into a structure, and also store in that structure the static variables from Figure 3.18. This was also done, and Figure 26.6 shows the new structure and new function prototypes.

```
typedef struct {
    int      read_fd;        /* caller's descriptor to read from */
    char     *read_ptr;      /* caller's buffer to read into */
    size_t   read_maxlen;    /* caller's max # bytes to read */
                      /* next three are used internally by the function */
    int      rl_cnt;         /* initialize to 0 */
    char     *rl_bufptr;     /* initialize to rl_buf */
    char     rl_buf[MAXLINE];
} Rline;

void    readline_rinit(int, void *, size_t, Rline *);
ssize_t readline_r(Rline *);
ssize_t Readline_r(Rline *);
```

Figure 26.6 Data structure and function prototype for re-entrant version of readline.

These new functions can be used on threaded and nonthreaded systems, but all applications that call readline must change.

- Restructure the interface to avoid any static variables so that the function is thread-safe. For the readline example, this would be the equivalent of ignoring the speedups introduced in Figure 3.18 and going back to the older version in Figure 3.17. Since we said the older version was "painfully slow," taking this option is not always viable.

Thread-specific data is a common technique for making an existing function thread-safe. Before describing the Pthread functions that work with thread-specific data, we describe the concept and a *possible* implementation, because the functions appear more complicated than they really are.

Part of the complication in many texts on using threads is that their descriptions of thread-specific data read like the Pthreads standard, talking about key-value pairs and keys being opaque objects. We describe thread-specific data in terms of *indexes* and *pointers* because common implementations use a small integer index for the key, and the value associated with the index is just a pointer to a region that the thread `malloc`s.

Each system supports a limited number of thread-specific data items. POSIX requires this limit be no less than 128 (per process), and we assume this limit in the following example. The system (probably the threads library) maintains one array of structures per process, which we call `Key` structures, as we show in Figure 26.7.

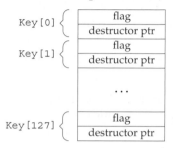

Figure 26.7 Possible implementation of thread-specific data.

The flag in the `Key` structure indicates whether this array element is currently in use, and all the flags are initialized to be "not in use." When a thread calls `pthread_key_create` to create a new thread-specific data item, the system searches through its array of `Key` structures and finds the first one not in use. Its index, 0 through 127, is called the *key*, and this index is returned to the calling thread. We will talk about the "destructor pointer," the other member of the `Key` structure, shortly.

In addition to the process-wide array of `Key` structures, the system maintains numerous pieces of information about each thread within a process. We call this a `Pthread` structure and part of this information is a 128-element array of pointers, which we call the `pkey` array. We show this in Figure 26.8.

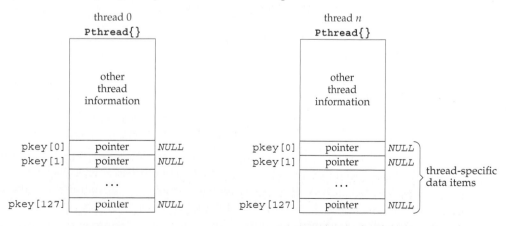

Figure 26.8 Information maintained by the system about each thread.

All entries in the `pkey` array are initialized to null pointers. These 128 pointers are the "values" associated with each of the possible 128 "keys" in the process.

When we create a key with `pthread_key_create`, the system tells us its key (index). Each thread can then store a value (pointer) for the key, and each thread normally obtains the pointer by calling `malloc`. Part of the confusion with thread-specific data is that the pointer is the value in the key-value pair, but the *real* thread-specific data is whatever this pointer points to.

We now go through an example of how thread-specific data is used, assuming that our `readline` function uses thread-specific data to maintain the per-thread state across successive calls to the function. Shortly we will show the code for this, modifying our `readline` function to follow these steps:

1. A process is started and multiple threads are created.

2. One of the threads will be the first to call `readline`, and it in turn calls `pthread_key_create`. The system finds the first unused `Key` structure in Figure 26.7 and returns its index (0–127) to the caller. We assume an index of 1 in this example.

   We will use the `pthread_once` function to guarantee that `pthread_key_create` is called only by the first thread to call `readline`.

3. `readline` calls `pthread_getspecific` to get the `pkey[1]` value (the "pointer" in Figure 26.8 for this key of 1) for this thread, and the returned value is a null pointer. Therefore, `readline` calls `malloc` to allocate the memory that it needs to keep the per-thread information across successive calls to `readline` for this thread. `readline` initializes this memory as needed and calls `pthread_setspecific` to set the thread-specific data pointer (`pkey[1]`) for this key to point to the memory it just allocated. We show this in Figure 26.9, assuming that the calling thread is thread 0 in the process.

   In this figure, we note that the `Pthread` structure is maintained by the system (probably the thread library), but the actual thread-specific data that we `malloc` is maintained by our function (`readline`, in this case). All that `pthread_setspecific` does is set the pointer for this key in the `Pthread` structure to point to our allocated memory. Similarly, all that `pthread_getspecific` does is return that pointer to us.

4. Another thread, say thread *n*, calls `readline`, perhaps while thread 0 is still executing within `readline`.

   `readline` calls `pthread_once` to initialize the key for this thread-specific data item, but since it has already been called, it is not called again.

5. `readline` calls `pthread_getspecific` to fetch the `pkey[1]` pointer for this thread, and a null pointer is returned. This thread then calls `malloc`, followed by `pthread_setspecific`, just like thread 0, initializing its thread-specific data for this key (1). We show this in Figure 26.10.

6. Thread *n* continues executing in `readline`, using and modifying its own thread-specific data.

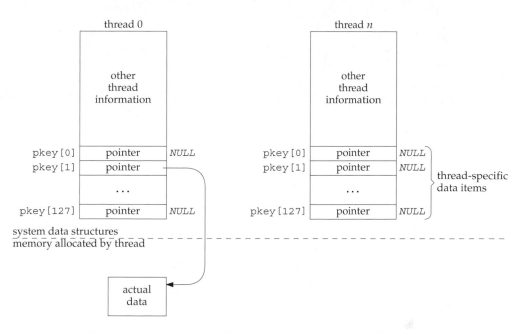

Figure 26.9 Associating `malloced` region with thread-specific data pointer.

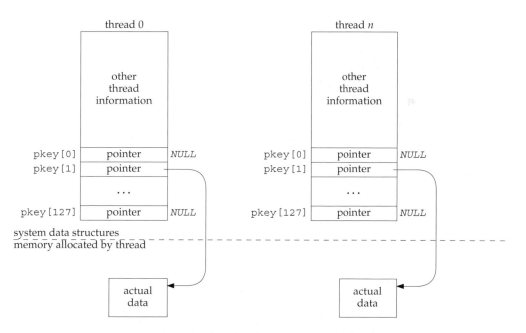

Figure 26.10 Data structures after thread *n* initializes its thread-specific data.

One item we have not addressed is: What happens when a thread terminates? If the thread has called our `readline` function, that function has allocated a region of memory that needs to be freed. This is where the "destructor pointer" from Figure 26.7 is used. When the thread that creates the thread-specific data item calls `pthread_key_create`, one argument to this function is a pointer to a *destructor* function. When a thread terminates, the system goes through that thread's `pkey` array, calling the corresponding destructor function for each non-null `pkey` pointer. What we mean by "corresponding destructor" is the function pointer stored in the `Key` array in Figure 26.7. This is how the thread-specific data is freed when a thread terminates.

The first two functions that are normally called when dealing with thread-specific data are `pthread_once` and `pthread_key_create`.

```
#include <pthread.h>

int pthread_once(pthread_once_t *onceptr, void (*init)(void));

int pthread_key_create(pthread_key_t *keyptr, void (*destructor)(void *value));
```
                                            Both return: 0 if OK, positive E*xx* value on error

`pthread_once` is normally called every time a function that uses thread-specific data is called, but `pthread_once` uses the value in the variable pointed to by *onceptr* to guarantee that the *init* function is called only one time per process.

`pthread_key_create` must be called only one time for a given key within a process. The key is returned through the *keyptr* pointer, and the *destructor* function, if the argument is a non-null pointer, will be called by each thread on termination if that thread has stored a value for this key.

Typical usage of these two functions (ignoring error returns) is as follows:

```
pthread_key_t    rl_key;
pthread_once_t   rl_once = PTHREAD_ONCE_INIT;

void
readline_destructor(void *ptr)
{
    free(ptr);
}

void
readline_once(void)
{
    pthread_key_create(&rl_key, readline_destructor);
}
```

```
ssize_t
readline( ... )
{
    ...

    pthread_once(&rl_once, readline_once);

    if ( (ptr = pthread_getspecific(rl_key)) == NULL) {
        ptr = Malloc( ... );
        pthread_setspecific(rl_key, ptr);
        /* initialize memory pointed to by ptr */
    }
    ...
    /* use values pointed to by ptr */
}
```

Every time `readline` is called, it calls `pthread_once`. This function uses the value pointed to by its *onceptr* argument (the contents of the variable `rl_once`) to make certain that its *init* function is called only one time. This initialization function, `readline_once`, creates the thread-specific data key that is stored in `rl_key`, and which `readline` then uses in calls to `pthread_getspecific` and `pthread_setspecific`.

The `pthread_getspecific` and `pthread_setspecific` functions are used to fetch and store the value associated with a key. This value is what we called the "pointer" in Figure 26.8. What this pointer points to is up to the application, but normally, it points to dynamically allocated memory.

```
#include <pthread.h>

void *pthread_getspecific(pthread_key_t key);
```

                         Returns: pointer to thread-specific data (possibly a null pointer)

```
int pthread_setspecific(pthread_key_t key, const void *value);
```

                         Returns: 0 if OK, positive E*xxx* value on error

---

Notice that the argument to `pthread_key_create` is a pointer to the key (because this function stores the value assigned to the key), while the arguments to the `get` and `set` functions are the key itself (probably a small integer index as discussed earlier).

Example: `readline` Function Using Thread-Specific Data

We now show a complete example of thread-specific data by converting the optimized version of our `readline` function from Figure 3.18 to be thread-safe, without changing the calling sequence.

Figure 26.11 shows the first part of the function: the `pthread_key_t` variable, the `pthread_once_t` variable, the `readline_destructor` function, the `readline_once` function, and our `Rline` structure that contains all the information we must maintain on a per-thread basis.

```
                                                                        threads/readline.c
 1 #include     "unpthread.h"

 2 static pthread_key_t rl_key;
 3 static pthread_once_t rl_once = PTHREAD_ONCE_INIT;

 4 static void
 5 readline_destructor(void *ptr)
 6 {
 7     free(ptr);
 8 }

 9 static void
10 readline_once(void)
11 {
12     Pthread_key_create(&rl_key, readline_destructor);
13 }

14 typedef struct {
15     int     rl_cnt;              /* initialize to 0 */
16     char    *rl_bufptr;          /* initialize to rl_buf */
17     char    rl_buf[MAXLINE];
18 } Rline;
                                                                        threads/readline.c
```

Figure 26.11   First part of thread-safe readline function.

Destructor

4–8   Our destructor function just frees the memory that was allocated for this thread.

One-time function

9–13   We will see that our one-time function is called one time by pthread_once, and it just creates the key that is used by readline.

Rline **structure**

14–18   Our Rline structure contains the three variables that caused the problem by being declared static in Figure 3.18. One of these structures will be dynamically allocated per thread and then released by our destructor function.

Figure 26.12 shows the actual readline function, plus the function my_read it calls. This figure is a modification of Figure 3.18.

my_read **function**

19–35   The first argument to the function is now a pointer to the Rline structure that was allocated for this thread (the actual thread-specific data).

Allocate thread-specific data

42   We first call pthread_once so that the first thread that calls readline in this process calls readline_once to create the thread-specific data key.

Fetch thread-specific data pointer

43–46   pthread_getspecific returns the pointer to the Rline structure for this thread. But if this is the first time this thread has called readline, the return value is a null pointer. In this case, we allocate space for an `Rline` structure and the `rl_cnt` member is initialized to 0 by `calloc`. We then store the pointer for this thread by calling `pthread_setspecific`. The next time this thread calls `readline`, `pthread_getspecific` will return this pointer that was just stored.

threads/readline.c

```
19  static ssize_t
20  my_read(Rline *tsd, int fd, char *ptr)
21  {
22      if (tsd->rl_cnt <= 0) {
23        again:
24          if ( (tsd->rl_cnt = read(fd, tsd->rl_buf, MAXLINE)) < 0) {
25              if (errno == EINTR)
26                  goto again;
27              return (-1);
28          } else if (tsd->rl_cnt == 0)
29              return (0);
30          tsd->rl_bufptr = tsd->rl_buf;
31      }
32      tsd->rl_cnt--;
33      *ptr = *tsd->rl_bufptr++;
34      return (1);
35  }

36  ssize_t
37  readline(int fd, void *vptr, size_t maxlen)
38  {
39      size_t  n, rc;
40      char    c, *ptr;
41      Rline   *tsd;
42      Pthread_once(&rl_once, readline_once);
43      if ( (tsd = pthread_getspecific(rl_key)) == NULL) {
44          tsd = Calloc(1, sizeof(Rline)); /* init to 0 */
45          Pthread_setspecific(rl_key, tsd);
46      }
47      ptr = vptr;
48      for (n = 1; n < maxlen; n++) {
49          if ( (rc = my_read(tsd, fd, &c)) == 1) {
50              *ptr++ = c;
51              if (c == '\n')
52                  break;
53          } else if (rc == 0) {
54              *ptr = 0;
55              return (n - 1);      /* EOF, n - 1 bytes read */
56          } else
57              return (-1);         /* error, errno set by read() */
58      }
59      *ptr = 0;
60      return (n);
61  }
```

threads/readline.c

Figure 26.12 Second part of thread-safe `readline` function.

26.6 Web Client and Simultaneous Connections (Continued)

We now revisit the Web client example from Section 16.5 and recode it using threads instead of nonblocking connects. With threads, we can leave the sockets in their default blocking mode and create one thread per connection. Each thread can block in its call to connect, as the kernel will just run some other thread that is ready.

Figure 26.13 shows the first part of the program, the globals, and the start of the main function.

Globals

1-16   We #include <thread.h>, in addition to the normal <pthread.h>, because we need to use Solaris threads in addition to Pthreads, as we will describe shortly.

10   We have added one member to the file structure: f_tid, the thread ID. The remainder of this code is similar to Figure 16.15. With this threads version, we do not use select and therefore do not need any descriptor sets or the variable maxfd.

36   The home_page function that is called is unchanged from Figure 16.16.

threads/web01.c

```
 1 #include    "unpthread.h"
 2 #include    <thread.h>          /* Solaris threads */

 3 #define MAXFILES    20
 4 #define SERV        "80"        /* port number or service name */

 5 struct file {
 6     char    *f_name;           /* filename */
 7     char    *f_host;           /* hostname or IP address */
 8     int     f_fd;              /* descriptor */
 9     int     f_flags;           /* F_xxx below */
10     pthread_t f_tid;           /* thread ID */
11 } file[MAXFILES];
12 #define F_CONNECTING    1      /* connect() in progress */
13 #define F_READING       2      /* connect() complete; now reading */
14 #define F_DONE          4      /* all done */

15 #define GET_CMD     "GET %s HTTP/1.0\r\n\r\n"

16 int     nconn, nfiles, nlefttoconn, nlefttoread;

17 void    *do_get_read(void *);
18 void    home_page(const char *, const char *);
19 void    write_get_cmd(struct file *);

20 int
21 main(int argc, char **argv)
22 {
23     int     i, n, maxnconn;
24     pthread_t tid;
25     struct file *fptr;

26     if (argc < 5)
27         err_quit("usage: web <#conns> <IPaddr> <homepage> file1 ...");
28     maxnconn = atoi(argv[1]);
```

```
29      nfiles = min(argc - 4, MAXFILES);
30      for (i = 0; i < nfiles; i++) {
31          file[i].f_name = argv[i + 4];
32          file[i].f_host = argv[2];
33          file[i].f_flags = 0;
34      }
35      printf("nfiles = %d\n", nfiles);

36      home_page(argv[2], argv[3]);

37      nlefttoread = nlefttoconn = nfiles;
38      nconn = 0;
```
——————————— threads/web01.c

Figure 26.13 Globals and start of `main` function.

Figure 26.14 shows the main processing loop of the `main` thread.

——————————————————————————————————— threads/web01.c
```
39      while (nlefttoread > 0) {
40          while (nconn < maxnconn && nlefttoconn > 0) {
41                  /* find a file to read */
42              for (i = 0; i < nfiles; i++)
43                  if (file[i].f_flags == 0)
44                      break;
45              if (i == nfiles)
46                  err_quit("nlefttoconn = %d but nothing found", nlefttoconn);

47              file[i].f_flags = F_CONNECTING;
48              Pthread_create(&tid, NULL, &do_get_read, &file[i]);
49              file[i].f_tid = tid;
50              nconn++;
51              nlefttoconn--;
52          }
53          if ( (n = thr_join(0, &tid, (void **) &fptr)) != 0)
54              errno = n, err_sys("thr_join error");

55          nconn--;
56          nlefttoread--;
57          printf("thread id %d for %s done\n", tid, fptr->f_name);
58      }
59      exit(0);
60  }
```
——————————————————————————————————— threads/web01.c

Figure 26.14 Main processing loop of `main` function.

If possible, create another thread

40–52   If we are allowed to create another thread (`nconn` is less than `maxnconn`), we do so. The function that each new thread executes is `do_get_read` and the argument is the pointer to the `file` structure.

Wait for any thread to terminate

53–54   We call the Solaris thread function `thr_join` with a first argument of 0 to wait for any one of our threads to terminate. Unfortunately, Pthreads does not provide a way to wait for *any* one of our threads to terminate; the `pthread_join` function makes us specify exactly which thread we want to wait for. We will see in Section 26.9 that the Pthreads solution for this problem is more complicated, requiring us to use a condition variable for the terminating thread to notify the main thread when it is done.

> The solution that we show, using the Solaris thread `thr_join` function, is not portable to all environments. Nevertheless, we want to show this version of our Web client example using threads without having to complicate the discussion with condition variables and mutexes. Fortunately, we can mix Pthreads with Solaris threads under Solaris.

Figure 26.15 shows the `do_get_read` function, which is executed by each thread. This function establishes the TCP connection, sends an HTTP `GET` command to the server, and reads the server's reply.

```
                                                                          threads/web01.c
61 void *
62 do_get_read(void *vptr)
63 {
64     int     fd, n;
65     char    line[MAXLINE];
66     struct file *fptr;

67     fptr = (struct file *) vptr;

68     fd = Tcp_connect(fptr->f_host, SERV);
69     fptr->f_fd = fd;
70     printf("do_get_read for %s, fd %d, thread %d\n",
71            fptr->f_name, fd, fptr->f_tid);

72     write_get_cmd(fptr);        /* write() the GET command */

73         /* Read server's reply */
74     for ( ; ; ) {
75         if ( (n = Read(fd, line, MAXLINE)) == 0)
76             break;              /* server closed connection */

77         printf("read %d bytes from %s\n", n, fptr->f_name);
78     }
79     printf("end-of-file on %s\n", fptr->f_name);
80     Close(fd);
81     fptr->f_flags = F_DONE;     /* clears F_READING */

82     return (fptr);             /* terminate thread */
83 }
                                                                          threads/web01.c
```

Figure 26.15 `do_get_read` function.

Create TCP socket, establish connection

68–71   A TCP socket is created and a connection is established by our `tcp_connect` function. The socket is a normal blocking socket, so the thread will block in the call to `connect` until the connection is established.

Write request to server

72   write_get_cmd builds the HTTP GET command and sends it to the server. We do not show this function again as the only difference from Figure 16.18 is that the threads version does not call FD_SET and does not use maxfd.

Read server's reply

73–82   The server's reply is then read. When the connection is closed by the server, the F_DONE flag is set and the function returns, terminating the thread.

We also do not show the home_page function, as it is identical to the version shown in Figure 16.16.

We will return to this example, replacing the Solaris thr_join function with the more portable Pthreads solution, but we must first discuss mutexes and condition variables.

26.7 Mutexes: Mutual Exclusion

Notice in Figure 26.14 that when a thread terminates, the main loop decrements both nconn and nlefttoread. We could have placed these two decrements in the function do_get_read, letting each thread decrement these two counters immediately before the thread terminates. But this would be a subtle, yet significant, concurrent programming error.

The problem with placing the code in the function that each thread executes is that these two variables are global, not thread-specific. If one thread is in the middle of decrementing a variable, that thread is suspended, and if another thread executes and decrements the same variable, an error can result. For example, assume that the C compiler turns the decrement operator into three instructions: load from memory into a register, decrement the register, and store from the register into memory. Consider the following possible scenario:

1.   Thread A is running and it loads the value of nconn (3) into a register.
2.   The system switches threads from A to B. A's registers are saved, and B's registers are restored.
3.   Thread B executes the three instructions corresponding to the C expression nconn--, storing the new value of 2.
4.   Sometime later, the system switches threads from B to A. A's registers are restored and A continues where it left off, at the second machine instruction in the three-instruction sequence. The value of the register is decremented from 3 to 2, and the value of 2 is stored in nconn.

The end result is that nconn is 2 when it should be 1. This is wrong.

These types of concurrent programming errors are hard to find for numerous reasons. First, they occur rarely. Nevertheless, it is an error and it will fail (Murphy's

Law). Second, the error is hard to duplicate since it depends on the nondeterministic timing of many events. Lastly, on some systems, the hardware instructions might be atomic; that is, there might be a hardware instruction to decrement an integer in memory (instead of the three-instruction sequence we assumed above) and the hardware cannot be interrupted during this instruction. But, this is not guaranteed by all systems, so the code works on one system but not on another.

We call threads programming *concurrent programming*, or *parallel programming*, since multiple threads can be running concurrently (in parallel), accessing the same variables. While the error scenario we just discussed assumes a single-CPU system, the potential for error also exists if threads A and B are running at the same time on different CPUs on a multiprocessor system. With normal Unix programming, we do not encounter these concurrent programming problems because with `fork`, nothing besides descriptors is shared between the parent and child. We will, however, encounter this same type of problem when we discuss shared memory between processes.

We can easily demonstrate this problem with threads. Figure 26.17 is a simple program that creates two threads and then has each thread increment a global variable 5,000 times.

We exacerbate the potential for a problem by fetching the current value of `counter`, printing the new value, and then storing the new value. If we run this program, we have the output shown in Figure 26.16.

```
4:  1
4:  2
4:  3
4:  4
                        continues as thread 4 executes
4:  517
4:  518
5:  518                 thread 5 now executes
5:  519
5:  520
                        continues as thread 5 executes
5:  926
5:  927
4:  519                 thread 4 now executes; stored value is wrong
4:  520
```

Figure 26.16 Output from program in Figure 26.17.

—————————————————————————— threads/example01.c

```
 1 #include    "unpthread.h"

 2 #define NLOOP 5000

 3 int     counter;               /* incremented by threads */

 4 void    *doit(void *);

 5 int
 6 main(int argc, char **argv)
 7 {
 8     pthread_t tidA, tidB;

 9     Pthread_create(&tidA, NULL, &doit, NULL);
10     Pthread_create(&tidB, NULL, &doit, NULL);

11         /* wait for both threads to terminate */
12     Pthread_join(tidA, NULL);
13     Pthread_join(tidB, NULL);

14     exit(0);
15 }

16 void *
17 doit(void *vptr)
18 {
19     int     i, val;

20     /*
21      * Each thread fetches, prints, and increments the counter NLOOP times.
22      * The value of the counter should increase monotonically.
23      */
24     for (i = 0; i < NLOOP; i++) {
25         val = counter;
26         printf("%d: %d\n", pthread_self(), val + 1);
27         counter = val + 1;
28     }

29     return (NULL);
30 }
```

—————————————————————————— threads/example01.c

Figure 26.17 Two threads that increment a global variable incorrectly.

Notice the error the first time the system switches from thread 4 to thread 5: The value 518 is stored by each thread. This happens numerous times through the 10,000 lines of output.

The nondeterministic nature of this type of problem is also evident if we run the program a few times: Each time, the end result is different from the previous run of the program. Also, if we redirect the output to a disk file, sometimes the error does not occur since the program runs faster, providing fewer opportunities to switch between the threads. The greatest number of errors occurs when we run the program interactively, writing the output to the (slow) terminal, but saving the output in a file using the Unix script program (discussed in detail in Chapter 19 of APUE).

The problem we just discussed, multiple threads updating a shared variable, is the simplest problem. The solution is to protect the shared variable with a *mutex* (which stands for "mutual exclusion") and access the variable only when we hold the mutex. In terms of Pthreads, a mutex is a variable of type `pthread_mutex_t`. We lock and unlock a mutex using the following two functions:

```
#include <pthread.h>

int pthread_mutex_lock(pthread_mutex_t *mptr);

int pthread_mutex_unlock(pthread_mutex_t *mptr);
```

Both return: 0 if OK, positive E*xx* value on error

If we try to lock a mutex that is already locked by some other thread, we are blocked until the mutex is unlocked.

If a mutex variable is statically allocated, we must initialize it to the constant `PTHREAD_MUTEX_INITIALIZER`. We will see in Section 30.8 that if we allocate a mutex in shared memory, we must initialize it at runtime by calling the `pthread_mutex_init` function.

> Some systems (e.g., Solaris) define `PTHREAD_MUTEX_INITIALIZER` to be 0, so omitting this initialization is acceptable, since statically allocated variables are automatically initialized to 0. But there is no guarantee that this is acceptable and other systems (e.g., Digital Unix) define the initializer to be nonzero.

Figure 26.18 is a corrected version of Figure 26.17 that uses a single mutex to lock the counter between the two threads.

threads/example02.c

```
 1 #include     "unpthread.h"

 2 #define NLOOP 5000

 3 int     counter;                    /* incremented by threads */
 4 pthread_mutex_t counter_mutex = PTHREAD_MUTEX_INITIALIZER;

 5 void    *doit(void *);

 6 int
 7 main(int argc, char **argv)
 8 {
 9     pthread_t tidA, tidB;

10     Pthread_create(&tidA, NULL, &doit, NULL);
11     Pthread_create(&tidB, NULL, &doit, NULL);

12         /* wait for both threads to terminate */
13     Pthread_join(tidA, NULL);
14     Pthread_join(tidB, NULL);

15     exit(0);
16 }
```

```
17 void *
18 doit(void *vptr)
19 {
20     int     i, val;

21     /*
22      * Each thread fetches, prints, and increments the counter NLOOP times.
23      * The value of the counter should increase monotonically.
24      */
25     for (i = 0; i < NLOOP; i++) {
26         Pthread_mutex_lock(&counter_mutex);

27         val = counter;
28         printf("%d: %d\n", pthread_self(), val + 1);
29         counter = val + 1;

30         Pthread_mutex_unlock(&counter_mutex);
31     }

32     return (NULL);
33 }
```
—— threads/example02.c

Figure 26.18 Corrected version of Figure 26.17 using a mutex to protect the shared variable.

We declare a mutex named `counter_mutex` and this mutex must be locked by the thread before the thread manipulates the `counter` variable. When we run this program, the output is always correct: The value is incremented monotonically and the final value printed is always 10,000.

How much overhead is involved with mutex locking? The programs in Figures 26.17 and 26.18 were changed to loop 50,000 times and were timed while the output was directed to `/dev/null`. The difference in CPU time from the incorrect version with no mutex to the correct version that used a mutex was 10%. This tells us that mutex locking is not a large overhead.

26.8 Condition Variables

A mutex is fine to prevent simultaneous access to a shared variable, but we need something else to let us go to sleep waiting for some condition to occur. Let's demonstrate this with an example. We return to our Web client in Section 26.6 and replace the Solaris `thr_join` with `pthread_join`. But, we cannot call the Pthread function until we know that a thread has terminated. We first declare a global variable that counts the number of terminated threads and protect it with a mutex.

```
int             ndone;          /* number of terminated threads */
pthread_mutex_t ndone_mutex = PTHREAD_MUTEX_INITIALIZER;
```

We then require that each thread increment this counter when it terminates, being careful to use the associated mutex.

```
void *
do_get_read(void *vptr)
{
    ...

    Pthread_mutex_lock(&ndone_mutex);
    ndone++;
    Pthread_mutex_unlock(&ndone_mutex);

    return(fptr);          /* terminate thread */
}
```

This is fine, but how do we code the main loop? It needs to lock the mutex continually and check if any threads have terminated.

```
while (nlefttoread > 0) {
    while (nconn < maxnconn && nlefttoconn > 0) {
        /* find a file to read */
        ...
    }

        /* See if one of the threads is done */
    Pthread_mutex_lock(&ndone_mutex);
    if (ndone > 0) {
        for (i = 0; i < nfiles; i++) {
            if (file[i].f_flags & F_DONE) {
                Pthread_join(file[i].f_tid, (void **) &fptr);

                /* update file[i] for terminated thread */
                ...
            }
        }
    }
    Pthread_mutex_unlock(&ndone_mutex);
}
```

While this is okay, it means the main loop *never* goes to sleep; it just loops, checking ndone every time around the loop. This is called *polling* and is considered a waste of CPU time.

We want a method for the main loop to go to sleep until one of its threads notifies it that something is ready. A *condition variable*, in conjunction with a mutex, provides this facility. The mutex provides mutual exclusion and the condition variable provides a signaling mechanism.

In terms of Pthreads, a condition variable is a variable of type pthread_cond_t. They are used with the following two functions:

```
#include <pthread.h>

int pthread_cond_wait(pthread_cond_t *cptr, pthread_mutex_t *mptr);

int pthread_cond_signal(pthread_cond_t *cptr);
```

Both return: 0 if OK, positive *Exxx* value on error

The term "signal" in the second function's name does not refer to a Unix SIG*xxx* signal.

An example is the easiest way to explain these functions. Returning to our Web client example, the counter ndone is now associated with both a condition variable and a mutex.

```
int             ndone;
pthread_mutex_t ndone_mutex = PTHREAD_MUTEX_INITIALIZER;
pthread_cond_t  ndone_cond  = PTHREAD_COND_INITIALIZER;
```

A thread notifies the main loop that it is terminating by incrementing the counter while its mutex lock is held and by signaling the condition variable.

```
Pthread_mutex_lock(&ndone_mutex);
ndone++;
Pthread_cond_signal(&ndone_cond);
Pthread_mutex_unlock(&ndone_mutex);
```

The main loop then blocks in a call to pthread_cond_wait, waiting to be signaled by a terminating thread.

```
while (nlefttoread > 0) {
    while (nconn < maxnconn && nlefttoconn > 0) {
            /* find file to read */
        ...
    }

        /* Wait for thread to terminate */
    Pthread_mutex_lock(&ndone_mutex);
    while (ndone == 0)
        Pthread_cond_wait(&ndone_cond, &ndone_mutex);

    for (i = 0; i < nfiles; i++) {
        if (file[i].f_flags & F_DONE) {
            Pthread_join(file[i].f_tid, (void **) &fptr);

            /* update file[i] for terminated thread */
            ...
        }
    }
    Pthread_mutex_unlock(&ndone_mutex);
}
```

Notice that the variable ndone is still checked only while the mutex is held. Then, if there is nothing to do, pthread_cond_wait is called. This puts the calling thread to sleep *and* releases the mutex lock it holds. Furthermore, when the thread returns from pthread_cond_wait (after some other thread has signaled it), the thread again holds the mutex.

Why is a mutex always associated with a condition variable? The "condition" is normally the value of some variable that is shared between the threads. The mutex is required to allow this variable to be set and tested by the different threads. For example, if we did not have the mutex in the example code just shown, the main loop would test it as follows:

```
                           /* Wait for thread to terminate */
                  while (ndone == 0)
                      Pthread_cond_wait(&ndone_cond, &ndone_mutex);
```

But, there is a possibility that the last of the threads increments ndone after the test of ndone == 0, but before the call to pthread_cond_wait. If this happens, this last "signal" is lost and the main loop would block forever, waiting for something that will never occur again.

This is the same reason that pthread_cond_wait must be called with the associated mutex locked, and why this function unlocks the mutex and puts the calling thread to sleep as a single, atomic operation. If this function did not unlock the mutex and then lock it again when it returns, the thread would have to unlock and lock the mutex and the code would look like the following:

```
                           /* Wait for thread to terminate */
                  Pthread_mutex_lock(&ndone_mutex);
                  while (ndone == 0) {
                      Pthread_mutex_unlock(&ndone_mutex);
                      Pthread_cond_wait(&ndone_cond, &ndone_mutex);
                      Pthread_mutex_lock(&ndone_mutex);
                  }
```

But again, there is a possibility that the final thread could terminate and increment the value of ndone between the call to pthread_mutex_unlock and pthread_cond_wait.

Normally, pthread_cond_signal awakens one thread that is waiting on the condition variable. There are instances when a thread knows that multiple threads should be awakened, in which case, pthread_cond_broadcast will wake up *all* threads that are blocked on the condition variable.

```
    #include <pthread.h>

    int pthread_cond_broadcast(pthread_cond_t *cptr);

    int pthread_cond_timedwait(pthread_cond_t *cptr, pthread_mutex_t *mptr,
                               const struct timespec *abstime);
```
                                              Both return: 0 if OK, positive E*xxx* value on error

pthread_cond_timedwait lets a thread place a limit on how long it will block. *abstime* is a timespec structure (as we defined with the pselect function, Section 6.9) that specifies the system time when the function must return, even if the condition variable has not been signaled yet. If this timeout occurs, ETIME is returned.

This time value is an *absolute time*; it is not a *time delta*. That is, *abstime* is the system time—the number of seconds and nanoseconds past January 1, 1970, UTC—when the function should return. This differs from both select and pselect, which specify the number of seconds and microseconds (nanoseconds for pselect) until some time in the future when the function should return. The normal procedure is to call gettimeofday to obtain the current time (as a timeval structure!), and copy this into a timespec structure, adding in the desired time limit. For example,

```
struct timeval  tv;
struct timespec ts;

if (gettimeofday(&tv, NULL) < 0)
    err_sys("gettimeofday error");
ts.tv_sec  = tv.tv_sec + 5;      /* 5 seconds in future */
ts.tv_nsec = tv.tv_usec * 1000;  /* microsec to nanosec */

pthread_cond_timedwait( ... , &ts);
```

The advantage in using an absolute time instead of a delta time is if the function prematurely returns (perhaps because of a caught signal), the function can be called again, without having to change the contents of the timespec structure. The disadvantage, however, is having to call gettimeofday before the function can be called the first time.

> The POSIX specification defines a clock_gettime function that returns the current time as a timespec structure.

26.9 Web Client and Simultaneous Connections (Continued)

We now recode our Web client from Section 26.6, removing the call to the Solaris thr_join function and replacing it with a call to pthread_join. As discussed in that section, we now must specify exactly which thread we are waiting for. To do this we will use a condition variable, as described in Section 26.8.

The only change to the globals (Figure 26.13) is to add one new flag and the condition variable.

```
#define   F_JOINED       8   /* main has pthread_join'ed */

int             ndone;         /* number of terminated threads */
pthread_mutex_t ndone_mutex = PTHREAD_MUTEX_INITIALIZER;
pthread_cond_t  ndone_cond  = PTHREAD_COND_INITIALIZER;
```

The only change to the do_get_read function (Figure 26.15) is to increment ndone and signal the main loop before the thread terminates.

```
        printf("end-of-file on %s\n", fptr->f_name);
        Close(fd);

        Pthread_mutex_lock(&ndone_mutex);
        fptr->f_flags = F_DONE;     /* clears F_READING */
        ndone++;
        Pthread_cond_signal(&ndone_cond);
        Pthread_mutex_unlock(&ndone_mutex);

        return(fptr);       /* terminate thread */
}
```

Most changes are in the main loop, Figure 26.14, the new version of which we show in Figure 26.19.

threads/web03.c

```
43          while (nlefttoread > 0) {
44              while (nconn < maxnconn && nlefttoconn > 0) {
45                      /* find a file to read */
46                  for (i = 0; i < nfiles; i++)
47                      if (file[i].f_flags == 0)
48                          break;
49                  if (i == nfiles)
50                      err_quit("nlefttoconn = %d but nothing found", nlefttoconn);
51                  file[i].f_flags = F_CONNECTING;
52                  Pthread_create(&tid, NULL, &do_get_read, &file[i]);
53                  file[i].f_tid = tid;
54                  nconn++;
55                  nlefttoconn--;
56              }
57                  /* Wait for thread to terminate */
58              Pthread_mutex_lock(&ndone_mutex);
59              while (ndone == 0)
60                  Pthread_cond_wait(&ndone_cond, &ndone_mutex);
61              for (i = 0; i < nfiles; i++) {
62                  if (file[i].f_flags & F_DONE) {
63                      Pthread_join(file[i].f_tid, (void **) &fptr);
64                      if (&file[i] != fptr)
65                          err_quit("file[i] != fptr");
66                      fptr->f_flags = F_JOINED;    /* clears F_DONE */
67                      ndone--;
68                      nconn--;
69                      nlefttoread--;
70                      printf("thread %d for %s done\n", fptr->f_tid, fptr->f_name);
71                  }
72              }
73              Pthread_mutex_unlock(&ndone_mutex);
74          }
75      exit(0);
76  }
```

threads/web03.c

Figure 26.19 Main processing loop of `main` function.

If possible, create another thread

44–56   This code has not changed.

Wait for thread to terminate

57–60   To wait for one of the threads to terminate, we wait for `ndone` to be nonzero. As discussed in Section 26.8, the test must be done while the mutex is locked. The sleep is performed by `pthread_cond_wait`.

Handle terminated thread

61–73   When a thread has terminated, we go through all the `file` structures to find the appropriate thread, call `pthread_join`, and then set the new `F_JOINED` flag.

Figure 16.20 shows the timing for this version, along with the timing of the version using nonblocking `connects`.

26.10 Summary

The creation of a new thread is normally faster than the creation of a new process with `fork`. This alone can be an advantage in heavily used network servers. Threads programming, however, is a new paradigm that requires more discipline.

All threads in a process share global variables and descriptors, allowing this information to be shared between different threads. But this sharing introduces synchronization problems and the Pthread synchronization primitives that we must use are mutexes and condition variables. Synchronization of shared data is a required part of almost every threaded application.

When writing functions that can be called by threaded applications, these functions must be thread-safe. Thread-specific data is one technique that helps with this, and we showed an example with our `readline` function.

We return to the threads model in Chapter 30 with another server design in which the server creates a pool of threads when it starts. An available thread from this pool handles the next client request.

Exercises

26.1   Compare the descriptor usage in a server using `fork` versus a server using a thread, assuming 100 clients are being serviced at the same time.

26.2   What happens in Figure 26.3 if the thread does not `close` the connected socket when `str_echo` returns?

26.3   In Figures 5.5 and 6.13, we print "server terminated prematurely" when we expect an echoed line from the server but receive an EOF instead (recall Section 5.12). Modify Figure 26.2 to print this message too, when appropriate.

26.4   Modify Figures 26.11 and 26.12 so that they can compile on a system that does not support threads.

26.5   To see the error with the `readline` function that is used in Figure 26.3, build that program and start the server. Then, build the TCP echo client from Figure 6.13 that works in a batch mode correctly. Find a large text file on your system and start the client three times in a batch mode, reading from the large text file and writing its output to a temporary file. If possible, run the clients on a different host from the server. If the three clients terminate correctly (often they hang), look at their temporary output files and compare them to the input file.

Now build a version of the server using the correct `readline` function from Section 26.5. Rerun the test with three clients; all three clients should now work. You should also put a `printf` in the `readline_destructor` function, the `readline_once` function, and in the call to `malloc` in `readline`. This shows that the key is created only one time, but the memory is allocated for every thread, and that the destructor function is called for every thread.

27

IP Options

27.1 Introduction

IPv4 allows up to 40 bytes of options to follow the fixed 20-byte header. Although 10 different options are defined, the most commonly used is the source route option. Access to these options is through the IP_OPTIONS socket option and we will demonstrate this with an example that uses source routing.

IPv6 allows extension headers to occur between the fixed 40-byte IPv6 header and the transport-layer header (e.g., ICMPv6, TCP, or UDP). Six different extension headers are currently defined. Unlike the IPv4 approach, access to the IPv6 extension headers is through a functional interface instead of forcing the user to understand the actual details of how the headers appear in the IPv6 packet.

27.2 IPv4 Options

In Figure A.1, we show options following the 20-byte IPv4 header. As noted there, the 4-bit header length field limits the total size of the IPv4 header to 15 32-bit words (60 bytes), so the size of the IP options is limited to 40 bytes. Ten different options are defined for IPv4:

1. NOP: no-operation—A one-byte option typically used for padding to make a later option fall on a four-byte boundary.

2. EOL: end-of-list—A one-byte option that terminates option processing. Since the total size of the IP options must be a multiple of four bytes, EOL bytes follow the final option.

3.   LSRR: loose source and record route (Section 8.5 of TCPv1)—We will show an example of this shortly.

4.   SSRR: strict source and record route (Section 8.5 of TCPv1)—We will show an example of this shortly.

5.   Timestamp (Section 7.4 of TCPv1).

6.   Record route (Section 7.3 of TCPv1).

7.   Basic security (obsolete).

8.   Extended security (obsolete).

9.   Stream identifier (obsolete).

10. Router alert—This option is described in RFC 2113 [Katz 1997]. This option is included in IP datagrams that should be examined by all routers that forward the datagram.

Chapter 9 of TCPv2 provides further details on the kernel processing of the first six options, and the indicated sections in TCPv1 provide examples of their use.

The `getsockopt` and `setsockopt` functions (with a *level* of `IPPROTO_IP` and an *optname* of `IP_OPTIONS`) fetch and set the IP options. The fourth argument to `getsockopt` and `setsockopt` is a pointer to a buffer (whose size is 44 bytes or less), and the fifth argument is the size of this buffer. The reason that the size of this buffer for `getsockopt` can be four bytes larger than the maximum size of the options is because of the way the source route option is handled, as we will describe shortly. Other than the two source route options, the format of what goes into the buffer is the format of the options when placed into the IP datagram.

When the IP options are set using `setsockopt`, the specified options will then be sent on all IP datagrams on that socket. This works for TCP, UDP, and raw IP sockets. To clear these options, call `setsockopt` and specify either a null pointer as the fourth argument or a value of 0 as the fifth argument (the length).

> Setting the IP options for a raw IP socket does not work on all implementations if the `IP_HDRINCL` socket option (which we will describe in the next chapter) is also set. Many Berkeley-derived implementations do not send the options set with `IP_OPTIONS` when `IP_HDRINCL` is enabled, because the application can set its own IP options in the IP header it builds (pp. 1056–1057 of TCPv2). Other systems (e.g., FreeBSD) allow the application to specify IP options using either the `IP_OPTIONS` socket option or by setting `IP_HDRINCL` and including them in the IP header that it builds, but not both.

When `getsockopt` is called to fetch the IP options for a connected TCP socket that was created by `accept`, all that is returned is the reversal of the source route option received with the client's SYN for the listening socket (p. 931 of TCPv2). The source route is automatically reversed by TCP because the source route specified by the client was from the client to the server, but the server needs to use the reverse of this route in datagrams it sends to the client. If no source route accompanied the SYN, then the value-result length returned by `getsockopt` through its fifth argument will be 0. For all other TCP sockets and for all UDP sockets and raw IP sockets, calling `getsockopt` to fetch the IP options just returns a copy of whatever IP options have been set by setsockopt for the socket. Note that for a raw IP socket, the received IP header, including any IP options, is always returned by the input functions, so the received IP options are always available.

> Berkeley-derived kernels have never returned a received source route, or any other IP options, for a UDP socket. The code shown on p. 775 of TCPv2 to return the IP options has existed since 4.3BSD Reno, but has always been commented out since it does not work. This makes it impossible for a UDP application to use the reverse of a received route for datagrams back to the sender.

27.3   IPv4 Source Route Options

A *source route* is a list of IP addresses specified by the sender of the IP datagram. If the source route is *strict*, then the datagram must pass through each listed node and only the listed nodes. That is, all the nodes listed in the source route must be neighbors. But if the source route is *loose*, the datagram must pass through each listed node, but can also pass through other nodes that do not appear in the source route.

> IPv4 source routing is controversial. While it can be very useful for network debugging, it can be used for "source address spoofing" and other types of attacks. [Cheswick, Bellovin, and Rubin 2003] advocate disabling the feature on all your routers, and many organizations and service providers do this. One legitimate use for source routing is to detect asymmetric routes using the traceroute program, as demonstrated on pp. 108–109 of TCPv1, although as more and more routers on the Internet disable source routing, even this use disappears. Nevertheless, specifying and receiving source routes is part of the sockets API and needs to be described.

IPv4 source routes are called *source and record routes* (LSRR for the loose option and SSRR for the strict option), because as a datagram passes through all the listed nodes, each one replaces its listed address with the address of the outgoing interface. This allows the receiver to take this new list and reverse it to follow the reverse path back to the sender. Examples of these two source routes, along with the corresponding tcpdump output, are found in Section 8.5 of TCPv1.

We specify a source route as an array of IPv4 addresses, prefixed by three one-byte fields, as shown in Figure 27.1. This is the format of the buffer that we will pass to setsockopt.

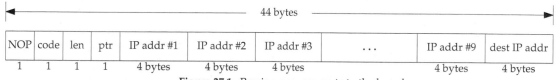

Figure 27.1 Passing a source route to the kernel.

We place an NOP before the source route option, which causes all the IP addresses to be aligned on a four-byte boundary. This is not required, but takes no additional space (the IP options are always padded to be a multiple of four bytes) and aligns the addresses.

In this figure, we show up to 10 IP addresses in the route, but the first listed address is removed from the source route option and becomes the destination address of the IP datagram when it leaves the source host. Although there is room for only 9 IP addresses in the 40-byte IP option space (do not forget the 3-byte option header that we are about to describe), there are actually 10 IP addresses in an IPv4 header when the destination address is included.

The *code* is either 0x83 for an LSRR option or 0x89 for an SSRR option. The *len* that we specify is the size of the option in bytes, including the three-byte header, and including the extra destination address at the end. It will be 11 for a route consisting of one IP address, 15 for a route consisting of two IP addresses, and so on, up to a maximum of 43. The NOP is not part of the option and is not included in the *len* field, but is included in the size of the buffer that we specify to setsockopt. When the first address in the list is removed from the source route option and placed into the destination address field of the IP header, this *len* value is decremented by four (Figures 9.32 and 9.33 of TCPv2). *ptr* is a pointer which contains the offset of the next IP address to be processed in the route, and we initialize it to 4, which points to the first IP address. The value of this field increases by four as the datagram is processed by each listed node.

We now develop three functions to initialize, create, and process a source route option. Our functions handle only a source route option. While it is possible to combine a source route with other IP options (such as router alert), such a combination is rare. Figure 27.2 is the first function, inet_srcrt_init, along with some static variables that are used as an option is being built.

ipopts/sourceroute.c

```
 1 #include     "unp.h"
 2 #include     <netinet/in_systm.h>
 3 #include     <netinet/ip.h>

 4 static u_char *optr;              /* pointer into options being formed */
 5 static u_char *lenptr;            /* pointer to length byte in SRR option */
 6 static int ocnt;                  /* count of # addresses */

 7 u_char *
 8 inet_srcrt_init(int type)
 9 {
10     optr = Malloc(44);            /* NOP, code, len, ptr, up to 10 addresses */
11     bzero(optr, 44);              /* guarantees EOLs at end */
12     ocnt = 0;
13     *optr++ = IPOPT_NOP;          /* NOP for alignment */
14     *optr++ = type ? IPOPT_SSRR : IPOPT_LSRR;
15     lenptr = optr++;              /* we fill in length later */
16     *optr++ = 4;                  /* offset to first address */

17     return (optr - 4);            /* pointer for setsockopt() */
18 }
```

ipopts/sourceroute.c

Figure 27.2 inet_srcrt_init function: initializes before storing a source route.

Initialize

10-17   We allocate a maximum sized buffer of 44 bytes and set it to 0. The value of the
EOL option is 0, so this initializes the entire option to EOL bytes. We then set up the
source route header. As shown in Figure 27.1, we first use an NOP for alignment, then
the type of source route (loose or strict), the length, and the pointer. We save a pointer
to the *len* field and will store this value as each address is added to the list. The pointer
to the option is returned to the caller and will be passed as the fourth argument to
setsockopt.

The next function, inet_srcrt_add, adds one IPv4 address to the source route
being constructed.

———————————————————————————————— ipopts/sourceroute.c
```
19 int
20 inet_srcrt_add(char *hostptr)
21 {
22     int      len;
23     struct addrinfo *ai;
24     struct sockaddr_in *sin;

25     if (ocnt > 9)
26         err_quit("too many source routes with: %s", hostptr);

27     ai = Host_serv(hostptr, NULL, AF_INET, 0);
28     sin = (struct sockaddr_in *) ai->ai_addr;
29     memcpy(optr, &sin->sin_addr, sizeof(struct in_addr));
30     freeaddrinfo(ai);

31     optr += sizeof(struct in_addr);
32     ocnt++;
33     len = 3 + (ocnt * sizeof(struct in_addr));
34     *lenptr = len;
35     return (len + 1);             /* size for setsockopt() */
36 }
```
———————————————————————————————— ipopts/sourceroute.c

Figure 27.3 inet_srcrt_add function: adds one IPv4 address to a source route.

Argument

19-20   The argument points to either a hostname or a dotted-decimal IP address.

Check for overflow

25-26   We check that too many addresses are not specified and then initialize if this is the
first address.

Obtain binary IP address and store in route

27-35   Our host_serv function handles either a hostname or a dotted-decimal string and
we store the resulting binary address in the list. We update the *len* field and return the
total size of the buffer (including the NOP) that the caller must pass to setsockopt.

When a received source route is returned to the application by getsockopt, the
format is different from Figure 27.1. We show the received format in Figure 27.4.

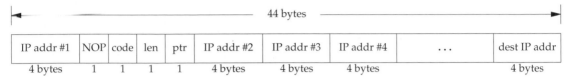

Figure 27.4 Format of source route option returned by getsockopt.

First, the order of the addresses has been reversed by the kernel from the ordering in the
received source route. What we mean by "reversed" is that if the received source route
contains the four addresses A, B, C, and D, in that order, the reverse of this route is D, C,
B, and then A. The first 4 bytes contain the first IP address in the list, followed by a
1-byte NOP (for alignment), followed by the 3-byte source route option header, followed by the remaining IP addresses. Up to 9 IP addresses can follow the 3-byte
header, and the *len* field in the returned header will have a maximum value of 39. Since
the NOP is always present, the length returned by getsockopt will always be a multiple of 4 bytes.

The format shown in Figure 27.4 is defined in <netinet/ip_var.h> as the following structure:

```
#define MAX_IPOPTLEN    40

struct ipoption {
  struct in_addr ipopt_dst;   /* first-hop dst if source routed */
  char           ipopt_list[MAX_IPOPTLEN];   /* options proper */
};
```

In Figure 27.5, we find it just as easy to parse the data ourselves, instead of using this structure.

This returned format differs from the format that we pass to setsockopt. If we
wanted to convert the format in Figure 27.4 to the format in Figure 27.1, we would have
to swap the first 4 bytes with the following 4 bytes and add 4 to the length field. Fortunately, we do not have to do this, as Berkeley-derived implementations automatically
use the reverse of a received source route for a TCP socket. That is, the information
shown in Figure 27.4 is returned by getsockopt for our information only. We do not
have to call setsockopt to tell the kernel to use this route for IP datagrams sent on the
TCP connection; the kernel does that automatically. We will see an example of this
shortly with our TCP server.

The next of our source route functions takes a received source route, in the format
shown in Figure 27.4, and prints the information. We show our inet_srcrt_print
function in Figure 27.5.

Save first IP address, skip any NOPs

43–45   The first IP address in the buffer is saved and any NOPs that follow are skipped.

```
                                                        ── ipopts/sourceroute.c
37 void
38 inet_srcrt_print(u_char *ptr, int len)
39 {
40     u_char   c;
41     char     str[INET_ADDRSTRLEN];
42     struct in_addr hop1;

43     memcpy(&hop1, ptr, sizeof(struct in_addr));
44     ptr += sizeof(struct in_addr);

45     while ( (c = *ptr++) == IPOPT_NOP) ; /* skip any leading NOPs */

46     if (c == IPOPT_LSRR)
47         printf("received LSRR: ");
48     else if (c == IPOPT_SSRR)
49         printf("received SSRR: ");
50     else {
51         printf("received option type %d\n", c);
52         return;
53     }
54     printf("%s ", Inet_ntop(AF_INET, &hop1, str, sizeof(str)));

55     len = *ptr++ - sizeof(struct in_addr);  /* subtract dest IP addr */
56     ptr++;                        /* skip over pointer */
57     while (len > 0) {
58         printf("%s ", Inet_ntop(AF_INET, ptr, str, sizeof(str)));
59         ptr += sizeof(struct in_addr);
60         len -= sizeof(struct in_addr);
61     }
62     printf("\n");
63 }
                                                        ── ipopts/sourceroute.c
```

Figure 27.5 inet_srcrt_print function: prints a received source route.

Check for source route option

46-62   We only print the information for a source route, and from the three-byte header, we check the *code*, fetch the *len*, and skip over the *ptr*. We then print all the IP addresses that follow the three-byte header, except the destination IP address.

Example

We now modify our TCP echo client to specify a source route and our TCP echo server to print a received source route. Figure 27.6 is our client.

Process command-line arguments

12-26   We call our inet_srcrt_init function to initialize the source route, with the type of route specified by either the -g option (loose) or the -G option (strict).

27-33   If the ptr pointer is set, a source route option was specified and we add all the specified intermediate hops to the source route that we allocated above with our inet_srcrt_add function. If ptr is not set, but there is more than one argument remaining on the command line, the user specified a route without specifying whether it is loose or strict, so we exit with an error.

—————————————————————————————— ipopts/tcpcli01.c

```
 1 #include    "unp.h"

 2 int
 3 main(int argc, char **argv)
 4 {
 5     int     c, sockfd, len = 0;
 6     u_char *ptr = NULL;
 7     struct addrinfo *ai;

 8     if (argc < 2)
 9         err_quit("usage: tcpcli01 [ -[gG] <hostname> ... ] <hostname>");
10     opterr = 0;                     /* don't want getopt() writing to stderr */
11     while ( (c = getopt(argc, argv, "gG")) != -1) {
12         switch (c) {
13         case 'g':                   /* loose source route */
14             if (ptr)
15                 err_quit("can't use both -g and -G");
16             ptr = inet_srcrt_init(0);
17             break;
18         case 'G':                   /* strict source route */
19             if (ptr)
20                 err_quit("can't use both -g and -G");
21             ptr = inet_srcrt_init(1);
22             break;
23         case '?':
24             err_quit("unrecognized option: %c", c);
25         }
26     }
27     if (ptr)
28         while (optind < argc - 1)
29             len = inet_srcrt_add(argv[optind++]);
30     else if (optind < argc - 1)
31         err_quit("need -g or -G to specify route");
32     if (optind != argc - 1)
33         err_quit("missing <hostname>");

34     ai = Host_serv(argv[optind], SERV_PORT_STR, AF_INET, SOCK_STREAM);

35     sockfd = Socket(ai->ai_family, ai->ai_socktype, ai->ai_protocol);

36     if (ptr) {
37         len = inet_srcrt_add(argv[optind]); /* dest at end */
38         Setsockopt(sockfd, IPPROTO_IP, IP_OPTIONS, ptr, len);
39         free(ptr);
40     }

41     Connect(sockfd, ai->ai_addr, ai->ai_addrlen);

42     str_cli(stdin, sockfd);    /* do it all */

43     exit(0);
44 }
```

—————————————————————————————— ipopts/tcpcli01.c

Figure 27.6 TCP echo client that specifies a source route.

Handle destination address and create socket

34–35 The final command-line argument is the hostname or dotted-decimal address of the server and our `host_serv` function processes it. We are not able to call our `tcp_connect` function because we must specify the source route between the calls to `socket` and `connect`. The latter initiates the three-way handshake and we want the initial SYN and all subsequent packets to use this source route.

36–42 If a source route is specified, we must add the server's IP address to the end of the list of IP addresses (Figure 27.1). `setsockopt` installs the source route for this socket. We then call `connect`, followed by our `str_cli` function (Figure 5.5).

Our TCP server is almost identical to the code shown in Figure 5.12, with the following changes. First, we allocate space for the options.

```
int      len;
u_char   *opts;

opts = Malloc(44);
```

We then fetch the IP options after the call to `accept`, but before the call to `fork`.

```
len = 44;
Getsockopt(connfd, IPPROTO_IP, IP_OPTIONS, opts, &len);
if (len > 0) {
    printf("received IP options, len = %d\n", len);
    inet_srcrt_print(opts, len);
}
```

If the received SYN from the client does not contain any IP options, the *len* variable will contain 0 on return from `getsockopt` (it is a value-result argument). As mentioned earlier, we do not have to do anything to cause TCP to use the reverse of the received source route: That is done automatically by TCP (p. 931 of TCPv2). All we are doing by calling `getsockopt` is obtaining a copy of the reversed source route. If we do not want TCP to use this route, we call `setsockopt` after `accept` returns, specifying a fifth argument (the length) of 0, and this removes any IP options currently in use. The source route has already been used by TCP for the second segment of the three-way handshake (Figure 2.5), but if we remove the options, IP will use whatever route it calculates for future packets to this client.

We now show an example of our client/server when we specify a source route. We run our client on the host `freebsd` as follows:

```
freebsd4 % tcpcli01 -g macosx freebsd4 macosx
```

After the appropriate configuration to handle source routes and forward IP, this sends the IP datagrams from `freebsd4` to the host `macosx`, back to `freebsd4`, and then finally to the host `macosx`, which is running the server. The two systems, `freebsd4` and `macosx`, must forward and accept source-routed datagrams for this example to work.

When the connection is established at the server, it outputs the following:

```
macosx % tcpserv01
received IP options, len = 16
received LSRR: 172.24.37.94 172.24.37.78 172.24.37.94
```

The first IP address printed is the first hop of the reverse path (freebsd4, as shown in Figure 27.4), and the next two addresses are in the order used by the server to send datagrams back to the client. If we watch the client/server exchange using tcpdump, we can see the source route option on every datagram in both directions.

> Unfortunately, the operation of the IP_OPTIONS socket option has never been documented, so you may encounter variations on systems that are not derived from the Berkeley source code. For example, under Solaris 2.5, the first address returned in the buffer by getsockopt (Figure 27.4) is not the first-hop address for the return route, but the address of the peer. Nevertheless, the reversed route used by TCP is correct. Also, Solaris 2.5 precedes all source route options with four NOPs, limiting the option to eight IP addresses instead of the real limit of nine.

Deleting Received Source Route

Unfortunately, source routes present a security hole to programs that perform authentication using only IP addresses (now known to be inadequate). If a hacker sends packets with a trusted address as the source, but his or her own address in the source route, the return packets using the reverse source route will get to the hacker without involving the system listed as the original source at all. Starting with the Net/1 release (1989), the rlogind and rshd servers had code similar to the following:

```
u_char  buf[44];
char    lbuf[BUFSIZ];
int     optsize;

optsize = sizeof(buf);
if (getsockopt(0, IPPROTO_IP, IP_OPTIONS,
               buf, &optsize) == 0 && optsize != 0) {
    /* format the options as hex numbers to print in lbuf[] */
    syslog(LOG_NOTICE,
           "Connection received using IP options (ignored):%s", lbuf);
    setsockopt(0, IPPROTO_IP, IP_OPTIONS, NULL, 0);
}
```

If a connection arrives with any IP options (the value of optsize returned by getsockopt is nonzero), a message is logged using syslog and setsockopt is called to clear the options. This prevents any future TCP segments sent on this connection from using the reverse of the received source route. This technique is now known to be inadequate, because by the time the application receives the connection, the TCP three-way handshake is complete, and the second segment (the server's SYN-ACK in Figure 2.5) has already followed the reverse of the source route back to the client (or at least to one of the intermediate hops listed in the source route, which is where the hacker is located). Since the hacker has seen TCP's sequence numbers in both directions, even if no more packets are sent with the source route, the hacker can still send packets to the server with the correct sequence number.

The only solution for this potential problem is to forbid all TCP connections that arrive with a source route when you are using the source IP address for some form of validation (as do `rlogind` and `rshd`). Replace the call to `setsockopt` in the code fragment just shown with a closing of the just-accepted connection and a termination of the newly spawned server. This way, the second segment of the three-way handshake has already been sent, but the connection should not be left open.

27.4 IPv6 Extension Headers

We do not show any options with the IPv6 header in Figure A.2 (it is always 40 bytes in length), but an IPv6 header can be followed by the following optional *extension headers*:

1. Hop-by-hop options must immediately follow the 40-byte IPv6 header. There are no hop-by-hop options currently defined that are usable by an application.

2. No destination options are currently defined that are usable by an application.

3. The routing header is a source routing option, similar in concept to what we described for IPv4 in Section 27.3.

4. The fragmentation header is automatically generated by a host that fragments an IPv6 datagram and then processed by the final destination when it reassembles the fragments.

5. The use of the authentication header (AH) is documented in RFC 2402 [Kent and Atkinson 1998b].

6. The use of the encapsulating security payload (ESP) header is documented in RFC 2406 [Kent and Atkinson 1998c].

We said the fragmentation header is handled entirely by the kernel, and the AH and ESP headers are automatically handled by the kernel based on the SADB and SPDB, which are maintained using `PF_KEY` sockets (Chapter 19). This leaves the first three options, which we will discuss in the next two sections. The API to specify these options is defined by RFC 3542 [Stevens et al. 2003].

27.5 IPv6 Hop-by-Hop Options and Destination Options

The hop-by-hop and destination options have a similar format, shown in Figure 27.7. The 8-bit *next header* field identifies the next header that follows this extension header. The 8-bit *header extension length* is the length of this extension header, in units of 8 bytes, but not including the first 8 bytes. For example, if this extension header occupies 8 bytes, then its header extension length is 0; if this extension header occupies 16 bytes, then its header extension length is 1, and so on. These two headers are padded to be a multiple of 8 bytes with either the `pad1` option or the `padN` option, which will be described shortly.

The hop-by-hop options header and destination options header each hold any number of individual options, which have the format shown in Figure 27.8.

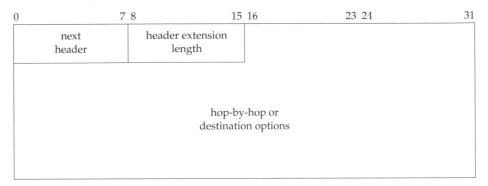

Figure 27.7   Format of hop-by-hop and destination options.

Figure 27.8   Format of individual hop-by-hop and destination options.

This is called *TLV coding* because each option appears with its type, length, and value. The 8-bit *type* field identifies the option type. Additionally, the two high-order bits specify what an IPv6 node does with this option if it does not understand the option:

00   Skip over this option and continue processing the header.

01   Discard the packet.

10   Discard the packet and send an ICMP parameter problem type 2 error (Figure A.16) to the sender, regardless of whether or not the packet's destination is a multicast address.

11   Discard the packet and send an ICMP parameter problem type 2 error (Figure A.16) to the sender. This error is sent only if the packet's destination is not a multicast address.

The next high-order bit specifies whether or not the option data changes en route:

0   The option data does not change en route.

1   The option data may change en route.

The low-order 5 bits then specify the option. Note that all 8 bits make up the option code; the low-order 5 bits do not by themselves identify the option. However, option value assignments are made to keep the low-order 5 bits unique for as long as possible.

The 8-bit *length* field specifies the length of the option data in bytes. The type field and this length field are not included in this length.

The two pad options are defined in RFC 2460 [Deering and Hinden 1998] and can be used in either the hop-by-hop options header or in the destination options header. The *jumbo payload length*, a hop-by-hop option, is defined in RFC 2675 [Borman, Deering, and Hinden 1999], and it is generated when needed and processed when received entirely by the kernel. *Router alert*, a hop-by-hop option, is described for IPv6 in RFC 2711 [Partridge and Jackson 1999] and is similar to the IPv4 router alert. We show these in Figure 27.9. Other options are also defined, for instance, for Mobile-IPv6, but we do not show them here.

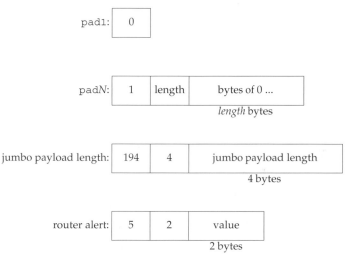

Figure 27.9 IPv6 hop-by-hop options.

The pad1 byte is the only option without a length and value. It provides 1 byte of padding. The padN option is used when 2 or more bytes of padding are required. For 2 bytes of padding, the length of this option would be 0 and the option would consist of just the type field and the length field. For 3 bytes of padding, the length would be 1, and 1 byte of 0 would follow this length. The jumbo payload length option provides a datagram length of 32 bits and is used when the 16-bit payload length field in Figure A.2 is inadequate. The router alert option indicates that this packet should be intercepted by certain routers along the path; the value in the router alert option indicates what routers should be interested.

We show the padding options because each hop-by-hop and destination option also has an associated *alignment requirement*, written as $xn + y$. This means that the option must appear at an integer multiple of x bytes from the start of the header, plus y bytes. For example, the alignment requirement of the jumbo payload option is $4n + 2$, and this is to force the 4-byte option value (the jumbo payload length) to be on a 4-byte boundary. The reason why the y value is 2 for this option is because of the 2 bytes that appear at the beginning of each hop-by-hop and destination options header (Figure 27.8). The alignment requirement of the router alert option is $2n + 0$, to force the 2-byte option value to be on a 2-byte boundary.

The hop-by-hop and destination options are normally specified as ancillary data with `sendmsg` and returned as ancillary data by `recvmsg`. Nothing special needs to be done by the application to send either or both of these options; just specify them in a call to `sendmsg`. To receive these options, the corresponding socket option must be enabled: `IPV6_RECVHOPOPTS` for the hop-by-hop options and `IPV6_RECVDSTOPTS` for the destination options. For example, to enable both options to be returned,

```
const int  on = 1;

setsockopt(sockfd, IPPROTO_IPV6, IPV6_RECVHOPOPTS, &on, sizeof(on));
setsockopt(sockfd, IPPROTO_IPV6, IPV6_RECVDSTOPTS, &on, sizeof(on));
```

Figure 27.10 shows the format of the ancillary data objects used to send and receive the hop-by-hop and destination options.

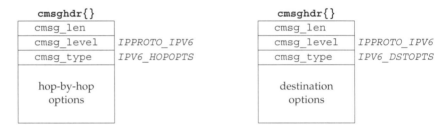

Figure 27.10   Ancillary data objects for hop-by-hop and destination options.

The actual contents of the IPv6 option header is passed between the user and the kernel as the `cmsg_data` portion of these objects. To reduce code duplication, seven functions are defined to create and process these data sections. The following four functions build an option to send:

```
#include <netinet/in.h>

int inet6_opt_init(void *extbuf, socklen_t extlen);
```

Returns: number of bytes required to hold empty extension header, −1 on error

```
int inet6_opt_append(void *extbuf, socklen_t extlen,
                     int offset, uint8_t type, socklen_t len,
                     uint_t align, void **databufp);
```

Returns: updated length of overall extension header after adding option, −1 on error

```
int inet6_opt_finish(void *extbuf, socklen_t extlen,
                     int offset);
```

Returns: updated length of finished extension header, −1 on error

```
int inet6_opt_set_val(void *databuf, int offset,
                      const void *val, socklen_t vallen);
```

Returns: new offset inside *databuf*

inet6_opt_init returns the number of bytes required to hold an empty extension header. If the *extbuf* argument is not NULL, it initializes the extension header. It fails and returns −1 if the *extbuf* argument is supplied but the *extlen* argument is not a multiple of 8. (All IPv6 hop-by-hop and destination options headers must be multiples of 8 bytes.)

inet6_opt_append returns the updated total length of the extension header after appending the specified option. If the *extbuf* argument is not NULL, it also initializes the option and inserts any necessary padding. It fails and returns −1 if the new option does not fit in the supplied buffer. The *offset* argument is the current running total length, and must be the return value from a previous call to inet6_opt_init or inet6_opt_append. The *type* and *len* arguments are the type and length of the option, and are copied directly into the option header. The *align* argument specifies the alignment requirement, that is, *x* from the function *x*n + *y*. The value of *y* is derived from *align* and *len*, so it does not need to be explicitly specified. The *databufp* argument is the address to a pointer that will be filled in with the location of the option value; the caller can then copy the option value into this location using the inet6_opt_set_val function or any other method.

inet6_opt_finish is called to complete an extension header, adding any needed padding to make the overall header a multiple of 8 bytes. As before, if the *extbuf* argument is non-NULL, the padding is actually inserted into the buffer; otherwise, the function simply computes the updated length. As with inet6_opt_append, the *offset* argument is the current running total length, the return value from a previous inet6_opt_init or inet6_opt_append. inet6_opt_finish returns the total length of the completed header, or −1 if the required padding will not fit in the supplied buffer.

`inet6_opt_set_val` copies an option value into the data buffer returned by `inet6_opt_append`. The *databuf* argument is the pointer returned from `inet6_opt_append`. *offset* is a running length within this option; it must be initialized to 0 for each option and then will be the return value from the previous `inet6_opt_set_val` as the option is built up. The *val* and *vallen* arguments specify the value to copy into the option value buffer.

The expected use of these functions is to make two passes through the list of options you intend to insert: the first to calculate the desired length, and the second to actually build the option into an appropriately sized buffer. During the first pass, we call `inet6_opt_init`, `inet6_opt_append` once for each option we will append, and `inet6_opt_finish`, passing NULL and 0 for the *extbuf* and *extlen* arguments, respectively. We then dynamically allocate the option buffer using the size returned by `inet6_opt_finish`, and we will pass this buffer as the *extbuf* argument during the second pass. During the second pass, we call `inet6_opt_init` and `inet6_opt_append`, either copying the data manually or using `inet6_opt_set_val` for each option value. Finally, we call `inet6_opt_finish`. Alternately, we can pre-allocate a buffer that should be large enough for our desired options and skip the first pass; however, this is vulnerable to failure if a change in the desired options would over-run the pre-allocated buffer.

The remaining three functions process a received option:

```
#include <netinet/in.h>

int inet6_opt_next(const void *extbuf, socklen_t extlen, int offset,
                   uint8_t *typep, socklen_t *lenp, void **databufp);
```
                                    Returns: offset of next option, –1 on end of options or error

```
int inet6_opt_find(const void *extbuf, socklen_t extlen, int offset,
                   uint8_t type, socklen_t *lenp, void **databufp);
```
                                    Returns: offset of next option, –1 on end of options or error

```
int inet6_opt_get_val(const void *databuf, int offset,
                      void *val, socklen_t vallen);
```
                                    Returns: new offset inside *databuf*

`inet6_opt_next` processes the next option in a buffer. *extbuf* and *extlen* specify the buffer containing the header. As with `inet6_opt_append`, *offset* is a running offset into the buffer. It is 0 for the first call to `inet6_opt_next`, and then it is the return value from the previous call for future calls. *typep*, *lenp*, and *databufp* return the type, length, and value of the option, respectively. `inet6_opt_next` returns –1 if the header is malformed or if it has reached the end of the buffer.

inet6_opt_find is similar to the previous function, but it lets the caller specify the option type to search for (the *type* argument) instead of always returning the next option.

inet6_opt_get_val is used to extract values from an option, using the *databuf* pointer returned by a previous inet6_opt_next or inet6_opt_find call. As with inet6_opt_set_val, the *offset* argument must start at 0 for each option, then must be the return value of a previous call to inet6_opt_get_val.

27.6 IPv6 Routing Header

The IPv6 routing header is used for source routing in IPv6. The first two bytes of the routing header are the same as we showed in Figure 27.7: a *next header* field followed by a *header extension length*. The next two bytes specify the *routing type* and the number of *segments left* (i.e., how many listed nodes are still to be visited). Only one type of routing header is specified, type 0, and we show its format in Figure 27.11.

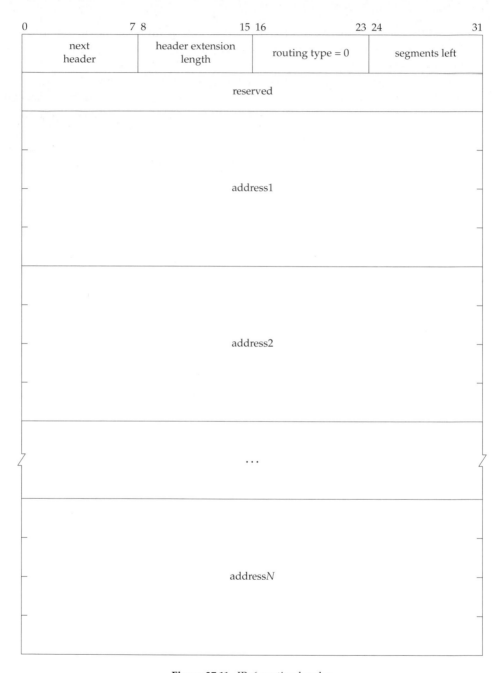

Figure 27.11 IPv6 routing header.

An unlimited number of addresses can appear in the routing header (limited only by packet length) and *segments left* must be equal to or less than the number of addresses in the header. RFC 2460 [Deering and Hinden 1998] specifies the details of how the header is processed as the packet travels to the final destination, along with a detailed example.

The routing header is normally specified as ancillary data with sendmsg and returned as ancillary data by recvmsg. Nothing special needs to be done by the application to send the header: just specify it as ancillary data in a call to sendmsg. To receive the routing header, the IPV6_RECVRTHDR socket option must be enabled, as in

```
const int  on = 1;

setsockopt(sockfd, IPPROTO_IPV6, IPV6_RECVRTHDR, &on, sizeof(on));
```

Figure 27.12 shows the format of the ancillary data object used to send and receive the routing header. Six functions are defined to create and process the routing header. The following three functions build an option to send:

```
#include <netinet/in.h>

socklen_t inet6_rth_space(int type, int segments);
```
                                     Returns: positive number of bytes if OK, 0 on error

```
void *inet6_rth_init(void *rthbuf, socklen_t rthlen,
                     int type, int segments);
```
                                     Returns: non-null pointer if OK, NULL on error

```
int inet6_rth_add(void *rthbuf, const struct in6_addr *addr);
```
                                     Returns: 0 if OK, –1 on error

inet6_rth_space returns the number of bytes required to hold a routing header of the specified *type* (normally specified as IPV6_RTHDR_TYPE_0) with the specified number of *segments*.

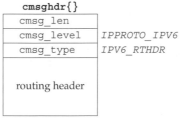

Figure 27.12   Ancillary data object for IPv6 routing header.

inet6_rth_init initializes the buffer pointed to by *rthbuf* to contain a routing header of the specified *type* and the specified number of *segments*. The return value is the pointer to the buffer, and this pointer is then used as an argument to the next function. inet6_rth_init returns NULL if an error occurs, for instance, when the supplied buffer is not large enough.

inet6_rth_add adds the IPv6 address pointed to by addr to the end of the routing header being constructed. When successful, the segleft member of the routing header is updated to account for the new address.

The following three functions deal with a received routing header:

```
#include <netinet/in.h>

int inet6_rth_reverse(const void *in, void *out);
```

Returns: 0 if OK, −1 on error

```
int inet6_rth_segments(const void *rthbuf);
```

Returns: number of segments in routing header if OK, −1 on error

```
struct in6_addr *inet6_rth_getaddr(const void *rthbuf, int index);
```

Returns: non-null pointer if OK, NULL on error

`inet6_rth_reverse` takes a routing header that was received (pointed to by *in*) and creates a new routing header (in the buffer pointed to by *out*) that sends datagrams along the reverse of that path. The reversal can occur in place; that is, the *in* and *out* pointers can point to the same buffer.

`inet6_rth_segments` returns the number of segments in the routing header described by *rthbuf*. When successful, the return value is greater than zero.

`inet6_rth_getaddr` returns a pointer to the IPv6 address specified by *index* in the routing header described by *rthbuf*. *index* must have a value between zero and one less than the value returned by `inet6_rth_segments`, inclusive.

To demonstrate these options, we create a UDP client and server. The client, shown in Figure 27.13, accepts a source route on the command line like the IPv4 TCP client we showed in Figure 27.6; the server prints the received source route and reverses it to send back to the client.

Create source route

11–21   If more than one argument was supplied, all but the final argument form the source route. We first determine how much space the route header will require with `inet6_rth_space`, then allocate the necessary space with `malloc`. We initialize the allocated buffer with `inet6_rth_init`. Then, for each address in the source route, we convert it to numeric form using `host_serv` and add it to the source route using `inet6_rth_add`. This is very similar to our IPv4 TCP client, except that instead of our own helper functions, these library functions are provided by the system.

Look up destination and create socket

22–23   We use `host_serv` to look up the destination, and create a socket to use.

Set sticky IPV6_RTHDR option and call worker function

24–27   As we will see in Section 27.7, instead of sending the same ancillary data with every packet, we can use `setsockopt` to apply the routing header to every packet in the session. We only set this option if `ptr` is non-NULL, meaning that we allocated a route header earlier. Finally, we call the worker function, `dg_cli`, which we defined in Figure 8.8.

```
                                                              ————— ipopts/udpcli01.c
 1 #include    "unp.h"

 2 int
 3 main(int argc, char **argv)
 4 {
 5     int     c, sockfd, len = 0;
 6     u_char *ptr = NULL;
 7     void   *rth;
 8     struct addrinfo *ai;

 9     if (argc < 2)
10         err_quit("usage: udpcli01 [ <hostname> ... ] <hostname>");

11     if (argc > 2) {
12         int     i;

13         len = Inet6_rth_space(IPV6_RTHDR_TYPE_0, argc - 2);
14         ptr = Malloc(len);
15         Inet6_rth_init(ptr, len, IPV6_RTHDR_TYPE_0, argc - 2);
16         for (i = 1; i < argc - 1; i++) {
17             ai = Host_serv(argv[i], NULL, AF_INET6, 0);
18             Inet6_rth_add(ptr,
19                         &((struct sockaddr_in6 *) ai->ai_addr)->sin6_addr);
20         }
21     }

22     ai = Host_serv(argv[argc - 1], SERV_PORT_STR, AF_INET6, SOCK_DGRAM);

23     sockfd = Socket(ai->ai_family, ai->ai_socktype, ai->ai_protocol);

24     if (ptr) {
25         Setsockopt(sockfd, IPPROTO_IPV6, IPV6_RTHDR, ptr, len);
26         free(ptr);
27     }

28     dg_cli(stdin, sockfd, ai->ai_addr, ai->ai_addrlen); /* do it all */

29     exit(0);
30 }
                                                              ————— ipopts/udpcli01.c
```

Figure 27.13 IPv6 UDP client with source route.

Our server is the same simple UDP server as before: open a socket and call dg_echo. The setup is trivial, so we do not show it. Instead, Figure 27.14 shows our dg_echo function, which prints the source route if one was received and reverses it for use in returning the packet.

Turn on IPV6_RECVRTHDR option and set up msghdr struct

12–13 To receive the incoming source route, we must set the IPV6_RECVRTHDR socket option. We must also use recvmsg, so we set up the unchanging fields of a msghdr structure.

Set up modifiable fields and call recvmsg

21–24 We set the length fields to the appropriate sizes and call recvmsg.

ipopts/dgechoprintroute.c

```
 1 #include    "unp.h"

 2 void
 3 dg_echo(int sockfd, SA *pcliaddr, socklen_t clilen)
 4 {
 5     int     n;
 6     char    mesg[MAXLINE];
 7     int     on;
 8     char    control[MAXLINE];
 9     struct msghdr msg;
10     struct cmsghdr *cmsg;
11     struct iovec iov[1];

12     on = 1;
13     Setsockopt(sockfd, IPPROTO_IPV6, IPV6_RECVRTHDR, &on, sizeof(on));

14     bzero(&msg, sizeof(msg));
15     iov[0].iov_base = mesg;
16     msg.msg_name = pcliaddr;
17     msg.msg_iov = iov;
18     msg.msg_iovlen = 1;
19     msg.msg_control = control;
20     for ( ; ; ) {
21         msg.msg_namelen = clilen;
22         msg.msg_controllen = sizeof(control);
23         iov[0].iov_len = MAXLINE;
24         n = Recvmsg(sockfd, &msg, 0);

25         for (cmsg = CMSG_FIRSTHDR(&msg); cmsg != NULL;
26              cmsg = CMSG_NXTHDR(&msg, cmsg)) {
27             if (cmsg->cmsg_level == IPPROTO_IPV6 &&
28                 cmsg->cmsg_type == IPV6_RTHDR) {
29                 inet6_srcrt_print(CMSG_DATA(cmsg));
30                 Inet6_rth_reverse(CMSG_DATA(cmsg), CMSG_DATA(cmsg));
31             }
32         }

33         iov[0].iov_len = n;
34         Sendmsg(sockfd, &msg, 0);
35     }
36 }
```

ipopts/dgechoprintroute.c

Figure 27.14 dg_echo function that prints and reverses IPv6 source route.

Find and process route header

25–32   We loop through the ancillary data using CMSG_FIRSTHDR and CMSG_NXTHDR. Even though we are only expecting one piece of ancillary data, it is good practice to loop like this. If we do find a routing header, we print it with our inet6_srcrt_print function (Figure 27.15). We then reverse the route with inet6_rth_reverse so that we can use it to return the packet along the same path. In this case, inet6_rth_reverse works on the route in place, so that we can use the same ancillary data to send the return packet.

Echo packet

33–34   We set the length of the data to send, and use sendmsg to return the packet.

ipopts/sourceroute6.c

```
 1 #include     "unp.h"

 2 void
 3 inet6_srcrt_print(void *ptr)
 4 {
 5     int     i, segments;
 6     char    str[INET6_ADDRSTRLEN];

 7     segments = Inet6_rth_segments(ptr);
 8     printf("received source route: ");
 9     for (i = 0; i < segments; i++)
10         printf("%s ", Inet_ntop(AF_INET6, Inet6_rth_getaddr(ptr, i),
11                                 str, sizeof(str)));
12     printf("\n");
13 }
```

ipopts/sourceroute6.c

Figure 27.15 inet6_srcrt_print function: prints a received IPv6 source route.

Our inet6_srcrt_print is almost trivial, thanks to the IPv6 route helper functions.

Determine number of segments in route

7   We first use inet6_rth_segments to determine the number of segments present in the route.

Loop through each segment

9-11   We loop through all the segments, calling inet6_rth_getaddr for each one and converting the address to presentation form using inet_ntop.

Our client and server that handle IPv6 source routes do not need to know how the source route is formatted in the packet. The library functions the API provides hide the details of the packet format from us, yet give us all the flexibility we had when we built the option from scratch in IPv4.

27.7 IPv6 Sticky Options

We have described the use of ancillary data with sendmsg and recvmsg to send and receive seven different ancillary data objects:

1. IPv6 packet information: the in6_pktinfo structure containing either the destination address and outgoing interface index, or the source address and the arriving interface index (Figure 22.21)

2. The outgoing hop limit or received hop limit (Figure 22.21)

3. The next-hop address (Figure 22.21)

4. The outgoing or received traffic class (Figure 22.21)

5. Hop-by-hop options (Figure 27.10)

6. Destination options (Figure 27.10)

7. Routing header (Figure 27.12)

We summarized the cmsg_level and cmsg_type values for these objects, along with the values for the other ancillary data object in Figure 14.11.

When the same value will be used for all packets sent on a socket, instead of sending these options in every call to sendmsg, we can set the corresponding socket options instead. The socket options use the same constants as the ancillary data, that is, the option level is always IPPROTO_IPV6 and the option name is IPV6_DSTOPTS, IPV6_HOPLIMIT, IPV6_HOPOPTS, IPV6_NEXTHOP, IPV6_PKTINFO, IPV6_RTHDR, or IPV6_TCLASS. But, these sticky options can be overridden on a per-packet basis for a UDP socket or for a raw IPv6 socket by specifying ancillary data in a call to sendmsg. If any ancillary data is specified in a call to sendmsg, the corresponding sticky options are not sent with that datagram.

The concept of sticky options can also be used with TCP because ancillary data is never sent or received by sendmsg or recvmsg on a TCP socket. Instead, a TCP application can set the corresponding socket option and specify any of the seven option types mentioned at the beginning of this section. These objects then affect all packets sent on this socket. However, retransmission of packets that were originally sent when other (or no) sticky options were set may use either the original or the new sticky options.

There is no way to retrieve options received via TCP since there is no relationship between received packets and user receive operations.

27.8 Historical IPv6 Advanced API

RFC 2292 [Stevens and Thomas 1998] defines an earlier version of the API described here, which is implemented and deployed in some systems. In this earlier version, the functions to deal with destination and hop-by-hop options are inet6_option_space, inet6_option_init, inet6_option_append, inet6_option_alloc, inet6_option_next and inet6_option_find. These functions dealt with struct cmsghdr objects directly, assuming that all options were contained in ancillary data. The routing header functions in that API were inet6_rthdr_space, inet6_rthdr_init, inet6_rthdr_add, inet6_rthdr_lasthop, inet6_rthdr_reverse, inet6_rthdr_segments, inet6_rthdr_getaddr and inet6_rthdr_getflags. These functions also operate directly on struct cmsghdr ancillary data objects.

In this API, sticky options were set with the IPV6_PKTOPTIONS socket option. The ancillary data objects that would have been passed to sendmsg were instead set as the data portion of the IPV6_PKTOPTIONS socket option. In that API, the IPV6_DSTOPTS, IPV6_HOPOPTS, and IPV6_RTHDR socket options were flag values to request reception of the respective headers via ancillary data.

For more information on these operations, refer to Sections 4 through 8 of RFC 2292 [Stevens and Thomas 1998].

27.9 Summary

The most commonly used of the 10 defined IPv4 options is the source route, but its use is dwindling these days because of security concerns. Access to IPv4 header options is through the `IP_OPTIONS` socket option.

IPv6 defines six extension headers. Access to IPv6 extension headers is through a functional interface, obviating the need to understand their actual format in the packet. These extension headers are written as ancillary data with `sendmsg` and returned as ancillary data with `recvmsg`.

Exercises

27.1 In our IPv4 source route example at the end of Section 27.3, what changes if we specify each intermediate node to the client with the `-G` option, instead of the `-g` option?

27.2 The length of the buffer specified to `setsockopt` for the `IP_OPTIONS` socket option must be a multiple of 4 bytes. What would we do if we did not place an NOP at the beginning of the buffer, as shown in Figure 27.1?

27.3 How does `ping` receive a source route when the IP record route option is used (described in Section 7.3 of TCPv1)?

27.4 In the example code from the `rlogind` server at the end of Section 27.3 that clears a received source route, why is the socket descriptor argument for `getsockopt` and `setsockopt` 0?

27.5 For many years, the code we showed at the end of Section 27.3 that clears a received source route looked like the following:

```
optsize = 0;
setsockopt(0, IPPROTO_IP, IP_OPTIONS, NULL, &optsize);
```

What is wrong with this code? Does it matter?

28

Raw Sockets

28.1 Introduction

Raw sockets provide three features not provided by normal TCP and UDP sockets:

- Raw sockets let us read and write ICMPv4, IGMPv4, and ICMPv6 packets. The ping program, for example, sends ICMP echo requests and receives ICMP echo replies. (We will develop our own version of the ping program in Section 28.5.) The multicast routing daemon, mrouted, sends and receives IGMPv4 packets.

  This capability also allows applications that are built using ICMP or IGMP to be handled entirely as user processes, instead of putting more code into the kernel. The router discovery daemon (in.rdisc under Solaris 2.x; Appendix F of TCPv1 describes how to obtain the source code for a publicly available version), for example, is built this way. It processes two ICMP messages (router advertisement and router solicitation) that the kernel knows nothing about.

- With a raw socket, a process can read and write IPv4 datagrams with an IPv4 protocol field that is not processed by the kernel. Recall the 8-bit IPv4 protocol field in Figure A.1. Most kernels only process datagrams containing values of 1 (ICMP), 2 (IGMP), 6 (TCP), and 17 (UDP). But many other values are defined for the protocol field: The IANA's "Protocol Numbers" registry lists all the values. For example, the OSPF routing protocol does not use TCP or UDP, but it uses IP directly, setting the protocol field of the IP datagram to 89. The gated program that implements OSPF must use a raw socket to read and write these IP datagrams since they contain a protocol field the kernel knows nothing about. This capability carries over to IPv6 also.

- With a raw socket, a process can build its own IPv4 header using the IP_HDRINCL socket option. This can be used, for example, to build UDP and TCP packets, and we will show an example of this in Section 29.7.

This chapter describes raw socket creation, input, and output. We will also develop versions of the ping and traceroute programs that work with both IPv4 and IPv6.

28.2 Raw Socket Creation

The steps involved in creating a raw socket are as follows:

1. The socket function creates a raw socket when the second argument is SOCK_RAW. The third argument (the protocol) is normally nonzero. For example, to create an IPv4 raw socket we would write

   ```
   int     sockfd;

   sockfd = socket(AF_INET, SOCK_RAW, protocol);
   ```

   where *protocol* is one of the constants, IPPROTO_*xxx*, defined by including the <netinet/in.h> header, such as IPPROTO_ICMP.

   Only the superuser can create a raw socket. This prevents normal users from writing their own IP datagrams to the network.

2. The IP_HDRINCL socket option can be set as follows:

   ```
   const int    on = 1;

   if (setsockopt(sockfd, IPPROTO_IP, IP_HDRINCL, &on, sizeof(on)) < 0)
       error
   ```

   We will describe the effect of this socket option in the next section.

3. bind can be called on the raw socket, but this is rare. This function sets only the local address: There is no concept of a port number with a raw socket. With regard to output, calling bind sets the source IP address that will be used for datagrams sent on the raw socket (but only if the IP_HDRINCL socket option is not set). If bind is not called, the kernel sets the source IP address to the primary IP address of the outgoing interface.

4. connect can be called on the raw socket, but this is rare. This function sets only the foreign address: Again, there is no concept of a port number with a raw socket. With regard to output, calling connect lets us call write or send instead of sendto, since the destination IP address is already specified.

28.3 Raw Socket Output

Output on a raw socket is governed by the following rules:

- Normal output is performed by calling `sendto` or `sendmsg` and specifying the destination IP address. `write`, `writev`, or `send` can also be called if the socket has been connected.

- If the `IP_HDRINCL` option is not set, the starting address of the data for the kernel to send specifies the first byte following the IP header because the kernel will build the IP header and prepend it to the data from the process. The kernel sets the protocol field of the IPv4 header that it builds to the third argument from the call to `socket`.

- If the `IP_HDRINCL` option is set, the starting address of the data for the kernel to send specifies the first byte of the IP header. The amount of data to write must include the size of the caller's IP header. The process builds the entire IP header, except: (i) the IPv4 identification field can be set to 0, which tells the kernel to set this value; (ii) the kernel always calculates and stores the IPv4 header checksum; and (iii) IP options may or may not be included; see Section 27.2.

- The kernel fragments raw packets that exceed the outgoing interface MTU.

> Raw sockets are documented to provide an identical interface to the one a protocol would have if it was resident in the kernel [McKusick et al. 1996] Unfortunately, this means that certain pieces of the API are dependent on the OS kernel, specifically with regard to the byte ordering of the fields in the IP header. On many Berkeley-derived kernels, all fields are in network byte order except `ip_len` and `ip_off`, which are in host byte order (pp. 233 and 1057 of TCPv2). On Linux and OpenBSD, however, all the fields must be in network byte order.

> The `IP_HDRINCL` socket option was introduced with 4.3BSD Reno. Before this, the only way for an application to specify its own IP header in packets sent on a raw IP socket was to apply a kernel patch that was introduced in 1988 by Van Jacobson to support `traceroute`. This patch required the application to create a raw IP socket specifying a *protocol* of `IPPROTO_RAW`, which has a value of 255 (and is a reserved value and must never appear as the protocol field in an IP header).

> The functions that perform input and output on raw sockets are some of the simplest in the kernel. For example, in TCPv2, each function requires about 40 lines of C code (pp. 1054–1057), compared to TCP input at about 2,000 lines and TCP output at about 700 lines.

Our description of the `IP_HDRINCL` socket option is for 4.4BSD. Earlier versions, such as Net/2, filled in more fields in the IP header when this option was set.

With IPv4, it is the responsibility of the user process to calculate and set any header checksums contained in whatever follows the IPv4 header. For example, in our `ping` program (Figure 28.14), we must calculate the ICMPv4 checksum and store it in the ICMPv4 header before calling `sendto`.

IPv6 Differences

There are a few differences with raw IPv6 sockets (RFC 3542 [Stevens et al. 2003]):

- All fields in the protocol headers sent or received on a raw IPv6 socket are in network byte order.

- There is nothing similar to the IPv4 `IP_HDRINCL` socket option with IPv6. Complete IPv6 packets (including the IPv6 header or extension headers) cannot be read or written on an IPv6 raw socket. Almost all fields in an IPv6 header and all extension headers are available to the application through socket options or ancillary data (see Exercise 28.1). Should an application need to read or write complete IPv6 datagrams, datalink access (described in Chapter 29) must be used.

- Checksums on raw IPv6 sockets are handled differently, as will be described shortly.

`IPV6_CHECKSUM` Socket Option

For an ICMPv6 raw socket, the kernel always calculates and stores the checksum in the ICMPv6 header. This differs from an ICMPv4 raw socket, where the application must do this itself (compare Figures 28.14 and 28.16). While ICMPv4 and ICMPv6 both require the sender to calculate the checksum, ICMPv6 includes a pseudoheader in its checksum (we will discuss the concept of a pseudoheader when we calculate the UDP checksum in Figure 29.14). One of the fields in this pseudoheader is the source IPv6 address, and normally the application lets the kernel choose this value. To prevent the application from having to try to choose this address just to calculate the checksum, it is easier to let the kernel calculate the checksum.

For other raw IPv6 sockets (i.e., those created with a third argument to `socket` other than `IPPROTO_ICMPV6`), a socket option tells the kernel whether to calculate and store a checksum in outgoing packets and verify the checksum in received packets. By default, this option is disabled, and it is enabled by setting the option value to a non-negative value, as in

```
int  offset = 2;

if (setsockopt(sockfd, IPPROTO_IPV6, IPV6_CHECKSUM,
                &offset, sizeof(offset)) < 0)
    error
```

This not only enables checksums on this socket, it also tells the kernel the byte offset of the 16-bit checksum: 2 bytes from the start of the application data in this example. To disable the option, it must be set to −1. When enabled, the kernel will calculate and store the checksum for outgoing packets sent on the socket and also verify the checksums for packets received on the socket.

28.4 Raw Socket Input

The first question that we must answer regarding raw socket input is: Which received IP datagrams does the kernel pass to raw sockets? The following rules apply:

- Received UDP packets and received TCP packets are *never* passed to a raw socket. If a process wants to read IP datagrams containing UDP or TCP packets, the packets must be read at the datalink layer, as described in Chapter 29.

- *Most* ICMP packets are passed to a raw socket after the kernel has finished processing the ICMP message. Berkeley-derived implementations pass all received ICMP packets to a raw socket other than echo request, timestamp request, and address mask request (pp. 302–303 of TCPv2). These three ICMP messages are processed entirely by the kernel.

- *All* IGMP packets are passed to a raw socket after the kernel has finished processing the IGMP message.

- *All* IP datagrams with a protocol field that the kernel does not understand are passed to a raw socket. The only kernel processing done on these packets is the minimal verification of some IP header fields: the IP version, IPv4 header checksum, header length, and destination IP address (pp. 213–220 of TCPv2).

- If the datagram arrives in fragments, nothing is passed to a raw socket until all fragments have arrived and have been reassembled.

When the kernel has an IP datagram to pass to the raw sockets, all raw sockets for all processes are examined, looking for all matching sockets. A copy of the IP datagram is delivered to *each* matching socket. The following tests are performed for each raw socket and only if all three tests are true is the datagram delivered to the socket:

- If a nonzero *protocol* is specified when the raw socket is created (the third argument to `socket`), then the received datagram's protocol field must match this value or the datagram is not delivered to this socket.

- If a local IP address is bound to the raw socket by `bind`, then the destination IP address of the received datagram must match this bound address or the datagram is not delivered to this socket.

- If a foreign IP address was specified for the raw socket by `connect`, then the source IP address of the received datagram must match this connected address or the datagram is not delivered to this socket.

Notice that if a raw socket is created with a *protocol* of 0, and neither `bind` nor `connect` is called, then that socket receives a copy of *every* raw datagram the kernel passes to raw sockets.

Whenever a received datagram is passed to a raw IPv4 socket, the entire datagram, including the IP header, is passed to the process. For a raw IPv6 socket, only the payload (i.e., no IPv6 header or any extension headers) is passed to the socket (e.g., Figures 28.11 and 28.22).

In the IPv4 header passed to the application, `ip_len`, `ip_off`, and `ip_id` are host byte ordered, and `ip_len` contains only the IP payload length (with the IP header length subtracted), but the remaining fields are network byte ordered. Under Linux, all fields are left in network byte order.

As previously mentioned, the raw socket interface is defined to provide an identical interface to the one a protocol would have if it was resident in the kernel, so the contents of the fields are dependent on the OS kernel.

We mentioned in the previous section that all fields in a datagram received on a raw IPv6 socket are left in network byte order.

ICMPv6 Type Filtering

A raw ICMPv4 socket receives most ICMPv4 messages received by the kernel. But ICMPv6 is a superset of ICMPv4, including the functionality of ARP and IGMP (Section 2.2). Therefore, a raw ICMPv6 socket can potentially receive many more packets compared to a raw ICMPv4 socket. But most applications using a raw socket are interested in only a small subset of all ICMP messages.

To reduce the number of packets passed from the kernel to the application across a raw ICMPv6 socket, an application-specified filter is provided. A filter is declared with a datatype of struct `icmp6_filter`, which is defined by including `<netinet/icmp6.h>`. The current filter for a raw ICMPv6 socket is set and fetched using `setsockopt` and `getsockopt` with a *level* of `IPPROTO_ICMPV6` and an *optname* of `ICMP6_FILTER`.

Six macros operate on the `icmp6_filter` structure.

```
#include <netinet/icmp6.h>
void ICMP6_FILTER_SETPASSALL(struct icmp6_filter *filt);
void ICMP6_FILTER_SETBLOCKALL(struct icmp6_filter *filt);
void ICMP6_FILTER_SETPASS(int msgtype, struct icmp6_filter *filt);
void ICMP6_FILTER_SETBLOCK(int msgtype, struct icmp6_filter *filt);
int  ICMP6_FILTER_WILLPASS(int msgtype, const struct icmp6_filter *filt);
int  ICMP6_FILTER_WILLBLOCK(int msgtype, const struct icmp6_filter *filt);
                   Both return: 1 if filter will pass (block) message type, 0 otherwise
```

The *filt* argument to all the macros is a pointer to an `icmp6_filter` variable that is modified by the first four macros and examined by the final two macros. The *msgtype* argument is a value between 0 and 255 and specifies the ICMP message type.

The `SETPASSALL` macro specifies that all message types are to be passed to the application, while the `SETBLOCKALL` macros specifies that no message types are to be passed. By default, when an ICMPv6 raw socket is created, all ICMPv6 message types are passed to the application.

The `SETPASS` macro enables one specific message type to be passed to the application while the `SETBLOCK` macro blocks one specific message type. The `WILLPASS` macro returns 1 if the specified message type is passed by the filter, or 0 otherwise; the `WILLBLOCK` macro returns 1 if the specified message type is blocked by the filter, or 0 otherwise.

As an example, consider the following application, which wants to receive only ICMPv6 router advertisements:

```
struct icmp6_filter  myfilt;

fd = Socket(AF_INET6, SOCK_RAW, IPPROTO_ICMPV6);

ICMP6_FILTER_SETBLOCKALL(&myfilt);
ICMP6_FILTER_SETPASS(ND_ROUTER_ADVERT, &myfilt);
Setsockopt(fd, IPPROTO_ICMPV6, ICMP6_FILTER, &myfilt, sizeof(myfilt));
```

We first block all message types (since the default is to pass all message types) and then pass only router advertisements. Despite our use of the filter, the application must be prepared to receive all types of ICMPv6 packets since any ICMPv6 packets that arrive between the `socket` and the `setsockopt` will be added to the receive queue. The `ICMP6_FILTER` option is simply an optimization.

28.5 `ping` Program

In this section, we will develop and present a version of the `ping` program that works with both IPv4 and IPv6. We will develop our own program instead of presenting the publicly available source code for two reasons. First, the publicly available `ping` program suffers from a common programming disease known as *creeping featurism*: It supports a dozen different options. Our goal in examining a `ping` program is to understand the network programming concepts and techniques without being distracted by all these options. Our version of `ping` supports only one option and is about five times smaller than the public version. Second, the public version works only with IPv4 and we want to show a version that also supports IPv6.

The operation of `ping` is extremely simple: An ICMP echo request is sent to some IP address and that node responds with an ICMP echo reply. These two ICMP messages are supported under both IPv4 and IPv6. Figure 28.1 shows the format of the ICMP messages.

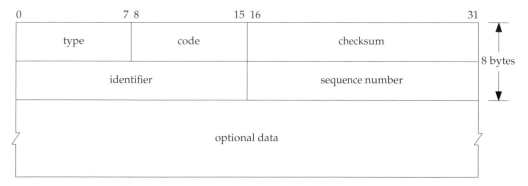

Figure 28.1   Format of ICMPv4 and ICMPv6 echo request and echo reply messages.

Figures A.15 and A.16 show the *type* values for these messages and also show that the *code* is 0. We will see that we set the *identifier* to the PID of the `ping` process and we increment the *sequence number* by one for each packet we send. We store the 8-byte timestamp of when the packet is sent as the *optional data*. The rules of ICMP require that the *identifier, sequence number,* and *any optional data* be returned in the echo reply. Storing the timestamp in the packet lets us calculate the RTT when the reply is received.

Figure 28.2 shows some examples of our program. The first uses IPv4 and the second uses IPv6. Note that we made our `ping` program set-user-ID, as it takes superuser privileges to create a raw socket.

```
freebsd % ping www.google.com
PING www.google.com (216.239.57.99): 56 data bytes
64 bytes from 216.239.57.99: seq=0, ttl=53, rtt=5.611 ms
64 bytes from 216.239.57.99: seq=1, ttl=53, rtt=5.562 ms
64 bytes from 216.239.57.99: seq=2, ttl=53, rtt=5.589 ms
64 bytes from 216.239.57.99: seq=3, ttl=53, rtt=5.910 ms

freebsd % ping www.kame.net
PING orange.kame.net (2001:200:0:4819:203:47ff:fea5:3085): 56 data bytes
64 bytes from 2001:200:0:4819:203:47ff:fea5:3085: seq=0, hlim=52, rtt=422.066 ms
64 bytes from 2001:200:0:4819:203:47ff:fea5:3085: seq=1, hlim=52, rtt=417.398 ms
64 bytes from 2001:200:0:4819:203:47ff:fea5:3085: seq=2, hlim=52, rtt=416.528 ms
64 bytes from 2001:200:0:4819:203:47ff:fea5:3085: seq=3, hlim=52, rtt=429.192 ms
```

Figure 28.2 Sample output from our `ping` program.

Figure 28.3 is an overview of the functions that comprise our `ping` program.

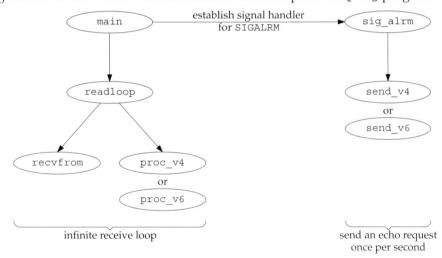

Figure 28.3 Overview of the functions in our `ping` program.

The program operates in two parts: One half reads everything received on a raw socket, printing the ICMP echo replies, and the other half sends an ICMP echo request once per second. The second half is driven by a `SIGALRM` signal once per second.

Figure 28.4 shows our `ping.h` header that is included by all our program files.

```
                                                                ─── ping/ping.h
 1 #include     "unp.h"
 2 #include     <netinet/in_systm.h>
 3 #include     <netinet/ip.h>
 4 #include     <netinet/ip_icmp.h>

 5 #define BUFSIZE     1500

 6               /* globals */
 7 char     sendbuf[BUFSIZE];

 8 int      datalen;                /* # bytes of data following ICMP header */
 9 char     *host;
10 int      nsent;                  /* add 1 for each sendto() */
11 pid_t    pid;                    /* our PID */
12 int      sockfd;
13 int      verbose;

14               /* function prototypes */
15 void     init_v6(void);
16 void     proc_v4(char *, ssize_t, struct msghdr *, struct timeval *);
17 void     proc_v6(char *, ssize_t, struct msghdr *, struct timeval *);
18 void     send_v4(void);
19 void     send_v6(void);
20 void     readloop(void);
21 void     sig_alrm(int);
22 void     tv_sub(struct timeval *, struct timeval *);

23 struct proto {
24     void     (*fproc) (char *, ssize_t, struct msghdr *, struct timeval *);
25     void     (*fsend) (void);
26     void     (*finit) (void);
27     struct sockaddr *sasend;     /* sockaddr{} for send, from getaddrinfo */
28     struct sockaddr *sarecv;     /* sockaddr{} for receiving */
29     socklen_t salen;             /* length of sockaddr{}s */
30     int      icmpproto;          /* IPPROTO_xxx value for ICMP */
31 } *pr;

32 #ifdef   IPV6

33 #include     <netinet/ip6.h>
34 #include     <netinet/icmp6.h>

35 #endif
                                                                ─── ping/ping.h
```

Figure 28.4 ping.h header.

Include IPv4 and ICMPv4 headers

1–22   We include the basic IPv4 and ICMPv4 headers, define some global variables, and our function prototypes.

Define proto structure

23–31   We use the proto structure to handle the differences between IPv4 and IPv6. This structure contains two function pointers, two pointers to socket address structures, the size of the socket address structures, and the protocol value for ICMP. The global pointer `pr` will point to one of the structures that we will initialize for either IPv4 or IPv6.

Include IPv6 and ICMPv6 headers

32–35   We include two headers that define the IPv6 and ICMPv6 structures and constants (RFC 3542 [Stevens et al. 2003]).

The `main` function is shown in Figure 28.5.

ping/main.c

```
 1 #include    "ping.h"

 2 struct proto proto_v4 =
 3     { proc_v4, send_v4, NULL, NULL, NULL, 0, IPPROTO_ICMP };

 4 #ifdef  IPV6
 5 struct proto proto_v6 =
 6     { proc_v6, send_v6, init_v6, NULL, NULL, 0, IPPROTO_ICMPV6 };
 7 #endif

 8 int     datalen = 56;           /* data that goes with ICMP echo request */

 9 int
10 main(int argc, char **argv)
11 {
12     int     c;
13     struct addrinfo *ai;
14     char    *h;

15     opterr = 0;                 /* don't want getopt() writing to stderr */
16     while ( (c = getopt(argc, argv, "v")) != -1) {
17         switch (c) {
18         case 'v':
19             verbose++;
20             break;

21         case '?':
22             err_quit("unrecognized option: %c", c);
23         }
24     }

25     if (optind != argc - 1)
26         err_quit("usage: ping [ -v ] <hostname>");
27     host = argv[optind];

28     pid = getpid() & 0xffff;    /* ICMP ID field is 16 bits */
29     Signal(SIGALRM, sig_alrm);

30     ai = Host_serv(host, NULL, 0, 0);

31     h = Sock_ntop_host(ai->ai_addr, ai->ai_addrlen);
32     printf("PING %s (%s): %d data bytes\n",
33             ai->ai_canonname ? ai->ai_canonname : h, h, datalen);

34         /* initialize according to protocol */
35     if (ai->ai_family == AF_INET) {
```

```
36          pr = &proto_v4;
37 #ifdef  IPV6
38      } else if (ai->ai_family == AF_INET6) {
39          pr = &proto_v6;
40          if (IN6_IS_ADDR_V4MAPPED(&(((struct sockaddr_in6 *)
41                                  ai->ai_addr)->sin6_addr)))
42              err_quit("cannot ping IPv4-mapped IPv6 address");
43 #endif
44      } else
45          err_quit("unknown address family %d", ai->ai_family);

46      pr->sasend = ai->ai_addr;
47      pr->sarecv = Calloc(1, ai->ai_addrlen);
48      pr->salen = ai->ai_addrlen;

49      readloop();

50      exit(0);
51 }
```
——— ping/main.c

Figure 28.5 main function.

Define `proto` structures for IPv4 and IPv6

2-7   We define a `proto` structure for IPv4 and IPv6. The socket address structure pointers are initialized to null pointers, as we do not yet know whether we will use IPv4 or IPv6.

Length of optional data

8   We set the amount of optional data that gets sent with the ICMP echo request to 56 bytes. This will yield an 84-byte IPv4 datagram (20-byte IPv4 header and 8-byte ICMP header) or a 104-byte IPv6 datagram. Any data that accompanies an echo request must be sent back in the echo reply. We will store the time at which we send an echo request in the first 8 bytes of this data area and then use this to calculate and print the RTT when the echo reply is received.

Handle command-line options

15-24   The only command-line option we support is -v, which will cause us to print most received ICMP messages. (We do not print echo replies belonging to another copy of ping that is running.) A signal handler is established for SIGALRM, and we will see that this signal is generated once per second and causes an ICMP echo request to be sent.

Process hostname argument

31-48   A hostname or IP address string is a required argument and it is processed by our host_serv function. The returned addrinfo structure contains the protocol family, either AF_INET or AF_INET6. We initialize the pr global to the correct proto structure. We also make certain that an IPv6 address is not really an IPv4-mapped IPv6 address by calling IN6_IS_ADDR_V4MAPPED, because even though the returned address is an IPv6 address, IPv4 packets will be sent to the host. (We could switch and use IPv4 when this happens.) The socket address structure that has already been allocated by the `getaddrinfo` function is used as the one for sending, and another socket address structure of the same size is allocated for receiving.

49   The function `readloop` is where the processing takes place. We will show this in Figure 28.6.

Create socket

12–13   A raw socket of the appropriate protocol is created. The call to `setuid` sets our effective user ID to our real user ID, in case the program was set-user-ID instead of being run by root. The program must have superuser privileges to create the raw socket, but now that the socket is created, we can give up the extra privileges. It is always best to give up an extra privilege when it is no longer needed, just in case the program has a latent bug that someone could exploit.

—————————————————————————————————— ping/readloop.c

```
 1 #include    "ping.h"

 2 void
 3 readloop(void)
 4 {
 5     int     size;
 6     char    recvbuf[BUFSIZE];
 7     char    controlbuf[BUFSIZE];
 8     struct msghdr msg;
 9     struct iovec iov;
10     ssize_t n;
11     struct timeval tval;

12     sockfd = Socket(pr->sasend->sa_family, SOCK_RAW, pr->icmpproto);
13     setuid(getuid());           /* don't need special permissions any more */
14     if (pr->finit)
15         (*pr->finit)();

16     size = 60 * 1024;           /* OK if setsockopt fails */
17     setsockopt(sockfd, SOL_SOCKET, SO_RCVBUF, &size, sizeof(size));

18     sig_alrm(SIGALRM);          /* send first packet */

19     iov.iov_base = recvbuf;
20     iov.iov_len = sizeof(recvbuf);
21     msg.msg_name = pr->sarecv;
22     msg.msg_iov = &iov;
23     msg.msg_iovlen = 1;
24     msg.msg_control = controlbuf;
25     for ( ; ; ) {
26         msg.msg_namelen = pr->salen;
27         msg.msg_controllen = sizeof(controlbuf);
28         n = recvmsg(sockfd, &msg, 0);
29         if (n < 0) {
30             if (errno == EINTR)
31                 continue;
32             else
33                 err_sys("recvmsg error");
34         }
```

```
35              Gettimeofday(&tval, NULL);
36              (*pr->fproc)(recvbuf, n, &msg, &tval);
37          }
38  }
```
—— *ping/readloop.c*

Figure 28.6 `readloop` function.

Perform protocol-specific initialization

14-15   If the protocol specified an initialization function, we call it. We show the IPv6 initialization function in Figure 28.10.

Set socket receive buffer size

16-17   We try to set the socket receive buffer size to 61,440 bytes (60×1024), which should be larger than the default. We do this in case the user `ping`s either the IPv4 broadcast address or a multicast address, either of which can generate lots of replies. By making the buffer larger, there is a smaller chance that the socket receive buffer will overflow.

Send first packet

18   We call our signal handler, which we will see sends a packet and schedules a SIGALRM for one second in the future. It is not common to see a signal handler called directly, as we do here, but it is acceptable. A signal handler is just a C function, even though it is normally called asynchronously.

Set up `msghdr` for `recvmsg`

19-24   We set up the unchanging fields in the `msghdr` and `iovec` structs that we will pass to `recvmsg`.

Infinite loop reading all ICMP messages

25-37   The main loop of the program is an infinite loop that reads all packets returned on the raw ICMP socket. We call `gettimeofday` to record the time that the packet was received and then call the appropriate protocol function (`proc_v4` or `proc_v6`) to process the ICMP message.

Figure 28.7 shows the `tv_sub` function, which subtracts two `timeval` structures, storing the result in the first structure.

—— *lib/tv_sub.c*
```
 1 #include      "unp.h"

 2 void
 3 tv_sub(struct timeval *out, struct timeval *in)
 4 {
 5     if ((out->tv_usec -= in->tv_usec) < 0) {     /* out -= in */
 6         --out->tv_sec;
 7         out->tv_usec += 1000000;
 8     }
 9     out->tv_sec -= in->tv_sec;
10 }
```
—— *lib/tv_sub.c*

Figure 28.7 `tv_sub` function: subtracts two `timeval` structures.

Figure 28.8 shows the proc_v4 function, which processes all received ICMPv4 messages. You may want to refer to Figure A.1, which shows the format of the IPv4 header. Also realize that when the ICMPv4 message is received by the process on the raw socket, the kernel has already verified that the basic fields in the IPv4 header and in the ICMPv4 header are valid (pp. 214 and 311 of TCPv2).

ping/proc_v4.c

```
 1 #include    "ping.h"

 2 void
 3 proc_v4(char *ptr, ssize_t len, struct msghdr *msg, struct timeval *tvrecv)
 4 {
 5     int     hlen1, icmplen;
 6     double  rtt;
 7     struct ip *ip;
 8     struct icmp *icmp;
 9     struct timeval *tvsend;

10     ip = (struct ip *) ptr;     /* start of IP header */
11     hlen1 = ip->ip_hl << 2;     /* length of IP header */
12     if (ip->ip_p != IPPROTO_ICMP)
13         return;                 /* not ICMP */

14     icmp = (struct icmp *) (ptr + hlen1);   /* start of ICMP header */
15     if ( (icmplen = len - hlen1) < 8)
16         return;                 /* malformed packet */

17     if (icmp->icmp_type == ICMP_ECHOREPLY) {
18         if (icmp->icmp_id != pid)
19             return;                 /* not a response to our ECHO_REQUEST */
20         if (icmplen < 16)
21             return;                 /* not enough data to use */

22         tvsend = (struct timeval *) icmp->icmp_data;
23         tv_sub(tvrecv, tvsend);
24         rtt = tvrecv->tv_sec * 1000.0 + tvrecv->tv_usec / 1000.0;

25         printf("%d bytes from %s: seq=%u, ttl=%d, rtt=%.3f ms\n",
26                 icmplen, Sock_ntop_host(pr->sarecv, pr->salen),
27                 icmp->icmp_seq, ip->ip_ttl, rtt);

28     } else if (verbose) {
29         printf("  %d bytes from %s: type = %d, code = %d\n",
30                 icmplen, Sock_ntop_host(pr->sarecv, pr->salen),
31                 icmp->icmp_type, icmp->icmp_code);
32     }
33 }
```

ping/proc_v4.c

Figure 28.8 proc_v4 function: processes ICMPv4 message.

Get pointer to ICMP header

10–16   The IPv4 header length field is multiplied by 4, giving the size of the IPv4 header in bytes. (Remember that an IPv4 header can contain options.) This lets us set icmp to point to the beginning of the ICMP header. We make sure that the IP protocol is ICMP

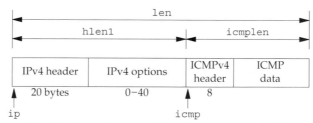

Figure 28.9 Headers, pointers, and lengths in processing ICMPv4 reply.

and that there is enough data echoed to look at the timestamp we included in the echo request. Figure 28.9 shows the various headers, pointers, and lengths used by the code.

Check for ICMP echo reply

17–21   If the message is an ICMP echo reply, then we must check the identifier field to see if this reply is in response to a request our process sent. If the ping program is running multiple times on this host, each process gets a copy of all received ICMP messages.

22–27   We calculate the RTT by subtracting the time the message was sent (contained in the optional data portion of the ICMP reply) from the current time (pointed to by the tvrecv function argument). The RTT is converted from microseconds to milliseconds and printed, along with the sequence number field and the received TTL. The sequence number field lets the user see if packets were dropped, reordered, or duplicated, and the TTL gives an indication of the number of hops between the two hosts.

Print all received ICMP messages if verbose option specified

28–32   If the user specified the -v command-line option, we print the type and code fields from all other received ICMP messages.

The processing of ICMPv6 messages is handled by the proc_v6 function, shown in Figure 28.12 (p. 751). It is similar to the proc_v4 function; however, since IPv6 raw sockets do not return the IPv6 header, it receives the hop limit as ancillary data. This was set up using the init_v6 function, shown in Figure 28.10.

The init_v6 function prepares the socket for use.

Set ICMPv6 receive filter

6–14   If the -v command-line option was not specified, install a filter that blocks all ICMP message types except for the expected echo reply. This reduces the number of packets received on the socket.

Request IPV6_HOPLIMIT ancillary data

15–22   The API to request reception of the hop limit with incoming packets has changed over time. We prefer the newer API: setting the IPV6_RECVHOPLIMIT socket option. However, if the constant for this option is not defined, we can try the older API: setting IPV6_HOPLIMIT as an option. We don't check the return value from setsockopt, since the program can still do useful work without receiving the hop limit.

——————————————————————————————————— *ping/init_v6.c*

```
 1 void
 2 init_v6()
 3 {
 4 #ifdef IPV6
 5     int     on = 1;
 6     if (verbose == 0) {
 7         /* install a filter that only passes ICMP6_ECHO_REPLY unless verbose */
 8         struct icmp6_filter myfilt;
 9         ICMP6_FILTER_SETBLOCKALL(&myfilt);
10         ICMP6_FILTER_SETPASS(ICMP6_ECHO_REPLY, &myfilt);
11         setsockopt(sockfd, IPPROTO_IPV6, ICMP6_FILTER, &myfilt,
12                     sizeof(myfilt));
13         /* ignore error return; the filter is an optimization */
14     }
15     /* ignore error returned below; we just won't receive the hop limit */
16 #ifdef IPV6_RECVHOPLIMIT
17     /* RFC 3542 */
18     setsockopt(sockfd, IPPROTO_IPV6, IPV6_RECVHOPLIMIT, &on, sizeof(on));
19 #else
20     /* RFC 2292 */
21     setsockopt(sockfd, IPPROTO_IPV6, IPV6_HOPLIMIT, &on, sizeof(on));
22 #endif
23 #endif
24 }
```

——————————————————————————————————— *ping/init_v6.c*

Figure 28.10 init_v6 function: initializes ICMPv6 socket.

The proc_v6 function (Figure 28.12) processes incoming packets.

Get pointer to ICMPv6 header

11–13   The ICMPv6 header is the data returned by the receive operation. (Recall that the IPv6 header and extension headers, if any, are never returned as normal data, but as ancillary data.) Figure 28.11 shows the various headers, pointers, and lengths used by the code.

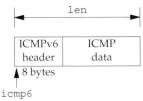

Figure 28.11 Headers, pointers, and lengths in processing ICMPv6 reply.

Check for ICMP echo reply

14–37   If the ICMP message type is an echo reply, we check the identifier field to see if the reply is for us. If so, we calculate the RTT and then print it along with the sequence number and IPv6 hop limit. We obtain the hop limit from the IPV6_HOPLIMIT ancillary data.

―― *ping/proc_v6.c*
```
 1 #include    "ping.h"

 2 void
 3 proc_v6(char *ptr, ssize_t len, struct msghdr *msg, struct timeval *tvrecv)
 4 {
 5 #ifdef  IPV6
 6     double  rtt;
 7     struct icmp6_hdr *icmp6;
 8     struct timeval *tvsend;
 9     struct cmsghdr *cmsg;
10     int     hlim;

11     icmp6 = (struct icmp6_hdr *) ptr;
12     if (len < 8)
13         return;                    /* malformed packet */

14     if (icmp6->icmp6_type == ICMP6_ECHO_REPLY) {
15         if (icmp6->icmp6_id != pid)
16             return;                    /* not a response to our ECHO_REQUEST */
17         if (len < 16)
18             return;                    /* not enough data to use */

19         tvsend = (struct timeval *) (icmp6 + 1);
20         tv_sub(tvrecv, tvsend);
21         rtt = tvrecv->tv_sec * 1000.0 + tvrecv->tv_usec / 1000.0;

22         hlim = -1;
23         for (cmsg = CMSG_FIRSTHDR(msg); cmsg != NULL;
24               cmsg = CMSG_NXTHDR(msg, cmsg)) {
25             if (cmsg->cmsg_level == IPPROTO_IPV6
26                 && cmsg->cmsg_type == IPV6_HOPLIMIT) {
27                 hlim = *(u_int32_t *) CMSG_DATA(cmsg);
28                 break;
29             }
30         }
31         printf("%d bytes from %s: seq=%u, hlim=",
32                 len, Sock_ntop_host(pr->sarecv, pr->salen), icmp6->icmp6_seq);
33         if (hlim == -1)
34             printf("???");      /* ancillary data missing */
35         else
36             printf("%d", hlim);
37         printf(", rtt=%.3f ms\n", rtt);
38     } else if (verbose) {
39         printf("  %d bytes from %s: type = %d, code = %d\n",
40                 len, Sock_ntop_host(pr->sarecv, pr->salen),
41                 icmp6->icmp6_type, icmp6->icmp6_code);
42     }
43 #endif  /* IPV6 */
44 }
```
―― *ping/proc_v6.c*

Figure 28.12 proc_v6 function: processes received ICMPv6 message.

Print all received ICMP messages if verbose option specified

38–41   If the user specified the -v command-line option, we print the type and code fields
from all other received ICMP messages.

Our signal handler for the SIGALRM signal is the sig_alrm function, shown in Figure 28.13. We saw in Figure 28.6 that our readloop function calls this signal handler once at the beginning to send the first packet. This function just calls the protocol-dependent function to send an ICMP echo request (send_v4 or send_v6) and then schedules another SIGALRM for one second in the future.

ping/sig_alrm.c
```
1 #include    "ping.h"

2 void
3 sig_alrm(int signo)
4 {
5     (*pr->fsend) ();

6     alarm(1);
7     return;
8 }
```
ping/sig_alrm.c

Figure 28.13 sig_alrm function: SIGALRM signal handler.

The function send_v4, shown in Figure 28.14, builds an ICMPv4 echo request message and writes it to the raw socket.

ping/send_v4.c
```
 1 #include    "ping.h"

 2 void
 3 send_v4(void)
 4 {
 5     int     len;
 6     struct icmp *icmp;

 7     icmp = (struct icmp *) sendbuf;
 8     icmp->icmp_type = ICMP_ECHO;
 9     icmp->icmp_code = 0;
10     icmp->icmp_id = pid;
11     icmp->icmp_seq = nsent++;
12     memset(icmp->icmp_data, 0xa5, datalen); /* fill with pattern */
13     Gettimeofday((struct timeval *) icmp->icmp_data, NULL);

14     len = 8 + datalen;          /* checksum ICMP header and data */
15     icmp->icmp_cksum = 0;
16     icmp->icmp_cksum = in_cksum((u_short *) icmp, len);

17     Sendto(sockfd, sendbuf, len, 0, pr->sasend, pr->salen);
18 }
```
ping/send_v4.c

Figure 28.14 send_v4 function: builds an ICMPv4 echo request message and sends it.

Build ICMPv4 message

7–13   The ICMPv4 message is built. The identifier field is set to our PID and the sequence number field is set to the global nsent, which is then incremented for the next packet. We store a pattern of 0xa5 in the data portion of the ICMP message. The current time-of-day is then stored in the beginning of the data portion.

Calculate ICMP checksum

14-16   To calculate the ICMP checksum, we set the checksum field to 0 and call the function in_cksum, storing the result in the checksum field. The ICMPv4 checksum is calculated from the ICMPv4 header and any data that follows.

Send datagram

17   The ICMP message is sent on the raw socket. Since we have not set the IP_HDRINCL socket option, the kernel builds the IPv4 header and prepends it to our buffer.

The Internet checksum is the one's complement of the one's complement sum of the 16-bit values to be checksummed. If the data length is an odd number, then 1 byte of 0 is logically appended to the end of the data, just for the checksum computation. Before computing the checksum, the checksum field itself is set to 0. This algorithm is used for the IPv4, ICMPv4, IGMPv4, ICMPv6, UDP, and TCP checksums. RFC 1071 [Braden, Borman, and Partridge 1988] contains additional information and some numeric examples. Section 8.7 of TCPv2 talks about this algorithm in more detail and shows a more efficient implementation. Our in_cksum function, shown in Figure 28.15, calculates the checksum.

———————————————————————————————— libfree/in_cksum.c

```
1 uint16_t
2 in_cksum(uint16_t * addr, int len)
3 {
4      int     nleft = len;
5      uint32_t sum = 0;
6      uint16_t *w = addr;
7      uint16_t answer = 0;

8      /*
9       * Our algorithm is simple, using a 32 bit accumulator (sum), we add
10      * sequential 16 bit words to it, and at the end, fold back all the
11      * carry bits from the top 16 bits into the lower 16 bits.
12      */
13     while (nleft > 1) {
14         sum += *w++;
15         nleft -= 2;
16     }

17         /* mop up an odd byte, if necessary */
18     if (nleft == 1) {
19         *(unsigned char *) (&answer) = *(unsigned char *) w;
20         sum += answer;
21     }

22         /* add back carry outs from top 16 bits to low 16 bits */
23     sum = (sum >> 16) + (sum & 0xffff); /* add hi 16 to low 16 */
24     sum += (sum >> 16);             /* add carry */
25     answer = ~sum;                  /* truncate to 16 bits */
26     return (answer);
27 }
```

———————————————————————————————— libfree/in_cksum.c

Figure 28.15 in_cksum function: calculate the Internet checksum.

Internet checksum algorithm

1-27   The first `while` loop calculates the sum of all the 16-bit values. If the length is odd, then the final byte is added in with the sum. The algorithm we show in Figure 28.15 is the simple algorithm. The kernel often has a specially optimized checksum algorithm due to the high volume of checksum computations performed by the kernel.

> This function is taken from the public domain version of `ping` by Mike Muuss.

The final function for our `ping` program is `send_v6`, shown in Figure 28.16, which builds and sends an ICMPv6 echo request.

—— *ping/send_v6.c*
```
 1 #include    "ping.h"

 2 void
 3 send_v6()
 4 {
 5 #ifdef  IPV6
 6     int     len;
 7     struct icmp6_hdr *icmp6;

 8     icmp6 = (struct icmp6_hdr *) sendbuf;
 9     icmp6->icmp6_type = ICMP6_ECHO_REQUEST;
10     icmp6->icmp6_code = 0;
11     icmp6->icmp6_id = pid;
12     icmp6->icmp6_seq = nsent++;
13     memset((icmp6 + 1), 0xa5, datalen); /* fill with pattern */
14     Gettimeofday((struct timeval *) (icmp6 + 1), NULL);

15     len = 8 + datalen;          /* 8-byte ICMPv6 header */

16     Sendto(sockfd, sendbuf, len, 0, pr->sasend, pr->salen);
17         /* kernel calculates and stores checksum for us */
18 #endif  /* IPV6 */
19 }
```
—— *ping/send_v6.c*

Figure 28.16   send_v6 function: builds and sends an ICMPv6 echo request message.

The `send_v6` function is similar to `send_v4`, but notice that it does not compute the ICMPv6 checksum. As we mentioned earlier in the chapter, since the ICMPv6 checksum uses the source address from the IPv6 header in its computation, this checksum is calculated by the kernel for us, after the kernel chooses the source address.

28.6 `traceroute` **Program**

In this section, we will develop our own version of the `traceroute` program. Like the `ping` program we developed in the previous section, we will develop and present our own version, instead of presenting the publicly available version. We do this because we need a version that supports both IPv4 and IPv6, and we do not want to be distracted with lots of options that are not germane to our discussion of network programming.

`traceroute` lets us determine the path that IP datagrams follow from our host to some other destination. Its operation is simple and Chapter 8 of TCPv1 covers it in detail with numerous examples of its usage. `traceroute` uses the IPv4 TTL field or the IPv6 hop limit field and two ICMP messages. It starts by sending a UDP datagram to the destination with a TTL (or hop limit) of 1. This datagram causes the first-hop router to return an ICMP "time exceeded in transit" error. The TTL is then increased by one and another UDP datagram is sent, which locates the next router in the path. When the UDP datagram reaches the final destination, the goal is to have that host return an ICMP "port unreachable" error. This is done by sending the UDP datagram to a random port that is (hopefully) not in use on that host.

Early versions of `traceroute` were able to set the TTL field in the IPv4 header only by setting the `IP_HDRINCL` socket option and then building their own IPv4 header. Current systems, however, provide an `IP_TTL` socket option that lets us specify the TTL to use for outgoing datagrams. (This socket option was introduced with the 4.3BSD Reno release.) It is easier to set this socket option than to build a complete IPv4 header (although we will show how to build IPv4 and UDP headers in Section 29.7). The IPv6 `IPV6_UNICAST_HOPS` socket option lets us control the hop limit field for IPv6 datagrams.

Figure 28.17 shows our `trace.h` header, which all our program files include.

1–11   We include the standard IPv4 headers that define the IPv4, ICMPv4, and UDP structures and constants. The `rec` structure defines the data portion of the UDP datagram that we send, but we will see that we never need to examine this data. It is sent mainly for debugging purposes.

Define `proto` structure

32–43   As with our `ping` program in the previous section, we handle the protocol differences between IPv4 and IPv6 by defining a `proto` structure that contains function pointers, pointers to socket address structures, and other constants that differ between the two IP versions. The global `pr` will be set to point to one of these structures that is initialized for either IPv4 or IPv6, after the destination address is processed by the `main` function (since the destination address is what specifies whether we use IPv4 or IPv6).

Include IPv6 headers

44–47   We include the headers that define the IPv6 and ICMPv6 structures and constants.

—— traceroute/trace.h

```
 1 #include      "unp.h"
 2 #include      <netinet/in_systm.h>
 3 #include      <netinet/ip.h>
 4 #include      <netinet/ip_icmp.h>
 5 #include      <netinet/udp.h>

 6 #define BUFSIZE      1500

 7 struct rec {                        /* of outgoing UDP data */
 8     u_short rec_seq;                /* sequence number */
 9     u_short rec_ttl;                /* TTL packet left with */
10     struct timeval rec_tv;          /* time packet left */
11 };

12              /* globals */
13 char    recvbuf[BUFSIZE];
14 char    sendbuf[BUFSIZE];

15 int     datalen;                    /* # bytes of data following ICMP header */
16 char    *host;
17 u_short sport, dport;
18 int     nsent;                      /* add 1 for each sendto() */
19 pid_t   pid;                        /* our PID */
20 int     probe, nprobes;
21 int     sendfd, recvfd;             /* send on UDP sock, read on raw ICMP sock */
22 int     ttl, max_ttl;
23 int     verbose;

24              /* function prototypes */
25 const char *icmpcode_v4(int);
26 const char *icmpcode_v6(int);
27 int     recv_v4(int, struct timeval *);
28 int     recv_v6(int, struct timeval *);
29 void    sig_alrm(int);
30 void    traceloop(void);
31 void    tv_sub(struct timeval *, struct timeval *);

32 struct proto {
33     const char *(*icmpcode) (int);
34     int     (*recv) (int, struct timeval *);
35     struct sockaddr *sasend;    /* sockaddr{} for send, from getaddrinfo */
36     struct sockaddr *sarecv;    /* sockaddr{} for receiving */
37     struct sockaddr *salast;    /* last sockaddr{} for receiving */
38     struct sockaddr *sabind;    /* sockaddr{} for binding source port */
39     socklen_t salen;            /* length of sockaddr{}s */
40     int     icmpproto;          /* IPPROTO_xxx value for ICMP */
41     int     ttllevel;           /* setsockopt() level to set TTL */
42     int     ttloptname;         /* setsockopt() name to set TTL */
43 } *pr;

44 #ifdef  IPV6

45 #include      <netinet/ip6.h>
46 #include      <netinet/icmp6.h>

47 #endif
```

—— traceroute/trace.h

Figure 28.17 trace.h header.

The main function is shown in Figure 28.18 (p. 759). It processes the command-line arguments, initializes the pr pointer for either IPv4 or IPv6, and calls our traceloop function.

Define proto structures

2-9   We define the two proto structures, one for IPv4 and one for IPv6, although the pointers to the socket address structures are not allocated until the end of this function.

Set defaults

10-13   The maximum TTL or hop limit that the program uses defaults to 30, although we provide the -m command-line option to let the user change this. For each TTL, we send three probe packets, but this could be changed with another command-line option. The initial destination port is 32768 + 666, which will be incremented by one each time we send a UDP datagram. We hope that these ports are not in use on the destination host when the datagrams finally reach the destination, but there is no guarantee.

Process command-line arguments

19-37   The -v command-line option causes most received ICMP messages to be printed.

Process hostname or IP address argument and finish initialization

38-58   The destination hostname or IP address is processed by our host_serv function, returning a pointer to an addrinfo structure. Depending on the type of returned address, IPv4 or IPv6, we finish initializing the proto structure, store the pointer in the pr global, and allocate additional socket address structures of the correct size.

59   The function traceloop, shown in Figure 28.19, sends the datagrams and reads the returned ICMP messages. This is the main loop of the program.

———————————————————————————————— traceroute/main.c

```
 1 #include    "trace.h"

 2 struct proto proto_v4 = { icmpcode_v4, recv_v4, NULL, NULL, NULL, NULL, 0,
 3     IPPROTO_ICMP, IPPROTO_IP, IP_TTL
 4 };

 5 #ifdef  IPV6
 6 struct proto proto_v6 = { icmpcode_v6, recv_v6, NULL, NULL, NULL, NULL, 0,
 7     IPPROTO_ICMPV6, IPPROTO_IPV6, IPV6_UNICAST_HOPS
 8 };
 9 #endif

10 int    datalen = sizeof(struct rec);   /* defaults */
11 int    max_ttl = 30;
12 int    nprobes = 3;
13 u_short dport = 32768 + 666;

14 int
15 main(int argc, char **argv)
16 {
17     int    c;
18     struct addrinfo *ai;
19     char   *h;

20     opterr = 0;                    /* don't want getopt() writing to stderr */
21     while ( (c = getopt(argc, argv, "m:v")) != -1) {
22         switch (c) {
23         case 'm':
24             if ( (max_ttl = atoi(optarg)) <= 1)
25                 err_quit("invalid -m value");
26             break;

27         case 'v':
28             verbose++;
29             break;

30         case '?':
31             err_quit("unrecognized option: %c", c);
32         }
33     }

34     if (optind != argc - 1)
35         err_quit("usage: traceroute [ -m <maxttl> -v ] <hostname>");
36     host = argv[optind];

37     pid = getpid();
38     Signal(SIGALRM, sig_alrm);

39     ai = Host_serv(host, NULL, 0, 0);

40     h = Sock_ntop_host(ai->ai_addr, ai->ai_addrlen);
41     printf("traceroute to %s (%s): %d hops max, %d data bytes\n",
42             ai->ai_canonname ? ai->ai_canonname : h, h, max_ttl, datalen);

43     /* initialize according to protocol */
44     if (ai->ai_family == AF_INET) {
45         pr = &proto_v4;
46 #ifdef  IPV6
```

```
47        } else if (ai->ai_family == AF_INET6) {
48            pr = &proto_v6;
49            if (IN6_IS_ADDR_V4MAPPED
50                    (&(((struct sockaddr_in6 *) ai->ai_addr)->sin6_addr)))
51                err_quit("cannot traceroute IPv4-mapped IPv6 address");
52 #endif
53        } else
54            err_quit("unknown address family %d", ai->ai_family);
55        pr->sasend = ai->ai_addr;     /* contains destination address */
56        pr->sarecv = Calloc(1, ai->ai_addrlen);
57        pr->salast = Calloc(1, ai->ai_addrlen);
58        pr->sabind = Calloc(1, ai->ai_addrlen);
59        pr->salen = ai->ai_addrlen;

60        traceloop();

61        exit(0);
62 }
```
—————————————————————————————————— traceroute/main.c

Figure 28.18 main function for traceroute program.

We next examine our function traceloop, shown in Figure 28.19 (p. 761).

Create raw socket

9-10   We need two sockets: a raw socket on which we read all returned ICMP messages and a UDP socket on which we send the probe packets with the increasing TTLs. After creating the raw socket, we reset our effective user ID to our real user ID since we no longer require superuser privileges.

Set ICMPv6 receive filter

11-20   If we are tracing the route to an IPv6 address and the -v command-line option was not specified, install a filter that blocks all ICMP message types except for the ones we expect: "time exceeded" or "destination unreachable." This reduces the number of packets received on the socket.

Create UDP socket and bind source port

21-25   We bind a source port to the UDP socket that is used for sending, using the low-order 16 bits of our PID with the high-order bit set to 1. Since it is possible for multiple copies of the traceroute program to be running at any given time, we need a way to determine if a received ICMP message was generated in response to one of our datagrams, or in response to a datagram sent by another copy of the program. We use the source port in the UDP header to identify the sending process because the returned ICMP message is required to include the UDP header from the datagram that caused the ICMP error.

Establish signal handler for SIGALRM

26   We establish our function sig_alrm as the signal handler for SIGALRM because each time we send a UDP datagram, we wait three seconds for an ICMP message before sending the next probe.

traceroute/traceloop.c

```
 1 #include     "trace.h"

 2 void
 3 traceloop(void)
 4 {
 5     int     seq, code, done;
 6     double  rtt;
 7     struct rec *rec;
 8     struct timeval tvrecv;

 9     recvfd = Socket(pr->sasend->sa_family, SOCK_RAW, pr->icmpproto);
10     setuid(getuid());          /* don't need special permissions anymore */

11 #ifdef  IPV6
12     if (pr->sasend->sa_family == AF_INET6 && verbose == 0) {
13         struct icmp6_filter myfilt;
14         ICMP6_FILTER_SETBLOCKALL(&myfilt);
15         ICMP6_FILTER_SETPASS(ICMP6_TIME_EXCEEDED, &myfilt);
16         ICMP6_FILTER_SETPASS(ICMP6_DST_UNREACH, &myfilt);
17         setsockopt(recvfd, IPPROTO_IPV6, ICMP6_FILTER,
18                     &myfilt, sizeof(myfilt));
19     }
20 #endif

21     sendfd = Socket(pr->sasend->sa_family, SOCK_DGRAM, 0);

22     pr->sabind->sa_family = pr->sasend->sa_family;
23     sport = (getpid() & 0xffff) | 0x8000;   /* our source UDP port # */
24     sock_set_port(pr->sabind, pr->salen, htons(sport));
25     Bind(sendfd, pr->sabind, pr->salen);

26     sig_alrm(SIGALRM);

27     seq = 0;
28     done = 0;
29     for (ttl = 1; ttl <= max_ttl && done == 0; ttl++) {
30         Setsockopt(sendfd, pr->ttllevel, pr->ttloptname, &ttl, sizeof(int));
31         bzero(pr->salast, pr->salen);

32         printf("%2d ", ttl);
33         fflush(stdout);

34         for (probe = 0; probe < nprobes; probe++) {
35             rec = (struct rec *) sendbuf;
36             rec->rec_seq = ++seq;
37             rec->rec_ttl = ttl;
38             Gettimeofday(&rec->rec_tv, NULL);

39             sock_set_port(pr->sasend, pr->salen, htons(dport + seq));
40             Sendto(sendfd, sendbuf, datalen, 0, pr->sasend, pr->salen);

41             if ( (code = (*pr->recv) (seq, &tvrecv)) == -3)
42                 printf(" *");   /* timeout, no reply */
43             else {
44                 char    str[NI_MAXHOST];

45                 if (sock_cmp_addr(pr->sarecv, pr->salast, pr->salen) != 0) {
```

```
46                          if (getnameinfo(pr->sarecv, pr->salen, str, sizeof(str),
47                                    NULL, 0, 0) == 0)
48                              printf(" %s (%s)", str,
49                                      Sock_ntop_host(pr->sarecv, pr->salen));
50                          else
51                              printf(" %s", Sock_ntop_host(pr->sarecv, pr->salen));
52                          memcpy(pr->salast, pr->sarecv, pr->salen);
53                      }
54                      tv_sub(&tvrecv, &rec->rec_tv);
55                      rtt = tvrecv.tv_sec * 1000.0 + tvrecv.tv_usec / 1000.0;
56                      printf("  %.3f ms", rtt);

57                      if (code == -1) /* port unreachable; at destination */
58                          done++;
59                      else if (code >= 0)
60                          printf(" (ICMP %s)", (*pr->icmpcode) (code));
61                  }
62              fflush(stdout);
63          }
64      printf("\n");
65  }
66 }
```
—————————————————— traceroute/traceloop.c

Figure 28.19 `traceloop` function: main processing loop.

Main loop; set TTL or hop limit and send three probes

27–38   The main loop of the function is a double nested `for` loop. The outer loop starts the TTL or hop limit at 1, and increases it by 1, while the inner loop sends three probes (UDP datagrams) to the destination. Each time the TTL changes, we call `setsockopt` to set the new value using either the `IP_TTL` or `IPV6_UNICAST_HOPS` socket option.

Each time around the outer loop, we initialize the socket address structure pointed to by `salast` to 0. This structure will be compared to the socket address structure returned by `recvfrom` when the ICMP message is read, and if the two structures are different, the IP address from the new structure will be printed. Using this technique, the IP address corresponding to the first probe for each TTL is printed, and should the IP address change for a given value of the TTL (say a route changes while we are running the program), the new IP address will then be printed.

Set destination port and send UDP datagram

39–40   Each time a probe packet is sent, the destination port in the `sasend` socket address structure is changed by calling our `sock_set_port` function. The reason for changing the port for each probe is that when we reach the final destination, all three probes are sent to a different port, and hopefully at least one of the ports is not in use. `sendto` sends the UDP datagram.

Read ICMP message

41–42   One of our functions, `recv_v4` or `recv_v6`, calls `recvfrom` to read and process the returned ICMP messages. These two functions return –3 if a timeout occurs (telling us to send another probe if we haven't sent three for this TTL), –2 if an ICMP "time exceeded in transit" error is received, –1 if an ICMP "port unreachable" error is received (which means we have reached the final destination), or the non-negative ICMP code if some other ICMP destination unreachable error is received.

Print reply

43–63   As we mentioned earlier, if this is the first reply for a given TTL, or if the IP address of the node sending the ICMP message has changed for this TTL, we print the hostname and IP address, or just the IP address (if the call to `getnameinfo` doesn't return the hostname). The RTT is calculated as the time difference from when we sent the probe to the time when the ICMP message was returned and printed.

Our `recv_v4` function is shown in Figure 28.20.

——————————————————————————— traceroute/recv_v4.c

```
 1 #include    "trace.h"
 2 extern int gotalarm;
 3 /*
 4  * Return: -3 on timeout
 5  *          -2 on ICMP time exceeded in transit (caller keeps going)
 6  *          -1 on ICMP port unreachable (caller is done)
 7  *       >= 0 return value is some other ICMP unreachable code
 8  */
 9 int
10 recv_v4(int seq, struct timeval *tv)
11 {
12     int     hlen1, hlen2, icmplen, ret;
13     socklen_t len;
14     ssize_t n;
15     struct ip *ip, *hip;
16     struct icmp *icmp;
17     struct udphdr *udp;
18     gotalarm = 0;
19     alarm(3);
20     for ( ; ; ) {
21         if (gotalarm)
22             return (-3);        /* alarm expired */
23         len = pr->salen;
24         n = recvfrom(recvfd, recvbuf, sizeof(recvbuf), 0, pr->sarecv, &len);
25         if (n < 0) {
26             if (errno == EINTR)
27                 continue;
28             else
29                 err_sys("recvfrom error");
30         }
31         ip = (struct ip *) recvbuf; /* start of IP header */
32         hlen1 = ip->ip_hl << 2; /* length of IP header */
33         icmp = (struct icmp *) (recvbuf + hlen1);   /* start of ICMP header */
34         if ( (icmplen = n - hlen1) < 8)
35             continue;           /* not enough to look at ICMP header */
36         if (icmp->icmp_type == ICMP_TIMXCEED &&
37             icmp->icmp_code == ICMP_TIMXCEED_INTRANS) {
38             if (icmplen < 8 + sizeof(struct ip))
```

```
39                      continue;        /* not enough data to look at inner IP */
40                  hip = (struct ip *) (recvbuf + hlen1 + 8);
41                  hlen2 = hip->ip_hl << 2;
42                  if (icmplen < 8 + hlen2 + 4)
43                      continue;        /* not enough data to look at UDP ports */
44                  udp = (struct udphdr *) (recvbuf + hlen1 + 8 + hlen2);
45                  if (hip->ip_p == IPPROTO_UDP &&
46                      udp->uh_sport == htons(sport) &&
47                      udp->uh_dport == htons(dport + seq)) {
48                      ret = -2;        /* we hit an intermediate router */
49                      break;
50                  }
51              } else if (icmp->icmp_type == ICMP_UNREACH) {
52                  if (icmplen < 8 + sizeof(struct ip))
53                      continue;        /* not enough data to look at inner IP */
54                  hip = (struct ip *) (recvbuf + hlen1 + 8);
55                  hlen2 = hip->ip_hl << 2;
56                  if (icmplen < 8 + hlen2 + 4)
57                      continue;        /* not enough data to look at UDP ports */
58                  udp = (struct udphdr *) (recvbuf + hlen1 + 8 + hlen2);
59                  if (hip->ip_p == IPPROTO_UDP &&
60                      udp->uh_sport == htons(sport) &&
61                      udp->uh_dport == htons(dport + seq)) {
62                      if (icmp->icmp_code == ICMP_UNREACH_PORT)
63                          ret = -1;    /* have reached destination */
64                      else
65                          ret = icmp->icmp_code;  /* 0, 1, 2, ... */
66                      break;
67                  }
68              }
69              if (verbose) {
70                  printf(" (from %s: type = %d, code = %d)\n",
71                          Sock_ntop_host(pr->sarecv, pr->salen),
72                          icmp->icmp_type, icmp->icmp_code);
73              }
74              /* Some other ICMP error, recvfrom() again */
75          }
76      alarm(0);                        /* don't leave alarm running */
77      Gettimeofday(tv, NULL);          /* get time of packet arrival */
78      return (ret);
79  }
```
———————————————————————— traceroute/recv_v4.c

Figure 28.20 recv_v4 function: reads and processes ICMPv4 messages.

Set alarm and read each ICMP message

19-30   An alarm is set for three seconds in the future and the function enters a loop that calls recvfrom, reading each ICMPv4 message returned on the raw socket.

> This function avoids the race condition we described in Section 20.5 by using a global flag.

Get pointer to ICMP header

31-35   ip points to the beginning of the IPv4 header (recall that a read on a raw socket always returns the IP header), and icmp points to the beginning of the ICMP header. Figure 28.21 shows the various headers, pointers, and lengths used by the code.

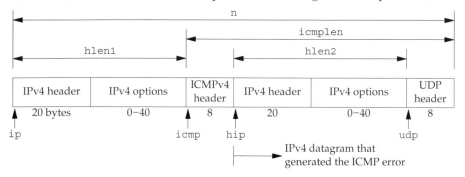

Figure 28.21 Headers, pointers, and lengths in processing ICMPv4 error.

Process ICMP "time exceeded in transit" message

36-50   If the ICMP message is a "time exceeded in transit" message, it is possibly a reply to one of our probes. hip points to the IPv4 header that is returned in the ICMP message following the 8-byte ICMP header. udp points to the UDP header that follows. If the ICMP message was generated by a UDP datagram and if the source and destination ports of that datagram are the values we sent, then this is a reply to our probe from an intermediate router.

Process ICMP "port unreachable" message

51-68   If the ICMP message is "destination unreachable," then we look at the UDP header returned in the ICMP message to see if the message is a response to our probe. If so, and if the ICMP code is "port unreachable," we return –1 as we have reached the final destination. If the ICMP message is from one of our probes but it is not a "port unreachable," then that ICMP code value is returned. A common example of this is a firewall returning some other unreachable code for the destination host we are probing.

Handle other ICMP messages

69-73   All other ICMP messages are printed if the -v flag was specified.

The next function, recv_v6, is shown in Figure 28.24 (p. 767) and is the IPv6 equivalent to the previously described function. This function is nearly identical to recv_v4 except for the different constant names and the different structure member names. Also, the IPv6 header is not part of the data received on an IPv6 raw socket; the data starts with the ICMPv6 header. Figure 28.22 shows the various headers, pointers, and lengths used by the code.

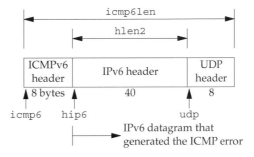

Figure 28.22 Headers, pointers, and lengths in processing ICMPv6 error.

We define two functions, icmpcode_v4 and icmpcode_v6, that can be called from the bottom of the traceloop function to print a description string corresponding to an ICMP "destination unreachable" error. Figure 28.25 (p. 767) shows just the IPv6 function. The IPv4 function is similar, albeit longer, as there are more ICMPv4 "destination unreachable" codes (Figure A.15).

The final function in our traceroute program is our SIGALRM handler, the sig_alrm function shown in Figure 28.23. All this function does is return, causing an error return of EINTR from the recvfrom in either recv_v4 or recv_v6.

―― *traceroute/sig_alrm.c*
```
1 #include     "trace.h"

2 int     gotalarm;

3 void
4 sig_alrm(int signo)
5 {
6     gotalarm = 1;                   /* set flag to note that alarm occurred */
7     return;                         /* and interrupt the recvfrom() */
8 }
```
―― *traceroute/sig_alrm.c*

Figure 28.23 sig_alrm function.

―――――――――――――――――――――――――――――――――――――― traceroute/recv_v6.c

```
 1 #include    "trace.h"

 2 extern int gotalarm;

 3 /*
 4  * Return: -3 on timeout
 5  *          -2 on ICMP time exceeded in transit (caller keeps going)
 6  *          -1 on ICMP port unreachable (caller is done)
 7  *        >= 0 return value is some other ICMP unreachable code
 8  */

 9 int
10 recv_v6(int seq, struct timeval *tv)
11 {
12 #ifdef  IPV6
13     int     hlen2, icmp6len, ret;
14     ssize_t n;
15     socklen_t len;
16     struct ip6_hdr *hip6;
17     struct icmp6_hdr *icmp6;
18     struct udphdr *udp;

19     gotalarm = 0;
20     alarm(3);
21     for ( ; ; ) {
22         if (gotalarm)
23             return (-3);        /* alarm expired */
24         len = pr->salen;
25         n = recvfrom(recvfd, recvbuf, sizeof(recvbuf), 0, pr->sarecv, &len);
26         if (n < 0) {
27             if (errno == EINTR)
28                 continue;
29             else
30                 err_sys("recvfrom error");
31         }

32         icmp6 = (struct icmp6_hdr *) recvbuf;   /* ICMP header */
33         if ( (icmp6len = n) < 8)
34             continue;           /* not enough to look at ICMP header */

35         if (icmp6->icmp6_type == ICMP6_TIME_EXCEEDED &&
36             icmp6->icmp6_code == ICMP6_TIME_EXCEED_TRANSIT) {
37             if (icmp6len < 8 + sizeof(struct ip6_hdr) + 4)
38                 continue;       /* not enough data to look at inner header */

39             hip6 = (struct ip6_hdr *) (recvbuf + 8);
40             hlen2 = sizeof(struct ip6_hdr);
41             udp = (struct udphdr *) (recvbuf + 8 + hlen2);
42             if (hip6->ip6_nxt == IPPROTO_UDP &&
43                 udp->uh_sport == htons(sport) &&
44                 udp->uh_dport == htons(dport + seq))
45                 ret = -2;       /* we hit an intermediate router */
46             break;

47         } else if (icmp6->icmp6_type == ICMP6_DST_UNREACH) {
48             if (icmp6len < 8 + sizeof(struct ip6_hdr) + 4)
49                 continue;       /* not enough data to look at inner header */
```

```
50                  hip6 = (struct ip6_hdr *) (recvbuf + 8);
51                  hlen2 = sizeof(struct ip6_hdr);
52                  udp = (struct udphdr *) (recvbuf + 8 + hlen2);
53                  if (hip6->ip6_nxt == IPPROTO_UDP &&
54                      udp->uh_sport == htons(sport) &&
55                      udp->uh_dport == htons(dport + seq)) {
56                      if (icmp6->icmp6_code == ICMP6_DST_UNREACH_NOPORT)
57                          ret = -1;   /* have reached destination */
58                      else
59                          ret = icmp6->icmp6_code;    /* 0, 1, 2, ... */
60                      break;
61                  }
62              } else if (verbose) {
63                  printf(" (from %s: type = %d, code = %d)\n",
64                          Sock_ntop_host(pr->sarecv, pr->salen),
65                          icmp6->icmp6_type, icmp6->icmp6_code);
66              }
67              /* Some other ICMP error, recvfrom() again */
68          }
69      alarm(0);                       /* don't leave alarm running */
70      Gettimeofday(tv, NULL);         /* get time of packet arrival */
71      return (ret);
72 #endif
73 }
```
—— *traceroute/recv_v6.c*

Figure 28.24   recv_v6 function: reads and processes ICMPv6 messages.

—— *traceroute/icmpcode_v6.c*

```
 1 #include     "trace.h"

 2 const char *
 3 icmpcode_v6(int code)
 4 {
 5 #ifdef  IPV6
 6     static char errbuf[100];
 7     switch (code) {
 8     case ICMP6_DST_UNREACH_NOROUTE:
 9         return ("no route to host");
10     case ICMP6_DST_UNREACH_ADMIN:
11         return ("administratively prohibited");
12     case ICMP6_DST_UNREACH_NOTNEIGHBOR:
13         return ("not a neighbor");
14     case ICMP6_DST_UNREACH_ADDR:
15         return ("address unreachable");
16     case ICMP6_DST_UNREACH_NOPORT:
17         return ("port unreachable");
18     default:
19         sprintf(errbuf, "[unknown code %d]", code);
20         return errbuf;
21     }
22 #endif
23 }
```
—— *traceroute/icmpcode_v6.c*

Figure 28.25   Return the string corresponding to an ICMPv6 unreachable code.

Example

We first show an example using IPv4.

```
freebsd % traceroute www.unpbook.com
traceroute to www.unpbook.com (206.168.112.219): 30 hops max, 24 data bytes
 1   12.106.32.1 (12.106.32.1)  0.799 ms  0.719 ms  0.540 ms
 2   12.124.47.113 (12.124.47.113)  1.758 ms  1.760 ms  1.839 ms
 3   gbr2-p27.sffca.ip.att.net (12.123.195.38)  2.744 ms  2.575 ms  2.648 ms
 4   tbr2-p012701.sffca.ip.att.net (12.122.11.85)  3.770 ms  3.689 ms  3.848 ms
 5   gbr3-p50.dvmco.ip.att.net (12.122.2.66)  26.202 ms  26.242 ms  26.102 ms
 6   gbr2-p20.dvmco.ip.att.net (12.122.5.26)  26.255 ms  26.194 ms  26.470 ms
 7   gar2-p370.dvmco.ip.att.net (12.123.36.141)  26.443 ms  26.310 ms  26.427 ms
 8   att-46.den.internap.ip.att.net (12.124.158.58)  26.962 ms  27.130 ms
                                                                      27.279 ms
 9   border10.ge3-0-bbnet2.den.pnap.net (216.52.40.79)  27.285 ms  27.293 ms
                                                                      26.860 ms
10   coop-2.border10.den.pnap.net (216.52.42.118)  28.721 ms  28.991 ms
                                                                      30.077 ms
11   199.45.130.33 (199.45.130.33)  29.095 ms  29.055 ms  29.378 ms
12   border-to-141-netrack.boulder.co.coop.net (207.174.144.178)  30.875 ms
                                                       29.747 ms  30.142 ms
13   linux.unpbook.com (206.168.112.219)  31.713 ms  31.573 ms  33.952 ms
```

We have wrapped the long lines for a more readable output.

Here is an example using IPv6.

```
freebsd % traceroute www.kame.net
traceroute to orange.kame.net (2001:200:0:4819:203:47ff:fea5:3085):
          30 hops max, 24 data bytes
 1   3ffe:b80:3:9ad1::1 (3ffe:b80:3:9ad1::1)  107.437 ms  99.341 ms  103.477 ms
 2   Viagenie-gw.int.ipv6.ascc.net (2001:288:3b0::55)
          105.129 ms  89.418 ms  90.016 ms
 3   gw-Viagenie.int.ipv6.ascc.net (2001:288:3b0::54)
          302.300 ms  291.580 ms  289.839 ms
 4   c7513-gw.int.ipv6.ascc.net (2001:288:3b0::c)
          296.088 ms  298.600 ms  292.196 ms
 5   m160-c7513.int.ipv6.ascc.net (2001:288:3b0::1e)
          296.266 ms  314.878 ms  302.429 ms
 6   m20jp-m160tw.int.ipv6.ascc.net (2001:288:3b0::1b)
          327.637 ms  326.897 ms  347.062 ms
 7   hitachi1.otemachi.wide.ad.jp (2001:200:0:1800::9c4:2)
          420.140 ms  426.592 ms  422.756 ms
 8   pc3.yagami.wide.ad.jp (2001:200:0:1c04::1000:2000)
          415.471 ms  418.308 ms  461.654 ms
 9   gr2000.k2c.wide.ad.jp (2001:200:0:8002::2000:1)
          416.581 ms  422.430 ms  427.692 ms
10   2001:200:0:4819:203:47ff:fea5:3085 (2001:200:0:4819:203:47ff:fea5:3085)
          417.169 ms  434.674 ms  424.037 ms
```

We have wrapped the long lines for a more readable output.

28.7 An ICMP Message Daemon

Receiving asynchronous ICMP errors on a UDP socket has been, and continues to be, a problem. ICMP errors are received by the kernel, but are rarely delivered to the application that needs to know about them. In the sockets API, we have seen that it requires connecting the UDP socket to one IP address to receive these errors (Section 8.11). The reason for this limitation is that the only error returned from `recvfrom` is an integer `errno` code, and if the application sends datagrams to multiple destinations and then calls `recvfrom`, this function cannot tell the application which datagram encountered an error.

In this section, we will provide a solution that does not require any kernel changes. We will provide an ICMP message daemon, `icmpd`, that creates a raw ICMPv4 socket and a raw ICMPv6 socket and receives all ICMP messages the kernel passes to these two raw sockets. It also creates a Unix domain stream socket, `binds` it to the pathname `/tmp/icmpd`, and listens for incoming client `connects` to this pathname. We will show this in Figure 28.26.

A UDP application (which is a client to the daemon) first creates its UDP socket, the socket for which it wants to receive asynchronous errors. The application must `bind` an ephemeral port to this socket, for reasons we will discuss later. It then creates a Unix domain socket and `connects` to this daemon's well-known pathname. We will show this in Figure 28.27.

The application next "passes" its UDP socket to the daemon across the Unix domain connection using *descriptor passing*, as we described in Section 15.7. This gives the daemon a copy of the socket so that it can call `getsockname` and obtain the port number bound to the socket. We will show this passing of the socket in Figure 28.28.

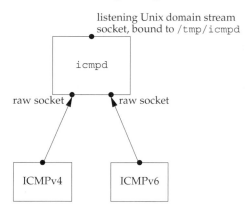

Figure 28.26 `icmpd` daemon: initial sockets created.

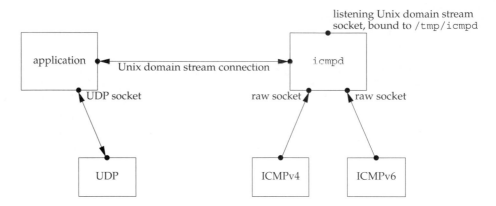

Figure 28.27   Application creates its UDP socket and a Unix domain connection to the daemon.

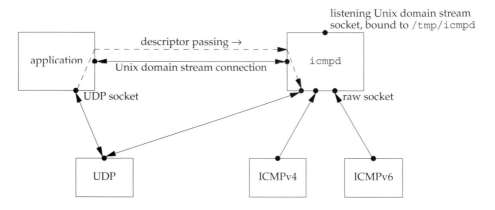

Figure 28.28   Passing UDP socket to daemon across Unix domain connection.

After the daemon obtains the port number bound to the UDP socket, it closes its copy of the socket, taking us back to the arrangement shown in Figure 28.27.

> If the host supports credential passing (Section 15.8), the application could also send its cre-
> dentials to the daemon. The daemon could then check whether this user should be allowed
> access to this facility.

From this point on, any ICMP errors the daemon receives in response to UDP data-grams sent from the port bound to the application's UDP socket cause the daemon to send a message (which we will describe shortly) across the Unix domain socket to the application. The application must therefore use `select` or `poll`, awaiting data on either the UDP socket or the Unix domain socket.

We now look at the source code for an application using this daemon, and then the daemon itself. We start with Figure 28.29, our header that is included by both the appli-cation and the daemon.

—————————————————————— icmpd/unpicmpd.h

```
 1 #ifndef  __unpicmp_h
 2 #define  __unpicmp_h

 3 #include    "unp.h"

 4 #define ICMPD_PATH      "/tmp/icmpd"   /* server's well-known pathname */

 5 struct icmpd_err {
 6     int     icmpd_errno;        /* EHOSTUNREACH, EMSGSIZE, ECONNREFUSED */
 7     char    icmpd_type;         /* actual ICMPv[46] type */
 8     char    icmpd_code;         /* actual ICMPv[46] code */
 9     socklen_t icmpd_len;        /* length of sockaddr{} that follows */
10     struct sockaddr_storage icmpd_dest; /* sockaddr_storage handles any size */
11 };

12 #endif  /* __unpicmp_h */
```

—————————————————————— icmpd/unpicmpd.h

Figure 28.29 unpicmpd.h header.

4-11   We define the server's well-known pathname and the icmpd_err structure that is passed from the server to the application whenever an ICMP message is received that should be passed to this application.

6-8   A problem is that the ICMPv4 message types differ numerically (and sometimes conceptually) from the ICMPv6 message types (Figures A.15 and A.16). The actual ICMP *type* and *code* values are returned, but we also map these into an errno value (icmpd_errno), similar to the final columns in Figures A.15 and A.16. The application can deal with this value instead of the protocol-dependent ICMPv4 or ICMPv6 values. Figure 28.30 shows the ICMP messages that are handled, plus their mapping into an errno value.

icmpd_errno	ICMPv4 error	ICMPv6 error
ECONNREFUSED	port unreachable	port unreachable
EMSGSIZE	fragmentation needed but DF set	packet too big
EHOSTUNREACH	time exceeded	time exceeded
EHOSTUNREACH	source quench	
EHOSTUNREACH	All other destination unreachables	All other destination unreachables

Figure 28.30 icmpd_errno mapping from ICMPv4 and ICMPv6 errors.

The daemon returns five types of ICMP errors.

- "port unreachable," indicating that no socket is bound to the destination port at the destination IP address.

- "packet too big," which is used with path MTU discovery. Currently, there is no API defined to allow a UDP application to perform path MTU discovery. What often happens on kernels that support path MTU discovery for UDP is that the receipt of this ICMP error causes the kernel to record the new path MTU value in the kernel's routing table, but the UDP application that sent the datagram that got discarded is not notified. Instead, the application must time out and retransmit the datagram, in which case, the kernel will find the new (and smaller) MTU in its routing table, and the kernel will then fragment the datagram. Passing this error back to the application lets the application retransmit sooner, and perhaps lets the application reduce the size of the datagrams it sends.

- The "time exceeded" error is normally seen with a code of 0, indicating that either the IPv4 TTL or IPv6 hop limit reached 0. This often indicates a routing loop, which might be a transient error.

- ICMPv4 "source quenches," while deprecated by RFC 1812 [Baker 1995], may be sent by routers (or by misconfigured hosts acting as routers). They indicate that a packet has been discarded, and we therefore treat them like a "destination unreachable" message. Note that IPv6 does not have a "source quench" error.

- All other destination unreachable messages indicate that a packet has been discarded.

10   The icmpd_dest member is a socket address structure containing the destination IP address and port of the datagram that generated the ICMP error. This member will be either a sockaddr_in structure for IPv4 or a sockaddr in6 structure for IPv6. If the application is sending datagrams to multiple destinations, it probably has one socket address structure per destination. By returning this information in a socket address structure, the application can compare it against its own structures to find the one that caused the error. It is a sockaddr_storage to allow storage of any sockaddr type the system supports.

UDP Echo Client That Uses Our `icmpd` Daemon

We now modify our UDP echo client, the dg_cli function, to use our icmpd daemon. Figure 28.31 shows the first half of the function.

2-3   The function arguments are the same as all previous versions of this function.

bind wildcard address and ephemeral port

12   We call our sock_bind_wild function to bind the wildcard IP address and an ephemeral port to the UDP socket. We do this so that the copy of this socket that we pass to the daemon has bound a port, as the daemon needs to know this port.

> The daemon could also do this bind if a local port has not already been bound to the socket that it receives, but this does not work in all environments. Certain SVR4 implementations, such as Solaris 2.5, in which sockets are not part of the kernel, have a bug when one process binds a port to a shared socket; the other process with a copy of that socket gets strange errors when it tries to use the socket. The easiest solution is to require the application to bind the local port before passing the socket to the daemon.

Establish Unix domain connection to daemon

13-16   We create an AF_LOCAL socket and connect to the daemon's well-known pathname.

```
                                                  ———————————————— icmpd/dgcli01.c
 1 #include      "unpicmpd.h"

 2 void
 3 dg_cli(FILE *fp, int sockfd, const SA *pservaddr, socklen_t servlen)
 4 {
 5     int     icmpfd, maxfdp1;
 6     char    sendline[MAXLINE], recvline[MAXLINE + 1];
 7     fd_set  rset;
 8     ssize_t n;
 9     struct timeval tv;
10     struct icmpd_err icmpd_err;
11     struct sockaddr_un sun;

12     Sock_bind_wild(sockfd, pservaddr->sa_family);

13     icmpfd = Socket(AF_LOCAL, SOCK_STREAM, 0);
14     sun.sun_family = AF_LOCAL;
15     strcpy(sun.sun_path, ICMPD_PATH);
16     Connect(icmpfd, (SA *) &sun, sizeof(sun));
17     Write_fd(icmpfd, "1", 1, sockfd);
18     n = Read(icmpfd, recvline, 1);
19     if (n != 1 || recvline[0] != '1')
20         err_quit("error creating icmp socket, n = %d, char = %c",
21                  n, recvline[0]);

22     FD_ZERO(&rset);
23     maxfdp1 = max(sockfd, icmpfd) + 1;
                                                  ———————————————— icmpd/dgcli01.c
```

Figure 28.31 First half of dg_cli application.

Send UDP socket to daemon, await daemon's reply

17-21   We call our `write_fd` function from Figure 15.13 to send a copy of our UDP socket to the daemon. We also send a single byte of data, the character "1," because some implementations do not like passing a descriptor without any data. The daemon sends back a single byte of data, consisting of the character "1" to indicate success. Any other reply indicates an error.

22-23   We initialize a descriptor set and calculate the first argument for `select` (the maximum of the two descriptors, plus one).

The last half of our client is shown in Figure 28.32. This is the loop that reads a line from standard input, sends the line to the server, reads back the server's reply, and writes the reply to standard output.

```
                                                                      icmpd/dgcli01.c
24     while (Fgets(sendline, MAXLINE, fp) != NULL) {
25         Sendto(sockfd, sendline, strlen(sendline), 0, pservaddr, servlen);

26         tv.tv_sec = 5;
27         tv.tv_usec = 0;
28         FD_SET(sockfd, &rset);
29         FD_SET(icmpfd, &rset);
30         if ( (n = Select(maxfdp1, &rset, NULL, NULL, &tv)) == 0) {
31             fprintf(stderr, "socket timeout\n");
32             continue;
33         }

34         if (FD_ISSET(sockfd, &rset)) {
35             n = Recvfrom(sockfd, recvline, MAXLINE, 0, NULL, NULL);
36             recvline[n] = 0;      /* null terminate */
37             Fputs(recvline, stdout);
38         }

39         if (FD_ISSET(icmpfd, &rset)) {
40             if ( (n = Read(icmpfd, &icmpd_err, sizeof(icmpd_err))) == 0)
41                 err_quit("ICMP daemon terminated");
42             else if (n != sizeof(icmpd_err))
43                 err_quit("n = %d, expected %d", n, sizeof(icmpd_err));
44             printf("ICMP error: dest = %s, %s, type = %d, code = %d\n",
45                     Sock_ntop(&icmpd_err.icmpd_dest, icmpd_err.icmpd_len),
46                     strerror(icmpd_err.icmpd_errno),
47                     icmpd_err.icmpd_type, icmpd_err.icmpd_code);
48         }
49     }
50 }
                                                                      icmpd/dgcli01.c
```

Figure 28.32 Last half of dg_cli application.

Call select

26–33   Since we are calling select, we can easily place a timeout on our wait for the echo server's reply. We set this to five seconds, enable both descriptors for readability, and call select. If a timeout occurs, we print a message and go back to the top of the loop.

Print server's reply

34–38   If a datagram is returned by the server, we print it to standard output.

Handle ICMP error

39–48   If our Unix domain connection to the icmpd daemon is readable, we try to read an icmpd_err structure. If this succeeds, we print the relevant information the daemon returns.

> strerror is an example of a simple, almost trivial, function that should be more portable than it is. First, ANSI C says nothing about an error return from the function. The Solaris man page says that the function returns a null pointer if the argument is out of range. But this means code like
>
> ```
> printf("%s", strerror(arg));
> ```

is incorrect because `strerror` can return a null pointer. But the FreeBSD implementation, along with all the source code implementations the authors could find, handle an invalid argument by returning a pointer to a string such as "Unknown error." This makes sense and means the code above is fine. But POSIX changes this and says that because no return value is reserved to indicate an error, if the argument is out of range, the function sets `errno` to `EINVAL`. (POSIX does not say anything about the returned pointer in the case of an error.) This means that completely conforming code must set `errno` to 0, call `strerror`, test whether `errno` equals `EINVAL`, and print some other message in case of an error.

UDP Echo Client Examples

We now show some examples of this client before looking at the daemon source code. We first send datagrams to an IP address that is not connected to the Internet.

```
freebsd % udpcli01 192.0.2.5 echo
hi there
socket timeout
and hello
socket timeout
```

We assume `icmpd` is running and expect ICMP "host unreachable" errors to be returned by some router, but none are received. Instead, our application times out. We show this to reiterate that a timeout is still required and the generation of ICMP messages such as "host unreachable" may not occur.

Our next example sends a datagram to the standard echo server on a host that is not running the server. We receive an ICMPv4 "port unreachable" as expected.

```
freebsd % udpcli01 aix-4 echo
hello, world
ICMP error: dest = 192.168.42.2:7, Connection refused, type = 3, code = 3
```

We try again with IPv6 and receive an ICMPv6 "port unreachable" as expected.

```
freebsd % udpcli01 aix-6 echo
hello, world
ICMP error: dest = [3ffe:b80:1f8d:2:204:acff:fe17:bf38]:7,
                          Connection refused, type = 1, code = 4
```

We have wrapped the long line for readability.

`icmpd` Daemon

We start the description of our `icmpd` daemon with the `icmpd.h` header, shown in Figure 28.33.

`client` array

2-17   Since the daemon can handle any number of clients, we use an array of `client` structures to keep the information about each client. This is similar to the data structures we used in Section 6.8. In addition to the descriptor for the Unix domain connection to the client, we also store the address family of the client's UDP socket AF_INET or AF_INET6) and the port number bound to this socket. We also declare the function prototypes and the globals shared by these functions.

icmpd/icmpd.h

```
 1 #include     "unpicmpd.h"

 2 struct client {
 3     int     connfd;              /* Unix domain stream socket to client */
 4     int     family;              /* AF_INET or AF_INET6 */
 5     int     lport;              /* local port bound to client's UDP socket */
 6     /* network byte ordered */
 7 } client[FD_SETSIZE];

 8                         /* globals */
 9 int     fd4, fd6, listenfd, maxi, maxfd, nready;
10 fd_set  rset, allset;
11 struct sockaddr_un cliaddr;

12               /* function prototypes */
13 int     readable_conn(int);
14 int     readable_listen(void);
15 int     readable_v4(void);
16 int     readable_v6(void);
```

icmpd/icmpd.h

Figure 28.33 icmpd.h header for icmpd daemon.

icmpd/icmpd.c

```
 1 #include     "icmpd.h"

 2 int
 3 main(int argc, char **argv)
 4 {
 5     int     i, sockfd;
 6     struct sockaddr_un sun;

 7     if (argc != 1)
 8         err_quit("usage: icmpd");
 9     maxi = -1;                   /* index into client[] array */
10     for (i = 0; i < FD_SETSIZE; i++)
11         client[i].connfd = -1;  /* -1 indicates available entry */
12     FD_ZERO(&allset);
13     fd4 = Socket(AF_INET, SOCK_RAW, IPPROTO_ICMP);
14     FD_SET(fd4, &allset);
15     maxfd = fd4;
16 #ifdef  IPV6
17     fd6 = Socket(AF_INET6, SOCK_RAW, IPPROTO_ICMPV6);
18     FD_SET(fd6, &allset);
19     maxfd = max(maxfd, fd6);
20 #endif
21     listenfd = Socket(AF_UNIX, SOCK_STREAM, 0);
22     sun.sun_family = AF_LOCAL;
23     strcpy(sun.sun_path, ICMPD_PATH);
24     unlink(ICMPD_PATH);
25     Bind(listenfd, (SA *) &sun, sizeof(sun));
26     Listen(listenfd, LISTENQ);
27     FD_SET(listenfd, &allset);
28     maxfd = max(maxfd, listenfd);
```

icmpd/icmpd.c

Figure 28.34 First half of main function: creates sockets.

Figure 28.34 shows the first half of the `main` function.

Initialize `client` array

9-10   The `client` array is initialized by setting the connected socket member to –1.

Create sockets

12-28   Three sockets are created: a raw ICMPv4 socket, a raw ICMPv6 socket, and a Unix domain stream socket. We `unlink` any previously existing instance of the Unix domain socket, `bind` its well-known pathname to the socket, and call `listen`. This is the socket to which clients `connect`. The maximum descriptor is also calculated for `select` and a socket address structure is allocated for calls to `accept`.

Figure 28.35 shows the second half of the `main` function, which is an infinite loop that calls `select`, waiting for any of the daemon's descriptors to be readable.

```
                                                            icmpd/icmpd.c
29     for ( ; ; ) {
30          rset = allset;
31          nready = Select(maxfd + 1, &rset, NULL, NULL, NULL);

32          if (FD_ISSET(listenfd, &rset))
33               if (readable_listen() <= 0)
34                   continue;

35          if (FD_ISSET(fd4, &rset))
36               if (readable_v4() <= 0)
37                   continue;

38 #ifdef  IPV6
39          if (FD_ISSET(fd6, &rset))
40               if (readable_v6() <= 0)
41                   continue;
42 #endif

43          for (i = 0; i <= maxi; i++) {    /* check all clients for data */
44               if ( (sockfd = client[i].connfd) < 0)
45                   continue;
46               if (FD_ISSET(sockfd, &rset))
47                    if (readable_conn(i) <= 0)
48                        break;       /* no more readable descriptors */
49          }
50     }
51     exit(0);
52 }
                                                            icmpd/icmpd.c
```

Figure 28.35 Second half of `main` function: handles readable descriptor.

Check listening Unix domain socket

32-34   The listening Unix domain socket is tested first and if ready, `readable_listen` is called. The variable `nready`, the number of descriptors that `select` returns as readable, is a global variable. Each of our `readable_XXX` function decrements this variable and returns its new value as the return value of the function. When this value reaches 0, all the readable descriptors have been processed and `select` is called again.

Check raw ICMP sockets

35–42   The raw ICMPv4 socket is tested, and then the raw ICMPv6 socket.

Check connected Unix domain sockets

43–49   We next check whether any of the connected Unix domain sockets are readable. Readability on any of these sockets means that the client has sent a descriptor, or that the client has terminated.

Figure 28.36 shows the `readable_listen` function, called when the daemon's listening socket is readable. This indicates a new client connection.

—————————————————————————————————— icmpd/readable_listen.c
```
 1 #include    "icmpd.h"

 2 int
 3 readable_listen(void)
 4 {
 5     int     i, connfd;
 6     socklen_t clilen;

 7     clilen = sizeof(cliaddr);
 8     connfd = Accept(listenfd, (SA *) &cliaddr, &clilen);

 9         /* find first available client[] structure */
10     for (i = 0; i < FD_SETSIZE; i++)
11         if (client[i].connfd < 0) {
12             client[i].connfd = connfd;   /* save descriptor */
13             break;
14         }
15     if (i == FD_SETSIZE) {
16         close(connfd);            /* can't handle new client, */
17         return (--nready);        /* rudely close the new connection */
18     }
19     printf("new connection, i = %d, connfd = %d\n", i, connfd);

20     FD_SET(connfd, &allset);      /* add new descriptor to set */
21     if (connfd > maxfd)
22         maxfd = connfd;           /* for select() */
23     if (i > maxi)
24         maxi = i;                 /* max index in client[] array */

25     return (--nready);
26 }
```
—————————————————————————————————— icmpd/readable_listen.c

Figure 28.36 Handle new client connections.

7–25   The connection is accepted and the first available entry in the `client` array is used. The code in this function was copied from the beginning of Figure 6.22. If an entry couldn't be found in the client array, we simply closed the new client connection and remained to serve our current clients.

When a connected socket is readable, our `readable_conn` function is called (Figure 28.37). Its argument is the index of this client in the `client` array.

Read client data and possibly a descriptor

13–18   We call our `read_fd` function from Figure 15.11 to read the data and possibly a descriptor. If the return value is 0, the client has closed its end of the connection, possibly by terminating.

——————————————————————————— icmpd/readable_conn.c

```
 1 #include    "icmpd.h"

 2 int
 3 readable_conn(int i)
 4 {
 5     int     unixfd, recvfd;
 6     char    c;
 7     ssize_t n;
 8     socklen_t len;
 9     struct sockaddr_storage ss;

10     unixfd = client[i].connfd;
11     recvfd = -1;
12     if ( (n = Read_fd(unixfd, &c, 1, &recvfd)) == 0) {
13         err_msg("client %d terminated, recvfd = %d", i, recvfd);
14         goto clientdone;          /* client probably terminated */
15     }

16         /* data from client; should be descriptor */
17     if (recvfd < 0) {
18         err_msg("read_fd did not return descriptor");
19         goto clienterr;
20     }
```

——————————————————————————— icmpd/readable_conn.c

Figure 28.37 Read data and possible descriptor from client.

> One design decision was whether to use a Unix domain stream socket between the application and the daemon, or a Unix domain datagram socket. The application's UDP socket can be passed over either type of Unix domain socket. The reason why we used a stream socket was to detect when a client terminated. When a client terminates, all its descriptors are automatically closed, including its Unix domain connection to the daemon, which tells the daemon to remove this client from the `client` array. Had we used a datagram socket, we would not know when the client terminated.

16–20   If the client has not closed the connection, then we expect a descriptor.

The second half of our `readable_conn` function is shown in Figure 28.38.

Get port number bound to UDP socket

21–25   `getsockname` is called so the daemon can obtain the port number bound to the socket. Since we do not know what size buffer to allocate for the socket address structure, we use a `sockaddr_storage` structure, which is large enough and appropriately aligned to store any socket address structure the system supports.

26–33   The address family of the socket is stored in the `client` structure, along with the port number. If the port number is 0, we call our `sock_bind_wild` function to `bind` the wildcard address and an ephemeral port to the socket, but as we mentioned earlier, this does not work on some SVR4 implementations.

```
                                                                    ─── icmpd/readable_conn.c
21      len = sizeof(ss);
22      if (getsockname(recvfd, (SA *) &ss, &len) < 0) {
23          err_ret("getsockname error");
24          goto clienterr;
25      }

26      client[i].family = ss.ss_family;
27      if ((client[i].lport = sock_get_port((SA *) &ss, len)) == 0) {
28          client[i].lport = sock_bind_wild(recvfd, client[i].family);
29          if (client[i].lport <= 0) {
30              err_ret("error binding ephemeral port");
31              goto clienterr;
32          }
33      }
34      Write(unixfd, "1", 1);       /* tell client all OK */
35      Close(recvfd);               /* all done with client's UDP socket */
36      return (--nready);

37  clienterr:
38      Write(unixfd, "0", 1);       /* tell client error occurred */
39  clientdone:
40      Close(unixfd);
41      if (recvfd >= 0)
42          Close(recvfd);
43      FD_CLR(unixfd, &allset);
44      client[i].connfd = -1;
45      return (--nready);
46  }
                                                                    ─── icmpd/readable_conn.c
```

Figure 28.38 Get port number that client has bound to its UDP socket.

Indicate success to client

34   One byte consisting of the character "1" is sent back to the client.

`close` client's UDP socket

35   We are finished with the client's UDP socket and `close` it. This descriptor was
passed to us by the client and is therefore a copy; hence, the UDP socket is still open in
the client.

Handle errors and termination of client

37–45   If an error occurs, a byte of "0" is written back to the client. When the client terminates, our end of the Unix domain connection is closed, and the descriptor is removed
from the set of descriptors for `select`. The `connfd` member of the `client` structure is
set to –1, indicating it is available.

Our `readable_v4` function is called when the raw ICMPv4 socket is readable. We show the first half in Figure 28.39. This code is similar to the ICMPv4 code shown earlier in Figures 28.8 and 28.20.

```
                                                                    icmpd/readable_v4.c
 1 #include    "icmpd.h"
 2 #include    <netinet/in_systm.h>
 3 #include    <netinet/ip.h>
 4 #include    <netinet/ip_icmp.h>
 5 #include    <netinet/udp.h>

 6 int
 7 readable_v4(void)
 8 {
 9     int      i, hlen1, hlen2, icmplen, sport;
10     char     buf[MAXLINE];
11     char     srcstr[INET_ADDRSTRLEN], dststr[INET_ADDRSTRLEN];
12     ssize_t n;
13     socklen_t len;
14     struct ip *ip, *hip;
15     struct icmp *icmp;
16     struct udphdr *udp;
17     struct sockaddr_in from, dest;
18     struct icmpd_err icmpd_err;

19     len = sizeof(from);
20     n = Recvfrom(fd4, buf, MAXLINE, 0, (SA *) &from, &len);

21     printf("%d bytes ICMPv4 from %s:", n, Sock_ntop_host((SA *) &from, len));

22     ip = (struct ip *) buf;        /* start of IP header */
23     hlen1 = ip->ip_hl << 2;        /* length of IP header */

24     icmp = (struct icmp *) (buf + hlen1);   /* start of ICMP header */
25     if ( (icmplen = n - hlen1) < 8)
26         err_quit("icmplen (%d) < 8", icmplen);

27     printf(" type = %d, code = %d\n", icmp->icmp_type, icmp->icmp_code);
                                                                    icmpd/readable_v4.c
```

Figure 28.39 Handle received ICMPv4 datagram, first half.

This function prints some information about every received ICMPv4 message. This was done for debugging when developing this daemon and could be output based on a command-line argument.

Figure 28.40 shows the last half of our `readable_v4` function.

―― *icmpd/readable_v4.c*
```
28      if (icmp->icmp_type == ICMP_UNREACH ||
29          icmp->icmp_type == ICMP_TIMXCEED ||
30          icmp->icmp_type == ICMP_SOURCEQUENCH) {
31          if (icmplen < 8 + 20 + 8)
32              err_quit("icmplen (%d) < 8 + 20 + 8", icmplen);

33          hip = (struct ip *) (buf + hlen1 + 8);
34          hlen2 = hip->ip_hl << 2;
35          printf("\tsrcip = %s, dstip = %s, proto = %d\n",
36                  Inet_ntop(AF_INET, &hip->ip_src, srcstr, sizeof(srcstr)),
37                  Inet_ntop(AF_INET, &hip->ip_dst, dststr, sizeof(dststr)),
38                  hip->ip_p);
39          if (hip->ip_p == IPPROTO_UDP) {
40              udp = (struct udphdr *) (buf + hlen1 + 8 + hlen2);
41              sport = udp->uh_sport;

42                  /* find client's Unix domain socket, send headers */
43              for (i = 0; i <= maxi; i++) {
44                  if (client[i].connfd >= 0 &&
45                      client[i].family == AF_INET &&
46                      client[i].lport == sport) {

47                      bzero(&dest, sizeof(dest));
48                      dest.sin_family = AF_INET;
49 #ifdef  HAVE_SOCKADDR_SA_LEN
50                      dest.sin_len = sizeof(dest);
51 #endif
52                      memcpy(&dest.sin_addr, &hip->ip_dst,
53                          sizeof(struct in_addr));
54                      dest.sin_port = udp->uh_dport;

55                      icmpd_err.icmpd_type = icmp->icmp_type;
56                      icmpd_err.icmpd_code = icmp->icmp_code;
57                      icmpd_err.icmpd_len = sizeof(struct sockaddr_in);
58                      memcpy(&icmpd_err.icmpd_dest, &dest, sizeof(dest));

59                          /* convert type & code to reasonable errno value */
60                      icmpd_err.icmpd_errno = EHOSTUNREACH;  /* default */
61                      if (icmp->icmp_type == ICMP_UNREACH) {
62                          if (icmp->icmp_code == ICMP_UNREACH_PORT)
63                              icmpd_err.icmpd_errno = ECONNREFUSED;
64                          else if (icmp->icmp_code == ICMP_UNREACH_NEEDFRAG)
65                              icmpd_err.icmpd_errno = EMSGSIZE;
66                      }
67                      Write(client[i].connfd, &icmpd_err, sizeof(icmpd_err));
68                  }
69              }
70          }
71      }
72      return (--nready);
73 }
```
―― *icmpd/readable_v4.c*

Figure 28.40 Handle received ICMPv4 datagram, second half.

Check message type, notify application

29-31   The only ICMPv4 messages that we pass to the application are "destination unreachable," "time exceeded," and "source quench" (Figure 28.30).

Check for UDP error, find client

34-42   hip points to the IP header that is returned following the ICMP header. This is the IP header of the datagram that elicited the ICMP error. We verify that this IP datagram is a UDP datagram and then fetch the source UDP port number from the UDP header following the IP header.

43-55   A search is made of all the client structures for a matching address family and port. If a match is found, an IPv4 socket address structure is built containing the destination IP address and port from the UDP datagram that caused the error.

Build icmpd_err structure

56-70   An icmpd_err structure is built that is sent to the client across the Unix domain connection to this client. The ICMPv4 message type and code are first mapped into an errno value, as described with Figure 28.30.

```
                                                     ———————— icmpd/readable_v6.c
 1 #include     "icmpd.h"
 2 #include     <netinet/in_systm.h>
 3 #include     <netinet/ip.h>
 4 #include     <netinet/ip_icmp.h>
 5 #include     <netinet/udp.h>

 6 #ifdef   IPV6
 7 #include     <netinet/ip6.h>
 8 #include     <netinet/icmp6.h>
 9 #endif

10 int
11 readable_v6(void)
12 {
13 #ifdef   IPV6
14     int     i, hlen2, icmp6len, sport;
15     char    buf[MAXLINE];
16     char    srcstr[INET6_ADDRSTRLEN], dststr[INET6_ADDRSTRLEN];
17     ssize_t n;
18     socklen_t len;
19     struct ip6_hdr *ip6, *hip6;
20     struct icmp6_hdr *icmp6;
21     struct udphdr *udp;
22     struct sockaddr_in6 from, dest;
23     struct icmpd_err icmpd_err;

24     len = sizeof(from);
25     n = Recvfrom(fd6, buf, MAXLINE, 0, (SA *) &from, &len);

26     printf("%d bytes ICMPv6 from %s:", n, Sock_ntop_host((SA *) &from, len));

27     icmp6 = (struct icmp6_hdr *) buf;    /* start of ICMPv6 header */
28     if ( (icmp6len = n) < 8)
29         err_quit("icmp6len (%d) < 8", icmp6len);

30     printf(" type = %d, code = %d\n", icmp6->icmp6_type, icmp6->icmp6_code);
                                                     ———————— icmpd/readable_v6.c
```

Figure 28.41 Handle received ICMPv6 datagram, first half.

ICMPv6 errors are handled by our readable_v6 function, the first half of which is shown in Figure 28.41. The ICMPv6 handling is similar to the code in Figures 28.12 and 28.24.

The second half of our readable_v6 function is shown in Figure 28.42 (p. 785). This code is similar to Figure 28.40: It checks the type of ICMP error, checks that the datagram that caused the error was a UDP datagram, and then builds the icmpd_err structure, which is sent to the client.

icmpd/readable_v6.c

```
31     if (icmp6->icmp6_type == ICMP6_DST_UNREACH ||
32         icmp6->icmp6_type == ICMP6_PACKET_TOO_BIG ||
33         icmp6->icmp6_type == ICMP6_TIME_EXCEEDED) {
34         if (icmp6len < 8 + 8)
35             err_quit("icmp6len (%d) < 8 + 8", icmp6len);

36         hip6 = (struct ip6_hdr *) (buf + 8);
37         hlen2 = sizeof(struct ip6_hdr);
38         printf("\tsrcip = %s, dstip = %s, next hdr = %d\n",
39                 Inet_ntop(AF_INET6, &hip6->ip6_src, srcstr, sizeof(srcstr)),
40                 Inet_ntop(AF_INET6, &hip6->ip6_dst, dststr, sizeof(dststr)),
41                 hip6->ip6_nxt);
42         if (hip6->ip6_nxt == IPPROTO_UDP) {
43             udp = (struct udphdr *) (buf + 8 + hlen2);
44             sport = udp->uh_sport;

45                 /* find client's Unix domain socket, send headers */
46             for (i = 0; i <= maxi; i++) {
47                 if (client[i].connfd >= 0 &&
48                     client[i].family == AF_INET6 &&
49                     client[i].lport == sport) {

50                     bzero(&dest, sizeof(dest));
51                     dest.sin6_family = AF_INET6;
52 #ifdef  HAVE_SOCKADDR_SA_LEN
53                     dest.sin6_len = sizeof(dest);
54 #endif
55                     memcpy(&dest.sin6_addr, &hip6->ip6_dst,
56                             sizeof(struct in6_addr));
57                     dest.sin6_port = udp->uh_dport;

58                     icmpd_err.icmpd_type = icmp6->icmp6_type;
59                     icmpd_err.icmpd_code = icmp6->icmp6_code;
60                     icmpd_err.icmpd_len = sizeof(struct sockaddr_in6);
61                     memcpy(&icmpd_err.icmpd_dest, &dest, sizeof(dest));

62                         /* convert type & code to reasonable errno value */
63                     icmpd_err.icmpd_errno = EHOSTUNREACH;   /* default */
64                     if (icmp6->icmp6_type == ICMP6_DST_UNREACH &&
65                         icmp6->icmp6_code == ICMP6_DST_UNREACH_NOPORT)
66                         icmpd_err.icmpd_errno = ECONNREFUSED;
67                     if (icmp6->icmp6_type == ICMP6_PACKET_TOO_BIG)
68                         icmpd_err.icmpd_errno = EMSGSIZE;
69                     Write(client[i].connfd, &icmpd_err, sizeof(icmpd_err));
70                 }
71             }
72         }
73     }
74     return (--nready);
75 #endif
76 }
```

icmpd/readable_v6.c

Figure 28.42 Handle received ICMPv6 datagram, second half.

28.8   Summary

Raw sockets provide three capabilities:

- We can read and write ICMPv4, IGMPv4, and ICMPv6 packets.
- We can read and write IP datagrams with a protocol field that the kernel does not handle.
- We can build our own IPv4 header, normally used for diagnostic purposes (or by hackers, unfortunately).

Two commonly used diagnostic tools, `ping` and `traceroute`, use raw sockets, and we have developed our own versions of both that support IPv4 and IPv6. We also developed our own `icmpd` daemon that provides access to ICMP errors for a UDP socket. This example also provided an example of descriptor passing across a Unix domain socket between an unrelated client and server.

Exercises

28.1   We said that almost all fields in an IPv6 header and all extension headers are available to the application through socket options or ancillary data. What information in an IPv6 datagram is *not* available to an application?

28.2   What happens in Figure 28.40 if for some reason the client stops reading from its Unix domain connection to the `icmpd` daemon and lots of ICMP errors arrive for the client? What is the easiest solution?

28.3   If we specify the subnet-directed broadcast address to our `ping` program, it works. That is, a broadcast ICMP echo request is sent as a link-layer broadcast, even though we do not set the SO_BROADCAST socket option. Why?

28.4   What happens with our `ping` program if we ping the all-hosts multicast group, 224.0.0.1 on a multihomed host?

29

Datalink Access

29.1 Introduction

Providing access to the datalink layer for an application is a powerful feature that is available with most current operating systems. This provides the following capabilities:

- The ability to watch the packets received by the datalink layer, allowing programs such as tcpdump to be run on normal computer systems (as opposed to dedicated hardware devices to watch packets). When combined with the capability of the network interface to go into a *promiscuous mode*, this allows an application to watch all the packets on the local cable, not just the packets destined for the host on which the program is running.

  > This ability is less useful in switched networks, which have become quite common. This is because the switch only passes traffic to a port if it is addressed to the device or devices attached to that port (unicast, multicast, or broadcast). To monitor traffic carried on other ports of the switch, the switch port must be configured to receive other traffic, often called *monitor mode* or *port mirroring*. Note that many devices that you might not expect to be switches actually are, for example, a dual-speed 10/100Mbps hub is usually a two-port switch: one port for the 100Mbps systems and the other for the 10Mbps systems.

- The ability to run certain programs as normal applications instead of as part of the kernel. For example, most Unix versions of an RARP server are normal applications that read RARP requests from the datalink (RARP requests are not IP datagrams) and then write the reply back to the datalink.

The three common methods to access the datalink layer under Unix are the BSD Packet Filter (BPF), the SVR4 Datalink Provider Interface (DLPI), and the Linux SOCK_PACKET interface. We present an overview of these three, but then describe `libpcap`, the publicly available packet capture library. This library works with all three and using this library makes our programs independent of the actual datalink access provided by the OS. We describe this library by developing a program that sends DNS queries to a name server (we build our own UDP datagrams and write them to a raw socket) and reading the reply using `libpcap` to determine if the name server enables UDP checksums.

29.2 BSD Packet Filter (BPF)

4.4BSD and many other Berkeley-derived implementations support BPF, the BSD packet filter. The implementation of BPF is described in Chapter 31 of TCPv2. The history of BPF, a description of the BPF pseudomachine, and a comparison with the SunOS 4.1.x NIT packet filter is provided in [McCanne and Jacobson 1993].

Each datalink driver calls BPF right before a packet is transmitted and right after a packet is received, as shown in Figure 29.1.

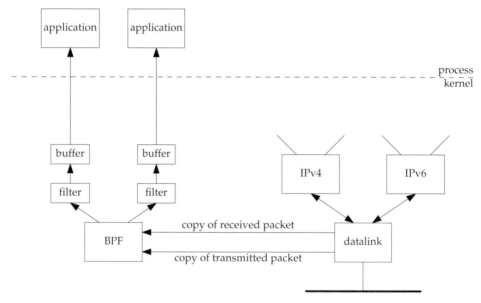

Figure 29.1 Packet capture using BPF.

Examples of these calls for an Ethernet interface are in Figures 4.11 and 4.19 of TCPv2. The reason for calling BPF as soon as possible after reception and as late as possible before transmission is to provide accurate timestamps.

While it is not hard to provide a tap into the datalink to catch all packets, the power of BPF is in its filtering capability. Each application that opens a BPF device can load its own filter, which is then applied by BPF to each packet. While some filters are simple (the filter "udp or tcp" receives only UDP or TCP packets), others can examine fields in the packet headers for certain values. For example,

```
tcp and port 80 and tcp[13:1] & 0x7 != 0
```

was used in Chapter 14 of TCPv3 to collect only TCP segments to or from port 80 that had either the SYN, FIN, or RST flags on. The expression tcp[13:1] refers to the 1-byte value starting at byte offset 13 from the start of the TCP header.

BPF implements a register-based filter machine that applies application-specific filters to each received packet. While one can write filter programs in the machine language of this pseudomachine (which is described on the BPF man page), the simplest interface is to compile ASCII strings (such as the one beginning with tcp that we just showed) into this machine language using the pcap_compile function that we will describe in Section 29.7.

Three techniques are used by BPF to reduce its overhead:

- The BPF filtering is within the kernel, which minimizes the amount of data copied from BPF to the application. This copy, from kernel space to user space, is expensive. If every packet was copied, BPF could have trouble keeping up with fast datalinks.

- Only a portion of each packet is passed by BPF to the application. This is called the *snapshot length*, or *snaplen*. Most applications need only the packet headers, not the packet data. This also reduces the amount of data copied by BPF to the application. tcpdump, for example, defaults this value to 96, which allows room for a 14-byte Ethernet header, a 40-byte IPv6 header, a 20-byte TCP header, and 22 bytes of data. But, to print additional information for other protocols (e.g., DNS and NFS) requires the user to increase this value when tcpdump is run.

- BPF buffers the data destined for an application and this buffer is copied to the application only when the buffer is full, or when the *read timeout* expires. This timeout value can be specified by the application. tcpdump, for example, sets the timeout to 1000 ms, while the RARP daemon sets it to 0 (since there are few RARP packets, and the RARP server needs to send a response as soon as it receives the request). The purpose of the buffering is to reduce the number of system calls. The same number of packets are still copied between BPF and the application, but each system call has an overhead, and reducing the number of system calls always reduces the overhead. (Figure 3.1 of APUE compares the overhead of the read system call, for example, when reading a given file in different chunk sizes varying between 1 byte and 131,072 bytes.)

  Although we show only a single buffer in Figure 29.1, BPF maintains two buffers for each application and fills one while the other is being copied to the application. This is the standard *double-buffering* technique.

In Figure 29.1, we show only the BPF reception of packets: packets received by the datalink from below (the network) and packets received by the datalink from above (IP). The application can also write to BPF, causing packets to be sent out the datalink, but most applications only read from BPF. There is no reason to write to BPF to send IP datagrams because the IP_HDRINCL socket option allows us to write any type of IP datagram desired, including the IP header. (We show an example of this in Section 29.7.) The only reason to write to BPF is to send our own network packets that are not IP datagrams. The RARP daemon does this, for example, to send its RARP replies, which are not IP datagrams.

To access BPF, we must open a BPF device that is not currently open. For example, we could try /dev/bpf0, and if the error return is EBUSY, then we could try /dev/bpf1, and so on. Once a device is opened, about a dozen ioctl commands set the characteristics of the device: load the filter, set the read timeout, set the buffer size, attach a datalink to the BPF device, enable promiscuous mode, and so on. I/O is then performed using read and write.

29.3   Datalink Provider Interface (DLPI)

SVR4 provides datalink access through DLPI. DLPI is a protocol-independent interface designed by AT&T that interfaces to the service provided by the datalink layer [Unix International 1991]. Access to DLPI is by sending and receiving STREAMS messages.

There are two styles of DLPI. In one style, there is a single device to open, and the desired interface is specified using a DLPI DL_ATTACH_REQ request. In the other style, the application simply opens the device (e.g., le0). But for efficient operation, two additional STREAMS modules are normally pushed onto the stream: pfmod, which performs packet filtering within the kernel, and bufmod, which buffers the data destined for the application. We show this in Figure 29.2.

Conceptually, this is similar to what we described in the previous section for BPF: pfmod supports filtering within the kernel using a pseudomachine and bufmod reduces the amount of data and number of system calls by supporting a snapshot length and a read timeout.

One interesting difference, however, is the type of pseudomachine supported by the BPF and pfmod filters. The BPF filter is a directed acyclic control flow graph (CFG), while pfmod uses a Boolean expression tree. The former maps naturally into code for a register machine while the latter maps naturally into code for a stack machine [McCanne and Jacobson 1993]. This paper shows that the CFG implementation used by BPF is normally 3 to 20 times faster than the Boolean expression tree, depending on the complexity of the filter.

Another difference is that BPF always makes the filtering decision before copying the packet, in order to not copy packets that the filter will discard. Depending on the DLPI implementation, the packet may be copied to give it to pfmod, which may then discard it.

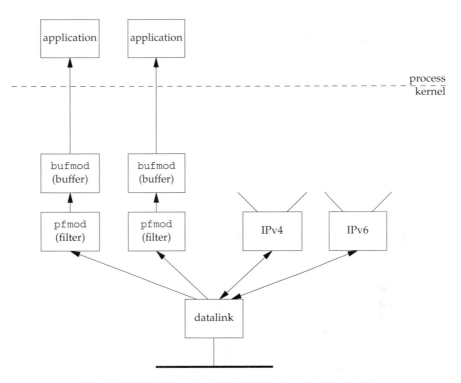

Figure 29.2 Packet capture using DLPI, `pfmod`, and `bufmod`.

29.4 Linux: `SOCK_PACKET` and `PF_PACKET`

There are two methods of receiving packets from the datalink layer under Linux. The original method, which is more widely available but less flexible, is to create a socket of type `SOCK_PACKET`. The newer method, which introduces more filtering and performance features, is to create a socket of family `PF_PACKET`. To do either, we must have sufficient privileges (similar to creating a raw socket), and the third argument to `socket` must be a nonzero value specifying the Ethernet frame type. When using `PF_PACKET` sockets, the second argument to `socket` can be `SOCK_DGRAM`, for "cooked" packets with the link-layer header removed, or `SOCK_RAW`, for the complete link-layer packet. `SOCK_PACKET` sockets only return the complete link layer packet. For example, to receive all frames from the datalink, we write

```
    fd = socket(PF_PACKET, SOCK_RAW, htons(ETH_P_ALL));         /* newer systems */
```

or

```
    fd = socket(AF_INET, SOCK_PACKET, htons(ETH_P_ALL));        /* older systems */
```

This would return frames for all protocols that the datalink receives.

If we wanted only IPv4 frames, the call would be

```
fd = socket(PF_PACKET, SOCK_RAW, htons(ETH_P_IP));        /* newer systems */
```

or

```
fd = socket(AF_INET, SOCK_PACKET, htons(ETH_P_IP));       /* older systems */
```

Other constants for the final argument are `ETH_P_ARP` and `ETH_P_IPV6`, for example.

Specifying a protocol of `ETH_P_xxx` tells the datalink which frame types to pass to the socket for the frames the datalink receives. If the datalink supports a promiscuous mode (e.g., an Ethernet), then the device must also be put into a promiscuous mode, if desired. This is done with a `PACKET_ADD_MEMBERSHIP` socket option, using a `packet_mreq` structure specifying an interface and an action of `PACKET_MR_PROMISC`. On older systems, this is done instead by an `ioctl` of `SIOCGIFFLAGS` to fetch the flags, setting the `IFF_PROMISC` flag, and then storing the flags with `SIOCSIFFLAGS`. Unfortunately, with this method, multiple promiscuous listeners can interfere with each other and a buggy program can leave promiscuous mode on even after it exits.

Some differences are evident when comparing this Linux feature to BPF and DLPI:

- The Linux feature provides no kernel buffering and kernel filtering is only available on newer systems (via the `SO_ATTACH_FILTER` socket option). There is a normal socket receive buffer, but multiple frames cannot be buffered together and passed to the application with a single `read`. This increases the overhead involved in copying the potentially voluminous amounts of data from the kernel to the application.

2. `SOCK_PACKET` provides no filtering by device. (`PF_PACKET` sockets can be linked to a device by calling `bind`.) If `ETH_P_IP` is specified in the call to `socket`, then all IPv4 packets from all devices (Ethernets, PPP links, SLIP links, and the loopback device, for example) are passed to the socket. A generic socket address structure is returned by `recvfrom`, and the `sa_data` member contains the device name (e.g., `eth0`). The application must then discard data from any device in which it is not interested. The problem again is too much data can be returned to the application, which can get in the way when monitoring a high-speed network.

29.5 `libpcap`: **Packet Capture Library**

The packet capture library, `libpcap`, provides implementation-independent access to the underlying packet capture facility provided by the OS. Currently, it supports only the reading of packets (although adding a few lines of code to the library lets one write datalink packets too on some systems). See the next section for a description of another library that supports not only writing datalink packets, but also constructing arbitrary packets.

Support currently exists for BPF under Berkeley-derived kernels, DLPI under HP-UX and Solaris 2.x, NIT under SunOS 4.1.x, the Linux `SOCK_PACKET` and `PF_PACKET` sockets, and a few other operating systems. This library is used by `tcpdump`. About 25 functions comprise the library, but rather than just describe the functions, we will show the actual use of the common functions in a complete example in a later section. All the library functions begin with the `pcap_` prefix. The `pcap` man page describes these functions in more detail.

> The library is publicly available from `http://www.tcpdump.org/`.

29.6   `libnet`: Packet Creation and Injection Library

`libnet` provides an interface to craft and inject arbitrary packets into the network. It provides both raw socket and datalink access modes in an implementation-independent manner.

The library hides many of the details of crafting the IP and UDP or TCP headers, and provides simple and portable access to writing datalink and raw packets. As with `libpcap`, the library is made up of quite a number of functions. We will show how to use a small group of the functions for accessing raw sockets in the example in the following section, as well as the code required to use raw sockets directly for comparison. All the library functions begin with the `libnet_` prefix; the `libnet` man page and online manual describe these functions in more detail.

> The library is publicly available from `http://www.packetfactory.net/libnet/`. The online manual is `http://www.packetfactory.net/libnet/manual/`. As of this writing, the only manual available is for the deprecated version 1.0; the supported version 1.1 has a *significantly* different API. This example uses the 1.1 API.

29.7   Examining the UDP Checksum Field

We will now develop an example that sends a UDP datagram containing a DNS query to a name server and reads the reply using the packet capture library. The goal of the example is to determine whether the name server computes a UDP checksum or not. With IPv4, the computation of a UDP checksum is optional. Most current systems enable these checksums by default, but unfortunately, older systems, notably SunOS 4.1.x, disable these checksums by default. All systems today, and especially a system running a name server, should *always* run with UDP checksums enabled, as corrupted datagrams can corrupt the server's database.

> Enabling or disabling UDP checksums is normally done on a systemwide basis, as described in Appendix E of TCPv1.

We will build our own UDP datagram (the DNS query) and write it to a raw socket. We will also show the same code using `libnet`. We could use a normal UDP socket to send the query, but we want to show how to use the `IP_HDRINCL` socket option to build a complete IP datagram.

We can never obtain the UDP checksum when reading from a normal UDP socket, and we can never read UDP or TCP packets using a raw socket (Section 28.4). Therefore, we must use the packet capture facility to obtain the entire UDP datagram containing the name server's reply.

We will also examine the UDP checksum field in the UDP header. If it is 0, the server does not have UDP checksums enabled.

Figure 29.3 summarizes the operation of our program.

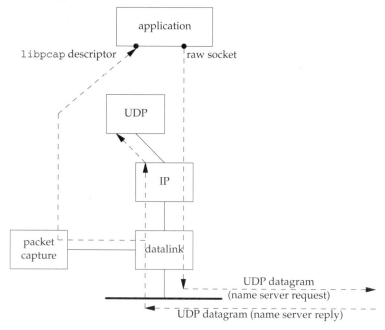

Figure 29.3 Our application to check if a name server has UDP checksums enabled.

We write our own UDP datagrams to the raw socket and read back the replies using `libpcap`. Notice that UDP also receives the name server reply, and it will respond with an ICMP "port unreachable" because it knows nothing about the source port number that our application chooses. The name server will ignore this ICMP error. We also note that it is harder to write a test program of this form that uses TCP, even though we are easily able to write our own TCP segments because any reply to the TCP segments we generate will normally cause our TCP to respond with an RST to whomever we sent the segment.

> One way around this is to send TCP segments with a source IP address that belongs to the attached subnet but is not currently assigned to some other node. Add an ARP entry to the sending host for this new IP address so that the sending host will answer ARP requests for this new address, but do not configure the new IP address as an alias. This will cause the IP stack on the sending host to discard packets received for this new IP address, assuming the sending host is not acting as a router.

Figure 29.4 is a summary of the functions that comprise our program.

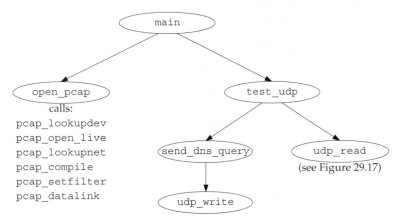

Figure 29.4 Summary of functions for our udpcksum program.

Figure 29.5 shows the header udpcksum.h, which includes our basic unp.h header along with the various system headers that are needed to access the structure definitions for the IP and UDP packet headers.

udpcksum/udpcksum.h

```
 1 #include     "unp.h"
 2 #include     <pcap.h>

 3 #include     <netinet/in_systm.h>    /* required for ip.h */
 4 #include     <netinet/in.h>
 5 #include     <netinet/ip.h>
 6 #include     <netinet/ip_var.h>
 7 #include     <netinet/udp.h>
 8 #include     <netinet/udp_var.h>
 9 #include     <net/if.h>
10 #include     <netinet/if_ether.h>

11 #define TTL_OUT      64               /* outgoing TTL */

12                          /* declare global variables */
13 extern struct sockaddr *dest, *local;
14 extern socklen_t destlen, locallen;
15 extern int datalink;
16 extern char *device;
17 extern pcap_t *pd;
18 extern int rawfd;
19 extern int snaplen;
20 extern int verbose;
21 extern int zerosum;

22                            /* function prototypes */
23 void    cleanup(int);
24 char    *next_pcap(int *);
25 void    open_output(void);
```

```
26 void     open_pcap(void);
27 void     send_dns_query(void);
28 void     test_udp(void);
29 void     udp_write(char *, int);
30 struct udpiphdr *udp_read(void);
```
——— *udpcksum/udpcksum.h*

Figure 29.5 udpcksum.h header.

3–10   Additional Internet headers are required to deal with the IP and UDP header fields.
11–29   We define some global variables and prototypes for our own functions that we will
show shortly.

The first part of the main function is shown in Figure 29.6.

——— *udpcksum/main.c*
```
 1 #include    "udpcksum.h"

 2                  /* define global variables */
 3 struct sockaddr *dest, *local;
 4 struct sockaddr_in locallookup;
 5 socklen_t destlen, locallen;

 6 int      datalink;              /* from pcap_datalink(), in <net/bpf.h> */
 7 char     *device;              /* pcap device */
 8 pcap_t *pd;                    /* packet capture struct pointer */
 9 int      rawfd;                /* raw socket to write on */
10 int      snaplen = 200;        /* amount of data to capture */
11 int      verbose;
12 int      zerosum;              /* send UDP query with no checksum */

13 static void usage(const char *);

14 int
15 main(int argc, char *argv[])
16 {
17     int     c, lopt = 0;
18     char    *ptr, localname[1024], *localport;
19     struct addrinfo *aip;
```
——— *udpcksum/main.c*

Figure 29.6 main function: definitions.

The next part of the main function, shown in Figure 29.7, processes the
command-line arguments.

Process command-line options

20–25   We call getopt to process the command-line arguments. The -0 option lets us
send our UDP query without a UDP checksum to see if the server handles this differently from a datagram with a checksum.

26–28   The -i option lets us specify the interface on which to receive the server's reply. If
this is not specified, the packet capture library chooses one, which might not be correct
on a multihomed host. This is one way that reading from a packet capture device

———————————————————————————————————— udpcksum/main.c

```
20     opterr = 0;                      /* don't want getopt() writing to stderr */
21     while ( (c = getopt(argc, argv, "0i:l:v")) != -1) {
22         switch (c) {

23         case '0':
24             zerosum = 1;
25             break;

26         case 'i':
27             device = optarg;     /* pcap device */
28             break;

29         case 'l':                        /* local IP address and port #: a.b.c.d.p */
30             if ( (ptr = strrchr(optarg, '.')) == NULL)
31                 usage("invalid -l option");

32             *ptr++ = 0;              /* null replaces final period */
33             localport = ptr;        /* service name or port number */
34             strncpy(localname, optarg, sizeof(localname));
35             lopt = 1;
36             break;

37         case 'v':
38             verbose = 1;
39             break;

40         case '?':
41             usage("unrecognized option");
42         }
43     }
```

———————————————————————————————————— udpcksum/main.c

Figure 29.7 main function: processes command-line arguments.

differs from reading from a normal socket: With a socket, we can wildcard the local address, allowing us to receive packets arriving on any interface, but with a packet capture device, we receive arriving packets on only one interface.

> We note that the Linux SOCK_PACKET feature does not limit its datalink capture to a single device. Nevertheless, libpcap provides this filtering based on either its default or on our -i option.

29-36   The -l option lets us specify the source IP address and port number. The port (or a service name) is taken as the string following the final period, and the source IP address is taken as everything before the final period.

―― *udpcksum/main.c*
```
44      if (optind != argc - 2)
45          usage("missing <host> and/or <serv>");

46          /* convert destination name and service */
47      aip = Host_serv(argv[optind], argv[optind + 1], AF_INET, SOCK_DGRAM);
48      dest = aip->ai_addr;          /* don't freeaddrinfo() */
49      destlen = aip->ai_addrlen;

50      /*
51       * Need local IP address for source IP address for UDP datagrams.
52       * Can't specify 0 and let IP choose, as we need to know it for
53       * the pseudoheader to calculate the UDP checksum.
54       * If -l option supplied, then use those values; otherwise,
55       * connect a UDP socket to the destination to determine the right
56       * source address.
57       */
58      if (lopt) {
59              /* convert local name and service */
60          aip = Host_serv(localname, localport, AF_INET, SOCK_DGRAM);
61          local = aip->ai_addr;    /* don't freeaddrinfo() */
62          locallen = aip->ai_addrlen;
63      } else {
64          int     s;
65          s = Socket(AF_INET, SOCK_DGRAM, 0);
66          Connect(s, dest, destlen);
67          /* kernel chooses correct local address for dest */
68          locallen = sizeof(locallookup);
69          local = (struct sockaddr *) &locallookup;
70          Getsockname(s, local, &locallen);
71          if (locallookup.sin_addr.s_addr == htonl(INADDR_ANY))
72              err_quit("Can't determine local address - use -l\n");
73          close(s);
74      }

75      open_output();                 /* open output, either raw socket or libnet */

76      open_pcap();                   /* open packet capture device */

77      setuid(getuid());              /* don't need superuser privileges anymore */

78      Signal(SIGTERM, cleanup);
79      Signal(SIGINT, cleanup);
80      Signal(SIGHUP, cleanup);

81      test_udp();

82      cleanup(0);
83  }
```
―― *udpcksum/main.c*

Figure 29.8 main function: converts hostnames and service names; creates socket.

The last part of the main function is shown in Figure 29.8.

Process destination name and port

46–49   We verify that exactly two command-line arguments remain: the destination host-name and service name. We call host_serv to convert these into a socket address structure, the pointer to which we save in dest.

Process local name and port

50–74   If specified on the command line, we then do the same conversion of the local hostname and port, saving the pointer to the socket address structure in `local`. Otherwise,
we determine the local IP address to use by connecting a datagram socket to the destination and storing the resulting local address in `local`. Since we will be building our
own IP and UDP headers, we must know the source IP address when we write the UDP
datagram. We cannot leave it as 0 and let IP choose the address, because the address is
part of the UDP pseudoheader (which we describe shortly) that we must use for the
UDP checksum computation.

Create raw socket and open packet capture device

75–76   The function `open_output` prepares the output method, whether raw sockets or
`libnet`. The function `open_pcap` opens the packet capture device; we will show this
function next.

Change permissions and establish signal handlers

77–80   We need superuser privileges to create a raw socket. We normally need superuser
privileges to open the packet capture device, but this depends on the implementation.
For example, with BPF, the administrator can set the permissions of the `/dev/bpf`
devices to whatever is desired for that system. We now give up these additional permissions, assuming the program file is set-user-ID. If the process has superuser privileges, calling `setuid` sets our real user ID, effective user ID, and saved set-user-ID to
our real user ID (`getuid`). We establish signal handlers in case the user terminates the
program before it is done.

Perform test and cleanup

81–82   The function `test_udp` (Figure 29.10) performs the test and then returns.
`cleanup` (Figure 29.18) prints summary statistics from the packet capture library and
terminates the process.

Figure 29.9 shows the `open_pcap` function, which we called from the `main` function to open the packet capture device.

Choose packet capture device

10–14   If the packet capture device was not specified (the `-i` command-line option), then
`pcap_lookupdev` chooses a device. It issues the `SIOCGIFCONF` ioctl and chooses
the lowest numbered device that is up, but not the loopback. Many of the `pcap` library
functions fill in an error string if an error occurs. The sole argument to this function is
an array that is filled in with an error string.

Open device

15–17   `pcap_open_live` opens the device. The term "live" refers to an actual device
being opened, instead of a save file containing previously saved packets. The first argument is the device name, the second is the number of bytes to save per packet
(`snaplen`, which we initialized to 200 in Figure 29.6), the third is a promiscuous flag,
the fourth is a timeout value in milliseconds, and the fifth is a pointer to an error message array.

—————————————————————————————— udpcksum/pcap.c

```
 1 #include    "udpcksum.h"

 2 #define CMD      "udp and src host %s and src port %d"

 3 void
 4 open_pcap(void)
 5 {
 6     uint32_t localnet, netmask;
 7     char    cmd[MAXLINE], errbuf[PCAP_ERRBUF_SIZE],
 8         str1[INET_ADDRSTRLEN], str2[INET_ADDRSTRLEN];
 9     struct bpf_program fcode;

10     if (device == NULL) {
11         if ( (device = pcap_lookupdev(errbuf)) == NULL)
12             err_quit("pcap_lookup: %s", errbuf);
13     }
14     printf("device = %s\n", device);

15         /* hardcode: promisc=0, to_ms=500 */
16     if ( (pd = pcap_open_live(device, snaplen, 0, 500, errbuf)) == NULL)
17         err_quit("pcap_open_live: %s", errbuf);

18     if (pcap_lookupnet(device, &localnet, &netmask, errbuf) < 0)
19         err_quit("pcap_lookupnet: %s", errbuf);
20     if (verbose)
21         printf("localnet = %s, netmask = %s\n",
22                 Inet_ntop(AF_INET, &localnet, str1, sizeof(str1)),
23                 Inet_ntop(AF_INET, &netmask, str2, sizeof(str2)));

24     snprintf(cmd, sizeof(cmd), CMD,
25             Sock_ntop_host(dest, destlen),
26             ntohs(sock_get_port(dest, destlen)));
27     if (verbose)
28         printf("cmd = %s\n", cmd);
29     if (pcap_compile(pd, &fcode, cmd, 0, netmask) < 0)
30         err_quit("pcap_compile: %s", pcap_geterr(pd));

31     if (pcap_setfilter(pd, &fcode) < 0)
32         err_quit("pcap_setfilter: %s", pcap_geterr(pd));

33     if ( (datalink = pcap_datalink(pd)) < 0)
34         err_quit("pcap_datalink: %s", pcap_geterr(pd));
35     if (verbose)
36         printf("datalink = %d\n", datalink);
37 }
```

—————————————————————————————— udpcksum/pcap.c

Figure 29.9 open_pcap function: opens and initializes packet capture device.

If the promiscuous flag is set, the interface is placed into promiscuous mode, causing it to receive all packets passing by on the wire. This is the normal mode for tcpdump. For our example, however, the DNS server replies will be sent to our host.

The timeout argument is a read timeout. Instead of having the device return a packet to the process every time a packet is received (which could be inefficient, invoking lots of copies of individual packets from the kernel to the process), a packet is returned only when either the device's read buffer is full or when the read timeout expires. If the read timeout is set to 0, every packet is returned as soon as it is received.

Obtain network address and subnet mask

18-23   pcap_lookupnet returns the network address and subnet mask for the packet capture device. We must specify the subnet mask in the call to pcap_compile that follows, because the packet filter needs this to determine if an IP address is a subnet-directed broadcast address.

Compile packet filter

24-30   pcap_compile takes a filter string (which we build in the cmd array) and compiles it into a filter program (stored in fcode). This will select the packets that we want to receive.

Load filter program

31-32   pcap_setfilter takes the filter program we just compiled and loads it into the packet capture device. This initiates the capturing of the packets we selected with the filter.

Determine datalink type

33-36   pcap_datalink returns the type of datalink for the packet capture device. We need this when receiving packets to determine the size of the datalink header that will be at the beginning of each packet we read (Figure 29.15).

After calling open_pcap, the main function calls test_udp, which we show in Figure 29.10. This function sends a DNS query and reads the server's reply.

———————————————————————————— udpcksum/udpcksum.c

```
12 void
13 test_udp(void)
14 {
15     volatile int nsent = 0, timeout = 3;
16     struct udpiphdr *ui;

17     Signal(SIGALRM, sig_alrm);
18     if (sigsetjmp(jmpbuf, 1)) {
19         if (nsent >= 3)
20             err_quit("no response");
21         printf("timeout\n");
22         timeout *= 2;              /* exponential backoff: 3, 6, 12 */
23     }
24     canjump = 1;                   /* siglongjmp is now OK */

25     send_dns_query();
26     nsent++;

27     alarm(timeout);
28     ui = udp_read();
29     canjump = 0;
30     alarm(0);

31     if (ui->ui_sum == 0)
32         printf("UDP checksums off\n");
33     else
34         printf("UDP checksums on\n");
35     if (verbose)
36         printf("received UDP checksum = %x\n", ntohs(ui->ui_sum));
37 }
```

———————————————————————————— udpcksum/udpcksum.c

Figure 29.10 `test_udp` function: sends queries and reads responses.

`volatile` **variables**

50   We want the two automatic variables, `nsent` and `timeout`, to retain their values after a `siglongjmp` from the signal handler back to this function. An implementation is allowed to restore automatic variables back to what their value was when `sigsetjmp` was called (p. 178 of APUE), but adding the `volatile` qualifier prevents this from happening.

Establish signal handler and jump buffer

52–53   A signal handler is established for `SIGALRM` and `sigsetjmp` establishes a jump buffer for `siglongjmp`. (These two functions are described in detail in Section 10.15 of APUE.) The second argument of 1 to `sigsetjmp` tells it to save the current signal mask since we will call `siglongjmp` from our signal handler.

Handle `siglongjmp`

54–58   This code is executed only when `siglongjmp` is called from our signal handler. This indicates that a timeout occurred: We sent a request and never received a reply. If we have sent three requests, we terminate. Otherwise, we print a message and multiply the timeout value by 2. This is an *exponential backoff*, which we described in Section 22.5. The first timeout will be for 3 seconds, then 6, and then 12.

The reason we use `sigsetjmp` and `siglongjmp` in this example, rather than just catching `EINTR` (as in Figure 14.1), is because the packet capture library reading functions (which are called by our `udp_read` function) restart a `read` operation when `EINTR` is returned. Since we do not want to modify the library functions to return this error, our only solution is to catch the `SIGALRM` signal and perform a nonlocal goto, returning control to our code instead of the library code.

Send DNS query and read reply

60-65   `send_dns_query` (Figure 29.12) sends a DNS query to a name server. `udp_read` (Figure 29.15) reads the reply. We call `alarm` to prevent the read from blocking forever. If the specified timeout period (in seconds) expires, `SIGALRM` is generated and our signal handler calls `siglongjmp`.

Examine received UDP checksum

66-71   If the received UDP checksum is 0, the server did not calculate and send a checksum.

Figure 29.11 shows our signal handler, `sig_alrm`, which handles the `SIGALRM` signal.

```
                                                                ——— udpcksum/udpcksum.c
 1 #include     "udpcksum.h"
 2 #include     <setjmp.h>

 3 static sigjmp_buf jmpbuf;
 4 static int canjump;

 5 void
 6 sig_alrm(int signo)
 7 {
 8     if (canjump == 0)
 9         return;
10     siglongjmp(jmpbuf, 1);
11 }
                                                                ——— udpcksum/udpcksum.c
```

Figure 29.11 `sig_alrm` function: handles `SIGALRM` signal.

8-10   The flag `canjump` was set in Figure 29.10 after the jump buffer was initialized by `sigsetjmp`. If the flag has been set, we call `siglongjmp`, which causes the flow of control to act as if the `sigsetjmp` in Figure 29.10 had returned with a value of 1.

Figure 29.12 shows the `send_dns_query` function that sends a UDP query to a DNS server using a raw socket. This function builds the application data, a DNS query.

```
                                                          ──────── udpcksum/senddnsquery-raw.c
  6 void
  7 send_dns_query(void)
  8 {
  9     size_t  nbytes;
 10     char    *buf, *ptr;

 11     buf = Malloc(sizeof(struct udpiphdr) + 100);
 12     ptr = buf + sizeof(struct udpiphdr);    /* leave room for IP/UDP headers */

 13     *((uint16_t *) ptr) = htons(1234);  /* identification */
 14     ptr += 2;
 15     *((uint16_t *) ptr) = htons(0x0100);    /* flags: recursion desired */
 16     ptr += 2;
 17     *((uint16_t *) ptr) = htons(1); /* # questions */
 18     ptr += 2;
 19     *((uint16_t *) ptr) = 0;    /* # answer RRs */
 20     ptr += 2;
 21     *((uint16_t *) ptr) = 0;    /* # authority RRs */
 22     ptr += 2;
 23     *((uint16_t *) ptr) = 0;    /* # additional RRs */
 24     ptr += 2;

 25     memcpy(ptr, "\001a\014root-servers\003net\000", 20);
 26     ptr += 20;
 27     *((uint16_t *) ptr) = htons(1); /* query type = A */
 28     ptr += 2;
 29     *((uint16_t *) ptr) = htons(1); /* query class = 1 (IP addr) */
 30     ptr += 2;

 31     nbytes = (ptr - buf) - sizeof(struct udpiphdr);
 32     udp_write(buf, nbytes);
 33     if (verbose)
 34         printf("sent: %d bytes of data\n", nbytes);
 35 }
                                                          ──────── udpcksum/senddnsquery-raw.c
```

Figure 29.12 send_dns_query function: sends a query to a DNS server.

Allocate buffer and initialize pointer

11–12   We use `malloc` to allocate `buf` with room for a 20-byte IP header, an 8-byte UDP header, and 100 bytes of user data. `ptr` is set to point to the first byte of user data.

Build DNS query

13–24   To understand the details of the UDP datagram built by this function requires an understanding of the DNS message format. This is found in Section 14.3 of TCPv1. We set the identification field to 1234, the flags to 0, the number of questions to 1, and the number of answer resource records (RRs), the number of authority RRs, and the number of additional RRs to 0.

25–30   We form the single question that follows in the message: an A query for the IP addresses of the host a.root-servers.net. This domain name is stored in 20 bytes and consists of 4 labels: the 1-byte label a, the 12-byte label root-servers (remember that \014 is an octal character constant), the 3-byte label net, and the root label whose length is 0. The query type is 1 (called an A query) and the query class is also 1.

Write UDP datagram

31–32   This message consists of 36 bytes of user data (eight 2-byte fields and the 20-byte domain name), but we calculate the message length by subtracting the beginning of the buffer from the current pointer within the buffer to avoid having to change a constant if we change the format of the message we're sending. We call our function `udp_write` to build the UDP and IP headers and write the IP datagram to our raw socket.

Figure 29.13 shows the `open_output` function for use with raw sockets.

Declare raw socket descriptor

2   We declare a global variable in which to hold the descriptor for the raw socket.

Create raw socket and enable `IP_HDRINCL`

7–13   We create a raw socket and enable the `IP_HDRINCL` socket option. This option lets us write complete IP datagrams, including the IP header.

```
                                                              ─ udpcksum/udpwrite.c
 2 int      rawfd;                      /* raw socket to write on */

 3 void
 4 open_output(void)
 5 {
 6     int     on = 1;
 7     /*
 8      * Need a raw socket to write our own IP datagrams to.
 9      * Process must have superuser privileges to create this socket.
10      * Also must set IP_HDRINCL so we can write our own IP headers.
11      */

12     rawfd = Socket(dest->sa_family, SOCK_RAW, 0);

13     Setsockopt(rawfd, IPPROTO_IP, IP_HDRINCL, &on, sizeof(on));
14 }
                                                              ─ udpcksum/udpwrite.c
```

Figure 29.13 `open_output` function: prepares a raw socket.

Figure 29.14 shows our function, `udp_write`, which builds the IP and UDP headers and then writes the datagram to the raw socket.

Initialize packet header pointers

24–26   `ip` points to the beginning of the IP header (an `ip` structure) and `ui` points to the same location, but the structure `udpiphdr` is the combined IP and UDP headers.

Zero header

27   We explicitly set the header area to zeros, to avoid checksumming any leftover data that might be in the buffer.

> Previous versions of this code explicitly set every element of the `struct udpiphdr` to zero; however, this struct contains some implementation details so it may be different from system to system. This is a typical portability problem when building headers explicitly.

Update lengths

28-31   `ui_len` is the UDP length: the number of bytes of user data plus the size of the UDP header (8 bytes). `userlen` (the number of bytes of user data that follows the UDP header) is incremented by 28 (20 bytes for the IP header and 8 bytes for the UDP header) to reflect the total size of the IP datagram.

Fill in UDP header and calculate UDP checksum

32-45   When the UDP checksum is calculated, it includes not only the UDP header and UDP data, but also fields from the IP header. These additional fields from the IP header form what is called the *pseudoheader*. The inclusion of the pseudoheader provides additional verification that if the checksum is correct, then the datagram was delivered to the correct host and to the correct protocol code. These statements initialize the fields in the IP header that form the pseudoheader. The code is somewhat obtuse, but is explained in Section 23.6 of TCPv2. The result is storing the UDP checksum in the `ui_sum` member if the `zerosum` flag (the `-0` command-line argument) is not set.

     If the calculated checksum is 0, the value `0xffff` is stored instead. In one's-complement arithmetic, the two values are the same, but UDP sets the checksum to 0 to indicate that the sender did not store a UDP checksum. Notice that we did not check for a calculated checksum of 0 in Figure 28.14 because the ICMPv4 checksum is required: The value of 0 does not indicate the absence of a checksum.

> We note that Solaris 2.x, for x < 6, has a bug with regard to checksums for TCP segments or UDP datagrams sent on a raw socket with the `IP_HDRINCL` socket option set. The kernel calculates the checksum and we must set the `ui_sum` field to the UDP length.

Fill in IP header

46-59   Since we have set the `IP_HDRINCL` socket option, we must fill in most fields in the IP header. (Section 28.3 discusses these writes to a raw socket when this socket option is set.) We set the identification field to 0 (`ip_id`), which tells IP to set this field. IP also calculates the IP header checksum. `sendto` writes the IP datagram.

> Note that we set the `ip_len` field in either host or network byte order, depending on the OS we're using. This is a typical portability problem when using raw sockets.

     The next function is `udp_read`, shown in Figure 29.15, which was called from Figure 29.10.

```
                                                     ─ udpcksum/udpwrite.c
19 void
20 udp_write(char *buf, int userlen)
21 {
22     struct udpiphdr *ui;
23     struct ip *ip;

24         /* fill in and checksum UDP header */
25     ip = (struct ip *) buf;
26     ui = (struct udpiphdr *) buf;
27     bzero(ui, sizeof(*ui));
28             /* add 8 to userlen for pseudoheader length */
29     ui->ui_len = htons((uint16_t) (sizeof(struct udphdr) + userlen));
30             /* then add 28 for IP datagram length */
31     userlen += sizeof(struct udpiphdr);

32     ui->ui_pr = IPPROTO_UDP;
33     ui->ui_src.s_addr = ((struct sockaddr_in *) local)->sin_addr.s_addr;
34     ui->ui_dst.s_addr = ((struct sockaddr_in *) dest)->sin_addr.s_addr;
35     ui->ui_sport = ((struct sockaddr_in *) local)->sin_port;
36     ui->ui_dport = ((struct sockaddr_in *) dest)->sin_port;
37     ui->ui_ulen = ui->ui_len;
38     if (zerosum == 0) {
39 #if 1                                  /* change to if 0 for Solaris 2.x, x < 6 */
40         if ( (ui->ui_sum = in_cksum((u_int16_t *) ui, userlen)) == 0)
41             ui->ui_sum = 0xffff;
42 #else
43         ui->ui_sum = ui->ui_len;
44 #endif
45     }

46         /* fill in rest of IP header; */
47         /* ip_output() calcuates & stores IP header checksum */
48     ip->ip_v = IPVERSION;
49     ip->ip_hl = sizeof(struct ip) >> 2;
50     ip->ip_tos = 0;
51 #if defined(linux) || defined(__OpenBSD__)
52     ip->ip_len = htons(userlen);    /* network byte order */
53 #else
54     ip->ip_len = userlen;         /* host byte order */
55 #endif
56     ip->ip_id = 0;                /* let IP set this */
57     ip->ip_off = 0;               /* frag offset, MF and DF flags */
58     ip->ip_ttl = TTL_OUT;

59     Sendto(rawfd, buf, userlen, 0, dest, destlen);
60 }
                                                     ─ udpcksum/udpwrite.c
```

Figure 29.14 udp_write function: builds UDP and IP headers and writes IP datagram to raw socket.

—————————————————————————————————— udpcksum/udpread.c

```
 7 struct udpiphdr *
 8 udp_read(void)
 9 {
10     int      len;
11     char     *ptr;
12     struct ether_header *eptr;

13     for ( ; ; ) {
14         ptr = next_pcap(&len);

15         switch (datalink) {
16         case DLT_NULL:              /* loopback header = 4 bytes */
17             return (udp_check(ptr + 4, len - 4));

18         case DLT_EN10MB:
19             eptr = (struct ether_header *) ptr;
20             if (ntohs(eptr->ether_type) != ETHERTYPE_IP)
21                 err_quit("Ethernet type %x not IP", ntohs(eptr->ether_type));
22             return (udp_check(ptr + 14, len - 14));

23         case DLT_SLIP:              /* SLIP header = 24 bytes */
24             return (udp_check(ptr + 24, len - 24));

25         case DLT_PPP:               /* PPP header = 24 bytes */
26             return (udp_check(ptr + 24, len - 24));

27         default:
28             err_quit("unsupported datalink (%d)", datalink);
29         }
30     }
31 }
```

—————————————————————————————————— udpcksum/udpread.c

Figure 29.15 udp_read function: reads next packet from packet capture device.

14–29   Our function next_pcap (Figure 29.16) returns the next packet from the packet capture device. Since the datalink headers differ depending on the actual device type, we branch based on the value returned by the pcap_datalink function.

> These magic offsets of 4, 14, and 24 are shown in Figure 31.9 of TCPv2. The 24-byte offsets shown for SLIP and PPP are for BSD/OS 2.1.

> Despite having the qualifier "10MB" in the name DLT_EN10MB, this datalink type is also used for 100 Mbit/sec Ethernet.

Our function udp_check (Figure 29.19) examines the packet and verifies fields in the IP and UDP headers.

Figure 29.16 shows the next_pcap function, which returns the next packet from the packet capture device.

43–44   We call the library function pcap_next, which returns the next packet or NULL if a timeout occurs. If the timeout occurs, we simply loop and call pcap_next again. A pointer to the packet is the return value of the function and the second argument points to a pcap_pkthdr structure, which is also filled in on return.

—————————————————————————————— *udpcksum/pcap.c*

```
38 char *
39 next_pcap(int *len)
40 {
41     char   *ptr;
42     struct pcap_pkthdr hdr;

43         /* keep looping until packet ready */
44     while ( (ptr = (char *) pcap_next(pd, &hdr)) == NULL) ;

45     *len = hdr.caplen;            /* captured length */
46     return (ptr);
47 }
```

—————————————————————————————— *udpcksum/pcap.c*

Figure 29.16 next_pcap function: returns next packet.

```
struct pcap_pkthdr {
  struct timeval ts;      /* timestamp */
  bpf_u_int32    caplen;  /* length of portion captured */
  bpf_u_int32    len;     /* length of this packet (off wire) */
};
```

The timestamp is when the packet capture device read the packet, as opposed to the actual delivery of the packet to the process, which could be sometime later. `caplen` is the amount of data that was captured (recall that we set our variable `snaplen` to 200 in Figure 29.6, and then this was the second argument to `pcap_open_live` in Figure 29.9). The purpose of the packet capture facility is to capture the packet headers and not all the data in each packet. `len` is the full length of the packet on the wire. `caplen` will always be less than or equal to `len`.

45–46   The captured length is returned through the pointer argument and the return value of the function is the pointer to the packet. Keep in mind that the "pointer to the packet" points to the datalink header, which is the 14-byte Ethernet header in the case of an Ethernet frame, or a 4-byte pseudolink header in the case of the loopback interface.

If we look at the implementation of `pcap_next` in the library, it shows the division of labor between the different functions. We show this in Figure 29.17. Our application calls the `pcap_` functions, and some of these functions are device-independent, while others are dependent on the type of packet capture device. For example, we show that the BPF implementation calls `read`, while the DLPI implementation calls `getmsg` and the Linux implementation calls `recvfrom`.

Our function `udp_check` verifies numerous fields in the IP and UDP headers. It is shown in Figure 29.19. We must do these verifications because when the packet is passed to us by the packet capture device, the IP layer has not yet seen the packet. This differs from a raw socket.

44–61   The packet length must include at least the IP and UDP headers. The IP version is verified along with the IP header length and the IP header checksum. If the protocol field indicates a UDP datagram, the function returns the pointer to the combined IP/UDP header. Otherwise, the program terminates since the packet capture filter that we specified in our call to `pcap_setfilter` in Figure 29.9 should not return any other type of packet.

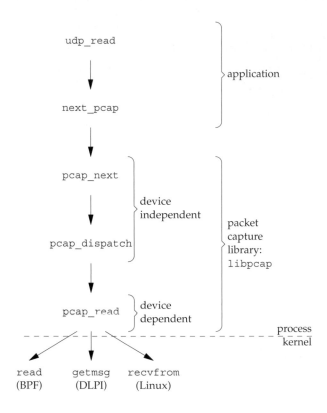

Figure 29.17 Arrangement of function calls to read from packet capture library.

udpcksum/cleanup.c
```
 2 void
 3 cleanup(int signo)
 4 {
 5     struct pcap_stat stat;

 6     putc('\n', stdout);

 7     if (verbose) {
 8         if (pcap_stats(pd, &stat) < 0)
 9             err_quit("pcap_stats: %s\n", pcap_geterr(pd));
10         printf("%d packets received by filter\n", stat.ps_recv);
11         printf("%d packets dropped by kernel\n", stat.ps_drop);
12     }

13     exit(0);
14 }
```
udpcksum/cleanup.c

Figure 29.18 cleanup function.

The cleanup function shown in Figure 29.18 is called by the main function immediately before the program terminates, and also as the signal handler if the user aborts the program (Figure 29.8).

————————————————————————— udpcksum/udpread.c

```
38 struct udpiphdr *
39 udp_check(char *ptr, int len)
40 {
41     int     hlen;
42     struct ip *ip;
43     struct udpiphdr *ui;

44     if (len < sizeof(struct ip) + sizeof(struct udphdr))
45         err_quit("len = %d", len);

46         /* minimal verification of IP header */
47     ip = (struct ip *) ptr;
48     if (ip->ip_v != IPVERSION)
49         err_quit("ip_v = %d", ip->ip_v);
50     hlen = ip->ip_hl << 2;
51     if (hlen < sizeof(struct ip))
52         err_quit("ip_hl = %d", ip->ip_hl);
53     if (len < hlen + sizeof(struct udphdr))
54         err_quit("len = %d, hlen = %d", len, hlen);

55     if ( (ip->ip_sum = in_cksum((uint16_t *) ip, hlen)) != 0)
56         err_quit("ip checksum error");

57     if (ip->ip_p == IPPROTO_UDP) {
58         ui = (struct udpiphdr *) ip;
59         return (ui);
60     } else
61         err_quit("not a UDP packet");
62 }
```

————————————————————————— udpcksum/udpread.c

Figure 29.19 udp_check function: verifies fields in IP and UDP headers.

Fetch and print packet capture statistics

7–12   pcap_stats fetches the packet capture statistics: the total number of packets received by the filter and the number of packets dropped by the kernel.

Example

We first run our program with the -0 command-line option to verify that the name server responds to datagrams that arrive with no checksum. We also specify the -v flag.

```
macosx # udpcksum -i en1 -0 -v bridget.rudoff.com domain
device = en1
localnet = 172.24.37.64, netmask = 255.255.255.224
cmd = udp and src host 206.168.112.96 and src port 53
datalink = 1
sent: 36 bytes of data
UDP checksums on
received UDP checksum = 9d15

3 packets received by filter
0 packets dropped by kernel
```

Next, we run our program to a local name server (our system `freebsd4`) that does not have UDP checksums enabled. (Note that it's increasingly rare to find a name server without UDP checksums enabled.)

```
macosx # udpcksum -i en1 -v freebsd4.unpbook.com domain
device = en1
localnet = 172.24.37.64, netmask = 255.255.255.224
cmd = udp and src host 172.24.37.94 and src port 53
datalink = 1
sent: 36 bytes of data
UDP checksums off
received UDP checksum = 0

3 packets received by filter
0 packets dropped by kernel
```

`libnet` Output Functions

We now show versions of `open_output` and `send_dns_query` that use `libnet` instead of raw sockets. As we will see, `libnet` takes care of many details for us, including the portability problems with checksums and IP header byte order that we mentioned. The `open_output` function for `libnet` is shown in Figure 29.20.

Declare `libnet` descriptor

7   `libnet` uses an opaque type, `libnet_t`, as a linkage to the library. The `libnet_init` function returns a `libnet_t` pointer, which is then passed to further `libnet` functions to indicate which instance is desired. In this way, it is similar to both socket and pcap descriptors.

Initialize `libnet`

12–16   We call the `libnet_init` function, asking it to open an IPv4 raw socket by supplying `LIBNET_RAW4` as its first argument. If an error is encountered, `libnet_init` returns an error in its *errbuf* argument, which we print if `libnet_init` returns NULL.

———————————————————————————————————— udpcksum/senddnsquery-libnet.c
```
 7 static libnet_t *l;              /* libnet descriptor */

 8 void
 9 open_output(void)
10 {
11     char    errbuf[LIBNET_ERRBUF_SIZE];

12     /* Initialize libnet with an IPv4 raw socket */
13     l = libnet_init(LIBNET_RAW4, NULL, errbuf);
14     if (l == NULL) {
15         err_quit("Can't initialize libnet: %s", errbuf);
16     }
17 }
```
———————————————————————————————————— udpcksum/senddnsquery-libnet.c

Figure 29.20 `open_output` function: prepares to use `libnet`.

```
                                                    udpcksum/senddnsquery-libnet.c
18 void
19 send_dns_query(void)
20 {
21     char    qbuf[24], *ptr;
22     u_int16_t one;
23     int     packet_size = LIBNET_UDP_H + LIBNET_DNSV4_H + 24;
24     static libnet_ptag_t ip_tag, udp_tag, dns_tag;
25     /* build query portion of DNS packet */
26     ptr = qbuf;
27     memcpy(ptr, "\001a\014root-servers\003net\000", 20);
28     ptr += 20;
29     one = htons(1);
30     memcpy(ptr, &one, 2);        /* query type = A */
31     ptr += 2;
32     memcpy(ptr, &one, 2);        /* query class = 1 (IP addr) */
33     /* build DNS packet */
34     dns_tag = libnet_build_dnsv4(1234 /* identification */ ,
35                                  0x0100 /* flags: recursion desired */ ,
36                                  1 /* # questions */ , 0 /* # answer RRs */ ,
37                                  0 /* # authority RRs */ ,
38                                  0 /* # additional RRs */ ,
39                                  qbuf /* query */ ,
40                                  24 /* length of query */ , 1, dns_tag);
41     /* build UDP header */
42     udp_tag = libnet_build_udp(((struct sockaddr_in *) local)->
43                                sin_port /* source port */ ,
44                                ((struct sockaddr_in *) dest)->
45                                sin_port /* dest port */ ,
46                                packet_size /* length */ , 0 /* checksum */ ,
47                                NULL /* payload */ , 0 /* payload length */ ,
48                                1, udp_tag);
49     /* Since we specified the checksum as 0, libnet will automatically */
50     /* calculate the UDP checksum.  Turn it off if the user doesn't want it. */
51     if (zerosum)
52         if (libnet_toggle_checksum(l, udp_tag, LIBNET_OFF) < 0)
53             err_quit("turning off checksums: %s\n", libnet_geterror(l));
54     /* build IP header */
55     ip_tag = libnet_build_ipv4(packet_size + LIBNET_IPV4_H /* len */,
56             0 /* tos */, 0 /* IP ID */, 0 /* fragment */,
57             TTL_OUT /* ttl */, IPPROTO_UDP /* protocol */,
58             0 /* checksum */,
59             ((struct sockaddr_in *) local)->sin_addr.s_addr /* source */,
60             ((struct sockaddr_in *) dest)->sin_addr.s_addr /* dest */,
61             NULL /* payload */, 0 /* payload length */, 1, ip_tag);
62     if (libnet_write(l) < 0) {
63         err_quit("libnet_write: %s\n", libnet_geterror(l));
64     }
65     if (verbose)
66         printf("sent: %d bytes of data\n", packet_size);
67 }
                                                    udpcksum/senddnsquery-libnet.c
```

Figure 29.21 send_dns_query function using libnet: sends a query to a DNS server.

The `send_dns_query` function for `libnet` is shown in Figure 29.21. Compare it against the `send_dns_query` (Figure 29.12) and `udp_write` (Figure 29.14) functions for raw sockets.

Build DNS query

25–32   We build the query portion of the DNS packet first, just as in lines 25–30 of Figure 29.12.

34–40   We then call the `libnet_build_dnsv4` function, which accepts each field in the DNS packet as a separate function argument. We only need to know the layout of the query portion; the details of how to put together the DNS packet header are taken care of for us.

Fill in UDP header and arrange for UDP checksum calculation

42–48   Similarly, we build the UDP header by calling `libnet_build_udp` function. This also accepts each header field as a separate function argument. When passing a checksum field in as 0, `libnet` automatically calculates the checksum for that field. This is comparable to lines 29–45 of Figure 29.14.

49–52   If the user requested that the checksum not be calculated, we must specifically turn checksum calculation off.

Fill in IP header

53–65   To complete the packet, we build the IPv4 header using the `libnet_build_ipv4` function. As with other `libnet_build` functions, we supply only the field contents and `libnet` puts the header together for us. This is comparable to lines 46–58 of Figure 29.14.

> Note that `libnet` automatically takes care of whether or not the `ip_len` field is in network byte order. This is a sample of a portability improvement gained by using `libnet`.

Write UDP datagram

66–70   We call the function `libnet_write` to write the assembled datagram to the network.

Note that the `libnet` version of `send_dns_query` is only 67 lines, while the raw socket version (`send_dns_query` and `udp_write` combined) is 96 lines and contains at least 2 portability "gotchas."

29.8 Summary

With raw sockets, we have the capability to read and write IP datagrams that the kernel does not understand, and with access to the datalink layer, we can extend that capability to read and write *any* type of datalink frame, not just IP datagrams. `tcpdump` is probably the most commonly used program that accesses the datalink layer directly.

Different operating systems have different ways of accessing the datalink layer. We looked at the Berkeley-derived BPF, SVR4's DLPI, and the Linux SOCK_PACKET. But we can ignore all their differences and still write portable code using the freely available packet capture library, `libpcap`.

Writing raw datagrams can be different on different systems. The freely available `libnet` library hides these differences and provides an interface to output both via raw sockets and directly on the datalink.

Exercises

29.1 What is the purpose of the `canjump` flag in Figure 29.11?

29.2 In our `udpcksum` program, common error replies are an ICMP "port unreachable" (the destination is not running a name server) or an ICMP "host unreachable." In either case, we need not wait for a timeout of our `udp_read` in Figure 29.10 because the ICMP error is essentially a reply to our DNS query. Modify the program to catch these ICMP errors.

30

Client/Server Design Alternatives

30.1 Introduction

We have several choices for the type of process control to use when writing a Unix server:

- Our first server, Figure 1.9, was an *iterative server*, but there are a limited number of scenarios where this is recommended because the server cannot process a pending client until it has completely serviced the current client.

- Figure 5.2 was our first *concurrent server* and it called `fork` to spawn a child process for every client. Traditionally, most Unix servers fall into this category.

- In Section 6.8, we developed a different version of our TCP server consisting of a single process using `select` to handle any number of clients.

- In Figure 26.3, we modified our concurrent server to create one thread per client instead of one process per client.

There are two other modifications to the concurrent server design that we will look at in this chapter:

- *Preforking* has the server call `fork` when it starts, creating a pool of child processes. One process from the currently available pool handles each client request.

- *Prethreading* has the server create a pool of available threads when it starts, and one thread from the pool handles each client.

There are numerous details with preforking and prethreading that we will examine in this chapter: What if there are not enough processes or threads in the pool? What if there are too many processes or threads in the pool? How can the parent and its children or threads synchronize with each other?

Clients are typically easier to write than servers because there is less process control in a client. Nevertheless, we have already examined various ways to write our simple echo client and we summarize these in Section 30.2.

In this chapter, we will look at nine different server designs and we will run each server against the same client. Our client/server scenario is typical of the Web: The client sends a small request to the server and the server responds with data back to the client. Some of the servers we have already discussed in detail (e.g., the concurrent server with one `fork` per client), while the preforked and prethreaded servers are new and therefore discussed in detail in this chapter.

We will run multiple instances of a client against each server, measuring the CPU time required to service a fixed number of client requests. Instead of scattering all our CPU timings throughout the chapter, we summarize them in Figure 30.1 and refer to this figure throughout the chapter. We note that the times in this figure measure the CPU time required *only for process control* and the iterative server is our baseline we subtract from actual CPU time because an iterative server has no process control overhead. We include the baseline time of 0.0 in this figure to reiterate this point. We use the term *process control CPU time* in this chapter to denote this difference from the baseline for a given system.

Row	Server description	Process control CPU time, seconds (difference from baseline)
0	Iterative server (baseline measurement; no process control)	0.0
1	Concurrent server, one `fork` per client request	20.90
2	Prefork with each child calling `accept`	1.80
3	Prefork with file locking to protect `accept`	2.07
4	Prefork with thread mutex locking to protect `accept`	1.75
5	Prefork with parent passing socket descriptor to child	2.58
6	Concurrent server, create one thread per client request	0.99
7	Prethreaded with mutex locking to protect `accept`	1.93
8	Prethreaded with main thread calling `accept`	2.05

Figure 30.1 Timing comparisons of the various servers discussed in this chapter.

All these server timings were obtained by running the client shown in Figure 30.3 on two different hosts on the same subnet as the server. For all tests, both clients spawned five children to create five simultaneous connections to the server, for a maximum of 10 simultaneous connections at the server at any time. Each client requested 4,000 bytes from the server across the connection. For those tests involving a preforked or a prethreaded server, the server created 15 children or 15 threads when it started.

| child # | # clients serviced | | | |
| or thread # | Preforked, | Preforked, | Preforked, | Prethreaded, |
	no locking around accept (row 2)	file locking around accept (row 3)	descriptor passing (row 5)	thread locking around accept (row 7)
0	333	347	1006	333
1	340	328	950	323
2	335	332	720	333
3	335	335	582	328
4	332	338	485	329
5	331	340	457	322
6	333	335	385	324
7	333	343	250	360
8	332	324	105	341
9	331	315	32	348
10	334	326	14	358
11	333	340	9	331
12	334	330	4	321
13	332	331	1	329
14	332	336	0	320
	5000	5000	5000	5000

Figure 30.2 Number of clients or threads serviced by each of the 15 children or threads.

Some server designs involve creating a pool of child processes or a pool of threads. An item to consider in these cases is the distribution of the client requests to the available pool. Figure 30.2 summarizes these distributions and we will discuss each column in the appropriate section.

30.2 TCP Client Alternatives

We have already examined various client designs, but it is worth summarizing their strengths and weaknesses:

- Figure 5.5 was the basic TCP client. There were two problems with this program. First, while it is blocked awaiting user input, it does not see network events such as the peer closing the connection. Additionally, it operates in a stop-and-wait mode, making it inefficient for batch processing.

- Figure 6.9 was the next iteration, and by using select, the client was notified of network events while waiting for user input. However, this program did not handle batch mode correctly. Figure 6.13 corrected this problem by using the shutdown function.

- Figure 16.3 began the presentation of our client using nonblocking I/O.

- The first of our clients that went beyond the single-process, single-thread design was Figure 16.10, which used `fork` with one process handling the client-to-server data and the other process handling the server-to-client data.

- Figure 26.2 used two threads instead of two processes.

At the end of Section 16.2, we summarized the timing differences between these various versions. As we noted there, although the nonblocking I/O version was the fastest, the code was more complex and using either two processes or two threads simplifies the code.

30.3 TCP Test Client

Figure 30.3 shows the client that we will use to test all the variations of our server.

10–12   Each time we run the client, we specify the hostname or IP address of the server, the server's port, the number of children for the client to `fork` (allowing us to initiate multiple connections to the same server concurrently), the number of requests each child should send to the server, and the number of bytes to request the server to return each time.

17–30   The parent calls `fork` for each child, and each child establishes the specified number of connections with the server. On each connection, the child sends a line specifying the number of bytes for the server to return, and then the child reads that amount of data from the server. The parent just `waits` for all the children to terminate. Notice that the client closes each TCP connection, so TCP's TIME_WAIT state occurs on the client, not on the server. This is a difference between our client/server and normal HTTP connections.

When we measure the various servers in this chapter, we execute the client as

```
% client 192.168.1.20 8888 5 500 4000
```

This creates 2,500 TCP connections to the server: 500 connections from each of five children. On each connection, 5 bytes are sent from the client to the server ("4000\n") and 4,000 bytes are transferred from the server back to the client. We run the client from two different hosts to the same server, providing a total of 5,000 TCP connections, with a maximum of 10 simultaneous connections at the server at any given time.

> Sophisticated benchmarks exist for testing various Web servers. One is called WebStone and is available from `http://www.mindcraft.com/webstone`. However, we do not need anything this sophisticated to make some general comparisons of the various server design alternatives that we will examine in this chapter.

We now present the nine different server designs.

———————————————————————————————— server/client.c

```
 1 #include    "unp.h"

 2 #define MAXN    16384              /* max # bytes to request from server */

 3 int
 4 main(int argc, char **argv)
 5 {
 6     int     i, j, fd, nchildren, nloops, nbytes;
 7     pid_t   pid;
 8     ssize_t n;
 9     char    request[MAXLINE], reply[MAXN];

10     if (argc != 6)
11         err_quit("usage: client <hostname or IPaddr> <port> <#children> "
12                    "<#loops/child> <#bytes/request>");

13     nchildren = atoi(argv[3]);
14     nloops = atoi(argv[4]);
15     nbytes = atoi(argv[5]);
16     snprintf(request, sizeof(request), "%d\n", nbytes); /* newline at end */

17     for (i = 0; i < nchildren; i++) {
18         if ( (pid = Fork()) == 0) {   /* child */
19             for (j = 0; j < nloops; j++) {
20                 fd = Tcp_connect(argv[1], argv[2]);

21                 Write(fd, request, strlen(request));

22                 if ( (n = Readn(fd, reply, nbytes)) != nbytes)
23                     err_quit("server returned %d bytes", n);

24                 Close(fd);        /* TIME_WAIT on client, not server */
25             }
26             printf("child %d done\n", i);
27             exit(0);
28         }
29         /* parent loops around to fork() again */
30     }

31     while (wait(NULL) > 0)       /* now parent waits for all children */
32         ;
33     if (errno != ECHILD)
34         err_sys("wait error");

35     exit(0);
36 }
```

———————————————————————————————— server/client.c

Figure 30.3 TCP client program for testing our various servers.

30.4 TCP Iterative Server

An iterative TCP server processes each client's request completely before moving on to
the next client. Iterative TCP servers are rare, but we showed one in Figure 1.9: a simple
daytime server.

We do, however, have a use for an iterative server in comparing the various servers in this chapter. If we run the client as

```
% client 192.168.1.20 8888 1 5000 4000
```

to an iterative server, we get the same number of TCP connections (5,000) and the same amount of data transferred across each connection. But since the server is iterative, there is *no process control whatsoever* performed by the server. This gives us a baseline measurement of the CPU time required to handle this number of clients that we can then subtract from all the other server measurements. From a process control perspective, the iterative server is the fastest possible because it performs no process control. We then compare the *differences* from this baseline in Figure 30.1.

We do not show our iterative server as it is a trivial modification to the concurrent server that we will present in the next section.

30.5   TCP Concurrent Server, One Child per Client

Traditionally, a concurrent TCP server calls `fork` to spawn a child to handle each client. This allows the server to handle numerous clients at the same time, one client per process. The only limit on the number of clients is the OS limit on the number of child processes for the user ID under which the server is running. Figure 5.12 is an example of a concurrent server and most TCP servers are written in this fashion.

The problem with these concurrent servers is the amount of CPU time it takes to `fork` a child for each client. Years ago (the late 1980s), when a busy server handled hundreds or perhaps even a few thousand clients per day, this was acceptable. But the explosion of the Web has changed this attitude. Busy Web servers measure the number of TCP connections per day in the millions. This is for an individual host, and the busiest sites run multiple hosts, distributing the load among the hosts. (Section 14.2 of TCPv3 talks about a common way to distribute this load using what is called "DNS round robin.") Later sections will describe various techniques that avoid the per-client `fork` incurred by a concurrent server, but concurrent servers are still common.

Figure 30.4 shows the `main` function for our concurrent TCP server.

```
                                                                  ——— server/serv01.c
 1 #include    "unp.h"

 2 int
 3 main(int argc, char **argv)
 4 {
 5     int     listenfd, connfd;
 6     pid_t   childpid;
 7     void    sig_chld(int), sig_int(int), web_child(int);
 8     socklen_t clilen, addrlen;
 9     struct sockaddr *cliaddr;

10     if (argc == 2)
11         listenfd = Tcp_listen(NULL, argv[1], &addrlen);
12     else if (argc == 3)
13         listenfd = Tcp_listen(argv[1], argv[2], &addrlen);
14     else
15         err_quit("usage: serv01 [ <host> ] <port#>");
16     cliaddr = Malloc(addrlen);

17     Signal(SIGCHLD, sig_chld);
18     Signal(SIGINT, sig_int);

19     for ( ; ; ) {
20         clilen = addrlen;
21         if ( (connfd = accept(listenfd, cliaddr, &clilen)) < 0) {
22             if (errno == EINTR)
23                 continue;       /* back to for() */
24             else
25                 err_sys("accept error");
26         }

27         if ( (childpid = Fork()) == 0) { /* child process */
28             Close(listenfd);    /* close listening socket */
29             web_child(connfd);  /* process request */
30             exit(0);
31         }
32         Close(connfd);           /* parent closes connected socket */
33     }
34 }
                                                                  ——— server/serv01.c
```

Figure 30.4 main function for TCP concurrent server.

This function is similar to Figure 5.12: It calls `fork` for each client connection and handles the `SIGCHLD` signals from the terminating children. This function, however, we have made protocol-independent by calling our `tcp_listen` function. We do not show the `sig_chld` signal handler: It is the same as Figure 5.11, with the `printf` removed.

We also catch the `SIGINT` signal, generated when we type our terminal interrupt key. We type this key after the client completes, to print the CPU time required for the program. Figure 30.5 shows the signal handler. This is an example of a signal handler that does not return.

server/serv01.c

```
35 void
36 sig_int(int signo)
37 {
38     void    pr_cpu_time(void);
39     pr_cpu_time();
40     exit(0);
41 }
```

server/serv01.c

Figure 30.5 Signal handler for SIGINT.

Figure 30.6 shows the pr_cpu_time function that is called by the signal handler.

server/pr_cpu_time.c

```
 1 #include    "unp.h"
 2 #include    <sys/resource.h>

 3 #ifndef HAVE_GETRUSAGE_PROTO
 4 int     getrusage(int, struct rusage *);
 5 #endif

 6 void
 7 pr_cpu_time(void)
 8 {
 9     double  user, sys;
10     struct rusage myusage, childusage;

11     if (getrusage(RUSAGE_SELF, &myusage) < 0)
12         err_sys("getrusage error");
13     if (getrusage(RUSAGE_CHILDREN, &childusage) < 0)
14         err_sys("getrusage error");

15     user = (double) myusage.ru_utime.tv_sec +
16         myusage.ru_utime.tv_usec / 1000000.0;
17     user += (double) childusage.ru_utime.tv_sec +
18         childusage.ru_utime.tv_usec / 1000000.0;
19     sys = (double) myusage.ru_stime.tv_sec +
20         myusage.ru_stime.tv_usec / 1000000.0;
21     sys += (double) childusage.ru_stime.tv_sec +
22         childusage.ru_stime.tv_usec / 1000000.0;

23     printf("\nuser time = %g, sys time = %g\n", user, sys);
24 }
```

server/pr_cpu_time.c

Figure 30.6 pr_cpu_time function: prints total CPU time.

The getrusage function is called twice to return the resource utilization of both the calling process (RUSAGE_SELF) and all the terminated children of the calling process (RUSAGE_CHILDREN). The values printed are the total user time (CPU time spent in the user process) and total system time (CPU time spent within the kernel, executing on behalf of the calling process).

The `main` function in Figure 30.4 calls the function `web_child` to handle each client request. Figure 30.7 shows this function.

```
                                                           ———————— server/web_child.c
 1 #include     "unp.h"

 2 #define MAXN     16384              /* max # bytes client can request */

 3 void
 4 web_child(int sockfd)
 5 {
 6     int     ntowrite;
 7     ssize_t nread;
 8     char    line[MAXLINE], result[MAXN];

 9     for ( ; ; ) {
10         if ( (nread = Readline(sockfd, line, MAXLINE)) == 0)
11             return;                 /* connection closed by other end */

12             /* line from client specifies #bytes to write back */
13         ntowrite = atol(line);
14         if ((ntowrite <= 0) || (ntowrite > MAXN))
15             err_quit("client request for %d bytes", ntowrite);

16         Writen(sockfd, result, ntowrite);
17     }
18 }
                                                           ———————— server/web_child.c
```

Figure 30.7 `web_child` function to handle each client's request.

After the client establishes the connection with the server, the client writes a single line specifying the number of bytes the server must return to the client. This is somewhat similar to HTTP: The client sends a small request and the server responds with the desired information (often an HTML file or a GIF image, for example). In the case of HTTP, the server normally closes the connection after sending back the requested data, although newer versions are using *persistent connections*, holding the TCP connection open for additional client requests. In our `web_child` function, the server allows additional requests from the client, but we saw in Figure 30.3 that our client sends only one request per connection and the client then closes the connection.

Row 1 of Figure 30.1 shows the timing result for this concurrent server. When compared to the subsequent lines in this figure, we see that the concurrent server requires the most CPU time, which is what we expect with one `fork` per client.

> One server design that we do not measure in this chapter is one invoked by `inetd`, which we covered in Section 13.5. From a process control perspective, a server invoked by `inetd` involves a `fork` and an `exec`, so the CPU time will be even greater than the times shown in row 1 of Figure 30.1.

30.6   TCP Preforked Server, No Locking Around `accept`

Our first of the "enhanced" TCP servers uses a technique called *preforking*. Instead of generating one `fork` per client, the server preforks some number of children when it starts, and then the children are ready to service the clients as each client connection arrives. Figure 30.8 shows a scenario where the parent has preforked N children and two clients are currently connected.

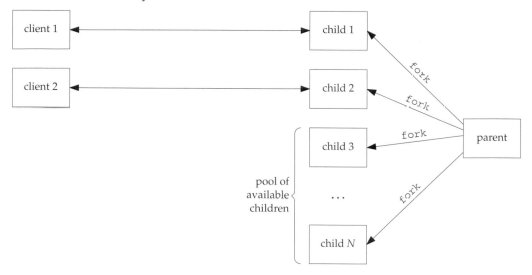

Figure 30.8   Preforking of children by server.

The advantage of this technique is that new clients can be handled without the cost of a `fork` by the parent. The disadvantage is that the parent must guess how many children to prefork when it starts. If the number of clients at any time ever equals the number of children, additional clients are ignored until a child is available. But recall from Section 4.5 that the clients are not completely ignored. The kernel will complete the three-way handshake for any additional clients, up to the `listen` backlog for this socket, and then pass the completed connections to the server when it calls `accept`. But, the client application can notice a degradation in response time because even though its `connect` might return immediately, its first request might not be handled by the server for some time.

With some extra coding, the server can always handle the client load. What the parent must do is continually monitor the number of available children, and if this value drops below some threshold, the parent must `fork` additional children. Also, if the number of available children exceeds another threshold, the parent can terminate some of the excess children, because as we'll see later in this chapter, having too many available children can degrade performance, too.

But before worrying about these enhancements, let's examine the basic structure of this type of server. Figure 30.9 shows the `main` function for the first version of our preforked server.

```
──────────────────────────────────────────────── server/serv02.c
 1 #include    "unp.h"

 2 static int nchildren;
 3 static pid_t *pids;

 4 int
 5 main(int argc, char **argv)
 6 {
 7     int     listenfd, i;
 8     socklen_t addrlen;
 9     void    sig_int(int);
10     pid_t   child_make(int, int, int);

11     if (argc == 3)
12         listenfd = Tcp_listen(NULL, argv[1], &addrlen);
13     else if (argc == 4)
14         listenfd = Tcp_listen(argv[1], argv[2], &addrlen);
15     else
16         err_quit("usage: serv02 [ <host> ] <port#> <#children>");
17     nchildren = atoi(argv[argc - 1]);
18     pids = Calloc(nchildren, sizeof(pid_t));

19     for (i = 0; i < nchildren; i++)
20         pids[i] = child_make(i, listenfd, addrlen); /* parent returns */

21     Signal(SIGINT, sig_int);

22     for ( ; ; )
23         pause();                    /* everything done by children */
24 }
──────────────────────────────────────────────── server/serv02.c
```

Figure 30.9 main function for preforked server.

11-18   An additional command-line argument is the number of children to prefork. An array is allocated to hold the PIDs of the children, which we need when the program terminates to allow the main function to terminate all the children.

19-20   Each child is created by child_make, which we will examine in Figure 30.11.

Our signal handler for SIGINT, which we show in Figure 30.10, differs from Figure 30.5.

30-34   getrusage reports on the resource utilization of *terminated* children, so we must terminate all the children before calling pr_cpu_time. We do this by sending SIGTERM to each child, and then we wait for all the children.

Figure 30.11 shows the child_make function, which is called by main to create each child.

7-9   fork creates each child and only the parent returns. The child calls the function child_main, which we show in Figure 30.12 and which is an infinite loop.

server/serv02.c

```
25 void
26 sig_int(int signo)
27 {
28     int      i;
29     void     pr_cpu_time(void);

30         /* terminate all children */
31     for (i = 0; i < nchildren; i++)
32         kill(pids[i], SIGTERM);
33     while (wait(NULL) > 0)        /* wait for all children */
34         ;
35     if (errno != ECHILD)
36         err_sys("wait error");

37     pr_cpu_time();
38     exit(0);
39 }
```

server/serv02.c

Figure 30.10 Signal handler for `SIGINT`.

server/child02.c

```
 1 #include    "unp.h"

 2 pid_t
 3 child_make(int i, int listenfd, int addrlen)
 4 {
 5     pid_t   pid;
 6     void    child_main(int, int, int);

 7     if ( (pid = Fork()) > 0)
 8         return (pid);            /* parent */

 9     child_main(i, listenfd, addrlen);   /* never returns */
10 }
```

server/child02.c

Figure 30.11 `child_make` function: creates each child.

server/child02.c

```
11 void
12 child_main(int i, int listenfd, int addrlen)
13 {
14     int      connfd;
15     void     web_child(int);
16     socklen_t clilen;
17     struct sockaddr *cliaddr;

18     cliaddr = Malloc(addrlen);

19     printf("child %ld starting\n", (long) getpid());
20     for ( ; ; ) {
21         clilen = addrlen;
22         connfd = Accept(listenfd, cliaddr, &clilen);

23         web_child(connfd);       /* process the request */
24         Close(connfd);
25     }
26 }
```

server/child02.c

Figure 30.12 `child_main` function: infinite loop executed by each child.

20-25   Each child calls accept, and when this returns, the function web_child (Figure 30.7) handles the client request. The child continues in this loop until terminated by the parent.

4.4BSD Implementation

If you have never seen this type of arrangement (multiple processes calling accept on the same listening descriptor), you probably wonder how it can even work. It's worth a short digression on how this is implemented in Berkeley-derived kernels (e.g., as presented in TCPv2).

The parent creates the listening socket before spawning any children, and if you recall, all descriptors are duplicated in each child each time fork is called. Figure 30.13 shows the arrangement of the proc structures (one per process), the one file structure for the listening descriptor, and the one socket structure.

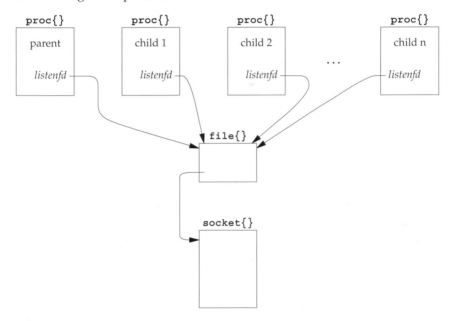

Figure 30.13   Arrangement of proc, file, and socket structures.

Descriptors are just an index in an array in the proc structure that reference a file structure. One of the properties of the duplication of descriptors in the child that occurs with fork is that a given descriptor in the child references the same file structure as that same descriptor in the parent. Each file structure has a reference count that starts at one when the file or socket is opened and is incremented by one each time fork is called or each time the descriptor is duped. In our example with N children, the reference count in the file structure would be $N + 1$ (don't forget the parent that still has the listening descriptor open, even though the parent never calls accept).

When the program starts, N children are created, and all N call accept and all are put to sleep by the kernel (line 140, p. 458 of TCPv2). When the first client connection arrives, all N children are awakened. This is because all N have gone to sleep on the same "wait channel," the `so_timeo` member of the `socket` structure, because all N share the same listening descriptor, which points to the same `socket` structure. Even though all N are awakened, the first of the N to run will obtain the connection and the remaining $N-1$ will all go back to sleep, because when each of the remaining $N-1$ execute the statement on line 135 of p. 458 of TCPv2, the queue length will be 0 since the first child to run already took the connection.

This is sometimes called the *thundering herd* problem because all N are awakened even though only one will obtain the connection. Nevertheless, the code works, with the performance side effect of waking up too many processes each time a connection is ready to be `accepted`. We now measure this performance effect.

Effect of Too Many Children

The CPU time of 1.8 for the server in row 2 of Figure 30.1 is for 15 children and a maximum of 10 simultaneous clients. We can measure the effect of the thundering herd problem by just increasing the number of children for the same maximum number of clients (10). We don't show the results of increasing the number of children because the individual test results aren't that interesting. Since any number greater than 10 introduces superfluous children, the thundering herd problem worsens and the timing results increase.

> Some Unix kernels have a function, often named `wakeup_one`, that wakes up only one process that is waiting for some event, instead of waking up all processes waiting for the event [Schimmel 1994].

Distribution of Connections to the Children

The next thing to examine is the distribution of the client connections to the pool of available children that are blocked in the call to `accept`. To collect this information, we modify the `main` function to allocate an array of long integer counters in shared memory, one counter per child. This is done with the following:

```
long    *cptr, *meter(int);    /* for counting # clients/child */

cptr = meter(nchildren);       /* before spawning children */
```

Figure 30.14 shows the `meter` function.

We use anonymous memory mapping, if supported (e.g., 4.4BSD), or the mapping of `/dev/zero` (e.g., SVR4). Since the array is created by `mmap` before the children are spawned, the array is then shared between this process (the parent) and all its children created later by `fork`.

We then modify our `child_main` function (Figure 30.12) so that each child increments its counter when `accept` returns and our `SIGINT` handler prints this array after all the children are terminated.

server/meter.c
```
 1 #include    "unp.h"
 2 #include    <sys/mman.h>

 3 /*
 4  * Allocate an array of "nchildren" longs in shared memory that can
 5  * be used as a counter by each child of how many clients it services.
 6  * See pp. 467-470 of "Advanced Programming in the Unix Environment."
 7  */

 8 long *
 9 meter(int nchildren)
10 {
11     int     fd;
12     long    *ptr;

13 #ifdef   MAP_ANON
14     ptr = Mmap(0, nchildren * sizeof(long), PROT_READ | PROT_WRITE,
15                 MAP_ANON | MAP_SHARED, -1, 0);
16 #else
17     fd = Open("/dev/zero", O_RDWR, 0);

18     ptr = Mmap(0, nchildren * sizeof(long), PROT_READ | PROT_WRITE,
19                 MAP_SHARED, fd, 0);
20     Close(fd);
21 #endif

22     return (ptr);
23 }
```
server/meter.c

Figure 30.14 meter function to allocate an array in shared memory.

Figure 30.2 shows the distribution. When the available children are blocked in the call to accept, the kernel's scheduling algorithm distributes the connections uniformly to all the children.

select **Collisions**

While looking at this example under 4.4BSD, we can also examine another poorly understood, but rare phenomenon. Section 16.13 of TCPv2 talks about *collisions* with the select function and how the kernel handles this possibility. A collision occurs when multiple processes call select on the same descriptor, because room is allocated in the socket structure for only one process ID to be awakened when the descriptor is ready. If multiple processes are waiting for the same descriptor, the kernel must wake up *all* processes that are blocked in a call to select since it doesn't know which processes are affected by the descriptor that just became ready.

We can force select collisions with our example by preceding the call to accept in Figure 30.12 with a call to select, waiting for readability on the listening socket. The children will spend their time blocked in this call to select instead of in the call to accept. Figure 30.15 shows the portion of the child_main function that changes, using plus signs to note the lines that have changed from Figure 30.12.

```
        printf("child %ld starting\n", (long) getpid());
+       FD_ZERO(&rset);
        for ( ; ; ) {
+           FD_SET(listenfd, &rset);
+           Select(listenfd+1, &rset, NULL, NULL, NULL);
+           if (FD_ISSET(listenfd, &rset) == 0)
+               err_quit("listenfd readable");
+
            clilen = addrlen;
            connfd = Accept(listenfd, cliaddr, &clilen);

            web_child(connfd);       /* process request */
            Close(connfd);
        }
```

Figure 30.15   Modification to Figure 30.12 to block in `select` instead of `accept`.

If we make this change and then examine the kernel's `select` collision counter before and after, we see 1,814 collisions one time we run the sever and 2,045 collisions the next time. Since the two clients create a total of 5,000 connections for each run of the server, this corresponds to about 35–40% of the calls to `select` invoking a collision.

If we compare the server's CPU time for this example, the value of 1.8 in Figure 30.1 increases to 2.9 when we add the call to `select`. Part of this increase is probably because of the additional system call (since we are calling `select` and `accept` instead of just `accept`), and another part is probably because of the kernel overhead in handling the collisions.

The lesson to be learned from this discussion is when multiple processes are blocking on the same descriptor, it is better to block in a function such as `accept` instead of blocking in `select`.

30.7   TCP Preforked Server, File Locking Around `accept`

The implementation that we just described for 4.4BSD, which allows multiple processes to call `accept` on the same listening descriptor, works only with Berkeley-derived kernels that implement `accept` within the kernel. System V kernels, which implement `accept` as a library function, may not allow this. Indeed, if we run the server from the previous section on such a system, soon after the clients start connecting to the server, a call to `accept` in one of the children returns EPROTO, which means a protocol error.

> The reasons for this problem with the SVR4 library version of `accept` arise from the STREAMS implementation (Chapter 31) and the fact that the library `accept` is not an atomic operation. Solaris fixes this, but the problem still exists in most other SVR4 implementations.

The solution is for the application to place a *lock* of some form around the call to `accept`, so that only one process at a time is blocked in the call to `accept`. The remaining children will be blocked trying to obtain the lock.

There are various ways to provide this locking around the call to accept, as we described in the second volume of this series. In this section, we will use POSIX file locking with the fcntl function.

The only change to the main function (Figure 30.9) is adding a call to our my_lock_init function before the loop that creates the children.

```
    +   my_lock_init("/tmp/lock.XXXXXX");  /* one lock file for all children */
        for (i = 0; i < nchildren; i++)
            pids[i] = child_make(i, listenfd, addrlen); /* parent returns */
```

The child_make function remains the same as Figure 30.11. The only change to our child_main function (Figure 30.12) is to obtain a lock before calling accept and release the lock after accept returns.

```
        for ( ; ; ) {
            clilen = addrlen;
    +       my_lock_wait();
            connfd = Accept(listenfd, cliaddr, &clilen);
    +       my_lock_release();

            web_child(connfd);         /* process request */
            Close(connfd);
        }
```

Figure 30.16 shows our my_lock_init function, which uses POSIX file locking.

server/lock_fcntl.c
```
 1 #include    "unp.h"

 2 static struct flock lock_it, unlock_it;
 3 static int lock_fd = -1;
 4                    /* fcntl() will fail if my_lock_init() not called */

 5 void
 6 my_lock_init(char *pathname)
 7 {
 8     char    lock_file[1024];

 9         /* must copy caller's string, in case it's a constant */
10     strncpy(lock_file, pathname, sizeof(lock_file));
11     lock_fd = Mkstemp(lock_file);

12     Unlink(lock_file);          /* but lock_fd remains open */

13     lock_it.l_type = F_WRLCK;
14     lock_it.l_whence = SEEK_SET;
15     lock_it.l_start = 0;
16     lock_it.l_len = 0;

17     unlock_it.l_type = F_UNLCK;
18     unlock_it.l_whence = SEEK_SET;
19     unlock_it.l_start = 0;
20     unlock_it.l_len = 0;
21 }
```
server/lock_fcntl.c

Figure 30.16 my_lock_init function using POSIX file locking.

9–12   The caller specifies a pathname template as the argument to `my_lock_init`, and the `mktemp` function creates a unique pathname based on this template. A file is then created with this pathname and immediately `unlinked`. By removing the pathname from the directory, if the program crashes, the file completely disappears. But as long as one or more processes have the file open (i.e., the file's reference count is greater than 0), the file itself is not removed. (This is the fundamental difference between removing a pathname from a directory and closing an open file.)

13–20   Two `flock` structures are initialized: one to lock the file and one to unlock the file. The range of the file that is locked starts at byte offset 0 (a `l_whence` of `SEEK_SET` with `l_start` set to 0). Since `l_len` is set to 0, this specifies that the entire file is locked. We never write anything to the file (its length is always 0), but that is fine. The advisory lock is still handled correctly by the kernel.

> It may be tempting to initialize these structures using
>
> ```
> static struct flock  lock_it = { F_WRLCK, 0, 0, 0, 0 };
> static struct flock  unlock_it = { F_UNLCK, 0, 0, 0, 0 };
> ```
>
> but there are two problems. First, there is no guarantee that the constant `SEEK_SET` is 0. But more importantly, there is no guarantee by POSIX as to the order of the members in the structure. The `l_type` member may be the first one in the structure, but not on all systems. All POSIX guarantees is that the members that POSIX requires are present in the structure. POSIX does not guarantee the order of the members, and POSIX also allows additional, non-POSIX members to be in the structure. Therefore, initializing a structure to anything other than all zeros should always be done by actual C code, and not by an initializer when the structure is allocated.
>
> An exception to this rule is when the structure initializer is provided by the implementation. For example, when initializing a Pthread mutex lock in Chapter 26, we wrote
>
> ```
> pthread_mutex_t  mlock = PTHREAD_MUTEX_INITIALIZER;
> ```
>
> The `pthread_mutex_t` datatype is often a structure, but the initializer is provided by the implementation and can differ from one implementation to the next.

Figure 30.17 shows the two functions that lock and unlock the file. These are just calls to `fcntl`, using the structures that were initialized in Figure 30.16.

This new version of our preforked server now works on SVR4 systems by assuring that only one child process at a time is blocked in the call to `accept`. Comparing rows 2 and 3 in Figure 30.1 shows that this type of locking adds to the server's process control CPU time.

> The Apache Web server, `http://www.apache.org`, preforks its children and then uses either the technique in the previous section (all children blocked in the call to `accept`), if the implementation allows this, or file locking around the `accept`.

Effect of Too Many Children

We can check this version to see if the same thundering herd problem exists, which we described in the previous section. We check by increasing the number of (unneeded) children and noticing that the timing results get worse proportionally.

```
                                                                    ——— server/lock_fcntl.c
22  void
23  my_lock_wait()
24  {
25      int     rc;

26      while ( (rc = fcntl(lock_fd, F_SETLKW, &lock_it)) < 0) {
27          if (errno == EINTR)
28              continue;
29          else
30              err_sys("fcntl error for my_lock_wait");
31      }
32  }

33  void
34  my_lock_release()
35  {
36      if (fcntl(lock_fd, F_SETLKW, &unlock_it) < 0)
37          err_sys("fcntl error for my_lock_release");
38  }
                                                                    ——— server/lock_fcntl.c
```

Figure 30.17 my_lock_wait and my_lock_release functions using fcntl.

Distribution of Connections to the Children

We can examine the distribution of the clients to the pool of available children by using the function we described with Figure 30.14. Figure 30.2 shows the result. The OS distributes the file locks uniformly to the waiting processes (and this behavior was uniform across several operating systems we tested).

30.8 TCP Preforked Server, Thread Locking Around accept

As we mentioned, there are various ways to implement locking between processes. The POSIX file locking in the previous section is portable to all POSIX-compliant systems, but it involves filesystem operations, which can take time. In this section, we will use thread locking, taking advantage of the fact that this can be used not only for locking between the threads within a given process, but also for locking between different processes.

Our main function remains the same as in the previous section, as do our child_make and child_main functions. The only thing that changes is our three locking functions. To use thread locking between different processes requires that: (i) the mutex variable must be stored in memory that is shared between all the processes; and (ii) the thread library must be told that the mutex is shared among different processes.

Also, the thread library must support the PTHREAD_PROCESS_SHARED attribute.

There are various ways to share memory between different processes, as we described in the second volume of this series. In our example, we will use the mmap function with the /dev/zero device, which works under Solaris and other SVR4 kernels. Figure 30.18 shows our my_lock_init function.

—— *server/lock_pthread.c*

```
 1 #include     "unpthread.h"
 2 #include     <sys/mman.h>

 3 static pthread_mutex_t *mptr;    /* actual mutex will be in shared memory */

 4 void
 5 my_lock_init(char *pathname)
 6 {
 7     int      fd;
 8     pthread_mutexattr_t mattr;

 9     fd = Open("/dev/zero", O_RDWR, 0);

10     mptr = Mmap(0, sizeof(pthread_mutex_t), PROT_READ | PROT_WRITE,
11               MAP_SHARED, fd, 0);
12     Close(fd);

13     Pthread_mutexattr_init(&mattr);
14     Pthread_mutexattr_setpshared(&mattr, PTHREAD_PROCESS_SHARED);
15     Pthread_mutex_init(mptr, &mattr);
16 }
```
—— *server/lock_pthread.c*

Figure 30.18 my_lock_init function using Pthread locking between processes.

9–12   We open /dev/zero and then call mmap. The number of bytes that are mapped is equal to the size of a pthread_mutex_t variable. The descriptor is then closed, which is fine, because the memory mapped to /dev/zero will remain mapped.

13–15   In our previous Pthread mutex examples, we initialized the global or static mutex variable using the constant PTHREAD_MUTEX_INITIALIZER (e.g., Figure 26.18). But with a mutex in shared memory, we must call some Pthread library functions to tell the library that the mutex is in shared memory and that it will be used for locking between different processes. We first initialize a pthread_mutexattr_t structure with the default attributes for a mutex and then set the PTHREAD_PROCESS_SHARED attribute. (The default for this attribute is PTHREAD_PROCESS_PRIVATE, allowing use only within a single process.) pthread_mutex_init then initializes the mutex with these attributes.

Figure 30.19 shows our my_lock_wait and my_lock_release functions. Each is now just a call to a Pthread function to lock or unlock the mutex.

Comparing rows 3 and 4 in Figure 30.1 for the Solaris server shows that thread mutex locking is faster than file locking.

30.9 TCP Preforked Server, Descriptor Passing

The final modification to our preforked server is to have only the parent call accept and then "pass" the connected socket to one child. This gets around the possible need

———————————————————————————————————— server/lock_pthread.c
```
17 void
18 my_lock_wait()
19 {
20      Pthread_mutex_lock(mptr);
21 }

22 void
23 my_lock_release()
24 {
25      Pthread_mutex_unlock(mptr);
26 }
```
———————————————————————————————————— server/lock_pthread.c

Figure 30.19 my_lock_wait and my_lock_release functions using Pthread locking.

for locking around the call to accept in all the children, but requires some form of descriptor passing from the parent to the children. This technique also complicates the code somewhat because the parent must keep track of which children are busy and which are free to pass a new socket to a free child.

In the previous preforked examples, the process never cared which child received a client connection. The OS handled this detail, giving one of the children the first call to accept, or giving one of the children the file lock or the mutex lock. The first two columns of Figure 30.2 also show that the OS that we are measuring does this in a fair, round-robin fashion.

With this example, we need to maintain a structure of information about each child. We show our child.h header that defines our Child structure in Figure 30.20.

—— server/child.h
```
1 typedef struct {
2     pid_t    child_pid;         /* process ID */
3     int      child_pipefd;      /* parent's stream pipe to/from child */
4     int      child_status;      /* 0 = ready */
5     long     child_count;       /* # connections handled */
6 } Child;

7 Child  *cptr;                   /* array of Child structures; calloc'ed */
```
—— server/child.h

Figure 30.20 Child structure.

We store the child's PID, the parent's stream pipe descriptor that is connected to the child, the child's status, and a count of the number of clients the child has handled. We will print this counter in our SIGINT handler to see the distribution of the client requests among the children.

Let us first look at the child_make function, which we show in Figure 30.21. We create a stream pipe, a Unix domain stream socket (Chapter 15), before calling fork. After the child is created, the parent closes one descriptor (sockfd[1]) and the child closes the other descriptor (sockfd[0]). Furthermore, the child duplicates its end of the stream pipe (sockfd[1]) onto standard error, so that each child just reads and writes to standard error to communicate with the parent. This gives us the arrangement shown in Figure 30.22.

```
                                                                    ─ server/child05.c
 1 #include    "unp.h"
 2 #include    "child.h"

 3 pid_t
 4 child_make(int i, int listenfd, int addrlen)
 5 {
 6     int      sockfd[2];
 7     pid_t    pid;
 8     void     child_main(int, int, int);

 9     Socketpair(AF_LOCAL, SOCK_STREAM, 0, sockfd);
10     if ( (pid = Fork()) > 0) {
11         Close(sockfd[1]);
12         cptr[i].child_pid = pid;
13         cptr[i].child_pipefd = sockfd[0];
14         cptr[i].child_status = 0;
15         return (pid);              /* parent */
16     }
17     Dup2(sockfd[1], STDERR_FILENO); /* child's stream pipe to parent */
18     Close(sockfd[0]);
19     Close(sockfd[1]);
20     Close(listenfd);               /* child does not need this open */
21     child_main(i, listenfd, addrlen);   /* never returns */
22 }
                                                                    ─ server/child05.c
```

Figure 30.21 child_make function descriptor passing preforked server.

Figure 30.22 Stream pipe after parent and child both close one end.

After all the children are created, we have the arrangement shown in Figure 30.23. We close the listening socket in each child, as only the parent calls accept. We show that the parent must handle the listening socket along with all the stream sockets. As you might guess, the parent uses select to multiplex all these descriptors.

Figure 30.24 shows the main function. The changes from previous versions of this function are that descriptor sets are allocated and the bits corresponding to the listening socket along with the stream pipe to each child are turned on in the set. The maximum descriptor value is also calculated. We allocate memory for the array of Child structures. The main loop is driven by a call to select.

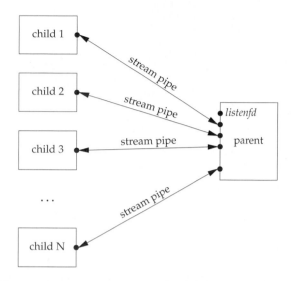

Figure 30.23 Stream pipes after all children have been created.

── *server/serv05.c*
```
 1 #include    "unp.h"
 2 #include    "child.h"

 3 static int nchildren;

 4 int
 5 main(int argc, char **argv)
 6 {
 7     int     listenfd, i, navail, maxfd, nsel, connfd, rc;
 8     void    sig_int(int);
 9     pid_t   child_make(int, int, int);
10     ssize_t n;
11     fd_set  rset, masterset;
12     socklen_t addrlen, clilen;
13     struct sockaddr *cliaddr;

14     if (argc == 3)
15         listenfd = Tcp_listen(NULL, argv[1], &addrlen);
16     else if (argc == 4)
17         listenfd = Tcp_listen(argv[1], argv[2], &addrlen);
18     else
19         err_quit("usage: serv05 [ <host> ] <port#> <#children>");

20     FD_ZERO(&masterset);
21     FD_SET(listenfd, &masterset);
22     maxfd = listenfd;
23     cliaddr = Malloc(addrlen);

24     nchildren = atoi(argv[argc - 1]);
25     navail = nchildren;
26     cptr = Calloc(nchildren, sizeof(Child));
```

```
27            /* prefork all the children */
28      for (i = 0; i < nchildren; i++) {
29          child_make(i, listenfd, addrlen);    /* parent returns */
30          FD_SET(cptr[i].child_pipefd, &masterset);
31          maxfd = max(maxfd, cptr[i].child_pipefd);
32      }

33      Signal(SIGINT, sig_int);

34      for ( ; ; ) {
35          rset = masterset;
36          if (navail <= 0)
37              FD_CLR(listenfd, &rset);    /* turn off if no available children */
38          nsel = Select(maxfd + 1, &rset, NULL, NULL, NULL);

39              /* check for new connections */
40          if (FD_ISSET(listenfd, &rset)) {
41              clilen = addrlen;
42              connfd = Accept(listenfd, cliaddr, &clilen);

43              for (i = 0; i < nchildren; i++)
44                  if (cptr[i].child_status == 0)
45                      break;          /* available */

46              if (i == nchildren)
47                  err_quit("no available children");
48              cptr[i].child_status = 1;   /* mark child as busy */
49              cptr[i].child_count++;
50              navail--;

51              n = Write_fd(cptr[i].child_pipefd, "", 1, connfd);
52              Close(connfd);
53              if (--nsel == 0)
54                  continue;           /* all done with select() results */
55          }

56              /* find any newly-available children */
57          for (i = 0; i < nchildren; i++) {
58              if (FD_ISSET(cptr[i].child_pipefd, &rset)) {
59                  if ( (n = Read(cptr[i].child_pipefd, &rc, 1)) == 0)
60                      err_quit("child %d terminated unexpectedly", i);
61                  cptr[i].child_status = 0;
62                  navail++;
63                  if (--nsel == 0)
64                      break;          /* all done with select() results */
65              }
66          }
67      }
68  }
```
                                                                              server/serv05.c

Figure 30.24 main function that uses descriptor passing.

Turn off listening socket if no available children

36–37   The counter `navail` keeps track of the number of available children. If this counter is 0, the listening socket is turned off in the descriptor set for `select`. This prevents us from `accepting` a new connection for which there is no available child. The kernel still queues these incoming connections, up to the `listen` backlog, but we do not want to `accept` them until we have a child ready to process the client.

`accept` **new connection**

39–55   If the listening socket is readable, a new connection is ready to `accept`. We find the first available child and pass the connected socket to the child using our `write_fd` function from Figure 15.13. We write one byte along with the descriptor, but the recipient does not look at the contents of this byte. The parent closes the connected socket.

We always start looking for an available child with the first entry in the array of `Child` structures. This means the first children in the array always receive new connections to process before later elements in the array. We will verify this when we discuss Figure 30.2 and look at the `child_count` counters after the server terminates. If we didn't want this bias toward earlier children, we could remember which child received the most recent connection and start our search one element past that each time, circling back to the first element when we reach the end. There is no advantage in doing this (it really doesn't matter which child handles a client request if multiple children are available), unless the OS scheduling algorithm penalizes processes with longer total CPU times. Spreading the load more evenly among all the children would tend to average out their total CPU times.

Handle any newly available children

56–66   We will see that our `child_main` function writes a single byte back to the parent across the stream pipe when the child has finished with a client. That makes the parent's end of the stream pipe readable. We `read` the single byte (ignoring its value) and then mark the child as available. Should the child terminate unexpectedly, its end of the stream pipe will be closed, and the `read` returns 0. We catch this and terminate, but a better approach is to log the error and spawn a new child to replace the one that terminated.

Our `child_main` function is shown in Figure 30.25.

Wait for descriptor from parent

32–33   This function differs from the ones in the previous two sections because our child no longer calls `accept`. Instead, the child blocks in a call to `read_fd`, waiting for the parent to pass it a connected socket descriptor to process.

Tell parent we are ready

38   When we have finished with the client, we `write` one byte across the stream pipe to tell the parent we are available.

Comparing rows 4 and 5 in Figure 30.1, we see that this server is slower than the version in the previous section that used thread locking between the children. Passing a descriptor across the stream pipe to each child and writing a byte back across the stream

server/child05.c
```
23 void
24 child_main(int i, int listenfd, int addrlen)
25 {
26     char    c;
27     int     connfd;
28     ssize_t n;
29     void    web_child(int);

30     printf("child %ld starting\n", (long) getpid());
31     for ( ; ; ) {
32         if ( (n = Read_fd(STDERR_FILENO, &c, 1, &connfd)) == 0)
33             err_quit("read_fd returned 0");
34         if (connfd < 0)
35             err_quit("no descriptor from read_fd");

36         web_child(connfd);      /* process request */
37         Close(connfd);

38         Write(STDERR_FILENO, "", 1);    /* tell parent we're ready again */
39     }
40 }
```
server/child05.c

Figure 30.25 child_main function: descriptor passing, preforked server.

pipe from the child takes more time than locking and unlocking either a mutex in shared memory or a file lock.

Figure 30.2 shows the distribution of the child_count counters in the Child structure, which we print in the SIGINT handler when the server is terminated. The earlier children do handle more clients, as we discussed with Figure 30.24.

30.10 TCP Concurrent Server, One Thread per Client

The last five sections have focused on one process per client, both one fork per client and preforking some number of children. If the server supports threads, we can use threads instead of child processes.

Our first threaded version is shown in Figure 30.26. It is a modification of Figure 30.4 that creates one thread per client, instead of one process per client. This version is very similar to Figure 26.3.

Main thread loop

19-23   The main thread blocks in a call to accept and each time a client connection is returned, a new thread is created by pthread_create. The function executed by the new thread is doit and its argument is the connected socket.

Per-thread function

25-33   The doit function detaches itself so the main thread does not have to wait for it and calls our web_client function (Figure 30.3). When that function returns, the

```
                                                               ——— server/serv06.c
 1 #include      "unpthread.h"

 2 int
 3 main(int argc, char **argv)
 4 {
 5     int      listenfd, connfd;
 6     void     sig_int(int);
 7     void     *doit(void *);
 8     pthread_t tid;
 9     socklen_t clilen, addrlen;
10     struct sockaddr *cliaddr;

11     if (argc == 2)
12         listenfd = Tcp_listen(NULL, argv[1], &addrlen);
13     else if (argc == 3)
14         listenfd = Tcp_listen(argv[1], argv[2], &addrlen);
15     else
16         err_quit("usage: serv06 [ <host> ] <port#>");
17     cliaddr = Malloc(addrlen);

18     Signal(SIGINT, sig_int);

19     for ( ; ; ) {
20         clilen = addrlen;
21         connfd = Accept(listenfd, cliaddr, &clilen);

22         Pthread_create(&tid, NULL, &doit, (void *) connfd);
23     }
24 }

25 void *
26 doit(void *arg)
27 {
28     void     web_child(int);

29     Pthread_detach(pthread_self());
30     web_child((int) arg);
31     Close((int) arg);
32     return (NULL);
33 }
                                                               ——— server/serv06.c
```

Figure 30.26 main function for TCP threaded server.

connected socket is closed.

We note from Figure 30.1 that this simple threaded version is faster than even the fastest of the preforked versions. This one-thread-per-client version is also many times faster than the one-child-per-client version (row 1).

> In Section 26.5 we noted three alternatives for converting a function that is not thread-safe into one that is thread-safe. Our web_child function calls our readline function, and the version shown in Figure 3.18 is not thread-safe. Alternatives 2 and 3 from Section 26.5 were timed with the example in Figure 30.26. The speedup from alternative 3 to alternative 2 was less than one percent, probably because readline is used only to read the five-character count from the client. Therefore, for simplicity we use the less efficient version from Figure 3.17 for the threaded server examples in this chapter.

30.11 TCP Prethreaded Server, per-Thread `accept`

We found earlier in this chapter that it is faster to prefork a pool of children than to create one child for every client. On a system that supports threads, it is reasonable to
expect a similar speedup by creating a pool of threads when the server starts, instead of
creating a new thread for every client. The basic design of this server is to create a pool
of threads and then let each thread call `accept`. Instead of having each thread block in
the call to `accept`, we will use a mutex lock (similar to Section 30.8) that allows only
one thread at a time to call `accept`. There is no reason to use file locking to protect the
call to `accept` from all the threads, because with multiple threads in a single process,
we know that a mutex lock can be used.

Figure 30.27 shows the `pthread07.h` header that defines a `Thread` structure that
maintains some information about each thread.

```
———————————————————————————————————————————————————— server/pthread07.h
 1 typedef struct {
 2      pthread_t thread_tid;          /* thread ID */
 3      long      thread_count;        /* # connections handled */
 4 } Thread;
 5 Thread *tptr;                       /* array of Thread structures; calloc'ed */

 6 int      listenfd, nthreads;
 7 socklen_t addrlen;
 8 pthread_mutex_t mlock;
———————————————————————————————————————————————————— server/pthread07.h
```

Figure 30.27 `pthread07.h` header.

We also declare a few globals, such as the listening socket descriptor and a mutex
variable that all the threads need to share.

Figure 30.28 shows the `main` function.

```
———————————————————————————————————————————————————————— server/serv07.c
 1 #include    "unpthread.h"
 2 #include    "pthread07.h"

 3 pthread_mutex_t mlock = PTHREAD_MUTEX_INITIALIZER;

 4 int
 5 main(int argc, char **argv)
 6 {
 7      int    i;
 8      void   sig_int(int), thread_make(int);

 9      if (argc == 3)
10          listenfd = Tcp_listen(NULL, argv[1], &addrlen);
11      else if (argc == 4)
12          listenfd = Tcp_listen(argv[1], argv[2], &addrlen);
13      else
14          err_quit("usage: serv07 [ <host> ] <port#> <#threads>");
15      nthreads = atoi(argv[argc - 1]);
16      tptr = Calloc(nthreads, sizeof(Thread));
```

```
17      for (i = 0; i < nthreads; i++)
18          thread_make(i);              /* only main thread returns */

19      Signal(SIGINT, sig_int);

20      for ( ; ; )
21          pause();                     /* everything done by threads */
22 }
```
――――――――――――――――――――――――――――――――――――――― server/serv07.c

Figure 30.28 main function for prethreaded TCP server.

The thread_make and thread_main functions are shown in Figure 30.29.

――――――――――――――――――――――――――――――――――――――― server/pthread07.c
```
 1 #include     "unpthread.h"
 2 #include     "pthread07.h"

 3 void
 4 thread_make(int i)
 5 {
 6     void    *thread_main(void *);

 7     Pthread_create(&tptr[i].thread_tid, NULL, &thread_main, (void *) i);
 8     return;                   /* main thread returns */
 9 }

10 void *
11 thread_main(void *arg)
12 {
13     int      connfd;
14     void     web_child(int);
15     socklen_t clilen;
16     struct sockaddr *cliaddr;

17     cliaddr = Malloc(addrlen);

18     printf("thread %d starting\n", (int) arg);
19     for ( ; ; ) {
20         clilen = addrlen;
21         Pthread_mutex_lock(&mlock);
22         connfd = Accept(listenfd, cliaddr, &clilen);
23         Pthread_mutex_unlock(&mlock);
24         tptr[(int) arg].thread_count++;

25         web_child(connfd);      /* process request */
26         Close(connfd);
27     }
28 }
```
――――――――――――――――――――――――――――――――――――――― server/pthread07.c

Figure 30.29 thread_make and thread_main functions.

Create thread

7   Each thread is created and executes the thread_main function. The only argument is the index number of the thread.

21-23 The thread_main function calls the functions pthread_mutex_lock and pthread_mutex_unlock around the call to accept.

Comparing rows 6 and 7 in Figure 30.1, we see that this latest version of our server is faster than the create-one-thread-per-client version. We expect this, since we create the pool of threads only once, when the server starts, instead of creating one thread per client. Indeed, this version of our server is the fastest on these two hosts.

Figure 30.2 shows the distribution of the thread_count counters in the Thread structure, which we print in the SIGINT handler when the server is terminated. The uniformity of this distribution is caused by the thread scheduling algorithm that appears to cycle through all the threads in order when choosing which thread receives the mutex lock.

> On a Berkeley-derived kernel, we do not need any locking around the call to accept and can make a version of Figure 30.29 without any mutex locking and unlocking. Doing so, however, increases the process control CPU time. If we look at the two components of the CPU time, the user time and the system time, without any locking, the user time decreases (because the locking is done in the threads library, which executes in user space), but the system time increases (the kernel's thundering herd as all threads blocked in accept are awakened when a connection arrives). Since some form of mutual exclusion is required to return each connection to a single thread, it is faster for the threads to do this themselves than for the kernel.

30.12 TCP Prethreaded Server, Main Thread accept

Our final server design using threads has the main thread create a pool of threads when it starts, and then only the main thread calls accept and passes each client connection to one of the available threads in the pool. This is similar to the descriptor passing version in Section 30.9.

The design problem is how does the main thread "pass" the connected socket to one of the available threads in the pool? There are various ways to implement this. We could use descriptor passing, as we did earlier, but there's no need to pass a descriptor from one thread to another since all the threads and all the descriptors are in the same process. All the receiving thread needs to know is the descriptor number. Figure 30.30 shows the pthread08.h header that defines a Thread structure, which is identical to Figure 30.27.

server/pthread08.h

```
1 typedef struct {
2     pthread_t  thread_tid;        /* thread ID */
3     long       thread_count;      /* # connections handled */
4 } Thread;
5 Thread *tptr;                     /* array of Thread structures; calloc'ed */

6 #define MAXNCLI 32
7 int       clifd[MAXNCLI], iget, iput;
8 pthread_mutex_t clifd_mutex;
9 pthread_cond_t clifd_cond;
```

server/pthread08.h

Figure 30.30 pthread08.h header.

Define shared array to hold connected sockets

6-9   We also define a `clifd` array in which the main thread will store the connected socket descriptors. The available threads in the pool take one of these connected sockets and service the corresponding client. `iput` is the index into this array of the next entry to be stored into by the main thread and `iget` is the index of the next entry to be fetched by one of the threads in the pool. Naturally, this data structure that is shared between all the threads must be protected and we use a mutex along with a condition variable.

Figure 30.31 is the `main` function.

Create pool of threads

23-25   `thread_make` creates each of the threads.

Wait for each client connection

27-38   The main thread blocks in the call to `accept`, waiting for each client connection to arrive. When one arrives, the connected socket is stored in the next entry in the `clifd` array, after obtaining the mutex lock on the array. We also check that the `iput` index has not caught up with the `iget` index, which indicates that our array is not big enough. The condition variable is signaled and the mutex is released, allowing one of the threads in the pool to service this client.

The `thread_make` and `thread_main` functions are shown in Figure 30.32. The former is identical to the version in Figure 30.29.

Wait for client descriptor to service

17-26   Each thread in the pool tries to obtain a lock on the mutex that protects the `clifd` array. When the lock is obtained, there is nothing to do if the `iget` and `iput` indexes are equal. In that case, the thread goes to sleep by calling `pthread_cond_wait`. It will be awakened by the call to `pthread_cond_signal` in the main thread after a connection is accepted. When the thread obtains a connection, it calls `web_child`.

The times in Figure 30.1 show that this server is slower than the one in the previous section, in which each thread called `accept` after obtaining a mutex lock. The reason is that this section's example requires both a mutex and a condition variable, compared to just a mutex in Figure 30.29.

If we examine the histogram of the number of clients serviced by each thread in the pool, it is similar to the final column in Figure 30.2. This means the threads library cycles through all the available threads when doing the wakeup based on the condition variable when the main thread calls `pthread_cond_signal`.

server/serv08.c

```
 1 #include     "unpthread.h"
 2 #include     "pthread08.h"

 3 static int nthreads;
 4 pthread_mutex_t clifd_mutex = PTHREAD_MUTEX_INITIALIZER;
 5 pthread_cond_t clifd_cond = PTHREAD_COND_INITIALIZER;

 6 int
 7 main(int argc, char **argv)
 8 {
 9     int      i, listenfd, connfd;
10     void     sig_int(int), thread_make(int);
11     socklen_t addrlen, clilen;
12     struct sockaddr *cliaddr;

13     if (argc == 3)
14         listenfd = Tcp_listen(NULL, argv[1], &addrlen);
15     else if (argc == 4)
16         listenfd = Tcp_listen(argv[1], argv[2], &addrlen);
17     else
18         err_quit("usage: serv08 [ <host> ] <port#> <#threads>");
19     cliaddr = Malloc(addrlen);

20     nthreads = atoi(argv[argc - 1]);
21     tptr = Calloc(nthreads, sizeof(Thread));
22     iget = iput = 0;

23         /* create all the threads */
24     for (i = 0; i < nthreads; i++)
25         thread_make(i);           /* only main thread returns */

26     Signal(SIGINT, sig_int);

27     for ( ; ; ) {
28         clilen = addrlen;
29         connfd = Accept(listenfd, cliaddr, &clilen);

30         Pthread_mutex_lock(&clifd_mutex);
31         clifd[iput] = connfd;
32         if (++iput == MAXNCLI)
33             iput = 0;
34         if (iput == iget)
35             err_quit("iput = iget = %d", iput);
36         Pthread_cond_signal(&clifd_cond);
37         Pthread_mutex_unlock(&clifd_mutex);
38     }
39 }
```

server/serv08.c

Figure 30.31 main function for prethreaded server.

```
                                                            ──── server/pthread08.c
 1 #include     "unpthread.h"
 2 #include     "pthread08.h"

 3 void
 4 thread_make(int i)
 5 {
 6     void   *thread_main(void *);

 7     Pthread_create(&tptr[i].thread_tid, NULL, &thread_main, (void *) i);
 8     return;                        /* main thread returns */
 9 }

10 void *
11 thread_main(void *arg)
12 {
13     int     connfd;
14     void    web_child(int);

15     printf("thread %d starting\n", (int) arg);
16     for ( ; ; ) {
17         Pthread_mutex_lock(&clifd_mutex);
18         while (iget == iput)
19             Pthread_cond_wait(&clifd_cond, &clifd_mutex);
20         connfd = clifd[iget];   /* connected socket to service */
21         if (++iget == MAXNCLI)
22             iget = 0;
23         Pthread_mutex_unlock(&clifd_mutex);
24         tptr[(int) arg].thread_count++;

25         web_child(connfd);      /* process request */
26         Close(connfd);
27     }
28 }
```
                                                            ──── server/pthread08.c

Figure 30.32 `thread_make` and `thread_main` functions.

30.13 Summary

In this chapter, we looked at nine different server designs and ran them all against the same Web-style client, comparing the amount of CPU time spent performing process control:

    0. Iterative server (baseline measurement; no process control)
    1. Concurrent server, one `fork` per client
    2. Preforked, with each child calling `accept`
    3. Preforked, with file locking to protect `accept`
    4. Preforked, with thread mutex locking to protect `accept`
    5. Preforked, with parent passing socket descriptor to child
    6. Concurrent server, create one thread per client request
    7. Prethreaded with mutex locking to protect `accept`
    8. Prethreaded with main thread calling `accept`

We can make a few summary comments:

- First, if the server is not heavily used, the traditional concurrent server model, with one fork per client, is fine. This can even be combined with inetd, letting it handle the accepting of each connection. The remainder of our comments are meant for heavily used servers, such as Web servers.

- Creating a pool of children or a pool of threads reduces the process control CPU time compared to the traditional one-fork-per-client design by a factor of 10 or more. The coding is not complicated, but what is required, above and beyond the examples that we have shown, is monitoring the number of free children and increasing or decreasing this number as the number of clients being served changes dynamically.

- Some implementations allow multiple children or threads to block in a call to accept, while on other implementations, we must place some type of lock around the call to accept. Either file locking or Pthread mutex locking can be used.

- Having all the children or threads call accept is normally simpler and faster than having the main thread call accept and then pass the descriptor to the child or thread.

- Having all the children or threads block in a call to accept is preferable over blocking in a call to select because of the potential for select collisions.

- Using threads is normally faster than using processes. But, the choice of one-child-per-client or one-thread-per-client depends on what the OS provides and can also depend on what other programs, if any, are invoked to service each client. For example, if the server that accepts the client's connection calls fork and exec, it can be faster to fork a single threaded process than to fork a multithreaded process.

Exercises

30.1   In Figure 30.13, why does the parent keep the listening socket open instead of closing it after all the children are created?

30.2   Can you recode the server in Section 30.9 to use a Unix domain datagram socket instead of a Unix domain stream socket? What changes?

30.3   Run the client and as many of the servers as your environment will support and compare your results with those reported in this chapter.

31

STREAMS

31.1 Introduction

In this chapter, we will provide an overview of the STREAMS system and the functions used by an application to access a stream. Our goal is to understand the implementation of networking protocols within the STREAMS framework. We will also develop a simple TCP client using the Transport Provider Interface (TPI), the interface into the transport layer that sockets normally use on a system based on STREAMS. Additional information on STREAMS, including information on writing kernel routines that utilize STREAMS, can be found in [Rago 1993].

> STREAMS were designed by Dennis Ritchie [Ritchie 1984] and were first made widely available with SVR3 in 1986. The POSIX specification defines STREAMS as an *option group*, which means a system may not implement STREAMS, but if it does, the implementation must comply with the POSIX specification. Any system derived from System V should provide POSIX, but the various 4.xBSD releases do not provide POSIX.

> Be careful to distinguish between STREAMS, the stream I/O system that we are describing in this chapter, versus "standard I/O streams." The latter term is used when talking about the standard I/O library (e.g., functions such as `fopen`, `fgets`, `printf`, and the like).

31.2 Overview

STREAMS provide a full-duplex connection between a process and a *driver*, as shown in Figure 31.1. Although we describe the bottom box as a driver, this does not need to be

851

associated with a hardware device; it can also be a pseudo-device driver (e.g., a software driver).

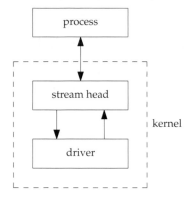

Figure 31.1 A stream shown between a process and a driver.

The *stream head* consists of the kernel routines that are invoked when the application makes a system call for a STREAMS descriptor (e.g., read, putmsg, ioctl, and the like).

A process can dynamically add and remove intermediate processing *modules* between the stream head and the driver. A module performs some type of filtering on the messages going up and down a stream. We show this in Figure 31.2.

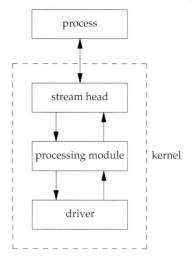

Figure 31.2 A stream with a processing module.

Any number of modules can be pushed onto a stream. When we say *"push,"* we mean that each new module gets inserted just below the stream head.

A special type of pseudo-device driver is a *multiplexor*, which accepts data from multiple sources. A STREAMS-based implementation of the TCP/IP protocol suite, as found on SVR4, for example, could be set up as shown in Figure 31.3.

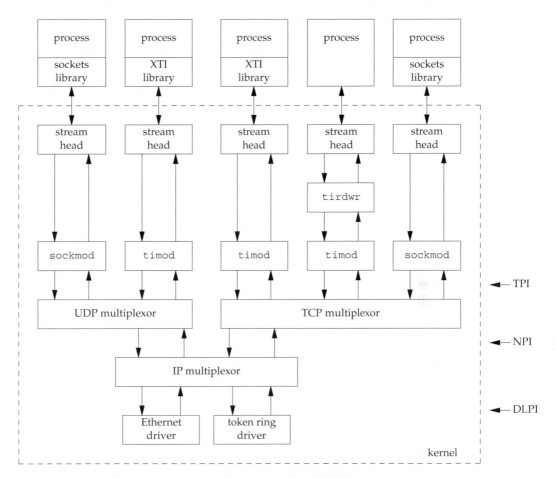

Figure 31.3 A potential implementation of TCP/IP using STREAMS.

- When a socket is created, the module `sockmod` is pushed onto the stream by the sockets library. It is the combination of the sockets library and the `sockmod` STREAMS module that provides the sockets API to the process.

- When an XTI endpoint is created, the module `timod` is pushed onto the stream by the XTI library. It is the combination of the XTI library and the `timod` STREAMS module that provides the X/Open Transport Interface (XTI) API to the process.

> This is one of the few places where we mention XTI. An earlier edition of this book described the XTI API in great detail, but it fell out of common use and even the POSIX specification no longer covers it, so we dropped the coverage from this book. Figure 31.3 shows where the XTI implemention typically lives and we touch on it briefly in this chapter, but we stop short of providing any detail since there's rarely a reason to use XTI anymore.

- The STREAMS module `tirdwr` must normally be pushed onto a stream to use `read` and `write` with an XTI endpoint. The middle process using TCP in Figure 31.3 has done this. This process has probably abandoned the use of XTI by doing this, so we have not shown the XTI library there.

- Various service interfaces define the format of the networking messages exchanged up and down a stream. We describe the three most common. TPI [Unix International 1992b] defines the interface provided by a transport-layer provider (e.g., TCP and UDP) to the modules above it. The *Network Provider Interface* (NPI) [Unix International 1992a] defines the interface provided by a network-layer provider (e.g., IP). DLPI is the *Data Link Provider Interface* [Unix International 1991]. An alternate reference for TPI and DLPI, which contains sample C code, is [Rago 1993].

Each component in a stream—the stream head, all processing modules, and the driver—contains at least one pair of *queues*: a write queue and a read queue. We show this in Figure 31.4.

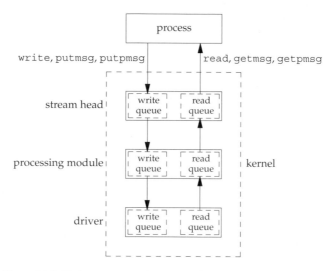

Figure 31.4   Each component in a stream has at least one pair of queues.

Message Types

STREAMS messages can be categorized as *high priority*, *priority band*, or *normal*. There are 256 different priority bands, between 0 and 255, with normal messages in band 0. The priority of a STREAMS message is used for both queueing and flow control. By convention, high-priority messages are unaffected by flow control.

Figure 31.5 shows the ordering of the messages on a given queue.

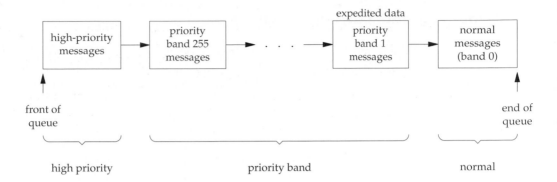

Figure 31.5 Ordering of STREAMS messages on a queue, based on priority.

Although the STREAMS system supports 256 different priority bands, networking protocols often use band 1 for expedited data and band 0 for normal data.

> TCP's out-of-band data is not considered true expedited data by TPI. Indeed, TCP uses band 0
> for both normal data and its out-of-band data. The use of band 1 for expedited data is for pro-
> tocols in which the expedited data (not just the urgent pointer, as in TCP) is sent ahead of nor-
> mal data.
>
> Beware of the term "*normal.*" In releases before SVR4, there were no priority bands; there were
> just normal messages and priority messages. SVR4 implemented priority bands, requiring the
> `getpmsg` and `putpmsg` functions, which we will describe shortly. The older priority messages
> were renamed high-priority. The question is what to call the new messages, with priority
> bands between 1 and 255. Common terminology [Rago 1993] refers to everything other than
> high-priority messages as normal-priority messages and then subdivides these normal-priority
> messages into priority bands. The term "*normal message*" should always refer to a message
> with a band of 0.

Although we talk about normal-priority messages and high-priority messages,
there are about a dozen normal-priority message types and around 18 high-priority
message types. From an application's perspective, and the `getmsg` and `putmsg` functions we are about to describe, we are interested in only three different types of messages: M_DATA, M_PROTO, and M_PCPROTO (PC stands for "priority control" and implies
a high-priority message). Figure 31.6 shows how these three different message types
are generated by the `write` and `putmsg` functions.

Function	Control?	Data?	Flags	Message type generated
`write`		Yes		M_DATA
`putmsg`	No	Yes	0	M_DATA
`putmsg`	Yes	Don't care	0	M_PROTO
`putmsg`	Yes	Don't care	MSG_HIPRI	M_PCPROTO

Figure 31.6 STREAMS message types generated by `write` and `putmsg`.

31.3   `getmsg` and `putmsg` Functions

The data transferred up and down a stream consists of messages, and each message contains *control*, *data*, or both. If we use `read` and `write` on a stream, these transfer only data. To allow a process to read and write both data and control information, two new functions were added.

```
#include <stropts.h>

int getmsg(int fd, struct strbuf *ctlptr, struct strbuf *dataptr, int *flagsp);

int putmsg(int fd, const struct strbuf *ctlptr,
           const struct strbuf *dataptr, int flags);
```

Both return: non-negative value if OK (see text), −1 on error

Both the control and data portions of the message are described by the following `strbuf` structure:

```
struct strbuf {
    int    maxlen;    /* maximum size of buf */
    int    len;       /* actual amount of data in buf */
    char   *buf;      /* data */
};
```

> Note the similarity between the `strbuf` structure and the `netbuf` structure. The names of the three elements in each structure are identical.

> But the two lengths in the `netbuf` structure are unsigned integers, while the two lengths in the `strbuf` structure are signed integers. The reason why is that some of the STREAMS functions use a `len` or `maxlen` value of −1 to indicate something special.

We can send only control information, only data, or both using `putmsg`. To indicate the absence of control information, we can either specify *ctlptr* as a null pointer or set *ctlptr->len* to −1. The same technique is used to indicate no data.

If there is no control information, an M_DATA message is generated by `putmsg` (Figure 31.6); otherwise, either an M_PROTO or an M_PCPROTO message is generated, depending on the *flags*. The *flags* argument to `putmsg` is 0 for a normal message or RS_HIPRI for a high-priority message.

The final argument to `getmsg` is a value-result argument. If the integer pointed to by *flagsp* is 0 when the function is called, the first message on the stream is returned (which can be normal- or high-priority). If the integer value is RS_HIPRI when the function is called, the function waits for a high-priority message to arrive at the stream head. In both cases, the value stored in the integer pointed to by *flagsp* will be 0 or RS_HIPRI, depending on the type of message returned.

Assuming we pass non-null *ctlptr* and *dataptr* values to `getmsg`, if there is no control information to return (i.e., an M_DATA message is being returned), this is indicated by setting *ctlptr->len* to −1 on return. Similarly, *dataptr->len* is set to −1 if there is no data to return.

The return value from putmsg is 0 if all is okay, or −1 on an error. But, getmsg returns 0 only if the entire message was returned to the caller. If the control buffer is too small for all the control information, the return value is MORECTL (which is guaranteed to be non-negative). Similarly, if the data buffer is too small, MOREDATA can be returned. If both are too small, the logical OR of these two flags is returned.

31.4 getpmsg **and** putpmsg **Functions**

When support for different priority bands was added to STREAMS with SVR4, the following two variants of getmsg and putmsg were added:

```
#include <stropts.h>

int getpmsg(int fd, struct strbuf *ctlptr,
            struct strbuf *dataptr, int *bandp, int *flagsp);

int putpmsg(int fd, const struct strbuf *ctlptr,
            const struct strbuf *dataptr, int band, int flags);
```

Both return: non-negative value if OK, −1 on error

The *band* argument to putpmsg must be between 0 and 255, inclusive. If the *flags* argument is MSG_BAND, then a message is generated in the specified priority band. Setting *flags* to MSG_BAND and specifying a band of 0 is equivalent to calling putmsg. If *flags* is MSG_HIPRI, *band* must be 0, and a high-priority message is generated. (Note that this flag is named differently from the RS_HIPRI flag for putmsg.)

The two integers pointed to by *bandp* and *flagsp* are value-result arguments for getpmsg. The integer pointed to by *flagsp* for getpmsg can be MSG_HIPRI (to read a high-priority message), MSG_BAND (to read a message whose priority band is at least equal to the integer pointed to by *bandp*), or MSG_ANY (to read any message). On return, the integer pointed to by *bandp* contains the band of the message that was read and the integer pointed to by *flagsp* contains MSG_HIPRI (if a high-priority message was read) or MSG_BAND (if some other message was read).

31.5 ioctl **Function**

With STREAMS, we again encounter the ioctl function that was described in Chapter 17.

```
#include <stropts.h>

int ioctl(int fd, int request, ... /* void *arg */ );
```

Returns: 0 if OK, −1 on error

The only change from the function prototype shown in Section 17.2 is the headers that must be included when dealing with STREAMS.

There are about 30 requests that affect a stream head. Each request begins with I_ and they are normally documented on the streamio man page.

31.6 Transport Provider Interface (TPI)

In Figure 31.3, we showed that TPI is the service interface into the transport layer from above. Both sockets and XTI use this interface in a STREAMS environment. In Figure 31.3, it is a combination of the sockets library and sockmod, along with a combination of the XTI library and timod, that exchange TPI messages with TCP and UDP.

TPI is a *message-based* interface. It defines the messages that are exchanged up and down a stream between the application (e.g., the sockets library) and the transport layer: the format of these messages and what operation each message performs. In many instances, the application sends a request to the provider (such as "bind this local address") and the provider sends back a response ("OK" or "error"). Some events occur asynchronously at the provider (the arrival of a connection request for a server), causing a message or a signal to be sent up the stream.

We are able to bypass both sockets and XTI and use TPI directly. In this section, we will rewrite our simple daytime client using TPI instead of sockets (Figure 1.5). Using programming languages as an analogy, using sockets is like programming in a high-level language such as C or Pascal, while using TPI directly is like programming in assembly language. We are not advocating the use of TPI directly in real applications. But examining how TPI works and developing this example give us a better understanding of how the sockets library works in a STREAMS environment.

Figure 31.7 is our tpi_daytime.h header.

```
                                                           streams/tpi_daytime.h
1 #include    "unpxti.h"
2 #include    <sys/stream.h>
3 #include    <sys/tihdr.h>

4 void    tpi_bind(int, const void *, size_t);
5 void    tpi_connect(int, const void *, size_t);
6 ssize_t tpi_read(int, void *, size_t);
7 void    tpi_close(int);
                                                           streams/tpi_daytime.h
```

Figure 31.7 Our tpi_daytime.h header.

We need to include one additional STREAMS header along with <sys/tihdr.h>, which contains the definitions of the structures for all TPI messages.

Figure 31.8 is the `main` function for our daytime client.

streams/tpi_daytime.c

```
 1 #include    "tpi_daytime.h"

 2 int
 3 main(int argc, char **argv)
 4 {
 5     int     fd, n;
 6     char    recvline[MAXLINE + 1];
 7     struct sockaddr_in myaddr, servaddr;

 8     if (argc != 2)
 9         err_quit("usage: tpi_daytime <IPaddress>");

10     fd = Open(XTI_TCP, O_RDWR, 0);

11         /* bind any local address */
12     bzero(&myaddr, sizeof(myaddr));
13     myaddr.sin_family = AF_INET;
14     myaddr.sin_addr.s_addr = htonl(INADDR_ANY);
15     myaddr.sin_port = htons(0);

16     tpi_bind(fd, &myaddr, sizeof(struct sockaddr_in));

17         /* fill in server's address */
18     bzero(&servaddr, sizeof(servaddr));
19     servaddr.sin_family = AF_INET;
20     servaddr.sin_port = htons(13);  /* daytime server */
21     Inet_pton(AF_INET, argv[1], &servaddr.sin_addr);

22     tpi_connect(fd, &servaddr, sizeof(struct sockaddr_in));

23     for ( ; ; ) {
24         if ( (n = tpi_read(fd, recvline, MAXLINE)) <= 0) {
25             if (n == 0)
26                 break;
27             else
28                 err_sys("tpi_read error");
29         }
30         recvline[n] = 0;           /* null terminate */
31         fputs(recvline, stdout);
32     }
33     tpi_close(fd);
34     exit(0);
35 }
```

streams/tpi_daytime.c

Figure 31.8 `main` function for our daytime client written to TPI.

Open transport provider, bind local address

10-16   We open the device corresponding to the transport provider (normally `/dev/tcp`). We fill in an Internet socket address structure with `INADDR_ANY` and a port of 0, telling TCP to bind any local address to our endpoint. We call our own function `tpi_bind` (shown shortly) to do the bind.

Fill in server's address, establish connection

17–22   We fill in another Internet socket address structure with the server's IP address (taken from the command line) and port (13). We call our `tpi_connect` function to establish the connection.

Read data from server, copy to standard output

23–33   As in our other daytime clients, we just copy data from the connection to standard output, stopping when we receive the EOF from the server (e.g., the FIN). We then call our `tpi_close` function to close our endpoint.

Our `tpi_bind` function is shown in Figure 31.9.

Fill in `T_bind_req` structure

16–20   The `<sys/tihdr.h>` header defines the `T_bind_req` structure.

```
struct T_bind_req {
  t_scalar_t      PRIM_type;      /* T_BIND_REQ */
  t_scalar_t      ADDR_length;    /* address length */
  t_scalar_t      ADDR_offset;    /* address offset */
  t_uscalar_t     CONIND_number;  /* connect indications requested */
      /* followed by the protocol address for bind */
};
```

All TPI requests are defined as a structure that begins with a long integer type field. We define our own `bind_req` structure that begins with the `T_bind_req` structure, followed by a buffer containing the local address to be bound. TPI says nothing about the contents of this buffer; it is defined by the provider. TCP providers expect this buffer to contain a `sockaddr_in` structure.

We fill in the `T_bind_req` structure, setting the `ADDR_length` member to the size of the address (16 bytes for an Internet socket address structure) and `ADDR_offset` to the byte offset of the address (it immediately follows the `T_bind_req` structure). We are not guaranteed that this location is suitably aligned for the `sockaddr_in` structure that is stored there, so we call `memcpy` to copy the caller's structure into our `bind_req` structure. We set `CONIND_number` to 0 because we are a client, not a server.

Call `putmsg`

21–23   TPI requires the structure that we just built to be passed to the provider as one `M_PROTO` message. We therefore call `putmsg`, specifying our `bind_req` structure as the control information, with no data and with a flag of 0.

Call `getmsg` to read high-priority message

24–30   The response to our `T_BIND_REQ` request will be either a `T_BIND_ACK` message or a `T_ERROR_ACK` message. These acknowledgment messages are sent as high-priority messages (`M_PCPROTO`) so we read them using `getmsg` with a flag of `RS_HIPRI`. Since the reply is a high-priority message, it will bypass any normal-priority messages on the stream.

streams/tpi_bind.c

```
 1 #include    "tpi_daytime.h"

 2 void
 3 tpi_bind(int fd, const void *addr, size_t addrlen)
 4 {
 5     struct {
 6         struct T_bind_req msg_hdr;
 7         char    addr[128];
 8     } bind_req;
 9     struct {
10         struct T_bind_ack msg_hdr;
11         char    addr[128];
12     } bind_ack;
13     struct strbuf ctlbuf;
14     struct T_error_ack *error_ack;
15     int     flags;

16     bind_req.msg_hdr.PRIM_type = T_BIND_REQ;
17     bind_req.msg_hdr.ADDR_length = addrlen;
18     bind_req.msg_hdr.ADDR_offset = sizeof(struct T_bind_req);
19     bind_req.msg_hdr.CONIND_number = 0;
20     memcpy(bind_req.addr, addr, addrlen);   /* sockaddr_in{} */

21     ctlbuf.len = sizeof(struct T_bind_req) + addrlen;
22     ctlbuf.buf = (char *) &bind_req;
23     Putmsg(fd, &ctlbuf, NULL, 0);

24     ctlbuf.maxlen = sizeof(bind_ack);
25     ctlbuf.len = 0;
26     ctlbuf.buf = (char *) &bind_ack;
27     flags = RS_HIPRI;
28     Getmsg(fd, &ctlbuf, NULL, &flags);

29     if (ctlbuf.len < (int) sizeof(long))
30         err_quit("bad length from getmsg");

31     switch (bind_ack.msg_hdr.PRIM_type) {
32     case T_BIND_ACK:
33         return;

34     case T_ERROR_ACK:
35         if (ctlbuf.len < (int) sizeof(struct T_error_ack))
36             err_quit("bad length for T_ERROR_ACK");
37         error_ack = (struct T_error_ack *) &bind_ack.msg_hdr;
38         err_quit("T_ERROR_ACK from bind (%d, %d)",
39                 error_ack->TLI_error, error_ack->UNIX_error);

40     default:
41         err_quit("unexpected message type: %d", bind_ack.msg_hdr.PRIM_type);
42     }
43 }
```

streams/tpi_bind.c

Figure 31.9 tpi_bind function: binds a local address to an endpoint.

These two messages are as follows:

```
struct T_bind_ack {
  t_scalar_t    PRIM_type;      /* T_BIND_ACK */
  t_scalar_t    ADDR_length;    /* address length */
  t_scalar_t    ADDR_offset;    /* address offset */
  t_uscalar_t   CONIND_number;  /* connect ind to be queued */
      /* followed by the bound address */
};

struct T_error_ack {
  t_scalar_t    PRIM_type;      /* T_ERROR_ACK */
  t_scalar_t    ERROR_prim;     /* primitive in error */
  t_scalar_t    TLI_error;      /* TLI error code */
  t_scalar_t    UNIX_error;     /* UNIX error code */
};
```

All these messages begin with the type, so we can read the reply assuming it is a
T_BIND_ACK message, look at the type, and process the message accordingly. We do
not expect any data from the provider, so we specify a null pointer as the third argument to getmsg.

> When we verify that the amount of control information returned is at least the size of a long
> integer, we must be careful to cast the sizeof value to an integer. The sizeof operator
> returns an unsigned integer value, but it is possible for the returned len field to be −1. But
> since the less-than comparison is comparing a signed value on the left to an unsigned value on
> the right, the compiler casts the signed value to an unsigned value. On a two's-complement
> architecture, −1, considered as an unsigned value, is very large, causing −1 to be greater than 4
> (if we assume a long integer occupies 4 bytes).

Process reply

31-33   If the reply is T_BIND_ACK, the bind was successful and we return. The actual
address that was bound to the endpoint is returned in the addr member of our
bind_ack structure, which we ignore.

34-39   If the reply is T_ERROR_ACK, we verify that the entire message was received and
then print the three return values in the structure. In this simple program, we terminate
when an error occurs; we do not return to the caller.

We can see these errors from the bind request by changing our main function to
bind some port other than 0. For example, if we try to bind port 1 (which requires
superuser privileges, since it is a port less than 1024), we get

```
solaris % tpi_daytime 127.0.0.1
T_ERROR_ACK from bind (3, 0)
```

The error TACCES has the value 3 on this system. If we change the port to a value
greater than 1023, but one that is currently in use by another TCP endpoint, we get

```
solaris % tpi_daytime 127.0.0.1
T_ERROR_ACK from bind (23, 0)
```

The error TADDRBUSY has the value 23 on this system.

The next function, shown in Figure 31.10, is `tpi_connect`, which establishes the connection with the server.

Fill in request structure and send to provider

18-26   TPI defines a `T_conn_req` structure that contains the protocol address and options for the connection.

```
struct T_conn_req {
   t_scalar_t      PRIM_type;    /* T_CONN_REQ */
   t_scalar_t      DEST_length;  /* destination address length */
   t_scalar_t      DEST_offset;  /* destination address offset */
   t_scalar_t      OPT_length;   /* options length */
   t_scalar_t      OPT_offset;   /* options offset */
      /* followed by the protocol address and options for connection */
};
```

As in our `tpi_bind` function, we define our own structure named `conn_req`, which includes a `T_conn_req` structure along with room for the protocol address. We fill in our `conn_req` structure, setting the two members dealing with options to 0. We call `putmsg` with only control information and a flag of 0 to send an `M_PROTO` message down the stream.

─────────────────────────────────────── *streams/tpi_connect.c*

```
 1 #include     "tpi_daytime.h"

 2 void
 3 tpi_connect(int fd, const void *addr, size_t addrlen)
 4 {
 5     struct {
 6         struct T_conn_req msg_hdr;
 7         char     addr[128];
 8     } conn_req;
 9     struct {
10         struct T_conn_con msg_hdr;
11         char     addr[128];
12     } conn_con;
13     struct strbuf ctlbuf;
14     union T_primitives rcvbuf;
15     struct T_error_ack *error_ack;
16     struct T_discon_ind *discon_ind;
17     int      flags;

18     conn_req.msg_hdr.PRIM_type = T_CONN_REQ;
19     conn_req.msg_hdr.DEST_length = addrlen;
20     conn_req.msg_hdr.DEST_offset = sizeof(struct T_conn_req);
21     conn_req.msg_hdr.OPT_length = 0;
22     conn_req.msg_hdr.OPT_offset = 0;
23     memcpy(conn_req.addr, addr, addrlen);   /* sockaddr_in{} */

24     ctlbuf.len = sizeof(struct T_conn_req) + addrlen;
25     ctlbuf.buf = (char *) &conn_req;
26     Putmsg(fd, &ctlbuf, NULL, 0);

27     ctlbuf.maxlen = sizeof(union T_primitives);
28     ctlbuf.len = 0;
29     ctlbuf.buf = (char *) &rcvbuf;
```

```
30      flags = RS_HIPRI;
31      Getmsg(fd, &ctlbuf, NULL, &flags);

32      if (ctlbuf.len < (int) sizeof(long))
33          err_quit("tpi_connect: bad length from getmsg");

34      switch (rcvbuf.type) {
35      case T_OK_ACK:
36          break;

37      case T_ERROR_ACK:
38          if (ctlbuf.len < (int) sizeof(struct T_error_ack))
39              err_quit("tpi_connect: bad length for T_ERROR_ACK");
40          error_ack = (struct T_error_ack *) &rcvbuf;
41          err_quit("tpi_connect: T_ERROR_ACK from conn (%d, %d)",
42                  error_ack->TLI_error, error_ack->UNIX_error);

43      default:
44          err_quit("tpi_connect: unexpected message type: %d", rcvbuf.type);
45      }

46      ctlbuf.maxlen = sizeof(conn_con);
47      ctlbuf.len = 0;
48      ctlbuf.buf = (char *) &conn_con;
49      flags = 0;
50      Getmsg(fd, &ctlbuf, NULL, &flags);

51      if (ctlbuf.len < (int) sizeof(long))
52          err_quit("tpi_connect2: bad length from getmsg");

53      switch (conn_con.msg_hdr.PRIM_type) {
54      case T_CONN_CON:
55          break;

56      case T_DISCON_IND:
57          if (ctlbuf.len < (int) sizeof(struct T_discon_ind))
58              err_quit("tpi_connect2: bad length for T_DISCON_IND");
59          discon_ind = (struct T_discon_ind *) &conn_con.msg_hdr;
60          err_quit("tpi_connect2: T_DISCON_IND from conn (%d)",
61                  discon_ind->DISCON_reason);

62      default:
63          err_quit("tpi_connect2: unexpected message type: %d",
64                  conn_con.msg_hdr.PRIM_type);
65      }
66  }
```
—— *streams/tpi_connect.c*

Figure 31.10 tpi_connect function: establishes connection with server.

Read response

27-45   We call getmsg, expecting to receive either a T_OK_ACK message if the connection establishment was started, or a T_ERROR_ACK message (which we showed earlier).

```
struct T_ok_ack {
  t_scalar_t    PRIM_type;      /* T_OK_ACK   */
  t_scalar_t    CORRECT_prim;   /* correct primitive */
};
```

In case of an error, we terminate. Since we do not know what type of message we will receive, a `union` named `T_primitives` is defined as the union of all the possible requests and replies, and we allocate one of these that we use as the input buffer for the control information when we call `getmsg`.

Wait for connection to be established

46–65   The successful `T_OK_ACK` message that was just received only tells us that the connection establishment was started. We must now wait for a `T_CONN_CON` message to tell us that the other end has confirmed the connection request.

```
struct T_conn_con {
  t_scalar_t      PRIM_type;       /* T_CONN_CON */
  t_scalar_t      RES_length;      /* responding address length */
  t_scalar_t      RES_offset;      /* responding address offset */
  t_scalar_t      OPT_length;      /* option length */
  t_scalar_t      OPT_offset;      /* option offset */
      /* followed by peer's protocol address and options */
};
```

We call `getmsg` again, but the expected message is sent as an `M_PROTO` message, not an `M_PCPROTO` message, so we set the flags to 0. If we receive the `T_CONN_CON` message, the connection is established and we return, but if the connection was not established (either the peer process was not running, a timeout occurred, or whatever), a `T_DISCON_IND` message is sent up the stream instead.

```
struct T_discon_ind {
  t_scalar_t      PRIM_type;       /* T_DISCON_IND */
  t_scalar_t      DISCON_reason;   /* disconnect reason */
  t_scalar_t      SEQ_number;      /* sequence number */
};
```

We can see the different errors that are returned by the provider. We first specify the IP address of a host that is not running the daytime server.

```
solaris % tpi_daytime 192.168.1.10
tpi_connect2: T_DISCON_IND from conn (146)
```

The error of 146 corresponds to `ECONNREFUSED`. Next, we specify an IP address that is not connected to the Internet.

```
solaris % tpi_daytime 192.3.4.5
tpi_connect2: T_DISCON_IND from conn (145)
```

The error this time is `ETIMEDOUT`. But if we run our program again, specifying the same IP address, we get a different error.

```
solaris % tpi_daytime 192.3.4.5
tpi_connect2: T_DISCON_IND from conn (148)
```

The error this time is `EHOSTUNREACH`. The difference in the last two results is that the first time, no ICMP "host unreachable" errors were returned, while the next time, this error was returned.

The next function is `tpi_read`, shown in Figure 31.11. It reads data from a stream.

streams/tpi_read.c

```
 1 #include    "tpi_daytime.h"

 2 ssize_t
 3 tpi_read(int fd, void *buf, size_t len)
 4 {
 5     struct strbuf ctlbuf;
 6     struct strbuf datbuf;
 7     union T_primitives rcvbuf;
 8     int    flags;

 9     ctlbuf.maxlen = sizeof(union T_primitives);
10     ctlbuf.buf = (char *) &rcvbuf;

11     datbuf.maxlen = len;
12     datbuf.buf = buf;
13     datbuf.len = 0;

14     flags = 0;
15     Getmsg(fd, &ctlbuf, &datbuf, &flags);

16     if (ctlbuf.len >= (int) sizeof(long)) {
17         if (rcvbuf.type == T_DATA_IND)
18             return (datbuf.len);
19         else if (rcvbuf.type == T_ORDREL_IND)
20             return (0);
21         else
22             err_quit("tpi_read: unexpected type %d", rcvbuf.type);
23     } else if (ctlbuf.len == -1)
24         return (datbuf.len);
25     else
26         err_quit("tpi_read: bad length from getmsg");
27 }
```

streams/tpi_read.c

Figure 31.11 `tpi_read` function: reads data from a stream.

Read control and data; process reply

9–26   This time, we call `getmsg` to read both control information and data. The `strbuf` structure for the data points to the caller's buffer. Four different scenarios can occur on the stream:

- The data can arrive as an `M_DATA` message, which is indicated by the returned control length being set to –1. The data was copied into the caller's buffer by `getmsg`, and we just return the length of this data as the return value of the function.

- The data can arrive as a `T_DATA_IND` message, in which case, the control information will be a `T_data_ind` structure.

```
struct T_data_ind {
  t_scalar_t   PRIM_type;  /* T_DATA_IND */
  t_scalar_t   MORE_flag;  /* more data */
};
```

If this message is returned, we ignore the MORE_flag member (it will never be set for a stream protocol such as TCP) and just return the length of the data that was copied into the caller's buffer by getmsg.

- A T_ORDREL_IND message is returned if all the data has been consumed and the next item is a FIN.

```
struct T_ordrel_ind {
  t_scalar_t    PRIM_type;      /* T_ORDREL_IND */
};
```

This is the orderly release. We just return 0, indicating to the caller that the EOF has been encountered on the connection.

- A T_DISCON_IND message is returned if a disconnect has been received.

Our final function is tpi_close, shown in Figure 31.12.

streams/tpi_close.c

```
 1 #include    "tpi_daytime.h"

 2 void
 3 tpi_close(int fd)
 4 {
 5     struct T_ordrel_req ordrel_req;
 6     struct strbuf ctlbuf;

 7     ordrel_req.PRIM_type = T_ORDREL_REQ;

 8     ctlbuf.len = sizeof(struct T_ordrel_req);
 9     ctlbuf.buf = (char *) &ordrel_req;
10     Putmsg(fd, &ctlbuf, NULL, 0);

11     Close(fd);
12 }
```

streams/tpi_close.c

Figure 31.12 tpi_close function: sends an orderly release to the peer.

Send orderly release to peer

7-10   We build a T_ordrel_req structure

```
struct T_ordrel_req {
  long  PRIM_type;   /* T_ORDREL_REQ */
};
```

and send it as an M_PROTO message using putmsg.

This example has given us a flavor for TPI. The application sends messages down a stream to the provider (requests) and the provider sends messages up the stream (replies). Some exchanges follow a simple request-reply scenario (binding a local address), while others may take a while (establishing a connection), allowing us to do something while we wait for the reply. Our choice of writing a TCP client using TPI was done for simplicity; writing a TCP server and handling connections are much harder.

We can compare the number of system calls required for the network operations that we have seen in this chapter when using TPI versus a kernel that implements sockets within the kernel. Binding a local address takes two system calls with TPI, but only one with kernel sockets (TCPv2, p. 454). To establish a connection on a blocking descriptor takes three system calls with TPI, but only one with kernel sockets (TCPv2, p. 466).

31.7 Summary

Sockets are sometimes implemented using STREAMS. Four new functions are provided to access the STREAMS subsystem: `getmsg`, `getpmsg`, `putmsg`, and `putpmsg`, plus the existing `ioctl` function is heavily used by the STREAMS subsystem also.

TPI is the SVR4 STREAMS interface from the upper layers into the transport layer. It is used by both sockets and XTI, as shown in Figure 31.3. We developed a version of our daytime client using TPI directly as an example to show the message-based interface that TPI uses.

Exercises

31.1   In Figure 31.12, we call `putmsg` to send the orderly release request down the stream and then immediately `close` the stream. What happens if our orderly release request is lost by the STREAMS subsystem when the stream is closed?

Appendix A

IPv4, IPv6, ICMPv4, and ICMPv6

A.1 Introduction

This appendix is an overview of IPv4, IPv6, ICMPv4, and ICMPv6. This material provides additional background that may be helpful in understanding the discussion of TCP and UDP in Chapter 2. Some features of IP and ICMP are also used in some of the later chapters: IP options (Chapter 27), along with the `ping` and `traceroute` programs (Chapter 28), for example.

A.2 IPv4 Header

The IP layer provides a connectionless best-effort datagram delivery service (RFC 791 [Postel 1981a]). IP makes its best effort to deliver an IP datagram to the specified destination, but there is no guarantee that the datagram will arrive, will arrive in order relative to other packets, or will arrive only once. Any desired reliability, ordering, and duplicate suppression must be added by the upper layers. In the case of a TCP or SCTP application, this is performed by the transport layer. In the case of a UDP application, this must be done by the application since UDP is unreliable; we show an example of this in Section 22.5.

One of the most important functions of the IP layer is *routing*. Every IP datagram contains a source and destination address. Figure A.1 shows the format of an IPv4 header.

- The 4-bit *version* field is 4. This has been the version of IP in use since the early 1980s.

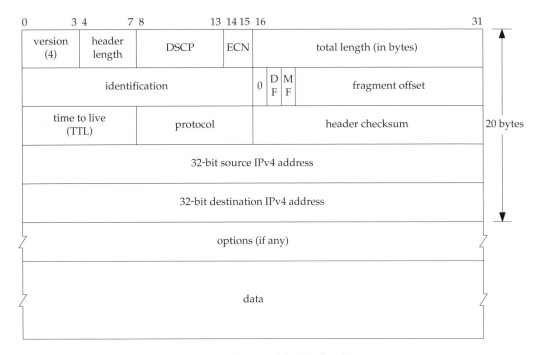

Figure A.1 Format of the IPv4 header.

- The *header length* field is the length of the entire IP header, including any options, in whole 32-bit words. The maximum value for this 4-bit field is 15 (0xf), giving a maximum IP header length of 60 bytes. Therefore, with the fixed portion of the header occupying 20 bytes, this allows for up to 40 bytes of options.

- The 6-bit *Differentiated Services Code Point* (DSCP) field (RFC 2474 [Nichols et al. 1998]) and the 2-bit *Explicit Congestion Notification* (ECN) field (RFC 3168 [Ramakrishnan, Floyd, and Black 2001]) replace the historical 8-bit *type-of-service* (TOS) field, which was described in RFC 1349 [Almquist 1992]. We can set all 8 bits of this field with the IP_TOS socket option (Section 7.6), although the kernel may overwrite any value we set to enforce Diffserv policy or implement ECN.

- The 16-bit *total length* field is the total length in bytes of the IP datagram, including the IPv4 header. The amount of data in the datagram is this field minus 4 times the header length (recall that the header length is in units of whole 32-bit words, or 4 bytes). This field is required because some datalinks pad the frame to some minimum length (e.g., Ethernet) and it is possible for the size of a valid IP datagram to be less than the datalink minimum.

- The 16-bit *identification* field is set to a different value for each IP datagram and enables fragmentation and reassembly (Section 2.11). The value must be unique for the packet's source, destination, and protocol, for the length of time that the datagram could be in transit. If there is no chance that the packet will be fragmented, for instance, the *DF* bit is set, there is no need to set this field.

- The *DF* (don't fragment) bit, the *MF* (more fragments) bit, and the 13-bit *fragment offset* field are also used with fragmentation and reassembly. The *DF* bit is also used with path MTU discovery (Section 2.11).

- The 8-bit *time-to-live* (TTL) field is set by the sender and then decremented by 1 each time a router forwards the datagram. The datagram is discarded by any router that decrements the value to 0. This limits the lifetime of any IP datagram to 255 hops. A common default for this field is 64, but we can query and change this default with the `IP_TTL` and `IP_MULTICAST_TTL` socket options (Section 7.6).

- The 8-bit *protocol* field specifies the next layer protocol contained in the IP datagram. Typical values are 1 (ICMPv4), 2 (IGMPv4), 6 (TCP), and 17 (UDP). These values are specified in the IANA's "Protocol Numbers" registry [IANA].

- The 16-bit *header checksum* is calculated over just the IP header (including any options). The algorithm is the standard Internet checksum algorithm, a simple 16-bit one's-complement addition, which we show in Figure 28.15.

- The *source IPv4 address* and the *destination IPv4 address* are both 32-bit fields.

- We describe the *options* field in Section 27.2 and show an example of the IPv4 source route option in Section 27.3.

A.3   IPv6 Header

Figure A.2 shows the format of an IPv6 header (RFC 2460 [Deering and Hinden 1998]).

- The 4-bit *version* field is 6. Since this field occupies the first 4 bits of the first byte of the header (just like the IPv4 version, Figure A.1), it allows a receiving IP stack to differentiate between the two versions. This differentiation is already done by most link layers by using different encapsulation for IPv4 and IPv6.

  During the development of IPv6 in the early 1990s, before the version number of 6 was assigned, the protocol was called *IPng*, for "IP next generation." You may still encounter references to IPng.

- The 6-bit DSCP field (RFC 2474 [Nichols et al. 1998]) and the 2-bit ECN field (RFC 3168 [Ramakrishnan, Floyd, and Black 2001]) replace the historical 8-bit *traffic class* field, which was described in RFC 2460. We can set all 8 bits of this field with the `IPV6_TCLASS` socket option (Section 22.8), although the kernel may overwrite any value we set to enforce Diffserv policy or implement ECN.

- The 20-bit *flow label* field can be chosen by the application or kernel for a given socket. A *flow* is a sequence of packets from a particular source to a particular destination for which the source desires special handling by intervening routers. For a given flow, once the flow label is chosen by the source, it does not change. A flow label of 0 (the default) identifies packets that do not belong to a flow. The flow label does not change while flowing through the network. [Rajahalme et al. 2003] describes the usage of the flow label more completely.

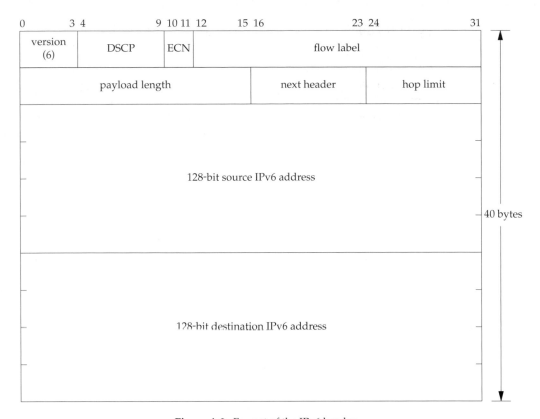

Figure A.2 Format of the IPv6 header.

The interface for the flow label is yet to be completely defined. The `sin6_flowinfo` member of the `sockaddr_in6` socket address structure (Figure 3.4) is reserved for future use. Some systems copy the lower 28 bits from the `sin6_flowinfo` directly into the IPv6 packet header, overwriting the DSCP and ECN fields.

- The 16-bit *payload length* field is the length in bytes of everything following the 40-byte IPv6 header. Note that unlike IPv4, the *payload length* field does not include the IPv6 header. A value of 0 means the length requires more than 16 bits to describe and is contained in a jumbo payload option (Figure 27.9). This is called a *jumbogram*.

- The 8-bit *next header* field is similar to the IPv4 protocol field. Indeed, when the upper layer protocol is basically unchanged from IPv4 to IPv6, the same values are used, such as 6 for TCP and 17 for UDP. There were so many changes from ICMPv4 to ICMPv6 that the latter was assigned a new value of 58.

  An IPv6 datagram can have numerous headers following the 40-byte IPv6 header. That is why the field is called the "next header" and not the "protocol."

- The 8-bit *hop limit* field is similar to the IPv4 TTL field. The hop limit is decremented by 1 each time a router forwards the datagram and the datagram is discarded by any router that decrements the value to 0. The default value for this field can be set and fetched with the `IPV6_UNICAST_HOPS` and `IPV6_MULTICAST_HOPS` (Sections 7.8 and 21.6) socket options. The `IPV6_HOPLIMIT` socket option also lets us set this field and the `IPV6_RECVHOPLIMIT` socket option lets us obtain its value from a received datagram.

> Early specifications of IPv4 had routers decrement the TTL by either one or the number of seconds that the router held the datagram, whichever was greater. Hence the name "time-to-live." In reality, however, the field was always decremented by one. IPv6 calls for its hop limit field to always be decremented by one, hence the name change from IPv4.

- The *source IPv6 address* and the *destination IPv6 address* are both 128-bit fields.

The most significant change from IPv4 to IPv6 is, of course, the larger IPv6 address fields. Another change is simplifying the IPv6 header as follows, to facilitate faster processing as a datagram traverses the network:

- There is no IPv6 header length field since the IPv6 header length is fixed at 40 bytes. Optional headers may follow the fixed 40-byte IPv6 header, but each of these has its own length field.

- The two IPv6 addresses end up aligned on a 64-bit boundary when the header itself is 64-bit aligned. This can speed up processing on 64-bit architectures. IPv4 addresses are only 32-bit aligned in a 64-bit aligned IPv4 header.

- There are no fragmentation fields in the IPv6 header because there is a separate fragmentation header for this purpose. This design decision was made because fragmentation is the exception, and exceptions should not slow down normal processing.

- The IPv6 header does not include its own checksum. This is because all the upper layers—TCP, UDP, and ICMPv6—have their own checksum that includes the upper-layer header, the upper-layer data, and the following fields from the IPv6 header: IPv6 source address, IPv6 destination address, payload length, and next header (RFC 2460 [Deering and Hinden 1998]). By omitting the checksum from the header, routers that forward the datagram need not recalculate a header checksum after they modify the hop limit. Again, speed of forwarding by routers is the key point.

In case this is your first encounter with IPv6, we also note the following major differences from IPv4 to IPv6:

- There is no broadcasting with IPv6 (Chapter 20). Multicasting (Chapter 21), which is optional with IPv4, is mandatory with IPv6. The case of sending to all systems on a subnet is handled with the all-nodes multicast group.

- IPv6 routers do not fragment packets they forward. If fragmentation is required, the router drops the packet and sends an ICMPv6 error (Section A.6). Fragmentation is performed only by the originating host with IPv6.

- IPv6 requires support for path MTU discovery (Section 2.11). Technically, this support is optional and could be omitted from minimal implementations such as bootstrap loaders, but if a node does not implement this feature, it must not send datagrams larger than the IPv6 minimum link MTU (1280 bytes). Section 22.9 describes socket options to control path MTU discovery behavior.

- IPv6 requires support for authentication and security options. These options appear after the fixed header.

A.4   IPv4 Addresses

IPv4 addresses are 32 bits long and are usually written as 4 decimal numbers, separated by dots ("."). This is called *dotted-decimal notation*, and each decimal number represents one of the 4 bytes of the 32-bit address. The first of the 4 decimal numbers identifies the address type, as shown in Figure A.3. Although historically IPv4 addresses were divided into five classes, as shown in Figure A.3, the three classes used for unicast addresses are functionally equivalent, so we show them as one range.

Usage	Class	Range
Unicast	A, B, C	**0**.0.0.0 to **223**.255.255.255
Multicast	D	**224**.0.0.0 to **239**.255.255.255
Experimental	E	**240**.0.0.0 to **255**.255.255.255

Figure A.3   Ranges for the five different classes of IPv4 addresses.

Whenever we talk about an IPv4 network or subnet address, we talk about a 32-bit network address and a corresponding 32-bit mask. Bits of 1 in the mask cover the network address and bits of 0 in the mask cover the host. Since the bits of 1 in the mask are usually contiguous from the leftmost bit, and the bits of 0 in the mask are always contiguous from the rightmost bit, this address mask can also be specified as a *prefix length* that denotes the number of contiguous bits of 1 starting from the left. For example, a mask of 255.255.255.0 corresponds with a prefix length of 24. These are known as *classless* addresses, so called because the mask is explicitly specified instead of being implied by the address class. IPv4 network addresses are normally written as a dotted-decimal number, followed by a slash, followed by the prefix length. Figure 1.16 showed examples of this.

> Discontiguous subnet masks were never ruled out by any RFC, but they are confusing and cannot be represented in prefix notation. BGP4, the Internet interdomain routing protocol, cannot represent discontiguous masks. IPv6 also requires that all address masks be contiguous starting at the leftmost bit.

Using classless addresses requires classless routing, and this is normally called *classless interdomain routing* (CIDR) (RFC 1519 [Fuller et al. 1993]). CIDR usage decreases the size of the Internet backbone routing tables and reduces the rate of IPv4 address depletion. All routes in CIDR must be accompanied by a mask or a prefix length. The class of the address no longer implies the mask. Section 10.8 of TCPv1 talks more about CIDR.

Subnet Addresses

IPv4 addresses are often *subnetted* (RFC 950 [Mogul and Postel 1985]). This adds another level to the address hierarchy:

- Network ID (assigned to site)
- Subnet ID (chosen by site)
- Host ID (chosen by site)

The boundary between the network ID and the subnet ID is fixed by the prefix length of the assigned network address. This prefix length is normally assigned by the organization's Internet service provider (ISP). But, the boundary between the subnet ID and the host ID is chosen by the site. All the hosts on a given subnet share a common *subnet mask*, and this mask specifies the boundary between the subnet ID and the host ID. Bits of 1 in the subnet mask cover the network ID and subnet ID, and bits of 0 cover the host ID.

As an example, consider a site that is assigned the prefix 192.168.42.0/24 by its ISP. If it chooses to use a 3-bit subnet ID, 5 bits are left for the host ID, as shown in Figure A.4.

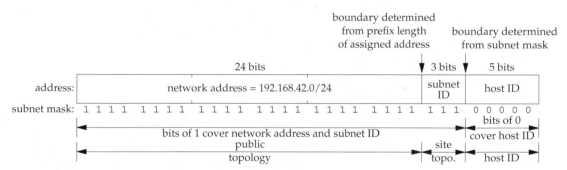

Figure A.4 24-bit network address with 3-bit subnet ID and 5-bit host ID.

This division results in the subnets shown in Figure A.5.

Subnet	Prefix
0	192.168.42.0/27 †
1	192.168.42.32/27
2	192.168.42.64/27
3	192.168.42.96/27
4	192.168.42.128/27
5	192.168.42.160/27
6	192.168.42.192/27
7	192.168.42.224/27 †

Figure A.5 Subnet list for 3-bit subnet ID and 5-bit host ID.

This gives us 6 to 8 subnets (subnet IDs 1−6 or 0−7), each supporting 30 systems (host IDs 1−30). RFC 950 recommends not using the two subnets with a subnet ID of all zero bits or all one bits (the ones marked with a dagger in Figure A.5). Most systems today support these two forms of subnet IDs. The highest host ID (31, in this case) is reserved for the broadcast address. The host ID 0 is reserved for identifying the network and to avoid problems with old systems that used host ID 0 as the broadcast address. However, on controlled networks with no such systems, it may be possible to use host ID 0. In general, network programs need not care about specific subnet or host IDs and should treat IP addresses as opaque values.

Loopback Addresses

By convention, the address 127.0.0.1 is assigned to the loopback interface. Anything sent to this IP address loops around and becomes IP input without ever leaving the machine. We often use this address when testing a client and server on the same host. This address is normally known by the name INADDR_LOOPBACK.

> Any address on the network 127/8 can be assigned to the loopback interface, but 127.0.0.1 is common and is often configured automatically by the IP stack.

Unspecified Address

The address consisting of 32 zero bits is the IPv4 unspecified address. In an IPv4 packet, it is only permitted to appear as the source address in packets sent by a node that is bootstrapping before the node learns its IP address. In the sockets API, this address is called the wildcard address and is normally known by the name INADDR_ANY. Also, specifying it in the sockets API, for example, to bind for a listening TCP socket, indicates that the socket will accept client connections destined to any of the node's IPv4 addresses.

Private Addresses

RFC 1918 [Rekhter et al. 1996] sets aside three address ranges for "private Internets," that is, networks that do not connect to the public Internet without a NAT or proxies in between. These address ranges are shown in Figure A.6:

Number of addresses	Prefix	Range
16,777,216	10/8	10.0.0.0 to 10.255.255.255
1,048,576	172.16/12	172.16.0.0 to 172.31.255.255
65,536	192.168/16	192.168.0.0 to 192.168.255.255

Figure A.6 Ranges for private IPv4 addresses.

These addresses must never appear on the Internet; they are reserved for use in private networks. Many small sites use these private addresses and NAT to a single public IP address visible to the Internet.

Multihoming and Address Aliases

Traditionally, the definition of a *multihomed* host has been a host with multiple interfaces: two Ethernets, for example, or an Ethernet and a point-to-point link. Each interface must generally have a unique IPv4 address. When counting interfaces to determine if a host is multihomed, the loopback interface does not count.

A router, by definition, is multihomed since it forwards packets that arrive on one interface out another interface. But, a multihomed host is not a router unless it forwards packets. Indeed, a multihomed host must not assume it is a router just because the host has multiple interfaces; it must not act as a router unless it has been configured to do so (typically by the administrator enabling a configuration option).

The term "multihoming," however, is more general and covers two different scenarios (Section 3.3.4 of RFC 1122 [Braden 1989]):

- A host with multiple interfaces is multihomed and each interface must in general have its own IP address. ("Unnumbered" interfaces need not have IP addresses, but we mostly encounter these on routers.) This is the traditional definition.

- Newer hosts have the capability of assigning multiple IP addresses to a given physical interface. Each additional IP address, after the first (primary), is called an *alias* or *logical interface*. Often, aliased IP addresses share the same subnet address as the primary address but have different host IDs. But, it is also possible for aliases to have a completely different network address or subnet addresses from the primary. We show an example of aliased addresses in Section 17.6.

Hence, the definition of a multihomed host is one with multiple interfaces visible to the IP layer, regardless of whether those interfaces are physical or logical.

> It is common to give a high-usage server multiple connections to the same Ethernet switch, and to aggregate these connections to appear as one higher bandwidth interface. Although such a system has multiple physical interfaces, it is not considered to be multihomed since only one logical interface is visible to IP.
>
> The term "multihoming" is also used in another context. A network that has multiple connections to the Internet is also called multihomed. For example, some sites have two connections to the Internet instead of one, providing a backup capability. The SCTP transport protocol can potentially take advantage of these multiple connections by communicating that the site is multihomed to its peer.

A.5   IPv6 Addresses

IPv6 addresses are 128 bits long and are usually written as eight 16-bit hexadecimal numbers. The high-order bits of the 128-bit address imply the type of address (RFC 3513 [Hinden and Deering 2003]). Figure A.7 shows the different values of the high-order bits and what type of address these bits imply.

Allocation	Interface ID size	Format prefix	Reference
Unspecified	n/a	`0000 0000 ... 0000 0000` *(128 bits)*	RFC 3513
Loopback	n/a	`0000 0000 ... 0000 0001` *(128 bits)*	RFC 3513
Global unicast address	any	`000`	RFC 3513
Global NSAP-based address	any	`0000001`	RFC 1888
Aggregatable global unicast address	64-bit	`001`	RFC 3587
Global unicast address	64-bit	*(anything not otherwise mentioned)*	RFC 3513
Link-local unicast address	64-bit	`1111 1110 10`	RFC 3513
Site-local unicast address	64-bit	`1111 1110 11`	RFC 3513
Multicast address	n/a	`1111 1111`	RFC 3513

Figure A.7   Meaning of high-order bits of IPv6 addresses.

These high-order bits are called the *format prefix*. For example, if the high-order 3 bits are `001`, the address is called a *global unicast address*. If the high-order 8 bits are `11111111` (`0xff`), it is a multicast address.

Global Unicast Addresses

The IPv6 addressing architecture has evolved based on lessons learned from deployment and from IPv4. The original definition of aggregatable global unicast addresses, which in Figure A.7 begin with a 3-bit prefix of `001`, had a fixed structure built into the address. This structure was removed by RFC 3587 [Hinden, Deering, and Nordmark 2003], and while the addresses beginning with the `001` prefix will be the first ones assigned, there is no difference between them and any other global address. These addresses will be used where IPv4 unicast addresses are used today.

The format of aggregation-based unicast addresses is defined in RFC 3513 [Hinden and Deering 2003] and RFC 3587 [Hinden, Deering, and Nordmark 2003] and contains the following fields, starting at the leftmost bit and going right:

- Global routing prefix (*n* bits)
- Subnet ID (64–*n* bits)
- Interface identifier (64 bits)

Figure A.8 illustrates the format of a global unicast address.

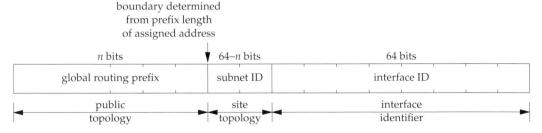

Figure A.8   IPv6 aggregatable global unicast addresses.

The interface ID must be constructed in modified *EUI-64* format. This is a variation of IEEE *EUI-64* format [IEEE 1997], which is a superset of the 48-bit IEEE 802 MAC addresses that are assigned to most LAN interface cards. This identifier should be automatically assigned for an interface based on its hardware MAC address when possible. Details for constructing modified EUI-64-based interface identifiers are in Appendix A of RFC 3513 [Hinden and Deering 2003].

Since a modified EUI-64 can be a globally unique identifier for a given interface, and an interface can identify a user, the modified EUI-64 format raises certain privacy concerns. It may be possible to track the actions and movements of a given user, for example, where they bring their roaming laptop, just from the modified EUI-64 value in their IPv6 address. RFC 3041 [Narten and Draves 2001] describes privacy extensions to generate interface identifiers that change several times per day to avoid this privacy concern.

6bone Test Addresses

The 6bone is a virtual network used for early testing of the IPv6 protocols (Section B.3). Although aggregatable global unicast addresses are being assigned, sites that do not qualify for address space based on the rules used by regional registries can use a special format of these addresses on the 6bone (RFC 2471 [Hinden, Fink, and Postel 1998]), as shown in Figure A.9.

3ffe	6bone site ID	subnet ID	interface ID
16 bits	32 bits	16 bits	64 bits

Figure A.9 IPv6 test addresses for 6bone.

These addresses are considered temporary, and nodes using these addresses will have to renumber when aggregatable global unicast addresses are assigned.

The high-order two bytes are 0x3ffe. The *6bone site ID* is assigned by the chair of the 6bone activity. These assignments are meant to reflect how IPv6 addresses would be assigned in real-world environments. 6bone activity is winding down [Fink and Hinden 2003] now that IPv6 production deployment is well underway (in 2002, more production address allocations were made than the 6bone had allocated in eight years). The *subnet ID* and *interface ID* are used as above for subnet and node identification.

In Section 11.2, we showed the IPv6 address for the host freebsd in Figure 1.16 as 3ffe:b80:1f8d:1:a00:20ff:fea7:686b. The 6bone site ID is 0x0b801f8d and the subnet ID is 0x1. The low-order 64 bits are the modified EUI-64 constructed from the MAC address of the host's Ethernet card.

IPv4-Mapped IPv6 Addresses

IPv4-mapped IPv6 addresses allow IPv6 applications on hosts supporting both IPv4 and IPv6 to communicate with IPv4-only hosts during the transition of the Internet to IPv6. These addresses are automatically created by DNS resolvers (Figure 11.8) when a query is made by an IPv6 application for the IPv6 addresses of a host that has only IPv4 addresses.

We saw in Figure 12.4 that using this type of address with an IPv6 socket causes an IPv4 datagram to be sent to the IPv4 host. These addresses are not stored in any DNS data files; they are created when needed by a resolver.

Figure A.10 shows the format of these addresses The low-order 32 bits contain an IPv4 address.

0000 0000	FFFF	IPv4 address
80 bits	16	32

Figure A.10   IPv4-mapped IPv6 address.

When writing an IPv6 address, a consecutive string of zeros can be abbreviated with two colons. Also, the embedded IPv4 address is written using dotted-decimal notation. For example, we can abbreviate the IPv4-mapped IPv6 address `0:0:0:0:0:FFFF:12.106.32.254` as `::FFFF:12.106.32.254`.

IPv4-Compatible IPv6 Addresses

IPv4-compatible IPv6 addresses were also planned to be used during the transition from IPv4 to IPv6 (RFC 2893 [Gilligan and Nordmark 2000]). The administrator for a host supporting both IPv4 and IPv6 that does not have a neighbor IPv6 router should create a DNS AAAA record containing an IPv4-compatible IPv6 address. Any other IPv6 host with an IPv6 datagram to send to an IPv4-compatible IPv6 address will then *encapsulate* the IPv6 datagram with an IPv4 header; this is called an *automatic tunnel*. However, deployment concerns have reduced the usage of this feature. We will talk more about tunneling in Section B.3 and show an example of this type of IPv6 datagram encapsulated within an IPv4 header in Figure B.2.

Figure A.11 shows the format of an IPv4-compatible IPv6 address.

0000 0000	0000	IPv4 address
80 bits	16	32

Figure A.11   IPv4-compatible IPv6 address.

An example of this type of address is `::12.106.32.254`.

IPv4-compatible IPv6 addresses can also appear in the source or destination of non-tunnelled IPv6 packets when using the SIIT IPv4/IPv6 transition mechanism (RFC 2765 [Nordmark 2000]).

Loopback Address

An IPv6 address consisting of 127 zero bits and a single one bit, written as `::1`, is the IPv6 loopback address. In the sockets API, it is referenced as `in6addr_loopback` or `IN6ADDR_LOOPBACK_INIT`.

Unspecified Address

An IPv6 address consisting of 128 zero bits, written as `0::0`, or just `::`, is the IPv6 unspecified address. In an IPv6 packet, the unspecified address can appear only as the source address in packets sent by a node that is bootstrapping, before the node learns its IPv6 address.

In the sockets API, this address is called the wildcard address. Specifying it, for example, to `bind` for a listening TCP socket, indicates that the socket will accept client connections destined to any of the node's addresses. It is referenced as `in6addr_any` or `IN6ADDR_ANY_INIT`.

Link-Local Address

A link-local address is used on a single link when it is known that the datagram will not be forwarded beyond the local network. Example uses are automatic address configuration at bootstrap time and neighbor discovery (similar to IPv4's ARP). Figure A.12 shows the format of these addresses.

1111111010	0000 0000	interface ID
10 bits	54	64

Figure A.12 IPv6 link-local address.

These addresses always begin with `0xfe80`. An IPv6 router must not forward a datagram with a link-local source or destination address to another link. In Section 11.2, we show the link-local address associated with the name `aix-611`.

Site-Local Address

As of this writing, the IETF IPv6 working group has decided to deprecate site-local addresses in their current form. The forthcoming replacement may or may not finally use the same address range as was originally defined for site-local addresses (`fec0/10`). Site-local addresses were meant to be used for addressing within a site without the need for a global prefix. Figure A.13 shows the originally defined format of these addresses.

1111111011	0000 . . . 0000	subnet ID	interface ID
10 bits	38	16	64

Figure A.13 IPv6 site-local address.

An IPv6 router must not forward a datagram with a site-local source or destination address outside of that site.

A.6   Internet Control Message Protocols (ICMPv4 and ICMPv6)

ICMP is a required and integral part of any IPv4 or IPv6 implementation. ICMP is normally used to communicate error or informational messages between IP nodes, both routers and hosts, but it is occasionally used by applications. The ping and traceroute applications (Chapter 28), for example, both use ICMP.

The first 32 bits of both ICMPv4 and ICMPv6 messages are the same and are shown in Figure A.14. RFC 792 [Postel 1981b] documents ICMPv4 and RFC 2463 [Conta and Deering 1998] documents ICMPv6.

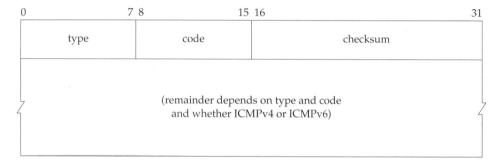

Figure A.14   Format of ICMPv4 and ICMPv6 messages.

The 8-bit *type* is the type of the ICMPv4 or ICMPv6 message and some types have an 8-bit *code* with additional information. The *checksum* is the standard Internet checksum, although in ICMPv4, the checksum covers only the ICMP payload starting with the type field, while the ICMPv6 checksum also includes the IPv6 pseudoheader.

From a network programming perspective, we need to understand which ICMP messages can be returned to an application, what causes an error, and how an error is returned to the application. Figure A.15 lists all the ICMPv4 messages and how they are handled by FreeBSD. Figure A.16 lists the ICMPv6 messages. The third column indicates the errno value returned by those messages that trigger an error to be returned to the application. When using TCP, the error is noted but is not immediately returned. If TCP later gives up on the connection due to a timeout, any ICMP error indication is then returned. When using UDP, the next send or receive operation receives the error, but only when using a connected socket, as described in Section 8.9.

type	*code*	Description	Handled by or `errno`	See also RFC
0	0	echo reply (Ping)	User process (Ping)	792
3		destination unreachable:		
	0	network unreachable	`EHOSTUNREACH`	792
	1	host unreachable	`EHOSTUNREACH`	792
	2	protocol unreachable	`ECONNREFUSED`	792
	3	port unreachable (∗)	`ECONNREFUSED`	792
	4	fragmentation needed but DF bit set	`EMSGSIZE`	792, 1191
	5	source route failed	`EHOSTUNREACH`	792
	6	destination network unknown	`EHOSTUNREACH`	1122
	7	destination host unknown	`EHOSTUNREACH`	1122
	8	source host isolated (obsolete)	`EHOSTUNREACH`	1122
	9	destination network administratively prohibited	`EHOSTUNREACH`	1108, 1122
	10	destination host administratively prohibited	`EHOSTUNREACH`	1108, 1122
	11	network unreachable for TOS	`EHOSTUNREACH`	1122
	12	host unreachable for TOS	`EHOSTUNREACH`	1122
	13	communication administratively prohibited	`ECONNREFUSED`	1812
	14	host precedence violation	`ECONNREFUSED`	1812
	15	precedence cutoff in effect	`ECONNREFUSED`	1812
4	0	source quench	Kernel for TCP, ignored by UDP	792, 1812
5		redirect:		
	0	redirect for network	Kernel updates routing table (†)	792
	1	redirect for host	Kernel updates routing table (†)	792
	2	redirect for TOS and network	Kernel updates routing table (†)	792
	3	redirect for TOS and host	Kernel updates routing table (†)	792
8	0	echo request (Ping)	Kernel generates reply	792
9		router advertisement:		
	0	normal router	User process	1256
	16	mobile-IP-only router	User process	2002
10		router solicitation:		
	0	normal router	User process	1256
	16	mobile-IP-only router	User process	2002
11		time exceeded:		
	0	TTL equals 0 during transit	User process	792
	1	timeout during reassembly	User process	792
12		parameter problem:		
	0	IP header bad (catchall error)	`ENOPROTOOPT`	792
	1	required option missing	`ENOPROTOOPT`	1108, 1122
13	0	timestamp request	Kernel generates reply	792
14	0	timestamp reply	User process	792
15	0	information request (obsolete)	User process	792
16	0	information reply (obsolete)	User process	792
17	0	address mask request	Kernel generates reply	950
18	0	address mask reply	User process	950

Figure A.15 Handling of the ICMP message types by FreeBSD.

∗ - "port unreachable" is only used by transport protocols that do not have their own mechanism for signalling that no process is listening on a port. For example, TCP sends an RST message so it does not need the "port unreachable" message.
† - redirects are ignored by systems acting as routers by forwarding packets.

type	*code*	Description	Handled by or `errno`	See also RFC
1		destination unreachable:		
	0	no route to destination	EHOSTUNREACH	2463
	1	administratively prohibited (firewall filter)	EHOSTUNREACH	2463
	2	beyond scope of source address	ENOPROTOOPT	2463bis (**)
	3	address unreachable	EHOSTDOWN	2463
	4	port unreachable (*)	ECONNREFUSED	2463
2	0	packet too big	Kernel does PMTU discovery	2463
3		time exceeded:		
	0	hop limit exceeded in transit	User process	2463
	1	fragment reassembly time exceeded	User process	2463
4		parameter problem:		
	0	erroneous header field	ENOPROTOOPT	2463
	1	unrecognized next header	ENOPROTOOPT	2463
	2	unrecognized option	ENOPROTOOPT	2463
128	0	echo request (Ping)	Kernel generates reply	2463
129	0	echo reply (Ping)	User process (Ping)	2463
130	0	multicast listener query	User process	2710
131	0	multicast listener report	User process	2710
132	0	multicast listener done	User process	2710
133	0	router solicitation	User process	2461
134	0	router advertisement	User process	2461
135	0	neighbor solicitation	User process	2461
136	0	neighbor advertisement	User process	2461
137	0	redirect	Kernel updates routing table (†)	2461
141	0	inverse neighbor solicitation	User process	3122
142	0	inverse neighbor advertisement	User process	3122

Figure A.16 ICMPv6 messages.

** - "RFC2463bis" designates the revision in progress of RFC 2463—[Conta and Deering 2001].

The notation "user process" means that the kernel does not process the message and it is up to a user process with a raw socket to handle the message. No error return is triggered for these messages. We must also note that different implementations may handle certain messages differently. For example, although Unix systems normally handle router solicitations and router advertisements in a user process, other implementations might handle these messages in the kernel.

ICMPv6 clears the high-order bit of the *type* field for the error messages (*types* 1–4) and sets this bit for the informational messages (*types* 128–137).

Appendix B

Virtual Networks

B.1 Introduction

When a new feature is added to TCP, such as the long fat pipe support defined in RFC 1323, support is required only in the hosts using TCP; no changes are required in the routers. These RFC 1323 changes, for example, are slowly appearing in host implementations of TCP, and when a new TCP connection is established, each end can determine if the other end supports the new feature. If both hosts support the feature, it can be used.

This differs from changes being made to the IP layer, such as multicasting at the end of the 1980s and IPv6 in the mid-1990s, because these new features require changes in all the hosts *and* all the routers. But, what if people want to start using the new features without having to wait for all the systems to be upgraded? To do this, a *virtual network* is established on top of the existing IPv4 Internet using *tunnels*.

B.2 The MBone

Our first example of a virtual network that is built using tunnels is the MBone, which started around 1992 [Eriksson 1994]. If two or more hosts on a LAN support multicasting, multicast applications can be run on all these hosts and communicate with each other. To connect this LAN to some other LAN that also has multicast-capable hosts, a tunnel is configured between one host on each of the LANs, as shown in Figure B.1. We show the following numbered steps in this figure:

1. An application on the source host, MH1, sends a multicast datagram to a class D address.

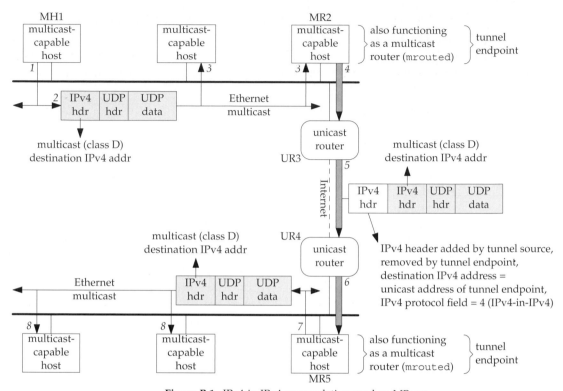

Figure B.1 IPv4-in-IPv4 encapsulation used on MBone.

2. We show this as a UDP datagram, since most multicast applications use UDP. We talk more about multicasting and how to send and receive multicast datagrams in Chapter 21.

3. The datagram is received by all the multicast-capable hosts on the LAN, including MR2. We note that MR2 is also functioning as a multicast router, running the mrouted program, which performs multicast routing.

4. MR2 prepends another IPv4 header at the front of the datagram with the destination IPv4 address of this new header set to the unicast address of the tunnel endpoint, MR5. This unicast address is configured by the administrator of MR2 and is read by the mrouted program when it starts up. Similarly, the unicast address of MR2 is configured for MR5, the other end of the tunnel. The protocol field in the new IPv4 header is set to 4, which is the value for IPv4-in-IPv4 encapsulation. The datagram is sent to the next-hop router, UR3, which we explicitly denote as a unicast router. That is, UR3 does not understand multicasting, which is the whole reason why we are using a tunnel. The shaded portion of the IPv4 datagram has not changed from what was sent in Step 1, other than the decrementing of the TTL field in the shaded IPv4 header.

5. UR3 looks at the destination IPv4 address in the outermost IPv4 header and forwards the datagram to the next-hop router, UR4, another unicast router.

6. UR4 delivers the datagram to its destination, MR5, the tunnel endpoint.

7. MR5 receives the datagram, and since the protocol field indicates IPv4-in-IPv4 encapsulation, it removes the first IPv4 header and then outputs the remainder of the datagram (a copy of what was multicast on the top LAN) as a multicast datagram on its LAN.

8. All the multicast-capable hosts on the lower LAN receive the multicast datagram.

The result is that the multicast datagram sent on the top LAN also gets transmitted as a multicast datagram on the lower LAN. This occurs even though the two routers that we show attached to these two LANs, and all the Internet routers between these two routers, are not multicast-capable.

In this example, we show the multicast routing function being performed by the `mrouted` program running on one host on each LAN. This is how the MBone started. But around 1996, multicast routing functionality started appearing in the routers from most major router vendors. If the two unicast routers UR3 and UR4 in Figure B.1 were multicast-capable, then we would not need to run `mrouted` at all, and UR3 and UR4 would function as multicast routers. But if there are still other routers between UR3 and UR4 that are not multicast-capable, then a tunnel is required. The tunnel endpoints would then be MR3 (a multicast-capable replacement for UR3) and MR4 (a multicast-capable replacement for UR4), not MR2 and MR5.

> In the scenario that we show in Figure B.1, every multicast packet appears twice on the top LAN and twice on the bottom LAN: once as a multicast packet, and again as a unicast packet within the tunnel as the packet goes between the host running `mrouted` and the next-hop unicast router (e.g., between MR2 and UR3, and between UR4 and MR5). This extra copy is the cost of tunneling. The advantage in replacing the two unicast routers UR3 and UR4 in Figure B.1 with multicast-capable routers (what we called MR3 and MR4) is to avoid this extra copy of every multicast packet from appearing on the LANs. Even if MR3 and MR4 must establish a tunnel between themselves because some intermediate routers between them (that we do not show) are not multicast-capable, this is still advantageous since it avoids the duplicate copies on each LAN.

In fact, the MBone is virtually nonexistent at this point, having been replaced with native multicast in this manner. There are probably still tunnels present in the Internet's multicast infrastructure, but they are commonly between native multicast routers inside a service provider's network and are invisible to the end-user.

B.3   The 6bone

The 6bone is a virtual network that was created in 1996 for reasons similar to the MBone: users with islands of IPv6-capable hosts wanted to connect them together using a virtual network without waiting for all the intermediate routers to become IPv6-capable. As of this writing, it is being phased out in favor of native IPv6 deployment; it is expected that the 6bone will cease to operate by June 2006 [Fink and Hinden 2003]. We cover the 6bone here because the examples still demonstrate configured tunnels. We will expand the example to include dynamic tunnels in Section B.4.

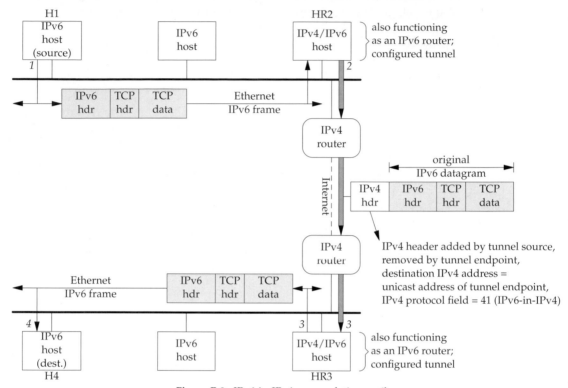

Figure B.2   IPv6-in-IPv4 encapsulation on 6bone.

Figure B.2 shows an example of two IPv6-capable LANs connected with a tunnel across IPv4-only routers. We show the following numbered steps in this figure:

1. Host H1 on the top LAN sends an IPv6 datagram containing a TCP segment to host H4 on the bottom LAN. We designate these two hosts as "IPv6 hosts," but both probably run IPv4 also. The IPv6 routing table on H1 specifies that host HR2 is the next-hop router and an IPv6 datagram is sent to this host.

2. Host HR2 has a configured tunnel to host HR3. This configured tunnel allows IPv6 datagrams to be sent between the two tunnel endpoints across an IPv4 Internet by encapsulating the IPv6 datagram in an IPv4 datagram (called "IPv6-in-IPv4 encapsulation"). The IPv4 protocol field has a value of 41. We note that the two IPv4/IPv6 hosts at the ends of the tunnel, HR2 and HR3, are both acting as IPv6 routers since they are forwarding IPv6 datagrams that they receive on one interface out another interface. The configured tunnel counts as an interface, even though it is a virtual interface and not a physical interface.

3. The tunnel endpoint, HR3, receives the encapsulated datagram, strips off the IPv4 header, and sends the IPv6 datagram onto its LAN.

4. The destination, H4, receives the IPv6 datagram.

B.4   IPv6 Transition: 6to4

The 6to4 transition mechanism, fully described in "Connection of IPv6 Domains via IPv4 Clouds" (RFC 3056 [Carpenter and Moore 2001]), is a method of dynamically creating the tunnels shown in Figure B.2. Unlike previously designed dynamic tunnel mechanisms, which required that each host involved have an IPv4 address and be aware of the tunneling mechanism, 6to4 only involves routers in the tunneling process. This allows for simpler configuration and a central location to enforce security policy. It also permits colocation of 6to4 functionality with the common NAT/firewall function that is often at the edge of a network (e.g., a small NAT/firewall device at the customer's end of a DSL or cable-modem connection).

6to4 addresses are in the range 2002/16. The IPv4 address follows in the next four bytes of the address, as shown in Figure B.3; the 16-bit 2002 prefix and the 32-bit IPv4 address create a 48-bit public topology identifier. This leaves two bytes for the subnet ID before the 64-bit interface ID. For example, the 6to4 prefix corresponding to our host freebsd, with IPv4 address 12.106.32.254, is 2002:c6a:20fe/48.

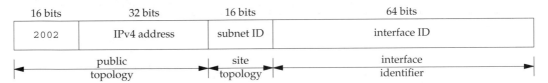

Figure B.3 6to4 addresses.

The advantage of 6to4 over the 6bone is that the tunnels making up the 6to4 infrastructure are built automatically; there is no prearranged configuration required. A site using 6to4 configures a default router using a well-known IPv4 anycast address, 192.88.99.1 (RFC 3068 [Huitema 2001]). This corresponds to the IPv6 address 2002:c058:6301::. Routers in the native IPv6 infrastructure that are willing to act as 6to4 gateways advertise a route to 2002/16 and encapsulate any traffic to the IPv4 address embedded in the 6to4 address. Such routers can be local to a site, regional, or global, depending on the scope of their route advertisements.

The goal for these virtual networks is that over time, as intermediate routers gain the required functionality (e.g., IPv6 routing in terms of the 6bone and other IPv6 transition mechanisms), the virtual networks will disappear.

Appendix C

Debugging Techniques

This appendix contains some hints and techniques for debugging network applications. No single technique is the answer for everyone; instead, there are various tools that we should be familiar with, and then use whatever works in our environment.

C.1 System Call Tracing

Many versions of Unix provide a system call tracing facility. This can often provide a valuable debugging technique.

Working at this level, we need to differentiate between a *system call* and a *function*. The former is an entry point into the kernel, and that is what we are able to trace with the tools we will look at in this section. POSIX and most other standards use the term "function" to describe what appears to the user to be functions, even though on some implementations, they may be system calls. For example, on a Berkeley-derived kernel, `socket` is a system call even though it appears to be a normal C function to the application programmer. But under SVR4, we will see shortly that it is a library function in the sockets library that issues calls to `putmsg` and `getmsg`, these latter two being actual system calls.

In this section, we will examine the system calls involved in running our daytime client. We showed this client in Figure 1.5.

BSD Kernel Sockets

We start with FreeBSD, a Berkeley-derived kernel in which all the socket functions are system calls. The `ktrace` program is provided by FreeBSD to run a program and trace the system calls that are executed. This writes the trace information to a file (whose default name is `ktrace.out`), which we print with `kdump`. We execute our sockets client as

```
freebsd % ktrace daytimetcpcli 192.168.42.2
Tue Aug 19 23:35:10 2003
```

We then execute `kdump` to output the trace information to standard output.

```
3211 daytimetcpcli CALL  socket(0x2,0x1,0)
3211 daytimetcpcli RET   socket 3

3211 daytimetcpcli CALL  connect(0x3,0x7fdfffe820,0x10)
3211 daytimetcpcli RET   connect 0

3211 daytimetcpcli CALL  read(0x3,0x7fdfffe830,0x1000)
3211 daytimetcpcli GIO   fd 3 read 26 bytes
     "Tue Aug 19 23:35:10 2003
     "
3211 daytimetcpcli RET   read 26/0x1a

 . . .

3211 daytimetcpcli CALL  write(0x1,0x204000,0x1a)
3211 daytimetcpcli GIO   fd 1 wrote 26 bytes
     "Tue Aug 19 23:35:10 2003\r
     "
3211 daytimetcpcli RET   write 26/0x1a

3211 daytimetcpcli CALL  read(0x3,0x7fdfffe830,0x1000)
3211 daytimetcpcli GIO   fd 3 read 0 bytes
     " "
3211 daytimetcpcli RET   read 0

3211 daytimetcpcli CALL  exit(0)
```

3211 is the PID. `CALL` identifies a system call, `RET` is the return, and `GIO` stands for generic process I/O. We see the calls to `socket` and `connect`, followed by the call to `read` that returns 26 bytes. Our client writes these bytes to standard output and the next call to `read` returns 0 (EOF).

Solaris 9 Kernel Sockets

Solaris 2.x is based on SVR4 and all the releases before 2.6 have implemented sockets as shown in Figure 31.3. One problem, however, with all SVR4 implementations that implement sockets in this fashion is that they rarely provide 100% compatibility with Berkeley-derived kernel sockets. To provide additional compatibility, versions starting with Solaris 2.6 changed the implementation technique and implemented sockets using a `sockfs` filesystem. This provides kernel sockets, as we can verify using `truss` on our sockets client.

```
solaris % truss -v connect daytimetcpcli 127.0.0.1
Mon Sep  8 12:16:42 2003
```

After the normal library linking, the first system call we see is to `so_socket`, a system call invoked by our call to `socket`.

```
so_socket(PF_INET, SOCK_STREAM, IPPROTO_IP, "", 1) = 3
connect(3, 0xFFBFDEF0, 16, 1)                       = 0
        AF_INET  name = 127.0.0.1  port = 13
read(3, " M o n   S e p     8   1".., 4096)    = 26
Mon Sep  8 12:48:06 2003
write(1, " M o n   S e p     8   1".., 26)     = 26
read(3, 0xFFBFDF03, 4096)                      = 0
_exit(0)
```

The first three arguments to so_socket are our three arguments to socket.

We see that connect is a system call, and truss, when invoked with the -v connect flag, prints the contents of the socket address structure pointed to by the second argument (the IP address and port number). The only system calls that we have replaced with ellipses are a few dealing with standard input and standard output.

C.2   Standard Internet Services

Be familiar with the standard Internet services described in Figure 2.18. We have used the daytime service many times for testing our clients. The discard service is a convenient port to which we can send data. The echo service is similar to the echo server we have used throughout this text.

> Many sites now prevent access to these services through their firewalls because of some denial-of-service attacks using these services in 1996 (Exercise 13.3). Nevertheless, you can hopefully use these services within your own network.

C.3   sock **Program**

Stevens' sock program first appeared in TCPv1, where it was frequently used to generate special case conditions, most of which were then examined in the text using tcpdump. The handy thing about the program is that it generates so many different scenarios, saving us from having to write special test programs.

We do not show the source code for the program in this text (it is over 2,000 lines of C), but the source code is freely available (see the Preface).

The program operates in one of four modes, and each mode can use either TCP or UDP:

- Standard input, standard output client (Figure C.1):

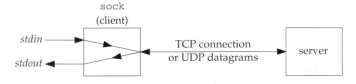

Figure C.1   sock client, standard input, standard output.

In the client mode, everything read from standard input is written to the network, and everything received from the network is written to standard output. The server's IP address and port must be specified, and in the case of TCP, an active open is performed.

- Standard input, standard output server—This mode is similar to the previous mode, except the program binds a well-known port to its socket, and in the case of TCP, performs a passive open.

- Source client (Figure C.2):

Figure C.2 sock program as source client.

The program performs a fixed number of writes to a network of some specified size.

- Sink server (Figure C.3):

Figure C.3 sock program as sink server.

The program performs a fixed number of reads from a network.

These four operating modes correspond to the following four commands:

```
sock [ options ] hostname service
sock [ options ] -s [ hostname ] service
sock [ options ] -i hostname service
sock [ options ] -is [ hostname ] service
```

where *hostname* is a hostname or IP address and *service* is a service name or port number. In the two server modes, the wildcard address is bound, unless the optional *hostname* is specified.

About 40 command-line options can also be specified, and these drive the optional features of the program. We will not detail these options here, but many of the socket options described in Chapter 7 can be set. Executing the program without any arguments prints a summary of the options.

```
-b n  bind n as client's local port number
-c    convert newline to CR/LF & vice versa
-f a.b.c.d.p  foreign IP address = a.b.c.d, foreign port # = p
-g a.b.c.d  loose source route
-h    issue TCP half-close on standard input EOF
-i    "source" data to socket, "sink" data from socket (w/-s)
-j a.b.c.d  join multicast group
-k    write or writev in chunks
-l a.b.c.d.p  client's local IP address = a.b.c.d, local port # = p
-n n  # buffers to write for "source" client (default 1024)
-o    do NOT connect UDP client
-p n  # ms to pause before each read or write (source/sink)
-q n  size of listen queue for TCP server (default 5)
-r n  # bytes per read() for "sink" server (default 1024)
-s    operate as server instead of client
-t n  set multicast ttl
-u    use UDP instead of TCP
-v    verbose
-w n  # bytes per write() for "source" client (default 1024)
-x n  # ms for SO_RCVTIMEO (receive timeout)
-y n  # ms for SO_SNDTIMEO (send timeout)
-A    SO_REUSEADDR option
-B    SO_BROADCAST option
-C    set terminal to cbreak mode
-D    SO_DEBUG option
-E    IP_RECVDSTADDR option
-F    fork after connection accepted (TCP concurrent server)
-G a.b.c.d  strict source route
-H n  IP_TOS option (16=min del, 8=max thru, 4=max rel, 2=min cost)
-I    SIGIO signal
-J n  IP_TTL option
-K    SO_KEEPALIVE option
-L n  SO_LINGER option, n = linger time
-N    TCP_NODELAY option
-O n  # ms to pause after listen, but before first accept
-P n  # ms to pause before first read or write (source/sink)
-Q n  # ms to pause after receiving FIN, but before close
-R n  SO_RCVBUF option
-S n  SO_SNDBUF option
-T    SO_REUSEPORT option
-U n  enter urgent mode before write number n (source only)
-V    use writev() instead of write(); enables -k too
-W    ignore write errors for sink client
-X n  TCP_MAXSEG option (set MSS)
-Y    SO_DONTROUTE option
-Z    MSG_PEEK
```

C.4   Small Test Programs

Another useful debugging technique, one that the authors use all the time, is writing small test programs to see how one specific feature works in a carefully constructed test case. It helps when writing small test programs to have a set of library wrapper functions and some simple error functions, such as the ones we have used throughout this text. This reduces the amount of code that we have to write, but still provides the required testing for errors.

C.5   `tcpdump` Program

An invaluable tool when dealing with network programming is a tool like `tcpdump`. This program reads packets from a network and prints lots of information about the packets. It also has the capability of printing only those packets that match some criteria that we specify. For example,

```
% tcpdump '(udp and port daytime) or icmp'
```

prints only the UDP datagrams with a source or destination port of 13 (the daytime server), or ICMP packets. The following command:

```
% tcpdump 'tcp and port 80 and tcp[13:1] & 2 != 0'
```

prints only the TCP segments with a source or destination port of 80 (the HTTP server) that have the SYN flag set. The SYN flag has a value of 2 in the byte with an offset of 13 from the start of the TCP header. The following command:

```
% tcpdump 'tcp and tcp[0:2] > 7000 and tcp[0:2] <= 7005'
```

prints only TCP segments with a source port between 7001 and 7005. The source port starts at byte offset 0 in the TCP header and occupies 2 bytes.

Appendix A of TCPv1 details the operation of this program in more detail.

> This program is available from `http://www.tcpdump.org/` and works under many different flavors of Unix. It was originally written by Van Jacobson, Craig Leres, and Steven McCanne at LBL, and is now maintained by a team at `tcpdump.org`.
>
> Some vendors supply a program of their own with similar functionality. For example, Solaris 2.x provides the `snoop` program. The advantage of `tcpdump` is that it works under so many versions of Unix, and using a single tool in a heterogeneous environment, instead of a different tool for each environment, is a big advantage.

C.6   `netstat` Program

We have used the `netstat` program many times throughout the text. This program serves multiple purposes:

- It shows the status of networking endpoints. We showed this in Section 5.6, when we followed the status of our endpoint as we started our client and server.

- It shows the multicast groups that a host belongs to on each interface. The -ia flags are the normal way to show this, or the -g flag under Solaris 2.x.

- It shows the per-protocol statistics with the -s option. We showed this in Section 8.13, when looking at the lack of flow control with UDP.

- It displays the routing table with the -r option and the interface information with the -i option. We showed this in Section 1.9, where we used netstat to discover the topology of our network.

There are other uses of netstat and most vendors have added their own features. Check the man page on your system.

C.7 lsof **Program**

The name lsof stands for "list open files." Like tcpdump, it is a publicly available tool that is handy for debugging and has been ported to many versions of Unix.

One common use for lsof with networking is to find which process has a socket open on a specified IP address or port. netstat tells us which IP addresses and ports are in use, and the state of the TCP connections, but it does not identify the process. For example, to find out which process provides the daytime server, we execute the following:

```
freebsd % lsof -i TCP:daytime
COMMAND    PID USER    FD    TYPE             DEVICE SIZE/OFF NODE NAME
inetd      561 root     5u   IPv4 0xfffff8003027a260     0t0   TCP *:daytime (LISTEN)
inetd      561 root     7u   IPv6 0xfffff800302b6720     0t0   TCP *:daytime
```

This tells us the command (this service is provided by the inetd server), its PID, the owner, descriptor (5 for IPv4 and 7 for IPv6, and the u means it is open for read/write), type of socket, address of the protocol control block, size or offset of the file (not meaningful for a socket), protocol type, and name.

One common use for this program is when we start a server that binds its well-known port and get the error that the address is already in use. We then use lsof to find the process that is using the port.

Since lsof reports on open files, it cannot report on network endpoints that are not associated with an open file: TCP endpoints in the TIME_WAIT state.

> ftp://lsof.itap.purdue.edu/pub/tools/unix/lsof/ is the location for this program. It was written by Vic Abell.
>
> Some vendors supply their own utility that does similar things. For example, FreeBSD supplies the fstat program. The advantage in lsof is that it works under so many versions of Unix, and using a single tool in a heterogeneous environment, instead of a different tool for each environment, is a big advantage.

Appendix D

Miscellaneous Source Code

D.1   `unp.h` Header

Almost every program in the text includes our `unp.h` header, shown in Figure D.1. This header includes all the standard system headers that most network programs need, along with some general system headers. It also defines constants such as MAXLINE, ANSI C function prototypes for the functions we define in the text (e.g., `readline`), and all the wrapper functions we use. We do not show these prototypes.

```
                                                                    lib/unp.h
 1 /* Our own header.  Tabs are set for 4 spaces, not 8 */

 2 #ifndef __unp_h
 3 #define __unp_h

 4 #include    "../config.h"        /* configuration options for current OS */
 5                                  /* "../config.h" is generated by configure */

 6 /* If anything changes in the following list of #includes, must change
 7    acsite.m4 also, for configure's tests. */

 8 #include    <sys/types.h>        /* basic system data types */
 9 #include    <sys/socket.h>       /* basic socket definitions */
10 #include    <sys/time.h>         /* timeval{} for select() */
11 #include    <time.h>             /* timespec{} for pselect() */
12 #include    <netinet/in.h>       /* sockaddr_in{} and other Internet defns */
13 #include    <arpa/inet.h>        /* inet(3) functions */
14 #include    <errno.h>
15 #include    <fcntl.h>            /* for nonblocking */
16 #include    <netdb.h>
17 #include    <signal.h>
18 #include    <stdio.h>
```

```
19 #include      <stdlib.h>
20 #include      <string.h>
21 #include      <sys/stat.h>        /* for S_xxx file mode constants */
22 #include      <sys/uio.h>         /* for iovec{} and readv/writev */
23 #include      <unistd.h>
24 #include      <sys/wait.h>
25 #include      <sys/un.h>          /* for Unix domain sockets */

26 #ifdef  HAVE_SYS_SELECT_H
27 # include    <sys/select.h>       /* for convenience */
28 #endif

29 #ifdef  HAVE_SYS_SYSCTL_H
30 # include    <sys/sysctl.h>
31 #endif

32 #ifdef  HAVE_POLL_H
33 # include    <poll.h>             /* for convenience */
34 #endif

35 #ifdef  HAVE_SYS_EVENT_H
36 # include    <sys/event.h>        /* for kqueue */
37 #endif

38 #ifdef  HAVE_STRINGS_H
39 # include    <strings.h>          /* for convenience */
40 #endif

41 /* Three headers are normally needed for socket/file ioctl's:
42  * <sys/ioctl.h>, <sys/filio.h>, and <sys/sockio.h>.
43  */
44 #ifdef  HAVE_SYS_IOCTL_H
45 # include    <sys/ioctl.h>
46 #endif
47 #ifdef  HAVE_SYS_FILIO_H
48 # include    <sys/filio.h>
49 #endif
50 #ifdef  HAVE_SYS_SOCKIO_H
51 # include    <sys/sockio.h>
52 #endif

53 #ifdef  HAVE_PTHREAD_H
54 # include    <pthread.h>
55 #endif

56 #ifdef HAVE_NET_IF_DL_H
57 # include    <net/if_dl.h>
58 #endif

59 #ifdef HAVE_NETINET_SCTP_H
60 #include     <netinet/sctp.h>
61 #endif

62 /* OSF/1 actually disables recv() and send() in <sys/socket.h> */
63 #ifdef  __osf__
64 #undef  recv
65 #undef  send
```

```
66 #define recv(a,b,c,d)    recvfrom(a,b,c,d,0,0)
67 #define send(a,b,c,d)    sendto(a,b,c,d,0,0)
68 #endif

69 #ifndef INADDR_NONE
70 #define INADDR_NONE 0xffffffff  /* should have been in <netinet/in.h> */
71 #endif

72 #ifndef SHUT_RD                    /* these three POSIX names are new */
73 #define SHUT_RD    0               /* shutdown for reading */
74 #define SHUT_WR    1               /* shutdown for writing */
75 #define SHUT_RDWR  2               /* shutdown for reading and writing */
76 #endif

77 #ifndef INET_ADDRSTRLEN
78 #define INET_ADDRSTRLEN     16  /* "ddd.ddd.ddd.ddd\0"
79                                    1234567890123456 */
80 #endif

81 /* Define following even if IPv6 not supported, so we can always allocate
82    an adequately sized buffer without #ifdefs in the code. */
83 #ifndef INET6_ADDRSTRLEN
84 #define INET6_ADDRSTRLEN    46  /* max size of IPv6 address string:
85                      "xxxx:xxxx:xxxx:xxxx:xxxx:xxxx:xxxx:xxxx" or
86                      "xxxx:xxxx:xxxx:xxxx:xxxx:xxxx:ddd.ddd.ddd.ddd\0"
87                       1234567890123456789012345678901234567890123456 */
88 #endif

89 /* Define bzero() as a macro if it's not in standard C library. */
90 #ifndef HAVE_BZERO
91 #define bzero(ptr,n)        memset(ptr, 0, n)
92 #endif

93 /* Older resolvers do not have gethostbyname2() */
94 #ifndef HAVE_GETHOSTBYNAME2
95 #define gethostbyname2(host,family)    gethostbyname((host))
96 #endif

97 /* The structure returned by recvfrom_flags() */
98 struct unp_in_pktinfo {
99     struct in_addr ipi_addr;    /* dst IPv4 address */
100    int     ipi_ifindex;        /* received interface index */
101 };

102 /* We need the newer CMSG_LEN() and CMSG_SPACE() macros, but few
103    implementations support them today.  These two macros really need
104    an ALIGN() macro, but each implementation does this differently. */
105 #ifndef CMSG_LEN
106 #define CMSG_LEN(size)      (sizeof(struct cmsghdr) + (size))
107 #endif
108 #ifndef CMSG_SPACE
109 #define CMSG_SPACE(size)    (sizeof(struct cmsghdr) + (size))
110 #endif

111 /* POSIX requires the SUN_LEN() macro, but not all implementations define
112    it (yet).  Note that this 4.4BSD macro works regardless whether there is
113    a length field or not. */
```

```
114 #ifndef SUN_LEN
115 # define    SUN_LEN(su) \
116     (sizeof(*(su)) - sizeof((su)->sun_path) + strlen((su)->sun_path))
117 #endif

118 /* POSIX renames "Unix domain" as "local IPC."
119    Not all systems define AF_LOCAL and PF_LOCAL (yet). */
120 #ifndef AF_LOCAL
121 #define AF_LOCAL    AF_UNIX
122 #endif
123 #ifndef PF_LOCAL
124 #define PF_LOCAL    PF_UNIX
125 #endif

126 /* POSIX requires that an #include of <poll.h> define INFTIM, but many
127    systems still define it in <sys/stropts.h>.  We don't want to include
128    all the STREAMS stuff if it's not needed, so we just define INFTIM here.
129    This is the standard value, but there's no guarantee it is -1. */
130 #ifndef INFTIM
131 #define INFTIM          (-1)     /* infinite poll timeout */
132 #ifdef  HAVE_POLL_H
133 #define INFTIM_UNPH             /* tell unpxti.h we defined it */
134 #endif
135 #endif

136 /* Following could be derived from SOMAXCONN in <sys/socket.h>, but many
137    kernels still #define it as 5, while actually supporting many more */
138 #define LISTENQ    1024        /* 2nd argument to listen() */

139 /* Miscellaneous constants */
140 #define MAXLINE     4096        /* max text line length */
141 #define BUFFSIZE    8192        /* buffer size for reads and writes */

142 /* Define some port number that can be used for our examples */
143 #define SERV_PORT        9877   /* TCP and UDP */
144 #define SERV_PORT_STR    "9877" /* TCP and UDP */
145 #define UNIXSTR_PATH     "/tmp/unix.str" /* Unix domain stream */
146 #define UNIXDG_PATH      "/tmp/unix.dg"  /* Unix domain datagram */

147 /* Following shortens all the typecasts of pointer arguments: */
148 #define SA  struct sockaddr

149 #define HAVE_STRUCT_SOCKADDR_STORAGE
150 #ifndef HAVE_STRUCT_SOCKADDR_STORAGE
151 /*
152  * RFC 3493: protocol-independent placeholder for socket addresses
153  */
154 #define __SS_MAXSIZE    128
155 #define __SS_ALIGNSIZE  (sizeof(int64_t))
156 #ifdef HAVE_SOCKADDR_SA_LEN
157 #define __SS_PAD1SIZE   (__SS_ALIGNSIZE - sizeof(u_char) - sizeof(sa_family_t))
158 #else
159 #define __SS_PAD1SIZE   (__SS_ALIGNSIZE - sizeof(sa_family_t))
160 #endif
161 #define __SS_PAD2SIZE   (__SS_MAXSIZE - 2*__SS_ALIGNSIZE)

162 struct sockaddr_storage {
```

```
163 #ifdef HAVE_SOCKADDR_SA_LEN
164     u_char   ss_len;
165 #endif
166     sa_family_t ss_family;
167     char     __ss_pad1[__SS_PAD1SIZE];
168     int64_t  __ss_align;
169     char     __ss_pad2[__SS_PAD2SIZE];
170 };
171 #endif

172 #define FILE_MODE    (S_IRUSR | S_IWUSR | S_IRGRP | S_IROTH)
173                      /* default file access permissions for new files */
174 #define DIR_MODE     (FILE_MODE | S_IXUSR | S_IXGRP | S_IXOTH)
175                      /* default permissions for new directories */

176 typedef void Sigfunc(int);     /* for signal handlers */

177 #define min(a,b)    ((a) < (b) ? (a) : (b))
178 #define max(a,b)    ((a) > (b) ? (a) : (b))

179 #ifndef HAVE_ADDRINFO_STRUCT
180 # include   "../lib/addrinfo.h"
181 #endif

182 #ifndef HAVE_IF_NAMEINDEX_STRUCT
183 struct if_nameindex {
184     unsigned int if_index;     /* 1, 2, ... */
185     char  *if_name;            /* null-terminated name: "le0", ... */
186 };
187 #endif

188 #ifndef HAVE_TIMESPEC_STRUCT
189 struct timespec {
190     time_t  tv_sec;            /* seconds */
191     long    tv_nsec;           /* and nanoseconds */
192 };
193 #endif
```

——— *lib/unp.h*

Figure D.1 Our header unp.h.

D.2   `config.h` **Header**

The GNU `autoconf` tool was used to aid in the portability of all the source code in this text. It is available from `http://ftp.gnu.org/gnu/autoconf`. This tool generates a shell script named `configure` that you must run after downloading the software onto your system. This script determines the features provided by your Unix system: Do socket address structures have a length field? Is multicasting supported? Are datalink socket address structures supported? and so on, generating a header named `config.h`. This header is the first header included by our `unp.h` header in the previous section. Figure D.2 shows the `config.h` header for FreeBSD 5.1.

The lines beginning with `#define` in column 1 are for features that the system provides. The lines that are commented out and contain #undef are features that the system does not provide.

sparc64-unknown-freebsd5.1/config.h

```
 1 /* config.h.  Generated automatically by configure.  */
 2 /* config.h.in.  Generated automatically from configure.in by autoheader.  */

 3 /* CPU, vendor, and operating system */
 4 #define CPU_VENDOR_OS "sparc64-unknown-freebsd5.1"

 5 /* Define if <netdb.h> defines struct addrinfo */
 6 #define HAVE_ADDRINFO_STRUCT 1

 7 /* Define if you have the <arpa/inet.h> header file. */
 8 #define HAVE_ARPA_INET_H 1

 9 /* Define if you have the bzero function. */
10 #define HAVE_BZERO 1

11 /* Define if the /dev/streams/xtiso/tcp device exists */
12 /* #undef HAVE_DEV_STREAMS_XTISO_TCP */

13 /* Define if the /dev/tcp device exists */
14 /* #undef HAVE_DEV_TCP */

15 /* Define if the /dev/xti/tcp device exists */
16 /* #undef HAVE_DEV_XTI_TCP */

17 /* Define if you have the <errno.h> header file. */
18 #define HAVE_ERRNO_H 1

19 /* Define if you have the <fcntl.h> header file. */
20 #define HAVE_FCNTL_H 1

21 /* Define if you have the getaddrinfo function. */
22 #define HAVE_GETADDRINFO 1

23 /* define if getaddrinfo prototype is in <netdb.h> */
24 #define HAVE_GETADDRINFO_PROTO 1

25 /* Define if you have the gethostbyname2 function. */
26 #define HAVE_GETHOSTBYNAME2 1

27 /* Define if you have the gethostbyname_r function. */
28 /* #undef HAVE_GETHOSTBYNAME_R */
```

```
29 /* Define if you have the gethostname function. */
30 #define HAVE_GETHOSTNAME 1

31 /* define if gethostname prototype is in <unistd.h> */
32 #define HAVE_GETHOSTNAME_PROTO 1

33 /* Define if you have the getnameinfo function. */
34 #define HAVE_GETNAMEINFO 1

35 /* define if getnameinfo prototype is in <netdb.h> */
36 #define HAVE_GETNAMEINFO_PROTO 1

37 /* define if getrusage prototype is in <sys/resource.h> */
38 #define HAVE_GETRUSAGE_PROTO 1

39 /* Define if you have the hstrerror function. */
40 #define HAVE_HSTRERROR 1

41 /* define if hstrerror prototype is in <netdb.h> */
42 #define HAVE_HSTRERROR_PROTO 1

43 /* Define if <net/if.h> defines struct if_nameindex */
44 #define HAVE_IF_NAMEINDEX_STRUCT 1

45 /* Define if you have the if_nametoindex function. */
46 #define HAVE_IF_NAMETOINDEX 1

47 /* define if if_nametoindex prototype is in <net/if.h> */
48 #define HAVE_IF_NAMETOINDEX_PROTO 1

49 /* Define if you have the inet_aton function. */
50 #define HAVE_INET_ATON 1

51 /* define if inet_aton prototype is in <arpa/inet.h> */
52 #define HAVE_INET_ATON_PROTO 1

53 /* Define if you have the inet_pton function. */
54 #define HAVE_INET_PTON 1

55 /* define if inet_pton prototype is in <arpa/inet.h> */
56 #define HAVE_INET_PTON_PROTO 1

57 /* Define if you have the kevent function. */
58 #define HAVE_KEVENT 1

59 /* Define if you have the kqueue function. */
60 #define HAVE_KQUEUE 1

61 /* Define if you have the nsl library (-lnsl). */
62 /* #undef HAVE_LIBNSL */

63 /* Define if you have the pthread library (-lpthread). */
64 /* #undef HAVE_LIBPTHREAD */

65 /* Define if you have the pthreads library (-lpthreads). */
66 /* #undef HAVE_LIBPTHREADS */

67 /* Define if you have the resolv library (-lresolv). */
68 /* #undef HAVE_LIBRESOLV */
```

```
 69 /* Define if you have the xti library (-lxti). */
 70 /* #undef HAVE_LIBXTI */

 71 /* Define if you have the mkstemp function. */
 72 #define HAVE_MKSTEMP 1

 73 /* define if struct msghdr contains the msg_control element */
 74 #define HAVE_MSGHDR_MSG_CONTROL 1

 75 /* Define if you have the <netconfig.h> header file. */
 76 #define HAVE_NETCONFIG_H 1

 77 /* Define if you have the <netdb.h> header file. */
 78 #define HAVE_NETDB_H 1

 79 /* Define if you have the <netdir.h> header file. */
 80 /* #undef HAVE_NETDIR_H */

 81 /* Define if you have the <netinet/in.h> header file. */
 82 #define HAVE_NETINET_IN_H 1

 83 /* Define if you have the <net/if_dl.h> header file. */
 84 #define HAVE_NET_IF_DL_H 1

 85 /* Define if you have the poll function. */
 86 #define HAVE_POLL 1

 87 /* Define if you have the <poll.h> header file. */
 88 #define HAVE_POLL_H 1

 89 /* Define if you have the pselect function. */
 90 #define HAVE_PSELECT 1

 91 /* define if pselect prototype is in <sys/stat.h> */
 92 #define HAVE_PSELECT_PROTO 1

 93 /* Define if you have the <pthread.h> header file. */
 94 #define HAVE_PTHREAD_H 1

 95 /* Define if you have the <signal.h> header file. */
 96 #define HAVE_SIGNAL_H 1

 97 /* Define if you have the snprintf function. */
 98 #define HAVE_SNPRINTF 1

 99 /* define if snprintf prototype is in <stdio.h> */
100 #define HAVE_SNPRINTF_PROTO 1

101 /* Define if <net/if_dl.h> defines struct sockaddr_dl */
102 #define HAVE_SOCKADDR_DL_STRUCT 1

103 /* define if socket address structures have length fields */
104 #define HAVE_SOCKADDR_SA_LEN 1

105 /* Define if you have the sockatmark function. */
106 #define HAVE_SOCKATMARK 1

107 /* define if sockatmark prototype is in <sys/socket.h> */
108 #define HAVE_SOCKATMARK_PROTO 1
```

```
109 /* Define if you have the <stdio.h> header file. */
110 #define HAVE_STDIO_H 1

111 /* Define if you have the <stdlib.h> header file. */
112 #define HAVE_STDLIB_H 1

113 /* Define if you have the <strings.h> header file. */
114 #define HAVE_STRINGS_H 1

115 /* Define if you have the <string.h> header file. */
116 #define HAVE_STRING_H 1

117 /* Define if you have the <stropts.h> header file. */
118 /* #undef HAVE_STROPTS_H */

119 /* Define if ifr_mtu is member of struct ifreq. */
120 #define HAVE_STRUCT_IFREQ_IFR_MTU 1

121 /* Define if the system has the type struct sockaddr_storage. */
122 #define HAVE_STRUCT_SOCKADDR_STORAGE 1

123 /* Define if you have the <sys/event.h> header file. */
124 #define HAVE_SYS_EVENT_H 1

125 /* Define if you have the <sys/filio.h> header file. */
126 #define HAVE_SYS_FILIO_H 1

127 /* Define if you have the <sys/ioctl.h> header file. */
128 #define HAVE_SYS_IOCTL_H 1

129 /* Define if you have the <sys/select.h> header file. */
130 #define HAVE_SYS_SELECT_H 1

131 /* Define if you have the <sys/socket.h> header file. */
132 #define HAVE_SYS_SOCKET_H 1

133 /* Define if you have the <sys/sockio.h> header file. */
134 #define HAVE_SYS_SOCKIO_H 1

135 /* Define if you have the <sys/stat.h> header file. */
136 #define HAVE_SYS_STAT_H 1

137 /* Define if you have the <sys/sysctl.h> header file. */
138 #define HAVE_SYS_SYSCTL_H 1

139 /* Define if you have the <sys/time.h> header file. */
140 #define HAVE_SYS_TIME_H 1

141 /* Define if you have the <sys/types.h> header file. */
142 #define HAVE_SYS_TYPES_H 1

143 /* Define if you have the <sys/uio.h> header file. */
144 #define HAVE_SYS_UIO_H 1

145 /* Define if you have the <sys/un.h> header file. */
146 #define HAVE_SYS_UN_H 1

147 /* Define if you have the <sys/wait.h> header file. */
148 #define HAVE_SYS_WAIT_H 1
```

```
149 /* Define if <time.h> defines struct timespec */
150 #define HAVE_TIMESPEC_STRUCT 1

151 /* Define if you have the <time.h> header file. */
152 #dcfinc HAVE_TIME_II 1

153 /* Define if you have the <unistd.h> header file. */
154 #define HAVE_UNISTD_H 1

155 /* Define if you have the vsnprintf function. */
156 #define HAVE_VSNPRINTF 1

157 /* Define if you have the <xti.h> header file. */
158 /* #undef HAVE_XTI_H */

159 /* Define if you have the <xti_inet.h> header file. */
160 /* #undef HAVE_XTI_INET_H */

161 /* Define if the system supports IPv4 */
162 #define IPV4 1

163 /* Define if the system supports IPv6 */
164 #define IPV6 1

165 /* Define if the system supports IPv4 */
166 #define IPv4 1

167 /* Define if the system supports IPv6 */
168 #define IPv6 1

169 /* Define if the system supports IP Multicast */
170 #define MCAST 1

171 /* the size of the sa_family field in a socket address structure */
172 /* #undef SA_FAMILY_T */

173 /* Define if you have the ANSI C header files. */
174 #define STDC_HEADERS 1

175 /* Define if you can safely include both <sys/time.h> and <time.h>. */
176 #define TIME_WITH_SYS_TIME 1

177 /* Define if the system supports UNIX domain sockets */
178 #define UNIXDOMAIN 1

179 /* Define if the system supports UNIX domain sockets */
180 #define UNIXdomain 1

181 /* 16 bit signed type */
182 /* #undef int16_t */

183 /* 32 bit signed type */
184 /* #undef int32_t */

185 /* the type of the sa_family struct element */
186 /* #undef sa_family_t */

187 /* unsigned integer type of the result of the sizeof operator */
188 /* #undef size_t */
```

```
189 /* a type appropriate for address */
190 /* #undef socklen_t */

191 /* define to __ss_family if sockaddr_storage has that instead of ss_family */
192 /* #undef ss_family */

193 /* a signed type appropriate for a count of bytes or an error indication */
194 /* #undef ssize_t */

195 /* scalar type */
196 #define t_scalar_t int32_t

197 /* unsigned scalar type */
198 #define t_uscalar_t uint32_t

199 /* 16 bit unsigned type */
200 /* #undef uint16_t */

201 /* 32 bit unsigned type */
202 /* #undef uint32_t */

203         /* -bit unsigned type */
204 /* #undef uint8_t */
```
sparc64-unknown-freebsd5.1/config.h

Figure D.2 Our config.h header for FreeBSD 5.1.

D.3   Standard Error Functions

We define our own set of error functions that are used throughout the text to handle error conditions. The reason for using our own error functions is to let us write our error handling with a single line of C code, as in

```
if  (error condition)
        err_sys (printf format with any number of arguments) ;
```

instead of

```
if  (error condition)  {
        char   buff[200];
        snprintf(buff, sizeof(buff), printf format with any number of arguments) ;
        perror(buff);
        exit(1);
}
```

Our error functions use the variable-length argument list facility from ANSI C. See Section 7.3 of [Kernighan and Ritchie 1988] for additional details.

Figure D.3 lists the differences between the various error functions. If the global integer daemon_proc is nonzero, the message is passed to syslog with the indicated level; otherwise, the error is output to standard error.

Function	strerror (errno) ?	Terminate ?	syslog level
err_dump	yes	abort();	LOG_ERR
err_msg	no	return;	LOG_INFO
err_quit	no	exit(1);	LOG_ERR
err_ret	yes	return;	LOG_INFO
err_sys	yes	exit(1);	LOG_ERR

Figure D.3   Summary of our standard error functions.

Figure D.4 shows the first five functions from Figure D.3.

lib/error.c
```
 1 #include    "unp.h"

 2 #include    <stdarg.h>          /* ANSI C header file */
 3 #include    <syslog.h>          /* for syslog() */

 4 int     daemon_proc;            /* set nonzero by daemon_init() */

 5 static void err_doit(int, int, const char *, va_list);

 6 /* Nonfatal error related to system call
 7  * Print message and return */

 8 void
 9 err_ret(const char *fmt, ...)
10 {
11      va_list ap;

12      va_start(ap, fmt);
```

```
13       err_doit(1, LOG_INFO, fmt, ap);
14       va_end(ap);
15       return;
16 }

17 /* Fatal error related to system call
18  * Print message and terminate */

19 void
20 err_sys(const char *fmt, ...)
21 {
22       va_list ap;

23       va_start(ap, fmt);
24       err_doit(1, LOG_ERR, fmt, ap);
25       va_end(ap);
26       exit(1);
27 }

28 /* Fatal error related to system call
29  * Print message, dump core, and terminate */

30 void
31 err_dump(const char *fmt, ...)
32 {
33       va_list ap;

34       va_start(ap, fmt);
35       err_doit(1, LOG_ERR, fmt, ap);
36       va_end(ap);
37       abort();                          /* dump core and terminate */
38       exit(1);                          /* shouldn't get here */
39 }

40 /* Nonfatal error unrelated to system call
41  * Print message and return */

42 void
43 err_msg(const char *fmt, ...)
44 {
45       va_list ap;

46       va_start(ap, fmt);
47       err_doit(0, LOG_INFO, fmt, ap);
48       va_end(ap);
49       return;
50 }

51 /* Fatal error unrelated to system call
52  * Print message and terminate */

53 void
54 err_quit(const char *fmt, ...)
55 {
56       va_list ap;

57       va_start(ap, fmt);
58       err_doit(0, LOG_ERR, fmt, ap);
```

```
59      va_end(ap);
60      exit(1);
61  }

62  /* Print message and return to caller
63   * Caller specifies "errnoflag" and "level" */

64  static void
65  err_doit(int errnoflag, int level, const char *fmt, va_list ap)
66  {
67      int     errno_save, n;
68      char    buf[MAXLINE + 1];

69      errno_save = errno;         /* value caller might want printed */
70  #ifdef  HAVE_VSNPRINTF
71      vsnprintf(buf, MAXLINE, fmt, ap);   /* safe */
72  #else
73      vsprintf(buf, fmt, ap);     /* not safe */
74  #endif
75      n = strlen(buf);
76      if (errnoflag)
77          snprintf(buf + n, MAXLINE - n, ": %s", strerror(errno_save));
78      strcat(buf, "\n");

79      if (daemon_proc) {
80          syslog(level, buf);
81      } else {
82          fflush(stdout);         /* in case stdout and stderr are the same */
83          fputs(buf, stderr);
84          fflush(stderr);
85      }
86      return;
87  }
```
—— *lib/error.c*

Figure D.4 Our standard error functions.

Appendix E

Solutions to Selected Exercises

Chapter 1

1.3 Under Solaris, we get the following:

```
solaris % daytimetcpcli 127.0.0.1
socket error: Protocol not supported
```

To find more information on this error, we first use grep to search for the string Protocol not supported in the <sys/errno.h> header.

```
solaris % grep 'Protocol not supported' /usr/include/sys/errno.h
#define EPROTONOSUPPORT 120    /* Protocol not supported */
```

This is the errno returned by socket. We then look at the man page:

```
aix % man socket
```

Most man pages give additional, albeit terse, information toward the end under a heading of the form "Errors."

1.4 We change the first declaration to be the following:

```
int    sockfd, n, counter = 0;
```

We add the statement

```
counter++;
```

as the first statement of the while loop. Finally, we execute

```
printf("counter = %d\n", counter);
```

before terminating. The value printed is always 1.

1.5   We declare an int named i and change the call to write to be the following:

```
for (i = 0; i < strlen(buff); i++)
    Write(connfd, &buff[i], 1);
```

The results vary, depending on the client host and server host. If the client and server are on the same host, the counter is normally 1, which means even though the server does 26 writes, the data is returned by a single read. But, one combination of client and server may produce two packets, and another combination 26 packets. (Our discussion of the Nagle algorithm in Section 7.9 explains one reason for this.)

The purpose of this example is to reiterate that different TCPs do different things with the data and our application must be prepared to read the data as a stream of bytes until the end of the data stream is encountered.

Chapter 2

2.1   Visit http://www.iana.org/numbers.htm and find the registry called "IP Version Number." Version 0 is reserved, versions 1–3 are unassigned, and version 5 is the Internet Stream Protocol.

2.2   All RFCs are available at no charge through electronic mail, anonymous FTP, or the Web. A starting point is http://www.ietf.org. The directory ftp://ftp.rfc-editor.org/in-notes is one location for RFCs. To start, fetch the current RFC index, normally the file rfc-index.txt, also available in an HTML version at http://www.rfc-editor.org/rfc-index.html. If we search the RFC index (see the solution to the previous exercise) with an editor of some form, looking for the term "Stream," we find that RFC 1819 defines Version 2 of the Internet Stream Protocol. Whenever looking for information that might be covered by an RFC, the RFC index should be searched.

2.3   With IPv4, this generates a 576-byte IP datagram (20 bytes for the IPv4 header and 20 bytes for the TCP header), the minimum reassembly buffer size with IPv4.

2.4   In this example, the server performs the active close, not the client.

2.5   The host on the token ring cannot send packets with more than 1,460 bytes of data because the MSS it received was 1,460. The host on the Ethernet can send packets with up to 4,096 bytes of data, but it will not exceed the MTU of the outgoing interface (the Ethernet) to avoid fragmentation. TCP cannot exceed the MSS announced by the other end, but it can always send less than this amount.

2.6   The "Protocol Numbers" section of the Assigned Numbers Web page (http://www.iana.org/numbers.htm) shows a value of 89 for OSPF.

2.7   A selective acknowledgment only indicates that the data covered by the sequence numbers reflected in the selective acknowledgment message was received. Only a cumulative acknowledgment says that the data up to and including the sequence number in the cumulative acknowledgment message was received. When freeing data from the send buffer based on a selective acknowledgment, the system may only free the exact data that was acknowledged, and not any before or after the selective acknowledgment.

Chapter 3

3.1 In C, a function cannot change the value of an argument that is passed by value. For a called function to modify a value passed by the caller requires that the caller pass a pointer to the value to be modified.

3.2 The pointer must be incremented by the number of bytes read or written, but C does not allow a void pointer to be incremented (since the compiler does not know the datatype pointed to).

Chapter 4

4.1 Look at the definitions for the constants beginning with INADDR_ except INADDR_ANY (which is all zero bits) and INADDR_NONE (which is all one bits). For example, the class D multicast address INADDR_MAX_LOCAL_GROUP is defined as 0xe00000ff with the comment "224.0.0.255," which is clearly in host byte order.

4.2 Here are the new lines added after the call to connect:

```
len = sizeof(cliaddr);
Getsockname(sockfd, (SA *) &cliaddr, &len);
printf("local addr: %s\n",
        Sock_ntop((SA *) &cliaddr, len));
```

This requires a declaration of len as a socklen_t and a declaration of cliaddr as a struct sockaddr_in. Notice that the value-result argument for getsockname (len) must be initialized before the call to the size of the variable pointed to by the second argument. The most common programming error with value-result arguments is to forget this initialization.

4.3 When the child calls close, the reference count is decremented from 2 to 1, so a FIN is not sent to the client. Later, when the parent calls close, the reference count is decremented to 0 and the FIN is sent.

4.4 accept returns EINVAL, since the first argument is not a listening socket.

4.5 Without a call to bind, the call to listen assigns an ephemeral port to the listening socket.

Chapter 5

5.1 The duration of the TIME_WAIT state should be between 1 and 4 minutes, giving an MSL between 30 seconds and 2 minutes.

5.2 Our client/server programs do not work with a binary file. Assume the first 3 bytes in the file are binary 1, binary 0, and a newline. The call to fgets in

Figure 5.5 reads up to MAXLINE-1 characters, or until a newline is encountered, or up through the EOF. In this example, it will read the first three characters and then terminate the string with a null byte. But, our call to strlen in Figure 5.5 returns 1, since it stops at the first null byte. One byte is sent to the server, but the server blocks in its call to readline, waiting for a newline character. The client blocks waiting for the server's reply. This is called a *deadlock*: Both processes are blocked waiting for something that will never arrive from the other one. The problem here is that fgets signifies the end of the data that it returns with a null byte, so the data that it reads cannot contain any null bytes.

5.3   Telnet converts the input lines into NVT ASCII (Section 26.4 of TCPv1), which terminates every line with the two-character sequence of a CR (carriage return) followed by an LF (linefeed). Our client adds only a newline, which is actually a linefeed character. Nevertheless, we can use the Telnet client to communicate with our server as our server echoes back every character, including the CR that precedes each newline.

5.4   No, the final two segments of the connection termination sequence are not sent. When the client sends the data to the server, after we kill the server child (the "another line"), the server TCP responds with an RST. The RST aborts the connection and also prevents the server end of the connection (the end that did the active close) from passing through the TIME_WAIT state.

5.5   Nothing changes because the server process that is started on the server host creates a listening socket and is waiting for new connection requests to arrive. What we send in Step 3 is a data segment destined for an ESTABLISHED TCP connection. Our server with the listening socket never sees this data segment, and the server TCP still responds to it with an RST.

5.6   Figure E.1 shows the program. Running this program under Solaris generates the following:

```
solaris % tsigpipe 192.168.1.10
SIGPIPE received
write error: Broken pipe
```

The initial sleep of two seconds is to let the daytime server send its reply and close its end of the connection. Our first write sends a data segment to the server, which responds with an RST (since the daytime server has completely closed its socket). Note that our TCP allows us to write to a socket that has received a FIN. The second sleep lets the server's RST be received, and our second write generates SIGPIPE. Since our signal handler returns, write returns an error of EPIPE.

5.7   Assuming the server host supports the *weak end system model* (which we describe in Section 8.8), everything works. That is, the server host will accept an incoming IP datagram (which contains a TCP segment in this case) arriving on the leftmost datalink, even though the destination IP address is the address of the rightmost datalink. We can test this by running our server on our host linux (Figure 1.16) and then starting the client on our host solaris, but specifying the other IP

—————————————————————————————— tcpcliserv/tsigpipe.c

```
 1 #include     "unp.h"

 2 void
 3 sig_pipe(int signo)
 4 {
 5     printf("SIGPIPE received\n");
 6     return;
 7 }

 8 int
 9 main(int argc, char **argv)
10 {
11     int     sockfd;
12     struct sockaddr_in servaddr;

13     if (argc != 2)
14         err_quit("usage: tcpcli <IPaddress>");

15     sockfd = Socket(AF_INET, SOCK_STREAM, 0);

16     bzero(&servaddr, sizeof(servaddr));
17     servaddr.sin_family = AF_INET;
18     servaddr.sin_port = htons(13);   /* daytime server */
19     Inet_pton(AF_INET, argv[1], &servaddr.sin_addr);

20     Signal(SIGPIPE, sig_pipe);

21     Connect(sockfd, (SA *) &servaddr, sizeof(servaddr));

22     sleep(2);
23     Write(sockfd, "hello", 5);
24     sleep(2);
25     Write(sockfd, "world", 5);

26     exit(0);
27 }
```

—————————————————————————————— tcpcliserv/tsigpipe.c

Figure E.1 Generate `SIGPIPE`.

address of the server (206.168.112.96) to the client. After the connection is established, if we run `netstat` on the server, we see that the local IP address is the destination IP address from the client's SYN, not the IP address of the datalink on which the SYN arrived (as we mentioned in Section 4.4).

5.8   Our client was on a little-endian Intel system, where the 32-bit integer with a value of 1 was stored as shown in Figure E.2.

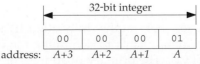

Figure E.2 Representation of the 32-bit integer 1 in little-endian format.

The 4 bytes are sent across the socket in the order *A*, *A+1*, *A+2*, and *A+3* where they are stored in the big-endian format, as shown in Figure E.3.

01	00	00	00
A	*A+1*	*A+2*	*A+3*

Figure E.3 Representation of the 32-bit integer from Figure E.2 in big-endian format.

This value of `0x01000000` is interpreted as 16,777,216. Similarly, the integer 2 sent by the client will be interpreted at the server as `0x02000000`, or 33,554,432. The sum of these two integers is 50,331,648, or `0x03000000`. When this big-endian value on the server is sent to the client, it is interpreted on the client as the integer value 3.

The 32-bit integer value of −22 is represented on the little-endian system as shown in Figure E.4, assuming a two's-complement representation of negative numbers.

ff	ff	ff	ea
A+3	*A+2*	*A+1*	*A*

Figure E.4 Representation of the 32-bit integer −22 in little-endian format.

This is interpreted on the big-endian server as `0xeaffffff`, or −352,321,537. Similarly, the little-endian representation of −77 is `0xffffffb3`, but this is represented on the big-endian server as `0xb3ffffff`, or −1,275,068,417. The addition on the server yields a binary result of `0x9efffffe`, or −1,627,389,954. This big-endian value is sent across the socket to the client where it is interpreted as the little-endian value `0xfefffff9e`, or −16,777,314, which is the value printed in our example.

5.9   The technique is correct (converting the binary values to network byte order), but the two functions `htonl` and `ntohl` cannot be used. Even though the `l` in these functions once meant "long," these functions operate on 32-bit integers (Section 3.4). On a 64-bit system, a `long` will probably occupy 64 bits and these two functions will not work correctly. One might define two new functions, `hton64` and `ntoh64`, to solve this problem, but this will not work on systems that represent `long`s using 32 bits.

5.10   In the first scenario, the server blocks forever in the call to `readn` in Figure 5.20 because the client sends two 32-bit values but the server is waiting for two 64-bit values. Swapping the client and server between the two hosts causes the client to send two 64-bit values, but the server reads only the first 64 bits, interpreting them as two 32-bit values. The second 64-bit value remains in the server's socket receive buffer. The server writes back one 32-bit value and the client will block forever in its call to `readn` in Figure 5.19, waiting to read one 64-bit value.

5.11   IP's routing function looks at the destination IP address (the server's IP address) and searches the routing table to determine the outgoing interface and next hop (Chapter 9 of TCPv1). The primary IP address of the outgoing interface is used as the source IP address, assuming the socket has not already bound a local IP address.

Chapter 6

6.1   The array of integers is contained within a structure and C allows structures to be assigned across an equals sign.

6.2   If `select` tells us that the socket is writable, the socket send buffer has room for 8,192 bytes, but when we call `write` for this blocking socket with a buffer length of 8,193 bytes, `write` can block, waiting for room for the final byte. Read operations on a blocking socket will always return a short count if some data is available, but write operations on a blocking socket will block until all the data can be accepted by the kernel. Therefore, when using `select` to test for writability, we must set the socket to nonblocking to avoid blocking.

6.3   If both descriptors are readable, only the first test is performed, the test of the socket. But this does not break the client; it just makes it less efficient. That is, if `select` returns with both descriptors readable, the first `if` is true, causing a `readline` from the socket followed by an `fputs` to standard output. The next `if` is skipped (because of the `else` we prepended), but `select` is then called again and immediately finds standard input readable and returns immediately. The key concept here is that what clears the condition of "standard input being readable" is not `select` returning, but reading from the descriptor.

6.4   Use the `getrlimit` function to fetch the values for the `RLIMIT_NOFILE` resource and then call `setrlimit` to set the current soft limit (`rlim_cur`) to the hard limit (`rlim_max`). For example, under Solaris 2.5, the soft limit is 64 but any process can increase this to the default hard limit of 1,024.

`getrlimit` and `setrlimit` are not part of POSIX.1, but are required by Unix 98.

6.5   The server application continually sends data to the client, which the client TCP acknowledges and throws away.

6.6   `shutdown` with `SHUT_WR` or `SHUT_RDWR` always sends a FIN, while `close` sends a FIN only if the descriptor reference count is 1 when `close` is called.

6.7   `read` returns an error, and our `Read` wrapper function terminates the server. Servers must be more robust than this. Notice that we handle this condition in Figure 6.26, although even that code is inadequate. Consider what happens if connectivity is lost between the client and server and one of the server's responses eventually times out. The error returned could be `ETIMEDOUT`.

In general, a server should not abort for errors like these. It should log the error, close the socket, and continue servicing other clients. Realize that handling an error of this type by aborting is unacceptable in a server such as this one, where one process is handling all clients. But if the server was a child handling just one client, then having that one child abort would not affect the parent (which we assume handles all new connections and spawns the children), or any of the other children that are servicing other clients.

Chapter 7

7.2   Figure E.5 shows one solution to this exercise. We have removed the printing of
the data string returned by the server as that value is not needed.

————————————————————————————————— sockopt/rcvbuf.c

```
 1 #include    "unp.h"
 2 #include    <netinet/tcp.h>      /* for TCP_MAXSEG */

 3 int
 4 main(int argc, char **argv)
 5 {
 6     int     sockfd, rcvbuf, mss;
 7     socklen_t len;
 8     struct sockaddr_in servaddr;

 9     if (argc != 2)
10         err_quit("usage: rcvbuf <IPaddress>");

11     sockfd = Socket(AF_INET, SOCK_STREAM, 0);

12     len = sizeof(rcvbuf);
13     Getsockopt(sockfd, SOL_SOCKET, SO_RCVBUF, &rcvbuf, &len);
14     len = sizeof(mss);
15     Getsockopt(sockfd, IPPROTO_TCP, TCP_MAXSEG, &mss, &len);
16     printf("defaults: SO_RCVBUF = %d, MSS = %d\n", rcvbuf, mss);

17     bzero(&servaddr, sizeof(servaddr));
18     servaddr.sin_family = AF_INET;
19     servaddr.sin_port = htons(13);   /* daytime server */
20     Inet_pton(AF_INET, argv[1], &servaddr.sin_addr);

21     Connect(sockfd, (SA *) &servaddr, sizeof(servaddr));

22     len = sizeof(rcvbuf);
23     Getsockopt(sockfd, SOL_SOCKET, SO_RCVBUF, &rcvbuf, &len);
24     len = sizeof(mss);
25     Getsockopt(sockfd, IPPROTO_TCP, TCP_MAXSEG, &mss, &len);
26     printf("after connect: SO_RCVBUF = %d, MSS = %d\n", rcvbuf, mss);

27     exit(0);
28 }
```

————————————————————————————————— sockopt/rcvbuf.c

Figure E.5   Print socket receive buffer size and MSS before and after connection establishment.

First, there is no "correct" output from this program. The results vary from system to system. Some systems (notably Solaris 2.5.1 and earlier) always return 0
for the socket buffer sizes, preventing us from seeing what happens with this
value across the connection.

With regard to the MSS, the value printed before connect is the implementation
default (often 536 or 512), while the value printed after connect depends on a
possible MSS option from the peer. On a local Ethernet, for example, the value
after connect could be 1,460. After a connect to a server on a remote network,
however, the MSS may be similar to the default, unless your system supports path

MTU discovery. If possible, run a tool like `tcpdump` (Section C.5) while the program is running to see the actual MSS option on the SYN segment from the peer.

With regard to the socket receive buffer size, many implementations round this value up after the connection is established to a multiple of the MSS. Another way to see the socket receive buffer size after the connection is established is to watch the packets using a tool like `tcpdump` and look at TCP's advertised window.

7.3   Allocate a `linger` structure named `ling` and initialize it as follows:

```
str_cli(stdin, sockfd);

ling.l_onoff = 1;
ling.l_linger = 0;
Setsockopt(sockfd, SOL_SOCKET, SO_LINGER, &ling, sizeof(ling));

exit(0);
```

This should cause the client TCP to terminate the connection with an RST instead of the normal four-segment exchange. The server child's call to `readline` returns an error of ECONNRESET and the message printed is as follows:

```
readline error: Connection reset by peer
```

The client socket should not go through the TIME_WAIT state, even though the client did the active close.

7.4   The first client calls `setsockopt`, `bind`, and `connect`. But between the first client's calls to `bind` and `connect`, if the second client calls `bind`, EADDRINUSE is returned. But as soon as the first client connects to the peer, the second client's `bind` will work, since the first client's socket is then connected. The only way to handle this is for the second client to try calling `bind` multiple times if EADDRINUSE is returned, and not give up the first time the error is returned.

7.5   We run the program on a host with multicast support (MacOS X 10.2.6).

```
macosx % sock -s 9999 &                           start first server with wildcard
[1]     29697
macosx % sock -s 172.24.37.78 9999                try second server, but without -A
can't bind local address: Address already in use
macosx % sock -s -A 172.24.37.78 9999 &           try again with -A; works
[2]     29699
macosx % sock -s -A 127.0.0.1 9999 &              third server with -A; works
[3]     29700
macosx % netstat -na | grep 9999
tcp4    0     0  127.0.0.1.9999        *.*              LISTEN
tcp4    0     0  172.24.37.78.9999     *.*              LISTEN
tcp4    0     0  *.9999                *.*              LISTEN
```

7.6   We first try on a host that supports multicasting, but does not support the SO_REUSEPORT option (Solaris 9).

```
solaris % sock -s -u 8888 &                            first one starts
[1]     24051
solaris % sock -s -u 8888
can't bind local address: Address already in use
solaris % sock -s -u -A 8888 &                         try second again with -A; works
solaris % netstat -na | grep 8888                      we can see the duplicate bindings
       *.8888                        Idle
       *.8888                        Idle
```

On this system, we do not need to specify SO_REUSEADDR for the first bind, only for the second.

Finally, we run this scenario under MacOS X 10.2.6, which supports multicasting and the SO_REUSEPORT option. We first try SO_REUSEADDR for both servers, but this does not work.

```
macosx % sock -u -s -A 7777 &
[1]     17610
macosx % sock -u -s -A 7777
can't bind local address: Address already in use
```

Next we try SO_REUSEPORT, but only for the second server, not for the first. This does not work since a completely duplicate binding requires the option for all sockets that share the binding.

```
macosx % sock -u -s 8888 &
[1]     17612
macosx % sock -u -s -T 8888
can't bind local address: Address already in use
```

Finally we specify SO_REUSEPORT for both servers, and this works.

```
macosx % sock -u -s -T 9999 &
[1]     17614
macosx % sock -u -s -T 9999 &
[2]     17615
macosx % netstat -na | grep 9999
udp4       0       0  *.9999                      *.*
udp4       0       0  *.9999                      *.*
```

7.7   This does nothing because ping uses an ICMP socket and the SO_DEBUG socket option affects only TCP sockets. The description for the SO_DEBUG socket option has always been something generic such as "this option enables debugging in the respective protocol layer," but the only protocol layer to implement the option has been TCP.

7.8   Figure E.6 shows the timeline.

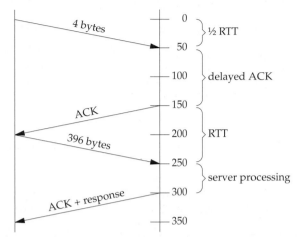

Figure E.6 Interaction of Nagle algorithm with delayed ACK.

7.9   Setting the `TCP_NODELAY` socket option causes the data from the second `write` to be sent immediately, even though the connection has a small packet outstanding. We show this in Figure E.7. The total time in this example is just over 150 ms.

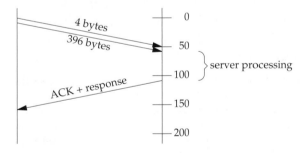

Figure E.7 Avoidance of Nagle algorithm by setting `TCP_NODELAY` socket option.

7.10 The advantage to this solution is reducing the number of packets, as we show in Figure E.8.

7.11 Section 4.2.3.2 states: "The delay MUST be less than 0.5 seconds, and in a stream of full-sized segments, there SHOULD be an ACK for at least every second segment." Berkeley-derived implementations delay an ACK by at most 200 ms (p. 821 of TCPv2).

7.12 The server parent in Figure 5.2 spends most of its time blocked in the call to `accept` and the child in Figure 5.3 spends most of its time blocked in the call to `read`, which is called by `readline`. The keep-alive option has no effect on a listening socket so the parent is not affected should the client host crash. The child's

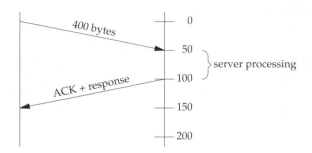

Figure E.8 Using `writev` instead of setting the `TCP_NODELAY` socket option.

read will return an error of ETIMEDOUT, sometime around two hours after the last data exchange across the connection.

7.13 The client in Figure 5.5 spends most of its time blocked in the call to `fgets`, which in turn is blocked in some type of read operation on standard input within the standard I/O library. When the keep-alive timer expires around two hours after the last data exchange across the connection, and all the keep-alive probes fail to elicit a response from the server, the socket's pending error is set to ETIMEDOUT. But the client is blocked in the call to `fgets` on standard input and will not see this error until it performs a read or write on the socket. This is one reason why we modified Figure 5.5 to use `select` in Chapter 6.

7.14 This client spends most of its time blocked in the call to `select`, which will return the socket as readable as soon as the pending error is set to ETIMEDOUT (as we described in the previous solution).

7.15 Only two segments are exchanged, not four. There is a very low probability that the two systems will have timers that are exactly synchronized; hence, one end's keep-alive timer will expire shortly before the other's. The first one to expire sends the keep-alive probe, causing the other end to ACK this probe. But the receipt of the keep-alive probe causes the keep-alive timer on the host with the (slightly) slower clock to be reset for two hours in the future.

7.16 The original sockets API did not have a `listen` function. Instead, the fourth argument to `socket` contained socket options, and SO_ACCEPTCON was used to specify a listening socket. When `listen` was added, the flag stayed around, but it is now set only by the kernel (p. 456 of TCPv2).

Chapter 8

8.1 Yes, `read` returns 4,096 bytes of data, but the `recvfrom` returns 2,048 (the first of the two datagrams). A `recvfrom` on a datagram socket never returns more than one datagram, regardless of how much the application asks for.

8.2 If the protocol uses variable-length socket address structures, `clilen` could be too large. We will see in Chapter 15 that this is acceptable with Unix domain socket address structures, but the correct way to code the function is to use the actual length returned by `recvfrom` as the length for `sendto`.

8.4   Running `ping` like this is an easy way to see ICMP messages that are received by the host on which `ping` is being run. We reduce the number of packets sent from the normal one per second just to reduce the output. If we run our UDP client on our host `aix`, specifying the server's IP address as 192.168.42.1, and also run the `ping` program, we get the following output:

```
aix % ping -v -i 60 127.0.0.1
PING 127.0.0.1: (127.0.0.1): 56 data bytes
64 bytes from 127.0.0.1: icmp_seq=0 ttl=255 time=0 ms
36 bytes from 192.168.42.1: Destination Port Unreachable
Vr HL TOS  Len   ID Flg  off TTL Pro  cks      Src        Dst Data
 4  5  00 0022 0007    0 0000  1e  11 c770 192.168.42.2  192.168.42.1
UDP: from port 40645, to port 9877 (decimal)
```

Note that not all `ping` clients print received ICMP errors, even with the -v flag.

8.5   It probably has a socket receive buffer size, but data is never accepted for a listening TCP socket. Most implementations do not preallocate memory for socket send buffers or socket receive buffers. The socket buffer sizes specified with the SO_SNDBUF and SO_RCVBUF socket options are just upper limits for that socket.

8.6   We run the `sock` program on the multihomed host `freebsd`, specifying the -u option (use UDP) and the -l option (specifying the local IP address and port).

```
freebsd % sock -u -l 12.106.32.254.4444 192.168.42.2 8888
hello
```

The local IP address is the Internet-side interface in Figure 1.16, but the datagram must go out the other interface to get to the destination. Watching the network with `tcpdump` shows that the source IP address is the one that was bound by the client, not the outgoing interface address.

```
14:28:29.614846 12.106.32.254.4444 > 192.168.42.2.8888: udp 6
14:28:29.615225 192.168.42.2 > 12.106.32.254: icmp: 192.168.42.2
                                          udp port 8888 unreachable
```

8.7   Putting a `printf` in the client should introduce a delay between each datagram, allowing the server to receive more datagrams. Putting a `printf` in the server should cause the server to lose more datagrams.

8.8   The largest IPv4 datagram is 65,535 bytes, limited by the 16-bit total length field in Figure A.1. The IP header requires 20 bytes and the UDP header requires 8 bytes, leaving a maximum of 65,507 bytes for user data. With IPv6 without jumbogram support, the size of the IPv6 header is 40 bytes, leaving a maximum of 65,487 bytes for user data.

Figure E.9 shows the new version of `dg_cli`. If you forget to set the send buffer size, Berkeley-derived kernels return an error of EMSGSIZE from `sendto`, since the size of the socket send buffer is normally less than required for a maximum-sized UDP datagram (be sure to do Exercise 7.1). But if we set the client's socket

udpcliserv/dgclibig.c

```
 1 #include    "unp.h"

 2 #undef  MAXLINE
 3 #define MAXLINE 65507

 4 void
 5 dg_cli(FILE *fp, int sockfd, const SA *pservaddr, socklen_t servlen)
 6 {
 7     int     size;
 8     char    sendline[MAXLINE], recvline[MAXLINE + 1];
 9     ssize_t n;

10     size = 70000;
11     Setsockopt(sockfd, SOL_SOCKET, SO_SNDBUF, &size, sizeof(size));
12     Setsockopt(sockfd, SOL_SOCKET, SO_RCVBUF, &size, sizeof(size));

13     Sendto(sockfd, sendline, MAXLINE, 0, pservaddr, servlen);

14     n = Recvfrom(sockfd, recvline, MAXLINE, 0, NULL, NULL);

15     printf("received %d bytes\n", n);
16 }
```

udpcliserv/dgclibig.c

Figure E.9 Writing the maximum-sized UDP/IPv4 datagram.

buffer sizes as shown in Figure E.9 and run the client program, nothing is returned by the server. We can verify that the client's datagram is sent to the server by running `tcpdump`, but if we put a `printf` in the server, its call to `recvfrom` does not return the datagram. The problem is that the server's UDP socket receive buffer is smaller than the datagram we are sending, so the datagram is discarded and not delivered to the socket. On a FreeBSD system, we can verify this by running `netstat -s` and looking at the "dropped due to full socket buffers" counter before and after our big datagram is received. The final solution is to modify the server, setting its socket send and receive buffer sizes.

On most networks, a 65,535-byte IP datagram is fragmented. Recall from Section 2.11 that an IP layer must support a reassembly buffer size of only 576 bytes. Therefore, you may encounter hosts that will not receive the maximum-sized datagrams sent in this exercise. Also, many Berkeley-derived implementations, including 4.4BSD-Lite2, have a sign bug that prevents UDP from accepting a datagram larger than 32,767 bytes (line 95 of p. 770 of TCPv2).

Chapter 9

9.1   There are a number of situations where `sctp_peeloff` can play an important role. An example application that might use this function is a traditional UDP-like server that responds to requests such as small transactions, but occasionally is requested to do a long-term audit. In most cases, you only need to send one or two small messages and no more; but when a audit request arrives, a long-term conversation is invoked, sending audit information. In this situation, you would peel off the audit into its own thread or process to do the audit.

In summary, any application that has mainly small requests but on occasion needs to have a long-term conversation can take advantage of `sctp_peeloff`.

9.2   The server side closes automatically when the client closes the association. This is because SCTP does not support the half-closed state, so when the client calls close, the shutdown sequence will flush any pending data the server had queued for the client and complete the shutdown, closing the association.

9.3   In the one-to-one style, a connect call must be performed first, and so when the COOKIE is sent to the peer, no data is pending. For the one-to-many style, an application can send data to a peer to set up an association. This means that when the COOKIE is sent, the DATA is available to send to the peer.

9.4   The only time a peer that you would be setting up an association with would be able to send back data is if it had DATA pending BEFORE the connection was set up. This would occur if each side was using the one-to-many style and each side did a send to implicitly set up the association. This type of association setup is called an INIT collision, and details on it can be found in Chapter 4 of [Stewart and Xie 2001].

9.5   In some cases, not all addresses that are bound may be passed to a peer endpoint. In particular, when addresses that an application has bound contain both private and public IP addresses, only the public addresses may be shared with a peer endpoint. Another example is found in IPv6, where link-local addresses cannot necessarily be shared with a peer.

Chapter 10

10.1   If the `sctp_sendmsg` function returns an error, no message will be sent and the application would then do a blocking `sctp_recvmsg`, waiting for a response message that would never be sent to it.

A way to fix this is to check the error return codes, and if an error occurs on sending, the client should NOT do the receive, but instead should report an error.

If the `sctp_recvmsg` function returns an error, no message will arrive and the server will still attempt to send a message, possibly setting up an association. To avoid this, the error code should be checked, and depending on the error, you may wish to report the error and close the socket, letting the server also then receive an error; or, if the error is transient, you could retry the `sctp_recvmsg` call.

10.2   If the server receives a request and then exits, the client in its current form will hang forever waiting for a message that will never come. A method that can be used by the client to detect this is to enable association events. This will allow the client application to receive a message when the server exits, telling the client that the association is now gone. This would allow the client to then take a recovery action such as contacting a different server.

An alternative method the client could use is to set up a timer and abort after some time period.

10.3   We choose 800 bytes to attempt to get each chunk in a single packet. A better way would be to get or set the SCTP_MAXSEG socket option to determine the size that will fit in one chunk.

10.4   The Nagle algorithm (controlled by the SCTP_NODELAY socket option; see Section 7.10) will cause a problem only if we choose a small data transfer size. So as long as we send a size that forces SCTP to send immediately, no harm will occur. However, choosing a smaller size for out_sz would skew the results, holding some transmissions awaiting SACKs from the remote endpoint. So if a smaller size is to be used, turning off the Nagle algorithm (i.e., turning on the SCTP_NODELAY socket option) would be a good idea.

10.5   If an application sets up an association and then changes the number of streams, the association will not have a different number of streams, it will have the original number before the change. This is because changing the number of streams only affects new associations, not existing ones.

10.6   The one-to-many style allows implicit setup of associations. To use ancillary data to change the setup of an association, you need to use the sendmsg call to provide the data before the association is set up. Thus, you must use an implicit association setup.

Chapter 11

11.1   Figure E.10 shows our program that calls gethostbyaddr. This program works fine for a host with a single IP address. If we run the program in Figure 11.3 for a host with four IP addresses, we get the following:

```
freebsd % hostent cnn.com
official hostname: cnn.com
        address: 64.236.16.20
        address: 64.236.16.52
        address: 64.236.16.84
        address: 64.236.16.116
        address: 64.236.24.4
        address: 64.236.24.12
        address: 64.236.24.20
        address: 64.236.24.28
```

But if we run the program in Figure E.10 for the same host, only the first IP address is output as follows:

```
freebsd % hostent2 cnn.com
official hostname: cnn.com
        address: 64.236.24.4
        name = www1.cnn.com
```

——————————————————————————— names/hostent2.c

```
 1 #include    "unp.h"

 2 int
 3 main(int argc, char **argv)
 4 {
 5     char    *ptr, **pptr;
 6     char    str[INET6_ADDRSTRLEN];
 7     struct hostent *hptr;

 8     while (--argc > 0) {
 9         ptr = *++argv;
10         if ( (hptr = gethostbyname(ptr)) == NULL) {
11             err_msg("gethostbyname error for host: %s: %s",
12                     ptr, hstrerror(h_errno));
13             continue;
14         }
15         printf("official hostname: %s\n", hptr->h_name);

16         for (pptr = hptr->h_aliases; *pptr != NULL; pptr++)
17             printf("    alias: %s\n", *pptr);

18         switch (hptr->h_addrtype) {
19         case AF_INET:
20 #ifdef  AF_INET6
21         case AF_INET6:
22 #endif
23             pptr = hptr->h_addr_list;
24             for ( ; *pptr != NULL; pptr++) {
25                 printf("\taddress: %s\n",
26                        Inet_ntop(hptr->h_addrtype, *pptr, str, sizeof(str)));
27                 if ( (hptr = gethostbyaddr(*pptr, hptr->h_length,
28                                           hptr->h_addrtype)) == NULL)
29                     printf("\t(gethostbyaddr failed)\n");
30                 else if (hptr->h_name != NULL)
31                     printf("\tname = %s\n", hptr->h_name);
32                 else
33                     printf("\t(no hostname returned by gethostbyaddr)\n");
34             }
35             break;

36         default:
37             err_ret("unknown address type");
38             break;
39         }
40     }
41     exit(0);
42 }
```

——————————————————————————— names/hostent2.c

Figure E.10 Modification to Figure 11.3 to call gethostbyaddr.

The problem is that the two functions, gethostbyname and gethostbyaddr, share the same hostent structure, as we show at the beginning of Section 11.18. When our new program calls gethostbyaddr, it reuses this structure, along with the storage that the structure points to (i.e., the h_addr_list array of pointers), wiping out the remaining three IP addresses returned by gethostbyname.

11.2   If your system does not supply the re-entrant version of gethostbyaddr (which we describe in Section 11.19), then you must make a copy of the array of pointers returned by gethostbyname, along with the data pointed to by this array, before calling gethostbyaddr.

11.3   The chargen server sends data to the client until the client closes the connection (i.e., until you abort the client).

11.4   This is a feature of some resolvers, but you cannot rely on it in a portable program because POSIX leaves the behavior unspecified. Figure E.11 shows the modified version. The order of the tests on the hostname string is important. We call inet_pton first, as it is a fast, in-memory test for whether or not the string is a valid dotted-decimal IP address. Only if this fails do we call gethostbyname, which typically involves some network resources and some time.

If the string is a valid dotted-decimal IP address, we make our own array of pointers (addrs) to the single IP address, allowing the loop using pptr to remain the same.

Since the address has already been converted to binary in the socket address structure, we change the call to memcpy in Figure 11.4 to call memmove instead, because when a dotted-decimal IP address is entered, the source and destination fields are the same in this call.

———————————————————————— names/daytimetcpcli2.c

```
 1 #include    "unp.h"

 2 int
 3 main(int argc, char **argv)
 4 {
 5     int      sockfd, n;
 6     char     recvline[MAXLINE + 1];
 7     struct sockaddr_in servaddr;
 8     struct in_addr **pptr, *addrs[2];
 9     struct hostent *hp;
10     struct servent *sp;

11     if (argc != 3)
12         err_quit("usage: daytimetcpcli2 <hostname> <service>");

13     bzero(&servaddr, sizeof(servaddr));
14     servaddr.sin_family = AF_INET;

15     if (inet_pton(AF_INET, argv[1], &servaddr.sin_addr) == 1) {
16         addrs[0] = &servaddr.sin_addr;
17         addrs[1] = NULL;
18         pptr = &addrs[0];
19     } else if ((hp = gethostbyname(argv[1])) != NULL) {
20         pptr = (struct in_addr **) hp->h_addr_list;
21     } else
```

```
22          err_quit("hostname error for %s: %s", argv[1], hstrerror(h_errno));
23      if ( (n = atoi(argv[2])) > 0)
24          servaddr.sin_port = htons(n);
25      else if ((sp = getservbyname(argv[2], "tcp")) != NULL)
26          servaddr.sin_port = sp->s_port;
27      else
28          err_quit("getservbyname error for %s", argv[2]);
29      for ( ; *pptr != NULL; pptr++) {
30          sockfd = Socket(AF_INET, SOCK_STREAM, 0);
31          memmove(&servaddr.sin_addr, *pptr, sizeof(struct in_addr));
32          printf("trying %s\n", Sock_ntop((SA *) &servaddr, sizeof(servaddr)));
33          if (connect(sockfd, (SA *) &servaddr, sizeof(servaddr)) == 0)
34              break;                  /* success */
35          err_ret("connect error");
36          close(sockfd);
37      }
38      if (*pptr == NULL)
39          err_quit("unable to connect");
40      while ( (n = Read(sockfd, recvline, MAXLINE)) > 0) {
41          recvline[n] = 0;            /* null terminate */
42          Fputs(recvline, stdout);
43      }
44      exit(0);
45 }
```
———————————————————————————————— *names/daytimetcpcli2.c*

Figure E.11   Allow dotted-decimal IP address or hostname, port number, or service name.

11.5   Figure E.12 shows the program.

———————————————————————————————— *names/daytimetcpcli3.c*
```
 1 #include     "unp.h"
 2 int
 3 main(int argc, char **argv)
 4 {
 5      int     sockfd, n;
 6      char    recvline[MAXLINE + 1];
 7      struct sockaddr_in servaddr;
 8      struct sockaddr_in6 servaddr6;
 9      struct sockaddr *sa;
10      socklen_t salen;
11      struct in_addr **pptr;
12      struct hostent *hp;
13      struct servent *sp;
14      if (argc != 3)
15          err_quit("usage: daytimetcpcli3 <hostname> <service>");
16      if ( (hp = gethostbyname(argv[1])) == NULL)
17          err_quit("hostname error for %s: %s", argv[1], hstrerror(h_errno));
18      if ( (sp = getservbyname(argv[2], "tcp")) == NULL)
19          err_quit("getservbyname error for %s", argv[2]);
```

```
20      pptr = (struct in_addr **) hp->h_addr_list;
21      for ( ; *pptr != NULL; pptr++) {
22          sockfd = Socket(hp->h_addrtype, SOCK_STREAM, 0);

23          if (hp->h_addrtype == AF_INET) {
24              sa = (SA *) &servaddr;
25              salen = sizeof(servaddr);
26          } else if (hp->h_addrtype == AF_INET6) {
27              sa = (SA *) &servaddr6;
28              salen = sizeof(servaddr6);
29          } else
30              err_quit("unknown addrtype %d", hp->h_addrtype);

31          bzero(sa, salen);
32          sa->sa_family = hp->h_addrtype;
33          sock_set_port(sa, salen, sp->s_port);
34          sock_set_addr(sa, salen, *pptr);

35          printf("trying %s\n", Sock_ntop(sa, salen));

36          if (connect(sockfd, sa, salen) == 0)
37              break;                  /* success */
38          err_ret("connect error");
39          close(sockfd);
40      }
41      if (*pptr == NULL)
42          err_quit("unable to connect");

43      while ( (n = Read(sockfd, recvline, MAXLINE)) > 0) {
44          recvline[n] = 0;        /* null terminate */
45          Fputs(recvline, stdout);
46      }
47      exit(0);
48  }
```
———————————————————————————————————— *names/daytimetcpcli3.c*

Figure E.12 Modification of Figure 11.4 to work with IPv4 and IPv6.

We use the h_addrtype value returned by gethostbyname to determine the
type of address. We also use our sock_set_port and sock_set_addr functions (Section 3.8) to set these two fields in the appropriate socket address structure.

Although this program works, it has two limitations. First, we must handle all
the differences, looking at h_addrtype and then setting sa and salen appropriately. A better solution is to have a library function that not only looks up the
hostname and service name, but also fills in the entire socket address structure
(e.g., getaddrinfo in Section 11.6). Second, this program compiles only on
hosts that support IPv6. To make this compile on an IPv4-only host would add
numerous #ifdefs to the code, thus complicating it.

We return to the concept of protocol independence in Chapter 11 and see better
ways to accomplish it.

11.7 Allocate a big buffer (larger than any socket address structure) and call
getsockname. The third argument is a value-result argument that returns the

actual size of the protocol's addresses. Unfortunately, this works only for protocols with fixed-length socket address structures (e.g., IPv4 and IPv6), but is not
guaranteed to work with protocols that can return variable-length socket address
structures (e.g., Unix domain sockets, Chapter 15).

11.8   We first allocate arrays to hold the hostname and service name as follows:

```
char    host[NI_MAXHOST], serv[NI_MAXSERV];
```

After `accept` returns, we call `getnameinfo` instead of `sock_ntop` as follows:

```
if (getnameinfo(cliaddr, len, host, NI_MAXHOST, serv, NI_MAXSERV,
            NI_NUMERICHOST | NI_NUMERICSERV) == 0)
    printf("connection from %s.%s\n", host, serv);
```

Since this is a server, we specify the `NI_NUMERICHOST` and `NI_NUMERICSERV`
flags to avoid a DNS query and a lookup of `/etc/services`.

11.9   The first problem is that the second server cannot `bind` the same port as the first
server because the `SO_REUSEADDR` socket option is not set. The easiest way to
handle this is to make a copy of the `udp_server` function, rename it
`udp_server_reuseaddr`, have it set the socket option, and call this new function from the server.

11.10   When the client outputs "Trying 206.62.226.35...", `gethostbyname` has returned
the IP address. Any client pause before this is the time taken by the resolver to
look up the hostname. The output "Connected to bsdi.kohala.com." means
`connect` has returned. Any pause between these two lines of output is the time
taken by `connect` to establish the connection.

Chapter 12

12.1   Here are the relevant excepts (e.g., with the login and directory listings omitted).
Note that the FTP client on the system `freebsd` *always* tries the EPRT command,
whether it is using IPv4 or IPv6, and falls back to the PORT command when it
doesn't work.

```
freebsd % ftp aix-4
Connected to aix-4.unpbook.com.
220 aix FTP server ...
...
230 Guest login ok, access restrictions apply.
ftp> debug
Debugging on (debug=1).
ftp> passive
Passive mode: off; fallback to active mode: off.
ftp> dir
---> EPRT |1|192.168.42.1|50484|
500 'EPRT |1|192.168.42.1|50484|': command not understood.
disabling epsv4 for this connection
---> PORT 192,168,42,1,197,52
200 PORT command successful.
---> LIST
```

```
150 Opening ASCII mode data connection for /bin/ls.

...

freebsd % ftp ftp.kame.net
Trying 2001:200:0:4819:203:47ff:fea5:3085...
Connected to orange.kame.net.
220 orange.kame.net FTP server ...
...
230 Guest login ok, access restrictions apply.
ftp> debug
Debugging on (debug=1).
ftp> passive
Passive mode: off; fallback to active mode: off.
ftp> dir
---> EPRT |2|3ffe:b80:3:9ad1::2|50480|
200 EPRT command successful.
---> LIST
150 Opening ASCII mode data connection for '/bin/ls'.
```

Chapter 13

13.1   The startup error due to an invalid command-line argument count would be logged using `syslog`.

13.2   The TCP versions of the `echo`, `discard`, and `chargen` servers all run as a child process after being `forked` by `inetd` because these three run until the client terminates the connection. The other two TCP servers, `time` and `daytime`, do not require a `fork` because their service is trivial to implement (get the current time and date, format it, write it, and close the connection), so these two are handled directly by `inetd`. All five UDP services are handled without a `fork` because each generates at most a single datagram in response to the client datagram that triggers the service. These five are therefore handled directly by `inetd`.

13.3   This is a well-known denial-of-service attack ([CERT 1996a]). The first datagram from port 7 causes the `chargen` server to send a datagram back to port 7. This is echoed and sends another datagram to the `chargen` server. This loop continues. One solution, implemented in FreeBSD, is to refuse datagrams to any of the internal servers if the source port of the incoming datagram belongs to any of the internal servers. Another solution is to disable these internal services, either through `inetd` on each host or at an organization's router to the Internet.

13.4   The client's IP address and port are obtained from the socket address structure filled in by `accept`.

The reason `inetd` does not do this for a UDP socket is because the `recvfrom` to read the datagram is performed by the actual server that is `execed`, not by `inetd` itself.

`inetd` could read the datagram specifying the `MSG_PEEK` flag (Section 14.7), just to obtain the client's IP address and port, but leaving the datagram in place for the actual server to read.

Chapter 14

14.1   If no handler had been set, the return from the first call to `signal` would be
`SIG_DFL` and the call to `signal` to reset the handler would just set it back to its
default.

14.3   Here is just the `for` loop:

```
for ( ; ; ) {
    if ( (n = Recv(sockfd, recvline, MAXLINE, MSG_PEEK)) == 0)
        break;        /* server closed connection */

    Ioctl(sockfd, FIONREAD, &npend);
    printf("%d bytes from PEEK, %d bytes pending\n", n, npend);

    n = Read(sockfd, recvline, MAXLINE);
    recvline[n] = 0;    /* null terminate */
    Fputs(recvline, stdout);
}
```

14.4   The data is still output because falling off the end of the `main` function is the
same as returning from this function, and the `main` function is called by the C
startup routine as follows:

```
exit(main(argc, argv));
```

Hence, `exit` is called, plus the standard I/O cleanup routine is called.

Chapter 15

15.1   `unlink` removes the pathname from the filesystem, and when the client calls
`connect` at a later time, the `connect` will fail. The server's listening socket is
not affected, but no clients will be able to `connect` after the `unlink`.

15.2   The client cannot `connect` to the server even if the pathname still exists, because
for the `connect` to succeed, a Unix domain socket must be currently open and
bound to that pathname (Section 15.4).

15.3   When the server prints the client's protocol address by calling `sock_ntop`, the
output is "datagram from (no pathname bound)" because no pathname is bound
to the client's socket by default.

One solution is to specifically check for a Unix domain socket in `udp_client`
and `udp_connect` and `bind` a temporary pathname to the socket. This puts the
protocol dependency in the library function where it belongs, not in our application.

15.4   Even though we force 1-byte `writes` by the server for its 26-byte reply, putting
the `sleep` in the client guarantees that all 26 segments are received before `read`
is called, causing `read` to return the entire reply. This is just to confirm (again)
that TCP is a byte stream with no inherent record markers.

To use the Unix domain protocols, we start the client and server with the two command-line arguments /local (or /unix) and /tmp/daytime (or any other temporary pathname you wish to use). Nothing changes: 26 bytes are returned by read each time the client runs.

Since the server specifies the MSG_EOR flag for each send, each byte is considered a logical record and read returns 1 byte each time it is called. What is happening here is that Berkeley-derived implementations support the MSG_EOR flag by default. This is undocumented, however, and should not be used in production code. We use it here as an example of the difference between a byte stream and a record-oriented protocol. From an implementation perspective, each output operation goes into a memory buffer (mbuf) and the MSG_EOR flag is retained by the kernel with the mbuf as the mbuf goes from the sending socket to the receiving socket's receive buffer. When read is called, the MSG_EOR flag is still attached to each mbuf, so the generic kernel read routine (which supports the MSG_EOR flag since some protocols use the flag) returns each byte by itself. Had we used recvmsg instead of read, the MSG_EOR flag would be returned in the msg_flags member each time recvmsg returned 1 byte. This does not work with TCP because the sending TCP never looks at the MSG_EOR flag in the mbuf that it is sending, and even if it did, there is no way to pass this flag to the receiving TCP in the TCP header. (Thanks to Matt Thomas for pointing out this undocumented "feature.")

15.5 Figure E.13 shows an implementation of this program.

debug/backlog.c

```
 1 #include     "unp.h"

 2 #define PORT        9999
 3 #define ADDR        "127.0.0.1"
 4 #define MAXBACKLOG  100

 5               /* globals */
 6 struct sockaddr_in serv;
 7 pid_t    pid;                       /* of child */

 8 int      pipefd[2];
 9 #define pfd pipefd[1]               /* parent's end */
10 #define cfd pipefd[0]               /* child's end */

11               /* function prototypes */
12 void     do_parent(void);
13 void     do_child(void);

14 int
15 main(int argc, char **argv)
16 {
17     if (argc != 1)
18         err_quit("usage: backlog");

19     Socketpair(AF_UNIX, SOCK_STREAM, 0, pipefd);

20     bzero(&serv, sizeof(serv));
21     serv.sin_family = AF_INET;
22     serv.sin_port = htons(PORT);
```

```
23      Inet_pton(AF_INET, ADDR, &serv.sin_addr);

24      if ( (pid = Fork()) == 0)
25          do_child();
26      else
27          do_parent();

28      exit(0);
29  }

30  void
31  parent_alrm(int signo)
32  {
33      return;                         /* just interrupt blocked connect() */
34  }

35  void
36  do_parent(void)
37  {
38      int     backlog, j, k, junk, fd[MAXBACKLOG + 1];

39      Close(cfd);
40      Signal(SIGALRM, parent_alrm);

41      for (backlog = 0; backlog <= 14; backlog++) {
42          printf("backlog = %d: ", backlog);
43          Write(pfd, &backlog, sizeof(int));  /* tell child value */
44          Read(pfd, &junk, sizeof(int));  /* wait for child */

45          for (j = 1; j <= MAXBACKLOG; j++) {
46              fd[j] = Socket(AF_INET, SOCK_STREAM, 0);
47              alarm(2);
48              if (connect(fd[j], (SA *) &serv, sizeof(serv)) < 0) {
49                  if (errno != EINTR)
50                      err_sys("connect error, j = %d", j);
51                  printf("timeout, %d connections completed\n", j - 1);
52                  for (k = 1; k <= j; k++)
53                      Close(fd[k]);
54                  break;          /* next value of backlog */
55              }
56              alarm(0);
57          }
58          if (j > MAXBACKLOG)
59              printf("%d connections?\n", MAXBACKLOG);
60      }
61      backlog = -1;                   /* tell child we're all done */
62      Write(pfd, &backlog, sizeof(int));
63  }

64  void
65  do_child(void)
66  {
67      int     listenfd, backlog, junk;
68      const int on = 1;

69      Close(pfd);

70      Read(cfd, &backlog, sizeof(int));   /* wait for parent */
```

```
71        while (backlog >= 0) {
72            listenfd = Socket(AF_INET, SOCK_STREAM, 0);
73            Setsockopt(listenfd, SOL_SOCKET, SO_REUSEADDR, &on, sizeof(on));
74            Bind(listenfd, (SA *) &serv, sizeof(serv));
75            Listen(listenfd, backlog);  /* start the listen */

76            Write(cfd, &junk, sizeof(int)); /* tell parent */

77            Read(cfd, &backlog, sizeof(int));   /* just wait for parent */
78            Close(listenfd);           /* closes all queued connections, too */
79        }
80  }
```
debug/backlog.c

Figure E.13   Determine actual number of queued connections for different *backlog* values.

Chapter 16

16.1   The descriptor is shared between the parent and child, so it has a reference count of 2. If the parent calls close, this just decrements the reference count from 2 to 1, and since it is still greater than 0, a FIN is not sent. This is another reason for the shutdown function: to force a FIN to be sent even if the descriptor's reference count is greater than 0.

16.2   The parent will keep writing to the socket that has received a FIN, and the first segment sent to the server will elicit an RST in response. The next write after this will send SIGPIPE to the parent as we discussed in Section 5.12.

16.3   When the child calls getppid to send SIGTERM to the parent, the returned PID will be 1, the init process, which inherits all children whose parents terminate while their children are still running. The child will try to send the signal to the init process, but will not have adequate permission. But if there is a chance that this client could run with superuser privileges, allowing it to send this signal to init, then the return value of getppid should be tested before sending the signal.

16.4   If these two lines are removed, select is called. But select will return immediately because with the connection established, the socket is writable. This test and goto are to avoid the unnecessary call to select.

16.5   This can happen when the server immediately sends data when its accept returns, and when the client host is busy when the second packet of the three-way handshake arrives to complete the connection at the client end (Figure 2.5). SMTP servers, for example, immediately write to a new connection before reading from it, to send a greeting message to the client.

Chapter 17

17.1   No, it does not matter, because the first three members of the `union` in Figure 17.2 are socket address structures.

Chapter 18

18.1   The `sdl_nlen` member will be 5 and the `sdl_alen` member will be 8. This requires 21 bytes, so the size is rounded up to 24 bytes (p. 89 of TCPv2), assuming a 32-bit architecture.

18.2   The kernel's response is never sent to this socket. This socket option determines whether the kernel sends its reply to the sending process, as discussed on pp. 649–650 of TCPv2. It defaults to ON, since most processes want replies. But, disabling the option prevents replies from being sent to the sender.

Chapter 20

20.1   If you get more than a few replies, they should not be in the same order each time. The sending host, however, is normally the first reply since the datagrams to and from it loop back internally and do not appear on the actual network.

20.2   Under FreeBSD, when the signal handler writes the byte to the pipe and then returns, `select` returns `EINTR`. It is called again and returns readability on the pipe.

Chapter 21

21.1   When we run the program, there is no output. To prevent accidental reception of multicast datagrams that a server is not expecting, the kernel does not deliver multicast groups to a socket that has never performed any multicast operations (e.g., joining a group). What is happening here is that the destination address of the UDP datagram is 224.0.0.1, the all-hosts group that all multicast-capable nodes must join. The UDP datagram is sent as a multicast Ethernet frame and all the multicast-capable nodes receive the datagram since they all belong to the group. However, the kernel drops the received datagram since the process bound to the daytime port has not set any multicast options.

21.2   Figure E.14 shows a simple modification to the `main` function to `bind` the multicast address and port 0.

—— *mcast/udpcli06.c*
```
 1 #include    "unp.h"

 2 int
 3 main(int argc, char **argv)
 4 {
 5     int      sockfd;
 6     socklen_t salen;
 7     struct sockaddr *cli, *serv;

 8     if (argc != 2)
 9         err_quit("usage: udpcli06 <IPaddress>");

10     sockfd = Udp_client(argv[1], "daytime", (void **) &serv, &salen);

11     cli = Malloc(salen);
12     memcpy(cli, serv, salen);   /* copy socket address struct */
13     sock_set_port(cli, salen, 0);   /* and set port to 0 */
14     Bind(sockfd, cli, salen);

15     dg_cli(stdin, sockfd, serv, salen);

16     exit(0);
17 }
```
—— *mcast/udpcli06.c*

Figure E.14   UDP client `main` function that `binds` a multicast address.

Unfortunately, on the three systems on which this was tried—FreeBSD 4.8, MacOS X, and Linux 2.4.7—all allowed the `bind` and then sent the UDP datagrams with a multicast source IP address.

21.3   If we do this from our host `aix`, which is multicast-capable, we get the following:

```
aix % ping 224.0.0.1
PING 224.0.0.1: 56 data bytes
64 bytes from 192.168.42.2: icmp_seq=0 ttl=255 time=0 ms
64 bytes from 192.168.42.1: icmp_seq=0 ttl=64 time=1 ms (DUP!)
^C
----224.0.0.1 PING Statistics----
1 packets transmitted, 1 packets received, +1 duplicates, 0% packet loss
round-trip min/avg/max = 0/0/0 ms
```

Both systems on the right-hand Ethernet in Figure 1.16 respond.

> To prevent certain denial-of-service attacks, some systems do not respond to broadcast or multicast pings by default. To get `freebsd` to respond, we had to configure it with
>
> ```
> freebsd % sysctl net.inet.icmp.bmcastecho=1
> ```

21.5   The value 1,073,741,824 is converted to a floating-point number and divided by 4,294,967,296, yielding 0.250. This is multiplied by 1,000,000, yielding 250,000, which in microseconds is one-quarter of a second.

The largest fraction is 4,294,967,295, which divided by 4,294,967,296 yields 0.99999999976716935634. Multiplying this by 1,000,000 and truncating to an integer yields 999,999, the largest value for the number of microseconds.

Chapter 22

22.1 Recall that sock_ntop uses its own static buffer to hold the result. If we call it twice as arguments in a call to printf, the second call overwrites the result of the first call.

22.2 Yes, if the reply contains 0 bytes of user data (i.e., just an hdr structure).

22.3 Since select does not modify the timeval structure that specifies its time limit, you need to note the time when the first packet is sent (this is already returned in units of milliseconds by rtt_ts). If select returns with the socket being readable, note the current time, and if recvmsg is called again, calculate the new timeout for select.

22.4 The common technique is to create one socket per interface address, as we did in Section 22.6, and send the reply from the same socket on which the request arrived.

22.5 Calling getaddrinfo without a hostname argument and without the AI_PASSIVE flag set causes it to assume the local host address: 0::1 (IPv6) and 127.0.0.1 (IPv4). Recall that an IPv6 socket address structure is returned before an IPv4 socket address structure by getaddrinfo, assuming IPv6 is supported. If both protocols are supported on the host, the call to socket in udp_client will succeed with the family equal to AF_INET6.

Figure E.15 is the protocol-independent version of this program.

advio/udpserv04.c

```
 1 #include     "unpifi.h"

 2 void    mydg_echo(int, SA *, socklen_t);

 3 int
 4 main(int argc, char **argv)
 5 {
 6     int     sockfd, family, port;
 7     const int on = 1;
 8     pid_t   pid;
 9     socklen_t salen;
10     struct sockaddr *sa, *wild;
11     struct ifi_info *ifi, *ifihead;

12     if (argc == 2)
13         sockfd = Udp_client(NULL, argv[1], (void **) &sa, &salen);
14     else if (argc == 3)
15         sockfd = Udp_client(argv[1], argv[2], (void **) &sa, &salen);
16     else
17         err_quit("usage: udpserv04 [ <host> ] <service or port>");
18     family = sa->sa_family;
19     port = sock_get_port(sa, salen);
```

```
20      Close(sockfd);                  /* we just want family, port, salen */
21      for (ifihead = ifi = Get_ifi_info(family, 1);
22           ifi != NULL; ifi = ifi->ifi_next) {
23              /* bind unicast address */
24          sockfd = Socket(family, SOCK_DGRAM, 0);
25          Setsockopt(sockfd, SOL_SOCKET, SO_REUSEADDR, &on, sizeof(on));
26          sock_set_port(ifi->ifi_addr, salen, port);
27          Bind(sockfd, ifi->ifi_addr, salen);
28          printf("bound %s\n", Sock_ntop(ifi->ifi_addr, salen));
29          if ( (pid = Fork()) == 0) {  /* child */
30              mydg_echo(sockfd, ifi->ifi_addr, salen);
31              exit(0);                /* never executed */
32          }
33          if (ifi->ifi_flags & IFF_BROADCAST) {
34                  /* try to bind broadcast address */
35              sockfd = Socket(family, SOCK_DGRAM, 0);
36              Setsockopt(sockfd, SOL_SOCKET, SO_REUSEADDR, &on, sizeof(on));
37              sock_set_port(ifi->ifi_brdaddr, salen, port);
38              if (bind(sockfd, ifi->ifi_brdaddr, salen) < 0) {
39                  if (errno == EADDRINUSE) {
40                      printf("EADDRINUSE: %s\n",
41                              Sock_ntop(ifi->ifi_brdaddr, salen));
42                      Close(sockfd);
43                      continue;
44                  } else
45                      err_sys("bind error for %s",
46                              Sock_ntop(ifi->ifi_brdaddr, salen));
47              }
48              printf("bound %s\n", Sock_ntop(ifi->ifi_brdaddr, salen));
49              if ( (pid = Fork()) == 0) {  /* child */
50                  mydg_echo(sockfd, ifi->ifi_brdaddr, salen);
51                  exit(0);            /* never executed */
52              }
53          }
54      }
55      /* bind wildcard address */
56      sockfd = Socket(family, SOCK_DGRAM, 0);
57      Setsockopt(sockfd, SOL_SOCKET, SO_REUSEADDR, &on, sizeof(on));
58      wild = Malloc(salen);
59      memcpy(wild, sa, salen);    /* copy family and port */
60      sock_set_wild(wild, salen);
61      Bind(sockfd, wild, salen);
62      printf("bound %s\n", Sock_ntop(wild, salen));
63      if ( (pid = Fork()) == 0) {  /* child */
64          mydg_echo(sockfd, wild, salen);
65          exit(0);                 /* never executed */
66      }
67      exit(0);
68  }
```

```
69 void
70 mydg_echo(int sockfd, SA *myaddr, socklen_t salen)
71 {
72     int       n;
73     char      mesg[MAXLINE];
74     socklen_t len;
75     struct sockaddr *cli;

76     cli = Malloc(salen);

77     for ( ; ; ) {
78         len = salen;
79         n = Recvfrom(sockfd, mesg, MAXLINE, 0, cli, &len);
80         printf("child %d, datagram from %s", getpid(), Sock_ntop(cli, len));
81         printf(", to %s\n", Sock_ntop(myaddr, salen));

82         Sendto(sockfd, mesg, n, 0, cli, len);
83     }
84 }
```
—— *advio/udpserv04.c*

Figure E.15 Protocol-independent version of program from Section 22.6.

Chapter 24

24.1   Yes, in the first example, 2 bytes are sent with a single urgent pointer that points
to the byte following the b. But in the second example (the two function calls),
first the a is sent with an urgent pointer that points just beyond it, and this is followed by another TCP segment containing the b with a different urgent pointer
that points just beyond it.

24.2   Figure E.16 shows the version using poll.

—— *oob/tcprecv03p.c*
```
 1 #include    "unp.h"

 2 int
 3 main(int argc, char **argv)
 4 {
 5     int      listenfd, connfd, n, justreadoob = 0;
 6     char     buff[100];
 7     struct pollfd pollfd[1];

 8     if (argc == 2)
 9         listenfd = Tcp_listen(NULL, argv[1], NULL);
10     else if (argc == 3)
11         listenfd = Tcp_listen(argv[1], argv[2], NULL);
12     else
13         err_quit("usage: tcprecv03p [ <host> ] <port#>");

14     connfd = Accept(listenfd, NULL, NULL);

15     pollfd[0].fd = connfd;
16     pollfd[0].events = POLLRDNORM;
17     for ( ; ; ) {
18         if (justreadoob == 0)
19             pollfd[0].events |= POLLRDBAND;
```

```
20              Poll(pollfd, 1, INFTIM);

21          if (pollfd[0].revents & POLLRDBAND) {
22              n = Recv(connfd, buff, sizeof(buff) - 1, MSG_OOB);
23              buff[n] = 0;          /* null terminate */
24              printf("read %d OOB byte: %s\n", n, buff);
25              justreadoob = 1;
26              pollfd[0].events &= ~POLLRDBAND;    /* turn bit off */
27          }

28          if (pollfd[0].revents & POLLRDNORM) {
29              if ( (n = Read(connfd, buff, sizeof(buff) - 1)) == 0) {
30                  printf("received EOF\n");
31                  exit(0);
32              }
33              buff[n] = 0;          /* null terminate */
34              printf("read %d bytes: %s\n", n, buff);
35              justreadoob = 0;
36          }
37      }
38  }
```
————————————————————————————————— *oob/tcprecv03p.c*

Figure E.16 Version of Figure 24.6 using `poll` instead of `select`.

Chapter 25

25.1 No, the modification introduces an error. The problem is that nqueue is decremented before the array entry dg[iget] is processed, allowing the signal handler to read a new datagram into this array element.

Chapter 26

26.1 In the fork example, there will be 101 descriptors in use, one listening socket,
and 100 connected sockets. But each of the 101 processes (one parent, 100 children) has just one descriptor open (ignoring any others, such as standard input,
if the server is not daemonized). In the threaded server, however, there are 101
descriptors in the single process. Each thread (including the main thread) is handling one descriptor.

26.2 The final two segments of the TCP connection termination—the server's FIN
and the client's ACK of this FIN—will not be exchanged. This leaves the client's
end of the connection in the FIN_WAIT_2 state (Figure 2.4). Berkeley-derived
implementations will time out the client's end when it remains in this state for
just over 11 minutes (pp. 825–827 of TCPv2). The server will also run out of
descriptors (eventually).

26.3 This message should be printed by the main thread when it reads an EOF from
the socket *and* the other thread is still running. A simple way to do this is to
declare another external named done that is initialized to 0. Before the thread
copyto returns, it sets this variable to 1. The main thread checks this variable,

and if 0, prints the error message. Since only one thread sets the variable, there is no need for any synchronization.

Chapter 27

27.1   Nothing changes; all the systems are neighbors, so a strict source route is identical to a loose source route.

27.2   We would place an EOL (a byte of 0) at the end of the buffer.

27.3   Since `ping` creates a raw socket (Chapter 28), it receives the complete IP header, including any IP options, on every datagram it reads with `recvfrom`.

27.4   `rlogind` is invoked by `inetd` (Section 13.5), so descriptor 0 is the socket to the client.

27.5   The problem is that the fifth argument to `setsockopt` is the pointer to the length, instead of the length. This bug was probably fixed when ANSI C prototypes were first used.

As it turns out, the bug is harmless, because as we mentioned, to clear the `IP_OPTIONS` socket option, we can specify either a null pointer as the fourth argument or a fifth argument (the length) of 0 (p. 269 of TCPv2).

Chapter 28

28.1   The version number field and the next header field in the IPv6 header are not available. The payload length field is available as either an argument to one of the output functions or as the return value from one of the input functions. But, if a jumbo payload option is required, that actual option itself is not available to an application. The fragment header is also not available to an application.

28.2   Eventually, the client's socket receive buffer will fill, causing the daemon's `write` to block. We do not want this to happen, as that stops the daemon from handling any more data on any of its sockets. The easiest solution is for the daemon to set its end of the Unix domain connection to the client to nonblocking. The daemon must then call `write` instead of the wrapper function `Write` and just ignore an error of `EWOULDBLOCK`.

28.3   Berkeley-derived kernels, by default, allow broadcasting on a raw socket (p. 1057 of TCPv2). The `SO_BROADCAST` socket option needs to be specified only for UDP sockets.

28.4   Our program does not check for a multicast address and does not set the `IP_MULTICAST_IF` socket option. Therefore, the kernel chooses the outgoing interface, probably by searching the routing table for 224.0.0.1. We also do not set the `IP_MULTICAST_TTL` field, so it defaults to 1, which is acceptable.

Chapter 29

29.1 This flag indicates that the jump buffer has been set by `sigsetjmp` (Figure 29.10). While the flag may seem superfluous, there is a chance that the signal can be delivered after the signal handler is established, but before the call to `sigsetjmp`. Even if the program doesn't cause the signal to be generated, signals can be generated in other ways, such as with the `kill` command.

Chapter 30

30.1 The parent keeps the listening socket open in case it needs to `fork` additional children at some later time (which would be an enhancement to our code).

30.2 Yes, a datagram socket can be used to pass a descriptor instead of using a stream socket. With a datagram socket, the parent does not receive an EOF on its end of the stream pipe when a child terminates prematurely, but the parent could use SIGCHLD for this purpose. One difference in this scenario, where SIGCHLD can be used versus our `icmpd` daemon in Section 28.7, is that in the latter, there was no parent/child relationship between the client and server so the EOF on the stream pipe was the only way for the server to detect the disappearance of a client.

Chapter 31

31.1 We are assuming here that the default for the protocol is an orderly release when the stream is closed, which is true for TCP.

Bibliography

All RFCs are available at no charge through electronic mail, anonymous FTP, or the World Wide Web. A starting point is `http://www.ietf.org`. The directory `ftp://ftp.rfc-editor.org/in-notes` is one location for RFCs. URLs are not specified for RFCs.

Items marked "Internet Draft" are works in progress of the IETF. These drafts expire six months after publication. The appropriate version of the draft may change after this book is published, or the draft may be published as an RFC. They are available at no charge via the Internet, similar to the RFCs. `http://www.ietf.org` is a major repository for Internet Drafts. We include the filename portion of the URL for each Internet Draft, since the filename contains the version number.

Whenever an electronic copy was found of a paper or report referenced in this bibliography, its URL is included. Be aware that these URLs can change over time, and readers are encouraged to check the Errata for this text on the book's home page for any changes (`http://www.unpbook.com/`). A terrific online database of papers can be found at `http://citeseer.nj.nec.com/cs`. Entering the title of a paper or report will not only find other papers that refer to the one entered, but will also point to known online versions.

Albitz, P. and Liu, C. 2001. *DNS and Bind, Fourth Edition.* O'Reilly & Associates, Sebastopol, CA.

Allman, M., Floyd, S., and Partridge, C. 2002. "Increasing TCP's Initial Window," RFC 3390.

Allman, M., Ostermann, S., and Metz, C. W. 1998. "FTP Extensions for IPv6 and NATs," RFC 2428.

Allman, M., Paxson, V., and Stevens, W. R. 1999. "TCP Congestion Control," RFC 2581.

Almquist, P. 1992. "Type of Service in the Internet Protocol Suite," RFC 1349 (obsoleted by RFC 2474).

> Original definition of how to use the type-of-service field in the IPv4 header. Obsoleted by RFC 2474 [Nichols et al. 1998] and RFC 3168 [Ramakrishnan, Floyd, and Black 2001].

Baker, F. 1995. "Requirements for IP Version 4 Routers," RFC 1812.

Borman, D. A. 1997a. "Re: Frequency of RST Terminated Connections," end2end-interest mailing list (http://www.unpbook.com/borman.97jan30.txt).

Borman, D. A. 1997b. "Re: SYN/RST cookies," tcp-impl mailing list (http://www.unpbook.com/borman.97jun06.txt).

Borman, D. A., Deering, S. E., and Hinden, R. 1999. "IPv6 Jumbograms," RFC 2675.

Braden, R. T. 1989. "Requirements for Internet Hosts—Communication Layers," RFC 1122.

> The first half of the host requirements RFC. This half covers the link layer, IPv4, ICMPv4, IGMPv4, ARP, TCP, and UDP.

Braden, R. T. 1992. "TIME-WAIT Assassination Hazards in TCP," RFC 1337.

Braden, R. T., Borman, D. A., and Partridge, C. 1988. "Computing the Internet checksum," RFC 1071.

Bradner, S. 1996. "The Internet Standards Process—Revision 3," RFC 2026.

Bush, R. 2001. "Delegation of IP6.ARPA," RFC 3152.

Butenhof, D. R. 1997. *Programming with POSIX Threads.* Addison-Wesley, Reading, MA.

Cain, B., Deering, S. E., Kouvelas, I., Fenner, B., and Thyagarajan, A. 2002. "Internet Group Management Protocol, Version 3," RFC 3376.

Carpenter, B. and Moore, K. 2001. "Connection of IPv6 Domains via IPv4 Clouds," RFC 3056.

CERT, 1996a. "UDP Port Deinal-of-Service Attack," Advisory CA-96.01, Computer Emergency Response Team, Pittsburgh, PA.

CERT, 1996b. "TCP SYN Flooding and IP Spoofing Attacks," Advisory CA-96.21, Computer Emergency Response Team, Pittsburgh, PA.

Cheswick, W. R., Bellovin, S. M., and Rubin, A. D. 2003. *Firewalls and Internet Security: Repelling the Wily Hacker, Second Edition.* Addison-Wesley, Reading, MA.

Conta, A. and Deering, S. E. 1998. "Internet Control Message Protocol (ICMPv6) for the Internet Protocol Version 6 (IPv6) Specification," RFC 2463.

Conta, A. and Deering, S. E. 2001. "Internet Control Message Protocol (ICMPv6) for the Internet Protocol Version 6 (IPv6) Specification," draft-ietf-ipngwg-icmp-v3-02.txt (Internet Draft).

> This is a revision of [Conta and Deering 1998] and is expected to eventually replace it.

Crawford, M. 1998a. "Transmission of IPv6 Packets over Ethernet Networks," RFC 2464.

Crawford, M. 1998b. "Transmission of IPv6 Packets over FDDI Networks," RFC 2467.

Crawford, M., Narten, T., and Thomas, S. 1998. "Transmission of IPv6 Packets over Token Ring Networks," RFC 2470.

Deering, S. E. 1989. "Host extensions for IP multicasting," RFC 1112.

Deering, S. E. and Hinden, R. 1998. "Internet Protocol, Version 6 (IPv6) Specification," RFC 2460.

Draves, R. 2003. "Default Address Selection for Internet Protocol version 6 (IPv6)," RFC 3484.

Eriksson, H. 1994. "MBONE: The Multicast Backbone," *Communications of the ACM*, vol. 37, no. 8, pp. 54–60.

Fink, R. and Hinden, R. 2003. "6bone (IPv6 Testing Address Allocation) Phaseout," draft-fink-6bone-phaseout-04.txt (Internet Draft).

Fuller, V., Li, T., Yu, J. Y., and Varadhan, K. 1993. "Classless Inter-Domain Routing (CIDR): an Address Assignment and Aggregation Strategy," RFC 1519.

Garfinkel, S. L., Schwartz, A., and Spafford, E. H. 2003. *Practical UNIX & Internet Security, 3rd Edition.* O'Reilly & Associates, Sebastapol, CA.

Gettys, J. and Nielsen, H. F. 1998. *SMUX Protocol Specification* (http://www.w3.org/TR/WD-mux).

Gierth, A. 1996. *Private communication.*

Gilligan, R. E. and Nordmark, E. 2000. "Transition Mechanisms for IPv6 Hosts and Routers," RFC 2893.

Gilligan, R. E., Thomson, S., Bound, J., McCann, J., and Stevens, W. R. 2003. "Basic Socket Interface Extensions for IPv6," RFC 3493.

Gilligan, R. E., Thomson, S., Bound, J., and Stevens, W. R. 1997. "Basic Socket Interface Extensions for IPv6," RFC 2133 (obsoleted by RFC 2553).

Gilligan, R. E., Thomson, S., Bound, J., and Stevens, W. R. 1999. "Basic Socket Interface Extensions for IPv6," RFC 2553 (obsoleted by RFC 3493).

Haberman, B. 2002. "Allocation Guidelines for IPv6 Multicast Addresses," RFC 3307.

Haberman, B. and Thaler, D. 2002. "Unicast-Prefix-based IPv6 Multicast Addresses," RFC 3306.

Handley, M. and Jacobson, V. 1998. "SDP: Session Description Protocol," RFC 2327.

Handley, M., Perkins, C., and Whelan, E. 2000. "Session Announcement Protocol," RFC 2974.

Harkins, D. and Carrel, D. 1998. "The Internet Key Exchange (IKE)," RFC 2409.

Hinden, R. and Deering, S. E. 2003. "Internet Protocol Version 6 (IPv6) Addressing Architecture," RFC 3513.

Hinden, R., Deering, S. E., and Nordmark, E. 2003. "IPv6 Global Unicast Address Format," RFC 3587.

Hinden, R., Fink, R., and Postel, J. B. 1998. "IPv6 Testing Address Allocation," RFC 2471.

Holbrook, H. and Cheriton, D. 1999. "IP multicast channels: EXPRESS support for large-scale single-source applications," *Computer Communication Review*, vol. 29, no. 4, pp. 65–78.

Huitema, C. 2001. "An Anycast Prefix for 6to4 Relay Routers," RFC 3068.

IANA, 2003. *Protocol/Number Assignments Directory* (http://www.iana.org/numbers.htm).

IEEE, 1996. "Information Technology—Portable Operating System Interface (POSIX)—Part 1: System Application Program Interface (API) [C Language]," IEEE Std 1003.1, 1996 Edition, Institute of Electrical and Electronics Engineers, Piscataway, NJ.

> This version of POSIX.1 contains the 1990 base API, the 1003.1b realtime extensions (1993), the 1003.1c pthreads (1995), and the 1003-1i technical corrections (1995). This is also International Standard ISO/IEC 9945–1: 1996 (E). Ordering information on IEEE standards and draft standards is available at http://www.ieee.org.

IEEE, 1997. *Guidelines for 64-bit Global Identifier (EUI-64) Registration Authority.* Institute of Electrical and Electronics Engineers, Piscataway, NJ (http://standards.ieee.org/regauth/oui/tutorials/EUI64.html).

Jacobson, V. 1988. "Congestion Avoidance and Control," *Computer Communication Review*, vol. 18, no. 4, pp. 314–329 (ftp://ftp.ee.lbl.gov/papers/congavoid.ps.Z).

> A classic paper describing the slow start and congestion avoidance algorithms for TCP.

Jacobson, V., Braden, R. T., and Borman, D. A. 1992. "TCP Extensions for High Performance," RFC 1323.

> Describes the window scale option, the timestamp option, and the PAWS algorithm, along with the reasons why these modifications were needed.

Jacobson, V., Braden, R. T., and Zhang, L. 1990. "TCP Extension for High-Speed Paths," RFC 1185 (obsoleted by RFC 1323).

Josey, A., ed. 1997. *Go Solo 2: The Authorized Guide to Version 2 of the Single UNIX Specification.* Prentice Hall, Uppser Saddle River, NJ.

Josey, A., ed. 2002. *The Single UNIX Specification—The Authorized Guide to Version 3.* The Open Group, Berkshire, UK.

Joy, W. N. 1994. *Private communication.*

Karn, P. and Partridge, C. 1991. "Improving Round-Trip Time Estimates in Reliable Transport Protocols," *ACM Transactions on Computer Systems*, vol. 9, no. 4, pp. 364–373.

Katz, D. 1993. "Transmission of IP and ARP over FDDI Networks," RFC 1390.

Katz, D. 1997. "IP Router Alert Option," RFC 2113.

Kent, S. T. 1991. "U. S. Department of Defense Security Options for the Internet Protocol," RFC 1108.

Kent, S. T. 2003a. "IP Authentication Header," draft-ietf-ipsec-rfc2402bis-04.txt (Internet Draft).

Kent, S. T. 2003b. "IP Encapsulating Security Payload (ESP)," draft-ietf-ipsec-esp-v3-06.txt (Internet Draft).

Kent, S. T. and Atkinson, R. J. 1998a. "Security Architecture for the Internet Protocol," RFC 2401.

Kent, S. T. and Atkinson, R. J. 1998b. "IP Authentication Header," RFC 2402.

As of this writing, this RFC is being updated by the IETF IPsec Working Group (see [Kent 2003a]).

Kent, S. T. and Atkinson, R. J. 1998c. "IP Encapsulating Security Payload (ESP)," RFC 2406.

As of this writing, this RFC is being updated by the IETF IPsec Working Group (see [Kent 2003b]).

Kernighan, B. W. and Pike, R. 1984. *The UNIX Programming Environment.* Prentice Hall, Englewood Cliffs, NJ.

Kernighan, B. W. and Ritchie, D. M. 1988. *The C Programming Language, Second Edition.* Prentice Hall, Englewood Cliffs, NJ.

Lanciani, D. 1996. "Re: sockets: AF_INET vs. PF_INET," Message-ID: <3561@news.IPSWITCH.COM>, USENET comp.protocols.tcp-ip Newsgroup (http://www.unpbook.com/lanciani.96apr10.txt).

Maslen, T. M. 1997. "Re: gethostbyXXXX() and Threads," Message-ID: <maslen.862463630@shellx>, USENET comp.programming.threads Newsgroup (http://www.unpbook.com/maslen.97may01.txt).

McCann, J., Deering, S. E., and Mogul, J. C. 1996. "Path MTU Discovery for IP version 6," RFC 1981.

McCanne, S. and Jacobson, V. 1993. "The BSD Packet Filter: A New Architecture for User-Level Packet Capture," *Proceedings of the 1993 Winter USENIX Conference*, San Diego, CA, pp. 259–269.

McDonald, D. L., Metz, C. W., and Phan, B. G. 1998. "PF_KEY Key Management API, Version 2," RFC 2367.

McKusick, M. K., Bostic, K., Karels, M. J., and Quarterman, J. S. 1996. *The Design and Implementation of the 4.4BSD Operating System.* Addison-Wesley, Reading, MA.

Meyer, D. 1998. "Administratively Scoped IP Multicast," RFC 2365.

Mills, D. L. 1992. "Network Time Protocol (Version 3) Specification, Implementation," RFC 1305.

Mills, D. L. 1996. "Simple Network Time Protocol (SNTP) Version 4 for IPv4, IPv6 and OSI," RFC 2030.

Mogul, J. C. and Deering, S. E. 1990. "Path MTU discovery," RFC 1191.

Mogul, J. C. and Postel, J. B. 1985. "Internet Standard Subnetting Procedure," RFC 950.

Narten, T. and Draves, R. 2001. "Privacy Extensions for Stateless Address Autoconfiguration in IPv6," RFC 3041.

Nemeth, E. 1997. *Private communication.*

Nichols, K., Blake, S., Baker, F., and Black, D. 1998. "Definition of the Differentiated Services Field (DS Field) in the IPv4 and IPv6 Headers," RFC 2474.

Nordmark, E. 2000. "Stateless IP/ICMP Translation Algorithm (SIIT)," RFC 2765.

Ong, L., Rytina, I., Garcia, M., Schwarzbauer, H., Coene, L., Lin, H., Juhasz, I., Holdrege, M., and Sharp, C. 1999. "Framework Architecture for Signaling Transport," RFC 2719.

Ong, L. and Yoakum, J. 2002. "An Introduction to the Stream Control Transmission Protocol (SCTP)," RFC 3286.

The Open Group, 1997. *CAE Specification, Networking Services (XNS), Issue 5.* The Open Group, Berkshire, UK.

> This is the specification for sockets and XTI in Unix 98, now superseded by *The Single UNIX Specification, Version 3.* This manual also has appendices describing the use of XTI with NetBIOS, the OSI protocols, SNA, and the Netware IPX and SPX protocols. Three appendices cover the use of both sockets and XTI with ATM.

Partridge, C. and Jackson, A. 1999. "IPv6 Router Alert Option," RFC 2711.

Partridge, C., Mendez, T., and Milliken, W. 1993. "Host Anycasting Service," RFC 1546.

Partridge, C. and Pink, S. 1993. "A Faster UDP," *IEEE/ACM Transactions on Networking,* vol. 1, no. 4, pp. 429–440.

Paxson, V. 1996. "End-to-End Routing Behavior in the Internet," *Computer Communication Review,* vol. 26, no. 4, pp. 25–38 (ftp://ftp.ee.lbl.gov/papers/routing.SIGCOMM.ps.Z).

Paxson, V. and Allman, M. 2000. "Computing TCP's Retransmission Timer," RFC 2988.

Plauger, P. J. 1992. *The Standard C Library.* Prentice Hall, Englewood Cliffs, NJ.

Postel, J. B. 1980. "User Datagram Protocol," RFC 768.

Postel, J. B. 1981a. "Internet Protocol," RFC 791.

Postel, J. B. 1981b. "Internet Control Message Protocol," RFC 792.

Postel, J. B. 1981c. "Transmission Control Protocol," RFC 793.

Pusateri, T. 1993. "IP Multicast over Token-Ring Local Area Networks," RFC 1469.

Rago, S. A. 1993. *UNIX System V Network Programming.* Addison-Wesley, Reading, MA.

Rajahalme, J., Conta, A., Carpenter, B., and Deering, S. E. 2003. "IPv6 Flow Label Specification," draft-ietf-ipv6-flow-label-07.txt (Internet Draft).

Ramakrishnan, K., Floyd, S., and Black, D. 2001. "The Addition of Explicit Congestion Notification (ECN) to IP," RFC 3168.

Rekhter, Y., Moskowitz, B., Karrenberg, D., de Groot, G. J., and Lear, E. 1996. "Address Allocation for Private Internets," RFC 1918.

Reynolds, J. K. 2002. "Assigned Numbers: RFC 1700 is Replaced by an On-line Database," RFC 3232.

> The database referred to in this RFC is [IANA 2003].

Reynolds, J. K. and Postel, J. B. 1994. "Assigned Numbers," RFC 1700 (obsoleted by RFC 3232).

> This RFC is the last in the series of "Assigned Numbers" RFCs. Since the information changed so often, it was decided to simply keep the directory online. See [Reynolds 2002] for more explanation or [IANA 2003] for the database itself.

Ritchie, D. M. 1984. "A Stream Input-Output System," *AT&T Bell Laboratories Technical Journal*, vol. 63, no. 8, pp. 1897–1910.

Salus, P. H. 1994. *A Quarter Century of Unix*. Addison-Wesley, Reading, MA.

Salus, P. H. 1995. *Casting the Net: From ARPANET to Internet and Beyond*. Addison-Wesley, Reading, MA.

Schimmel, C. 1994. *UNIX Systems for Modern Architectures: Symmetric Multiprocessing and Caching for Kernel Programmers*. Addison-Wesley, Reading, MA.

Spero, S. 1996. *Session Control Protocol (SCP)* (`http://www.w3.org/Protocols/HTTP-NG/http-ng-scp.html`).

Srinivasan, R. 1995. "XDR: External Data Representation Standard," RFC 1832.

Stevens, W. R. 1992. *Advanced Programming in the UNIX Environment*. Addison-Wesley, Reading, MA.

> All the details of Unix programming. Referred to in this text as APUE.

Stevens, W. R. 1994. *TCP/IP Illustrated, Volume 1: The Protocols*. Addison-Wesley, Reading, MA.

> A complete introduction to the Internet protocols. Referred to in this text as TCPv1.

Stevens, W. R. 1996. *TCP/IP Illustrated, Volume 3: TCP for Transactions, HTTP, NNTP, and the UNIX Domain Protocols*. Addison-Wesley, Reading, MA.

> Referred to in this text as TCPv3.

Stevens, W. R. and Thomas, M. 1998. "Advanced Sockets API for IPv6," RFC 2292 (obsoleted by RFC 3542).

Stevens, W. R., Thomas, M., Nordmark, E., and Jinmei, T. 2003. "Advanced Sockets Application Program Interface (API) for IPv6," RFC 3542.

Stewart, R. R., Bestler, C., Jim, J., Ganguly, S., Shah, H., and Kashyap, V. 2003a. "Stream Control Transmission Protocol (SCTP) Remote Direct Memory Access (RDMA) Direct Data Placement (DDP) Adaptation," draft-stewart-rddp-sctp-02.txt (Internet Draft).

Stewart, R. R., Ramalho, M., Xie, Q., Tuexen, M., Rytina, I., Belinchon, M., and Conrad, P. 2003b. "Stream Control Transmission Protocol (SCTP) Dynamic Address Reconfiguration," draft-ietf-tsvwg-addip-sctp-07.txt (Internet Draft).

Stewart, R. R. and Xie, Q. 2001. *Stream Control Transmission Protocol (SCTP): A Reference Guide*. Addison-Wesley, Reading, MA.

Stewart, R. R., Xie, Q., Morneault, K., Sharp, C., Schwarzbauer, H., Taylor, T., Rytina, I., Kalla, M., Zhang, L., and Paxson, V. 2000. "Stream Control Transmission Protocol," RFC 2960.

Stone, J., Stewart, R. R., and Otis, D. 2002. "Stream Control Transmission Protocol (SCTP) Checksum Change," RFC 3309.

Tanenbaum, A. S. 1987. *Operating Systems Design and Implementation*. Prentice Hall, Englewood Cliffs, NJ.

Thomson, S. and Huitema, C. 1995. "DNS Extensions to support IP version 6," RFC 1886.

Torek, C. 1994. "Re: Delay in re-using TCP/IP port," Message-ID: <199501010028.QAA16863 @elf.bsdi.com>, USENET comp.unix.wizards Newsgroup (http://www.unpbook.com/ torek.94dec31.txt).

Touch, J. 1997. "TCP Control Block Interdependence," RFC 2140.

Unix International, 1991. *Data Link Provider Interface Specification*. Unix International, Parsippany, NJ, Revision 2.0.0 (http://www.unpbook.com/dlpi.2.0.0.ps).

> A newer version of this specification is available online from The Open Group at http://www.rdg.opengroup.org/pubs/catalog/web.htm.

Unix International, 1992a. *Network Provider Interface Specification*. Unix International, Parsippany, NJ, Revision 2.0.0 (http://www.unpbook.com/npi.2.0.0.ps).

Unix International, 1992b. *Transport Provider Interface Specification*. Unix International, Parsippany, NJ, Revision 1.5 (http://www.unpbook.com/tpi.1.5.ps).

> A newer version of this specification is available online from The Open Group at http://www.rdg.opengroup.org/pubs/catalog/web.htm.

Vixie, P. A. 1996. *Private communication*.

Wright, G. R. and Stevens, W. R. 1995. *TCP/IP Illustrated, Volume 2: The Implementation*. Addison-Wesley, Reading, MA.

> The implementation of the Internet protocols in the 4.4BSD-Lite operating system. Referred to in this text as TCPv2.

Index

Networking is a field that is pockmarked with acronyms. Rather than provide a separate glossary (with most of the entries being acronyms), this index also serves as a glossary for all the acronyms used in the book. The primary entry for the acronym appears under the acronym name. For example, all references to the Internet Control Message Protocol appear under ICMP. The entry under the compound term "Internet Control Message Protocol" refers back to the main entry under ICMP.

The notation "definition of" appearing with a C function refers to the boxed function prototype for that function, its primary description. The "definition of" notation for a structure refers to its primary definition. Some functions also contain the notation "source code" if the source code implementation for that function appears in the text.

Structure Definitions